Western Hemisphere

Eastern Hemisphere

Multiple images from satellites *Terra*, *Aqua*, *Radarsat*, and *Defense Meteorological Satellite*, and from Space Shuttle *Endeavor's* radar data of topography, all merge in a dramatic composite to show the Western Hemisphere and Eastern Hemisphere of Earth. What indications do you see on these images that tell you the time of year? These are part of NASA's Blue Marble Next Generation image collection.

[NASA images by Reto Stöckli, based on data from NASA and NOAA.]

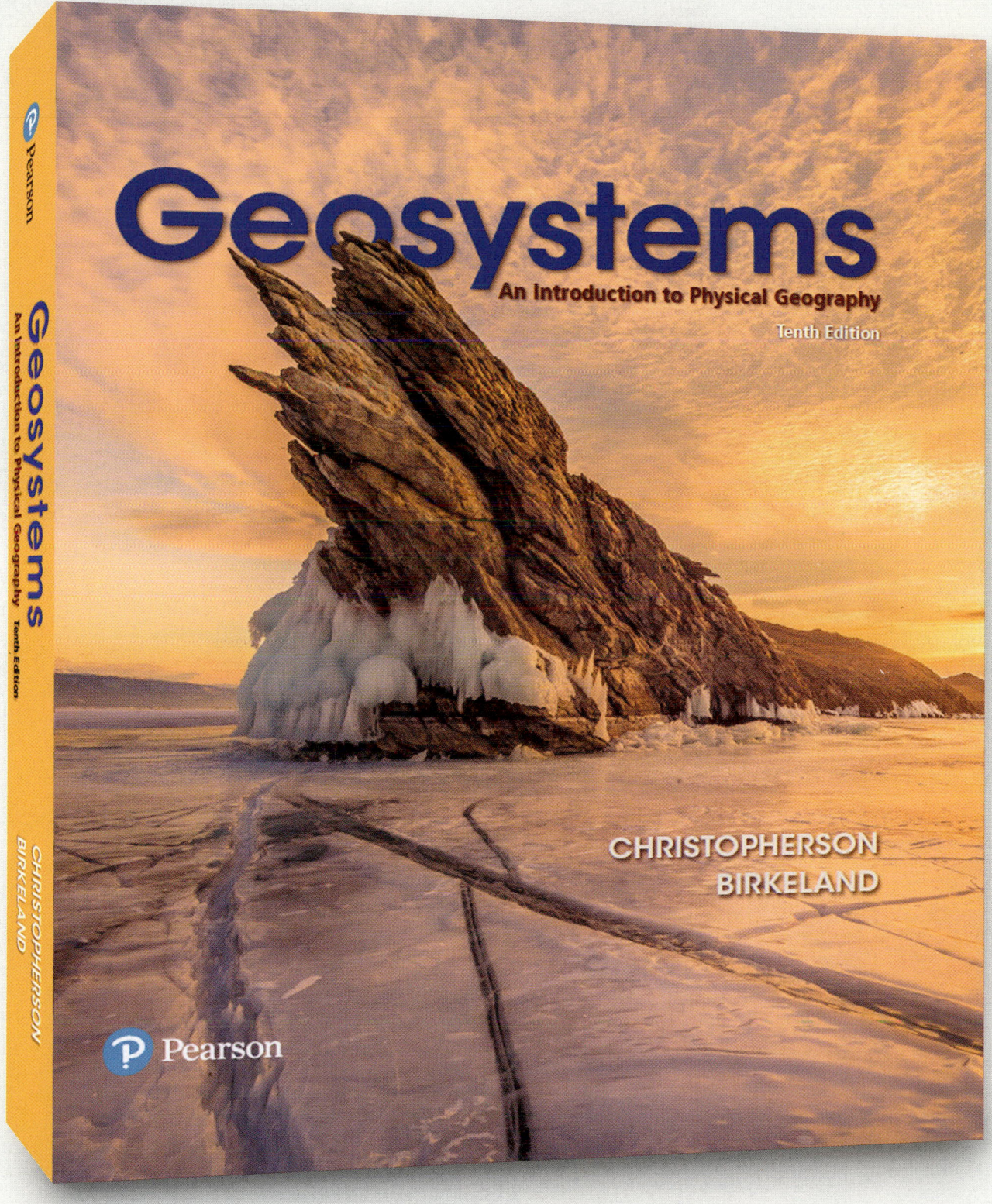

Geosystems

An Introduction to Physical Geography

Tenth Edition

CHRISTOPHERSON
BIRKELAND

Pearson

Real-World Physical Geography

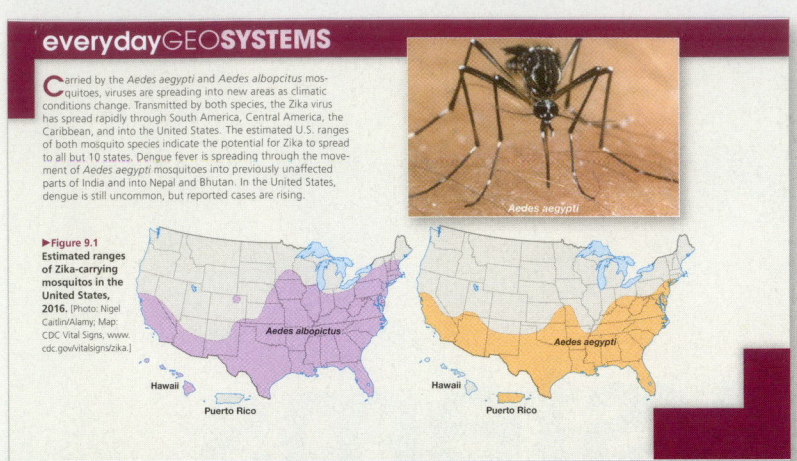

everydayGEOSYSTEMS

Carried by the *Aedes aegypti* and *Aedes albopictus* mosquitoes, viruses are spreading into new areas as climatic conditions change. Transmitted by both species, the Zika virus has spread rapidly through South America, Central America, the Caribbean, and into the United States. The estimated U.S. ranges of both mosquito species indicate the potential for Zika to spread to all but 10 states. Dengue fever is spreading through the movement of *Aedes aegypti* mosquitoes into previously unaffected parts of India and into Nepal and Bhutan. In the United States, dengue is still uncommon, but reported cases are rising.

▶ Figure 9.1
Estimated ranges of Zika-carrying mosquitos in the United States, 2016. [Photo: Nigel Caitlin/Alamy; Map: CDC Vital Signs, www. cdc.gov/vitalsigns/zika.]

Aedes albopictus

Aedes aegypti

Hawaii

Puerto Rico

NEW! Everyday Geosystems features at the beginning of each chapter invite the reader to explore the "why" and "how" application of physical geography concepts to everyday phenomena.

NEW! Mobile Field Trips by acclaimed geoscientist, photographer, and pilot Michael Collier transport students out into the field to explore the patterns and processes of North America's physical geography.

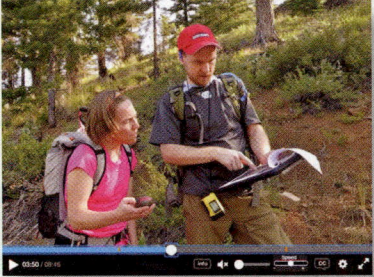

NEW! Condor Quadcopter Videos capture stunning footage of the Mountain West region with a quadcopter and a GoPro camera. Annotation, sketching, and narrations help students learn about monoclines, streams, terraces, and much more.

Radial dike

Shiprock

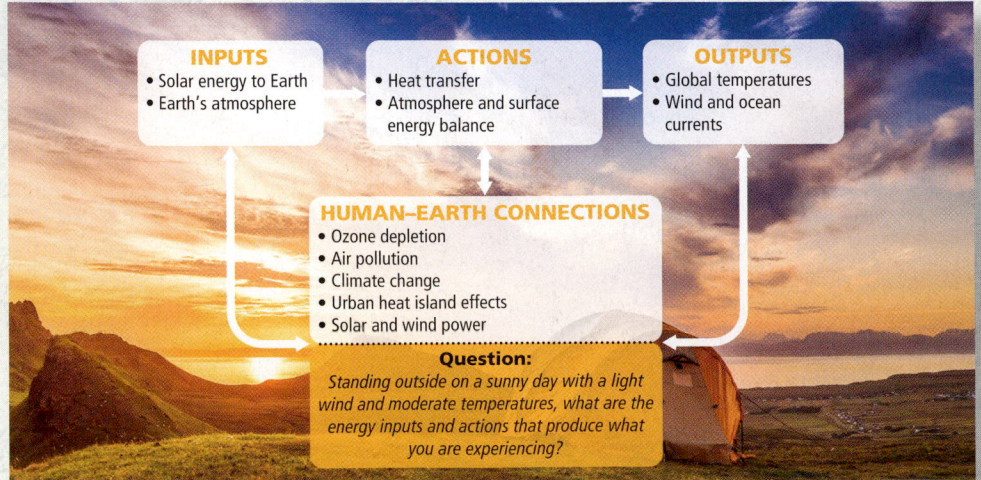

INPUTS
• Solar energy to Earth
• Earth's atmosphere

ACTIONS
• Heat transfer
• Atmosphere and surface energy balance

OUTPUTS
• Global temperatures
• Wind and ocean currents

HUMAN–EARTH CONNECTIONS
• Ozone depletion
• Air pollution
• Climate change
• Urban heat island effects
• Solar and wind power

Question:
Standing outside on a sunny day with a light wind and moderate temperatures, what are the energy inputs and actions that produce what you are experiencing?

UPDATED! Systems Diagrams on all part-opener and chapter-opener pages emphasize the interactions and flow of Earth systems' concepts relative to each part and chapter. These pages now include questions that make readers reflect on the topics they are about to explore within their real-world context.

Applying the Tools & Practices of Science

NEW! **Geospatial Analysis exercises** at the end of each chapter are capstone mini-lab activities, sending students outside of the book to primary science tools and data sets from organizations such as NASA, USGS, and NOAA, to perform critical geospatial data analysis.

GEO**SPATIAL** ANALYSIS

Citizen Science

Citizens collecting high quality data can make a big contribution to the science community. These data are used by scientists to fill in gaps in the data and improve forecasts.

Activities

Go to the CoCoRaHS website at http://www.cocorahs.org/ and find a county near you with a CoCoRaHS station. Click on "View Data" and then click on "Daily Precipitation Reports." Enter the name of the state and county. Choose a start date of one week ago and an end date of today so you can examine the last 7 days of data. Click "Search" to display the stations in your county. If there are multiple stations enter the Station Number for one of the stations in the "Station Fields" box and check "Station Number." Click "Search."

1. During the last seven days, how many days had precipitation reports?

2. What is the precipitation total for the week? If applicable, how many inches of snow?

3. Do these reports reflect what you experienced during those same days? Explain and analyze.

Go back and find a county that is reporting precipitation and has multiple CoCoRaHS observation stations.

4. Notice that for a given day not all of the stations report the same amount of precipitation. What might be an explanation for this?

5. What is the precipitation total for the week? How many inches of snow?

GEO**SPATIAL** ANALYSIS

Recent Volcanic Activity

The Smithsonian Institution Global Volcanism Program and the USGS report new and changing volcanic activity worldwide. NOAA issues Volcanic Ash Advisories to alert aircraft downwind from volcanic eruptions.

Activities

Go to the Weekly Volcanic Activity Report page at http://volcano.si.edu/reports_weekly.cfm.

1. Where is volcanic activity occurring according to the map?

2. Click on "Criteria and Disclaimers." Why are some volcanoes not displayed on the map?

3. Click on "Weekly Report." List the new volcanic activity locations and list at least 3 locations of ongoing activity.

Click on a volcano under "New Activity Highlights."

1. List the city, country, volcanic region, latitude and longitude, and dates of recent volcanic activity.

2. What are the key features for this type of volcano?

3. Is this volcano located near a tectonic plate boundary or hot spot? Explain.

4. Click on "Archive." Click on this volcano, and summarize its eruptive history.

Go to the Volcanic Ash Advisory Center (VAAC) page at: http://www.ssd.noaa.gov/VAAC/washington.html.

1. List the 9 VAAC locations.

2. Click on "Current Volcanic Ash Advisories." According to the list for the present year, what is the most active VAAC region? What is the name of the volcano with the most ash advisories?

NEW! *Work It Out* **activities** integrated throughout each chapter give students a chance to practice basic conceptual or quantitative reasoning as they read.

 WORKIT**OUT 4.1**
Coastal and Inland Temperatures

Using the map, graphs, and other data in Figures 4.27 and 4.28, complete the following:

1. Using the graphs in Figure 4.27, determine the lowest minimum average monthly temperatures for San Francisco and Wichita. Explain the difference between the two temperatures.
2. Why does San Francisco's average monthly temperature peak occur later in the summer than that of Wichita?
3. Determine the annual temperature ranges for Verkhoyansk and Wichita. Which location has the larger temperature range, and why?

 WORKIT**OUT 17.1**
Identify Glacial Features

The Colony Glacier is located in Alaska's Chugach Mountains (**Figure WIO 17.1**).

1. Using the figures in this chapter as a guide, identify the features that correspond with each letter on the photo. (*Hint:* Choose among cirque, arête, horn, erratic, medial moraine, lateral moraine, terminal moraine, crevasses, piedmont glacier, and valley glacier.)

| A. _____ | C. _____ | E. _____ |
| B. _____ | D. _____ | F. _____ |

2. Does this glacier appear to have a positive or negative mass balance? Explain.

▲Figure WIO 17.1 Erosional features of alpine glaciation.
[P.A. Lawrence, LLC/Alamy.]

NEW! *Apply Concepts* **features,** part of the text's hallmark *Focus Studies*, are active learning tasks and short activities that compel students to reflect on the information they have learned from these rich case studies.

APPLYconcepts Determine the suitability of wind power in your state, based on wind speed (see Figure 5.2.1) and site-specific conditions (described in "Conditions for Wind Power"). Write a sentence summarizing your state's overall wind power potential.

Suitability for wind power		
Highest wind speed	_____	
Lowest wind speed	_____	
Site-specific conditions	a. _____	b. _____

APPLYconcepts Referring to the map in Figure 7.1.1b and the chapter's sections "Storm Development" and "Physical Structure," explain key events in the life cycle of Hurricane Patricia.

October 23, atmospheric pressure reading	a. How did Patricia's 872 mb pressure on October 23 affect the storm's intensity? Explain._____
October 23, landfall	b. What area(s) probably experienced the strongest winds as Patricia came ashore? Explain.
October 24, moving inland	c. How and why did Patricia's intensity change after the storm made landfall?_____

Our Changing Earth, Changing Content

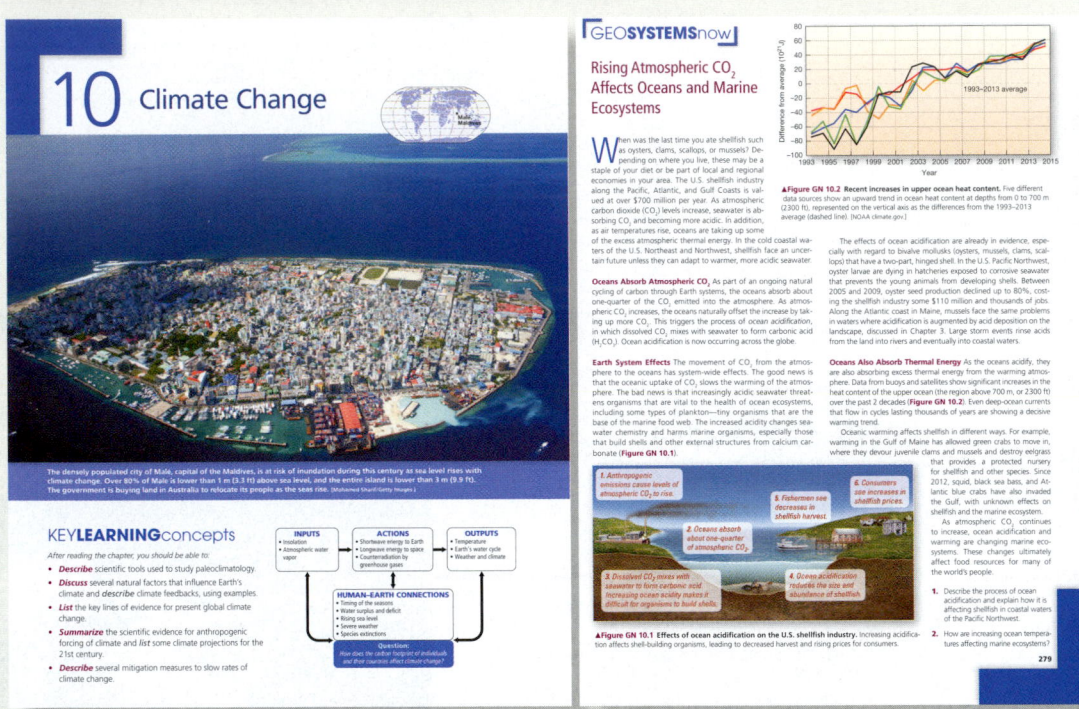

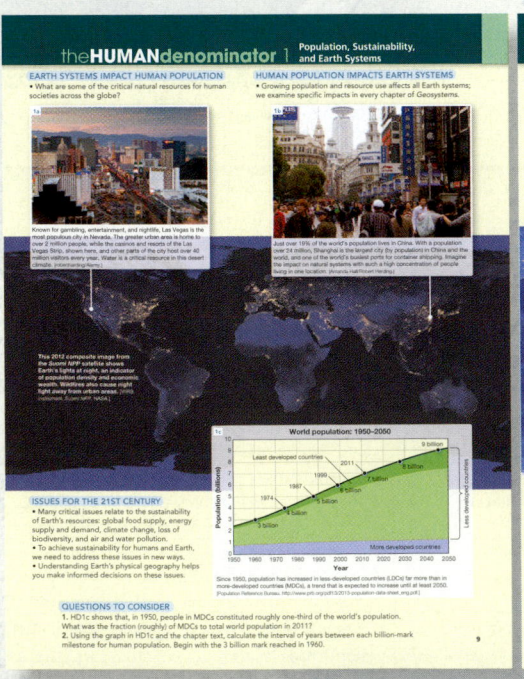

... with the New Tenth Edition

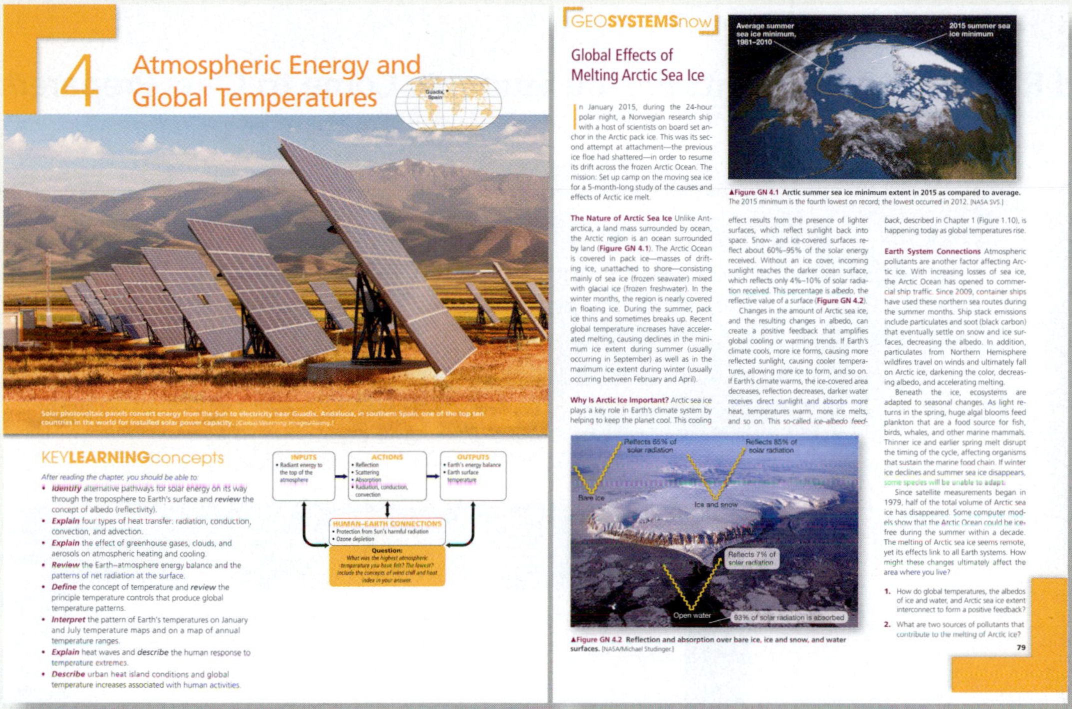

4 Atmospheric Energy and Global Temperatures

Solar photovoltaic panels convert energy from the Sun to electricity near Guadix, Andalusia, in southern Spain, one of the top ten countries in the world for installed solar power capacity. [Global Warming Images/Alamy.]

KEY LEARNING concepts

After reading the chapter, you should be able to:

- *Identify* alternative pathways for solar energy on its way through the troposphere to Earth's surface and *review* the concept of albedo (reflectivity).
- *Explain* four types of heat transfer: radiation, conduction, convection, and advection.
- *Explain* the effect of greenhouse gases, clouds, and aerosols on atmospheric heating and cooling.
- *Review* the Earth–atmosphere energy balance and the patterns of net radiation at the surface.
- *Define* the concept of temperature and *review* the principle temperature controls that produce global temperature patterns.
- *Interpret* the pattern of Earth's temperatures on January and July temperature maps and on a map of annual temperature ranges.
- *Explain* heat waves and *describe* the human response to temperature extremes.
- *Describe* urban heat island conditions and global temperature increases associated with human activities.

INPUTS
- Radiant energy to the top of the atmosphere

ACTIONS
- Reflection
- Scattering
- Absorption
- Radiation, conduction, convection

OUTPUTS
- Earth's energy balance
- Earth surface temperature

HUMAN–EARTH CONNECTIONS
- Protection from Sun's harmful radiation
- Ozone depletion

Question:
What was the highest atmospheric temperature you have felt? The lowest? Include the concepts of wind chill and heat index in your answer.

GEOSYSTEMS now

Global Effects of Melting Arctic Sea Ice

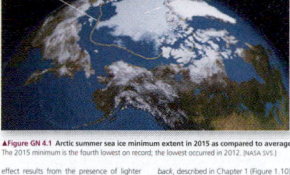

In January 2015, during the 24-hour polar night, a Norwegian research ship with a host of scientists on board set anchor in the Arctic pack ice. This was its second attempt at attachment—the previous ice floe had shattered—in order to resume its drift across the frozen Arctic Ocean. The mission: Set up camp on the moving sea ice for a 5-month-long study of the causes and effects of Arctic ice melt.

The Nature of Arctic Sea Ice Unlike Antarctica, a land mass surrounded by ocean, the Arctic region is an ocean surrounded by land (Figure GN 4.1). The Arctic Ocean is covered in pack ice—masses of drifting ice, unattached to shore—consisting mainly of sea ice (frozen seawater) mixed with glacial ice (frozen freshwater). In the winter months, the region is nearly covered in floating ice. During the summer, pack ice thins and sometimes breaks up. Recent global temperature increases have accelerated melting, causing declines in the minimum ice extent during summer (usually occurring in September) as well as in the maximum ice extent during winter (usually occurring between February and April).

Why is Arctic Ice Important? Arctic sea ice plays a key role in Earth's climate system by helping to keep the planet cool. This cooling

▲Figure GN 4.1 Arctic summer sea ice minimum extent in 2015 as compared to average. The 2015 minimum is the fourth lowest on record; the lowest occurred in 2012. [NASA SVS.]

effect results from the presence of lighter surfaces, which reflect sunlight back into space. Snow- and ice-covered surfaces reflect about 60%–95% of the solar energy received. Without an ice cover, incoming sunlight reaches the darker ocean surface, which reflects only 4%–10% of solar radiation received. This percentage is albedo, the reflective value of a surface (Figure GN 4.2).

Changes in the amount of Arctic sea ice, and the resulting changes in albedo, can create a positive feedback that amplifies global cooling or warming trends. If Earth's climate cools, more ice forms, causing more reflected sunlight, causing cooler temperatures, allowing more ice to form, and so on. If Earth's climate warms, the ice-covered area decreases, reflection decreases, darker water receives direct sunlight and absorbs more heat, temperatures warm, more ice melts, and so on. This so-called ice-albedo feedback, described in Chapter 1 (Figure 1.10), is happening today as global temperatures rise.

Earth System Connections Atmospheric pollutants are another factor affecting Arctic ice. With increasing losses of sea ice, the Arctic Ocean has opened to commercial ship traffic. Since 2009, container ships have used these northern sea routes during the summer months. Ship stack emissions include particulates and soot (black carbon) that eventually settle on snow and ice surfaces, decreasing the albedo. In addition, particulates from Northern Hemisphere wildfires travel on winds and ultimately fall on Arctic ice, darkening the color, decreasing albedo, and accelerating melting.

Beneath the ice, ecosystems are adapted to seasonal changes. As light returns in the spring, huge algal blooms feed plankton that are a food source for fish, birds, whales, and other marine mammals. Thinner ice and earlier spring melt disrupt the timing of the cycle, affecting organisms that sustain the marine food chain. If winter ice declines and summer sea ice disappears, some species will be unable to adapt.

Since satellite measurements began in 1979, half of the total volume of Arctic sea ice has disappeared. Some computer models show that the Arctic Ocean could be ice-free during the summer within a decade. The melting of Arctic sea ice seems remote, yet its effects link to all Earth systems. How might these changes ultimately affect the area where you live?

1. How do global temperatures, the albedos of ice and water, and Arctic sea ice extent interconnect to form a positive feedback?

2. What are two sources of pollutants that contribute to the melting of Arctic ice?

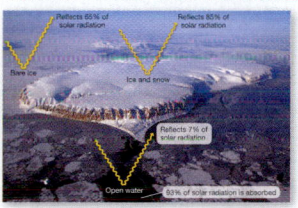

▲Figure GN 4.2 Reflection and absorption over bare ice, ice and snow, and water surfaces. [NASA/Michael Studinger.]

Reflects 85% of solar radiation — Bare ice

Reflects 85% of solar radiation — Ice and snow

Reflects 7% of solar radiation — Open water — 83% of solar radiation is absorbed

79

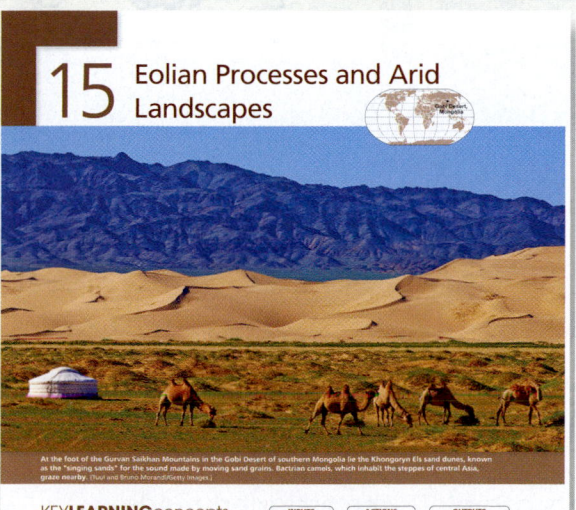

15 Eolian Processes and Arid Landscapes

At the foot of the Gurvan Saikhan Mountains in the Gobi Desert of southern Mongolia lie the Khongoryn Els sand dunes, known as the "singing sands" for the sound made by moving sand grains. Bactrian camels, which inhabit the steppes of central Asia, graze nearby. [Paul and Bruno Morandi/Getty Images.]

KEY LEARNING concepts

After reading the chapter, you should be able to:

- *Describe* eolian transport of dust and sand.
- *Discuss* eolian erosion and the resultant landforms.
- *Explain* the formation of sand dunes and *describe* loess deposits and their origins.
- *Discuss* the causes and human impacts of desertification.
- *List* some landforms unique to arid regions and *explain* their formation.

INPUTS
- Solar energy
- Earth materials
- Wind

ACTIONS
- Weathering
- Erosion
- Deposition

OUTPUTS
- Sand seas and sand dunes
- Loess deposits
- Basin and Range topography
- Badlands

HUMAN–EARTH CONNECTIONS
- Dune stabilization and restoration
- Desertification
- Climate change

Question:
What changes are underway on Earth's arid and semi-arid regions?

GEOSYSTEMS now

Sliding Rocks on Death Valley's Racetrack Playa

In a remote, low-elevation basin between mountain ranges in southern California and Nevada, rocks are moving with no obvious cause. From year to year, unseen by humans, the rocks shift position along a flat, hard-surfaced playa, a dry lakebed. The rocks leave trails behind them, furrows in the silty lakebed sediments, as proof of their movement (Figure GN 15.1). The tracks are hundreds of meters in length, and some of the rocks weigh hundreds of kilograms. The movement is episodic and unpredictable—years, even decades, can pass between movement events.

Possible Causes for Movement The rock trails on Racetrack Playa suggest that movement happens when the playa is wet from infrequent rains and the sediments form a soft mud. If animals or humans were moving the rocks, they would leave tracks on the playa's surface. If gravity were moving the rocks, a slope would be present, but the playa surface is nearly flat. If streams were moving the rocks, a channel would be present, as well as other alluvial material. Eliminating these factors leaves two possibilities: the forces of wind and ice.

For years, scientists sought an explanation for the sliding rocks. The dominant hypothesis was that strong winds were the force for rock movement. The prevailing winds on Racetrack Playa blow from the southwest, parallel to most of the rock tracks. However, some of the heaviest sliding rocks were embedded several centimeters into the playa sediments. Could strong winds alone be enough to force their movement?

On Racetrack Playa, winter rains sometimes produce a shallow lake that lasts for weeks or months. Every few years, conditions are such that a shallow lake forms and then freezes so that a thin layer of ice on the surface covers the water below. During the day, the ice breaks up and melts, and then at night it refreezes. If the rocks become embedded in the ice layer, could wind work together with ice to move the rocks over the wet, slippery surface?

Solving the Mystery In 2011, researchers set up a weather station and time-lapse cameras on Racetrack Playa to test this hypothesis. On the playa surface, they placed rocks with GPS trackers designed to record position and speed at the onset of movement. Then they waited, and in December 2013, rock movement occurred.

Measurements and observations in 2013 and 2014 showed that the rocks slide across the wet surface of the playa on sunny days that follow nights with subfreezing temperatures. At night, the shallow water on the playa freezes to form a thin layer of ice at the surface (Figure GN 15.2). During the late morning, as the sun warms the basin, the ice breaks up into thin panes. Then wind—both light breezes and strong gusts—moves the ice panels, effectively "bulldozing" the rocks across the saturated, muddy surface of the playa.

The conditions necessary for rock movement occur infrequently at Racetrack Playa. A shallow lake must be present at the same time that nighttime temperatures dip below freezing to initiate surface freeze. The winters of 2010–2011 and 2011–2012 included infrequent snow and rain events but not enough moisture to form a lake. Once formed, a lake that persists over weeks or months in combination with temperature conditions that promote nighttime freezing and daytime ice breakup can have numerous rock sliding events. (For more information, see http://journals.plos.org/plosone/article?id=10.1371/journal.pone.0105948.)

1. What conditions did scientists observe at the playa surface when rock movement occurred?

2. Why do the rocks on Racetrack Playa move in some years and not in others?

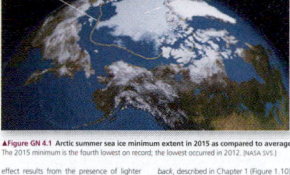

▲Figure GN 15.1 A sliding rock at rest on Racetrack Playa, Death Valley National Park, California. When in motion, the rocks slide over the wet playa at slow speeds for brief periods of time, sometimes only for seconds. [Daniel Osterkamp/Getty Images.]

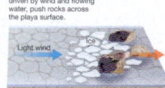

1. Rain creates a shallow water layer on the dry lakebed.

2. Water freezes overnight. In the morning, ice breaks into thin sheets.

3. The floating ice panels, driven by wind and flowing water, push rocks across the playa surface.

▲Figure GN 15.2 The observed process for rock movement on Racetrack Playa. [Based on R.D. Norris et al. 2014, Sliding Rocks on Racetrack Playa, Death Valley National Park: First Observation of Rocks in Motion. PLoS ONE 9(8): e105948.]

439

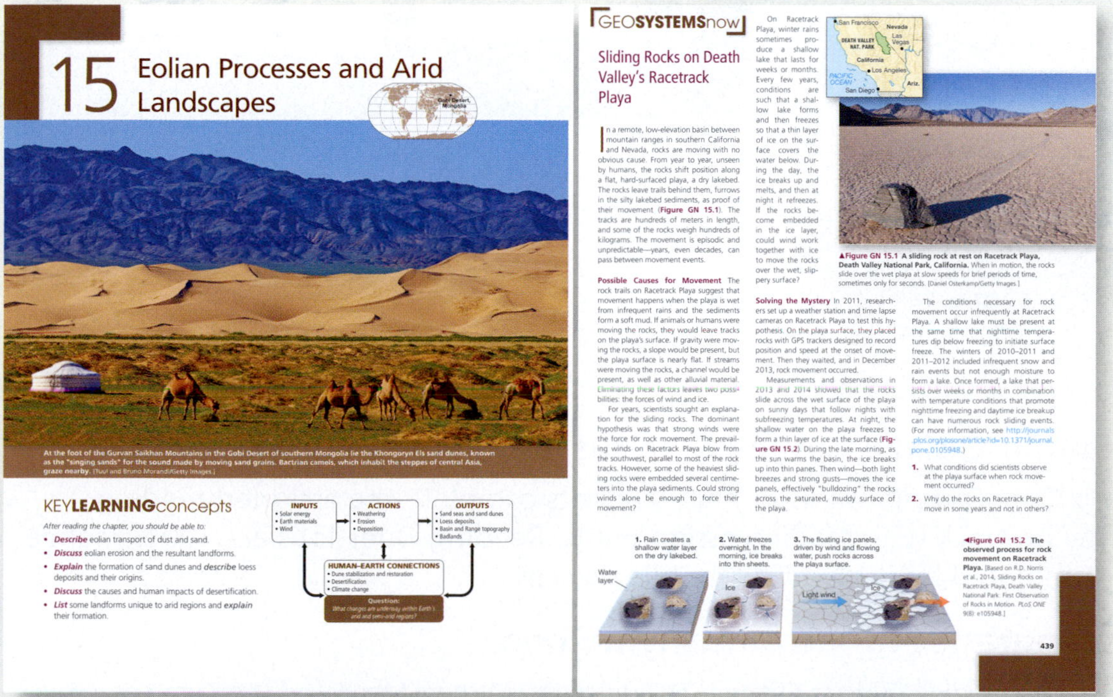

Continuous Learning
Before, During, and After Class

BEFORE CLASS

Mobile Media and Reading Assignments Ensure Students Come to Class Prepared

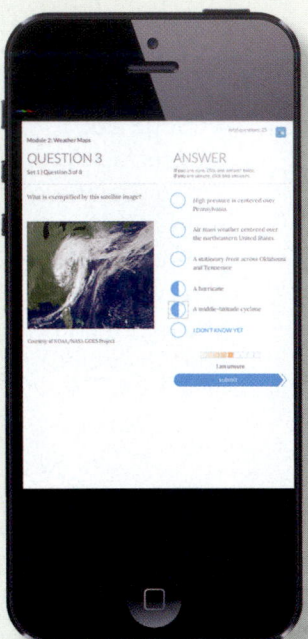

UPDATED! Dynamic Study Modules help students study more effectively by continuously assessing student performance and providing practice in areas where students struggle the most. Each Dynamic Study Module, accessed by computer, smartphone, or tablet, promotes fast learning and long-term retention.

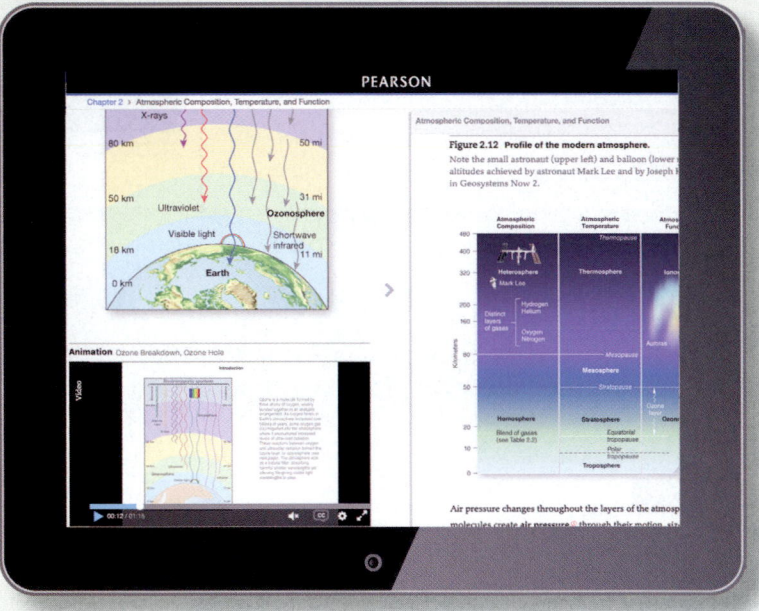

NEW! Interactive eText 2.0 gives students access to the text whenever they can access the Internet. eText features include:

- Available on smartphones and tablets.
- Seamlessly integrated videos and animations.
- Accessible (screen-reader ready).
- Configurable reading settings, including resizable type and night reading mode.
- Instructor and student note taking, highlighting, bookmarking, and searching.

Pre-Lecture Reading Quizzes are easy to customize and assign

UPDATED! Reading Quiz Questions ensure that students complete the assigned reading before class and stay on track with reading assignments. Reading Questions are 100% mobile ready and can be completed by students on mobile devices.

Optional eText upgrades for accompanying books

- *Dire Predictions: Understanding Climate Change*, 2nd Edition, by Michael Mann and Lee Kump
- *Goode's World Atlas*, 23rd Edition by Rand McNally

. . . with MasteringGeography™

DURING CLASS

Engage Students with Learning Catalytics

What has teachers and students excited? Learning Cataltyics, a "bring your own device" student engagement, assessment, and classroom intelligence system, allows students to use their smartphone, tablet, or laptop to respond to questions in class. With Learning Catalytics, you can:

- Assess students in real time using open-ended question formats, such as word clouds, sketching, and image upload, to uncover student misconceptions and adjust lectures accordingly.

- Automatically create groups for peer instruction based on student response patterns to optimize discussion.

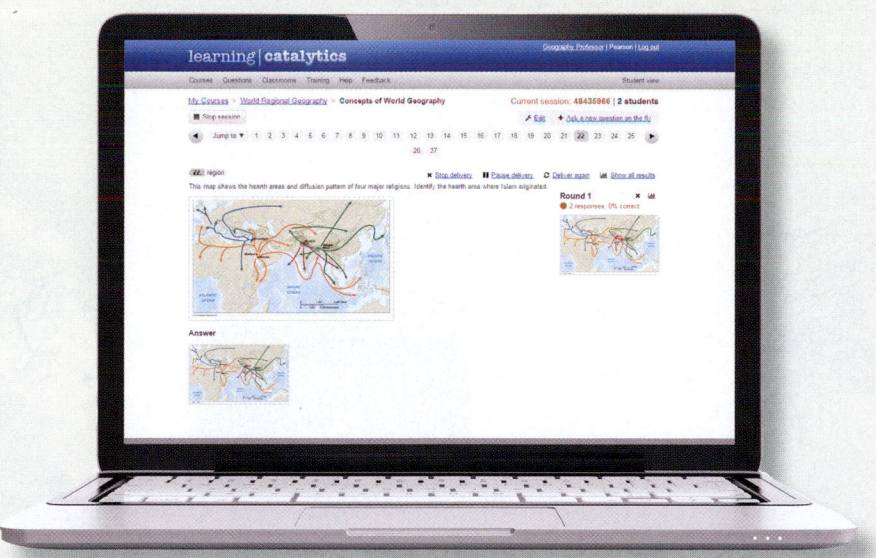 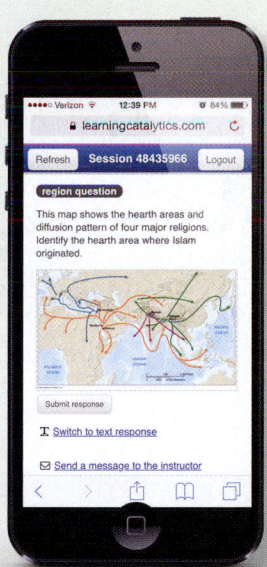

"My students are so busy and engaged answering Learning Catalytics questions during the lecture that they don't have time for Facebook."

Declan De Paor, Old Dominion University

Continuous Learning
Before, During, and After Class

AFTER CLASS

Easy to Assign, Customizable, Media-Rich, and Automatically Graded Assignments

Why is what where?

01:58 / 08:46

NEW! Mobile Field Trips by acclaimed geoscientist, photographer, and pilot Michael Collier transport students out into the field to explore the patterns and processes of North America's physical geography. Teachers can assign the videos with quizzes in MasteringGeography to assess student understanding.

NEW! Condor Quadcopter Videos capture stunning footage of the Mountain West region with a quadcopter and a GoPro camera. Annotation, sketching, and narrations help students learn about monoclines, streams, terraces, and so much more. Teachers can assign the videos with quizzes in MasteringGeography to assess student understanding.

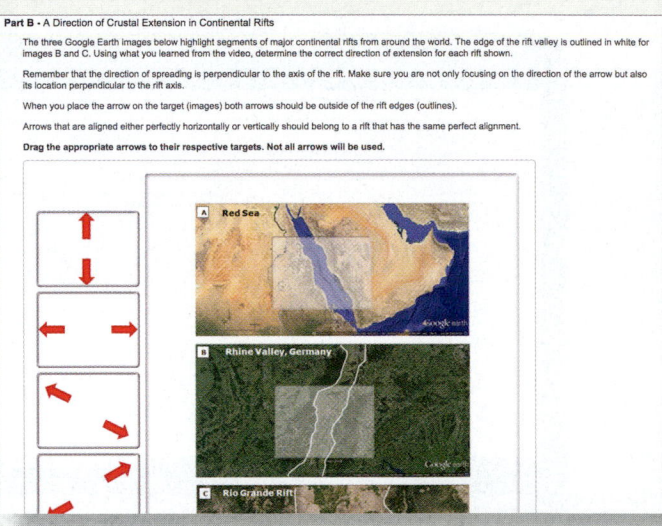

Part B - A Direction of Crustal Extension in Continental Rifts

The three Google Earth images below highlight segments of major continental rifts from around the world. The edge of the rift valley is outlined in white for images B and C. Using what you learned from the video, determine the correct direction of extension for each rift shown.

Remember that the direction of spreading is perpendicular to the axis of the rift. Make sure you are not only focusing on the direction of the arrow but also its location perpendicular to the rift axis.

When you place the arrow on the target (images) both arrows should be outside of the rift edges (outlines).

Arrows that are aligned either perfectly horizontally or vertically should belong to a rift that has the same perfect alignment.

Drag the appropriate arrows to their respective targets. Not all arrows will be used.

A Red Sea

B Rhine Valley, Germany

C Rio Grande Rift

Drag the appropriate labels to their respective targets.

very cold and dry | cooler with low to average precipitation | | warmer and drier

Weber Lake, northeastern Minnesota

(a) transition from a warmer to cooler climate with variable precipitation

Radiocarbon dates

Depth (meters)

Spruce Larch Ash Birch Alder Fir Pine Elm Oak Grasses Sedges Sage Ragweed Chenopods

7300—

White pine

Jack/red pine

9150—

10,300—
14,700—

0 20%

The Percentage of total Pollen by Plants

reset help

Submit Hints My Answers Give Up Review Part

HALLMARK! GeoTutor Activities help students master the most challenging physical geoscience concepts with highly visual, kinesthetic, and data-rich activities focused on critical thinking and the application of core geoscience concepts.

www.masteringgeography.com

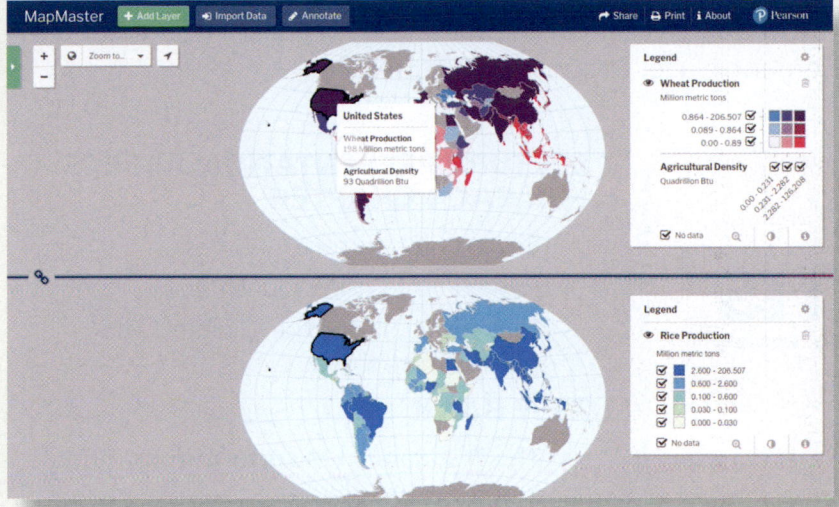

New! MapMaster 2.0 Interactive Map Activities are inspired by GIS, allowing students to layer various thematic maps to analyze spatial patterns and data at regional and global scales. The maps are now fully mobile, with enhanced analysis tools, such as split screen, allowing students to geolocate themselves in the data and upload their own data for advanced mapmaking. This tool includes zoom and annotation functionality, with hundreds of map layers leveraging recent data from sources such as the PRB, the World Bank, NOAA, NASA, USGS, United Nations, the CIA, and more.

NEW! GeoLab Activities augment the chapters with online, automatically graded, and data-rich applied lab activities.

NEW! Video Activities from sources such as the BBC, Financial Times, and Television for the Environment's *Life* and *Earth Report* series provide students with applied real-world examples of physical geography in action, giving a sense of place, and allowing students to explore a range of locations and topics.

Resources for YOU, the Instructor

MasteringGeography provides you with everything you need to prep for your course and deliver a dynamic lecture, in one convenient place. Resources include:

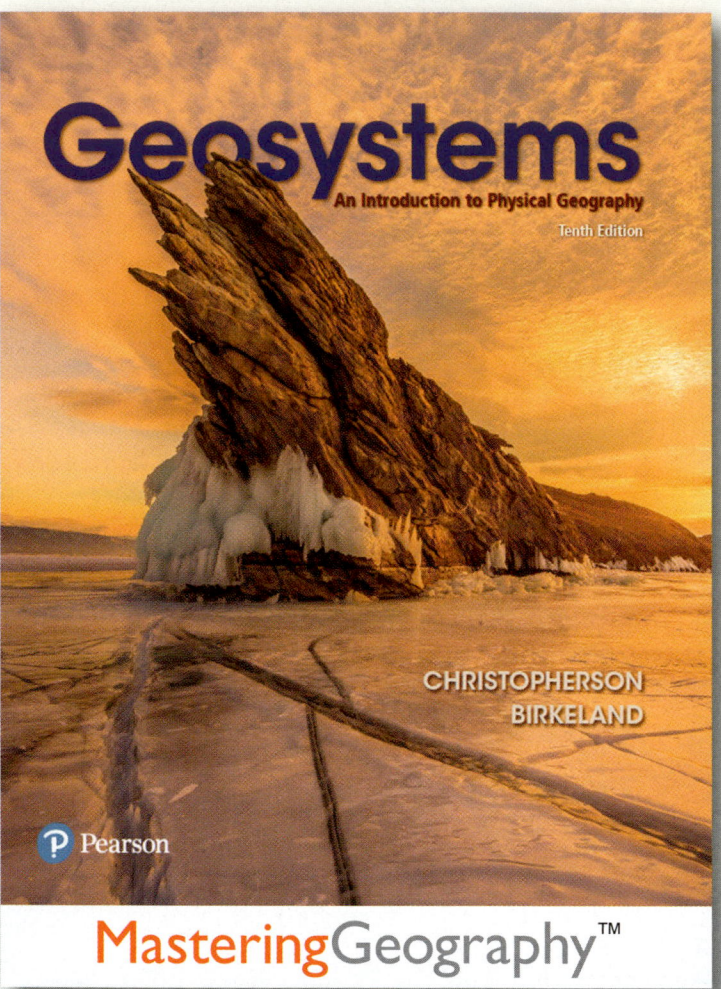

LECTURE PRESENTATION ASSETS FOR EACH CHAPTER

- PowerPoint Lecture Outlines
- PowerPoint Clicker Questions
- Files for all illustrations, tables, and photos from the text

TEST BANK

- The *Test Bank* in Microsoft Word formats
- TestGen Computerized Test Bank, which includes all the questions from the printed test bank in a format that allows you to easily and intuitively build exams and quizzes

TEACHING RESOURCES

- *Instructor Resource Manual* in Microsoft Word and PDF formats
- Pearson Community Website (https://communities.pearson.com /northamerica/s/)
- Goode's *World Atlas*, 23rd Edition
- Mann/Kump, *Dire Predictions: Understanding Climate Change*, 2nd Edition
- *Applied Physical Geography: Geosystems in the Lab*, 10th Edition

Measuring Student Learning Outcomes

All of the MasteringGeography assignable content is tagged to key learning concepts from the book, the National Geography Standards, and Bloom's Taxonomy. You also have the ability to add your own learning outcomes, helping you track student performance against your course goals. You can view class performance against the specified learning outcomes and share those results quickly and easily by exporting to a spreadsheet.

GEOSYSTEMS

AN INTRODUCTION TO PHYSICAL GEOGRAPHY

Tenth Edition

GEOSYSTEMS

AN INTRODUCTION TO PHYSICAL GEOGRAPHY

Tenth Edition

ROBERT W. CHRISTOPHERSON

GINGER H. BIRKELAND

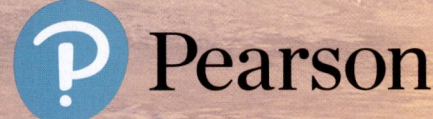

330 Hudson Street, NY, NY 10013

Executive Editor, Geosciences Courseware: Christian Botting
Content Producer: Anton Yakovlev
Courseware Specialist: Jonathan Cheney
Courseware Analyst: Jay McElroy
Editorial Assistant: Emily Bornhop
Courseware Director, Portfolio Management: Beth Wilbur
Courseware Director, Content Development: Ginnie Simione Jutson
Managing Producer, Science: Mike Early
Production Management: Jeanine Furino, Cenveo® Publisher Services
Copyeditor: Kathy Pruno

Compositor: Cenveo® Publisher Services
Design Manager: Mark Ong
Interior/Cover Designer: Preston Thomas
Illustrators: Lachina and International Mapping Associates
Rights & Permissions Manager: Ben Ferrini
Photo Researchers: Kristin Piljay, Danny Meldung
Manufacturing Buyer: Maura Zaldivar-Garcia
Executive Product Marketing Manager: Neena Bali
Senior Field Marketing Manager: Mary Salzman
Associate Media Content Producer: Mia Sullivan
Cover Photo: *Island in Lake Baikal*, by Chalermkiat Seedokmai/Getty Images.

Library of Congress Cataloging-in-Publication Data

Names: Christopherson, Robert W., author. | Birkeland, Ginger H., author.
Title: An introduction to physical geography : geosystems / Robert W. Christopherson, Ginger H. Birkeland.
Description: Tenth edition. | Hoboken, NJ : Pearson, 2017. | Includes index.
Identifiers: LCCN 2016051486| ISBN 9780134597119 (alk. paper) | ISBN 0134597117 (alk. paper)
Subjects: LCSH: Physical geography.
Classification: LCC GB54.5 .C48 2017 | DDC 910/.02--dc23
LC record available at https://lccn.loc.gov/2016051486

1   16

ISBN-10: 0-134-59711-7; ISBN-13: 978-0-134-59711-9

DEDICATION

To the students and teachers of Earth, and to all the children and grandchildren, for it is their future and home planet.

The land still provides our genesis, however we might like to forget that our food comes from dank, muddy Earth, that the oxygen in our lungs was recently inside a leaf, and that every newspaper or book we may pick up is made from the hearts of trees that died for the sake of our imagined lives. What you hold in your hands right now, beneath these words, is consecrated air and time and sunlight.

—Barbara Kingsolver

BRIEF CONTENTS

CONTENTS

I The Energy–Atmosphere System   34

II The Water, Weather, and Climate Systems 152

6 Water and Atmospheric Moisture 154

7 Weather 182

III   The Earth–Atmosphere Interface   314

12 Tectonics, Earthquakes, and Volcanism 348

13 Weathering, Karst Landscapes, and Mass Movement 380

14 River Systems 408

15 Eolian Processes and Arid Landscapes 438

16 Oceans and Coastal Systems 462

17   Glacial Landscapes and the Cryosphere   490

IV   Soils, Ecosystems, and Biomes   520

18   The Geography of Soils   522

MasteringGeography Mobile-Ready Animations & Videos

MasteringGeography Mobile-Ready Animations & Videos

Mobile Field Trip
Introduction to Physical Geography

https://goo.gl/pRdrGU

everydayGEOSYSTEMS & GEOreports

Welcome to the tenth edition of *Geosystems*! This edition features updated content, new active learning activities to engage students, and many new photos and illustrations. We continue to build on the success of the first nine editions, as well as the companion texts, *Elemental Geosystems*, now in its eighth edition; *Geosystems*, *Canadian Edition*, fourth edition; and the newest *Geosystems Core*, first edition. Students and teachers appreciate the systems organization, integration of figures and text, and overall relevance to what is happening to Earth systems in real time. *Geosystems* continues to tell Earth's story in student-friendly language.

New to the Tenth Edition

Nearly every page of *Geosystems*, tenth edition, presents new content in text and figures, and new features. Significant content changes include:

- **Chapter 4, Atmospheric Energy and Global Temperatures:** We consolidated content from Chapters 4 and 5 in previous editions into a new chapter. The discussion of atmospheric and surface energy balances now leads into the material on global temperatures, with improved connections between the two topics.
- **Chapter 6, Water and Atmospheric Moisture:** We updated, reorganized, and clarified content and added a new section on precipitation processes.
- **Chapter 15, Eolian Processes and Arid Landscapes:** We restored our coverage of wind processes and desert landscapes as a stand-alone chapter, with updated and expanded coverage from previous editions.
- **Chapter 10, Climate Change:** This edition features extensive updates to our stand-alone chapter on climate change, offering an overview of climate change science. The chapter explores paleoclimatology, climate feedbacks, evidence and causes of present climate change, climate models and projections, and steps we can take to moderate Earth's changing climate.
- **Mobile Field Trip Videos** have students accompany acclaimed photographer and pilot Michael Collier in the air and on the ground to explore iconic landscapes of North America and beyond. Readers scan Quick Response (QR) links in the book to access the 20 videos as they read. Also available within MasteringGeography.
- **Project Condor Quadcopter Videos**, linked via QR codes, take students out into the field through narrated quadcopter footage, exploring the physical processes that have helped shape North American landscapes. Readers scan Quick Response (QR) links in the book to access the 10 videos as they read. Also available within MasteringGeography.

- **New systems diagrams** on all chapter-opener pages emphasize the inputs, actions, outputs, and human–Earth connections relevant to each chapter. These chapter-specific diagrams expand on the systems diagrams on part-opener pages that remain a hallmark of this text.
- **New and revised illustrations and maps** improve student learning in every chapter. More than 250 new photos and images bring real-world scenes into the classroom.

Also new to the tenth edition are features that help students relate physical geography topics to the real world and apply concepts as they learn.

- A new *Everyday Geosystems* feature at the beginning of each chapter invites students to explore the "why" and "how" application of physical geography concepts to everyday phenomena. Example topics are:

  - *How much water is needed to produce the food I eat?* (Chapter 8)
  - *What kind of damage occurs when a river floods?* (Chapter 14)
  - *Have you noticed fewer bees in your neighborhood?* (Chapter 19)

- New *Work It Out* activities in each chapter give students a chance to practice basic conceptual or quantitative reasoning. Integrated into appropriate sections of each chapter, these activities give students the opportunity to demonstrate understanding of learned concepts and practice critical thinking as they read.
- New *Geospatial Analysis* exercises at the end of each chapter are summative mini-lab activities, sending students outside of the book to access and explore online science tools and data sets from sources such as NASA, USGS, and NOAA, to perform critical geospatial data analysis.
- New *Apply Concepts* features, part of the text's hallmark Focus Studies, are active learning tasks that compel students to reflect on the information they have learned and perform short activities.
- New *Questions to Consider* within the *Human Denominator* feature in each chapter ask students to interpret graphs and maps in the feature and connect information to topics within the chapter.

Hallmark Features and Content Updates

- Twenty **Focus Studies**, with either updated or new content, explore relevant applied topics in greater depth and are a popular feature of the *Geosystems* texts. These features are grouped by topic into categories: Pollution, Sustainable Resources, Environmental Extremes,

Climate Change, Natural Hazards, and Environmental Restoration. Eleven new Focus Study topics include:

- Forms of Energy (Chapter 1)
- Geographic Information Systems (Chapter 1)
- Summer Fog Protects the World's Tallest Trees (Chapter 6)
- The 2015 Northern Hemisphere Tropical Cyclone Season (Chapter 7)
- Melting Permafrost Releases Greenhouse Gases in the Arctic (Chapter 10)
- Human-caused Earthquakes on the Increase (Chapter 12)
- Is Summer Heat a Trigger for Yosemite Rockfalls? (Chapter 13)
- Petra, Jordan—Human Impacts on an Ancient City in an Arid Land (Chapter 15)
- Sand Dunes Protect Coastlines during Superstorm Sandy (Chapter 16)
- Greenland and Antarctica: Melting at the Edges of the Continental Ice (Chapter 17)
- The 1930s Dust Bowl: Regional-Scale Soil Erosion (Chapter 18)

- The chapter-opening **Geosystems Now** features present brief original case studies and current issues in geography and Earth systems science. The 20 new *Geosystems Now* topics in the tenth edition include citizen science in the 21st century (Chapter 1), storm chasing (Chapter 7), the U.S. Pacific Northwest earthquake hazard (Chapter 12), and coral reefs in decline (Chapter 16). Many of these features emphasize linkages across Earth systems, exemplifying the Geosystems approach.
- **Geosystems In Action** features focus on key topics, processes, systems, or human–Earth connections. In every chapter, these features offer a one- to two-page highly visual presentation of a topic central to the chapter, with active learning questions and links to media in *MasteringGeography*, as well as a GeoQuiz to aid student learning. The feature is updated and streamlined from the past edition and includes two new topics: atmospheric temperature (Chapter 3) and precipitation processes (Chapter 6).
- **The Human Denominator** feature at the end of every chapter links chapter topics to human examples and applications. The feature includes updated maps, photos, graphs, and other diagrams to provide visual examples of many human–Earth interactions. In this edition, all Human Denominators end with two new *Questions to Consider*.
- **GeoReports** continue to describe timely and relevant events related to the discussion in the chapter, and offer new sources of information and citizen science opportunities. Example topics from the more than 40 *GeoReports* in this edition include:

- Crowdsourcing precipitation with the free MPING app (Chapter 6)
- Citizen science using satellite imagery to assess tropical cyclones (Chapter 7)

- A luxury cruise ship crosses the Northern Passage (Chapter 17)
- Rising sea level causes the first mammal extinction (Chapter 19)

- **Key Learning Concepts** appear at the outset of each chapter, helping students prioritize chapter learning objectives. Each chapter concludes with the *Key Learning Concepts Review*, which summarizes the chapter using the opening objectives.
- *Geosystems* continues to embed URLs within the text, linking to original science sources. More than 60 appear in this edition. These allow students to pursue topics of interest to greater depth, or to obtain the latest information about weather and climate, tectonic events, or floods
- The book is supported by MasteringGeography™, the most widely used and effective online homework, tutorial, and assessment system with resources for before, during, and after class. Assignable media and activities include Geoscience Animations, videos, *Mobile Field Trip* videos, *Project Condor* Quadcopter videos, *Encounter Physical Geography* Google Earth™ explorations, GIS-inspired MapMaster™ interactive maps, Hazard City context-rich problems, GeoTutor coaching activities on the toughest topics in geography, end-of-chapter questions and exercises, reading quizzes, and Test Bank questions. Students have access to *Dynamic Study Modules* that provide each student with a customized learning experience. Students also have access to a text-specific Study Area with study resources, including a Pearson eText version of *Geosystems*—all at www.masteringgeography.com.
- *Learning Catalytics*, a "bring your own device" student engagement, assessment, and classroom intelligence system, is integrated with *MasteringGeography*.

Author Acknowledgments

After all these years, the strength of a publishing team remains ever essential. Continuing thanks to President Paul Corey for his leadership since 1990 and to Beth Wilbur, Senior Vice-President and Editorial Director for Geosciences, for her vision. Thanks to Executive Geosciences Editor Christian Botting for his guidance and for the attention devoted to the *Geosystems* texts and to his newest edition, a son, Lucas Lockwood Botting. Thanks to Content Producer Anton Yakovlev and Editorial Assistant Emily Bornhop for their careful attention. We offer special thanks to development editors Jonathan Cheney and Jay McElroy for advice and suggestions that improved many aspects of this edition.

Our appreciation to designers Preston Thomas and Mark Ong for such skill in a complex book design. Thanks to Marketing Managers Neena Bali and Mary Salzman, and the many publisher representatives who spend months in the field communicating the *Geosystems* approach. Our gratitude is extended to the entire "*Geosystems* Team" for allowing us to participate in the publishing process.

Our sincere appreciation for production coordination goes to Editorial Director for Higher Education Cindy Miller of Cenveo LLC for the sustaining care through nine books and to Jeanine Furino, our Cenveo production manager, for her ability to oversee manuscript, copy editing, complex compositing, and page proofs. With so many changes in this edition, her skills make it work. To photo researchers Kristin Piljay and Danny Meldung, copy editor Jane Loftus, proofreader Denne Wesolowski, and indexer Pam Reigeluth we give thanks for quality work. Our appreciation also goes to Redina Herman, who contributed the *Geospatial Analysis* activities for this edition as well as the second Chapter 1 Focus Study. Thanks to all the colleagues who served as reviewers on one or more editions of each book or who offered helpful suggestions in conversations at our national and regional geography meetings. Thanks to the accuracy reviewers of all tenth edition chapters: Todd Fagin, *Oklahoma University*, and Ricardo Nogueira, *Georgia State University*. Thanks also to Todd Fagin for authoring the Test Bank for this edition and to Charlie Thomsen, *American River College*, for authoring the *Instructor Resource Manual*, the Lecture PowerPoints, and the Clicker questions.

We are grateful for the generosity of ideas and sacrifice of time. Thanks to all reviewers who have provided valuable feedback on *Geosystems* over the years:

Jason Allard, *Valdosta State University*
Michael Allen, *Kent State University*
Philip P. Allen, *Frostburg State University*
Ted J. Alsop, *Utah State University*
Nathaniel Amador, *Ohio Wesleyan University*
Ward Barrett, *University of Minnesota*
Steve Bass, *Mesa Community College*
Stefan Becker, *University of Wisconsin–Oshkosh*
Daniel Bedford, *Weber State University*
Bradley Bereitschaft, *University of Nebraska—Omaha*
David Berner, *Normandale Community College*
Trent Biggs, *San Diego State University*
Franco Biondi, *University of Nevada, Reno*
Peter D. Blanken, *University of Colorado, Boulder*
Patricia Boudinot, *George Mason University*
Anthony Brazel, *Arizona State University*
David R. Butler, *Southwest Texas State University*
Mary-Louise Byrne, *Wilfred Laurier University*
Janet Cakir, *Rappahannock Community College*
Ian A. Campbell, *University of Alberta–Edmonton*
Randall S. Cerveny, *Arizona State University*
Fred Chambers, *University of Colorado, Boulder*
Philip Chaney, *Auburn University*
Muncel Chang, *Butte College* Emeritus
Jordan Clayton, *Georgia State University*
Andrew Comrie, *University of Arizona*
C. Mark Cowell, *Indiana State University*
Richard A. Crooker, *Kutztown University*
Stephen Cunha, *Humboldt State University*
Armando M. da Silva, *Towson State University*
Dennis Dahms, *University of Northern Iowa*
J. Michael Daniels, *University of Denver*
Shawna Dark, *California State University, Northridge*
Stephanie Day, *University of Kansas*
Dirk H. de Boer, *University of Saskatchewan*
Lisa DeChano-Cook, *Western Michigan University*

Mario P. Delisio, *Boise State University*
Joseph R. Desloges, *University of Toronto*
Lee R. Dexter, *Northern Arizona University*
Vicki Drake, *Santa Monica College*
Don W. Duckson, Jr., *Frostburg State University*
Daniel Dugas, *New Mexico State University*
Anthony Dzik, *Shawnee State University*
Kathryn Early, *Metropolitan State College*
Christopher H. Exline, *University of Nevada–Reno*
Todd Fagin, *Oklahoma University*
Michael M. Folsom, *Eastern Washington University*
Mark Francek, *Central Michigan University*
Glen Fredlund, *University of Wisconsin–Milwaukee*
Dorothy Friedel, *Sonoma State University*
William Garcia, *University of N. Carolina–Charlotte*
Doug Goodin, *Kansas State University*
Mark Goodman, *Grossmont College*
David E. Greenland, *University of N. Carolina–Chapel Hill*
Duane Griffin, *Bucknell University*
Barry N. Haack, *George Mason University*
Roy Haggerty, *Oregon State University*
John W. Hall, *Louisiana State University–Shreveport*
Vern Harnapp, *University of Akron*
John Harrington, *Kansas State University*
Blake Harrison, *Southern Connecticut University*
Jason "Jake" Haugland, *University of Colorado, Boulder*
James Hayes, *University of Nebraska—Omaha*
Gail Hobbs, *Pierce College*
Thomas W. Holder, *University of Georgia*
David H. Holt, *University of Southern Mississippi*
Robert Hordon, *Rutgers University*
David A. Howarth, *University of Louisville*
Patricia G. Humbertson, *Youngstown State University*
David W. Icenogle, *Auburn University*
Philip L. Jackson, *Oregon State University*
J. Peter Johnson, Jr., *Carleton University*
Gabrielle Katz, *Appalachian State University*
Guy King, *California State University–Chico*
David Kitchen, *University of Richmond*
Ronald G. Knapp, *SUNY–The College at New Paltz*
Peter W. Knightes, *Central Texas College*
Jean Kowal, *University of Wisconsin – Whitewater*
Thomas Krabacher, *California State University–Sacramento*
Hsiang-te Kung, *University of Memphis*
Richard Kurzhals, *Grand Rapids Junior College*
Kara Kuvakas, *Hartnell College*
Steve Ladochy, *California State University, Los Angeles*
Charles W. Lafon, *Texas A & M University*
Paul R. Larson, *Southern Utah University*
Robert D. Larson, *Southwest Texas State University*
Derek Law, *University of Kentucky*
Elena Lioubimtseva, *Grand Valley State University*
Joyce Lundberg, *Carleton University*
Scott Mandia, *Suffolk County Community College, Long Island*
W. Andrew Marcus, *Montana State University*
Giraldo Mario, *California State University, Northridge*
Brian Mark, *Ohio State University*

Nadine Martin, *University of Arizona*
Elliot G. McIntire, *California State University, Northridge*
Norman Meek, *California State University, San Bernardino*
Leigh W. Mintz, *California State University–Hayward*, Emeritus
Sherry Morea-Oaks, Boulder, CO
Debra Morimoto, *Merced College*
Patrick Moss, *University of Wisconsin – Madison*
Steven Namikas, *Louisiana State University*
Lawrence C. Nkemdirim, *University of Calgary*
Ricardo Noguaira, *Georgia State University*
Sherry Oaks, Front Range Community College—Westminster
Andrew Oliphant, *San Francisco State University*
John E. Oliver, *Indiana State University*
Bradley M. Opdyke, *Michigan State University*
Richard L. Orndorff, *University of Nevada, Las Vegas*
FeiFei Pan, *University of North Texas*
Patrick Pease, *East Carolina University*
James Penn, *Southeastern Louisiana University*
Rachel Pinker, *University of Maryland, College Park*
Greg Pope, *Montclair State University*
Robin J. Rapai, *University of North Dakota*
Philip Reeder, *University of South Florida*
Philip D. Renner, *American River College*
William C. Rense, *Shippensburg University*
Leslie Rigg, *Northern Illinois University*
Dar Roberts, *University of California–Santa Barbara*
Wolf Roder, *University of Cincinnati*
Robert Rohli, *Louisiana State University*
Bill Russell, *L.A. Pierce College*
Dorothy Sack, *Ohio University*
Erinanne Saffell, *Arizona State University*
Randall Schaetzl, *Michigan State University*
Glenn R. Sebastian, *University of South Alabama*
Daniel A. Selwa, *U.S.C. Coastal Carolina College*
Debra Sharkey, *Cosumnes River College*
Marshall Shepherd, *University of Georgia*
Peter Siska, *Austin Peay State University*
Lee Slater, *Rutgers University*
Thomas W. Small, *Frostburg State University*
Daniel J. Smith, *University of Victoria*
Richard W. Smith, *Hartford Community College*
Stephen J. Stadler, *Oklahoma State University*
Michael Talbot, *Pima Community College*
Paul E. Todhunter, *University of North Dakota*
Susanna T.Y. Tong, *University of Cincinnati*
Liem Tran, *Florida Atlantic University*
Suzanne Traub-Metlay, *Front Range Community College*
Jill Trepanier, *Louisiana State University*
Alice V. Turkington, *The University of Kentucky*
Jon Van de Grift, *Metropolitan State College*
David Weide, *University of Nevada–Las Vegas*
Forrest Wilkerson, *Minnesota State University, Mankato*
Thomas B. Williams, *Western Illinois University*
Brenton M. Yarnal, *Pennsylvania State University*
Catherine H. Yansa, *Michigan State University*
Keith Yearwood, *Georgia State University*
Stephen R. Yool, *University of Arizona*
Kenneth Young, *University of Texas—Austin*
Don Yow, *Eastern Kentucky University*
Susy Svatek Ziegler, *University of Minnesota*

From Robert: The tenth edition marks the 25th anniversary since the first edition in 1992. I thank my family for believing in this work, and especially the next generation: Chavon, Bryce, Payton, Brock, Trevor, Blake, Chase, Téyenna, and Cade. When I look into our grandchildren's faces, I see the reason we work toward a sustainable future.

I give special gratitude to all the students during my 30 years teaching at American River College, for it is in the classroom crucible that the *Geosystems* books were forged. Special continued thanks to Charlie Thomsen for his creative work and collaboration on *Encounter Geosystems*, the *Applied Physical Geography* lab manual, work on *MasteringGeography* media and assessments, and ancillaries, and the new *Geosystems Core* text, with Stephen Cunha. I offer a special thanks to Ginger Birkeland, Ph.D., my continuing coauthor on the *Geosystems* texts, for her essential work, attention to detail, and original thinking. Ginger understands the *Geosystems* approach as a different way to teach physical geography and influenced the power of this tenth edition from our first preplanning meetings. She has worked as a river guide operating boats on the Colorado River, and I feel her at the helm of *Geosystems*! I believe the future of the *Geosystems* franchise looks bright.

As you read this book, you will learn from many content-specific photographs made by my wife, photographer, and expedition partner, Bobbé Christopherson. Bobbé is my colleague, wife, and best friend.

From Ginger: Many thanks to my husband, Karl Birkeland, and my daughters, Erika and Kelsey, for their ongoing patience, support, and inspiration. Special thanks to Robert Christopherson for inviting and supporting me on this *Geosystems* journey. I hope our raft runs smoothly and stays upright on the voyage ahead!

From us both: We thank the many authors and scientists who published research that enriches this work. Thanks for all the dialogue received from students and teachers shared through e-mails from across the globe.

Physical geography teaches us a holistic view of the intricate supporting web that is Earth's environment and our place in it. Dramatic global change is underway in human–Earth relations as we alter physical, chemical, and biological systems. Our attention to climate change science and applied topics is in response to the impacts we are experiencing and the future we are shaping. All things considered, this is a critical time for you to be enrolled in a physical geography course! The best to you in your studies—and ***carpe diem!***

Robert W. Christopherson
Roseville, CA
E-mail: bobobbe@aol.com

Ginger H. Birkeland
Bozeman, Montana

About Our **Sustainability Initiatives**

Pearson recognizes the environmental challenges facing this planet, as well as acknowledges our responsibility in making a difference. This book is carefully crafted to minimize environmental impact. The binding, cover, and paper come from facilities that minimize waste, energy consumption, and the use of harmful chemicals. Pearson closes the loop by recycling every out-of-date text returned to our warehouse. Along with developing and exploring digital solutions to our market's needs, Pearson has a strong commitment to achieving carbon-neutrality. As of 2009, Pearson became the first carbon- and climate-neutral publishing company, having reduced our absolute carbon footprint by 22% since then. Pearson has protected over 1,000 hectares of land in Columbia, Costa Rica, the United States, the UK and Canada. In 2015, Pearson formally adopted The Global Goals for Sustainable Development, sponsoring an event at the United Nations General Assembly and other ongoing initiatives. Pearson sources 100% of the electricity we use from green power and invests in renewable energy resources in multiple cities where we have operations, helping make them more sustainable and limiting our environmental impact for local communities. The future holds great promise for reducing our impact on Earth's environment, and Pearson is proud to be leading the way. We strive to publish the best books with the most up-to-date and accurate content, and to do so in ways that minimize our impact on Earth. To learn more about our initiatives, please visit https://www.pearson.com/sustainability.html.

For Students & Teachers

MasteringGeography™ *with Pearson eText.* The *Mastering* platform is the most widely used and effective online homework, tutorial, and assessment system with resources for before, during, and after class. It delivers self-paced tutorials that provide individualized coaching, focus on course objectives, and are responsive to each student's progress. The *Mastering* system helps teachers maximize class time with customizable, easy-to-assign, and automatically graded assessments that motivate students to learn outside of class and arrive prepared for lecture. MasteringGeography™ offers:

- **Assignable activities** that include GIS-inspired Map-Master™ interactive map activities, *Encounter* Google Earth™ Explorations, video activities, *Mobile Field Trips, Project Condor* Quadcopter videos, Geoscience Animation activities, map projections activities, Hazard City context-rich problems, GeoTutor coaching activities on the toughest topics in geography, Dynamic Study Modules that provide each student with a customized learning experience, end-of-chapter questions and exercises, reading quizzes, *Test Bank* questions, and more.
- **A student Study Area** with MapMaster™ interactive maps, videos, *Mobile Field Trips, Project Condor* Quadcopter videos, Geoscience Animations, web links, glossary flashcards, "In the News" articles, chapter quizzes, PDF downloads of regional outline maps, an optional Pearson eText and more.

Pearson eText gives students access to the text whenever and wherever they can access the Internet. Features of Pearson eText include:

- Now available on smartphones and tablets.
- Seamlessly integrated videos and other rich media.
- Fully accessible (screen-reader ready).
- Configurable reading settings, including resizable type and night reading mode.
- Instructor and student note-taking, highlighting, bookmarking, and search. **www.masteringgeography.com**

Television for the Environment Earth Report Geography Videos, DVD (0321662989). This three-DVD set helps students visualize how human decisions and behavior have affected the environment and how individuals are taking steps toward recovery. With topics ranging from the poor land management promoting the devastation of river systems in Central America to the struggles for electricity in China and Africa, these 13 videos from Television for the Environment's global *Earth Report* series recognize the efforts of individuals around the world to unite and protect the planet.

Geoscience Animation Library, 5th edition, DVD (0321716841). Created through a unique collaboration among Pearson's leading geoscience authors, this resource offers over 100 animations covering the most difficult-to-visualize topics in physical geography, meteorology, earth science, physical geology, and oceanography.

Practicing Geography: Careers for Enhancing Society and the Environment by Association of American Geographers (0321811151). This book examines career opportunities for geographers and geospatial professionals in the business, government, nonprofit, and education sectors. A diverse group of academic and industry professionals shares insights on career planning, networking, transitioning between employment sectors, and balancing work and home life.

Teaching College Geography: A Practical Guide for Graduate Students and Early Career Faculty by Association of American Geographers (0136054471). This two-part resource provides a starting point for becoming an effective geography teacher from the very first day of class. Part One addresses "nuts-and-bolts" teaching issues. Part Two explores being an effective teacher in the field, supporting critical thinking with GIS and mapping technologies, engaging learners in large geography classes, and promoting awareness of international perspectives and geographic issues.

Aspiring Academics: A Resource Book for Graduate Students and Early Career Faculty by Association of American Geographers (0136048919). Drawing on several years of research, this set of essays is designed to help graduate students and early career faculty start their careers in geography and related social and environmental sciences.

Hazard City for MasteringGeography (0321970349) is a collection of eleven online problem-solving assignments that demonstrate the work of practicing geoscientists and environmental professionals. The activities allow the student to step into the role of a practicing geoscientist to analyze potential disasters in the fictional town of *Hazard City*. Students learn to research and explore on their own in areas such as Map Reading, Ground Water Contamination, Volcanic Hazard Assessment, Earthquake Damage Assessment, Shoreline Property Assessment, and much more. **www.masteringgeography.com**

For Students

Applied Physical Geography—Geosystems in the Laboratory, **Tenth Edition** by Charlie Thomsen and Robert Christopherson (0134686365). A variety of exercises provides flexibility in lab assignments. Each exercise includes key terms and learning concepts linked to *Geosystems*. The Tenth Edition includes exercises on climate change, soils, and rock identification, a fully updated exercise on basic GIS using ArcGIS online, and more integrated media, including Google Earth™ and Quick Response (QR) codes linking to Pre-Lab videos. Supported with online worksheets as well as KMZ files for all of the Google Earth™ exercises found in the lab manual.

Goode's World Atlas, 23rd Edition (0133864642). First published by Rand McNally in 1923, *Goode's World Atlas* is the gold standard for college reference atlases. It features hundreds of physical, political, and thematic maps, graphs, and tables, as well as a comprehensive pronouncing index. The 23rd Edition introduces dozens of new maps, incorporating the latest geographic scholarship and technologies, with expanded coverage of the Canadian Arctic, Europe's microstates, Africa's island states, and U.S. cities. It introduces several new thematic maps on critical topics such as: oceanic environments, earthquakes and tsunamis, desertification vulnerability, maritime political claims, megacities, human trafficking, labor migration . . . and many other topics important to contemporary geography. Available in eText formats from Pearson.

Pearson's Encounter Series provides rich, interactive explorations of geoscience concepts through Google Earth™ activities. For those who do not use *MasteringGeography*™, all chapter explorations are available in print workbooks, as well as in online quizzes at **www.mygeoscienceplace.com**. Each exploration consists of a worksheet, online quizzes whose results can be emailed to teachers, and a corresponding Google Earth™ KMZ file.

- *Encounter Physical Geography* by Jess C. Porter and Stephen O'Connell (0321672526)
- *Encounter World Regional Geography* by Jess C. Porter (0321681754)
- *Encounter Human Geography* by Jess C. Porter (0321682203)

Dire Predictions: Understanding Global Climate Change 2nd Edition by Michael Mann, Lee R. Kump (0133909778). Periodic reports from the Intergovernmental Panel on Climate Change (IPCC) evaluate the risk of climate change brought on by humans. In just over 200 pages, this practical text presents and expands upon the essential findings of the IPCC in a visually stunning and undeniably powerful way to the lay reader. Scientific findings that provide validity to the implications of climate change are presented in clear-cut graphic elements, striking images, and understandable analogies. The Second Edition covers the latest climate change data and scientific consensus from the IPCC *Fifth Assessment Report* and integrates mobile media links to online media. The text is also available in various eText formats, including an eText upgrade option from Mastering-Geography courses.

For Teachers

Learning Catalytics is a "bring your own device" student engagement, assessment, and classroom intelligence system. With Learning Catalytics, you can:

- Assess students in real time, using open-ended tasks to probe student understanding.
- Understand immediately where students are and adjust your lecture accordingly.
- Improve your students' critical-thinking skills.
- Access rich analytics to understand student performance.
- Add your own questions to make Learning Catalytics fit your course exactly.
- Manage student interactions with intelligent grouping and timing.

Learning Catalytics is a technology that has grown out of twenty years of cutting-edge research, innovation, and implementation of interactive teaching and peer instruction. Available integrated with *MasteringGeography*™.

Instructor Resource Manual (Download) by Charlie Thomsen (0134700244). The manual includes lecture outlines and key terms, additional source materials, teaching tips, and a complete annotation of chapter review questions. Available from **www.pearsonhighered.com/irc** and in the Instructor Resources area of *MasteringGeography*™.

TestGen® Test Bank (Download) by Todd Fagin (013470021X). TestGen® is a computerized test generator that lets you view and edit *Test Bank* questions, transfer questions to tests, and print tests in a variety of customized formats. This *Test Bank* includes around 3,000 multiple-choice and short answer/essay questions. All questions are correlated against the National Geography Standards, textbook key learning concepts, and Bloom's Taxonomy. The *Test Bank* is also available in Microsoft Word® and importable into Blackboard. Available from **www.pearsonhighered.com/irc** and in the Instructor Resources area of *MasteringGeography*™.

Instructor Resource Materials (Download) (0134700252). The *Instructor Resource Materials* provide a collection of resources to help teachers make efficient and effective use of their time. All digital resources can be found in one well-organized, easy-to-access place. The IRM includes:

- All textbook images as JPEGs, and PowerPoint™ Presentations
- Pre-authored Lecture Outline PowerPoint® Presentations which outline the concepts of each chapter with embedded art and can be customized to fit teachers' lecture requirements
- CRS "Clicker" Questions in PowerPoint™
- The TestGen software, *Test Bank* questions, and electronic files of the *Instructor Resource Manual* and *Test Bank*

This *Instructor Resource* content is also available online via the Instructor Resources section of *MasteringGeography*™ and **www.pearsonhighered.com/irc**.

1

Essentials of Geography

Queenstown, New Zealand

Queenstown, New Zealand, is known for snowsports, rafting, fishing, mountain biking, and boating on Lake Wakatipu, the country's longest lake. The city is also the tourist gateway to the glacial landscapes of the Southern Lakes region of the South Island.
[Beerpix/Getty Images.]

KEY**LEARNING**concepts

After reading the chapter, you should be able to:

- **Define** geography and physical geography, and **describe** spatial analysis.
- **Summarize** the scientific process and **discuss** human population growth as it relates to geographic science.
- **Describe** open and closed systems, feedback, and equilibrium concepts as they relate to Earth systems.
- **Explain** Earth's shape and reference grid: latitude, longitude, latitudinal geographic zones, and time zones.
- **Define** cartography and mapping basics: map scale and map projections.
- **Describe** three geoscience tools—the Global Positioning System (GPS), remote sensing, and geographic information systems (GIS)—and **explain** how these tools are used in geographic analysis.

A Geosystems schematic diagram appears in this space in all subsequent chapters. The content of each chapter is laid out as a system to demonstrate chapter organization. The Geosystems approach studies content in this sequence:

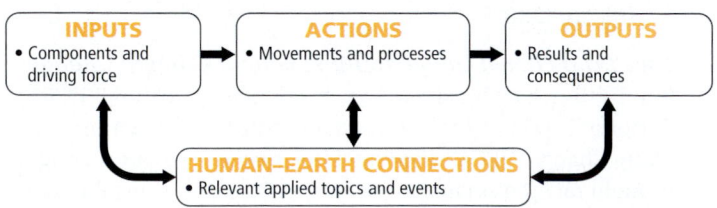

INPUTS
- Components and driving force

ACTIONS
- Movements and processes

OUTPUTS
- Results and consequences

HUMAN–EARTH CONNECTIONS
- Relevant applied topics and events

Citizen Science in the 21st Century

Is weather your go-to conversation starter when an awkward silence sets in? Would you be interested in expanding your inventory of weather small talk by observing and reporting weather in your own backyard? If the answer is yes, then you won't be alone. In one national effort, the *Community Collaborative Rain, Hail, and Snow Network* (CoCoRaHS), about 20,000 volunteers post daily rain and snow amounts, measured in their own yard, to http://www.cocorahs.org (**Figure GN 1.1**). Volunteers are everyday citizens with a range of age and experience, from elementary students to retirees. The result of this grassroots effort, part of a growing movement called citizen science, is a vast precipitation database used for education, research, and natural resource management.

What Is Citizen Science? *Citizen science* is the practice of using public participation for scientific data collection and monitoring. It is a form of *crowdsourcing* because it uses small contributions from a large number of people. CoCoRaHS, like many other organized efforts, offers training through its interactive website. The necessary equipment—for example, precipitation gauges and hail pads—is simple and inexpensive. Volunteers record their measurements on data sheets and submit them online, then turn in equipment such as used hail pads at the nearest CoCoRaHS office.

Citizen science occurs over a wide-ranging spatial scale. CoCoRaHS, for example, is a national network of precipitation data. The effort began in 1998 in Fort Collins, Colorado, a year after a flood killed five people and caused $200 million in damage—the city's worst natural disaster. *BioBlitz*, an international effort focusing on biodiversity, is an example of a community project. The goal of BioBlitz is for volunteers to find and identify as many species as possible in a specific area over a short time period (**Figures GN 1.2 and 1.3**).

Public participation in scientific research is not new. For example, community wildlife surveys began well over 100 years ago. However, in the last decade or so, citizen science has greatly expanded with advances in technology, in particular the prevalence of smartphones that allow easy and convenient online information sharing. Smartphones have built-in GPS receivers that enable real-time location, essential for reporting species sightings and weather observations. (We discuss the Global Positioning System in this chapter.) Evolving technology may soon add air quality and temperature sensors to mobile devices, expanding citizen science possibilities.

Citizen Science and Geosystems One of the strengths of citizen science is the production of a large dataset that allows for spatial analysis, the study of phenomena across spaces, areas, and locations—issues at the heart of geographic science. In Chapter 1 we present the framework for our study of Earth systems and physical geography: spatial concepts, the scientific process, human–Earth connections, Earth systems thinking, and geographic tools. Throughout *Geosystems*, we look at citizen science news and opportunities (check the GeoReports in each chapter).

1. What types of Earth systems science interest you?

2. As you read the chapter, make a list of physical geography topics you might like to investigate as a citizen scientist volunteer.

DAILY PRECIPITATION (inches)

- 2.78–3.09
- 1.85–2.77
- 0.77–1.84
- 0.31–0.76
- 0.16–0.30
- 0.01–0.15
- Trace
- 0.00

▲Figure GN 1.1 **Map of precipitation reported to CoCoRaHS on April 11, 2016.** [www.cocorahs.org]

◄Figure GN 1.2 **Inventory of insects.** Volunteers inventory insects at Lily Lake in Rocky Mountain National Park, Colorado, as part of a national Park Service BioBlitz in 2012. [Karine Aigner/NPS]

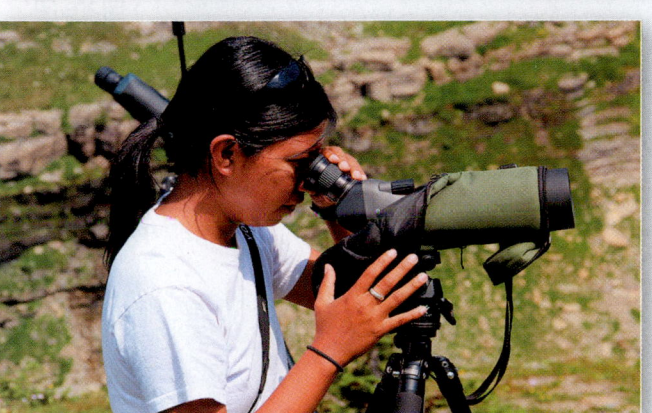

◄Figure GN 1.3 **Citizen scientist looks for mountain goats, Glacier National Park, Montana, gathering data for a species count.** [Melissa Sladek/NPS.]

Welcome to *Geosystems* and the study of physical geography! In this text, we examine Earth's natural environments, including their living and nonliving elements, the processes that shape them, and their connections to human societies. Physical geography studies environments across and within landscapes, including processes in the atmosphere, at Earth's surface, and within living ecosystems. Throughout *Geosystems*, we emphasize the study of Earth *systems*, the interconnected parts that make up the whole. In the 21st century, as our natural world changes with the growing influence of humans, the scientific study of physical geography and Earth systems is more exciting and relevant than ever.

Think back to some recent events in the news, for example, a flood in the U.S. Midwest, a tropical storm in the Pacific or hitting the U.S. Southeast coast, or dangerous air pollution in China. What processes caused these events and how did they impact human lives? Why do these processes occur in some places and not others? These questions, typical for physical geographers, are *spatial* in nature, meaning that they seek to understand physical processes across spaces, locations, and regions (Figure 1.1). Such questions encompass the connections between humans and their environment, from the air we breathe to the water we drink to the soils we plant with crops to the natural disasters that take human lives.

Consider these specific examples and the question they raise for the study of physical geography and Earth systems. This text provides tools for answering these questions and understanding the underlying issues.

- In April 2015, a magnitude 7.8 earthquake devastated the small Himalayan nation of Nepal, causing more than 8800 deaths and 18,000 injuries. Why do earthquakes occur in particular locations across the globe?
- In 2014, the U.S. National Park Service finished the deconstruction of two dams on the Elwha River in Washington—the largest dam removals in the world to date. The project has restored a free-flowing river for fisheries and associated ecosystems. How do dams change river environments? Can other rivers be restored with dam removal?
- In 2016, carbon dioxide—the primary greenhouse gas emitted by human activities such as the burning of fossil fuels—reached its highest concentrations in Earth's atmosphere in over 800,000 years, and continues to rise. What is the role of this gas in our atmosphere, and how will rising concentrations affect life on Earth?
- During the winter of 2014–2015, the city of Boston, Massachusetts, received over 110 inches of snow—their highest yearly snowfall since record-keeping began in the 1800s. This snow accumulation occurred

everyday GEOSYSTEMS

Where and how far do pollutants move in the atmosphere?

Pollutants are carried by winds, affecting human health and living ecosystems over a wide region. Smoke and particulates, emerging from the smokestack at right, are by-products of burning coal to produce power. Water vapor, emerging from the towers at left, is another by-product that combines with pollutants to form acid precipitation. Carbon dioxide gas from fossil fuel burning traps heat in the atmosphere near Earth's surface, contributing to climate change. Physical geographers analyze air pollution and other environmental issues with a spatial focus on movement, distribution, and pattern, emphasizing human–Earth relationships.

Mobile Field Trip (MG)
Introduction to Physical Geography

https://goo.gl/pRdrGU

◀Figure 1.1 **Geography's spatial view.** Smoke and water vapor enter the air at the Bruce Mansfield Power Station near Shippingport, Pennsylvania. [Clarence Holmes Photography/Alamy.]

during the two warmest years on record for global temperature. What atmospheric processes explain the formation of winter storms? Why did heavy snow occur in the U.S. Northeast during a year when record high air temperatures occurred across the globe?

Perhaps more than any other issue, climate change has become an overriding focus of the study of Earth systems. Rising atmospheric concentrations of carbon dioxide and other greenhouse gases are changing Earth's energy balance and are linked to increasing global temperatures. Rising air and ocean temperatures affect the entire planet, from the poles to the equator. As a result, Arctic sea ice is declining and the Greenland and Antarctic Ice Sheets are melting at accelerating rates. Sea level is rising, affecting human populations living in coastal regions. Globally, intense weather events, droughts, and flooding continue to increase. In presenting the state of the planet, *Geosystems* surveys climate change evidence and considers its implications. How can your actions make a difference? In every chapter, we present up-to-date science and information to help you understand our dynamic Earth systems. Welcome to an exploration of physical geography!

The Science of Geography

Geographic science is concerned with much more than place names. **Geography** (from *geo*, "Earth," and *graphein*, "to write") is the science that studies the relationships among natural systems, geographic areas, human culture, and the interdependence of all of these, *over space*. These last two words are important, for geography is a science that is in part defined by its method—analyzing phenomena in relation to space.

In geography, the term *spatial* refers to the nature and character of physical space and the distribution of things within it. The unifying method of geography is **spatial analysis**, the view of phenomena as occurring across space. The language of geography—territory, zone, pattern, distribution, place, location, region, sphere, province, and distance—reflects this spatial view.

Given this spatial perspective, geographic teaching and research has traditionally been divided into five themes: **Location**, **place**, **movement**, **region**, and **human–Earth relationships**, with examples illustrated and defined in **Figure 1.2**. These themes provide a framework for understanding geographic concepts and asking geographic questions.

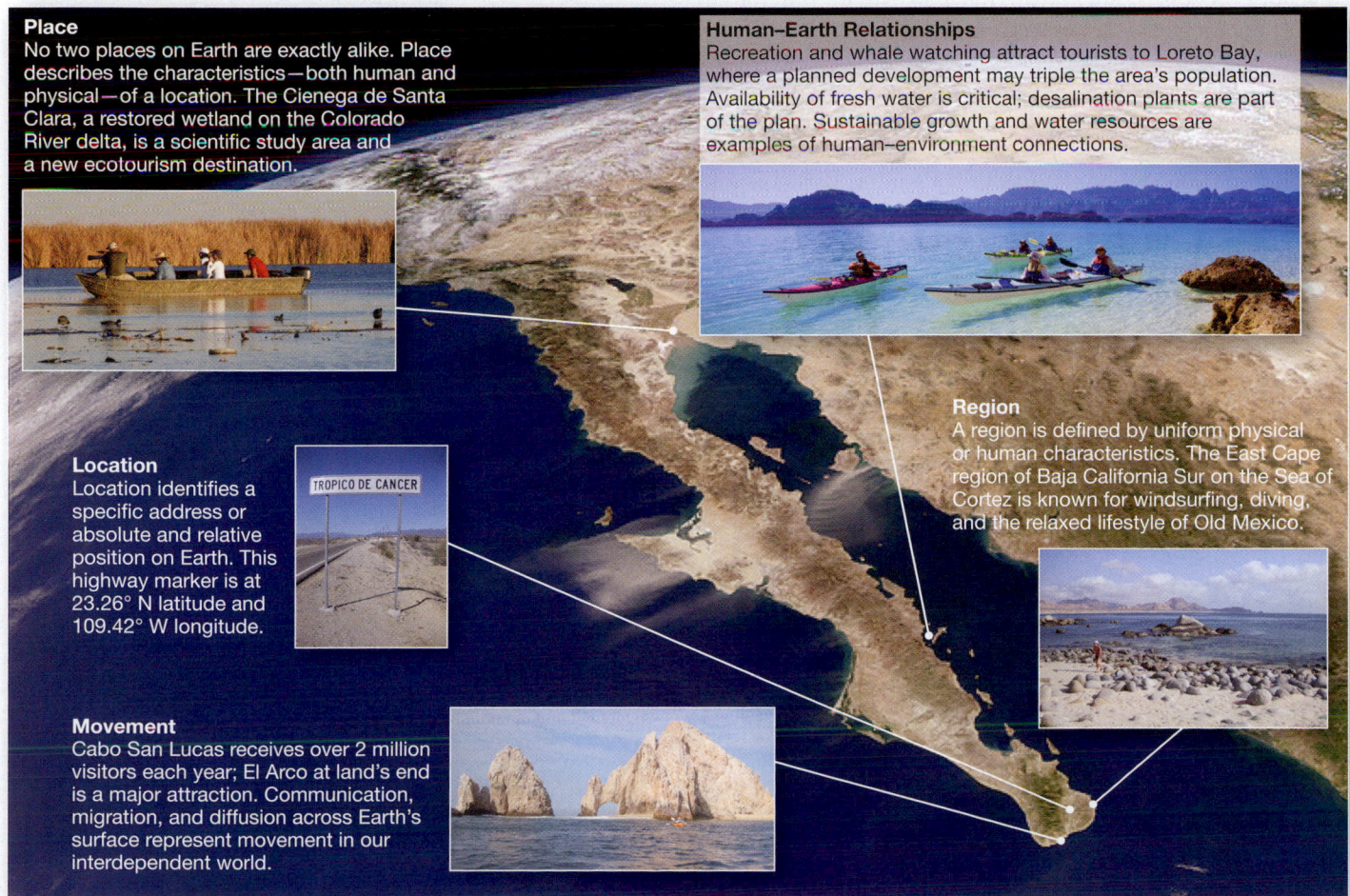

Place
No two places on Earth are exactly alike. Place describes the characteristics—both human and physical—of a location. The Cienega de Santa Clara, a restored wetland on the Colorado River delta, is a scientific study area and a new ecotourism destination.

Human–Earth Relationships
Recreation and whale watching attract tourists to Loreto Bay, where a planned development may triple the area's population. Availability of fresh water is critical; desalination plants are part of the plan. Sustainable growth and water resources are examples of human–environment connections.

Location
Location identifies a specific address or absolute and relative position on Earth. This highway marker is at 23.26° N latitude and 109.42° W longitude.

Region
A region is defined by uniform physical or human characteristics. The East Cape region of Baja California Sur on the Sea of Cortez is known for windsurfing, diving, and the relaxed lifestyle of Old Mexico.

Movement
Cabo San Lucas receives over 2 million visitors each year; El Arco at land's end is a major attraction. Communication, migration, and diffusion across Earth's surface represent movement in our interdependent world.

▲**Figure 1.2** **Five themes of geographic science.** This 2011 satellite image shows the entire length of Mexico's Baja peninsula, including Earth's curvature. [Photos by Karl Birkeland, except Place by Cheryl Zook/National Geographic and Human–Earth by Gary Luhm/garyluhm.net. Image from *Aqua* satellite/Norman Kuring, Ocean Color Team, NASA/GSFC.]

Although geography is not limited to place names, maps and location are central to the discipline and are important tools for conveying geographic data. Evolving technologies such as the Global Positioning System (GPS) and geographic information systems (GIS) are widely used for scientific and everyday applications as hundreds of millions of people access maps and locations on smartphones, tablets, and computers. We discuss these geospatial tools, including remote sensing and geovisualization, later in this chapter.

Geographic Subfields

Because many subjects can be examined geographically, geography is a diverse science that integrates subject matter from a wide range of disciplines. Even so, it splits broadly into two primary subfields: *physical geography*, comprising specialty areas that draw largely on the physical and life sciences, and *human geography*, comprising specialty areas that draw largely on the social and cultural sciences (**Figure 1.3**). With the increasing complexity of human–Earth connections, the focus of most geographic research has moved toward the overlapping areas of these two broad fields.

Physical geography is the spatial study of all the elements, processes, and systems that make up the natural environment: energy, air, water, weather, climate, landforms, soils, animals, plants, microorganisms, and Earth itself. Within physical geography, research in all specialty areas now emphasizes human influences on natural systems. For example, physical geographers examine the vulnerability of human populations to landslides, participate in ecosystems restoration projects, and examine the effects of drought and changing climate on regional water supplies.

Geographic Investigation

In addition to spatial analysis, the concepts of process, scale, and systems are central to physical geography investigations. **Process** refers to a set of actions or mechanisms that operate in some special order. In *Geosystems*, we examine processes in every chapter: for example, those involved in Earth's weather patterns, in continental crust movements and earthquake occurrences, and in the spread of invasive plants and animals.

Geographers often use the concept of scale, both over space and time, to examine patterns and processes. We define scale for this purpose as the relative size or extent of some attribute; for example, a *spatial scale* of analysis may range from global to regional to local (**Figure 1.4**). A

▶**Figure 1.4**
Viewing Hurricane Patricia, 2015, at global, regional, and local scales.
[(a) *GOES-13* satellite, NOAA. (b) NASA/NOAA via NOAA Environmental Visualization Laboratory. (c) Omar Torres/AFP/Getty Images.]

(a) Global scale: Western Hemisphere

(b) Regional scale: Mexico's Pacific Coast

(c) Local scale: Damaged restaurant in Las Manzanillas, Jalisco state, Mexico

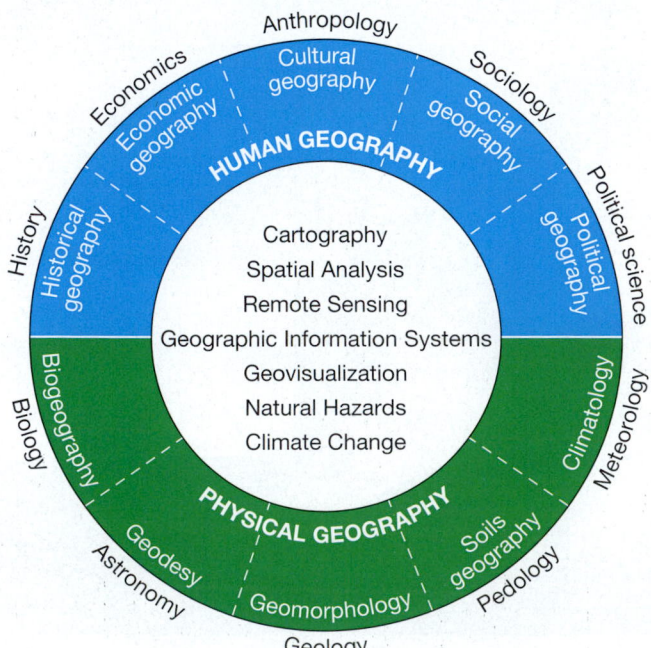

▲**Figure 1.3 The scope of geography.** Geography combines Earth topics and human topics, blending ideas from many different sciences. Numerous subfields, especially those focused on geographic techniques, fall into the overlap between physical and human geography.

process operating at a global scale, such as the jet stream winds in the upper atmosphere, can affect those occurring at regional and local scales, bringing storms to a particular region and causing heavy precipitation or flooding in a particular community.

Many processes have different effects according to the *temporal scale* at which they are studied. For example, a landslide into a river channel has dramatic effects over a short time scale (days, months, years) by creating a temporary dam that alters habitat and channel processes. But over a long time scale (decades, centuries, millennia), a landslide is a temporary disturbance as the river eventually loosens the material and carries it away. Note that later in this chapter, we discuss *map scale*, which is a slightly different concept that relates the size of a unit of distance on a map to the size of the same unit of distance on the ground.

Systems analysis is fundamental to physical geography, and we discuss systems at length later in this chapter. Physical geography encompasses the field of **Earth systems science**, the area of study that seeks to understand Earth as an interacting set of physical, chemical, and biological systems. We now discuss the general process and methods used by scientists, including geographers.

The Scientific Process

In *Geosystems Now*, we introduced "citizen science" in which volunteers participate in data collection. These efforts assist scientists, but data collection alone does not define scientific research. The process of science consists of observing, questioning, testing, and understanding elements of the natural world. The **scientific method** is the traditional recipe of a scientific investigation; it can be thought of as simple, organized steps leading toward concrete, objective conclusions (**Figure 1.5**). There is no single, definitive method for scientific inquiry; scientists in different fields and even in different subfields of physical geography may approach their scientific testing in different ways. However, the end result must be a conclusion that is reproducible by other scientists, that can be tested repeatedly, and that possibly can be shown to be true or false. Without these characteristics, the result of an inquiry is not science.

Forming and Testing the Hypothesis
After making observations and exploring relevant scientific literature, scientists formulate a *hypothesis*—a tentative explanation for the phenomena observed. In forming the hypothesis, they ask questions and identify *variables*, the conditions that change in an experiment or model. Because natural systems are complex, reducing the number of variables helps simplify research questions.

Scientists then test the hypothesis using an experimental study in a laboratory or natural settings. Data collected by citizen scientists can strengthen a study by expanding the database from which to draw results. The methods used for these studies must be reproducible so

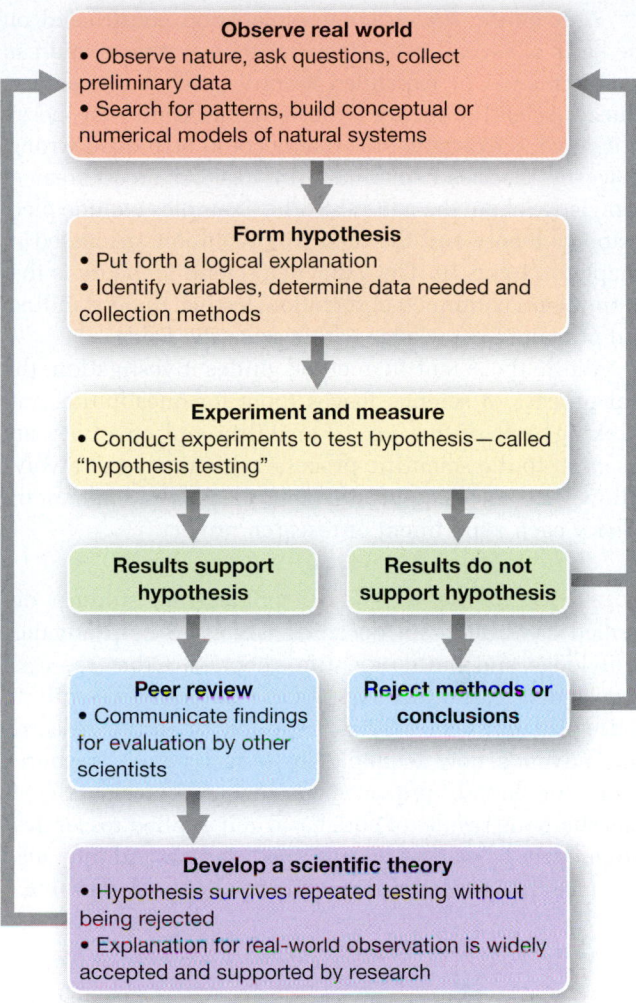

▲Figure 1.5 **Scientific method flow chart.**

that repeat testing can occur. Results may support the hypothesis or not, or predictions made according to the hypothesis may prove accurate or inaccurate. If the results do not support the hypothesis, the researcher will need to adjust data-collection methods or refine the hypothesis statement. If the results support the hypothesis, repeated testing and verification may lead to its elevation to the status of a *theory*.

Developing a Scientific Theory
For scientific work to reach other scientists and eventually the public at large, it should be described in a scientific paper and published in one of the many scientific journals—another part of the scientific method. When a scientist submits a paper to a scientific journal, that journal sends it out for *peer review*. During this critical process, other members of the scientific or professional community critique the methods and interpretation of results set out in the paper. This process also helps detect any personal or political bias on the part of the scientist. The reviewers may recommend rejecting the paper or accepting and revising it for publication. Once a number of papers are published with similar results and conclusions, the building of a theory begins.

A scientific *theory* is an explanation constructed on the basis of several extensively tested hypotheses and can be reevaluated or expanded according to new evidence. Thus, a scientific theory is not absolute truth—the possibility always exists that the theory could be proved wrong. However, theories explain and tie together broad areas of knowledge about the natural world. Examples include plate tectonics theory and the theory of evolution, discussed in Chapters 11 and 19. The value of a scientific theory is that it stimulates continued observation, testing, understanding, and pursuit of knowledge within scientific fields.

While the scientific method guides investigation, the real process of science leaves room for questioning and thinking "out of the box." Flexibility and creativity are essential to the scientific process, which may not always follow the same sequence of steps or use the same methods for each experiment or research project.

Applying Scientific Results Scientific studies described as "basic" are designed largely to help advance knowledge and build scientific theories. Other research is designed to produce "applied" results tied directly to real-world problem solving. Applied scientific research may advance new technologies, affect natural resource policy, or directly impact management strategies. Scientists share the results of both basic and applied research at conferences as well as in published papers, and they may take leadership roles in developing policy and planning.

Human–Earth Interactions in the 21st Century

Issues surrounding the growing influence of humans on Earth systems are central concerns of physical geography that we discuss in every chapter of *Geosystems*. More people are alive today than at any previous moment in the planet's long history. The human influence on Earth is now pervasive.

The Human Denominator One way to consider the sum of the human impact on Earth is to think in terms of fractions. The denominator in a fraction tells how many parts a whole is divided into, for example 4/8 means that the whole is divided into 8 parts. In *Geosystems*, we refer to the *human denominator* as the growing human population and its demand for Earth's resources. The numerator in the fraction is Earth's resource base, which remains relatively fixed. As the human denominator grows, the stresses on Earth systems increase.

We emphasize the connections between humans and Earth systems in the Human Denominator feature in each chapter (see Figure HD 1). This illustration shows important examples of human–Earth interactions using a base map, photos, and graphs with explanatory text, all organized to show that Earth systems impact humans, for example through weather or natural hazards, at the same time that humans impact Earth systems, such as by harvesting forests or polluting water sources.

Human Population Trends The global human population reached 1 billion people in 1804, and doubled to 2 billion in 1927. The time interval to add 1 billion people steadily decreased, as population passed 6 billion in August 1999 and 7 billion in 2011. At present, population growth rates are declining, a trend expected to continue. Yet despite this decline, projections show world population reaching 9 billion in the 2040s. Virtually all new population growth is in the less-developed countries (LDCs), which now possess 81% of the total population.

The population in just two countries (both categorized as LDCs with rapidly developing economies) makes up 37% of Earth's human count: 19.2% live in China and 17.5% in India—2.7 billion people combined. Considered overall, the planetary population is young, with some 26% still under the age of 15 years (for more information, see http://www.census.gov/popclock).

Although population in most of the more-developed countries (MDCs) is no longer increasing, people in the MDCs have a greater impact on the planet per person than those in the LDCs. The United States and Canada, with about 5% of the world's population, produce about 25% of the world's gross domestic product. These two countries use more energy per person than Europeans, Latin Americans, and Asians, and up to 20 times more than Africans. Therefore, the impact of this 5% on natural resources and Earth systems is critical.

Global Sustainability Recently, **sustainability science** has emerged as a new, integrative discipline. The concept of sustainability refers to the ability of something to be sustained—to keep going, continue, or endure. The basic question underlying sustainability science is: How can we live well over the long term using the resources of one planet Earth? Sustainable development seeks to advance the condition of human society while maintaining functioning Earth systems. Geographic concepts are fundamental to this new science, with its emphasis on human well-being, Earth systems, and human–environment interactions.

GEOreport 1.1   Welcome to the Anthropocene

The human population on Earth reached 7 billion in 2011 and may reach 8 billion in 2024. Many scientists now agree that the *Anthropocene* is an appropriate name for the most recent years of geologic history, when humans have influenced Earth's climate and ecosystems. Most scientists mark the start of the Anthropocene as either the beginning of agriculture, more than 5000 years ago, or the dawn of the Industrial Revolution, in the 18th century (see http://www.anthropocene.info).

EARTH SYSTEMS IMPACT HUMAN POPULATION

• What are some of the critical natural resources for human societies across the globe?

1a

Known for gambling, entertainment, and nightlife, Las Vegas is the most populous city in Nevada. The greater urban area is home to over 2 million people, while the casinos and resorts of the Las Vegas Strip, shown here, and other parts of the city host over 40 million visitors every year. Water is a critical resource in this desert climate. [robertharding/Alamy.]

HUMAN POPULATION IMPACTS EARTH SYSTEMS

• Growing population and resource use affects all Earth systems; we examine specific impacts in every chapter of *Geosystems*.

1b

Just over 19% of the world's population lives in China. With a population over 24 million, Shanghai is the largest city (by population) in China and the world, and one of the world's busiest ports for container shipping. Imagine the impact on natural systems with such a high concentration of people living in one location. [Amanda Hall/Robert Harding.]

This 2012 composite image from the *Suomi NPP* satellite shows Earth's lights at night, an indicator of population density and economic wealth. Wildfires also cause night light away from urban areas. [VIIRS instrument, *Suomi NPP*, NASA.]

ISSUES FOR THE 21ST CENTURY

• Many critical issues relate to the sustainability of Earth's resources: global food supply, energy supply and demand, climate change, loss of biodiversity, and air and water pollution.
• To achieve sustainability for humans and Earth, we need to address these issues in new ways.
• Understanding Earth's physical geography helps you make informed decisions on these issues.

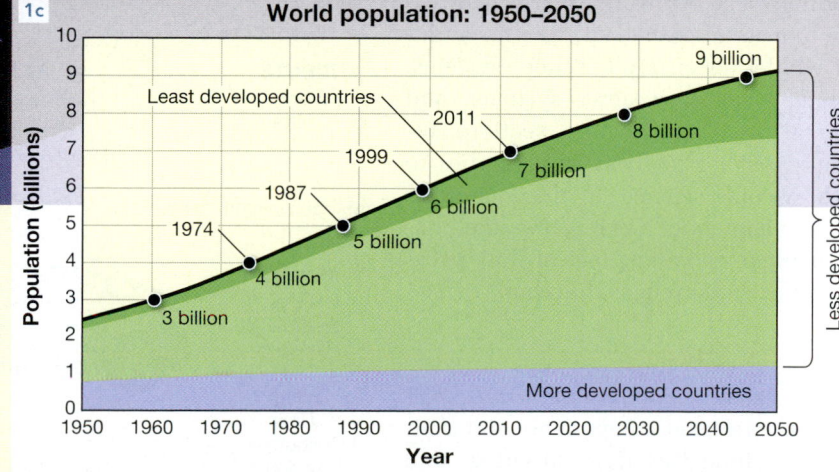

1c

World population: 1950–2050

Since 1950, population has increased in less-developed countries (LDCs) far more than in more-developed countries (MDCs), a trend that is expected to increase until at least 2050. [Population Reference Bureau, http://www.prb.org/pdf13/2013-population-data-sheet_eng.pdf.]

QUESTIONS TO CONSIDER

1. HD1c shows that, in 1950, people in MDCs constituted roughly one-third of the world's population. What was the fraction (roughly) of MDCs to total world population in 2011?

2. Using the graph in HD1c and the chapter text, calculate the interval of years between each billion-mark milestone for human population. Begin with the 3 billion mark reached in 1960.

A common concept related to sustainability is the human "footprint," representing the human impact on Earth systems. When the population of over 7 billion is taken into account, the human footprint on Earth is enormous in its strength and spatial influence. Shrinking this footprint ties to sustainability science and can be accomplished at levels ranging from the global community to nations, regions, neighborhoods, and individuals.

Earth Systems Concepts

We often hear the word *system* in reference to a set of parts that make up a unified whole: for example, school systems, heating systems, weather systems, and political systems. In this section, we discuss systems analysis as it applies to Earth systems science. In the four parts and 20 chapters of *Geosystems*, the content is organized along logical flow paths consistent with systems thinking.

Systems Theory

Simply stated, a **system** is any set of ordered, interrelated components and their attributes, linked by flows of energy and matter, as distinct from the surrounding environment outside the system. The elements within a system may be arranged in a series or intermingled. A system may be simple or complex, and it may comprise any number of subsystems.

Within Earth's systems, both matter and energy are stored and retrieved, and energy is transformed from one type to another. *Matter* is mass that assumes a physical shape and occupies space. *Energy* is the capacity to change the motion of, or to do work on, matter. Focus Study 1.1 explains forms of energy, providing the basis for numerous processes throughout this book.

Open Systems Systems in nature are generally not self-contained: Inputs of energy and matter flow into the system, and outputs of energy and matter flow from the system. Such a system is an **open system** (Figure 1.6). Within a system, the parts function together in a way that gives each system its operational character. The human body, a pot of coffee, and a houseplant are all open systems, with energy and matter flowing in and out. Earth is an open system in terms of energy because solar energy enters freely and heat energy leaves, going back into space.

Within the Earth system, many subsystems are interconnected. Free-flowing rivers are open systems: Inputs consist of solar energy, precipitation, and soil and rock particles; outputs are water and sediments to the ocean. Changes to a river system may affect the nearby coastal system; for example, an increase in a river's sediment load may spread pollutants along a coastline. Most natural systems and subsystems are open in terms of energy. Examples of open atmospheric subsystems include hurricanes and tornadoes.

Closed Systems A system that is shut off from the surrounding environment so that it is self-contained is a **closed system**. An example is a thermos of coffee, which can be viewed as a closed system because it does not allow the transfer of energy or matter to the surroundings. Although such closed systems are rarely found in nature, Earth is essentially a closed system in terms of physical

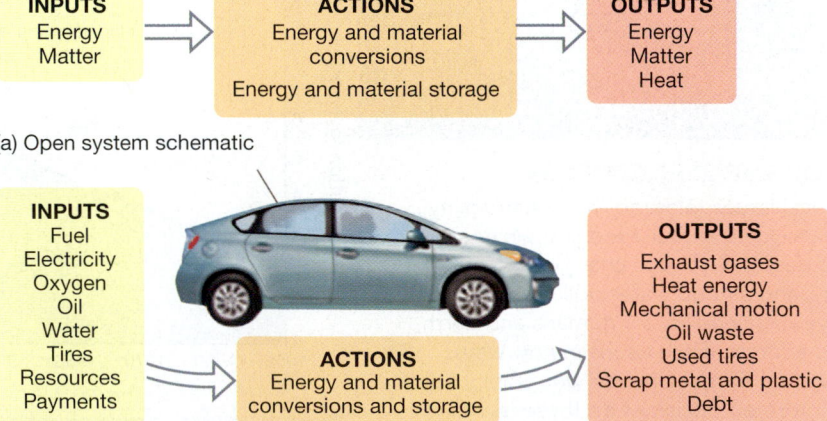

(a) Open system schematic

INPUTS	ACTIONS	OUTPUTS
Energy Matter	Energy and material conversions — Energy and material storage	Energy Matter Heat

(b) Open system example: a car

INPUTS	ACTIONS	OUTPUTS
Fuel Electricity Oxygen Oil Water Tires Resources Payments	Energy and material conversions and storage	Exhaust gases Heat energy Mechanical motion Oil waste Used tires Scrap metal and plastic Debt

▲Figure 1.6 **An open system.** Note the inputs (energy and matter) and outputs (energy, matter, and heat as waste) in terms of a car as an open system. Expand your thinking to the entire system of auto production, from raw materials to assembly to sales to car accidents to junkyards. What other open systems do you encounter in your daily life?

FOCUSstudy 1.1 Forms of Energy

Scientists define *energy* as the capacity to do work, or move matter. Therefore, energy accomplishes work when it moves matter. Energy takes many forms, such as radiant energy, kinetic energy, potential energy, and chemical energy, and when doing work, energy is often converted to another form (**Figure 1.1.1**).

Energy released from the Sun is *radiant energy*, which travels in waves through space. As this energy passes through the outermost edge of Earth's atmosphere, it is transformed into the various kinds of energy that power Earth systems. Eventually, Earth radiates this energy back to space as *heat energy*. We discuss these energy forms at length in Chapters 2 and 4.

Kinetic energy is the energy of motion, and is produced, for example, when you run, walk, or ride a bicycle. Kinetic energy

has several forms, including the *vibrational* energy of molecules and the translational energy of objects moving from one place to another (for example, a ball flying through the air). **Potential energy** is stored energy (stored either due to composition or position) that has the capacity to do work under the right conditions. Potential energy of position is also called *gravitational potential energy* because it relates to height. Gravitational potential energy is directly proportional to the mass of an object (or substance) and its elevation or distance from Earth's surface. A book on a shelf has potential energy because it will fall if the shelf moves. The water in the reservoir above a hydropower dam has potential energy that is released when gravity pulls it through the turbines and into the river downstream. Both kinetic energy and po-

tential energy produce work, in which matter is moved into a new position or location.

Chemical energy is stored in the molecular bonds of all substances. It is released, absorbed, or converted into another form when the substance undergoes a chemical reaction. Humans have learned to manipulate chemical and other types of energy to work for our benefit, such as the chemical energy used to burn petroleum that runs motor vehicles, or the gravitational energy used within dams for hydropower production. We discuss these different forms of energy throughout *Geosystems*.

1. What is the difference between kinetic energy and potential energy?

2. What characteristics of energy are important to the ways in which humans use energy?

APPLYconcepts Classify each example of energy in Earth systems according to the form of energy involved and describe the work that is done.

Example	Form of Energy	Work
Ocean waves pounding a beach	a _____	b _____
Boulder on a steep hillside	a _____	b _____
Dead leaves decaying on a forest floor	a _____	b _____
Sunlight drying up a puddle	a _____	b _____

(a) Radiant energy travels from Sun to Earth in waves

A runner converts chemical energy stored in her cells to kinetic energy

(b) Kinetic energy is energy of motion

As the book falls, potential energy is converted to kinetic energy

(c) Potential energy is stored energy, such as the gravitational energy related to vertical position

As the car burns gasoline, chemical energy is converted to kinetic energy

(d) Chemical energy is stored in molecular bonds and converted during chemical reactions

▲**Figure 1.1.1 Forms of energy.** [(a) Alexandra Lande/Shutterstock. (b) Daniel S Edwards/Shutterstock. (c) Volt Collection/Shutterstock. (d) Tomas Urbelionis/Shutterstock.]

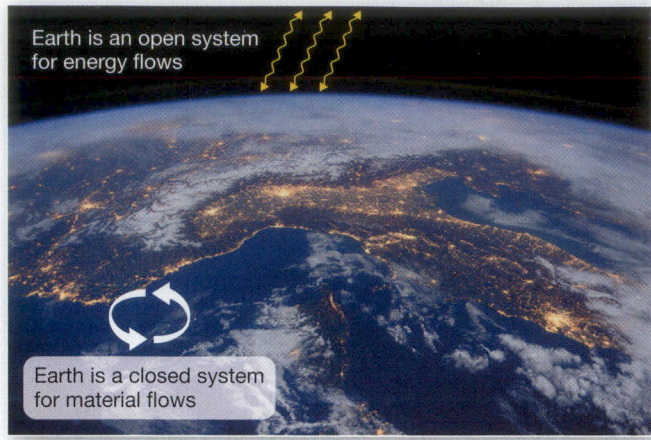

Earth is an open system for energy flows

Earth is a closed system for material flows

▲**Figure 1.7** **Earth as a system.** Earth, here showing Italy and the Mediterranean Sea in January 2016 viewed from the International Space Station, is an open system for energy flows and a closed system for material flows. [ESA/NASA.]

sugars (carbohydrates), releasing oxygen that we breathe. The process of respiration uses oxygen to convert the chemical energy of sugars to energy used for plant growth, releasing carbon dioxide. Figure 1.8a illustrates these inputs, actions, and outputs at the scale of a houseplant.

Figure 1.8b shows system interactions at the scale of a forest. Forest outputs include products and activities that link to other Earth systems. For example, forests store carbon and are thus referred to as "carbon sinks." Forests absorb about one third of the carbon dioxide released through the burning of fossil fuels, making them a critical part of Earth's climate system as global carbon dioxide levels rise. Forest roots stabilize soil on hillslopes and stream banks, connecting trees to land and water systems. Finally, forests produce food, habitat, and human resources, such as lumber, paper products, and medicine.

matter and resources, such as air, water, and most materials (**Figure 1.7**). The only exceptions are the slow escape of lightweight gases (such as hydrogen) from the atmosphere into space and the input of frequent, but tiny, meteors and cosmic dust. The fact that Earth is a closed material system makes recycling efforts unavoidable if we want a sustainable global economy.

Natural System Example A houseplant and a forest are examples of open systems (**Figure 1.8**). Trees and other plants use sunlight as an energy input and water, nutrients, and carbon dioxide as material inputs. The process of photosynthesis converts these inputs to stored chemical energy in the form of plant

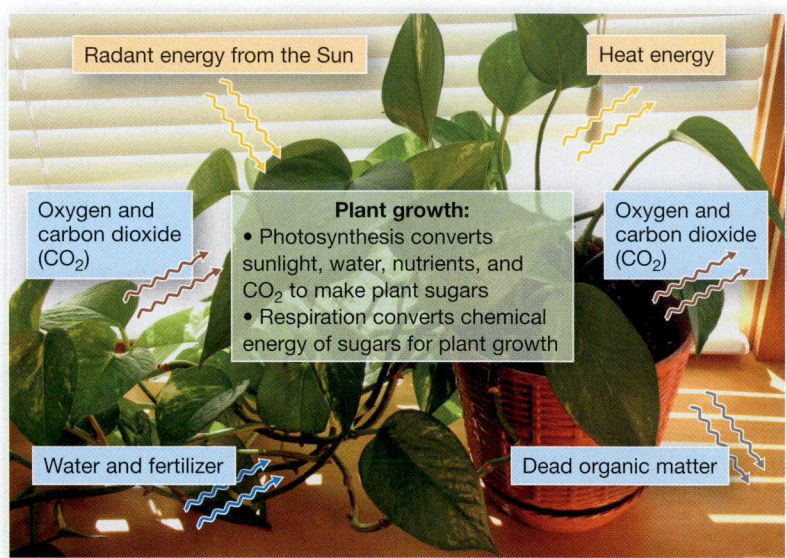

Radiant energy from the Sun

Heat energy

Oxygen and carbon dioxide (CO_2)

Plant growth:
• Photosynthesis converts sunlight, water, nutrients, and CO_2 to make plant sugars
• Respiration converts chemical energy of sugars for plant growth

Oxygen and carbon dioxide (CO_2)

Water and fertilizer

Dead organic matter

(a) A houseplant is an open system with inputs (radiant energy, oxygen and carbon dioxide, water, and fertilizer), actions (photosynthesis and respiration), and outputs (heat energy, oxygen and carbon dioxide, and organic matter).

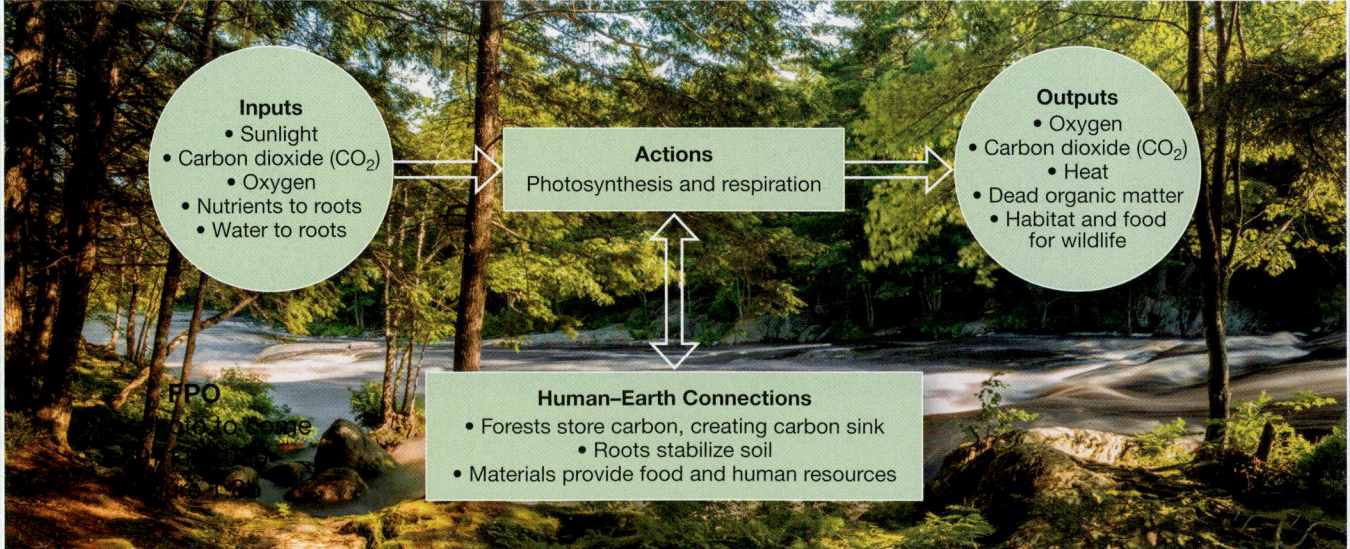

Inputs
• Sunlight
• Carbon dioxide (CO_2)
• Oxygen
• Nutrients to roots
• Water to roots

Actions
Photosynthesis and respiration

Outputs
• Oxygen
• Carbon dioxide (CO_2)
• Heat
• Dead organic matter
• Habitat and food for wildlife

Human–Earth Connections
• Forests store carbon, creating carbon sink
• Roots stabilize soil
• Materials provide food and human resources

FPO

(b) The inputs, actions, outputs, and human–Earth connections of a forest as an open system.

▲**Figure 1.8** **Natural open systems: a houseplant and a forest.** [(a) Shutterstock/Andrew F. Kazmierski. (b) Vadim Petrov/Shutterstock.]

The double-headed arrow in Figure 1.8b indicates two causal directions for the human–Earth connection. Forest processes affect humans by storing carbon (reducing carbon uptake by the atmosphere and oceans), stabilizing soils (reducing sediment inputs into source areas for drinking water), and providing food and resources. Human influences on forests include direct impacts such as logging for wood resources, burning to make way for agriculture, and clearing for development. Indirect impacts include pollution, which affects tree health, and the effects of human-caused climate change, as rising temperatures enhance the spread of disease and insects.

System Feedback As a system operates, it generates outputs that influence its own operations. These outputs function as "information" that returns to various points in the system. Feedback information can guide, and sometimes control, further system operations, often forming pathways called **feedback loops**.

If the feedback information discourages change in the system, it is **negative feedback**. Stated another way, negative feedback happens when performing an action leads to fewer performances of that action. For example, if you e-mail your instructor with questions about this course, and your instructor e-mails back with clear answers, then you will have fewer questions and less need to write e-mails for clarification. In this case, negative feedback leads to stability in the classroom system, and reduces the need for extra help.

If feedback information encourages change in the system, it is **positive feedback**. For example, if you e-mail your course instructor with questions, and receive confusing answers that create more questions, then you will continue to send more e-mails as the number of questions increases. In this case, positive feedback causes instability in the classroom system as your confusion increases; if unchecked, this feedback loop could result in you dropping the class.

Note that negative feedback is not "bad," and positive feedback is not "good." Each type of feedback relates to system stability: Negative feedback opposes system changes and leads to stability; positive feedback leads to instability, and if unchecked can create a runaway ("snowballing") condition. In natural systems, such unchecked system changes can reach a critical limit, leading to system disruption or death of organisms.

In nature, negative feedback causes a system to regulate itself. In a mountain forest, for example, healthy trees produce roots that stabilize slopes and prevent erosion to streams, providing a negative feedback that maintains a stable ecosystem. If the forest is removed, as by a fire, slopes may become unstable and subject to landslides. Another example of negative feedback is the natural regulation of predators and prey in a stable ecosystem (**Figure 1.9**). Predators increase as their prey population increases. Eventually predators reduce the prey population, and as their food source dwindles, predator populations decrease. At this point prey populations recover as the system stabilizes.

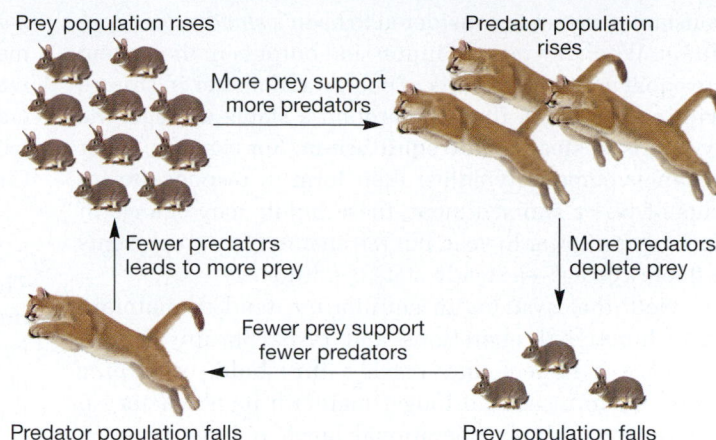

▲**Figure 1.9 The predator–prey negative feedback loop.** As prey populations rise, predators increase until the prey population becomes depleted. Then the predator population falls, until the prey population increases again.

An example of positive feedback is the melting of summer sea ice in the Arctic related to global climate. As arctic temperatures rise, summer sea ice and glacial melting accelerate. This causes a reduction in light-colored snow and sea-ice surfaces, which reflect sunlight and so remain cooler. Light-colored snow and ice surfaces are replaced by darker-colored open ocean surfaces, which absorb sunlight and become warmer. As a result, the ocean absorbs more solar energy, which raises the temperature, which, in turn, melts more ice, and so forth (**Figure 1.10**). This is a positive feedback loop because it further enhances the effects of higher temperatures and warming trends.

System Equilibrium Most systems maintain structure and character over time. An energy and material system that remains balanced over time, in which conditions are

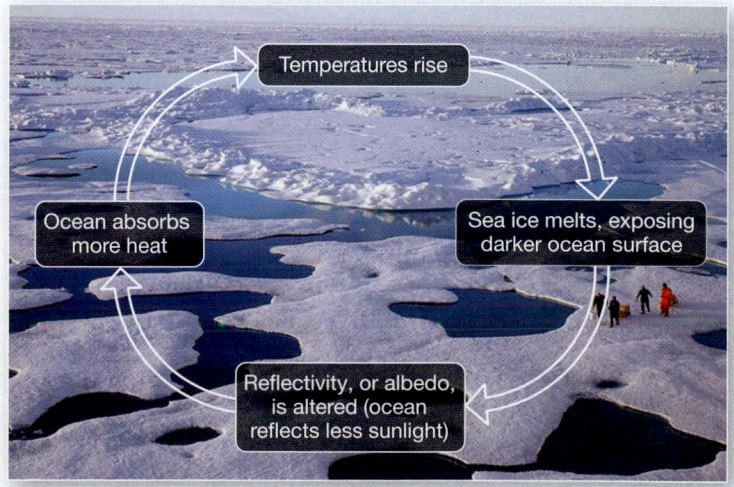

▲**Figure 1.10 The Arctic sea ice–albedo positive feedback loop.** Average ice thickness in the Arctic summer has dropped dramatically, leaving thinner ice that melts more easily. If the current rate of ice loss continues, the first ice-free Arctic September might happen before 2020. [NOAA.]

constant or recur, is considered to be in a *steady-state condition*. When the rates of inputs and outputs in the system are equal and the amounts of energy and matter in storage within the system fluctuate around a stable average, the system is in **steady-state equilibrium**. For example, river channels commonly adjust their form in response to inputs of water and sediment; these inputs may change in amount from year to year, but the channel form represents a stable average—a steady-state condition.

Note that systems in equilibrium tend to maintain their functional operations and resist abrupt change. However, a system may reach a **threshold**, or *tipping point*, where it can no longer maintain its character, so it lurches to a new operational level. A large flood in a river system may push the river channel to a threshold where it abruptly shifts, carving a new channel. A landslide may send a hillside or coastal bluff toward a new equilibrium form, balanced among slope, materials, and energy over time. Plant and animal communities can reach thresholds. For example, frogs are reaching a tipping point in response to a deadly fungus that has spread worldwide; extinctions of over 200 known species (about 3% of the total) have occurred since 1970. Scientists estimate that 10% of all frog species will be gone by 2100.

Models of Systems A **model** is a simplified, idealized representation of part of the real world that helps us understand complex processes. Scientists design models with varying degrees of specificity. A conceptual model is usually the most generalized and focuses on how processes interact within a system. A numerical model is more specific and is usually based on data collected from field or laboratory work. The simplicity of a model makes a system easier to understand and to simulate in experiments. An example is a model of the *hydrologic system*, which represents Earth's entire water system; its related energy flows; and the atmosphere, surface, and subsurface environments through which water moves (see Chapter 8, Figure 8.5).

Geosystems and Earth's Four "Spheres"

The part structure of Geosystems is designed around the four immense open systems that interact over Earth's surface, the "spheres" pertaining to air, water, land, and living organisms. The three *abiotic*, or nonliving, systems are the atmosphere, hydrosphere, and lithosphere. These systems overlap as the framework for the *biotic*, or living, system, the biosphere. Together, these spheres form a simplified model of Earth systems (**Figure 1.11**).

- The **atmosphere** is a thin, gaseous veil surrounding Earth, held to the planet by the force of gravity, and is the focus of Part I, Chapters 2–5. Formed by gases arising from within Earth's crust and interior combined with radiant energy from the Sun, the lower atmosphere is unique in the solar system. It is a combination of nitrogen, oxygen, argon, carbon dioxide, water vapor, and trace gases.

- The **hydrosphere** encompasses all of Earth's waters, existing in the atmosphere, on the surface, and in the crust near the surface, and is the focus of Part II, Chapters 6–10. That portion of the hydrosphere that is frozen is the **cryosphere**—ice sheets, ice caps and fields, glaciers, ice shelves, sea ice, and subsurface ground ice. Water of the hydrosphere exists as liquid, solid (the frozen cryosphere), and gaseous (water vapor) forms, and in two general chemical conditions, fresh and saline (salty).

- The **lithosphere** includes the Earth's crust and a portion of the upper mantle directly below the crust, and is the focus of Part III, Chapters 11–17. In a broad sense, the term *lithosphere* sometimes refers to the entire solid planet. The soil layer is the *edaphosphere* and generally covers Earth's land surfaces. In this text, soils represent the bridge between Parts III and IV.

- The **biosphere** includes all the living organisms on Earth taken together and linked with their physical environment, providing the focus of Part IV, Chapters 18–20.

▼Figure 1.11. **Earth's four spheres.** [Dennis Frates/Alamy.]

The biosphere, sometimes called the *ecosphere*, exists wherever life is sustainable, from the seafloor, to the upper layers of the crustal rock, to about 8 km (5 mi) into the atmosphere.

From the part structure to the chapter flow to the specific topics within each chapter, *Geosystems* follows a systems flow, focusing on inputs, actions, and outputs, with an emphasis on human–Earth interactions. Geosystems in Action 1 on the following pages outlines the part structure and chapter content corresponding to Earth's four spheres.

The Colorado River: A Systems Approach

Throughout *Geosystems*, we focus on the Colorado River as an example of how our systems approach helps us analyze geospatial issues. This vast river system encompasses parts of seven western states and supplies water and electricity to many of the fastest growing U.S. urban areas. The environmental challenges affecting the Colorado River focus on human–Earth connections and involve all Earth spheres. Water supply in this dry region links to the atmosphere, as rainfall declines owing to climate change. The river itself represents the hydrosphere, with water quality intimately tied to human activities such as mining and agriculture. Dams and reservoirs link to the lithosphere and biosphere, as they store and distribute water for human use but at the same time disrupt natural river system processes and environments. Specific examples throughout this book relate to the Colorado River system, serving as a reminder of the interconnectedness of all Earth systems.

Location and Time on Earth

Earth's *sphericity*, or roundness, was first determined more than two millennia ago by the Greek mathematician and philosopher Pythagoras (ca. 580–500 B.C.E.). The idea of a spherical rather than a flat Earth was generally accepted by the educated populace as early as the first century C.E. Christopher Columbus, for example, knew he was sailing around a sphere in 1492; this is one reason why he thought he had arrived in the East Indies.

Earth's Shape and Dimensions

Until 1687, the idea that Earth is a perfect sphere was a basic assumption of **geodesy**, the science that determines Earth's shape and size by surveys and mathematical calculations. But in that year, Sir Isaac Newton postulated that Earth, along with the other planets, could not be perfectly spherical. Newton reasoned that the more rapid rotational speed at the equator—the

part of the planet farthest from the central axis and therefore the fastest moving—produces an equatorial bulge as centrifugal force pulls Earth's surface outward. He was convinced that Earth is slightly misshapen into an *oblate spheroid*, or, more correctly, an *oblate ellipsoid* (*oblate* means "flattened"), with the oblateness occurring at the poles.

Earth's equatorial bulge and its polar oblateness are today universally accepted and confirmed with tremendous precision by satellite observations. The irregular shape of Earth's surface, coinciding with mean sea level and perpendicular to the direction of gravity, is described as a **geoid**. Imagine Earth's geoid as a constant sea-level surface that extends worldwide, beneath the continents. Both heights on land and depths in the oceans measure from this hypothetical surface. Think of the geoid surface as a balance among the gravitational attraction of Earth's mass, the distribution of water and ice upon its surface, and the outward centrifugal pull caused by Earth's rotation. **Figure 1.12** gives Earth's polar and equatorial circumferences and diameters.

Earth's Reference Grid

To determine location on our not-quite-spherical planet, we use a coordinated grid system that is internationally accepted. The terms *latitude* and *longitude* for the lines of this grid were in use on maps as early as the first century C.E. with the concepts themselves dating to earlier times.

The geographer, astronomer, and mathematician Ptolemy (ca. 90–168 C.E.) contributed greatly to the development of modern maps. Ptolemy divided the circle into 360 degrees (360°), with each degree having 60 minutes (60′) and each minute having 60 seconds (60″) in a manner adapted from the ancient Babylonians. He located places using these degrees, minutes, and seconds. However, the precise length of a degree of latitude and a degree of longitude remained unresolved for the next 17 centuries.

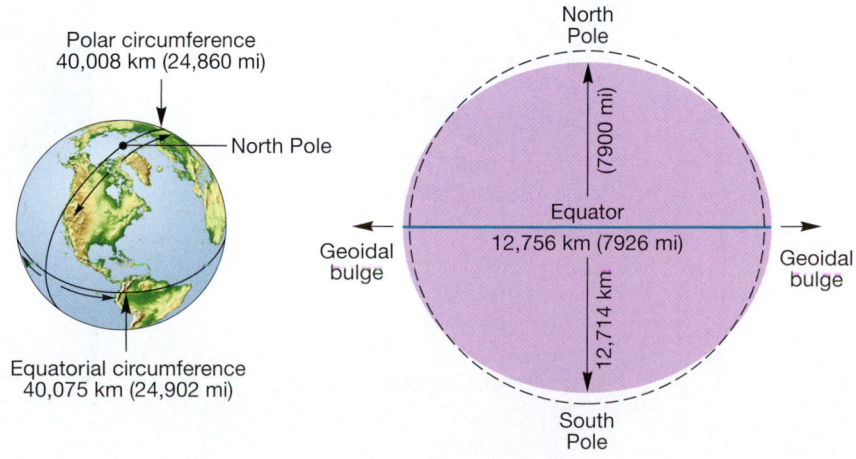

(a) Equatorial and polar circumferences

Polar circumference 40,008 km (24,860 mi)
North Pole
Equatorial circumference 40,075 km (24,902 mi)

(b) Equatorial and polar diameters

North Pole
(7900 mi)
Equator 12,756 km (7926 mi)
Geoidal bulge
Geoidal bulge
12,714 km
South Pole

▲**Figure 1.12 Earth's dimensions.** The dashed line is a perfect circle for comparison to Earth's geoid.

Throughout all four PARTs of *Geosystems*, we discuss connetions between the Colorado River system and interactions with all Earth systems. The increasing demands on river flows as a water resource is in stark contrast to declining discharge, lowering reservoir levels, and a western drought attributable to global climate change. Our systems organization guides you through this evolving condition.

PART I THE ENERGY–ATMOSPHERE SYSTEM

Incoming solar radiation provides the energy input that drives Earth's physical systems, determining weather and climate patterns and influencing living organisms.

ATMOSPHERE
Earth systems deliver energy and water to the headwater region of the Colorado River.

Headwaters of the Colorado River in northwest Colorado.

CHAPTER 2
Solar Energy to Earth and the Seasons

CHAPTER 3
Earth's Atmosphere

CHAPTER 4
Atmospheric Energy and Global Temperatures

CHAPTER 5
Atmospheric and Oceanic Circulations

INPUTS
• Solar energy to Earth
• Earth's modern atmosphere

ACTIONS
• Atmosphere and surface energy balances

OUTPUTS
• Global temperatures
• Wind and ocean currents

HUMAN-EARTH CONNECTION
• Ozone depletion
• Air pollution
• Urban environment
• Human temperature response
• Solar energy
• Wind power

PART II WATER, WEATHER, AND CLIMATE SYSTEMS

The distribution and circulation of water in Earth's atmosphere and hydrosphere are key influences on weather and determine the water available for humans and other living organisms.

HYDROSPHERE
River discharge through the basin provides a valuable water resource, now impacted by reduced flows related to climate change.

The Colorado river in Utah.

CHAPTER 6
Water and Atmospheric Moisture

CHAPTER 7
Weather

CHAPTER 8
Water Resources

CHAPTER 9
Earth's Climatic Regions

CHAPTER 10
Climate Change

INPUTS
• Water
• Atmospheric moisture

ACTIONS
• Cloud formation
• Air mass movement
• Atmospheric lifting

OUTPUTS
• Weather
• Water resources
• Climatic patterns

HUMAN-EARTH CONNECTION
• Weather hazards
• Water shortages
• Climate change

Video MG
The Changing Face of Earth

https://goo.gl/tRXOmC

MasteringGeography™

Visit the Study Area in MasteringGeography™ to explore Earth systems.

Visualize: Study geosciences animations of Earth's radiation balance and the rock cycle.

Assess: Demonstrate understanding of Earth system interactions (if assigned by instructor).

PART III — THE EARTH–ATMOSPHERE INTERFACE

Earth's surface is shaped by internal processes that build, warp, and break Earth's crust and by external processes that carve, shape, and wear down the landscape.

Lake Powell in Arizona.

LITHOSPHERE

The Colorado is an exotic stream that flows from humid to arid regions, sculpting the landscape, increasingly exposed by lowering reservoirs.

INPUTS
• Heat from within Earth
• Solar energy to Earth
• Precipitation
• Wind

ACTIONS
• Rock formation
• Tectonic processes
• Crustal deformation
• Weathering and erosion

OUTPUTS
• Folded and faulted landscapes
• Mountain chains
• Landforms related to water, wind, waves, ice

HUMAN-EARTH CONNECTION
• Geothermal energy
• Earthquakes and volcanism
• Floodplain management
• Desertification

PART IV — SOILS, ECOSYSTEMS, AND BIOMES

Solar energy powers the biosphere through photosynthesis, in which plants and algae convert sunlight into food. Soil is the essential link between plants, the lithosphere, and the rest of Earth's physical systems.

BIOSPHERE

The Colorado River affects ecosystems and the biogeography of the semiarid Southwest.

The Colorado River landscape near Imperial Dam in southern Arizona.

INPUTS
• Insolation
• Precipitation
• Biotic interactions
• Earth materials

ACTIONS
• Photosynthesis/respiration
• Biochemical cycling
• Food webs
• Evolution
• Disturbance and succession

OUTPUTS
• Soil types
• Species distributions
• Biodiversity
• Earth's biomes

HUMAN-EARTH CONNECTION
• Soil erosion
• Biodiversity losses
• Invasive species
• Ecosystem restoration

GEOquiz

1. Explain: Which spheres represent Earth's abiotic environment? How are these spheres distinct from one another?

2. Compare: What are two main sources of energy for processes in Earth's systems? Based on the illustration, give an example of processes that involve each form of energy.

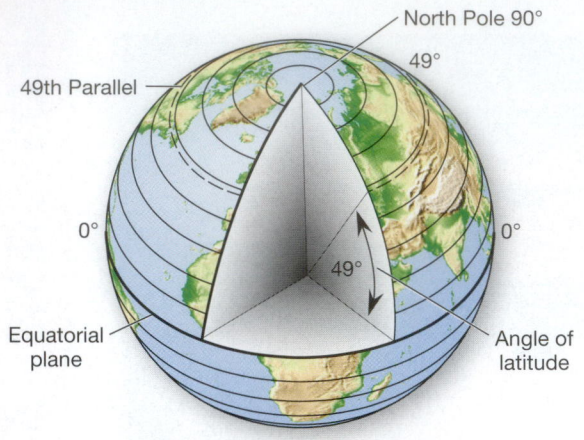

(a) Latitude is measured in degrees north or south of the Equator (0°). Earth's poles are at 90°. Note the measurement of 49° latitude.

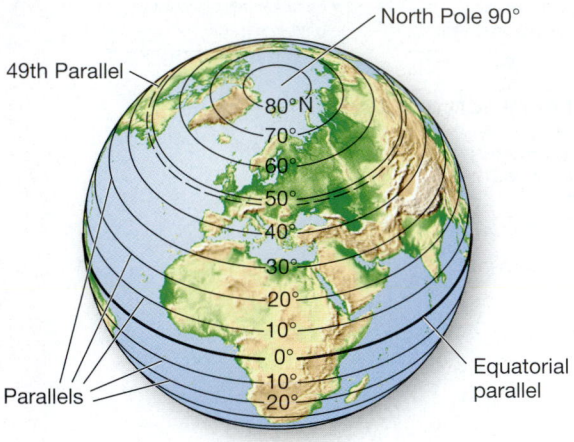

(b) These angles of latitude determine parallels along Earth's surface.

▲**Figure 1.13 Parallels of latitude.** Europe is north of the equator; therefore, it is in the Northern Hemisphere.

Latitude The angular distance north or south of the equator, measured from the center of Earth, is **latitude** (**Figure 1.13a**). On a map or globe, the lines designating these angles of latitude run east and west, parallel to the equator (**Figure 1.13b**). Because Earth's equator divides the distance between the North Pole and the South Pole exactly in half, it is assigned the value of 0° latitude. Thus, latitude increases from the equator northward to the North Pole, at 90° north latitude, and southward to the South Pole, at 90° south latitude.

A line connecting all points along the same latitudinal angle is a **parallel**. In Figure 1.13, an angle of 49° north latitude is measured, and by connecting all points at this latitude, we have the 49th parallel. Thus, *latitude* is the name of the angle (49° north latitude), *parallel* names the line (49th parallel), and both indicate distance north of the equator.

From equator to poles, the distance represented by a degree of latitude is fairly consistent, about 100 km (69 mi); at the poles, a degree of latitude is only slightly larger (about 1.12 km, or 0.70 mi) than at the equator (look ahead to Figure 1.15). To pinpoint location more precisely, we divide degrees into 60 minutes and minutes into 60 seconds. For example, Cabo San Lucas, Baja California, Mexico, in Figure 1.2 sits at 22 degrees, 53 minutes, 23 seconds (22° 53′ 23″) north latitude. Alternatively, many geographic information systems and geovisualization programs use decimal notation for latitude and longitude degrees. In decimal units, Cabo San Lucas is at 22.8897° latitude—the positive value indicates north latitude, a negative sign is for south latitude.

Physical geographers often use latitude to generalize the locations of different phenomena on Earth, such as weather patterns or plant and animal distributions. "Lower latitudes" are those nearer the equator, whereas "higher latitudes" are those nearer the poles. Other terms such as "the tropics" and "the Arctic" characterize environments that result from differing amounts of solar energy received throughout the year at different latitudes. **Figure 1.14** shows the names and locations

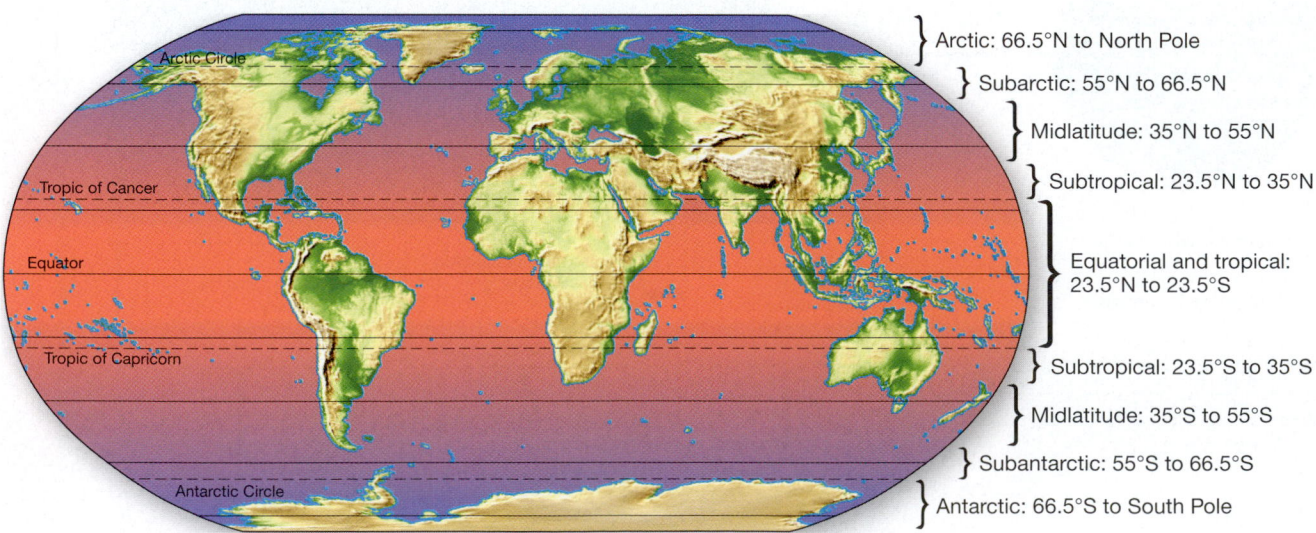

▲**Figure 1.14 Latitudinal geographic zones.** Temperature and other variables are the basis for geographic zones that characterize various regions by latitude.

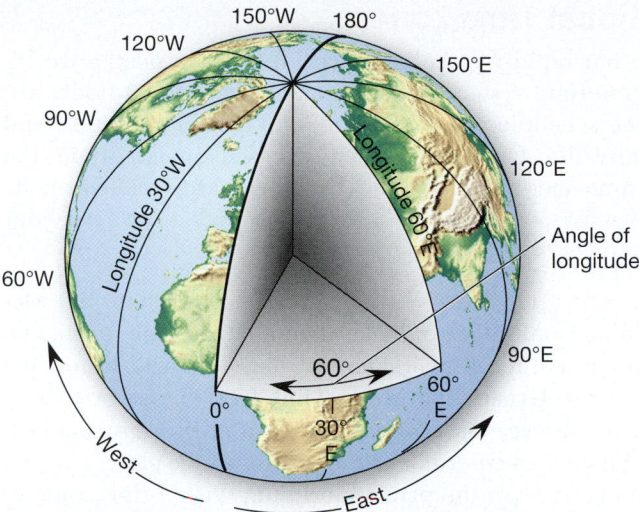

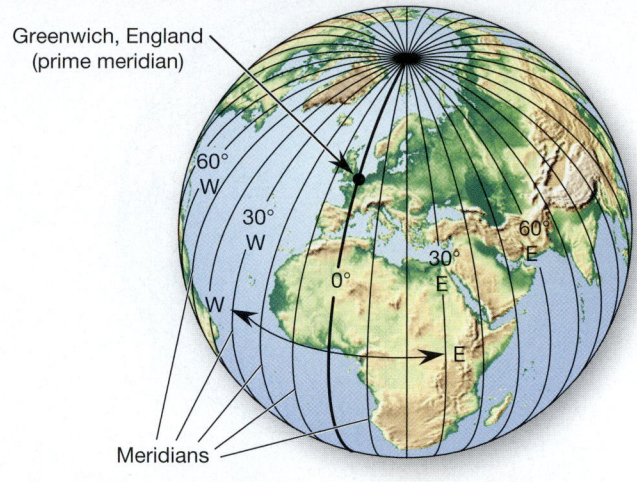

(a) Longitude is measured in degrees east or west of a 0° starting line, the prime meridian. Note the measurement of 60°E longitude

(b) Angles of longitude measured from the prime meridian determine other meridians.

▲**Figure 1.15 Meridians of longitude.** North America is west of Greenwich, England; therefore it is in the Western Hemisphere.

of the *latitudinal geographic zones* used by geographers: *equatorial and tropical*, *subtropical*, *midlatitude*, *subarctic* or *subantarctic*, and *Arctic* or *Antarctic*. These generalized latitudinal zones are useful for reference and comparison, but they do not have rigid boundaries; rather, they have wide transition areas from one to another. We discuss specific lines of latitude, such as the Tropic of Cancer and the Arctic Circle, in Chapter 2 as we learn about the seasons.

Longitude The angular distance east or west of a point on Earth's surface, measured from the center of Earth, is **longitude** (**Figure 1.15a**). On a map or globe, the lines designating these angles of longitude run north and south (**Figure 1.15b**). A **meridian** is a line connecting all points along the same longitude. Meridians run at right angles (90°) to all parallels, including the equator.

Thus, *longitude* is the name of the angle, *meridian* names the line, and both indicate distance east or west of an arbitrary **prime meridian**—a meridian designated as 0° (Figure 1.14b). Earth's prime meridian passes through the old Royal Observatory at Greenwich, England, as set by an 1884 treaty; this is the *Greenwich prime meridian*. Because meridians of longitude converge toward the poles, the actual distance on the ground spanned by a degree of longitude is greatest at the equator (where meridians separate to their widest distance apart) and diminishes to zero at the poles (where meridians converge;). As with latitude, longitude is expressed in degrees, minutes, and seconds or in decimal degrees. Cabo San Lucas in Figure 1.2 is located at 109° 54′ 56″ W longitude, or −109.9156°; east longitude has a positive decimal value, while west longitude is negative.

Figure 1.16 combines latitude and parallels with longitude and meridians to illustrate Earth's complete coordinate grid system. Note the red dot that marks 49° N and 60° E, a location in western Kazakhstan. Next time you click on a location on Google Earth or Google Maps, note the latitude and longitude.

WORK**IT**OUT 1.2
Locations on Earth

Select a location—for example, your campus, home, or a city you'd like to visit—and determine its latitude and longitude. (If you use Google Maps or Google Earth, right click the location to determine latitude/longitude; or use a GPS measurement.)

1. What is the geographic location (latitude and longitude) in degrees, minutes, and seconds, and as decimal degrees?

(To convert between the two, go to https://www.fcc.gov/media/radio/dms-decimal.)

2. In which latitudinal geographic zone does it fall? (Look back to Figure 1.13.)
3. What is the geographic location (latitude and longitude) of Fairbanks, Alaska? In which latitudinal zone is this city?
4. How many degrees of latitude and longitude separate your location from Fairbanks?

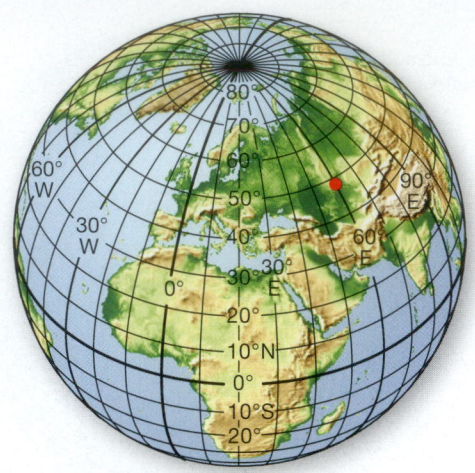

▲**Figure 1.16 Earth's coordinate grid system.** The red dot is at 49° N latitude and 60° E longitude.

Great Circles and Small Circles

Great circles and small circles are important navigational concepts that help summarize latitude and longitude (**Figure 1.17**). A **great circle** is any circle of Earth's circumference whose center coincides with the center of Earth. An infinite number of great circles can be drawn on Earth. Every meridian is one half of a great circle that passes through the poles. In contrast, only one parallel is a great circle—the equator. All other parallels diminish in length toward the poles and constitute **small circles**, which have centers that do not coincide with Earth's center.

Global Time Zones

In our rapidly globalizing world, humans need a world-wide time system to coordinate international trade, airline schedules, business and agricultural activities, and daily life. Our time system is based on longitude, the prime meridian, and the fact that Earth rotates on its own axis, revolving 360° every 24 hours, or 15° per hour ($360° \div 24 = 15°$).

Greenwich Mean Time   The 1884 International Meridian Conference in Washington, DC, set the prime meridian as the official standard for the world time zone system—**Greenwich Mean Time (GMT)** (see http://wwp .greenwichmeantime.com/). This standard time system established 24 *central meridians* around the globe at equal intervals from the prime meridian, with a time zone of 1 hour spanning 7.5° on either side. Before this universal system, time zones were problematic, especially in large countries. In 1870, railroad travelers going from Maine to San Francisco made 22 adjustments to their watches to stay consistent with local time! Today, only three adjustments are needed in the continental United States—from Eastern Standard Time to Central, Mountain, and Pacific—and four changes across Canada (**Figure 1.18**).

Figure 1.18 shows that when it is is 9:00 P.M. in Greenwich, then it is 1:00 P.M. in Seattle and Los Angeles (–8 hr), and 11:00 A.M. in Honolulu (–10 hr). To the east, it is midnight in Riyadh, Saudi Arabia (+3 hr). The designation A.M. is for *ante meridiem*, "before noon," whereas P.M. is for *post meridiem*, "after noon." Using a 24-hour clock, 3 A.M. is 3:00 hours and 3 P.M. is 15:00 hours, avoiding the use of A.M. and P.M. designations.

In a number of cases, national or state boundaries and political considerations distort time boundaries. For example, China spans four time zones, but its government decided to keep the entire country on the same time. Thus, in some parts of China clocks are several hours off solar time. In the United States, parts of Florida and west Texas are in the same time zone.

Notice in Figure 1.18 that some countries have nonstandard time zones that deviate by a half hour (Afghanistan, Venezuela, the Canadian province of Newfoundland) or 15 minutes (Nepal). The entire country of India, for example, is 5.5 hours offset from the time in Greenwich. The reasons for these offsets are usually political and are particular to each country or region.

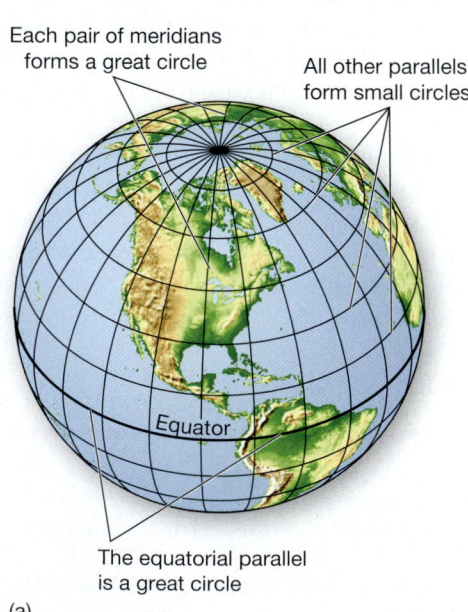

Each pair of meridians forms a great circle

All other parallels form small circles

Equator

The equatorial parallel is a great circle

(a)

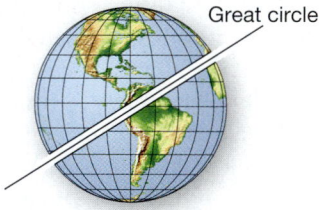

Great circle

(b) A plane intersecting the globe along a great circle divides the globe into equal halves and passes through its center.

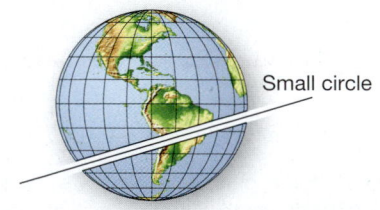

Small circle

(c) A plane that intersects the globe along a small circle splits the globe into unequal sections—this plane does not pass through the center of the globe.

▲**Figure 1.17 Great circles and small circles.**

▲**Figure 1.18** **Modern international standard time zones.** If it is 7 p.m. in Greenwich, determine the present time in Moscow, London, Halifax, Chicago, Winnipeg, Denver, Los Angeles, Fairbanks, Honolulu, Tokyo, and Singapore. [Adapted from Defense Mapping Agency; see http://aa.usno.navy.mil/faq/docs/world_tzones.html.]

Coordinated Universal Time GMT was originally determined using astronomical clocks that rely on Earth's rotation, which varies slightly over time (discussed in Chapters 2 and 10). The invention of atomic clocks in the early 1950s improved the accuracy of measuring time. In 1972, the **Coordinated Universal Time (UTC)** time-signal system replaced GMT and became the legal reference for official time in all countries. (The UTC acronym represents a compromise between the English (CUT) and French (TUC) word orders.) UTC is based on average time calculations from atomic clocks collected worldwide and is the recommended term for all timekeeping applications.

International Date Line An important corollary of the prime meridian is the 180° meridian on the opposite side of the planet. This meridian is the **International Date**

Line **(IDL)**, which marks the place where each day officially begins (at 12:01 a.m.). From this "line," the new day sweeps westward. This *westward* movement of time is created by Earth's turning *eastward* on its axis. Locating the date line in the sparsely populated Pacific Ocean minimizes most local confusion (**Figure 1.19**).

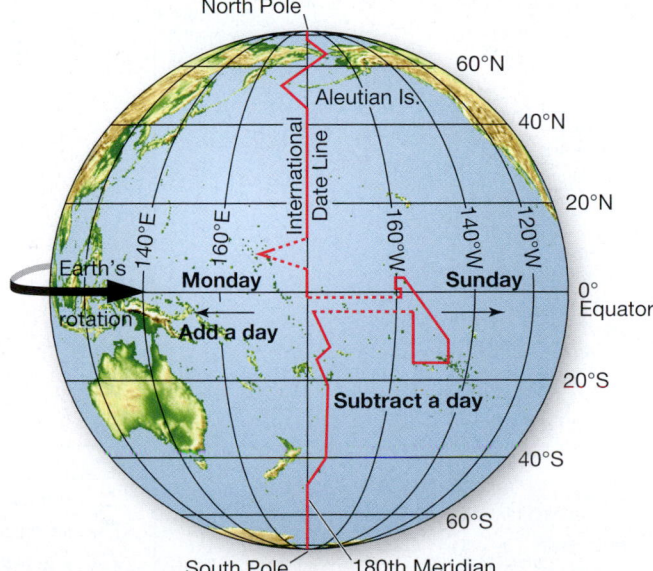

▲**Figure 1.19** **International Date Line.** The IDL location is approximately along the 180th meridian (see the IDL location on Figure 1.15). The dotted lines on the map show where island countries have set their own time zones, but their political control extends only 3.5 nautical miles (4 mi) offshore. Officially, you gain 1 day crossing the IDL from east to west.

WORKITOUT 1.3
Time Changes Across the Globe

Answer the following questions using the international time zones in Figure 1.18.

1. When it is 11:00 p.m. in Greenwich, England, what is the time in New York?
2. When it is 5 p.m. in Denver, Colorado, what is the time in Cairo, Egypt?
3. When it is 9 a.m. in Tokyo, Japan, what is the time in Mexico City? In New Delhi, India?

At the IDL, the west side of the line is always 1 day ahead of the east side. No matter what time of day it is when the line is crossed, the calendar changes a day. Note in the illustration the departures from the IDL and the 180° meridian; this deviation is due to local administrative and political preferences.

Daylight Saving Time In 70 countries, mainly in the subtropical and midlatitudes, time is set ahead 1 hour in the spring and set back 1 hour in the fall—a practice known as **daylight saving time**. The idea to extend daylight for early evening activities at the expense of daylight in the morning, first proposed by Benjamin Franklin, was not adopted until World War I and again in World War II, when Great Britain, Australia, Germany, Canada, and the United States used the practice to save energy (1 less hour of artificial lighting needed).

In 1986 and again in 2007, the United States and Canada extended the number of weeks of daylight saving time. Currently, time "springs forward" 1 hour on the second Sunday in March and "falls back" 1 hour on the first Sunday in November, except in a few places that do not use daylight saving time (Hawai'i, Arizona, and Saskatchewan). In Europe, the time changes occur on the last Sundays in March and October. (See http://www.timeanddate.com/time/dst/.)

Maps and Cartography

For centuries, geographers have used maps as tools to display spatial information and analyze spatial relationships. A **map** is a generalized view of an area, usually some portion of Earth's surface, as seen from above and greatly reduced in size. A map usually represents a specific characteristic of a place or area, such as rainfall, airline routes, or political features such as state boundaries and place names. **Cartography** is the science and art of mapmaking, often blending aspects of geography, engineering, mathematics, computer science, and art. **Digital cartography**, or *digital mapping*, refers to data collected and presented in a virtual image on a computer or mobile device. Digital maps rely on Global Positioning System (GPS) technology, which we discuss later in the chapter.

Representative fraction: 1:500,000 or 1/500,000
Written scale: 1 in. = 8 mi
1 cm = 5.0 km
Graphic scale: 8 MILES / 10 KILOMETERS

- ■ Point of interest
- 110 Interstate highway
- 441 U.S. highway
- 110 State highway
- —— Street

Representative fraction: 1:24,000 or 1/24,000
Written scale: 1 in. = 2000 ft
1 cm = 0.25 km
Graphic scale: 2000 FEET / 0.5 KILOMETERS

(a) Relatively small scale map of Miami area shows less detail.

(b) Relatively large scale map of the same area shows a higher level of detail.

▲**Figure 1.20 Map scale.** Examples of maps at different scales, with three common expressions of map scale—representative fraction, written scale, and graphic scale. Both maps are enlarged, so only the graphic scale is accurate. [USGS. Courtesy of University of Texas Libraries, University of Texas at Austin.]

The Scale of Maps

Architects, toy designers, and mapmakers have something in common: They all represent real things and places with the convenience of a model. In most cases, the model is smaller than the reality. For example, an architect renders a blueprint of a structure to guide the building contractors, preparing the drawing so that a centimeter (or inch) on the blueprint represents so many meters (or feet) on the proposed building.

The cartographer does the same thing in preparing a map. The ratio of the image on a map to the real world is the **map scale**; it relates the size of a unit on the map to the size of a similar unit on the ground. A 1:1 scale means that any unit (for example, a centimeter) on the map represents that same unit (a centimeter) on the ground, although this is an impractical map scale because the map is as large as the area mapped! A more appropriate scale for a local map is 1:24,000, in which 1 unit on the map represents 24,000 identical units on the ground.

Map scale can be a tricky concept. Maps rendered at a smaller scale cover a larger area and typically show less detail (**Figure 1.20a**). Conversely, maps rendered at a larger scale cover a smaller area and typically show more detail (**Figure 1.20b**). For physical geographers, a small-scale map of the world works well for illustrating global wind patterns or ocean currents, but is little help in finding an exact location. In contrast, a large-scale map is useful for applications needing precise location, but doesn't show regional or global patterns.

Cartographers express map scale as a representative fraction, a written scale, or a graphic scale (Figure 1.20). A *representative fraction* (*RF*, or *fractional scale*) is expressed with either a colon or a slash, as in 1:125,000 or 1/125,000. No actual units of measurement are mentioned because any unit is applicable as long as both parts of the fraction are in the same unit: 1 cm to 125,000 cm, 1 in. to 125,000 in., or 1 mile to 125,000 miles.

A *written scale* is a statement of the relationship between different, but related, units; for example, "1 centimeter equals 5 kilometers" or "1 inch equals 8 miles." In Figure 1.20b, note that the RF 1:24,000 converts to a written scale of "1 inch = 2000 feet" (divide 24,000 inches by 12 inches/1 ft for the conversion to feet).

A *graphic scale*, or *bar scale*, is a bar graph with units to allow measurement of distances on the map. An important advantage of a graphic scale is that, if the map is enlarged or reduced, the graphic scale enlarges or reduces along with the map. In contrast, written and fractional scales become incorrect with enlargement or reduction. As an example, if you shrink a map from 1:24,000 to 1:63,360, the written scale "1 in. to 2000 ft" is no longer correct. The new correct written scale is "1 in. to 5280 ft (1 mi)."

Map scale can be small, medium, or large, depending on the ratio described. In relative terms, an RF of 1:24,000 is a large scale, whereas an RF of 1:50,000,000 is a small scale. The greater the denominator in a fractional scale (or the number on the right in a ratio expression), the smaller the scale of the map.

Map Projections

Flat maps represent our three-dimensional Earth in two dimensions, a conversion that causes distortion. A globe can provide a fairly good representation of *distance*, *direction*, *area*, *shape*, and *proximity* on Earth. However, the properties of a globe cannot be reproduced simultaneously on a flat surface. Simply taking a globe apart and laying it flat on a table illustrates the challenge faced by cartographers (**Figure 1.21**).

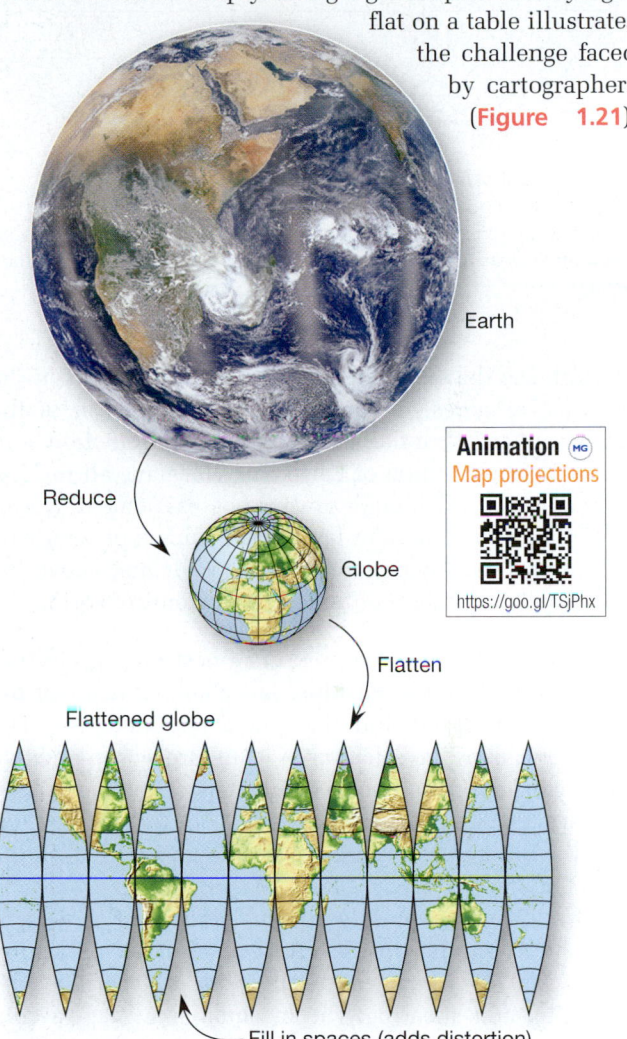

Earth

Animation (MG)
Map projections

https://goo.gl/TSjPhx

Reduce

Globe

Flatten

Flattened globe

Fill in spaces (adds distortion)

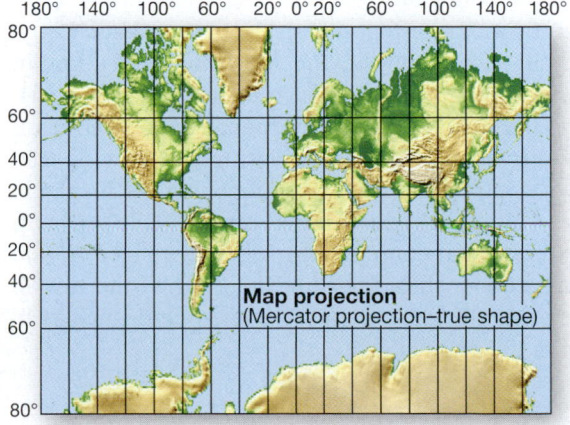

Map projection
(Mercator projection–true shape)

▲**Figure 1.21 From globe to flat map.** Conversion of the globe to a flat map projection requires a decision about which properties to preserve and the amount of distortion that is acceptable. [NASA/NOAA/GSFC/Suomi NPP/VIIRS/Norman Kuring.]

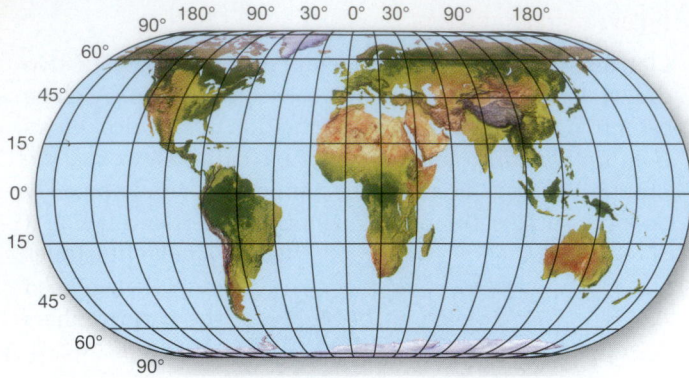

▲**Figure 1.22 An equal-area projection: The Eckert IV.** The Eckert IV is an equal-area pseudocylindrical map projection in which meridians are semiellipses (portions of ellipses) and parallels are spaced to preserve area. The length of the polar lines is half the length of the equator.

You can see the empty spaces that open up between the sections, or gores, of the globe. This reduction of the spherical Earth to a flat surface is a **map projection**, and no flat map projection of Earth can ever have all the features of a globe. Flat maps always possess some degree of distortion—much less for large-scale maps representing a few kilometers; much more for small-scale maps covering individual countries, continents, or the entire world.

Equal Area or True Shape? The best map projection is determined by the location and characteristics of the area being mapped and the map's intended use. The major decisions in selecting a map projection involve the properties of **equal area** (equivalence) and **true shape** (conformality). A decision favoring one property sacrifices the other, for they cannot be shown together on the same flat map.

If a cartographer selects equal area as the desired trait—for example, the Eckert IV equal-area projection in **Figure 1.22**—then true shape must be sacrificed by stretching and shearing. On an equal-area map, a coin covers the same amount of surface area no matter where you place it on the map.

In contrast, if a cartographer selects true shape as the desired trait—for example, the Mercator projection in Figure 1.21 at the bottom—then equal area must be sacrificed, and the scale will actually change from one region of the map to another. For centuries, maps showing true shape were important for navigation using a magnetic compass. Any straight line drawn on the Mercator map is a line of constant compass bearing, known as a *rhumb line*. Thus, once a ship navigator determined the rhumb line using the Mercator map, the course could be easily followed in the open ocean.

Classes of Projections Figure 1.23 illustrates four classes of map projections and the perspective from which each class is generated. Despite the fact that

modern cartographic technology uses mathematical constructions and computer-assisted graphics, we still use the word *projection*. The term comes from times past, when geographers actually projected the shadow of a wire-skeleton globe onto a geometric surface, such as a cylinder, plane, or cone. The wires represented parallels, meridians, and outlines of the continents. A light source casts a shadow pattern of these lines from the globe onto the chosen geometric surface.

The main map projection classes include the *cylindrical*, *planar* (also called azimuthal), and *conic*. Another class of projections, which cannot be derived from this physical-perspective approach, is the nonperspective oval shape. Still other projections derive from purely mathematical calculations.

With projections, the contact line or contact point between the wire globe and the projection surface—a *standard line* or *standard point*—is the only place where all globe properties are preserved, making a standard line true to scale along its entire length without any distortion. Areas away from this line or point become increasingly distorted.

The **Mercator projection** discussed earlier is a *cylindrical projection* invented by Gerardus Mercator in 1569 (Figure 1.23a). The Mercator is a true shape (conformal) projection, with meridians appearing as equally spaced straight lines and parallels appearing as straight lines that are spaced closer together near the equator. The poles are infinitely stretched, with the 84th N parallel and 84th S parallel fixed at the same length as that of the equator. The Mercator projection is cut off near the 80th parallel in each hemisphere because of the severe distortion at higher latitudes.

Although still used for navigation, Mercator projections are rarely used as world maps because they present false notions of the size (area) of some landmasses on Earth. A dramatic example on the Mercator projection is Greenland, which looks bigger than all of South America. In reality, Greenland is an island only one eighth the size of South America and is actually 20% smaller than Argentina alone.

The *gnomonic projection* in Figure 1.23b is a type of planar projection generated by projecting a light source at the center of a globe onto a plane that is tangent to (touching) the globe's surface. The resulting severe distortion prevents showing a full hemisphere on one projection.

Great Circle Routes on Map Projections The routes of long, international air flights illustrate the distortion that occurs when representing a spherical globe on a flat map. To save time and fuel, these routes follow *great circle routes*, the shortest distance between two points on a sphere (**Figure 1.24**). This distance falls along a great circle (see Figure 1.17). The gnomonic projection portrays a great circle route as a straight line (Figure 1.24a). By comparison, the Mercator projection

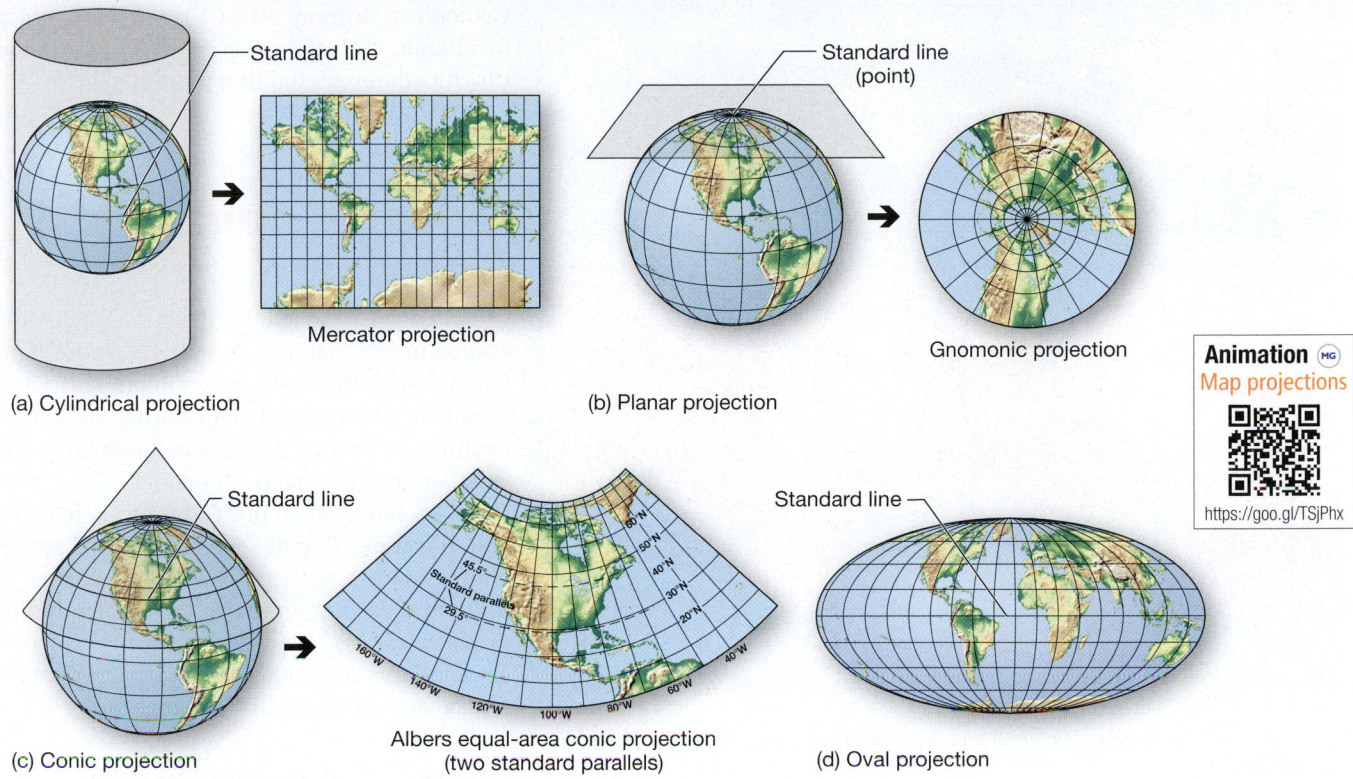

▲**Figure 1.23** **Classes of map projections.**

shows a great circle route as a curved line, making it appear longer (Figure 1.24b).

Types of Maps

Geographers and the general public use many different types of maps to portray a range of features—mountains and valleys, political borders, transportation systems—and a range of data, such as geology, climate, population, and development patterns. A *planimetric map* shows the horizontal position (latitude/longitude) of

political boundaries, bodies of water, and economic and cultural features. A highway map is a common example of a planimetric map, as are the maps in Figure 1.20.

The shape of a land surface also has a vertical component known as **topography** (the general term for the undulations and variations of a surface), which includes slope and **relief**, the vertical differences in local landscape elevation. A **topographic map**, or "topo" map, shows position and elevation on Earth's land surface

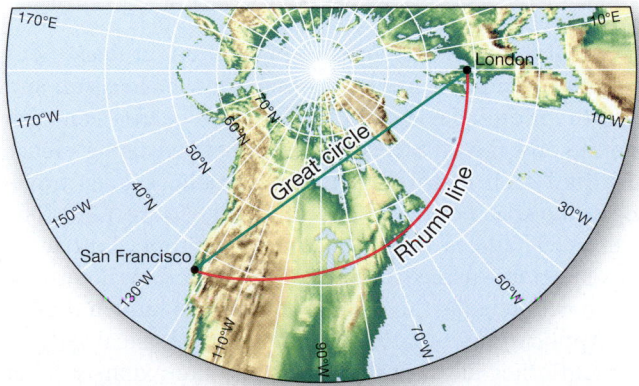

(a) The gnomonic projection is used to determine the shortest distance (great circle route) between San Francisco and London because on this projection the arc of a great circle is a straight line.

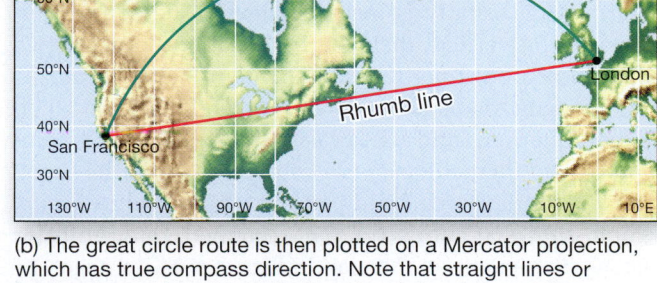

(b) The great circle route is then plotted on a Mercator projection, which has true compass direction. Note that straight lines or bearings on a Mercator projection (rhumb lines) are not the shortest route.

▲**Figure 1.24** **Determining great circle routes.**

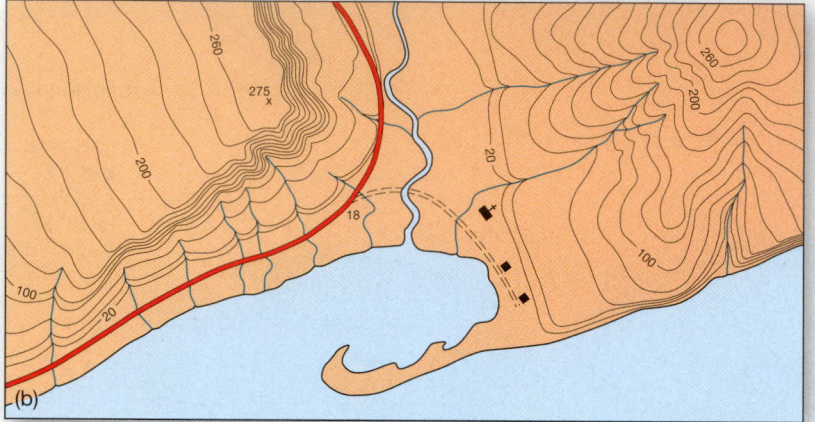

▲Figure 1.25 (a) Perspective view and (b) topographic map of a hypothetical landscape. [USGS.]

using **contour lines** connecting all points at the same elevation. A contour line is a type of *isoline*, a line on a map that connects points of equal value.

Figure 1.25 shows a hypothetical landscape and topographic (topo) map, demonstrating how contour lines and intervals depict slope and relief—the three-dimensional aspects of terrain. The pattern of lines and the spacing between them indicate slope. The steeper a slope or cliff, the closer together the contour lines appear. In the figure, note the narrowly spaced contours that represent the cliffs to the left of the highway (red line). A wider spacing of these contour lines portrays a more gradual slope, as you can see from the widely spaced lines on the beach and to the right of the river valley.

Scientists use topo maps for landscape analysis. Recreationists use topos, which are included with some GPS units, for navigation. On a topographic map, elevations are shown above or below a vertical datum, or reference level, which usually is mean sea level. The contour interval is the vertical distance in elevation between two adjacent contour lines (20 ft, or 6.1 m in Figure 1.25b).

Thematic maps show data of a specific subject, such as precipitation, land use, or earthquake hazard. A common type of thematic map is a *choropleth* (from the Greek *choro*, meaning "area," and *pleth*, meaning "value") *map*, which shows quantitative data grouped into units or classes. For example, the map in Figure 6.24 on page 171 shows the number of days with fog, with data grouped into classes. Another example is the temperature range map in Figure 4.31 on page 106, which uses different colors to show the temperature range intervals.

For more information on maps used in this text and standard map symbols, turn to Appendix A. The U.S.

Geological Survey (USGS) *National Map* (available at http://nationalmap.gov/) provides downloadable digital topographic data for the entire United States.

Modern Tools for Geoscience

When you use Google Earth or the navigation system in your car, you are relying on the same technologies that help geographers and Earth scientists analyse and map Earth: the Global Positioning System (GPS), remote sensing, and geographic information systems (GIS). GPS relies on satellites in orbit to provide location and elevation. Remote sensing utilizes spacecraft, aircraft, and ground-based sensors to provide data that enhance our understanding of Earth. GIS is a means for storing and processing large amounts of spatial data as separate layers of geographic information.

Global Positioning System

When location services are turned on in your smartphone, websites and apps use your location, for example for searches using Google Maps. How do these devices determine location? Smartphones have a number of different built-in location systems, the most accurate of which is GPS. The **Global Positioning System (GPS)** uses radio signals from satellites to accurately determine your location in terms of latitude, longitude, and elevation anywhere on or near the surface of Earth. The system comprises at least 27 orbiting satellites that transmit navigational signals to receivers on Earth. In areas where GPS satellites are inaccessible (such as in mountainous terrain or the urban "canyons" of the inner city), smartphones use Bluetooth, WiFi hotspots, and cell towers to determine location.

A GPS receiver senses signals from at least four satellites—a minimum of three satellites for location and a fourth for timing corrections. The distance between each satellite and the GPS receiver is calculated using clocks built into each instrument that time radio signals traveling at the speed of light between them (Figure 1.26). The receiver calculates its true position—latitude, longitude, and elevation—using trilateration, a method for determining a position using the distance from three known points.

Applications of GPS technology in physical geography and other Earth systems sciences are extensive. For example, on Mount St. Helens in Washington, a network of GPS stations measure ground deformation associated with earthquake activity (Figure 1.27). In southern California, a similar GPS system can record fault movement as small as 1 mm (0.04 in.). Another example occurs in the Mohave Desert of California, Nevada, and Arizona, where golden eagles are fitted with GPS "backpacks" to track movement and determine habitat, with the goal of

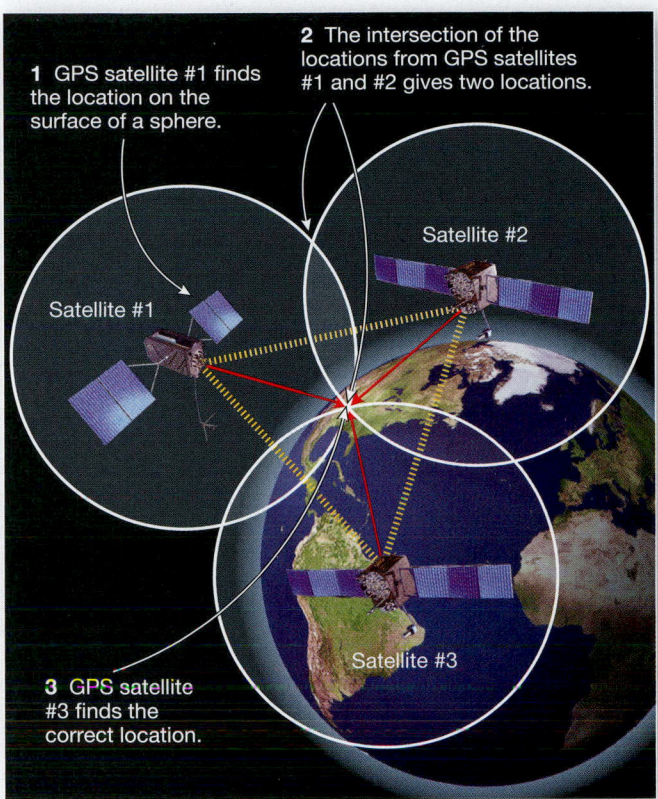

▲**Figure 1.26 Using GPS satellites to determine location.**

without having physical contact with the object, is **remote sensing**. Scientists collect these data from a distance using satellites, aircraft, and remote submersibles in the oceans. Remote sensing is nothing new to humans; we do it with our eyes as we scan the environment, sensing the shape, size, and color of objects from a distance by registering energy from the visible-wavelength portion of the electromagnetic spectrum (discussed in Chapter 2, see Figure 2.7). A camera is a remote-sensing instrument because it intercepts the wavelengths for which its film or sensor is designed.

Aerial photographs from balloons and aircraft were the first type of remote sensing, used for many years to improve the accuracy of surface maps. Later, remote sensors on satellites, the International Space Station, and other craft were used to sense a broader range of wavelengths beyond the visible range of our eyes. These sensors "see" wavelengths other than visible light (such as infrared and microwave radar). As examples, infrared sensing produces images based on the temperature of objects on the ground, microwave sensing reveals features below Earth's surface, and radar sensing shows land surface elevations, even in areas that are obscured by clouds.

species conservation as renewable energy expands rapidly in the region (**Figure 1.28**). For many kinds of scientists, GPS technology is both convenient and precise, reducing the need for traditional land surveys that require point-to-point line-of-sight measurements on the ground.

Remote Sensing

The science of obtaining information about distant objects through the emission or reflection of electromagnetic energy,

▼**Figure 1.28 A female Golden Eagle fitted with a GPS–GSM unit in California.** The GSM (global system for mobile communications) stores locations every 15 minutes and sends data once per day to a server over the cellular network. [Daniel Driscoll, American Eagle Research Institute/USGS.]

▼**Figure 1.27 GPS base station on Mount St. Helens volcano.** [Mike Poland/USGS.]

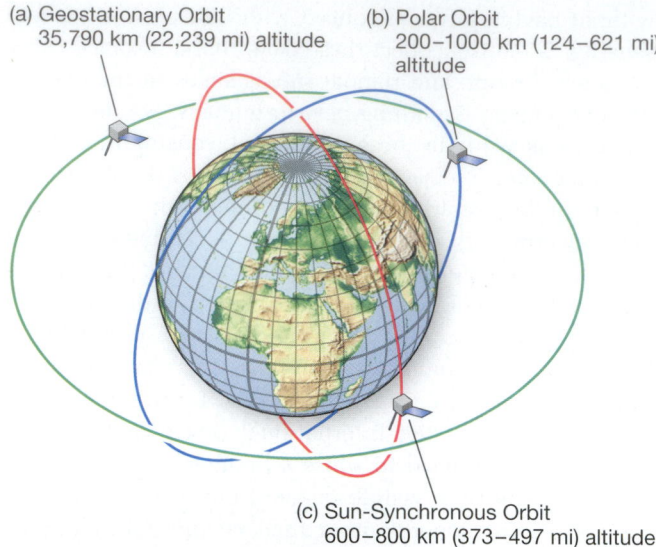

(a) Geostationary Orbit
35,790 km (22,239 mi) altitude

(b) Polar Orbit
200–1000 km (124–621 mi) altitude

(c) Sun-Synchronous Orbit
600–800 km (373–497 mi) altitude

▲**Figure 1.29 Three satellite orbital paths.** Satellites are set in specific orbital paths according to the type of data and imagery required. For example, weather satellites are in geostationary orbit so they remain "parked" over a certain area.

Satellite Imaging During the last 50 years, satellite remote sensing has transformed Earth observation. Different portions of Earth's surface emit energy in different wavelengths depending on the temperature and other physical characteristics of surface materials. Satellites and other craft sense and record these emissions and send the data to receiving stations on the ground. The receiving stations sort these wavelengths into specific bands, or ranges. Computers then process these data and produce a variety of digital images, including those with simulated natural color, "false" color to highlight a particular feature, and enhanced contrast.

Satellites are set in specific orbital paths that affect the type of data and imagery produced (**Figure 1.29**). Geostationary (or geosynchronous) orbits effectively match Earth's rotation speed so that one orbit is completed in about 24 hours (Figure 1.29a). These satellites remain in a "fixed" position so that satellite antennas on Earth can be pointed permanently at one position in the sky where the satellite is located.

The angle, or *inclination*, of a satellite's orbit in relation to Earth's equator affects remotely sensed data. Some satellites orbit near the equator to monitor Earth's tropical regions, acquiring data only from low latitudes. Monitoring the polar regions requires a satellite in polar orbit, with a higher inclination of about 90° (Figure 1.29b).

One type of polar orbit useful for scientific observation is a Sun-synchronous orbit (Figure 1.29c). This orbit is synchronous with the Sun, so that the satellite crosses the equator at the same local solar time each day. Ground observation is maximized in Sun-synchronous orbit because Earth surfaces viewed from the satellite are illuminated by the Sun at a consistent angle. This enables better comparison of images from year to year because lighting and shadows do not change.

Passive Remote Sensing Like the human eye, passive remote-sensing systems record wavelengths of energy radiated from a surface, particularly visible light and infrared. Thus, passive sensors detect energy that is naturally emitted by the object (such as heat energy) or that is reflected by sunlight.

A number of satellites carry passive remote sensors for weather forecasting. The *Geostationary Operational Environmental Satellites*, or *GOES*, provide information for weather monitoring, including the images you see in weather reports. Figure 1.4a showing Hurricane Patricia in the Western Hemisphere is a *GOES* image.

Geographers and other scientists use images from passive remote sensors for many applications (**Figure 1.30**). An example is tracking landscape change over time, often

Rio Doce

Brazil

Atlantic Ocean

Contaminant plume

5 km   N

▲**Figure 1.30** *Landsat* **image of the Rio Doce in Brazil, carrying contaminated water from an iron mine to the Atlantic Ocean.** This natural color image was captured on November 30, 2015, more than 3 weeks after a dam holding toxic pollutants in a tailings pond failed in southeastern Brazil. [Joshua Stevens, NASA/USGS.]

GEOreport 1.2 Polar-orbiting satellites predict Hurricane Sandy's path

Scientists reported in 2013 that polar-orbiting satellites, such as the *Suomi NPP*, were critical for predicting Hurricane Sandy's track in October 2012. Without data from these satellites, predictions for Sandy would have been off by hundreds of miles, showing the storm heading out to sea rather than turning toward the New Jersey coast. *Suomi* orbits Earth about 14 times each day, collecting data from nearly the entire planet and producing many of the beautiful NASA "Blue Marble" Earth images.

using data from *Landsat* satellites, which began imaging Earth in the 1970s (view more images at http://earthobservatory.nasa.gov). *Landsat-5* retired in 2012 after 29 years, the longest-running Earth-observing mission in history; *Landsat-8* launched in 2013, beginning the new *Landsat* program managed by the USGS.

Active Remote Sensing Instruments that direct a beam of energy at a surface and analyze the energy reflected back are active remote sensors. An example is *radar* (*radio detection and ranging*). A radar transmitter emits short bursts of energy toward the subject terrain, penetrating clouds and darkness, resulting in an image derived from the energy reflected back to the radar receiver. Another example is *sonar* (*sound navigation and ranging*), used for ocean floor mapping because sound waves travel farther distances in water than radar or light waves.

LIDAR (*light and radar*) is another active remote-sensing technology. LIDAR systems, typically fitted to aircraft, collect highly detailed and accurate data for surface terrain using a laser scanner with up to 150,000 pulses per second, 8 pulses or more per square meter, providing 15 m (49.2 ft) resolution (**Figure 1.31**). GPS systems onboard the aircraft determine the location of each pulse, resulting in a "point cloud" of data that can be used to generate different types of geospatial models, including digital elevation models (discussed ahead).

LIDAR is especially useful for mapping the ground surface in heavily forested areas because as each pulse of light is reflected, it can have multiple returns, the first return from the highest objects (trees) and later returns from lower objects and the ground. Thus the trees can be

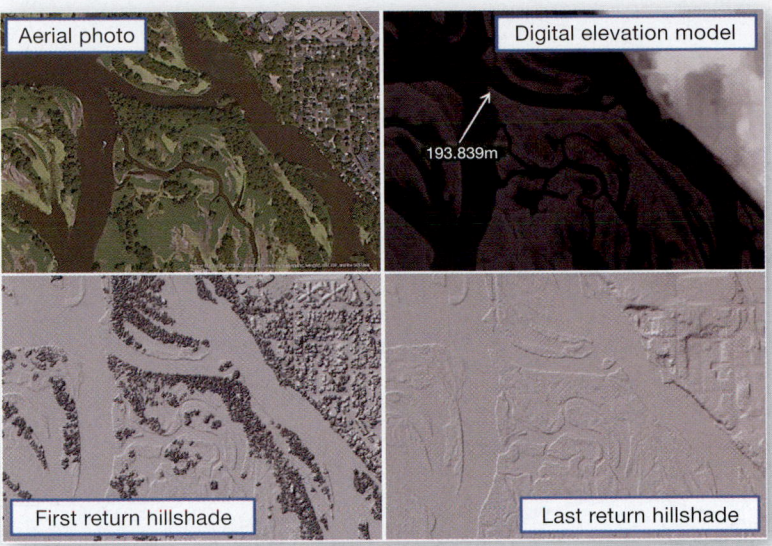

(a) Photograph and LIDAR maps of a section of the river channel. Note that the first return shows vegetation, while the last return shows bare ground.

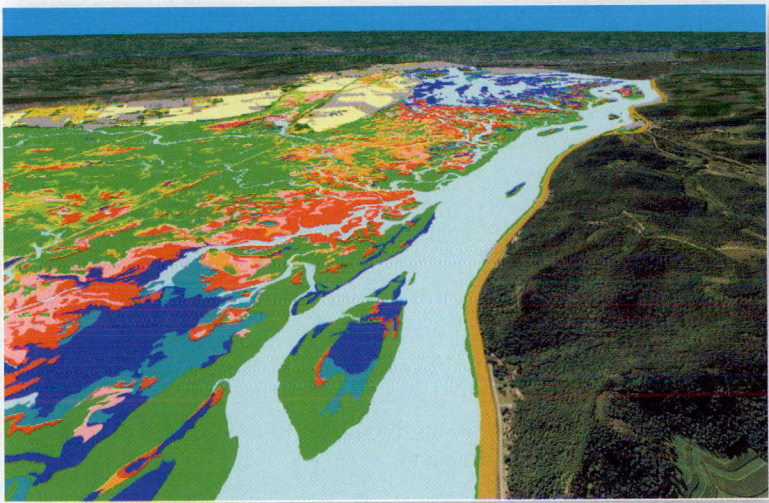

(b) Perspective view of the channel shows land cover data overlaid on aerial photography and LIDAR.

▲**Figure 1.32 LIDAR mapping of the Upper Mississippi River, Minnesota and Iowa.** [Upper Mississippi River Restoration Program, U.S. Army Corps of Engineers/USGS. http://www.umesc.usgs.gov/mapping/resource_mapping_ltrmp_lidar.html.]

"filtered out" to allow a view of ground surface topography and cultural sites.

LIDAR data sets are often shared among private, public, and scientific users for multiple applications. Scientists are presently collecting and distributing LIDAR data to assess river flows and habitat as part of the Upper Mississippi River Restoration Program (**Figure 1.32**).

Geospatial Data Analysis

Techniques such as remote sensing acquire large volumes of spatial data that must be processed for scientific applications. Scientists use a number of rapidly developing technologies for analysis and visualization of large data sets.

Geographic Information Systems A **geographic information system (GIS)** is a computer-based data-processing tool for gathering, manipulating, and analyzing

▲**Figure 1.31 Airborne LIDAR.** LIDAR surveys produce digital surface models showing the vegetation canopy or only the bare ground.

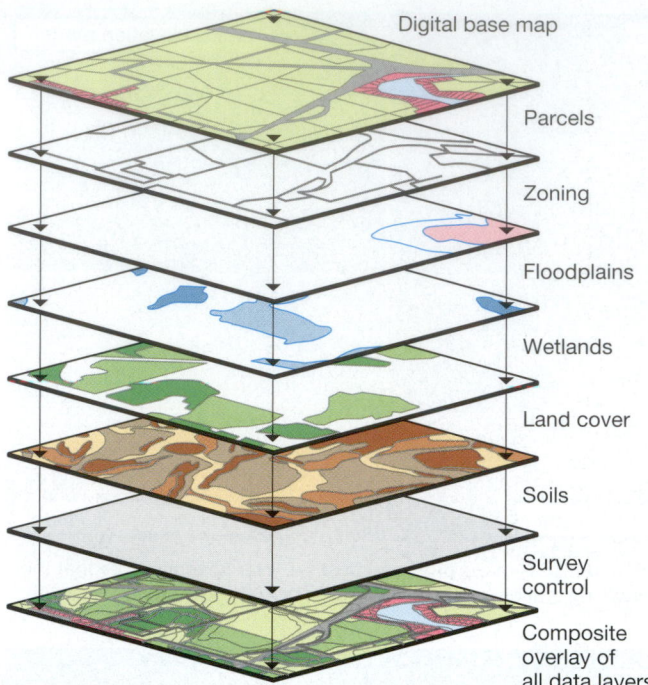

▲**Figure 1.33** **GIS model shows an example of layered spatial data used for geographic analyses.** [After USGS.]

geographic data. In a GIS, spatial data can be organized in layers, or planes, containing different kinds of information (**Figure 1.33**). The beginning component for any GIS is a base map, such as scanned or digitized paper maps or georeferenced aerial photos and satellite imagery (the top layer in Figure 1.33). This map establishes reference points against which to accurately position other data, such as remotely sensed imagery.

Geographic information science (GISci) is the field that develops the capabilities of GIS technology for use within geography and other disciplines. GISci analyzes Earth and human phenomena over time—for example, the study of diseases, the destruction from earthquakes, and the status of endangered species.

GIS technology is widely used in the creation of maps with a three-dimensional perspective. *Digital elevation models* (DEMs) of the land surface, such as shown in Figure 1.32a, provide base elevation data of the terrain, which can then be overlaid with satellite imagery. Data for DEMs can come from LIDAR or ground survey data, or from satellite radar. In 2000, the Shuttle Radar Topography Mission (SRTM) instruments on board the Space Shuttle *Endeavor* surveyed 80% of Earth's land surface, providing high-resolution data that are typically combined with image overlay to display topography (**Figure 1.34**). These data are then available for animations and other scientific analyses.

Geovisualization When you use Google Maps to find a restaurant or coffee shop, you are using a geovisualization tool. *Geovisualization* is a set of technologies for adjusting geospatial data sets in real time so that users can instantly make changes to maps and other visual models. An example is Google Earth, which uses satellite imagery to provide three-dimensional viewing of the globe and related geographic information. Google Earth and similar downloadable programs allow the user to instantly zoom in on landscapes and features of interest.

Access to GIS technology, geovisualization tools, and large scientific data sets is expanding and becoming more user-friendly. Public access to large remote-sensing data sets for analysis and display is now available, without the need to download large amounts of data (see examples of research applications at http://disc.sci.gsfc.nasa.gov/).

▶**Figure 1.34** **Digital elevation model of Mount St. Helens, Washington.** The view here is looking to the southeast. The 1989 volcanic eruption took out the north side of the mountain. DEM displays terrain elevation data with a satellite image overlay. [Shuttle Radar Topography Mission, courtesy of JPL/NGS/NASA-Cal Tech.]

FOCUSstudy 1.2
Using GIS to Prevent Aircraft Bird Strikes
By Redina Herman, Western Illinois University

Geographers use geospatial tools such as GPS, GIS, and remote sensing to solve real-world problems. One example is the hazard of bird strikes by aircraft. To address this problem, scientists and airport personnel combine information on bird habitats and migration paths, airport locations, and real-time bird movements into a layered GIS. Analyses of these spatial data can then help pilots minimize the number of aircraft collisions with birds.

Birds are hard to see from an aircraft in flight. If hit in midair, large birds (such as vultures and eagles) or large flocks of birds (such as geese and gulls) can damage aircraft. The January 2009 bird strike that caused engine failure on a commercial flight shortly after takeoff from LaGuardia Airport, forcing a water landing in the Hudson River, focused public attention on the bird-strike hazard. Bird strikes result in annual damage estimated at $650 million in the United States and $1.2 billion worldwide.

Several strategies can help aviation specialists reduce aircraft bird strikes. One strategy is to assess and manage bird habitats around airports. Trees, grassy fields, and water retention ponds make an area more attractive to flocks of birds. For example, at New York's John F. Kennedy International Airport, wetlands next to the airport are a major waystation for migratory birds. Removing these natural landscape elements can help reduce the bird-strike hazard. Another option is to scare birds away using loud noises produced by "bird cannons" that fire compressed air.

A second strategy is to track and map seasonal bird migration patterns with GPS transmitters similar to the one shown in Figure 1.28. The danger of bird strikes increases during seasonal migrations when many birds follow routes that take them near major airports (Figure 1.2.1). Using GIS, planners develop models of seasonal bird movements so that air traffic controllers can identify hazardous flight paths. The U.S. Air Force has created a database of bird migration around the country as part of its Avian Hazard Avoidance System (see http://www.usahas.com/).

Finally, air traffic controllers can track real-time bird movement near airports using remote sensing technology such as radar. The highest risk of bird strike occurs during takeoff and landing, or during low-altitude flight. If the aircraft path looks like it will intersect birds in flight, the pilot may

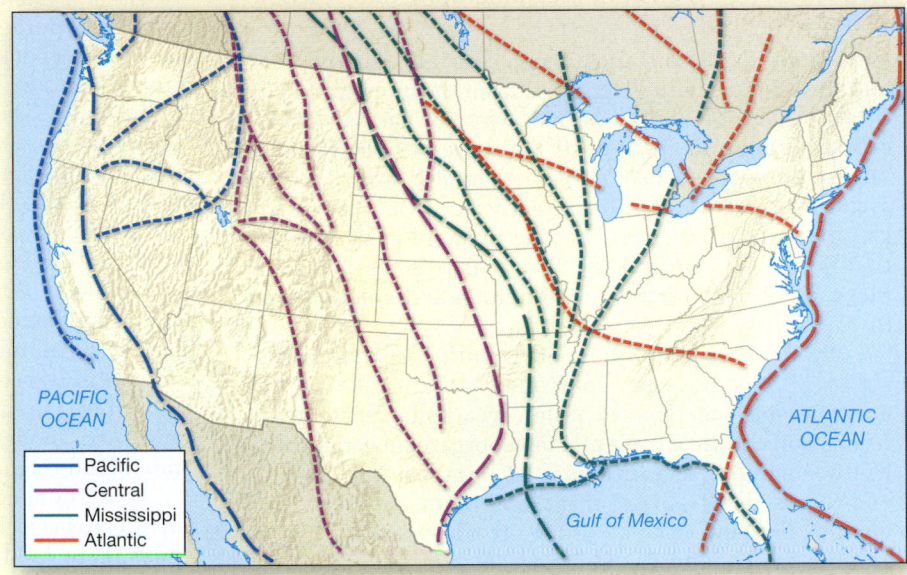

Pacific
Central
Mississippi
Atlantic

(a) Bird migration pathways of North America.

(b) Major airport locations in the United States.

▲**Figure 1.2.1 Migration pathways and airport locations.** [(a) NOAA/climate.gov (b) Federal Aviation Administration.]

be asked to delay takeoff or landing or to land on a different runway.

Airport personnel today consider bird strikes as a type of weather, and monitor "bird weather" as they monitor actual weather patterns. Using geospatial techniques such as GPS, GIS, and radar remote sensing, aviation analysts can predict bird weather and help pilots avoid the bird-strike hazard.

1. What airport features and landscapes are attractive to birds?

2. What kinds of data are needed to forecast "bird weather"?

APPLYconcepts Refer to the map in Figure 1.2.1 to answer the following questions.

Which airports have the greatest risk of bird strikes related to bird migration? Look for locations with multiple migration paths.	_____
Which airports have the least risk of bird strikes related to migrating birds?	_____

KEY**LEARNING**concepts**review**

Geography (p. 5) combines disciplines from the physical and life sciences with disciplines from the human and cultural sciences to attain a holistic view of Earth. Methods of **spatial analysis** (p. 5) unify this diverse field, focusing on the interdependence among geographic areas, natural systems, society, and cultural activities over space. Geographic science integrates a wide range of subject matter traditionally categorized into five major themes: **location**, **place**, **movement**, **region**, and **human–Earth relationships** (p. 5).

Physical geography (p. 6) applies spatial analysis to all the physical components that make up the environment—energy, air, water, weather, climate, landforms, soils, animals, plants, microorganisms, and Earth itself—including the influence of humans. The analysis of **process** (p. 6)—a set of actions or mechanisms that operate in some special order—is also central to geographic understanding. Physical geography is an essential aspect of **Earth systems science** (p. 7).

1. Define physical geography and review the type of analysis that characterizes the geographic sciences.

Scientists from all disciplines follow the *scientific process*, which relies on a general series of steps that make up the **scientific method** (p. 7). Results and conclusions from scientific experiments can lead to basic theories that advance scientific knowledge, as well as applied uses for the general public. Recently, **sustainability science** (p. 8) has become an important discipline integrating sustainable development and functioning Earth systems.

2. Sketch a flow diagram of the scientific method, beginning with observations and ending with the development of theories.
3. Summarize current population growth and sustainability issues in your own words: population size, global distribution, the impact per person, and future projections.

A **system** (p. 10) is any ordered set of interacting components and their attributes, as distinct from their surrounding environment. Earth is an **open system** (p. 10) in terms of energy, receiving energy from the Sun, but it is essentially a **closed system** (p. 10) in terms of matter and physical resources. *Energy* is the capacity to do work, and it takes many forms, such as radiant energy (energy that travels in waves through space), **kinetic energy**, (p. 11), (energy of motion), **potential energy**, (p. 11), (energy stored due to composition or position), and chemical energy (the energy stored in the molecular bonds of substances).

As a system operates, "information" is returned to various points in the operational process via pathways of **feedback loops** (p. 13). If the feedback information discourages change in the system, it is **negative feedback** (p. 13). Such negative feedback causes self-regulation in a natural system, stabilizing the system. If feedback information encourages change in the system, it is **positive feedback** (p. 13). When the rates of inputs and outputs in the system are equal and the amounts of energy and matter in storage within the system are constant or when they fluctuate around a stable average, the system is in **steady-state equilibrium** (p. 14). A **threshold** (p. 14), or tipping point, is the moment at which a system can no longer maintain its character and lurches to a new operational level. Geographers often construct a simplified **model** (p. 14) of natural systems to better understand them.

Four immense open systems powerfully interact at Earth's surface: three *abiotic*, or nonliving, systems—the **atmosphere** (p. 14), **hydrosphere**, (p. 14), (including the **cryosphere**, p. 14), and **lithosphere** (p. 14)—and a *biotic* (p. 14), or living, system—the **biosphere** (p. 14).

4. What is the difference between an open system and a closed system? Describe an example of an open system.
5. What is the difference between a positive feedback loop and a negative feedback loop?

The science that studies Earth's shape and size is **geodesy** (p. 15). Earth bulges slightly through the equator and is oblate (flattened) at the poles, making its surface a misshapened spheroid, or **geoid** (p. 15). Absolute location on Earth is described with a specific reference grid of **parallels** of **latitude** (measuring distances north and south of the equator), (p. 18), and **meridians** of **longitude** (measuring distances east and west of a prime meridian), (p. 19). A historic breakthrough in navigation occurred with the establishment of an international **prime meridian** (0° through Greenwich, England), (p. 19). A **great circle** (p. 20) is any circle of Earth's circumference whose center coincides with the center of Earth. **Small circles** are those whose centers do not coincide with Earth's center.

The prime meridian provided the basis for **Greenwich Mean Time (GMT)**, (p. 20), the world's first universal time system. Today, **Coordinated Universal Time (UTC)**, (p. 21), is the worldwide standard and the basis for international time zones. A corollary of the prime meridian is the 180° meridian, the **International Date Line (IDL)**, (p. 21) which marks the place where each day officially begins. **Daylight saving time** (p. 22) is a seasonal change of clocks by 1 hour in summer months.

6. In which latitudinal geographic zone do you live?
7. What and where is the prime meridian?

Define cartography and mapping basics: map scale and map projections.

A **map** (p. 22), is a generalized depiction of the layout of an area, usually some portion of Earth's surface, as seen from above and greatly reduced in size. **Cartography** (p. 22), is the science and art of mapmaking. **Digital cartography,** (p. 22) or *digital mapping*, refers to data collected and presented in a virtual image on a computer or mobile device. **Map scale** (p. 23), is the ratio of the image on a map to the real world; it relates a unit on the map to a corresponding unit on the ground. When creating a **map projection** (p. 24), cartographers select the class of projection that is the best compromise for the map's specific purpose. Relative abilities to portray **equal area**, (p. 24), (equivalence), **true shape** (conformality), (p. 24), true direction, and true distance are all considerations in selecting a projection. The **Mercator projection** (p. 24), is in the cylindrical class; it has true-shape qualities and straight lines that show constant direction.

Topography (p. 25) is the general term for the undulations and variations of a surface, including slope and **relief**, (p. 25) the vertical differences in local landscape elevation on Earth's surface. A **topographic map** (p. 25) shows the shape of the land surface using **contour lines** (p. 26) that connect all points at the same elevation.

8. What is map scale? In what three ways may it be expressed on a map?
9. What does a contour line represent on a topographic map?

Describe three geoscience tools—the Global Positioning System (GPS), remote sensing, and geographic information systems (GIS)—and *explain* how these tools are used in geographic analysis.

Latitude, longitude, and elevation are accurately measured using **Global Positioning System (GPS)** instrumentation (p. 26), that reads radio signals from satellites. Orbital and aerial **remote sensing** (p. 27), obtains information about Earth systems from great distances without the need for physical contact. Satellites receive radiant-energy data that are then transmitted to Earth-based receivers and recorded in digital form. Geospatial data may be analyzed using **geographic information system (GIS)** technology (p. 29). *Digital elevation models* are three-dimensional products of GIS technology.

10. How does a GPS find your location and elevation on Earth? Give an example of GPS technology used for scientific purposes.
11. What is remote sensing? What are you viewing when you observe a LIDAR image?

GEO**SPATIAL** ANALYSIS

Citizen Science

Citizens collecting high quality data can make a big contribution to the science community. These data are used by scientists to fill in gaps in the data and improve forecasts.

Activities

Go to the CoCoRaHS website at http://www.cocorahs.org/ and find a county near you with a CoCoRaHS station. Click on "View Data" and then click on "Daily Precipitation Reports." Enter the name of the state and county. Choose a start date of one week ago and an end date of today so you can examine the last 7 days of data. Click "Search" to display the stations in your county. If there are multiple stations enter the Station Number for one of the stations in the "Station Fields" box and check "Station Number." Click "Search."

1. During the last seven days, how many days had precipitation reports?

2. What is the precipitation total for the week? If applicable, how many inches of snow?

3. Do these reports reflect what you experienced during those same days? Explain and analyze.

Go back and find a county that is reporting precipitation and has multiple CoCoRaHS observation stations.

4. Notice that for a given day not all of the stations report the same amount of precipitation. What might be an explanation for this?

5. What is the precipitation total for the week? How many inches of snow?

MasteringGeography™

Looking for additional review and test prep materials? Visit the Study Area in MasteringGeography™ to enhance your geographic literacy, spatial reasoning skills, and understanding of this chapter's content by accessing a variety of resources, including MapMaster™ interactive maps, videos, *Mobile Field Trips*, *Project Condor* Quadcopter videos, *In the News* RSS feeds, flashcards, web links, self-study quizzes, and an eText version of *Geosystems*.

The Energy–Atmosphere System

Isle of Skye,
Scotland

▲ The sun rises over the rugged landscape of the Trotternish peninsula on the Isle of Skye in the Inner Hebrides archipelago, Scotland. [fotovoyager/Getty Images.]

Part I, the Energy–Atmosphere System, begins our study of Earth's physical and living systems. Radiant energy from the Sun provides the essential input that powers Earth systems. Because of Earth's curvature, the energy arriving from the Sun is unevenly distributed at the top of the atmosphere, creating energy imbalances over the surface. As a result, the equatorial region experiences surpluses, receiving more

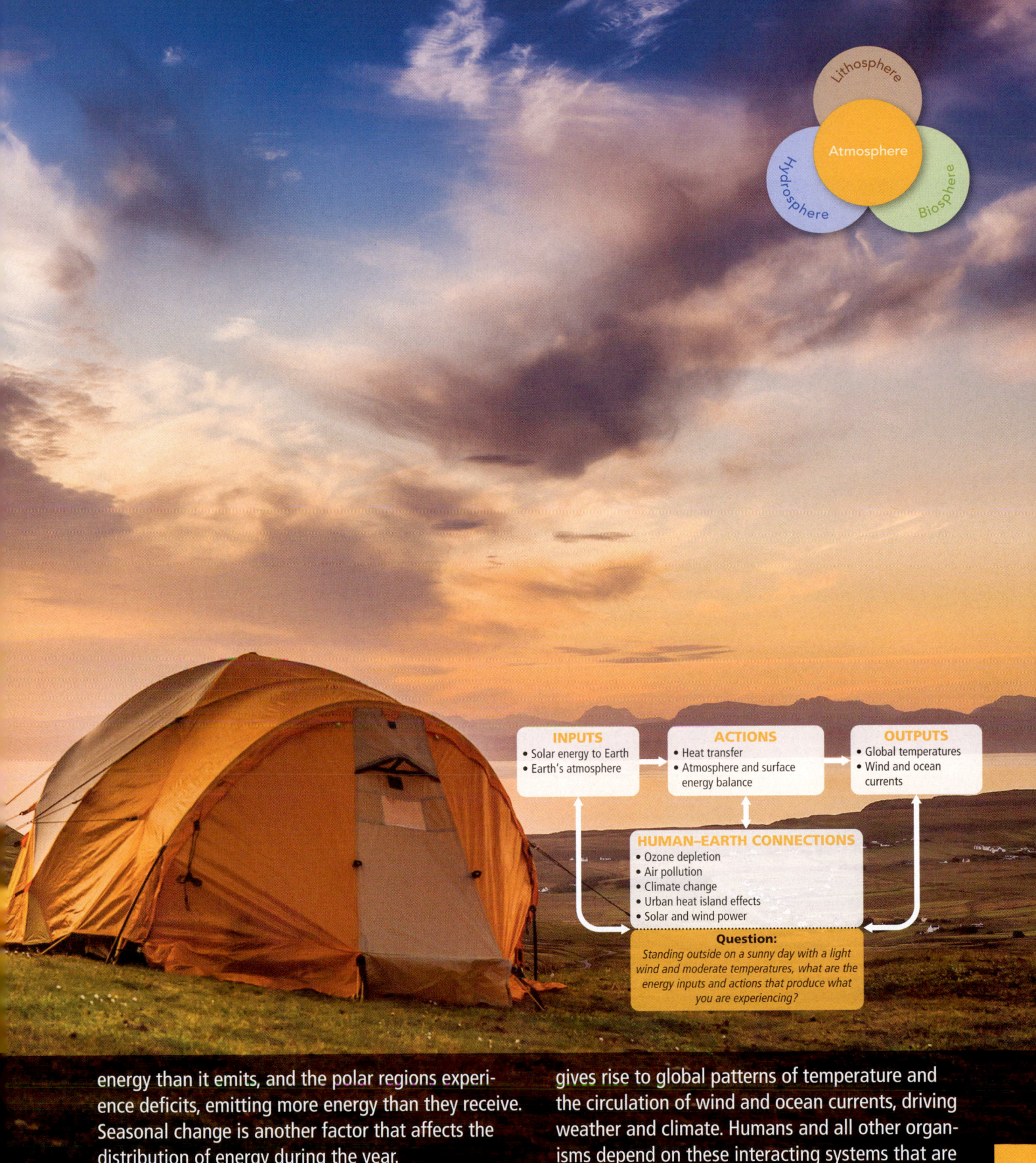

INPUTS
- Solar energy to Earth
- Earth's atmosphere

ACTIONS
- Heat transfer
- Atmosphere and surface energy balance

OUTPUTS
- Global temperatures
- Wind and ocean currents

HUMAN–EARTH CONNECTIONS
- Ozone depletion
- Air pollution
- Climate change
- Urban heat island effects
- Solar and wind power

Question:
Standing outside on a sunny day with a light wind and moderate temperatures, what are the energy inputs and actions that produce what you are experiencing?

energy than it emits, and the polar regions experience deficits, emitting more energy than they receive. Seasonal change is another factor that affects the distribution of energy during the year.

Earth's atmosphere acts as an efficient filter, absorbing most harmful radiation and charged particles so that they do not reach Earth's surface. In the lower atmosphere the unevenness of daily energy receipt gives rise to global patterns of temperature and the circulation of wind and ocean currents, driving weather and climate. Humans and all other organisms depend on these interacting systems that are set into motion by energy from the Sun.

2 Solar Energy to Earth and the Seasons

San Juan Mountains, Colorado, USA

Global climate change is affecting the timing of seasons on Earth. The spectacular leaf changes of autumn, shown here in southwest Colorado's San Juan Mountains, are happening later in the year as air temperatures rise. [Ron Niebrugge/Alamy.]

KEY**LEARNING**concepts

After reading the chapter, you should be able to:

- **Locate** Earth in the Universe, **describe** the formation of our Solar System, and **sketch** Earth's orbital path around the Sun.

- **Describe** the Sun's operation, and **explain** the solar wind and the electromagnetic spectrum of radiant energy.

- **Illustrate** the interception of solar energy and its uneven distribution at the top of the atmosphere.

- **Explain** the concept of seasonality, and **list** the five reasons for Earth's seasons.

- **Describe** the Earth–Sun relationships during the annual march of the seasons.

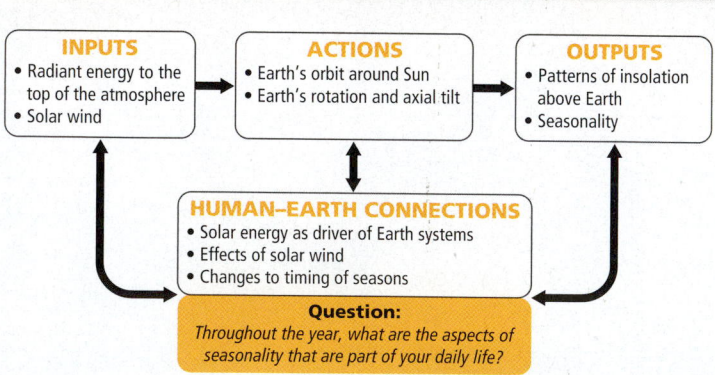

INPUTS
- Radiant energy to the top of the atmosphere
- Solar wind

ACTIONS
- Earth's orbit around Sun
- Earth's rotation and axial tilt

OUTPUTS
- Patterns of insolation above Earth
- Seasonality

HUMAN–EARTH CONNECTIONS
- Solar energy as driver of Earth systems
- Effects of solar wind
- Changes to timing of seasons

Question:
Throughout the year, what are the aspects of seasonality that are part of your daily life?

GEOSYSTEMSnow

Searching for Earthlike Planets in the Goldilocks Zone

Remember the children's story *Goldilocks and the Three Bears*? In the fairy tale, Goldilocks passes over the porridge that is "too hot" and "too cold," and the chairs that are "too small" and "too large." Instead, she chooses those that are "just right."

The Goldilocks concept is now used in astronomy and space science as humans search for another planet that is habitable, like Earth. Such a planet would exist in the *Goldilocks zone*, the area of orbit about a star where conditions make it "just right" for living organisms.

An Earth-Size Habitable Planet? In 2014, scientists reported the discovery of the first Earth-size potentially habitable planet. Found using NASA's orbiting Kepler telescope, the planet is in a system known as *Kepler-186*, located about 500 light-years away from Earth (**Figure GN 2.1**). In this system, five planets circle a star, just as the eight planets of our own Solar System

circle the Sun (**Figure GN 2.2**). One of those planets, dubbed *Kepler-186f*, is about the same size as Earth in the Goldilocks zone of its host star.

The Goldilocks zone, or habitable zone, is the part of space in which a planet lies at exactly the right distance from its host star to have temperatures that can support life as we know it. Earth lies within this zone, but Venus, at the inner edge, is too hot and Mars, at the outer edge, is too cold. In the Goldilocks zone, water exists as a liquid on the surface of the planet, rather than evaporating out to space as on a hot planet or remaining permanently frozen as on a cold planet.

Characteristics of Kepler-186f The planet Kepler-186f is about 10% larger than Earth and orbits its host star every 130 days, just as Earth orbits the Sun every 365 days. However, Kepler-186f receives only about half the energy from its star that Earth receives from the Sun. Whether the planet is habitable remains unknown, but the discovery of an "Earth cousin" remains a breakthrough. Although billions of planets exist in the Goldilocks zone, only a dozen are close in size to Earth.

Other than its "just right" distance from the Sun, what makes Earth habitable? Our

▲**Figure GN 2.1 Artists conception of Kepler-186f with its host star in the distance.** [NASA Ames/JPL/T. Pyle.]

home planet is protected from harmful solar radiation by Earth's magnetic field, is kept warm by an insulating atmosphere, and has the chemical ingredients necessary for life, mainly water and carbon. We discuss these characteristics in this chapter and throughout *Geosystems*. Earth systems constantly cycle the elements that sustain life and provide resources for our modern technological society.

In July 2015, scientists reported another Earth-size planet orbiting a star similar to our Sun; see http://www.nasa.gov /keplerbriefing0723. Do you think we will find an Earth-like planet that supports life?

1. What is the Goldilocks zone? Why is it important in the search for habitable planets?

2. What conditions on Kepler-186f might limit its suitability as a home for living organisms?

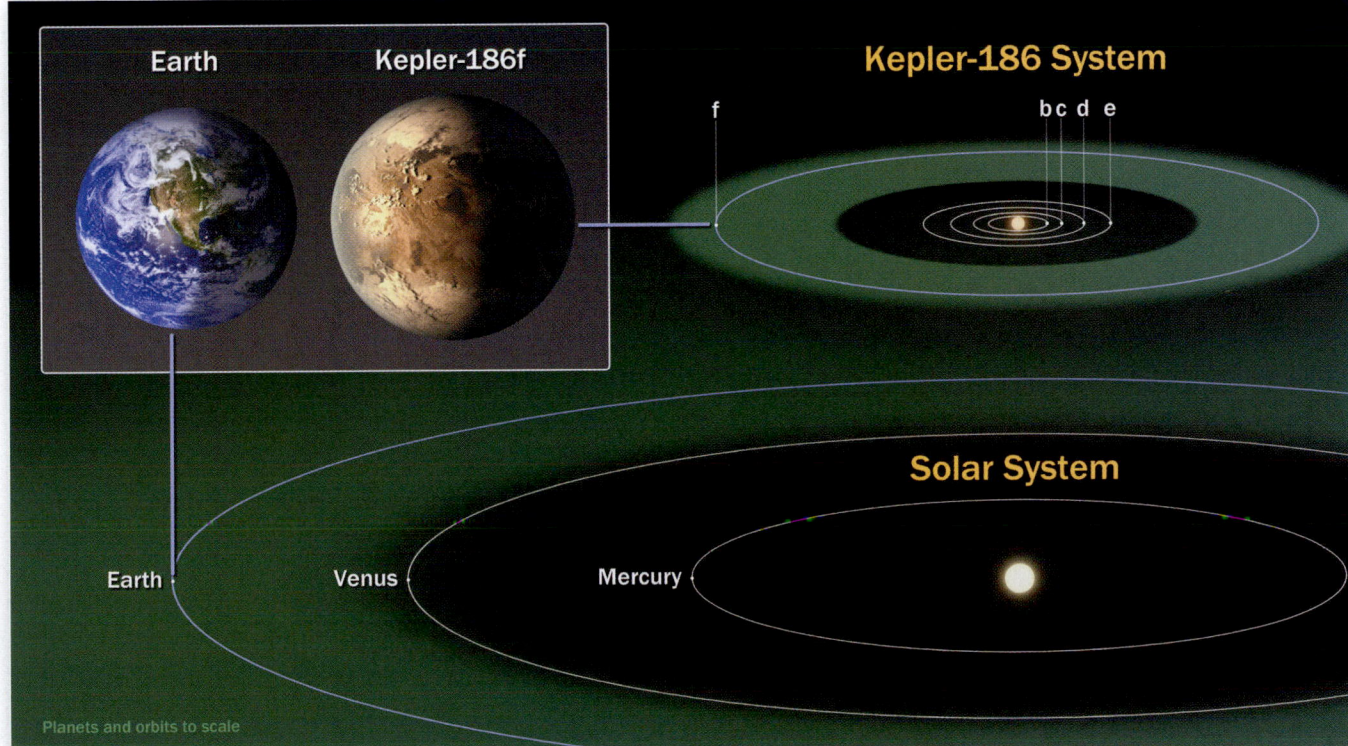

▲**Figure GN 2.2 Earth's inner Solar System compared to Kepler-186. The planets of Kepler-186 orbit a star that is half the size and mass of the Sun.** [NASA Ames/SETI Institute/JPL.]

To locate Earth in the Universe, we begin at the spatial scale of the Universe and work back toward our home planet. The Universe consists of all of time and space, including huge galaxies—collections of stars, gases, and dust—as well as the smallest particles. The Universe encompasses at least 125 billion galaxies, one of which is our own Milky Way Galaxy, containing over 300 billion stars. Among these stars is an average-size yellow star, the Sun, which radiates energy in all directions and upon its family of orbiting planets. Earth is the third planet from the Sun, centered in the *Goldilocks zone* where liquid water is available to support life (**Figure 2.1**). The Sun is the ultimate energy source that powers Earth's biosphere.

The Solar System

Our Solar System is located in the **Milky Way Galaxy**, a flattened, disk-shaped collection of stars in the form of a spiral with a slightly elongated core (**Figure 2.2**). Our Solar System is embedded more than halfway out from the galactic center, in one of the Milky Way's spiral arms—the Orion Spur of the Sagittarius Arm. A supermassive black hole some 2 million solar masses in size sits in the galactic center. The entire Galaxy rotates, with the rate depending on the distance from the galactic center. Our Sun and Solar System take about 200 million years to complete one full orbit around the center of the Milky Way Galaxy.

Solar System Formation

In our Solar System, a collection of eight planets orbit the Sun (**Figure 2.3a**). More than 100 moons (planetary satellites) orbit six of the eight planets. As of 2012, the new satellite count for the four outer planets was Jupiter, 67 moons; Saturn, 62 moons; Uranus, 27 moons; and Neptune, 14 moons. Also part of our Solar System are comets, asteroids, meteors, and four dwarf planets.

According to prevailing theory, our Solar System condensed from a *nebula*, a large, slowly rotating and collapsing cloud of dust and gas. **Gravity**, the mutual attraction exerted by every object upon all other objects in proportion to their mass, was a key force affecting this condensing solar nebula. As the nebular cloud organized and flattened into a disk shape, the early *protosun* grew in mass at the center, drawing in more matter through the force of gravity. Small eddies of accumulating material swirled at varying distances from the center of the solar nebula; these were the *protoplanets*.

The **planetesimal hypothesis**, or *dust-cloud hypothesis*, explains how suns condense from nebular clouds. In this hypothesis, the force of gravity pulls together small grains of cosmic dust and other solids to form planetesimals that may grow to become protoplanets and eventually planets, all orbiting the developing solar system's central mass.

Astronomers study this formation process in other parts of the Galaxy, where planets are observed orbiting distant stars. By 2016, scientists had discovered over 4700 of these *exoplanets* (planets that orbit a star outside our Solar System), with over 3375 confirmed.

Measuring Distances in Space

You may have heard distance in space expressed using the term *light-year*, a unit of measurement equivalent to the distance that light travels in 1 year. The **speed of light** is about 300,000 kmps (kilometers per second), or 186,000 mps (miles per second). Therefore, a light-year is about 9.5 trillion kilometers per year, or nearly 6 trillion miles per year.

---

everyday GEOSYSTEMS

Why is Earth so colorful when viewed from space?

The colors represent water, critical for a habitable Earth. Composite satellite images show the blue of Earth's deep oceans, the lighter blue of shallow coastal waters, the light white of clouds, and the bright white of ice in the polar regions. Even the green vegetation on land reflects the presence of water, Earth's most precious resource.

▲**Figure 2.1 Earth, the water planet.** [NASA image by Reto Stöckli.]

▶Figure 2.2 **Milky Way Galaxy and our Solar System.** The Milky Way contains over 300 billion stars, as well as gas and dust, and slowly rotates, with the speed of rotation depending on the distance from the center of the galaxy. (a) Artist's conception of the Milky Way, top view. (b) Image of Milky Way cross-section. [NASA/JPL.]

For spatial comparison, our Solar System is some 30,000 light-years from the black hole at the center of the Milky Way Galaxy, and about 15 light-years above the orbital plane of the Milky Way. The Milky Way itself is about 100,000 light-years from side to side, and the known Universe that is observable from Earth stretches approximately 12 billion light-years in all directions.

In terms of light speed, our Moon is about 1.28 seconds distant from Earth, an average distance of 384,400 km (238,866 mi); for the *Apollo* astronauts this was a 3-day space voyage. Earth's average distance from the Sun is approximately 150 million km (93 million mi), which means that light reaches Earth from the Sun in an average of 8 minutes and 20 seconds. Our entire Solar System is approximately 11 hours in diameter, measured by light speed. (See a Solar System simulator at http://space.jpl.nasa.gov/.)

Earth's orbit around the Sun is presently elliptical—a closed, oval path (**Figure 2.3b**). The point in Earth's orbit where it is closest to the Sun is **perihelion**, occurring on January 3 during the Northern Hemisphere winter. Earth's farthest position from the Sun is **aphelion**, occurring on July 4 during the Northern Hemisphere summer. The difference between Earth's perihelion and aphelion is 4,828,000 km, or 3,000,000 mi. This seasonal difference causes a slight variation in the solar energy incoming to Earth but is not an immediate reason for seasonal change.

The shape of Earth's elliptical orbit is not constant but varies slightly over long periods ranging from an oval to nearly circular orbital pattern. Earth's distance from the Sun varies more than 17 million km (11 million mi) during a 100,000-year cycle, changing the distance at perihelion and aphelion at different times in the cycle.

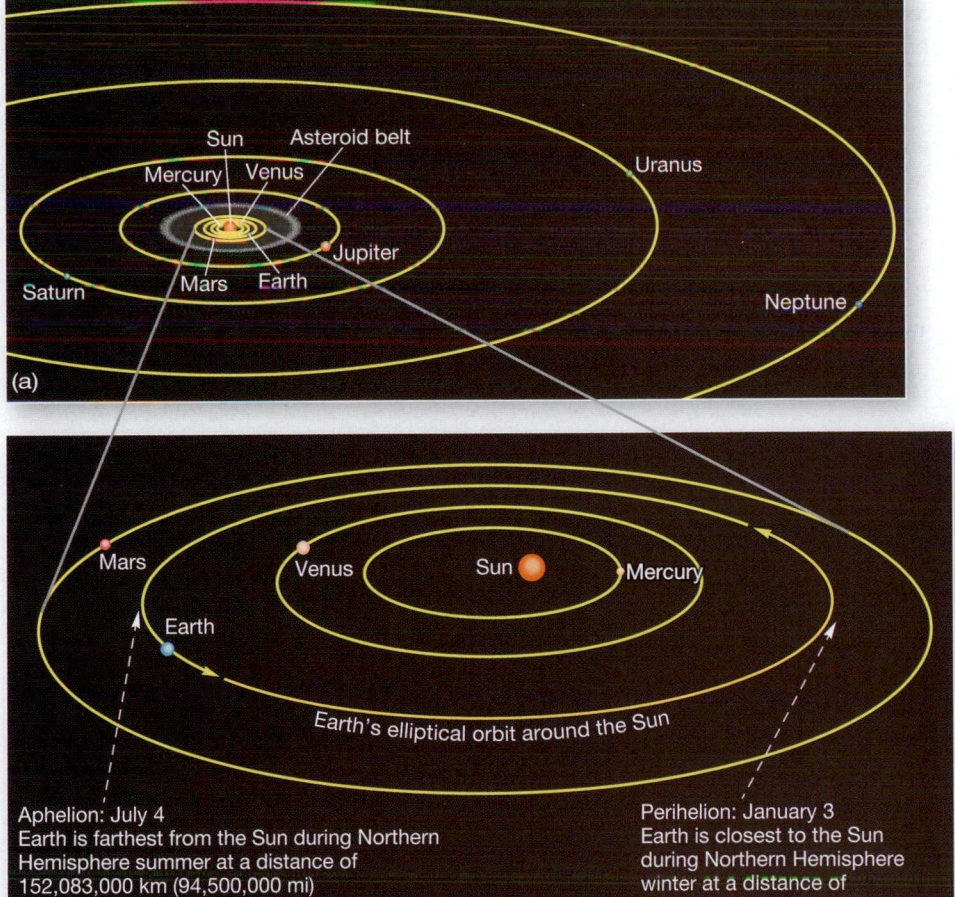

Aphelion: July 4
Earth is farthest from the Sun during Northern Hemisphere summer at a distance of 152,083,000 km (94,500,000 mi)

Perihelion: January 3
Earth is closest to the Sun during Northern Hemisphere winter at a distance of 147,255,000 km (91,500,000 mi)

▲Figure 2.3 **Planets of our Solar System and Earth's elliptical orbit.** (a) Note that all of the planets have a similar orbital plane. Pluto, considered the ninth planet for over 70 years, was reclassified as a dwarf planet in 2006. (b) The four inner terrestrial planets and Earth's orbital path. Earth's distance at perihelion and aphelion does not affect seasonal change.

Animation 🎬
Nebular Hypothesis

https://goo.gl/esDSak

Solar Energy: From Sun to Earth

Although the Sun is the dominant object in our region of space, it is a commonplace star in the Galaxy. It has average temperature, size, and color when compared with other stars. Yet from the perspective of humans on Earth, the Sun is the ultimate energy source, fueling most of the processes in our biosphere.

The Sun captured about 99.9% of the matter from the original solar nebula. The remaining 0.1% of the matter formed all the planets, their satellites, asteroids, comets, and debris. In the entire Solar System, the Sun is the only object having the enormous mass needed to sustain a nuclear reaction in its core and produce radiant energy.

The solar mass produces tremendous pressure and high temperatures deep in its dense interior. Under these conditions, the Sun's abundant hydrogen atoms are forced together and pairs of hydrogen nuclei are joined in the process of **fusion**. In the fusion reaction, hydrogen nuclei form helium, the second-lightest element in nature, and enormous quantities of energy are liberated—literally, disappearing solar mass becomes energy.

The Sun's principal outputs consist of the *solar wind* and radiant energy spanning portions of the *electromagnetic spectrum*. Let us now trace each of these emissions across space to Earth.

Solar Activity and Solar Wind

Telescopes and satellite images reveal solar activity to us in the form of sunspots and other surface disturbances (Figure 2.4). The *solar cycle* is the periodic variation in the Sun's activity and appearance over time. Since telescopes first allowed sunspot observation in the 1800s, scientists have used these solar surface features to define the solar cycle.

Sunspots The Sun's most conspicuous features are large **sunspots**, surface disturbances caused by magnetic storms. Sunspots appear as dark areas on the solar surface, with some as large as 160,000 km (100,000 mi), more than 12 times Earth's diameter. Sunspots are related to solar activity, with more sunspots representing increased solar radiation.

A *solar minimum* is a period of years when few sunspots are visible; a *solar maximum* is a period during which sunspots are numerous. Over the last 300 years, sunspot occurrences have cycled fairly regularly, reaching a maximum every 11 years on average (Figure 2.4b). The current cycle, *Sunspot Cycle 24*, began with a minimum in 2008, followed by little activity until 2010, a maximum in 2013, and finally a second, slightly larger maximum in 2014. (For more on the sunspot cycle, see http://solarscience.msfc.nasa.gov/SunspotCycle.shtml.) Although sunspot cycles are linked to long-term changes in Earth's climate, scientists have ruled out sunspots as a cause for increasing temperature trends on Earth over the past few decades.

Activity on the Sun is highest during solar maximum (Figure 2.4a). *Solar flares*, magnetic storms that cause surface explosions, and *prominence eruptions*, outbursts of gases from the surface, often occur in active regions near sunspots. Although much of the material from these eruptions is pulled back toward the Sun by gravity, some moves into space as part of the solar wind.

Relative size of Earth

(a) Solar eruption, December 31, 2012

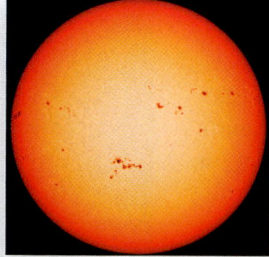

(b) Sunspot maximum in July 2000, part of Solar Cycle 23.

(c) Sunspot minimum in March 2009, the beginning of Solar Cycle 24.

▲**Figure 2.4 Image of the Sun and sunspots.** This relatively minor prominence eruption was about 20 times the diameter of Earth, shown for scale. Earth is actually far smaller than the average sunspot. [(a) NASA/*SDO*/Steele Hill, 2012. (b) SOHO/EIT Consortium (NASA and ESA).]

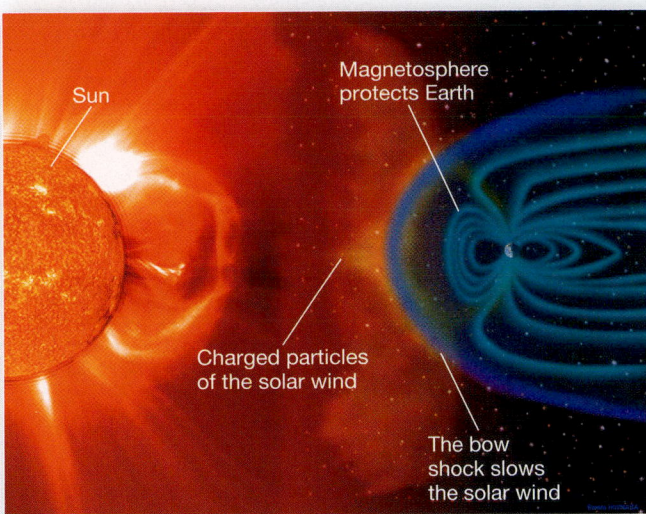

▲**Figure 2.5 Artist conception of solar wind and Earth's magnetosphere.** The bow shock is the boundary where the solar wind slows from supersonic (exceeding the speed of sound) to subsonic speeds as it nears the magnetosphere. [NASA.]

(a) *Aurora australis* as seen from orbit.

(b) *Aurora borealis* over Whitehorse, Yukon, in Canada. On August 31, 2012, a coronal mass ejection glanced off Earth's magnetosphere, causing this aurora four days later.

▲**Figure 2.6 Auroras from orbital and ground perspectives.** [(a) GSFC/NASA. (b) David Cartier, Sr., courtesy of GSFC/NASA.]

Solar Wind Effects The Sun constantly emits clouds of electrically charged particles (principally, hydrogen nuclei and free electrons) that surge outward in all directions from the Sun's surface. This stream of energetic material travels more slowly than light—at about 50 million km (31 million mi) a day—taking approximately 3 days to reach Earth. This phenomenon is the **solar wind**, originating from the Sun's extremely hot solar corona, or outer atmosphere. The corona is the Sun's rim, observable with the naked eye from Earth during a solar eclipse.

As the charged particles of the solar wind approach Earth, they interact with Earth's magnetic field. This **magnetosphere**, which surrounds the Earth and extends beyond Earth's atmosphere, is generated by dynamo-like motions within our planet. The magnetosphere deflects the solar wind toward both of Earth's poles so that only a small portion of it enters the upper atmosphere (**Figure 2.5**).

In addition, massive outbursts of charged material, referred to as *coronal mass ejections* (CMEs), contribute to the flow of solar wind material from the Sun into space. CMEs that are aimed toward Earth often cause spectacular **auroras** in the upper atmosphere near the poles. These lighting effects, known as the *aurora borealis* (northern lights) and *aurora australis* (southern lights), occur 80–500 km (50–300 mi) above Earth's surface through the interaction of the solar wind with the upper layers of Earth's atmosphere. Auroras typically occur at latitudes higher than 65° N and S (**Figure 2.6**). However, in 2012, auroras were visible as far south as Colorado and Arkansas (see http://www.gi.alaska.edu/auroraforecast).

GEOreport **2.1** The International Space Station in orbit above you

Since 2000, astronauts aboard the International Space Station (ISS) have carried on "normal" daily life, living and working in orbit. With length equivalent to a football field and solar arrays covering 0.4 hectares (1 acre), the ISS is an engineering marvel often unnoticed by the general public. The ISS is, in essence, an artificial satellite in low orbit around Earth, easily visible in the night sky. Several apps (ISS Spotter, NASA's SkyWatch) tell you when the ISS is overhead.

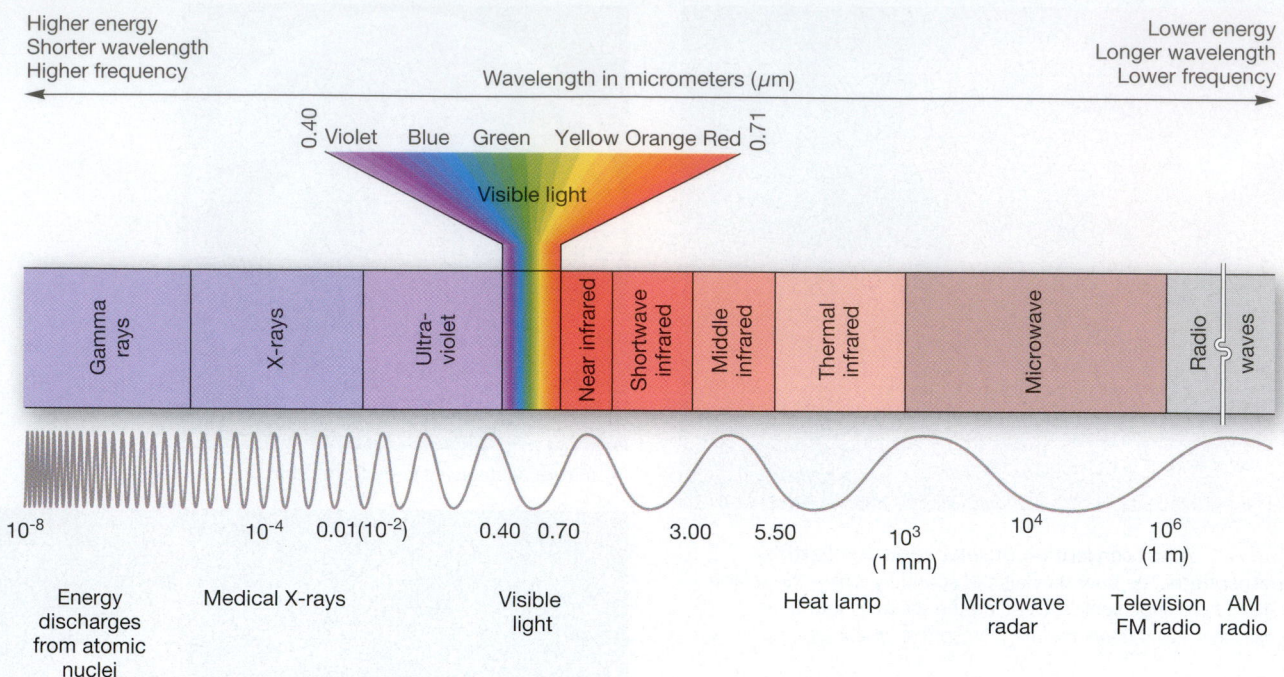

▲Figure 2.7 **A portion of the electromagnetic spectrum of radiant energy from the Sun.**

Radiant Energy Flows

Energy released from the Sun is *radiant energy*, which travels in waves through space. (Please review the different types of energy in Focus Study 1.1.) These *electromagnetic waves* have electrical and magnetic properties that allow them to travel long distances at the speed of light. Electromagnetic waves move like ocean waves, with crests (high points) and troughs (low points), but they do not move matter (as opposed to ocean waves, which require matter to move). Radiant energy is carried by atomic particles; when it is absorbed by an object, radiant energy is converted to heat.

The Electromagnetic Spectrum
Electromagnetic energy is the term for all energy traveling in waves through space, including light, heat, X-rays, radar, and radio waves. Each type of wave has a specific **wavelength**, the distance between corresponding points on any two successive waves. The number of waves passing a fixed point per unit time is the *frequency*. The spectrum of all possible wavelengths of electromagnetic energy is the **electromagnetic spectrum**.

The Sun emits radiant energy composed of 8% ultraviolet, X-ray, and gamma-ray wavelengths; 47% visible light wavelengths; and 45% infrared wavelengths. **Figure 2.7** shows a portion of the electromagnetic spectrum. Note the wavelengths at which various phenomena and human energy use occur.

Energy Emitted by Sun and Earth
An important physical law states that all objects radiate energy in wavelengths related to their individual surface temperatures:

The hotter the object, the shorter the wavelengths emitted. This law holds true for the Sun and Earth.

As we discuss temperature in this chapter, and throughout *Geosystems*, remember that temperature and heat are different, though related, concepts. By definition, **temperature** is a measure of the average kinetic energy of individual molecules in matter. In other words, temperature is the average speed of molecular movement. If molecular movement increases, temperature increases. We measure temperature in degrees Celsius (°C) or Fahrenheit (°F), or Kelvin (K); **Figure 2.8** shows boiling, freezing, and absolute zero on these temperature scales.

In contrast, heat is a form of energy that transfers between molecules and thus between bodies or substances. By definition, **heat** is the flow of kinetic energy between molecules or from one body or substance to another resulting from a temperature difference between them. We measure heat in joules (J) or in calories. A *calorie* is the amount of energy required to raise the temperature of 1 gram of water (at 15°C) 1 degree Celsius, and it is equal to 4.184 joules.

Heat is a form of energy, while temperature is related to the amount of energy in a substance. Because temperature is a measure of the average kinetic energy of individual molecules in matter, temperature is a measure of heat. An object with a "hot" temperature contains more heat energy; an object with a "cold" temperature contains less heat energy.

Heat always flows from matter at higher temperature to matter at lower temperature. An example is the transfer of heat when you wrap your warm hand around a snowball, or a piece of ice, and it melts. Another example

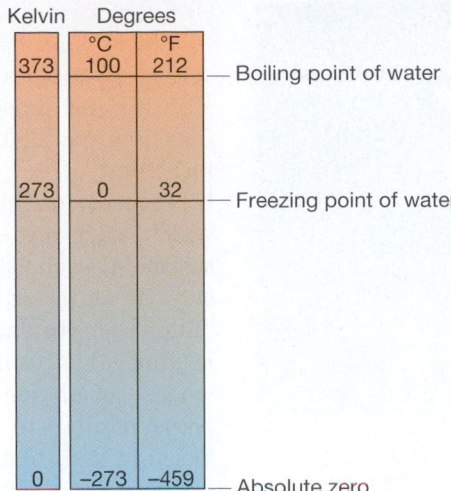

▲**Figure 2.8 Temperature scales.** Compare the boiling point of water, melting point of ice, and absolute zero on Kelvin, Celsius, and Fahrenheit temperature scales. A more detailed comparison of the scales is in Chapter 4.

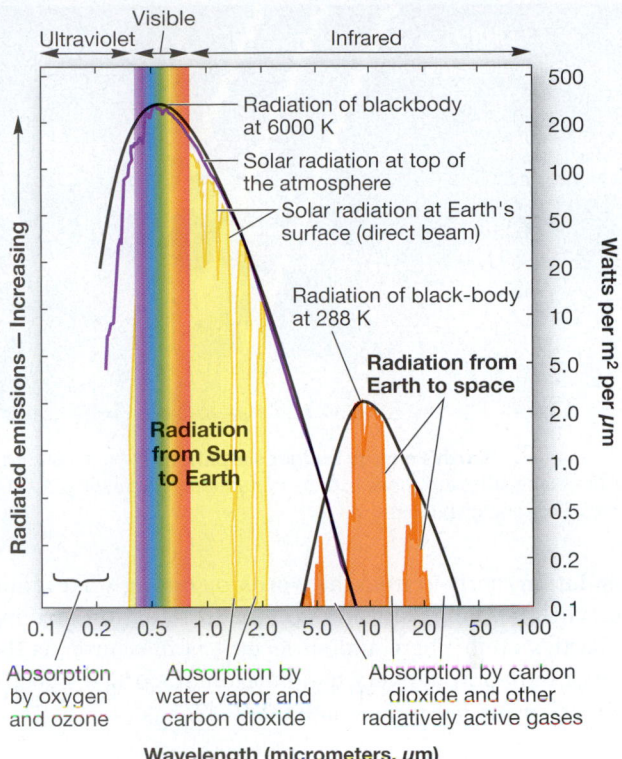

▲**Figure 2.9 Solar and terrestrial energy distribution by wavelength.** A hotter Sun radiates shorter wavelengths, whereas a cooler Earth emits longer wavelengths. Dark lines represent ideal blackbody curves for the Sun and Earth. The dropouts in the plot lines represent radiation absorbed by atmospheric gases, mainly oxygen, water vapor, carbon dioxide, and ozone (O_3). [Adapted from W. D. Sellers, *Physical Climatology* (Chicago: University of Chicago Press), p. 20. Used by permission.]

is the warming of your hand when you hold a hot mug of tea. Heat flow between objects or substances stops when the temperatures—that is, when the amounts of kinetic energy—become equal.

Applying these concepts to the Sun and Earth, we see that the hot Sun radiates shorter wavelength energy, concentrated around 0.5 μm (micrometer), with the majority falling in the visible region of the electromagnetic spectrum. Because Earth is a cooler radiating body, it emits longer wavelengths, mostly in the infrared portion of the spectrum, centered around 10 μm. **Figure 2.9** shows the distribution of radiant energy emitted by both Sun and Earth.

The Sun is a *blackbody radiator*, meaning that it absorbs and subsequently emits all the radiant energy that it receives with 100% efficiency. The Sun's surface temperature is about 6000 K (6273°C, 11,459°F), and its radiation emission curve is similar to that predicted for a blackbody at that temperature (shown in Figure 2.9). Although cooler than the Sun with a temperature of 288 K (15°C, 59°F), Earth is also a blackbody, radiating nearly all the energy that it absorbs.

As electromagnetic energy moves through Earth's atmosphere, gases such as water vapor and carbon dioxide absorb certain wavelengths. These gases vary in their response to radiation received, being transparent to some wavelengths while absorbing others (noted at the bottom of Figure 2.9). We discuss these gases further in Chapters 3 and 4.

To summarize, radiant energy is the transfer of heat energy in electromagnetic waves. A hotter object like the Sun emits a much greater amount of energy per unit area of its surface than does a similar area of a cooler object like Earth. **Figure 2.10** illustrates the flows of energy into

and out of Earth systems. The Sun emits *shortwave radiation* that peaks in the visible wavelengths, whereas Earth emits *longwave radiation* concentrated in the infrared wavelengths. In other chapters, we look at Earth's atmosphere and how it affects energy from Sun to Earth and Earth to space and we examine the overall Earth–atmosphere energy budget.

Incoming Energy at the Top of the Atmosphere

The region at the top of the atmosphere, approximately 480 km (300 mi) above Earth's surface, is the **thermopause** (see Geosystems in Action 3). It is the outer boundary of Earth's energy system and provides a useful point to assess the arriving solar radiation before it is diminished as it passes through the atmosphere.

Earth's distance from the Sun results in its interception of only 1 two-billionth of the Sun's total energy output. Nevertheless, this tiny fraction of energy from the Sun is an enormous amount of energy flowing into Earth's systems. Solar radiation that is intercepted by Earth is

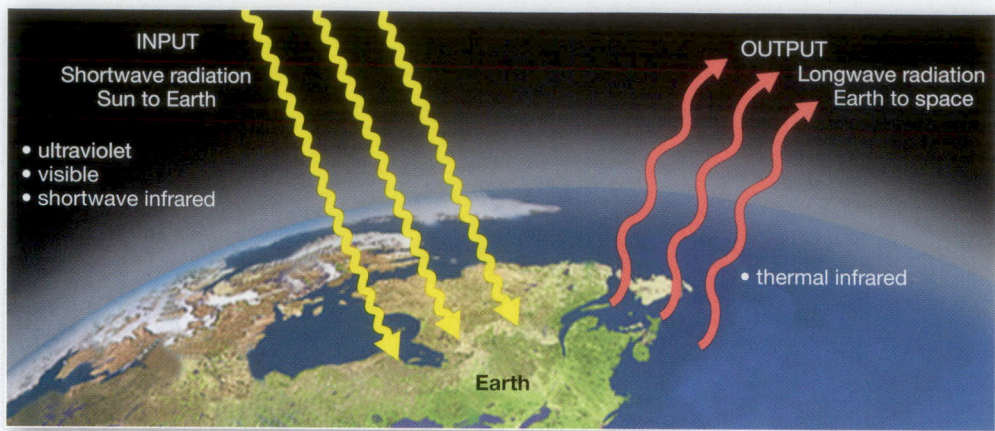

▲**Figure 2.10 Earth's energy budget simplified.** We build on this simplified figure in Chapter 3, as we examine Earth's atmosphere, and in Chapter 4, where we present a detailed discussion of the Earth–atmosphere energy budget.

insolation, derived from the words *in*coming *sol*ar radia*tion*. Insolation specifically applies to radiation arriving at Earth's atmosphere and surface; it is measured as the rate of radiation delivery to a horizontal surface, specifically, as watts per square meter (W/m²).

Solar Constant The **solar constant** is the average insolation received at the thermopause when Earth is at its average distance from the Sun, a value of 1372 W/m². (A *watt* is a unit of power equal to 1 joule per second.) As we follow insolation through the atmosphere to Earth's surface in Chapters 3 and 4, we will see that its amount is reduced as clouds and other atmospheric particles reflect and absorb radiation.

Uneven Distribution of Insolation Earth's curved surface presents a continually varying angle to the incoming parallel rays of insolation (**Figure 2.11**). Differences in the angle at which solar rays meet the surface at each latitude result in an uneven distribution of insolation and heating. The only point where insolation arrives perpendicular to the surface (hitting it from directly overhead, at a 90° angle) is the **subsolar point**.

During the year, the subsolar point occurs only at lower latitudes, between the tropics (about 23.5° N and 23.5° S). As a result, the energy received there is more concentrated. All other places, away from the subsolar point, receive insolation at an angle less than 90° and thus experience more diffuse energy; this effect becomes more pronounced at higher latitudes.

The varying angle of insolation results in the thermopause above the equatorial region receiving 2.5 times more insolation annually than the thermopause above the poles. As radiation passes through Earth's atmosphere, low-angle solar rays at Earth's highest latitudes must pass through a greater thickness of atmosphere, resulting in additional losses of energy due to scattering, reflection, and absorption.

Surface area receiving insolation

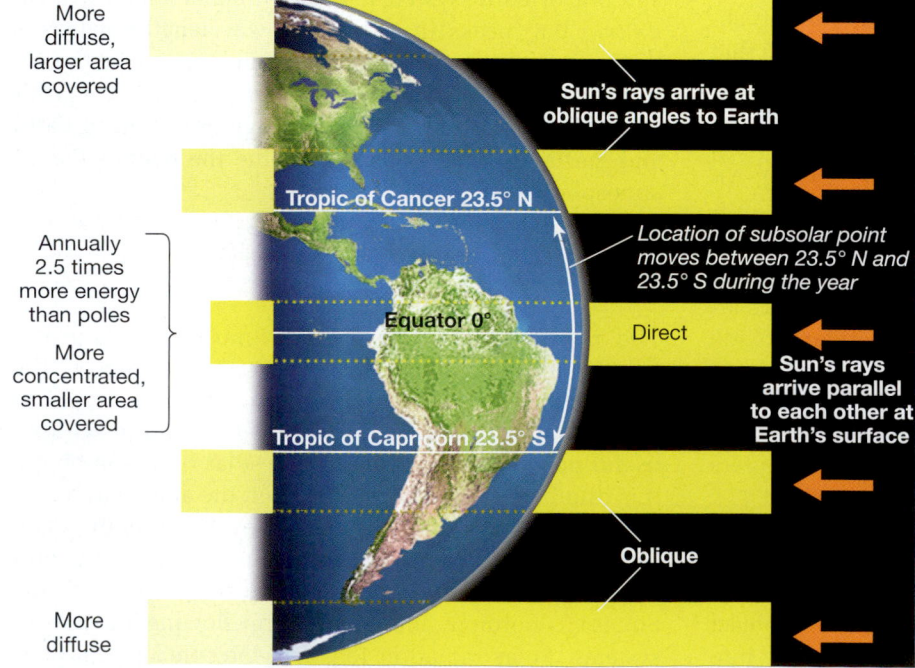

◄**Figure 2.11 Insolation receipts and Earth's curved surface.** The angle at which insolation arrives from the Sun determines the concentration of energy receipts by latitude. The subsolar point, where the Sun's rays arrive perpendicular to Earth, moves between the tropics during the year.

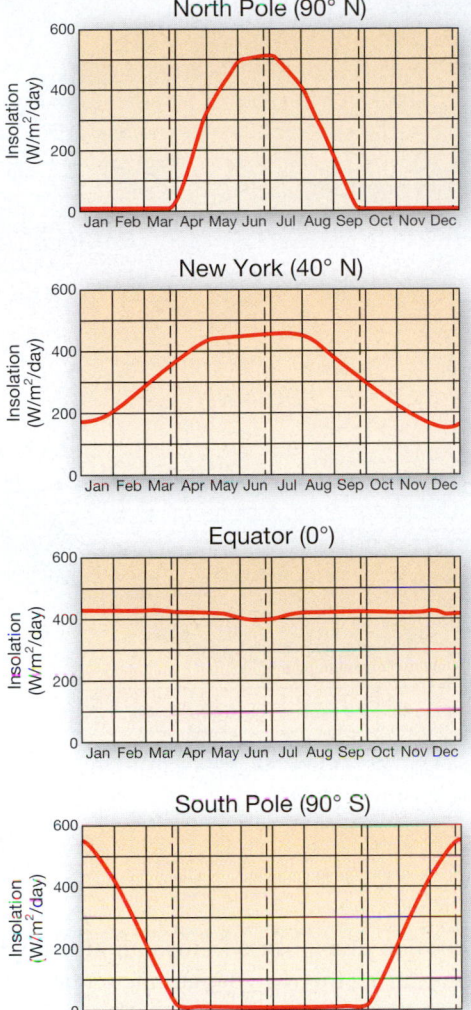

▲**Figure 2.12 Daily insolation received at the top of the atmosphere.** The total daily insolation received at the top of the atmosphere is charted in watts per square meter per day for four locations (1 W/m²/day = 2.064 cal/cm²/day). The vertical dashed lines mark the equinoxes and solstices, two of each during the year.

The energy received at the top of the atmosphere at different locations changes throughout the year. The graphs in **Figure 2.12** show the seasonal variations in insolation for four locations, ranging from the equator northward and southward to the poles. In June, the North Pole receives slightly more than 500 W/m² per day, which is more than is ever received at 40° N latitude or at the equator. Such high values result from long 24-hour daylengths at the poles in summer, compared with only 15 hours of daylight at 40° N latitude and 12 hours at the equator.

In December, the pattern reverses, as shown on the graphs. Note that the top of the atmosphere at the South Pole receives more than 550 W/m²—even more insolation than the North Pole does in June. This is a function of Earth's closer location to the Sun at perihelion (January 3 in Figure 2.3 b).

Global Net Radiation The balance between incoming shortwave energy from the Sun and all outgoing radiation from Earth and the atmosphere—energy inputs minus energy outputs—is *net radiation*. The map in **Figure 2.13** uses *isolines*, or lines connecting points of equal value, to show global net radiation patterns at the top of the atmosphere. Following the line for 70 W/m² on the map shows that the higher positive net radiation values are in equatorial regions, especially over oceans.

Note the latitudinal energy imbalance in net radiation on the map—positive values in lower latitudes and negative values toward the poles. Negative net radiation occurs in the higher latitudes because Earth's climate system loses more energy to space than it gains from the Sun, as measured at the top of the atmosphere. The largest positive net radiation values, averaging 80 W/m², are above the tropical oceans. Net radiation is lowest over Antarctica. The negative net radiation over the Sahara Desert region in Africa results from longwave radiation losses related to clear skies and reflective surfaces, processes we discuss further in Chapter 4.

This latitudinal imbalance in energy is critical because it drives global circulation in the atmosphere and the oceans, as discussed in later chapters. Having examined the flow of solar energy to the top of Earth's atmosphere, we now look at how seasonal changes affect the distribution of insolation as Earth orbits the Sun during the year.

WORK**IT**OUT 2.1
Daily Insolation Comparisons

Refer to the graphs in Figure 2.12 and assume insolation values (in W/m²/day) are for the top of the atmosphere at all locations.

1. How much insolation arrives over the North Pole (90° N) in June?
2. How much insolation arrives over the equator in June?
3. Calculate the difference in energy receipt in June for the two locations.
4. In June, daylength at the North Pole is 24 hours and daylength at the equator is 12 hours. Given that the length of daylight in June is twice as long at the North Pole (24 hours) as at the equator (12 hours), explain why the insolation difference is only 100 W/m²/day. (Use Figure 2.11 to help your thinking.)

The Seasons

Earth's cycles of warmth and cold and changing Sun angle throughout the year have fascinated humans for centuries. Many ancient societies marked the annual change in temperature and Sun angle with festivals, monuments,

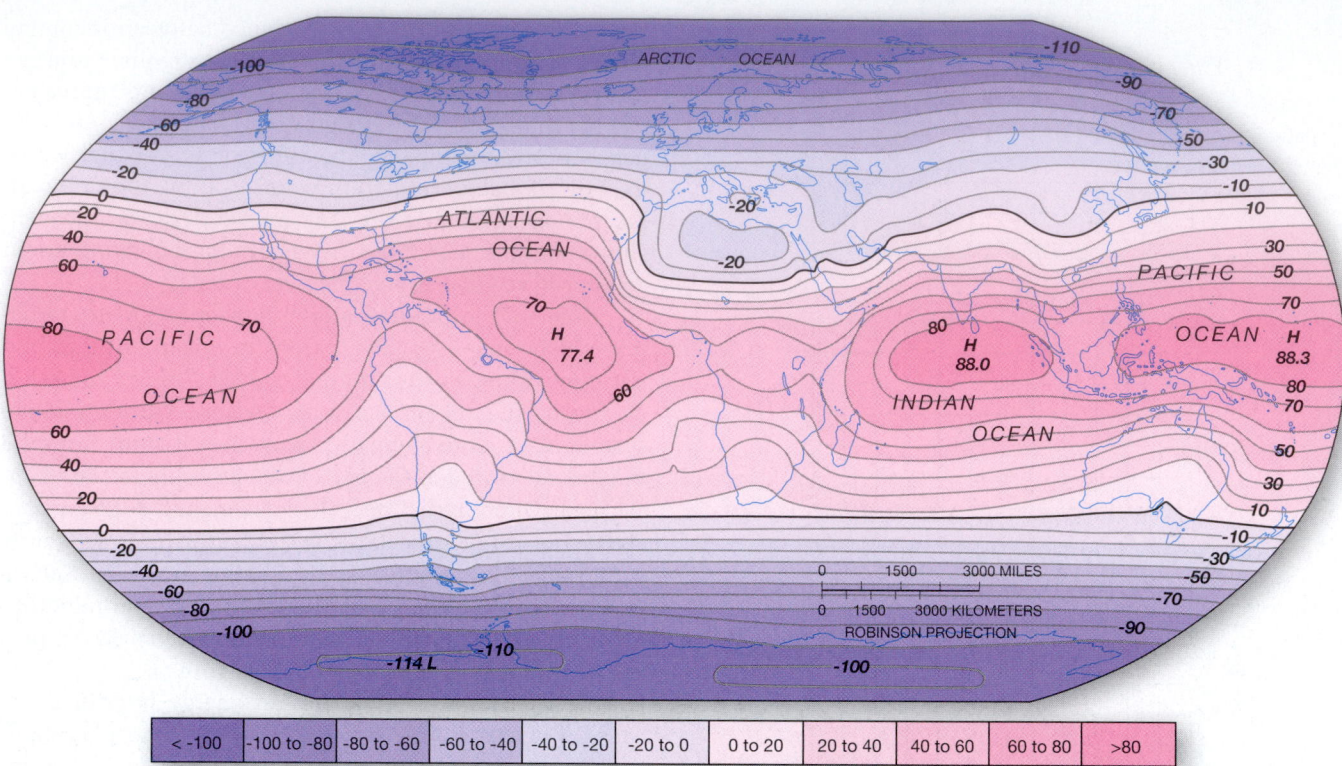

< -100	-100 to -80	-80 to -60	-60 to -40	-40 to -20	-20 to 0	0 to 20	20 to 40	40 to 60	60 to 80	>80

▲**Figure 2.13** **Daily net radiation patterns at the top of the atmosphere.** Averaged daily net radiation flows measured at the top of the atmosphere by the Earth Radiation Budget Experiment (ERBE). Units are W/m². [Data for map courtesy of GSFC/NASA.]

ground markings, and calendars (The Solar Observatory at Chankillo, Peru, is an example, see http://www.wmf .org/project/chankillo). Such monuments and calendar markings are found worldwide, including thousands of sites in North America, demonstrating an ancient awareness of seasonal timing and astronomical relations.

Seasonality

Seasonality refers to the variations in the Sun's position above the horizon and changing daylength during the year. The seasonal variations we observe on Earth are a response to changes in **Sun altitude**, the angle between the horizon and the Sun. At sunrise or sunset, the Sun is at the horizon, so its altitude is 0°. If during the day the Sun reaches halfway between the horizon and directly overhead, it is at 45° altitude. If the Sun reaches the point directly overhead, it is at 90° altitude.

The Sun is directly overhead (90° altitude, or *zenith*) only at the subsolar point, where insolation is at a maximum. At all other surface points, the Sun is at a lower altitude angle, producing more diffuse insolation.

The latitude of the subsolar point, known as the Sun's **declination**, annually migrates through 47° of latitude, moving between the Tropic of Cancer and Tropic of Capricorn parallels. Although it passes through Hawai'i, located between 19° N and 22° N, the subsolar point does not reach the continental United States or Canada; all other states and provinces are too far north.

The duration of exposure to insolation is **daylength**, which varies during the year, depending on latitude. Daylength is the interval between *sunrise*, the moment when the disk of the Sun first appears above the horizon in the east, and *sunset*, that moment when it totally disappears below the horizon in the west.

At the equator, daylength is always 12 hours long, with no variation throughout the year. At the North and South poles, the range of daylength is extreme, with a 6-month period of no insolation followed by daylight lasting for a 6-month period of continuous 24-hour insolation.

WORK**IT**OUT 2.2
Using a Solar Calculator

To calculate sunrise and sunset at any location, go to http:// www.esrl.noaa.gov/gmd/grad/solcalc/. Choose your location and select the DST box if you are on daylight saving time. Do the sunrise and sunset times match what you observe on a daily basis?

1. What is the solar declination on your selected date? What does it mean if the declination has a negative value?
2. Try changing the date to 6 months ahead. How has the solar declination changed?

Reasons for Seasons

The seasonal changes in Sun altitude, declination, and daylength result from several physical characteristics of Earth that operate together: Earth's *revolution* in orbit around the Sun, its daily *rotation* on its axis, its *tilted* axis, the unchanging *orientation of its axis*, and its *sphericity*. The essential ingredient is having a single source of radiant energy—the Sun.

Revolution Earlier we looked at Earth's elliptical orbit around the Sun (see Figure 2.3b). Earth's speed in orbit averages 107,280 kmph (66,660 mph), and each full orbit, or **revolution**, around the Sun takes 365.2422 days. This is the length of a year, encompassing the full duration of the seasons.

Recall that the Earth-to-Sun distance from aphelion to perihelion is not a significant factor in seasonal change. The distance varies about 3% (4.8 million km, or 3 million mi) during the year, amounting to only a slight (about 50 W/m²) difference in daily insolation between summers at the different poles (review Figure 2.12).

Earth's orbit varies in cycles over several time scales. Over a 100,000-year cycle, the shape of the ellipse varies by more than 17.7 million km (11 million mi), affecting Earth's climate. (See Chapter 10 for a full discussion.)

Rotation Earth's **rotation**, or turning on its axis, is a complex motion that averages slightly less than 24 hours in duration. Rotation determines daylength, creates the apparent deflection of winds and ocean currents, and produces the twice-daily rise and fall of the ocean tides in relation to the gravitational pull of the Sun and the Moon. Note in **Figure 2.14** the distinction between rotation—Earth's spinning on its axis—and revolution—Earth's travel around the Sun.

When viewed from above the North Pole, Earth rotates counterclockwise on its **axis**, an imaginary line extending through the planet from the geographic North Pole to the South Pole. Viewed from above the equator, Earth rotates west to east. This eastward rotation creates the Sun's *apparent* westward daily journey from sunrise in the east to sunset in the west. Of course, relative to the planets, the Sun actually remains in a fixed position in the center of our Solar System.

Although every point on Earth takes the same 24 hours to complete one rotation, the linear velocity of rotation at any point on Earth's surface varies dramatically with latitude (**Table 2.1**). The equator is 40,075 km (24,902 mi) long; therefore, rotational velocity at the equator must be approximately 1675 kmph (1041 mph) to cover that distance in 1 day. At 60°

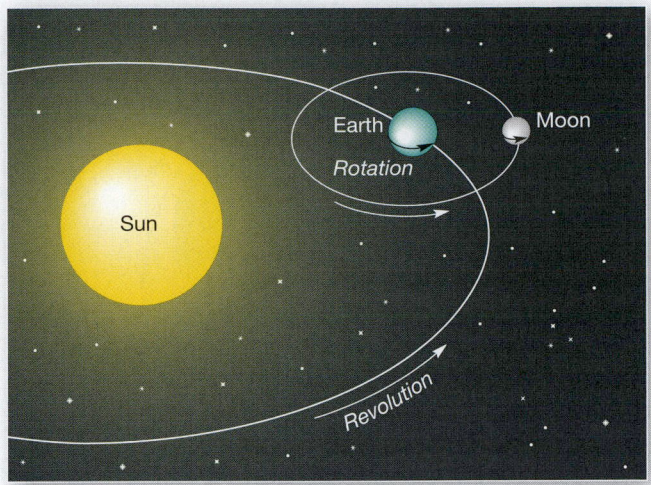

▲**Figure 2.14 Earth's revolution and rotation.** Earth's revolution about the Sun and rotation on its axis, viewed from above Earth's orbit. Note the Moon's revolution and rotation on its axis are counterclockwise, as well.

latitude, a parallel is only half the length of the equator, or 20,038 km (12,451 mi) long, so the rotational velocity there is 838 kmph (521 mph). This variation in rotational velocity establishes the effect of the Coriolis force, discussed in Chapter 5.

Earth's rotation produces the familiar pattern of day and night. The dividing line between day and night is the **circle of illumination** (as illustrated in Geosystems in Action 2). Because this day–night dividing circle of illumination intersects the equator (and because both are great circles and any two great circles on a sphere bisect one another), *daylength at the equator is always evenly*

TABLE 2.1 Speed of Rotation at Selected Latitudes

Latitude	Speed kmph	(mph)	Representative Geographic Location near Each Latitude
90°	0	(0)	North Pole
60°	838	(521)	Seward, Alaska
50°	1078	(670)	Chibougamau, Québec
40°	1284	(798)	Columbus, Ohio
30°	1452	(902)	New Orleans, Louisiana
0°	1675	(1041)	Quito, Ecuador

GEOreport **2.2** Why do we always see the same side of the Moon?

Note in Figure 2.14 that the Moon revolves around Earth and rotates counterclockwise on its axis. The timing for both these motions—revolution and rotation—is the same, about 27.3 days. Thus, we see only one side of the lunar surface—always the same side facing Earth.

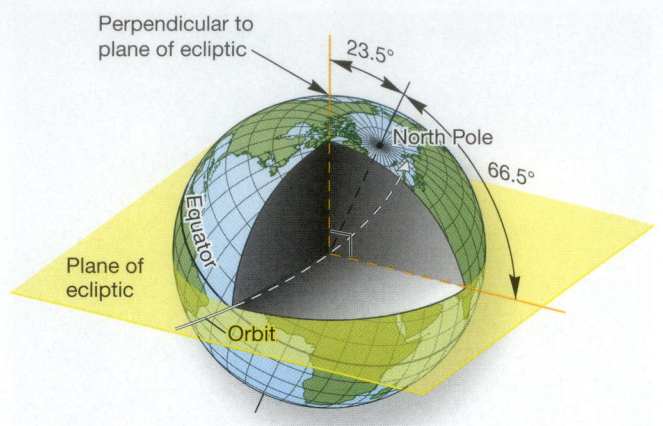

▲**Figure 2.15** **The plane of Earth's orbit—the ecliptic—and Earth's axial tilt.** Note on the illustration that the plane of the equator is inclined to the plane of the ecliptic at about 23.5°.

TABLE 2.2 Five Reasons for Seasons	
Factor	Description
Revolution	Orbit around the Sun; requires 365.24 days to complete
Rotation	Earth turning on its axis; takes approximately 24 hours to complete
Tilt	Axis aligned about 23.5° from perpendicular to the plane of the ecliptic (the plane of Earth's orbit)
Axial parallelism	Unchanging (fixed) axial alignment throughout the year
Sphericity	Oblate spheroidal shape lit by Sun's parallel rays

divided—12 hours of day and 12 hours of night. All other latitudes experience uneven daylength through the seasons, except for 2 days a year, on the equinoxes.

The length of a true day varies slightly from 24 hours throughout the year. However, by international agreement a day is defined as exactly 24 hours, or 86,400 seconds, an average called *mean solar time.* Since Earth's rotation is gradually slowing, partially owing to the drag of lunar tidal forces, a "day" on Earth today is many hours longer than it was 4 billion years ago.

Tilt of Earth's Axis To understand Earth's **axial tilt**, imagine a plane (a flat surface) that intersects Earth's elliptical orbit about the Sun, with half of the Sun and Earth above the plane and half below. Such a plane, touching all points of Earth's orbit, is the **plane of the ecliptic**. Earth's tilted axis remains fixed relative to this plane as Earth revolves around the Sun. Now, imagine a perpendicular (at a 90° angle) line passing through the plane. From this perpendicular, Earth's axis is tilted about 23.5° (**Figure 2.15**). It forms a 66.5° angle from the plane itself. The axis through Earth's two poles points just slightly off Polaris, which is named, appropriately, the *North Star.* The plane of the ecliptic is important to our discussion of Earth's seasons because it provides a frame of reference for analyzing Earth's orientation relative to the Sun over the course of a year.

The tilt angle is often described as "about" 23.5° because Earth's axial tilt changes over a complex 41,000-year cycle (see Figure 10.16). The axial tilt ranges roughly between 22° and 24.5°. The present tilt is 23.45°. For convenience, this is rounded off to a 23.5° tilt (or 66.5° from the plane) in most usage.

Axial Parallelism Throughout its orbit around the Sun, Earth's axis maintains the same alignment relative to the plane of the ecliptic and to Polaris and other stars. You can see this consistent alignment in Geosystems in Action, Figure GIA 2.2. If we compared the axis in different months, it would always appear parallel to itself, a condition known as **axial parallelism**.

Sphericity Even though Earth is not a perfect sphere, as discussed in Chapter 1, we can still refer to Earth's *sphericity* as contributing to seasonality. Earth's approximately spherical shape causes the parallel rays of the Sun to fall at different angles on Earth's surface, depending on latitude and time of year. As we saw in Figure 2.11, Earth's curvature means that insolation angles and net radiation received vary between the equator and the poles.

Table 2.2 presents a summary of the five reasons for seasons. Now, considering all these factors operating together, we explore the march of the seasons.

WORKITOUT 2.3
Consider Earth's Axial Tilt

Scientists have found that Earth's axial tilt and orbital path vary over long time periods (discussed in Chapter 11 regarding orbital factors that might affect climate change). Consider the following scenarios, and answer the questions.

1. What do you think the effect on Earth's seasons would be
   • If the tilt of the axis was decreased?
   • If the tilt was increased a little?
   • If Earth was lying on its side?
2. What if Earth's orbit was more circular as opposed to its present elliptical shape?

(Hint: To visualize these scenarios, take a ball or piece of round fruit, mark the poles, and then move it around a light bulb as if revolving it around the Sun. Change the axial tilt of your ball or fruit, and note where the light falls relative to the poles.)

Annual March of the Seasons

Geosystems in Action 2 summarizes the annual march of the seasons and Earth's relationship to the Sun during the year, using a side view (**Figure GIA 2.1**) and a top view (**Figure GIA 2.2**).

During the march of the seasons on Earth, daylength is the most obvious way of sensing changes in season at latitudes away from the equator. The extremes of daylength occur at the *solstices* in December and June, around December 21 and June 21. Strictly speaking, the solstices are specific points in time at which the Sun's declination is at its position farthest north at the **Tropic of Cancer**, or south at the **Tropic of Capricorn**. "Tropic" is from *tropicus*, meaning a turn or change, so a tropic latitude is where the Sun's declination appears to stand still briefly (Sun stance, or *sol stice*) and then "turn" and head toward the other tropic.

During the year, places on Earth outside of the equatorial region experience a continuous but gradual shift in daylength, a few minutes each day, and the Sun's altitude increases or decreases a small amount. You may have noticed that these daily variations become more pronounced in spring and autumn, when the Sun's declination changes at a faster rate. The seasonal differences in Earth landscapes between January and July reflect the different insolation receipts between the Northern and Southern Hemispheres (**Figure 2.16**).

December 21 or 22 marks the **December solstice**, or *winter solstice* in the Northern Hemisphere, the moment when the circle of illumination includes the South Pole region but leaves the North Pole region in darkness. The subsolar point is about 23.5° S latitude at the Tropic of Capricorn. The Northern Hemisphere is tilted away from these more direct rays of sunlight—our northern winter—thereby creating a lower angle for the incoming solar rays and thus a more diffuse pattern of insolation.

On the December solstice, the Sun remains below the horizon all day in the region from the **Arctic Circle** at about 66.5° N to the North Pole. In contrast, locations above the Antarctic Circle at about 66.5° S experience 24 hours of daylight.

During the following 3 months, daylength and solar angles gradually increase in the Northern Hemisphere as Earth completes one-fourth of its orbit. The moment of the **March equinox**, or *vernal equinox* in the Northern Hemisphere, occurs on March 20 or 21. At that time, Earth's orientation is such that the circle of illumination passes through both poles, thus all locations on Earth experience a 12-hour day and a 12-hour night. At the North Pole, the Sun peeks above the horizon for the first time since the previous September; at the South Pole, the Sun is setting. In the Northern Hemisphere, spring arrives.

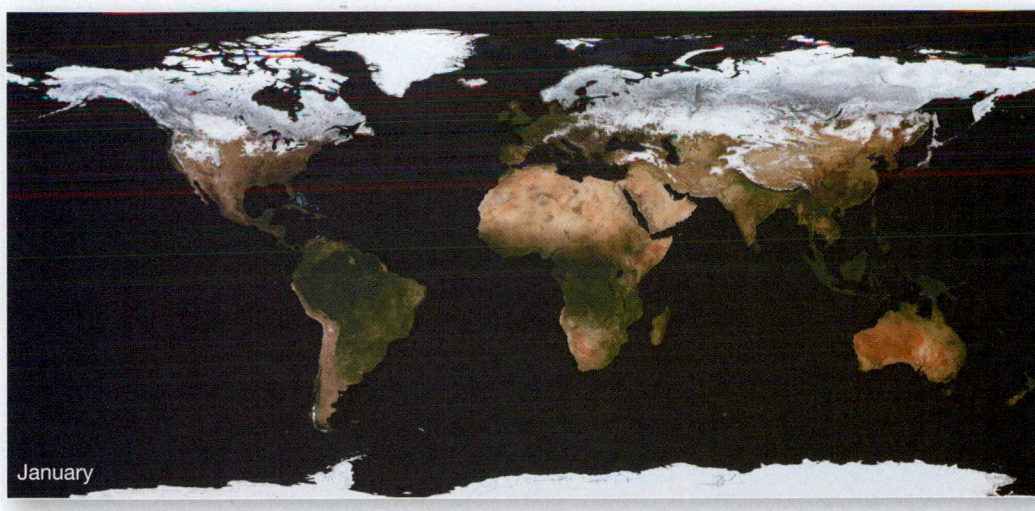

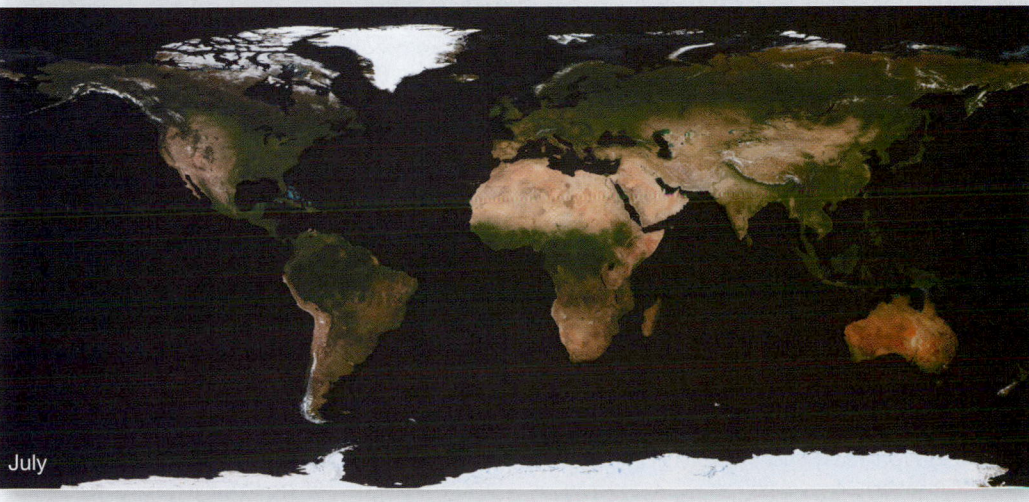

◀**Figure 2.16 Satellite images show seasonal changes.** Note the differences in ice cover (white) and vegetation (green), especially in the Northern Hemisphere, between these January and July composite images. [Blue Marble Next generation, Reto Stöckli/NASA Earth Observatory.]

Midnight Sun over Arctic Ocean, June

During the year, outside of the equatorial regions, the Sun's altitude changes slightly each day, and daylength gradually increases and decreases. These changes affect the amount of insolation received, which drives weather and climate. Taken together, these variations in Earth's relationship to the Sun produce the annual "march" of the seasons.

2.1 EARTH'S ORIENTATION AT SOLSTICES AND EQUINOXES

As Earth (seen in side view) orbits the Sun, the 23.5° tilt of Earth's axis remains constant. As a result, the area covered by the circle of illumination changes, along with the location of the subsolar point (red dot).

March 20 or 21 Equinox
The poles are at the very edge of the circle of illumination. At all latitudes in between, day and night are equal.

Subsolar point at 0° (Equator)

23.5° N
Arctic Circle
Tropic of Cancer
Equator
Tropic of Capricorn
Antarctic Circle
S 23.5°

December 21 or 22 Solstice
The North Pole points away from the Sun, excluding areas above the Arctic Circle from the circle of illumination.

June 20 or 21 Solstice
The North Pole points toward the Sun, bringing areas above the Arctic Circle into the circle of illumination.

23.5° N
Arctic Circle
Tropic of Cancer
Equator
Tropic of Capricorn
Antarctic Circle
S 23.5°

Subsolar point at 23.5°N (Tropic of Cancer)

Sun

Subsolar point at 23.5°S (Tropic of Capricorn)

23.5° N
Arctic Circle
Tropic of Cancer
Equator
Tropic of Capricorn
Antarctic Circle
S 23.5°

September 22 or 23 Equinox
The poles are at the very edge of the circle of illumination. At all latitudes in between, day and night are equal.

23.5° N
Arctic Circle
Tropic of Cancer
Equator
Tropic of Capricorn
Antarctic Circle
S 23.5°

Subsolar point at 0° (Equator)

Animation (MG)
Earth–Sun Relations
https://goo.gl/rMwMKz

MasteringGeography™

Visit the Study Area in MasteringGeography™ to explore Geosystems in Action.

Visualize: Study a geosciences animation of the Earth–Sun relations.

Assess: Demonstrate understanding of Earth–Sun relations (if assigned by instructor).

2.2 MARCH OF THE SEASONS

As Earth (visualized from above the North Pole) orbits the Sun, the 23.5° tilt of its axis produces continuous changes in daylength and Sun angle.

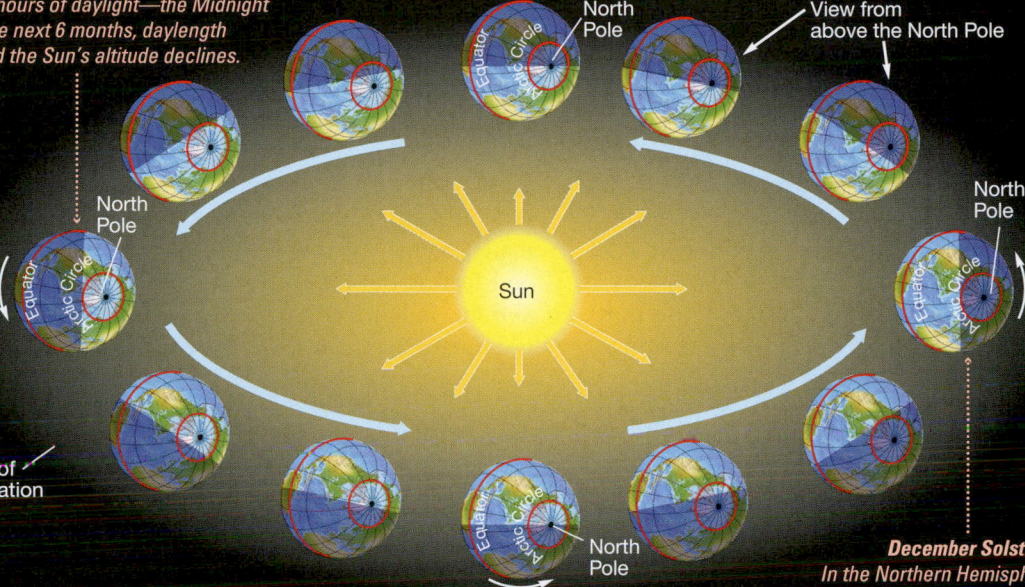

March Equinox
In the Northern Hemisphere, this is the vernal equinox, marking the beginning of spring. The circle of illumination passes through both poles, so that all locations on Earth experience 12 hours of day and night. At the North Pole, the Sun rises for the first time since the previous September.

June Solstice
In the Northern Hemisphere, this is the summer solstice, marking the beginning of summer. The circle of illumination includes the North Polar region, so everything north of the Arctic Circle receives 24 hours of daylight—the Midnight Sun. Over the next 6 months, daylength shortens and the Sun's altitude declines.

View from above the North Pole

North Pole

North Pole

Sun

North Pole

Circle of illumination

December Solstice
In the Northern Hemisphere, this is the winter solstice, marking the beginning of winter. Notice that the North Pole is dark. It lies outside the circle of illumination. Over the next 6 months, daylength and the Sun's altitude increase.

North Pole

September Equinox
In the Northern Hemisphere, this is the autumnal equinox, marking the beginning of autumn. As with the March equinox, days and nights are of equal length.

2.3 OBSERVING SUN DIRECTION AND ALTITUDE

As the seasons change, the Sun's altitude, or angle above the horizon, also changes, as does its position at sunrise and sunset along the horizon (illustrated below from the viewpoint of an observer).

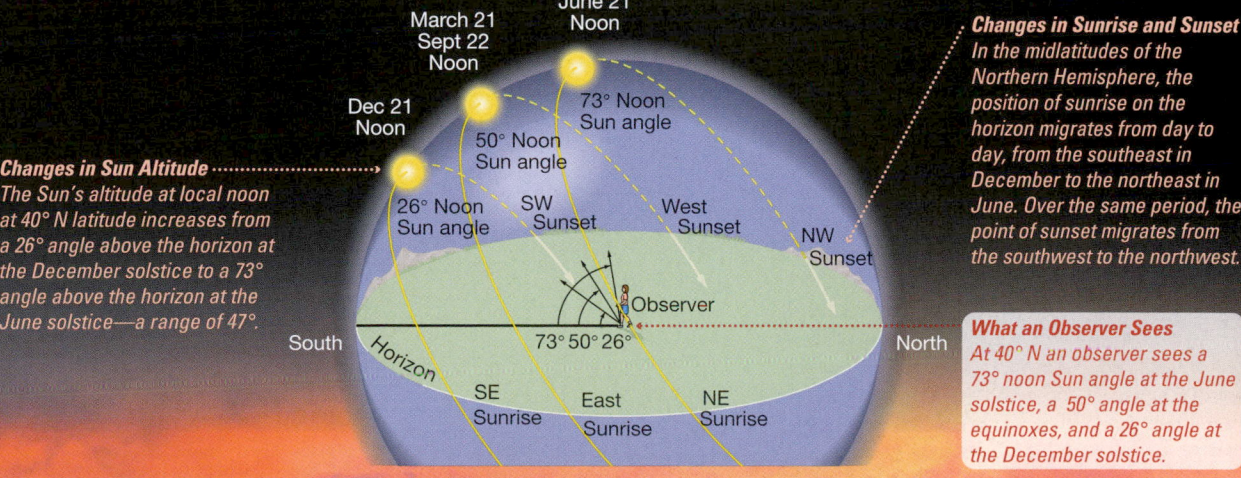

March 21 Sept 22 Noon

June 21 Noon

Dec 21 Noon

73° Noon Sun angle

50° Noon Sun angle

26° Noon Sun angle

SW Sunset

West Sunset

NW Sunset

Changes in Sun Altitude
The Sun's altitude at local noon at 40° N latitude increases from a 26° angle above the horizon at the December solstice to a 73° angle above the horizon at the June solstice—a range of 47°.

South

Horizon

73° 50° 26°

Observer

North

SE Sunrise

East Sunrise

NE Sunrise

Changes in Sunrise and Sunset
In the midlatitudes of the Northern Hemisphere, the position of sunrise on the horizon migrates from day to day, from the southeast in December to the northeast in June. Over the same period, the point of sunset migrates from the southwest to the northwest.

What an Observer Sees
At 40° N an observer sees a 73° noon Sun angle at the June solstice, a 50° angle at the equinoxes, and a 26° angle at the December solstice.

GEOquiz

1. Apply Concepts: Ushuaia, Argentina, is located at 55° S latitude near the southern tip of South America. Describe the march of the seasons for Ushuaia, explaining changes in daylength, Sun altitude, and the position of sunrise and sunset.

2. Explain: What happens to the amount of insolation an area on Earth's surface receives as you move away from the equator? What role does this play in producing the seasons?

Antarctic sunset, December 11:30 pm

June 20 or 21 marks the **June solstice**, or Northern Hemisphere *summer solstice*, the moment when the circle of illumination includes the North Pole region but leaves the South Pole in darkness. The Northern Hemisphere is tilted toward the more direct rays of the Sun— our northern summer—and the subsolar point is about 23.5° N latitude at the Tropic of Cancer. The North Polar region (66.5° N to 90° N) experiences 24 hours of daylight (known as the *Midnight Sun*). In contrast, locations between the **Antarctic Circle** at 66.5° S and the South Pole at 90° S experience 24 hours of darkness as the Sun remains below the horizon.

September 22 or 23 is the **September equinox**, or *autumnal equinox* in the Northern Hemisphere, when the circle of illumination again passes through both poles, so that all parts of the globe experience a 12-hour day and a 12-hour night. The subsolar point is at the equator, with days growing shorter to the north and longer to the south. In the Northern Hemisphere,

autumn arrives, whereas in the Southern Hemisphere it is spring.

Seasonal Change in Sun Altitude In the midlatitudes of the Northern Hemisphere, the Sun altitude at local noon changes seasonally, and the position of sunrise and sunset on the horizon migrates from day to day. At 40° N latitude, the Sun's altitude above the horizon at local noon increases by 47° from the December solstice to the June solstice (**Figure GIA 2.3**). Sunrise migrates from the southeast in December to the northeast in June. Over the same period, the point of sunset migrates from the southwest to the northwest.

Seasonal Timing Recently, the timing of seasonal patterns in the biosphere has begun shifting with global climate change. In the middle and high latitudes, spring and leafing out are occurring earlier than a century ago, and fall is happening later (see the graph in Human Denominator 2). Ecosystems are changing in response.

WORK**IT**OUT 2.4
Use the Analemma to Find the Subsolar Point

If you marked the location of the Sun in the sky at noon each day throughout the year, you would find that the Sun takes a figure-8–shaped path called an *analemma* (see http://www.analemma.com). On the analemma chart in **Figure WO 2.4.1**, you can locate any date, then trace horizontally to the *y*-axis and find the Sun's declination (the latitude of the subsolar point). Along the Tropic of Capricorn, the subsolar point occurs on December 21–22, at the lower end of the analemma. Following the chart, you see that by March 20–21, the Sun's declination reaches the equator, and then moves on to the Tropic of Cancer in June. Using the chart,

1. What is the location of the subsolar point on your birthday?
2. What is the location of the subsolar point today?

The shape of the analemma as the Sun's declination moves between the tropics is a result of Earth's axial tilt and elliptical orbit. As Earth revolves around the Sun, it moves faster during December and January (at perihelion) and slower in June and July (at aphelion). This is reflected in the *equation of time* at the top of the chart.

An average day of 24 hours (86,400 seconds) is the basis for *mean solar time*, time measured by a clock (and introduced earlier in the chapter). However, *observed solar time* is the observed movement of the Sun crossing your meridian each day at noon. The equation of time is the difference between mean solar time and observed solar time. You see on the chart that in October and November, *fast-Sun times* occur and the Sun arrives ahead of local noon (12:00). In February and March the Sun arrives later than local noon, causing *slow-Sun times*.

3. What was the equation of time on your birthday?

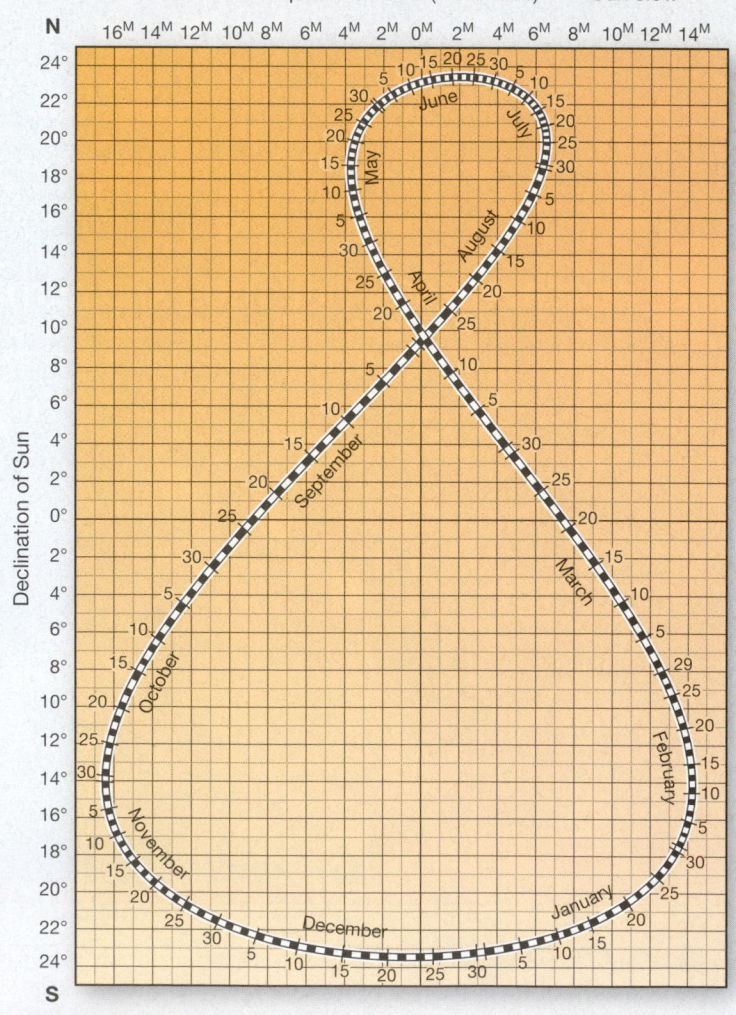

▲**Figure WO 2.4.1** The analemma chart.

SOLAR ENERGY/SEASONS IMPACT HUMANS

• Based on what you have learned in this chapter, list three ways solar energy and seasonal change affect humans.

Solar energy drives Earth systems, including winds, ocean currents, weather, and living ecosystems. [NASA/JSC.]

HUMANS IMPACT SOLAR ENERGY/SEASONS

• Climate change affects timing of the seasons. Changing temperature and rainfall patterns means that spring is coming earlier and fall is starting later. Prolonged summer temperatures heat water bodies, promote early thawing and later refreezing of seasonal ice cover, alter animal migrations, and shift vegetation patterns to higher latitudes—virtually all ecosystems on Earth are affected.

Pollinators such as honeybees, here shown on a crabapple (*Malus*) blossom, are becoming active earlier in the spring as seasonal timing shifts. [B LaRue/Alamy.]

In Africa, seasonal shifts in the subtropical high pressure belts are leading to decreased rainfall. New crops such as drought-tolerant maize will help farmers adapt to climate change. [Philimon Bulawayao/Reuters]

As summers get longer in Alaska, moose migrations no longer coincide with the hunting seasons of native peoples, who depend on the meat. Shifting animal migrations and vegetation patterns will affect ecosystems across the globe. [Steve Bower/Shutterstock.]

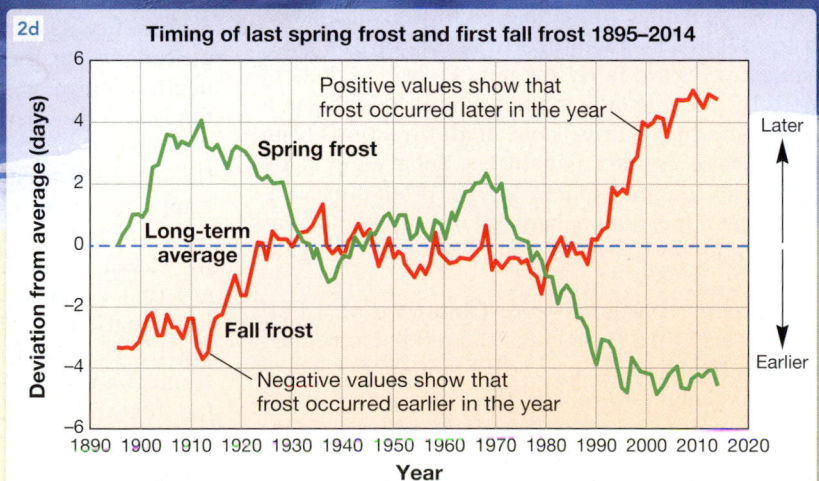

Timing of last spring frost and first fall frost 1895–2014

Deviation from average (days) vs *Year*

Positive values show that frost occurred later in the year

Spring frost

Long-term average

Fall frost

Negative values show that frost occurred earlier in the year

Later / Earlier

Data is for the contiguous United States. The overall trend is toward a longer growing season, with a longer fall and an earlier spring. [EPA, data courtesy K.E. Kunkel 2015; www.epa.gov/climatechange/indicators.]

ISSUES FOR THE 21ST CENTURY

• Ongoing climate change will continue to alter Earth systems. Societies will need to adapt their resource base as timing of seasonal patterns changes.

QUESTIONS TO CONSIDER

1. Based on the graph in HD 2d, did the final spring frost in 2010 occur earlier or later in the year? By how many days?

2. In 1910, did the final spring frost occur earlier or later in the year? By how many days?

KEY**LEARNING**concepts**review**

Locate Earth in the Universe, **describe** the formation of our Solar System, and **sketch** Earth's orbital path around the Sun.

Our Solar System—the Sun and eight planets—is located in the **Milky Way Galaxy** (p. 38), a flattened, disk-shaped collection estimated to contain up to 300 billion stars. **Gravity** (p. 38), the mutual attracting force exerted by all objects upon all other objects in proportion to their mass, is an organizing force in the Universe. The **planetesimal hypothesis** (p. 38) describes the formation of solar systems as a process in which stars (like our Sun) condense from nebular dust and gas, with planetesimals and then proto-planets forming in orbits around these central masses.

Distances in space are so vast that the **speed of light**, (p. 38) (300,000 kmps, or 186,000 mps, which is about 9.5 trillion km, or nearly 6 trillion mi, per year), is used to express distance.

In its orbit, Earth is at **perihelion** (p. 39), its closest position to the Sun, during our Northern Hemisphere winter (January 3 at 147,255,000 km, or 91,500,000 mi). It is at **aphelion** (p. 39), its farthest position from the Sun, during our Northern Hemisphere summer (July 4 at 152,083,000 km, or 94,500,000 mi).

1. Other than planets, what are the components of our Solar System?
2. Briefly describe Earth's origin as part of the Solar System.

Describe the Sun's operation, and **explain** the solar wind and the electromagnetic spectrum of radiant energy.

The **fusion** (p. 40) process—hydrogen nuclei forced together under tremendous temperature and pressure in the Sun's interior—generates incredible quantities of energy. **Sunspots** (p. 40) are magnetic disturbances on the solar surface; *solar cycles* are fairly regular, 11-year periods of sunspot activity. Solar energy in the form of charged particles of **solar wind** (p. 41) travels out in all directions from magnetic disturbances and solar storms. Solar wind is deflected by Earth's **magnetosphere** (p. 41), producing various effects in the upper atmosphere, including spectacular **auroras** (p. 41), the northern and southern lights at higher latitudes.

Radiant energy travels outward from the Sun in all directions, representing a portion of the total **electromagnetic spectrum** (p. 42) made up of different energy wavelengths. A **wavelength** (p. 43) is the distance between corresponding points on any two successive waves. Eventually, some of this radiant energy reaches Earth's surface. **Temperature** (p. 42) is a measure of the average kinetic energy of individual molecules in matter. **Heat** (p. 42) is the flow of kinetic energy between molecules and from one body to another because of a temperature difference between them.

3. What is the sunspot cycle? At what stage was the cycle in the year 2014?
4. Describe Earth's magnetosphere and its effects on the solar wind.
5. Describe the various segments of the electromagnetic spectrum, from shortest to longest wavelength. What are the main wavelengths emitted by the Sun? Which wavelengths does Earth radiate to space?

Illustrate the interception of solar energy and its uneven distribution at the top of the atmosphere.

Electromagnetic radiation from the Sun passes through Earth's magnetic field to the top of the atmosphere—the **thermopause** (p. 43), at approximately 500 km (300 mi) altitude. Incoming solar radiation is **insolation** (p. 44), measured as energy delivered to a horizontal surface area over some unit of time. The **solar constant** (p. 44) is a general measure of insolation at the top of the atmosphere, approximately 1372 W/m². The place receiving maximum insolation is the **subsolar point** (p. 44), where solar rays are perpendicular to the Earth's surface (radiating from directly overhead). All other locations away from the subsolar point receive slanting rays and more diffuse energy.

6. If Earth were flat and oriented at right angles to incoming solar radiation (insolation), what would be the latitudinal distribution of solar energy at the top of the atmosphere?

Explain the concept of seasonality, and **list** the five reasons for Earth's seasons.

Seasonality is the annual pattern of change in **Sun altitude** (p. 46), the angle between the Sun and the horizon, **declination** (p. 46), the latitude of the subsolar point, and **daylength** (p. 46), the duration of exposure to insolation.

Several factors related to Earth movement and position produce seasons. **Revolution** (p. 47) is Earth's annual orbit about the Sun. **Rotation** (p. 47) is Earth's turning on its **axis** (p. 47), an imaginary line running through the North and South Poles. As Earth rotates, the boundary that divides daylight and darkness is the **circle of illumination** (p. 47). Three other reasons for seasons are Earth's **axial tilt** (p. 48) at about 23.5° from a perpendicular to the **plane of the ecliptic** (p. 48); **axial parallelism** (p. 48), the consistent alignment of the Earth's axis throughout the year; and Earth's *sphericity*.

7. What phenomena define the concept of seasonality? How do these aspects of seasonality change during a year at 0° latitude? At 90°?
8. Describe Earth's revolution and rotation and differentiate between them.

Describe the Earth–Sun relationships during the annual march of the seasons.

The **Tropic of Cancer** (p. 49) parallel at 23.5° N latitude marks the farthest north the subsolar point migrates during the year. The **Tropic of Capricorn** (p. 49) parallel at about 23.5° S latitude marks the farthest south the subsolar point migrates during the year. Throughout the march of the seasons, Earth experiences the **December solstice**, (p. 49) **March equinox**, (p. 49) **June solstice**, (p. 52) and **September equinox**

(p. 52). The polar regions experience daylight extremes: Areas north of the **Arctic Circle**, (p. 49) (66.5° N), experience a 24-hour day on the June solstice and 24 hours of darkness on the December solstice. For areas south of the **Antarctic Circle**, (p. 52) (66.5° S), the June solstice brings 24 hours of darkness and December brings 24 hours of daylight.

9. What are the solstices and equinoxes, and what is the Sun's declination at these times?
10. Describe seasonal conditions in the Northern Hemisphere on each solstice and equinox date.

GEO**SPATIAL** ANALYSIS

Seasons in Tromsø, Norway

The number of daylight hours and solar radiation reaching the ground determine temperature at a particular location.

Activities

Go to the World Atlas Latitude & Longitude Finder at http://www.worldatlas.com/aatlas/findlatlong.htm.

1. The University of Tromsø in Tromsø, Norway, is at a high latitude. What is the latitude for Tromsø, Norway, to the nearest degree?

2. Where is the Arctic Circle in relation to Tromsø?

Go to University of Tromsø Weather Observations page at http://weather.cs.uit.no/ . Click on "Time Lapse Video" and choose a date to watch. Make note of any clouds and precipitation.

3. For the most recent day, how many hours of daylight are there? You may need to view the video in full screen to see the date and time.

4. How many hours of daylight are there in the most recent video for the vernal equinox? Summer solstice? Autumnal equinox? Winter solstice? Does the sun ever rise above the horizon on the winter solstice?

Mastering Geography™

Looking for additional review and test prep materials? Visit the Study Area in MasteringGeography™ to enhance your geographic literacy, spatial reasoning skills, and understanding of this chapter's content by accessing a variety of resources, including MapMaster™ interactive maps, videos, *Mobile Field Trips*, *Project Condor* Quadcopter videos, *In the News* RSS feeds, flashcards, web links, self-study quizzes, and an eText version of *Geosystems*.

3 Earth's Atmosphere

Brazil

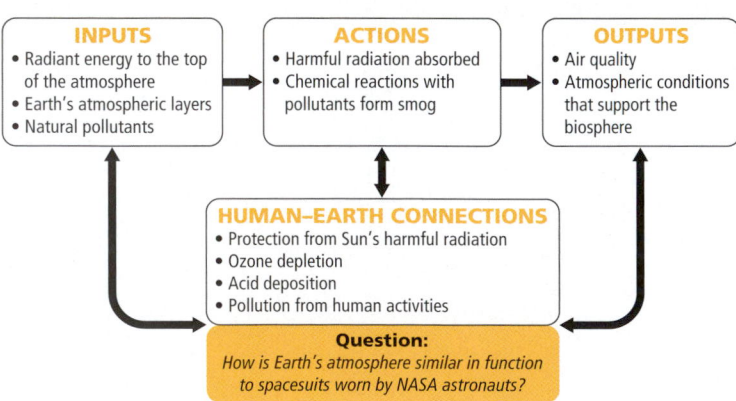

Sunset over Brazil and the Atlantic coastline. [Filipe Rhodes/EyeEm/Getty Images.]

KEY**LEARNING**concepts

After reading the chapter, you should be able to:

- **Explain** the relationship between air pressure, density, and altitude.
- **List** and **describe** the components of the atmosphere, giving their relative percentage contributions by volume.
- **Draw** a diagram showing atmospheric structure based on temperature.
- **Describe** the atmospheric profile on the basis of function, focusing on the status of the ozone layer.
- **Describe** natural and anthropogenic pollutants in the lower atmosphere, including pollution from photochemical reactions in vehicle exhaust and from industrial smog.

INPUTS
- Radiant energy to the top of the atmosphere
- Earth's atmospheric layers
- Natural pollutants

ACTIONS
- Harmful radiation absorbed
- Chemical reactions with pollutants form smog

OUTPUTS
- Air quality
- Atmospheric conditions that support the biosphere

HUMAN–EARTH CONNECTIONS
- Protection from Sun's harmful radiation
- Ozone depletion
- Acid deposition
- Pollution from human activities

Question:
How is Earth's atmosphere similar in function to spacesuits worn by NASA astronauts?

GEOSYSTEMSnow

Sun Safety and the UV Index

When you're in the sun, do you tan or burn? Do you protect your skin during the hot summer months? In 2013, the Centers for Disease Control and Prevention (CDC) reported that the vast majority of Americans do not regularly use sunscreen. Studies also suggest that more than 90% of college athletes do not use sunscreen, even though practices and competitions often occur midday when the Sun angle is highest. Those with fair skin probably know that the Sun's ultraviolet rays can burn in as little as 15 minutes.

Skin is the human body's largest organ. Ultraviolet radiation (UV), which causes sunburn, premature aging, and skin cancers, poses a threat to skin health. Fortunately, protection is simple and inexpensive: stay out of the midday sun, wear a hat, cover your skin, and use SPF 30 sunscreen. Also, you can check the daily *UV Index*, a simple guide to the danger of solar UV radiation intensity at your location (**Figure GN 3.1**).

UV and Ozone Because not all radiation from the Sun is beneficial, our atmosphere safeguards life on Earth by "filtering" some of the Sun's harmful rays. Ultraviolet radiation encompasses a range of wavelengths from shorter-wavelength UVC, to UVB, to longer-wavelength UVA. *Ozone* (O_3) is a gas concentrated in a layer in the stratosphere, far above Earth's surface, that absorbs UV wavelengths—generally all of the UVC, the most dangerous for living organisms, and some of the UVB (ozone does not absorb UVA). The presence and condition of the ozone layer affects the amount of UV reaching Earth. For the past 50 years, human activities have caused a depletion of this critical atmospheric gas. As the ozone layer has thinned, more UVB radiation is reaching Earth's surface.

Health Effects In humans, UVB causes sunburn, skin cancer, eye damage, and weakening of the immune system. UVA is less intense than UVB, but it penetrates human skin more deeply, causing significant damage in the outer layer of skin, where most skin cancers occur. UVA levels are fairly constant throughout the year during daylight hours and can penetrate glass and clouds. In contrast, UVB intensity varies by latitude, season, time of day, and the condition of the ozone layer.

The UV Index In 1992, in response to declining ozone, the National Weather Service (NWS) and Environmental Protection Agency (EPA) began reporting the UV Index to help people avoid UV overexposure and related health effects. The index, standardized worldwide in 2004, uses a scale from 1 to 11+. A higher number indicates a greater risk of UV exposure; an index of 0 indicates no risk, such as at night.

UV Index values vary according to the level of ozone present, Sun angle, and cloud cover. Lower ozone, high Sun angle, and clear skies yield the highest UV Index values. Areas of particularly high risk occur in the summer at high elevation, such as in the Rocky Mountain West (**Figure GN 3.2**).

What is the UV Index at your location today, and how can you minimize your risk? You can download the free EPA SunWise app for your smartphone at http://www.epa.gov/sunsafety/uv-index-1; in Canada, go to https://ec.gc.ca/uv/.

1. How is UV radiation harmful to human health?

2. What change in the atmosphere has affected human exposure to UV radiation?

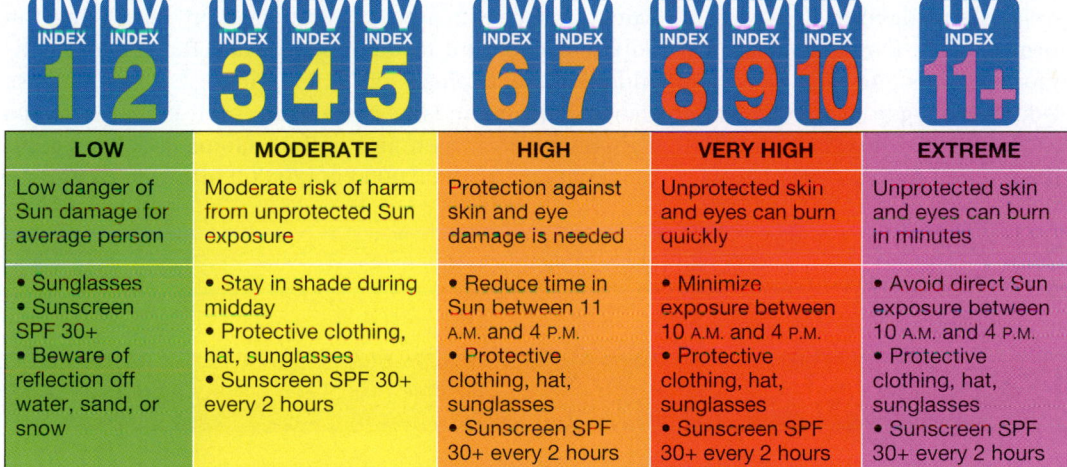

▲Figure GN 3.1 The UV Index. [EPA and WHO.]

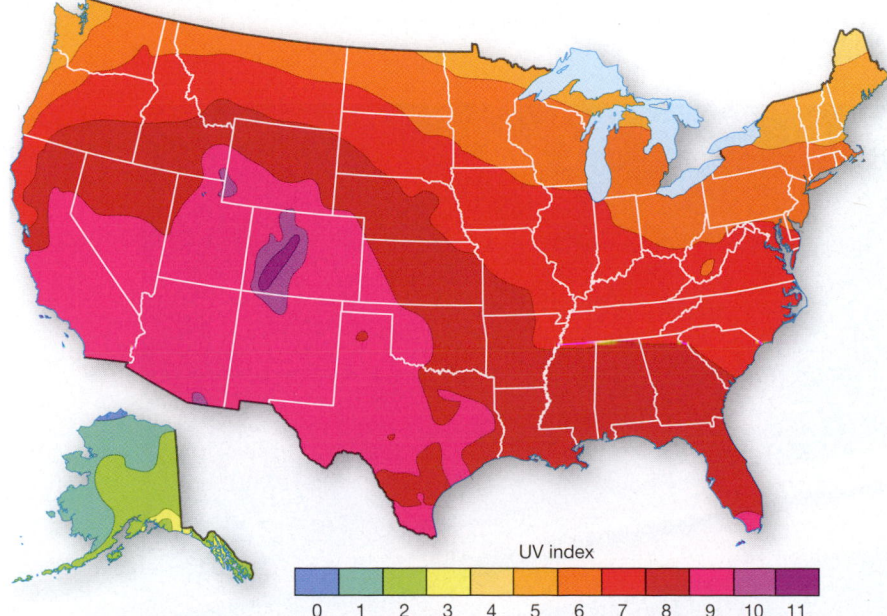

▲Figure GN 3.2 Average July UV Index for the United States. [EPA.]

57

Earth's atmosphere contains the gases that sustain life. Some of the gases are crucial components in biological processes; some protect us from hostile radiation and particles from the Sun and beyond. For humans to survive in space, away from the lower regions of the atmosphere, they need highly technical suits that maintain oxygen, temperature, and pressure conditions appropriate for human survival.

The principal substance of our atmosphere is air, the medium of life as well as a major industrial and chemical raw material. **Air** is a simple mixture of gases that is naturally odorless, colorless, tasteless, and formless, blended so thoroughly that it behaves as if it were a single gas.

The modern atmosphere evolved over 4.6 billion years and is probably the fourth general atmosphere in Earth's history. The first atmosphere most likely formed from *outgassing*, or the release of gases trapped within Earth's interior. We still see outgassing today in the form of volcanic activity. This atmosphere was high in sulfuric gases, low in nitrogen, and devoid of oxygen. The second atmosphere formed when Earth cooled and water vapor condensed to form clouds and rain. Oceans formed, nitrogen increased, but oxygen was still not present in the atmosphere. The third atmosphere developed slowly as oceanic life evolved and bacteria began the process of photosynthesis, using the Sun's energy to convert atmospheric carbon dioxide to oxygen. Oxygen became significant in the atmosphere about 2.2 billion years ago, but it took another billion years before atmospheric oxygen levels were stable. Our modern atmosphere formed when oxygen molecules absorbed sunlight and formed ozone, the protective layer in the stratosphere that shields all life from ultraviolet radiation.

Profile of the Atmosphere

Earth's atmosphere is a thin envelope of imperfectly shaped concentric "shells" or "spheres" that grade into one another, all bound to the planet by gravity (**Figure 3.1**). To study the atmosphere, we view it in layers, each with distinctive properties and processes. As a practical matter, we consider the top of our atmosphere to be around 480 km (300 mi) above Earth's surface, the same altitude we used in Chapter 2 for measuring the solar constant and insolation received. Beyond that altitude is the **exosphere**, or "outer sphere," where the less dense atmosphere is nearly a vacuum. It contains scarce lightweight hydrogen and helium atoms, weakly bound by gravity as far as 32,000 km (20,000 mi) from Earth.

everyday GEO**SYSTEMS**

Why do we see colored "shells" above Earth's curved surface in astronaut photographs?

Each layer of the atmosphere has distinctive characteristics related to molecular density, gas composition, particles, and temperature. The gases and particles of each layer filter out certain wavelengths of light, so that the "shells" appear different from one another. The troposphere, closest to Earth, is the area of clouds, weather, and other processes that support the biosphere.

◄**Figure 3.1 Earth's atmosphere.** [ISS astronaut photo/NASA.]

Outer space

Upper atmosphere

Stratosphere

Troposphere

Earth

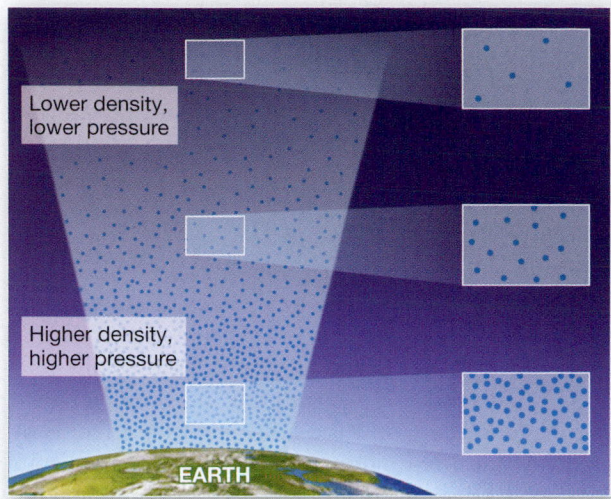

(a) Air density is higher near Earth's surface. (Density is mass per unit volume.)

▲**Figure 3.2 Density and pressure decreasing with altitude.** In part (b), pressure is in millibars (mb) and as a percentage of sea-level pressure. Note that the troposphere holds about 90% of the atmospheric mass (far right % column).

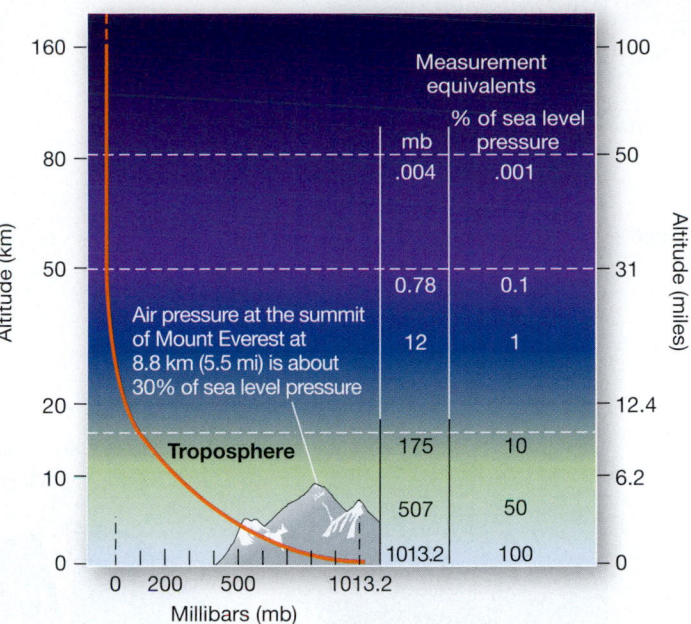

(b) Pressure profile shows that air pressure decreases with increasing altitude.

Air Pressure

In our atmosphere, air molecules create **air pressure** through their motion, size, and number. Air pressure is the force exerted from the ongoing collision of gas molecules on all surfaces they come in contact with. You have measured air pressure in your bicycle tire using a tire gauge. The pressure of air in our atmosphere (measured as force per unit area) pushes in on all of us. Fortunately, that same pressure also exists inside us, pushing outward; otherwise, we would be crushed by the mass of air around us.

Earth's atmosphere also presses downward under the pull of gravity and therefore has weight. **Atmospheric pressure** is the pressure exerted by the weight of air in Earth's atmosphere. In the upper atmosphere, far from Earth's surface, the low density of molecules means that they are far apart, making collisions between them less frequent and thereby reducing pressure (**Figure 3.2a**). Near Earth's surface, gravity compresses air, making it denser (meaning that there is a greater mass of molecules in a volume of air). At sea level, the atmosphere exerts an average pressure equivalent to that of a 1 kg weight resting on 1 cm² of area.

Figure 3.2b shows the atmospheric pressure profile in which air pressure decreases with increasing altitude (height above Earth's surface). This is the "thinning" of air that humans feel on high mountain summits as less oxygen is available in each breath a person takes. This makes breathing more difficult at the top of Mount Everest, where air pressure is about 30% of that at sea level.

The atmospheric pressure profile also explains why, in a descending airplane, passengers feel increasing air pressure as a "popping" sensation in their ears, reflecting the changing pressure balance in the eardrum.

Over half the total mass of the atmosphere, compressed by gravity, lies below 5.5 km (3.14 mi, or 18,000 ft) altitude. Only 0.1% of the atmosphere remains above an altitude of 50 km (31 mi), as shown in the pressure profile in Figure 3.2b (percentage column is farthest to the right).

Pressure is expressed as millibars (mb, a measure of force per square meter of surface area), inches of mercury (symbol, Hg), as measured by a barometer, or kilopascals (kPa). At sea level, the atmosphere exerts a pressure of 1013.2 mb, or 29.92 inches of mercury. In Canada and certain other countries, normal air pressure is expressed as 101.32 kPa (1 kPa = 10 mb). (See Chapter 5 for further discussion.)

Scientists use three atmospheric criteria—*composition*, *temperature*, and *function*—to define layers of the atmosphere. The criteria discussions ahead follow the path of incoming solar radiation as it travels through the atmosphere to Earth's surface.

Atmospheric Composition

By the criterion of chemical *composition*, the atmosphere divides into two broad regions, the *heterosphere* (80 to 480 km altitude) and the *homosphere* (Earth's surface to 80 km altitude).

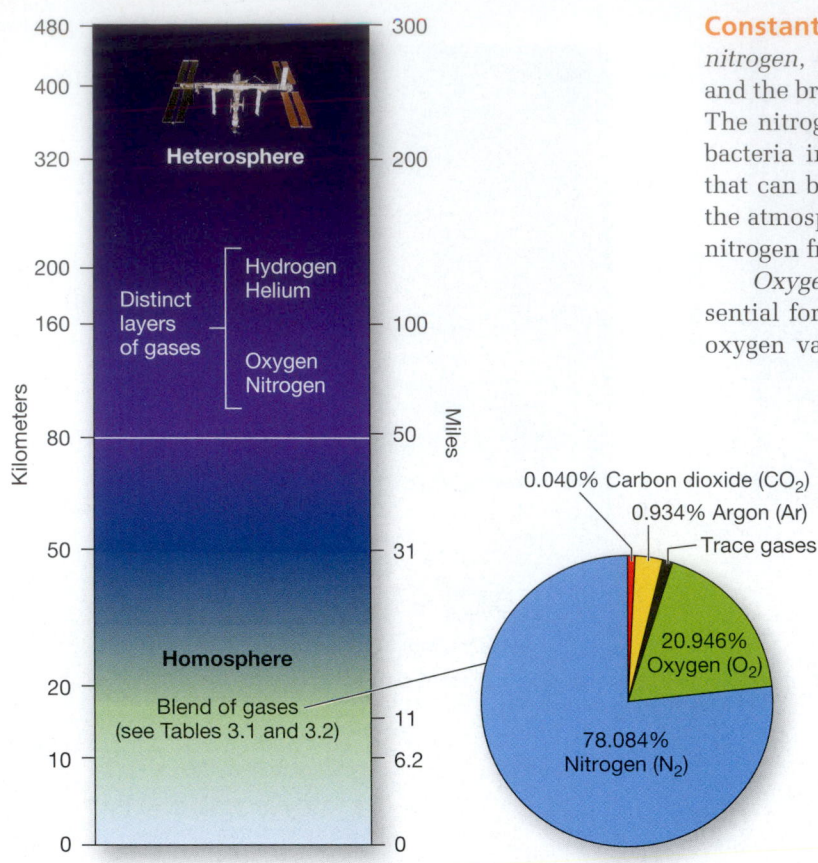

▲Figure 3.3 **Composition of the heterosphere and homosphere.**

Constant Gases Our atmosphere is 78% relatively inert *nitrogen*, originating principally from volcanic sources and the breakdown of organic material by bacteria in soil. The nitrogen cycle is a process whereby nitrogen-fixing bacteria incorporate nitrogen from air into compounds that can be used by plants. The nitrogen later returns to the atmosphere through the work of bacteria that remove nitrogen from decaying organic materials.

Oxygen, a by-product of photosynthesis, also is essential for life processes. The percentage of atmospheric oxygen varies slightly over different portions of Earth's surface, reflecting variations in plant photosynthesis related to seasonal change, latitude, and the associated lag time as atmospheric circulation slowly mixes the air. Oxygen readily reacts with many elements to form compounds that compose about half of Earth's crust. Both nitrogen and oxygen reserves in the atmosphere are so extensive that, at present, they far exceed human capabilities to disrupt or deplete them.

The gas *argon*, constituting less than 1% of the homosphere, is completely inert (an unreactive "noble" gas) and unusable in life processes. All the argon present in the modern atmosphere comes from slow accumulation over millions of years. Inert argon is extracted or "mined" from the atmosphere for commercial, medical, and industrial uses.

Heterosphere The **heterosphere** is the outer atmosphere in terms of composition. As the prefix *hetero-* implies, this region's composition is not uniform—its gases are not evenly mixed (**Figure 3.3**). Gases in the heterosphere occur in distinct layers sorted by gravity according to their atomic weight, with the lightest elements (hydrogen and helium) at the margins of outer space and the heavier elements (oxygen and nitrogen) dominant in the lower heterosphere.

The heterosphere begins at about 80 km (50 mi) altitude and extends outward to the exosphere and interplanetary space. Less than 0.001% of the atmosphere's mass is in this region.

Homosphere Below the heterosphere is the **homosphere**, extending from an altitude of 80 km (50 mi) to Earth's surface. **Table 3.1** lists by volume the gases that constitute dry, clean air in the homosphere. *Constant* gases have shown almost no change throughout the history of Earth's modern atmosphere. In contrast, *variable* gases are present in small amounts that may vary on a daily, monthly, or yearly time scale.

Within the homosphere, the blend of gases is nearly uniform throughout. The only exceptions are the concentration of ozone (O_3) in the "ozone layer," from 19 to 50 km (12 to 31 mi) above sea level, and the variations in water vapor, pollutants, and some trace chemicals in the lowest portion of the atmosphere.

Variable Gases Numerous variable gases exist in our atmosphere, most of which affect Earth's energy balance by absorbing or transmitting radiant energy. As electromagnetic energy from the Sun moves through Earth's atmosphere, gases such as water vapor and carbon dioxide absorb certain wavelengths. These gases vary in their response to radiation received, being transparent to some wavelengths while absorbing others. Gases that absorb and emit radiation are known as *greenhouse gases* because they trap heat in the lower atmosphere.

Table 3.2 lists by volume the variable greenhouse gases in the homosphere with their main sources. We discuss these gases in Chapter 10 with regard to climate

TABLE 3.1 Constant Gases of the Homosphere		
Gas (Symbol)	Percentage by Volume	Parts per Million (ppm)
Nitrogen (N_2)	78.084	780,840
Oxygen (O_2)	20.946	209,460
Argon (Ar)	0.934	9,340
Neon (Ne)	0.001818	18
Helium (He)	0.000525	5.2
Krypton (Kr)	0.00010	1.0
Xenon (Xe)	Trace	~0.1

TABLE 3.2 Variable Gases That Affect Earth's Radiation Budget

Gas (Symbol)	Percentage by Volume	Parts per Million (ppm)	Sources
Water vapor (H_2O)	0–4% (max. at tropics, min. at poles)		Evaporation, photosynthesis, volcanic eruptions
Carbon dioxide (CO_2)*	0.0408	408	Fossil fuel combustion, volcanic eruptions, plant respiration
Methane (CH_4)	0.00018	1.8	Bacterial activity
Nitrous oxide (N_2O)	Trace	~0.3	Soil bacteria, human activity
Ozone (O_3)	Variable		Ultraviolet radiation, fossil fuel combustion

*May 2016 average CO_2 measured at Mauna Loa, Hawai'i (see http://www.esrl.noaa.gov/gmd/ccgg/trends).

change. (We discuss ozone later in this chapter.) Although their overall percentage is small, these gases are today affecting global temperatures.

Water vapor is the most abundant variable gas, with concentrations varying over Earth's surface at any moment. A greenhouse gas, water vapor reaches its highest concentrations over warm, tropical oceans and lowest concentrations at high latitudes and over deserts (**Figure 3.4**; also see Chapter 6).

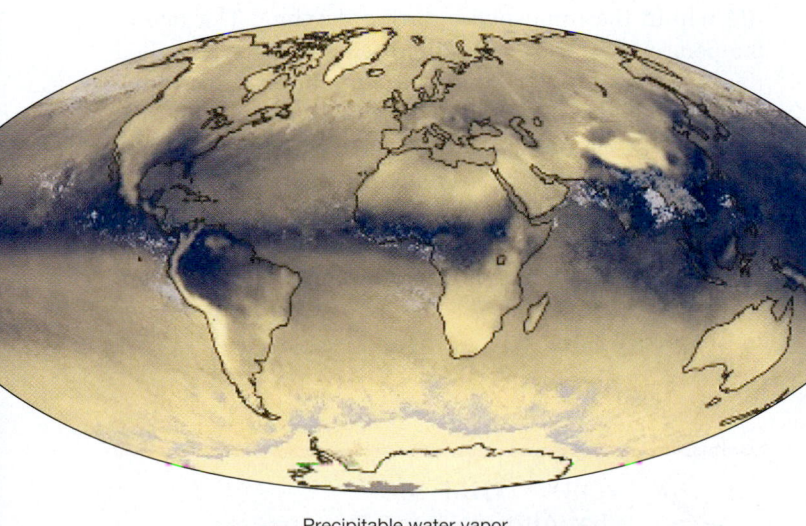

Precipitable water vapor

0   1   2   3   4   5   6 cm

▲**Figure 3.4 Atmospheric water vapor.** This July 2015 image shows *precipitable water vapor*, the total water vapor available in a column of air extending from the top of the atmosphere to Earth's surface. (This represents the depth of water that would accumulate if all the water vapor fell as precipitation to Earth's surface.)

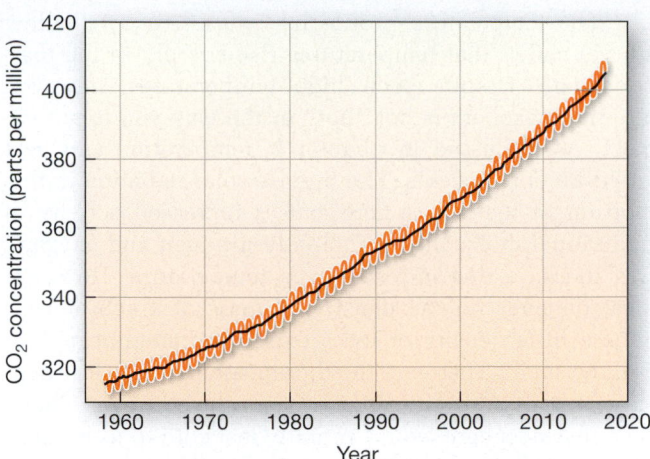

▲**Figure 3.5 Increasing atmospheric carbon dioxide since 1950.** Monthly average CO_2 measured at Mauna Loa Observatory in Hawai'i. The highest and lowest months (usually May and October) are plotted for each year; black line shows the 5-year running average.

Carbon dioxide (CO_2) is another variable gas that occurs naturally in the atmosphere as part of Earth's carbon cycle but is increasing rapidly as a result of human activities. As a greenhouse gas, CO_2 is critical for regulating the temperature of Earth's lower atmosphere so that it can support life.

The study of past atmospheres trapped in samples of glacial ice reveals that the present levels of atmospheric CO_2 are higher than at any time in the past 800,000 years. Over the past 200 years, and especially since the 1950s, the CO_2 percentage has increased steadily, primarily as a result of burning fossil fuels for energy and transportation (**Figure 3.5**).

Particulates The atmosphere also contains variable amounts of *particulates*, solids and liquid droplets that enter the air from natural and human sources. These particles range in size from the relatively large liquid water droplets, salt, and pollen visible with the naked eye to relatively small, even microscopic, dust and soot. Particulates are important for cloud formation and affect human health (discussed later in the chapter).

Atmospheric Temperature

By the criterion of temperature, the atmospheric profile can be divided into four distinct zones—thermosphere, mesosphere, stratosphere, and troposphere (see Geosystems in Action 3).

Thermosphere The atmosphere's outermost layer in terms of temperature, the **thermosphere** ("heat sphere") roughly corresponds to the heterosphere (from 80 km out to 480 km, or 50–300 mi). The upper limit of the thermosphere is the **thermopause** (the suffix *-pause* means "to change"). During periods of a less active Sun, with fewer sunspots and eruptions from the solar surface, the thermopause may lower in altitude from the average 480 km (300 mi) to only 250 km (155 mi). During periods of a more active Sun, the outer atmosphere swells to an altitude of 550 km (340 mi), where it can create frictional drag on satellites in low orbit.

The temperature profile in **Figure GIA 3.1** (yellow curve) shows that temperatures rise sharply in the thermosphere. Despite such high temperatures, however, the thermosphere is not "hot" in the way you might expect. As discussed in Chapter 2, temperature and heat are different concepts. The intense solar radiation in this portion of the atmosphere causes increased activity of individual molecules (principally nitrogen and oxygen). We measure this movement as temperature. However, heat depends on the density or mass of a substance—where little density or mass exists, the amount of heat will be small. Therefore the thermosphere, with low density of molecules and little heat produced, is not "hot." The thermosphere would actually feel cold to us because the number of molecules is not great enough to transfer heat to our skin.

Mesosphere Part of the homosphere, the **mesosphere** is the area from 50 to 80 km (30 to 50 mi) above Earth. The mesosphere's outer boundary, the *mesopause*, is the coldest portion of the atmosphere, averaging −90°C (−130°F), although that temperature may vary considerably. Air pressure in this region is extremely low (look back to Figure 3.2).

The mesosphere sometimes receives cosmic or meteoric dust particles, which act as nuclei around which fine ice crystals form. At high latitudes in the Northern Hemisphere, an observer at night may see these bands of ice crystals glow in rare and unusual **noctilucent clouds**, which are so high in altitude that they still catch sunlight after sunset.

Stratosphere Temperatures increase with altitude throughout the **stratosphere**, which extends from about 18 to 50 km (11 to 31 mi) above Earth's surface. Temperatures range from −57°C (−70°F) at the stratosphere's lower limit to 0°C (32°F) at the stratosphere's outer boundary, called the *stratopause*. The stratosphere is the location of the ozone layer. Stratospheric ozone (sometimes called "good ozone") converts ultraviolet energy to heat, causing the warming with altitude in this layer. Later in this chapter, we discuss ground-level ozone, the "bad ozone" associated with vehicle emissions that damages human health.

Troposphere The region of weather activity, the **troposphere**, also supports life and the biosphere. Approximately 90% of the total mass of the atmosphere and the bulk of all water vapor, clouds, and air pollution are within the troposphere. An average temperature of −57°C (−70°F) defines the **tropopause**, the troposphere's upper limit, but its exact altitude varies with the season, latitude, and surface temperatures and pressures. Near the equator, because of the expansion of air with intense solar heating at Earth's surface, the tropopause is at its highest altitude (18 km, or 11 mi). In the middle latitudes, its height averages 12 km (8 mi). At the North

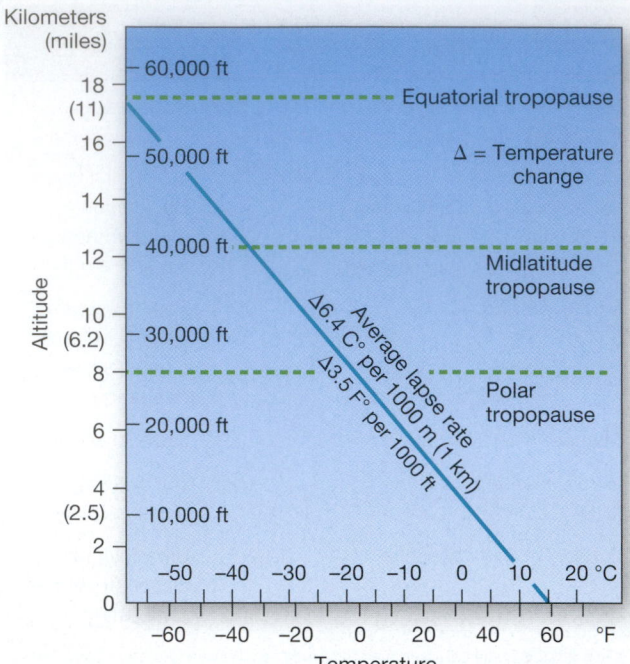

▲**Figure 3.6 Temperature, altitude, and average lapse rate in the troposphere.** Note that the altitude of the tropopause varies with latitude.

and South Poles, the tropopause averages only 8 km (5 mi) or less above Earth's surface, reflecting colder temperatures (**Figure 3.6**). The marked warming in the stratosphere above the tropopause causes the tropopause to act like a lid, generally preventing whatever is in the cooler (denser) air below from mixing into the warmer (less dense) stratosphere.

Figure 3.6 illustrates the normal temperature profile within the troposphere during daytime. The rate of temperature decrease with increasing altitude is called the **lapse rate**. As the graph shows, temperatures in the troposphere decrease rapidly with increasing altitude at an average lapse rate of 6.4°C per km (3.5°F per 1000 ft). The actual lapse rate, known as the **environmental lapse rate**, varies considerably over time and at different locations because of local weather conditions. This variation in the rate of temperature change in the lower troposphere is central to our discussion of weather processes in Chapters 6 and 7.

WORK**IT**OUT 3.1
What Altitude Is the Tropopause?

By definition, the tropopause is located at the upper limit of the troposphere, wherever the temperature reaches −57°C (−70°F).

1. In the midlatitudes, is the tropopause at a higher altitude in summer or in winter? Explain in your own words.

In terms of temperature, scientists divide the atmospheric profile into the thermosphere, mesosphere, stratosphere, and troposphere. Each zone has a different temperature profile, as shown in GIA 3.1. Humans continue to explore the atmosphere from the thermosphere (GIA 3.2) to the stratosphere (GIA 3.3).

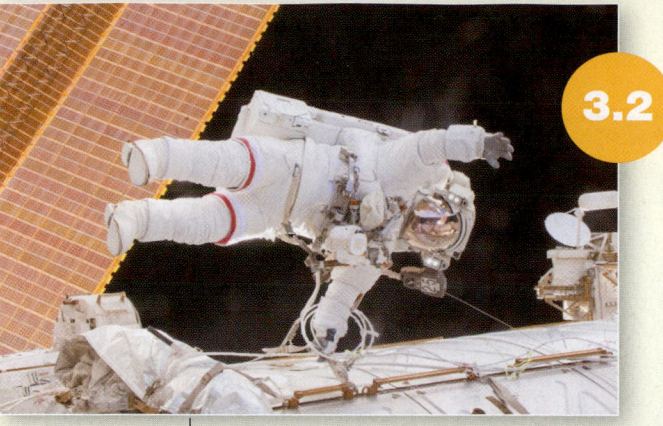

3.2 Astronaut Scott Kelly on a spacewalk in December 2015 during his yearlong mission aboard the International Space Station. His spacesuit replicates the services that the atmosphere provides humans on Earth; for example, protection from radiation and particle impacts, protection from temperature extremes, and regulation of air pressure against the vacuum of outer space. [NASA.]

3.1

Temperatures are hot in the thermosphere because intense solar radiation excites molecules into faster vibrational motion. However, little heat is produced because molecular density is so low.

The mesopause is the coldest region of the atmosphere.

Noctilucent clouds form as water molecules crystallize around debris from disintegrating meteors. They occur most often in summer when water vapor is lifted high in the atmosphere to mix with "meteor smoke."

The stratosphere is warmer because ozone molecules convert ultraviolet energy from the Sun into heat energy. Ozone protects Earth from harmful ultraviolet radiation.

In the troposphere, temperature decreases with altitude at the average lapse rate of 6.4 C°/km (3.5 F°/1000 ft).

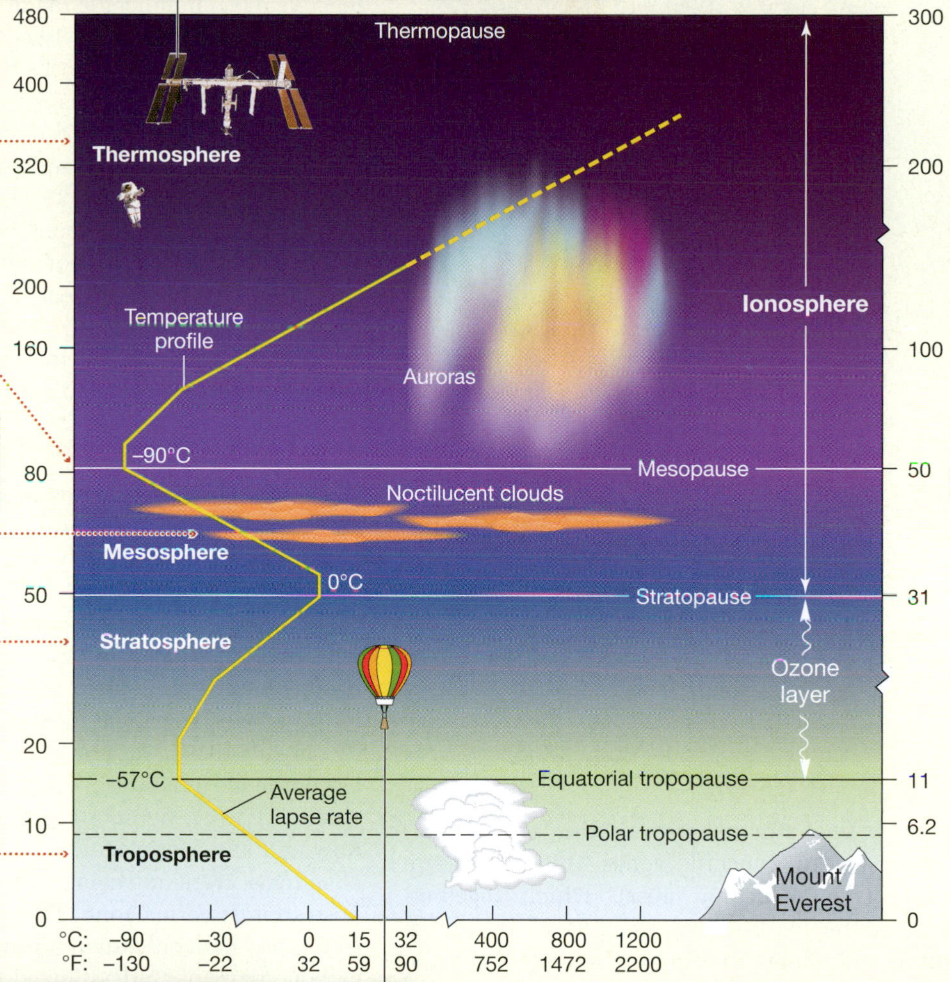

Thermopause
Thermosphere
Temperature profile
Auroras
Ionosphere
–90°C
Mesopause
Noctilucent clouds
Mesosphere
0°C
Stratopause
Stratosphere
Ozone layer
–57°C
Equatorial tropopause
Average lapse rate
Polar tropopause
Troposphere
Mount Everest
Kilometers
480
400
320
200
160
80
50
20
10
0
Miles
300
200
100
50
31
11
6.2
0
°C: –90 –30 0 15 32 400 800 1200
°F: –130 –22 32 59 90 752 1472 2200

3.3

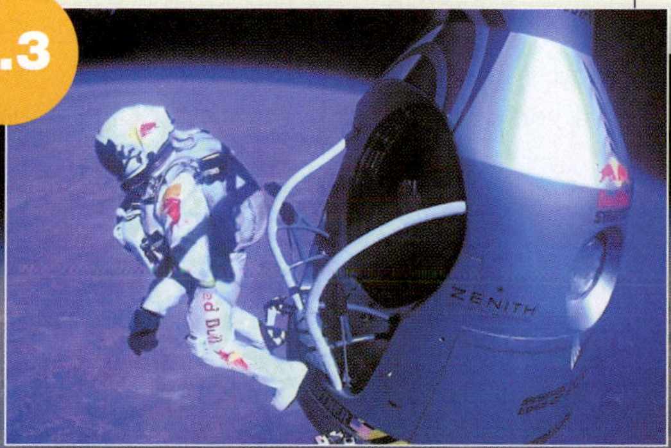

In 2012, Felix Baumgartner ascended by helium balloon to 39.0 km (24.3 mi) altitude and then jumped. Reaching a top free-fall speed of 1342 kmph (834 mph), his fall to Earth lasted 4 minutes, 20 seconds. In 2014, Alan Eustace set a new height record of 41.4 km (25.7 mi), an altitude more than halfway to the top of the stratosphere. [Red Bull Stratos/AP Images.]

MasteringGeography™

Visit the Study Area in MasteringGeography™ to explore atmospheric temperature.

Assess: Demonstrate understanding of atmospheric temperature (if assigned by instructor).

GEOquiz

1. Describe: How and at what rate does temperature change in the troposphere?

2. Explain: Why do temperatures rise in the stratosphere?

3. Analyze: Assuming you did not need to wear a space suit, would you feel hot or cold in the thermosphere? Give a reason for your answer.

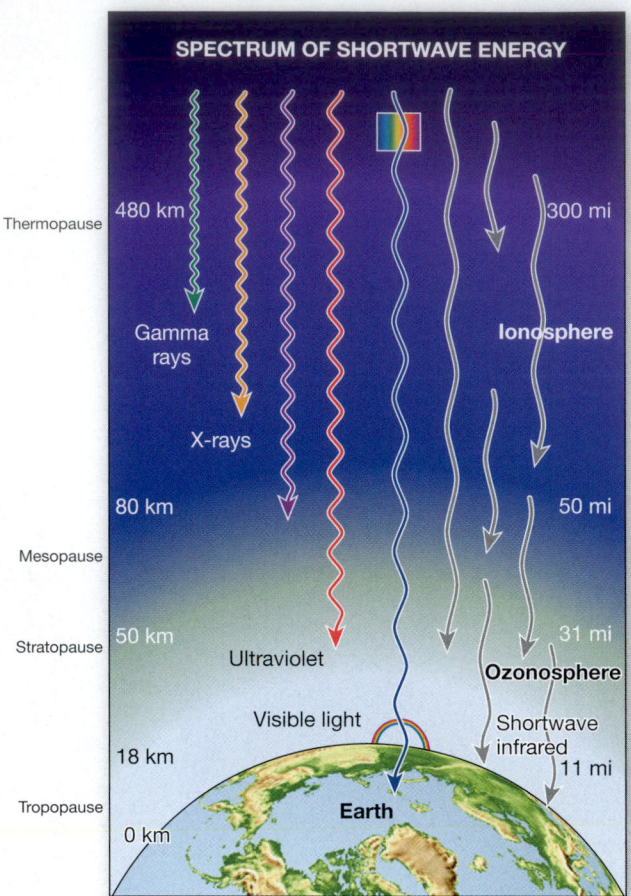

SPECTRUM OF SHORTWAVE ENERGY

Thermopause — 480 km — 300 mi

Gamma rays

Ionosphere

X-rays

80 km — 50 mi

Mesopause

50 km — 31 mi

Stratopause

Ultraviolet

Ozonosphere

Visible light

18 km — Shortwave infrared — 11 mi

Tropopause

Earth

0 km

▲**Figure 3.7 Absorption of wavelengths above Earth's surface.** As shortwave solar energy passes through the atmosphere, the shortest wavelengths are absorbed. Only a fraction of the ultraviolet radiation reaches Earth's surface, as does most of the visible light and shortwave infrared.

Atmospheric Function

According to our final atmospheric criterion of function, the atmosphere has two specific zones, the ionosphere and the ozonosphere (ozone layer), which together remove most of the harmful wavelengths of incoming solar radiation and charged particles. **Figure 3.7** gives a general depiction of the absorption of radiation by these functional layers of the atmosphere.

Ionosphere The outer functional layer, the **ionosphere**, extends throughout the thermosphere and into the mesosphere below (see Figure GIA 3.1). The ionosphere absorbs cosmic rays, gamma rays, X-rays, and shorter wavelengths of ultraviolet radiation, changing atoms to positively charged ions and giving the ionosphere its name. The glowing auroral lights discussed in Chapter 2 occur principally within the ionosphere.

Distinct regions within the ionosphere are important for broadcast communications and GPS signals. These regions reflect certain radio wavelengths, including AM radio and other shortwave radio broadcasts, especially at night. Activity such as solar flares can trigger radio blackouts. This also affects airplanes that fly over the Arctic; over the North Pole, these aircraft lose contact with

geosynchronous satellites and must rely on radio communications, which can be disrupted in a blackout.

Before they reach the ground, GPS satellite signals must first pass through the ionosphere, where gases bend and weaken radio waves. Solar and geomagnetic storms that disturb the ionosphere can cause GPS position errors as large as 100 m (328 ft).

Ozonosphere That portion of the stratosphere that contains a high concentration of ozone relative to other layers is the **ozonosphere**, or **ozone layer**. Ozone is a highly reactive oxygen molecule made up of three oxygen atoms (O_3) instead of the usual two atoms (O_2) that make up oxygen gas. As ozone absorbs the shorter wavelengths of UV radiation, UV energy is converted to heat energy.

Scientists have monitored the ozone layer from ground stations since the 1920s and using satellite instruments since 1978. For the past 35 years, increasingly accurate data show stratospheric ozone losses and the formation of an "ozone hole" (an area of severe ozone loss) over Antarctica for part of every year (**Figure 3.8**; also, see http://ozonewatch.gsfc.nasa.gov/). The depletion has surpassed the changes expected due to natural processes, and scientists have identified human causes for the ozone losses.

Stratospheric Ozone Depletion

If all the stratospheric ozone were brought down to Earth's surface and compressed to surface pressure, the ozone layer would be only 3 mm thick (about one tenth of an inch). At an altitude of 29 km (18 mi), where the ozone layer is densest, it contains only 1 part ozone per 4 million parts of air. Yet this relatively thin layer, which has been naturally stable over the past several hundred million years, is critical for protecting living organisms.

In the 1960s, experts began to express concern that human-made chemicals in the atmosphere may affect ozone. In 1974, two atmospheric chemists, F. Sherwood Rowland and Mario Molina, hypothesized that synthetic chemicals were releasing chlorine atoms that decompose stratospheric ozone. These **chlorofluorocarbons**, or **CFCs**, are molecules containing chlorine, fluorine, and carbon. Years of study showed the ozone breakdown hypothesis to be correct. For their work, Doctors Rowland and Molina and another colleague, Paul Crutzen, received the 1995 Nobel Prize for Chemistry.

Ozone Breakdown Process CFCs are used as propellants in aerosol sprays, foam for insulation and fire suppression, solvents in the electronics industry, and refrigerants. CFCs are stable, or inert, under conditions at Earth's surface, meaning that their molecules do not dissolve in water and do not break down in biological processes.

Stable CFC molecules slowly migrate into the stratosphere, where intense UV radiation splits them, freeing chlorine (Cl) atoms. This process produces a set of reactions that breaks up ozone molecules (O_3) and leaves oxygen gas molecules (O_2) in their place (**Figure 3.9**). Because chlorine atoms have a residence time of 40 to 100 years in the ozone layer, a single chlorine atom can decompose

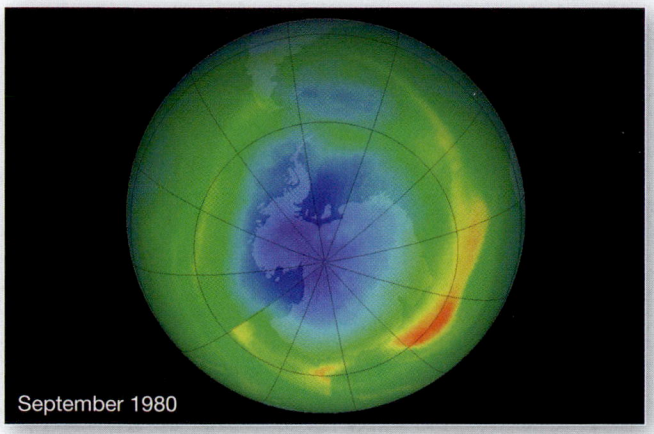

September 1980

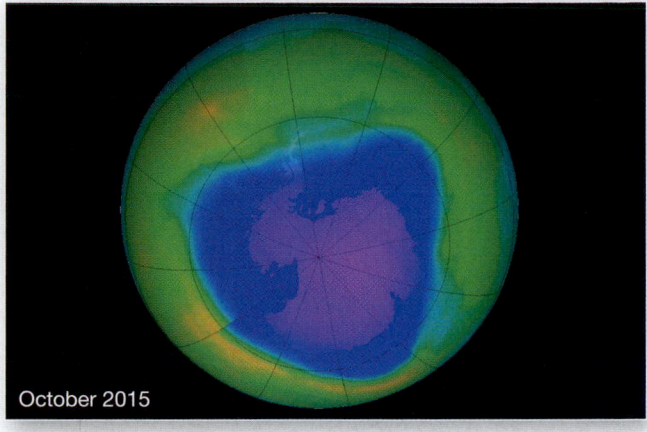

October 2015

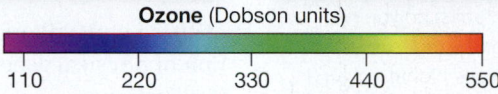

Ozone (Dobson units)

110   220   330   440   550

▲**Figure 3.8** **The Antarctic ozone hole.** Images show the extent of the ozone "hole" in 1980 and 2015. Blues and purples show low ozone (the "hole"); greens, yellows, and reds denote more ozone. The 2015 ozone hole was the second largest on record. [NASA; 1979 to 2015 yearly images are at http://earthobservatory.nasa.gov/Features/WorldOfChange/ozone.php.]

more than 100,000 ozone molecules. This long residence time also means that the chlorine already in place is likely to have long-term consequences.

Ozone Losses over the Poles In the 1980s, satellite measurements confirmed a large ozone "hole" above Antarctica from September through November (the Antarctic spring). Although many CFCs are produced in the Northern Hemisphere, the ozone hole forms over the South Pole because chlorine freed in the Northern Hemisphere midlatitudes concentrates over Antarctica through the work of stratospheric winds. Persistent cold temperatures during the winter create a region of air—the south polar vortex—contained by these winds that remains in place for several months. (We discuss the polar vortex further in Chapter 5.)

Within the south polar vortex, chemicals and water in the stratosphere freeze out to form thin, icy clouds. Within these clouds, ice particle surfaces allow the chemicals to react, releasing chlorine. The chlorine cannot destroy ozone without the addition of UV light, which arrives with the spring in September. UV light sets off the reaction that depletes ozone and forms the ozone hole. As wind patterns change and temperatures warm, ozone levels return to normal over the Antarctic region (see the South Pole ozone graph in Human Denominator 3).

Over the North Pole, stratospheric conditions and temperatures differ from those in the Antarctic. Arctic ozone depletion, first recorded in the 1980s, is smaller in scale than Antarctic ozone depletion. The largest Arctic ozone hole on record occurred in 2011 (see http://earthobservatory.nasa.gov/IOTD/view.php?id=49874).

The Montreal Protocol The United States banned selling and production of CFCs in 1978. However, sales increased again when a 1981 presidential order permitted the export and sale of banned products. In 1987, an international agreement—the *Montreal Protocol on Substances*

That Deplete the Ozone Layer (1987)—halted further sales growth. With 189 signatory countries, the protocol aims to reduce and eliminate all ozone-depleting substances (see http://ozone.unep.org/new_site/en/index.php).

CFC sales declined until all production of harmful CFCs ceased in 2010. In 2007, the protocol instituted an aggressive phasedown of HCFCs, or *hydrochlorofluorocarbons*, one of the CFC-replacement compounds. If the Montreal Protocol is fully enforced, global ozone should recover to the 1980 benchmark level by 2050. Antarctic ozone should reach that level by 2070.

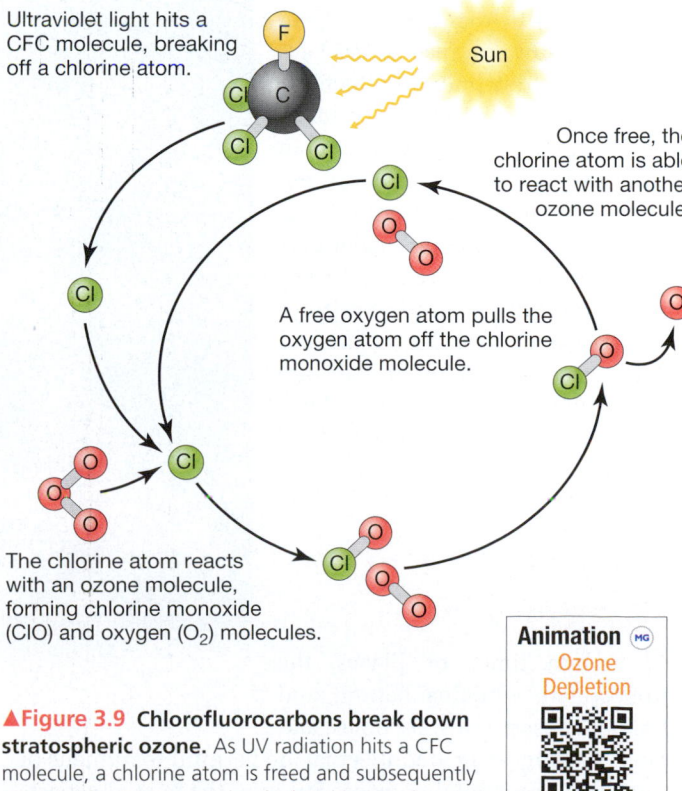

Ultraviolet light hits a CFC molecule, breaking off a chlorine atom.

Sun

Once free, the chlorine atom is able to react with another ozone molecule.

A free oxygen atom pulls the oxygen atom off the chlorine monoxide molecule.

The chlorine atom reacts with an ozone molecule, forming chlorine monoxide (ClO) and oxygen (O_2) molecules.

Animation (MG)
Ozone Depletion

https://goo.gl/0kIRAq

▲**Figure 3.9** **Chlorofluorocarbons break down stratospheric ozone.** As UV radiation hits a CFC molecule, a chlorine atom is freed and subsequently reacts with an ozone molecule, breaking its chemical bonds.

WORK**IT**OUT 3.2
Finding Your Local Ozone

To determine the total column ozone amount at your present location and at any point on Earth, go to "Ozone over your head" at https://ozoneaq.gsfc.nasa.gov/tools/ozonemap/. Total column ozone is the total amount of ozone in a column from the top of the atmosphere to Earth's surface.

Select a point on the map (or enter your latitude and longitude) and the date you want to check. The ozone column is currently measured by the Ozone Monitoring Instrument (OMI) sensor aboard the *Aqua* satellite and is mainly sensitive to stratospheric ozone.

1. Select a date in January 2015, and check some locations in Antarctica. What OMI values (in Dobson units) do you find?
2. Change the date to September 2015, and check similar locations in Antarctica. Are the OMI values higher, lower, or the same?

Explain your findings based on the chapter discussion.

Environmental Effects

As discussed in Geosystems Now, UV radiation can be subdivided into wavelengths of UVC, UVB, and UVA (which makes up about 95% of the UV radiation that reaches Earth). The effects of declining ozone vary according to the wavelength. UVC is absorbed by both oxygen and ozone, meaning that small changes in ozone concentrations do not affect UVC levels at Earth's surface. However, UVB is absorbed only by ozone. For every 1% decrease in stratospheric ozone levels, an estimated 1% increase in UVB occurs at Earth's surface.

In addition to the effects on human health discussed in Geosystems Now, increased UVB radiation has detrimental effects on plants and marine ecosystems. UVB alters plant physiology in complex ways that lead to decreased agricultural productivity. In marine ecosystems, scientists have documented 10% declines in phytoplankton productivity in areas of ozone depletion around Antarctica—these organisms are the primary producers that form the basis of the ocean's food chain.

Pollutants in the Atmosphere

At certain times or places, the troposphere contains natural and human-caused gases, particles, and other substances in amounts that are harmful to humans or cause environmental damage. Study of the spatial aspects

TABLE 3.3 Sources of Natural Pollutants

Source	Contribution
Volcanoes	Sulfur oxides, particulates
Forest fires	Carbon monoxide and dioxide, nitrogen oxides, particulates
Plants	Hydrocarbons, pollens
Decaying plants	Methane, hydrogen sulfides
Soil	Dust and viruses
Ocean	Salt spray, particulates

of these atmospheric **pollutants** is an important application of physical geography with far-reaching human health implications.

Recently, increasing human population and development has intensified air quality problems. Regulations to curb human-caused air pollution have had great success, although much remains to be done. Solutions require regional, national, and international strategies because pollution sources often are distant from the observed impact. Both natural and human-caused air pollution crosses political boundaries and even oceans.

Natural Sources of Air Pollution

Natural sources produce greater quantities of air pollutants—nitrogen oxides, carbon monoxide, hydrocarbons from plants and trees, and carbon dioxide—than

▲**Figure 3.10 Pavlof erupts on March 28, 2016, Aleutian Islands, Alaska.** Viewed here from an aircraft at 6100 m (20,000 ft) altitude, the eruption prompted an aviation warning as the ash cloud rose to 11,280 m (37,000 ft) and extended 650 km (400 mi) into interior Alaska. [Nahshon Almandmoss, U.S. Coast Guard.]

▲**Figure 3.11** **Smoke from California wildfires.** Wildfires related to drought and high temperatures in southern California regularly burn hundreds of thousands of hectares, usually in the late summer and fall when conditions are driest. In 2016, the Blue Cut fire near San Bernardino caused the evacuation of over 82,000 people from their homes. [*Terra* MODIS, NASA/GSFC.]

do sources attributable to humans. **Table 3.3** lists some of these natural sources and the substances they contribute to the air. Volcanoes, forest fires, and dust storms are the most significant sources, based on the volume of smoke and particulates produced and blown over large areas. However, pollen from crops, weeds, and other plants can also cause high amounts of particle pollution, triggering asthma as well as other adverse human health effects. The particulates produced by these events are also known as **aerosols** and include the liquid droplets and suspended solids that range in size from visible water droplets and pollen to microscopic dust. (Aerosols produced from human sources are discussed in the next section.)

Volcanoes Volcanic eruptions are dramatic natural sources of air pollution (**Figure 3.10**). The 1991 eruption of Mount Pinatubo in the Philippines, the 20th century's second-largest eruption, injected nearly 20 million tons of sulfur dioxide (SO_2) into the stratosphere. (The spread of these emissions is shown in satellite images in Focus Study 5.1 on page XXX.) Even small eruptions, such as on the Big Island of Hawai'i or in the Aleutian Island chain of Alaska, emit sulfur oxides in concentrations that affect living organisms.

Wildfires Another source of natural air pollution are wildfires, which occur frequently on several continents (**Figure 3.11**). Wind patterns spread the soot, ash, and gases from the fires to nearby cities, darkening skies, closing airports, and forcing evacuations to avoid the health-related dangers. Satellite images show smoke plumes traveling horizontally for distances up to 1600

km (1000 mi). Smoke, soot, and particulates can be propelled vertically as high as the stratosphere.

Wildfire smoke contains particulates (dust, soot, ash), nitrogen oxides, carbon monoxide, and volatile organic compounds. In southern California, recent wildfire smoke was linked to respiratory problems and increased hospital admissions, as well as lower birth weight for babies born to women living in smoke-exposed areas.

Since the early 2000s, scientists have linked increasing wildfire occurrence in the western United States with climate change, which is causing higher spring and summer temperatures and earlier snowmelt, resulting in a longer fire season. These connections occur across the globe, as in drought-plagued Australia, where thousands of wildfires burned millions of hectares in recent years.

Dust Defined as particles less than 62 μm, or 0.0025 in., in size, dust is another natural pollutant. Dust can come from soils, dry lakebeds, and the breakdown ofw rocks, especially in arid regions of the world. Dust is moved by wind, sometimes in dramatic dust storms known as *haboobs* (discussed in Chapter 15). Dust can travel with winds across oceans—the smaller the dust particle, the longer it can remain suspended in the air (see Figure 3.14). When dust enters the human respiratory system, it can exacerbate health conditions such as asthma. In 2015, a prolonged summer dust storm over the Middle East caused hundreds of people to seek medical attention for breathing disorders.

Anthropogenic Pollution

In addition to contaminants from volcanic eruptions, wildfires, and dust storms, the atmosphere contains increasing amounts of *anthropogenic* (human-caused) contaminants. Air pollution is closely linked to our production and consumption of energy and resources and has collected around population centers throughout history. Today, over half the world's population lives in urban areas, about one third with unhealthy levels of air pollution. A common pollutant over cities is **nitrogen dioxide (NO_2)**, a gas produced by cars, power plants, and industry.

As urban populations continue to grow, the exposure to air pollution represents a potentially massive public health issue. In 2016, scientists reported that 5.5 million people die every year from air pollution, with over 3 million of those deaths occurring in China and India. In the United States, although air quality is improving in many places, over 40% of the country's population lives with air pollution that poses a health risk.

Pollution from Transportation Most urban air pollutants result from combustion of fossil fuels in transportation—specifically, cars and light trucks. For example, **carbon monoxide (CO)** is a by-product of combustion that is dangerously toxic, as explained in GeoReport 3.1.

Photochemical smog from motor vehicles is a major component of anthropogenic air pollution, causing the hazy sky and reduced sunlight in many of our cities. **Photochemical smog** is a mixture of pollutants that results from the interaction of sunlight and the combustion products in automobile exhaust, primarily nitrogen oxides and **volatile organic compounds (VOCs)**, such as hydrocarbons that evaporate from gasoline.

Car exhaust becomes photochemical smog through the photochemical reaction of nitrogen dioxide (NO_2) with oxygen (O_2) and VOCs (**Figure 3.12**). Ultraviolet radiation liberates atomic oxygen (O) and a nitric oxide (NO) molecule from the NO_2. The free oxygen atom combines with an oxygen molecule, O_2, to form ozone, O_3. The ozone in photochemical smog is the same gas that is beneficial to us in the stratosphere in absorbing ultraviolet radiation. However, *ground-level ozone* is a reactive gas that damages biological tissues and has a variety of detrimental human health effects, including lung irritation, asthma, and susceptibility to respiratory illnesses. The NO molecule freed by sunlight combines with VOCs to produce **peroxyacetyl nitrates**, or **PANs**, the other

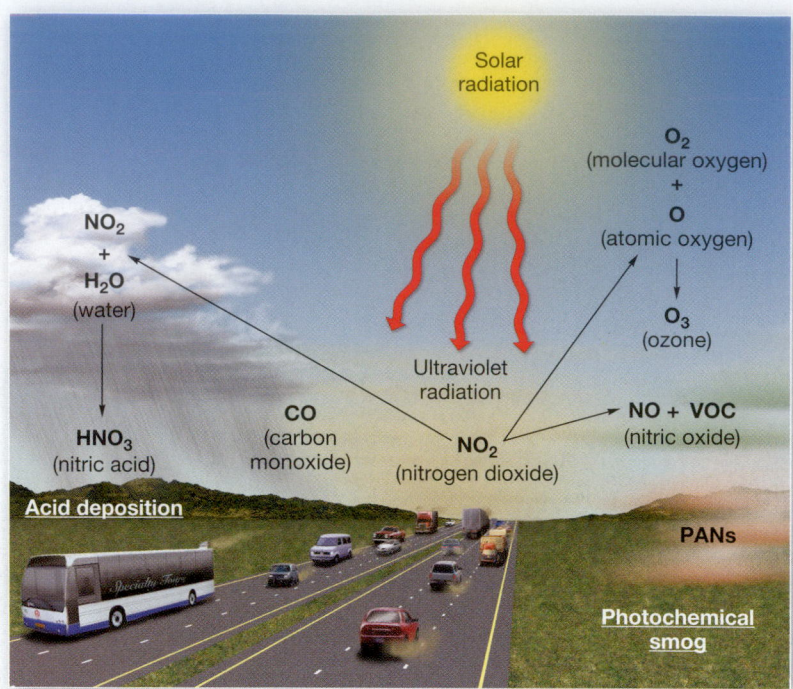

▲Figure 3.12 **Photochemical reactions and pollutants from car exhaust.**

principal component of photochemical smog. PANs irritate human eyes and respiratory system function and damage plants.

The NO_2 from car exhaust also interacts with water vapor to form nitric acid (HNO_3), a contributor to acid deposition by precipitation, the subject of Focus Study 3.1. **Table 3.4** summarizes major pollutants and their effects.

TABLE 3.4 Major Pollutants over Urban Areas			
Name	Symbol	Sources	Effects
Carbon monoxide	CO	Vehicle emissions	Toxic; causes headaches and vision loss.
Nitrogen oxides	NO_x (NO, NO_2)	Agriculture, fertilizers, vehicle emissions	Inflames respiratory system, destroys lung tissue. Leads to acid deposition.
Volatile organic compounds	VOCs	Combustion of fossil fuels; cleaning and paint solvents	Causes ground-level ozone formation.
Ground-level ozone	O_3	Photochemical reactions related to vehicle emissions	Highly reactive, unstable gas. Irritates eyes and respiratory system. Damages plants.
Peroxyacetyl nitrates	PANs	Photochemical reactions related to vehicle emissions	Irritates eyes and respiratory system. Major damage to plants, forests, crops.
Sulfur oxides	SO_x (SO_2, SO_3)	Combustion of sulfur-containing fuels	Irritating smell. Causes asthma, bronchitis, emphysema. Leads to acid deposition.
Particulate matter	PM	Vehicle and power-plant emissions; agriculture	Mixture of dust, soot, salt, metals, and organics causes bronchitis, lung problems.
Carbon dioxide	CO_2	Combustion of fossil fuels	Principal greenhouse gas (see Chapter 10).

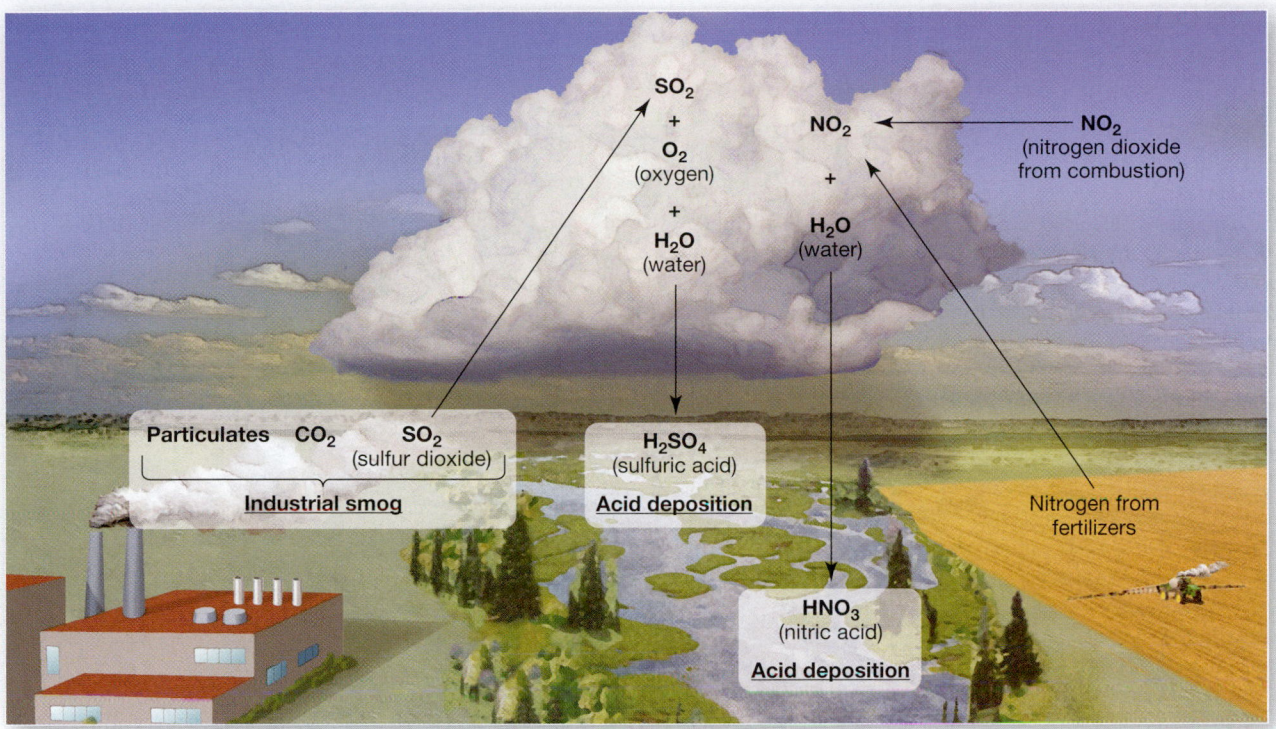

▲Figure 3.13 **Chemical reactions and pollutants from industrial smog.**

Industrial Pollution Coal-burning industries and electrical generation produces air pollution known as **industrial smog**, which has high concentrations of carbon dioxide, particulates, and sulfur oxides (Table 3.4; Figure 3.13). Once in the atmosphere, **sulfur dioxide** (SO_2) reacts with oxygen (O) to form sulfur trioxide (SO_3), which is highly reactive and, in the presence of water or water vapor, forms tiny particles known as sulfate aerosols. Sulfuric acid (H_2SO_4) can also form, even in moderately polluted air at normal temperatures. Coal-burning electric utilities and steel manufacturing are the main sources of sulfur dioxide.

Sulfur dioxide–laden air is dangerous to health, corrodes metals, and deteriorates stone building materials at accelerated rates. Sulfuric acid deposition, added to nitric acid deposition, has increased in severity since it was first described in the 1970s. Focus Study 3.1 discusses this vital atmospheric issue and recent progress.

Particulates/Aerosols The diverse mixture of fine particles, both solid and liquid, that pollute the air and affect human health is referred to as **particulate matter (PM)**, a term used by meteorologists and regulatory agencies such as the U.S. Environmental Protection Agency. Other scientists refer to these particulates as aerosols. Examples are haze, smoke, and dust, which are visible reminders of particulates in the air we breathe. Remote sensing now provides a global portrait of such aerosols—look ahead to the background image in The Human Denominator 3.

Black carbon, or "soot," is an aerosol having devastating health effects in developing countries, especially where people burn animal dung for cooking and heating. This fine particulate is not necessarily prevalent over urban areas; black carbon is mainly produced in small villages, but winds can spread it over the globe. In Africa, Asia, and South America, cooking stoves produce the highest concentrations, with diesel engines and coal plants having a smaller role. Black carbon is both an indoor and outdoor pollutant, made up of pure carbon in several forms; it absorbs heat in the atmosphere and changes the reflectivity of snow and ice surfaces, giving it a critical role in climate change (discussed in Chapters 4 and 10).

GEOreport 3.1 Carbon monoxide—the colorless, odorless pollutant

As your car idles at a downtown intersection or you walk through a parking garage, you may be exposed to 100 ppm of carbon monoxide (CO) without being aware of inhaling this colorless, odorless, toxic gas. The physiological effects are serious: CO combines with the oxygen-carrying hemoglobin of human blood, displacing the oxygen. The result is that the hemoglobin no longer transports adequate oxygen to vital organs such as the heart and brain; too much exposure to CO causes sudden illness and death (see http://www.cdc.gov/co/.)

FOCUSstudy 3.1 Pollution
Acid Deposition: Damaging to Ecosystems

Acid deposition is most familiar as "acid rain," but it also occurs as "acid snow" and in dry form as dust or aerosols. Acid deposition damages buildings, sculptures, and historic artifacts, and it is causally linked to serious environmental problems: declining fish populations, forest damage, and altered soil chemistry. Regions that have suffered most are the northeastern United States, southeastern Canada, Sweden, Norway, Germany, much of eastern Europe, and China.

Figure 3.13 shows the pollutants and chemical reactions that produce acid deposition. The acids fall as rain or snow (wet deposition) and attached to particulate matter (a form of dry deposition). The acid then settles on the landscape and eventually enters streams and lakes, carried by runoff and groundwater flows.

The acidity of precipitation is measured on the pH scale. The scale is logarithmic: Each whole number represents a tenfold change. Pure water has a neutral pH 7.0; lower values are acidic, and higher values are basic, or alkaline (**Figure 3.1.1**). (Vinegar and lemon juice are strongly acid at pH 3.0; ammonia is strongly alkaline at pH 11.0.)

Natural precipitation is slightly acidic, with a pH range from 5.3 to 6.0. Scientists have measured precipitation as acidic as pH 2.0 in the eastern United States, Scandinavia, and Europe. In lakes, aquatic plant and animal life dies when pH drops below 4.8.

Effects on Natural Systems

Tens of thousands of lakes and wetlands and some 100,000 km (62,000 mi) of streams in the United States and Canada are below pH 5.3, with several hundred lakes incapable of supporting any aquatic life. The effects of acid deposition are enhanced by soil chemistry—acidification causes the release of aluminum from soils, which moves into water bodies where it is toxic to fish and other aquatic animals.

Acid deposition also affects soils by killing microorganisms and causing a decline in soil nutrients, leading to declines in forest health. Some of the worst impacts are in the forests of eastern Europe, especially Germany and Poland, where forest damage reflects the long history of coal burning and industrial activity.

In the eastern United States, extensive forest decline has occurred in the spruce and fir forests of North Carolina and Tennessee (**Figure 3.1.2**). In the Adirondacks, red spruce and sugar maples have been especially hard hit. Affected trees are susceptible to winter cold, insects, and droughts.

Status of Sulfur and Nitrogen Oxide Emissions

In the United States, the 1990 Clean Air Act amendments targeted industrial emissions of sulfur dioxide and nitrogen oxides. Since 1990, sulfur emissions from power plants decreased almost 70%, and wet sulfate deposition rates dropped across the eastern United States (**Figure 3.1.3**). Reductions continue to the present day. Nitrogen emissions from agricultural operations, motor vehicles, and coal-combustion power plants have also declined dramatically since 2005. Western Europe shows a 50% decline in nitrogen emissions since 2005, mainly resulting from environmental regulations.

◄**Figure 3.1.2 Acid deposition damages trees.** Stressed forests on Mount Mitchell in the Appalachians. [Will and Deni McIntyre/Photo Researchers.]

▲**Figure 3.1.1 pH scale.** Lower pH corresponds to increasing acidity; higher pH corresponds to increasing alkalinity.

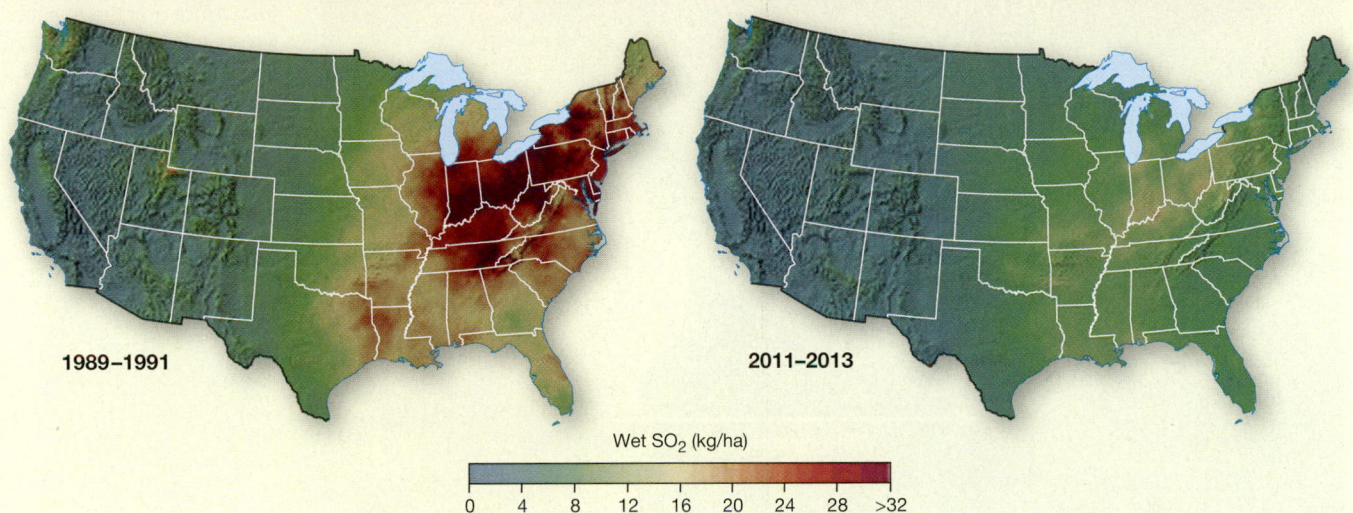

1989–1991   2011–2013

Wet SO$_2$ (kg/ha)

0 4 8 12 16 20 24 28 >32

▲**Figure 3.1.3 Improvement in U.S. annual average wet sulfate deposition.** Comparison of two separate 3-year periods shows a marked decrease since 1989 in the sulfate that falls as rain, snow, or fog. Improvements result from combined Canadian and U.S. regulatory action on emissions that add acids to the environment. [EPA 2014.]

In China, overuse of nitrogen fertilizers has led to acid deposition in soils, lessening crop production in some regions. Growth in manufacturing caused a 20% to 50% increase in nitrogen dioxide emissions from 2005 to 2014.

Addressing acid deposition requires international cooperation because wind and weather patterns carry pollution across borders. Research pinpointing nitrogen as the leading cause of acid deposition links this issue to food production and global sustainability issues. Recently, scientists have reported that acidification associated with increasing atmospheric CO_2 is altering water quality in the U.S.

Northeast (see http://www.hubbard-brook.org/). Renewable energy and energy conservation are potential ways to reduce emissions, thereby also mitigating climate change.

APPLYconcepts At which pH levels, and in which states on the map in **Figure 3.1.4**, are the described effects on plant and animal life in lakes, streams, and wetlands most likely to be found?

1. Summarize the causes and effects of acid precipitation.

2. Why are the effects of acid precipitation so widespread?

Conditions	pH range of precipitation	States
Few or no effects on plant and animal life	a. _____	b. _____
Declines in plant and animal life	a. _____	b. _____
Most plant and animal life severely affected or dead	a. _____	b. _____

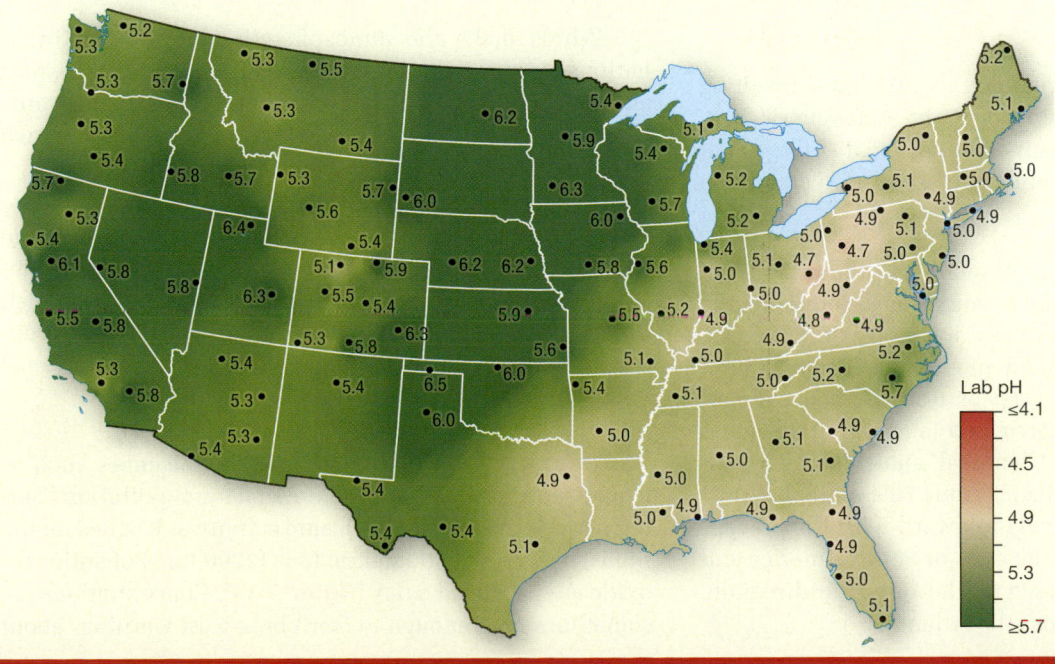

◀**Figure 3.1.4 Map of U.S. precipitation pH, 2014** The distribution of pH values below 5.3—the threshold for acidic precipitation—relates to the location of industries that release oxides of sulfur and nitrogen and prevailing winds that carry these pollutants in an easterly direction. [National Atmospheric Deposition Program/National Trends Network; http://napd.isws. illinois.edu.]

Lab pH

≤4.1
4.5
4.9
5.3
≥5.7

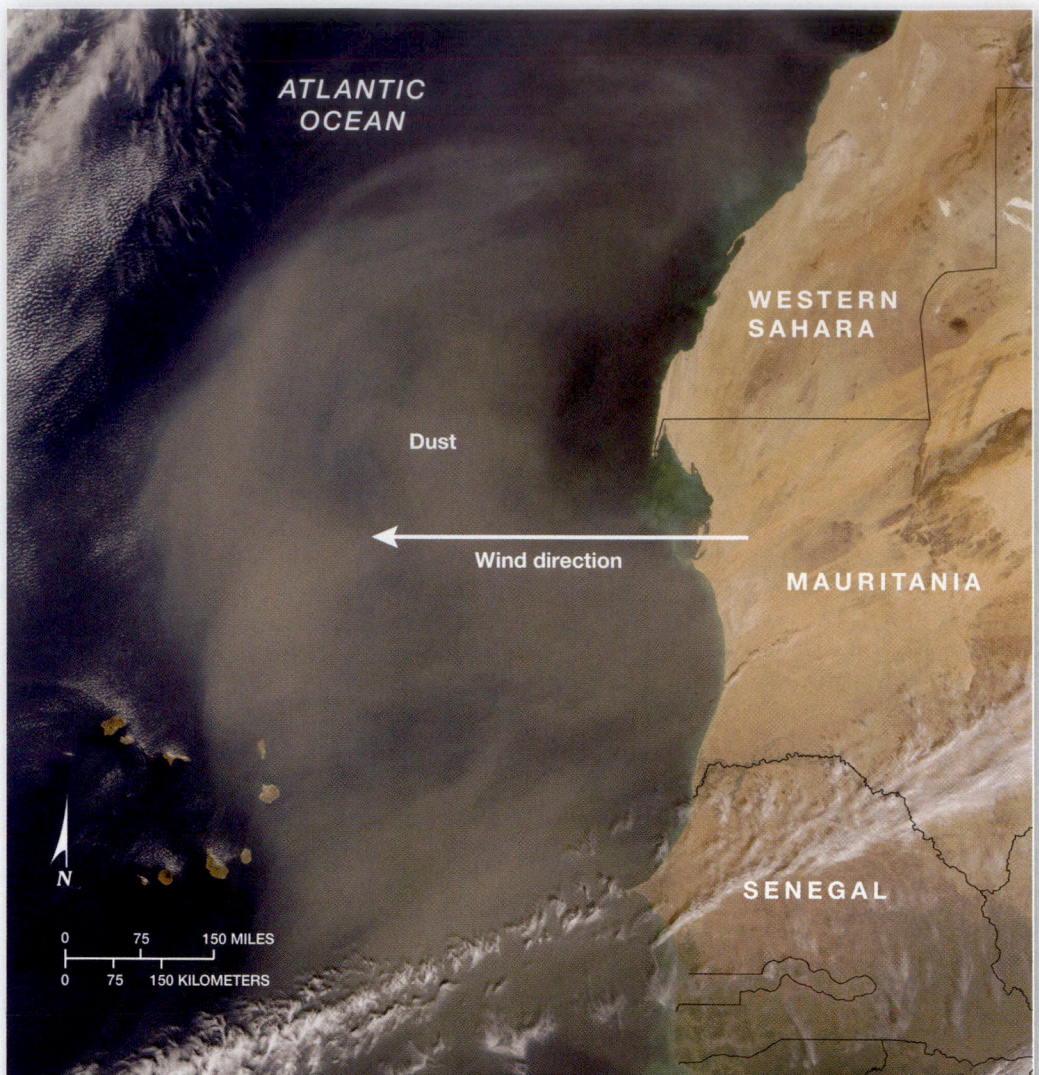

◄**Figure 3.14** **Winds carrying dust in the atmosphere.** Natural-color image shows dust blowing from Africa over the Atlantic Ocean in January 2016. [LANCE/EOSDIS Rapid Response Team, Jeff Schmaltz/NASA.]

Natural Factors That Affect Pollutants

Several natural factors worsen the problems resulting from both natural and anthropogenic atmospheric contaminants. These factors include wind, local and regional landscape characteristics, and temperature inversions in the troposphere.

Winds Previously, we mentioned the importance of winds in moving pollutants, sometimes reducing the concentration of pollution in one location while increasing it in another. Wind often moves dust from natural sources, such as dry lakebeds, or from human sources, such as overgrazed or overirrigated lands, long distances and even across oceans. Chemical analysis can determine the source areas of dust. About 70% of global dust comes from Africa and travels eastward with the prevailing winds, contributing to the soils of South America and Europe (**Figure 3.14**). Moving in the opposite direction, Texas dust can end up across the Atlantic.

Winds make the atmosphere's condition an international issue. For example, prevailing winds transport air pollution from the United States to Canada, causing much complaint and negotiation between the two governments.

Local Landscapes Topographic features can affect the movement and concentration of air pollutants. Mountains and hills can form barriers to air movement or can direct the movement of pollutants from one area to another. Some of the worst air quality results when local landscapes trap and concentrate air pollution.

Volcanic Activity Places with active volcanoes such as Iceland and Hawai'i have their own natural pollution. During periods of sustained volcanic activity at Kīlauea on the Big Island, some 2000 metric tons (2200 tons) of sulfur dioxide are produced a day (**Figure 3.15**). Concentrations are sometimes high enough to merit broadcast warnings about

▲**Figure 3.15 Halema'uma'u Crater vents sulfur dioxide.** The eruption sequence at this site began in March 2011 and is a major source for vog-forming chemicals. Halema'uma'u is within the Kīlauea Crater. [USGS/Hawaiian Volcano Observatory.]

Temperature Inversions Vertical differences in temperature and atmospheric density in the troposphere also can worsen pollution conditions. A **temperature inversion** occurs when the normal temperature decrease with altitude—the lapse rate—reverses trend and begins to increase. This can happen at any elevation from ground level to several thousand meters.

Figure 3.16 compares a normal temperature profile with that of a temperature inversion. Under normal conditions (Figure 3.16a), air at the surface can freely mix with the air above. (This occurs as warm, less dense surface air rises, discussed in Chapter 5.) This process moderates surface pollution. When an inversion occurs, a warmer air layer lies above the colder (more dense) air below, halting the vertical mixing of pollutants with other atmospheric gases (Figure 3.16b). Thus, instead of being carried away, pollutants are trapped under the inversion layer. Inversions most often result from certain weather conditions, discussed in Chapter 6, or from topographic situations such as when cool mountain air drains into valley bottoms at night (see discussion of local winds in Chapter 5).

health concerns. The resulting acid rain and volcanic smog, called *vog* by Hawaiians (for *v*olcanic sm*og*), cause losses to agriculture as well as other economic impacts.

(a) A normal temperature profile.

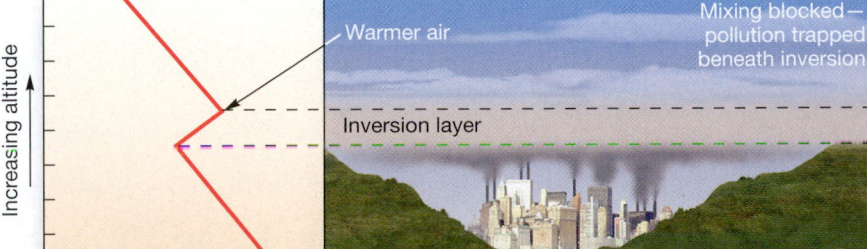

(b) A temperature inversion occurs when the lapse rate reverses direction, causing warmer air to "trap" cooler air below.

(c) An inversion layer traps pollution over a landscape.

▲**Figure 3.16 Normal and inverted temperature profiles.** [(c) Bobbé Christopherson.]

Air quality index, levels of health concern	Numerical value	Meaning
Good	0 to 50	Air quality is considered satisfactory, and air pollution poses little or no risk.
Moderate	51 to 100	Air quality is acceptable; however, for some pollutants a moderate health concern exists for the few people who are unusually sensitive.
Unhealthy for sensitive groups	101 to 150	Members of sensitive groups may experience health effects. The general public is not likely to be affected.
Unhealthy	151 to 200	Everyone may begin to experience health effects; members of sensitive groups may experience more serious health effects.
Very unhealthy	201 to 300	Health warnings of emergency conditions. The entire population is more likely to be affected.
Hazardous	301 to 500	Health alert: everyone may experience more serious health effects.

(a) The Air Quality Index.

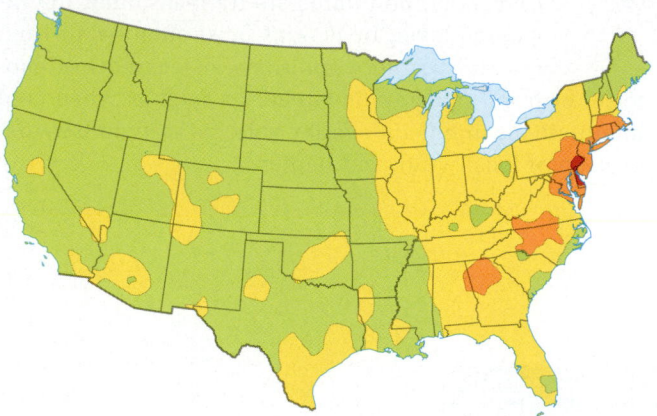

(b) Air quality conditions in the United States, May 2016.

▲**Figure 3.17** **The U.S. Air Quality Index.** The AQI map for May 26, 2016 is color-keyed to the health concerns table. Where are the areas "unhealthy for sensitive groups" on this day? [EPA.]

The Air Quality Index

Many countries monitor and report changes in air quality. In the United States, for example, the Environmental Protection Agency (EPA) reports daily air quality conditions as the Air Quality Index (AQI). In the same way that the UV Index reports the daily exposure risk for ultraviolet radiation (discussed in Geosystems Now), the AQI reports daily air pollution values and the related levels of health concern (**Figure 3.17**). The Air Quality Health Index in Canada (http://www.ec.gc.ca/cas-aqhi/) provides similar information.

The AQI is based on five criteria pollutants: carbon monoxide, nitrogen dioxide, sulfur dioxide, ground-level ozone, and particulate matter. The AQI runs from 0 to 500; higher values indicate greater air pollution and related health concerns. Any value over 300 is considered hazardous to human health and will affect the entire population. AQI maps and related information are published in local newspapers and are available online and as smartphone apps (for example, EPA AIRNow and UCLA AirForU; see https://www.airnow.gov/).

The Clean Air Act

In 1963, Congress passed the Clean Air Act (CAA) to control air pollution on a national level. The CAA was one of the first major environmental laws in the United States, and was expanded in 1970, 1977, and 1990. As a result of the CAA, air pollutant concentrations in the United States declined significantly, saving trillions of dollars in health, economic, and environmental losses (**Figure 3.18**). These remarkable reductions show the successful linking of science and public policy. Human Denominator 3 summarizes some of the issues and connections between humans and the shared global atmosphere.

▼**Figure 3.18** **Improved air quality in U.S. cities.** In 2013, New York City reported its cleanest air in 50 years, a result of dramatic reductions in sulfur dioxide and soot as part of the city's long-term sustainability blueprint, known as PlaNYC. [Andy Selinger/Alamy]

THE ATMOSPHERE IMPACTS HUMANS

- From the information in this chapter, in what ways does Earth's atmosphere protect humans?
- What natural processes produce pollutants that are detrimental to human health?

HUMANS IMPACT THE ATMOSPHERE

- Human-made chemicals deplete the ozone layer. Winds concentrate these pollutants over Antarctica, where the ozone hole is largest.
- Anthropogenic air pollution collects over urban areas, reaching dangerous levels in some regions, such as northern India and eastern China; other regions have improved air quality, as in the Los Angeles metropolitan area.

3a

London implemented new low emissions standards for diesel vehicles in 2012. Owners must comply or face a daily penalty fee. Stricter regulation is one strategy to control increasing air pollution from the transportation sector. [Steve Parsons/AP Images.]

3b

China's air pollution is severe, with PM2.5 levels regularly reaching harmful levels above cities. Despite a decrease in emissions from coal-burning power plants in 2014, China still burns more coal and emits more CO_2 than any country on Earth. [Hung Chung Chih/Shutterstock.]

This 2012 portrait of global aerosols shows dust lifted from the surface in red, sea salt in blue, smoke from fires in green, and sulfate particles from volcanoes and fossil fuel emissions in white. [NASA.]

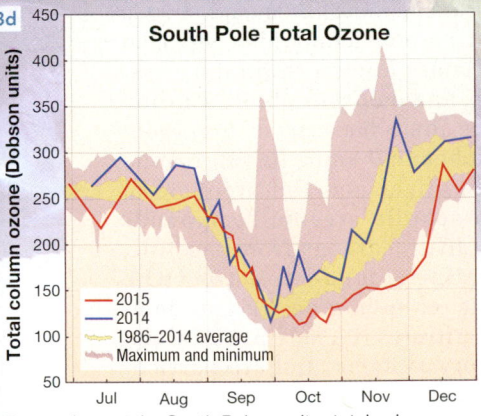

3d

South Pole Total Ozone

Total column ozone (Dobson units)

- 2015
- 2014
- 1986–2014 average
- Maximum and minimum

Jul Aug Sep Oct Nov Dec

Researchers at the South Pole monitor total column ozone using a radiosonde balloon that carries instruments to 32 km (20 mi) altitude. Significant seasonal ozone depletion still occurs, despite decreases in ozone-depleting chemicals. The month of greatest depletion is September, although depletion occurred through October in 2015. [NOAA.]

3c

In 2014, India was home to 7 of the top 10 most polluted cities in the world, as measured by the presence of fine particulate matter. Regular air quality monitoring began in India in 2015 as a first step in addressing the problem. [dbimages/Alamy.]

ISSUES FOR THE 21ST CENTURY

- Human-made emissions must be reduced to improve air quality in Asia. Air pollution will continue to improve in regions where emissions are regulated, such as in Europe, the United States, and Canada.
- Alternative, clean energy sources are vital for reducing industrial pollution worldwide.
- Fuel efficiency, vehicle-emissions regulations, and alternative and public transportation are pathways for reducing urban pollution and CO_2 emissions that drive climate change.

QUESTIONS TO CONSIDER

1. Based on the background image of global aerosols, what regions have high concentrations of sulfate particles from fossil fuel burning? Does this pattern make sense given what you learned in this chapter?
2. Do you see more evidence of smoke from fires in the Northern or Southern hemisphere? Across which ocean do you see dust traveling?

KEY**LEARNING**concepts**review**

Explain the relationship between air pressure, density, and altitude.

The principal substance of Earth's atmosphere is **air** (p. 58)—a mixture of gases that is naturally odorless, colorless, tasteless, and formless. The **exosphere** (p. 58) is the region above an altitude of 480 km (300 mi), where the atmosphere is nearly a vacuum. Below this region, gas molecules are in constant motion, creating **air pressure** (p. 59) by exerting a force on all surfaces they come in contact with. The weight (force over a unit area) of the atmosphere, exerted on all surfaces, is **atmospheric pressure** (p. 59). The density of air molecules, which creates air pressure, decreases rapidly with altitude.

1. Why does air pressure change with increasing altitude above Earth's surface?
2. What three distinct criteria are employed in dividing the atmosphere for study?

List and **describe** the components of the atmosphere, giving their relative percentage contributions by volume.

By *composition*, we divide the atmosphere into the **heterosphere** (p. 60), extending from 480 km (300 mi) to 80 km (50 mi), and the **homosphere** (p. 60), extending from 80 km to Earth's surface.

3. Name the five most prevalent gases in the homosphere. Where did each originate? Is the amount of any of these changing at this time?

Draw a diagram showing atmospheric structure based on temperature.

Using *temperature* as a criterion, we identify the **thermosphere** (p. 61) as the outermost layer, corresponding roughly to the heterosphere in location. Its upper limit, the **thermopause** (p. 61), is at an altitude of approximately 480 km. Below the thermosphere are the **mesosphere** (p. 62), **stratosphere** (p. 62), and **troposphere** (p. 62). Within the mesosphere, cosmic or meteoric dust particles act as nuclei around which fine ice crystals form to produce **noctilucent clouds** (p. 62).

The top of the troposphere is wherever a temperature of $-57°C$ ($-70°F$) is recorded, a transition known as the **tropopause** (p. 62). The normal temperature profile within the troposphere during the daytime decreases rapidly with increasing altitude at a specific **lapse rate** (p. 62), which averages 6.4 C° per km (3.5 F° per 1000 ft). The actual lapse rate at any particular time and place is the **environmental lapse rate** (p. 62), which varies because of local weather conditions.

4. Describe the overall temperature profile of the atmosphere and list the four layers defined by temperature.
5. Why does the height of the tropopause vary by latitude and throughout the year?

Describe the atmospheric profile on the basis of function, focusing on the status of the ozone layer.

The outermost region we distinguish by function is the **ionosphere** (p. 64). A functional region within the stratosphere is the **ozonosphere** (p. 64), or **ozone layer** (p. 64), which absorbs life-threatening ultraviolet radiation, subsequently raising the temperature of the stratosphere.

Since World War II, quantities of human-made **chlorofluorocarbons (CFCs)**, (p. 64), have made their way into the stratosphere. The increased ultraviolet light at those altitudes breaks down these stable chemical compounds, thus freeing chlorine atoms, which act as catalysts in reactions that destroy ozone molecules.

6. What is the primary function of the ionosphere?
7. Why is stratospheric ozone so important? Describe the chemical process whereby CFCs cause the breakdown of ozone.

Describe natural and anthropogenic pollutants in the lower atmosphere, including pollution from photochemical reactions in vehicle exhaust and from industrial smog.

Within the troposphere are both natural and human-caused **pollutants** (p. 66), gases, particles, and other chemicals in amounts that are harmful to human health or cause environmental damage. Volcanoes, fires, and dust storms are natural sources of pollutants. **Aerosols** (p. 67) are suspended solids and liquid droplets in the air, such as pollens, dust, and soot from natural and human sources.

Transportation is the major human-caused source for nitrogen dioxide and carbon monoxide. **Nitrogen dioxide (NO$_2$)**, (p. 67), inflames human respiratory systems, destroys lung tissue, and damages plants. **Carbon monoxide (CO)**, (p. 68), is toxic because it deoxygenates human blood. **Photochemical smog** (p. 68) results from the interaction of sunlight and the products of automobile exhaust. The **volatile organic compounds (VOCs)**, (p. 68), including hydrocarbons from gasoline, are important factors forming *ground-level ozone* (O$_3$), which has negative effects on human health and damages plants. **Peroxyacetyl nitrates (PANs)**, (p. 68), affect human eyes and respiratory systems, and are particularly harmful to plants, including both agricultural crops and forests.

Coal-burning power plants produce **industrial smog** (p. 69). Nitric oxides are part of reactions that produce nitric acid (HNO$_3$) in the atmosphere, forming both wet and dry acidic deposition. Industrial smog also contains **sulfur dioxide (SO$_2$)**, (p. 69), which reacts in the atmosphere to produce *sulfate aerosols*, which in turn produce sulfuric acid (H$_2$SO$_4$) deposition. **Particulate matter (PM)**, (p. 69), consists of dirt, dust, soot, and ash from industrial and natural sources. A **temperature inversion** (p. 73) occurs when the normal temperature decrease with altitude (the lapse rate) reverses, and temperature begins to increase at some altitude.

8. Define pollutant, and list several human activities that produce pollutants.

9. What is the difference between photochemical smog and industrial smog?

10. In what ways does a temperature inversion worsen an air pollution episode?

GEO**SPATIAL** ANALYSIS

Air Quality

The concentration of particulates and chemical compounds determines air quality, expressed as AQI. Related data are measured around the world, and alerts are issued when the air becomes unhealthy.

Activities

Go to the Real-time Air Quality Index Visual Map at http://aqicn.org/map/ to see current Air Quality Index (AQI) measurements. Zoom out to see the entire world.

1. Which regions have the highest AQI values? What are some of the highest values shown on the map?

2. Which regions have the lowest AQI values? Which regions are not reporting data on this site?

Click on a station that displays multiple pollutants and a very high AQI. Click the link to see the full report.

3. What is the name of this location and when was the station data updated?

4. What is the AQI value and what is the danger level?

5. Which types of air pollution are monitored at this station? What type of pollution is responsible for the high AQI value?

6. What are the sources for these pollutants and what are the adverse effects they cause? Consult Table 3.4.

7. Do any of the pollutants exhibit a daily cycle? If so, which one(s)?

8. What is air quality forecast for the next few days?

Mastering Geography™

Looking for additional review and test prep materials? Visit the Study Area in MasteringGeography™ to enhance your geographic literacy, spatial reasoning skills, and understanding of this chapter's content by accessing a variety of resources, including MapMaster™ interactive maps, videos, *Mobile Field Trips*, *Project Condor* Quadcopter videos, *In the News* RSS feeds, flashcards, web links, self-study quizzes, and an eText version of *Geosystems*.

4 Atmospheric Energy and Global Temperatures

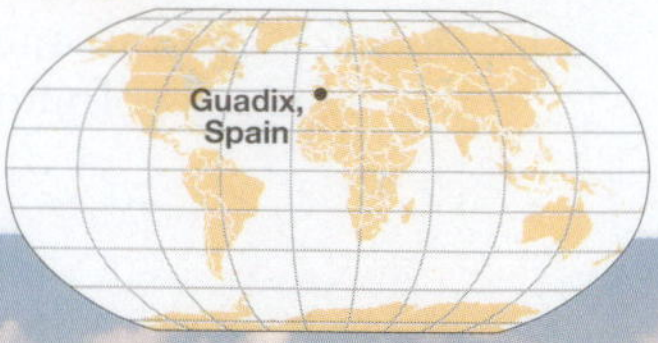

Guadix, Spain

Solar photovoltaic panels convert energy from the Sun to electricity near Guadix, Andalucia, in southern Spain, one of the top ten countries in the world for installed solar power capacity. [Global Warming Images/Alamy.]

KEY**LEARNING**concepts

After reading the chapter, you should be able to:

- *Identify* alternative pathways for solar energy on its way through the troposphere to Earth's surface and *review* the concept of albedo (reflectivity).
- *Explain* four types of heat transfer: radiation, conduction, convection, and advection.
- *Explain* the effect of greenhouse gases, clouds, and aerosols on atmospheric heating and cooling.
- *Review* the Earth–atmosphere energy balance and the patterns of net radiation at the surface.
- *Define* the concept of temperature and *review* the principle temperature controls that produce global temperature patterns.
- *Interpret* the pattern of Earth's temperatures on January and July temperature maps and on a map of annual temperature ranges.
- *Explain* heat waves and *describe* the human response to temperature extremes.
- *Describe* urban heat island conditions and global temperature increases associated with human activities.

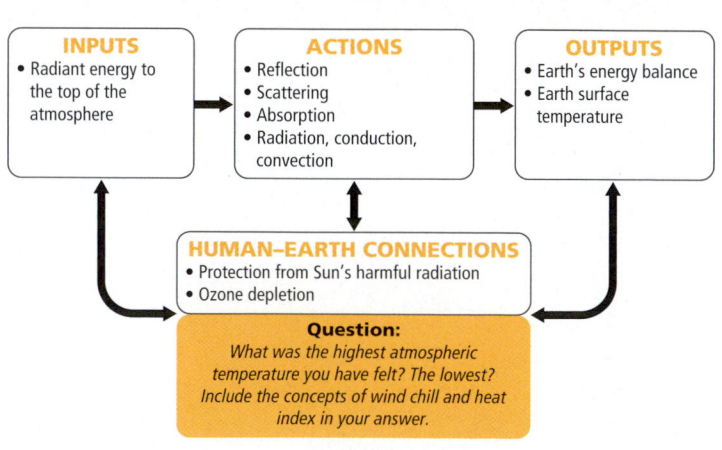

INPUTS
- Radiant energy to the top of the atmosphere

ACTIONS
- Reflection
- Scattering
- Absorption
- Radiation, conduction, convection

OUTPUTS
- Earth's energy balance
- Earth surface temperature

HUMAN–EARTH CONNECTIONS
- Protection from Sun's harmful radiation
- Ozone depletion

Question:
What was the highest atmospheric temperature you have felt? The lowest? Include the concepts of wind chill and heat index in your answer.

Global Effects of Melting Arctic Sea Ice

In January 2015, during the 24-hour polar night, a Norwegian research ship with a host of scientists on board set anchor in the Arctic pack ice. This was its second attempt at attachment—the previous ice floe had shattered—in order to resume its drift across the frozen Arctic Ocean. The mission: Set up camp on the moving sea ice for a 5-month-long study of the causes and effects of Arctic ice melt.

The Nature of Arctic Sea Ice Unlike Antarctica, a land mass surrounded by ocean, the Arctic region is an ocean surrounded by land (**Figure GN 4.1**). The Arctic Ocean is covered in pack ice—masses of drifting ice, unattached to shore—consisting mainly of sea ice (frozen seawater) mixed with glacial ice (frozen freshwater). In the winter months, the region is nearly covered in floating ice. During the summer, pack ice thins and sometimes breaks up. Recent global temperature increases have accelerated melting, causing declines in the minimum ice extent during summer (usually occurring in September) as well as in the maximum ice extent during winter (usually occurring between February and April).

Why Is Arctic Ice Important? Arctic sea ice plays a key role in Earth's climate system by helping to keep the planet cool. This cooling

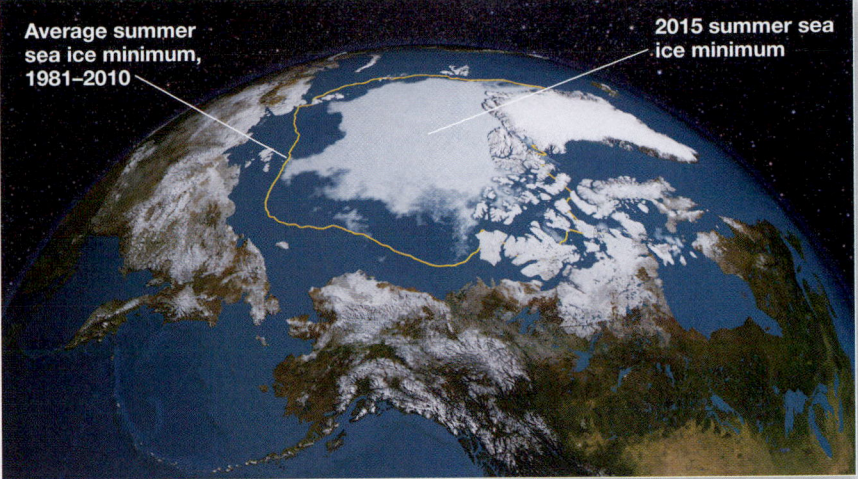

▲**Figure GN 4.1 Arctic summer sea ice minimum extent in 2015 as compared to average.** The 2015 minimum is the fourth lowest on record; the lowest occurred in 2012. [NASA SVS.]

effect results from the presence of lighter surfaces, which reflect sunlight back into space. Snow- and ice-covered surfaces reflect about 60%–95% of the solar energy received. Without an ice cover, incoming sunlight reaches the darker ocean surface, which reflects only 4%–10% of solar radiation received. This percentage is *albedo*, the reflective value of a surface (**Figure GN 4.2**).

Changes in the amount of Arctic sea ice, and the resulting changes in albedo, can create a positive feedback that amplifies global cooling or warming trends. If Earth's climate cools, more ice forms, causing more reflected sunlight, causing cooler temperatures, allowing more ice to form, and so on. If Earth's climate warms, the ice-covered area decreases, reflection decreases, darker water receives direct sunlight and absorbs more heat, temperatures warm, more ice melts, and so on. This so-called *ice–albedo feed-*

back, described in Chapter 1 (Figure 1.10), is happening today as global temperatures rise.

Earth System Connections Atmospheric pollutants are another factor affecting Arctic ice. With increasing losses of sea ice, the Arctic Ocean has opened to commercial ship traffic. Since 2009, container ships have used these northern sea routes during the summer months. Ship stack emissions include particulates and soot (black carbon) that eventually settle on snow and ice surfaces, decreasing the albedo. In addition, particulates from Northern Hemisphere wildfires travel on winds and ultimately fall on Arctic ice, darkening the color, decreasing albedo, and accelerating melting.

Beneath the ice, ecosystems are adapted to seasonal changes. As light returns in the spring, huge algal blooms feed plankton that are a food source for fish, birds, whales, and other marine mammals. Thinner ice and earlier spring melt disrupt the timing of the cycle, affecting organisms that sustain the marine food chain. If winter ice declines and summer sea ice disappears, some species will be unable to adapt.

Since satellite measurements began in 1979, half of the total volume of Arctic sea ice has disappeared. Some computer models show that the Arctic Ocean could be ice-free during the summer within a decade. The melting of Arctic sea ice seems remote, yet its effects link to all Earth systems. How might these changes ultimately affect the area where you live?

1. How do global temperatures, the albedos of ice and water, and Arctic sea ice extent interconnect to form a positive feedback?

2. What are two sources of pollutants that contribute to the melting of Arctic ice?

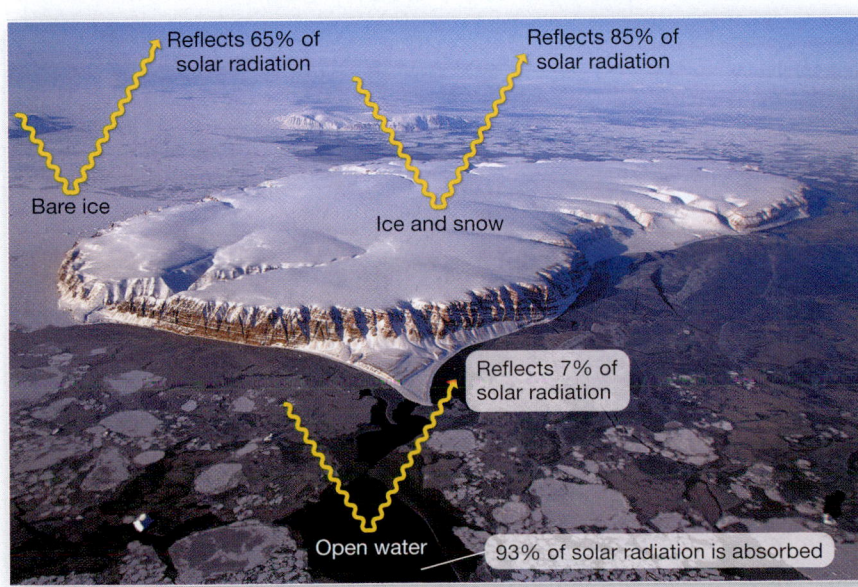

Reflects 65% of solar radiation

Reflects 85% of solar radiation

Bare ice

Ice and snow

Reflects 7% of solar radiation

Open water

93% of solar radiation is absorbed

▲**Figure GN 4.2 Reflection and absorption over bare ice, ice and snow, and water surfaces.** [NASA/Michael Studinger.]

The Sun is an important engine for the functioning systems on Earth. Radiant energy heats Earth's surface, drives wind and ocean currents, and induces water in the atmosphere to form clouds and precipitation. These energy and moisture exchanges between Earth's surface and its atmosphere are essential elements of weather and climate, discussed in later chapters.

In Chapter 2, we introduced the concept of Earth's energy balance—Earth's energy balance is the equilibrium between shortwave solar radiation to Earth and shortwave and longwave radiation to space. This energy balance is analogous to a *budget* that balances energy income and expenditure. For Earth, energy income is insolation, and energy expenditure is radiation to space, with an overall balance maintained between the two. Since solar energy is unevenly distributed by latitude and fluctuates seasonally, the energy budget is not the same at every location on Earth's surface, even though the overall energy system remains in steady-state equilibrium.

Earth's energy balance determines air and ocean temperatures. Air temperature plays a remarkable role in human life at all levels, affecting not only personal comfort but also environmental processes across Earth. Land temperatures interact with atmospheric moisture and precipitation to determine vegetation patterns and their associated habitats—for example, the high temperatures in deserts limit the presence of many plant and animal species. Ocean temperatures affect atmospheric moisture and weather, as well as ocean ecosystems such as coral reefs. Variations in average temperatures of air and water have far-ranging effects on Earth systems.

In addition to these considerations is the fact that temperatures are rising across the globe in response to greenhouse gas emissions, mainly from the burning of fossil fuels and removal of forests, as discussed in Chapter 3. Present CO_2 levels in the atmosphere are higher than at any time in the past 800,000 years, and they are steadily increasing. Thus, temperature concepts are at the forefront of understanding climate change and its far-reaching effects on Earth.

Energy-Balance Essentials

As discussed in Chapter 2, all objects emit radiation (energy that travels in waves). The temperature of the object or substance determines the wavelength of radiation it emits; the hotter an object, the shorter the wavelengths that are emitted. Thus, the Sun emits shorter wavelengths of energy and Earth emits longer wavelengths.

The *inputs* for our Earth–atmosphere energy budget consist of shortwave radiation (ultraviolet light, visible light, and near-infrared wavelengths). Only a portion of the insolation that enters Earth's atmosphere reaches Earth's surface; the remainder is either reflected back out to space or absorbed by Earth's atmosphere. Insolation arrives at Earth's surface as either direct or diffuse radiation—the direct sunlight that causes shadows or the diffuse, shadowless light cast in shaded areas or on cloudy days (**Figure 4.1**). This energy is absorbed by Earth's surface and converted to heat. The *outputs* of our energy budget consist of shortwave radiation (the light reflected before reaching Earth's surface) and

everyday GEOSYSTEMS

How does insolation reach Earth's surface on a sunny versus a cloudy day?

When the sky is clear, insolation travels directly to Earth's surface without changing direction. This type of radiation is direct, arriving from a single direction and causing shadows. When the sky is cloudy, insolation encounters water vapor molecules in clouds that cause it to change direction before reaching the ground. This type of radiation is diffuse, reaching Earth's surface from many directions so that it does not cause shadows. Different cloud types transmit varying amounts of solar radiation and affect Earth's overall energy budget, discussed later in this chapter.

◄**Figure 4.1 Direct and diffuse radiation.** Sunny and cloudy conditions over two coastal cities. [jovannig/Fotolia/. dinozzaver/Shutterstock.]

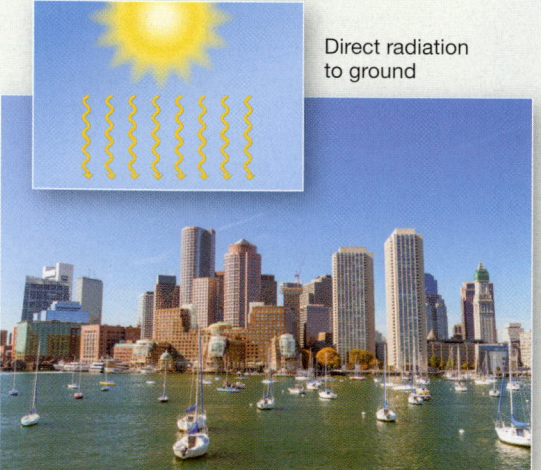

Direct radiation to ground

(a) Boston, Massachusetts

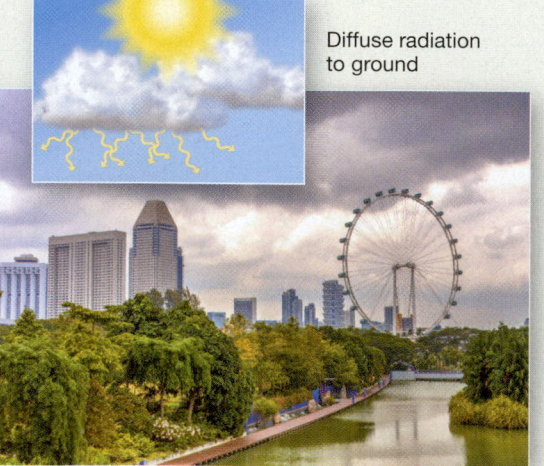

Diffuse radiation to ground

(b) Singapore, southeast Asia.

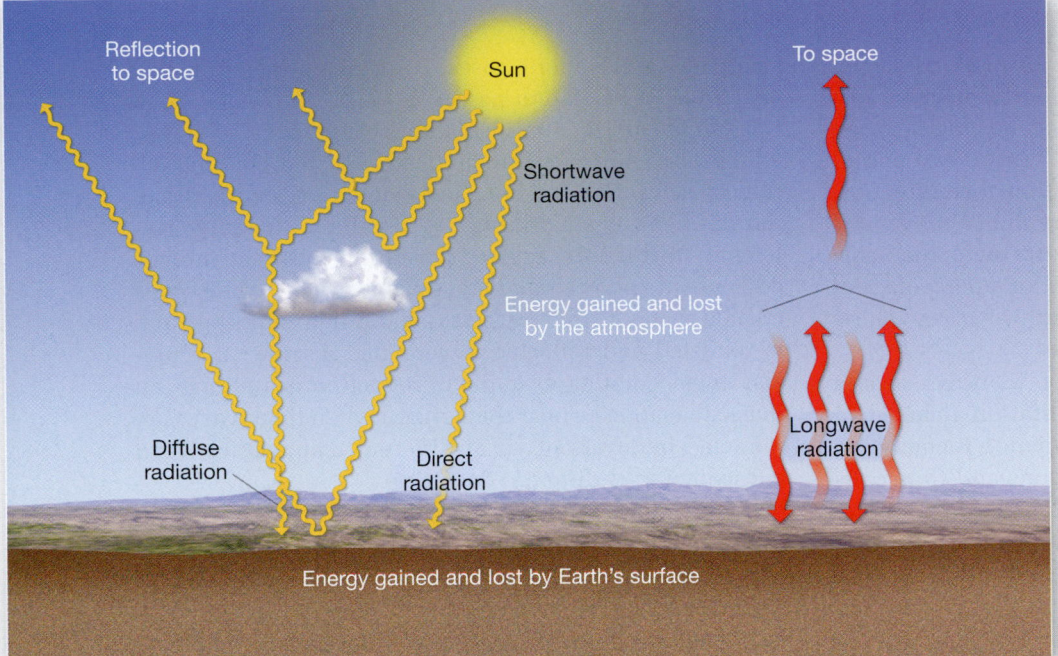

Animation Ⓜ️
Earth-Atmosphere Energy Balance

https://goo.gl/0xPDVa

Animation Ⓜ️
Global Warming, Climate Change

https://goo.gl/v6Xdgb

longwave radiation in thermal infrared wavelengths. A simplified energy system diagram is in **Figure 4.2**; a more detailed illustration of energy balance is in Geosystems in Action 4 on pages 88–89.

Solar Radiation: Pathways and Principles

Insolation, or incoming solar radiation, is the single energy input driving the Earth–atmosphere system, yet it is not equal at all surfaces across the globe (**Figure 4.3**). Throughout the equatorial and tropical latitudes, minor variations in daylength and high Sun altitude produce fairly consistent insolation values (about 180–220 watts per square meter, or W/m²). Insolation decreases toward the poles, from about 25° latitude in both the Northern and the Southern Hemispheres. In general, greater insolation at the surface (about 240–280 W/m²) occurs in low-latitude deserts worldwide because of frequently cloudless skies. Note this energy pattern in the subtropical deserts in both hemispheres.

Roughly half of the total insolation received at the top of the atmosphere arrives at Earth's surface. The other portion is either scattered and reflected back to space or absorbed by the atmosphere. For the purpose of studying Earth's energy budget, **transmission** refers to the uninterrupted passage of shortwave and longwave energy through either the atmosphere or water. *Direct radiation* arrives at Earth's surface by transmission. We now look at the pathways for energy flows that determine the amount and distribution of insolation at Earth's surface.

▲**Figure 4.3 Insolation at Earth's surface.** Average annual solar radiation received on a horizontal surface at ground level in watts per square meter (100 W/m² = 75 kcal/cm²/year). [Based on M. I. Budyko, *The Heat Balance of the Earth's Surface* (Washington, DC: U.S. Department of Commerce, 1958).]

Scattering and Diffuse Radiation Insolation encounters an increasing density of atmospheric molecules as it travels toward Earth's surface. These atmospheric gases, as well as dust, cloud droplets, water vapor, and pollutants, physically interact with insolation to redirect radiation, changing the direction of the light's movement without altering its wavelengths. **Scattering** is the name for this phenomenon, which accounts for a percentage of the insolation that does not reach Earth's surface, but is instead reflected back to space.

Incoming energy that reaches Earth's surface after scattering occurs is **diffuse radiation** (labeled in Figure 4.2). This weaker, dispersed radiation is composed of waves traveling in different directions and thus casts shadowless light on the ground. In contrast, *direct radiation* travels to Earth's surface without being scattered or otherwise affected by materials in the atmosphere. (The values on the surface-insolation map in Figure 4.3 combine both direct and diffuse radiation.)

Have you wondered why Earth's sky is blue? And why sunsets and sunrises are often red? We can answer these common questions using the principle of *Rayleigh scattering* (named for English physicist Lord Rayleigh). This principle applies to radiation scattered by small gas molecules and relates the amount of scattering in the atmosphere to wavelengths of light—shorter wavelengths are scattered more, whereas longer wavelengths are scattered less.

We learned in Chapter 2, Figure 2.7, that blues and violets are the shorter wavelengths of visible light. According to the Rayleigh scattering principle, these wavelengths are scattered more than longer wavelengths such as orange or red. When we look at the sky with the Sun overhead, we see the wavelengths that are scattered the most throughout the atmosphere. Our human eye perceives the scattered blues and violets as the color blue, resulting in the common observation of a blue sky (**Figure 4.4**).

Scattering by atmospheric particles larger than the wavelengths of light, such as cloud droplets and many pollutants, occurs by the process of *Mie scattering*. In a sky filled with smog and haze, the larger particles scatter all wavelengths of visible light evenly, making the sky appear almost white.

The colors we see at sunset and sunrise relate to the Sun's altitude, which determines the thickness of the atmosphere through which its rays must pass to Earth's surface. Direct rays (from overhead) pass through less atmosphere and experience less scattering than do low, oblique-angle rays, which must travel farther through the atmosphere. When the Sun is low on the horizon at dawn (the period of diffused light before sunrise) or twilight (the corresponding period after sunset), shorter wavelengths (blue and violet) are scattered out, leaving only the residual oranges and reds to reach our eyes.

Refraction As insolation enters the atmosphere, it passes from one medium to another, from virtually empty space into atmospheric gases. A change of medium also occurs when insolation passes from air into water. Such transitions subject the insolation to a change of speed, which also shifts its direction—this is the bending action of **refraction**. In the same way, a crystal or prism refracts light passing through it, bending different wavelengths to different angles, separating the light into its component colors to display the spectrum. A rainbow is created when visible light passes through raindrops and is refracted and reflected toward the observer at a precise angle. Another example of refraction is a *mirage*, an image that appears near the horizon when light waves are refracted by layers of air at different temperatures (and consequently of different densities).

Refraction produces the atmospheric distortion of the setting Sun (**Figure 4.5**). When the Sun is low in the sky, light must penetrate more air than when the Sun is high; thus, light is refracted through air layers of different densities on its way to the observer. This distortion means that we see the Sun's refracted image for about 4 minutes before the Sun actually peeks over the horizon in the morning and for about 4 minutes after the Sun sets in the evening. The extra 8 minutes of daylight caused by refraction vary with atmospheric temperature, moisture, and pollutants.

Reflection and Albedo A portion of arriving solar energy bounces directly back into space—this is **reflection**. Clouds reflect about 20% of insolation over the course of a year, far more than is reflected by Earth's surface. Air pollutants, either natural or anthropogenic, also reflect incoming energy. We discuss the role of clouds and aerosols in the Earth–atmosphere energy budget ahead.

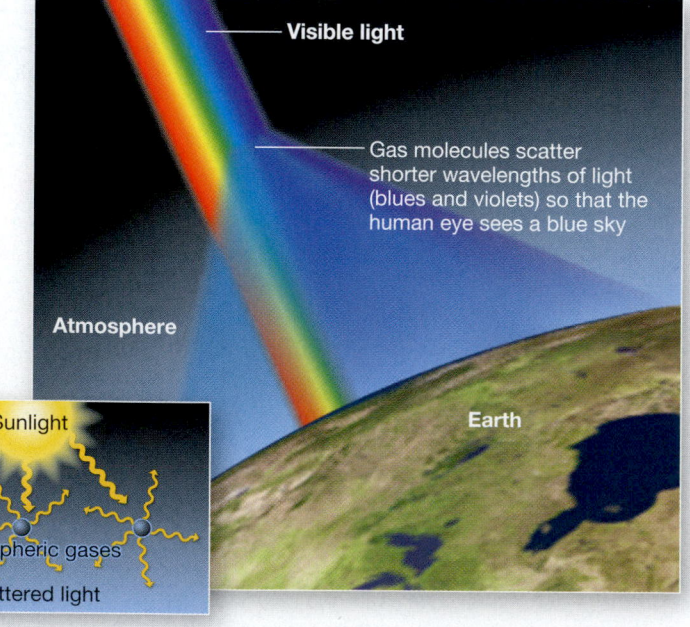

▲**Figure 4.4 Scattering.** When insolation interacts with atmospheric gases, scattering occurs in all directions. Shorter wavelengths of visible light, such as violets and blues, are scattered more than longer wavelengths, making the sky appear blue.

▲**Figure 4.5 Sun refraction.** The distorted appearance of the Sun as it sets over the ocean is produced by refraction of the Sun's image in the atmosphere. [Robert Christopherson.]

The reflective quality, or intrinsic brightness, of a surface is **albedo**, an important control over the amount of insolation that reaches Earth. We report albedo as the percentage of insolation that is reflected: 0% is total absorption; 100% is total reflectance.

In terms of visible wavelengths, darker-colored surfaces (such as asphalt) have lower albedos, and lighter-colored surfaces (such as snow) have higher albedos (**Figure 4.6**). Light-colored clouds have a higher albedo than much of Earth's surface. On water surfaces, the angle of the solar rays also affects albedo values: Lower angles produce more reflection than do higher angles. In addition, smooth surfaces increase albedo, whereas rougher surfaces reduce it.

Individual locations can experience highly variable albedo values during the year in response to changes in cloud and ground cover. Satellite data reveal that albedos average 19%–38% for all surfaces between the tropics (23.5° N to 23.5° S latitude), whereas albedos for the polar regions may be as high as 80% as a result of ice and snow. The tree cover of tropical forests are characteristically low in albedo (15%), whereas the sand and rock surfaces of deserts have higher albedos (35%).

Earth and its atmosphere reflect 31% of all insolation when averaged over a year. The glow of Earth's albedo, or the sunshine reflected off Earth, is called *earthshine*. By comparison, a full Moon, which is bright enough to read by under clear skies, has only a 6%–8% albedo value.

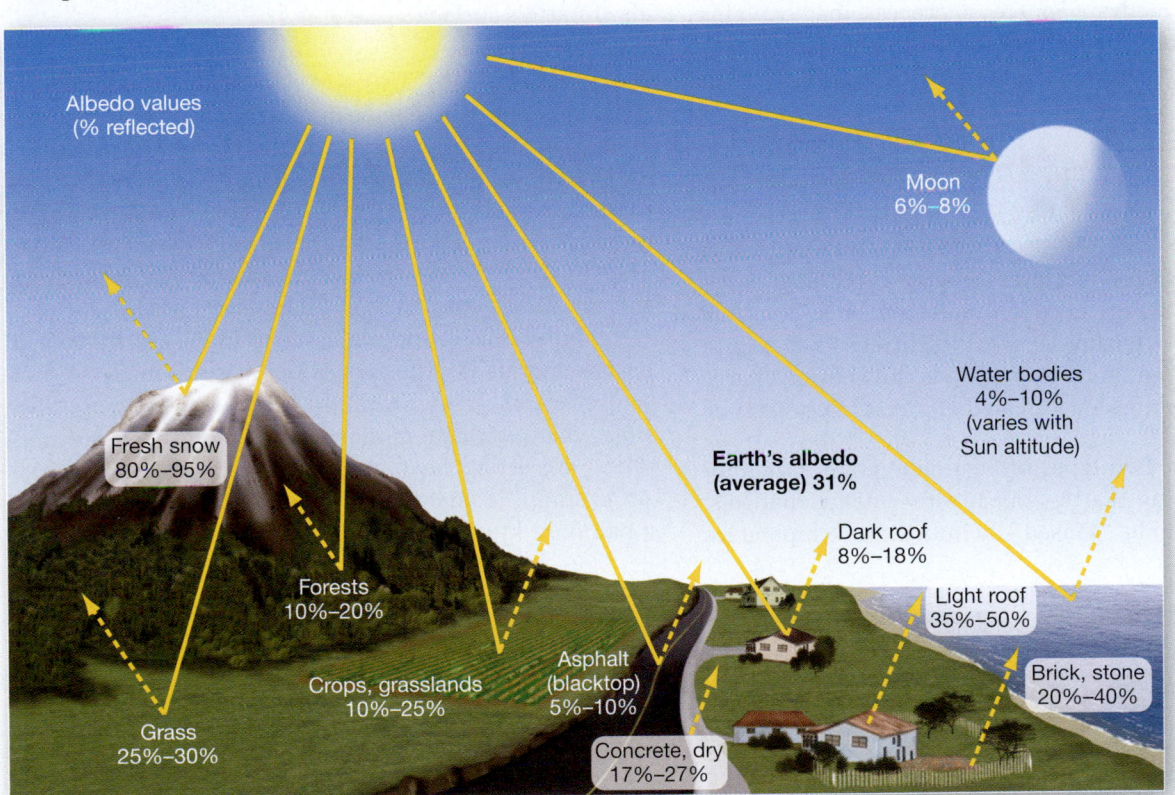

▲**Figure 4.6 Various albedo values.** In general, light surfaces are more reflective than dark surfaces and thus have higher albedo values. Note that the albedo for water surfaces varies with Sun angle and the roughness of the water surface. Low angle sunlight might have up to 60% reflected from a smooth surface.

GEOReport 4.1 Did light refraction sink the Titanic?

An unusual optical phenomenon called "super refraction" may explain why the *Titanic* struck an iceberg in 1912 and why the *California* did not come to her aid during that fateful April night. Recently, a British historian combined weather records, survivors' testimony, and ships' logs to determine that atmospheric conditions were conducive to a bending of light that causes objects to be obscured in a mirage in front of a "false" horizon. Under these conditions, the *Titanic*'s lookouts could not see the iceberg until too late to turn, and the nearby *California* could not identify the sinking ship. Read the full story at http://www.smithsonianmag.com/science-nature/Did-the-Titanic-Sink-Because-of-an-Optical-Illusion.html.

Absorption Insolation, both direct and diffuse, that is not part of the 31% reflected from Earth's surface and atmosphere is absorbed, either in the atmosphere or by Earth's surface. **Absorption** is the assimilation of radiation by molecules of matter, converting the radiation from one form of energy to another. Solar energy is absorbed by land and water surfaces (about 45% of insolation) as well as by atmospheric gases, dust, clouds, and stratospheric ozone (together about 24% of insolation; **Figure 4.7**). At Earth's surface, it is converted into either longwave radiation or chemical energy, such as by plants during photosynthesis. The process of absorption raises the temperature of the absorbing surface.

The atmosphere does not absorb as much insolation as Earth's surface because gases are selective about the wavelengths they absorb. For example, oxygen and ozone effectively absorb ultraviolet radiation in the stratosphere. None of the atmospheric gases absorb the wavelengths of visible light, which pass through the atmosphere to Earth as direct radiation. However, several gases—water vapor and carbon dioxide, in particular—are good absorbers of longwave radiation emitted by Earth. These gases absorb heat in the lower troposphere, a process that explains why Earth's atmosphere is warmer at the surface, acting somewhat like a natural greenhouse (discussed ahead in this chapter).

Heat Transfer at Earth's Surface

The solar energy absorbed by Earth's surface and atmosphere produces heat. For the purpose of studying Earth's energy budget, remember from Chapter 2 that **heat** is the flow of kinetic energy between molecules and from one body or substance to another resulting from a temperature difference between them. Heat always flows from an area of higher temperature into an area of lower temperature.

Types of Heat Two types of heat energy are important for understanding Earth–atmosphere energy budgets. **Sensible heat** can be "sensed" by humans as temperature because it comes from the kinetic energy of molecular motion. Radiant energy from the Sun must be absorbed before it can be felt as sensible heat. **Latent heat** ("hidden" heat) is the energy gained or lost when a substance changes from one state to another, such as from water to water vapor (liquid to gas) or from water to ice (liquid to solid). Latent heat transfer differs from sensible heat transfer in that as long as a physical change in state is taking place, the substance itself does not change temperature (although the surroundings do gain or lose heat). The latent heat absorbed in the process of evaporation is an important output of the Earth–atmosphere energy system.

Various substances differ in their ability to absorb heat and change temperature. *Specific heat* is the term for the heat capacity of a substance. Water, for example, has a higher specific heat than land, meaning that water can hold more heat than soil or rock and so it warms or cools more slowly. Put another way, more energy is needed to heat a given volume of water than is needed to heat the same volume of soil or rock. (We discuss this further later in the chapter.) For now, this concept applies to the rate of heat transfer through various materials at Earth's surface.

Methods of Heat Transfer Heat energy is known as *thermal energy*, and can be transferred throughout Earth's atmosphere, land, and water bodies by several processes. **Radiation** is the transfer of heat in electromagnetic waves. Examples are heat transfer from the Sun to Earth or from a fire or a burner on the stove (**Figure 4.8**). Waves of radiation do not need to travel through a medium, such as air or water, in order to transfer heat.

Conduction is the molecule-to-molecule transfer of heat energy as it diffuses through a substance. As molecules warm, their vibration increases, causing collisions that produce motion in neighboring molecules, thus transferring heat from warmer to cooler material. An example is energy conducted through the handle of a pan on a kitchen stove. Different materials (gases, liquids, and solids) conduct sensible heat directionally from areas of higher temperature to those of lower temperature. This heat flow transfers energy through matter at varying rates, depending on the conductivity of the material—Earth's land surface is a better conductor than air; moist air is a slightly better conductor than dry air.

Gases and liquids also transfer energy by **convection**, the transfer of heat by mixing or circulation. An example is a convection oven, in which a fan circulates heated air to uniformly cook food, or the movement of boiling water on a stove. In the atmosphere or in bodies of water, warmer (less dense) masses tend to rise, and cooler (denser) masses tend to sink, establishing patterns of convection. This physical mixing usually

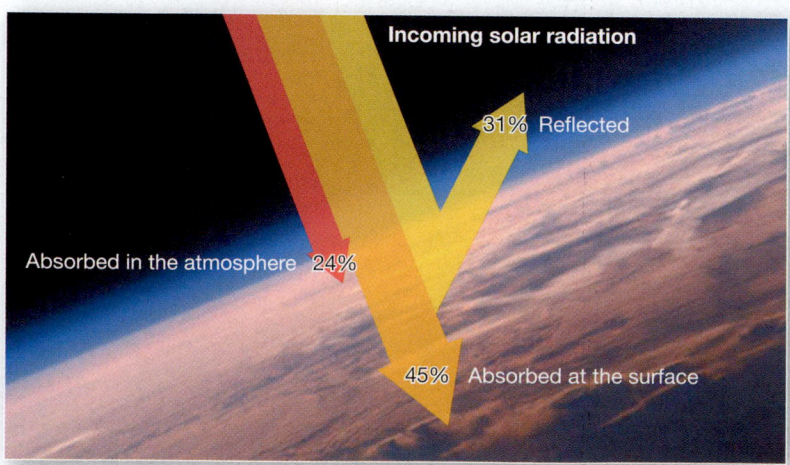

▲**Figure 4.7 Simplified view of the shortwave energy budget.**

(Image labels: Incoming solar radiation; 31% Reflected; Absorbed in the atmosphere 24%; 45% Absorbed at the surface)

◀Figure 4.8 Heat-transfer processes. Infrared energy *radiates* from the burner to the saucepan and the air. Energy *conducts* through the molecules of the pan and the handle. The water physically mixes, carrying heat energy by *convection*. Latent heat is the energy absorbed when liquid water changes to steam (water vapor).

involves a strong vertical motion. When horizontal motion dominates, the term **advection** applies.

These physical transfer mechanisms occur at all locations over varying scales; **Figure 4.9** shows an example at a coastal location. Over land, conduction transfers heat from within the warm ground to the cooler surface and convection transfers heat by vertical mixing in the atmosphere. Over water, convective heat transfer occurs as evaporation, in which water changes from liquid to gas, absorbing latent heat. Once in the atmosphere, water vapor mixes vertically by convection and horizontally by advection, always along a gradient from warmer to cooler temperatures.

Energy Balance in the Troposphere

The Earth–atmosphere energy system naturally balances itself in a steady-state equilibrium. The inputs of shortwave energy to Earth's atmosphere and surface from the Sun are eventually balanced by the outputs of shortwave energy reflected and longwave energy emitted from Earth's atmosphere and surface back to space. During times when this balance is not achieved, Earth can undergo a period of temporary warming or cooling that affects the overall climate (discussed further in Chapter 10).

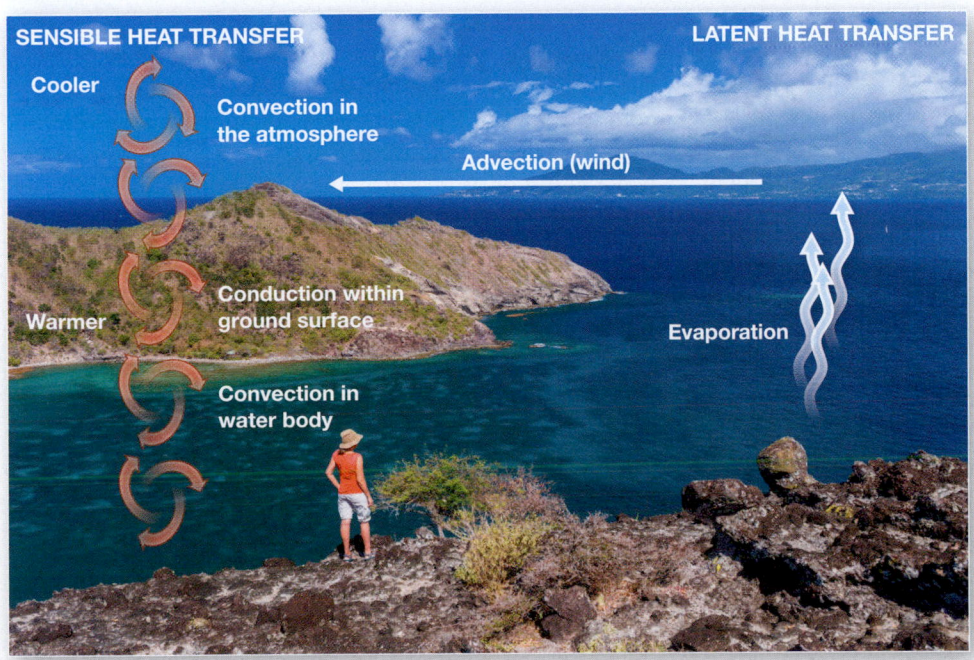

▲Figure 4.9 Heat transfer by conduction, radiation, and convection at a coastal location.
[Hemis/Alamy Stock Photo.]

Outgoing Radiation and the Greenhouse Concept

We saw in Chapter 2 that Earth constantly emits radiation, thus losing heat to the atmosphere and to space. However, as introduced in Chapter 3, some of this longwave radiation is absorbed by clouds and certain gases in the lower atmosphere and then emitted to space or *reradiated* back toward Earth. This process effectively delays longwave energy losses to space and acts to warm the lower atmosphere so that temperatures are habitable for living organisms. The rough similarity between this process and the way a greenhouse operates gives the process its name—the **greenhouse effect**.

The "Greenhouse" Analogy In a greenhouse, the glass is transparent to shortwave insolation, allowing light to pass through to the soil, plants, and materials inside. The absorbed energy is then emitted as longwave radiation, warming the air inside the greenhouse. The glass physically traps the warmed air inside the greenhouse, preventing it from mixing with cooler outside air. Thus, the glass acts as a one-way filter, allowing the shortwave energy in, but not allowing the longwave energy out except by opening the greenhouse's roof vents. This is the same effect you experience in a car parked in direct sunlight; the interior gets surprisingly hot with the windows closed, even on a day with mild temperatures outside.

In the atmosphere, the greenhouse analogy does not fully apply because longwave radiation is not trapped as in a greenhouse. Rather, its passage to space is delayed as the longwave radiation is absorbed by certain gases, clouds, and dust in the atmosphere and is reradiated back to Earth's surface before being eventually lost to space. The heat emitted from the atmosphere toward Earth's surface, called **counterradiation**, is significant, amounting to more energy than is absorbed at the surface from insolation.

In the lower atmosphere, gases that are mostly transparent to the passage of shortwave solar radiation but are effective at absorbing longwave infrared radiation emitted by Earth and the atmosphere are known as **greenhouse gases**—primarily water vapor, carbon dioxide, methane, nitrous oxide, and chlorofluorocarbons (CFCs). Greenhouse gases heat up the lower atmosphere, and are significant controls on Earth's temperature (**Figure 4.10**). Increasing concentrations of greenhouse gases, especially carbon dioxide, in the lower atmosphere since the Industrial Revolution (about 1850) have enhanced this natural greenhouse effect, producing a warming trend and related changes in the Earth–atmosphere energy system.

Clouds and Aerosols Clouds can cause cooling or heating of the lower atmosphere, affecting Earth's

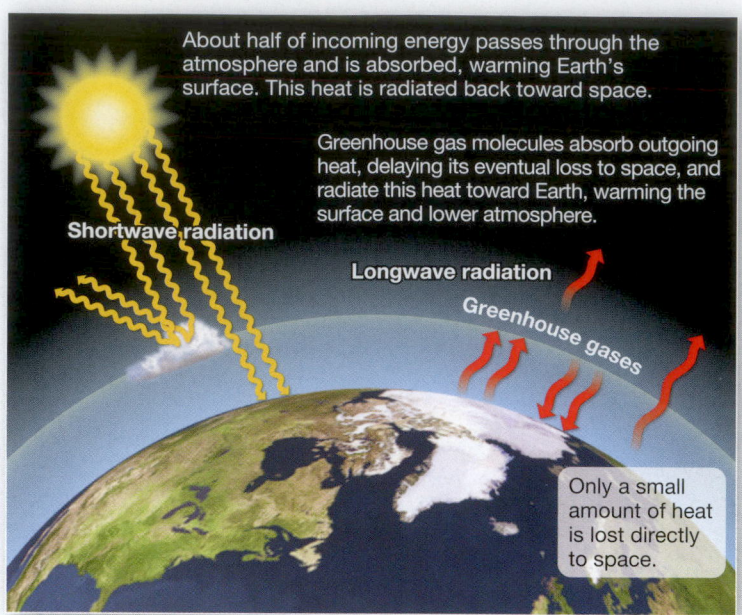

About half of incoming energy passes through the atmosphere and is absorbed, warming Earth's surface. This heat is radiated back toward space.

Greenhouse gas molecules absorb outgoing heat, delaying its eventual loss to space, and radiate this heat toward Earth, warming the surface and lower atmosphere.

Shortwave radiation

Longwave radiation

Greenhouse gases

Only a small amount of heat is lost directly to space.

▲Figure 4.10 **Greenhouse gases and Earth's energy budget.**

temperature. Because clouds reflect shortwave insolation, their presence or absence may make a 75% difference in the amount of energy that reaches Earth's surface. Clouds also absorb longwave radiation leaving Earth. Longwave radiation trapped by an insulating cloud layer creates warming of Earth's atmosphere as part of the greenhouse effect.

The effect of clouds is dependent on the percentage of cloud cover as well as cloud type, altitude, and thickness (water content and density). Low, thick stratus or cumulus clouds reflect about 90% of insolation. The term **cloud-albedo forcing** refers to an increase in albedo caused by such clouds and the resulting cooling of Earth's climate (here, albedo effects exceed greenhouse effects, shown in **Figure 4.11**, left side). High-altitude, ice-crystal clouds reflect only about 50% of incoming insolation. These cirrus clouds also act as insulation, trapping longwave radiation from Earth and raising minimum temperatures. This is **cloud-greenhouse forcing**, which causes warming of Earth's climate. Here, greenhouse effects exceed albedo effects, shown in Figure 4.11, right side.

Jet contrails produce high cirrus clouds related to aircraft exhaust—sometimes called *contrail cirrus* (**Figure 4.12**). Contrails, formed as the water vapor in jet exhaust condenses, both cool and warm the atmosphere, and these opposing effects make it difficult for scientists to determine their overall role in Earth's energy budget. Recent research indicates that contrail cirrus trap outgoing radiation from Earth at a slightly greater rate than they reflect insolation, suggesting that their overall effect is a warming of climate. When numerous contrails merge and spread in size, their effect on Earth's energy budget may be significant.

Aerosols from both natural and anthropogenic sources can also cause cooling or heating of Earth's atmosphere. The effect of aerosols on surface temperatures depends on whether they reflect or absorb insolation. For

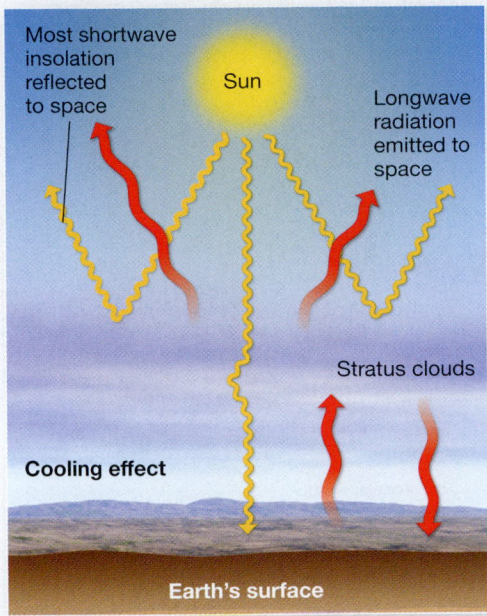

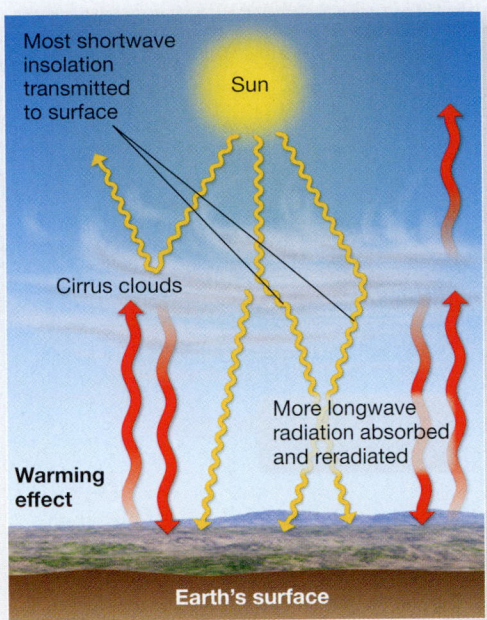

(a) Low, thick clouds lead to cloud-albedo forcing and atmospheric cooling.

(b) High, thin clouds lead to cloud-greenhouse forcing and atmospheric warming.

example, stratospheric aerosols from the 1991 eruption of Mount Pinatubo in the Philippines (shown in Figure 5.1.1) resulted in an increase in global atmospheric albedo and a temporary average cooling of 0.5 C° (0.9 F°). Scientists have correlated similar cooling trends with other large volcanic eruptions throughout history. Industrial pollutants such as sulfate aerosols are today increasing the reflectivity of the atmosphere, with a slight cooling effect at Earth's surface. However, darker aerosols (especially black carbon) readily absorb radiation and reradiate heat back toward Earth—with warming effects. Recent research suggests that the overall warming of the lower atmosphere associated with greenhouse gases is much greater than the slight cooling effect of anthropogenic aerosols.

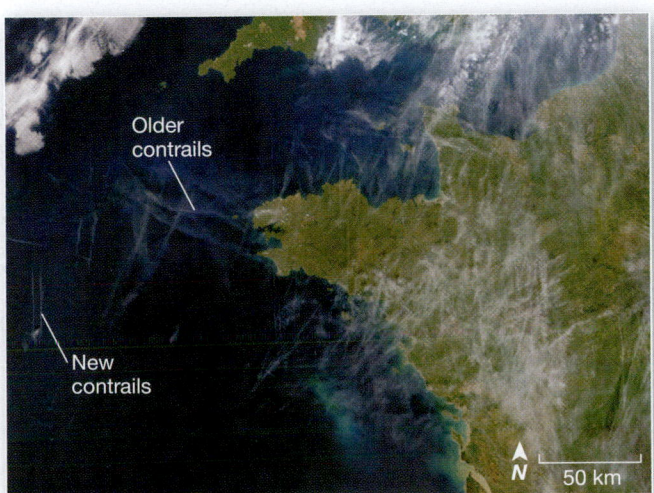

▲**Figure 4.12 Jet contrails form contrail cirrus over Brittany, France.** Newer contrails are thin; older contrails have widened and formed thin, high cirrus clouds, with an overall warming effect on Earth. [*Terra* MODIS, NASA/GSFC.]

Earth–Atmosphere Energy Balance

If Earth's surface and its atmosphere are considered separately, neither exhibits a balanced radiation budget in which inputs equal outputs. The average annual energy distribution is positive (an energy surplus, or gain) for Earth's surface and negative (an energy deficit, or loss) for Earth's atmosphere as it radiates energy to space. However, when considered together, these two equal each other, making it possible for us to construct an overall energy balance.

Geosystems in Action 4 summarizes the Earth–atmosphere radiation balance, bringing together all the elements previously discussed by following 100% of arriving insolation through the troposphere. Incoming energy is on the left in the illustration; outgoing energy is on the right.

Summary of Inputs and Outputs Out of 100% of the solar energy arriving at the top of the atmosphere, 31% is reflected back to space—this is Earth's average albedo. Another 24% of arriving solar energy is absorbed by the atmosphere. About 45% of the incoming insolation transmits through to Earth's surface as direct and diffuse shortwave radiation. In sum, Earth's atmosphere and surface absorb 69% of incoming shortwave radiation: 24% (atmosphere heating) + 45% (surface heating) = 69%. **Figure GIA 4.1** shows a detailed accounting of shortwave radiation inputs. Earth eventually emits this 69% as longwave radiation back into space.

Outgoing energy transfers from the surface are both *nonradiative* (involving physical, or mechanical, motion) and *radiative* (consisting of radiation). Nonradiative transfer processes include sensible heat transfer by convection and latent heat transfer—the energy absorbed as water changes from liquid to gas (evaporation) or ice to gas (sublimation). Radiative transfer is by longwave radiation from the surface to the atmosphere and then to space (represented in **Figure GIA 4.2** as the greenhouse effect and direct loss to space).

Incoming solar energy in the form of shortwave radiation interacts with both the atmosphere and Earth's surface (GIA 4.1). The surface reflects or absorbs some of the energy, reradiating the absorbed energy as longwave radiation (GIA 4.2). Averaged over a year, Earth's surface has an energy gain, or surplus, while the atmosphere has an energy deficit, or loss. These two amounts of energy equal each other, maintaining an overall balance in Earth's energy "budget."

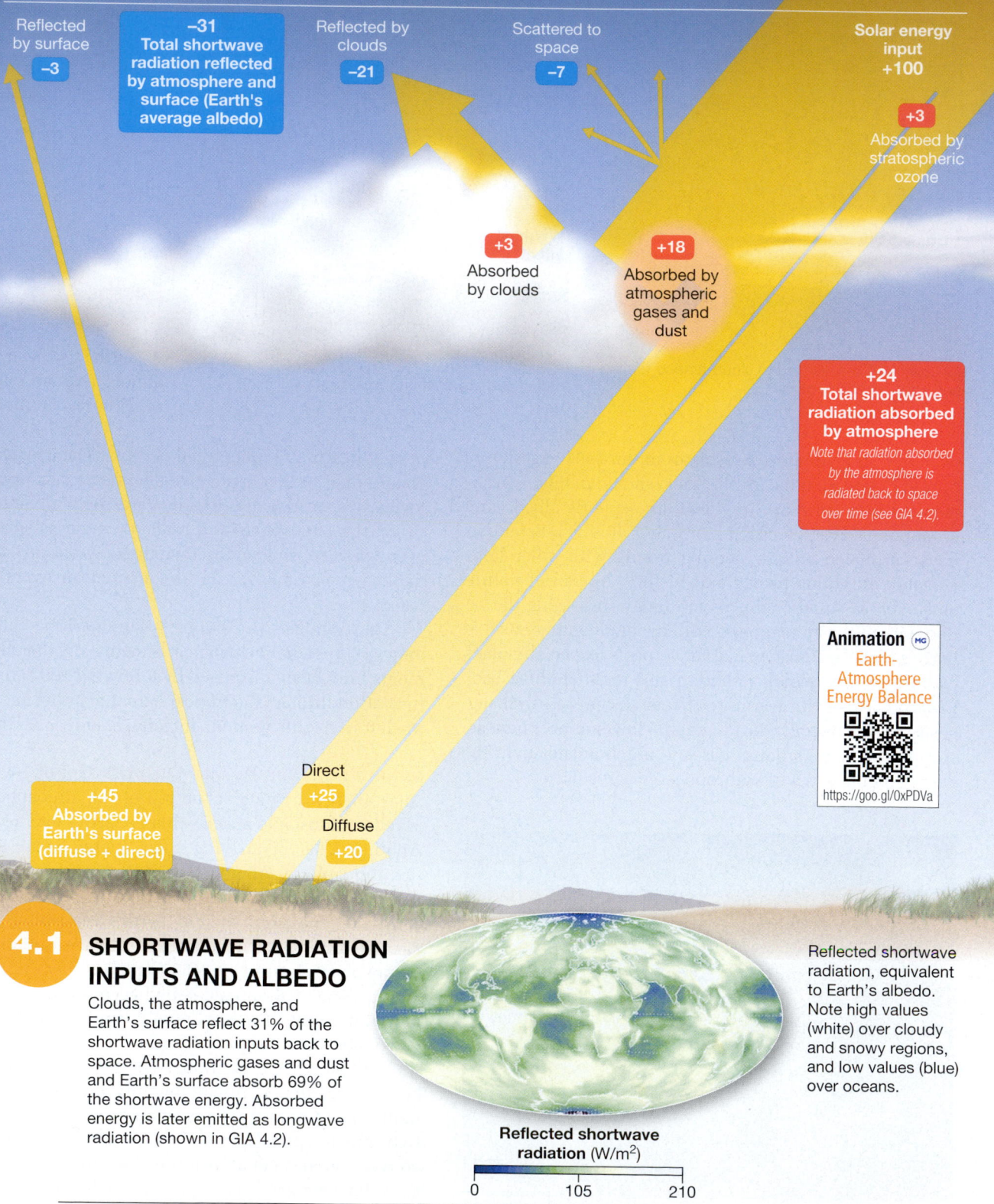

Reflected by surface
−3

−31
Total shortwave radiation reflected by atmosphere and surface (Earth's average albedo)

Reflected by clouds
−21

Scattered to space
−7

Solar energy input
+100

+3
Absorbed by stratospheric ozone

+3
Absorbed by clouds

+18
Absorbed by atmospheric gases and dust

+24
Total shortwave radiation absorbed by atmosphere
Note that radiation absorbed by the atmosphere is radiated back to space over time (see GIA 4.2).

Animation MG
Earth-Atmosphere Energy Balance
https://goo.gl/0xPDVa

+45
Absorbed by Earth's surface (diffuse + direct)

Direct
+25

Diffuse
+20

4.1 **SHORTWAVE RADIATION INPUTS AND ALBEDO**

Clouds, the atmosphere, and Earth's surface reflect 31% of the shortwave radiation inputs back to space. Atmospheric gases and dust and Earth's surface absorb 69% of the shortwave energy. Absorbed energy is later emitted as longwave radiation (shown in GIA 4.2).

Reflected shortwave radiation, equivalent to Earth's albedo. Note high values (white) over cloudy and snowy regions, and low values (blue) over oceans.

Reflected shortwave radiation (W/m²)

0   105   210

MasteringGeography™

Visit the Study Area in MasteringGeography™ to explore the Earth–atmosphere energy balance.

Visualize: Study geosciences animations of atmospheric energy balance.

Assess: Demonstrate understanding of the Earth–atmosphere energy balance (if assigned by instructor).

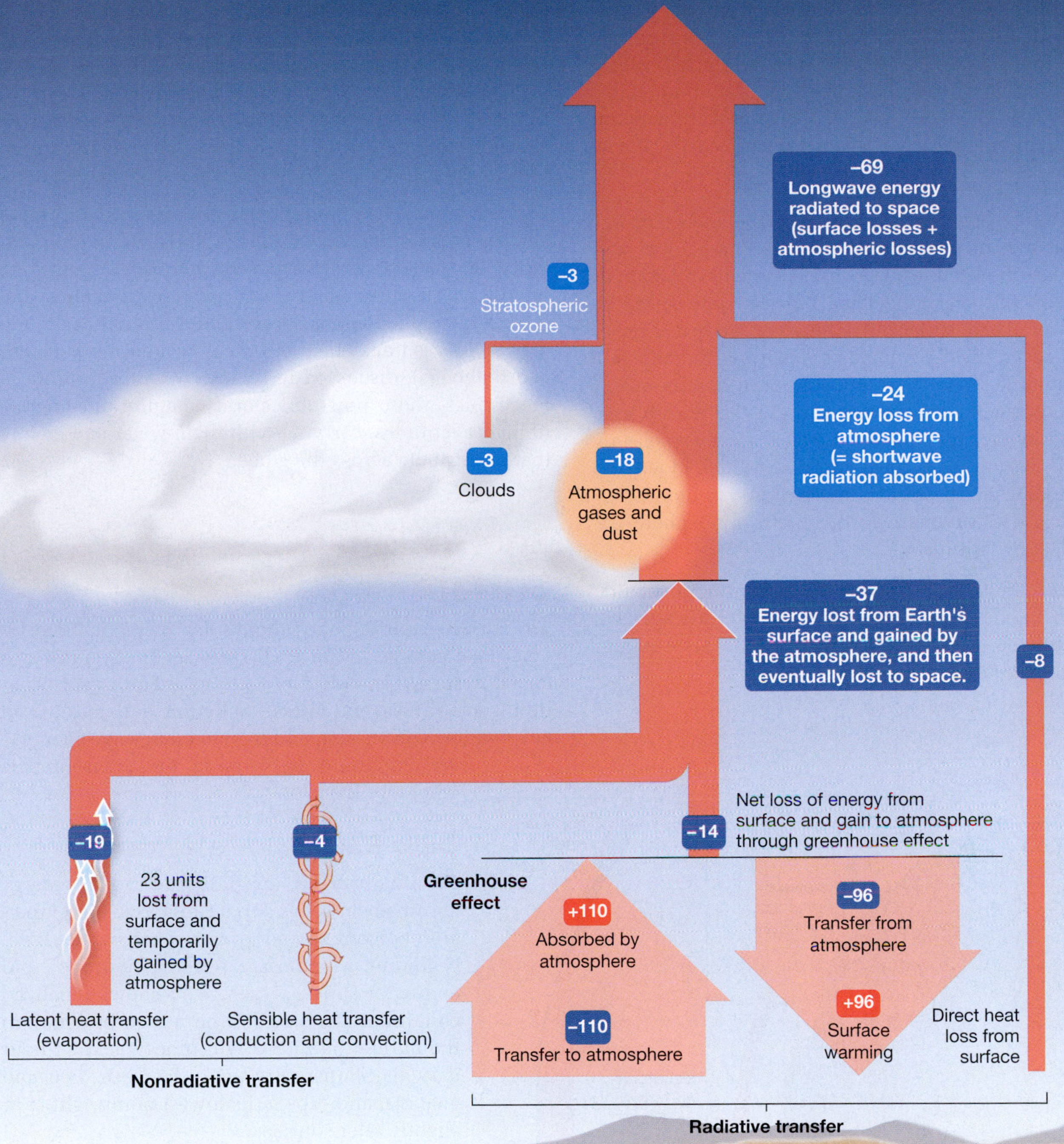

−69
Longwave energy radiated to space (surface losses + atmospheric losses)

−3
Stratospheric ozone

−24
Energy loss from atmosphere (= shortwave radiation absorbed)

−3
Clouds

−18
Atmospheric gases and dust

−8

−37
Energy lost from Earth's surface and gained by the atmosphere, and then eventually lost to space.

Net loss of energy from surface and gain to atmosphere through greenhouse effect

−19

−4

−14

23 units lost from surface and temporarily gained by atmosphere

Greenhouse effect

+110
Absorbed by atmosphere

−110
Transfer to atmosphere

−96
Transfer from atmosphere

+96
Surface warming

Direct heat loss from surface

Latent heat transfer (evaporation)

Sensible heat transfer (conduction and convection)

Nonradiative transfer

Radiative transfer

4.2 OUTGOING LONGWAVE RADIATION

Over time, Earth emits, on average, 69% of incoming energy to space. When added to the amount of energy reflected (31%), this equals the total energy input from the Sun (100%). Outgoing energy transfers from the surface are both *radiative* (consisting of longwave radiation directly to space) and *nonradiative* (involving convection and the energy released by latent heat transfer).

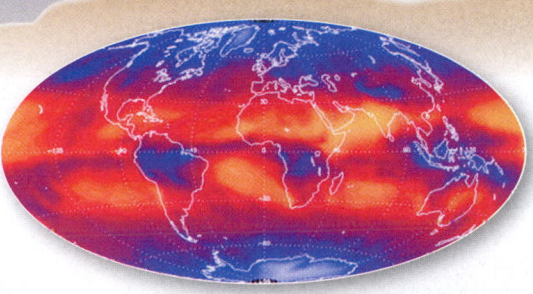

Outgoing longwave radiation emitted from Earth and the atmosphere. Note high values (yellow) over deserts and low values (white and blue) over the polar regions.

Outgoing longwave radiation (W/m²)

100   210   320

GEOquiz

1. Explain: Greenhouse gases emit longwave radiation toward the surface and into space. Explain the net effect of this process.

2. Infer: Which is more important in heating Earth's atmosphere: incoming shortwave radiation or outgoing longwave radiation? Explain.

3. Predict: Suppose that latent heat energy is released into the atmosphere as water evaporates from a lake. How is this energy involved in the atmosphere's energy balance and what eventually happens to it?

89

In total, the atmosphere radiates 61% of the absorbed energy back to space. Earth's surface emits 8% of absorbed radiation directly back to space. Note that atmospheric energy losses are greater than those from Earth. However, the energy is in balance overall: 61% atmospheric losses + 8% surface losses = 69%.

Latitudinal Energy Imbalances As stated earlier, energy budgets at specific places or times on Earth are not always the same (see the satellite images in Geosystems in Action 4). Greater amounts of sunlight are reflected into space by lighter-colored land surfaces (ice, snow, or sandy deserts) or by cloud cover. Greater amounts of longwave radiation are emitted from Earth to space in subtropical deserts, where little cloud cover is present over surfaces that absorb heat. Less longwave energy is emitted over the cooler polar regions and over tropical lands covered in thick clouds (in the equatorial Amazon region, in Africa, and in Indonesia).

Figure 4.13 summarizes the Earth–atmosphere energy budget by latitude.

- Between the tropics, the angle of incoming insolation is high and daylength is consistent, with little seasonal variation, so more energy is gained than lost—*energy surpluses dominate.*

- In the polar regions, the Sun is low in the sky, surfaces are light (ice and snow) and reflective, and for up to 6 months during the year, no insolation is received, so more energy is lost than gained—*energy deficits prevail.*
- At around 36° latitude, a balance exists between energy gains and losses for the Earth–atmosphere system.

The imbalance of energy from the tropical surpluses and the polar deficits drives a vast global circulation pattern. The meridional (north–south) transfer agents are winds, ocean currents, dynamic weather systems, and other related phenomena. Dramatic examples of such energy and mass transfers are tropical cyclones (hurricanes and typhoons), discussed in Chapter 7. After forming in the tropics, these powerful storms mature and migrate to higher latitudes, carrying with them water and energy that redistribute across the globe.

Energy Balance at Earth's Surface

The surface environment, where solar energy is the principal heat source, is the final stage in the Sun-to-Earth energy system. The radiation patterns at Earth's surface—inputs of diffuse and direct radiation and outputs of evaporation, convection, and radiated longwave energy—are important in forming the environments where we live.

Daily Radiation Patterns

On a daily basis, the timing of radiant energy absorbed at Earth's surface relates to air temperature. Incoming energy arrives during daylight, beginning at sunrise, peaking at noon, and ending at sunset. Figure 4.14 shows idealized conditions for bare soil on a cloudless day in the middle latitudes. Within a typical 24-hour day, air temperature peaks between 3:00 and 4:00 P.M. and dips to its lowest point right at or slightly after sunrise.

The shape and height of the insolation curve vary with season and latitude. The maximum heights for such a curve occur in summer, at the time of the June solstice in the Northern Hemisphere and the December solstice in the Southern Hemisphere. The air-temperature plot also responds to seasonal variations in insolation input.

Note the *lag* between the insolation curve and the air-temperature curve in Figure 4.14. The warmest time of day occurs not at the moment of maximum insolation, but at the moment when a maximum of insolation has been absorbed and emitted to the atmosphere from the ground. As long as the incoming energy exceeds the outgoing energy, air temperature continues to increase. However, owing to

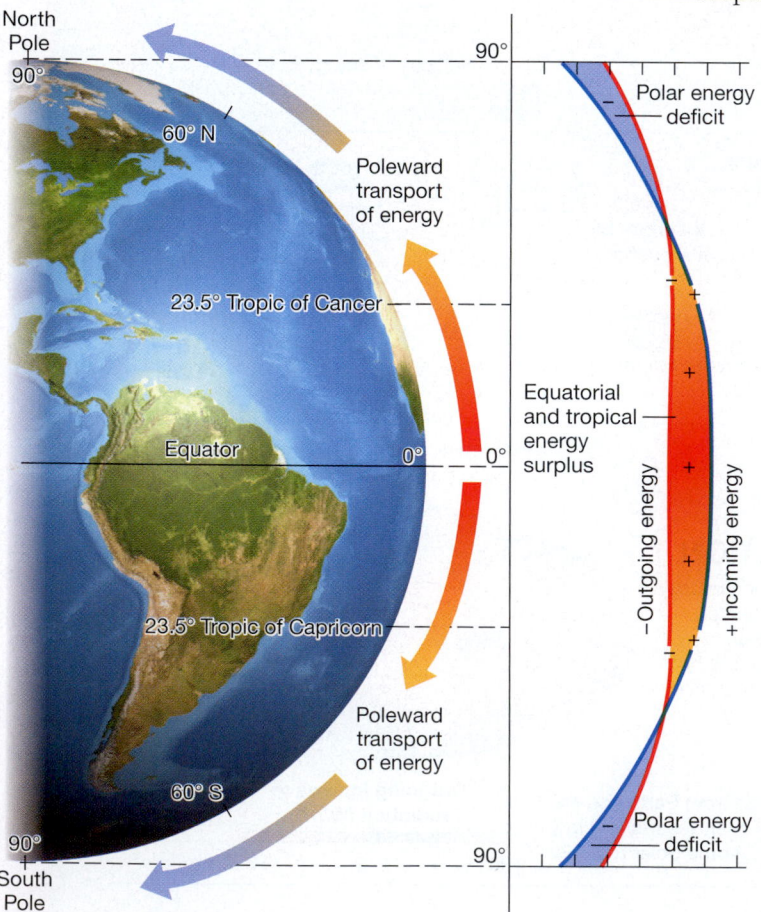

▲Figure 4.13 **Energy budget by latitude.** Low-latitude energy surpluses and high-latitude energy deficits produce the poleward transport of energy and mass in each hemisphere, through atmospheric circulation and ocean currents.

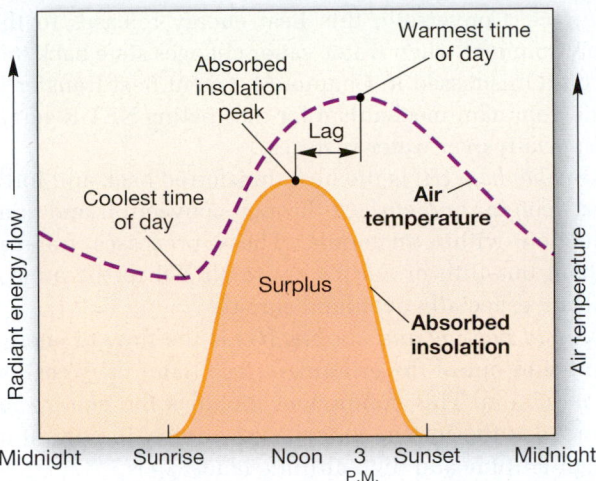

▲**Figure 4.14** **Daily radiation and temperature curves.** This sample radiation plot for a typical day shows the changes in absorbed insolation (solid line) and air temperature (dashed line). Comparing the curves reveals a lag between the insolation peak at local noon and the warmest time of day 3 hours later.

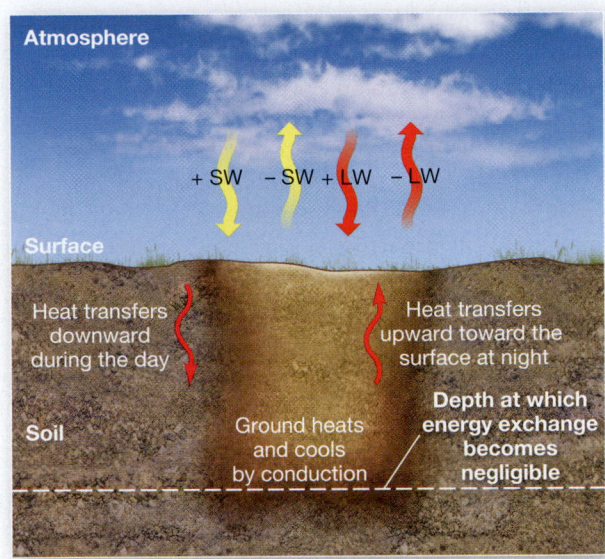

▲**Figure 4.15** **Surface energy-budget components over soil column.** Idealized input and output of energy at the surface and within a column of soil (SW = shortwave, LW = longwave).

the lag between the insolation and temperature curves, air temperature peaks *after* the incoming energy begins to diminish, as the afternoon Sun's altitude decreases.

The annual pattern of insolation and air temperature exhibits a similar lag. For the Northern Hemisphere, January is usually the coldest month, occurring after the December solstice and the shortest days. Similarly, the warmest months of July and August occur after the June solstice and the longest days.

A Simplified Surface Energy Budget

Energy and moisture are continually exchanged with the lower atmosphere at Earth's surface—this is the *boundary layer* (also known as the atmospheric, or planetary, boundary layer). Specific characteristics of Earth's surface, such as the presence or absence of vegetation and local topography, affect the energy balance in the boundary layer. The height of the boundary layer is not constant over time or space.

Microclimatology is the science of physical conditions, including radiation, heat, and moisture, in the boundary layer at or near Earth's surface. *Microclimates* are local climate conditions over a relatively small area, such as in a park, or on a particular slope, or in your backyard. Thus, our discussion now focuses on local-scale (the lowest few meters of the atmosphere) rather than global-scale (the troposphere) energy-budget components.

The surface in any given location receives and loses shortwave (SW) and longwave (LW) energy according to the following simple scheme:

$$+SW\downarrow - SW\uparrow + LW\downarrow - LW\uparrow = NET\ R$$
<small>(Insolation) (Reflection) (Infrared) (Infrared) (Net radiation)</small>

Net radiation (NET R) is the sum of all radiation gains and losses, and varies with daylength through the seasons, the amount of cloud cover, and latitude.

In and over most soil surfaces, heat is transferred by conduction through the soil, predominantly downward during the day (or in summer) and toward the surface at night (or in winter). Energy exchange with the surface or with surrounding materials becomes negligible at a certain depth, usually less than a meter (**Figure 4.15**). Energy moving from the atmosphere into the surface is reported as a positive value (a gain), and energy moving outward from the surface, through sensible and latent heat transfers, is reported as a negative value (a loss) in the surface account.

Figure 4.16 illustrates the surface energy components for a typical summer day at a midlatitude location.

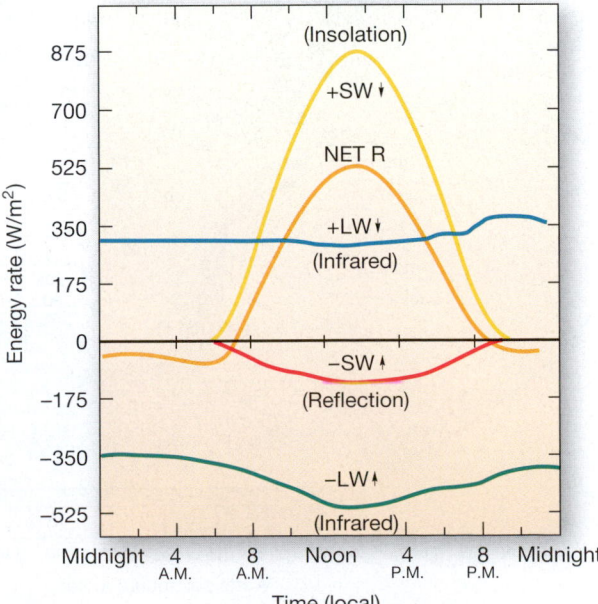

▲**Figure 4.16** **Daily radiation budget.** Radiation budget on a typical July summer day at a midlatitude location (Matador in southern Saskatchewan, about 51° N). [Based on T. R. Oke, *Boundary Layer Climates*, © 1978 Methuen & Co.]

Energy gains include shortwave from the Sun (both diffuse and direct) and longwave counterradiation (from the atmosphere downward to Earth). Energy losses include reflected shortwave and Earth's longwave emissions that pass through the atmosphere to space.

On a daily basis, NET R values are positive during the daylight hours, peaking just after noon with the peak in insolation; at night, values become negative because the shortwave component ceases at sunset and the surface continues to lose longwave radiation to the atmosphere. The surface rarely reaches a zero NET R value—a perfect balance—at any one moment. However, over time, Earth's total surface naturally balances incoming and outgoing energies.

Net Radiation Expenditure The net radiation available at Earth's surface is the final outcome of the entire energy-balance process discussed in this chapter. As we have learned, in order for the energy budget at Earth's surface to balance over time, areas that have positive net radiation must somehow dissipate, or lose, heat. This happens through nonradiative processes that move energy from the ground into the boundary layer.

- The *latent heat of evaporation* (*LE*) is the energy absorbed by water as it changes from liquid to gas, forming water vapor in the atmosphere. During evaporation, water absorbs large quantities of this latent heat, thereby removing this heat energy from the

surface. Conversely, this heat energy releases to the environment when water vapor changes state back to a liquid (discussed in Chapter 6). Latent heat transfer is the dominant mechanism for dissipating NET R gains, especially over water surfaces.

- *Sensible heat* (*H*) is the heat transferred back and forth between air and surface through convection and conduction within materials. These processes transfer about one-fifth of Earth's entire NET R to the atmosphere, especially over land surfaces.
- *Ground heating and cooling* (*G*) is the flow of energy into and out of the ground surface (land or water) by conduction. This component includes the energy absorbed at the surface to melt snow or ice, important in high-latitude and high-altitude landscapes.

On land, the highest annual values for *LE* occur in the tropics and decrease toward the poles (**Figure 4.17**). Over the oceans, the highest *LE* values are over subtropical latitudes, where hot, dry air comes into contact with warm ocean water. The values for *H* are highest in the subtropics. Here vast regions of subtropical deserts feature nearly waterless surfaces, cloudless skies, and almost vegetation-free landscapes. Through the processes of latent, sensible, and ground heat transfer, the energy from net radiation is able to do the "work" that ultimately produces the global climate system—work such as raising temperatures in the boundary layer, melting ice, or evaporating water from the oceans.

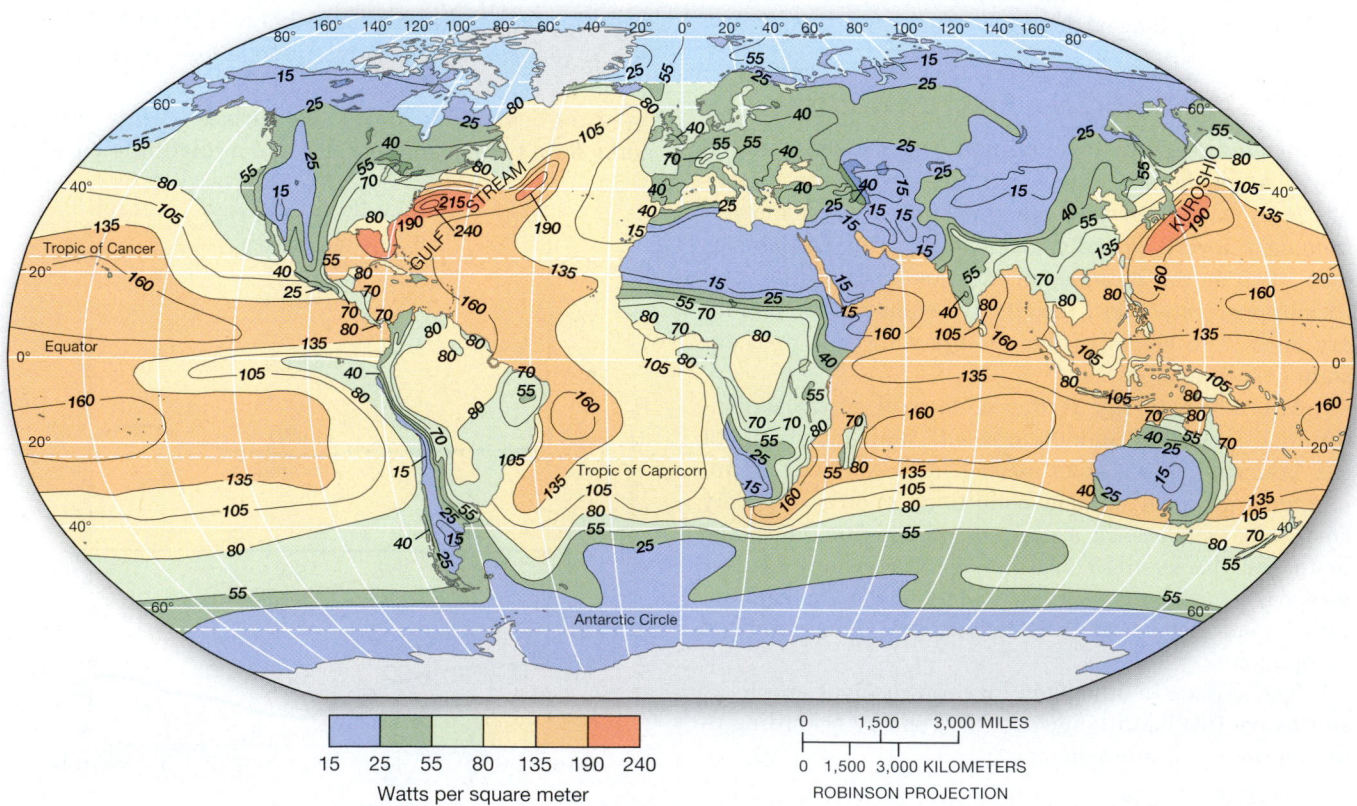

▲**Figure 4.17 Global latent heat of evaporation.** Annual energy dissipated as the latent heat of evaporation (LE) at the surface. Note the highest values over areas with high sea-surface temperatures associated with warm ocean currents—the Gulf Stream off the east coast of North America and the Kuroshio off the east coast of Japan. [Adapted from M. I. Budyko, *The Earth's Climate, Past and Future,* © 1982 Academic Press.]

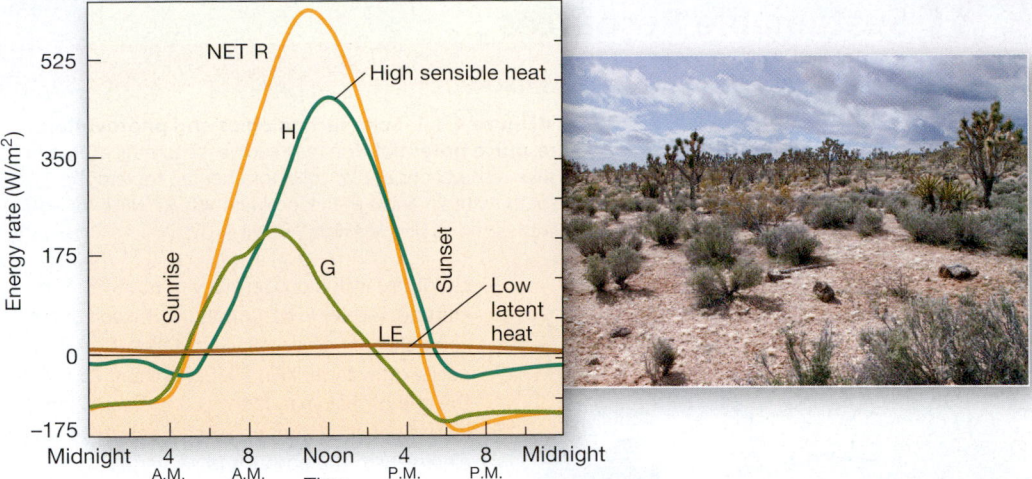

◀**Figure 4.18** **Radiation budgets for two stations.** *H* = turbulent sensible heat transfer; *LE* = latent heat of evaporation; *G* = ground heating and cooling. [(a) Based on W. D. Sellers, *Physical Climatology,* © 1965 University of Chicago. (b) Based on T. R. Oke, *Boundary Layer Climates,* © 1978 Methuen & Co. Photos by Bobbé Christopherson.]

(a) Daily net radiation budget at El Mirage, California, near 35°N latitude. Note the Mojave desert landscape near El Mirage in the photo.

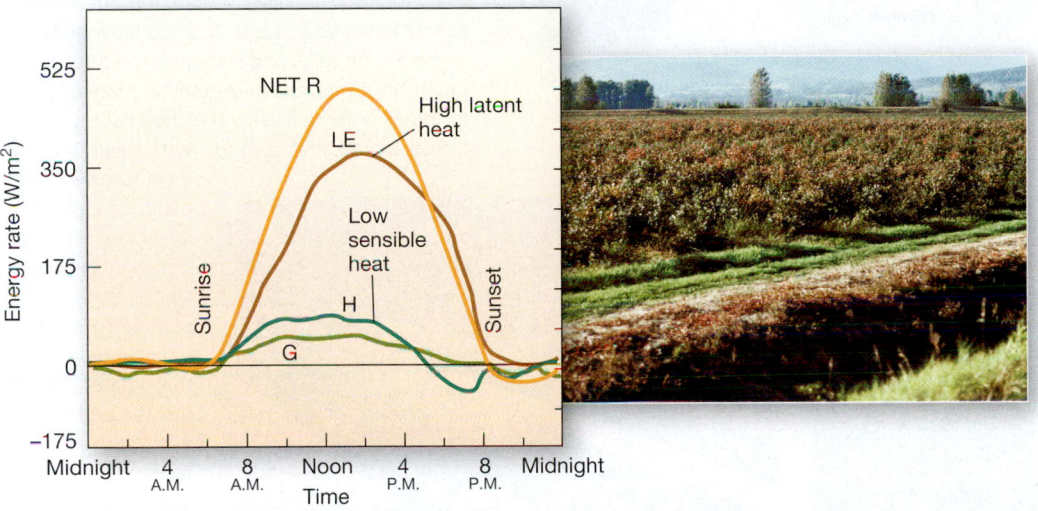

(b) Daily net radiation budget for Pitt Meadows, British Columbia, near 49°N latitude. Note the irrigated blueberry orchards near Pitt Meadows in the photo.

Two Sample Stations The daily radiation budgets at two locations, El Mirage in California and Pitt Meadows in British Columbia, provide an example of the portion of NET R dissipated by nonradiative heat transfer processes (**Figure 4.18**).

El Mirage, at 35° N, is a hot desert location characterized by bare, dry soil with sparse vegetation. The data in the graph is from a clear summer day, with a light wind in the late afternoon. NET R reflects the large amount of incoming energy (Sun close to zenith at the June solstice combined with absence of clouds) countered by the reflection from light-colored surfaces (with relatively high albedo) and the longwave radiation emitted from hot soil at the ground surface throughout the afternoon.

El Mirage has little or no energy loss through evaporation (*LE*). With little water and sparse vegetation, most of the available radiant energy dissipates through the transfer of sensible heat (*H*), warming air and soil to high temperatures. Over a 24-hour period, *H* is 90% of NET R expenditure; the remaining 10% is ground heating (*G*).

The *G* component is greatest in the morning, when winds are light and convective transfers are lowest. In the afternoon, heated air rises off the hot ground, and convective heat expenditures are accelerated as winds increase.

For comparison, Pitt Meadows is midlatitude (49° N), vegetated, and moist, and its energy expenditures differ greatly from those at El Mirage. The energy-balance data are from a cloudless summer day. The Pitt Meadows landscape is able to retain more of its energy because of lower albedo values (less reflection), the presence of more water and plants, and lower surface temperatures than those of El Mirage. Higher *LE* values result from the moist environment of rye grass and irrigated mixed orchards, contributing to the more moderate *H* levels during the day.

The principles and processes of net radiation at Earth's surface have a bearing on the design and use of solar energy technologies that concentrate shortwave energy for human use. Focus Study 4.1 reviews this application of surface energy budgets.

FOCUSstudy 4.1   Sustainable Resources
Solar Energy

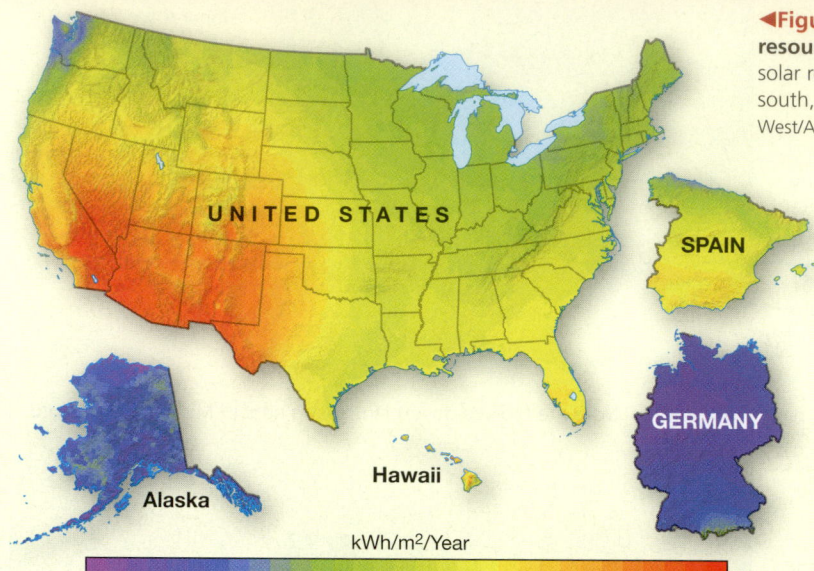

◄**Figure 4.1.1 Solar technologies and photovoltaic resource potential.** The map shows the annual average solar resource for a solar collector oriented toward the south, with tilt angle at the local latitude. [(a) NREL. (b) Jim West/Alamy. (c) Ellen McKnight/Alamy.]

(a) U.S. solar PV resource as compared to Germany and Spain.

(b) Rooftop solar panels, Denver, Colorado.

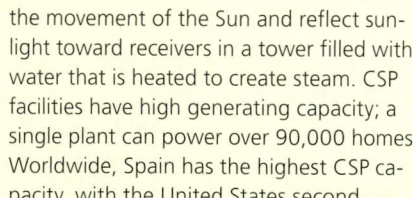

(c) Parabolic trough collectors, California.

The solar energy that Earth receives every hour is enough to meet world power needs for a year. In the United States, the solar energy that arrives every 35 minutes is equivalent to the energy produced by fossil fuels in a year. The potential for solar energy is tremendous; yet the resource remains underutilized as an energy resource.

Photovoltaic Solar Power

Electricity can be generated directly from sunlight using photovoltaic (PV) cells, first developed for spacecraft in the 1950s. You see solar PV technology in rooftop solar panels. When light shines on a semiconductor material in these cells, it stimulates a flow of electrons (an electrical current) in the cell. Numerous cells are wired together in solar panels, and the panels then arranged in arrays that can power homes and buildings (**Figure 4.1.1b**). New thin-film solar cells use layers of semiconductor materials that are only a few micrometers thick, making them suitable for use as rooftop tiles or shingles.

As the efficiency of PV cells improves and the cost drops, PV capacity worldwide is more than doubling every 2 years. Half the world's total PV capacity is in Europe. Germany is the world's leading producer of solar power, with an installed capacity of 38 GW at the end of 2015. Although the potential for solar PV in the United States is excellent (**Figure 4.1.1a**), growth of solar energy has lagged behind that of Europe—even though many European countries, including Germany at about 51° N latitude, receive lower amounts of insolation by comparison. However, U.S. installed solar PV capacity grew by 16% in 2015, reaching 25 GW by the end of that year. Many U.S. residential installations generate enough surplus energy to supply electricity to the power grid.

Concentrated Solar Power

Utility-scale solar power production often uses concentrated solar power (CSP), a technology that relies on reflecting sunlight onto a focal point that contains a heat-transfer material (often oil or molten salt). This material is collected, stored, and used to create steam to drive turbines that generate electricity. Numerous large CSP plants in the United States use *parabolic troughs*, long curved mirrors that rotate with the Sun and focus heat onto a tube in front of the mirror (**Figure 4.1.1c**). Another type of CSP uses mirrors called *heliostats* that track the movement of the Sun and reflect sunlight toward receivers in a tower filled with water that is heated to create steam. CSP facilities have high generating capacity; a single plant can power over 90,000 homes. Worldwide, Spain has the highest CSP capacity, with the United States second.

1. In which U.S. regions is solar PV potential highest?

2. What is the main difference between solar PV and CSP technologies?

APPLYconcepts Use Figure 4.1.1 to explore variations in solar potential across the United States. (If you need help locating the cities, refer to an atlas or online map.)

List these cities in order of their solar potential, from highest to lowest: Anchorage, AK, 61° N; Atlanta, GA, 34° N; Caribou, ME, 47° N; Casper, WY, 43° N; Chicago, IL, 42° N; Olympia, WA, 47° N; Phoenix, AZ, 33° N	a. _____ b. _____ c. _____ d. _____ e. _____ f. _____ g. _____

Based on the chapter discussion, explain the differences in solar potential between these locations._____

Temperature Concepts and Measurement

Earlier, we discussed types of heat and mechanisms of heat transfer, such as conduction, convection, and radiation. Recall from Chapter 2 that, unlike heat, temperature is not a form of energy but rather is related to the amount of energy in a substance. **Temperature** is a measure of the *average* kinetic energy of individual molecules in matter. Thus, temperature is a measure of heat.

Remember that heat always flows from matter at a higher temperature to matter at a lower temperature, and heat transfer usually results in a change in temperature.

For example, when you jump into a cool lake, kinetic energy leaves your body and flows to the water, causing a transfer of heat and a lowering of the temperature of your skin. Heat transfer can also occur without a change in temperature, when a substance changes state (as in latent heat transfer, discussed further in Chapter 6).

Temperature Scales

The lowest possible temperature (at which atomic and molecular motion in matter completely stops) is *absolute zero*, or *0 absolute temperature*. This value on three commonly encountered temperature-measuring scales is −273° Celsius (C), −459.67° Fahrenheit (F), and 0 Kelvin (K), as shown in **Figure 4.19**. Formulas for converting among Celsius, SI (Système International), and English units are in Appendix C.

The Fahrenheit temperature scale, named for German physicist Daniel G. Fahrenheit (1686–1736), places the melting point of ice at 32°F, separated by 180 subdivisions from the boiling point of water at 212°F. Note that ice has only one melting point, but water has many freezing points, ranging from 32°F down to −40°F, depending on its purity, its volume, and certain conditions in the atmosphere.

The Celsius scale (formerly centigrade), named after Swedish astronomer Anders Celsius (1701–1744), places the melting point of ice at 0°C and the boiling temperature of water at sea level at 100°C. The scale divides into 100 degrees using a decimal system.

The Kelvin scale, first proposed in 1848 by British physicist Lord Kelvin (born William Thomson, 1824–1907), starts at absolute zero. The Kelvin scale's melting point for ice is 273 K, and its boiling point of water is 373 K, 100 units higher. Therefore, the size of one Kelvin unit is the same size as one Celsius degree. Scientists often use this scale because its temperature readings are proportional to the actual kinetic energy in a material.

Most countries use the Celsius scale to express temperature—the United States is an exception. This textbook presents Celsius (with Fahrenheit equivalents in parentheses).

Measuring Temperature

A common instrument used to measure temperature is a thermometer, a sealed glass tube containing a fluid that expands with heating and contracts with cooling. Scientists use both *mercury thermometers* and *alcohol thermometers* to measure outdoor temperatures—however, mercury thermometers have the limitation that mercury freezes at −39°C (−38.2°F), making them ineffective for assessing Earth's colder climates. The principle of these thermometers is simple: A thermometer stores fluid in a small reservoir at one end and is marked with calibrations to measure the expansion or contraction of the fluid, which reflects the temperature of the thermometer's environment.

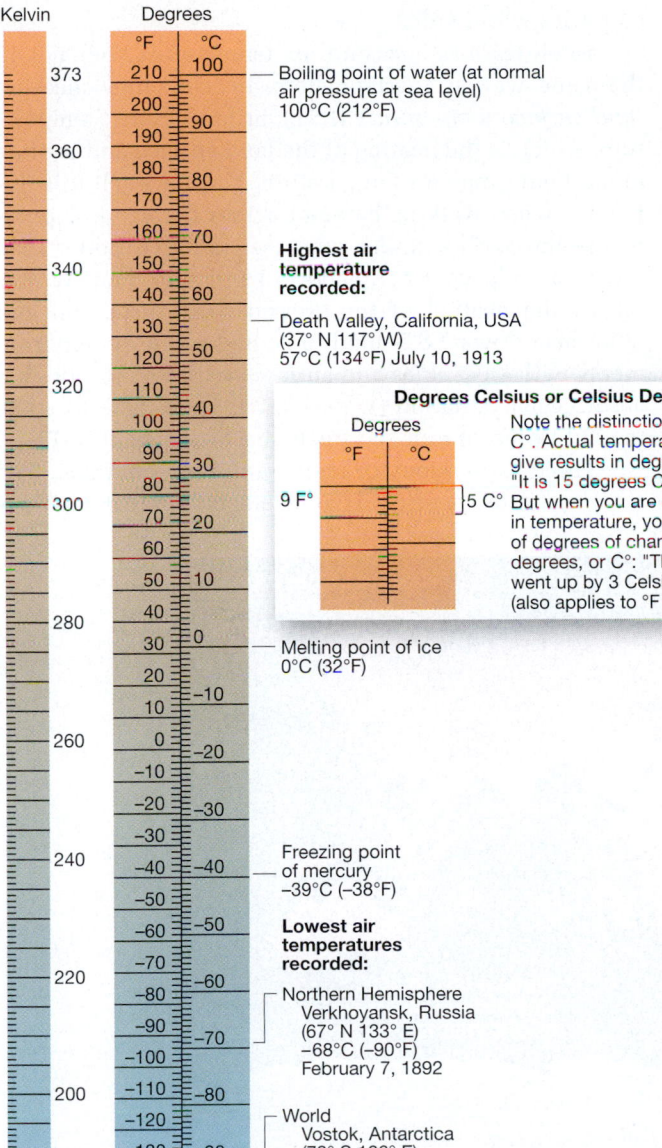

▲**Figure 4.19 Temperature scales.** Scales for expressing temperature in Kelvin (K) and degrees Celsius (°C) and Fahrenheit (°F), including significant temperatures and temperature records. Note the distinction between temperature (indicated by the color gradation on the scale) and units of temperature expression, and the placement of the degree symbol.

▲**Figure 4.20 Instrument shelter.** This standard thermistor shelter is louvered and installed above a level grass surface. [Bobbé Christopherson]

Devices for taking standardized official air temperature readings are placed outdoors in small shelters that are white (for high albedo) and louvered (for ventilation) to avoid overheating of the instruments (**Figure 4.20**). They are placed at least 1.2–1.8 m (4–6 ft) above a level ground surface, usually on turf, and in the shade but not too close to buildings or trees. Standard instrument shelters contain a *thermistor*, which measures temperature by sensing the electrical resistance of a semiconducting material, a measure that can be converted to temperature and reported electronically to the weather station.

Temperature readings occur daily, sometimes hourly, at more than 16,000 weather stations worldwide. Some stations also report the duration of a temperature, the rate of temperature rise or fall, and the temperature variation over time throughout the day and night. The Global Climate Observing System coordinates the reading and recording of temperature and other climate factors among countries worldwide.

Satellites also measure air temperature, but not in the same way as thermometers. Instead, they measure *land surface temperature* (LST), or land "skin" temperature, which is the heating of the land surface and is often much hotter than air temperature. You have felt this difference when walking barefoot across hot sand or pavement—the surface under your feet is much hotter than the air around your body above. Land skin temperatures record the heating of the ground from insolation and other heat flows; LSTs tend to be highest in dry environments with clear skies and surfaces with low albedo that absorb solar radiation (**Figure 4.21**). From 2003 to 2009, the Lut Desert of Iran had the highest consistent LST.

Three expressions of temperature are common: The *daily mean temperature* is an average of hourly readings

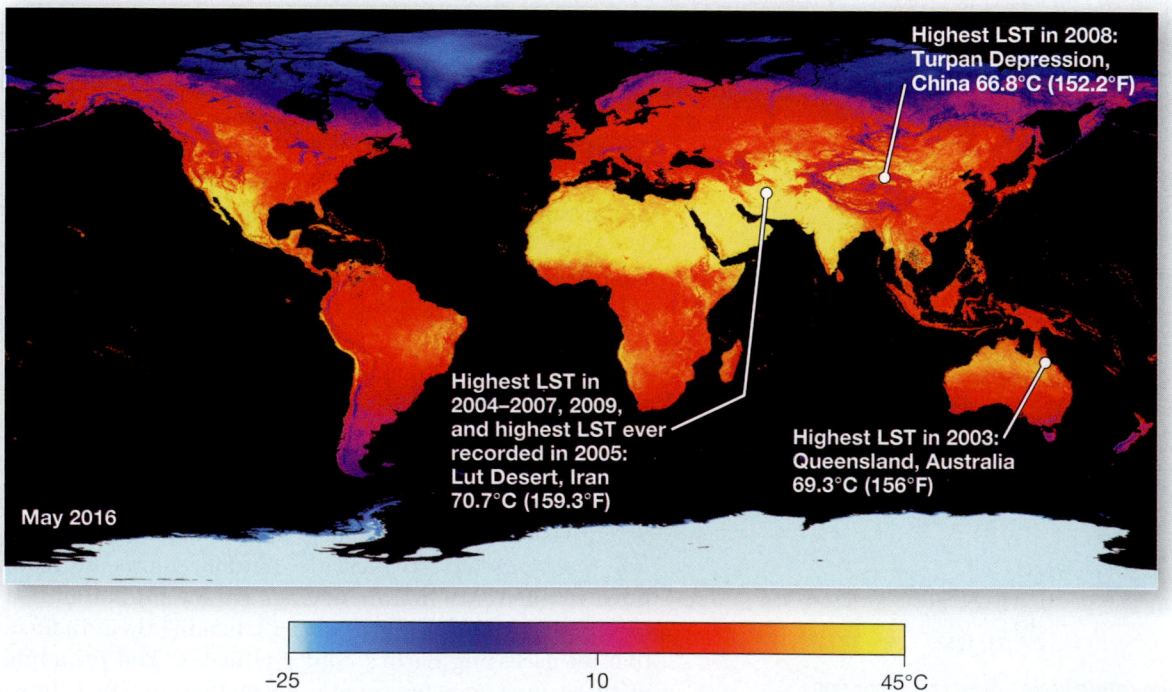

▲**Figure 4.21 Earth's hottest land temperatures.** The image shows land surface temperatures (LSTs), which are often higher than air temperatures, measured by satellites for May 2016. Yellow shows the warmest temperatures (up to 45°C, or 113°F) and light blue shows the coldest temperatures (down to -25°C, or -13°F). Earth's record air temperature as measured by instruments occurred at Death Valley, California. Earth's highest LSTs from 2003 to 2009 occurred at locations in Asia and Australia. More information is at http://earthobservatory.nasa.gov/Features/HottestSpot/page2.php. [NASA image by Reto Stockli, using LST data from the MODIS instrument aboard several satellites.]

taken over a 24-hour day, but may also be the average of the daily minimum–maximum readings. The *monthly mean temperature* is the total of daily mean temperatures for the month divided by the number of days in the month. An *annual temperature range* expresses the difference between the lowest and highest monthly mean temperatures for a given year.

Principal Temperature Controls

Insolation is the single most important influence on temperature variations. However, several other physical controls interact with it to produce Earth's temperature patterns. These include latitude, altitude and elevation, cloud cover, and land–water heating differences.

Latitude

We learned in Chapter 2 that between the Tropic of Cancer at 23.5° N latitude and the Tropic of Capricorn at 23.5° S latitude, insolation is more intense than at higher latitudes where the Sun is never directly overhead (at a 90° angle) during the year. The intensity of incoming solar radiation decreases away from the equator and toward the poles. Daylength also varies with latitude during the year, influencing the duration of insolation exposure. Variations in these two factors—Sun angle and daylength—throughout the year drive the seasonal effect of latitude on temperature.

Temperature patterns throughout the year for the four cities in **Figure 4.22** demonstrate the effects of latitudinal position. Note the range from near-constant warm temperatures at Salvador, Brazil, near the equator, to wide-ranging seasonal temperature variation at Barrow, Alaska, at 71° N latitude. From equator to poles, Earth ranges from continually warm, to seasonally variable, to continually cold.

Altitude and Elevation

From Chapter 3, remember that within the troposphere, temperatures decrease with increasing altitude above Earth's surface. (Recall from Figure 3.6 that the average lapse rate, or temperature decrease with altitude, is 6.4 C°/1000 m, or 3.5 F°/1000 ft.) The density of the atmosphere also diminishes with increasing altitude. In fact, the density of the atmosphere at an elevation of 5500 m (18,000 ft) is about half that at sea level. As the atmosphere thins, it contains less sensible heat. Thus, worldwide, mountainous areas experience lower temperatures than do regions nearer sea level, even at similar latitudes.

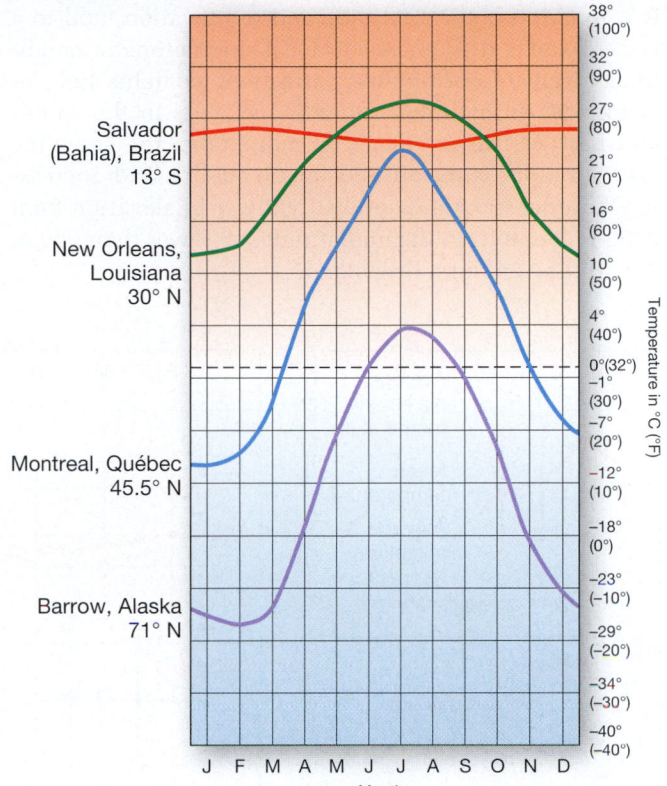

▲Figure 4.22 **Latitudinal effects on temperatures.** A comparison of five cities from near the equator to north of the Arctic Circle demonstrates changing seasonality and increasing differences between average minimum and maximum temperatures with increasing latitude. All cities have elevations near sea level.

Two terms, altitude and elevation, are commonly used to refer to heights on or above Earth's surface. *Altitude* refers to airborne objects or heights *above* Earth's surface. *Elevation* usually refers to the height of a point *on* Earth's surface above some plane of reference, such as elevation above sea level. Therefore, the height of a flying jet is expressed as altitude, whereas the height of a mountain ski resort is expressed as elevation.

In the thinner atmosphere at high elevations in mountainous regions or on high plateaus, surfaces lose energy rapidly to the atmosphere. The result is that average air temperatures are lower, nighttime cooling is greater, and the temperature range between day and night is greater than at low elevations.

The *snowline* seen on mountain slopes is the lower limit of permanent snow and indicates where winter snowfall exceeds the amount of snow lost through summer melting and evaporation. The snowline's location

GEOreport **4.2** The hottest temperature on Earth

The hottest temperature ever measured on Earth—a sweltering 57°C (134°F)—was recorded at Furnace Creek in Death Valley, California in 1913. The station where this temperature was recorded is one of the lowest on Earth, at −54.3 m, or −178 ft (the minus indicates meters or feet below sea level). One hundred years later on June 29, 2013, the official National Park Service thermometer in Death Valley reached 53.9°C (129°F)—a U.S. record for June, although 2.78 C° (5 F°) lower than 1913.

is a function both of latitude and of elevation, and to a lesser extent, it is related to local microclimatic conditions. Even at low latitudes, permanent ice fields and glaciers exist on mountain summits, such as in the Andes and East Africa. In equatorial mountains, the snowline occurs at approximately 5000 m (16,400 ft). With increasing latitude, snowlines gradually lower in elevation from 2700 m (8850 ft) in the midlatitudes to lower than 900 m (2950 ft) in southern Greenland.

The effects of latitude and elevation combine to create temperature characteristics at many locations. In Bolivia, two cities, both at about 16° S latitude, located less than 800 km (497 mi) apart, have quite different climates (**Figure 4.23**). Concepción is a low-elevation city at 490 m (1608 ft), with a warm, moist climate that is typical for many low-latitude locations with consistent Sun angle and daylength throughout the year. This city has an annual average temperature of 24°C (75°F).

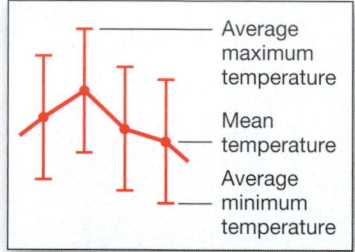

(a) Comparison of temperatures for two Bolivian cities.

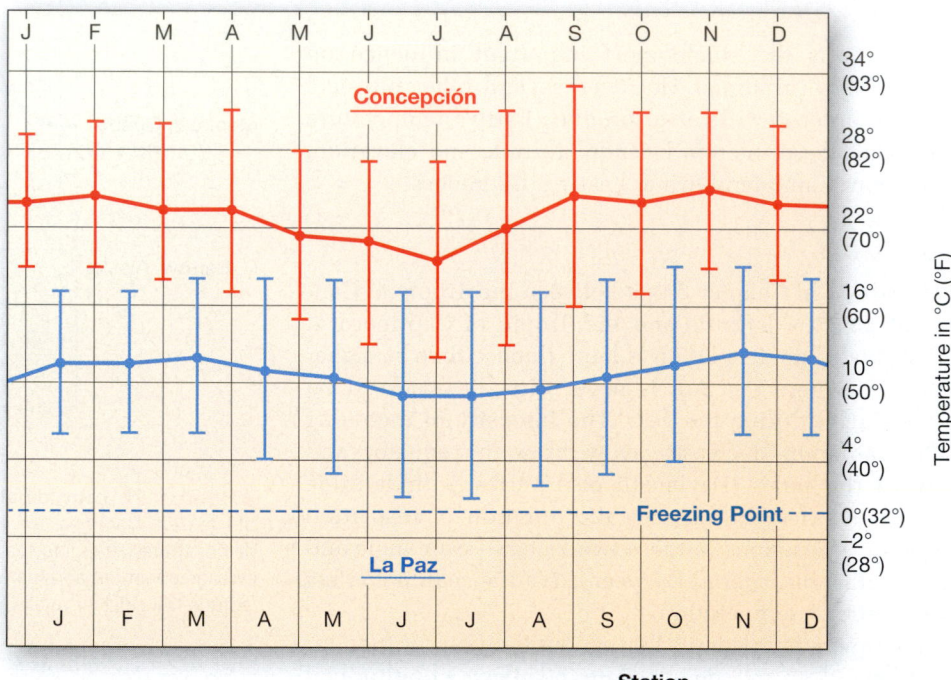

Station	Concepción, Bolivia	La Paz, Bolivia
Latitude/longitude	16° 15′ S 62° 03′ W	16° 30′ S 68° 10′ W
Elevation	**490 m (1608 ft)**	**4103 m (13,461 ft)**
Avg. ann. temperature	23°C (73.4°F)	11°C (51.8°F)
Ann. temperature range	6.5 C° (11.7 F°)	3.5 C° (6.3 F°)
Ann. precipitation	121.2 cm (47.7 in.)	55.5 cm (21.9 in.)
Population	10,000	810,300 (administrative division 1.6 million)

(b) Tropical dry forests cover the lower elevations of east-central Bolivia near Concepción; some forests have been cleared for farmland and ranching.

(c) High-elevation villages near La Paz are in view of permanent ice-covered peaks of the Bolivian Cordillera Real in the Andes Mountains.

▲**Figure 4.23** **Effects of latitude and elevation.** [(b) Design Pics/Alamy. (c) Seux Paule/AGE Fotostock America, Inc.]

La Paz, at an elevation of 4103 m (13,461 ft) above sea level, is situated on a high plateau with a cool, dry climate. La Paz has moderate annual temperatures, averaging about 11°C (51.8°F). Despite its high elevation, people living around La Paz are able to grow wheat, barley, and potatoes—crops characteristic of the midlatitudes—in the fertile highland soils. Compared to the harsh climates at similar elevations in the United States, such as the 4301-m (14,111-ft) summit of Pikes Peak at 38° N in Colorado or the 4392-m (14,410-ft) top of Mount Rainier at 46° N in Washington, La Paz has a mild and hospitable climate resulting from its low-latitude location.

Cloud Cover

At any given moment, approximately 50% of Earth is covered by clouds. We learned that clouds affect the Earth–atmosphere energy balance by reflecting and absorbing radiation and that their effects vary with cloud type, height, and density.

The presence of cloud cover at night has a moderating effect on temperature; you may have experienced the relatively colder temperatures outside on a clear night versus a cloudy night, especially before dawn, the coldest time of the day. At night, clouds act as an insulating layer that reradiates longwave energy back to Earth, preventing rapid energy loss to space. Thus, in general, the presence of clouds raises minimum nighttime temperatures. During the day, clouds reflect insolation, lowering daily maximum temperatures; this is the familiar shading effect you feel when clouds move in on a hot summer day. Clouds also reduce seasonal temperature differences as a result of these moderating effects.

Land–Water Heating Differences

An important control over temperature is the difference in the ways land and water surfaces respond to insolation. Land and water absorb and store energy differently, with the result that water bodies tend to have more-moderate temperature patterns, whereas continental interiors have more temperature extremes.

The physical differences between land (rock and soil) and water (oceans, seas, and lakes) are the reasons for **land–water heating differences**, the most basic of which is that land heats and cools faster than water. **Figure 4.24** summarizes these differences, which relate to the principles and processes of evaporation, transparency, specific heat, and movement. We include ocean currents and sea-surface temperatures in this section because of their effects on temperatures in coastal locations.

CONTINENTAL
Temperature conditions more extreme—land warms and cools rapidly

Insolation

Less evaporation

Surface is **opaque**

Land has a **lower specific heat**

Land has **no mixing** between layers

Land

MARINE
Temperature conditions more moderate—water warms and cools slowly

Insolation

More evaporaton

Surface is **transparent**

Water has a **higher specific heat**

Water has **mobility** and mixes in vast ocean currents

Ocean

◄**Figure 4.24 Land–water heating differences.** The differential heating of land and water produces contrasting marine (more moderate) and continental (more extreme) temperature regimes.

GEOreport **4.3** Alaska and Montana hold U.S. records for low temperatures

The lowest temperature ever recorded in the United States is –62°C (–80°F), which occurred on January 23, 1971, at Prospect Creek, Alaska, a small settlement located about 290 km (180 mi) northwest of Fairbanks at an elevation of 335 m (1100 ft). In the contiguous United States (the "lower 48"), a record cold temperature of –57°C (–70°F) occurred at Rogers Pass, Montana, on January 20, 1954, at an elevation of 1667 m (5470 ft).

Evaporation As discussed earlier, the process of *evaporation* dissipates significant amounts of the energy arriving at the ocean's surface, much more than over land surfaces where less water is available. An estimated 84% of all evaporation on Earth is from the oceans. When water evaporates, it changes from liquid to vapor, absorbing heat energy in the process and storing it as latent heat.

As surface water evaporates, it absorbs energy from the immediate environment; this cooling process results in a lowering of temperatures. (Remember that the water and vapor remain the same temperature throughout the process; the vapor stores the absorbed energy as latent heat.) Land temperatures are affected less by evaporative cooling than are temperatures over water.

Transparency Soil and water differ in their transmission of light: Solid ground is opaque; water is transparent. This difference affects the distribution of heat energy within land surfaces and water bodies.

Light striking a soil surface does not pass through, but is absorbed, heating the ground surface. That energy is accumulated during times of sunlight exposure and is rapidly lost at night or when shaded. Maximum and minimum daily temperatures for soil surfaces generally occur at the ground surface level. Below the surface, even at shallow depths, temperatures remain about the same throughout the day. You encounter this at a beach, where surface sand may be painfully hot to your feet, but as you dig in your toes and feel the sand a few centimeters below the surface, it is cooler, offering relief.

In contrast, when light reaches a body of water, it penetrates the surface because of water's **transparency**—water is clear, and light passes through it to an average depth of 60 m (200 ft) in the ocean. This illuminated zone occurs in some ocean waters to depths of 300 m (1000 ft). The transparency of water results in the distribution of available heat energy over a much greater depth and volume, forming a larger reservoir of energy storage than that which occurs on land.

Specific Heat The energy needed to increase the temperature of water is greater than for an equal volume of land. Overall, water can hold more heat than can soil or rock. The heat capacity of a substance is **specific heat**. On average, the specific heat of water is about four times that of soil. Therefore, a given volume of water represents a more substantial energy reservoir than does the same volume of soil or rock and consequently heats and cools more slowly. For

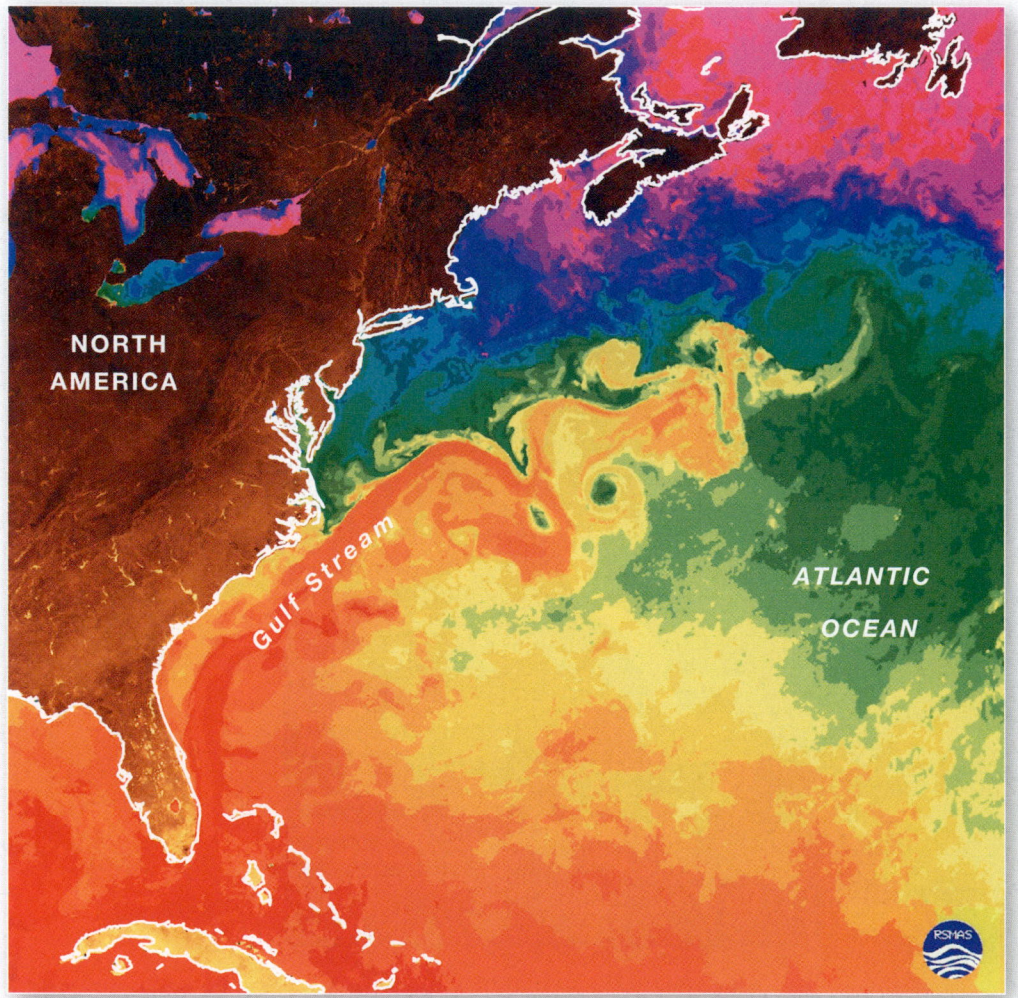

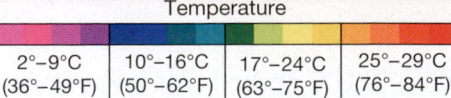

Temperature

| 2°–9°C (36°–49°F) | 10°–16°C (50°–62°F) | 17°–24°C (63°–75°F) | 25°–29°C (76°–84°F) |

▲**Figure 4.25 The Gulf Stream.** This thermal infrared image shows ocean temperatures in the Atlantic Ocean near the Gulf Stream. [Imagery by RSMAS, University of Miami.]

Animation (MG)
Gulf Stream

https://goo.gl/88N4Ml

this reason, day-to-day temperatures near large water bodies tend to be moderated rather than having large extremes.

Movement In contrast to solid land, water is fluid and capable of movement. The movement of currents results in a mixing of cooler and warmer waters, and that mixing spreads the available energy over an even greater volume than if the water was still. Surface water and deeper waters mix, redistributing energy in a vertical direction as well.

Ocean Currents and Sea-Surface Temperatures Ocean currents affect land temperatures in different ways, depending on whether the currents are warm or cold. Cool ocean currents flowing from higher latitudes toward the equator moderate summer air temperatures on land. For example, the cold Humboldt Current flowing offshore from Lima, Peru, at 12° S latitude moderates the tropical summer heat so that this city has a cooler climate than might be expected at that latitude.

The warm current known as the **Gulf Stream** moves northward off the east coast of North America, carrying warm water far into the North Atlantic (**Figure 4.25**). As a result, the southern third of Iceland experiences much milder winter temperatures than would be expected for a latitude of 65° N, just south of the Arctic Circle. In Reykjavík, on the southwestern coast of Iceland, monthly temperatures average above freezing during all months of the year. The Gulf Stream also moderates temperatures in coastal Scandinavia and northwestern Europe. In the western Pacific Ocean, the warm Kuroshio, or Japan Current, functions much the same as the Gulf Stream, having a warming effect on temperatures in Japan, in the Aleutian Islands, and along the northwestern margin of North America.

Ocean temperatures are typically measured at the surface and recorded as the *sea-surface temperature*, or SST. The maps of global average SSTs measured from satellites in **Figure 4.26** reveal that the region with the highest average ocean temperatures is the *Western Pacific Warm Pool* in the Pacific Ocean, where temperatures are often above 30°C (86°F). Although the difference in SSTs between the equator and the poles is apparent on both maps, note the seasonal changes in ocean temperatures, such as the northward shifting of the Western Pacific Warm Pool in July. The temperature effects of these currents are most clearly visible on the July map, where cool water extends into tropical latitudes along the west coasts of Africa and South America. Following the same recent trends as global air temperatures, average annual SSTs increased steadily since the 1970s and are now at record-high levels.

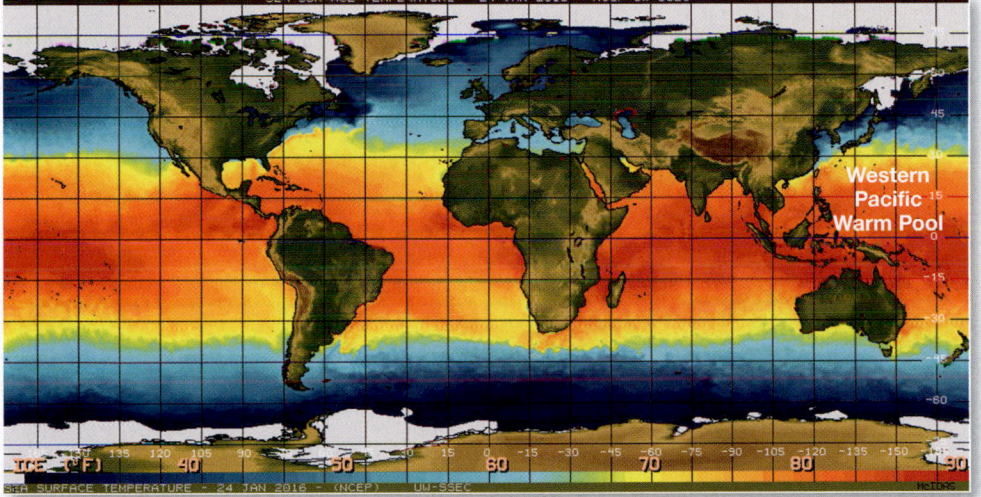

(a) January 24, 2016

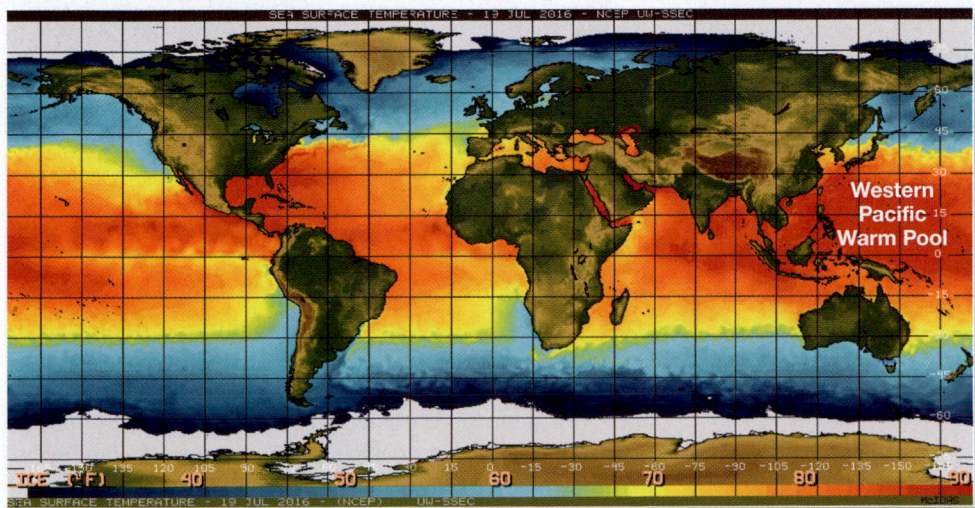

(b) July 19, 2016

▲**Figure 4.26 Average monthly sea-surface temperatures for January and July.** Red and orange indicate the warmest temperatures (greater than about 27°C (80°F). Darker blues indicate the coolest temperatures (less than about 4°C (40°F). [Satellite data courtesy of Space Science and Engineering Center, University of Wisconsin, Madison.]

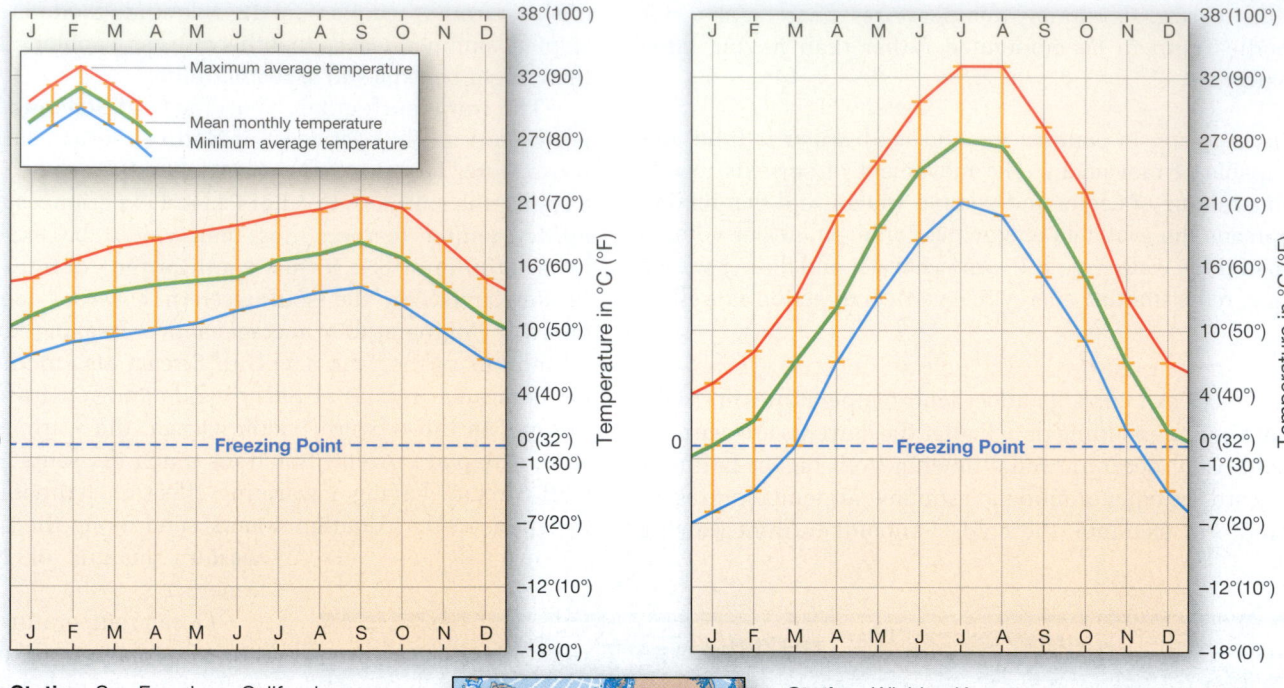

Station: San Francisco, California
Lat/long: 37° 46′ N 122° 23′ W
Avg. ann. temp.: 14.6°C (58.3°F)
Total ann. precip.:
    56.6 cm (22.3 in.)
Elevation: 5 m (16.4 ft)
Population: 777,000
Ann. temp. range:
    11.4 C° (20.5 F°)

Station: Wichita, Kansas
Lat/long: 37° 39′ N 97° 25′ W
Avg. ann. temp.: 13.7°C (56.6°F)
Total ann. precip.:
    72.2 cm (28.4 in.)
Elevation: 402.6 m (1321 ft)
Population: 327,000
Ann. temp. range:
    27 C° (48.6 F°)

▲**Figure 4.27 Marine and continental cities—United States.** Compare temperatures in coastal San Francisco, California, with those of continental Wichita, Kansas. [kropic1/Shutterstock; RGB Ventures/SuperStock/Alamy.]

WORK**IT**OUT 4.1
Coastal and Inland Temperatures

Using the map, graphs, and other data in Figures 4.27 and 4.28, complete the following:

1. Using the graphs in Figure 4.27, determine the lowest minimum average monthly temperatures for San Francisco and Wichita. Explain the difference between the two temperatures.
2. Why does San Francisco's average monthly temperature peak occur later in the summer than that of Wichita?
3. Determine the annual temperature ranges for Verkhoyansk and Wichita. Which location has the larger temperature range, and why?

Examples of Marine and Continental Temperature Differences Land–water heating differences result in temperature differences between marine and continental locations on Earth. The moderating influence of the ocean on climate, known as the *marine effect*, occurs along coastlines or on islands. The *continental effect*, or condition of *continentality*, refers to the greater range between maximum and minimum temperatures on both a daily and a yearly basis that occurs in areas that are inland from the ocean or distant from other large water bodies.

The monthly temperatures of San Francisco, California, and Wichita, Kansas, both at approximately 37° N latitude, illustrate these effects (**Figure 4.27**). In San

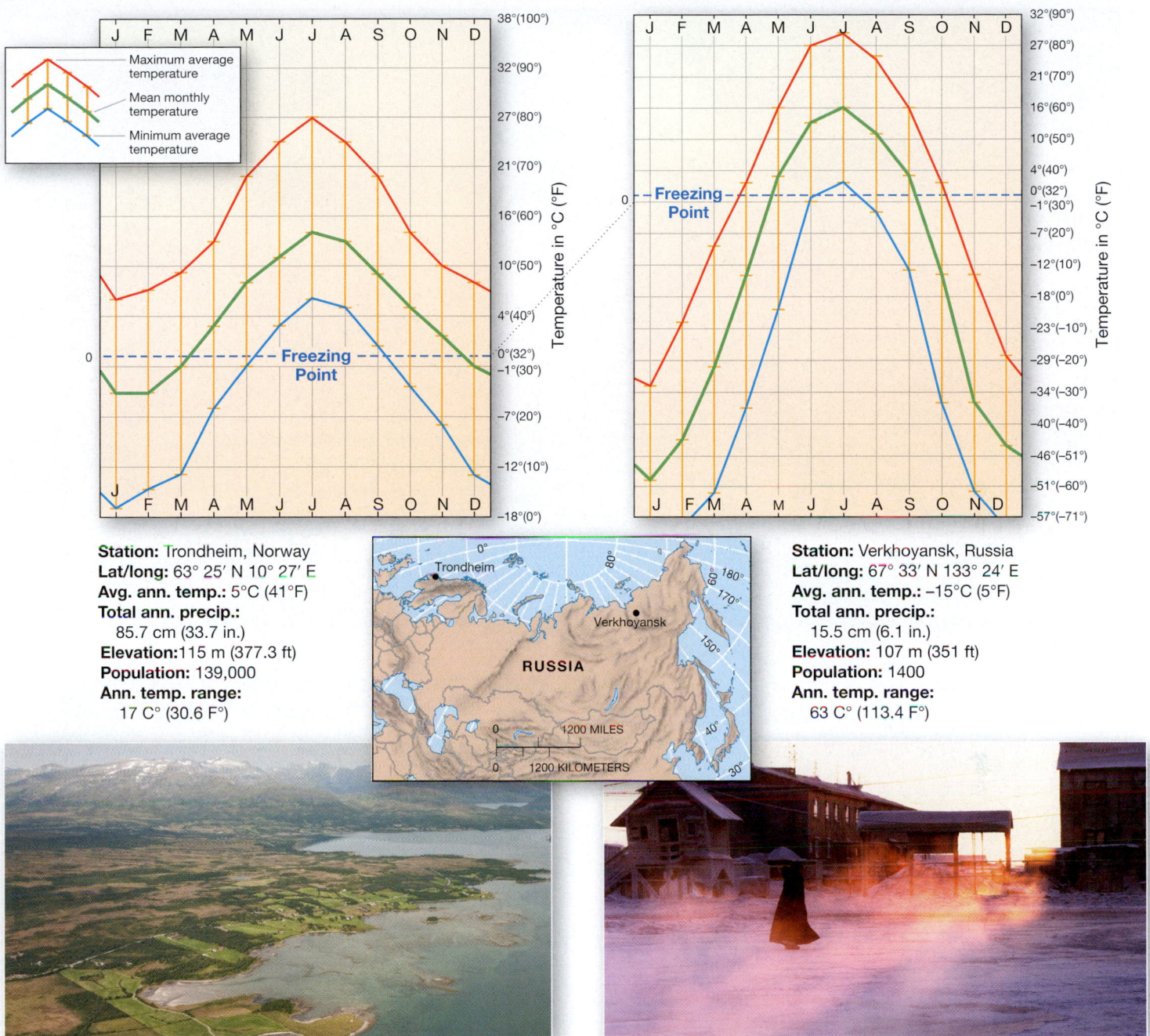

▲**Figure 4.28 Marine and continental cities—Eurasia.** Compare temperatures in coastal Trondheim, Norway, with continental Verkhoyansk, Russia. Note that the freezing levels on the two graphs are positioned differently to accommodate the contrasting data. [Bobbé Christopherson; Martin Hartley/Image Bank/Getty Images.]

Francisco, only a few days a year have summer maximums that exceed 32.2°C (90°F). Winter minimums rarely drop below freezing. In contrast, Wichita, Kansas, is susceptible to freezing temperatures from late October to mid-April—the record low temperature is −30°C (−22°F). Wichita's temperature reaches 32.2°C (90°F) or higher more than 65 days each year, with 46°C (114°F) as a record high. During the summer of 2012, temperatures exceeded 38°C (100°F) for a record 53 nonconsecutive days.

In Eurasia, similar trends exist for cities (at similar latitudes and elevations) in marine versus continental locations (**Figure 4.28**). The coastal location of Trondheim, Norway, moderates its annual temperature regime. The lowest minimum and highest maximum temperatures ever recorded in Trondheim are −30°C and +35°C (−22°F and +95°F). In contrast, Verkhoyansk, Russia, with a population of 1400, has a continental location. Temperature extremes reflect continental effects: Verkhoyansk recorded a record minimum temperature of −68°C (−90°F) in January and a record maximum temperature of +37°C (+98°F) in July—an incredible 105 C° (189 F°) minimum–maximum range for the record temperature extremes!

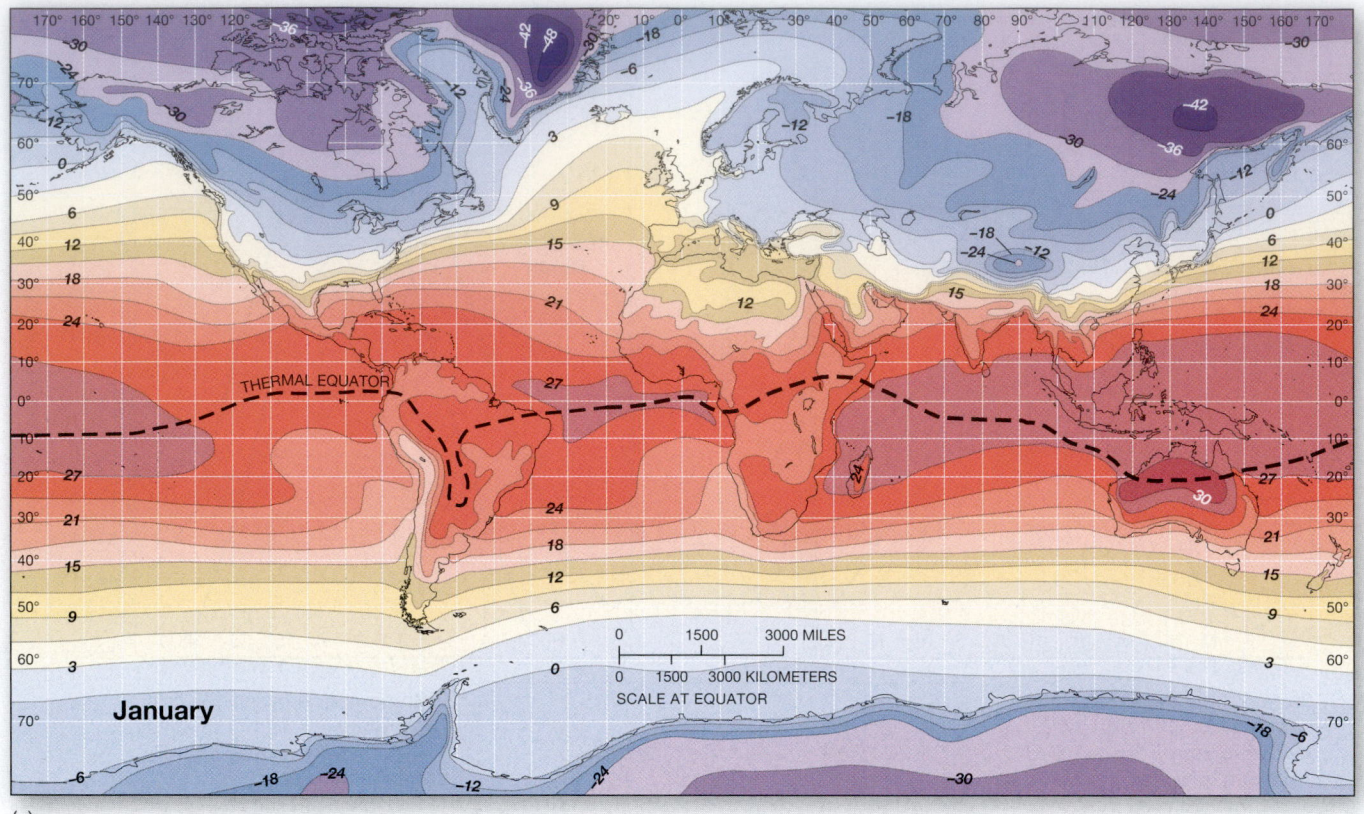

(a)

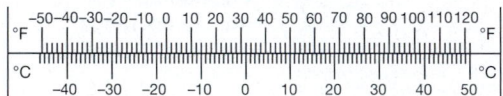

▲**Figure 4.29 Global average temperatures for January.**
(a) Temperatures are in Celsius (convertible to Fahrenheit by means of
the scale) as taken from separate air temperature databases for ocean
and land. (b) Note the equatorward-trending isotherms in the interior
of North America. [Adapted by author and redrawn from National Climatic
Data Center, *Monthly Climatic Data for the World*, 47 (January 1994), and WMO
and NOAA.]

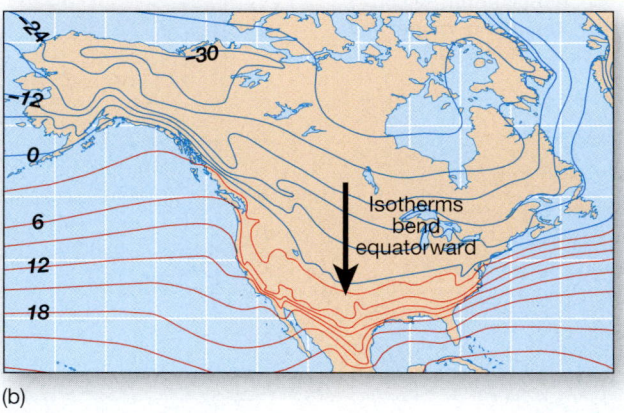

(b)

Earth's Temperature Patterns

Figures 4.29 through 4.32 are a series of maps to help us
visualize Earth's temperature patterns: global mean temperatures for January and July, global annual temperature
ranges (differences between the averages of the coolest
and warmest months), and polar region mean temperatures for January and July. Maps are for January and July
instead of the solstice months of December and June because of the lag that occurs between insolation received
and maximum or minimum temperatures experienced.

The lines on temperature maps are known as *isotherms*. An **isotherm** is an isoline—a line along which
there is a constant value—that connects points of equal
temperature to portray the temperature pattern, just as a

contour line on a topographic map illustrates points of
equal elevation. Isotherms are useful for the spatial analysis of temperatures.

Global January and July Temperature Comparison

In January, high Sun altitudes and longer days in the
Southern Hemisphere cause summer weather conditions;
lower Sun altitudes and shorter days in the Northern Hemisphere are associated with winter. Isotherms on the January average-temperature map mark the general decrease in
insolation and net radiation with distance from the equator (Figure 4.29). Isotherms generally trend east–west, and
are parallel to the equator, except where large landmasses
cause the isotherms to bend. This bending results from the
differential heating of land and water discussed earlier.

The **thermal equator** is a line around Earth connecting all points of highest mean temperature, roughly 27°C (80°F); it trends southward into the interior of South America and Africa, indicating higher temperatures over the interiors of landmasses. In the Northern Hemisphere, isotherms shift toward the equator as cold air chills the continental interiors. More moderate temperatures occur over oceans, with warmer conditions extending farther north than over land at comparable latitudes.

To see the temperature differences over land and water, follow along 50° N latitude (the 50th parallel) in Figure 4.29 and compare isotherms: 3°C to 6°C in the North Pacific and 3°C to 9°C in the North Atlantic, as contrasted with −18°C in the interior of North America and −24°C to −30°C in central Asia. Also, note the orientation of isotherms over areas with mountain ranges and how they illustrate the cooling effects of elevation— check the South American Andes as an example.

For a continental region other than Antarctica, Russia—and specifically, northeastern Siberia—is the coldest area (look back to Figure 4.28). The intense cold results from winter conditions of consistently clear, dry, calm air; small insolation input; and an inland location far from moderating maritime effects. Prevailing global winds prevent moderating effects from the Pacific Ocean to the east.

In July, the longer days of summer and higher Sun altitude are in the Northern Hemisphere (**Figure 4.30**). Winter dominates the Southern Hemisphere, although it is milder than winters north of the equator because continental landmasses, with their greater temperature ranges, are smaller. The thermal equator shifts northward with the high summer Sun and reaches the Persian Gulf–Pakistan–Iran area. The Persian Gulf is the site of the highest recorded sea-surface temperature—an astounding 36°C (96°F).

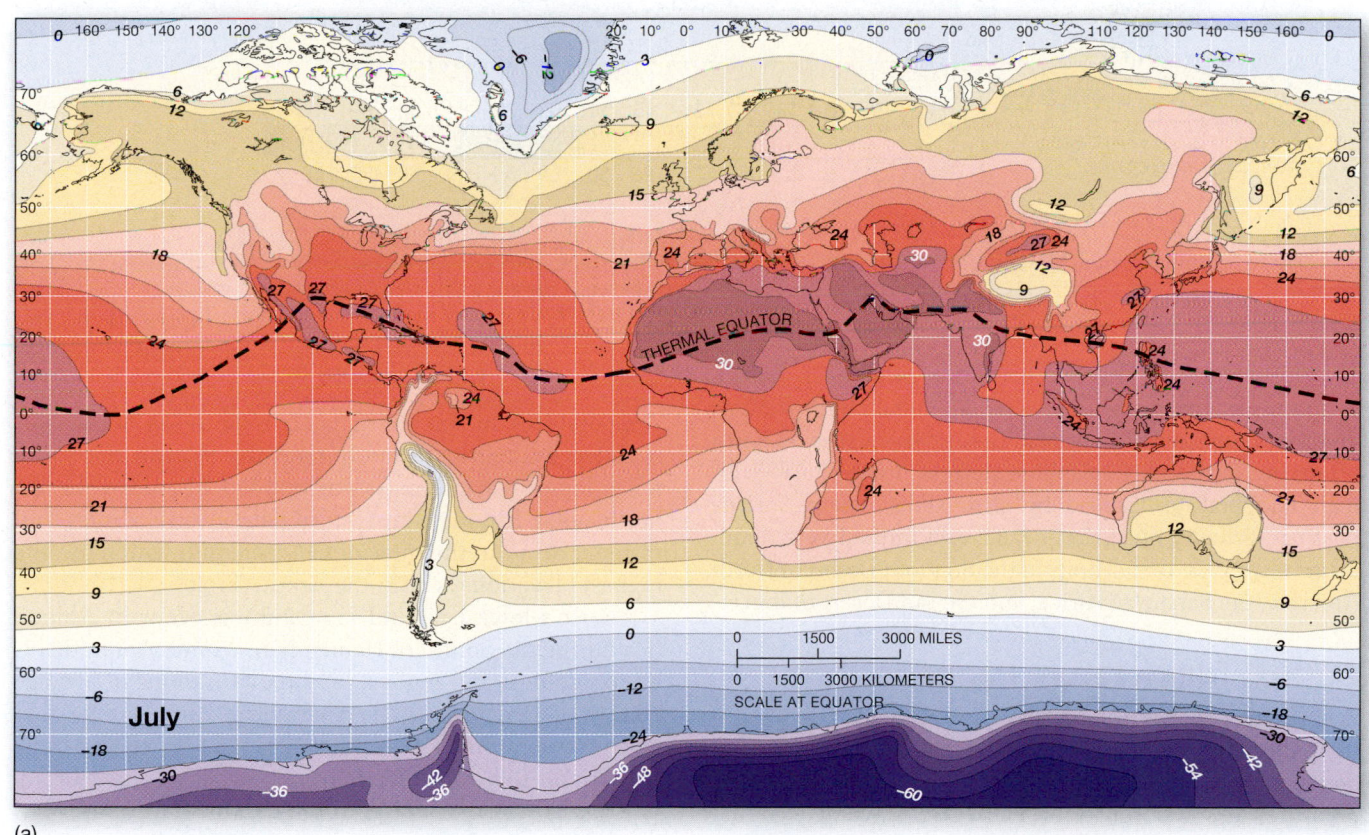

(a)

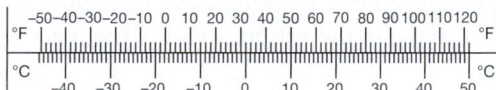

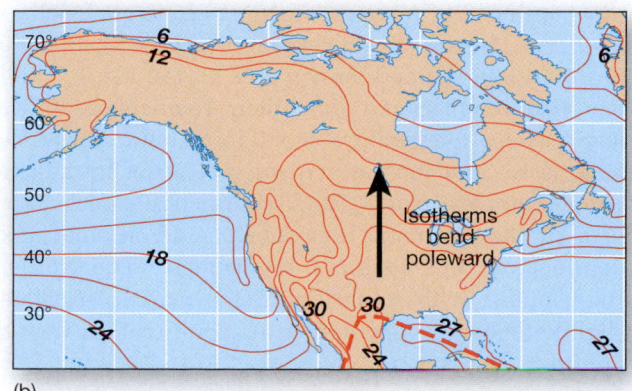

(b)

▲**Figure 4.30 Global average temperatures for July.** (a) Temperatures are in Celsius (convertible to Fahrenheit by means of the scale) as taken from separate air temperature databases for ocean and land. (b) Note the poleward-trending isotherms in the interior of North America. [Adapted by author and redrawn from National Climatic Data Center, *Monthly Climatic Data for the World,* 47 (July 1994), and WMO and NOAA.]

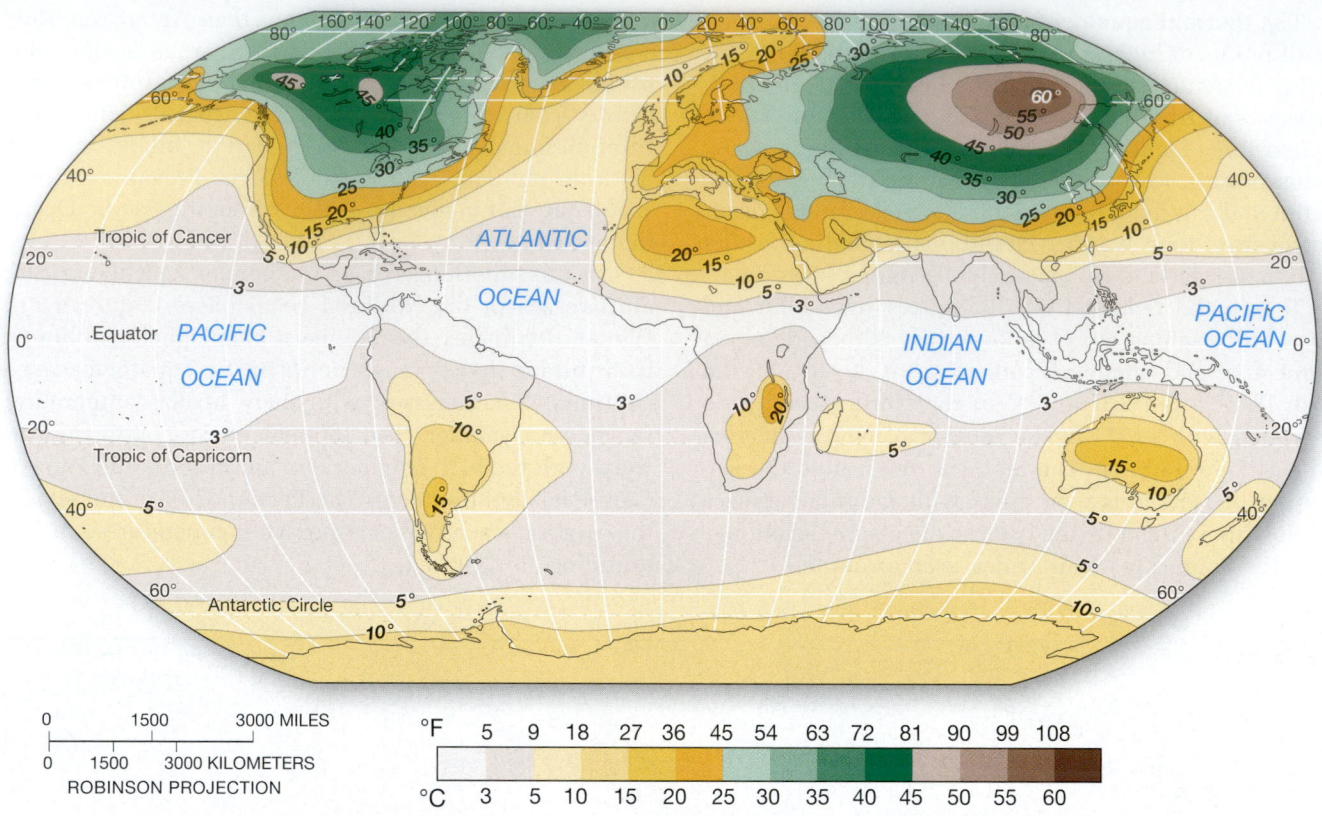

▲**Figure 4.31 Global annual temperature ranges.** The annual ranges of global temperatures in Celsius degrees, C°, with conversions to Fahrenheit degrees, F°, shown on scale. The mapped data show the difference between average January and July temperature maps.

During July in the Northern Hemisphere, isotherms shift toward the poles over land as higher temperatures dominate continental interiors. The hottest places on Earth occur in Northern Hemisphere deserts during July, with high temperatures caused by clear skies, strong surface heating, virtually no surface water, and limited vegetation. Prime examples are portions of the Sonoran Desert of North America, the Sahara of Africa, and the Lut Desert in Iran.

Annual Temperature Range

Temperature patterns are also indicated by the annual temperature range for a location—that is, the difference between the highest and lowest average annual temperatures for that location. The largest average annual temperature ranges occur at subpolar locations within the continental interiors of North America and Asia (**Figure 4.31**), where average ranges of 64 C° (115 F°) are recorded (see the dark brown area on the map). Smaller temperature ranges in the Southern Hemisphere indicate less seasonal temperature variation owing to fewer large landmasses and the vast expanses of water to moderate temperature extremes. Thus, continental effects dominate in the Northern Hemisphere, and marine effects dominate in the Southern Hemisphere. The Northern Hemisphere, with greater land area overall, registers a slightly higher average surface temperature than does the Southern Hemisphere.

Polar Region Temperatures

Temperatures in the north polar region—an ocean surrounded by land—are more moderate than in the south polar region—a landmass surrounded by ocean. In the north polar region, temperature extremes in winter and summer occur in the interior of Greenland, which has the highest elevations within the Arctic Circle.

Earth's lowest natural temperatures occur in Antarctica during the Southern Hemisphere winter. Antarctica is Earth's coldest and highest landmass (in terms of average elevation). Even during the Antarctic summer, January average temperatures range from −3°C (26.6°F) on the coast to −28°C (−18.4°F) at the South Pole (elevation 2835 m, or 9301 ft). Vostok Station in the continental interior has the coldest reported temperatures on Earth (**Figure 4.32**). Focus Study 4.2 examines some of the hazards of working or living in the extreme cold of the polar regions.

Cold Snaps and Heat Waves

Especially in the midlatitudes, regional patterns of pressure and winds can sometimes cause prolonged periods of unusually cold or warm temperatures. The term *cold snap*, or *cold wave*, as used by the news media, refers to a period of cold weather. More specifically, the U.S. National Weather Service defines a cold wave as a rapid fall in temperature during a 24-hour period that requires

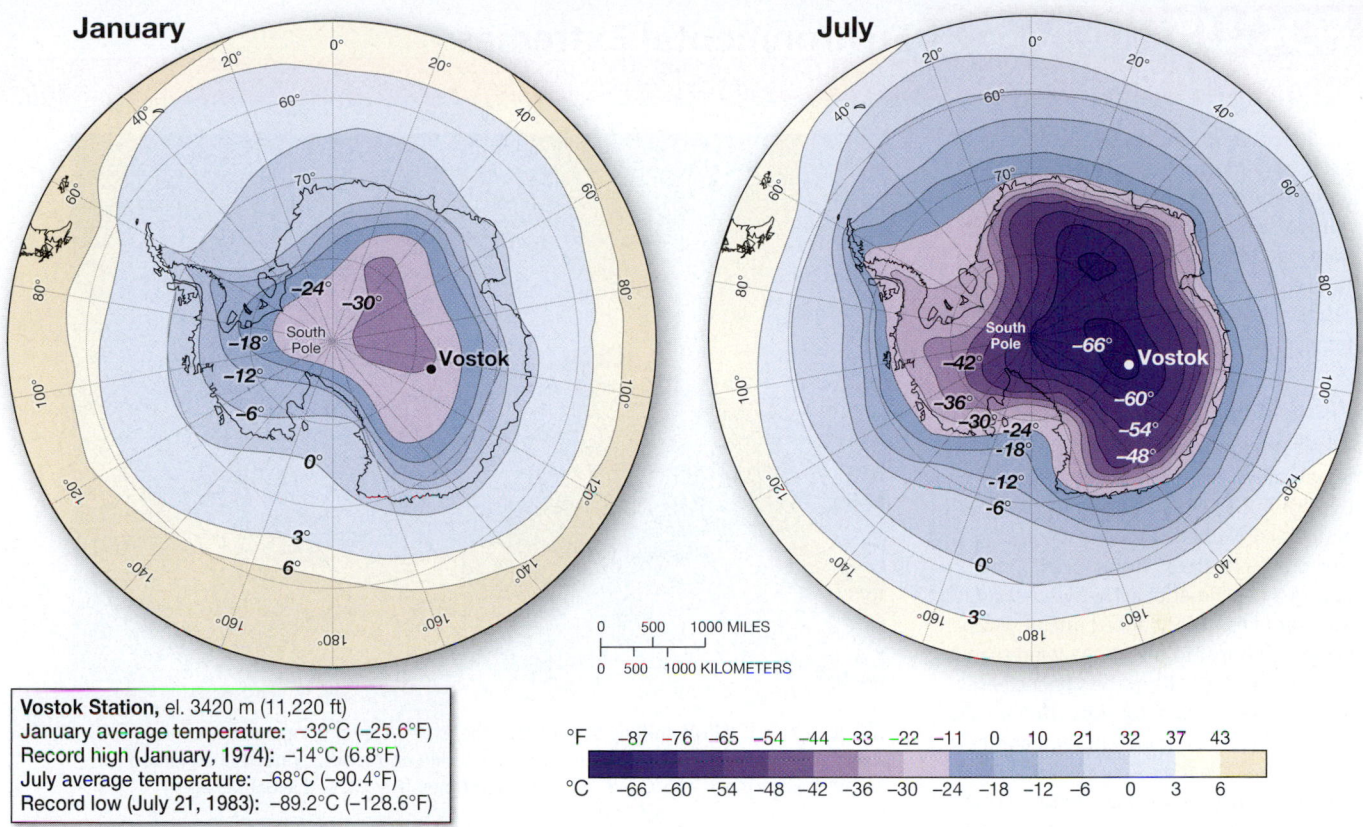

January

July

Vostok Station, el. 3420 m (11,220 ft)
January average temperature: −32°C (−25.6°F)
Record high (January, 1974): −14°C (6.8°F)
July average temperature: −68°C (−90.4°F)
Record low (July 21, 1983): −89.2°C (−128.6°F)

°F	−87	−76	−65	−54	−44	−33	−22	−11	0	10	21	32	37	43
°C	−66	−60	−54	−48	−42	−36	−30	−24	−18	−12	−6	0	3	6

▲**Figure 4.32 January and July average temperatures in the south polar region.** Note the average and record January and July temperatures at the Vostok station. [Map prepared by Robert Christopherson, using same sources as Figure 4.29.]

increased protection for agriculture, industry, commerce, and human activities. The minimum temperature criterion for a cold wave depends on time of year and location. Cold waves can damage crops, kill livestock, and cause human fatalities. For example, a February 2012 cold snap in eastern Europe with temperature below −35°C (−31°F) killed almost 600 people.

A **heat wave** is a prolonged period of abnormally high temperatures, often in association with humid weather. Heat waves can be deadly in midlatitude regions, where extremes of temperature and humidity lasting days or weeks can accompany unmoving, stable weather systems during the warmer months. As discussed in Focus Study 4.2, when humidity is high, the effects of hot temperatures are amplified, and can be fatal. Heat waves in developing countries are often worsened by electricity outages that prevent the use of air conditioners and fans, as well as water shortages that add dehydration to the list of human health effects. The following are some heat wave characteristics and examples:

- Heat waves can cause high numbers of human casualties. In Europe during the summer of 2003, when temperatures topped 40°C (104°F) in June, July, and

August, over 70,000 people died in numerous western European countries, with the highest number in France.

- Heat waves are often associated with increased wildfires. The 2010 Russian summer heat wave brought persistent high temperatures throughout eastern Europe, causing an estimated 55,000 heat-related deaths, massive crop losses, over 1 million hectares (2.5 million acres) of land burned by wildfires, and an overall estimated economic cost of US$15 billion (**Figure 4.33**).

▲**Figure 4.33 Wildfires in Russia, summer 2010.** American tourists in Moscow wear face masks to filter smoke from nearby forest fires as temperatures top 38°C (100°F). [Pavel Golovkin/AP.]

FOCUSstudy 4.2 Environmental Extremes
Human Responses to Wind Chill and Heat Stress

The human body senses temperature and reacts to temperature changes. *Apparent temperature* is the general term for the outdoor temperature as it is perceived by humans. Under extremes of air temperature, either cold or hot, the human body reacts in various ways to maintain its core temperature.

Wind Chill

When strong winds combine with cold temperature, the effects can be deadly (**Figure 4.2.1**). On a cold, windy day, the air feels colder because wind increases evaporative heat loss from our skin, producing a cooling effect. The *wind-chill factor* quantifies the enhanced rate at which body heat is lost to the air. As wind speeds increase, heat loss from the skin increases, and the wind-chill factor rises. To track the effects of wind on apparent temperature, the National Weather Service (NWS) uses the *Wind-Chill Temperature Index*, a chart plotting the temperature we feel as a function of actual air temperature and wind speed (**Figure 4.2.2**). The chart provides a simple, accurate tool for assessing the dangers to humans from winter winds and freezing temperatures.

▲Figure 4.2.1 **Wind chill in Antarctica.** The extreme cold temperatures of the polar regions pose serious challenges for human life and work. Wind-chill conditions in Antarctica can reach –46°C (–51°F) even in summer. [Gordon Wiltsie/Getty Images.]

The lower wind-chill values on the chart present a serious freezing hazard, called *frostbite*, to exposed flesh. Another danger is *hypothermia*, a condition of abnormally low body temperature that occurs when the human body is losing heat faster than it can be produced. Even without wind, frostbite and hypothermia are potential dangers in the extreme cold. Moreover, hypothermia can arise in any situation where humans become chilled; it is not exclusively related to freezing temperatures.

The Wind-Chill Temperature Index does not account for sunlight intensity, a person's physical activity, or the use of protective clothing, all of which mitigate wind-chill intensity. Imagine living in some of the coldest regions of the world. To what degree would you need to adjust your personal wardrobe?

Actual Air Temperature in °C (°F)

Calm	4°(40°)	–1°(30°)	–7°(20°)	–12°(10°)	–18°(0°)	–23°(–10°)	–29°(–20°)	–34°(–30°)	–40°(–40°)
8 (5)	2°(36°)	–4°(25°)	–11°(13°)	–17°(1°)	–24°(–11°)	–30°(–22°)	–37°(–34°)	–43°(–46°)	–49°(–57°)
16 (10)	1°(34°)	–6°(21°)	–13°(9°)	–20°(–4°)	–27°(–16°)	–33°(–28°)	–41°(–41°)	–47°(–53°)	–54°(–66°)
24 (15)	0°(32°)	–7°(19°)	–14°(6°)	–22°(–7°)	–28°(–19°)	–36°(–32°)	–43°(–45°)	–50°(–58°)	–57°(–71°)
32 (20)	–1°(30°)	–8°(17°)	–16°(4°)	–23°(–9°)	–30°(–22°)	–37°(–35°)	–44°(–48°)	–52°(–61°)	–59°(–74°)
40 (25)	–2°(29°)	–9°(16°)	–16°(3°)	–24°(–11°)	–31°(–24°)	–38°(–37°)	–46°(–51°)	–53°(–64°)	–61°(–78°)
48 (30)	–2°(28°)	–9°(15°)	–17°(–1°)	–24°(–12°)	–32°(–26°)	–39°(–39°)	–47°(–53°)	–55°(–67°)	–62°(–80°)
56 (35)	–2°(28°)	–10°(14°)	–18°(0°)	–26°(–14°)	–33°(–27°)	–41°(–41°)	–48°(–55°)	–56°(–69°)	–63°(–82°)
64 (40)	–3°(27°)	–11°(13°)	–18°(–1°)	–26°(–15°)	–34°(–29°)	–42°(–43°)	–49°(–57°)	–57°(–71°)	–64°(–84°)
72 (45)	–3°(26°)	–11°(12°)	–19°(–2°)	–27°(–16°)	–34°(–30°)	–42°(–44°)	–50°(–58°)	–58°(–72°)	–66°(–86°)
80 (50)	–3°(26°)	–11°(12°)	–19°(–3°)	–27°(–17°)	–35°(–31°)	–43°(–45°)	–51°(–60°)	–59°(–74°)	–67°(–88°)

Wind speed, kmph (mph)

Frostbite times: ☐ 30 min. ☐ 10 min. ☐ 5 min.

◄Figure 4.2.2 **The Wind-Chill Temperature Index.** This index uses wind speed and actual air temperature to determine apparent temperature and was developed by the NWS (http://www.nws.noaa.gov/os/windchill/) and the Meteorological Service of Canada.

Heat Stress

At the other extreme, hot temperatures—especially when combined with high humidity—also stress the human body. Through several complex mechanisms, the human body maintains an average internal temperature ranging within a degree of 36.8°C (98.2°F), although variations occur with exercise, time of day, and method of measurement. Perspiration is the body's first response for maintaining this core temperature under hot conditions.

Humidity is the presence of water vapor in the air and is commonly expressed as relative humidity (see the full discussion in Chapter 6); the higher the amount of water vapor, the higher the humidity. When humidity is high, perspiration evaporates at a slower rate and is not as effective a cooling mechanism as in dry environments.

When exposed to extreme heat and humidity, the human body is at risk of heat-related illness, or *heat stress*. Heat stress in humans takes such forms as heat cramps, heat exhaustion, and heat stroke, which is a life-threatening condition. A person with heat stroke has overheated to the point where the body is unable to cool itself—at this point, internal temperature may have risen to as high as 41°C (106°F), and the sweating mechanism has ceased to function.

The *Heat Index* uses values for temperature and relative humidity to indicate how the air feels to an average person—its apparent temperature—and gauge the human body's probable reaction (**Figure 4.2.3**). During appropriate months, the NWS reports the Heat Index in its daily weather summaries. For example, on a day when the temperature reaches 37.8°C (100°F) and relative humidity is 50%, the Heat Index is 48°C (118°F), in the "danger" zone where heat stress is probable with prolonged exposure or strenuous activity.

APPLYconcepts

Use the Wind-Chill Temperature Index chart in Figure 4.2.2 to analyze these scenarios.
a. If the air temperature is –23°C (–10°F) and the wind is blowing at 32 kmph (20 mph), what is the wind-chill temperature for exposed human skin?
b. Is frostbite a potential danger in this scenario? If so, then what is the estimated time frame within which frostbite might occur?
c. If the temperature remains the same, but the winds pick up to 48 kmph (30 mph), how does the wind chill index change?
d. Has the danger of frostbite changed under these new conditions?

Use the Heat Index chart in Figure 4.2.3 to answer these questions.
a. On a day when the temperature reaches 37.8°C (100°F) and relative humidity is 50%, what is the apparent temperature?
b. If the relative humidity is 80%, above what temperature do humans enter the "danger" zone where heat stroke is probable with strenuous exercise?

How does high humidity increase the risk of heat stress? Explain.

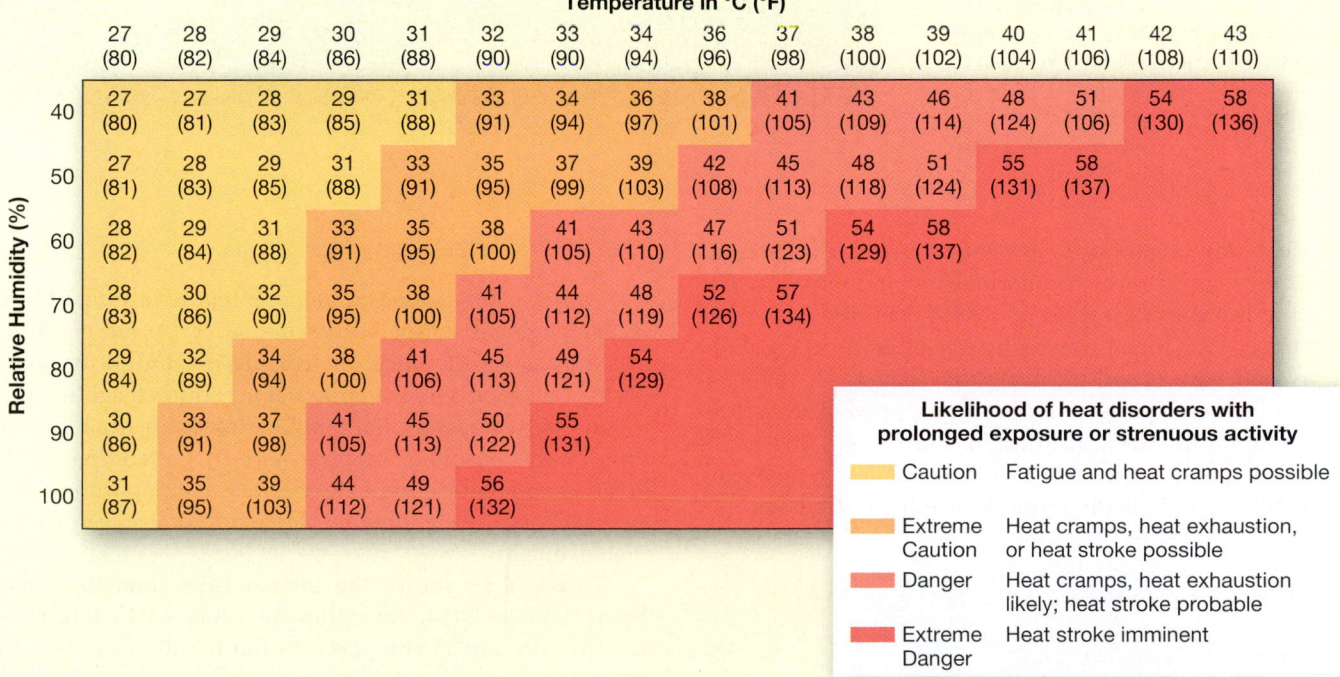

▲**Figure 4.2.3 The Heat Index.** This index uses relative humidity and actual air temperature to determine apparent temperature. For more information, see http://www.nws.noaa.gov/om/heat/index.shtml.

gases and present evidence for climate change in Chapter 10.) Thus, human actions are enhancing Earth's natural greenhouse effect, causing the "global warming" phenomenon that is related to complex changes now occurring in the lower atmosphere.

Humans are also affecting Earth's energy balance on a local scale in city environments. Characteristics of urban areas have caused temperatures to be higher in cities than in surrounding rural areas, a result of pollutants, urban surfaces, lack of plant cover, and output heat from homes, vehicles, and industry.

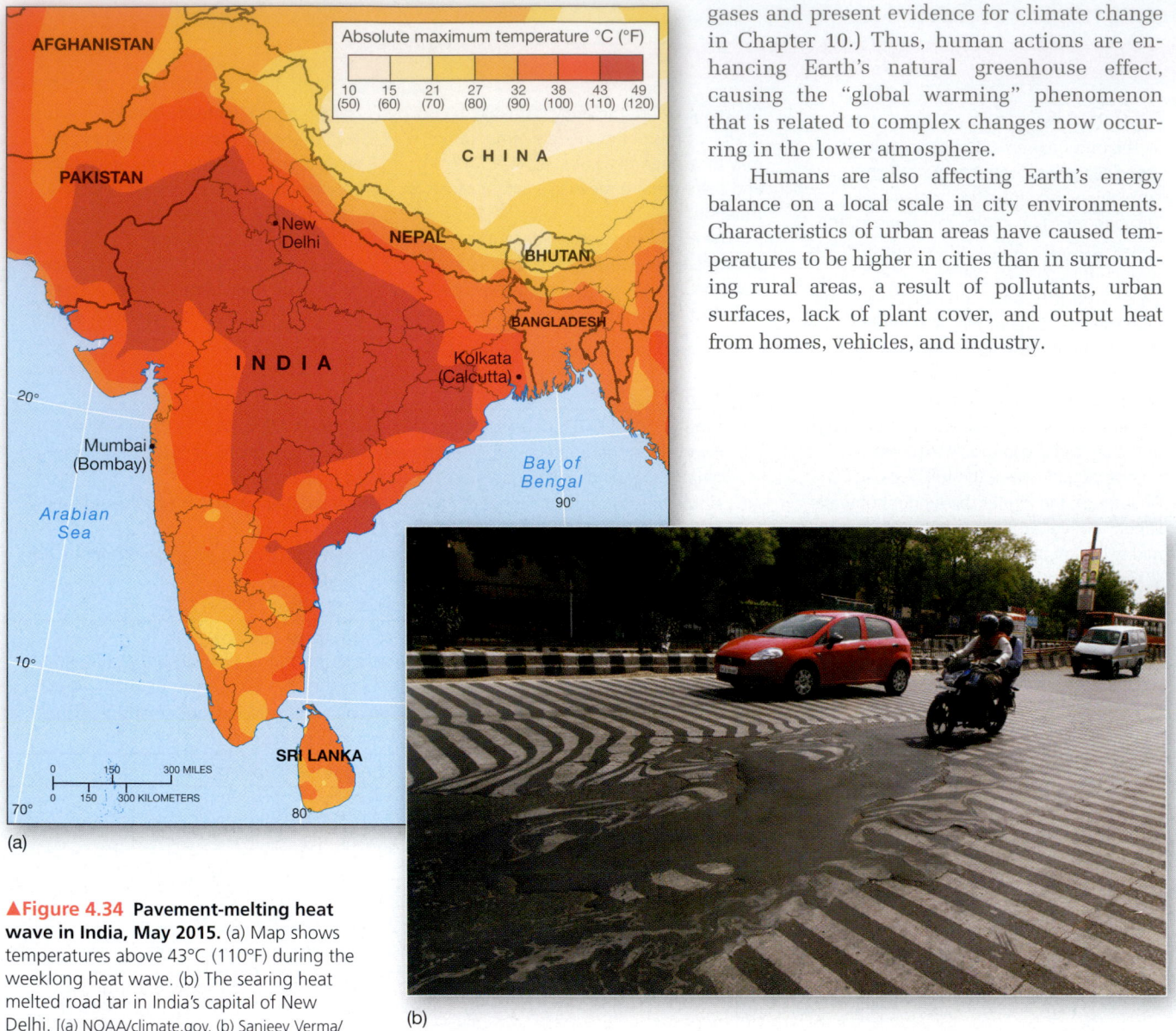

(a)

(b)

▲Figure 4.34 **Pavement-melting heat wave in India, May 2015.** (a) Map shows temperatures above 43°C (110°F) during the weeklong heat wave. (b) The searing heat melted road tar in India's capital of New Delhi. [(a) NOAA/climate.gov. (b) Sanjeev Verma/Hindustan Times via Getty Images.]

- Heat waves can occur in regions and during seasons when temperatures are normally extremely hot. The fifth deadliest heat wave on record occurred in India in May 2015, a time of year where temperatures regularly exceed 38°C (100°F). During the heat wave, temperatures in some parts of the country topped 46°C (115°F) for an entire week, leading to more than 2300 fatalities (**Figure 4.34**). In nearby Pakistan a few weeks later, over 1300 people died from heat-related illnesses.

Human Impacts on Earth's Energy Balance

Scientists agree that human activities, principally the burning of fossil fuels, are increasing atmospheric greenhouse gases that absorb longwave radiation, delaying losses of heat energy to space. (We discuss greenhouse

Global Temperature Increase

One way scientists assess changing temperature patterns is using global temperature anomalies. A temperature *anomaly* is a difference, or irregularity, found by comparing recorded average annual temperatures against the long-term average annual temperature for a time period (this is the *baseline*, or base period, for comparison). Positive anomalies indicate warmer temperatures than average; negative anomalies indicate cooler conditions than average.

Figure 4.35 shows the temperature anomaly trend from 1950 to 2014, revealing the changes in temperature per decade as compared to the baseline of 1951 to 1980. The overall trend toward warming temperatures is occurring worldwide, especially over the Northern Hemisphere. The map also shows that some regions are warming more than others. For example, the Arctic has experienced larger and more rapid temperature increases

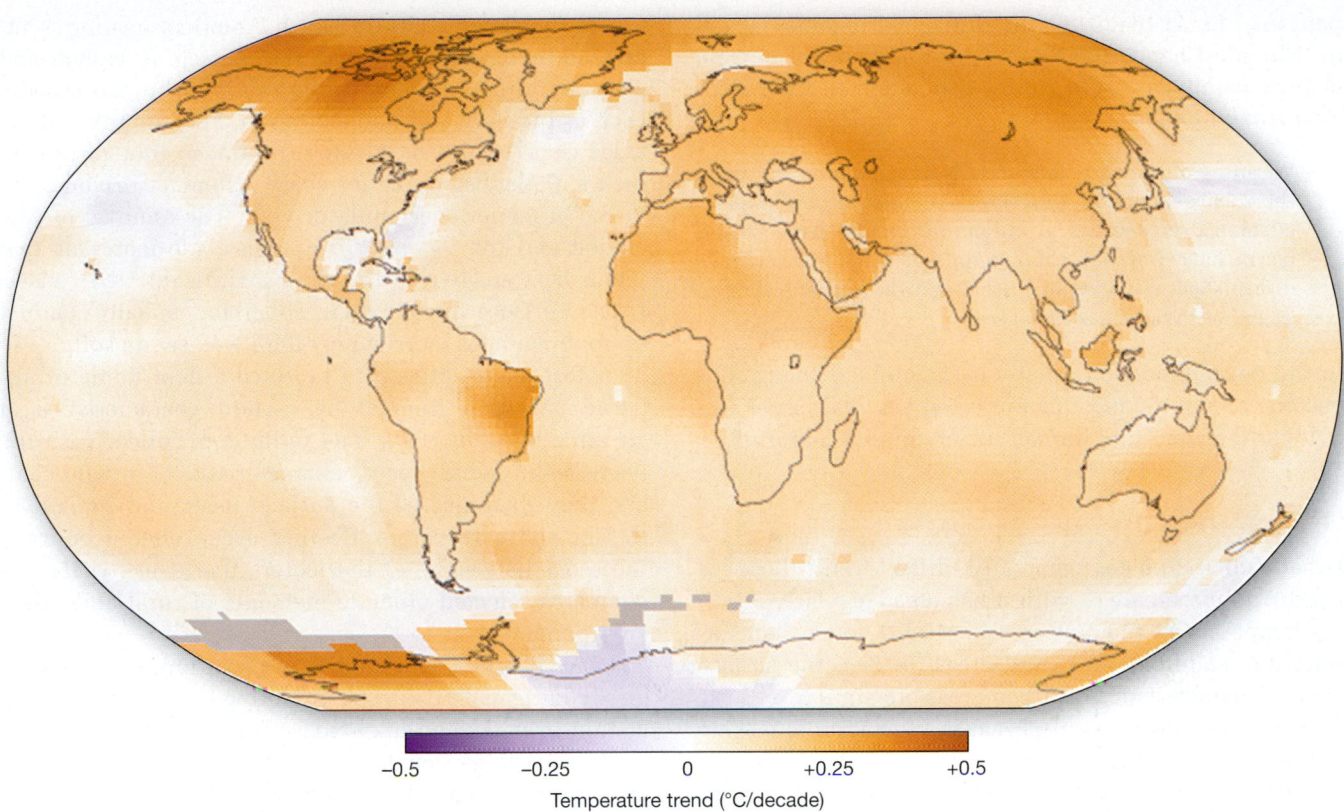

▲Figure 4.35 Surface-temperature anomalies from 1950 to 2014, compared to 1951–1980 baseline. Oranges indicate positive anomalies (warmer temperatures); purples indicate negative anomalies (cooler temperatures). Note the warming trend, especially in the Arctic region. By the end of 2015, 14 of the 15 warmest years on record had occurred since 2001. [GISS/NASA.]

than in the middle and lower latitudes. Since 1978, warming has increased in the Arctic region to a rate of 1.2 C° (2.2 F°) per decade, which means the last 20 years warmed at nearly seven times the rate of the last 100 years. **Arctic amplification**, also called *polar amplification*, refers to the tendency for polar latitudes, the north polar region in particular, to experience enhanced warming relative to the rest of the planet. This phenomenon is related to the presence of snow and ice and the positive feedback loops triggered by snow and ice melt, as discussed in Geosystems Now.

Since 1880, when the instrumental climate record began, Earth's average surface temperature has warmed about 0.8°C (1.4°F). Since 1970, global temperatures have increased an average of 0.17 C° (0.3 F°) per decade. As we discuss in detail in Chapter 10, temperatures today are higher than at any time during the past 125,000 years. According to the U.S. National Research Council of the National Academy of Sciences, each Celsius degree of global temperature increase can have far-reaching effects on Earth systems (**Figure 4.36**).

However, "global warming" (the recent, ongoing rise in global average surface temperature related to the greenhouse effect) is not the same thing as global climate change, and the two terms should not be considered interchangeable. Climate change (long-term alteration of the climate system, either natural or human-induced)

encompasses all the effects of atmospheric warming—these effects vary with location and relate to humidity, precipitation, sea-surface temperatures, severe storms, and many other Earth processes. An example of the effects of global warming is the positive ice–albedo feedback loop created by Arctic sea-ice melting and temperature rise. Other impacts will be discussed in chapters ahead—climate change affects almost all Earth systems.

The long-term climate records show that climates have varied over the last 5 million years. In essence, climate is always changing. However, many of the changes occurring today are beyond what can be explained by the natural variability of Earth's climate

Each **1 C°** increase in global temperatures results in:

↕ **5–10%** change in precipitation in many regions	↓ **25%** decrease in extent of Arctic summer sea ice
↑ **3–10%** increase in rainfall from heaviest precipitation events	↓ **5–15%** reduction in crop yields
↕ **5–10%** change in flow of streams and rivers (up or down)	↑ **200–400%** increase in area burned by wildfires in western United States

▲Figure 4.36 Projected impacts of global temperature increases on Earth systems. [Adapted from NCDC/NOAA *State of the Climate* reports and the National Research Council.]

patterns. In 2013–2014, the Intergovernmental Panel on Climate Change (IPCC), the leading body of climate change scientists in the world, concluded in their *Fifth Assessment Report*,

> Warming of the climate system is unequivocal, and since the 1950s, many of the observed changes are unprecedented over decades to millennia. The atmosphere and ocean have warmed, the amounts of snow and ice have diminished, sea level has risen, and the concentration of greenhouse gases has increased.

In the news almost on a daily basis, climate change has become one of the most complicated yet vital issues facing world leaders and human society in this century.

Urban Environments

Urban microclimates generally differ from those of nearby nonurban areas, with urban areas regularly reaching temperatures as much as 6 C° (10 F°) hotter than surrounding suburban and rural areas. In fact, the surface energy characteristics of urban areas are similar to those of desert locations, mainly because vegetation is lacking in both environments.

The physical characteristics of urbanized regions produce an **urban heat island (UHI)** that has, on average, both maximum and minimum temperatures higher than nearby rural settings (**Figure 4.37**). A UHI experiences higher temperatures toward the downtown central business district and lower temperatures over areas of trees and parks (**Figure 4.38**). Sensible heat is less in urban forests than in other parts of the city because of both shading from tree canopies and plant processes such as transpiration that move moisture into the air. In New York City, daytime temperatures average 5–10 C° (9–18 F°) cooler in Central Park than in the greater metropolitan area. UHI effects tend to be highest in cities with dense population and slightly lower in cities with more urban sprawl.

In the average city in North America, heating is increased by modified urban surfaces such as asphalt and glass, building geometry, pollution, and human activity such as industry and transportation. For example, an average car (10 km/l or 25 mpg) produces enough heat to melt a 4.5-kg bag of ice for every kilometer driven (a 14 lb bag of ice for every mile driven). The removal of vegetation and the increase in human-made materials that retain heat are two of the most significant UHI causes. Urban surfaces (metal, glass, concrete, asphalt) conduct up to three times more energy than wet, sandy soil.

Most major cities also produce a **dust dome** of airborne pollution trapped by certain characteristics of air circulation in UHIs: The pollutants collect with the decrease in wind speed characteristic of urban centers; they then rise as the surface heats and remain in the air above the city, affecting urban energy budgets. **Table 4.1** lists some of the factors that cause UHIs and compares selected climatic elements of rural and urban environments.

City planners and architects use a number of strategies to mitigate UHI effects, including the planting of vegetation in parks and open space (urban forests), "green" roofs (rooftop gardens), "cool" roofs (high-albedo roofs), and "cool" pavements (lighter-colored materials such as concrete or lighter surface coatings for asphalt). In addition to lowering urban outdoor temperatures, such strategies keep buildings' interiors cooler, thereby reducing energy consumption and greenhouse gases released by fossil-fuel combustion.

Studies show the effects of roof materials on temperature. During the hottest day of the 2011 New York City summer, temperature measurements for a white roof covering were 24 C° (42 F°) cooler than those for a traditional black roof nearby (**Figure 4.39**). Other research shows that for structures with solar panel arrays, the roof temperatures under the shade of the panels dropped dramatically.

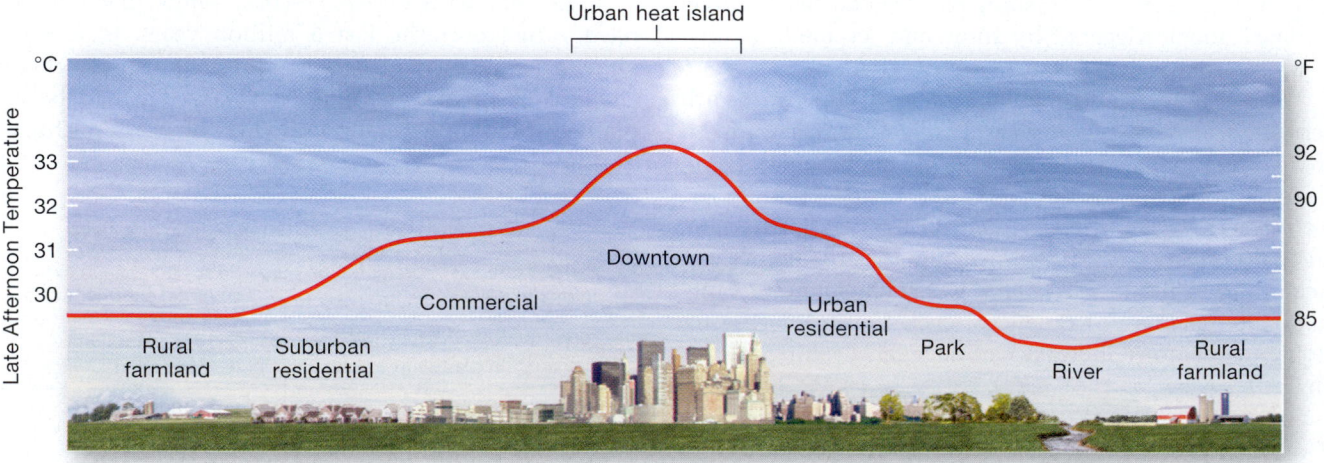

▲**Figure 4.37 Typical urban heat island profile.** On average, urban temperatures may be 1–3 C° (2–5 F°) warmer than nearby rural areas on a sunny summer day. Temperatures are highest at the urban core. Note the cooling over the park and rural areas. [Based on Heat Island, Urban Climatology and Air Quality, available at http://weather.msfc.nasa.gov/urban/urban_heat_island.html.]

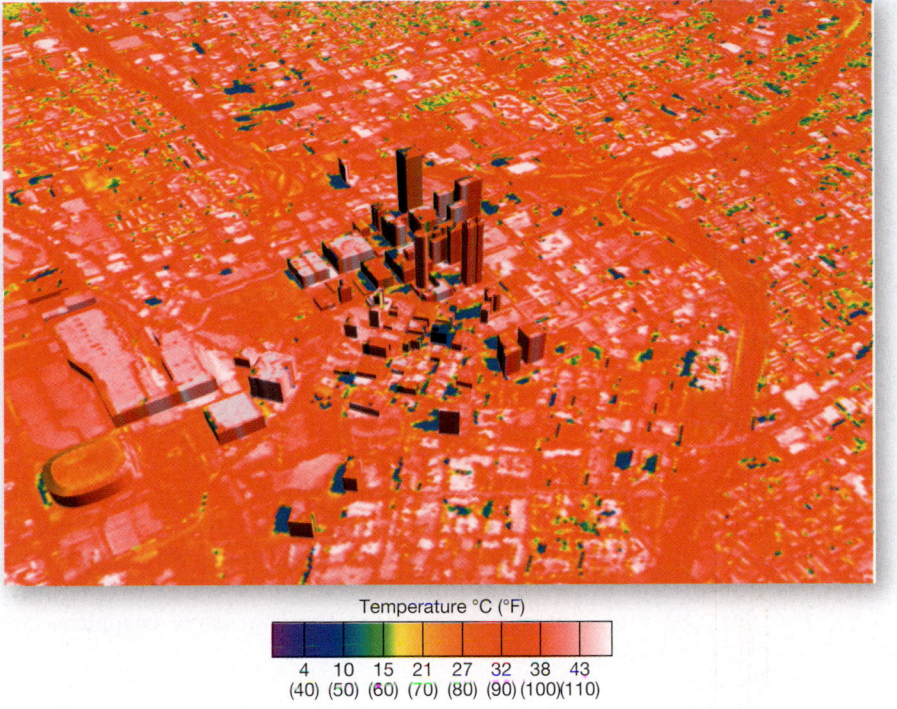

◀**Figure 4.38 Infrared image of downtown Atlanta, Georgia.** [NASA SVS/ GSFC.]

Temperature °C (°F)

4   10   15   21   27   32   38   43
(40) (50) (60) (70) (80) (90)(100)(110)

waterproof membrane for an effective insulating barrier. Living roof applications are simpler and less expensive when used on flat or shallow-slope roofs, but can also work on steep-slope roofs common in regions with heavy snowfall.

With predictions that 60% of the global population will live in cities by the year 2030 and with air and water temperatures rising because of climate change, UHI issues are emerging as a significant concern both for physical geographers and for the public at large. Studies have found a direct correlation between peaks in UHI intensity and heat-related illness and fatalities (more information is at http://www .epa.gov/hiri/).

A green roof, also called a "living roof," provides insulation for the building below, reducing heating and cooling costs by as much as 20% (**Figure 4.40**). Vegetation is planted in a lightweight growing medium over a

One of the challenges humans are facing with the environmental effects of urban landscapes and climate change is an increase in the frequency of heat waves, putting more people at risk from the effects of prolonged

TABLE 4.1 Urban Heat Islands: Driving Factors and Climatic Response

Driving Factor	Climatic Element and UHI Effect	Explanation
Thermal properties of urban surfaces: metal, glass, asphalt, concrete, brick	Higher net radiation	• Urban surfaces conduct more energy than natural surfaces such as soil.
Reflective properties of urban surfaces	Lower albedo	• Urban surfaces often have low albedo, so they absorb and retain heat, leading to high net radiation values.
Urban canyon effect	Lower wind speeds More calm periods	• Reflected insolation is conducted into surface materials, thus increasing temperatures. • Buildings interrupt wind flows, diminishing heat loss and blocking nighttime radiation to space. • Maximum UHI effects occur on calm, clear days and nights.
Anthropogenic heating	Higher temperatures • annual average • winter minima • summer maxima	• Homes, vehicles, and factories generate heat. • Heat output may surge with power for heating in winter and air conditioning in summer.
Urban dust dome	More pollutants More cloudiness, including fog More precipitation More thunderstorms Less snowfall, inner city	• Aerosols in urban dust dome raise temperatures by absorbing insolation and reradiating heat to surface. • Particulates are condensation nuclei for water vapor, increasing cloud formation and precipitation.
Urban desert effect: less plant cover and more sealed surfaces	Lower relative humidity Less infiltration More runoff Less evaporation	• Cooling effect of evaporation and plant transpiration is reduced or absent. • More water flows as runoff because it cannot infiltrate through sealed surfaces to soil. • Urban surfaces respond as desert landscapes—storms may cause "flash floods."

(a) Rooftops in Queens, New York, in September 2011

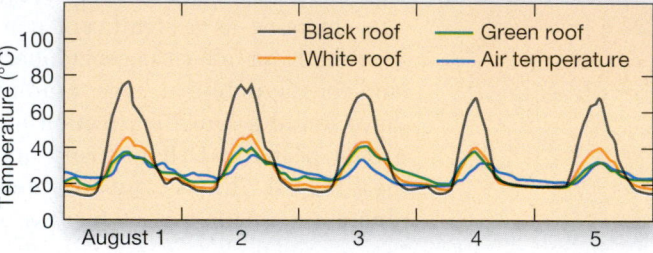

(b) Graph shows the higher temperature of black roofs as compared to bright white or green (vegetated) roofs.

◀**Figure 4.39** **Effects of rooftop materials on urban heat islands.** Research shows that reflective or living roof materials can lower heating and cooling costs by as much as 20% for the building below. [(a) Natural color image from Digital Globe's *Worldview-2* satellite. (b) Columbia University and NASA Goddard Institute for Space Studies.]

high temperatures during the summer season. According to the IPCC, recent heat waves relate to warming temperatures and global climate change. Over the last several decades, as global humidity has increased, high-humidity heat waves have become more common and the number of human casualties from heat stress has risen, making heat waves a major cause of weather-related deaths. The deadly effects of high temperatures, especially in cities, result from more frequent extreme daily temperature maximums combined with lack of nighttime cooling. Those most susceptible to heat-related illness are the young, the elderly, and people with preexisting medical conditions. Extreme heat can lead to heart attack or stroke, meaning the heat-wave casualties are often underreported.

▼**Figure 4.40** **Green roof in New York City.** A living roof helps mitigate the urban heat island effect on a New York University building near Washington Square Park in Greenwich Village, Lower Manhattan, New York. [Andrew Cribb/Alamy.]

ENERGY BALANCE AND TEMPERATURE IMPACT HUMANS

• The Earth–atmosphere system balances itself naturally, maintaining planetary systems that support Earth, life, and human society.
• Solar energy is harnessed for power production worldwide.

4a The International Maritime Organization, made up of 170 countries, is developing policies to improve energy efficiency and reduce diesel ship emissions, including black carbon. In the Arctic, soot and particulates darken ice surfaces, decrease albedo, and enhance ice melt. [Justin Kase zninez/Alamy Stock Photo.]

HUMANS IMPACT ENERGY BALANCE AND TEMPERATURE

• Humans produce atmospheric gases and aerosols that affect clouds and the Earth–atmosphere energy budget, which in turn affects temperature and climate. For example, fossil-fuel burning produces carbon dioxide and other greenhouse gases that warm the lower atmosphere.
• Urban heat island effects accelerate warming in cities, which house more than half the global human population.

4b The Gujarat Solar Park in western India is one of the world's largest photovoltaic solar facilities; expansion is ongoing, with a goal of 10 GW capacity by 2020. [Ajit Solanki/AP.]

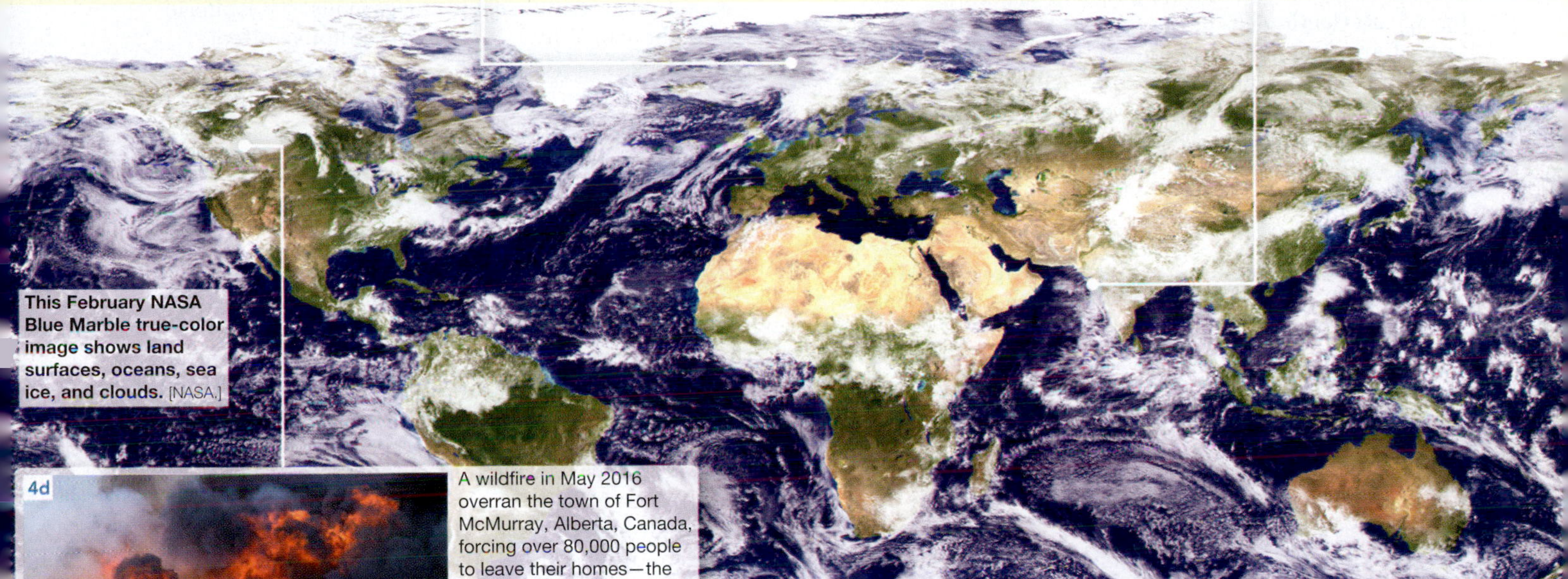

This February NASA Blue Marble true-color image shows land surfaces, oceans, sea ice, and clouds. [NASA.]

4d A wildfire in May 2016 overran the town of Fort McMurray, Alberta, Canada, forcing over 80,000 people to leave their homes—the largest evacuation in provincial history. Temperatures far above average for early May combined with a dry winter created conditions ripe for wildfire. [CBC News/Reuters.]

ISSUES FOR THE 21ST CENTURY

• Improved energy efficiency and renewable energy sources, such as solar, can reduce the use of energy from fossil fuels, thus slowing the addition of anthropogenic greenhouse gases to the atmosphere.
• Strategies to reduce urban heat island effects can help lessen the dangers of heat waves in cities and slow the general atmospheric warming trend.
• Continued increases in average global air and ocean temperatures will enhance climate change effects worldwide.

QUESTIONS TO CONSIDER

1. Based on the graph in HD 4c, around what year did annual temperature anomalies become consistently positive? Do positive anomalies indicate cooler or warmer temperatures?
2. Is "global warming" the same as "climate change"? Explain your answer.

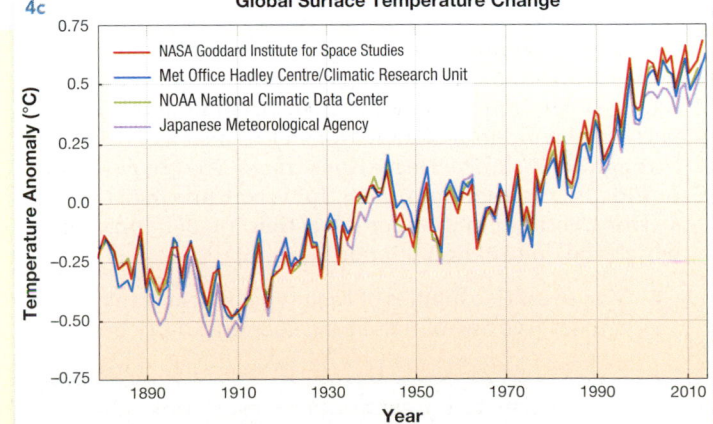

4c Global Surface Temperature Change

Temperature Anomaly (°C) vs. Year

— NASA Goddard Institute for Space Studies
— Met Office Hadley Centre/Climatic Research Unit
— NOAA National Climatic Data Center
— Japanese Meteorological Agency

Records from several international scientific agencies are in agreement as to the rising global temperatures over the past century. This graph shows temperature anomalies as compared to the base period from 1951–1980. [NASA Earth Observatory/Robert Simmon.]

KEY**LEARNING**concepts**review**

Identify alternative pathways for solar energy on its way through the troposphere to Earth's surface and ***review*** the concept of albedo (reflectivity).

Transmission (p. 81) is the uninterrupted passage of short-wave and longwave energy through either the atmosphere or water. In the process known as **scattering** (p. 82), the molecules and particles of the atmosphere may redirect radiation, changing the direction of the light's movement without altering its wavelengths. Some incoming insolation is scattered by clouds and atmosphere and is transmitted to Earth as **diffuse radiation** (p. 82), the downward component of scattered light.

The speed of insolation entering the atmosphere changes as it passes from one medium to another; this change of speed causes a bending action called **refraction** (p. 82). **Reflection** (p. 82) is the process in which a portion of arriving energy bounces directly back into space without reaching Earth's surface. **Albedo** (p. 83) is the reflective quality of a surface, reported as the percentage of reflected insolation. **Absorption** (p. 84) is the assimilation of radiation by molecules of a substance, converting the radiation from one form to another—for example, visible light to infrared radiation.

1. What factors explain the lower atmosphere's blue color? What process determines the beautiful colors of a sunset?
2. List six types of surfaces and their albedo values. Based on albedo alone, which surfaces are cooler? Which are warmer?

Explain four types of heat transfer: radiation, conduction, convection, and advection.

The flow of kinetic energy from one body to another resulting from a temperature difference between them is **heat** (p. 84). Two types are **sensible heat** (p. 84), energy that we can feel and measure, and **latent heat** (p. 84), "hidden" heat that is gained or lost in phase changes, such as from solid to liquid to gas and back, while the substance's temperature remains unchanged.

One mechanism of heat transfer is **radiation** (p. 84), which flows in electromagnetic waves and does not require a medium such as air or water. **Conduction** (p. 84) is the molecule-to-molecule transfer of heat as it diffuses through a substance. Heat also is transferred in gases and liquids by **convection**, (p. 84), (physical mixing that has a strong vertical motion) or **advection**, (p. 85), (mixing in which the dominant motion is horizontal).

3. Give several examples of each type of heat transfer. Do you observe any of these processes on a daily basis?

Explain the effect of greenhouse gases, clouds, and aerosols on atmospheric heating and cooling.

Carbon dioxide, water vapor, methane, and other gases in the lower atmosphere absorb infrared radiation that is then emitted to Earth, thus delaying energy loss to space—this process is the **greenhouse effect** (p. 86). **Counterradiation** (p. 86) is the heat emitted from the atmosphere back to Earth's surface. In the atmosphere, longwave radiation is not actually trapped, as it would be in a greenhouse, but its passage to space is delayed (heat energy is detained in the atmosphere) through absorption and reradiation by **greenhouse gases** (p. 86).

Cloud-albedo forcing (p. 86) is the increase in albedo (reflectivity) caused by clouds, resulting in a cooling effect at the surface. An increase in greenhouse warming caused by clouds is **cloud-greenhouse forcing** (p. 86). **Jet contrails**, or condensation trails, are produced by aircraft exhaust, particulates, and water vapor and can form high cirrus clouds, sometimes called *contrail cirrus*.

4. What are the similarities and differences between an actual greenhouse and the gaseous atmospheric greenhouse? Why is Earth's greenhouse effect changing?
5. What is counterradiation, and why is it important to life on Earth?

Review the Earth–atmosphere energy balance and the patterns of net radiation at the surface.

The Earth–atmosphere energy system naturally balances itself in a steady-state equilibrium. Of the incoming shortwave radiation, Earth and its atmosphere reflect 31% and Earth's atmosphere and surface absorb 69% of the total. Of the outgoing longwave radiation, Earth's surface emits 8% of absorbed radiation directly back to space, and the atmosphere ultimately radiates 61% of the absorbed energy back to space (after delays related to counterradiation and the greenhouse effect).

Microclimatology (p. 91) is the science focusing on physical conditions in the boundary layer at or near Earth's surface. **Net radiation (NET R)**, (p. 91), is the value reached by adding and subtracting the energy inputs and outputs at some location on the surface; it is the sum of all shortwave (SW) and longwave (LW) radiation gains and losses.

6. In terms of surface energy balance, what are the four components in the equation for net radiation (NET R)?
7. What are the nonradiative processes by which energy transfers from Earth's surface to the atmosphere?

Define the concept of temperature, and ***review*** the principle temperature controls that produce global temperature patterns.

Temperature (p. 95) is a measure of the average kinetic energy, or molecular motion, of individual molecules in matter. Principal controls and influences on temperature patterns include latitude (the distance north or south of the equator), altitude and elevation, cloud cover (reflection, absorption, and radiation of energy), and land–water heating differences.

Differences in the physical characteristics of land (rock and soil) compared to water (oceans, seas, and lakes) lead to **land–water heating differences** (p. 99) that affect temperatures. These physical differences, related to *evaporation*, *transparency*, *specific heat*, and *movement*, cause land surfaces to heat and cool faster than water surfaces. Because of water's **transparency** (p. 100), light passes through it to an average depth of 60 m (200 ft) in the ocean, distributing available heat energy through a much greater volume than is possible through land. At the same time, water has a higher **specific heat** (p. 100), or heat capacity, requiring far more energy to increase its temperature than does an equal volume of land. Ocean currents and *sea-surface temperatures* also affect land temperature. An example of the effect of ocean currents is the **Gulf Stream** (p. 100), which moves northward off the east coast of North America, carrying warm water far into the North Atlantic.

8. Why is it possible to grow moderate-climate-type crops such as wheat, barley, and potatoes at an elevation of 4103 m (13,460 ft) near La Paz, Bolivia?
9. How do marine effects on temperature differ from continental effects on temperature?

Interpret the pattern of Earth's temperatures on January and July temperature maps.

Each line on January and July temperature maps is an **isotherm** (p. 104), an isoline that connects points of equal temperature. Isotherms portray temperature patterns and generally trend east–west, marking the general decrease in insolation and net radiation with distance from the equator. The **thermal equator**, (p. 105), an isoline connecting all points of highest mean temperature, trends southward in January and shifts northward with the high summer Sun in July.

10. Why does the thermal equator shift position annually?
11. Where are the hottest places on Earth? Are they near the equator or elsewhere? Explain. Where is the coldest place on Earth?

Explain heat waves and describe the human response to temperature extremes.

Heat waves (p. 110) are prolonged periods of high temperatures lasting days or weeks, and they have caused thousands of fatalities in recent years. The *wind-chill factor* indicates the apparent temperature (how the air feels to an average person) in cold, windy conditions. *Heat stress* refers to the heat-related illnesses that can occur in hot, humid conditions.

12. What is the definition of a heat wave? Why is the frequency of heat waves on the rise?

Describe global temperature increases associated with human activities and urban heat island conditions.

Arctic amplification (p. 111), also called *polar amplification*, refers to the tendency for polar latitudes, the north polar region in particular, to experience enhanced warming relative to the rest of the planet. Altered microclimatic effects in cities produce an **urban heat island** (p. 112), where temperatures are higher than surrounding rural areas. Air pollution, including gases, dusts, and aerosols, is greater over urban areas, producing a **dust dome** (p. 113) that adds to the urban heat island effects.

13. How does temperature differ in cities as compared to rural areas? Name three reasons for the difference.

GEO**SPATIAL** ANALYSIS

Temperature trends

NASA's Goddard Institute for Space Studies (GISS) monitors global surface temperature change. These data are compiled from land-based meteorological stations and reconstructed sea surface temperatures worldwide.

Activities

Go to the GISS Surface Temperature Anomalies page at http://data .giss.nasa.gov/gistemp/maps/. Read the text at the bottom of the page to learn more about the information displayed. Leave all variables at their default values: "Map Type: Anomalies," "Mean Period: current full month," "Time interval: current year for both Begin and End." The anomalies are the difference between the current temperature and the 1951-1980 average temperature (Base Period.)

1. What is the global average temperature anomaly for the current month and year?
2. What is the temperature anomaly in your approximate location? (Give a range of temperatures.)
3. Where is the largest temperature anomaly and what is its value? And, the smallest?

Examine the "Zonal Mean versus Latitude graph." This graph displays the average temperature anomaly along latitude bands. Holding the mouse over a data point displays its latitude and temperature anomaly value.

4. What is the zonal mean temperature anomaly at the Equator?
5. What latitude recorded the largest anomaly and what is its value? And, the smallest?

Change the Mean Period to "Annual (Jan–Dec)" and the Time Interval to "Begin at 2001 and End at 2015." Click "Make Map." This creates the average annual temperature anomaly for the time interval specified.

6. In which hemisphere are temperature anomalies the greatest? Why?
7. Using the line graph, what relationship do you find between latitude and temperature anomaly in the Northern Hemisphere?

Change the Map Type to "Trends" then click "Make Map." This displays the temperature changes over the specified time interval.

8. Scientists prefer to use the term climate change instead of global warming because not all locations will warm. Which regions cooled over the 15-year time interval?
9. Change the time interval to the most recent 30 years. Where has most of the warming occurred and to what degree? How much has the global average temperature changed?

5 Atmospheric and Oceanic Circulations

Seattle

San Francisco

Los Angeles

Pacific Ocean

The cool currents off the coast of North America are some of the most biologically productive waters in the world. Shown here are green blooms of phytoplankton, a rich source of marine nutrients, in the southward flow of the California Current. [VIIRS instrument aboard Suomi NPP/Norman Kuring/NASA.]

KEYLEARNINGconcepts

After reading the chapter, you should be able to:

- **Define** wind and air pressure and **describe** instruments that measure each.

- **Explain** the driving forces within the atmosphere—gravity, pressure gradient force, Coriolis force, and friction force—that affect wind.

- **Locate** the primary high- and low-pressure areas and principal winds on Earth.

- **Describe** upper-air circulation and **define** the jet streams.

- **Explain** several types of local and regional winds, including the monsoons.

- **Sketch** the basic pattern of Earth's major surface ocean currents and deep thermohaline circulation.

- **Summarize** the El Niño and La Niña oscillations of air pressure and circulation in the Pacific Ocean.

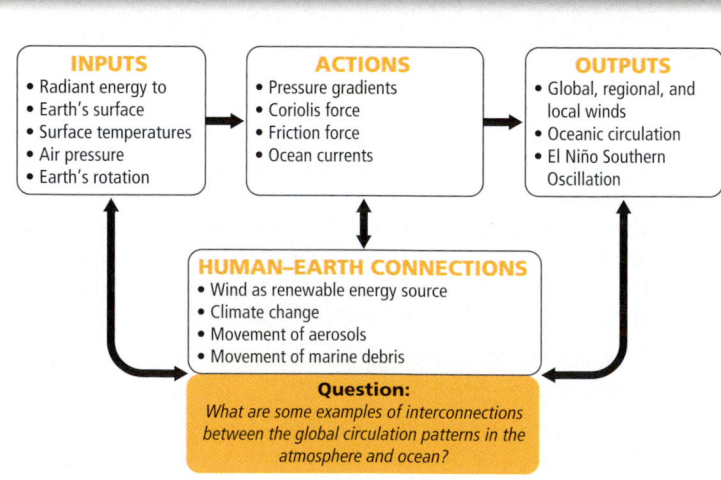

INPUTS
- Radiant energy to Earth's surface
- Surface temperatures
- Air pressure
- Earth's rotation

ACTIONS
- Pressure gradients
- Coriolis force
- Friction force
- Ocean currents

OUTPUTS
- Global, regional, and local winds
- Oceanic circulation
- El Niño Southern Oscillation

HUMAN–EARTH CONNECTIONS
- Wind as renewable energy source
- Climate change
- Movement of aerosols
- Movement of marine debris

Question:
What are some examples of interconnections between the global circulation patterns in the atmosphere and ocean?

California's Santa Ana Winds

In mid-January 2014, dangerously dry conditions in the San Gabriel Mountains outside Los Angeles prompted the National Weather Service (NWS) to issue a Red Flag Warning, the highest alert for fire danger. Throughout the region, soils and vegetation were desiccated from an extremely dry winter and a decade-long drought. In addition, the seasonal Santa Ana winds worsened the fire hazard. These winds concentrate below mountain passes and canyons in the rugged topography of southern California. The Santa Anas can gust over 129 kmph (80 mph) and are notorious for damaging buildings, felling trees, and, most importantly, spreading wildfires (**Figure GN 5.1**).

The Colby Wildfire Just before dawn on January 16, the gusty Santa Ana winds fanned the embers from an illegal campfire near the Colby Trail in the Angeles National Forest into flames. The fire quickly spread into the neighborhoods near Glendora—about 40 km (25 mi) northeast of downtown Los Angeles—where police and firefighters woke residents and asked them to evacuate.

At daybreak, the Santa Anas picked up speed and intensity, blowing the Colby fire downslope toward houses tucked onto steep slopes with difficult access for fighting wildfires. Winds averaged about 42 kmph (26 mph) through the day, with gusts reaching 98 kmph (61 mph). Over the next 5 days, 3700 residents evacuated their homes as the fire burned about 800 hectares (2000 acres).

Causes of the Santa Ana Winds Like most winds, the Santa Anas are driven by an atmospheric pressure gradient, a large difference in pressure between two locations (**Figure GN 5.2**). In winter, high pressure over the relatively cold, high-elevation Great Basin desert of Nevada and southern Utah contrasts with the lower pressure of the warm, moist southern California coastal areas, forming a pressure gradient.

As the atmospheric high pressure rotates, this cold air is swept downslope toward the coast, warming as it picks up speed and channels through mountain passes and canyons. With the rise in wind temperature, the relative humidity drops, resulting in a hot, dry wind in the coastal region. In fact, the hottest day ever recorded in downtown Los Angeles—45°C (113°F) on September 27, 2010—occurred during a Santa Ana wind. These winds can not only spread wildfire flames and embers, but also act as a drying agent for vegetation that fuels the fire on the ground.

The conditions that produce high pressure over the Great Basin desert usually occur between September and March, defining the season for Santa Ana winds. Thus, September typically marks the end of smog season in the Los Angeles Basin, as the winds blow smog out to sea. However, the Santa Anas are most strongly associated with wildfire in October, at the end of the dry summer typical of the southern California climate (**Figure GN 5.3**). Recently, dry winters have made this wind–wildfire association extend longer throughout the year.

▲**Figure GN 5.2** The Santa Anas blow from an area of high pressure over the Great Basin to one of low pressure over the Pacific coast.

▲**Figure GN 5.3** Santa Anas send smoke plumes over the Pacific Ocean. The October 2003 Cedar fire in San Diego was the largest in California's history. [Jacques Descloitres, MODIS Rapid Response Team, NASA/GSFC.]

These winds are now notorious for creating some of the most dangerous wind and wildfire conditions in the United States.

Regional and local winds affect Earth systems, influencing natural ecosystems and human societies. In this chapter, we look at the winds and ocean currents that drive Earth's general circulation patterns and produce such local effects.

1. What is the pattern and direction of wind in your area? Do your local winds affect daily life, as do the Santa Anas?

2. How do the Santa Anas affect temperatures in the Los Angeles area?

▲**Figure GN 5.1** Glendora, California, during the 2014 Colby fire. [Keith Birmingham/Zuma Press/Alamy.]

The global-scale circulation of winds and ocean currents across Earth has fascinated explorers, sailors, and scientists for centuries. Driven by the imbalance between energy surpluses at the equator and energy deficits at the poles, Earth's atmospheric circulation transfers both energy and mass on a global scale, determining Earth's weather patterns and the flow of ocean currents.

The atmosphere is the dominant medium for redistributing heat energy from about 35° latitude to the poles in each hemisphere. Near the equator, in the region between about 17° N and S latitude, ocean currents are the primary means of redistributing heat energy. Atmospheric circulation also spreads air pollutants, whether natural or human-caused, worldwide, far from their point of origin. As described in Geosystems Now, surface currents move marine debris in circular flow patterns within Earth's oceans.

Wind Essentials

Simply stated, **wind** is the generally horizontal motion of air across Earth's surface. Differences in air pressure between one location and another produce wind. These differences occur because of the differential heating of Earth surfaces described in previous chapters. Wind patterns on Earth can be characterized at global, regional, and local scales. For example, if you live in a coastal area, or are a surfer, windsurfer, or kitesurfer, you are probably familiar with local "onshore" and "offshore" winds. An offshore wind blows from the shore toward the ocean, so is at your back when standing on the beach. An onshore wind blows from the ocean directly toward shore. These local

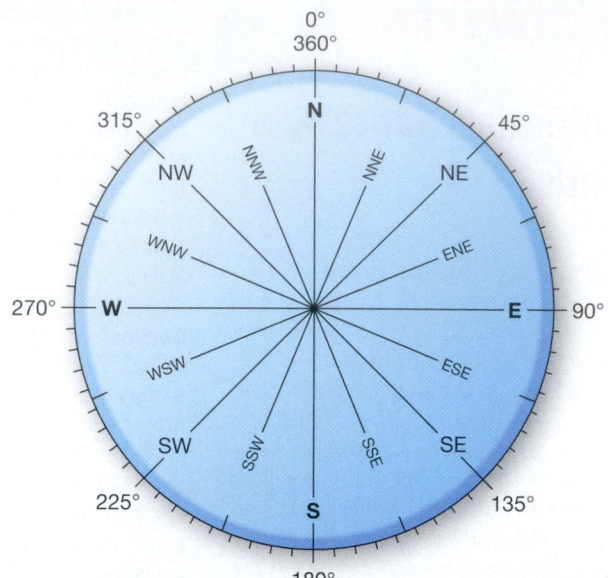

▲Figure 5.1 **Sixteen wind directions identified on a wind compass.** Winds are named for the direction from which they originate.

winds, discussed ahead in this chapter, are related to the different heat properties of land and water.

Winds are named for the direction from which they originate. For example, a wind from the west is a westerly wind (it blows eastward); a wind out of the south is a southerly wind (it blows northward). The term "prevailing wind" refers to the predominate wind direction at a certain location. For example, the prevailing winds in the United States during winter are from the west. **Figure 5.1** illustrates a simple wind compass, naming 16 principal wind directions used by meteorologists.

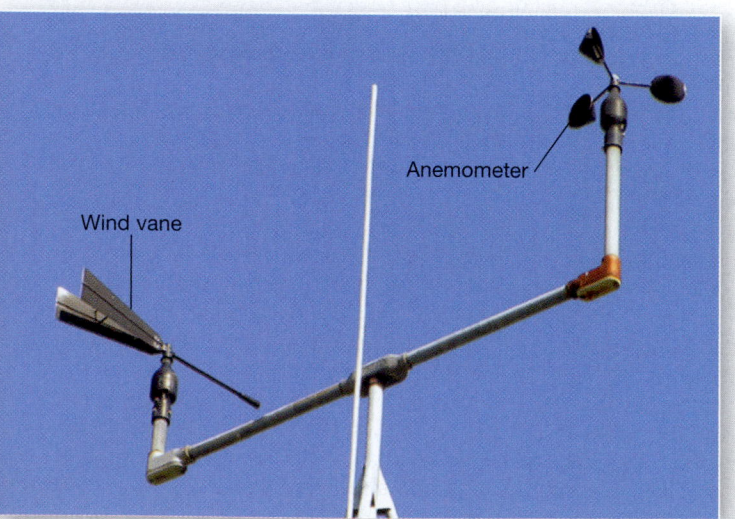

(a) Wind vane and anemometer at the top of a weather station.

(b) A Remote Automated Weather Station in northeast Washington, with vane anemometer at the top.

▲Figure 5.2 **Instruments that measure wind direction and speed: wind vane, anemometer, and vane anemometer.** [(a) NOAA Photo Library. (b) USFS.]

Wind Measurement

Wind's two principal properties are speed and direction, and instruments measure each. An **anemometer** measures wind speed in kilometers per hour (kmph), miles per hour (mph), meters per second (mps), or knots. (A knot is a nautical mile per hour, equivalent to 1.85 kmph, or 1.15 mph.) A **wind vane** determines wind direction. To reduce the effects of local topography and standardize the measurement of wind direction, wind vanes are placed a standard 10 m (33 ft) above the ground. A *vane anemometer* is a wind vane with a propeller attached to measure both wind speed and direction (**Figure 5.2**). Recently, tiny portable wind meters that attach to smartphones have become available to assess local wind conditions (one example is the Weatherflow Wind Meter). The accompanying app enables users to store and share data recorded by the wind meter, making these devices convenient for windsurfers, sailors, and others who measure daily winds.

The Beaufort wind scale (named after Admiral Beaufort of the British Navy, who introduced the scale in 1806) is a descriptive scale useful in visually estimating wind speed over oceans, but can also be applied over land. Even though most ships today use sophisticated equipment to measure wind, ocean charts still reference the Beaufort scale.

Wind measurements are represented on maps using streamlines, vectors, and wind barbs (examples and descriptions are in **Figure 5.3**). Later in this chapter and in Chapter 7, we see examples of these wind maps.

Atmospheric Pressure and Wind

Atmospheric pressure is key to understanding wind. In Chapter 3, we defined *atmospheric pressure* as the weight of the atmosphere described as force per unit area. The molecules of the different gases that constitute air create *air pressure* through their motion, size, and number, and this pressure is exerted on all surfaces in contact with air. As we saw in Chapter 3, the number of molecules and their motion are also the factors that determine the density and temperature of the air.

Pressure Relationships As discussed in Chapter 3, pressure and density decrease with altitude in the atmosphere. The low density in the upper atmosphere means the molecules are far apart, making collisions between them less frequent and thereby reducing pressure (review Figure 3.2).

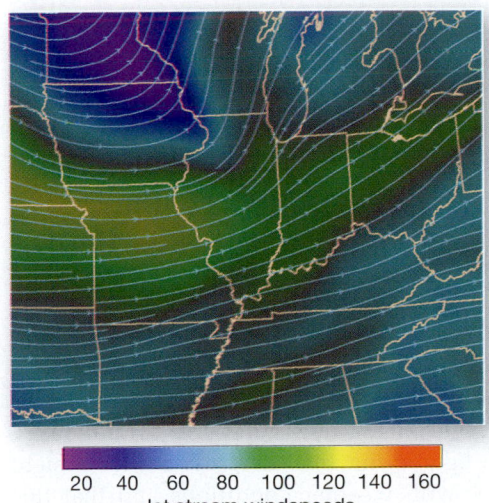

20 40 60 80 100 120 140 160
Jet stream windspeeds

(a) Streamlines are continuous; arrows show wind direction and background color indicates wind speed. The map shows jet stream winds in the central U.S. in November 2013, just before a tornado outbreak.

(b) Wind vectors are individual arrows showing direction; length of arrow indicates wind speed. (Figure 7.31b on page 212 shows wind maps that use vectors.)

Wind Speed Symbol	Miles per Hour	Knots
—	1–2	1–2
⌐	3–8	3–7
⌐	9–14	8–12
⌐	15–20	13–17
⌐	21–25	18–22
⌐	26–31	23–27

(c) Wind barbs point in the direction from which the wind blows (the example shows winds from the southwest over the ocean). The configuration of barb or flag shows wind speed.

▲Figure 5.3 **Winds represented on maps: streamlines, vectors, and barbs.**

everyday GEOSYSTEMS

What causes wind to blow from a certain direction?

The uneven heating of Earth's surface is the primary cause of wind. Differences in the amount of radiant energy received at different places on Earth affect air pressure. Variations in pressure set air in motion, always moving from areas of high pressure to areas of low pressure. Patterns of pressure and related winds occur at global, regional, and local scales, and vary daily or seasonally.

Wind moves from high pressure to low pressure

- Colder, drier air
- Higher density of molecules
- Higher pressure

- Warmer, humid air
- Lower density of molecules
- Lower pressure

▶Figure 5.4 **The Lincoln City Kite Festival,** held twice a year along the central Oregon coast, relies on consistent onshore winds to keep the kites aloft. [Larry Geddes/Alamy.]

Remember that temperature is a measure of the average kinetic energy of molecular motion. When air in the atmosphere is heated, molecular activity increases and temperature rises. With increased activity, the spacing between molecules increases so that density is reduced and air pressure decreases. Therefore, warmer air is less dense, or lighter, than colder air, and exerts less pressure.

The amount of water vapor in the air also affects its density. Moist air is lighter because the molecular weight of water is less than that of the molecules making up dry air (Table 5.1). If the same total number of molecules has a higher percentage of water vapor, mass will be less than if the air were dry (that is, than if it were made up entirely of oxygen and nitrogen molecules). As water vapor in the air increases, density decreases, so humid air exerts less pressure than dry air.

The end result over Earth's surface is that *warm, humid air is associated with low pressure* and *cold, dry air is associated with high pressure* (Figure 5.4). These relationships between air pressure, density, temperature, and moisture are important to the discussion ahead.

Atmospheric Pressure Measurement In 1643, work by Evangelista Torricelli, a pupil of Galileo, on a mine-drainage problem led to the first method for measuring air pressure (Figure 5.5a). Torricelli knew that pumps in the mine were able to "pull" water upward about 10 m (33 ft) but no higher, and that this level fluctuated from day to day. Careful observation revealed that the limitation was not the fault of the pumps but a property of the atmosphere itself. He figured out that air pressure, the weight of the air, varies with weather conditions and that this weight determined the height of the water in the pipe.

To simulate the problem at the mine, Torricelli devised an instrument using a much denser fluid than water—mercury (Hg)—and a glass tube 1 m (3.3 ft) high. He sealed the glass tube at one end, filled it with mercury, and inverted it into a dish containing mercury, at which point a small space containing a vacuum was formed in the tube's closed end (Figure 5.5b). Torricelli found that the average height of the column of mercury remaining in the tube was 760 mm (29.92 in.), depending on

TABLE 5.1 Molecular Weights of Common Atmospheric Gases	
Gas	Molecular Weight
Water vapor (H_2O)	18.02
Nitrogen (N_2)	28.02
Oxygen (O_2)	32.00
Carbon dioxide (CO_2)	44.01

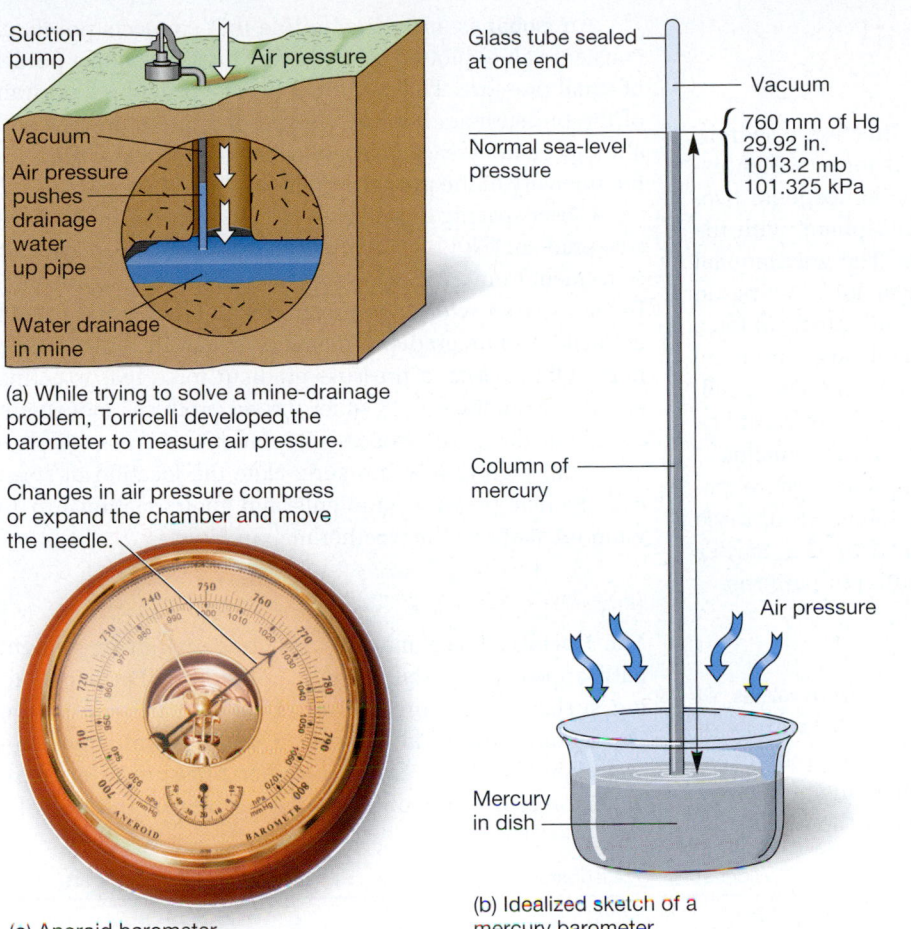

(a) While trying to solve a mine-drainage problem, Torricelli developed the barometer to measure air pressure.

Changes in air pressure compress or expand the chamber and move the needle.

(c) Aneroid barometer.

(b) Idealized sketch of a mercury barometer.

◄**Figure 5.5 Developing the barometer.** Have you used a barometer? If so, what type was it? [(c) Kirillica/Fotolia.]

Torricelli developed a **mercury barometer**. A more compact barometer design, which works without a meter-long tube of mercury, is the **aneroid barometer** (**Figure 5.5c**). Aneroid means "using no liquid." The aneroid barometer principle is simple: Imagine a small chamber, partially emptied of air, which is sealed and connected to a mechanism attached to a needle on a dial. As the air pressure outside the chamber increases, it presses inward on the chamber; as the outside air pressure decreases, it relieves the pressure on the chamber—in both cases causing changes in the chamber that move the needle. An aircraft altimeter is a type of aneroid barometer.

the weather. He concluded that the mass of surrounding air was exerting pressure on the mercury in the dish and thus counterbalancing the weight of the column of mercury in the tube.

Any instrument that measures atmospheric pressure is a barometer (from the Greek *baros*, meaning "weight").

Today, atmospheric pressure is measured at weather stations by electronic sensors that provide continuous measurement over time using millibars (mb, which express force per square meter of a surface area) or hectopascals (1 millibar = 1 hectopascal). To compare pressure conditions from one place to another, pressure measurements are adjusted to a standard of normal sea-level pressure, which is 1013.2 mb or 29.92 in. of mercury (Hg). In Canada and certain other countries, normal sea-level pressure is expressed as 101.32 kilopascal, or kPa (1 kPa = 10 mb). The adjusted pressure is known as *barometric pressure*.

Figure 5.6 shows comparative scales in millibars and inches of mercury for air pressure. Note that the normal range of Earth's atmospheric pressure from strong high pressure to deep low pressure is about 1050 to 980 mb (31.00 to 29.00 in.). The figure also indicates pressure extremes recorded for the United States and worldwide.

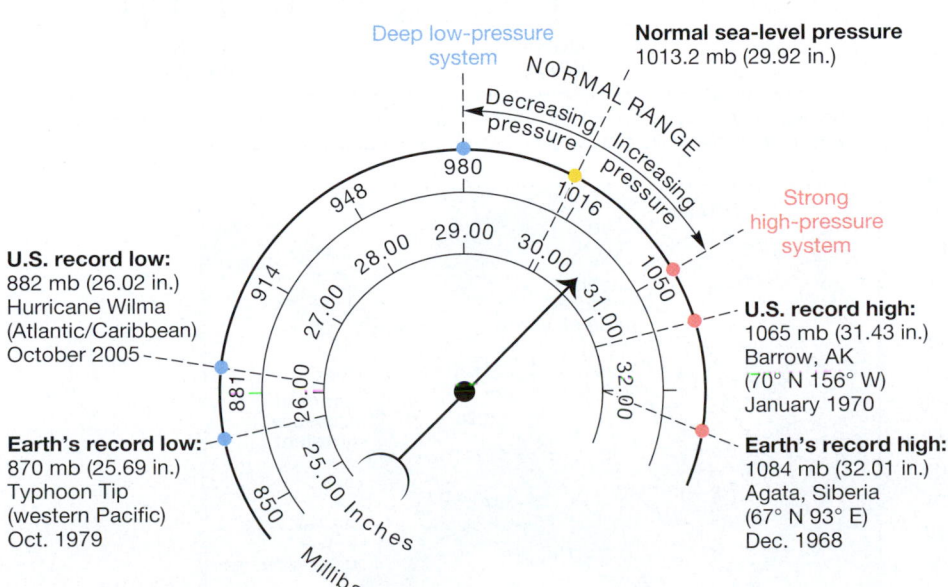

U.S. record low:
882 mb (26.02 in.)
Hurricane Wilma
(Atlantic/Caribbean)
October 2005

Earth's record low:
870 mb (25.69 in.)
Typhoon Tip
(western Pacific)
Oct. 1979

Normal sea-level pressure
1013.2 mb (29.92 in.)

Strong high-pressure system

U.S. record high:
1065 mb (31.43 in.)
Barrow, AK
(70° N 156° W)
January 1970

Earth's record high:
1084 mb (32.01 in.)
Agata, Siberia
(67° N 93° E)
Dec. 1968

▲**Figure 5.6 Atmospheric pressure readings and conversions.** Scales express barometric air pressure in millibars and inches of mercury (Hg), with average air pressure values and recorded pressure extremes.

Driving Forces Within the Atmosphere

Four forces determine both speed and direction of winds. The first of these is Earth's *gravitational force*, which exerts a virtually uniform pressure on the atmosphere over all of Earth. Gravity compresses the atmosphere, with the density decreasing as altitude increases. The gravitational force counteracts the outward centrifugal force acting on Earth's spinning surface and atmosphere. (Centrifugal force is the apparent force drawing a rotating body away from the center of rotation; it is equal and opposite to the centripetal, or "center-seeking," force.) Without gravity, there would be no atmospheric pressure—or atmosphere, for that matter.

The other forces affecting winds are the pressure gradient force, Coriolis force, and friction force. All of these forces operate on moving air and ocean currents at Earth's surface and influence global wind-circulation patterns.

Pressure Gradient Force

The **pressure gradient force** drives air from areas of higher barometric pressure (more-dense air) to areas of lower barometric pressure (less-dense air), thereby causing winds. A *gradient* is the rate of change in some property over distance. A *pressure gradient* is the change in pressure over some distance; stated another way, it is the change in pressure from point A to point B, divided by the distance from point A to point B. Without a pressure gradient force, there would be no wind.

High- and low-pressure areas exist in the atmosphere principally because Earth's surface is unequally heated. For example, cold, dry, dense air at the poles exerts greater pressure than warm, humid, less-dense air along the equator. On a regional scale, high- and low-pressure areas are associated with specific masses of air that have varying characteristics. When these air masses are near each other, a pressure gradient develops, and the pressure gradient force leads to horizontal air movement.

In addition, vertical air movement can create pressure gradients. This happens when air descends from the upper atmosphere and diverges at the surface or when air converges at the surface and ascends into the upper atmosphere. Strongly subsiding and diverging air is associated with high pressure, and strongly converging and rising air is associated with low pressure. These horizontal and vertical pressure differences establish a pressure gradient force that is a causal factor for winds.

An **isobar** is an isoline (a line that connects points of constant value) plotted on a weather map to connect points of equal pressure. The pattern of isobars provides a portrait of the pressure gradient between a high-pressure area and a low-pressure area. The spacing between isobars indicates the intensity of the pressure gradient.

Closer spacing of isobars denotes steepness in the pressure gradient (**Figure 5.7a**). A steep gradient causes faster air movement from a high-pressure area to a low-pressure area. Isobars spaced wider apart from one another mark a more gradual pressure gradient, creating slower airflow. Along a horizontal surface, a pressure gradient force that is acting alone (uncombined with other forces) produces movement at right angles to the isobars, so wind blows across the isobars from high to low pressure. Note the location of steep and gradual pressure gradients and their relationship to wind intensity on the weather map in **Figure 5.7b**.

Coriolis Force

The **Coriolis force** makes wind traveling in a straight path appear to be deflected in relation to Earth's rotating surface. This force is an effect of Earth's rotation. On a nonrotating Earth, surface winds would move in a straight line from areas of higher pressure to areas of lower pressure. But on our rotating planet, the Coriolis

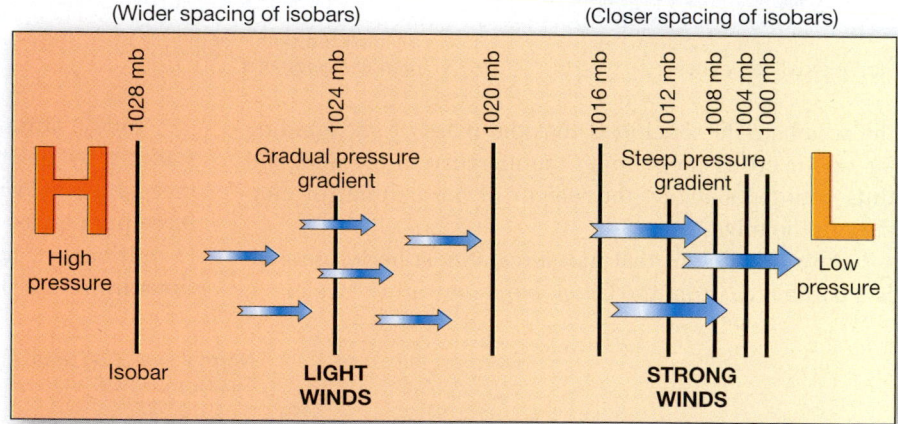

(a) The spacing of isobars indicates the pressure gradient. A gradual pressure gradient causes light winds, while a steep pressure gradient causes strong winds.

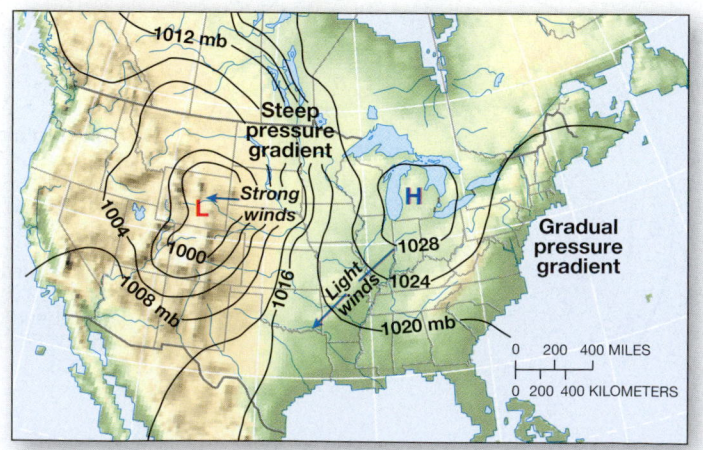

(b) Pressure gradient and wind strength in areas of high and low pressure portrayed on a weather map.

◀Figure 5.7
Effect of pressure gradient on wind speed.

force deflects anything that flies or flows across Earth's surface—wind, an airplane, or ocean currents—from a straight path. Because Earth rotates eastward, such objects appear to curve to the right in the Northern Hemisphere and to the left in the Southern Hemisphere (**Figure 5.8a**). Because the speed of Earth rotation varies with latitude, the strength of this deflection varies, being weakest at the equator and strongest at the poles.

Coriolis Force Example A simple example of an airplane helps explain this subtle but significant force. From the viewpoint of a person standing on Earth's surface looking at an airplane passing overhead, the airplane appears to curve off course. The airplane does not actually deviate from a straight path, but it appears to do so because we are standing on Earth's rotating surface. Because of this apparent deflection, the airplane must make constant corrections in flight path to maintain its "straight" heading relative to a rotating Earth (see **Figure 5.8b** and **c**).

Distribution and Significance Several factors contribute to the Coriolis force on Earth. First, the strength of this deflection varies with the speed of Earth's rotation, which varies with latitude (please review Table 2.1). Second, the deflection occurs regardless of the direction in which the object is moving and does not change the speed of the moving object. Third, the deflection increases as the speed of the moving object increases; thus, the faster the wind speed, the greater its apparent deflection. Although the Coriolis force affects all moving objects on Earth to some degree, its effects are negligible for small-scale motions that cover insignificant distance and time, such as a Frisbee or an arrow.

How does the Coriolis force affect wind? As air rises from the surface through the lowest levels of the atmosphere, it leaves the drag of surface friction behind and increases speed (the friction force is discussed just ahead). This increases the Coriolis force, bending the winds to the right in the Northern Hemisphere or to the left in the Southern Hemisphere, generally producing upper-air westerly winds from the subtropics to the poles. In the upper troposphere, the Coriolis force just balances the pressure gradient force. Consequently, the winds between higher-pressure and lower-pressure areas in the upper troposphere flow parallel to the isobars, along lines of equal pressure.

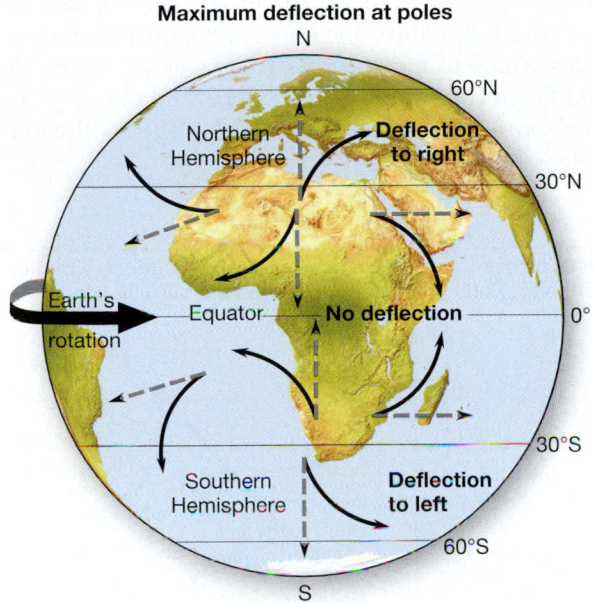

(a) Distribution of the Coriolis force on Earth. Apparent deflection is to the right in the Northern Hemisphere and to the left in the Southern Hemisphere; dashed lines show intended route and solid lines show actual movement.

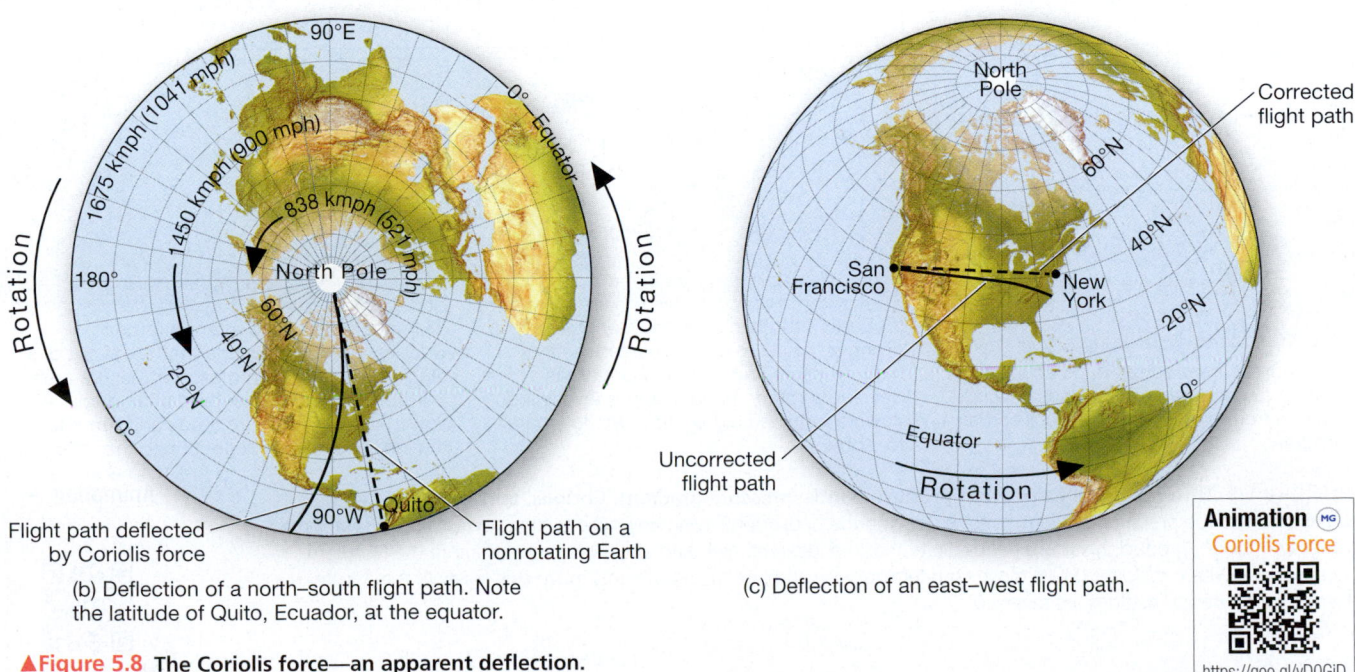

(b) Deflection of a north–south flight path. Note the latitude of Quito, Ecuador, at the equator.

(c) Deflection of an east–west flight path.

▲**Figure 5.8** The Coriolis force—an apparent deflection.

Friction Force

The **friction force** drags on wind as it moves across Earth's surfaces, but decreases with height above the surface. At the surface, the effect of friction varies with surface texture, wind speed, time of day and year, and atmospheric conditions. In general, rougher surfaces produce more friction. The friction force counters the Coriolis force so that surface winds cross isobars at an angle. The effect of surface friction extends to a height of about 500 m (around 1600 ft) so that it does not affect upper-air winds.

Summary of Physical Forces on Winds

Winds are a result of the combination of the pressure gradient, Coriolis, and friction forces (**Figure 5.9**). When the pressure gradient acts alone, shown in Figure 5.9a, winds flow from areas of high pressure to areas of low pressure. Note the descending, diverging air associated with high pressure and the ascending, converging air associated with low pressure in the side view.

Figure 5.9b illustrates the combined effect of the pressure gradient force and the Coriolis force on air currents in the upper atmosphere, above about 1000 m (3300 ft). Together, they produce winds that do not flow directly from high to low, but that flow around the pressure areas, remaining parallel to the isobars. Such winds are **geostrophic winds** and are characteristic of upper tropospheric circulation. (The suffix -*strophic* means "to turn.") Geostrophic winds produce the characteristic pattern shown on the upper-air weather map just ahead (see Figure 5.15).

Near the surface, friction prevents the equilibrium between the pressure gradient and Coriolis forces that results in geostrophic wind flows in the upper atmosphere (Figure 5.9c). Because surface friction decreases wind speed, it reduces the effect of the Coriolis force and causes winds to move across isobars at an angle. Thus, wind flows around pressure centers form enclosed areas called *pressure systems*, or *pressure cells*, as illustrated in Figure 5.9c.

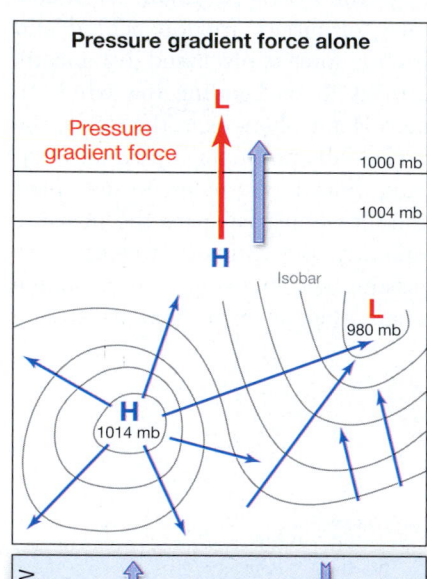

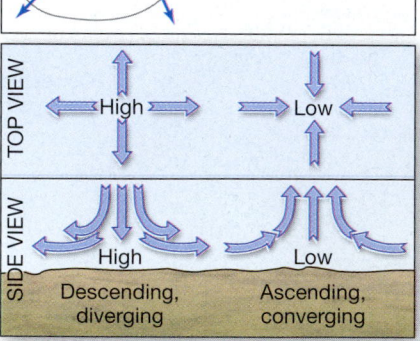

(a) The pressure gradient force acting by itself on a nonrotating Earth causes winds to move from high to low pressure across isobars.

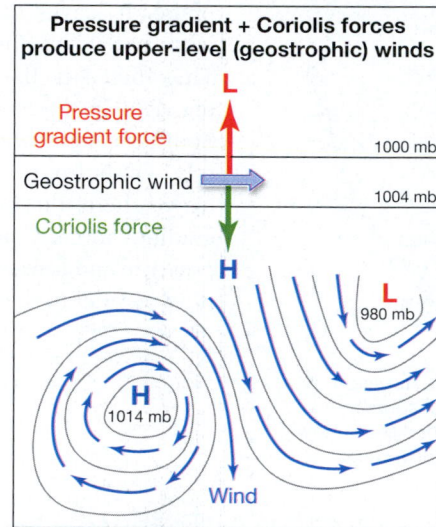

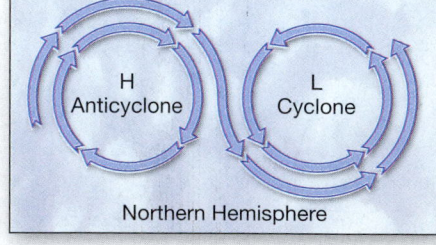

(b) Earth's rotation adds the Coriolis force, giving a "twist" to air movements so that high-pressure and low-pressure areas develop a rotary motion. Upper-level winds flowing between highs and lows flow parallel to isobars.

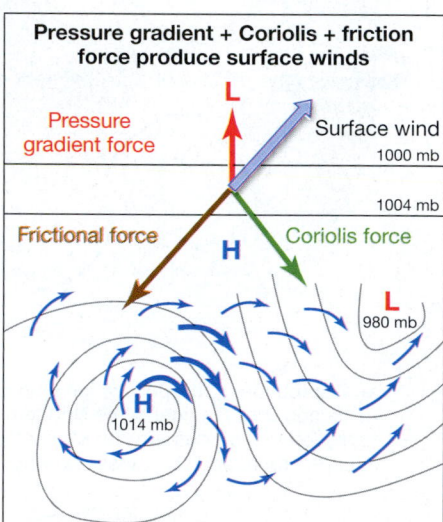

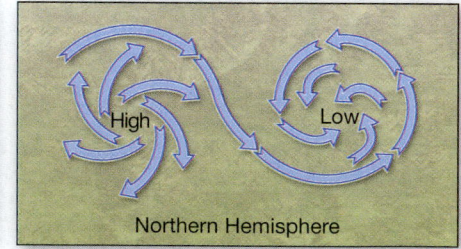

(c) Friction adds a countering force to Coriolis, producing winds that spiral out of a high-pressure area into a low-pressure area. Surface winds cross isobars at an angle. Air flows into low-pressure areas and turns to the left, because of deflection to the right.

▲**Figure 5.9 Three physical forces that produce winds: pressure gradient, Coriolis, and friction.** The Coriolis force counters the pressure gradient force, producing the geostrophic wind flow. The friction force combines with the other two forces, producing surface winds. Note that the idealized high and low pressure areas are in the Northern Hemisphere, where cyclones (lows) move counterclockwise and anticyclones (highs) move clockwise. In the Southern Hemisphere, these directions are reversed.

Animation MG
Global Wind Patterns

https://goo.gl/KXSJvR

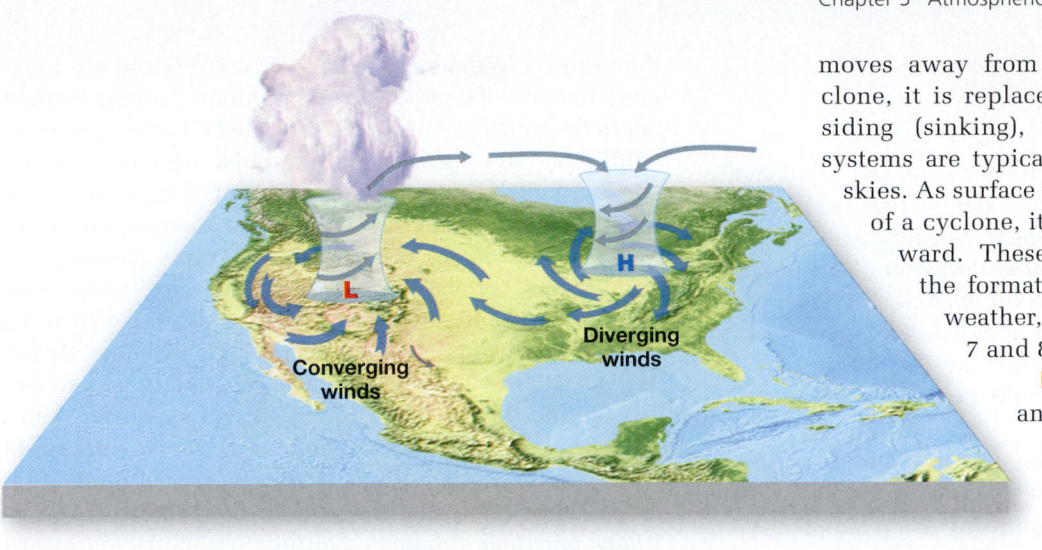

▲Figure 5.10 **High- and low-pressure cells and associated wind movement.** Side view of high- and low-pressure cells over the United States. Note surface winds spiraling clockwise out of the high-pressure area toward the low pressure, where winds spiral counterclockwise into the low.

High- and Low-Pressure Systems

In the Northern Hemisphere, surface winds spiral out from a *high-pressure area* in a clockwise direction, forming an **anticyclone**, and spiral into a *low-pressure area* in a counterclockwise direction, forming a **cyclone** (Figure 5.9). In the Southern Hemisphere these circulation patterns are reversed, with winds flowing counterclockwise out of anticyclonic high-pressure cells and clockwise into cyclonic low-pressure cells.

Anticyclones and cyclones have vertical air movement in addition to these horizontal patterns. As air moves away from the center of an anticyclone, it is replaced by descending, or subsiding (sinking), air. These high-pressure systems are typically characterized by clear skies. As surface air flows toward the center of a cyclone, it converges and moves upward. These rising motions promote the formation of cloudy and stormy weather, as discussed in Chapters 7 and 8.

Figure 5.10 shows high- and low-pressure systems over the United States, with a side view of the wind movement around and within each pressure cell. Strong low-pressure systems in the tropics can form destructive *tropical cyclones*, also called hurricanes and typhoons (see discussion in Chapter 7). In the midlatitudes and high latitudes, these low-pressure systems are *extratropical cyclones*, or *midlatitude cyclones*, associated with strong winds, heavy precipitation, and extreme weather in both hemispheres. **Figure 5.11** shows a pressure map and satellite view of an extratropical cyclone over North America in October 2010.

You may have noticed that on weather maps, pressure systems vary in size and shape. Often these cells have elongated shapes and are called low-pressure "troughs" or high-pressure "ridges" (see Figure 5.15 ahead).

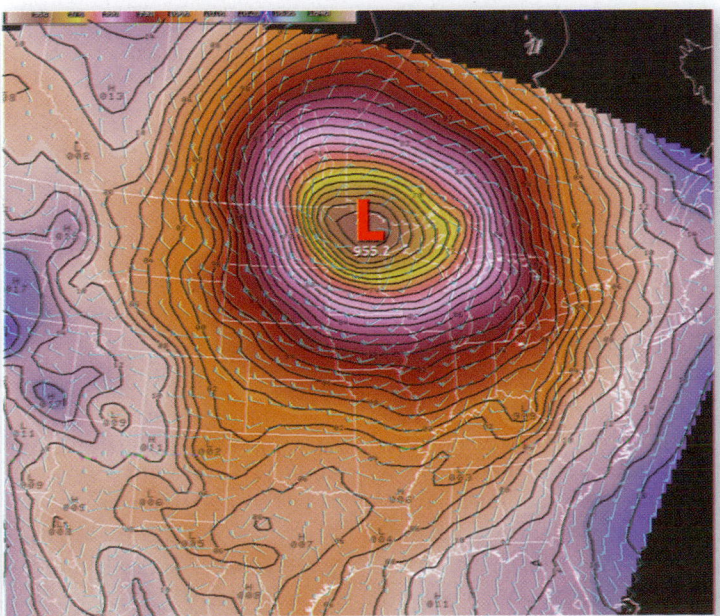

(a) Sea level pressure readings for the midlatitude cyclone, centered over Minnesota and Wisconsin.

(b) Satellite image shows the cyclone's counterclockwise flow.

▲Figure 5.11 **Midlatitude cyclone over North America.** Surface-pressure and satellite image of an unusually large cyclonic storm on October 26, 2010 (see http://www.weather.gov/dlh/101026_extratropicallow). [(a) NWS. (b) NASA/NOAA *GOES* project.]

Atmospheric Patterns of Motion

With the concepts related to pressure and wind movement in mind, we are ready to examine Earth's circulation patterns. Physical geographers categorize atmospheric circulation at several spatial scales, from the global patterns known as *primary circulation*, to the regional winds related to migrating high-pressure and low-pressure systems (also called *secondary circulation*), to the local winds in valleys, on mountain passes, or along certain coastlines.

To begin our study of global circulation, we should remember the relationships between pressure, density, and temperature as they apply to the unequal heating of Earth's surface (energy surpluses at the equator and energy deficits at the poles). The warmer, less-dense air along the equator rises, creating low pressure at the surface, and the colder, more-dense air at the poles sinks, creating high pressure at the surface. If Earth did not rotate, the result would be a simple wind flow from the poles to the equator. This meridional flow—in which winds move north or south along meridians of longitude—would relate solely by the pressure gradient. However, Earth does rotate, creating a more complex flow system. On a rotating Earth, the poles-to-equator flow is broken up into latitudinal zones, both at the surface and aloft in the upper-air winds. Winds moving generally east or west along parallels of latitude are *zonal* flows.

Primary Pressure Areas and Associated Winds

Global circulation is dominated by high- and low-pressure centers, or cells, that form uneven latitudinal belts of similar pressure interrupted by landmasses (**Figure 5.12**). The pressure cells within these belts range in size and shift slightly in location from January to July, producing changing weather patterns in the regions over which they pass. Between these pressure areas flow the primary surface winds, which are suggested by the isobars on the pressure maps.

Four broad primary pressure areas cover the Northern and Southern Hemispheres (**Table 5.2**). The formation of the **equatorial low** (marked by the ITCZ line on the maps) and the weak **polar highs** at the North and South poles

(not shown, as the maps are cut off at 80° N and 80° S) relates to *thermal* (temperature) conditions. The warm, light air in the equatorial region is associated with low pressure, while the cold, dense air in the polar regions is associated with high pressure. The formation of the **subtropical highs** (marked with an H on the map) and **subpolar lows** (marked with an L) relate to *dynamic* (mechanical) factors. Remember that converging, rising air is associated with low pressure, whereas subsiding, diverging air is associated with high pressure—these are dynamic factors because they result from the physical displacement of air.

Within the subtropical high-pressure area, the dominant pressure cells in the Atlantic region are the **Bermuda High** in July, which shifts to become the **Azores High** in January. In the Pacific region, the **Pacific High**, or *Hawaiian High*, dominates in July and shifts southward in January. In the Southern Hemisphere, three large high-pressure centers dominate the Pacific, Atlantic, and Indian Oceans.

Within the subpolar low-pressure area, two cyclonic cells exist in January over the oceans near their namesake islands: the North Pacific **Aleutian Low** and the North Atlantic **Icelandic Low**. Both cells are dominant in winter and weaken or disappear in summer with the strengthening of high-pressure systems in the subtropics.

Of the two polar regions, the Antarctic has the stronger and more persistent high-pressure system, the **Antarctic High**, forming over the Antarctic landmass (shown ahead in Figure GIA 5.1.). Less consistent is a polar high-pressure cell over the Arctic Ocean, which, when present, tends to locate over the colder northern continental areas in winter (Canadian and Siberian Highs) rather than directly over the relatively warmer Arctic Ocean.

Geosystems in Action 5 illustrates the pressure areas and wind patterns that determine Earth's atmospheric circulation. We now briefly discuss the characteristics of each pressure region and its associated winds.

Equatorial Low or ITCZ: Warm and Rainy Constant high Sun altitude and consistent daylength (12 hours a day, year-round) create energy surpluses in the equatorial region throughout the year. The associated warming in this region leads to lighter, less-dense, rising air, with surface winds converging along the entire extent of the low-pressure trough. This converging air is extremely moist and full of latent heat energy. As it rises, the air expands and cools, producing heavy rainfall throughout this zone (**Figure 5.13**; we discuss precipitation in Chapter 6).

The equatorial low, or *equatorial trough*, forms the **intertropical convergence zone (ITCZ)**, which is identified by bands of clouds along the equator (see dashed line in Figure 5.12 and **Figure GIA 5.1**). The ITCZ shifts southward in January in response to high Sun altitudes in the Southern Hemisphere and northward in July as high Sun altitudes shift to the Tropic of Cancer in the Northern Hemisphere. Within the ITCZ, winds are calm or mildly variable because of the weak pressure gradient and the rising air. These equatorial calms are called the *doldrums*

TABLE 5.2 Four Hemispheric Pressure Areas

Name	Cause	Location	Characteristics
Equatorial low	Thermal	10° N to 10° S	Warm/wet
Subtropical high	Dynamic	20°–35° N, 20°–35° S	Hot/dry
Subpolar low	Dynamic	60° N, 60° S	Cool/wet
Polar high	Thermal	90° N, 90° S	Cold/dry

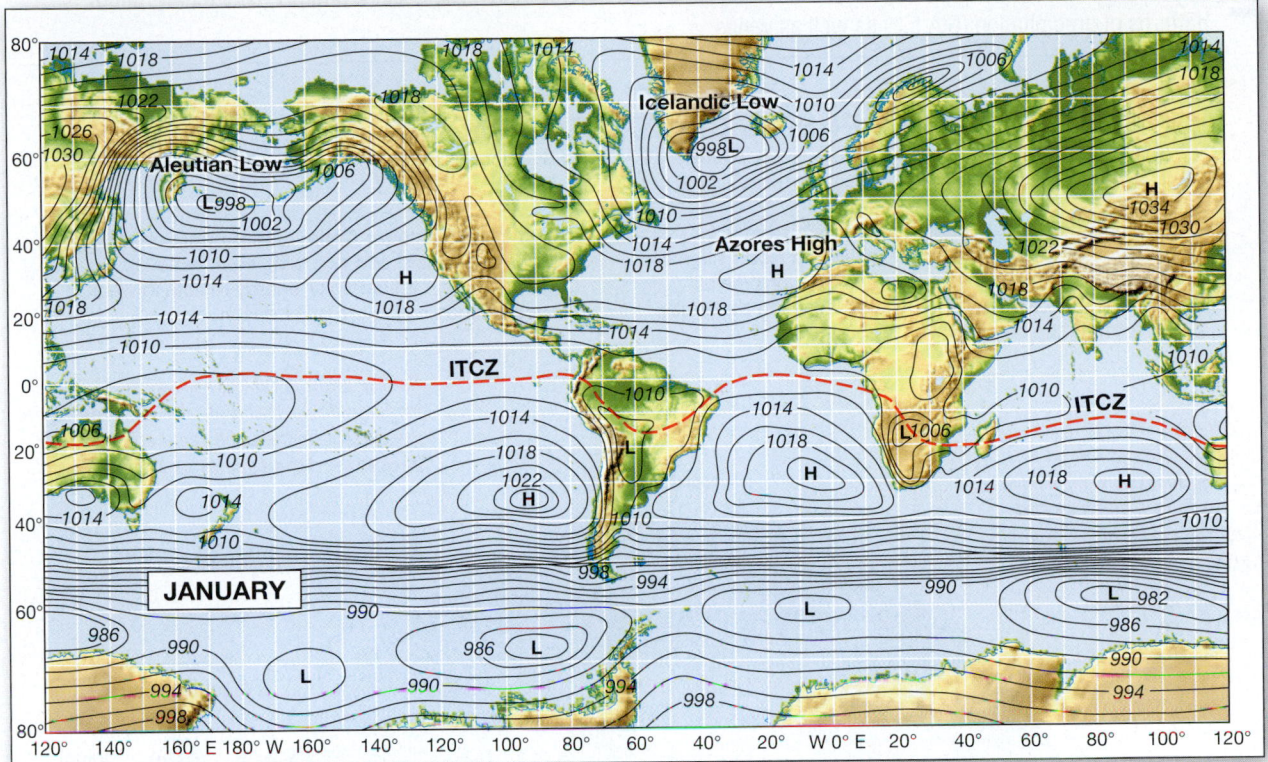

(a) January average surface barometric pressures (millibars); dashed line marks the general location of the intertropical convergence zone (ITCZ).

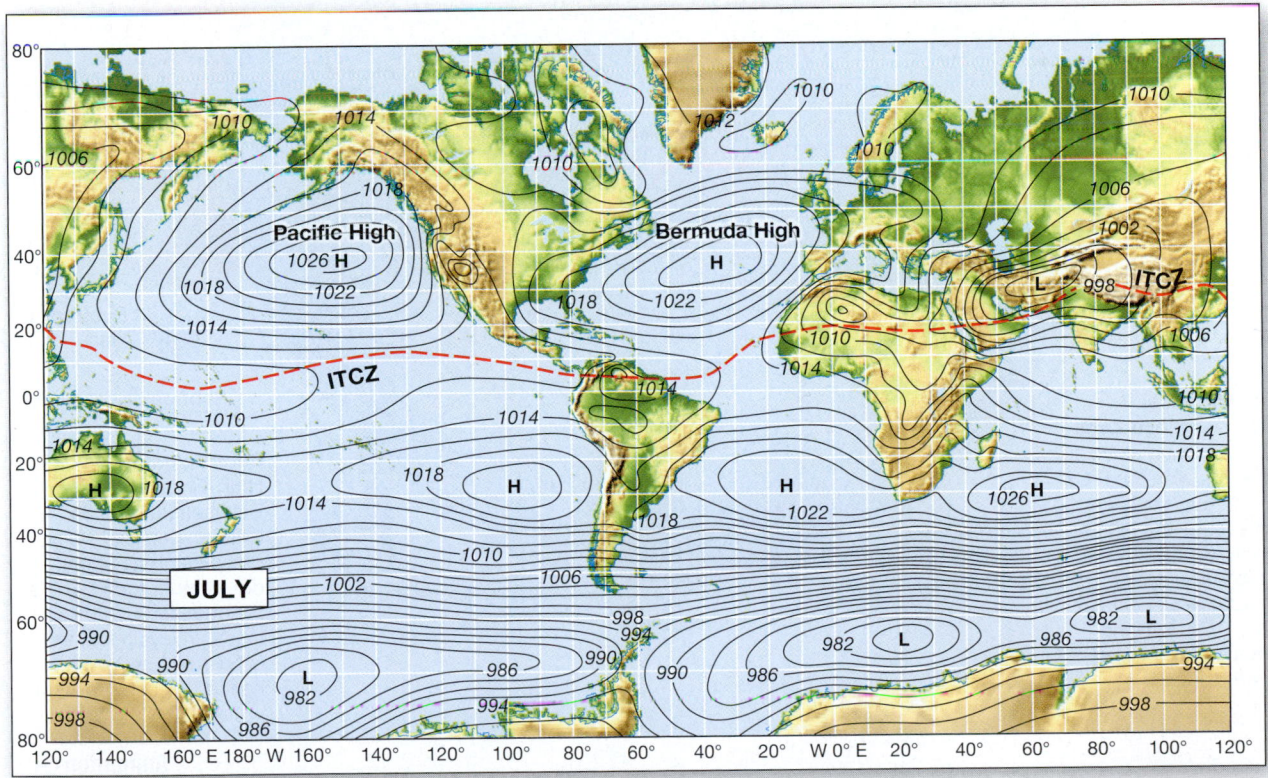

(b) July average surface barometric pressures. Compare pressures in the North Pacific, the North Atlantic, and the central Asian landmass with the January map above.

▲**Figure 5.12 Global barometric pressures for January and July.** [Adapted by author and redrawn from National Climatic Data Center, Monthly Climatic Data for the World, 46 (January and July 1993), and WMO and NOAA.]

Animation (MG)
Global Patterns of Pressure

https://goo.gl/UAe4pU

Earth's atmospheric circulation transfers thermal energy from the equator toward the poles. The overall pattern of the atmospheric circulation (GIA 5.1) arises from the distribution of high- and low-pressure regions, which determines patterns of precipitation (GIA 5.2) as well as winds.

5.1 GENERAL ATMOSPHERIC CIRCULATION MODEL

In both the Northern and Southern Hemispheres, zones of converging, rising air (lows), and diverging, sinking air (highs), form circulation cells.

Subpolar Low-Pressure Cells Persistent lows (cyclones) over the North Pacific and North Atlantic cause cool, moist conditions. Cold, northern air masses clash with warmer air masses to the south, forming the *polar front*.

Polar High-Pressure Cells A small atmospheric polar mass is cold and dry, with weak anticyclonic high pressure. Limited solar energy results in weak, variable winds called the *polar easterlies*.

Hadley cells Winds rise along the ITCZ and sweep poleward at high altitude, then sink to the surface in the subtropics and circulate back toward the equator as the trade winds.

Westerlies In the mid-latitudes, the westerlies are the prevailing surface winds, formed where air sinks and diverges along the poleward border of the Hadley cells.

North Pole

Polar front

Polar jet stream

Polar easterlies

Westerlies

Westerlies

Subtropical jet stream

Sub-tropical high

Tropic of Cancer

Northeast trade winds

Trade winds

ITCZ

Equator

Hadley cells

Southeast trade winds

Tropic of Capricorn

Intertropical Convergence Zone (ITCZ) Lying along the equator, the ITCZ is a trough of low pressure and light or calm winds—the doldrums. Moist, unstable air rises in the ITCZ, causing heavy precipitation year-round.

Westerlies

Polar front

South Pole

Subtropical high

Subtropical jet stream

Polar jet stream

Subtropical High-Pressure Cells Between 20° and 35° latitude, persistent high pressure areas of hot, dry weather form Earth's major deserts. Within these anticyclones, air is pushed downward, heating by compression.

MasteringGeography™

Visit the Study Area in MasteringGeography™ to explore atmospheric circulation.

Visualize: Study geoscience animations of atmospheric circulation patterns.

Assess: Demonstrate understanding of Earth's atmospheric circulation (if assigned by instructor).

Animation (MG)
Global Atmospheric Circulation

https://goo.gl/RqR5L5

5.2 PRECIPITATION PATTERNS AND ATMOSPHERIC CIRCULATION

Areas of higher precipitation in green, yellow, and orange are zones of low pressure and moist, rising air. Areas of lower precipitation, shown in white on the maps, are zones of high pressure, where air sinks and dries out. Notice the band of heavy rainfall along the ITCZ.

Converging air along the ITCZ rises and cools, producing clouds and heavy rainfall.

ITCZ

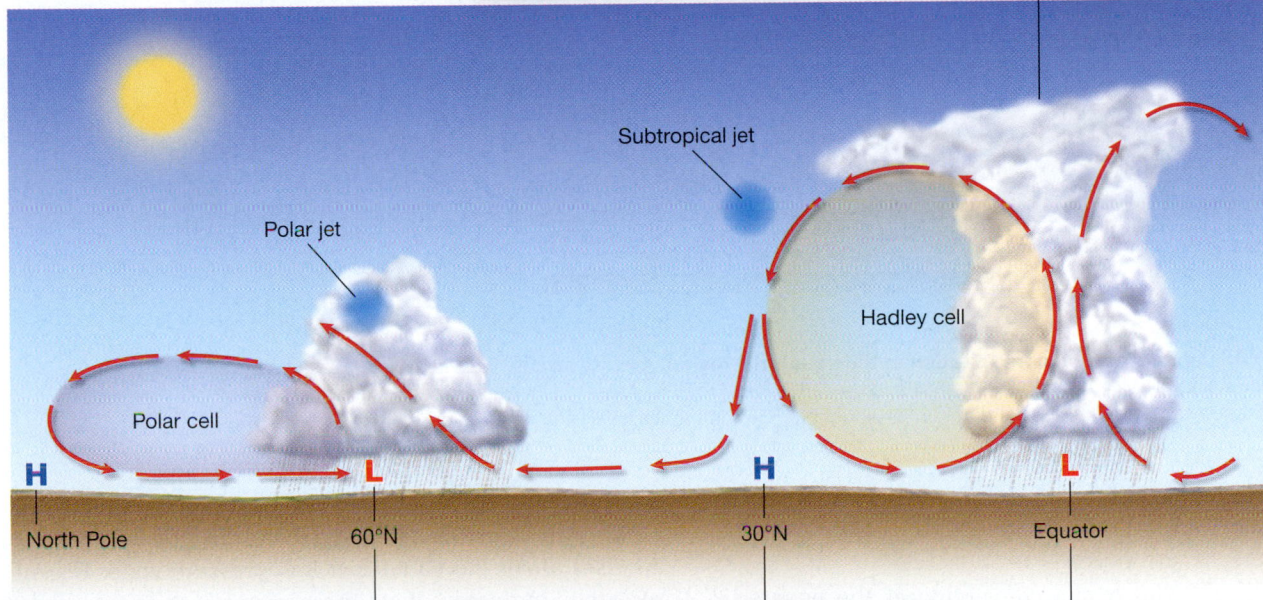

Polar jet

Subtropical jet

Polar cell

Hadley cell

H   L   H   L

North Pole   60°N   30°N   Equator

Cyclonic storms associated with the Aleutian and Icelandic low pressure cells produce winter precipitation in the cool, moist climates of northwest North America (such as in Oregon and British Columbia) and northwest Europe (such as in coastal Norway, shown here).

Subtropical high pressure in the south Atlantic Ocean and offshore cool currents produce the dry climate of southern Africa's Namib Desert; pictured here is the Sossusvlei area of Namib Naukluft National Park, Namibia.

Consistent precipitation characterizes the zone of low pressure in the equatorial region.

GEOquiz

1. Explain: The position of subtropical highs and subpolar lows shifts with the seasons. Explain how this shift affects climate patterns of the midlatitudes.

2. Compare: Describe surface air movements where a Hadley cell meets a midlatitude cell and where two Hadley cells meet the ITCZ. How do these movements explain the climate patterns along these boundaries?

3. Infer: In what directions would the westerlies and northeast trade winds blow if there were no Coriolis force?

4. Explain: What causes the difference in precipitation between the dry and rainy seasons?

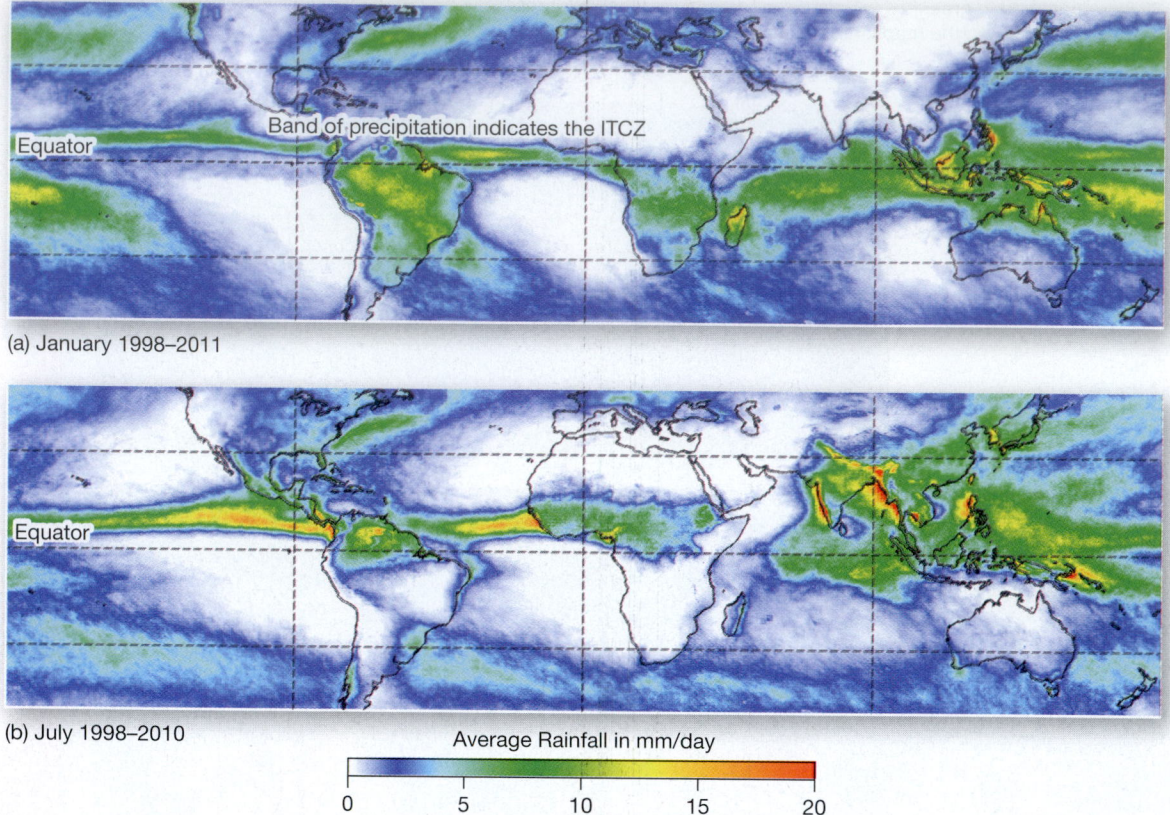

(a) January 1998–2011

(b) July 1998–2010

Average Rainfall in mm/day

0   5   10   15   20

▲**Figure 5.13** **January and July precipitation in the equatorial region.** Average rainfall (1998–2010) as measured by NASA's Tropical Rainfall Measuring Mission satellite for (a) January and (b) July. Areas of highest precipitation are orange/red; zero precipitation is white. Note the band of rainfall along the ITCZ and the seasonal variation in its position. [GSFC/NASA.]

because of the difficulty sailing ships encountered when attempting to move through this zone.

Trade Winds The winds converging at the equatorial low are known generally as the **trade winds**, or trades, named during the era of sailing ships that carried merchandise for trade across the seas. *Northeast trade winds* blow in the Northern Hemisphere and *southeast trade winds* in the Southern Hemisphere. These are the most consistent winds on Earth.

Circulation cells known as *Hadley cells* (after the 18th-century English scientist George Hadley) in each hemisphere begin with air rising along the low-pressure trough of the ITCZ. Within these cells, upper-air flow moves northward and southward into the subtropics, descending to the surface in the high-pressure systems of the subtropical latitudes, and returning to the ITCZ as the trade winds.

Subtropical Highs: Hot and Dry Between 20° and 35° latitude in both hemispheres, broad high-pressure zones of hot, dry air brings clear, frequently cloudless skies over the Sahara and the Arabian Deserts and portions of the Indian Ocean (see Figure GIA 5.2). These subtropical anticyclones generally form as air above the subtropics heats by compression on its descent to the surface. Warmer air has a greater capacity to absorb water vapor than does cooler air, making this descending warm air

relatively dry (discussed in Chapter 6). The air is also dry because moisture is removed as heavy precipitation as air rises along the equatorial low-pressure zone. Recent research indicates that these semi-permanent high-pressure areas may intensify with climate change, with impacts on droughts and extreme weather events such as tropical cyclones.

The subtropical highs are zones of windless, hot, dry air. Sailors dubbed these regions the *horse latitudes*, a name of uncertain origin that is popularly attributed to becalmed and stranded sailing crews of past centuries who destroyed the horses on board, not wanting to share food or water with the livestock.

The entire high-pressure system migrates with the summer high Sun, fluctuating about 5°–10° in latitude. The eastern sides of these anticyclonic systems are drier, with subsiding air, and associated with cool ocean currents, producing arid climates (**Figure 5.14**). Earth's major deserts generally occur within the subtropical belt and extend to the west coast of several continents. The western sides of these systems have weaker subsidence and produce surface winds that pass over warm ocean currents, gathering moisture from evaporation and carrying it toward landmasses where it falls as precipitation; the U.S. Southeast coast is an example.

Westerlies Surface air diverging within the subtropical high-pressure cells generates Earth's principal surface

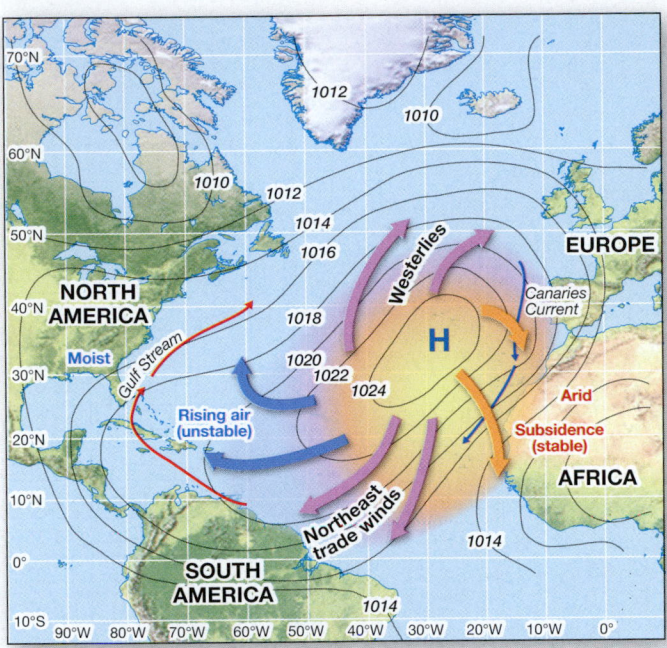

▲Figure 5.14 **Subtropical high-pressure system in the Atlantic.** In the Northern Hemisphere, subsiding air on the east side produces dry, stable conditions. On the west side, rising air is associated with wetter conditions, enhanced by the presence of warm offshore currents (shown in Figure 5.22).

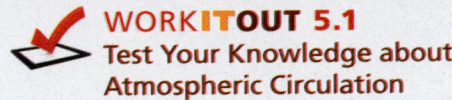

WORK**IT**OUT 5.1
Test Your Knowledge about Atmospheric Circulation

Using Figure 5.12, Geosystems in Action 5, and the chapter text, answer the following questions.

1. Which two pressure systems dominate in winter at about 60° N latitude? How do these low-pressure cyclonic storms affect weather and climate in North America and in Europe?
2. Within the Hadley cell circulation, at about what latitude is air rising? At about what latitude is air subsiding? Which surface winds are associated with the Hadley cell circulation?
3. Does the Coriolis force have a greater effect on the direction of the trade winds or the westerlies? Explain your answer.

Upper Atmospheric Circulation

Circulation in the middle and upper troposphere is an important component of the atmosphere's general circulation. For surface-pressure maps, we plot air pressure using the fixed elevation of sea level as a reference datum—a *constant height surface*. For upper-atmosphere pressure maps, we use a fixed pressure value of 500 mb as a reference datum and plot its elevation above sea level throughout the map to produce a **constant isobaric surface**.

Figure 5.15a illustrates the undulating surface elevations of a 500-mb constant isobaric surface for an April day. Similar to surface-pressure maps, closer spacing of the height contours indicates faster winds; wider spacing indicates slower winds. On this map, altitude variations in the isobaric surface are ridges for high pressure (with height contours on the map bending poleward) and troughs for low pressure (with height contours on the map bending equatorward).

The pattern of ridges and troughs in the upper-air wind flow is important in sustaining surface cyclonic (low-pressure) and anticyclonic (high-pressure) circulation. Along ridges, winds slow and converge (pile up); along troughs, winds accelerate and diverge (spread out). (Note the wind barbs indicating speed and direction in Figure 5.15a.)

Figure 5.15b shows convergence and divergence in the upper-air flow. Divergence aloft is important to cyclonic circulation at the surface because it creates an outflow of air aloft that stimulates an inflow of air into the low-pressure cyclone (like what happens when you open an upstairs window to create an upward draft). Similarly, convergence aloft is important to anticyclonic circulation at the surface, driving descending airflows and causing airflow to diverge from high-pressure anticyclones.

Rossby Waves Within the westerly flow of geostrophic winds are great waving undulations, the **Rossby waves**, named for meteorologist Carl G. Rossby, who first described them mathematically in 1938. Rossby waves occur along the polar front, where colder air meets warmer air, and bring tongues of cold air southward, with warmer tropical air moving northward. The development

winds: the trade winds that flow toward the equator and the **westerlies**, which are the dominant winds flowing from the subtropics toward higher latitudes. The westerlies diminish somewhat in summer and are stronger in winter in both hemispheres. These winds are less consistent than the trade winds, with variability resulting from migrating midlatitude pressure systems and topographic barriers that can change wind direction.

Subpolar Lows: Cool and Moist The area of contrast between cold air from higher latitudes and warm air from lower latitudes forms the **polar front**, where masses of air with different characteristics meet (discussed in Chapter 7). This front encircles Earth at about the latitude of the subpolar lows.

Figure GIA 5.2 illustrates the polar front, where warm, moist air from the westerlies meets cold, dry air from the polar and Arctic regions. Warm air is displaced upward above the cool air at this front, leading to condensation and precipitation (we discuss frontal precipitation in Chapter 7). In the Southern Hemisphere, a discontinuous belt of subpolar low-pressure systems surrounds Antarctica.

Polar Highs: Frigid and Dry Polar high-pressure cells are weak because the polar atmospheric receives little energy from the Sun to put it into motion. Variable winds, cold and dry, move away from the polar region in an anticyclonic direction. They descend and diverge clockwise in the Northern Hemisphere (counterclockwise in the Southern Hemisphere) and form weak, variable winds of the **polar easterlies** (Figure GIA 5.2).

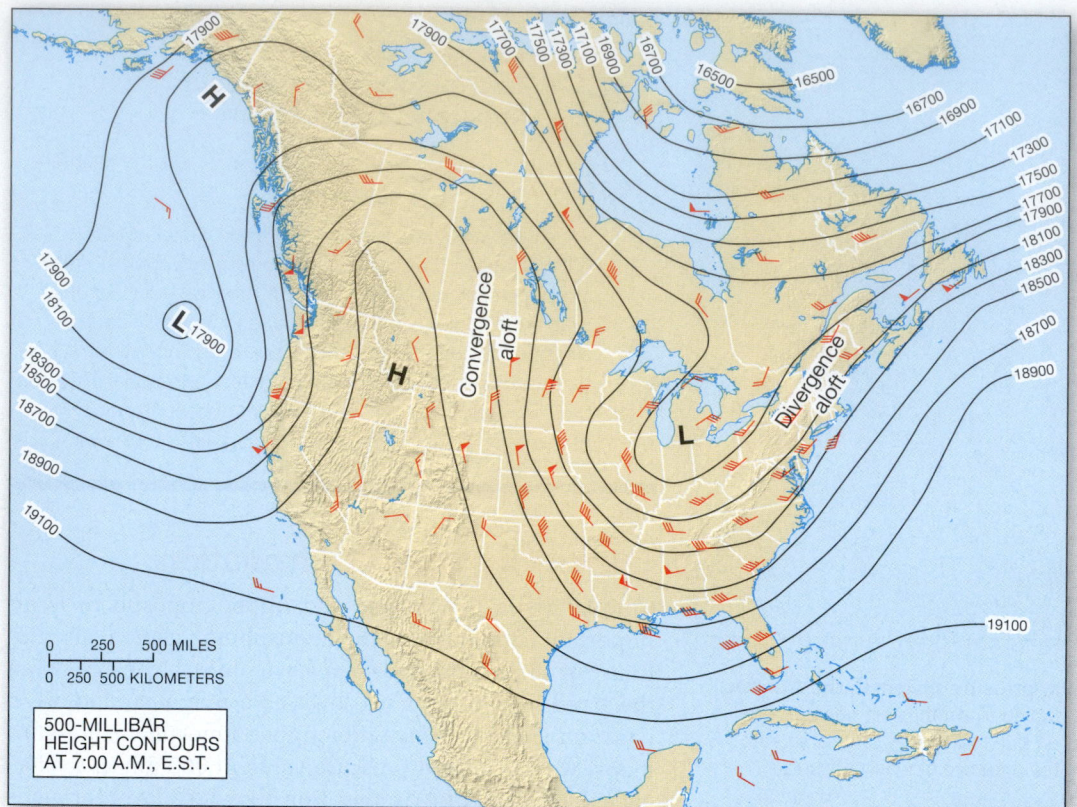

Wind Speed Symbol	Miles (statute) per Hour	Knots
◎	Calm	Calm
─	1–2	1–2
╲	3–8	3–7
╲	9–14	8–12
╲	15–20	13–17
╲	21–25	18–22
╲	26–31	23–27
╲	32–37	28–32
╲	38–43	33–37
╲	44–49	38–42
╲	50–54	43–47
╲	55–60	48–52
╲	61–66	53–57
╲	67–71	58–62
╲	72–77	63–67
╲	78–83	68–72
╲	84–89	73–77
╲	119–123	103–107

(a) Contours show height (in feet) at which 500-mb pressure occurs—a constant isobaric surface. The pattern of contours reveals geostrophic wind patterns in the troposphere ranging from 16,500 to 19,100 ft in elevation.

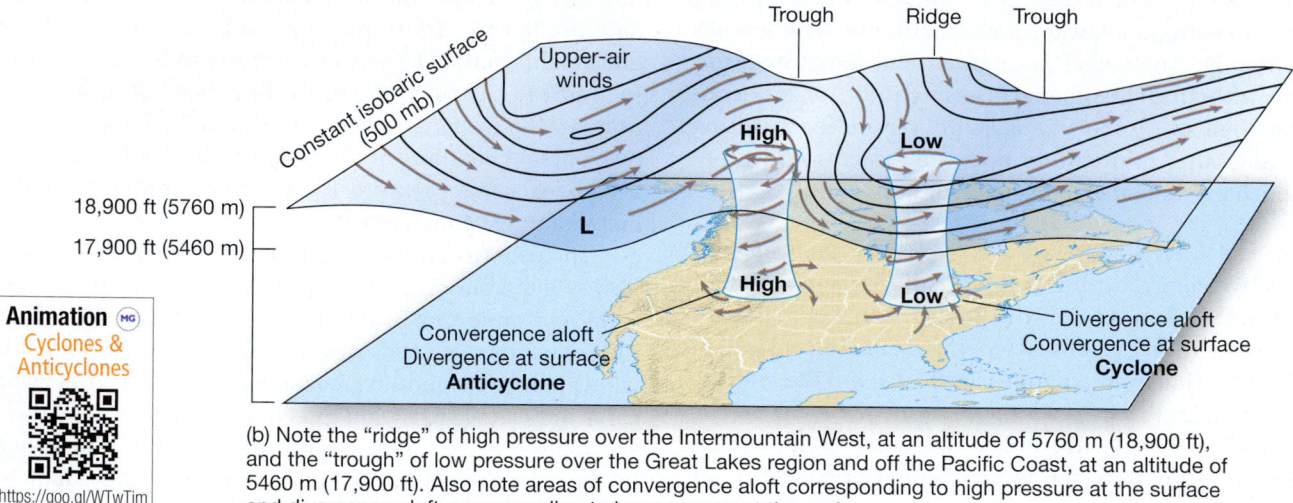

Animation Ⓜ
Cyclones & Anticyclones

https://goo.gl/WTwTim

(b) Note the "ridge" of high pressure over the Intermountain West, at an altitude of 5760 m (18,900 ft), and the "trough" of low pressure over the Great Lakes region and off the Pacific Coast, at an altitude of 5460 m (17,900 ft). Also note areas of convergence aloft corresponding to high pressure at the surface and divergence aloft corresponding to low pressure at the surface.

▲Figure 5.15 **Analysis of a constant isobaric surface for an April day.**

of Rossby waves begins with undulations that then increase in amplitude to form waves (**Figures 5.16** and **5.17**).

The extremely cold temperatures in the United States during the winter of 2014, dubbed the "polar vortex," occurred when one of these waves meandered farther south than usual. However, this term does not actually refer to a weather event. The *polar vortex* is the semipermanent area of low pressure in the upper atmosphere at Earth's two poles. The polar vortex has cyclonic flow aloft, and anticyclonic flow at the surface (the polar high), usually strongest in winter. (The rotation is caused by the

Coriolis force.) When it pushes southward or breaks up, extremely cold air can move into Europe and the United States, as happened again in 2016.

Rossby waves produce upper-air ridges and troughs of high and low air pressure. Upper-air troughs, with diverging air, support cyclonic storm systems, with converging air, at the surface. Rossby waves develop along the flow axis of a jet stream.

Jet Streams The most prominent movement in the upper-level westerly geostrophic wind flows are the

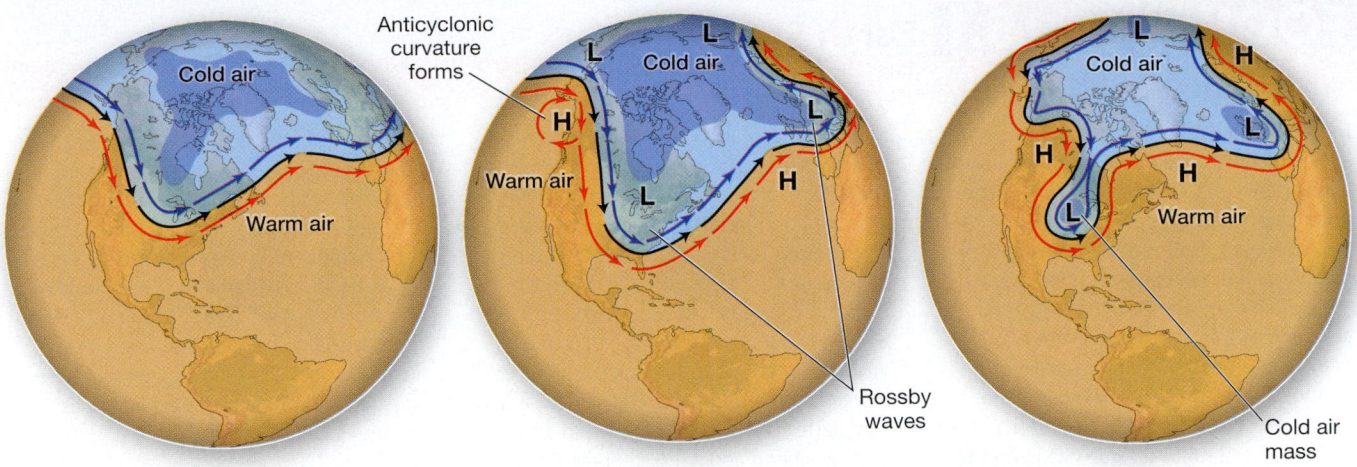

(a) Upper-air circulation and jet stream begin to gently undulate within the westerlies.

(b) Undulations increase in amplitude (height) in north–south direction, forming Rossby waves.

(c) Strong development of waves produces cells of cold and warm air—high pressure ridges and low-pressure troughs.

▲Figure 5.16 **Rossby wave formation in the upper atmosphere.**

Animation 🅜🅖
Jet Stream and Rossby Waves

https://goo.gl/gFWGvP

jet streams, irregular, concentrated bands of wind occurring at several different locations that influence surface weather systems (Figures 5.17a and GIA 5 show jet stream location). The jet streams normally are 160–480 km (100–300 mi) wide by 900–2150 m (3000–7000 ft) thick, with core speeds that can exceed 300 kmph (190 mph), as shown in Figure 5.17b. Jet streams in each hemisphere tend to weaken during the hemisphere's summer and strengthen during its winter as the streams shift closer to the equator. The pattern of high-pressure ridges and low-pressure troughs in the meandering jet streams causes variation in jet-stream speeds.

The *polar jet stream* meanders between 30° and 70° N latitude, at the tropopause along the polar front, at altitudes between 7600 and 10,700 m (24,900 and 35,100 ft). The polar jet stream can migrate as far south as Texas, steering colder air masses into North America and influencing

surface storm paths traveling eastward. In the summer, the polar jet stream remains at higher latitudes and exerts less influence on midlatitude storms.

In the subtropical latitudes, near the boundary between tropical and midlatitude air, the *subtropical jet stream* flows near the tropopause. The subtropical jet stream meanders from 20° to 50° latitude and may occur over North America simultaneously with the polar jet stream—sometimes the two will actually merge for brief episodes.

An excellent example illustrating Earth's global atmospheric circulation is the Mount Pinatubo volcanic eruption in 1991. Focus Study 5.1 illustrates the global movement of aerosols in the days following this event, the second greatest eruption during the 20th century.

(a) Average locations of the two jet streams over North America.

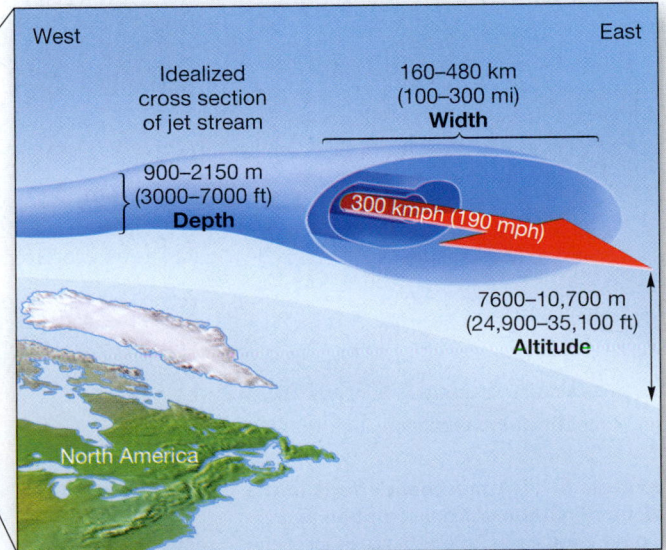

(b) Width, depth, altitude, and core speed of an idealized polar jet stream.

▲Figure 5.17 **Jet stream position and characteristics over North America.**

FOCUSstudy 5.1 Earth Systems
Global Impacts of the Mount Pinatubo Volcanic Eruption

More than any other Earth system, our atmosphere is shared by all humanity, as winds move pollutants worldwide, unconfined by political borders. The 1991 eruption of Mount Pinatubo in the Philippines provided a unique opportunity to assess the dynamics of atmospheric circulation as scientists tracked contaminants from the volcanic explosion using satellite monitoring (**Figure 5.1.1a**). The Mount Pinatubo event ejected 15–20 million tons of ash, dust, and sulfur dioxide (SO_2) into the atmosphere. As the sulfur dioxide rose into the stratosphere, it quickly formed sulfuric acid (H_2SO_4) aerosols, which concentrated at an altitude of 16–25 km (10–15.5 mi).

In a satellite image from the first few days after the eruption (**Figure 5.1.1b**), we see the atmospheric aerosols borne by global winds: millions of tons of dust from African soils crossing the Atlantic Ocean, the effects of smoke from Kuwaiti oil well fires set during the 1990 Persian Gulf War, smoke from forest fires in Siberia, and haze off the East Coast of the United States. During the weeks following (**Figures 5.1.1c** and **d**), Mount Pinatubo's aerosols, mixed with this airborne dust, smoke, and haze, were carried around Earth by global circulation patterns. This debris increased atmospheric albedo about 1.5%. Some 60 days after the eruption, the aerosol cloud covered about 42% of the globe, from 20° S to 30° N. For almost 2 years, a small temporary lowering of average temperatures followed.

As aerosols travel freely over Earth, international concerns about transboundary air pollution and nuclear weapons testing illustrate how the fluid movement of the atmosphere links humanity more than perhaps any other natural or cultural factor. The global spread of low-level radioactive contamination from Japan's nuclear disaster associated with the 2011 earthquake and tsunami, which reached the U.S. West Coast in 2014, is another example of this linkage. In our shared global atmosphere, one person's or country's exhalation is another's inhalation.

1. Which consistent global winds helped spread Mount Pinatubo's aerosols worldwide?

2. What is a possible explanation related to global circulation for the beautiful sunrises and sunsets during the summer of 1992 in North America?

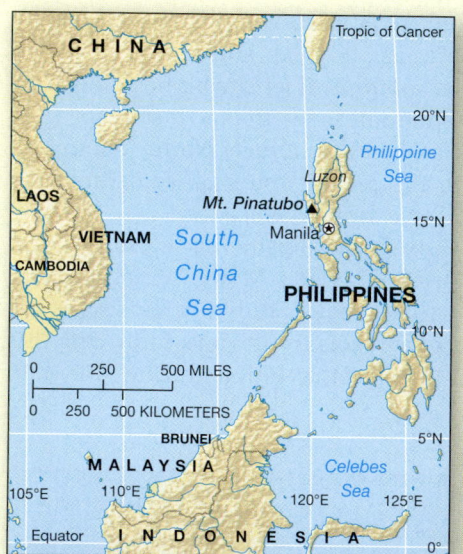

(a) Mount Pinatubo erupts on June 15, 1991.

▲**Figure 5.1.1 Atmospheric effects of the Mount Pinatubo volcanic eruption and global winds.** [(a) USGS. (b–d) AOT images from the advanced very high resolution radiometer (AVHRR) instrument aboard *NOAA-11; NESDIS/NOAA.*]

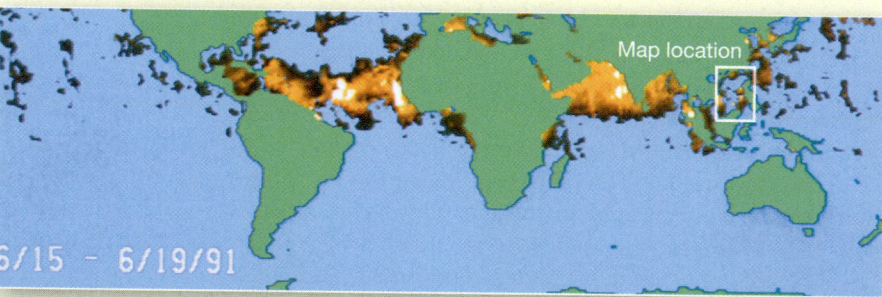

(b) False-color images show aerosol optical thickness: White has the highest concentration of aerosols; yellow shows medium values; and brown shows the lowest values. Note dust, smoke from fires, and haze in the atmosphere at the time of the eruption.

(c) The aerosol layer circles the entire globe 21 days after the eruption.

(d) The effects of the eruption cover 42% of the globe after 2 months.

Local and Regional Winds

Compared to the global winds just discussed, local and regional winds occur on a smaller scale. Such winds occur as several types, each related to a specific topographic setting.

Land and Sea Breezes Along coastlines, the different heating characteristics of land and water surfaces produce **land and sea breezes** (**Figure 5.18**). Land gains heat energy and warms faster than the water offshore during the day. Because warm air is less dense, it rises and triggers an onshore flow of cooler marine air to replace the rising warm air—the flow is usually strongest in the afternoon, forming a sea breeze. At night, land cools by radiating heat energy faster than offshore waters do. As a result, the cooler air over the land subsides (sinks) and flows offshore toward the lower-pressure area over the warmer water, where the air is lifted. This nighttime land-breeze pattern reverses the process that developed during the day.

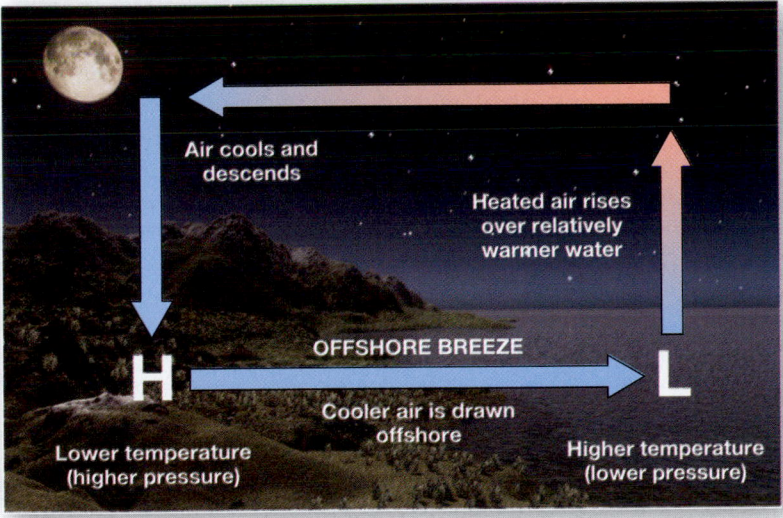

(a) Daytime sea-breeze conditions.

(b) Nighttime land-breeze conditions.

▲**Figure 5.18** **Temperature and pressure patterns for daytime sea breezes and nighttime land breezes.**

Mountain and Valley Breezes Local winds produced when mountain air cools rapidly at night and when valley air gains heat energy rapidly during the day are **mountain and valley breezes** (**Figure 5.19**). Valley slopes are heated sooner during the day than valley floors. As the slopes heat up and warm the air above, this warm, less-dense air rises and creates an area of low pressure. By the afternoon, winds blow out of the valley in an upslope direction along this slight pressure gradient, forming a valley breeze. At night, heat is lost from the slopes, and the cooler, denser air then subsides downslope in a mountain breeze.

Santa Ana Winds As discussed in Geosystems Now, *Santa Ana winds* result from a pressure gradient generated when high pressure builds over the Great Basin of the western United States. A strong, dry wind flows out across this region to southern California coastal areas. Compression heats the air as it flows from higher to lower elevations, and with increasing speed, it moves through constricting valleys to the southwest. These winds bring dust, dryness, and heat to populated areas near the coast and create dangerous wildfire conditions.

Katabatic Winds Drainage winds that are of larger regional scale and usually stronger than local winds are **katabatic winds**. They develop on elevated plateaus or highlands where layers of air at the surface cool, become denser, and flow downslope. Such drainage winds are not specifically related to the pressure gradient. The ferocious winds that can blow off the ice sheets of Antarctica and Greenland are katabatic in nature.

GEOreport 5.1 Icelandic ash caught in the jet stream

Although smaller than the Mount Pinatubo 1991 eruption, the 2010 eruption of Eyjafjallajökull volcano in Iceland injected about a tenth of a cubic kilometer of volcanic debris into the jet-stream flow. The ash cloud from Iceland was swept toward the European mainland and the United Kingdom. Aircraft cannot risk ingesting volcanic ash into jet engines; therefore, airports were shut down and thousands of flights canceled.

(a) Daytime valley-breeze conditions.

As valley slopes heat up, rising air creates low pressure so that a breeze blows upslope.

Warmer air

(b) Nighttime mountain-breeze conditions.

As valley slopes cool, denser air sinks to the valley bottom, creating a light downslope breeze.

Cooler air

▲Figure 5.19 **Conditions for daytime upslope valley breezes and nighttime downslope mountain breezes.**

Names for Local Winds

Names for Local Winds Worldwide, various terrains produce distinct types of local winds that are known by local names. The *mistral* of the Rhône Valley in southern France is a cold north wind that can cause frost damage to vineyards as it moves over the region on its way to the Gulf of Lions and the Mediterranean Sea. The frequently stronger *bora*, driven by the cold air of winter high-pressure systems occurring inland over the Balkans and southeastern Europe, flows across the Adriatic Coast to the west and south. In the U.S. West, *chinook winds* are dry, warm downslope winds occurring on the leeward side of mountain ranges such as the Cascades in Washington or the Rockies in Montana.

Regionally, wind represents a significant and increasingly important source of renewable energy. Focus Study 5.2 explores wind as a sustainable resource.

Monsoonal Winds

A number of regional wind systems change direction on a seasonal basis. Such regional wind flows occur in the tropics over Southeast Asia, Indonesia, India, northern Australia, and equatorial Africa. A mild regional flow also occurs in the extreme southwestern United States in Arizona during the summer. These seasonally shifting wind systems are **monsoons** (from the Arabic word *mausim*, meaning "season") and involve an annual cycle of returning precipitation with the summer Sun.

The Asian Monsoon Pattern The unequal heating between the Asian landmass and the Indian Ocean drives the monsoons of southern and eastern Asia (**Figure 5.20**). This process is heavily influenced by the shifting migration of the ITCZ during the year, which brings moisture-laden air northward during the Northern Hemisphere summer (look back to Figure 5.13).

A large difference occurs between summer and winter temperatures over the large Asian landmass—a result of the continental effect on temperature discussed in Chapter 4. During the Northern Hemisphere winter (November to March), an intense high-pressure cell dominates this continental landmass (Figure 5.20a). At the same time, the ITCZ is present over the central area of the Indian Ocean. The resulting pressure gradient produces cold, dry winds from the Asian interior that flow from high pressure over the Himalayas southward toward low pressure over the ocean.

During the Northern Hemisphere summer, the ITCZ shifts northward over southern Asia, and the Asian continental interior develops low pressure associated with hot temperatures (remember the summer warmth in Verkhoyansk, Siberia, from Chapter 4). Meanwhile, high pressure dominates over the Indian Ocean, causing warming of sea-surface temperatures (Figure 5.20b). The resulting pressure gradient is reversed from the winter pattern as hot subtropical air sweeps over the warm ocean toward India.

This air reaches the Indian subcontinent laden with moisture, which produces the monsoonal rains from about June to September (Figure 5.20c). These rains are welcome relief from the dust, heat, and parched land of Asia's springtime. World-record rainfalls occur in this region: Cherrapunji, India, holds the record for both the second highest average annual rainfall (1143 cm, or 450 in.) and the highest single-year rainfall (2647 cm, or 1042 in.) on Earth. In the Himalayas, the monsoon brings snowfall.

Heavy monsoon precipitation can cause devastating floods and damage arable land. For example, record-breaking monsoon rains in August 2010 caused flooding in Pakistan, inundating productive farmland and leaving 20 million people homeless.

Recent Changes in the Asian Monsoon The wet monsoon supplies nearly 70% of the annual precipitation for the entire south Asian region, making it a vital water resource for about 20% of the world's population.

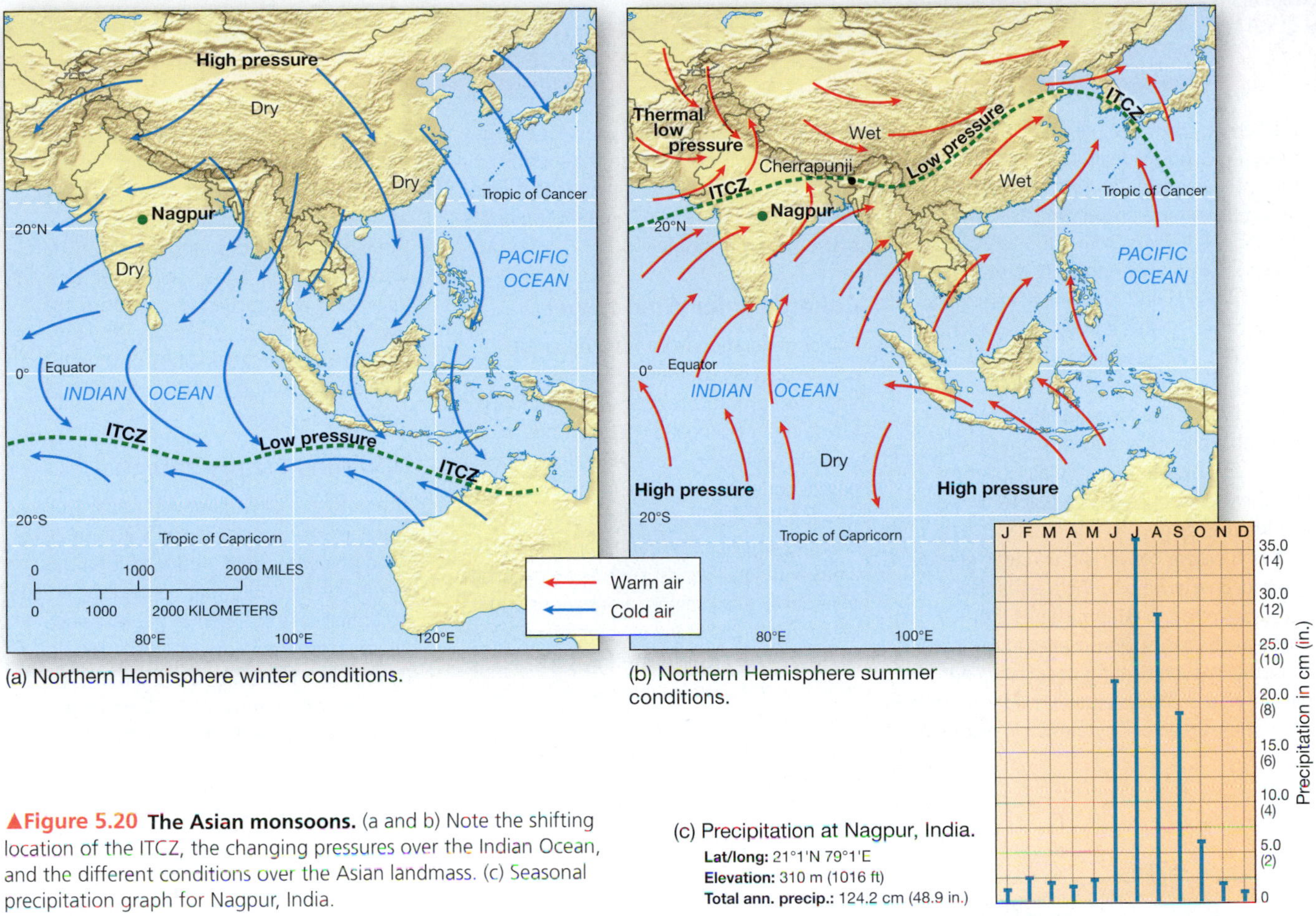

(a) Northern Hemisphere winter conditions.

(b) Northern Hemisphere summer conditions.

Warm air
Cold air

(c) Precipitation at Nagpur, India.
Lat/long: 21°1'N 79°1'E
Elevation: 310 m (1016 ft)
Total ann. precip.: 124.2 cm (48.9 in.)

▲**Figure 5.20 The Asian monsoons.** (a and b) Note the shifting location of the ITCZ, the changing pressures over the Indian Ocean, and the different conditions over the Asian landmass. (c) Seasonal precipitation graph for Nagpur, India.

Studies indicate that the Asian monsoon circulation has weakened during the past several decades, reducing rainfall over parts of South Asia. The decline appears linked to changes in air quality (aerosol pollution) and warming temperatures in the equatorial Indian Ocean owing to climate change.

Research shows complicated interactions between air pollution and ocean warming on monsoon circulation. Recent studies suggest that rising concentrations of aerosols—principally sulfur compounds and black carbon—reduce sunlight and surface heating of land areas. This combines with rising ocean temperatures attributable to climate change to cause an overall decrease in the pressure differences at the heart of monsoonal flows. The result is a drop in monsoon precipitation. However, some studies indicate that warmer air and ocean temperatures have increased monsoon precipitation in the Northern Hemisphere over the past few decades.

The North American Monsoon A monsoon season occurs in North America during the late summer months. Although not as strong or persistent as the Asian monsoon, it brings episodes of heavy rainfall to Arizona, New Mexico, and northwest Mexico from late June to late September. The shift in regional wind patterns is similar to the Asian pattern—warm summer air creates low pressure over land surfaces and draws moist air from the oceans.

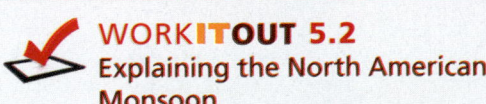

WORKITOUT 5.2
Explaining the North American Monsoon

Based on your knowledge of pressure, winds, and the Asian monsoon, explain the details of the North American monsoon.

1. With rising summer temperatures in the deserts of the U.S. Southwest, how does barometric pressure change over land surfaces?
2. Do these changes in pressure affect regional wind direction? Explain.
3. In Arizona, from 2005 to 2015, 68 people died in flash floods (sudden floods resulting from intense rainfall). The vast majority of those events occurred during the months of August and September. Does this statistic have a connection to the North American monsoon? Explain your answer.

FOCUSstudy 5.2 Sustainable Resources
Wind Power: An Energy Resource for the Future

Wind energy is growing in the United States and worldwide. In the United States, the capacity for electricity generation from wind power increased by 517% in the 7 years from 2005 to 2012. Globally, wind power grew 22% in 2015 alone. Overall, wind power is a leading source of *renewable energy*, that which is collected from resources that renew, or replenish, themselves naturally over a short time scale. Transitioning toward renewable energy and away from fossil fuels is essential to reducing air pollution and the greenhouse gas emissions linked to climate change.

Wind power converts the kinetic energy in atmospheric wind to the mechanical energy of rotating wind turbines that produce electricity. Because wind results from the uneven heating of surfaces on Earth, wind energy is essentially a form of solar energy. Wind is a renewable resource because increasing use of wind for energy production will not deplete the supply. Wind energy is clean, meaning that it does not produce pollution or greenhouse gases, and is widely available.

Conditions for Wind Power

Power generation from wind depends on site-specific conditions. Several settings are favorable for consistent wind: (1) Coastlines influenced by trade winds and westerly winds; (2) areas where mountain passes constrict air flow and interior valleys develop thermal low-pressure areas, thus drawing air across the landscape; and (3) areas with local winds, such as an expanse of relatively flat prairies, or locations with katabatic winds. Many developing countries are located in areas blessed by such steady winds, such as the trade winds across the tropics.

In areas of sufficient winds, power generation comes from single wind turbines or from multiple-turbine installations known as *wind farms*. Wind turbines consist of three rotating blades atop a tubular shaft. Winds turn the blades, which then turn an internal shaft attached to a gearbox that ultimately produces electricity. If winds are reliable less than 25%–30% of the time, only small-scale use of wind power is economically feasible.

U.S. Wind Energy Potential

The potential of wind power in the United States is enormous (**Figure 5.2.1**). In 2015, wind power provided 4.5% of total U.S. electricity. By 2050, that percentage could potentially rise to 35%. In the Midwest, energy from the winds of North and South Dakota and Texas alone could meet all U.S. electrical needs. In the California Coast Ranges, land and sea breezes blow

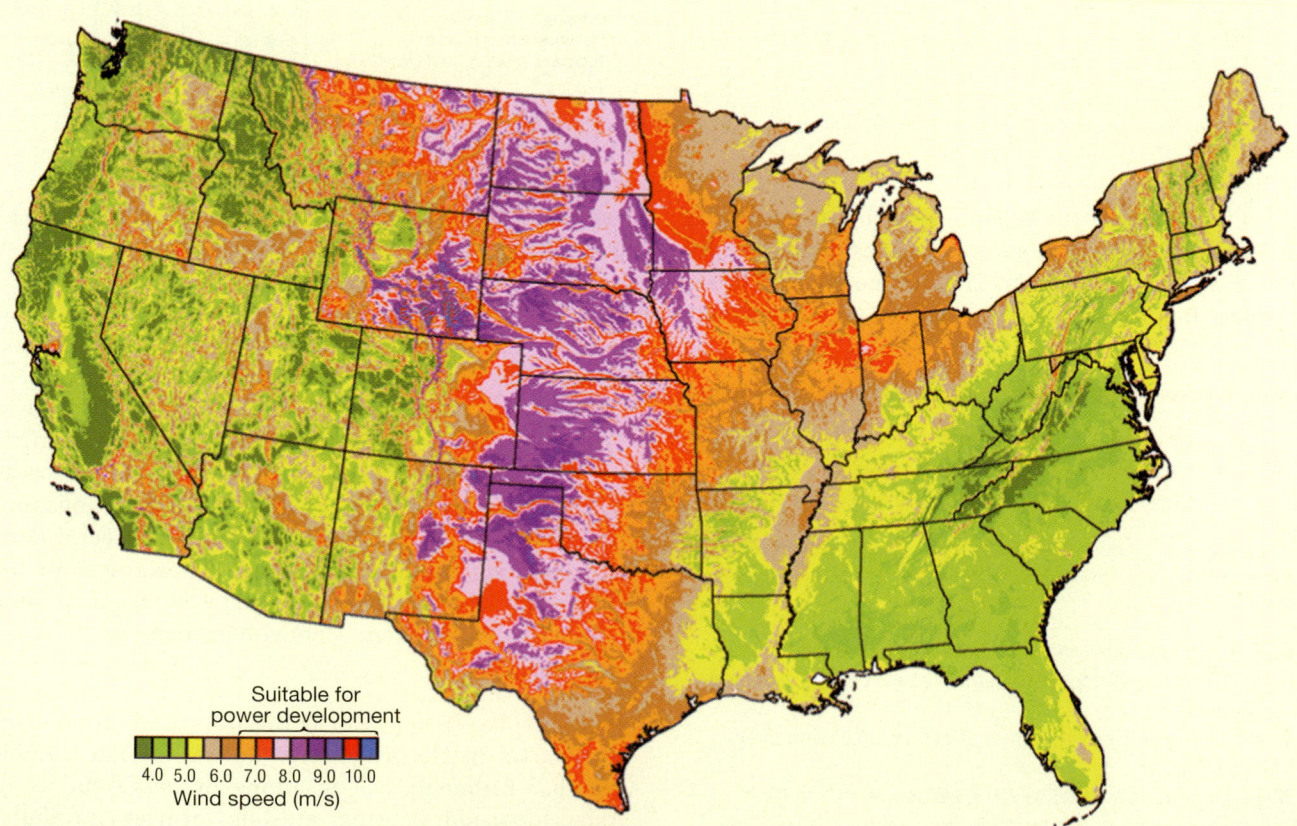

Suitable for power development

4.0 5.0 6.0 7.0 8.0 9.0 10.0
Wind speed (m/s)

▲Figure 5.2.1 **Wind-speed map of the contiguous United States.** The map shows predicted average wind speeds at a height of 80 m (164 ft) above the ground. Areas with wind speeds greater than 6.5 m/s (21 ft/s) are considered suitable for power development. The map has a spatial resolution of 2.5 km (1.6 mi). [NREL and AWS Truepower.]

▲**Figure 5.2.2 Wind turbines at Tehachapi Pass, southern California.** The Tehachapi Pass Wind Farm, located at the mountain pass between the southern Sierra Nevada and the Tehachapi Mountains, is one of the largest in the United States. [Patrick Poendl/Shutterstock.]

between the Pacific and Central Valley, peaking in intensity from April to October, which happens to match peak electrical demands for air conditioning during the hot summer months.

Wind installations are currently operating in 39 U.S. states (**Figure 5.2.2**). Texas has more than double the wind energy capacity of any other state. On December 20, 2015, wind provided 45% of the state's electricity for over 15 consecutive hours—an important milestone. During this time, natural gas plants adjusted their production to offset the rise in wind energy production. Although most U.S. wind power is land-based, offshore wind development also has high potential. At least 10 offshore projects are currently under consideration, most of them on the East Coast.

In addition to reducing the use of fossil fuels, wind energy development benefits local economies. On the eastern shore of Lake Erie, a former steel town recently used wind power to lift itself out of an economic depression. The Bethlehem Steel mill was contaminated with industrial waste until the site was redeveloped with eight wind-power turbines in 2007, followed by six more in 2012. Using the slogan "Turning the Rust Belt into the Wind Belt," developers have reinvented this former waste site, and it now supplies

enough electricity to power 15,000 homes in western New York. In nearby Cleveland, Ohio, a proposed offshore wind project in Lake Erie includes six turbines to be completed in 2018—the first freshwater wind project in North America.

Global Wind-Power Status and Benefits

Wind power capacity continues to rise worldwide, growing about 16% each year. In Europe, wind fulfills over 15% of total energy needs. Wind energy comes from installations in over 80 countries, including Ethiopia, home to sub-Saharan Africa's first commercial wind farm built in 2013. Overall, China has the highest installed wind capacity, with the United States second, followed by Germany and India.

The economic and social benefits from using wind resources are numerous. With all costs considered, wind energy is cheaper than oil, coal, natural gas, and nuclear power. However, wind power causes some environmental degradation from land clearing as well as habitat fragmentation from power facilities and transmission lines. Research has linked bat and bird fatalities—including federally protected Golden Eagles—to collisions with wind turbines. Other challenges of wind-generated power are the high initial financial investment required to build the turbines and the cost of building transmission lines to bring electricity from rural wind farms to urban locations.

1. Why is wind power a renewable resource?

2. Describe an example of how wind power can benefit local economies.

APPLYconcepts Determine the suitability of wind power in your state, based on wind speed (see Figure 5.2.1) and site-specific conditions (described in "Conditions for Wind Power"). Write a sentence summarizing your state's overall wind power potential.

Suitability for wind power		
Highest wind speed		_____
Lowest wind speed		_____
Site-specific conditions	a. _____	b. _____

Oceanic Currents

The atmospheric and oceanic systems are intimately connected in that the driving force for ocean currents is the frictional drag of the winds. Also important in shaping ocean currents is the interplay of the Coriolis force, density differences caused by temperature and salinity (the amount of dissolved salts in the water), the configuration of the continents and ocean floor, and the astronomical forces that cause tides.

Surface Currents

The atmospheric circulation around subtropical high-pressure cells in both hemispheres drives Earth's major surface ocean currents (**Figure 5.21**). Because ocean currents flow over long distances, the Coriolis force deflects them. However, their pattern of deflection is not as tightly circular as that of the atmosphere (compare Figure 5.21 ocean currents with pressure cells in Figure 5.12). The oceanic circulation systems are known as *gyres* and generally appear to be offset toward the western side of each ocean basin. Remember, in the Northern Hemisphere, winds and ocean currents move clockwise about high-pressure cells; in the Southern Hemisphere, circulation is counterclockwise, as shown on the map.

The North Atlantic Gyre features clear, warm waters and large quantities of *Sargassum* (a seaweed) that gives the area its name—the Sargasso Sea. Roughly corresponding with the Azores high-pressure cell, this sea is defined not by land masses, as are other seas of the world, but by ocean currents—the Gulf Stream, the North Atlantic Current, the Canary Current, and the North Atlantic Equatorial Current.

Examples of Gyre Circulation In the early 1990s, a letter in a glass bottle traveled the vast clockwise-circulating gyre around the Pacific High for 3 years, from its starting point in Dana Point, California (33.5° N) to the island of Mogmog in the Caroline Islands of Micronesia (7° N) in the western Pacific (**Figure 5.22**).

In January 1992, a powerful storm damaged a container ship, dumping nearly 30,000 toy rubber ducks, turtles, and frogs into the North Pacific. Westerly winds and the North Pacific Current swept this floating cargo (today known as the Friendly Floatees) at up to 29 km (18 mi) a day across the ocean to the coast of Alaska, Canada, Oregon, and California. Other toys drifted through the Bering Sea and into the Arctic Ocean (see dashed red line in Figure 5.22).

Marine debris circulating in the North Pacific Gyre is the subject of ongoing scientific study. Although plastics, especially small-sized plastic fragments, are predominant, this debris also consists of metals, fishing gear, and abandoned vessels. Some of the debris remains in circulation within the gyre and some makes landfall (**Figure 5.23**). Over time, larger plastics break down into smaller pieces that are ingested by fish, birds, and other marine life, damaging their internal organs (often causing death) and releasing harmful chemicals that work their way up the food chain from fish to seabirds, marine mammals, and humans (see http://marinedebris.noaa.gov/info/patch.html).

Animation MG
Ocean Circulation

https://goo.gl/WtTyQt

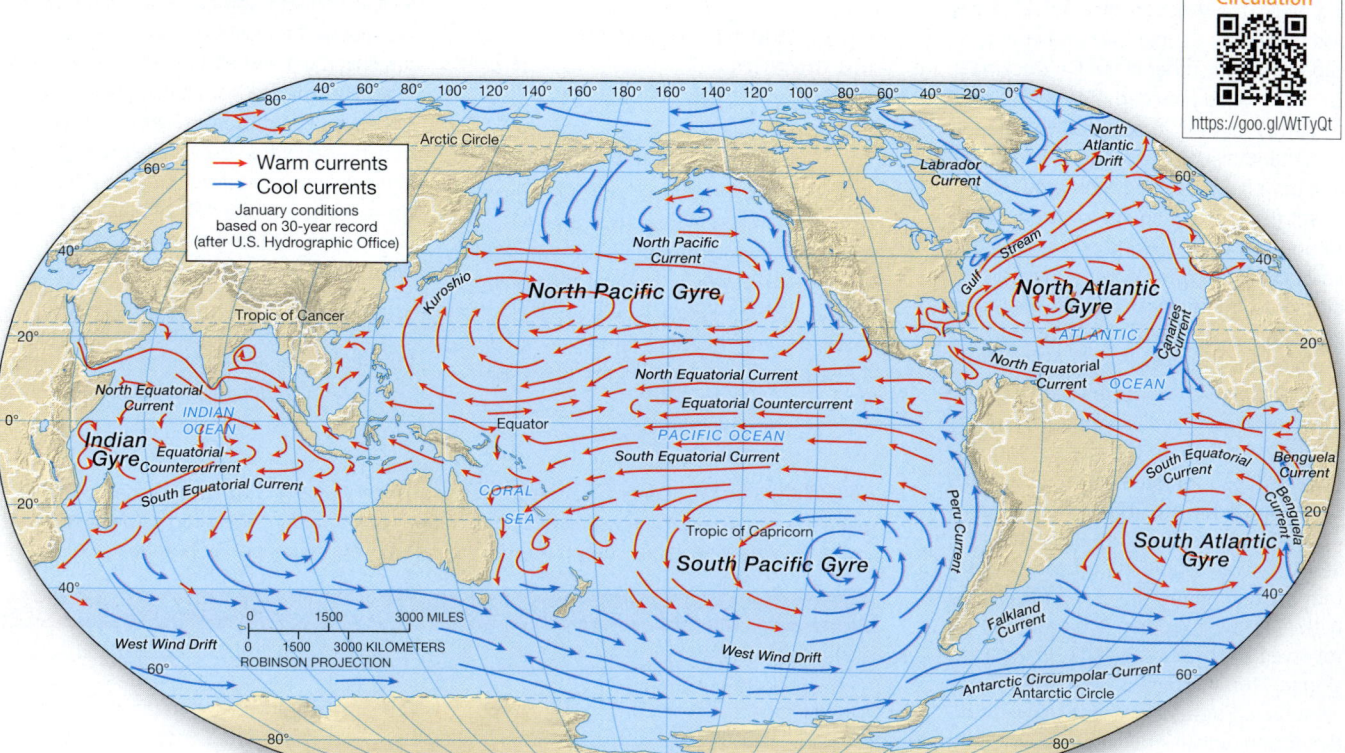

▲Figure 5.21 **Major ocean currents and the five subtropical gyres.** [After the U.S. Naval Oceanographic Office.]

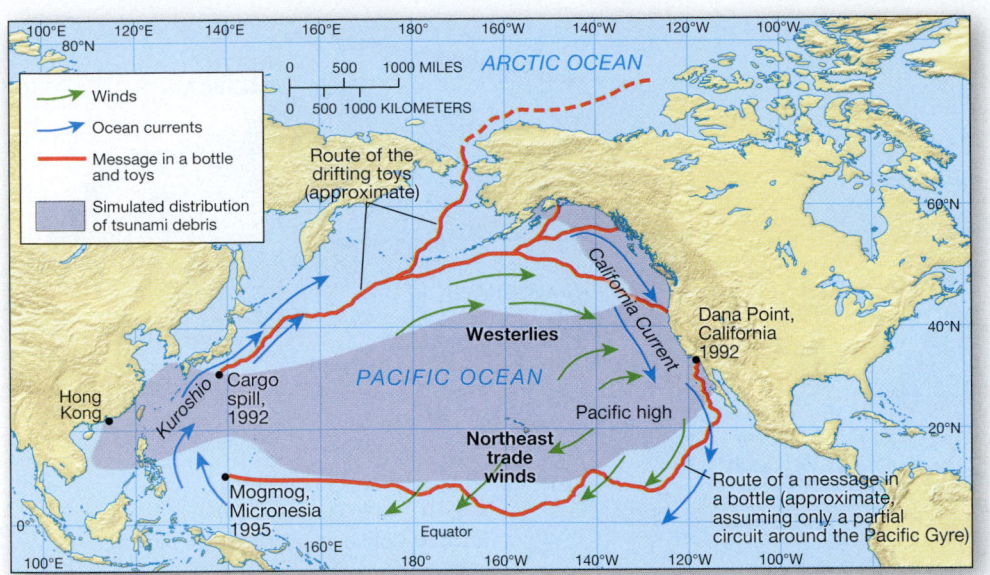

▲**Figure 5.22** **Transport of marine debris by Pacific Ocean currents.** The paths of a message in a bottle and toy rubber duckies show the movement of currents around the North Pacific Gyre. The distribution of debris from the 2011 Japan tsunami is a computer simulation based on expected winds and currents through January 7, 2012. [NOAA.]

Debris from the 2011 Japan tsunami added more material into the North Pacific; computer models based on winds and currents estimate the extent of the debris, some of which has already washed up on the U.S. coastlines (Figure 5.23 and Human Denominator 5a). See http://marinedebris.noaa.gov/tsunamidebris for more information.

Equatorial Currents Trade winds drive the ocean-surface waters westward in a concentrated channel along the equator (Figure 5.21). These equatorial currents remain near the equator because of the weakness of the Coriolis force, which diminishes to zero at that latitude. As these surface currents approach the western margins of the oceans, the water actually piles up against the eastern shores of the continents. The average height of this pileup is 15 cm (6 in.). This phenomenon is the **western intensification**.

The piled-up ocean water then spills northward and southward in strong currents, flowing in tight channels along the eastern shorelines. In the Northern Hemisphere, the Gulf Stream and the Kuroshio (a current east of Japan) move forcefully northward as a result of western intensification. Their speed and depth increase with the constriction of the area they occupy. The warm, deep, clear water of the ribbon-like Gulf Stream (see Figure 4.25) usually is 50–80 km (30–50 mi) wide and 1.5–2.0 km (0.9–1.2 mi) deep, moving at 3–10 kmph (1.8–6.2 mph). In 24 hours, ocean water can move 70–240 km (40–150 mi) in the Gulf Stream.

Upwelling Where surface water is swept away from a coast, either by surface divergence (induced by the Coriolis force) or by offshore winds, **upwelling** occurs. Upwelling is the upward movement of cold, nutrient-rich water from great depths to replace the vacating surface water. Upwelling occurs off the Pacific coasts of North and South America and the subtropical and midlatitude west coast of Africa. These areas are some of Earth's prime fishing regions.

WORK**IT**OUT 5.3
Subtropical and Subpolar Gyres

Noted on Figure 5.21, in the Northern Hemisphere are two clockwise-flowing subtropical gyres—the North Pacific and North Atlantic Gyres. Looking closely at the figure in the Northern Hemisphere, you can see two small subpolar gyres—one south of Alaska and one between Greenland and Europe (the North Atlantic Drift). Note that the flow of these subpolar gyres is counterclockwise.

1. Given your knowledge about pressure, winds, and ocean currents, explain why the subtropical gyres flow clockwise in the Northern Hemisphere while the subpolar gyres flow counterclockwise.

(a) Some ocean waste makes landfall, shown here on the island of Kahoʻolawe, Hawaiʻi. Located near the center of the North Pacific Gyre, the Hawaiian islands are hotspots for marine debris accumulation.

(b) Most marine debris consists of microplastics that are not readily visible on the surface but create a "soup" of floating debris in the water column below.

▲**Figure 5.23** **Marine debris in the North Pacific.** [(a) NOAA. (b) Zuma Press, Inc./Alamy.]

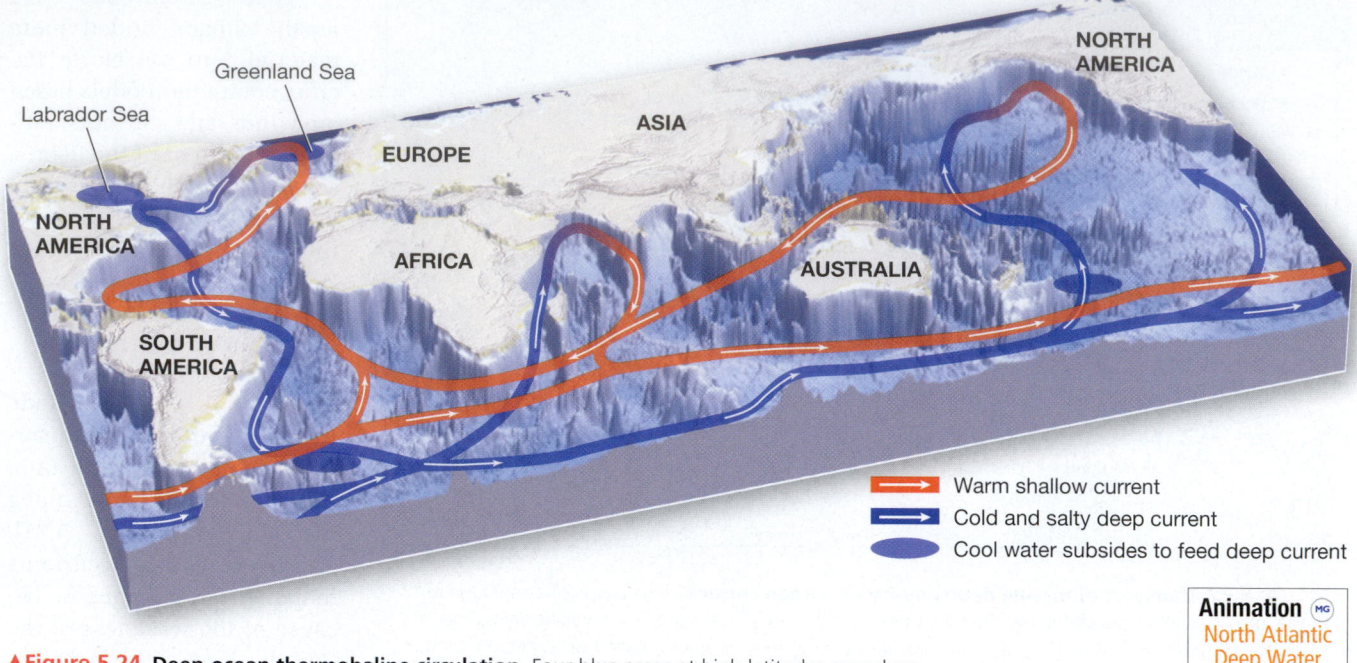

▲**Figure 5.24 Deep-ocean thermohaline circulation.** Four blue areas at high latitudes are where surface water cools, increases in salinity, sinks, and feeds the deep circulation. This vast conveyor belt of water draws heat energy from warm, shallow currents and transports it to higher latitudes for release in the depths of the ocean basins in cold, deep, salty currents.

Animation 🅜🅖
North Atlantic
Deep Water
Circulation

https://goo.gl/5legyz

Thermohaline Circulation—The Deep Currents

Differences in water density, driven by differences in temperatures and salinity (the amount of salts dissolved in water), drive the flow of deep currents on Earth known as **thermohaline circulation**, or THC (*thermo-* refers to temperature and *-haline* refers to salinity). Traveling at slower speeds than wind-driven surface currents, the thermohaline circulation moves larger volumes of water. (Figure 16.X illustrates the ocean's physical structure; note that temperature and salinity vary with depth.)

To picture the THC, imagine a continuous channel of water beginning with the surface currents of the Gulf Stream and the North Atlantic Drift shown in Figure 5.21. When this warm, salty water mixes with the cold water of the Arctic Ocean, it cools, increases in density, and sinks. In addition, the cold ocean temperatures enhance the formation of sea ice. When salt water freezes, the salt is essentially squeezed out of the ice structure and released into the surrounding water. As the seawater gets saltier, it increases in density and sinks. The denser, sinking water pulls in surface water to replace it, thus triggering a current that continues as the surface water freezes, becomes saltier, and sinks. Thus temperature and salinity work together to trigger the thermohaline circulation.

The sinking of cold water in the North Atlantic, on either side of Greenland, produces the deep current sometimes called the *global conveyor belt* that then flows southward. Such sinking also occurs in the high southern latitudes as warm equatorial surface currents meet cold Antarctic waters (**Figure 5.24**). As water then moves northward, it warms and rises, as occurs in the Indian Ocean and North Pacific. A complete circuit of these surface and subsurface currents may require 1000 years.

Global climate change may disrupt the flow of these deep currents. In the polar regions, warmer land and water temperatures are causing a "freshening" of ocean waters through the melting of sea ice and increased rates of glacial and ice sheet melting. The resulting fresh, lower-density surface waters ride on top of the denser saline water. In theory a large input of freshwater into the North Atlantic could reduce the density of seawater enough that the sinking of cold water would no longer occur there—effectively shutting down the THC.

Ongoing scientific research shows the effects of climate change in the Arctic: rising temperatures, melting sea ice, thawing permafrost, melting glaciers, increased runoff in rivers, increased rainfall, all adding to an overall increase in the amount of freshwater entering the Arctic Ocean. Current models suggest that a weakening of the THC is possible by the end of the 21st century and perhaps much sooner.

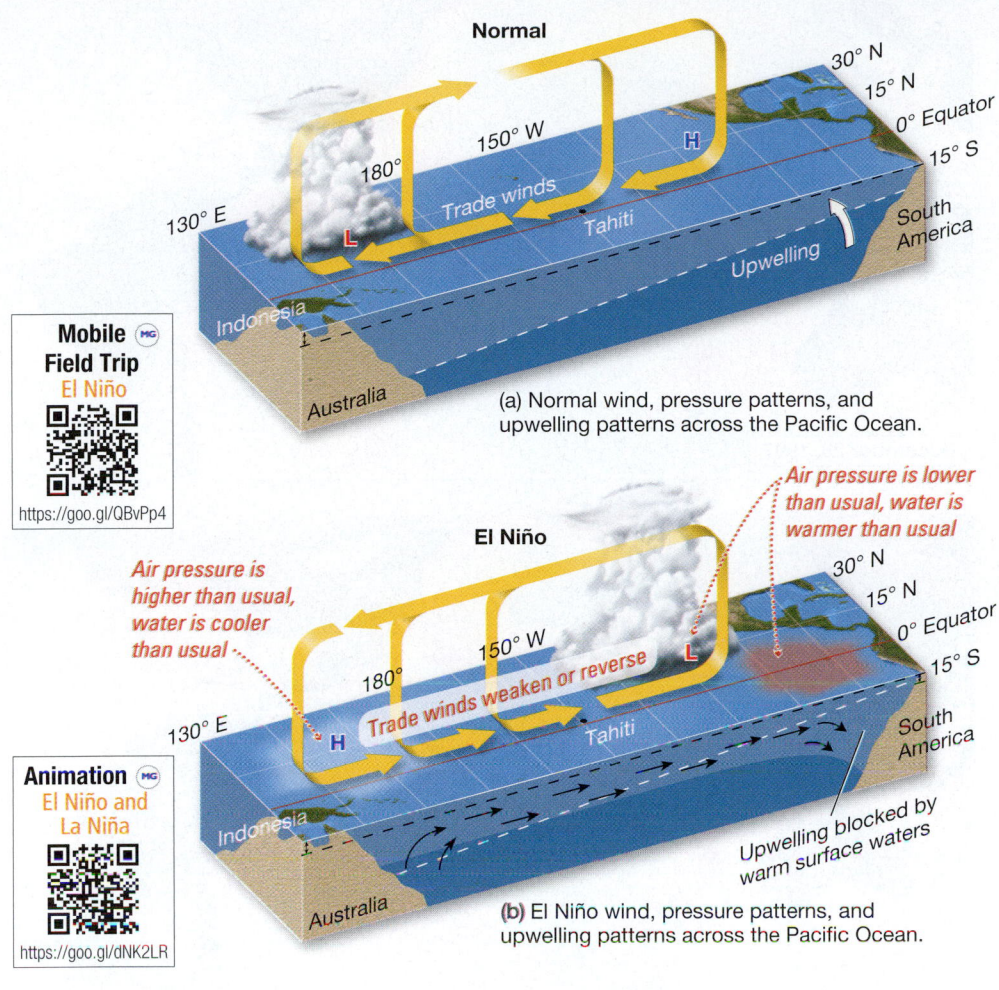

Normal

(a) Normal wind, pressure patterns, and upwelling patterns across the Pacific Ocean.

El Niño

Air pressure is higher than usual, water is cooler than usual

Air pressure is lower than usual, water is warmer than usual

Trade winds weaken or reverse

Upwelling blocked by warm surface waters

(b) El Niño wind, pressure patterns, and upwelling patterns across the Pacific Ocean.

▲**Figure 5.25 Normal and El Niño conditions in the Pacific.** [Adapted and corrected from C. S. Ramage, "El Niño." © 1986 by *Scientific American, Inc.*]

ocean temperatures that temporarily lowers the productivity of local fisheries. This event is now known as *El Niño* ("the boy child"), since it usually happens in December, coinciding with the Christmas holiday. Actually, El Niños can occur as early as spring and summer and persist throughout the year.

In the South Pacific Ocean, the cold Humboldt Current (also called the Peru Current) flows northward off South America's coast, joining the westward movement of the South Equatorial Current near the equator (**Figure 5.25**). The Humboldt Current is part of the normal counterclockwise circulation of winds and surface ocean currents around the subtropical high-pressure cell dominating the eastern Pacific in the Southern Hemisphere. As a result, the coastal city of Guayaquil, Ecuador, normally receives 91.4 cm (36 in.) of precipitation each year under dominant high pressure and colder SSTs. In the western Pacific, in contrast, islands in the Indonesian archipelago receive more than 254 cm (100 in.) under dominant low pressure and warmer SSTs. This normal alignment of pressure and SSTs is shown in Figure 5.25a.

Natural Oscillations in Global Circulation

In some regions, global circulation patterns can oscillate, or swing back and forth, causing fluctuations in temperature and air pressure that can last years. The most famous of these is the **El Niño–Southern Oscillation (ENSO)**, a shifting of sea-surface temperatures (SSTs), air pressure, and winds across the equatorial Pacific. This shift influences marine ecosystems as well as global precipitation and storm movement, ultimately affecting global climates. Here, we describe ENSO and introduce three other hemisphere-scale oscillations that affect North America.

El Niño–Southern Oscillation (ENSO)

In the equatorial Pacific, consistent trade winds drag warm surface water away from the South American coast, causing upwelling of colder, nutrient-rich water from below. Yet, for thousands of years, fishermen in this region have observed a periodic warming of coastal

El Niño—ENSO's Warm Phase Occasionally, for unexplained reasons, pressure patterns and surface ocean temperatures shift from their usual locations in the Pacific. Higher pressure than normal develops over the western Pacific, and lower pressure develops over the eastern Pacific. Trade winds normally moving from east to west weaken and can be reduced or even replaced by an eastward (west-to-east) flow (Figure 5.25b). The shifting of atmospheric pressure and wind patterns across the Pacific is the *Southern Oscillation.*

As winds and ocean currents no longer pull warm surface waters westward, the *thermocline* (the transition layer between surface water and colder, deeper water beneath it) lowers in depth in the eastern Pacific Ocean, and upwelling stops. The associated loss of nutrients deprives fish, marine mammals, and predatory birds of nourishment.

SSTs may increase to more than 8 C° (14 F°) above normal. Such ocean-surface warming, creating the "warm pool," may extend from South America to the International Date Line. This surface pool of warm water is the El Niño, leading to the designation ENSO, or El Niño–Southern Oscillation.

ENSO events recur roughly every 3 to 7 years, although the interval can range from 2 to 12 years. Each event can last many months, or years, before conditions return to normal. The frequency and intensity of ENSO events increased through the 20th century, a topic of extensive scientific research looking for a link to global climate change. Although recent studies suggest that this phenomenon might be more responsive to global climate change than previously thought, scientists have found no definitive connection.

The two strongest ENSO events in 120 years occurred in 1997–1998 and 2015–2016 (**Figure 5.26**). These two ENSO events each recorded 2.3°C above average SSTs at their peak during October–December. However, the patterns of sea-surface temperature were different: the 1997–1998 event was stronger in the eastern Pacific, while the 2015–2016 event was stronger in the central Pacific.

La Niña—ENSO's Cool Phase

When surface waters in the central and eastern Pacific cool to below normal by 0.4 C° (0.7 F°) or more, the condition is dubbed *La Niña*, Spanish for "the girl." This condition is weaker and less consistent than El Niño; otherwise, there is no correlation in strength or weakness between the two phases. For instance, following the record 1997–1998 ENSO event, the lingering warm water in the Pacific resulted in the subsequent La Niña being not as strong as predicted. In contrast, the 2010–2011 La Niña was one of the strongest on record.

Global Effects Related to ENSO

Although the phenomenon was first recognized for its effects on fisheries, scientists have linked ENSO to unusually intense weather and short-term climate effects across the globe. El Niño correlates with droughts in South Africa and Australia; strong hurricanes in the Pacific; and heavy precipitation in the southwestern United States and Peru (**Figure 5.27**). One of California's wettest years on record occurred during the the strong 1997–1998 ENSO. The 2015–2016 event produced a record-breaking Pacific hurricane season (discussed in Chapter 8). In India, every drought for more than 400 years seems linked to this warm phase of ENSO.

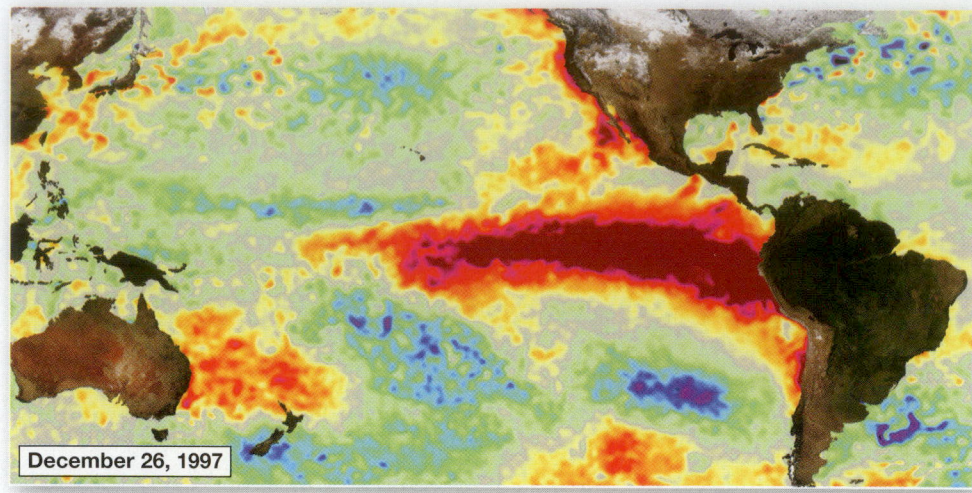

December 26, 1997

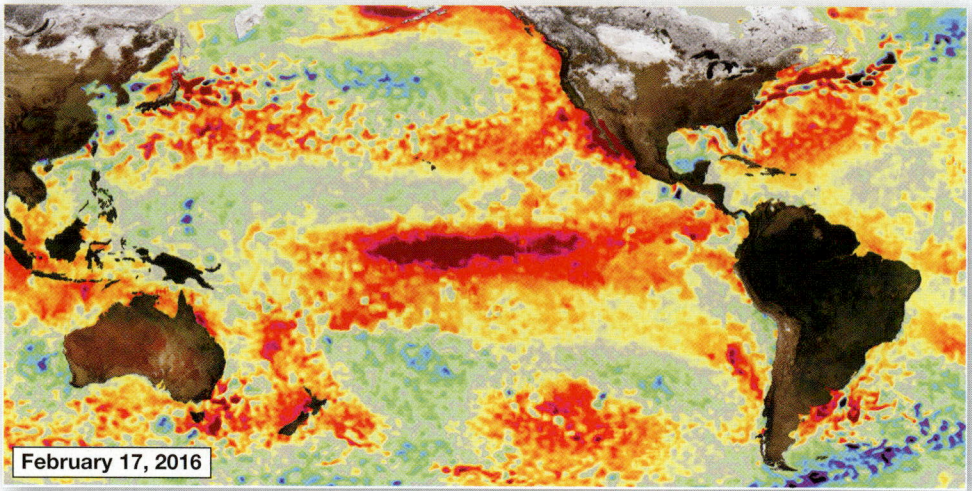

February 17, 2016

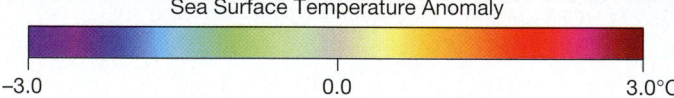

Sea Surface Temperature Anomaly

−3.0   0.0   3.0°C

▲**Figure 5.26** **Strong El Niños in 1997 and 2016.** Sea-surface temperature anomalies represent the difference between (a) December 1997 and (b) February 2016 SSTs (as measured by satellites) and average conditions. Positive anomalies (warmer than average conditions) are orange/red. [NASA Jet Propulsion Laboratory.]

La Niña often brings wetter conditions throughout Indonesia, the South Pacific, and northern Brazil. The 2010–2011 La Niña corresponded with the wettest December in history in Queensland and across eastern Australia, where months of rainfall led to the country's worst flooding in 50 years. The Atlantic hurricane season weakens during El Niño years and strengthens during La Niña years. (More information is at http://www.pmel.noaa.gov/toga-tao/el-nino/nino-home.html.)

Pacific Decadal Oscillation

The *Pacific Decadal Oscillation* (*PDO*) is a pattern of sea-surface temperatures, air pressure, and winds that shift between the northern and tropical western Pacific Ocean (off the coast of Asia) and the northern and

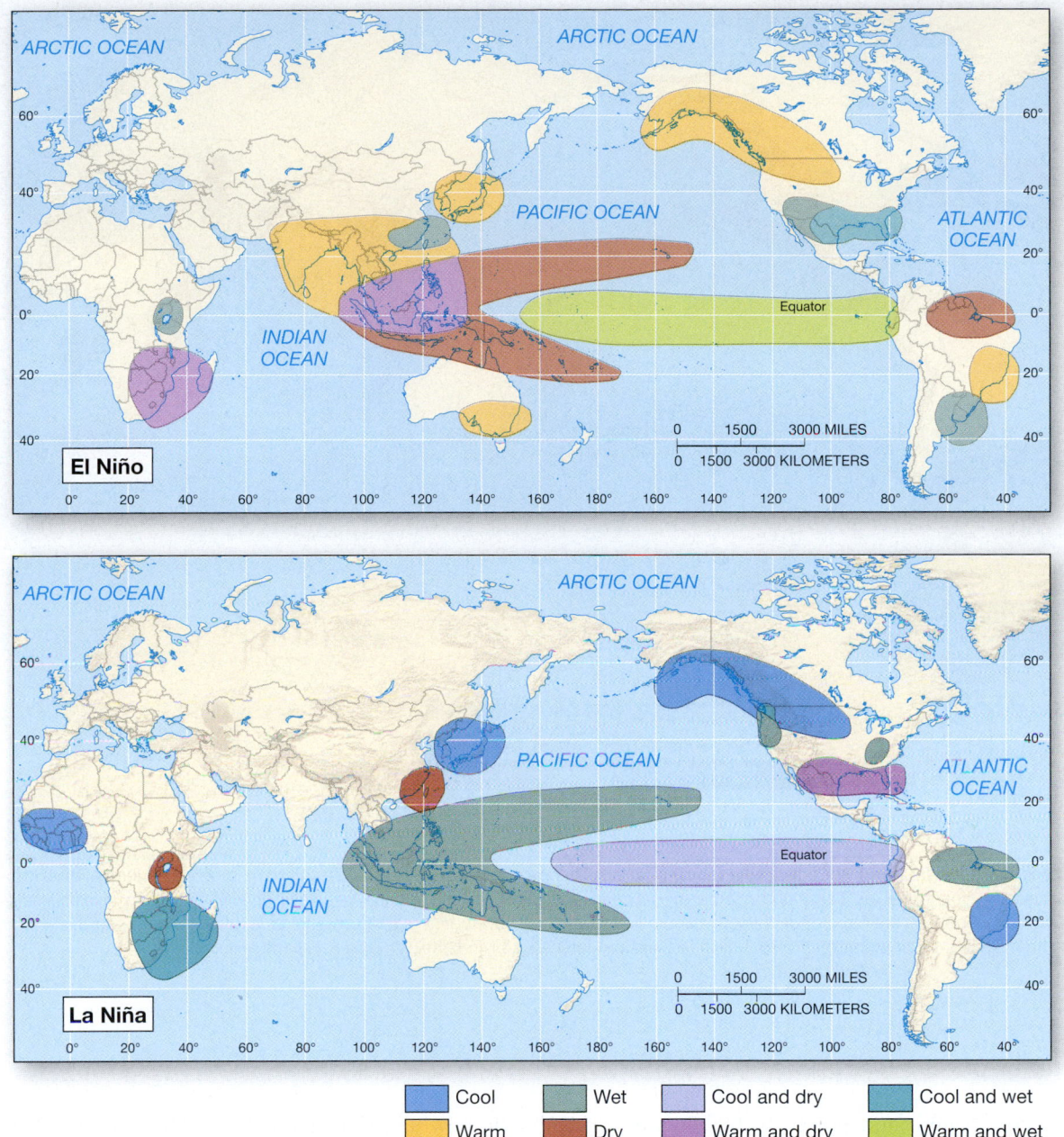

Cool

Warm

Wet

Dry

Cool and dry

Warm and dry

Cool and wet

Warm and wet

▲**Figure 5.27** **Global impacts of El Niño (top) and La Niña (bottom) from December–February (Northern Hemisphere winter).**
[NOAA PMEL, http://www.pmel.noaa.gov/elnino/impacts-of-el-nino.]

tropical eastern Pacific (along the U.S. West Coast). The PDO is longer-lived than the 2- to 12-year variation in the ENSO. The PDO is strongest in the North Pacific, rather than in the tropical Pacific, another distinction from the ENSO.

The PDO positive phase, or warm phase, occurs when higher-than-normal sea-surface temperatures occur near the U.S. West Coast; such conditions occurred consistently from 1977 to the 1990s. In 2008, the PDO switched to a consistent negative phase, in which lower sea-surface temperatures occur off the U.S. West Coast (**Figure 5.28**). This PDO negative phase may be related to the recent drought conditions in the U.S.

West. In 2015, signs began to point to a shift to a positive PDO.

The PDO affects fisheries along the U.S. Pacific coast, with more productive regions shifting northward toward Alaska during PDO warm phases and southward along the California coast during cool phases. For more information, see https://sealevel.jpl.nasa.gov/science/elninopdo/pdo/.

Arctic and North Atlantic Oscillations

A north–south hemispheric fluctuation of atmospheric pressure marks the *Arctic Oscillation* (*AO*). In the AO positive, or warm, phase, lower pressure than normal is

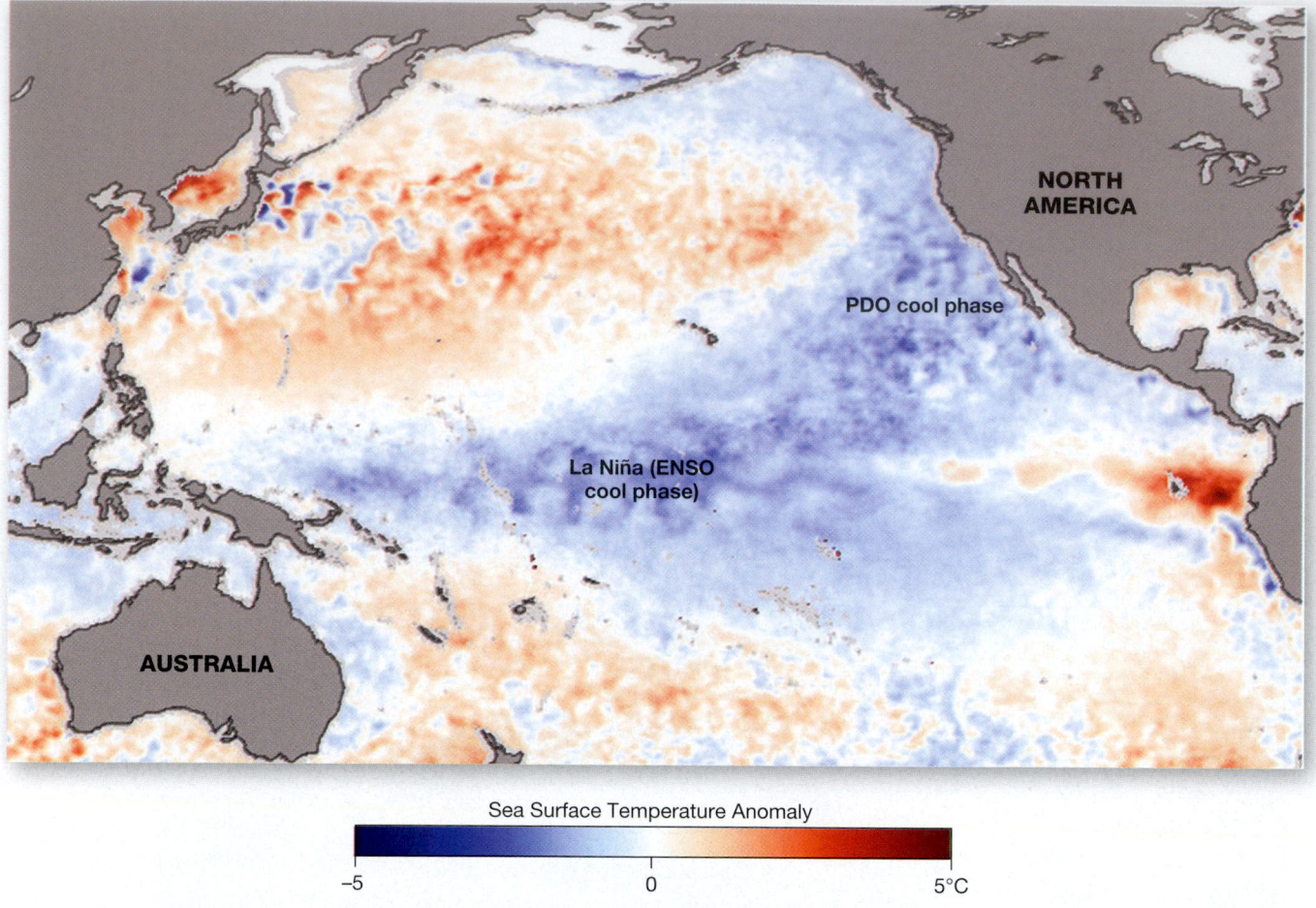

Sea Surface Temperature Anomaly

−5   0   5°C

▲Figure 5.28 **Weakening La Niña and PDO negative (cool) phase in the Pacific Ocean in 2008.** Sea-surface temperature anomalies reveal differences in sea-surface temperatures (as measured by satellites) between April 2008 and the baseline period from 1985–1997. Positive anomalies (warmer than average temperatures) are red/orange; negative anomalies (cooler than average temperatures) are blue; average temperatures are white. The PDO can remain in the same phase for 2 to 3 decades, and can intensify La Niña effects. [*Aqua* AMSR instrument/NASA.]

over the North Pole region, and relatively higher pressures are present at lower latitudes. This sets up stronger westerly winds and a consistently strong jet stream. Cold air masses are confined to the polar region, and winters are colder than normal in Greenland.

In the AO negative, or cold, phase, higher-than-normal pressure is over the polar region, and relatively lower pressure is over the central Atlantic. In winter, cold air masses migrate into the eastern United States, northern Europe, and Asia, and sea ice in the Arctic Ocean becomes a bit thicker. Greenland, Siberia, northern Alaska, and the Canadian Archipelago are all warmer than normal (see Figure HD 5b; more information is at http://nsidc.org/arcticmet/patterns/arctic _oscillation.html).

The *North Atlantic Oscillation* (*NAO*) is associated with the AO, but is confined to the North Atlantic Ocean, specifically the shifting pressure gradient between the Icelandic Low and the Azores High. Phases of the NAO correlate with phases of the AO, and their influence on weather patterns is strongest in winter.

Recent research shows that melting sea ice in the Arctic region may be forcing a negative AO. As sea ice melts, the open ocean retains heat, which it releases to the atmosphere in the fall, warming the arctic air. This reduces the temperature difference between the poles and the midlatitudes and reduces the strength of the polar vortex, strong wind patterns that trap arctic air masses at the poles. Weakening of the polar vortex causes a weaker jet stream, which then meanders in a north -south direction. This forces a negative AO, leading to mostly colder winters over the Northern Hemisphere and the presence of a blocking high-pressure system over Greenland. The Human Denominator 5 illustrates this phenomenon as well as other examples of interactions between humans and Earth's circulation patterns.

GLOBAL CIRCULATION IMPACTS HUMANS

• Wind and pressure contribute to Earth's general atmospheric circulation. In what ways does global circulation affect human activities and provide resources?
• Ocean currents carry human debris into remote areas and spread oil spills across the globe.

HUMANS IMPACT GLOBAL CIRCULATION

• Climate change may be altering patterns of atmospheric circulation, especially in relation to Arctic sea-ice melting and the jet stream as well as possible intensification of subtropical high-pressure cells.
• Air pollution in Asia affects monsoonal wind flow; weaker flow could reduce rainfall and affect water availability.

5a In June 2012, a dock washed ashore in Oregon, 15 months after a tsunami swept it out to sea from Misawa, Japan. The dock traveled about 7280 km (4524 mi) on ocean currents across the Pacific. [Rick Bowmer/AP Images.]

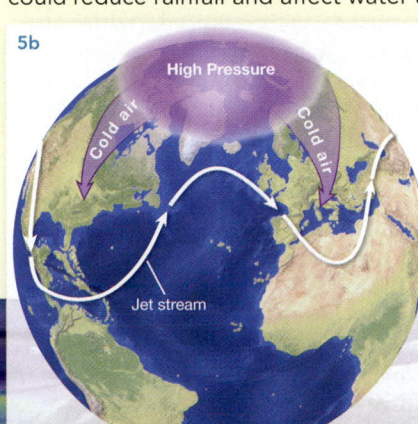

5b High pressure over the polar region associated with the Arctic Oscillation negative phase weakens the jet stream, creating large meanders that bring colder conditions to the United States and Europe. High pressure and warmer conditions occur over Greenland. [After C.H. Greene and B.C. Monger (2012), Rip current: An Arctic wild card in the weather, *Oceanography* 25(2): 7–9.]

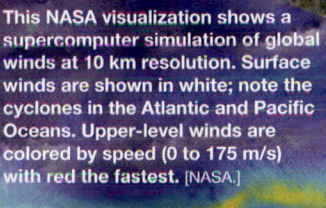

This NASA visualization shows a supercomputer simulation of global winds at 10 km resolution. Surface winds are shown in white; note the cyclones in the Atlantic and Pacific Oceans. Upper-level winds are colored by speed (0 to 175 m/s) with red the fastest. [NASA.]

5d Windsurfers enjoy the effects of the mistral winds off the coast of southern France. These cold, dry winds driven by pressure gradients blow southward across Europe through the Rhône River valley. [Gardel Bertrand/Hemis/Alamy.]

5c In August 2010, monsoon rainfall caused flooding in Pakistan that affected 20 million people and led to over 2000 fatalities. The rains came from an unusually strong monsoonal flow, worsened by La Niña conditions. [Adrees Latif/Thomson Reuters.]

ISSUES FOR THE 21ST CENTURY

• Wind energy is a renewable resource, expanding in use. Further development of wind power is key for reducing dependence on fossil fuels.
• Ongoing climate change may affect ocean currents, including the thermohaline circulation as well as natural oscillations in circulation, such as the Arctic and Pacific Decadal Oscillations.

QUESTIONS TO CONSIDER

1. HD 5b shows the meandering jet stream associated with a negative Arctic Oscillation. Do jet streams exist in the Southern Hemisphere? Why or why not? (Hint: Review GIA 5.)
2. What were the temperature and pressure conditions over South Asia during the monsoon flooding in August 2010?

KEY**LEARNING**concepts**review**

Define **wind and air pressure and** *describe* **instruments that measure each.**

Wind (p. 120) is the horizontal movement of air across Earth's surface. Wind speed is measured with an **anemometer**, (p. 121) (a device with cups that are pushed by the wind), and its direction with a **wind vane**, (p. 121) (a flat blade or surface that is directed by the wind). An *aerovane* is a wind vane with a propeller that measures both wind speed and direction

The motion, size, and number of air molecules create air pressure. A **mercury barometer** (p. 123) measures air pressure at the surface (mercury in a tube—closed at one end and open at the other, with the open end placed in a vessel of mercury—that changes level in response to pressure changes), as does an **aneroid barometer**, (p. 123) (a closed cell, partially evacuated of air, that detects changes in pressure).

1. Explain two instruments used to measure wind and describe the basic instruments used to measure air pressure.
2. What is the relationship between air pressure and density, and between air pressure and temperature?

Explain **the driving forces within the atmosphere— gravity, pressure gradient force, Coriolis force, and friction force—that affect wind.**

The pressure that Earth's *gravitational force* exerts on the atmosphere is virtually uniform worldwide. The **pressure gradient force** (p. 124) drives winds, as air moves from areas of high pressure to areas of low pressure. Maps portray air pressure patterns using the **isobar** (p. 124)—an isoline that connects points of equal pressure. The **Coriolis force** (p. 124) causes an apparent deflection in the path of winds or ocean currents, owing to the rotation of Earth. This force deflects objects to the right in the Northern Hemisphere and to the left in the Southern Hemisphere. The **friction force** (p. 126) drags winds along Earth's varied surfaces in opposition to the pressure gradient. The pressure gradient and Coriolis force in combination (absent the friction force) produce **geostrophic winds** (p. 126), which move parallel to isobars, characteristic of winds above the surface frictional layer.

In a high-pressure system, or **anticyclone** (p. 127), winds descend and diverge, spiraling outward in a clockwise direction in the Northern Hemisphere. In a low-pressure system, or **cyclone** (p. 127), winds converge and ascend, spiraling upward in a counterclockwise direction in the Northern Hemisphere. (The rotational directions are reversed for each in the Southern Hemisphere.)

3. How does the spacing of isobars on a weather map relate to wind speed?
4. How does the Coriolis force appear to deflect atmospheric and oceanic circulations?
5. Describe the horizontal and vertical air motions in a high-pressure anticyclone and in a low-pressure cyclone.

Locate **the primary high- and low-pressure areas and principal winds on Earth.**

The primary pressure regions on Earth are the **equatorial low** (p. 128), the weak **polar highs**, (p. 128) (at both the North and the South Poles), the **subtropical highs** (p. 128), and the **subpolar lows** (p. 128). The subtropical high-pressure cells are generally between 20° and 35° in each hemisphere. In the Northern Hemisphere, they include the **Bermuda High** (p. 128), **Azores High** (p. 128), and **Pacific High** (p. 128). In January, at about 60° N latitude, two low-pressure cells known as the **Aleutian Low** (p. 128) and **Icelandic Low** (p. 128) dominate the North Pacific and Atlantic, respectively. Weak high-pressure cells occur at each pole, the stronger of which is the **Antarctic High** (p. 128).

All along the equator, winds converge into the equatorial low, creating the **intertropical convergence zone (ITCZ)**, p. 128. Air rises in this zone and descends in the subtropics in each hemisphere. The winds returning to the ITCZ from the northeast in the Northern Hemisphere and from the southeast in the Southern Hemisphere produce the **trade winds** (p. 132). Winds flowing out of the subtropics to higher latitudes produce the **westerlies** (p. 133) in each hemisphere. The region of contrast between cold polar air and the warmer air toward the equator is the **polar front** (p. 133). The weak and variable **polar easterlies** (p. 133) diverge from the polar highs.

6. Construct a simple diagram of Earth's general circulation; begin by labeling the four principal pressure belts or zones, and then add arrows between these pressure systems to denote the three principal wind systems.
7. At what latitude is the intertropical convergence zone (ITCZ) located? Does it maintain the same location throughout the year?

Describe **upper-air circulation and** *define* **the jet streams.**

A **constant isobaric surface** (p. 133)—a surface that varies in altitude from place to place according to where a given air pressure, such as 500 mb, occurs—is useful for visualizing geostrophic wind patterns. Vast wave motions in the upper-air westerlies are known as **Rossby waves** (p. 133). Prominent streams of high-speed westerly winds in the upper-level troposphere are the **jet streams** (p. 135). Depending on their latitudinal position in either hemisphere, they are termed the *polar jet stream* or the *subtropical jet stream*.

8. How is upper-air circulation, especially the ridges and troughs, related to surface-pressure systems? Explain the connections between divergence aloft and surface lows, and convergence aloft and surface highs.
9. Describe the jet streams. How might they affect airline schedules for the trip from New York to San Francisco and for the return trip to New York?

Explain **several types of local and regional winds, including the monsoons.**

The difference in the heating characteristics of land and water surfaces creates **land and sea breezes** (p. 137). Temperature differences during the day and evening between valleys and mountain summits cause **mountain and valley breezes** (p. 137). *Santa Ana winds* result from the pressure gradient between high pressure over the Great Basin of the western United States and low pressure over the southern California coastal areas. **Katabatic winds** (p. 137) are drainage winds of larger regional scale and are usually stronger than local winds. They develop on elevated plateaus or highlands where layers of air at the surface cool, become denser, and flow downslope.

Intense, seasonally shifting wind systems occur in the tropics over South Asia, equatorial Africa, and the U.S. Southwest and northern Mexico. These winds, the **monsoons**, (p. 137) are associated with seasonal changes in temperature and pressure over tropical oceans and nearby land masses.

10. Explain the causes of changing wind patterns between day and night in coastal areas. What similar patterns can develop in mountains and valleys?
11. Describe the seasonal pressure patterns that produce the Asian monsoon circulation.

Sketch **the basic pattern of Earth's major surface ocean currents and deep thermohaline circulation.**

Ocean currents are caused by the frictional drag of wind and variations in seawater density. The trade winds converge along the ITCZ and push enormous quantities of water that pile up along the eastern shore of continents in a process known as the **western intensification** (p. 143). Where surface water is swept away from a coast, either by surface divergence (induced by the Coriolis force) or by offshore winds, **upwelling** (p. 143) brings cold, nutrient-rich water from great depths to replace the water at the surface.

Variations in temperatures and salinity produce seawater density differences important to the flow of deep currents; this is Earth's **thermohaline circulation** (p. 144). Powered by currents created as cold, saline (denser) water sinks in the polar regions, the thermohaline circulation moves large volumes of water over the globe.

12. What causes upwelling and where does it occur?
13. What is the process related to temperature and salinity that powers the deep-ocean thermohaline circulation?

Summarize **the El Niño and La Niña oscillations of air pressure and circulation in the Pacific Ocean.**

The most famous multiyear oscillation in global circulation patterns is the **El Niño–Southern Oscillation (ENSO)**, p. 145, in the Pacific Ocean, which affects weather and climate on a global scale. During El Niño, ENSO's warm phase, low pressure and warm sea-surface temperatures occur in the eastern Pacific, blocking upwelling off the coast of South America. During La Niña, ENSO's cool phase, sea-surface temperatures cool to below normal in the eastern Pacific, enhancing upwelling off South America.

The *Pacific Decadal Oscillation* (*PDO*) is a pattern in which sea-surface temperatures and related air pressure vary back and forth between two regions of the Pacific Ocean. The *Arctic Oscillation* (*AO*) is the variable fluctuation in pressure between the polar and midlatitude regions of the Northern Hemisphere. The *North Atlantic Oscillation* (*NAO*) results from changes in the pressure gradient between the Icelandic Low and the Azores High.

14. Describe the changes in atmospheric pressure and sea-surface temperatures during El Niño and La Niña.
15. How might El Niño affect winter weather in North America? What locations can expect wet weather from December to February during a La Niña event?

GEO**SPATIAL** ANALYSIS

Sea Surface Temperatures

Satellites observe sea-surface temperatures (SST) in the Equatorial Pacific Ocean. These data are useful toward the prediction and of El Niño and La Niña events.

Activities

Go to the Unisys Weather page at http://weather.unisys.com/. Click on "Surface Data" under Analyses, and then click on "Daily Plots" under Other Pages. Click on "SST Data" under Plots to bring up a current sea surface temperature map.

1. Based on sea surface temperatures, where do you think warm ocean currents are located? Cold ocean currents? Compare your answers to the ocean current map in Figure 5.21.

2. Are temperatures off the west coast of Equatorial South America slightly warmer or slightly colder than surrounding water to the west? Based on the temperature pattern, which

direction are surface winds blowing from in the Equatorial Pacific Ocean? How can you tell?

Click on "SST Anom" to display the sea surface temperature anomalies map. These anomalies are the difference between the current temperature and the 1981–2010 average temperature.

3. Are the temperatures in the western part of the Equatorial Pacific Ocean warmer or colder than average? Central part? Eastern part?

4. Based on what you know about the Southern Oscillation, is the eastern Equatorial Pacific Ocean currently exhibiting El Niño, La Niña, or normal characteristics?

Another reference to check and compare to the last site is: NOAA's Southern Oscillation Index (SOI) page at https://www.ncdc.noaa.gov/teleconnections/enso/indicators/soi/ . What do you find?

II The Water, Weather, and Climate Systems

Bahía de Corrientes, Cuba

▲ A storm rolls across Cuba's Bahía de Corrientes, located at the western tip of the island on the Guanahacabibes Peninsula. [Michael&Amp Jennifer Lewis/Getty Images]

In Part II, we examine water in the atmosphere, where it produces energy that drives weather, and at Earth's surface, where it is the essential resource needed for living organisms. Chapter 6 describes the remarkable properties water possesses. It also examines the daily dynamics of the atmosphere—the powerful interaction of moisture and energy in the form of latent heat, the resulting stability and instability of atmospheric conditions, the

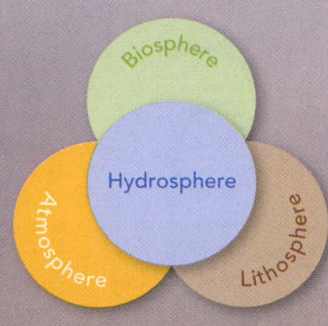

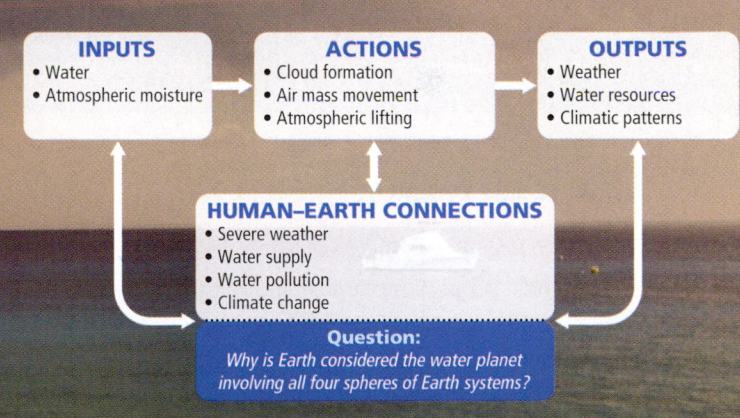

INPUTS
- Water
- Atmospheric moisture

ACTIONS
- Cloud formation
- Air mass movement
- Atmospheric lifting

OUTPUTS
- Weather
- Water resources
- Climatic patterns

HUMAN–EARTH CONNECTIONS
- Severe weather
- Water supply
- Water pollution
- Climate change

Question:
Why is Earth considered the water planet involving all four spheres of Earth systems?

varieties of cloud forms, and types of precipitation—all important to understanding weather. Chapter 7 examines weather, including the movement of air masses and severe weather phenomena such as thunderstorms, tornadoes, and hurricanes.

Chapter 8 describes the distribution of water on Earth, including water circulation in the hydrologic cycle. We examine surface and groundwater resources, outputs of the water–weather system. In Chapter 9, we survey Earth's climates, the outputs of the energy–atmosphere and water–weather systems. This discussion interconnects all the system elements from Chapters 2 through 9. Part II closes with a discussion of global climate change science, a look at present conditions, and a forecast of future climate trends.

6 Water and Atmospheric Moisture

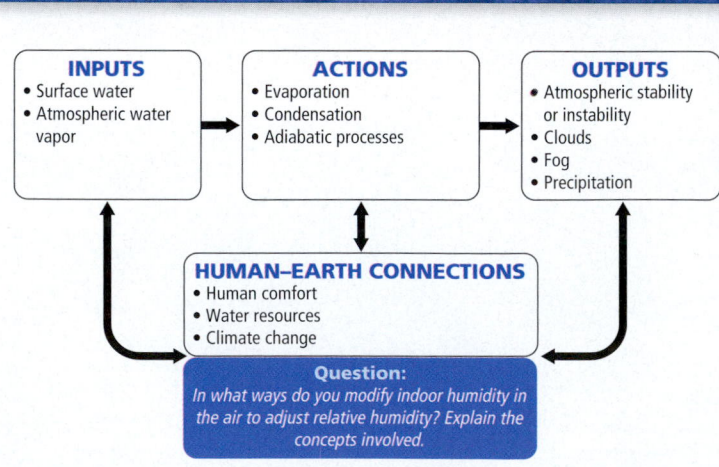

River Avon, UK

Frost covers the landscape along the Avon River at dusk near Worcestershire, England, in the United Kingdom. [Nagelstock/Alamy.]

KEY**LEARNING**concepts

After reading the chapter, you should be able to:

- **Describe** the heat properties of water, including the heat energy transferred during phase changes between solid, liquid, and gas.

- **Describe** expressions of humidity: vapor pressure, specific humidity, relative humidity, and dew-point temperature.

- **Explain** adiabatic lapse rates and *discuss* unstable, conditionally unstable, and stable atmospheric conditions.

- **Identify** the requirements for cloud formation and *explain* the major cloud types, including fog.

- **Describe** the processes that form precipitation in the atmosphere and *list* the types of precipitation at the ground surface.

INPUTS
- Surface water
- Atmospheric water vapor

ACTIONS
- Evaporation
- Condensation
- Adiabatic processes

OUTPUTS
- Atmospheric stability or instability
- Clouds
- Fog
- Precipitation

HUMAN–EARTH CONNECTIONS
- Human comfort
- Water resources
- Climate change

Question:
In what ways do you modify indoor humidity in the air to adjust relative humidity? Explain the concepts involved.

GEOSYSTEMSnow

Atmospheric Rivers Transport Water Vapor

In February 2015, a fast-moving band of moisture-laden air streaming northward from the tropical Pacific Ocean caused a series of storms along the U.S. West Coast (**Figure GN 6.1**). The resulting rain and mountain snow accumulation brought temporary relief from a multi-year drought, but intense precipitation also caused mudslides and flooding in many California communities. On the other side of the globe, 11 months later, moist tropical air from the Caribbean Sea streamed toward Europe, fueling a fierce storm over the North Atlantic Ocean that brought heavy rain, landslides, and flooding to Northern Ireland and the United Kingdom (**Figure GN 6.2**). Both of these storm systems tapped into the energy and moisture of what scientists call an atmospheric river.

Rivers of Water Vapor An *atmospheric river* is a narrow band in the atmosphere, usually 400 to 600 km wide (248 to 373 mi), where winds transport vast amounts of moisture in the form of water vapor from a warm ocean source region with conditions that favor evaporation. Molecules of water vapor, the gas phase of water, are everywhere in the atmosphere, invisible until the vapor cools, condenses, and forms clouds and precipitation. Although the total amount of water vapor in the air at any moment in time is relatively small, the movement of water vapor through the atmosphere is critical to the functioning of Earth systems. Atmospheric rivers are a key transport mechanism for global water vapor.

An atmospheric river originates over warm, tropical oceans, where it picks up large quantities of moisture and then moves

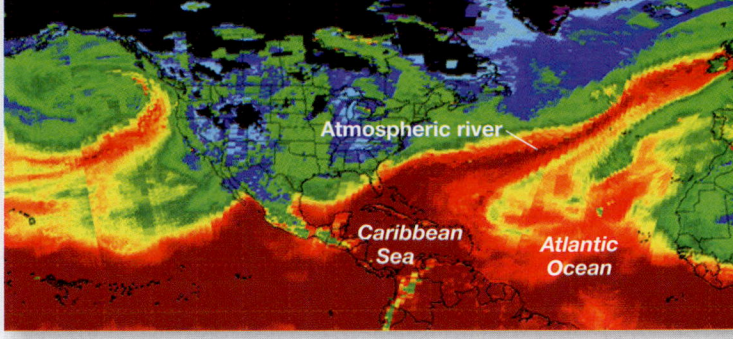

▲**Figure GN 6.2** **Moist air flows from the Caribbean region toward Europe.** On December 5, 2015, an atmospheric river carried moisture across the Atlantic Ocean to Northern Europe, causing heavy rainfall and flooding In Ireland and the United Kingdom. [NWS.]

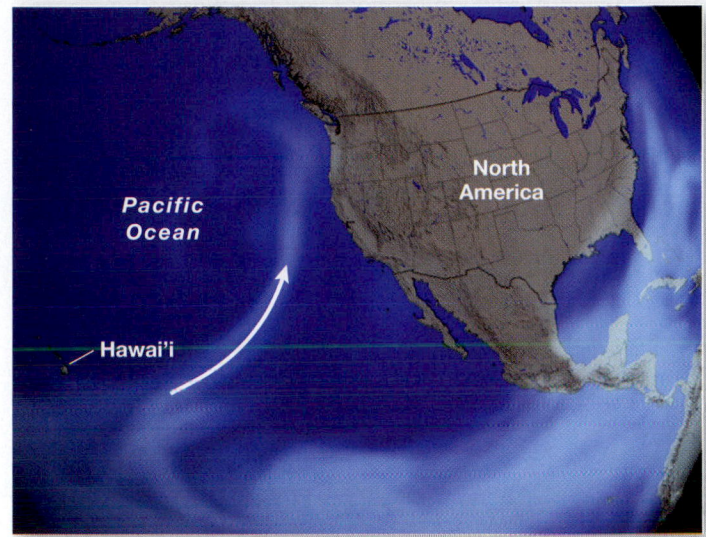

▲**Figure GN 6.3** **Satellite image shows water vapor over the North American region.** Note the moisture plume (white arrow) in the Pacific Ocean flowing from warm subtropical waters northeastward toward the west coast of the U.S. and Canada. [NASA/GSFC.]

with the prevailing winds toward land in the midlatitudes. Atmospheric rivers can be thousands of kilometers long, especially in the Atlantic Ocean, where water vapor from the Caribbean Sea can travel as far as Norway. Specialized remote-sensing instruments detect atmospheric rivers, producing images in which the moisture plumes are easily visible (**Figure GN 6.3**). Over the past decade, scientific understanding of these features grew exponentially using these data.

Global Importance Atmospheric rivers transport moisture from the tropics toward the poles, making them an essential part of Earth's water cycle. The amount of water vapor moved in a strong atmospheric river is massive, roughly 7 to 10 times the average flow of liquid water at the Mississippi River's mouth. Along the U.S. West Coast, a few strong atmospheric river storms can provide 30%–50% of the annual precipitation that forms this region's water supply.

Water-vapor transport through the atmosphere drives weather and provides water for Earth systems. For real-time water-vapor images, see the Atmospheric River Portal at http://mead.ucsd.edu/.

1. Describe three characteristics of an atmospheric river.

2. In Figure GN 6.2, where does the atmospheric river originate? Where does precipitation occur as a result?

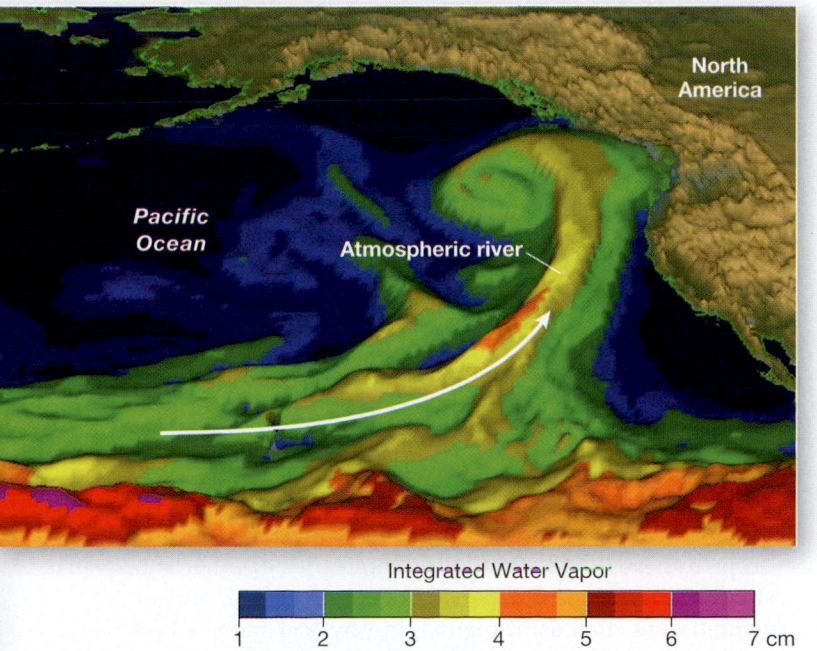

Integrated Water Vapor

| 1 | 2 | 3 | 4 | 5 | 6 | 7 cm |

▲**Figure GN 6.1** **Water vapor flows from the equatorial region toward the west coast of North America.** In February 2015, this moisture plume caused several storms along the U.S. West Coast. [NOAA.]

Water is in the atmosphere in visible forms—clouds, fog, and precipitation—and in microscopic forms, such as water vapor. Of all the water present in Earth systems, only a tiny percentage (less than 0.03%) is stored in the atmosphere. If this amount fell to Earth as rain, it would cover the surface to a depth of 2.5 cm (1.0 in.). However, this relatively small amount of water in the atmosphere is critical for all Earth systems, and the atmosphere is a key pathway of water movement around the globe.

This chapter begins our study of the *hydrologic cycle*, or *water cycle*, defined as the movement of water throughout the atmosphere, hydrosphere, lithosphere, and biosphere. This movement includes evaporation from oceans and the formation of clouds and precipitation over land and water. Our study continues in Chapter 8, where we discuss the surface and subsurface components of the cycle, summarizing them in Figure 8.5. Together, these are the processes that power weather systems on Earth.

everyday GEO**SYSTEMS**

Why does water form beads on a leaf?

On the leaf surface, cohesion between the water molecules is stronger than adhesion between the water molecules and the leaf. Thus, water molecules stick tightly together and contract to the smallest possible surface area, forming droplets, or beads. Surface tension holds each bead together in a spherical shape and also produces the effect of a thin "skin" across the bead surface. Some plants, such as the nasturtium shown here, have leaves that are highly water repellent (an adaptation known as "superhydrophobicity"). As droplets roll off the leaf, they pick up dirt particles and pathogens by adhesion, effectively cleaning the leaves and protecting the plant from disease.

▲**Figure 6.1 Water beads on a nasturtium leaf.** [kristof lauwers/ Alamy Stock Photo]

Water's Unique Properties

Water is an extraordinary compound. It is the only common substance on Earth that naturally occurs in all three states of matter: liquid, solid, and vapor. Unlike other liquids, water expands when it freezes, making its solid form less dense than its liquid form. In addition, water readily dissolves a range of other substances and is sometimes called the "universal solvent." Finally, when water changes from one state of matter to another (as from liquid to gas or solid), the large amount of energy absorbed or released helps power the general circulation of the atmosphere, which drives daily weather patterns.

Each water molecule is made up of two atoms of hydrogen and one of oxygen, which readily bond. Once the hydrogen and oxygen atoms join in covalent bonds, they are difficult to separate, thereby producing a water molecule that remains stable in Earth's environment.

The nature of the hydrogen–oxygen bond gives the hydrogen side of a water molecule a positive charge and the oxygen side a negative charge. As a result of this *polarity*, water molecules attract each other: The positive (hydrogen) side of a water molecule attracts the negative (oxygen) side of another—an interaction called *hydrogen bonding*. The polarity of water molecules also explains why water is able to dissolve many substances—specifically, substances that are also polar. Pure water is rare in nature because of its ability to dissolve other substances within it.

The effects of hydrogen bonding in water create **cohesion**, the attraction of molecules for other molecules of the same kind. Cohesion allows you to slightly overfill a glass with water; webs of millions of hydrogen bonds hold the water slightly above the rim. Cohesive forces also cause water to form beads on hydrophobic surfaces that repel water, such as a freshly waxed car or a plant leaf (**Figure 6.1**). Cohesion creates water's *surface tension*, the capacity of a substance to hold together rather than rupture under tension or stress. Surface tension allows a steel needle to float lengthwise on the surface of water, even though steel is much denser than water.

Water molecules are also attracted to molecules of other substances, creating **adhesion**—the attraction of molecules of one kind for molecules of another kind. Adhesion is the cause of capillary action, observed when you "dry" something with a paper towel. The towel draws water through its fibers because of cohesion between water molecules and adhesion between water and the charged cellulose molecules of the paper. *Capillary action*, the upward movement of water against gravity, occurs because water molecules stick together (forming drops or beads) and stick to the molecules of other substances (the fibers of a paper towel, glass, soil, and organic tissues such as in plants). In physical science labs, students can observe the adhesion between water and glass in a cylinder or test tube. The *meniscus*, or curved surface of liquid in the tube, is concave because adhesion allows the water to slightly "climb" the glass sides. In nature, capillary action is part of the process that pulls

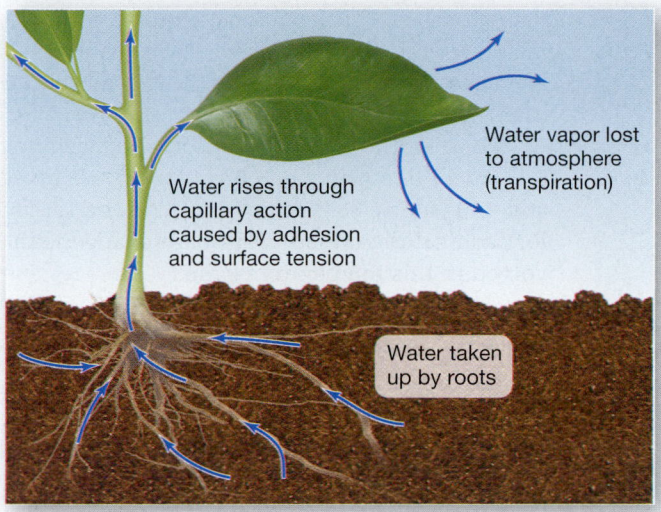

▲**Figure 6.2 Capillary action.** Water moves upward through the plant structure by capillary action.

water from plant roots upward through the narrow, porous stem and into the body of the plant (**Figure 6.2**).

Phase Changes and Heat Exchange

For water to change from one state to another, known as a **phase change**, heat energy must be added to it (absorbed) or removed from it (released). The amount of heat energy absorbed or released must be sufficient to affect the hydrogen bonds between molecules. The energy for each phase change is measured in calories. A calorie (cal) is the amount of heat energy required to raise the temperature of 1 g of water (at 15°C) by 1 degree Celsius. The heat exchanged by water during phase changes provides more than 30% of the energy that powers the general circulation of the atmosphere.

Figure 6.3 shows the three states of water and the six phase changes between them. Note that the molecular arrangement differs between solid, liquid, and gas: Ice has a regular arrangement, with molecules close together; water has a more random arrangement and wider spacing between molecules; and water vapor has the most random arrangement, with molecules the farthest apart.

- *Freezing* and *melting* describe the familiar phase changes between solid and liquid.
- *Condensation* is the process through which water vapor

in the air becomes liquid water—this is the basis of the process that forms clouds.

- *Evaporation* is the process through which liquid water becomes water vapor. This phase change is called *vaporization* when water is at boiling temperature.
- *Deposition* is the process through which water vapor changes directly to a solid, as when it attaches to an ice crystal in the formation of *frost*. You may have seen this on your car windshield on a cold morning or inside your freezer.
- **Sublimation** is the process by which ice changes directly to water vapor. A classic sublimation example is the production of water-vapor clouds through the vaporization of dry ice (frozen carbon dioxide) when it is exposed to air.

As discussed in Chapter 4, the heat energy of a phase change is **latent heat**, which is heat that is "hidden" within the structure of water's physical state and does not produce a change in temperature. Instead, the heat energy is used to break the hydrogen bonds between molecules. Because the hydrogen bonds of ice molecules are stronger and harder to break than those in liquid water, latent heat energy must be absorbed, or added, for phase changes from solid to liquid, and again for phase changes from liquid to gas. Energy is released, or removed, for phase changes in the opposite direction, gas to liquid to solid.

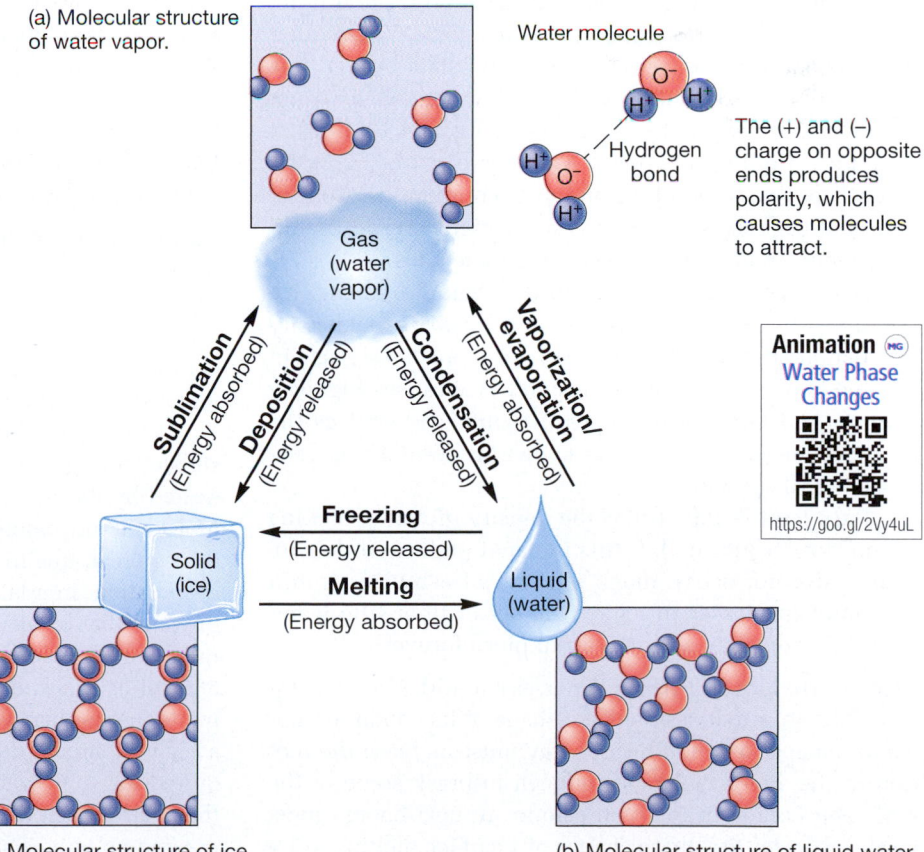

(a) Molecular structure of water vapor.

Water molecule

Hydrogen bond

The (+) and (−) charge on opposite ends produces polarity, which causes molecules to attract.

Gas (water vapor)

Sublimation (Energy absorbed)

Deposition (Energy released)

Condensation (Energy released)

Vaporization/ evaporation (Energy absorbed)

Freezing (Energy released)

Melting (Energy absorbed)

Solid (ice)

Liquid (water)

Animation ⓜⒼ
Water Phase Changes

https://goo.gl/2Vy4uL

(c) Molecular structure of ice.

(b) Molecular structure of liquid water.

▲**Figure 6.3 Three physical states of water (solid, liquid, and gas) and the phase changes between them.** Note the diagram showing a hydrogen bond in a water molecule. Of the three states, ice has the most rigid molecular structure. Heat energy is either added or released during a phase change.

▲**Figure 6.4 The buoyancy of ice.** Most solid compounds are more dense than liquid compounds, so they sink. Water reaches its greatest density in the liquid state, explaining why solid ice floats in cold water. Because ice usually contains air bubbles, most icebergs are about 0.86 the density of water. Here, a kayaker paddles past an iceberg in the Tracy Arm–Fords Terror Wilderness, southeast Alaska. [Design Pics Inc./Alamy.]

Ice, the Solid Phase Ice is a solid with a rigid, crystalline structure in which molecules are held firmly together by their hydrogen bonds. Ice is a unique solid because it is less dense than liquid water, so it floats.

As water cools from room temperature, it contracts in volume and increases in density because the same number of molecules now occupy a smaller space. When other liquids cool, they congeal into the solid state by the time they reach their greatest density. However, when water has cooled to the point of greatest density, at 4°C (39°F), it is still in a liquid state. Below a temperature of 4°C (39°F), water behaves differently from other compounds. Continued cooling makes it expand as the rigid crystalline arrangement forms among the slowing molecules.

As temperatures descend further below freezing, ice continues to expand in volume and decrease in density to a temperature of −29°C (−20°F); up to a 9% increase in volume is possible. This expansion of ice causes highway damage and burst water pipes in winter, as well as the physical breakdown of rocks known as *weathering* (discussed in Chapter 13).

Pure ice has 0.91 times the density of water, making it buoyant (**Figure 6.4**). If this unusual pattern of density change did not occur, much of Earth's freshwater would be bound in masses of ice on the ocean floor (the water would freeze, sink, and remain in place forever).

Water, the Liquid Phase Water, as a liquid, is a noncompressible fluid that assumes the shape of its container. For ice to change to water, heat energy must increase the motion of the water molecules enough to break some of the hydrogen bonds. In total, 80 calories of heat energy must be absorbed for the phase change of 1 g of ice melting to 1 g of water—this transfer of latent heat occurs despite the fact that the temperature remains the same: Both ice and water measure 0°C (32°F). When the phase change is reversed and a gram of water freezes, latent heat is released rather

than absorbed. The latent heat required for melting, known as the *latent heat of fusion*, and the latent heat released during freezing are each 80 cal/g, as shown in **Figure 6.5a**.

To raise the temperature of 1 g of water at 0°C (32°F) to boiling at 100°C (212°F), we must add 100 calories (an increase of 1 C°, or 1.8 F°, for each calorie added). No phase change is involved in this temperature gain.

Water Vapor, the Gas Phase Water vapor is an invisible and compressible gas in which each molecule moves independently of the others. When the phase change from liquid to vapor is induced by boiling, it requires the addition of 540 cal for each gram, under normal sea-level pressure; this amount of energy is the **latent heat of vaporization** (Figure 6.5). When water vapor condenses to a liquid, each gram gives up its hidden 540 cal as the **latent heat of condensation**. We see water vapor in the atmosphere after condensation has occurred in the form of clouds, fog, and steam. If you have noticed the heat on your skin from steam when you drained steamed vegetables or pasta, you have felt the release of the latent heat of condensation.

In summary, the changing of 1 g of ice at 0°C to water and then to water vapor at 100°C—from a solid to a liquid to a gas—*absorbs* 720 cal (80 cal + 100 cal + 540 cal). Reversing the process, or changing the phase of 1 g of water vapor at 100°C to water and then to ice at 0°C, *releases* 720 cal into the surrounding environment.

In contrast, the **latent heat of sublimation** absorbs 680 cal as a gram of ice transforms directly into vapor. Water vapor freezing directly to ice releases a comparable amount of energy.

Latent Heat Transfer under Natural Conditions In nature, the number of calories absorbed or released during a phase change varies with the environmental conditions such as temperature. Both evaporation and condensation are always occurring over water and other moist surfaces on Earth.

Figure 6.5b shows an example of the latent heat absorbed during evaporation. As water at Earth's surface is heated by the Sun's radiant energy, the temperature rises, molecular movement increases, and some liquid water molecules break free to become water vapor, in the process of evaporation. In a lake or stream at 20°C (68°F), every gram of water that breaks away from the surface through evaporation must absorb from the environment approximately 585 cal as the *latent heat of evaporation*. This is slightly more energy than would be required if the water were at a higher temperature (if the water is boiling, 540 cal is required for vaporization). Because energy is removed from the environment during the phase change, *evaporation is a cooling process*. This is the same type of cooling you feel as the water evaporates from your skin when you step out of a swimming pool or lake on a warm summer day. As we learned in Chapter 4, the latent heat of evaporation is the dominant cooling process in Earth's energy budget.

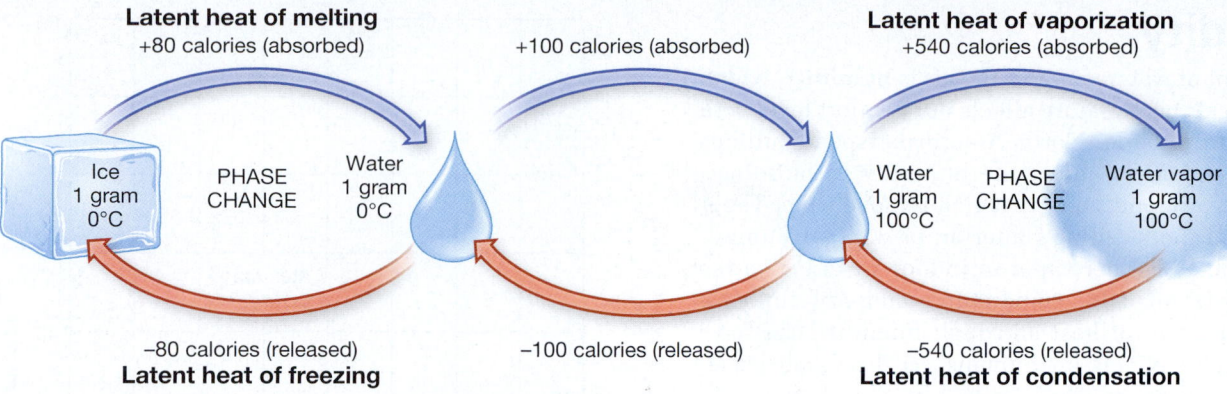

Latent heat of melting
+80 calories (absorbed)

+100 calories (absorbed)

Latent heat of vaporization
+540 calories (absorbed)

Ice 1 gram 0°C | PHASE CHANGE | Water 1 gram 0°C

Water 1 gram 100°C | PHASE CHANGE | Water vapor 1 gram 100°C

−80 calories (released)
Latent heat of freezing

−100 calories (released)

−540 calories (released)
Latent heat of condensation

(a) Latent heat absorbed or released in phase changes between ice and water and water vapor. To transform 1 g of ice at 0°C to 1 g of water vapor at 100°C requires 720 cal: 80 + 100 + 540.

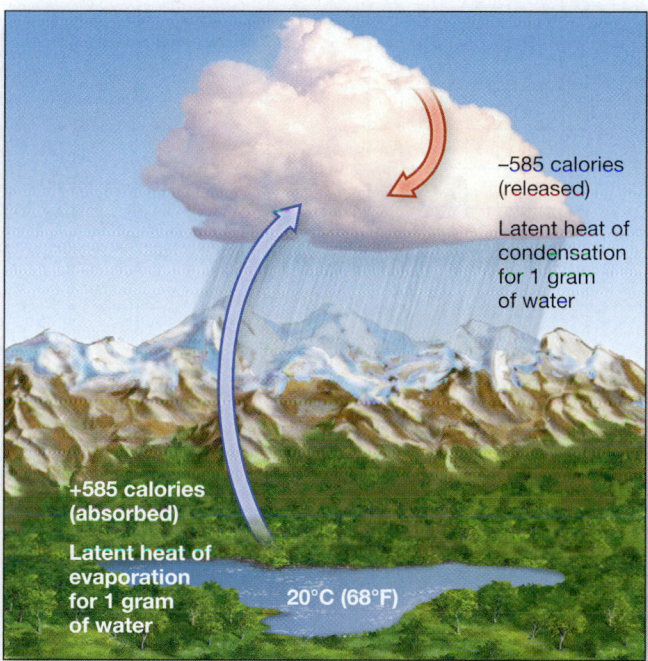

−585 calories (released)

Latent heat of condensation for 1 gram of water

+585 calories (absorbed)

Latent heat of evaporation for 1 gram of water

20°C (68°F)

(b) Latent heat exchange between water in a lake at 20°C and water vapor in the atmosphere, under typical conditions.

◄**Figure 6.5** Latent heat energy absorbed and released during phase changes of water.

Animation ᴹᴳ
Water Phase Changes

https://goo.gl/2Vy4uL

In Figure 6.5b, we see the process reverse when air cools and water vapor condenses into the liquid state, releasing 585 cal for every gram of water as the *latent heat of condensation*. We see the result of condensation as clouds, in which water vapor has condensed onto microscopic particles in the air to form liquid droplets. The condensation occurring in one small cloud can release tremendous amounts of energy as condensation forms millions of cloud droplets. Because heat energy is added to the environment, *condensation is a warming process*. In the tropics, where water vapor is abundant, the warming of condensation can result in towering storm clouds, discussed later in this chapter.

Rates of Evaporation and Condensation

The phase changes of evaporation and condensation are occurring simultaneously at all times in the lower atmosphere and over ground and water surfaces. When the rate of evaporation exceeds the rate of condensation, *net evaporation* occurs. Higher evaporation rates often occur over warm water or in areas with warm air temperature. Wind also enhances evaporation rates. When the rate of condensation exceeds the rate of evaporation, *net condensation* occurs.

The point at which evaporation and condensation are in balance is *saturation equilibrium*, or **saturation**. At the point of saturation, the amount of water vapor in the air has reached full capacity (the maximum possible amount). Beyond this point any addition of water vapor will cause net condensation. We discuss saturation and condensation in the next section.

WORKITOUT 6.1
Phase Changes and Latent Heat

Explain in your own words:

1. Why is the latent heat of sublimation greater than the latent heat of evaporation?
2. Why does the process of condensation release rather than absorb energy?
3. Why is evaporation a cooling process?

🌍 **GEO**report **6.1**   Water vapor: an important greenhouse gas

Water vapor is different from other greenhouse gases in that its concentration is tied to temperature. As global temperatures rise with climate change, evaporation increases from lakes, oceans, and land surfaces, increasing the amount of water vapor in the atmosphere and strengthening the greenhouse effect over Earth. Scientists have measured an increase in average global water vapor in recent decades. As atmospheric water vapor increases, precipitation patterns are changing, the amount of rainfall is increasing during the heaviest events, and the frequency of severe storm events is rising.

Humidity

The amount of water vapor in the air is **humidity**, which along with air temperature affects our comfort level both indoors and outside. North Americans spend billions of dollars a year to adjust the humidity in buildings, either with air conditioners, which remove water vapor as they cool the building's interior, or with air humidifiers, which add water vapor to indoor air to lessen the drying effects of cold temperatures and dry climates. The combination of heat and high humidity can have serious health effects on humans, as discussed previously in Focus Study 4.2.

You may have noticed that your hair changes in character on a humid day or when you travel to a more humid environment. Human hair expands and lengthens when humidity increases, changing as much as 4% in length between completely dry and extremely humid air. This relationship is the basis for the *hair hygrometer*, or hair-tension hygrometer, an instrument developed in the 1700s to measure humidity using bundled strands of human hair connected to a mechanism that records changes in tension. Modern hygrometers include *sling psychrometers*, small instruments that use two thermometers side by side (one wet and one dry), deriving the level of humidity from the temperature difference between them, and *electric hygrometers*, which measure changes in electrical conductivity or resistance of certain materials under changing humidity. In addition, satellites using infrared sensors monitor water vapor in the lower atmosphere, as discussed in Geosystems Now.

Humidity is an important measurement for understanding weather because the amount of water vapor in the air affects condensation, cloud formation, and the possibility of precipitation. The capacity of air for water vapor is primarily a function of the temperatures of both the air and the water vapor, which are usually the same. We express humidity using measures of actual water-vapor content—vapor pressure, specific humidity, and dew-point temperature—and a measure of water-vapor content relative to water-vapor capacity—relative humidity.

Vapor Pressure

One way to measure humidity is by the pressure exerted by water-vapor molecules. As water molecules evaporate from surfaces into the atmosphere, they become water vapor. As part of the air, water-vapor molecules exert a portion of the air pressure along with nitrogen and oxygen molecules. The share of air pressure that is made up of water-vapor molecules at a given temperature is **vapor pressure**, expressed in millibars (mb). Vapor pressure increases with the concentration of water-vapor molecules present (the greater mass of molecules exerts more pressure) and the temperature of the air (higher temperature means that molecules move more rapidly and exert more pressure).

Air that is saturated (carrying the maximum possible amount of water vapor for the current temperature) is

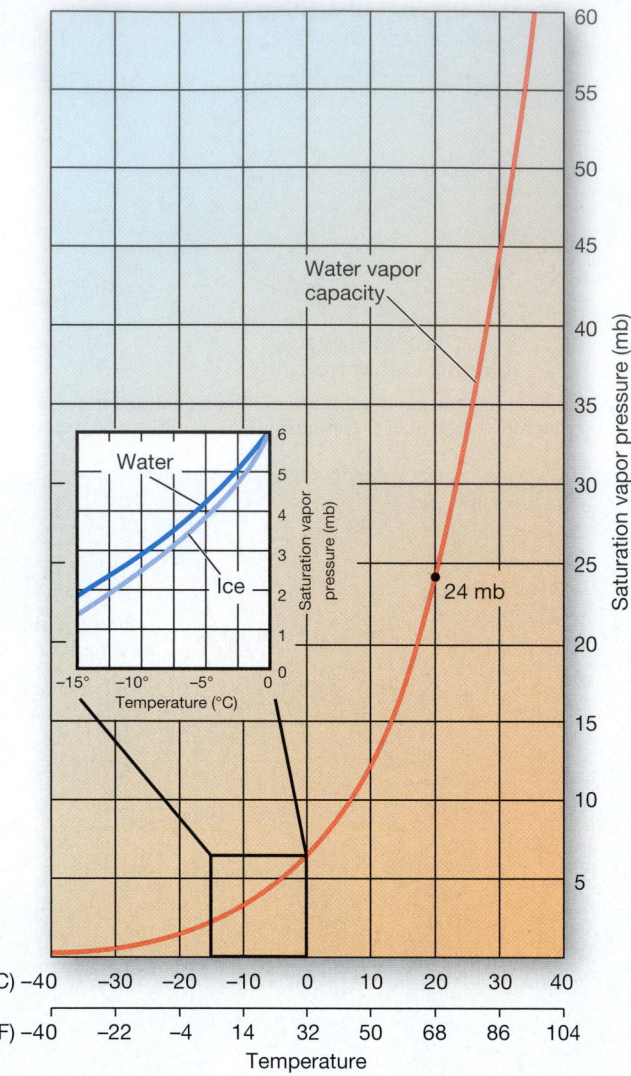

▲Figure 6.6 **Saturation vapor pressure at various temperatures.** Saturation vapor pressure is the maximum possible water vapor as measured by the pressure it exerts (mb). Inset graph compares saturation vapor pressures over water surfaces with those over ice surfaces at subfreezing temperatures.

at **saturation vapor pressure**. As temperature increases, saturation vapor pressure increases (**Figure 6.6**). For the temperatures commonly found at Earth's surface (from about 0°C to 25°C), every air temperature increase of 10 C° (18 F°) means that the saturation vapor pressure nearly doubles. Therefore, warm air at temperatures around 30°C (86°F) has nearly four times the water-vapor capacity as cooler air at 10°C (50°F).

Applying this relationship to Earth systems, we see that in the warm, humid equatorial regions, warm air has a high capacity for water vapor. When this moist air cools, net condensation can release the tremendous latent heat that powers tropical storms (discussed in Chapter 7). Conversely, in polar regions, cold air has less capacity for water vapor, producing the "polar deserts" discussed in Chapters 17 and 20.

The inset in Figure 6.6 shows that, at temperatures below 0°C (32°F), saturation vapor pressure is slightly higher over a "supercooled" water surface than over an ice surface. (Supercooled water, as discussed ahead, has a temperature below the temperature at which water normally freezes.) This fact is important for precipitation, as described later in this chapter.

Specific Humidity

Another measure of humidity is **specific humidity**, the mass of water vapor (in grams) per mass of air (in kilograms). This is nearly equivalent to the *mixing ratio*, another humidity measure (mixing ratio is the mass of water vapor per mass of dry air, in grams per kilograms). Because specific humidity is measured in mass, it changes only if the amount of water vapor changes. Specific humidity does not change with temperature or as air expands and contracts with changes in pressure (as long as water vapor is not added or removed). Specific humidity is often used to describe the conditions in large air masses.

The maximum mass of water vapor possible in a kilogram of air at a given temperature is the *saturation specific humidity*, plotted in **Figure 6.7**. Note the similar relationships on the graphs in Figures 6.6 and 6.7. Both show that as air temperature increases, the capacity for water vapor increases, with the rate of increase more pronounced at higher temperatures.

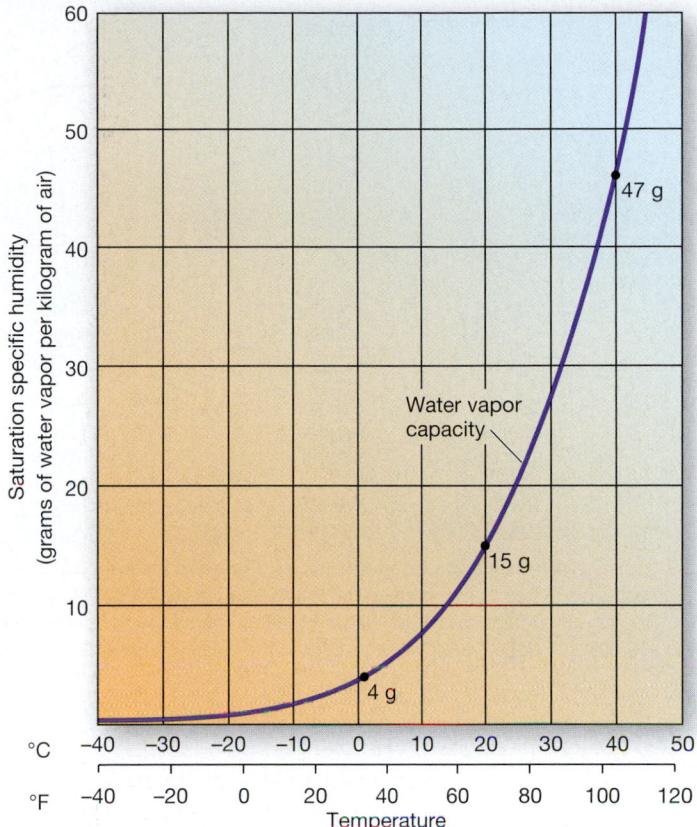

▲**Figure 6.7 Saturation specific humidity at various temperatures.** Saturation specific humidity is the maximum possible water vapor in a mass of water vapor per unit mass of air (g/kg).

Relative Humidity

A common measure of humidity in weather reports is **relative humidity**, which compares the actual water-vapor content to the maximum possible amount of water-vapor content in a body of air. Meteorologists use relative humidity to determine the Heat Index, discussed in Focus Study 4.2.

We define relative humidity as the ratio of vapor pressure to saturation vapor pressure. It is expressed as a percentage, and calculated as:

$$\text{Relative humidity} = \frac{\text{Vapor pressure}}{\text{Saturation vapor pressure}} \times 100$$

We can use the graph in Figure 6.6 to calculate relative humidity values. As marked on the graph, air at 20°C (68°F) has a saturation vapor pressure of 24 mb. If the vapor pressure of an air sample at that temperature is 12 mb, we can calculate the relative humidity (RH) as:

$$\text{At } 20°C \ (68°F)\text{: RH} = \frac{12 \text{ mb}}{24 \text{ mb}} = 0.50 \times 100 = 50\%$$

Similarly, if we know that an air sample at 15°C (59°F) has a vapor pressure of 12 mb, we can again use the graph in Figure 6.6 to find the saturation vapor pressure (16 mb). We can then calculate the relative humidity of the sample as:

$$\text{At } 15°C \ (59°F)\text{: RH} = \frac{12 \text{ mb}}{16 \text{ mb}} = 0.75 \times 100 = 75\%$$

Note from these examples that relative humidity increases with a decrease in temperature.

 **WORKITOUT 6.2**
Relative Humidity

Using the graph in Figure 6.6 to look up the saturation vapor pressure for different temperatures, solve these problems:

1. For air at 10°C (50°F) at a vapor pressure of 10 mb, what is the relative humidity?
2. For air at 20°C (68°F) at the same vapor pressure of 10 mb, what is the relative humidity?
3. If the temperature of the air rises to 30°C (86°F) and vapor pressure remains the same, what is the relative humidity?
4. At what temperature will the air be at 100% relative humidity if the vapor pressure remains the same?

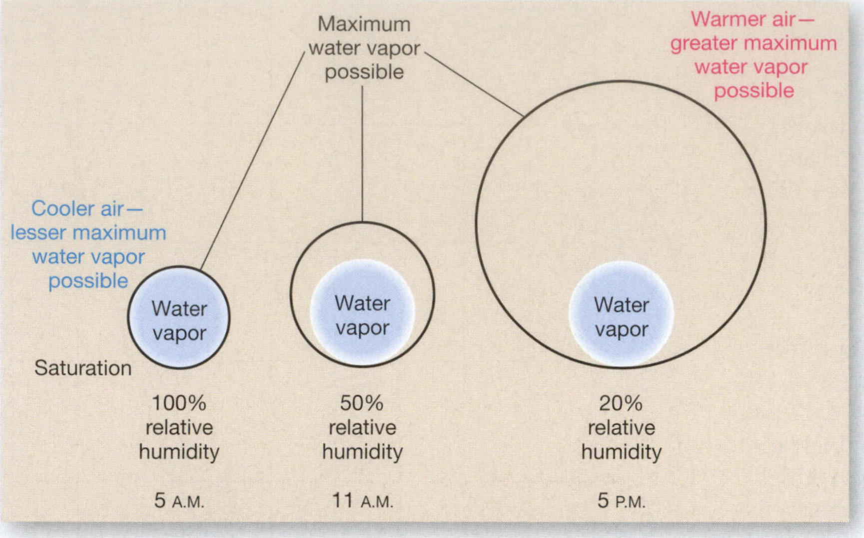

Maximum
water vapor
possible

Warmer air—
greater maximum
water vapor
possible

Cooler air—
lesser maximum
water vapor
possible

Saturation

Water
vapor

Water
vapor

Water
vapor

100%
relative
humidity

50%
relative
humidity

20%
relative
humidity

5 A.M.

11 A.M.

5 P.M.

▲**Figure 6.8 Water vapor, temperature, and relative humidity.** The maximum water vapor possible in warm air is greater (net evaporation more likely) than that possible in cold air (net condensation more likely), so relative humidity changes with temperature, even though in this example the actual water vapor present in the air stays the same during the day.

To illustrate the relationship between relative humidity and temperature, **Figure 6.8** compares water-vapor content and capacity at three times during a typical day. At 5 A.M., the cool morning air is at saturation equilibrium, and any further cooling or addition of water vapor produces net condensation. At this point, the relative humidity is 100%. At 11 A.M., the air temperature is rising, so the evaporation rate exceeds the condensation rate; as a result, the same volume of water vapor now occupies only 50% of the maximum possible capacity. At 5 P.M., the air temperature is just past its daily peak, so the evaporation rate exceeds condensation by an even greater amount, and relative humidity is at 20%.

Dew-Point Temperature We learned earlier that at saturation, any further addition of water vapor results in net condensation. We also learned that as temperature decreases, relative humidity increases, until the point of saturation at 100% relative humidity. The temperature at which air becomes saturated and condensation begins to form water droplets is the **dew-point temperature**, or simply, the *dew point*. When temperatures are below freezing, the *frost point* is the temperature at which the air becomes saturated, leading to the formation of frost (ice) on exposed surfaces.

A cold drink in a glass provides a familiar example of dew-point temperature conditions (**Figure 6.9**). Condensation in the form of *dew* (observed on lawns, bicycles, or tents on cool mornings) indicates that temperatures have fallen below the dew point. In winter, when surfaces such as car windshields cool to temperatures below freezing, *frost* forms when water condenses on the cold surface and then freezes, or when water vapor deposits on the cold surface and forms ice crystals (remember that deposition is the phase change from gas directly to solid).

Dew-point temperature is commonly included on weather maps as an absolute (rather than relative) indicator of humidity. A high dew point indicates air with higher water-vapor content, while a low dew point indicates drier air. (Go to http://graphical.weather.gov/sectors/conus.php to view real-time dew-point temperature maps.)

Daily Relative Humidity Patterns
Figure 6.10 illustrates the relationship between relative humidity and temperature throughout a typical day. Relative humidity is highest at dawn, when air temperature is lowest. If you park outdoors, you know about the wetness of the dew that condenses on your car or bicycle overnight. You have probably also noticed that the morning dew on windows, cars, and lawns evaporates by late morning as air temperature increases. Relative humidity is lowest in the late afternoon, when temperatures are higher. As shown in Figure 6.8, the actual water vapor present in the air may remain the same throughout the day. However, relative humidity changes because the temperature varies from morning to afternoon.

Cold glass chills the
surrounding air layer
to the dew-point
temperature

Dew
(active
condensation)

▲**Figure 6.9 Dew-point temperature example.** When the air reaches the dew-point temperature, water vapor condenses out of the air and forms water droplets on the glass.

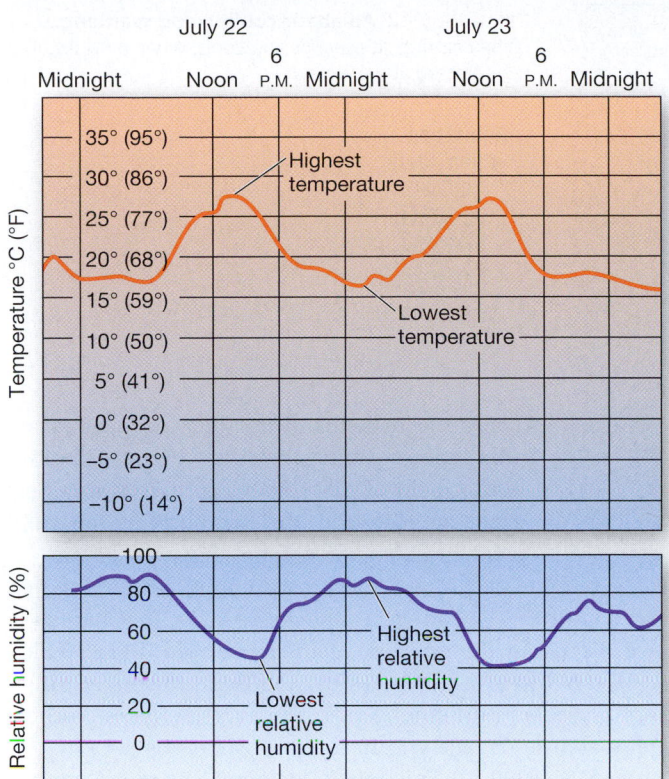

▲**Figure 6.10 Daily relative humidity patterns.** Typical daily variations demonstrate temperature and relative humidity relations.

stability of air parcels in the atmosphere is an indicator of weather conditions.

The opposing forces of buoyancy and gravity decide the vertical position of a parcel of air. These forces are closely related to the parcel's density—a measure of the spacing between molecules (wider spacing means lower density and more buoyancy, tight spacing means higher density and less buoyancy). The density of an air parcel depends on its temperature: Warm air has lower density than cold air and thus more buoyancy, causing a parcel that is warmer than the surrounding atmosphere to rise. Conversely, a parcel that is cooler than the surrounding atmosphere will sink with gravity. The density of an air parcel also depends on its moisture content: Moist air has a lower density than dry air. (Recall from Chapter 5 that moist air is lighter than dry air because the molecular weight of water is less than that of the oxygen and nitrogen molecules that make up dry air.)

In the atmosphere, a parcel is *stable* if it resists displacement upward or, when disturbed, tends to return to its starting place. An air parcel is *unstable* if it continues to rise until it reaches an altitude where the surrounding air has a density and temperature similar to its own. Note that the stability or instability of an air parcel depends on the difference between the temperature inside the parcel and the temperature of the air surrounding the parcel (**Figure 6.11**).

Atmospheric Stability

Air rises (ascends) or falls (descends) vertically in the atmosphere depending on its density. **Atmospheric stability** refers to the tendency of the atmosphere to either encourage or discourage vertical air motion. Stable air tends to resist movement; unstable air tends to rise. When describing the processes related to atmospheric stability, meteorologists use the term *parcel* to describe a pocket of air that has specific temperature and humidity characteristics. Although an air parcel has no fixed size, we assume that it retains its general shape and character as it rises or falls in the atmosphere. The relative

▲**Figure 6.11 Hot air balloons illustrate principles of air stability.** As a balloon fills with hot (less dense) air, it rises with the buoyancy force. When air in the balloon cools (becomes more dense), the balloon sinks with gravity. This scene is near Albuquerque, New Mexico. [Chad Ehlers/Alamy.]

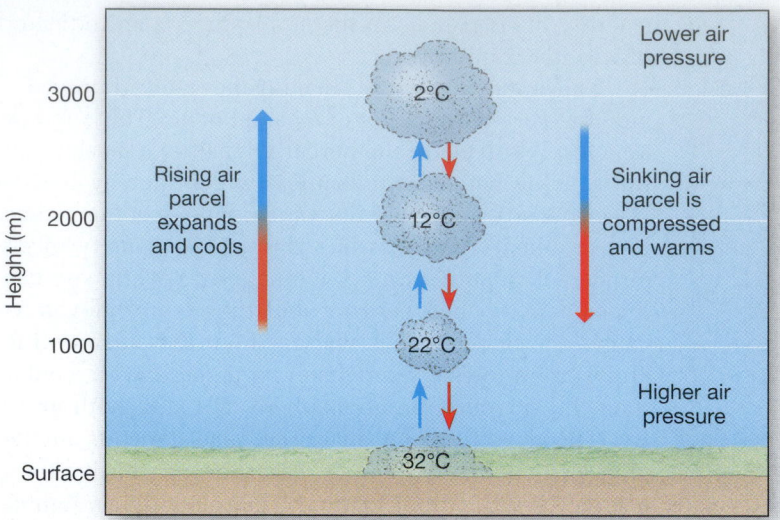

◀**Figure 6.12** **Adiabatic cooling and warming.**
When air rises, it expands and cools; when air sinks, it is
compressed and warms.

Animation
Atmospheric
Stability

https://goo.gl/lo2VYR

Adiabatic Processes

We learned in Chapter 3 that atmospheric pressure decreases as altitude increases, causing the effect of "thin air" at higher altitude above Earth's surface. The change in atmospheric pressure with altitude affects the temperature and vertical movement of an air parcel. As illustrated in **Figure 6.12**, a rising air parcel expands as atmospheric pressure decreases with altitude. As the parcel expands, air within it pushes outward, using up some of the kinetic energy of motion and causing cooling within the parcel. In contrast, a falling parcel compresses as external air pressure increases, causing warming within it.

Thus, *an ascending air parcel tends to cool by expansion*, responding to the reduced pressure at higher altitudes, and *a descending air parcel tends to heat by compression*.

These mechanisms of cooling and heating are **adiabatic**, meaning that they occur without a loss or gain of heat—that is, without any heat exchange between the surrounding environment and the vertically moving parcel of air.

The rate at which atmospheric temperature decreases with altitude is known as the *lapse rate*. In Chapter 3, we discussed the *environmental lapse rate* (ELR), which can vary by several degrees per thousand meters at different places and different times. The average rate of vertical temperature change within the troposphere is 6.4 C°/1000 m (3.5 F°/1000 ft). This rate is for nonrising air. When we consider adiabatic temperature changes within a rising air parcel, we use one of two specific *adiabatic lapse rates*, depending on moisture conditions in the parcel: dry adiabatic rate (DAR) and moist adiabatic rate (MAR).

Dry Adiabatic Rate The **dry adiabatic rate (DAR)** is the rate at which "dry" air cools by expansion as it rises or heats by compression as it falls (**Figure 6.13**). "Dry" refers to air that is less than saturated (relative humidity is less than 100%). The average DAR is 10 C°/1000 m (5.5 F°/1000 ft).

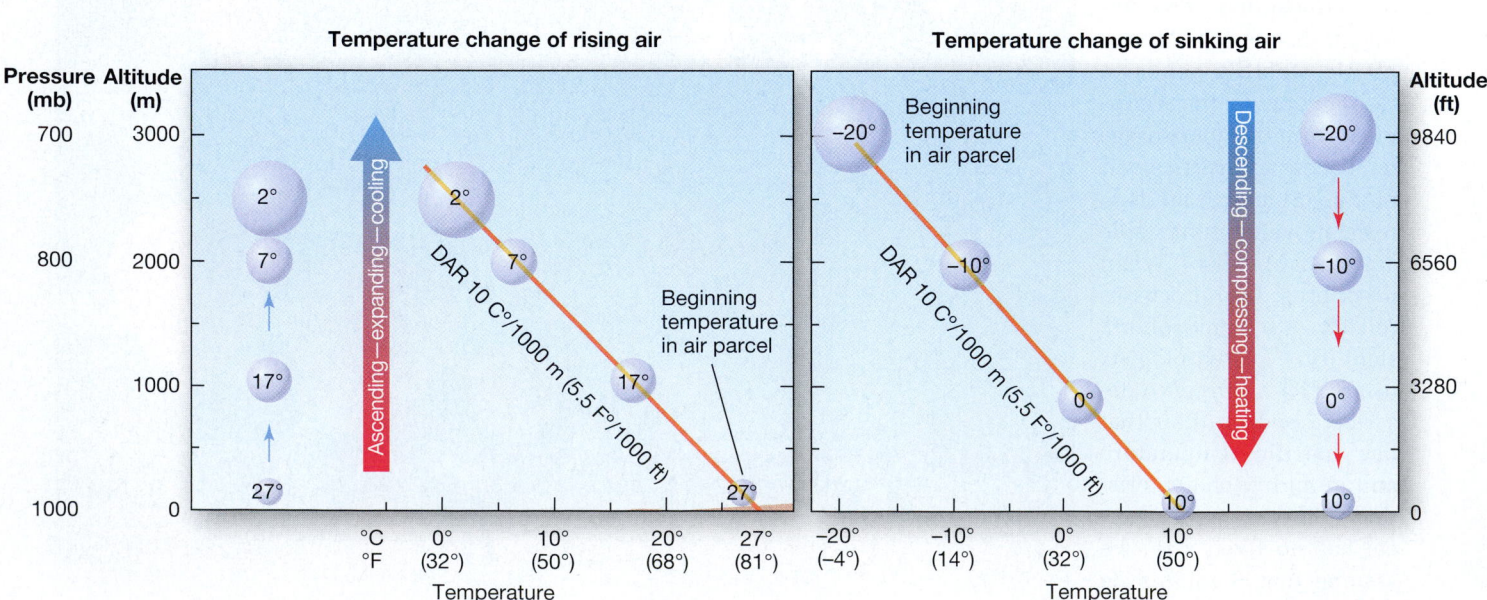

(a) Temperature change as rising air cools adiabatically.

(b) Temperature change as sinking air heats adiabatically.

▲**Figure 6.13** **Examples of adiabatic cooling and warming at the dry adiabatic rate.**

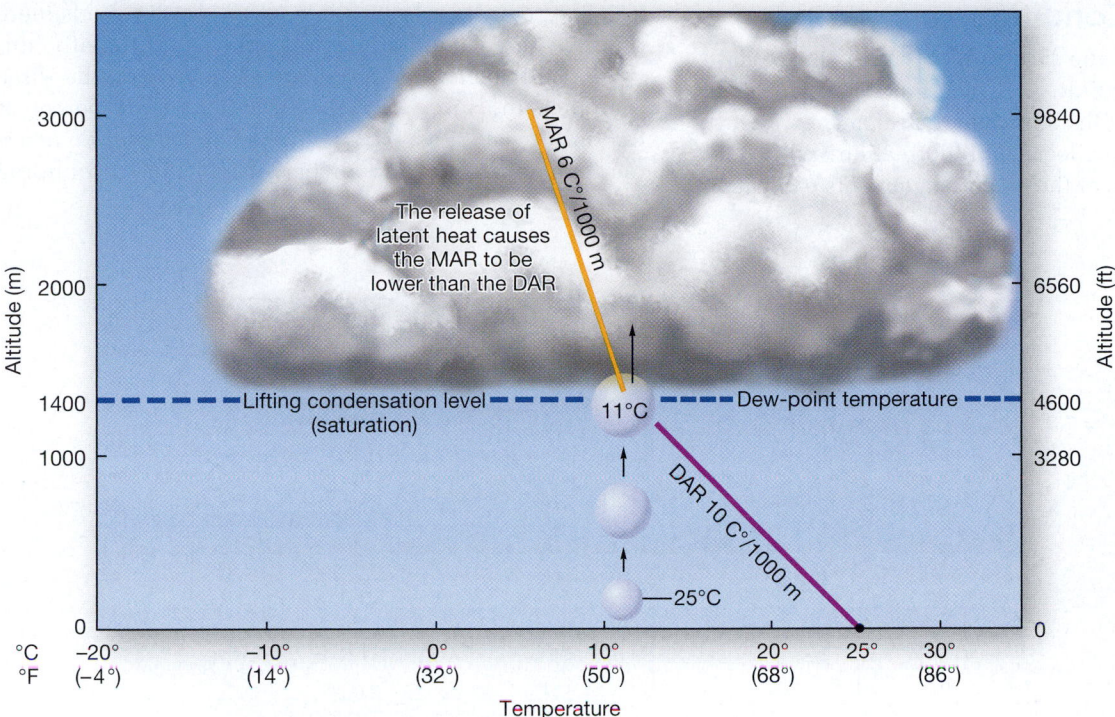

▲Figure 6.14 Unstable atmospheric conditions. The rising air parcel reaches dew point at 1400 m (4600 ft) after 14 C° of adiabatic cooling at the DAR. Above the lifting condensation level, the parcel cools at the MAR. In this example, the environmental lapse rate is 12 C°/1000 m; we discuss unstable conditions and the environmental lapse rate in the next section.

To see how a specific example of dry air behaves, consider an unsaturated parcel of air at the surface with a temperature of 27°C (81°F), shown in Figure 6.13a. It rises, expands, and cools adiabatically at the DAR, reaching a temperature of 2°C (36°F) at an altitude of 2500 m (approximately 8000 ft). In Figure 6.13b, assume that an unsaturated air parcel with a temperature of −20°C at 3000 m (24°F at 9800 ft) descends to the surface, heating adiabatically. According to the DAR, the temperature of the air parcel when it arrives at the surface is 10°C (50°F).

Moist Adiabatic Rate The **moist adiabatic rate (MAR)** is the rate at which an ascending air parcel that is moist, or saturated, cools by expansion. The average MAR is 6 C°/1000 m (3.3 F°/1000 ft). This is roughly 4 C° (2 F°) less than the dry adiabatic rate. From this average, the MAR varies with moisture content and temperature and can range from 4 C° to 10 C° per 1000 m (2 F° to 5.5 F° per 1000 ft). Note that a descending parcel of saturated air warms at the MAR as well, because the evaporation of liquid droplets absorbs latent heat and offsets the rate of compressional warming.

The cause of this variability, and the reason that the MAR is lower than the DAR, relates to the latent heat of condensation (**Figure 6.14**). As an air parcel rises and cools, it may eventually achieve saturation at the dew-point temperature, followed by active condensation. This is the *lifting condensation level*, an altitude that you

sometimes see in the sky as the flat bottoms of clouds. Figure 6.14 shows an example of a rising air parcel that cools at the DAR until it reaches the lifting condensation level, at which point it becomes saturated and continues to cool at the MAR. As water vapor condenses in the saturated air, the release of latent heat causes the parcel to cool more slowly, decreasing the adiabatic rate. The release of latent heat may vary with temperature and water-vapor content. The MAR is much lower than the DAR in warm air with higher water-vapor content, whereas the two rates are more similar in cold air.

WORKITOUT 6.3
Adiabatic Lapse Rates

Using Figures 6.13 and 6.14 for guidance, calculate the temperature change of an air parcel under the following conditions:

1. If an unsaturated air parcel at 25°C (77°F) at sea level rises and cools at the DAR, what is its temperature at 1500 m (4921 ft)?
2. If an unsaturated parcel at −15°C (5°F) at 3000 m (9842 ft) descends and warms at the DAR, what is its temperature at sea level?
3. If an unsaturated parcel at 30°C (86°F) at sea level rises and cools, what is its temperature at 2000 m (6562 ft)? If at that point the parcel becomes saturated and continues to rise, what will its temperature be at 3000 m (9842 ft)?

Atmospheric Conditions

The relationship of the DAR and MAR to the environmental lapse rate, or ELR, at a given time and place determines the stability of the atmosphere over an area. In turn, atmospheric stability affects cloud formation and precipitation patterns, some of the essential elements of weather.

Temperature relationships in the lower atmosphere produce three conditions: unstable, conditionally unstable, and stable. For the sake of illustration, the three examples in **Figure 6.15** begin with an air parcel at the surface at 25°C (77°F). In each example, compare the temperatures of the air parcel and the surrounding

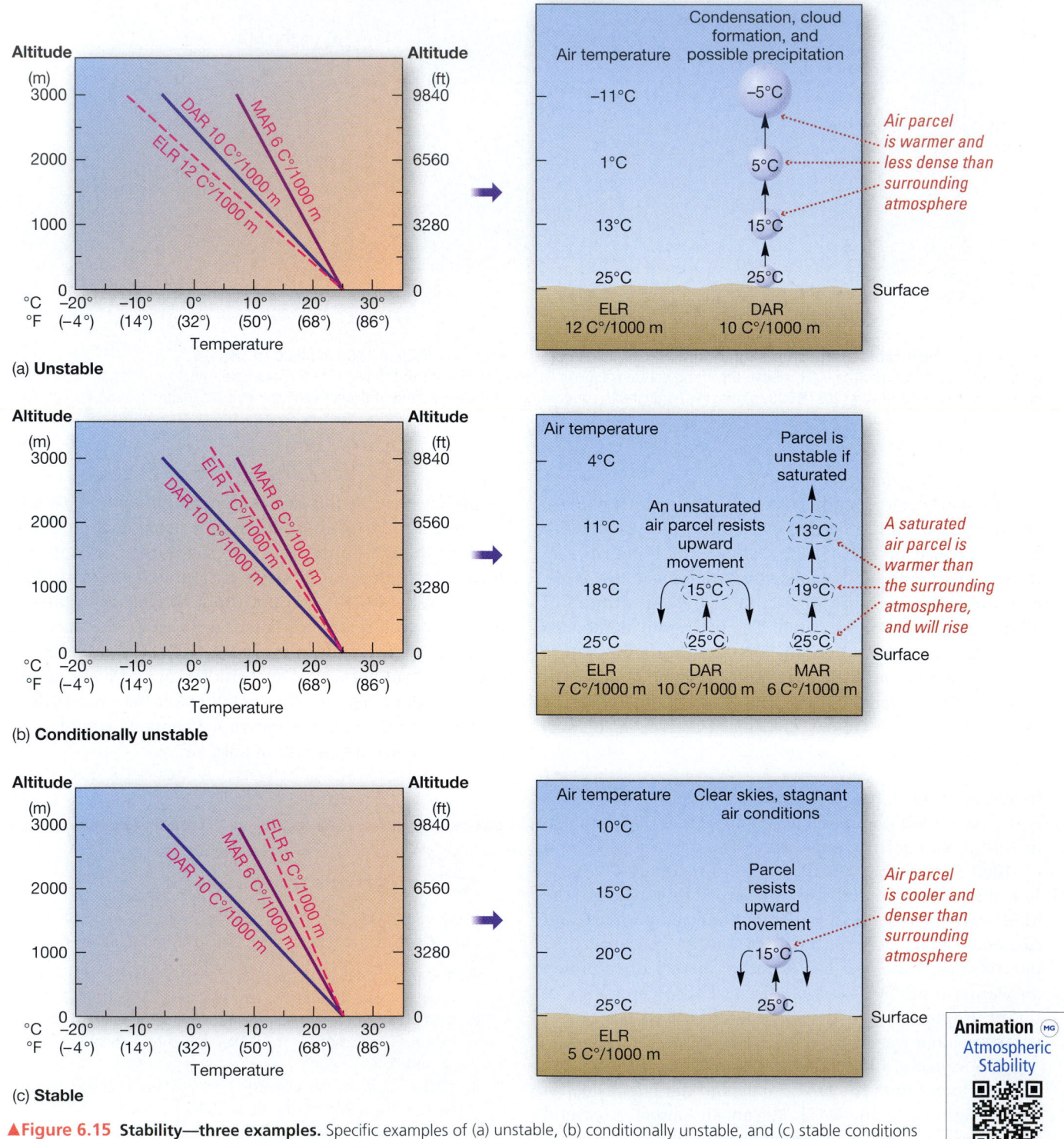

▲**Figure 6.15 Stability—three examples.** Specific examples of (a) unstable, (b) conditionally unstable, and (c) stable conditions in the lower atmosphere. Note the response to these three conditions in the air parcel on the right side of each diagram.

Animation
Atmospheric Stability

https://goo.gl/lo2VYR

environment. Assume that a lifting mechanism, such as surface heating, a mountain range, or weather fronts, is present to get the parcel started (we examine lifting mechanisms in Chapter 7).

Unstable Conditions When the ELR exceeds the DAR, the atmosphere is unstable. The example in Figure 6.15a shows unstable conditions resulting when the ELR is 12 C°/1000 m (6.6 F°/1000 ft). Under these conditions, the air parcel continues to rise through the atmosphere because it is warmer (less dense and more buoyant) than the surrounding environment. By 1000 m (3300 ft), the rising air parcel has cooled adiabatically by expansion at the DAR from 25° to 15°C, while the surrounding air has cooled from 25°C at the surface to 13°C. By comparing the temperatures in the air parcel and the surrounding environment, you see that the temperature in the parcel is 2 C° (3.6 F°) warmer than the surrounding air at 1000 m (3300 ft).

Under unstable atmospheric conditions, a rising parcel of air may reach the lifting condensation level, where it becomes saturated and continues to rise at the MAR. Conditions like these frequently occur when the Sun's radiant energy heats surfaces, causing air to rise by convectional lifting that ultimately produces clouds and precipitation.

Conditionally Unstable Conditions If the ELR is somewhere between the DAR and the MAR, the atmosphere is neither unstable nor stable, a situation known as conditional instability (Figure 6.15b shows an example where the ELR is 7 C°/1000 m). Under these conditions, if an air parcel is less than saturated, it will resist upward movement, unless forced. But if the air parcel becomes saturated at the lifting condensation level, it will now be unstable and continue to rise and cool at the MAR.

One example of such conditionally unstable air occurs when stable air is forced to lift as it passes over a mountain range (discussed in Chapter 7). As the air parcel lifts and cools to the dew point, the air becomes saturated and condensation begins. Now the MAR is in effect, and the air parcel behaves in an unstable manner. The sky over a valley or plain may be clear and without a cloud, yet huge clouds may develop over a nearby mountain range.

Stable Conditions When the ELR is less than both the DAR and MAR, the lower atmosphere is stable. The example in Figure 6.15c shows stable conditions resulting when the ELR is 5 C°/1000 m (3 F°/1000 ft). Under these conditions, the air parcel has a lower temperature (is more dense and less buoyant) than the surrounding environment. The relatively cooler air parcel tends to resist lifting unless forced by updrafts or a topographic barrier, and the sky remains generally cloud free. If clouds form, they tend to be

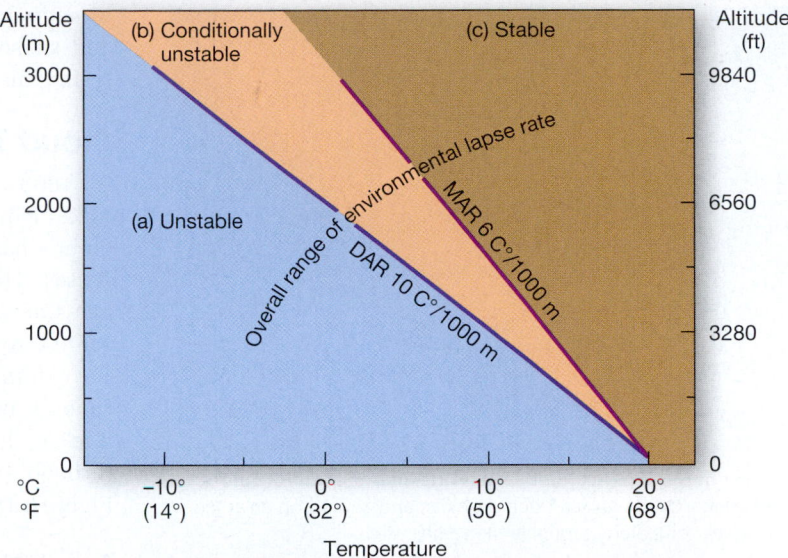

▲**Figure 6.16 Temperature relationships and atmospheric stability.** The relationship between dry and moist adiabatic rates and environmental lapse rates produces three atmospheric conditions: (a) unstable (ELR exceeds the DAR), (b) conditionally unstable (ELR is between the DAR and MAR), and (c) stable (ELR is less than the DAR and MAR).

stratiform (flat clouds) or cirroform (wispy), lacking vertical development. In regions experiencing air pollution, stable conditions in the atmosphere worsen the pollution by slowing exchanges in the surface air.

The overall relationships between the dry and moist adiabatic rates and environmental lapse rates that produce conditions of instability, conditional instability, and stability are summarized in **Figure 6.16**. We work more with lapse rates and adiabatic cooling and heating in Chapter 7, where we discuss atmospheric lifting.

Clouds and Fog

A **cloud** is an aggregation of tiny water droplets and ice crystals that are suspended in air and are great enough in volume and concentration to be visible. Clouds are lovely and sometimes striking indicators of overall atmospheric conditions, including moisture content and atmospheric stability. *Fog* is a low-lying cloud, often in contact with the ground. Clouds and fog form when air becomes saturated and water vapor condenses or deposits onto tiny particles in the air.

Cloud Formation

The formation and composition of a cloud depends on temperature. The *warm clouds* of the tropics, which have temperatures above 0°C (32°F) from top to bottom, are great masses of tiny liquid droplets, each invisible without magnification. The *cold clouds* of the midlatitudes, which have temperatures below −40°C (−40°F), are masses of ice crystals, typically occurring above 6,000 m (20,000 ft) in altitude. *Mixed-phase clouds*, such as a cumulonimbus thunderhead (discussed ahead in this section), contain both liquid cloud droplets and solid ice crystals.

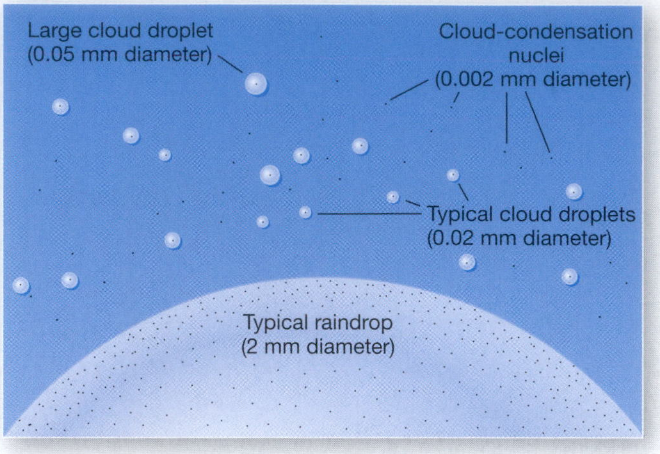

▲**Figure 6.17 Cloud-condensation nuclei and cloud droplets.** Cloud-condensation nuclei, cloud droplets, and a raindrop enlarged many times compared at roughly the same scale.

As previously discussed, a rising air parcel may cool to the dew-point temperature, where saturation occurs. More lifting of the air parcel cools it further, producing condensation of water vapor into liquid water—a **cloud droplet**. For a cloud droplet to form, condensation must occur on **cloud-condensation nuclei**, microscopic particles that always are present in the lower atmosphere. These nuclei typically come from dust, soot, and ash from volcanoes and forest fires, and particles from burned fuel, such as sulfate aerosols. Masses of air over continents average 10 billion cloud-condensation nuclei per cubic meter. In air masses that form over oceans, sea salts derived from ocean sprays act as nuclei, averaging 1 billion per cubic meter. Cloud droplets range in size, from the typical diameter of 0.02 mm (0.0008 in.) up to about 0.05 mm (0.002 in.). The largest cloud droplets can form on *giant cloud condensation nuclei* (having a diameter greater than 0.01 mm), such as sea salt (**Figure 6.17**).

In cold clouds, with temperatures at or below −40°C (−40°F), the highly ordered lattice structure of ice crystals can form spontaneously from liquid water droplets. In mixed-phase clouds with slightly higher temperatures, ice crystals can form in the presence of **freezing nuclei**, tiny atmospheric particles upon which water vapor deposits. Freezing nuclei include certain bacteria, particles of clay and other minerals, and other compounds that mimic the hexagonal (six-sided) crystalline structure of ice—an example is silver iodide, used for cloud seeding (a method for artificially promoting precipitation). In the presence of these nuclei, ice crystals form by deposition, in which water vapor changes directly to ice without passing through the liquid phase.

Freezing nuclei are less common than cloud-condensation nuclei, so that mixed-phase clouds contain some ice crystals and many more liquid droplets. Because temperatures are below freezing, these liquid water droplets are *supercooled*, meaning that they are in a liquid state at temperatures below 0°C (32°F). Supercooled water droplets initiate the growth of ice crystals either by freezing directly onto freezing nuclei or by evaporating into vapor and subsequently depositing onto an ice crystal. We describe this process later in the chapter.

Cloud Types and Identification

In 1803, English biologist and amateur meteorologist Luke Howard established a classification system for clouds based on their physical form and formation processes. His grouping of clouds into three basic forms has since been expanded to include 10 cloud types, presented in **Table 6.1** and **Figure 6.18**.

Altitude and *shape* are key to cloud classification. Clouds occur in four primary altitude classes—low, middle, high, and clouds that are vertically developed through the troposphere (illustrated at the far right in Figure 6.18) and in three basic forms: flat, puffy, and wispy.

- Flat and layered clouds with horizontal development are classed as *stratiform*.
- Puffy and globular clouds with vertical development are *cumuliform*.
- Wispy clouds, usually high in altitude and made of ice crystals, are *cirroform*.

Combinations of altitude and shape result in 10 basic cloud types.

For example, low clouds, ranging from the surface up to 2000 m (6500 ft) in the middle latitudes, are *stratus* or *cumulus*, depending on their general shape. **Stratus** clouds appear dull, gray, and featureless. When they yield precipitation, they become *nimbostratus*, and their showers typically fall as drizzling rain. **Cumulus** clouds appear bright and puffy, like cotton balls. When they do not cover the sky, they float by in infinitely varied shapes. Sometimes near the end of the day **stratocumulus** may fill the sky in patches of lumpy, grayish, low-level clouds.

The prefix *alto-* (meaning "high") denotes middle-level clouds. They contain water droplets, mixed, when temperatures are cold enough, with ice crystals. *Altostratus* clouds often cover the entire sky in a gray sheet.

TABLE 6.1 Cloud Classes and Types	
Altitude and Midlatitude Composition	**Cloud Type**
Low clouds	Stratus
• Up to 2000 m (6500 ft)	Stratocumulus
• Water	Nimbostratus
Middle clouds	Altostratus
• 2000–6000 m (6500–20,000 ft)	Altocumulus
• Ice and water	
High clouds	Cirrus
• 6000–13,000 m (20,000–43,000 ft)	Cirrostratus
• Ice	Cirrocumulus
Vertically developed clouds	Cumulus
• Near surface to 13,000 m (43,000 ft)	Cumulonimbus
• Mix of ice and water	

(a) Altocumulus

(b) Cirrostratus

(c) Cirrus

(d) Cirrostratus

High clouds

Cirrocumulus

Cirrus

6000 m—

Cirrostratus (halo)

Anvil-shaped head

Altocumulus

Cirrostratus

Middle clouds

Altostratus

Clouds with vertical development

Cumulonimbus

Lenticular

Nimbostratus

Cumulus (fair weather)

Stratus

Stratocumulus

2000 m—
Low clouds

(e) Nimbostratus

(f) Stratus

(g) Cumulus

(h) Cumulonimbus

▲**Figure 6.18 Principal cloud types and special cloud forms.** Cloud types according to form and altitude (low, middle, high, and vertically developed). [(a), (c), and (h) Bobbé Christopherson. (d), (e), and (f) Robert Christopherson. (b) Teerawat Sumrantin/Shutterstock. (g) Brian Kinney/Shutterstock.]

Prevailing wind

▲**Figure 6.19 Lenticular clouds over the Sierra Nevada range, California.** Westerly winds form lenticular clouds, shown here near Tioga Pass in Yosemite National Park. [Gary Crabbe/Alamy.]

Altocumulus clouds may form patchy rows, wave patterns, a "mackerel sky," or lens-shaped (lenticular) clouds.

High clouds, above 6000 m (20,000 ft), consist of ice crystals. These wispy filaments, usually white except when colored by sunrise or sunset, are **cirrus** clouds, sometimes dubbed "mares' tails." Cirrus clouds can indicate an oncoming storm, especially if they thicken and lower in elevation. The prefix *cirro-*, as in *cirrostratus* and *cirrocumulus*, indicates other high clouds that form a thin veil or have a puffy appearance.

Lenticular, or lens-shaped, clouds often form over mountain ranges, where stable, moist air passing over the terrain develops a wave pattern (**Figure 6.19**). These clouds often appear stationary, but they are not. The flow of moist air continuously resupplies the cloud on the windward side as air evaporates from the cloud on the leeward side. Under the right conditions, multiple layers of lenticular clouds may be stacked on top of one another. Lenticular clouds can also form over flat terrain with the movement of fronts (discussed in Chapter 7).

A cumulus cloud can develop into a towering giant called **cumulonimbus** (**Figure 6.20**). Such clouds are known as *thunderheads* because of their shape and associated lightning and thunder. Notable characteristics are surface wind gusts, updrafts and downdrafts, heavy rain, and ice crystals present at the top of the rising cloud column. High-altitude winds may shear the top of the cloud into the signature anvil shape of the mature thunderhead. Turbulent mixing of water droplets and ice crystals within the cloud leads to the formation of several types of precipitation, all described later in the chapter.

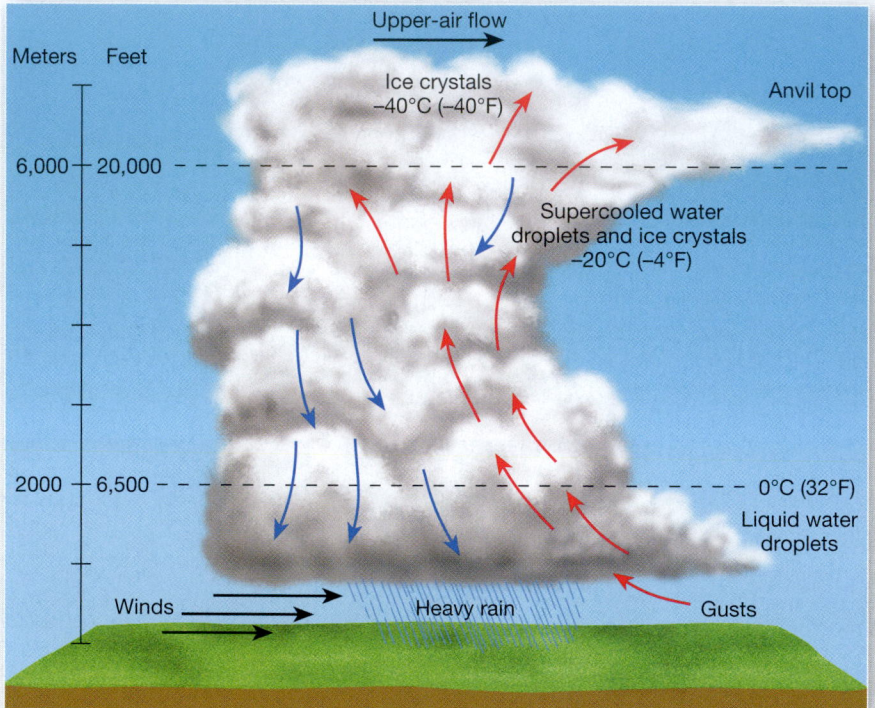

(a) Violent updrafts and downdrafts mark the circulation within the cumulonimbus cloud. Note the areas of liquid water droplets, supercooled water droplets, and ice crystal within the cloud.

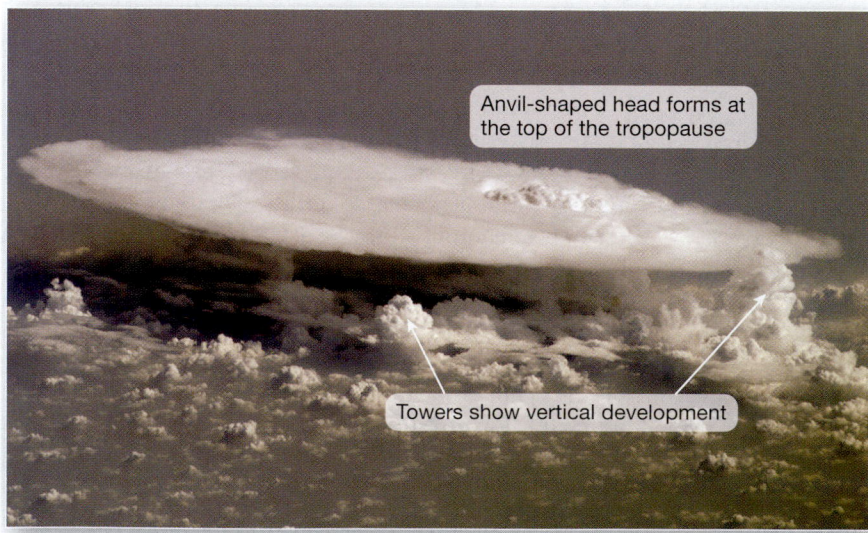

(b) A dramatic cumulonimbus thunderhead over Africa at 13.5° N latitude near the Senegal–Mali border.

▲**Figure 6.20** **Cumulonimbus thunderhead.** [(b) ISS Astronaut photograph, NASA.]

Processes That Form Fog

By international definition, **fog** is a cloud layer on the ground, with visibility restricted to less than 1 km (3300 ft). The presence of fog tells us that the air temperature and the dew-point temperature at ground level are nearly identical, indicating saturated conditions. A temperature inversion is often in effect with fog formation, meaning that the cooler temperatures of the fog layer are capped by warmer temperatures and sunny skies above it—with a difference in air temperature as much as 22 C° (40 F°) between ground level and the top of the inversion.

Almost all fog is warm; that is, its moisture droplets are above freezing. Freezing fog (or supercooled fog), in which the moisture droplets remain liquid below freezing, is less common, as is ice fog, consisting of ice crystals and only forming at temperatures around −40°C (−40°F).

Radiation When radiative cooling of the ground chills the air layer directly above to the dew-point temperature, a **radiation fog** forms. This fog occurs over moist ground, especially on clear nights; it does not occur over water because water does not cool appreciably overnight. As daytime temperatures warm the ground, the fog evaporates from the bottom up.

Winter radiation fog is typical in the Central Valley of California and is locally known as a *tule fog* (pronounced "toolee") after the tule (bulrush) plants that line the marshes of the Sacramento River and San Joaquin River delta regions (**Figure 6.21**). Tule fog can reduce visibility to 3 m (10 ft) or less and is a leading cause of weather-related traffic accidents in California.

Scientists have noted a decline in the number of fog days in the Central Valley between November and February since 1981. Radiation fog in this region forms over ground surfaces that are moist from winter rains and under cold temperature conditions that cause condensation. When conditions are dry and warm, as has occurred recently with ongoing drought and warming temperatures related to climate change, fewer fog days occur. Decline in fog days affects fruit and nut trees, staples of California's multibillion

▲**Figure 6.21 Winter radiation fog.** This January 2014 image shows fog in California's Central Valley, trapped by the topographic barriers of the Cascades to the north, the Sierra Nevada to the east, and the Coastal Ranges to the west. Once a frequent winter occurrence, radiation fog days in California are declining with warming temperatures and ongoing drought [*Terra* MODIS image, NASA.]

▲**Figure 6.22 Advection fog.** San Francisco's Golden Gate Bridge is shrouded by an invading advection fog characteristic of summer conditions along a western coast. [Brad Perks Lightscapes/Alamy.]

dollar agricultural industry. Without cold temperatures and fog, the trees have a shorter dormant period, allowing less time for the trees to reach their most productive yields.

Advection When unsaturated air migrates to a new place where conditions cause it to reach saturation, an **advection fog** forms. For example, when warm, moist air moves over cooler ocean currents, lake surfaces, or snow masses, the layer of migrating air directly above the surface becomes chilled to the dew point and fog develops. Off all subtropical west coasts in the world, summer fog forms in the manner just described (**Figure 6.22**). Focus Study 6.1 discusses the effects of advection fog on northern California's coast redwood forests.

One type of advection fog forms when moist air flows to higher elevations along a hill or mountain. This upslope lifting leads to adiabatic cooling by expansion as the air rises. The resulting **upslope fog** forms a cloud at the lifting condensation level where saturation occurs. Along the Appalachians and the eastern slopes of the Rockies, such fog is common in winter and spring.

Another advection fog associated with topography is **valley fog**. Because cool air is denser than warm air, it settles in low-lying areas, producing a fog in the chilled, saturated layer near the ground in the valley.

Evaporation Another type of fog, one related to both advection and evaporation, forms when cold air lies over warm water in a lake, an ocean surface, or even a swimming pool. This wispy **evaporation fog**, or *steam fog*, may form as water molecules evaporate from the warm water surface, adding water vapor to the cold overlying air. This process effectively humidifies the air to saturation, at which point condensation begins to form fog (**Figure 6.23**). When evaporation fog happens at sea, it is a shipping hazard called *sea smoke*.

▲**Figure 6.23 Evaporation fog.** Morning fog over Devil's Lake, Wisconsin. Later that morning as air temperatures rose, what do you think happened to the evaporation fog? [Terry Donnelly/Alamy.]

FOCUSstudy 6.1 Climate Change
Summer Fog Protects the World's Tallest Trees

Along the Pacific coast of California live the world's tallest trees, the coast redwoods (*Sequoia sempervirens*), which can grow to heights over 91 m (300 ft). The coastal habitat of these trees is often enshrouded in summer advection fog, formed over the cold waters of the California Current (**Figure 6.1.1**). Local winds carry this moist air across the Coast Ranges where the trees live. The fog provides a cool, humid summer climate for the coast redwoods, which depend on this seasonal moisture.

Decline in Summer Fog

Recently, University of California, Berkeley, researchers examined a variety of factors affecting summer fog along California's coast. The scientists found, first, that the average number of hours of daily fog in summer has dropped by about 14% since 1901, which amounts to about 3 hours per day less fog. Second, they found that frequent coastal fog was almost always associated with a large temperature gradient between coastal and inland areas, and that this gradient has decreased since 1950 along the entire coast from Seattle to San Diego. One comparison between temperature stations showed that a coastal–inland temperature difference of 9.5 C° (17 F°) at the beginning of the 20th century had

dropped to a 6.1 C° (11 F°) difference in 2008. Overall, the study found a 33% reduction in fog frequency within the range of the coast redwoods.

Decreased coastal fog is linked to warmer sea-surface temperatures, caused in part by climate change but also related to shifting pressure and wind patterns over the northern Pacific Ocean (discussed in Chapter 5). In addition, the scientists linked fog frequency to the presence of a strong temperature inversion that traps fog between the coast and the coastal mountains during the summer, preventing it from passing across the Coast Ranges into the interior. This temperature inversion has weakened with the decline in the coastal–inland temperature gradient, causing warmer and drier coastal conditions.

Fog Drip and Redwood Ecology

Because coast redwoods evolved within a narrow range of coastal habitat with consistent climatic conditions, these trees have specific temperature and humidity requirements. As fog moves into the forest, water droplets accumulate on branches and needles, eventually falling onto the vegetation and ground beneath (**Figure 6.1.2**). This "fog drip" reduces temperature and raises humidity in the forest, an important process during California's typically dry summer when temperatures are higher and rainfall scant. Redwood roots, which may spread 24 m (80 ft) out from the tree's base, absorb about 35% of the fog drip, drawing moisture up into the tree's internal water system.

Fog Helps Redwoods Conserve Water

Redwoods depend on humid conditions to properly regulate their water use. Redwood

▲Figure 6.1.2 **California coast redwoods in fog.** [NPS.]

needle leaves, like other plant leaves, have openings called stomata through which the tree loses water to the atmosphere by *transpiration* (a process similar to evaporation). Redwoods are unusual in that their stomata remain open at night as well as during the day, making them vulnerable to excessive transpiration during hot, dry conditions.

As in previous studies, the Berkeley scientists found significantly reduced redwood transpiration rates in the presence of summer fog, indicating the importance of fog for water conservation in these trees. A decline in this summer moisture increases drought stress, with unknown consequences for tree health.

1. What two trends did scientists find regarding the timing and frequency of fog along California's Pacific coast?
2. Why is fog important for coast redwood trees?

▲Figure 6.1.1 **Coast redwood forest and distribution.** [Will Goldenberg/Moment Open/Getty Images. Map after USGS.]

APPLYconcepts For each Earth system component, list the changes that ultimately impact the redwood forests.

Earth Systems Component	Changes
Hydrosphere: Ocean	_____, leading to . . .
Atmosphere: Daily hours of fog	_____, leading to . . .
Atmosphere: Temperature	_____, leading to . . .
Biosphere: Redwood forest	_____

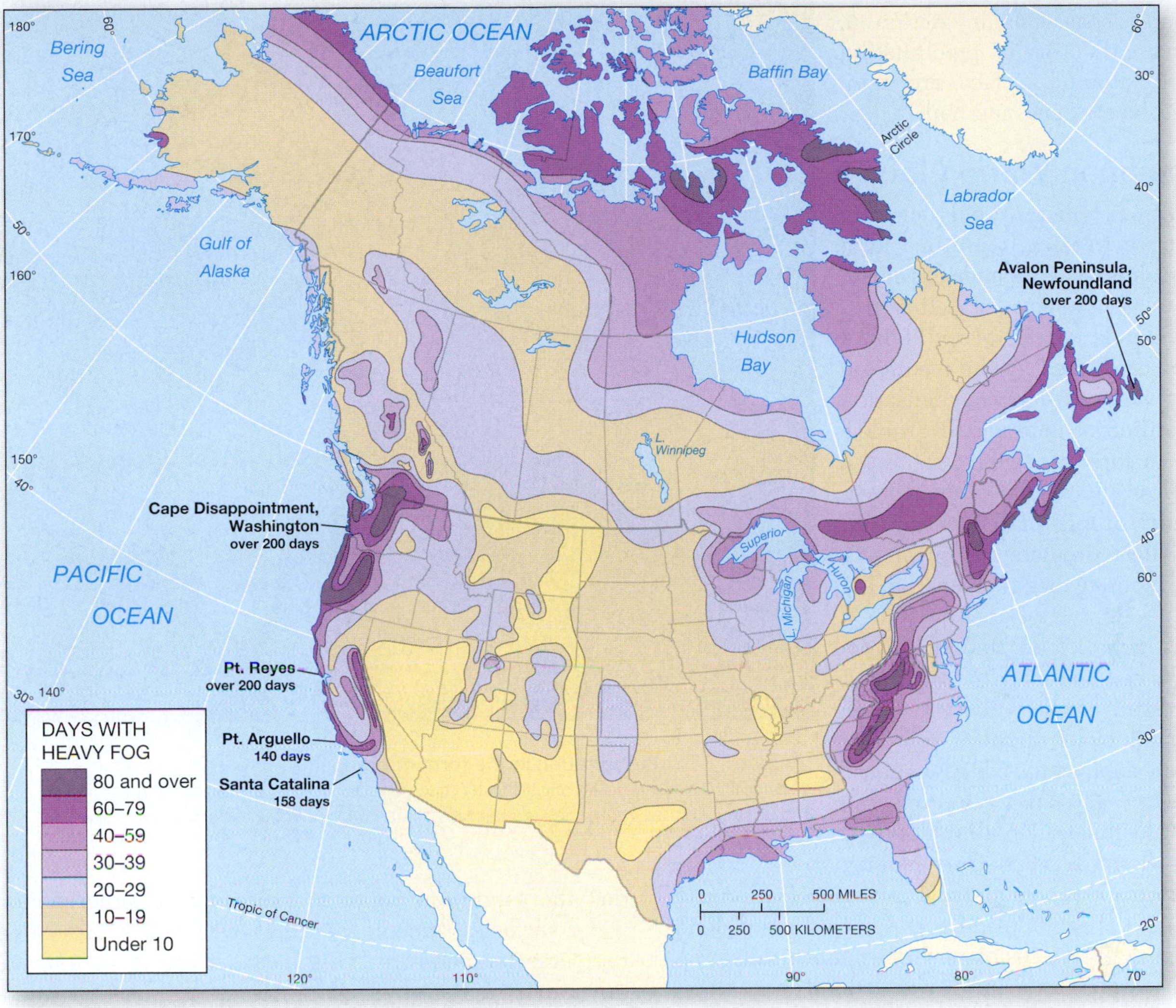

DAYS WITH HEAVY FOG
- 80 and over
- 60–79
- 40–59
- 30–39
- 20–29
- 10–19
- Under 10

Cape Disappointment, Washington over 200 days

Pt. Reyes over 200 days

Pt. Arguello 140 days

Santa Catalina 158 days

Avalon Peninsula, Newfoundland over 200 days

▲**Figure 6.24** **Mean annual number of days with heavy fog in the United States and Canada.** The foggiest spot in the United States is the mouth of the Columbia River, where it enters the Pacific Ocean at Cape Disappointment, Washington. One of the foggiest places in the world is Newfoundland's Avalon Peninsula, which regularly exceeds 200 days of fog each year. [Data courtesy of NWS; *Climatic Atlas of Canada*, Atmospheric Environment Service Canada; and *The Climates of Canada*, Environment Canada, 1990.]

The prevalence of fog throughout the United States and Canada is shown in **Figure 6.24**. Every year, multicar pileups occur on stretches of highway where vehicles drive at high speed in foggy conditions. Fog is a hazard to drivers, pilots, sailors, pedestrians, and cyclists, even though its conditions of formation are quite predictable. The distribution of regional fog occurrence should be a planning consideration for any proposed airport, harbor facility, or highway.

Fog is an important moisture source for many organisms (see Focus Study 6.1). Humans are increasingly using fog as a water resource in some regions. Throughout history, people have harvested water from fog, perhaps taking a cue from insects and other organisms that do so. For centuries, coastal villages in the deserts of Oman collected water drips deposited on trees by coastal fogs. In the Atacama Desert of Chile and Peru, residents stretch large nets to intercept advection fog; moisture condenses on the netting, drips into trays, and then flows through pipes into a reservoir. At least 30 countries across the globe experience foggy conditions suitable for harvesting water (see Human Denominator 6d).

Mobile Field Trip
Clouds: Earth's Dynamic Atmosphere

https://goo.gl/npztSJ

WORKITOUT 6.4
Condensation and Fog

Use your knowledge of condensation and fog formation to explain the following situations:

1. What process is occurring when you can see your warm breath on a cold day? Is your breath creating a type of cloud or fog? If yes, then what type?
2. You may have heard people say that a morning fog "lifts" as the day goes on. What is happening when a fog "lifts?"

Precipitation

Precipitation over land and water is a major component of Earth's water cycle, replenishing surface and subsurface freshwater across the planet. **Precipitation** occurs when condensed water droplets or ice crystals in a cloud become large enough to fall with gravity. Two primary mechanisms form precipitation: the collision–coalescence process for raindrops in warm clouds and the Bergeron process for snowflakes in cold clouds, illustrated in Geosystems in Action 6. Common general forms of precipitation reaching the ground surface are rain, freezing rain, sleet, snow, and hail.

Precipitation in Warm Clouds

In warm regions where cloud temperatures are above freezing, raindrops form by the **collision–coalescence process**, illustrated in Geosystems in Action 6.1. Recall that clouds consist of millions of liquid droplets, formed by the condensation of water vapor onto tiny condensation nuclei. A million or more cloud droplets are needed to form an average raindrop, which is larger and visible to the human eye. All cloud droplets fall with gravity, but the smallest droplets fall so slowly that they evaporate before reaching the ground.

Within a warm cloud, updrafts of rising air force condensation to occur and then carry cloud droplets aloft. As these varied sizes of cloud droplets mix and bump into one another, the collisions cause them to coalesce into larger raindrops that eventually "precipitate," or fall under their own weight (**Figure GIA 6.1**). Once moving downward through the cloud, these raindrops continue to grow in size as they collide and coalesce with more cloud droplets. The collision–coalescence mechanism for forming raindrops is most efficient in warm clouds over tropical oceans, where warm, moist air rises rapidly and where numerous giant condensation nuclei are available to form large cloud droplets.

Precipitation in Cold Clouds

In areas outside the tropics, precipitation often begins with the formation of ice crystals within clouds where temperatures are below freezing, conditions that can occur either at high altitudes within towering cumulonimbus clouds or during winter in low clouds. Such precipitation, frequent in the mid to high latitudes, occurs by means of the **Bergeron process** of ice crystal formation (the full name is the *Wegener–Bergeron–Findeisen process*, named for the three scientists that developed the theory).

When cloud temperatures are below about −10°C (14°F), clouds contain a mix of ice crystals and supercooled cloud droplets composed of water that has remained in the liquid state even though temperatures are below freezing. The Bergeron process occurs as water vapor evaporates from supercooled water droplets and deposits onto ice crystals, which eventually grow in size and fall with gravity (**Figure GIA 6.2**).

The transfer of water vapor from liquid cloud droplets to ice crystals depends on the saturation vapor pressure conditions discussed earlier. We saw in Figure 6.6

▲**Figure 6.25 Precipitation in the form of graupel.** The process of riming, in which supercooled cloud droplets stick directly to ice crystals, forms soft pellets that can form the nucleus for hail when they are held aloft in a cumulonimbus cloud. [Howard Bluestein/Science Source.]

that the saturation vapor pressure over a supercooled water surface is greater than that over an ice surface at the same temperature. This means that, at saturation, the vapor pressure gradient (or difference) between water and ice surfaces causes water vapor to move *away* from supercooled water droplets (where vapor pressure is slightly higher) and move *toward* ice crystals (where vapor pressure is slightly lower). The result is that supercooled cloud droplets become smaller by evaporation and ice crystals become larger by deposition, a net transfer of water-vapor molecules that leads to the growth of ice crystals into snowflakes.

This molecule-by-molecule growth of ice crystals into snowflakes explains their delicate and varied forms, such as plates, columns, needles, and dendrites. As snowflakes fall, they collide and merge in the process of *aggregation*, eventually reaching the ground as snow.

If there is turbulence, such as in a cumulonimbus cloud, ice crystals may be suspended aloft and become freezing nuclei for supercooled cloud droplets. *Riming* is the process whereby supercooled cloud droplets freeze directly onto an ice crystal, causing it to grow. Riming differs from the Bergeron process in that water droplets freeze on contact with an ice crystal (in contrast to water-vapor molecules depositing on an ice crystal to form a snowflake). The riming of an ice crystal forms *graupel*, precipitation that reaches the surface in the form of "soft hail," or pellets (rather than flakes) that fall apart when touched (**Figure 6.25**). Hail also forms by the process of riming, discussed ahead.

Precipitation occurs primarily through two mechanisms, one forming raindrops and one causing the growth of ice crystals into snowflakes. In warm clouds, raindrops form when updrafts of rising air cause water vapor to condense onto tiny nuclei. The resulting cloud droplets mix and collide to form raindrops that fall under their own weight and continue to grow in size (GIA 6.1). In cold clouds, ice crystal growth occurs as water evaporates from supercooled cloud droplets and deposits onto ice crystals, which grow and eventually fall with gravity (GIA 6.2).

6.1 PRECIPITATION IN WARM CLOUDS: THE COLLISION–COALESCENCE PROCESS

The collision–coalescence process produces raindrops in *warm* clouds where temperatures are *above* freezing.

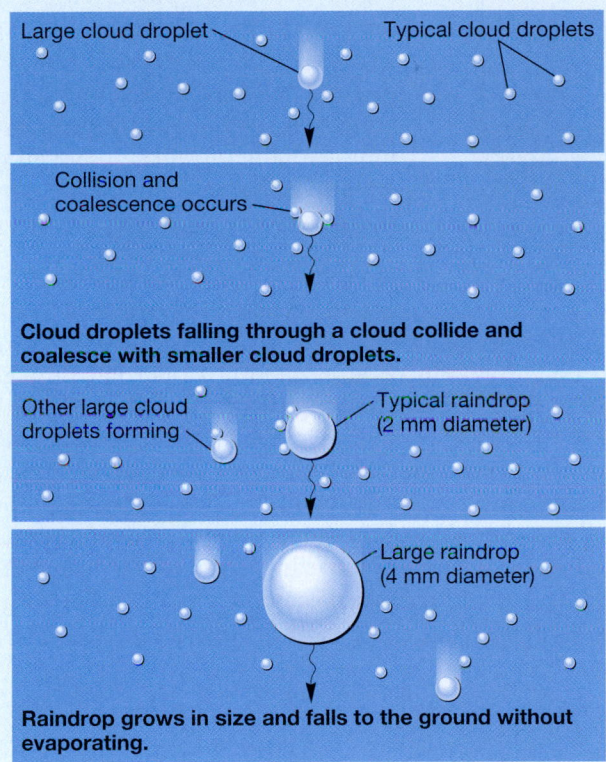

Large cloud droplet Typical cloud droplets

Collision and coalescence occurs

Cloud droplets falling through a cloud collide and coalesce with smaller cloud droplets.

Other large cloud droplets forming Typical raindrop (2 mm diameter)

Large raindrop (4 mm diameter)

Raindrop grows in size and falls to the ground without evaporating.

6.2 PRECIPITATION IN COLD CLOUDS: THE BERGERON PROCESS

The Bergeron process produces ice crystals in *cold* clouds where temperatures are *below* freezing.

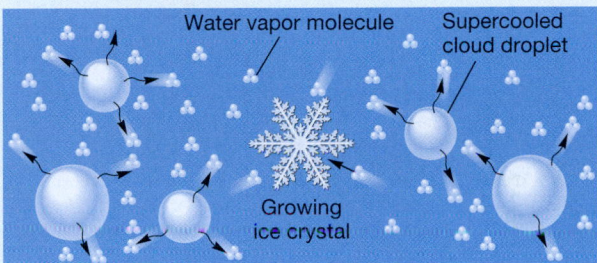

Water vapor molecule Supercooled cloud droplet

Growing ice crystal

Ice crystal continues to grow

Water evaporates from supercooled cloud droplets, which then shrink in size. Water vapor deposits onto the ice crystal, which then grows in size.

Snowflake

The net transfer of water vapor from cloud droplet to ice crystal continues until the snowflake falls with gravity to the ground.

MasteringGeography™

Visit the Study Area in MasteringGeography™ to explore precipitation processes.

Visualize: Study videos of the collision–coalescence and Bergeron processes.

Assess: Demonstrate understanding of precipitation processes (if assigned by instructor).

Animation (MG)
Atmospheric Stability

https://goo.gl/lo2VYR

This snowflake shows the typical six-sided crystal structure of ice.

GEOquiz

1. Describe: What environmental conditions determine whether precipitation forms by the collision–coalescense and Bergeron processes? Explain.

2. Compare and contrast: How are the two processes that increase the size of raindrops and snowflakes similar? How are they different?

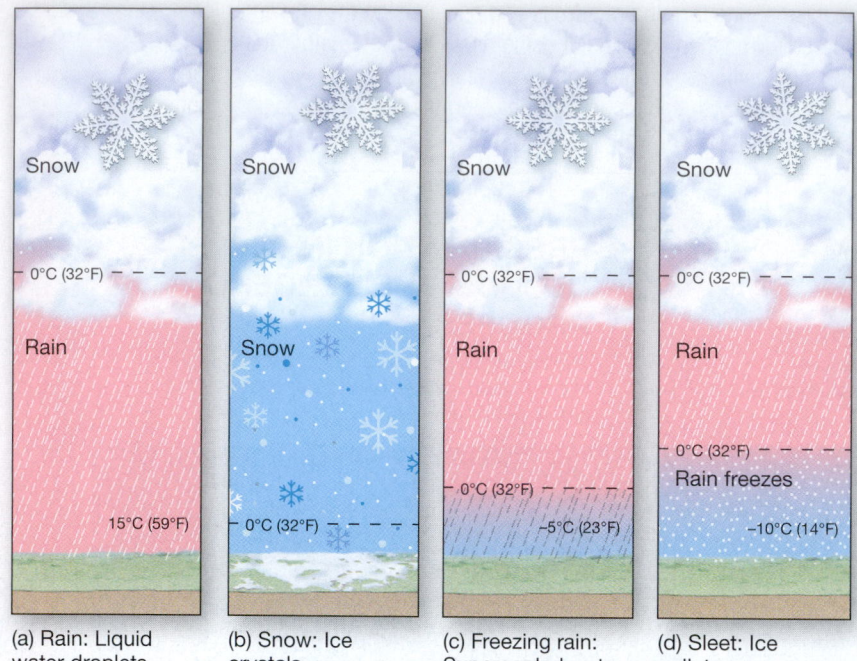

			Temperature (°C)
			■ < 0
			■ > 0

Snow — Snow — Snow — Snow

— 0°C (32°F) — — —   — 0°C (32°F) — — —   — 0°C (32°F) — — —   — 0°C (32°F) — — —

Rain   Snow   Rain   Rain

— 0°C (32°F) —
Rain freezes
15°C (59°F)   — 0°C (32°F) — — —   — −5°C (23°F)   −10°C (14°F)

(a) Rain: Liquid water droplets.

(b) Snow: Ice crystals.

(c) Freezing rain: Supercooled water droplets.

(d) Sleet: Ice pellets.

▲Figure 6.26 **Precipitation at the ground surface.** The arrival of rain, snow, freezing rain, and sleet at the ground relates to temperature conditions in the lower atmosphere.

Precipitation Reaching the Surface

The type of precipitation that reaches the ground surface depends on air temperature (**Figure 6.26**). **Rain** is precipitation in the form of liquid water droplets that forms by condensation and precipitation in air with a temperature above freezing or by melting of ice crystals as they pass through a warm layer of the atmosphere. In cold and mixed-phase clouds, precipitation begins as **snow**—precipitation in the form of ice crystals, pellets, or aggregates of ice crystals known as snowflakes (Figure 6.26b). Precipitation can also take several intermediate forms, depending on atmospheric temperature and turbulence.

Freezing Rain and Sleet As noted, when precipitation falls through a thick, warm layer of air, snowflakes melt into raindrops. But if these raindrops then fall through a thin layer of subfreezing temperatures, they will become supercooled and, upon reaching the ground, will instantly freeze onto cold surfaces—vegetation, roads, cars, and power lines (**Figure 6.27**). This is *freezing rain*, sometimes known as glaze (Figure 6.26c). If the raindrops fall through a thick, subfreezing layer of air nearer the ground, they will refreeze, becoming ice pellets known as **sleet** (Figure 6.26d).

Hail Ice pellets larger than 0.5 cm (0.20 in) that form within a cumulonimbus cloud are known as **hail**—or *hailstones*, after they fall to the ground. During hail formation, graupel (small snow pellets) circulate in the cloud, moving repeatedly above and below the freezing level, adding layers of ice in the process of riming. Eventually the graupel forms hail, which falls when the circulation in the

◀Figure 6.27 **Freezing rain.** A layer of ice covers trees in Postojna, Slovenia, in February 2014. A blizzard followed by freezing rain knocked out power to over 250,000 households. Freezing rain, also called glaze, forms when supercooled raindrops freeze onto cold objects. [Srdjan Zivulovic/Reuters.]

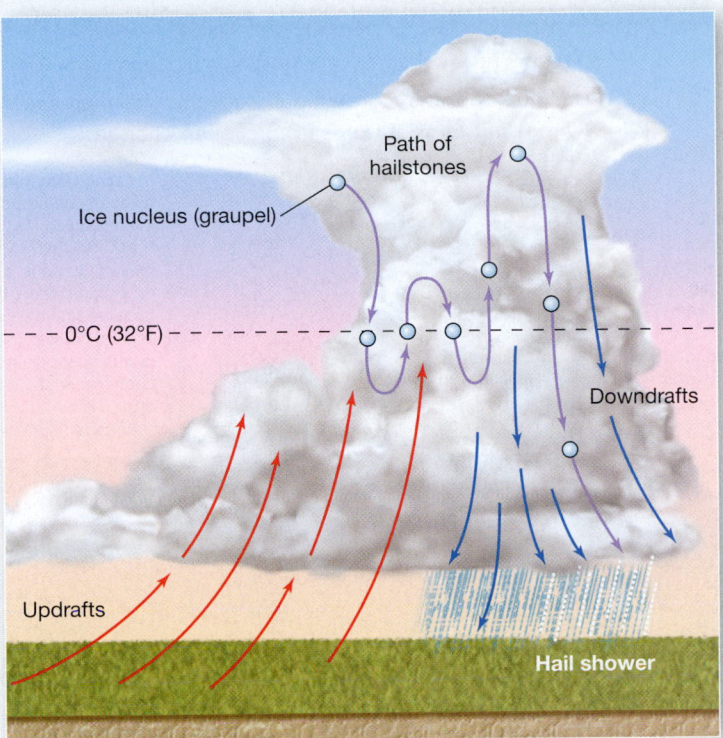

(a) The path of a hailstone within a cumulonimbus cloud.

▲Figure 6.28 Formation of a hailstone. [(b) Warren Faidley/Corbis Documentary/Getty Images. (c) Khampha Bouaphanh/Star-Telegram via AP.]

(b) Hailstone found after the 2001 Joplin, Missouri, tornado shows ice layers accumulated as it circulated above and below the freezing level within the cloud.

(c) Hail damage to an ambulance response vehicle in Fort Worth, Texas, in March 2016. Golf ball-sized hail coated parts of North Texas, breaking windows, damaging police vehicles, and killing exotic birds at the Fort Worth Zoo.

cloud can no longer support the weight. Hail only occurs in cumulonimbus clouds with strong updrafts and abundant supercooled cloud droplets (**Figure 6.28**).

Pea-sized hail (0.63 cm, or 0.25 in., in diameter) is common, although hail can range from the size of quarters (2.54 cm, or 1.00 in.) to softballs (11.43 cm, or 4.50 in.). Baseball-sized hail fell a half dozen times in 2010 in the United States alone. For larger hail to form, the graupel must stay aloft for longer periods; the largest hail is formed during severe storms with intense updrafts. One

of the largest authenticated hailstones, which fell from a thunderstorm in Aurora, Nebraska, in June 2003, measured 47.62 cm (18.75 in.) in circumference. However, the largest hailstone by diameter and weight fell in Vivian, South Dakota, in July 2010.

Hail is most common in the continental interiors of midlatitude landmasses. In the United States, hail is most common in Colorado, Nebraska, and Wyoming, a region sometimes called "Hail Alley." Annual U.S. hail damage to property and crops exceeds $1 billion.

GEOreport **6.2** Crowdsourcing precipitation with the free mPING app

Scientists at NOAA's National Severe Storms Laboratory have developed a smartphone app called mPING—Meteorological Phenomena Identification Near the Ground—that enables citizen scientists to submit weather reports. Participants simply select the type of weather (tornadoes, flooding, fog) or precipitation (rain, freezing rain, drizzle, snow, ice pellets, and mixed rain) occurring at their location and press "Submit." The crowdsourced data are used to improve forecasts for roadwork, aviation, and severe weather, and to verify radar observations (see http://mping.nssl.noaa.gov/).

ATMOSPHERIC MOISTURE IMPACTS HUMANS

• Based on what you have learned in this chapter, how does water in the atmosphere affect humans?

6a To reduce the frequency of deadly fog-related traffic accidents in parts of California's Central Valley, electronic freeway signs warn drivers when potentially hazardous road conditions exist. [Jeremy Walker/Getty Images.]

HUMANS IMPACT ATMOSPHERIC MOISTURE

• Water vapor is a greenhouse gas that will increase with rising temperatures from climate change.

6b Morning Glory clouds are rare, tubular clouds that form in only several locations on Earth. Northern Australia's Gulf of Carpentaria is the only place where they are observed on a regular basis. Gliders flock to this area to ride the associated winds. Learn more at http://www.morninggloryaust ralia.com/. [Mick Pertroff/NASA.]

6d A net captures moisture from advection fog that forms over the cold Humboldt Current in the Pacific Ocean and creeps toward the Andes Mountains of Chile and Peru. Nets such as this can collect up to 5 L/m² of water, which translates to 200 L/day per net, a significant amount in this dry region. [Mariana Bazo/Reuters.]

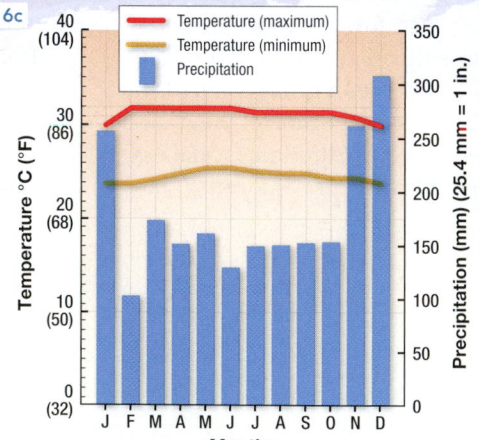

6c

Temperature °C (°F) / Precipitation (mm) (25.4 mm = 1 in.)

- Temperature (maximum)
- Temperature (minimum)
- Precipitation

Months: J F M A M J J A S O N D

The tropical climate of Singapore is hot and humid all year, with daily relative humidity averaging 84% and often exceeding 90% at night. Rain falls on most days, and dramatic afternoon thunderstorms can occur throughout the year. [GoSingapore/Alamy. Climate data from WeatherWise Singapore.]

ISSUES FOR THE 21ST CENTURY

• Fog is a potential water resource that can supplement drinking water supplies in some regions of the world.
• Rising global temperatures increase evaporation rates, which increases atmospheric water vapor, which increases greenhouse warming as water vapor absorbs heat in the lower atmosphere. Does this process produce a positive or negative feedback loop? Explain your answer.

QUESTIONS TO CONSIDER

1. Based on the graph for Singapore temperature and precipitation in HD 6c, which three months have the highest precipitation?
2. Why would relative humidity in Singapore be highest at night rather than during the day?

KEY**LEARNING**concepts**review**

Describe the heat properties of water, including the heat energy transferred during phase changes between solid, liquid, and gas.

The effects of *hydrogen bonding* in water create **cohesion** (p. 156), the attraction of molecules for other molecules of the same kind (causing water beading and surface tension). Water molecules also bond strongly to other molecules, creating **adhesion** (p. 156)—the attraction of molecules of one kind for molecules of another kind (causing capillary action). Water exists naturally on Earth in all three states: solid, liquid, and gas. A change from one state to another is a **phase change** (p. 157). The change from liquid to solid is freezing; from solid to liquid, melting; from vapor to liquid, condensation; from liquid to vapor, vaporization or evaporation; from vapor to solid, deposition; and from solid to vapor, **sublimation** (p. 157).

The heat energy required for water to change phase is **latent heat** (p. 157) because, once absorbed, it is hidden within the structure of the water, ice, or water vapor; the temperature of the water does not alter during the change. For 1 g of water to become 1 g of water vapor by boiling requires the addition of 540 cal, or the **latent heat of vaporization** (p. 158). When this 1 g of water vapor condenses, the same amount of heat energy, 540 calories, is released and is the **latent heat of condensation** (p. 158). The **latent heat of sublimation** (p. 158) is the energy exchanged in the phase change from ice to vapor and vapor to ice.

1. Describe the molecular structure of water's three physical states: ice, water, and water vapor.
2. What is latent heat? How is it involved in the phase changes of water?

Describe several expressions of humidity: vapor pressure, specific humidity, relative humidity, and dew-point temperature.

Air is said to be at **saturation** (p. 159) when the rate of evaporation and the rate of condensation reach equilibrium; any further addition of water vapor or temperature decrease will result in active condensation. The amount of water vapor in the atmosphere is **humidity** (p. 160). The capacity for water vapor in air is principally a function of the temperature of the air and of the water vapor (usually these temperatures are the same). **Vapor pressure** (p. 160) is that portion of the atmospheric pressure produced by the presence of water vapor; it increases with the concentration of water-vapor molecules present and the temperature of the air. **Saturation vapor pressure** (p. 160) is the point at which air is saturated (in which water vapor has reached the maximum possible amount) at a given temperature. **Specific humidity** (p. 161) is the mass of water vapor (in grams) per mass of air (in kilograms) at any specified temperature. **Relative humidity** (p. 161) is a ratio of the vapor pressure (the water-vapor content of the air) to the saturation vapor pressure (the maximum amount of water vapor possible) at a given temperature. The

temperature at which air achieves saturation is the **dew-point temperature** (p. 162).

3. What is meant by *dew-point temperature* and how does it relate to the formation of dew?
4. How does the daily trend in relative humidity values compare with the daily trend in air temperature?

Explain adiabatic lapse rates and **discuss** unstable, conditionally unstable, and stable atmospheric conditions.

Atmospheric stability (p. 163) refers to the tendency of the atmosphere to either encourage or discourage vertical air motion. An air parcel is *stable* if it resists displacement upward or, when disturbed, tends to return to its starting place. An air parcel is *unstable* if it continues to rise until it reaches an altitude where the surrounding air has a density (air temperature) similar to its own. Temperature changes in ascending and descending air parcels are **adiabatic** (p. 164), meaning they occur as a result of expansion or compression, without any significant heat exchange between the surrounding environment and the vertically moving parcel of air.

The **dry adiabatic rate (DAR)**, (p. 164), is the rate at which "dry" (less than saturated) air cools by expansion (if ascending) or heats by compression (if descending). The DAR is 10 C°/1000 m (5.5 F°/1000 ft). The **moist adiabatic rate (MAR)**, (p. 165), is the average rate at which moist (saturated) air cools by expansion on ascent or warms by compression on descent. The average MAR is 6 C°/1000 m (3.3 F°/1000 ft); however, the MAR varies slightly with moisture content and temperature. A simple comparison of the DAR and MAR in a vertically moving parcel of air with the *environmental lapse rate* (ELR) in the surrounding air reveals the atmosphere's stability—whether it is unstable (air parcel continues lifting), stable (air parcel resists vertical displacement), or conditionally unstable (air parcel behaves as though unstable if the MAR is in operation and stable otherwise).

5. Explain the different behaviors of a stable and unstable parcel of air lifted vertically in the atmosphere.
6. Why is there a difference between the dry adiabatic rate (DAR) and the moist adiabatic rate (MAR)?

Identify the requirements for cloud formation and **explain** the major cloud classes and types, including fog.

A **cloud** (p. 167) is an aggregation of tiny water droplets and ice crystals suspended in the air. As lifting air cools, water vapor condenses to form a **cloud droplet** (p. 168) of liquid water, a process that requires **cloud-condensation nuclei** (p. 168), microscopic particles that always are present in the atmosphere. Ice crystals form as water vapor deposits or supercooled water freezes onto **freezing nuclei** (p. 168), tiny particles that are less abundant than cloud-condensation nuclei.

Low clouds, ranging from surface levels up to 2000 m (6500 ft) in the middle latitudes, are **stratus**, (p. 168) (flat clouds, in layers), or **cumulus**, (p. 168) (puffy clouds, in heaps). When stratus clouds yield precipitation, they are *nimbostratus*. Sometimes near the end of the day, lumpy, grayish, low-level clouds called **stratocumulus** (p. 168) may fill the sky in patches. **Altocumulus** (p. 169) clouds are middle-level clouds and include many different types. Clouds at high altitude, principally composed of ice crystals, are called **cirrus** (p. 169). A cumulus cloud can develop into a towering giant **cumulonimbus** (p. 170) cloud, sometimes called a *thunderhead*.

Fog (p. 170) is a cloud that occurs at ground level. Radiative cooling of a surface that chills the air layer directly above the surface to the dew-point temperature creates saturated conditions and a **radiation fog** (p. 170). **Advection fog** (p. 171) forms when unsaturated air migrates to a new place where conditions bring it to the point of saturation—for example, when warm, moist air moves over cooler ocean currents. **Upslope fog** (p. 171) is produced when moist air is forced to higher elevations along a hill or mountain. Another fog caused by topography is **valley fog** (p. 171), formed because cool, denser air settles in low-lying areas, producing fog in the chilled, saturated layer near the ground. **Evaporation fog** (p. 171), or steam fog, forms when cold air flows over the warm water, resulting in evaporation of water molecules from the water surface into the cold overlying air.

7. What are the basic forms of clouds? Describe the components of clouds at different altitudes.
8. What type of cloud is fog? List and define the principal types of fog.

Describe the processes that form precipitation in the atmosphere and **list** the types of precipitation at the ground surface.

Precipitation (p. 173) occurs when cloud droplets or ice crystals in a cloud become large enough to fall with gravity. In clouds with temperatures above freezing, raindrops form by the **collision–coalescence process** (p. 174) in which updrafts of rising air force condensation of water vapor onto condensation nuclei. The resulting cloud droplets move aloft, mixing and colliding to form raindrops that eventually fall under their own weight. The raindrops continue to coalesce with cloud droplets as they move downward through the cloud. The **Bergeron process** (p. 174) of ice crystal growth occurs as water evaporates from supercooled cloud droplets and deposits onto ice crystals, which grow and eventually fall under their own weight.

The type of precipitation that reaches the ground surface depends on air temperature. In cold and mixed-phase clouds, precipitation begins as **snow** (p. 176), composed of ice crystals or aggregates of ice crystals known as snowflakes. If ice crystals pass through a warm layer in the atmosphere, they melt and become raindrops. **Rain** (p. 176) is precipitation in the form of liquid water droplets (raindrops) that falls from a cloud. *Freezing rain*, also called *glaze*, forms when raindrops fall through a thin layer of subfreezing temperatures and become supercooled, freezing instantly to cold surfaces when they reach the ground. If the raindrops fall through a thick, subfreezing layer of air nearer the ground, they will refreeze, becoming ice pellets known as **sleet** (p. 176).

Ice pellets larger than 0.5 cm (0.20 in.) that form within a cumulonimbus cloud are **hail** (p. 176)—or *hailstones*, after they fall to the ground. Hail is formed by the process of *riming*, in which supercooled water droplets freeze directly onto ice crystals. Graupel (small ice pellets) is carried by updrafts to circulate within a cumulonimbus cloud, accumulating layers of ice and growing in size, ultimately forming hail that falls under its own weight.

9. Describe the process of ice crystal growth that commonly occurs in cold and mixed-phase clouds.
10. What is the difference between freezing rain, sleet, and hail? Explain in your own words.

GEO**SPATIAL** ANALYSIS

Cloud Climatology

The International Satellite Cloud Climatology Project (ISCCP) collects global cloud data from several satellites. The role of clouds in climate is a subject of great interest and research.

Activities

Go to the ISCCP Monthly Means and Climatology page at http://isccp .giss.nasa.gov/products/browsed2.html. Retain the variable "Total Cloud Amount (%)" and time period "Mean Annual," then click "View".

1. The map indicates the average annual percentage of cloud-covered sky. What is the range of cloud cover amounts for the United States?

2. In general, is the cloud cover amount higher over oceans or land? What factors contribute to this distribution?

Go back and view the mean "Total Cloud Amount (%) for the current month by selecting the month in the Time Period menu. Also, look outside and examine the actual sky.

3. According to the ISCCP data, what is the mean cloud amount for your location during the current month?

4. How does the actual amount of cloud cover in the sky compare to the monthly average for your location?

5. What types of clouds are currently in the sky? Do the clouds indicate that the atmosphere is stable or unstable? Compare this to what you see in the sky in real time.

Go back and compare the variables "VIS-IR Low Cloud Amount (%)," "VIS-IR Low Middle Cloud Amount (%)," and "VIS-IR High Cloud Amount (%)," and examine cloud amounts derived from visible and infrared satellite data.

6. Examine the annual mean low clouds globally. Where are most of these clouds? What elements contribute to this pattern? (Hint: Compare the cloud pattern to the major ocean currents in Figure 5.18.)

Go back and select the variable "Mean Precipitable Water for 1000-680 mb"; then click "View."

7. The map indicates how much moisture is available for precipitation in the lower half of the troposphere. Notice that "precipitable water amounts" are high in the equatorial region and decrease poleward. Why does precipitable water vary in this way?

Go back and select the variable "Mean Precipitable Water for 680-310 mb"; then click "View."

8. The map indicates how much moisture is available for precipitation in the upper half of the troposphere. Again, precipitable water is most abundant in the equatorial region. What type of clouds are likely to form there? It may help to refer to the principle cloud types in Figure 6.17.

MasteringGeography™

Looking for additional review and test prep materials? Visit the Study Area in MasteringGeography™ to enhance your geographic literacy, spatial reasoning skills, and understanding of this chapter's content by accessing a variety of resources, including MapMaster™ interactive maps, videos, *Mobile Field Trips*, *Project Condor* Quadcopter Videos, *In the News* RSS feeds, flashcards, web links, self-study quizzes, and an eText version of *Geosystems*.

7 Weather

State of Kansas, US

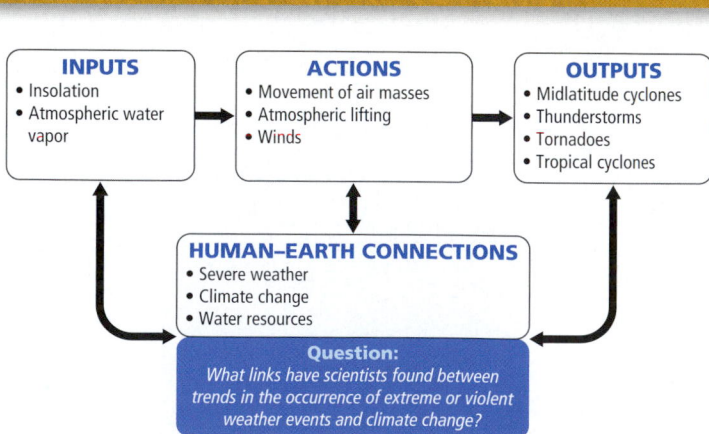

A storm chaser photographs the largest supercell of the day at sunset in north–central Kansas. [John Finney Photography/Getty Images.]

KEY**LEARNING**concepts

After reading the chapter, you should be able to:

- **Describe** the characteristics of air masses that affect North America.
- **Identify** and **describe** four types of atmospheric lifting mechanisms.
- **Describe** the life cycle of a midlatitude cyclonic storm system.
- **Describe** several types of data and imagery used for weather forecasting.
- **Review** various forms of violent weather—ice storms, thunderstorms, derechos, tornadoes, and tropical cyclones—by their formation and characteristics.

INPUTS
- Insolation
- Atmospheric water vapor

ACTIONS
- Movement of air masses
- Atmospheric lifting
- Winds

OUTPUTS
- Midlatitude cyclones
- Thunderstorms
- Tornadoes
- Tropical cyclones

HUMAN–EARTH CONNECTIONS
- Severe weather
- Climate change
- Water resources

Question:
What links have scientists found between trends in the occurrence of extreme or violent weather events and climate change?

Storm Chasers

On May 31, 2013, three experienced storm chasers, including well-known tornado field researcher Tim Samaras, were killed by a violent tornado near El Reno, Oklahoma. The El Reno tornado was 4.2 km (2.6 mi) wide, the widest ever recorded, with multiple vortices—the twisting funnels that make contact with the ground (**Figure GN 7.1**). On that fateful spring evening, the monstrous storm turned sharply and accelerated in speed just before it engulfed the storm chasers' car. The event shook the storm chasing community and ignited an ongoing conversation about safety and risk.

Who Chases Storms? *Storm chasing* is generally defined as the pursuit of severe weather for purposes that include scientific investigation, news reporting, photography, and thrill-seeking. Whereas tornadoes are often the ultimate goal, storm chasers pursue a range of severe weather, including supercell thunderstorms, hail, and lightning. Some storm chasers are scientists; many others seek video footage to sell to media outlets. Recently, an increasing percentage are part of a guided storm-chasing adventure. These tour companies emphasize safety and insist that they maintain safe distances from the storms they observe. At the same time, scientists and photographers are moving ever closer to the centers of violent storms (**Figure GN 7.2**).

Tornado Science: Worth the Risk? Meteorologists rely on "storm spotter" reports, radar images, and weather data to understand and forecast severe storms. Since the 1970s, the SKYWARN program of the National Weather Service (NWS) has offered free training for volunteers, a group that today includes over 350,000 severe weather observers. For storm chasing, scientists use radar and weather data, mixed with their own experience, to get as close as possible. Once in position, they can obtain

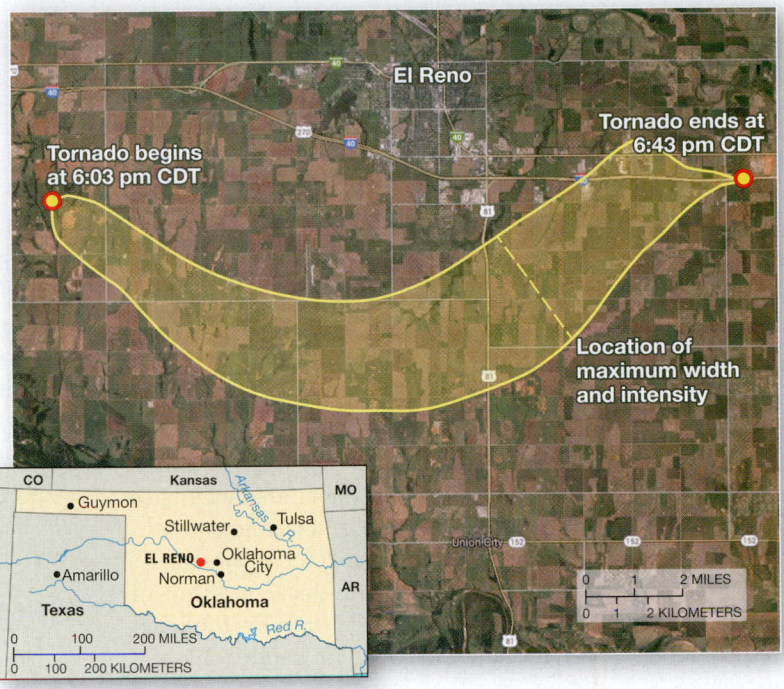

▲**Figure GN 7.2** **The path of the 2013 El Reno tornado.**
[NWS, Norman, Oklahoma.]

key ground measurements of temperature, pressure, wind, and humidity. The placement of sensors and probes directly in the path of a tornado yields valuable data that advances science and improves warning times. Unsurprisingly, such practices place researchers at risk, begging the question: How close is too close?

Despite the danger, storm chasing has proven its worth. The NWS issues a tornado warning only when a tornado appears on a radar image or if a trained spotter reports a tornado on the ground. In Oklahoma, storm chasers from local television stations have provided early warnings and saved lives. Warning times average about 15 minutes; researchers hope to improve this to 30 minutes.

A Growing Community The fatalities near El Reno in 2013 brought unprecedented attention to storm chasing and prompted scientists to reevaluate the danger. Yet, in spite of, and perhaps because of, the risk, the storm-chasing community is growing. Across parts of the U.S. Midwest, especially in the core region of tornado activity known as "Tornado Alley," storm chasing is no longer a fad but has become a full-fledged industry. Oklahoma, with its extensive plains and frequent summer thunderstorms, is a particularly good region for observing severe weather. On a given spring day with conditions ripe for the development of tornadoes, hundreds of storm chasers are in pursuit. As observers increase, so does crowding along roads and highways, inhibiting the ability of vehicles to make a quick getaway in the path of an oncoming storm.

Have you observed a violent storm or tornado? Your chances of observing a tornado are high in Tornado Alley, centered on Texas, Oklahoma, Kansas, and Nebraska. The U.S. Southeast is another area of consistent tornado activity.

1. Describe the purposes of storm chasing and the types of severe weather that storm chasers investigate.

2. What are the risks and benefits of storm chasing in tornado-prone areas?

▲**Figure GN 7.1** **Storm chasers with the Center for Severe Weather Research watch an approaching supercell thunderstorm near Hays, Kansas in 2012.** [Ryan McGinnis/Moment/Getty Images.]

The weather is often a topic of daily discussion. Extreme weather events impact humans and ecosystems. Almost on a daily basis, we see images of the beauty, power, and destructive capability of atmospheric events (**Figure 7.1**). Storm chasing, including the data and images it produces, has become an interest of scientists and the general public.

Radiant energy and water, with its ability to absorb and release vast quantities of heat energy, drive the daily conditions in the atmosphere. The spatial patterns of weather as they link to human activities make meteorology, weather, and weather forecasting important concerns of physical geography.

Meteorology is the scientific study of the atmosphere. (*Meteor* means "heavenly" or "of the atmosphere.") Meteorologists study the atmosphere's physical characteristics and motions and the complex linkages of the atmosphere to other Earth systems. Meteorologists also forecast weather.

Weather is the short-term, day-to-day condition of the atmosphere, as differentiated from *climate*—the long-term average (over decades) of weather conditions and extremes in a region. Weather is both a "snapshot" of atmospheric conditions and a status report of the Earth–atmosphere heat-energy budget.

The cost of weather-related destruction can be staggering. Since 1980, over 188 weather events—droughts, floods, hail, tornadoes, derechos, tropical storms, storm surges, blizzards, and ice storms—exceeded $1 billion each in cost (see http://www.ncdc.noaa.gov/billions/events.pdf). Studies estimate that annual losses from weather-related damage could exceed $1 trillion by 2040. Extreme weather events fueled by global climate change are driving this increasing total at a pace that is accelerating.

Air Masses

Weather forecasts often refer to movement of the "cold Canadian air mass" and the "moist tropical air mass" from the Gulf of Mexico. These terms refer to the temperature and moisture characteristics of air overlying specific regions of Earth's surface. Such a distinctive body of air is an **air mass**, and it initially reflects the characteristics of its *source region*. The conditions of the source region create a homogenous mix of temperature, humidity, and stability that extend into the lower atmosphere. The various masses of air over Earth's surface interact to produce weather patterns.

Air Masses Affecting North America

We classify air masses according to the general moisture and temperature characteristics of their source regions: *Moisture* is designated **m** for maritime (wet) or **c** for continental (dry). *Temperature* is directly related to latitude and is designated **A** for arctic, **P** for polar, **T** for tropical, **E** for equatorial, and **AA** for antarctic. **Figure 7.2** shows the principal air masses that affect North America in winter and summer.

Continental polar (cP) air masses form only in the Northern Hemisphere and are most developed in winter and cold-weather conditions. An area covered by cP air

everydayGEOSYSTEMS

What kinds of damage, other than rain and hail, results from thunderstorms?

A fast-moving band of thunderstorms can create a swath of strong, destructive winds that moves across an entire region. If wind speeds exceed 93 kmph (58 mph) and the swath of damage is at least 386 km (240 mi) long, such a windstorm is known as a derecho (pronounced "deh-REY-cho"). In June 2012, a strong derecho moved 1126 km (700 mi) in 12 hours, averaging 96 kmph (60 mph), from Iowa to the mid-Atlantic coast, producing gusts over 129 kmph (80 mph) and causing widespread power outages. In parts of suburban Washington D.C. and Baltimore, more than a week passed before power was restored. Both land lines and cell service were down for several days.

◄**Figure 7.1 Derechos in the United States.** An uprooted tree blocks a street in the American University neighborhood of Washington, D.C. after the 2012 derecho. [Mandel Ngan/AFP-Getty Images.]

Derecho frequency in the continental U.S.

- 4 per 3 years
- 1 per year
- 1 per 2 years
- 1 per 4 years

0   300   600 MILES

0   300   600 KILOMETERS

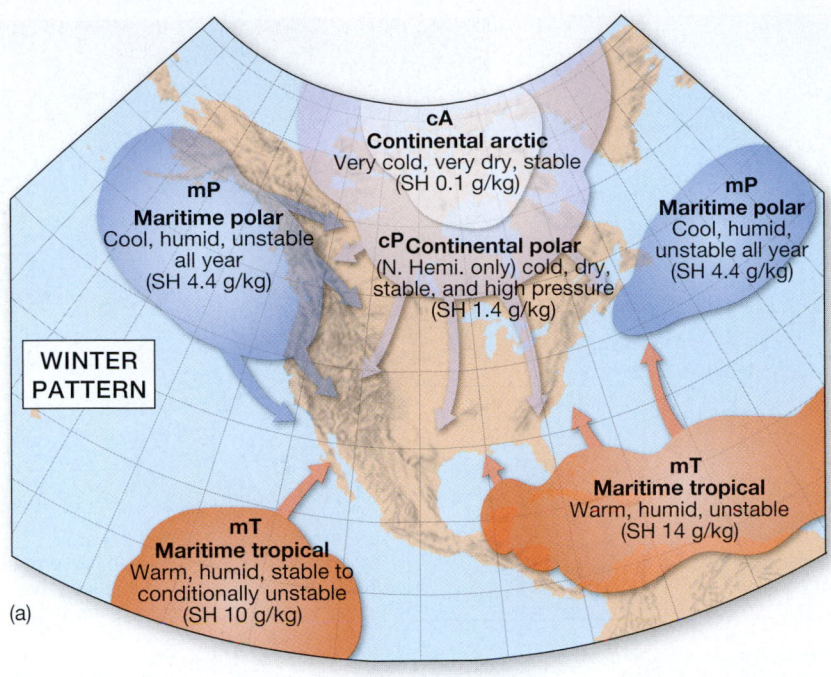

(a)

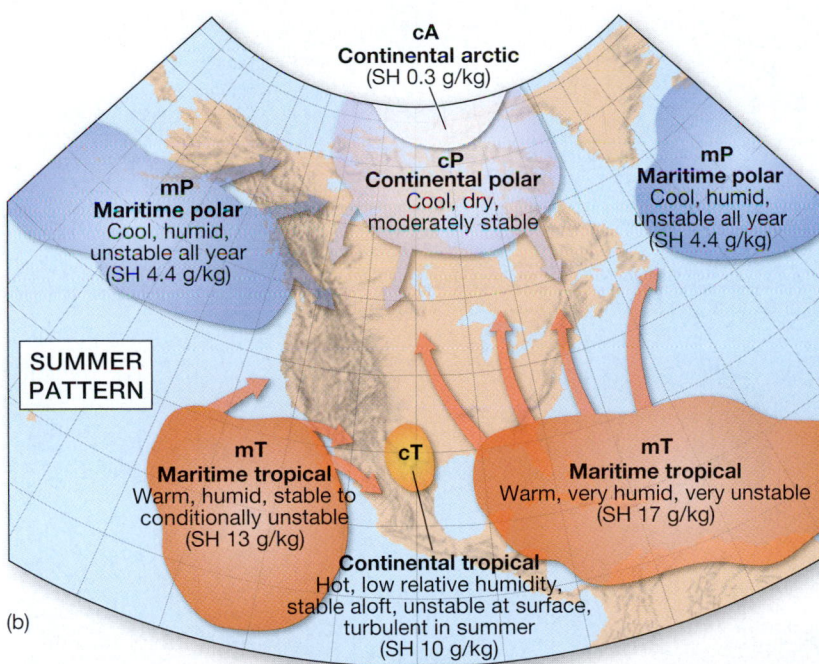

(b)

▲**Figure 7.2 Principal air masses affecting North America.** Air masses and their source regions influencing North America during (a) winter and (b) summer. Specific humidity (SH) are average values.

Two *maritime tropical* (mT) air masses—the mT Gulf/Atlantic and the mT Pacific—influence North America. The humidity experienced in the North American East and Midwest is created by the mT Gulf/Atlantic air mass, which is particularly unstable and active from late spring to early fall. In contrast, the mT Pacific is stable to conditionally unstable and generally lower in moisture content and available energy. As a result, the western United States, influenced by this weaker Pacific air mass, receives lower average precipitation than the rest of the country.

Air Mass Modification

The longer an air mass remains stationary over a region, the more definite its physical attributes become. As air masses migrate from source regions, their temperature and moisture characteristics slowly change to the characteristics of the land over which they pass. For example, an mT Gulf/Atlantic air mass may carry humidity to Chicago and on to Winnipeg, but it gradually loses its initial high humidity and warmth with each day's passage northward.

Similarly, below-freezing temperatures occasionally reach into southern Texas and Florida, brought by an invading winter cP air mass from the north. However, that air mass warms to above the −50°C (−58°F) of its winter source region in central Canada, especially after it leaves areas covered by snow.

Modification of cP air as it moves south and east produces snowbelts that lie to the east of each of the Great Lakes. As below-freezing cP air passes over the warmer Great Lakes, it absorbs heat energy and moisture from the lake surfaces and becomes *humidified*. In what is called the *lake effect*, this enhancement produces heavy snowfall downwind of the lakes, into Ontario, Québec, Michigan, northern Pennsylvania, and New York—some areas receiving in excess of 250 cm (100 in.) in average snowfall a year (**Figure 7.3**).

The severity of the lake effect also depends on the presence of a low-pressure system positioned north of the Great Lakes, with counterclockwise winds pushing air across the lakes. Climate change is expected to enhance lake-effect snowfall over the next several decades. Warmer water temperatures enhance evaporation, and warmer air can absorb more water vapor. In contrast, some climate models show that later in this century, lake-effect snowfall will decrease as temperatures rise, but that rainfall totals will continue to increase over the regions leeward of the Great Lakes. Research is ongoing as to the effects of climate change on precipitation in this region.

in winter experiences cold, stable air; clear skies; high pressure; and anticyclonic wind flow. The Southern Hemisphere lacks the necessary continental landmasses at high latitudes to create this type of air mass.

Maritime polar (mP) air masses in the Northern Hemisphere sit over the northern oceans. Within them, cool, moist, unstable conditions prevail throughout the year. The Aleutian and Icelandic subpolar low-pressure cells reside within these mP air masses, especially in their well-developed winter pattern (see the January pressure map in Figure 5.12a).

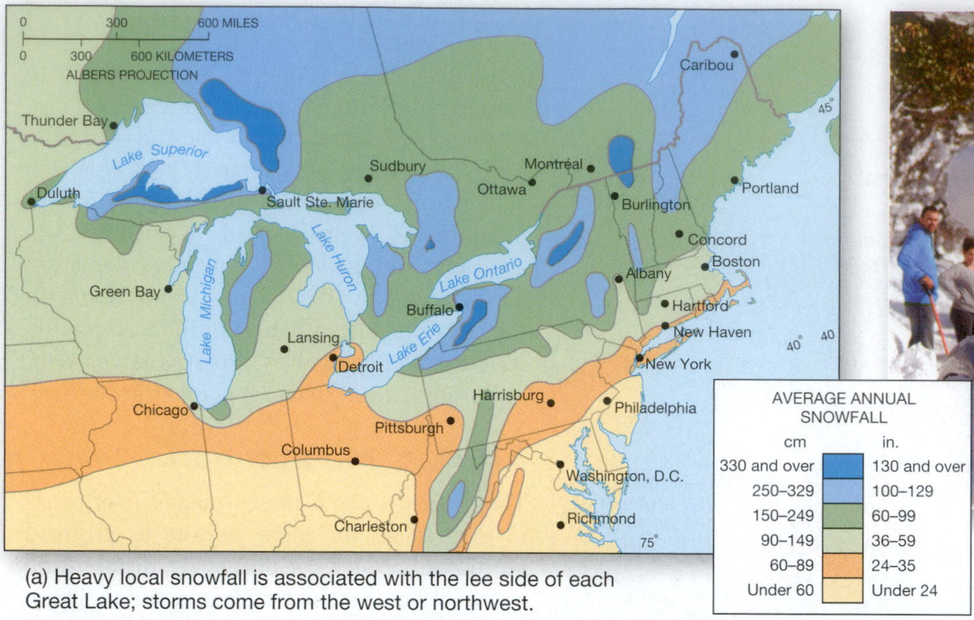

(a) Heavy local snowfall is associated with the lee side of each Great Lake; storms come from the west or northwest.

AVERAGE ANNUAL SNOWFALL		
cm		in.
330 and over		130 and over
250–329		100–129
150–249		60–99
90–149		36–59
60–89		24–35
Under 60		Under 24

(d) Heavy snowfall buried the area around Buffalo, New York, in November 2014, dropping over 7 feet in less than a week during back-to-back storms.

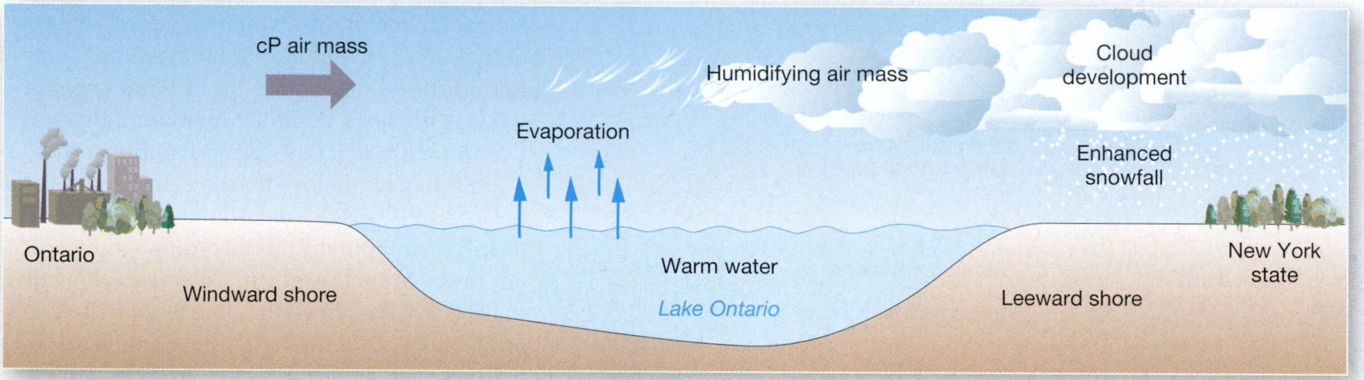

(b) Processes causing lake-effect snowfall are generally limited to about 50 km (30 mi) to 100 km (60 mi) inland.

(c) Satellite image shows lake-effect weather in December.

▲**Figure 7.3** **Lake-effect snowbelts of the Great Lakes.** [(a) NCDC's *Climatic Atlas of the United States*, p. 53. (c) *Terra* MODIS image, NASA/GSFC. (d) John Normile/Stringer/Getty Images.]

Atmospheric Lifting Mechanisms

When an air mass is lifted, it cools adiabatically (by expansion). When the cooling reaches the dew-point temperature, moisture in the saturated air can condense, forming clouds and perhaps precipitation. Four principal lifting mechanisms, illustrated in **Figure 7.4**, operate in the atmosphere:

- Convergent lifting results when air flows toward an area of low pressure.
- Convectional lifting happens when air is stimulated by local surface heating.
- Orographic lifting occurs when air is forced over a barrier such as a mountain range.

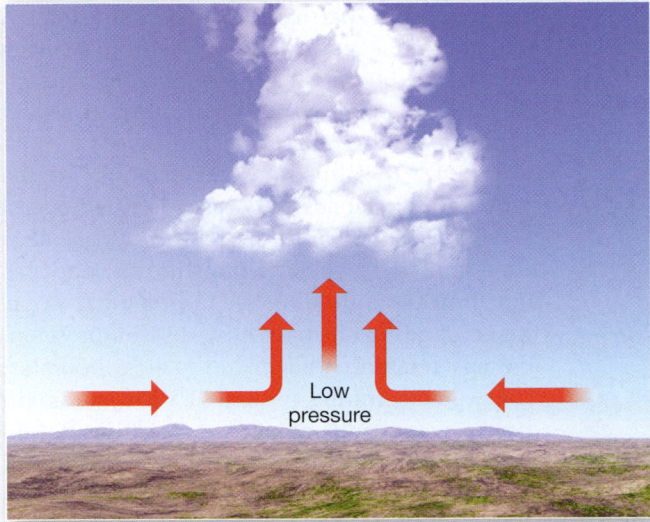

(a) Convergent lifting

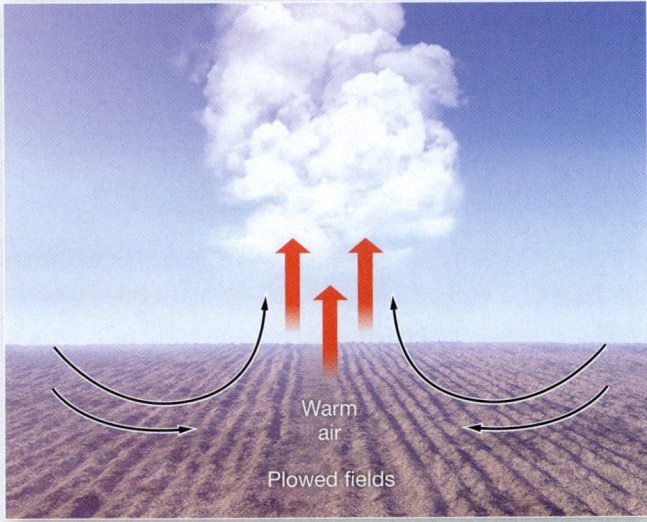

(b) Convectional lifting

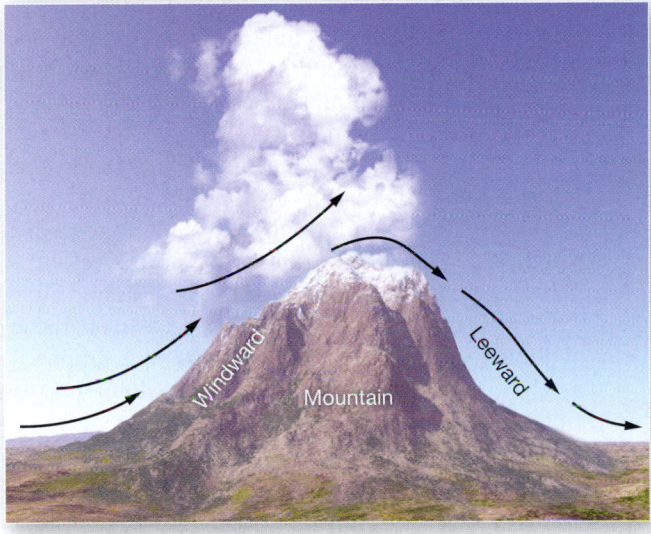

(c) Orographic lifting

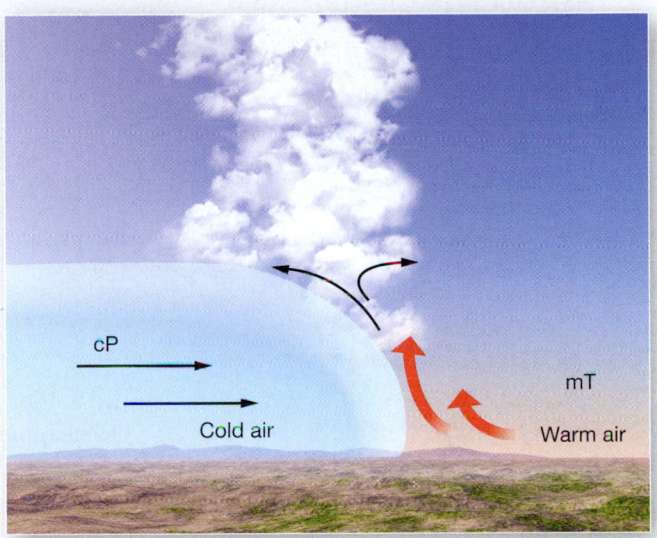

(d) Frontal lifting, cold-front example

▲Figure 7.4 **Four atmospheric lifting mechanisms.**

Mobile ᴹᴳ
Field Trip
Clouds: Earth's
Dynamic
Atmosphere

https://goo.gl/npztSJ

- Frontal lifting occurs as air is displaced upward along the leading edges of contrasting air masses.

Convergent Lifting

Air flowing from different directions into the same low-pressure area is converging, displacing air upward in **convergent lifting** (Figure 7.4a). All along the equatorial region, the southeast and northeast trade winds converge, forming the intertropical convergence zone (ITCZ) and areas of extensive convergent uplift, towering cumulonimbus cloud development, and high average annual precipitation.

Convectional Lifting

When an air mass passes from a maritime source region to a warmer continental region, heating from the warmer land surface causes lifting and convection in the air mass. Other sources of surface heating might include an urban heat island or the dark soil in a plowed field; the warmer

surfaces produce **convectional lifting**. If conditions are unstable, initial lifting continues and clouds develop. Figure 7.4b illustrates convectional action stimulated by local heating with unstable conditions present in the atmosphere.

Florida's precipitation generally illustrates both convergent and convectional lifting mechanisms. Heating of the land produces convergence of onshore winds from the Atlantic and the Gulf of Mexico. **Figure 7.5** depicts a day on which the landmass of Florida was warmer than the surrounding Gulf of Mexico and Atlantic Ocean, creating sea breeze conditions and convergent lifting. Because the Sun's radiation gradually heats the land throughout the day and warms the air above it, convectional lifting produces showers in the afternoon and early evening. Thus, Florida has the highest frequency of days with thunderstorms in the United States.

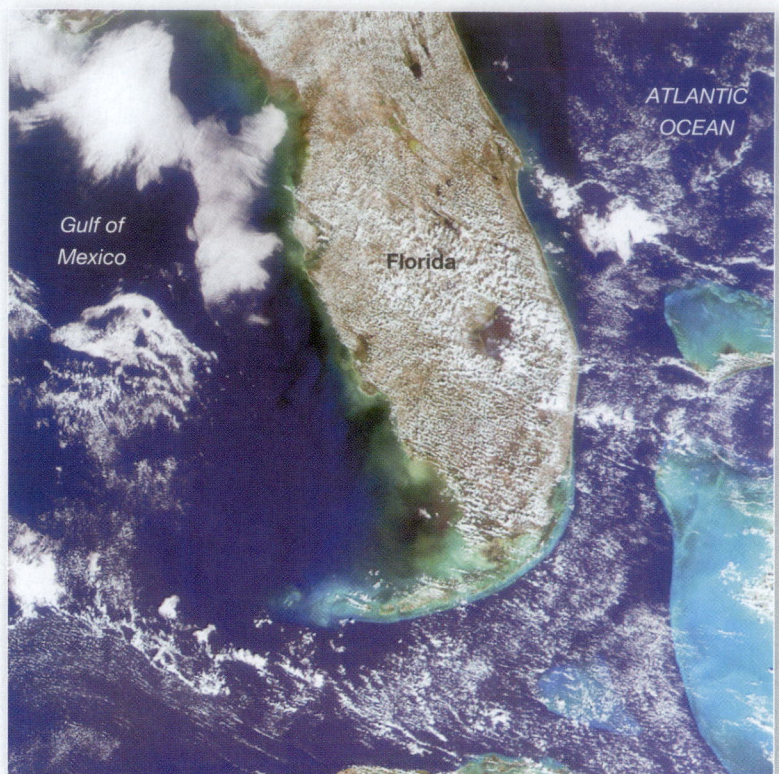

▲**Figure 7.5 Convectional activity over the Florida peninsula.**
Cumulus clouds cover the land, with several cells developing into cumulonimbus thunderheads. [*Terra* MODIS image, NASA/GSFC.]

Orographic Lifting

The physical presence of a mountain acts as a topographic barrier to migrating air masses. **Orographic lifting** (*oro* means "mountain") occurs when air is forcibly lifted upslope as it is pushed against a mountain (Figure 7.4c). The lifting air cools adiabatically. Stable air forced upward in this manner may produce stratiform clouds, whereas unstable or conditionally unstable air usually forms a line of cumulus and cumulonimbus clouds.

An orographic barrier enhances convectional activity and causes additional lifting during the passage of weather fronts, thereby extracting more moisture from passing air masses and resulting in *orographic precipitation*.

Figure 7.6 illustrates an example of the temperature changes of air as it is lifted over a mountain range. On the *windward slope*, air is lifted and cools, causing moisture to condense and form precipitation; on the *leeward slope*, the descending air mass heats by compression, and any remaining water in the air evaporates. Thus, air beginning its ascent up a mountain can be warm and moist, but finishing its descent on the leeward slope, it becomes hot and dry. The term **rain shadow** is applied to this dry, leeward side of mountains.

In North America, **chinook winds** (called *föhn* or *foehn* winds in Europe) are the warm, downslope airflows characteristic of the leeward side of mountains. Such winds can bring a 20 C° (36 F°) jump in temperature and greatly reduce relative humidity.

The state of Washington provides an excellent illustration of this concept. **Figure 7.7** shows data from four climate stations presented as *climographs*, specialized graphs that portray monthly precipitation (as bars) and temperature (as a line). Climographs are often used to present these two basic characteristics of climate. (Chapter 9 includes many such graphs.)

The Olympic Mountains and Cascade Mountains are topographic barriers that cause orographic lifting of the mP air masses from the North Pacific Ocean, resulting in high annual precipitation on the windward slopes. The cities of Sequim, in the Puget Trough, and Yakima, in the Columbia Basin, are in the rain shadows (on the leeward sides) of these mountain ranges and have characteristically low annual precipitation.

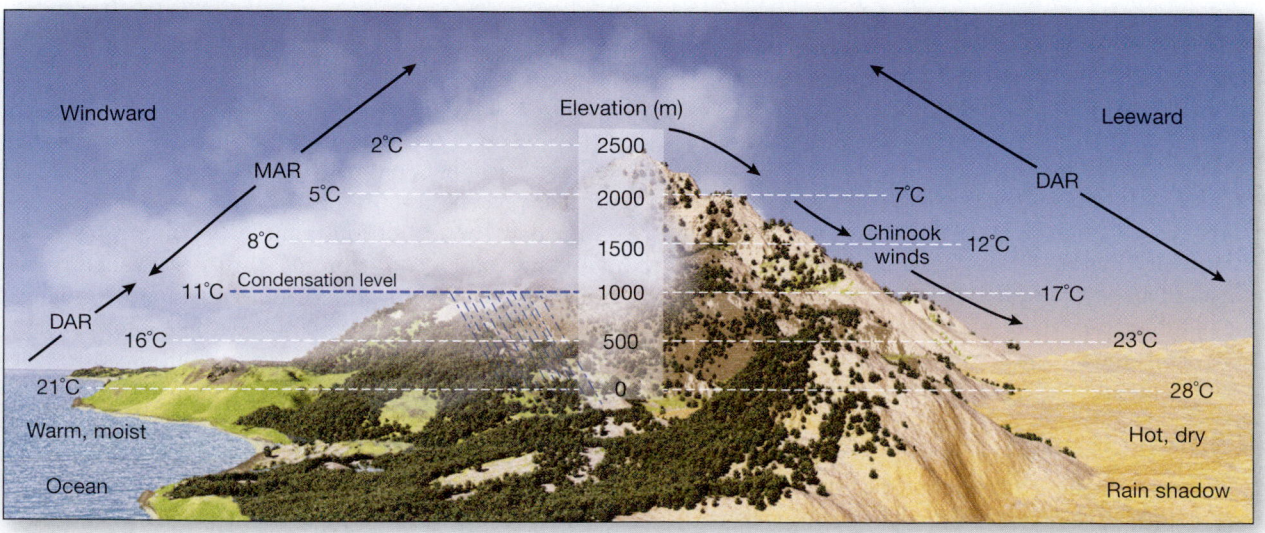

▲**Figure 7.6 Orographic precipitation, unstable conditions assumed.** As prevailing winds force warm, moist air upward over a mountain range, the air cools, condenses, and forms clouds and precipitation. On the leeward slope, "dry" air descends and warms by compression. Recall that the DAR is 10°C/1000 m and the MAR is 6°C/1000 m.

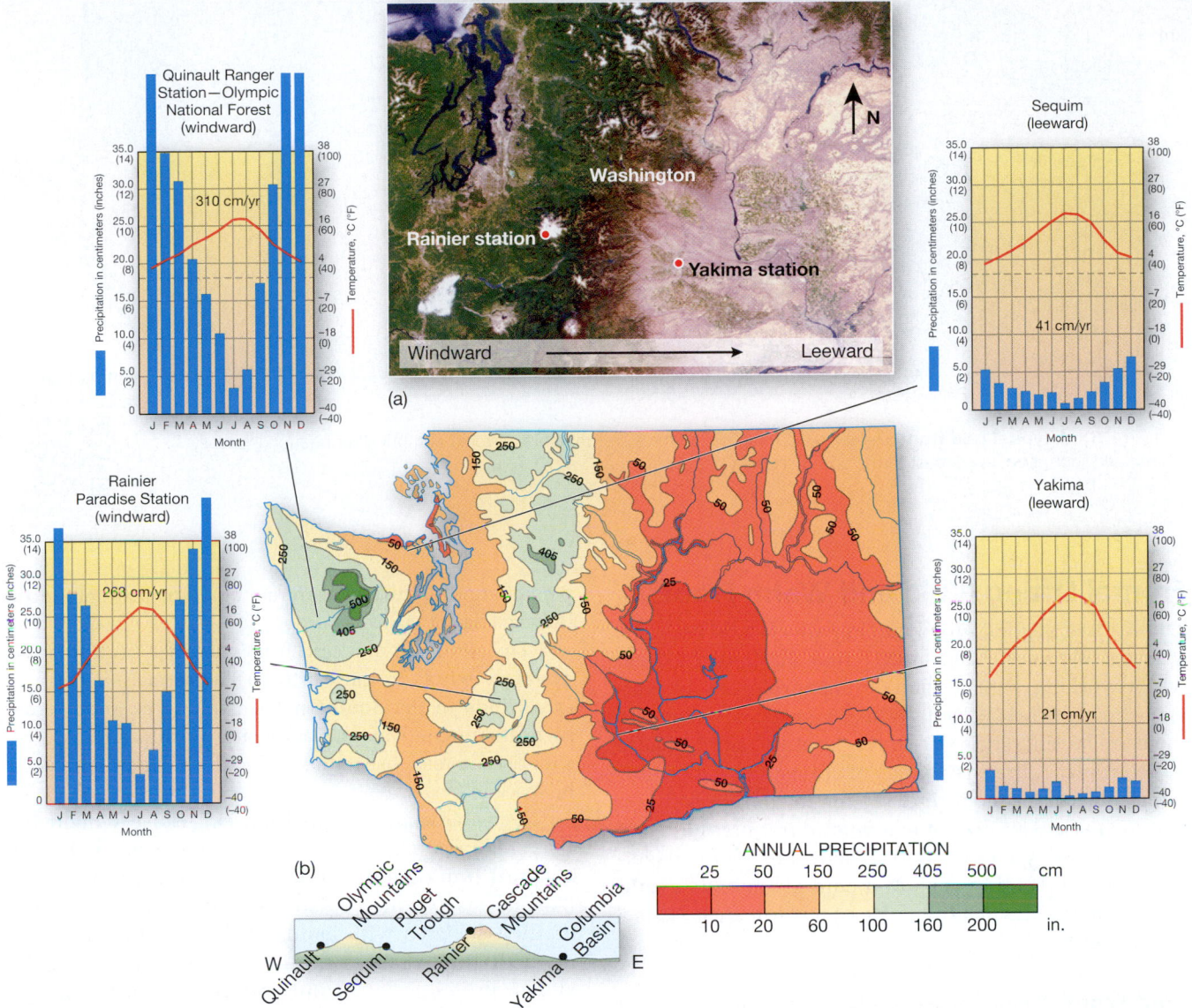

▲**Figure 7.7 Orographic patterns in Washington State.** Four stations in Washington provide examples of orographic effects: windward precipitation and leeward rain shadows. Isohyets (isolines of equal precipitation amounts) on the map indicate rainfall (in inches). Note each station on the landscape profile at bottom. [(a) *Terra* MODIS, NASA/GSFC. (b) Data from J. W. Scott and others, 1989, *Washington: A Centennial Atlas*, Center for Pacific Northwest Studies, Western Washington University.]

In the United States, rain-shadow conditions also occur east of the Sierra Nevada and the Rocky Mountains and on the islands of Hawai'i. On Kaua'i, in the rain shadow of Mount Wai'ale'ale, only 50 cm (20 in.) of rain falls each year. In contrast, annual rainfall on the windward slope averaged 1234 cm (486 in., or 40.5 ft) from 1940 to 1992, making it one of the world's wettest locations. Recently, geographers from the University of Hawai'i at Manoa reported data indicating that Big Bog on the east slope of Haleakalā National Park on Maui is another of Earth's wettest spots with an average of 1026 cm (404 in.) of annual rainfall (http://rainfall.geography.hawaii.edu/rainfall.html). The precipitation pattern of windward and leeward slopes is seen worldwide (see the world precipitation map in Chapter 9, Figure 9.1).

GEOreport 7.1 Orographic lifting causes record rains

The South Asian summer monsoon brings moisture to the windward slopes of the Himalayas, creating some of the wettest conditions on Earth. Cherrapunji, India, located at 1313 m (4309 ft) elevation in the Assam Hills south of the Himalayas, holds the record for the highest rainfall in 1 month—930 cm (366 in., or 30.5 ft)—and for a single year—2647 cm (1042 in., or 86.8 ft).

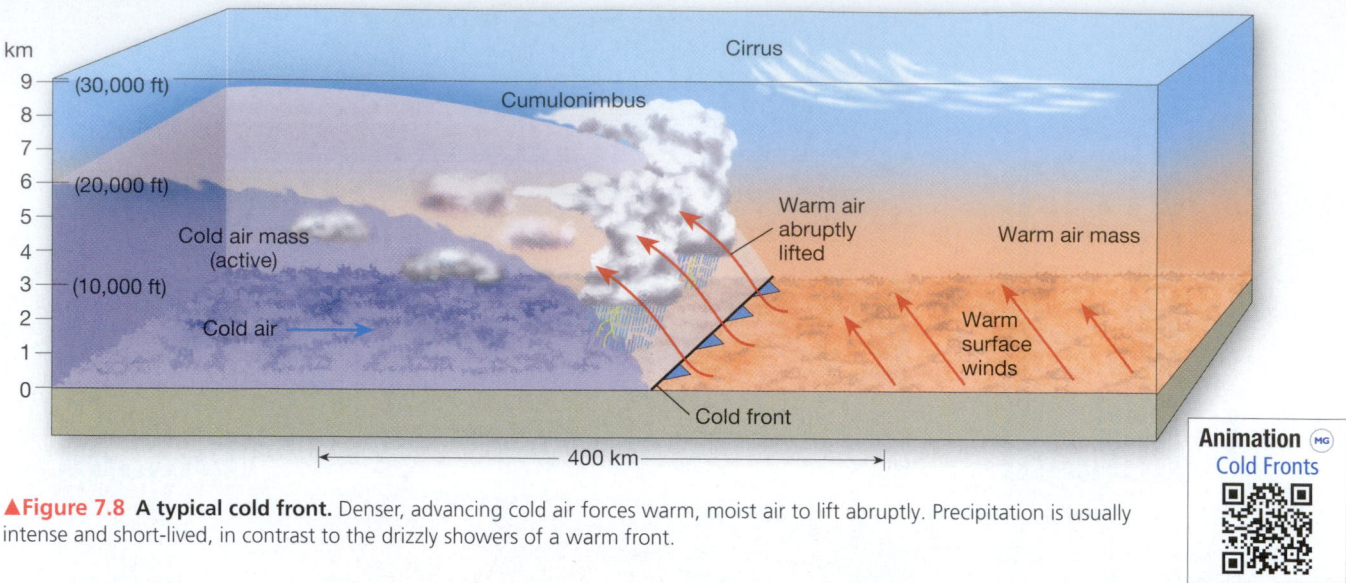

▲**Figure 7.8 A typical cold front.** Denser, advancing cold air forces warm, moist air to lift abruptly. Precipitation is usually intense and short-lived, in contrast to the drizzly showers of a warm front.

Animation ᴹᴳ
Cold Fronts

https://goo.gl/MD7YE6

Frontal Lifting (Cold and Warm Fronts)

The leading edge of an advancing air mass is its *front*. Vilhelm Bjerknes (1862–1951) first applied the term while working with a team of meteorologists in Norway during World War I. Weather systems seemed to them to be migrating air mass "armies" doing battle along fronts. A front is a place of atmospheric discontinuity, a narrow zone forming a line of conflict between two air masses of different temperature, pressure, humidity, wind direction and speed, and cloud development. The leading edge of a cold air mass is a **cold front**, whereas the leading edge of a warm air mass is a **warm front**.

Cold Front A cold air mass advancing into an area of warm air tends to hug the ground because of the greater density of cold air. Friction at the ground surface slows the advance of the cold air relative to the air aloft so that the front steepens as it moves (**Figure 7.8**). Cumulonimbus clouds form as the cold, dense air displaces moist, warm air, lifting and cooling the warm air and causing its vapor to condense. Cold fronts can move at speeds up to 80 kmph (50 mph), causing rapid lifting and more violent weather than is associated with warm fronts. On weather maps, the ground-surface position of a cold front is depicted as a line with triangular spikes that point in the direction of frontal movement along an advancing air mass.

The cP air masses are major players in middle- and high-latitude weather. A day or two ahead of a cold front's arrival, high cirrus clouds appear. Shifting winds, dropping temperature, and lowering barometric pressure mark the front's advance due to lifting of the displaced warmer air along the front's leading edge. At the line of most intense lifting, usually traveling just ahead of the front itself, air pressure drops to a local low. Clouds and intense precipitation usually concentrate along or just behind the leading edge of the front.

The aftermath of a cold front's passage usually brings northerly winds in the Northern Hemisphere and southerly winds in the Southern Hemisphere as anticyclonic high pressure advances. Temperatures drop and air pressure rises in response to the cooler, denser air. Cloud cover breaks and clears.

A fast-advancing cold front can cause violent lifting, creating a narrow line of thunderstorms known as a **squall line** right along or slightly ahead of the front. (A *squall* is a sudden episode of high winds that is generally associated with bands of thunderstorms.) Along a squall line, such as the one in the Gulf of Mexico shown in **Figure 7.9**, wind patterns are turbulent and wildly changing, and precipitation is intense. The well-defined frontal clouds in the photograph rise abruptly, feeding the formation of new thunderstorms along the front.

Warm Front In the U.S. Midwest and Southeast, mT air from the Gulf of Mexico often moves northward into areas with colder air. The leading edge of an advancing warm air mass is unable to displace cooler, denser air along the surface. Instead, the warm air tends to slide up and over the cooler air, forming a gentle slope and a large area of atmospheric lifting and precipitation. A line with semicircles facing in the direction of frontal movement denotes a warm front on weather maps.

Figure 7.10 illustrates a typical warm front, in which gentle lifting of mT air leads to cloud development and drizzly precipitation. High cirrus and cirrostratus clouds announce the advancing frontal system; then come lower and thicker altostratus clouds; and finally, still lower and thicker stratus clouds appear within several hundred kilometers of the front.

Warm air masses can be carried by the jet stream into regions with colder air, such as when an atmospheric river of water vapor called the "Pineapple Express" carries warm, moist air from Hawai'i and the Pacific into California. Warm air also advances during monsoonal flow conditions, such as when mT air moves from the Pacific Ocean into the low-pressure areas over the heated landmasses of the U.S. Southwest during July and August.

At times, two air masses may meet and form a **stationary front**, one that remains in place for an extended period. Along a stationary front, airflow on either side is almost parallel to the front, although in opposite directions, and gentle lifting might produce light to moderate precipitation. Eventually, the stationary front will begin to move, as one of the air masses assumes dominance, evolving into a warm or a cold front.

▲Figure 7.9 **Cold front and squall line.** A sharp line of cumulonimbus clouds near the Texas coast and Gulf of Mexico marks the squall line and front. The clouds rise to 17,000 m (56,000 ft). [NASA.]

WORK**IT**OUT 7.1
Cold Fronts and Warm Fronts

Using the text description and Figures 7.8 and 7.10, answer the following questions.

1. Which type of front is associated with a sharp drop in barometric pressure?
2. Thinking back to what you learned about precipitation in Chapter 6, which type of front favors the formation of freezing rain in winter?
3. What two characteristics of a cold front produce more severe weather than is associated with a warm front?

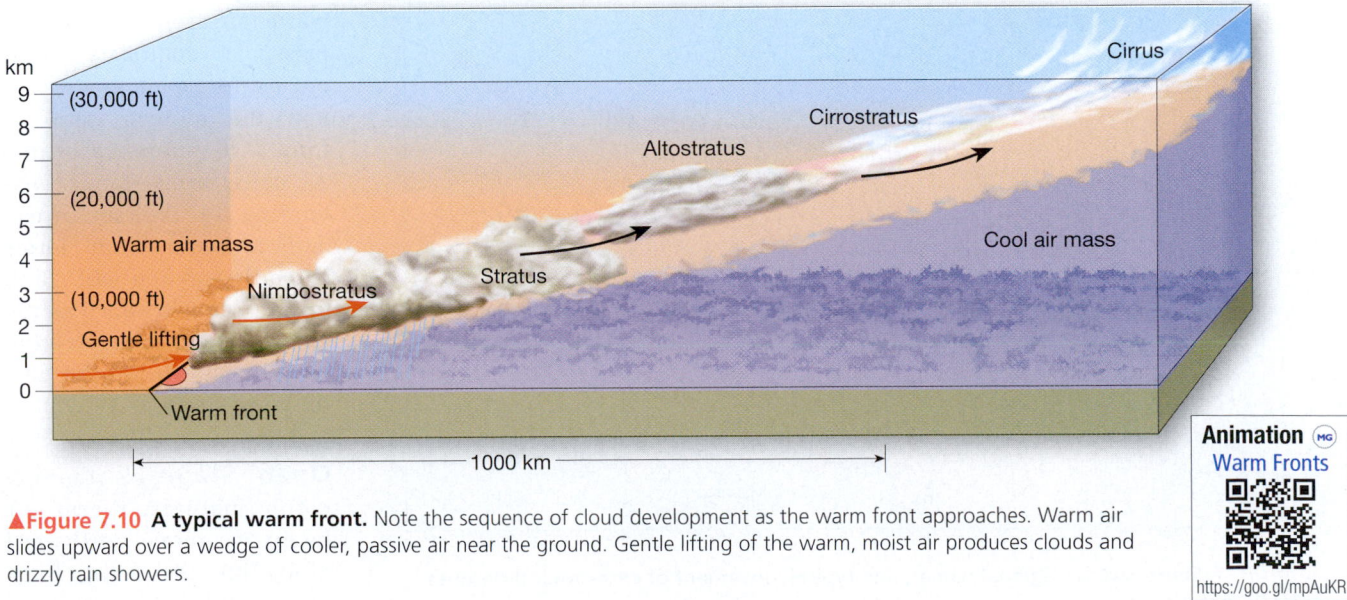

▲Figure 7.10 **A typical warm front.** Note the sequence of cloud development as the warm front approaches. Warm air slides upward over a wedge of cooler, passive air near the ground. Gentle lifting of the warm, moist air produces clouds and drizzly rain showers.

Animation ᴹᴳ
Warm Fronts

https://goo.gl/mpAuKR

Midlatitude Cyclonic Systems

The meeting of two contrasting air masses can develop a **midlatitude cyclone**, also called an **extratropical cyclone** or *wave cyclone*. Midlatitude cyclones are migrating low-pressure weather systems that occur in the middle latitudes, outside the tropics. They have a low-pressure center with converging, ascending air spiraling inward counterclockwise in the Northern Hemisphere and inward clockwise in the Southern Hemisphere. These systems, which can be 1600 km (1000 mi) wide, move with the flow of the westerly winds and dominate midlatitude weather patterns.

Source Areas and Movement

A midlatitude cyclone can originate along the polar front, particularly in the region of the Icelandic and Aleutian low-pressure cells in the Northern Hemisphere. Certain other areas are associated with cyclone development and intensification: the eastern slope of the Rocky Mountains, home of the Colorado Low in the United States and of the Alberta Clipper in Canada; the Gulf Coast, home of the Gulf Low; and the eastern seaboard, home of the Hatteras Low and the nor'easter (**Figure 7.11**).

The intense high-speed winds of the jet streams guide midlatitude cyclonic systems across the continent (review the jet stream paths in Figure 5.17). These paths are typically farther northward in summer and farther southward in winter. The most severe weather associated with these systems usually occurs in winter, when the temperature difference between converging air masses is greatest.

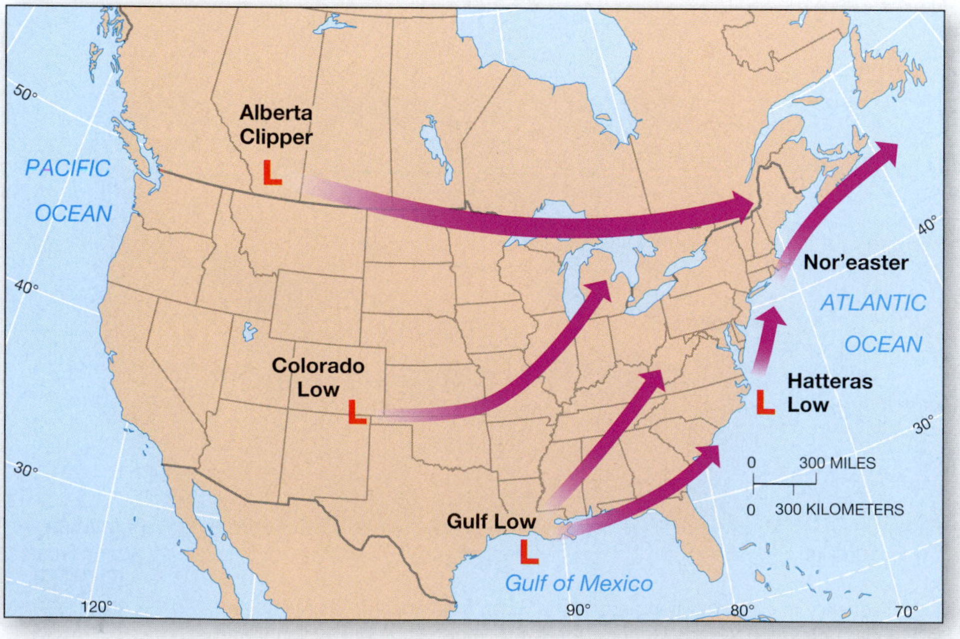

Nor'easters are midlatitude cyclonic systems notorious for bringing heavy snows to the northeastern United States. In March 2014, a massive nor'easter brought blizzard conditions to Massachusetts, Maine, and the Canadian Maritime provinces (**Figure 7.12**). Pressure at the center of this storm dropped to 957 mb, and winds gusted to 183 kmph (114 mph). In January 2016, a nor'easter (nicknamed Winter Storm Jonas by The Weather Channel) dumped 0.6 to 0.9 m (2 to 3 ft) of snow along the U.S. East Coast. The associated high winds and storm surge of this storm affected 52 million people, caused 55 fatalities, and led to its ranking as a "crippling" category 4 storm on the Northeast Snowfall Impact Scale (see The Human Denominator 7 at the end of the chapter).

Life Cycle of a Midlatitude Cyclone

Geosystems in Action 7 shows the formation and development of a typical midlatitude cyclone in several stages. On average, a midlatitude cyclonic system takes 3–10 days to progress through its life cycle from the area where it develops to the area where it finally dissolves.

For a wave cyclone to form along the polar front, a compensating area of divergence aloft must match a surface point of air convergence. Even a slight disturbance along the polar front, such as a small change in the path of the jet stream, can initiate the converging, ascending flow of air and thus a surface low-pressure system.

Cyclogenesis The development and strengthening of a midlatitude cyclone is **cyclogenesis**. This process usually begins along the polar front, where cold and warm air masses converge, creating potentially unstable conditions. In the Northern Hemisphere, as cold air from the cP air mass meets warm air from the mT air mass, a stationary front begins to develop a wave, and the system starts to form a low-pressure center. A cold front forms, extending to the southwest, and a warm front forms extending to the east. Both of the fronts advance as the entire system migrates from west to east within the flow of the westerlies.

Open Stage As the cyclone matures, warm air begins to move northward along an advancing front and cold air advances

▲Figure 7.11 **Source areas, regional names, and typical movement of extratropical cyclones over North America.**

Counterclockwise flow in the Northern Hemisphere

Canada

United States

Low pressure center

Atlantic Ocean

▲**Figure 7.12 A midlatitude cyclonic system off the U.S/Canadian Atlantic coast in March 2014.** This nor'easter brought blizzard conditions to Massachusetts, Maine, and the Canadian Maritime provinces. [VIIRS instrument aboard *Suomi NPP*/NOAA.]

moisture. Remnants of the cyclonic system then dissipate in the atmosphere.

Although the actual patterns of cyclonic passage over North America are widely varied in shape and duration, you can apply this general model of the stages of a midlatitude cyclone, along with your understanding of warm and cold fronts, to your reading of the daily weather map.

Weather Forecasting

A typical weather map synthesizes the vast amounts of information needed for a reliable weather forecast. *Synoptic analysis* is the observation and recording of weather data at a specific time at many different locations. Building a database of wind, pressure, temperature, and moisture conditions is key to weather prediction and the development of weather-forecasting models. Weather data necessary for the preparation of a surface weather map and forecast include:

southward to the west of the center. The system maintains its counterclockwise flow as the low pressure strengthens. Precipitation occurs in association with each of the fronts. The region between the warm and cold fronts, known as the warm sector, is characterized by relatively warm temperature and calm weather.

Occluded Stage Occlusion begins within the cyclonic circulation as the faster-moving cold front (with cooler, denser air) overtakes the warm front (with warmer, less-dense air), eventually wedging beneath it. Cold fronts can travel at an average 40 kmph (25 mph), whereas warm fronts average roughly half that, 16–24 kmph (10–15 mph). Thus, this process may take several days, during which time an **occluded front** (*occlude* means "to close") develops. Precipitation and wind are most intense during the occluded stage, with intensity tapering off as the warm air mass is forced aloft.

Dissolving Stage The midlatitude cyclone dissolves when its lifting mechanism is completely cut off from the warm air mass, which was its source of energy and

- Barometric pressure
- Surface air temperature
- Dew-point temperature
- Wind speed, direction, and character (gusts)
- Cloud cover and type
- Current sky conditions
- Visibility (fog, haze)
- Precipitation

Data Sources

Meteorologists acquire weather data mainly from satellites, weather balloons, ground-based weather stations, and Doppler radar. Together, these data can provide the basis for a weather forecast.

Satellites Environmental satellites are one of the key tools in forecasting weather and analyzing climate. The National Oceanic and Atmospheric Administration (NOAA) operates *GOES*, or *Geostationary Operational Environmental Satellites*, which provide imagery and data from two locations over the equator: *GOES East*, at 75° W longitude over South America, and *GOES West*, at about 135° W longitude over the Pacific Ocean.

A midlatitude cyclone is a low-pressure system that forms when a cool air mass (cP) collides with a warm, moist air mass (mT). Steered by the jet stream, these storms typically migrate from west to east. On these pages, a cyclonic system of air mass interactions is represented both in the established Norwegian model (GIA 7.1), and in the new conveyor belt model (GIA 7.2). Remote sensing from satellite platforms is essential for analyzing cyclonic structure (GIA 7.3).

7.1 AIR MASS MODEL

The life cycle of a midlatitude cyclone has four stages that unfold at the meeting point between cold and warm air masses.

Open stage cross-section

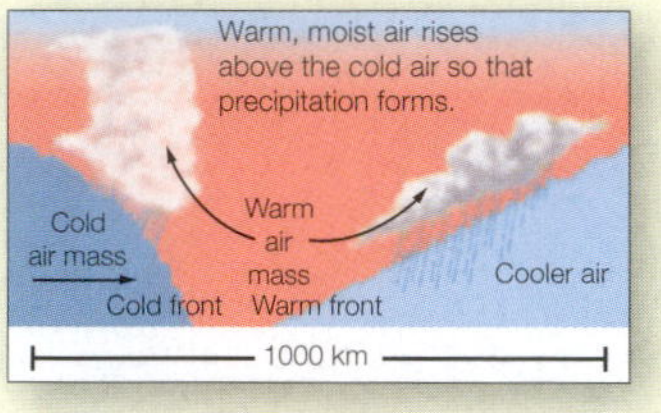

Warm, moist air rises above the cold air so that precipitation forms.
Cold air mass — Warm air mass — Cooler air
Cold front — Warm front
1000 km

Stage ❶ Cyclogenesis
A disturbance develops, usually along the polar front. Warm air converges near the surface and begins to rise, creating instability.

Stage ❷ Open stage
Cyclonic, counterclockwise flow pulls warm, moist air from the south into the low-pressure center while cold air advances southward west of the center.

Stage ❸ Occluded stage
The faster-moving cold front overtakes the slower warm front and wedges beneath it. This forms an occluded front, along which cold air pushes warm air upward, causing precipitation.

Stage ❹ Dissolving stage
The midlatitude cyclone dissolves when the cold air mass completely cuts off the warm air mass from its source of energy and moisture.

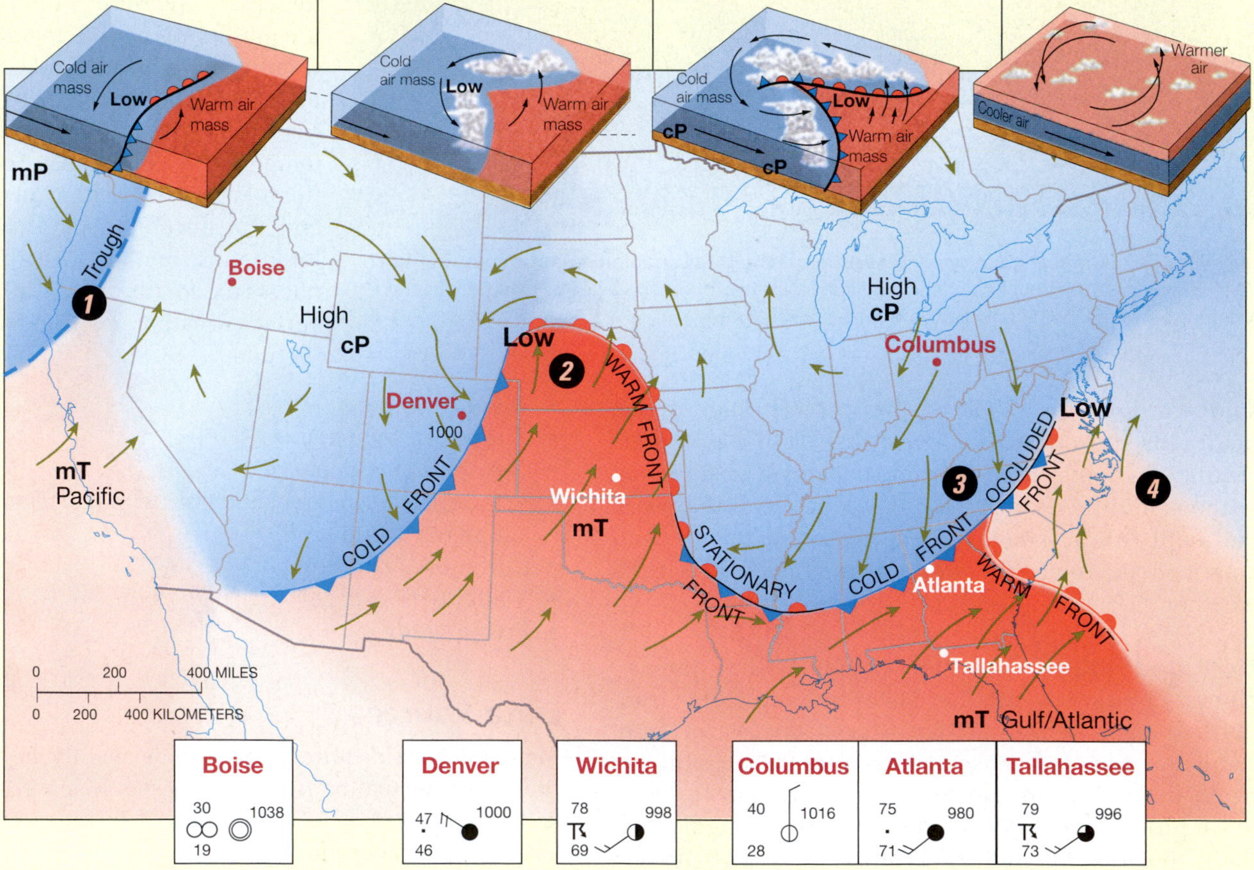

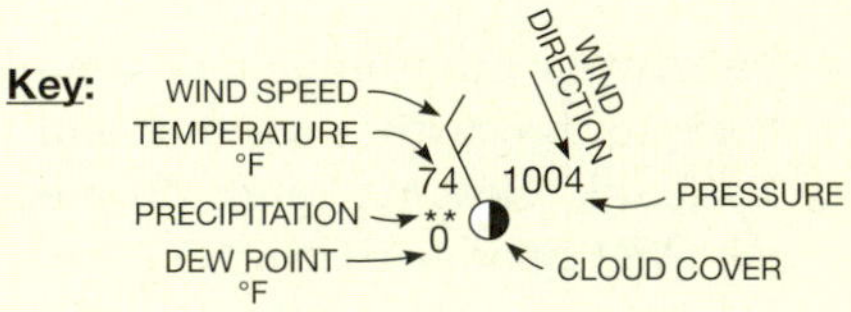

Boise	Denver	Wichita	Columbus	Atlanta	Tallahassee
30 1038	47 1000	78 998	40 1016	75 980	79 996
19	46	69	28	71	73

Key:
WIND SPEED
WIND DIRECTION
TEMPERATURE °F
PRECIPITATION
DEW POINT °F
74 1004 PRESSURE
CLOUD COVER

See MasteringGeography™ for a detailed explanation of weather station symbols. See Figure 5.15 for explanation of wind speed symbols.

MasteringGeography™

Visit the Study Area in MasteringGeography™ to explore midlatitude cyclones.

Visualize: Study geoscience animations of a midlatitude cyclone.

Assess: Demonstrate understanding of midlatitude cyclones (if assigned by instructor).

7.2 CONVEYOR BELT MODEL

Three conveyors of air and moisture, one aloft and two initially along the surface, interact to produce a midlatitude cyclone and sustain it as a dynamic system.

Animation (MG)
Midlatitude Cyclones
https://goo.gl/RSV3gl

Dry conveyor belt
Dry, cold air aloft flows from the west, with some descending behind the cold front as clear, cold air. Another branch of this flow moves cyclonically toward the low. This generally cloud-free dry sector can form a "dry slot," separating warm and cold cloud bands, clearly visible on satellite images.

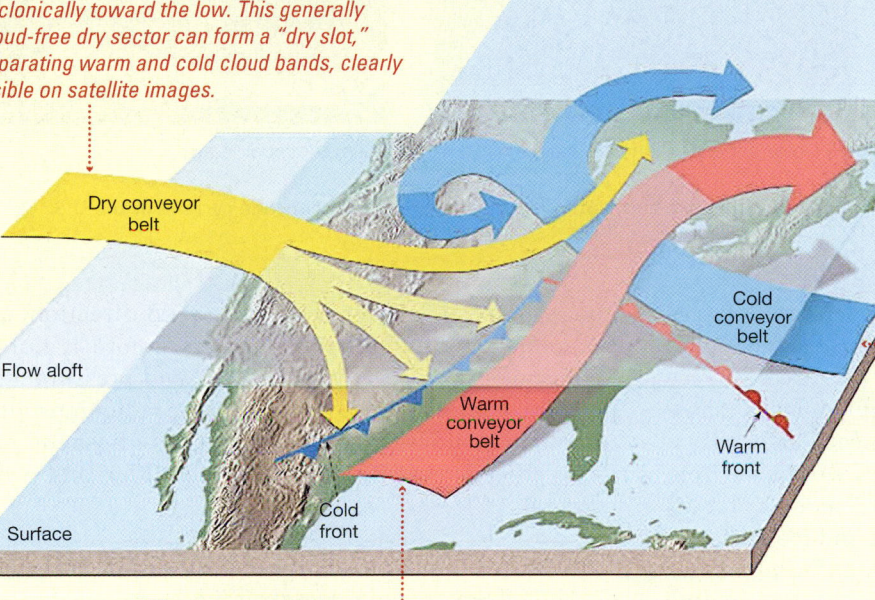

Dry conveyor belt

Flow aloft

Cold conveyor belt

Warm conveyor belt

Warm front

Cold front

Surface

Cold conveyor belt
Cold surface air flows from the east beneath the less dense air. As the cold air converges with the low, lifting occurs, with one lifted stream turning counterclockwise around the low. Another stream moves clockwise to join the westerly flow aloft. As the cold conveyor passes beneath the warm channel, it picks up moisture and becomes saturated as it rises. Thus, this cold conveyor can be an important snow producer northwest of the low; an area labeled in GIA 7.3a as a "comma head."

Warm conveyor belt
Warm, moist air moves as a surface flow into the system, riding upward over cooler air to the north. A warm front structure results, with gentle lifting and stratus clouds. During its passage, moisture is delivered ahead of the cold front. This flow is the principal moisture source for the frontal systems. Eventually, the warm air conveyor turns eastward and joins the westerly flow aloft.

7.3 OBSERVING A MIDLATITUDE CYCLONE

Satellite images reveal the flow of moist and dry air that drives a midlatitude cyclone, as well as how the storm changes over time.

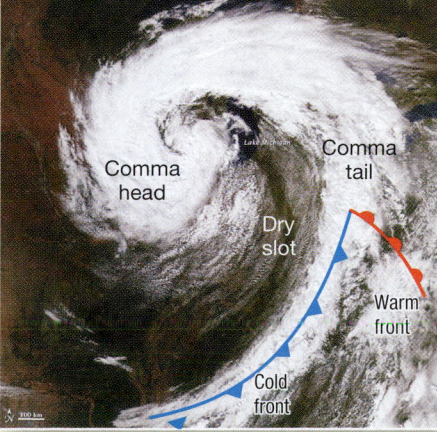

(a) September 26, 2011: Occluded stage.
A midlatitude cyclone over the U.S. Midwest.

Comma head

Comma tail

Dry slot

Warm front

Cold front

(b) September 26, 2011: Water vapor image.
The cold conveyor belt delivers cold, dry air (in yellow) that will soon cut off the storm's supply of warm, moist air.

Cold, dry air

GEOquiz

1. Summarize: In your own words, summarize the life cycle of a midlatitude cyclone.

2. Analyze: Which of the three conveyor belts is most critical in maintaining a midlatitude cyclone? Explain. Hint: Review stages 3 and 4 of the air-mass model.

3. Explain: How do the conveyor belts interact to produce precipitation north of the warm front?

4. From the sources given in this chapter, find several satellite images of midlatitude cyclones and identify the basic elements described here. List the dates you found.

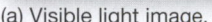

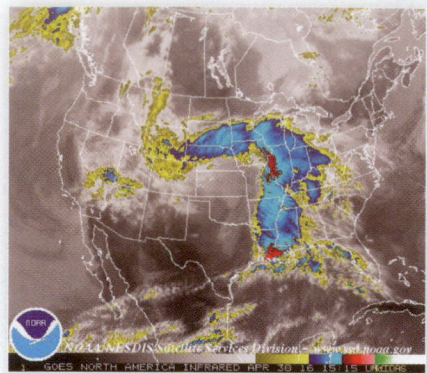

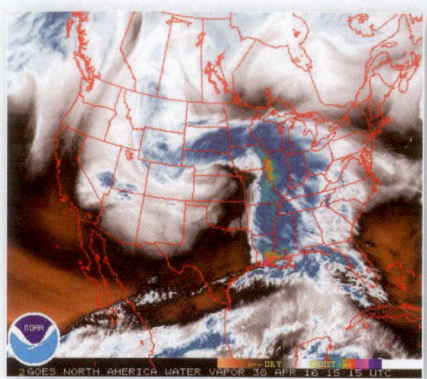

(a) Visible light image.

(b) Color-enhanced infrared image.

(c) Water vapor image.

▲**Figure 7.13** *GOES East* **satellite images—visible light, infrared, and water vapor—featuring a midlatitude cyclone in the U.S. Midwest on April 30, 2016.** [NOAA.]

GOES East provides most of the data and images for the United States, including cloud cover, cloud height, and atmospheric water vapor (**Figure 7.13**; see http://www.goes.noaa.gov/). Visible light images show sunlight reflected off surfaces on or near Earth, essentially representing what the human eye would see from the satellite. Objects at higher altitude (such as clouds) and with higher albedo (such as snow and ice surfaces) tend to look brightest (Figure 7.13a). Infrared images (IR) show thermal infrared longwave radiation emitted from Earth or from clouds in the atmosphere. IR images show the relative temperature of objects, with colder objects appearing brighter and warmer objects appearing darker. Color-enhanced IR images show the colder tops of high-altitude clouds in colors and low-altitude, warmer clouds as gray (Figure 7.13b). Water vapor images display wavelengths absorbed by water vapor, showing areas with greater atmospheric moisture as colored and bright white (Figure 7.13c).

Other satellites provide data and imagery for precipitation (see the TRMM images in Chapter 5, Figure 5.13) and surface temperature. The CERES sensor aboard several satellites measures Earth's outgoing longwave energy, indicating the heat leaving Earth's surface, which is useful for measuring and mapping the extreme temperatures during heat waves.

Weather Balloons Small, expendable instrument packages suspended below unmanned, hydrogen- or helium-filled balloons that ascend to the upper atmosphere are *radiosondes*, often called weather balloons. A radiosonde ascends at a constant rate, providing data for wind speed and direction, and can remain aloft for up to 2 hours before it bursts. Radiosondes also carry sensors that send pressure, temperature, and relative humidity data by radio transmitter to ground stations. Meteorologists use radiosonde data for weather forecasting, as well as pollution and ozone research.

Ground Installations Surface weather information in the United States comes mainly from the Automated Surface Observing System (ASOS), which is installed at over 900 airports across the country. An ASOS instrument array is made up of numerous sensors that supply continuous on-the-ground weather data, helping the National Weather Service (NWS) increase the timeliness and accuracy of its forecasts (**Figure 7.14**).

(a) A radar antenna is within the dome structure of the NWS weather installation at the Indianapolis International Airport.

(b) ASOS weather-instrument station.

▲**Figure 7.14** **NWS weather installation and ASOS weather instruments.** [Bobbé Christopherson.]

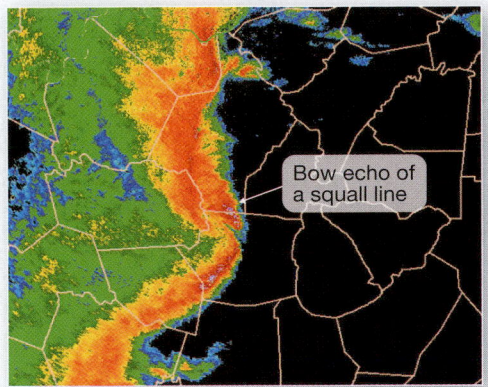

(a) Doppler radar shows the "bow echo" indicating strong winds along a squall line in central Kentucky.

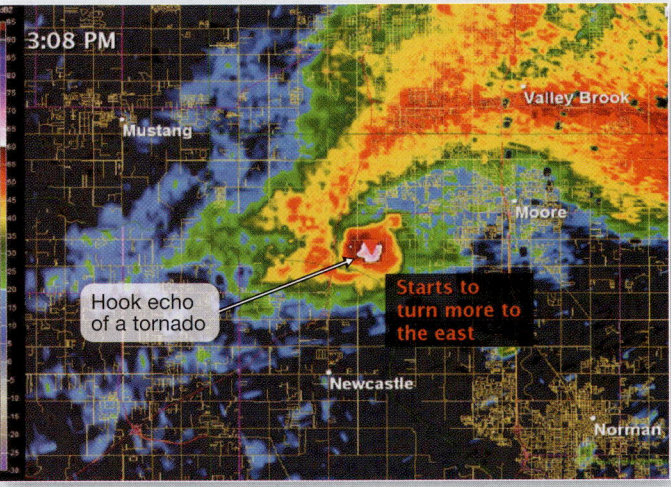

(b) Doppler radar shows the hook signature of the EF-5 tornado that hit Moore, Oklahoma, in 2013.

(c) A storm chaser repairs the DOW dish near Kimball, Nebraska.

◀Figure 7.15 **Doppler radar signatures and Doppler on Wheels (DOW) truck.** [(a) NWS. (b) NWS, Norman, OK, Weather Forecast Office. (c) Ryan McGinnis/Alamy.]

Doppler Radar Doppler radar is an essential element of severe weather forecasting. A radar antenna, typically housed in a radar dish, sends out short pulses of radar waves that are reflected by objects in the atmosphere, such as water droplets and ice crystals. The intensity of the reflected pulse and the time delay between the pulse and its return reveal the distance and direction of movement of the intercepted objects. Thus the reflected energy, called the return echo, indicates the rate of precipitation, as well as wind direction and speed, in the scanned area.

Many radar images you see online show reflectivity measured in values of decibels, or dBZ. These equate to rainfall rates and are assigned color groups: Higher decibels mean more intense rainfall, represented by red and yellow on radar images, while lower decibels mean less intense rainfall, shown by greens and blues (look ahead to Figure 7.18). Radar images show either base reflectivity, from the lowest elevation radar scan, or composite reflectivity, from all elevations scanned. Composite reflectivity images can reveal storm structure, an important feature for assessing severity.

Doppler radar yields critical information for issuing accurate severe storm warnings. A squall line has a distinct radar signature called a "bow echo" that indicates high winds (**Figure 7.15a**). A tornado signature forms a hook, or "hook echo," produced by the strong counterclockwise winds carrying precipitation around the updraft at the center of the storm (**Figure 7.15b**).

The NWS operates 155 Doppler radar systems in the United States. In addition, the Center for Severe Weather Research in Boulder, Colorado, maintains a fleet of Doppler radar trucks, known as Doppler on Wheels (DOW). The DOW units collect data for thunderstorms, hurricanes, and tornadoes (**Figure 7.15c**).

Forecasting Technology

The accuracy of forecasts continues to improve with technological advancements in instruments and software and with our increasing knowledge of the atmospheric interactions that produce weather. In 2015, NOAA's next-generation Advanced Weather Interactive Processing System (AWIPS II) was fully implemented at NWS stations. The new system features seamless integration of data from satellites, radar, and other sensors, in addition to laptop capability that enables forecasters to work on location with emergency responders. A goal of this updated system is to improve forecast accuracy and severe weather warnings. However, because the atmosphere tends toward chaotic, or random, behavior, slight variations in the input data or slight changes to a weather model's basic assumptions can produce widely varying forecasts.

In the United States, the NWS provides current satellite images and weather forecasts (see http://www.weather.gov/). In Canada, the Meteorological Service of Canada provides forecasts at https://weather.gc.ca/index_e.html. Internationally, the World Meteorological Organization coordinates weather information (see http://public.wmo.int/en).

Violent Weather

Weather is a continuous reminder that the flow of energy across the latitudes can at times set into motion destructive, violent events. In the United States, government research and monitoring of violent weather is

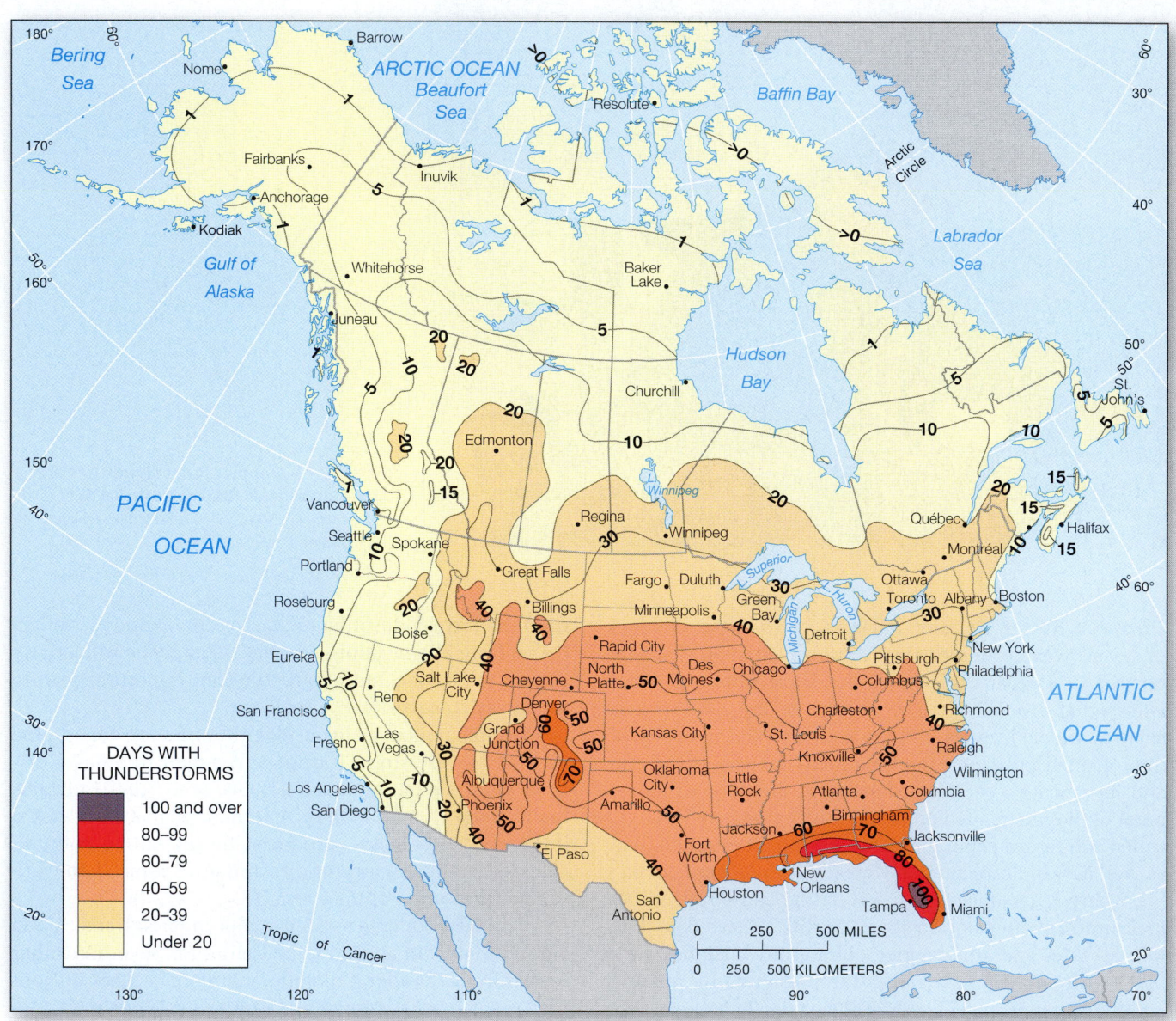

▲**Figure 7.16** **Thunderstorm occurrence.** Average annual number of days experiencing thunderstorms. Compare this map with the location of mT air masses in Figure 7.2. [Data courtesy of NWS; *Climatic Atlas of Canada,* Atmospheric Environment Service, Canada.]

centered at NOAA's National Severe Storms Laboratory and Storm Prediction Center (see http://www.nssl.noaa .gov/ and http://www.spc.noaa.gov/). We focus in this chapter on ice storms, thunderstorms, derechos, tornadoes, and tropical cyclones; coverage of floods appears in Chapter 14 and coastal hazards in Chapter 16.

Ice Storms and Blizzards

Ice storms and blizzards are types of violent weather that are generally confined to the mid- to high-latitude regions of the world. According to the National Weather Service, an *ice storm* is a winter storm in which at least 6.4 mm (0.25 in.) of ice accumulates on exposed surfaces. Ice storms occur when a layer of warm air is between two layers of cold air, promoting the formation of freezing rain and sleet.

Ice storms occur every winter in the U.S. Midwest, South, and Northeast. In 2009, a 3-day ice storm caused power outages in 609,000 homes and businesses; area schools were closed for a week. In 2015, the worst ice storm in 20 years hit Tennessee and left 300,000 homes without power as it moved across the South.

As discussed earlier, midlatitude cyclonic systems often bring heavy snowfall across the United States. *Blizzards* are snowstorms with frequent gusts or sustained winds greater than 56 kmph (35 mph) for a period of time longer than 3 hours and blowing snow that reduces visibility to 400 m (0.25 mi) or less. The snow accumulation from these storms can paralyze regional transportation both during the storm and for days afterward. (see an example in the Human Denominator feature at the end of the chapter)

Thunderstorms

By definition, a *thunderstorm* is a type of turbulent weather accompanied by lightning and thunder. Such storms are characterized by a buildup of giant cumulonimbus clouds that can be associated with squall lines of heavy rain, including sleet, blustery winds, hail, and tornadoes. Thunderstorms may develop within an air mass, in a line along a front (particularly a cold front), or where mountain slopes cause orographic lifting.

Thousands of thunderstorms occur on Earth at any given moment. Equatorial regions and the ITCZ experience many of them, exemplified by the city of Kampala, Uganda, in East Africa, which sits virtually on the equator and averages a record 242 days a year with thunderstorms. In North America, most thunderstorms occur in areas dominated by mT air masses (**Figure 7.16**).

Short-lived Thunderstorms
Isolated, short-lived thunderstorms fueled by the rapid upward movement of warm, moist air are **single-cell thunderstorms**, also called *air mass thunderstorms*. As the air rises, cools, and condenses to form clouds and precipitation, tremendous energy is released by the condensation of large quantities of water vapor. This process locally heats the air, causing updrafts and downdrafts as rising parcels of air pull surrounding air into the column and as the frictional drag of raindrops pulls air toward the ground.

Single-cell thunderstorms typically pass through three stages. In the *cumulus stage*, warm moist air rises to form a cumulus cloud. Water droplets form within the cloud, but evaporate into the cool, dry surrounding air, creating unstable conditions. In the *mature stage*, updrafts can extend cloud tops as high as the troposphere. Strong downdrafts cause heavy precipitation at the ground surface, as well as strong, gusty winds (**Figure 7.17**). In the *dissipating stage*, downdrafts pull cooler air into the cloud, inhibiting convective lifting and release of latent heat. Precipitation tapers off as the energy for the storm dissipates.

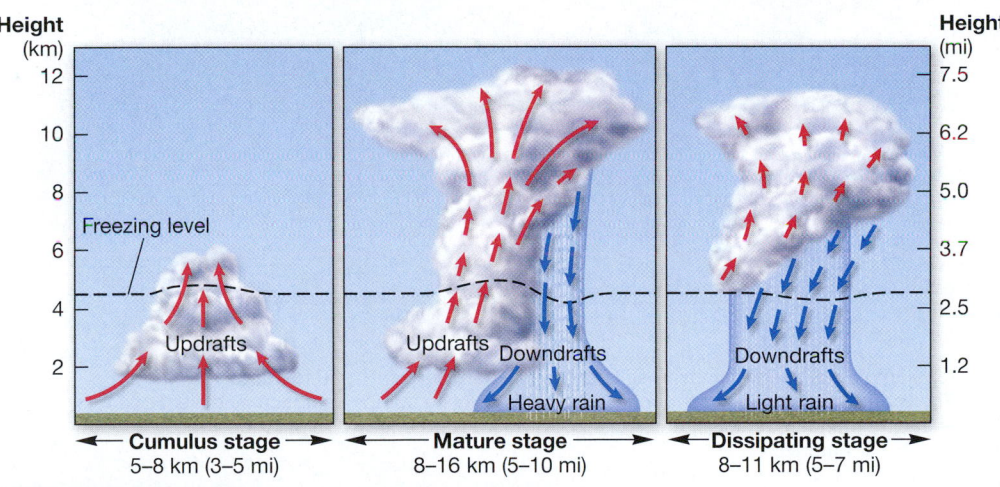

(a) Thunderstorm formation.

(b) Single-cell thunderstorm, cumulus stage, over Elko, Nevada.

▲**Figure 7.17 Stages of a single-cell thunderstorm.** [(b) Dennis Frates/Alamy..]

Lightning and Thunder Within a cumulonimbus cloud, turbulent mixing of air of different densities, water, and ice pellets can create areas of positive and negative charge. **Lightning** refers to the flashes of light resulting from the discharge of electricity that has built up between areas within a cumulonimbus cloud or between the cloud and the ground. Such discharges can contain tens of millions to hundreds of millions of volts that briefly superheat the air. The process begins as updrafts and downdrafts cause ice crystals and water droplets to collide within the cloud, creating electrical charges. Positively charged particles collect in one area and negatively charged particles in another. Eventually the charged areas reach a threshold and discharge as lightning. The ground underneath the cloud also builds up an electrical charge, so that sometimes the discharge occurs from cloud to ground (**Figure 7.18a**).

The boom of **thunder** that follows a lightning flash comes from the sound wave produced by the violent expansion of the abruptly heated air as it sends shock waves through the atmosphere. Although lightning and thunder occur at the same time, the sound waves of thunder travel more slowly than the light waves of lightning. Thus the crack of thunder we hear is delayed—a 5-second delay means that the thunder is about 1.6 km, or 1 mile, away.

An estimated 8 million lightning strikes occur each day on Earth. Lightning poses a hazard to aircraft and causes an average of 48 deaths each year in the United States. People caught outdoors as a lightning charge builds should not seek shelter beneath a tree, as trees are a high point on the landscape and are good conductors of electricity because of their internal moisture. Data from NASA's Lightning Imaging Sensor (LIS) show that about 90% of all strikes occur over land in response to increased convection over relatively warmer continental surfaces (**Figure 7.18b**).

(a) The electrical flashes of lightning, shown here near Arlee, Montana, are caused by the buildup of negative charge in the bottom of the cloud and positive charge on the ground.

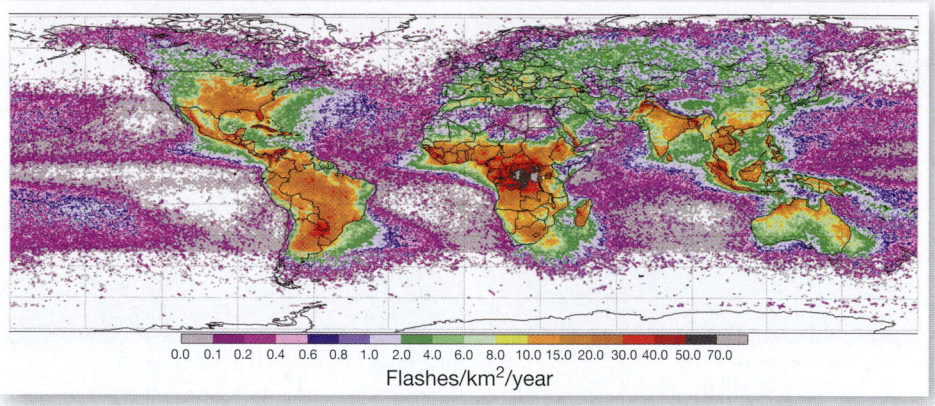

(b) Map of total annual lightning strikes (flashes) from January 1998 to February 2012. The lightning imaging sensor aboard the *TRMM* satellite combines optical and electronic elements that can detect lightning within individual storms, day or night, between 35° N and 35° S latitudes.

▲**Figure 7.18 Lightning and global lightning strikes, 1998 to 2012.** [(a) Design Pics, Inc./Alamy. (b) Lightning Imaging Sensor-Optical Transient Detector (LIS-OTD) global lightning image obtained from the NASA EOSDIS Global Hydrology Resource Center DAAC, Huntsville, AL. Reprinted by permission of Richard Blakeslee.]

Severe Thunderstorms Longer-lived thunderstorms with several cells (more than one main updraft), lines of cells (squall lines), or supercells (strong rotating updrafts) can be classified as severe. A defining characteristic is *wind shear*, the variation of wind speed and direction with altitude. High wind shear (extreme and sudden variation) is needed to produce hail and tornadoes, two by-products of severe thunderstorm activity.

Severe thunderstorms can produce enormous turbulence in the form of *downbursts*, which are strong downdrafts that cause exceptionally strong winds near the ground. Downbursts are classified by size: A *macroburst*

(a) A shelf cloud over LaPorte, Indiana, indicates the strong winds of the advancing derecho.

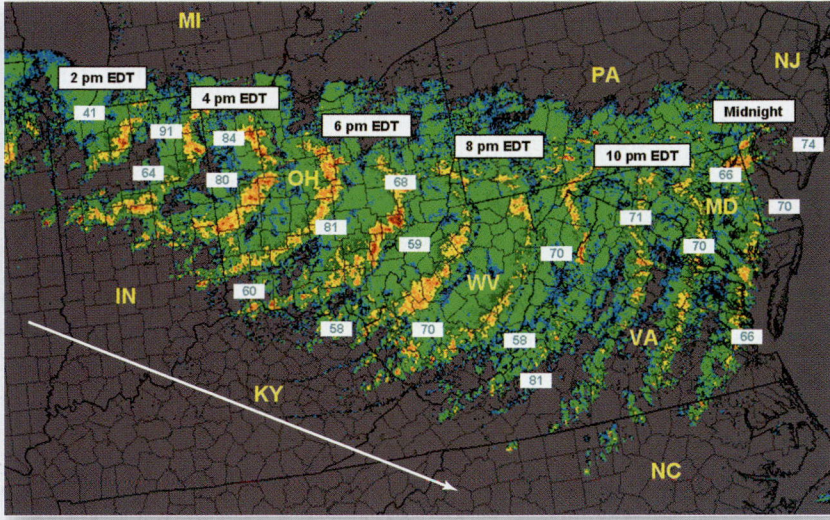

(b) Composite of hourly radar reflectivity imagery shows the development of the June 29, 2012, derecho event, including selected wind gusts (mph), beginning at 2 P.M. Eastern Daylight Time (far left) and ending at midnight (far right).

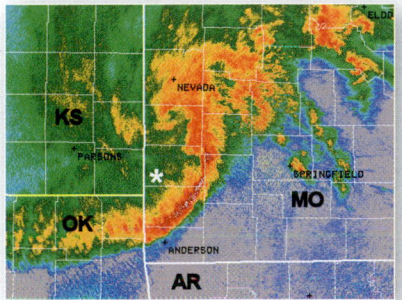

(c) Radar reflectivity image of the May 2009 super derecho over Kansas and Missouri, showing the early stages of the developing eyelike structure.

▲Figure 7.19 **Derecho events in 2009 and 2012.** [(a) Kevin Gould, NOAA. (b) Base image by G. Carbin, NOAA Storm Prediction Center.]

is at least 4.0 km (2.5 mi) wide and in excess of 210 kmph (130 mph); a *microburst* is smaller in size and speed. Downbursts are characterized by the dreaded high-wind-shear conditions that can bring down aircraft. Such turbulence events are short-lived and hard to predict or detect.

The strongest thunderstorms are known as **supercell thunderstorms**, or *supercells*. Supercells often contain a deep, persistently rotating updraft, range up to 10 km (6 mi) in diameter, and can produce heavy rain, large hail, and tornadoes (as discussed and illustrated later in this chapter). The conditions conducive to forming thunderstorms and more intense supercells—lots of warm, moist air and strong convective activity—are enhanced by climate change. However, wind shear, another important factor in thunderstorm and supercell formation, will likely lessen in the midlatitudes as Arctic warming reduces overall temperature differences across the globe. Research is ongoing as to which of these effects will be more important for determining severe thunderstorm frequency in different regions of the world.

Derechos

Straight-line winds associated with fast-moving, severe thunderstorms are known as **derechos**—or *plow winds*, in Canada. These strong, linear winds—produced by

powerful thunderstorm downbursts—travel in straight paths fanning out along wide, curved-wind fronts. By definition, a derecho has winds or wind gusts exceeding 93 kmph (58 mph) that cause a swath of damage extending 386 km (240 mi) across the landscape. The name derives from a Spanish word meaning "direct" or "straight ahead." Researchers identified 377 derechos between 1986 and 2003, an average of about 21 per year. For more information, see http://www.spc.noaa.gov/misc/AbtDerechos/derechofacts.htm.

Derechos pose distinct hazards to summer outdoor activities by overturning boats, hurling flying objects, and breaking tree trunks and limbs. About 70% of derechos occur between May and August in the U.S. Midwest, from Iowa to Illinois and into the Ohio River Valley. In June 2012, a derecho originated near Chicago and traveled southeastward toward Washington, D.C., causing damage and power outages for millions of people, as well as several fatalities (**Figure 7.19**). From September through April, areas of derecho activity shift southward toward Texas and Alabama.

In May 2009, a fierce windstorm crossed Kansas, Missouri, Illinois, and Kentucky, with 160 kmph (100 mph) winds and a path of destruction over 450 km (280 mi) wide. Scientists coined the term *super derecho* to describe this new phenomenon: a derecho with an eyelike structure similar to a hurricane that spun off 18 tornadoes as it moved across Kansas (Figure 7.19c).

Tornadoes

A **tornado** is a violently rotating column of air, a *vortex*, that extends downward from a cumulonimbus cloud. The vortex is usually visible as a spinning cloud of water vapor, dust, and debris. A tornado can range from a few meters to over 4 kilometers in diameter and can last anywhere from a few moments to tens of minutes.

Tornado development begins when wind shear produces a rotating body of air that resembles a rolling pin (**Figure 7.20a**). This spinning tube, or vortex, is lifted when it encounters the moist rising air of an updraft and shifts to a vertical position (**Figure 7.20b**). This forms a **mesocyclone**, a spinning, cyclonic, rising column of air associated with a convective storm. Mesocyclones range up to 10 km (6 mi) in diameter and are characteristic of the rotating thunderstorms called supercells (**Figure 7.20c**). However, fewer than half of supercells produce tornadoes.

As moisture-laden air is drawn up into the circulation of a mesocyclone, it spirals upward until it merges with the airflow within the thunderstorm of the cumulonimbus cloud. As the mesocyclone stretches out in a vertical direction, the rotation of air increases speed. The narrower the mesocyclone, the faster the spin of converging parcels of air being sucked into the rotation. The slowly rotating *wall cloud* is formed as the narrowing mesocyclone protrudes beneath the base of the parent cloud. From the base of the wall cloud emerges the twisting **funnel cloud**. If the spinning cloud makes contact with the ground, it is a tornado (**Figure 7.20d**). The funnel cloud is usually visible as a condensation funnel, formed as air is sucked into the storm, expands, cools, and condenses. Sometimes, when the air is dry, the funnel cloud is made visible from dust and debris. When tornado circulation occurs over water, surface water is drawn some 3–5 m (10–16 ft) up into the funnel, forming a **waterspout**.

Sometimes a tornado will have multiple vortices, appearing as several tornadoes at once. These small and intense vortices move around the tornado center and can cause severe and apparently random damage paths on the ground. The deaths of several storm chasers in 2013 near El Reno, Oklahoma, were caused by a multiple-vortex tornado (discussed in Geosystems Now).

Tornado Classification Pressures inside a tornado usually measure about 10% less than those in the surrounding air. The inrushing convergence created by such a pressure gradient causes high wind speeds, sometimes exceeding 482 kmph (300 mph). In 1971, meteorologist Theodore Fujita designed the Fujita Scale, which classifies tornadoes according to estimated wind speed as indicated by related property damage. The 2007 refinement of this scale is the Enhanced Fujita Scale, or EF scale (**Table 7.1**). To assist with wind estimates, the EF Scale includes damage indicators, representing types of structures and vegetation affected, along with degree of damage ratings, both of which are available at http://www.spc.noaa.gov/faq/tornado/ef-scale.html.

From 1950 to 2010 in the United States, tornadoes caused over 5000 deaths (about 85 deaths per year) and property damage of over $28 billion. The yearly average cost of tornado damage is rising each year. In 2011, Joplin, Missouri, was hit by an EF-5 tornado that killed at least 159 people and cost an estimated $3 billion in damages, the most expensive in U.S. history.

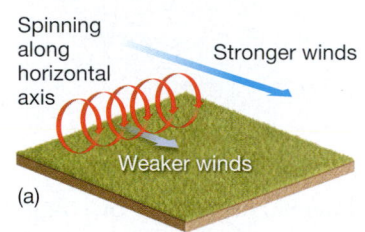

Spinning along horizontal axis

Stronger winds

Weaker winds

(a)

Thunderstorm forming

Updraft

(b)

Animation MG
Tornado Wind Patterns

https://goo.gl/Jck973

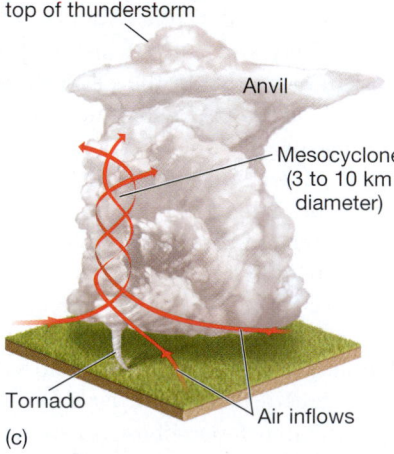

Clouds overshoot top of thunderstorm

Anvil

Mesocyclone (3 to 10 km diameter)

Tornado

Air inflows

(c)

(d) A tornado descends from the base of a supercell on May 30, 2015, near the town of Dora in eastern New Mexico.

▲**Figure 7.20 Mesocyclone and tornado formation.** Strong wind aloft establishes spinning, and updraft from thunderstorm development tilts the rotating air, causing a mesocyclone to form as a rotating updraft within the thunderstorm. If one forms, a tornado will descend from the lower portion of the mesocyclone. [(d) Novarc Images/Alamy.]

TABLE 7.1 The Enhanced Fujita Scale

EF-Number	3-Second-Gust Wind Speed; Damage
EF-0 Gale	105–137 kmph (65–85 mph); *light damage*: branches broken, chimneys damaged.
EF-1 Weak	138–177 kmph (86–110 mph); *moderate damage*: beginning of hurricane wind-speed designation, roof coverings peeled off, mobile homes pushed off foundations.
EF-2 Strong	178–217 kmph (111–135 mph); *considerable damage*: roofs torn off frame houses, large trees uprooted or snapped, boxcars pushed over, small missiles generated.
EF-3 Severe	218–266 kmph (136–165 mph); *severe damage*: roofs torn off well-constructed houses, trains overturned, trees uprooted, cars thrown.
EF-4 Devastating	267–322 kmph (166–200 mph); *devastating damage*: well-built houses leveled, cars thrown, large missiles generated.
EF-5 Incredible	>322 kmph (>200 mph); *incredible damage*: houses lifted and carried, car-sized missiles fly farther than 100 m, bark removed from trees.

Tornado Forecasting The Storm Prediction Center in Kansas City, Missouri, issues daily forecasts for thunderstorm activity and severe weather (http://www.spc.noaa.gov/). If conditions are right for tornadoes, they may issue a *tornado watch*, lasting from 4 to 6 hours. If tornadoes are sighted on the ground or observed on Doppler radar, local NWS forecast offices issue a *tornado warning*. People in potentially affected areas should take shelter immediately. Warning times are about 15 minutes with current technology; however, scientists are actively working to extend lead times to 30 minutes.

Tornado Frequency North America experiences more tornadoes than anywhere on Earth, because its latitudinal position and topography are conducive to the meeting of contrasting air masses and the formation of frontal precipitation and thunderstorms. Tornado occurrence in the United States is highest in Texas and Oklahoma (the southern part of the region known as "tornado alley"), Indiana, and Florida (**Figure 7.21a**). Tornadoes have struck all 50 states and all the Canadian provinces and territories.

According to records since 1950, May and June are the peak months for tornadoes in the United States (**Figure 7.21b**). A comparison of average monthly tornadoes per month for 1950 to 2000 and for 1991 to 2010 shows an apparent trend toward increasing tornado frequency. However, scientists agree that these data are unreliable indicators of actual changes in tornado occurrence because they correspond with the larger number of storm chaser and storm spotter reports. Any actual increases in tornado occurrence may in part relate to rising sea-surface temperatures. Warmer oceans increase evaporation rates, which increase the availability of moisture in the mT air masses, thus producing more intense thunderstorm activity over certain areas of the United States. Other factors in tornado development, such as wind shear, are not as well understood and cannot be definitively linked to climate change.

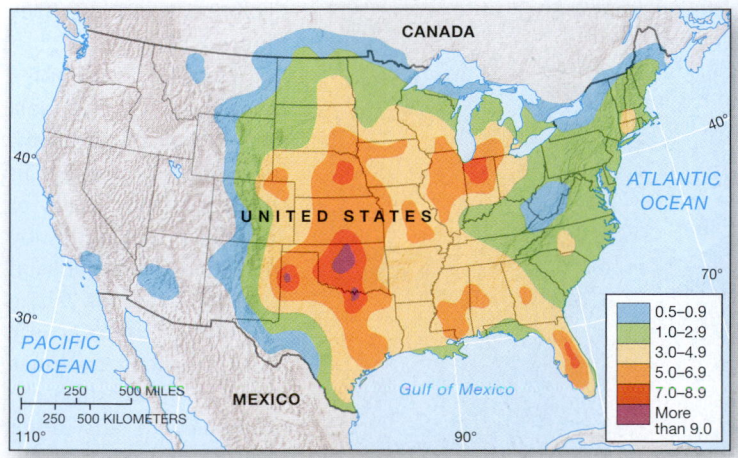

(a) Average number of tornadoes per 26,000 km² (10,000 mi²). Tornado numbers in Alaska and Hawai'i are negligible.

▲**Figure 7.21 Tornado occurrence in the United States.** [Data courtesy of the Storm Prediction Center, NWS, and NOAA.]

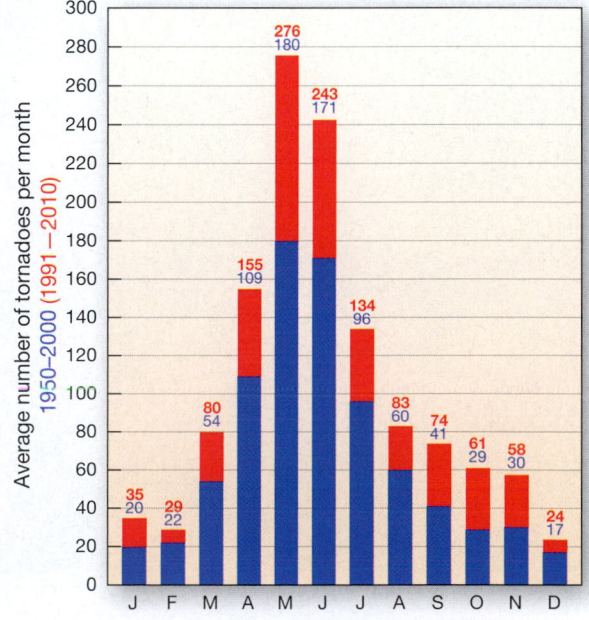

(b) Average number of U.S. tornadoes per month from 1950 to 2000, with additional updated statistics from 1991 to 2010 (in red).

However, recent research has found that the occurrence of tornado outbreaks—consisting of multiple tornado sightings in a day or within a period of days—is on the rise. On April 27, 2011, 319 tornadoes were sighted, the third highest number ever recorded on a single day. In April 2014, a tornado outbreak occurred across the southern plains, centered on Arkansas and Mississippi. Over a 3-day period, 84 tornadoes ranging from EF-0 to EF-3 took 17 lives (**Figure 7.22**). The number of tornadoes per outbreak is also increasing. Further research is needed as to the cause of these changes.

Canada experiences an average of 80 observed tornadoes per year, but those in sparsely populated rural areas can go unreported. In South America, particularly Argentina and Brazil, tornadoes and hailstorms cause damage every year. Tornadoes also occur in Europe, Australia, and Africa—South Africa in particular. Other continents experience a small number of tornadoes annually.

TABLE 7.2 Tropical Cyclone Classification		
	Winds	Features
Tropical disturbance	Variable, low	Definite area of surface low pressure; patches of clouds
Tropical depression	Up to 61 kmph (38 mph, 33 knots)	Gale force; organizing circulation; light to moderate rain
Tropical storm	62–118 kmph (39–73 mph, 34–63 knots)	Closed isobars; definite circular organization; heavy rain; assigned a name
Hurricane (Atlantic and East Pacific) Typhoon (West Pacific) Cyclone (Indian Ocean, Australia)	Greater than 119 kmph (74 mph, 64 knots)	Circular, closed isobars; heavy rain, storm surges; tornadoes in right-front quadrant
Super typhoon (West Pacific)	Greater than 241 kmph (150 mph, 130 knots)	

Tropical Cyclones

A **tropical cyclone** is a rotating low-pressure storm system, with strong winds and thunderstorms that produce heavy rainfall, originating over warm tropical or subtropical waters. Tropical cyclones are classified according to wind speed (**Table 7.2**). The most powerful are **hurricanes**, **typhoons**, or *cyclones*, which are different regional names for the same type of tropical storm. The three names are based on location: Hurricanes occur around North America, typhoons in the western Pacific (mainly in Japan and the Philippines), and cyclones in Indonesia, Bangladesh, and India. A full-fledged hurricane, typhoon, or cyclone has sustained wind speeds greater than 119 kmph (74 mph, or 64 knots).

In the western Pacific, a strong tropical cyclone is designated a *super typhoon* when winds speeds reach 241 kmph (150 mph, or 130 knots). In November 2013, Super Typhoon Haiyan hit the Philippines with sustained winds at 306–314 kmph (190–195 mph), the strongest ever recorded for a tropical cyclone at landfall (see Figure 7.25a).

Tropical cyclones—hurricanes, typhoons, and cyclones—form during specific months in seven primary areas, or "basins," identified by the actual storm tracks of tropical cyclones since the 1850s (**Figure 7.23**). More tropical cyclones occur in the western Pacific than in any other basin worldwide.

In the Atlantic basin, tropical depressions (low-pressure areas) tend to intensify into tropical storms as they cross the Atlantic toward North and Central America.

▲**Figure 7.22** **Destroyed houses in a cul-de-sac in Mayflower, Arkansas, caused by an EF-3 tornado on April 28, 2014.** Over 75 million Americans in six states were under tornado warnings on the day that this storm occurred. [Danny Johnston/AP.]

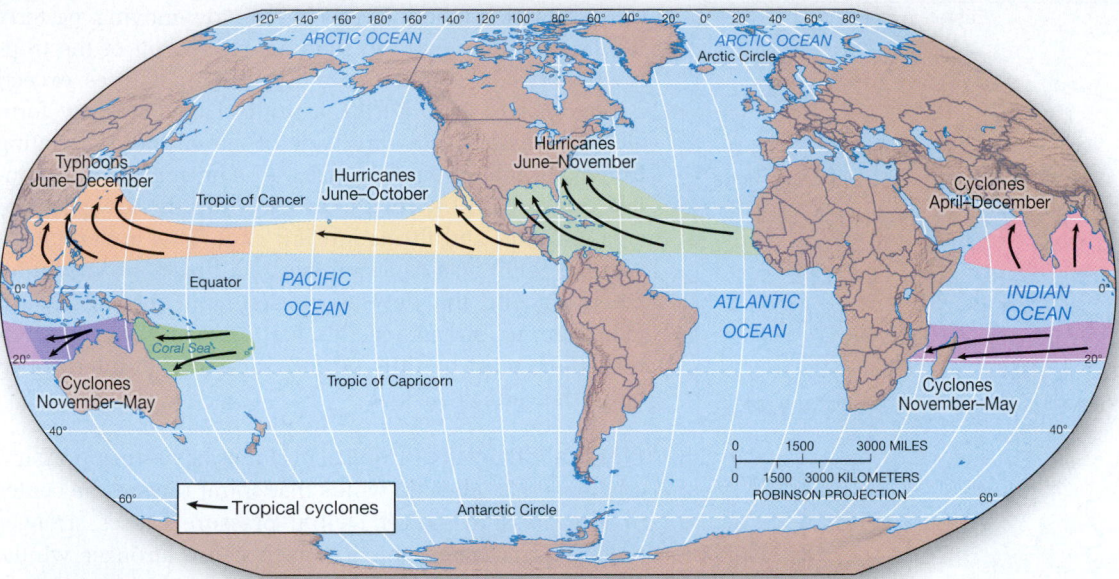

(a) Seven primary areas of tropical cyclone formation, with regional names and principal months of occurrence.

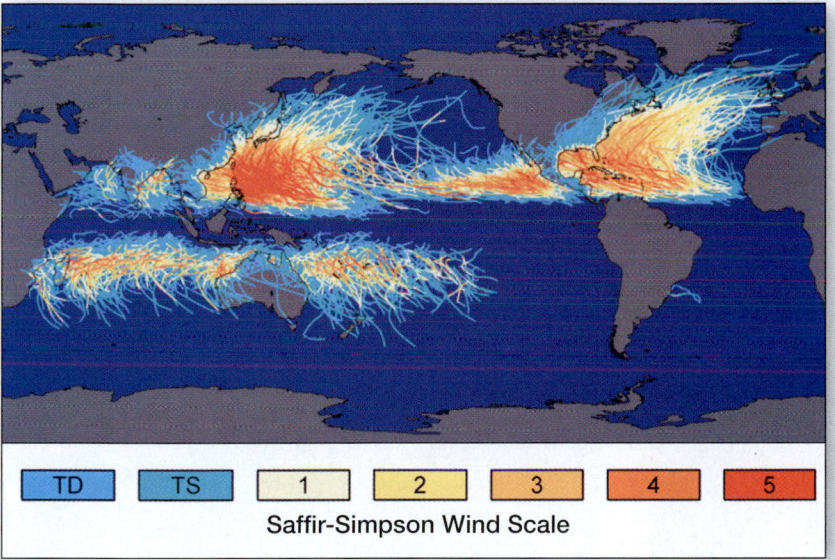

Saffir-Simpson Wind Scale

(b) Global tropical cyclone tracks from 1856 to 2006. Note the track of Hurricane Catarina in 2004, the only recorded hurricane in the south Atlantic Ocean.

▲**Figure 7.23** **Tropical cyclone formation areas and storm tracks.** [(b) R. Rohde/ NASA/GSFC.]

The number of Atlantic hurricanes broke records in 2005, including the most named tropical storms in a single year and the highest number of major hurricanes (category 3 or higher, explained just ahead). The 2005 season was also the first time that three intense category 5 storms (Katrina, Rita, and Wilma) occurred in the Gulf of Mexico. In 2015, a record number of hurricanes occurred in the Northern Hemisphere Pacific basin; Focus Study 7.1 gives details of this remarkable season.

Storm Development Cyclonic systems forming in the tropics are quite different from midlatitude cyclones because the air of the tropics is essentially homogeneous, with no fronts or converging air masses of differing temperatures. In addition, the warm air and warm seas ensure abundant water vapor and thus the necessary latent heat to fuel these storms. Tropical cyclones convert heat energy from the ocean into mechanical energy in the wind—the warmer the ocean and atmosphere, the more intense the conversion and powerful the storm.

If tropical storms mature early along their track, before reaching approximately 40° W longitude, they tend to curve northward toward the north Atlantic and miss the United States. If a tropical storm matures after it reaches the longitude of the Dominican Republic (70° W), then it has a higher probability of hitting the U.S. coast.

GEOreport 7.2 Citizen science using satellite imagery to assess tropical cyclones

Cyclone Center is a citizen science project launched in 2012 that puts volunteers to work analyzing tropical cyclones using infrared imagery from weather satellites since 1978. The objective is to assess cloud temperatures and patterns on the image in order to answer specific questions regarding the storm center, the cloud pattern type, and the change in cloud characteristics over time. The goal of the method, developed in the 1970s, is to make a reasonable approximation of storm intensity and thereby expand the global database, an important objective as climate change affects the frequency and strength of tropical storms (see https://www.cyclonecenter.org/).

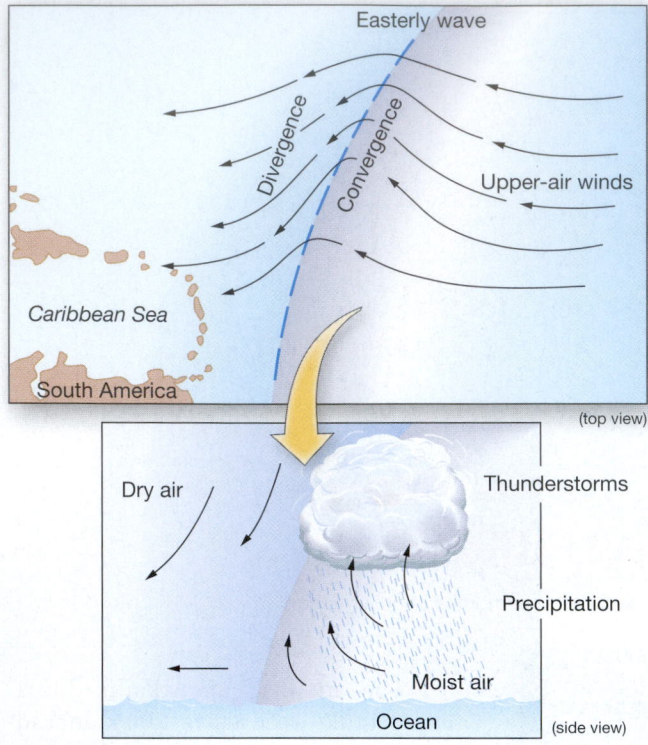

▲Figure 7.24 Easterly wave in the tropics. A low-pressure center develops along an easterly (westward-moving) wave. Moist air rises in an area of convergence at the surface to the east of the wave trough. Wind flows bend and converge before the trough and diverge downwind from the trough.

Cyclonic motion begins with slow-moving easterly waves of low pressure in the trade-wind belt of the tropics (**Figure 7.24**). If the sea-surface temperatures exceed approximately 26°C (79°F), a tropical cyclone may form along the eastern (leeward) side of one of these migrating troughs of low pressure, a place of convergence and rainfall. Surface airflow then converges into the low-pressure area, ascends, and flows outward aloft. This important divergence aloft acts as a chimney, pulling more moisture-laden air into the developing system (**Figure 7.25**). To maintain and strengthen this vertical convective circulation, there must be little or no wind shear to interrupt or block the vertical airflow.

Physical Structure Tropical cyclones have steep pressure gradients that generate winds that spiral toward the center of low pressure—lower central pressure causes stronger pressure gradients, which in turn cause stronger winds. However, other factors come into play so that the storms with lowest central pressure are not always the strongest nor do they cause the most damage. The minimum central pressure ever measured in a tropical cyclone is 870 mb, recorded in 1979 for Typhoon Tip in the western Pacific.

As winds rush toward the center of a tropical cyclone, they turn upward, forming a wall of dense rain bands called the *eyewall*—this is the zone of most intense precipitation. The central area is designated the *eye*

(a) Super Typhoon Haiyan made landfall in the central Phillipines on November 7, 2013, with sustained winds over 306 kmph (190 mph), the strongest ever recorded for a tropical cyclone at landfall using satellite measurements.

▲Figure 7.25 Super Typhoon Haiyan and tropical cyclone structure. [(a) NOAA Forecast Systems Laboratory. (c) NASA and Natalie Tourville/Colorado State University.]

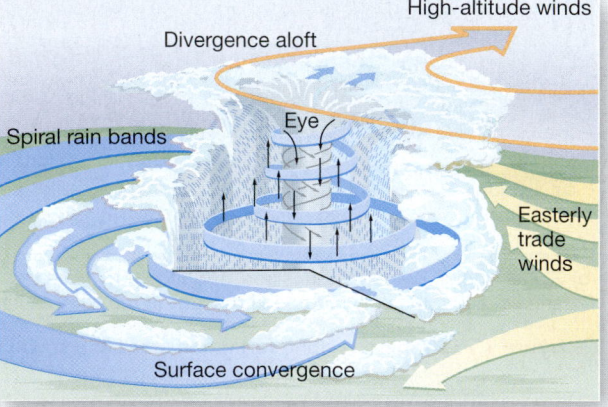

(b) A stylized portrait of a mature hurricane, drawn from an oblique perspective (cutaway view shows the eye, rain bands, and wind-flow patterns).

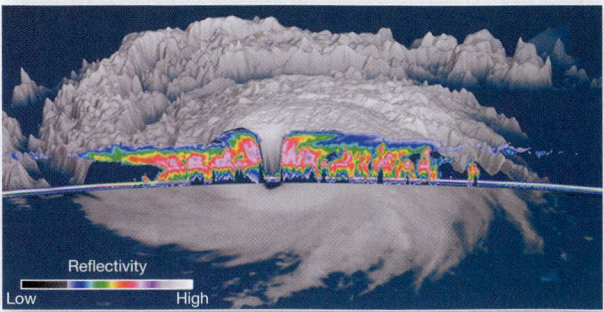

(c) A side view radar image of Typhoon Dolphin in the West Pacific on May 16, 2015. Note the clear sky in the central eye. Red and purple areas indicate large amounts of cloud droplets or precipitation.

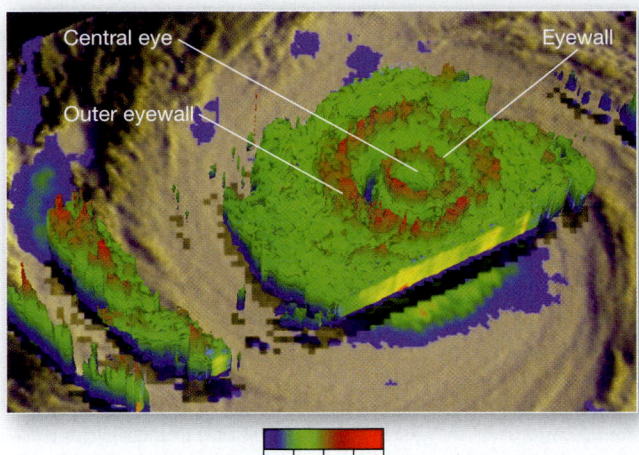

0 5 10 15 20 km

▲**Figure 7.26 Vertical structure of Super Typhoon Lekima over the western Pacific Ocean.** Data from TRMM's Precipitation Radar instrument are overlaid on infrared images to produce this visualization of Lekima on October 24, 2013. Note the well-defined eye and eyewall at the center. In the second, outer eyewall, rain fell at a rate greater than 130 mm/hour (5.2 in./hour). [NASA/GSFC.]

of the storm, where wind and precipitation subside; this is the warmest area of the storm. Although clear skies can appear in the eye, they may not always be present, as commonly believed. The structure of the rain bands, eyewall, and central eye are clearly visible in satellite images (**Figure 7.26**).

Tropical cyclones range in diameter from a compact 160–1000 km (100–600 mi) to the 1300–1600 km (800–1000 mi) attained by some western Pacific super typhoons. Vertically, a tropical cyclone dominates the full height of the troposphere. These storms move along over water at about 16–40 kmph (10–25 mph). The strongest winds are usually recorded in the right-front quadrant (relative to the storm's directional path) of the storm. At **landfall**, where the eye moves ashore, dozens of fully developed tornadoes may be located in this high-wind sector.

▲**Figure 7.27 Storm surge on the rise in New York City just ahead of Superstorm Sandy's arrival in 2012.** The combination of storm surge and high tide caused flooding of 17% of the city's land surface. [John G. Wilbanks/Alamy.]

TABLE 7.3 Saffir–Simpson Hurricane Wind Scale

Category	Wind Speed	Types of Damage
1	119–153 kmph (74–95 mph, 65–82 knots)	Some damage to homes
2	154–177 kmph (96–110 mph, 83–95 knots)	Extensive damage to homes; major roof and siding damage
3	178–208 kmph (111–129 mph, 96–112 knots)	Devastating damage; removal of roofs and gables
4	209–251 kmph (130–156 mph, 113–136 knots)	Catastrophic damage; severe damage to roofs and walls
5	>252 kmph (>157 mph, >137 knots)	Catastrophic damage; total roof failure and wall collapse on high percentage of homes

Damage Potential When you hear meteorologists speak of a category 4 hurricane, they are using the Saffir–Simpson Hurricane Wind Scale to estimate possible damage from hurricane-force winds. The scale uses sustained wind speed at certain locations to rank hurricanes and typhoons in five categories, from smaller category 1 storms to extremely dangerous category 5 storms (**Table 7.3**). The rating can vary for different locations; for example, Hurricane Charley in 2004 hit the coastal area of Punta Gorda, Florida, with category 4 winds, with the rest of the city experiencing only category 3 winds. Often, the rating category decreases after the storm moves inland. This scale does not address other potential hurricane impacts, such as storm surge, flooding, and tornadoes. Damage depends on the degree of property development at a storm's landfall site, how prepared citizens are for the blow, and the local building codes in effect.

Storm Surge When a tropical cyclone makes landfall, additional hazards arise from storm surge and the flooding associated with heavy rainfall. In fact, the impact of hurricanes on human population centers is as much connected to storm surge as it is to damaging winds. **Storm surge** is the seawater that is pushed inland during a hurricane and can combine with the normal tide to create a *storm tide* of 4.5 m (15 ft) or more in height. The landfall of Hurricane Sandy in 2012 coincided with high tide to create a record storm surge in New York City—as high as 4.2 m (13.9 ft) at the southern tip of Manhattan (**Figure 7.27**). Rainfall and flooding can cause devastation and loss of life, making even a weak, slow-moving tropical cyclone quite dangerous and destructive. In 2012, rainfall totals associated with Hurricane Sandy were greater than 180 mm (7.0 in.) over some coastal areas from South Carolina to New Jersey, and snowfall topped 76 cm (30 in.) in parts of Tennessee and West Virginia.

FOCUSstudy 7.1 Climate Change
The 2015 Northern Hemisphere Tropical Cyclone Season

Midday on October 22, 2015, Tropical Storm Patricia reached hurricane strength in the eastern Pacific Ocean near the coast of Mexico. Over the following 24 hours, the storm's low pressure center fell 100 mb—a remarkable and explosive deepening that occurred in response to low wind shear, high moisture, and unusually warm sea-surface temperatures. Patricia's minimum pressure of 872 mb is the lowest on record for the Western Hemisphere, and the second lowest measured for any tropical cyclone. With maximum sustained winds of 346 kmph (215 mph), Patricia became the strongest hurricane on record in either the

eastern Pacific or Atlantic basins (**Figure 7.1.1a**). The category 5 hurricane weakened before making landfall near Manzanillo, Mexico, at category 4 strength. The storm caused severe damage and two fatalities throughout this sparsely populated region.

Hurricane Patricia was the ninth tropical cyclone to reach category 4 or 5 status in the east Pacific basin during the 2015 season. The energy for these storms came from higher-than-average Pacific Ocean temperatures throughout the summer caused by a strong El Niño —a shifting of pressure, winds, and sea-surface temperatures (SSTs) over the equatorial Pacific Ocean —in combination with

global climate change, which is forcing higher temperatures for the oceans and atmosphere (**Figure 7.1.2**). By October, SSTs in both the eastern and central Pacific were more than 2.5 C° (4.4 F°) higher than the historical baseline. In the specific area where Patricia intensified, average mid-October SSTs were the highest in the 67-year record beginning in 1948 (**Figure 7.1.1b**).

As the El Niño pattern established in the Pacific, unusually strong tropical cyclone activity broke records for the Northern Hemisphere. The 2015 season, which runs from June 1 to November 30, included 30 category 3 or higher tropical cyclones, breaking

(a) Hurricane Patricia at category 5 strength off the coast of Mexico on October 23, 2015.

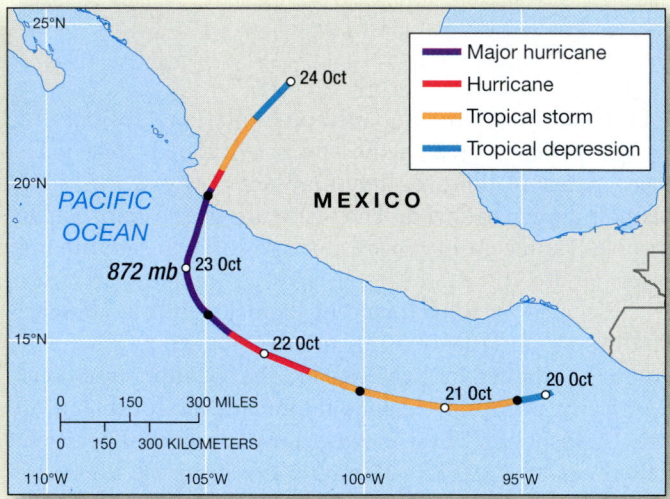

(b) Patricia's track and stages of development from October 20–24, 2015.

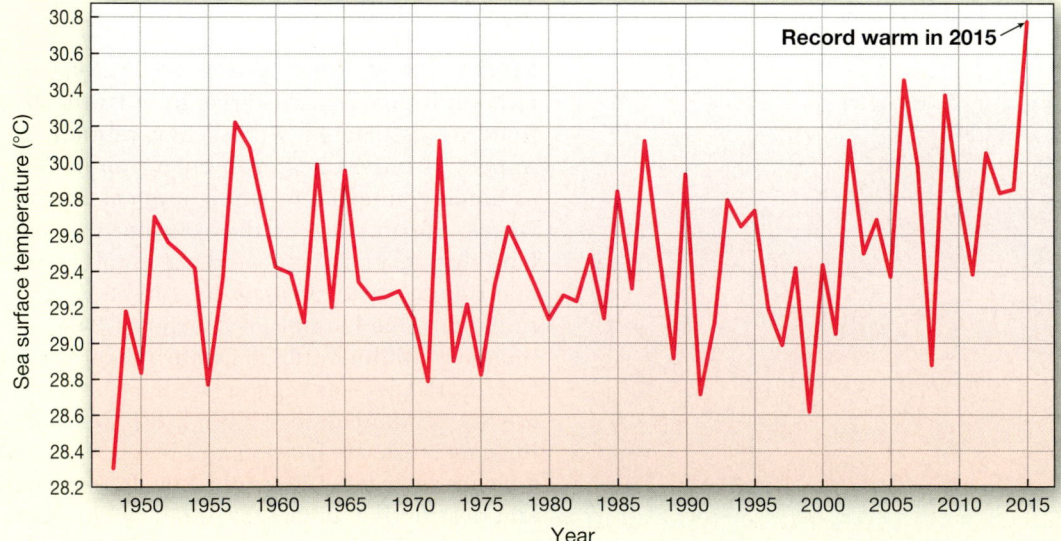

(c) Average mid-October sea-surface temperatures from 1948 to 2015 for the area 13°–17° N and 100°–105° W.

▲**Figure 7.1.1 Hurricane Patricia: Storm track and regional sea-surface temperatures during storm intensification.** [(a) Jeff Schmaltz LANCE EOSDIS Rapid Response/NASA. (b) National Hurricane Center. (c) NOAA, NCEP/NCAR Reanalysis database.]

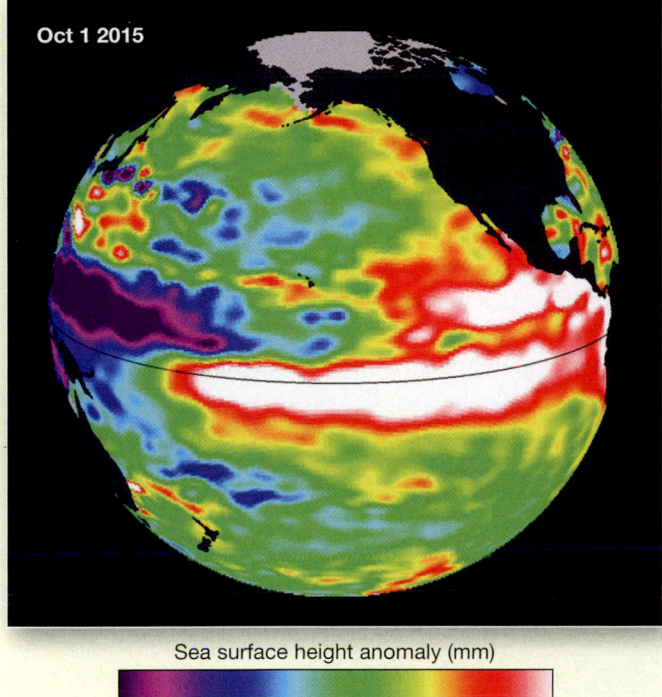

Oct 1 2015

Sea surface height anomaly (mm)

−180 −120   −60   0   60   120   180

◄**Figure 7.1.2** **October 2015 El Niño in the central and eastern Pacific Ocean.** Pacific Ocean sea-surface height anomalies correspond with sea-surface temperatures—greater heights indicate warmer temperatures (warm water expands, causing sea level to increase). White indicates the warmest water; blue and magenta indicate the coldest. [*OSTM Jason–2* image courtesy of JPL/NASA.]

hurricanes, 9 of which were category 3 or higher (see a map at http://earthobservatory.nasa.gov/IOTD/view.php?id=87092).

In the central Pacific, eight tropical cyclones, five of which reached category 3 or higher, occurred in the most active season since 1971 when record-keeping began. For the first time ever, three tropical cyclones at category 3 or higher occurred at the same time east of the International Dateline (**Figure 7.1.3**).

In the West Pacific region, where the El Niño pattern causes slightly reduced SSTs, the number of tropical cyclones was not unusual. However, winds pushed the formation areas of storms farther east, away from the continental land masses, so that storms traveling longer distances over water strengthened to greater intensity. In all, 15 typhoons reached category 3 or higher, tying records set in 1958 and 1965.

1. What conditions in the eastern Pacific combined to help Patricia develop into a category 5 hurricane?

2. Based on what you learned in Chapter 5, explain how El Niño affected the number and strength of tropical cyclones in the Atlantic and Pacific basins in 2015.

the previous record of 23. Twenty-five of the 30 became category 4 or 5 storms, eclipsing the previous record of 18 set in 2004.

The 2015 season saw distinct contrasts between the Atlantic and east Pacific basins. The Atlantic basin had below normal hurricane activity, with 11 tropical storms, only 4 of which became hurricanes. This pattern is typical during an El Niño, which tends to produce stable conditions with strong wind shear over the Atlantic Ocean, inhibiting the formation of tropical storms. In the eastern and central Pacific, activity was far above normal. The eastern Pacific saw 13

APPLYconcepts Referring to the map in Figure 7.1.1b and the chapter's sections "Storm Development" and "Physical Structure," explain key events in the life cycle of Hurricane Patricia.

October 23, atmospheric pressure reading	a. How did Patricia's 872 mb pressure on October 23 affect the storm's intensity? Explain._____ _____
October 23, landfall	b. What area(s) probably experienced the strongest winds as Patricia came ashore? Explain. _____
October 24, moving inland	c. How and why did Patricia's intensity change after the storm made landfall? _____

▲**Figure 7.1.3** **Four tropical cyclones in the Pacific, September 1, 2015.** Typhoon Kilo, Hurricane Ignacio, Hurricane Jimena, and Tropical Depression 14E moved across the Pacific Ocean at the same time in 2015. [NASA/NOAA *GOES* Project.]

WORKITOUT 7.2
Hurricanes as Heat Engines

Answer these questions using your knowledge from Chapters 6 and 7.

1. Why are hurricanes referred to as atmospheric "heat engines"?

2. What is the fuel that produces the engine's heat, and how is the heat dissipated?

Devastation Tropical cyclones are potentially the most destructive storms experienced by humans, claiming thousands of lives each year worldwide. The tropical cyclone that struck Bangladesh in 1970 killed an estimated 300,000 people, and the one in 1991 claimed over 200,000. In Central and North America, death tolls are much lower, but still significant. Hurricane Mitch (October 26–November 4, 1998) was the deadliest Atlantic hurricane in two centuries, killing more than 12,000 people, mainly in Honduras and Nicaragua.

Despite these statistics, the risk of human fatalities is decreasing in most parts of the world owing to better warning and rescue systems and ongoing improvements in the forecasting of these storms. At the same time, especially in the United States, the damage caused by tropical cyclones is increasing as more and more development occurs along susceptible coastlines (Figure 7.28). No matter how accurate storm forecasts become, coastal and lowland property damage will continue to increase until better hazard zoning and development restrictions are in place.

(a) September 9, 2008

◄Figure 7.28. The Bolivar Peninsula in Texas, before and after Hurricane Ike in September 2008. Hurricane Ike made landfall along the Texas coast on September 13 at category 2 strength. Sustained winds and storm surge destroyed over 80% of the homes on the Bolivar Peninsula. Ike was the third costliest hurricane in U.S. history. [USGS.]

(b) September 15, 2008

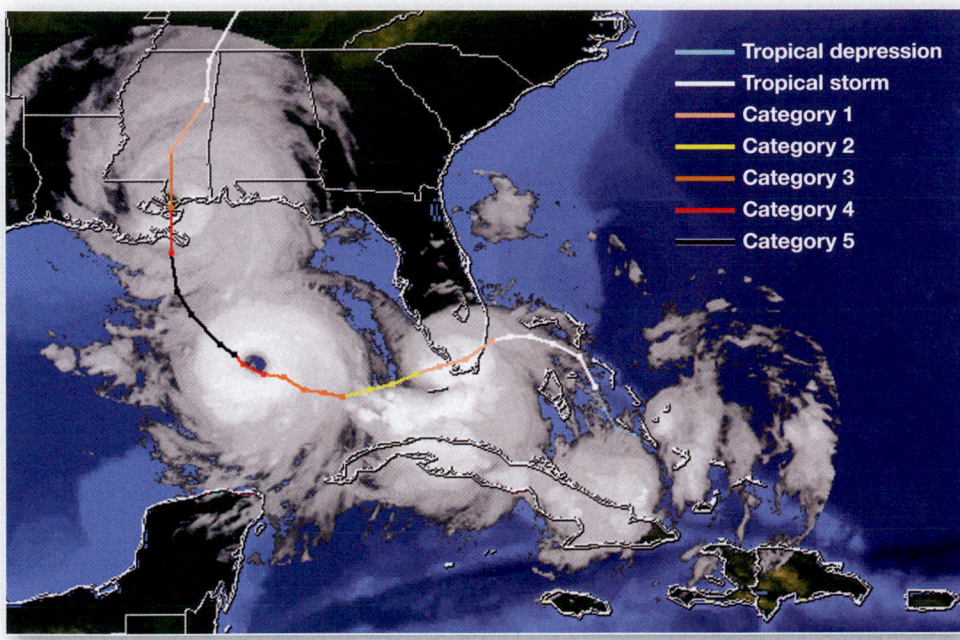

Animation
Hurricane Wind
Patterns

https://goo.gl/z6cFWd

▲**Figure 7.29** **Hurricane Katrina.** Katrina's track and development over a 7-day period. [Courtesy of NOAA and SSEC CIMSS, University of Wisconsin–Madison.]

Hurricane Katrina Hurricane Katrina was the most expensive hurricane in United States history, causing $152 billion (adjusted to current dollars) in damage, and was one of the five deadliest, killing over 1830 people between the storm itself and the storm surge. On August 28, 2005, Katrina reached category 5 strength over the Gulf of Mexico (**Figure 7.29**). The next day, the storm made landfall near New Orleans as a strong category 3 hurricane, with sustained wind speeds over 200 kmph (125 mph) along the Louisiana coast. High rainfall and storm surges caused extensive flooding in New Orleans. About half of the city is below sea level in elevation, the result of years of draining wetlands, compacting soils, and overall land subsidence. In addition, a system of canals, built throughout the 20th century for drainage and navigation, runs through the city. As Katrina moved ashore, water moved into the city through the canals. As the level in nearby Lake Pontchartrain rose from rainfall and storm surge, floodwalls and levees (earthen embankments constructed along the banks of waterways to prevent overflow of the channel) either failed or were breached (**Figure 7.30**). Some neighborhoods were submerged up to 6.1 m (20 ft), and the polluted water remained for weeks.

Although the flooding from Hurricane Katrina resulted more from human engineering and construction errors than from the storm itself, the failure of the flood protection system was a valuable lesson. Since Katrina, the Army Corps of Engineers has strengthened levees, floodwalls, floodgates, and pumping stations in preparation for future hurricanes, at a cost of over $12 billion.

▶**Figure 7.30** **New Orleans on August 30, 2005, after Hurricane Katrina.** [David J. Phillip/AP Photo.]

(a) Just before landfall, Sandy covered 4.7 million square kilometers (1.8 million square miles), from the mid-Atlantic coast west to the Ohio Valley and the Great Lakes and north into Canada.

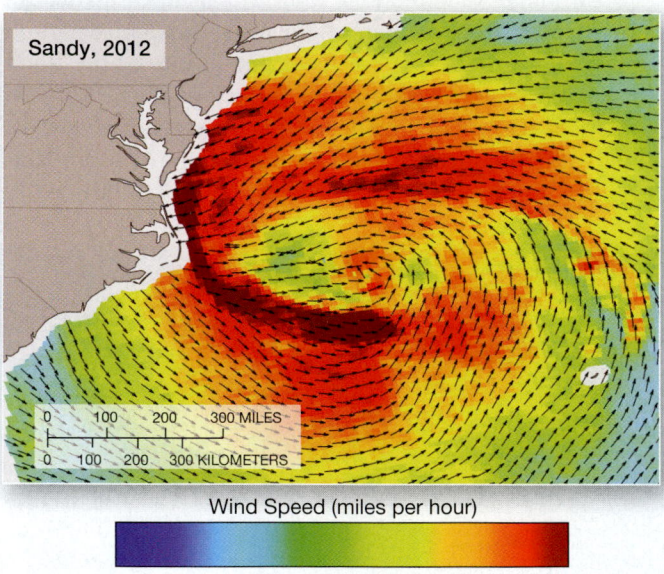

Wind Speed (miles per hour)

0   20   40   60

(b) Wind speed map shows weaker winds to the east, indicating the influence of nearby air masses and associated pressure systems.

▲**Figure 7.31 Hurricane Sandy just before landfall.** Sandy's circulation and wind speeds on October 29, 2012, as the storm moved northward with maximum sustained winds of 150 kmph (90 mph). [(a) *Suomi NPP*, NASA/GSFC. (b) *QuickSat*, NASA/JPL.]

Video (MG)
Superstorm Sandy

https://goo.gl/ELdFAM

"Superstorm" Sandy Hurricane Sandy, often called "Superstorm" Sandy owing to its unusual characteristics, caused an estimated $75 billion in damage—the second most expensive hurricane in U.S. history. The storm affected an estimated 20% of the U.S. population and resulted in over 100 fatalities. Hurricane Sandy began as tropical depression in the Caribbean Sea, reaching hurricane strength on October 23, 2012. Sandy moved northward toward the mid-Atlantic coast, where it was expected to move offshore and dissipate. Instead, an area of high pressure centered on Greenland blocked its path, causing Sandy to veer westward, turning sharply and unexpectedly toward land. The center of the storm hit the New Jersey shoreline just after 11 P.M. on October 29 (**Figure 7.31a**).

According to the National Hurricane Center's criteria for storm classification, Hurricane Sandy transitioned into a *post-tropical*, or *extratropical*, storm just before making landfall. At this point, Sandy departed from the classic tropical cyclone pattern and was instead gathering energy from sharp temperature contrasts between air masses. The storm now exhibited characteristics more closely aligned with nor'easters, midlatitude cyclonic winter storms that typically cover a large area, with strong winds and precipitation far from the center of the storm. Just before landfall, Sandy's wind patterns were asymmetrical, with a broad wind and cloud field shaped like a comma (rather than a circle), but retaining strong, hurricane-force winds (**Figure 7.31b**). Superstorm Sandy is the largest-diameter hurricane ever to form in the Atlantic basin.

Tropical Cyclones and Climate Change Higher sea-surface temperatures caused by climate change have affected tropical cyclone intensity, frequency, and duration. As oceans warm, the energy available to fuel tropical cyclones is increasing. In addition, the latitude at which hurricanes are reaching their greatest intensity is shifting toward the poles, at a rate of 1° per decade. Scientists project that with continued warming of air and ocean temperatures, storm intensity and rainfall rates will increase. Models suggest that the number of category 4 and 5 storms in the Atlantic basin may double by the end of this century. In addition, rising sea levels associated with climate change have worsened the damage from hurricane storm surge.

In the United States, the current trend of increasing coastal population—combined with continued ocean warming—will likely result in substantial hurricane-related property losses. Eventually, though, the more intense storms and rising sea level could lead to shifts in population along U.S. coasts and even to the abandonment of some coastal resort communities, such as those along North Carolina's outer banks and the New Jersey shore.

WEATHER IMPACTS HUMANS

• Frontal activity and midlatitude cyclones bring severe weather that affects transportation systems and daily life.
• Violent weather events—ice storms, thunderstorms, tornadoes, tropical cyclones—cause destruction and human casualties.

HUMANS IMPACT WEATHER

• Rising temperatures with climate change have caused less snowfall in the Northern Hemisphere.
• Sea-level rise is increasing tropical cyclone storm surge on the U.S. East Coast and other locations worldwide.

7a

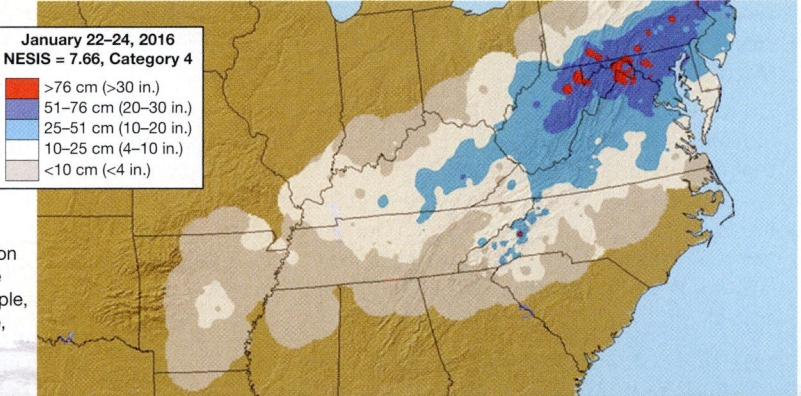

January 22–24, 2016
NESIS = 7.66, Category 4

■	>76 cm (>30 in.)
■	51–76 cm (20–30 in.)
■	25–51 cm (10–20 in.)
□	10–25 cm (4–10 in.)
□	<10 cm (<4 in.)

NOAA's Northeast Snowfall Index Scale ranks winter storms from 1 to 5 based on the amount of snow (at least 25 cm, or 10 in.) and the size and population of the impacted area. The January 22–24, 2016, blizzard affected over 100 million people, and ranked as category 4—a "crippling" storm. Washington, D.C., pictured here, recorded 46 cm (18 in.) of snow. Of 58 ranked blizzards since 1950, only two—occurring in 1993 and 1996—rank as category 5, "extreme." [MLADEN ANTONOV/Staff/AFP/Getty Images.]

Blue Marble–Next Generation image shows land surface, ocean, sea ice, and clouds.

7c

In late December 2015, a tornado outbreak across north and central Texas produced 12 confirmed tornadoes, highly unusual for the month with the lowest average tornado count. The storms killed 13 people, and produced the damage seen here in the city of Garland. [Stewart F. House/Getty Images.]

7b

Tropical Cyclone Pam, a category 5, hit the South Pacific island nation of Vanuatu in March 2015, killing 15 people and causing devastating damage. The most intense Southern Hemisphere cyclone of 2015, the storm leveled over 90% of the structures on several islands. [Dave Hunt/Getty Images.]

ISSUES FOR THE 21ST CENTURY

• Changing climate will cause global snowfall to decrease, with less snow falling during a shorter winter season; however, extreme snowfall events (blizzards) will increase in intensity.
• Increasing ocean temperatures with climate change will strengthen the intensity and frequency of tropical cyclones by the end of the century.

QUESTIONS TO CONSIDER

1. Why does the January 2016 storm qualify as a blizzard (rather than a snowstorm)? What is the difference between a blizzard and an ice storm?
2. How is climate change expected to affect winter storms and tropical cyclones during this century?

KEY**LEARNING**concepts**review**

Meteorology (p. 184) is the scientific study of the atmosphere. **Weather** (p. 184) is the short-term condition of the atmosphere.

Describe the characteristics of air masses that affect North America.

An **air mass** (p. 184) is a regional volume of air that is homogenous in humidity, stability, and cloud coverage and that may extend through the lower half of the troposphere. Air masses are categorized by their moisture content—**m** for maritime (wetter) and **c** for continental (drier)—and their temperature, a function of latitude—designated **A** (arctic), **P** (polar), **T** (tropical), **E** (equatorial), and **AA** (antarctic).

1. How does a source region influence the type of air mass that forms over it? Give specific examples of each basic classification.
2. What happens to air masses as they migrate to locations different from their source regions?

Identify and *describe* four types of atmospheric lifting mechanisms.

Air masses can rise through **convergent lifting** (p. 187), in which air flows converge and force some of the air to lift; **convectional lifting** (p. 187), in which air passing over warm surfaces gains buoyancy; **orographic lifting** (p. 186), in which air passes over a topographic barrier; and *frontal lifting*. Orographic lifting creates wetter windward slopes and drier leeward slopes situated in the **rain shadow** (p. 188) of the mountain. In North America, **chinook winds**, (p. 188) (called föhn or foehn winds in Europe), are the warm, downslope airflows characteristic of the leeward side of mountains. Conflicting air masses may produce a **cold front**, (p. 190) (and sometimes a zone of strong wind and rain), or a **warm front** (p. 190). A narrow band of thunderstorms, called a **squall line** (p. 190), often forms right along or slightly ahead of the front. Sometimes a **stationary front** (p. 191) develops between conflicting air masses, where airflow is parallel to the front on both sides.

3. What happens to air that is lifted as it passes over a mountain range? Describe the patterns of precipitation on the windward and leeward sides of the mountain range.
4. Differentiate between frontal lifting at an advancing cold front and at an advancing warm front, and describe the weather you would experience with each one.

Describe the life cycle of a midlatitude cyclonic storm system.

A **midlatitude cyclone** (p. 192), also known as an **extratropical cyclone** or *wave cyclone*, is a vast low-pressure system that forms along a front between cold and warm air masses and migrates with the westerly winds. **Cyclogenesis** (p. 192), the birth of the low-pressure circula-

tion, can occur off the west coast of North America, along the polar front, along the lee slopes of the Rockies, in the Gulf of Mexico, and along the East Coast. An **occluded front** (p. 193) is produced when a cold front overtakes a warm front in the maturing cyclone.

5. What is cyclogenesis? In what areas does it occur?
6. Describe the formation of an occluded front in the life cycle of a midlatitude cyclone and the associated weather.

Describe several types of data and imagery used for weather forecasting.

Synoptic analysis involves the collection of weather data at a specific time. Data needed for a surface weather map and forecast include barometric pressure, surface air temperatures, dew-point temperatures, wind speed and direction, clouds, sky conditions, and visibility. Weather data mainly come from satellites, weather balloons, ground-based weather stations, and Doppler radar.

7. What data is available from the *GOES* weather satellites? Name three types of GOES imagery you could use for a weather forecast.
8. Describe and explain the characteristic shape that signifies a tornado on a Doppler radar map.

Review various forms of violent weather—ice storms, thunderstorms, derechos, tornadoes, and tropical cyclones—by their formation and characteristics.

Ice storms are winter storms that involve freezing rain and sleet that can form ice coatings on roads, power lines, and crops. Isolated, short-lived **single-cell thunderstorms** (p. 199), also called *air mass thunderstorms*, are fueled by the rapid upward movement of warm, moist air that forms a towering cumulonimbus cloud. Such thunderstorms produce **lightning**, (p. 200) (electrical discharges in the atmosphere), and **thunder**, (p. 200) (sonic bangs produced by the rapid expansion of air after intense heating by lightning). Severe thunderstorms have multiple cells and are characterized by enormous turbulence and wind shear. **Supercell thunderstorms** (p. 201), or *supercells*, contain a deep, persistently rotating updraft, can range up to 10 km (6 mi) in diameter, and may produce heavy rain, large hail, and tornadoes. Strong linear winds in excess of 26 m/s (58 mph), known as **derechos** (p. 201), are associated with thunderstorms and bands of showers crossing a region.

A **tornado** (p. 202) is a violently rotating column of air in contact with the ground surface. In supercell thunderstorms, a cyclonic updraft—a **mesocyclone** (p. 202)— forms within a cumulonimbus cloud, sometimes rising to the mid-troposphere. The rising air and water vapor in the updraft is often visible as a **funnel cloud** (p. 202) pulsing from the bottom side of the parent cloud. A **waterspout** (p. 202) forms when a tornado circulation occurs over water.

Within tropical air masses, large low-pressure centers can form along easterly wave troughs. Under the right conditions, a tropical cyclone is produced. A **tropical cyclone** (p. 204) becomes a **hurricane**, **typhoon**, or *cyclone* (p. 204) when winds exceed 64 knots (119 kmph, 74 mph). Great damage occurs to coastal areas when hurricanes make **landfall** (p. 207) and when winds drive ocean water inland to form a **storm surge** (p. 207).

9. Briefly describe how lightning and thunder develop in association with a thunderstorm.
10. Describe the formation process of a mesocyclone.
11. Where are the seven primary areas for tropical cyclone formation?

GEO**SPATIAL** ANALYSIS

Current Weather Conditions

Weather data are collected worldwide to give forecasters the information they need to determine weather conditions ahead. These data keep people informed about what to wear, whether to bring an umbrella, and inform scheduling activities.

Activities

Go to the National Weather Service page at http://www.weather.gov/ to display a map of current weather-related watches and warnings.

1. What are the three current weather alerts that cover the largest geographic area?

2. Below the map click on the name of the alert next to its color square. Briefly describe the current weather situation for each alert.

3. Click on your current location to see a larger map. What weather advisories, if any, are currently active in your region? Click on each and give a brief description.

4. Click on your exact location on the Watches/Warnings map to get a local forecast. What weather advisories, if any, are currently active at your location?

5. How is your weather expected to change over the next 48-hours?

Go to http://www.wpc.ncep.noaa.gov/national_forecast/natfcst.php to bring up the National Forecast Charts showing fronts and regions of precipitation. The default map is "Today's Forecast" which is the first tab above the map.

6. Where are the midlatitude cyclones, if any, located on the map? How are the midlatitude cyclones on the map similar to and different from the idealized cyclone shown in Geosystems in Action 7? Be sure to compare the types of fronts, frontal orientation and any precipitation.

7. Click on the "Tomorrow's Forecast" tab. How has each of the fronts moved?

8. Click on the "Day 3 Forecast" tab. How has each of the fronts moved?

MasteringGeography™

Looking for additional review and test prep materials? Visit the Study Area in MasteringGeography™ to enhance your geographic literacy, spatial reasoning skills, and understanding of this chapter's content by accessing a variety of resources, including MapMaster™ interactive maps, videos, *Mobile Field Trips*, *Project Condor* Quadcopter videos, *In the News* RSS feeds, flashcards, web links, self-study quizzes, and an eText version of *Geosystems*.

8 Water Resources

Los Algodones,
Baja, Mexico

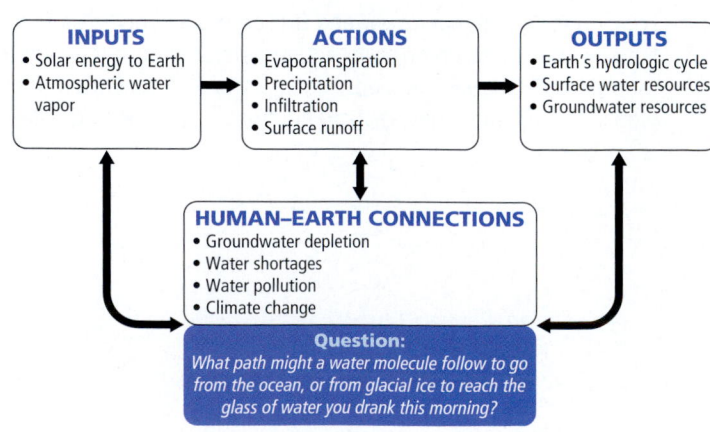

Morelos Dam, located on the U.S.–Mexico border, is the final dam on the Colorado River, which in most years does not reach its outlet in the Gulf of California. The dam diverts river flows into a canal that carries water westward to irrigate fields in the Mexicali Valley, the southern extension of California's Imperial Valley. [Peter McBride/Getty Images.]

KEY**LEARNING**concepts

After reading the chapter, you should be able to:

- **Describe** the origin of Earth's waters and *list* the locations of Earth's freshwater supply.

- **Illustrate** the hydrologic cycle with a simple sketch that labels each water pathway.

- **Construct** the water-budget equation and *explain* each of the components.

- **Discuss** water storage in lakes, reservoirs, and wetlands and *describe* the nature of hydroelectric power production.

- **List** and *describe* the elements of the groundwater environment.

- **Identify** critical aspects of present freshwater supplies, and *discuss* the U.S. water budget.

INPUTS
- Solar energy to Earth
- Atmospheric water vapor

ACTIONS
- Evapotranspiration
- Precipitation
- Infiltration
- Surface runoff

OUTPUTS
- Earth's hydrologic cycle
- Surface water resources
- Groundwater resources

HUMAN–EARTH CONNECTIONS
- Groundwater depletion
- Water shortages
- Water pollution
- Climate change

Question:
What path might a water molecule follow to go from the ocean, or from glacial ice to reach the glass of water you drank this morning?

▲**Figure GN 8.1 Fountains at the Bellagio.** The fountain's water supply is a privately owned 8.5-acre lake holding 22 million gallons of water. Although the water cycles, every year about 12 million gallons are lost to evaporation and leaky pipes. [Dave Stamboulis/Alamy.]

GEOSYSTEMSnow

Toward a Sustainable Water Future in Las Vegas, Nevada

The desert city of Las Vegas, Nevada, known for its casinos and entertainment, has more than 2 million residents and hosts over 40 million tourists every year. The 6.4 km (4.0 mi) Las Vegas strip is home to 15 of the world's largest resort hotels, including the Venetian, the MGM Grand, and the Bellagio, with over 60,000 rooms (**Figure GN 8.1**).

More than 90% of the city's water supply comes from the Colorado River—specifically, from Lake Mead, the largest reservoir in the United States. Is the supply for this vast amount of water, which runs through hotel and residential faucets, funnels into artificial lakes and swimming pools, and irrigates golf courses, sustainable? Given population growth and drought in the Colorado River watershed, the simple answer is no.

Water in the Desert Las Vegas sits in the middle of the driest, hottest region of the U.S. Southwest. Known for its abundant sunshine, the city receives an average 10.7 cm (4.2 in.) of precipitation each year—less than Phoenix, Arizona, by about half. In the summer, triple-digit temperatures are the norm, worsened by an urban heat island effect that raises summer nighttime temperatures 5 to 15 F° above the surrounding rural areas. Water arrives from the mountains of Colorado, Wyoming, and Utah via the Colorado River, which passes through numerous dams before entering Lake Mead, from which a portion is transferred by pipeline to Las Vegas.

Water Conservation As the city's population increased in the 1990s, water experts began to plan for water shortages. They focused first on resorts, requiring water-efficient technologies such as low-flow showerheads and launching an extensive water-recycling program. However, resorts account for only about 7% of the city's total water consumption. In the early 2000s, with the onset of drought conditions across the U.S. Southwest, water planners targeted residential developments, banning grass lawns in front yards, implementing mandatory watering schedules, and imposing water waste fees.

Despite water conservation efforts, water use in Las Vegas in 2015 was about 219 gallons per person per day. For comparison, per person consumption in Seattle is half that rate, and in San Francisco water use averages only 46 gallons per person per day. Las Vegas now relies on extensive water recycling: All used indoor water is piped to treatment plants where it is filtered, disinfected, and channeled back into Lake Mead. However, as metropolitan growth continues and river flows decline, the city's present level of overall water consumption cannot last.

A Sustainable Future? In 2008, as river flows declined and Lake Mead's water level dropped, the Southern Nevada Water Authority began constructing a new pipeline to draw water from the deepest part of the reservoir. Completed in 2015, the pipeline will allow the faucets to keep flowing in Las Vegas when Lake Mead drops to lower levels (**Figures GN 8.2 and 8.3**). Still underway is construction of a new pumping station to power the water transfer at an estimated cost of $1.5 billion.

How will Las Vegas, and other similar cities, achieve water sustainability? As world population grows, societies face ongoing challenges to turn water scarcity into water security.

1. What are two reasons that current water-use levels in Las Vegas are not sustainable?

2. Describe water conservation measures in Las Vegas. Are they sufficient to solve the city's water scarcity problems?

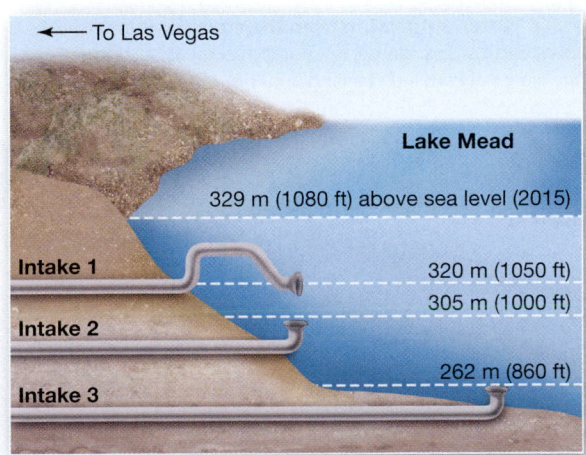

▲**Figure GN 8.2 Elevations of intake pipelines for water transfers from Lake Mead to Las Vegas.** The third intake, known as the "third straw," is 67 m (220 ft) below the 2015 surface level of the reservoir. [Source: NOAA U.S. Climate Resilience Toolkit and the Southern Nevada Water Authority.]

▲**Figure GN 8.3 Lake Mead "bathtub ring" shows higher reservoir levels.** During summer 2016, the reservoir dropped to 36% capacity, its lowest elevation since the 1930s just after dam construction. [Jim West/Alamy.]

Earth's physical processes are dependent on water, the essence of all life. Humans are about 70% water, as are plants and other animals. We use water to cook, bathe, wash clothes, dilute wastes, and run industrial processes. We use water to produce food, from the scale of small gardens to vast agricultural tracts (**Figure 8.1**). Water is Earth's most critical resource.

In the Solar System, water occurs in significant quantities only on our planet, covering 71% of Earth by area. Yet freshwater that people need for drinking, agriculture, and industry is not always naturally available where and when we want it. Consequently, we rearrange water resources to suit our needs. We drill wells to tap groundwater and dam and divert streams to redirect surface water, either across space (geographically, from one area to another) or over time (from one part of the calendar to another). All of this activity constitutes water-resource management. **Hydrology** is the science of water and its global circulation, distribution, and properties—focusing on water at and below Earth's surface.

Fortunately, water is a renewable resource, constantly cycling through the environment in the hydrologic cycle. Even so, people in 80 countries face impending water shortages owing to either water quantity or water quality, or both. Even when sufficient water is present, it may be unsuitable for drinking or other human needs. For many parts of the world, the question of water quantity and quality looms as the most important resource issue in this century.

Water on Earth

Earth's hydrosphere contains over 1 billion cubic kilometers of water. Much of Earth's water originated from icy comets and from hydrogen- and oxygen-laden debris within the planetesimals that coalesced to form the planet. As a planet forms, water from within migrates to its surface and outgasses.

Outgassing on Earth is a continuing process in which water and water vapor emerge from layers deep within and below the crust, 25 km (15.5 mi) or more below the surface, and are released in the form of gas (**Figure 8.2**). In the early atmosphere, massive quantities of outgassed water vapor condensed and then fell to Earth in torrential rains. For water to remain on Earth's surface, land temperatures had to drop below the boiling point of 100°C (212°F), something that occurred about 3.8 billion years ago. The lowest places across the face of Earth then began to fill with water—first forming ponds, then lakes and seas, and eventually ocean-sized bodies of water. Massive flows of water washed over the landscape, carrying both dissolved and solid materials to these early seas and oceans. Outgassing of water has continued ever since and is visible in volcanic eruptions, geysers, and seepage to the surface.

▼Figure 8.1 **The water we use.** Shoppers at a supermarket in Detroit, Michigan. [Jim West/Alamy.]

▼Figure 8.2 **Water outgassing from the crust.** Outgassing of water from Earth's crust occurs in geothermal areas such as Yellowstone National Park in Wyoming and Montana. [Zoonar GmbH/Alamy.]

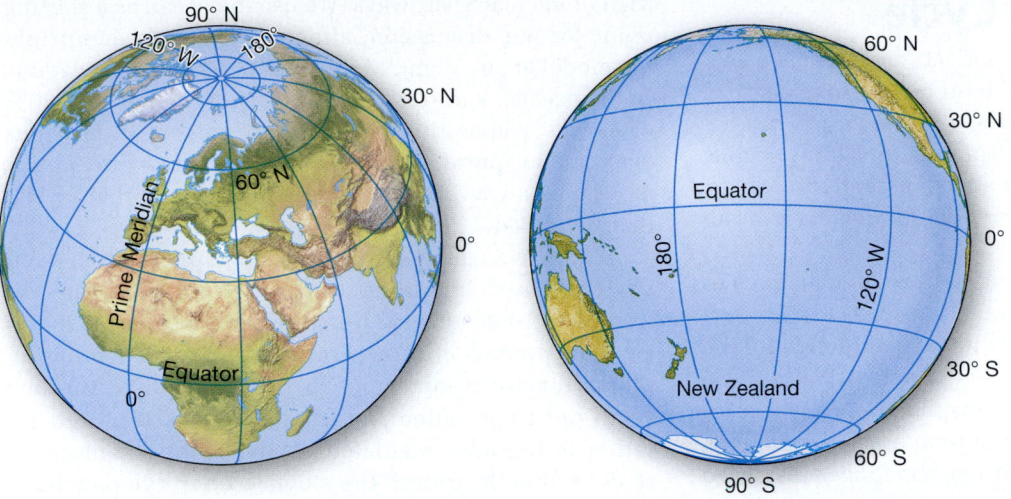

▲Figure 8.3 **Land and water hemispheres.** Two perspectives that roughly illustrate Earth's ocean hemisphere and land hemisphere.

Worldwide Equilibrium

Today, water is the most common compound on the surface of Earth. The present volume of water circulating throughout Earth's surface systems was attained approximately 2 billion years ago, and this quantity has remained relatively constant even though water is continuously gained and lost. Gains occur as water not previously at the surface emerges from within Earth's crust. Losses occur when water dissociates into hydrogen and oxygen and the hydrogen escapes Earth's gravity to space or when it breaks down and forms new compounds with other elements. The net result of these water inputs and outputs is that Earth's hydrosphere is in a steady-state equilibrium in terms of quantity.

Within this overall balance, the amount of water stored in glaciers and ice sheets varies, leading to periodic global changes in sea level (discussed in Chapters 10 and 16). The term **eustasy** refers to changes in global sea level caused by changes in the volume of water in the oceans. During cooler global climatic conditions, when more water is bound up in glaciers (at high latitudes and at high elevations worldwide) and in ice sheets (on Greenland and Antarctica), sea level lowers. During warmer periods, less water is stored as ice, so sea level

rises. Today, sea level is rising worldwide at an accelerating pace as higher temperatures melt more ice and, in addition, cause ocean water to thermally expand.

Distribution of Earth's Water Today

From a geographic point of view, ocean and land surfaces are distributed unevenly on Earth. If you examine a globe, it is obvious that most of Earth's continental land is in the Northern Hemisphere, whereas water dominates the surface in the Southern Hemisphere. In fact, when you look at Earth from certain angles, it appears to have an *oceanic hemisphere* and a *land hemisphere* (**Figure 8.3**).

The present distribution of all of Earth's water between the liquid and frozen states, between fresh and saline, and between surface and underground, is shown in **Figure 8.4**. The oceans contain 97.22% of all water, with about 48% of that water in the Pacific Ocean (as measured by ocean surface area). The remaining 2.78% is freshwater (nonoceanic) and is either surface or subsurface water. Ice sheets and glaciers contain the greatest amount of Earth's freshwater. Groundwater, either shallow or deep, is the second largest amount. The remaining freshwater, which resides in lakes and rivers, actually represents less than 1% of freshwater.

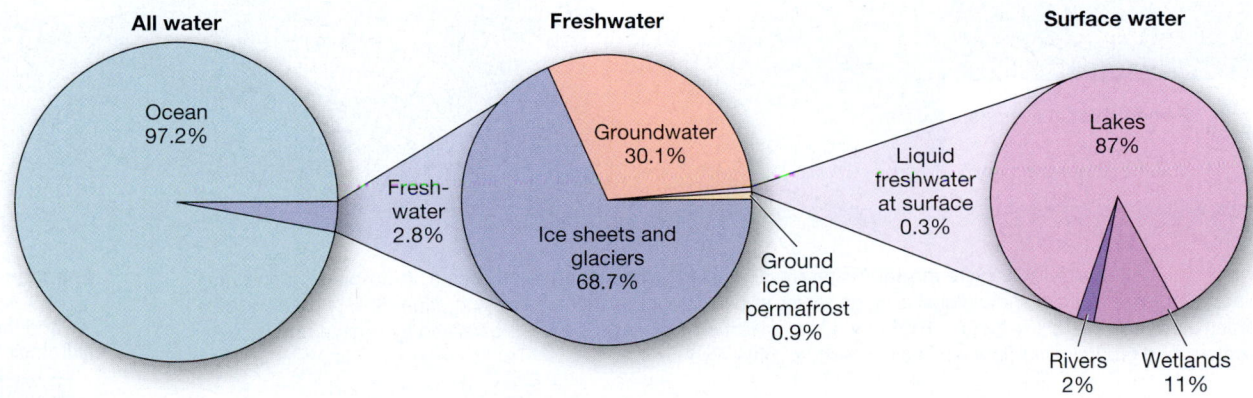

▲Figure 8.4 **Ocean and freshwater distribution on Earth.** The locations and percentages of all water on Earth, with detail of the freshwater portion (surface and subsurface) and a breakdown of the surface water component.

The Hydrologic Cycle

Vast currents of water, water vapor, ice, and associated energy are flowing continuously in an open, global system. Together, they form the **hydrologic cycle**, which has operated for billions of years, circulating and transforming water throughout Earth's lower atmosphere, hydrosphere, biosphere, and lithosphere to several kilometers beneath the surface.

The water cycle can be divided into three main components: atmosphere, surface, and subsurface. The residence time for a water molecule in any component of the cycle, and its effect on climate, is variable. Water has a short residence time in the atmosphere—an average of 10 days—where it plays a role in temporary fluctuations in regional weather patterns. Water has longer residence times in deep-ocean circulation, groundwater, and glacial ice (as long as 3000–10,000 years), where it acts to moderate temperature and climatic changes. These slower parts of the hydrologic cycle, the parts where water is stored and released over long periods, can have a "buffering" effect during periods of water shortage.

Water in the Atmosphere

Figure 8.5 is a simplified model of the hydrologic system, including global average values as percentages for each of the main pathways. We use the ocean as a starting point for our discussion, although we could jump into the model at any point. More than 97% of Earth's water is in the oceans, and it is over these water bodies that 86% of Earth's evaporation occurs. As discussed in previous chapters, **evaporation** is the net movement of free water molecules away from a wet surface into air that is less than saturated.

Water also moves into the atmosphere from land environments, including water moving from the soil into plant roots and passing through their leaves to the air. This process is **transpiration**. During transpiration, plants release water vapor to the atmosphere through small openings called stomata in their leaves. Transpiration is partially regulated by the plants themselves, as control cells around the stomata conserve or release water. On a hot day, a single tree can transpire hundreds of liters of water, and a forest, millions of liters. Evaporation and transpiration from Earth's land surfaces together make up **evapotranspiration**, which represents 14% of the water entering Earth's atmosphere in Figure 8.5.

The different parts of the cycle vary over different regions on Earth, depending on the local climate. This results in imbalances that lead to water surpluses in one place and water shortages in another.

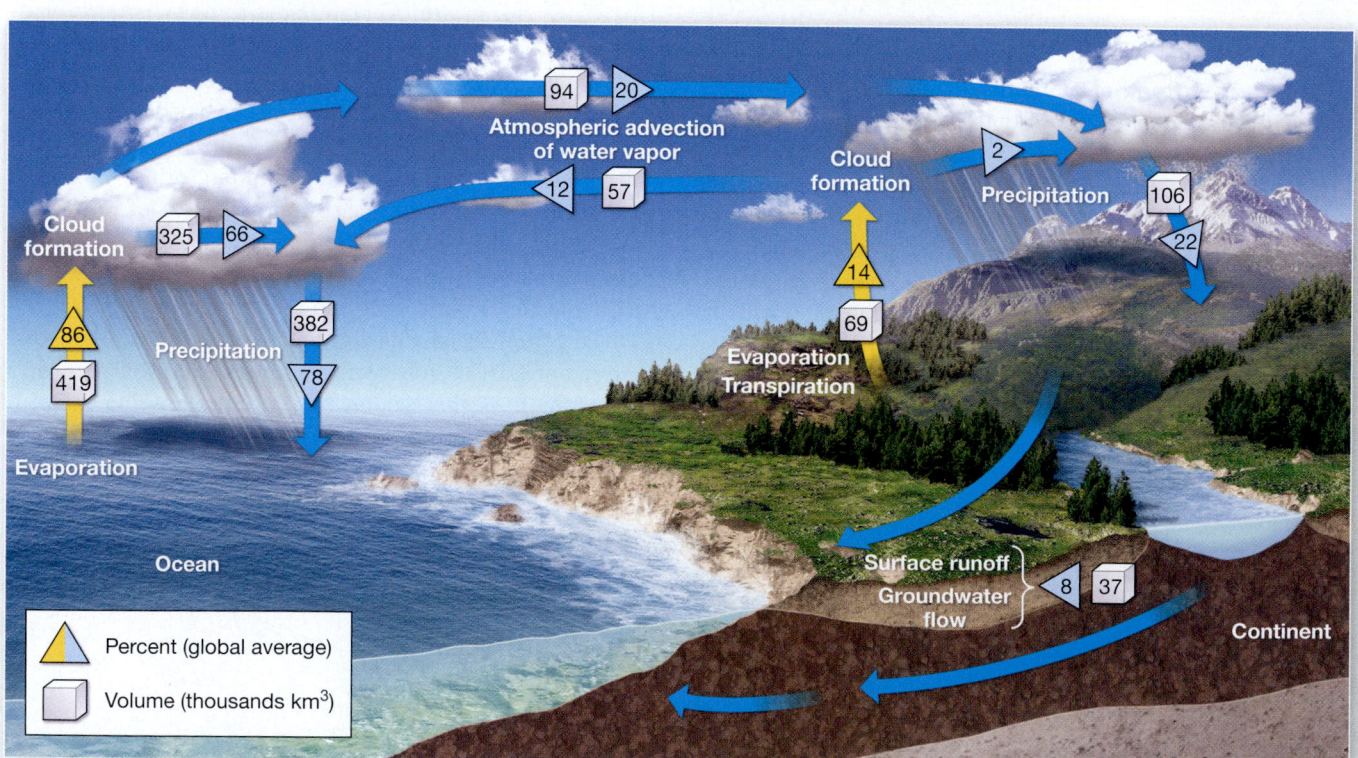

▲**Figure 8.5 The hydrologic cycle model.** Water travels endlessly through the hydrosphere, atmosphere, lithosphere, and biosphere. The triangles show global average values as percentages. Note that all evaporation (86% + 14% = 100%) equals all precipitation (78% + 22% = 100%) and that advection in the atmosphere is balanced by surface runoff, streamflow, and groundwater flow when all of Earth is considered.

Water at the Surface

Precipitation that reaches Earth's surface as rain follows two basic pathways: It either flows overland or soaks into the soil. Along the way, **interception** also occurs, in which precipitation lands on vegetation or other ground cover before reaching the surface. Intercepted water that drains across plant leaves and down their stems to the ground is known as *stem flow*. Precipitation that falls directly to the ground, including drips from vegetation that are not stem flow, is *throughfall*. Precipitation that reaches Earth's surface as snow may accumulate for a period of hours or days before melting, or it may accumulate as part of the snowpack that remains throughout winter and melts in the spring.

After reaching the ground surface as rain, or after snowmelt, water may soak into the subsurface through **infiltration**, or penetration of the soil surface (**Figure 8.6**). If the ground surface is impermeable (does not permit the passage of liquids), then the water will begin to flow downslope as **overland flow**, also known as **surface runoff**. Overland flow will also occur if the soil has been infiltrated to full capacity and is saturated. Excess water may remain in place on the surface in puddles or ponds, or it may flow until it forms channels—at this point, it becomes *streamflow*, a term that describes surface water flow in streams, rivers, and other channels.

Figure 8.5 shows that 8% of the water in the cycle is moving on or through land. Most of this movement—about 95%—comes from surface waters that wash across land as overland flow and streamflow. Only 5% of water movement is slow-moving subsurface groundwater. The surface component in rivers and streams is dynamic and fast moving compared to its sluggish subsurface counterpart.

Water in the Subsurface

Water that infiltrates into the subsurface moves downward into soil or rock by **percolation**, the slow passage of water through a porous substance (shown in Figure 8.6). The **soil-moisture zone** contains the volume of subsurface water stored in the soil that is accessible to plant roots. An estimated 76% of precipitation over land infiltrates the subsurface, and about 85% of this water returns to the atmosphere either by evaporation from soil or by transpiration from plants.

If the soil is saturated, then any water surplus within the soil body percolates downward into the deeper groundwater. At the point where the groundwater flow intersects a stream channel, water naturally discharges at the surface, producing **base flow**, which refers to the portion of streamflow that consists of groundwater.

Under natural conditions, streams and groundwater ultimately flow into oceans, thus continuing movement through the hydrologic cycle. In some cases, streams flow into closed lake basins, where water evaporates or soaks into the ground. Many streams flow into reservoirs behind dams, where water is stored until it evaporates or is released into the channel downstream. Groundwater flows slowly toward the sea, intersecting the surface or seeping from underground after reaching the coast, sometimes mixing with seawater in coastal wetlands and estuaries (bodies of water near the mouths of rivers). We discuss groundwater later in the chapter.

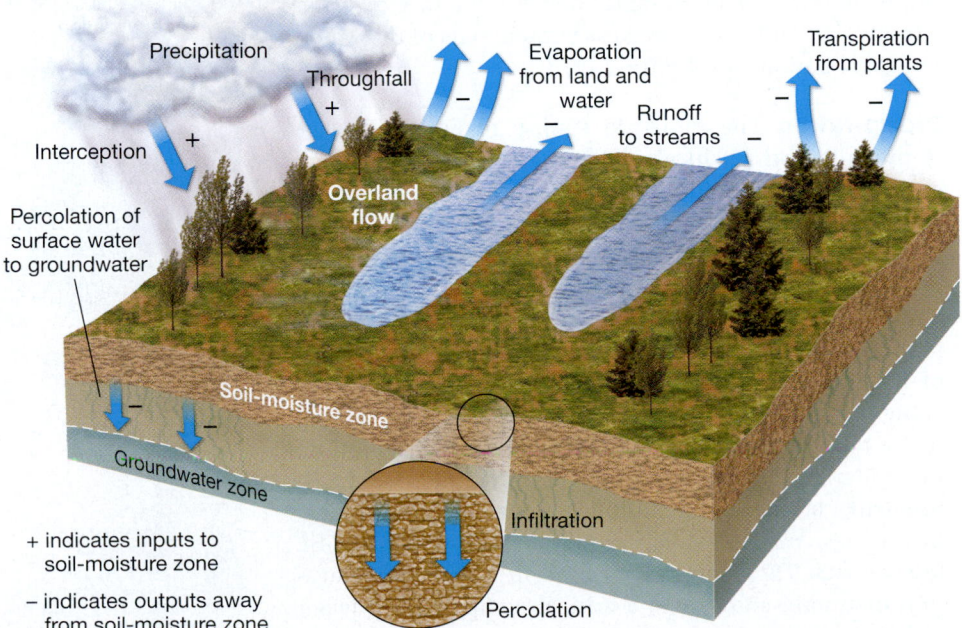

▲**Figure 8.6 Pathways for precipitation on Earth's surface.** The principal pathways for precipitation include interception by plants, throughfall to the ground, collection on the surface and overland flow to streams, transpiration from plants, evaporation from land and water, and gravitational water moving to subsurface groundwater.

Water Budgets and Resource Analysis

An effective method for assessing portions of the water cycle as they apply to water resources is to establish a **water budget** for any area of Earth's surface—a continent, country, region, field, or front yard. A water budget is derived from measuring the input of precipitation and its distribution and the outputs of evapotranspiration—including evaporation from ground surfaces and transpiration from plants—and surface runoff. Also included in this budget is moisture that is stored in the soil-moisture zone. Such a budget can cover any time frame, from minutes to years.

A water budget functions like a money budget: Precipitation is the income that must balance against expenditures for evaporation and transpiration. Soil-moisture storage acts as a savings account, accepting precipitation deposits and yielding withdrawals of water. Sometimes all expenditure demands are met, and any extra water results in a **surplus**. This water surplus often becomes surface runoff, feeding surface streams and lakes and recharging groundwater. At other times, precipitation and soil-moisture savings are inadequate to meet demands, and a **deficit**, or water shortage, results. Deficits cause drought conditions, discussed ahead in this chapter.

Components of the Water Budget

In its simplest form, a water budget shows that, for any area functioning as the accounting unit, the amount of water flowing into that unit is balanced by rate of water flowing out, plus or minus the change in water storage in the soil. To understand water-budget methodology, we begin by defining terms and concepts relating to water supply, demand, and storage as components of the water-budget equation (see Figure 8.11).

Precipitation The moisture supply to Earth's surface is precipitation (P) in all its forms, such as rain, sleet, snow, or hail. Precipitation is usually measured with an automated precipitation gauge at a weather station (**Figure 8.7a**). A common type of gauge contains a collection bucket sitting on an electronic weighing device. A wind shield around the top disrupts wind flow so that precipitation enters the bucket instead of crossing over the top of it. Antifreeze added to the collection bucket causes snow to melt to liquid, and a thin layer of oil floats on top of the water inside the bucket to prevent evaporation. Precipitation data come from regular precipitation measurements at more than 100,000 locations worldwide. In the U.S. West, snowfall is measured at 730 SNOTEL (SNOwpack TELemetry) sites used to assess high-elevation mountain snowpack, a critical component of water supply in this region (**Figure 8.7b**).

Figure 8.8 shows a map of precipitation patterns in the United States and Canada; note the influence of air masses and lifting mechanisms presented in Chapter 7.

For global annual precipitation patterns, see the map in Chapter 9, Figure 9.1.

Evapotranspiration The moisture demand at a given location is evapotranspiration, an actual expenditure of water to the atmosphere. For water budget analyses and other applications, this is called **actual evapotranspiration** (AE).

In contrast, **potential evapotranspiration** (PE) is the amount of water that would evaporate and transpire under optimum moisture conditions when adequate precipitation and soil moisture are present. We can illustrate this concept by filling a bowl with water and letting the water

(a) A standard precipitation gauge has an interior collection bucket sitting in an electronic weighing mechanism that registers weight gain from rain or snow accumulation.

(b) A SNOTEL site near Cordova, Alaska includes a rain gauge (left) and weather station (right).

▲Figure 8.7 **Measuring precipitation: A rain gauge and SNOTEL station.** [(a) Bobbé Christopherson. (b) Daniel Fisher/NRCS/USDA.]

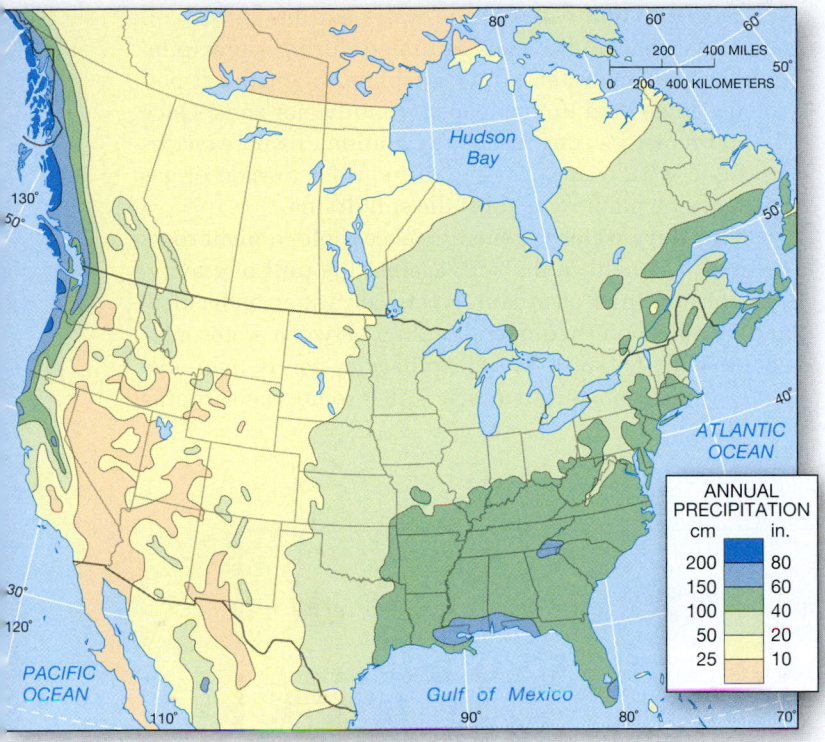

▲Figure **8.8 Precipitation in North America—the water supply.**
[Based on NWS, U.S. Department of Agriculture, and Environment Canada.]

geographer Charles Thornthwaite (1899–1963), who pioneered applied water-resource analysis. Note that higher values occur in the South, with the highest readings in the Southwest, a region with relatively high average air temperature and low relative humidity. Lower PE values are found at higher latitudes and elevations, which have lower average temperatures.

WORK**IT**OUT 8.2
Comparing Precipitation and Evapotranspiration Maps

Use the maps in Figures 8.8 and 8.9 to answer the following questions.

1. In which U.S state(s) is precipitation and evapotranspiration relatively high (as compared to the rest of the country)?
2. In which U.S. state(s) is annual precipitation less than 25 cm (10 in.) and annual evapotranspiration greater than 107 cm (42 in.)? Do you think this region generally has a water surplus or a water deficit?
3. In an area with low rainfall and high evapotranspiration all year, what is one way that farmers can increase water inputs to meet demand and avoid a water deficit?

evaporate: When the bowl becomes dry, some degree of evaporation demand remains. If the bowl could be constantly replenished with water, the amount of water that would evaporate given this constant supply is PE—the total water demand.

During the period when PE is greater than AE, the water demand must be met by moisture stored in the soil or by artificial irrigation. A deficit, or moisture shortage, results when PE cannot be satisfied by precipitation inputs, soil moisture storage, or additional inputs of water by irrigation. Under ideal conditions for plants, potential and actual amounts of evapotranspiration are about the same, so plants do not experience a water shortage.

Precise measurement of evapotranspiration is difficult. One method employs an *evaporation pan*, or evaporimeter. As evaporation occurs, water in measured amounts is automatically replaced in the pan, equaling the amount that evaporated. A more elaborate measurement device is a *lysimeter*, which isolates a representative volume of soil, subsoil, and plant cover to allow measurement of the moisture moving through the sampled area.

Figure 8.9 presents PE values for the United States and Canada derived by

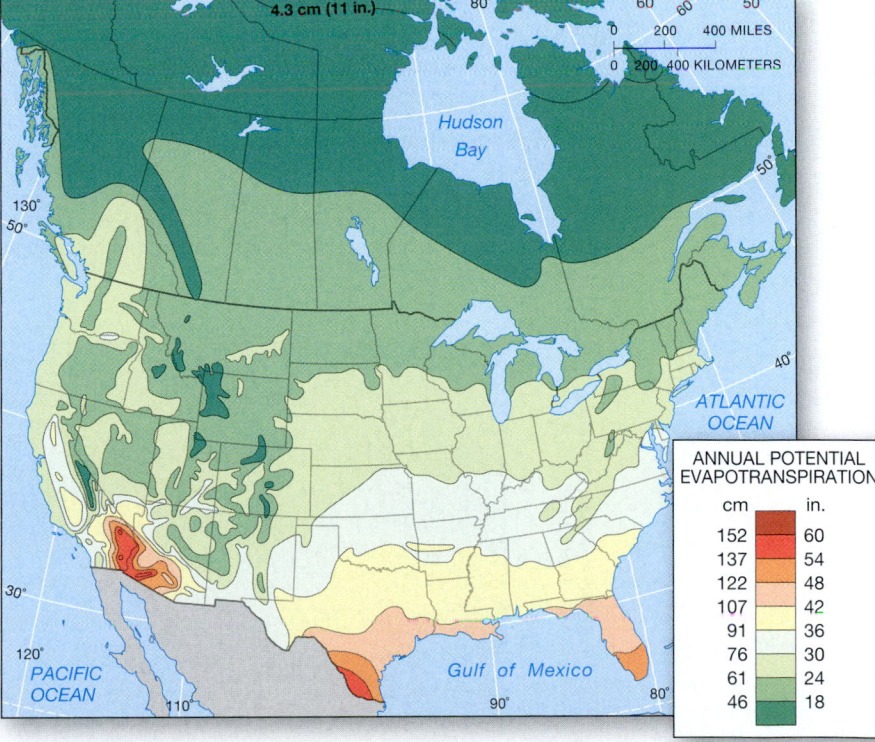

▲Figure **8.9 Potential evapotranspiration for the United States and Canada—the water demand.** [From C. W. Thornthwaite, "An approach toward a rational classification of climate," *Geographical Review* 38 (1948): 64, © American Geographical Society. Canadian data adapted from M. Sanderson, "The climates of Canada according to the new Thornthwaite classification," *Scientific Agriculture* 28 (1948): 501–517.]

Soil Moisture: Water Storage As part of the water budget, the volume of water in the subsurface soil-moisture zone that is accessible to plant roots is **soil-moisture storage** (S). This is the savings account of water that receives deposits (recharge) and provides for withdrawals (utilization).

The soil-moisture environment includes three categories of water—gravitational, capillary, and hygroscopic. Gravitational water fills the soil pore spaces and then drains downward under the force of gravity. Capillary water and hygroscopic water remain in the soil-moisture zone, but only capillary water is accessible to plants (**Figure 8.10a**).

Gravitational water is the water surplus in the soil body after the soil becomes saturated during a precipitation event. This water is unavailable to plants, as it percolates downward to the deeper groundwater zone. Once the soil-moisture zone reaches saturation, the pore spaces are filled with water, leaving no room for oxygen or gas exchange by plant roots until the soil drains.

Capillary water is generally accessible to plant roots because it is held in the soil, against the pull of gravity, by cohesion (hydrogen bonds between water molecules) and by adhesion (hydrogen bonding between water molecules and the soil). Most capillary water is *available water* in soil-moisture storage. After some water drains

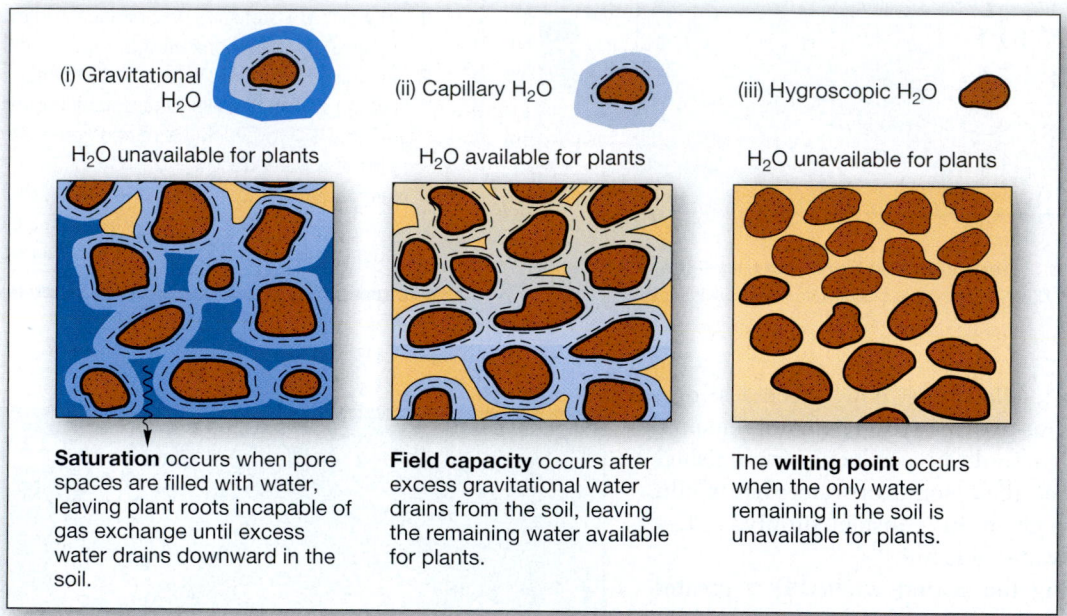

(a) The (i) gravitational, (ii) capillary, and (iii) hygroscopic categories of water exist in the soil moisture environment. Note that some capillary water is bound to hygroscopic water on soil particles and is not available to plants.

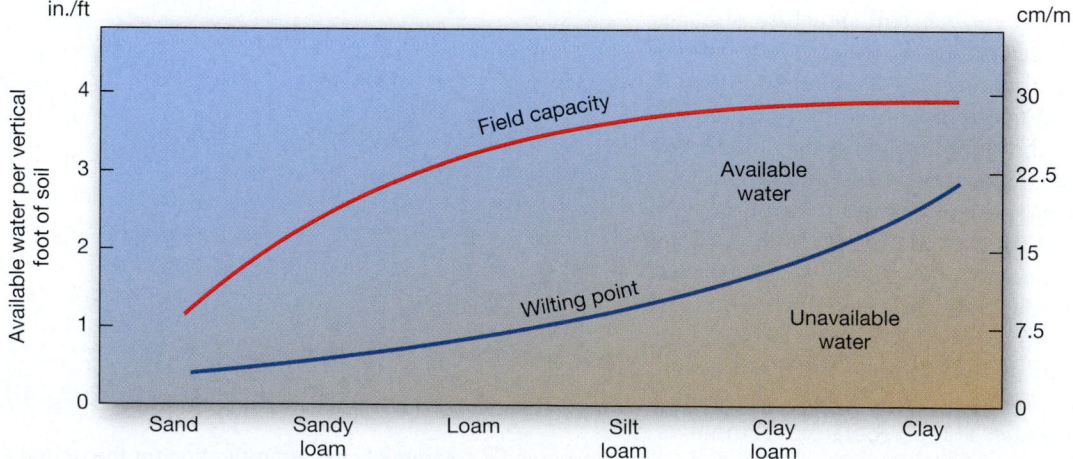

(b) The relationship between soil-moisture availability and soil texture determines the distance between the two curves that show field capacity and wilting point. A loam soil (one-third each of sand, silt, and clay) has roughly the most available water per vertical foot of soil exposed to plant roots.

▲**Figure 8.10 Types and availability of soil moisture.** [(b) NRCS/USDA.]

from the larger pore spaces, the amount of available water remaining for plants is termed **field capacity**, or storage capacity. This water can meet PE demands through the capillary action of plant roots and surface evaporation.

Field capacity is specific to each soil type and depends on **porosity**, which refers to the spaces, or voids, between particles in a given volume of soil. These voids contain the liquids and gases in the soil (as opposed to the soil particles or organic matter). The texture and structure of the soil dictate the percentage of pore spaces. A sandy soil has relatively large particles and large pore spaces, but the total overall volume of pore space is small. A clay soil has smaller particles, creating numerous small pore spaces so that the overall volume of pore space is large. Thus we say that clay soil has higher porosity than sandy soil. (Further discussion is in Chapter 18.)

When only a small amount of soil moisture is present, it may be unavailable to plants. **Hygroscopic water** is inaccessible to plants because it is a molecule-thin layer that is tightly bound to each soil particle by the hydrogen bonding of water molecules. Hygroscopic water exists in all climates, even in deserts, but it is unavailable to meet PE demands. Soil moisture is at the **wilting point** for plants when all that remains is this inaccessible water; plants wilt and eventually die after a prolonged period at this degree of moisture stress. In agriculture, farmers use irrigation to avoid a deficit and enhance plant growth with adequate amounts of available water.

Figure 8.10b shows the relation of soil texture to soil-moisture content. Different plant species send roots to different depths and therefore reach different amounts of soil moisture. A soil blend that maximizes available water is best for plants.

When water demand exceeds the precipitation supply, **soil-moisture utilization**—usage by plants of the available moisture in the soil—occurs. As water is removed from the soil, plants have increased difficulty extracting the amount of moisture they need. Eventually, even though a small amount of water may remain in the soil, plants may be unable to use it.

When water infiltrates the soil and replenishes available water, whether from natural precipitation or artificial irrigation, **soil-moisture recharge** occurs. The property of the soil that determines the rate of soil-moisture recharge is its **permeability**, the ability of water to flow through rock or soil, which depends on particle sizes and the shape and packing of soil grains.

The Water-Budget Equation

Figure 8.11 presents the water-budget equation, which states that, for any given location or portion of the hydrologic cycle, the water inputs are equal to the water outputs plus or minus the change in water storage. The delta symbol, Δ, means "change"—in this case, the change in soil-moisture storage, which includes both recharge and utilization.

In summary, precipitation (mostly rain and snow) provides the moisture input. This supply is distributed as actual water undergoing evaporation and plant transpiration, extra water running into streams and subsurface groundwater, and water that moves in and out of soil-moisture storage. As in all equations, the two sides must balance; that is, the precipitation input (left side) must equal the outputs (right side).

Ultimately, the climatic factors of precipitation and temperature (as it affects evapotranspiration) determine the water budget. However, local vegetation, soils, and land use also influence the movement of water through the hydrologic cycle in a given area.

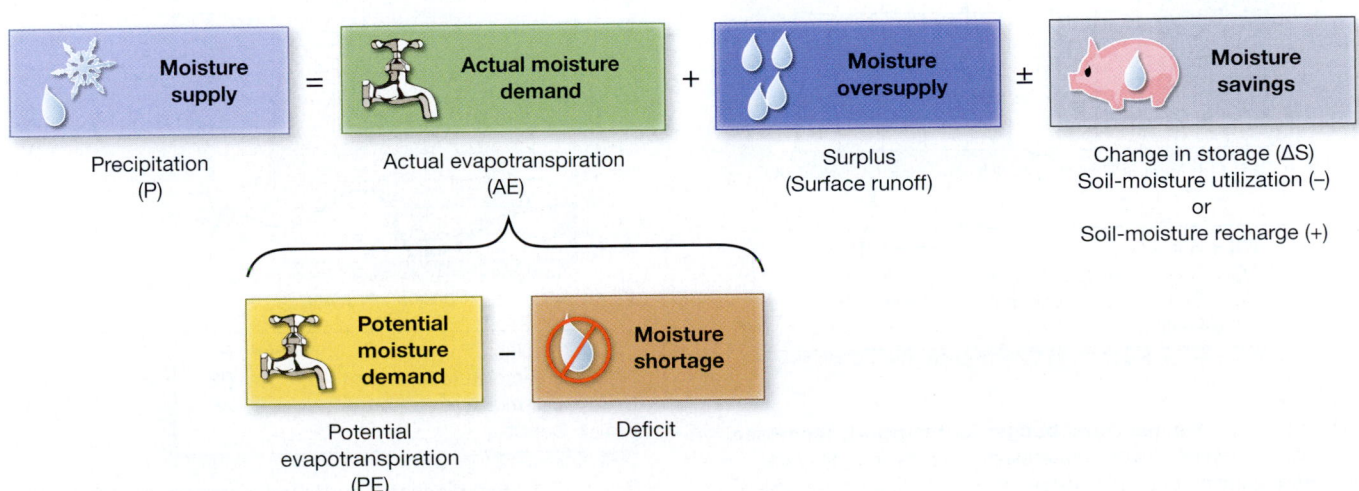

▲**Figure 8.11** The water-budget equation explained.

Sample Water Budgets

Water budgets can be used to assess water supply and demand for any spatial scale over any period of time (minutes to years to millennia). As an example, the water-budget graph for the city of Kingsport, Tennessee, shows a net surplus during the cooler time from October to May (**Figure 8.12**). The surplus disappears during the warm days from June through September. During this time, water demand is satisfied through soil-moisture utilization, with a small summer soil-moisture deficit.

The Kingsport water budget is typical of a humid continental region. **Figure 8.13** presents water-budget graphs for two other climatic regimes: the cities of Berkeley, California, which has a summer minimum in precipitation, and Phoenix, Arizona, which has low precipitation throughout the year. Compare the size and timing of the water deficits at these locations with the Kingsport graph.

Drought: The Water Deficit

In simplest terms, **drought** is an extended period of dry conditions caused by lower precipitation and higher temperatures. During a drought, dry conditions last long enough to cause environmental problems, such as declining fish populations associated with low streamflow, or socioeconomic problems, such as the financial losses resulting from crop failure. Yet drought is a complex concept. Meteorologists use drought to refer to dry weather conditions. Farmers use drought to refer to soil-moisture shortages as they affect crop yields. Hydrologists use drought in the context of snowpack declines, lowered

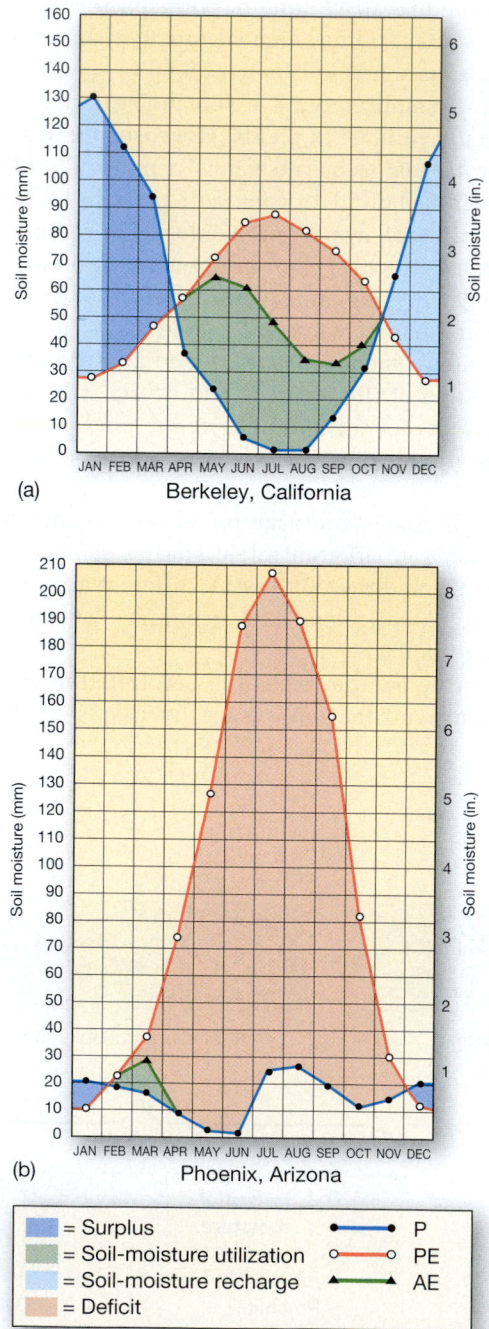

(a)   Berkeley, California

(b)   Phoenix, Arizona

= Surplus   ● P
= Soil-moisture utilization   ○ PE
= Soil-moisture recharge   ▲ AE
= Deficit

▲**Figure 8.13 Sample water budgets for stations near Berkeley and Phoenix.** Note the difference in the size of the water deficit between Berkeley and Phoenix, and compare it to the Kingsport deficit in Figure 8.12.

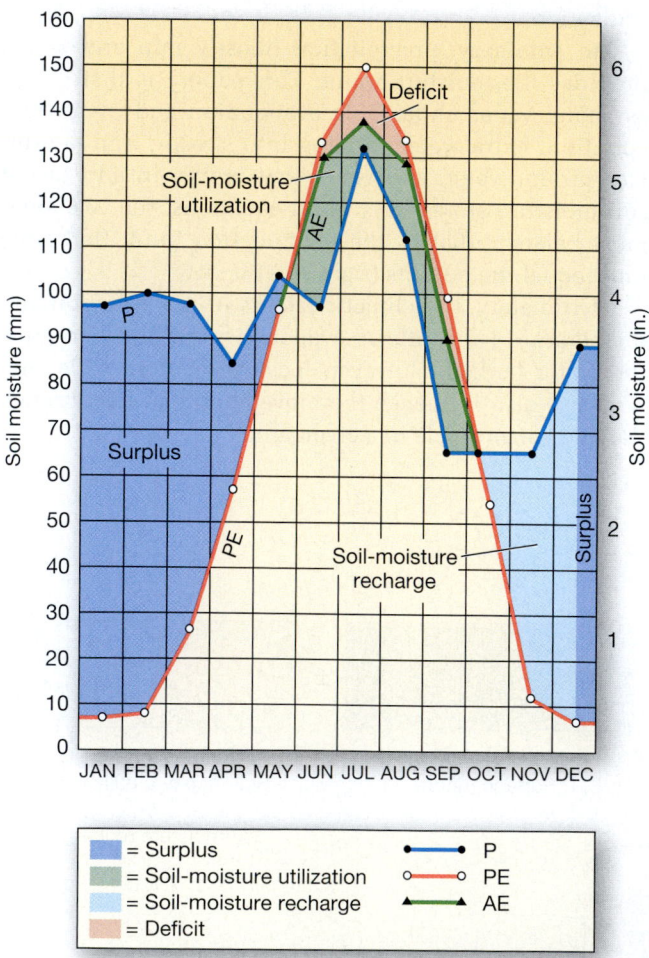

= Surplus   ● P
= Soil-moisture utilization   ○ PE
= Soil-moisture recharge   ▲ AE
= Deficit

▲**Figure 8.12 Sample water budget for Kingsport, Tennessee.** Compare the average plots for precipitation inputs and potential evapotranspiration outputs to determine the condition of the soil-moisture environment. A typical pattern for Kingsport exhibits a spring surplus, summer soil-moisture utilization, a small summer deficit, autumn soil-moisture recharge, and a year-ending surplus.

streamflows and reservoir levels, and groundwater removal. Drought also operates on a variety of different time scales, from weeks to months to years.

In July of 2012, the U.S. Department of Agriculture declared almost one-third of all U.S. counties federal disaster areas owing to drought conditions—the largest natural disaster area ever declared. According to the National Climatic Data Center, 23 drought events that occurred from 1980 to 2015 cost over $1 billion each, making drought one of the costliest U.S. weather-related events. In the United States, scientists and resource managers use the Palmer Drought Indices to assess drought conditions. See http://www.drought.unl.edu/ for a weekly Drought Monitor map.

California's Ongoing Drought Ongoing since 2011, California's drought has led to water restrictions for urban communities and economic losses for farmers. Precipitation in California is typically highest from December through March, when an average 66% of total precipitation arrives. Snowpack in the Sierra Nevada normally accounts for about 30% of the state's total water supply. In 2012, meteorologists identified a persistent ridge of high pressure, dubbed the "ridiculously resilient ridge," as a main cause of decreased precipitation. Drought conditions worsened during the 2014–2015 winter, when the overall Sierra Nevada snowpack measured only 5% of normal. On April 1, 2015, the date when snowpack is typically at its highest level before the spring melt begins, some mountain weather stations recorded no snow.

In early 2014, water shortages led to conditions so severe that California's governor declared a state of emergency, calling for all Californians to voluntarily conserve water. In 2015, the governor officially ordered cities to cut water use by 25%—the first mandatory water restrictions in state history. Suggested strategies were to impose higher rates and fees for water use; restrict watering of golf courses, campuses, and cemeteries; use only nonpotable water for median strips on streets; remove millions of square meters of grass lawns throughout the state; and impose fines for violating water use restrictions. For many California residents, this meant shorter and less frequent showers, fewer loads of laundry, and watching outdoor lawns turn brown. Drought continued into 2016, even after the 2015 El Niño–Southern Oscillation (ENSO) event. Rain and snowmelt filled northern California reservoirs, providing some drought relief, but the southern part of the state remained dry (**Figure 8.14**).

Drought and Climate Change Scientists suggest that multiple years of higher-than-average precipitation are necessary to alleviate the prolonged effects of the California drought. As climate change alters temperature and precipitation patterns, and if California remains under persistent high pressure, today's "drought" (usually a temporary condition) may become part of a new and drier permanent climate. Even if the drought ends, water experts are now wondering if California's water supply can meet the state's total water demand from agriculture and urban use.

Drought is a natural and recurrent feature of climate. However, scientists are finding mounting evidence that in many world regions increased aridity, or climatic dryness, links to global climate change and the expansion of the subtropical dry zones to higher latitudes. The effects of lasting drought are worsened by steady population growth and ever-increasing demand on regional water supplies. Focus Study 8.1 discusses water supply, drought, and increasing water demand in the Colorado River watershed.

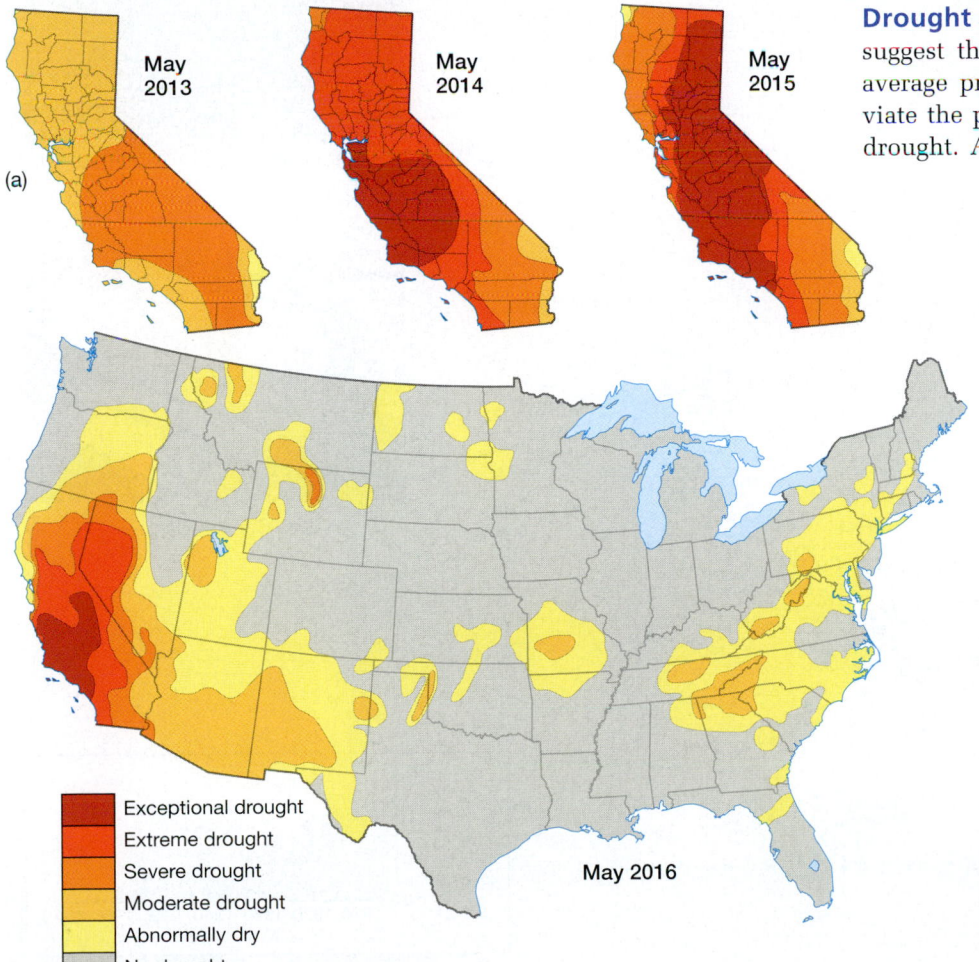

(a)

May 2013

May 2014

May 2015

Exceptional drought
Extreme drought
Severe drought
Moderate drought
Abnormally dry
No drought

May 2016

(b)

▲**Figure 8.14 California drought map, May 2013 to May 2015 and U.S. drought map for 2016.**
[(a) National Drought Mitigation Center, U.S. Drought Monitor archives, NOAA/NWS/NCEP/CPC. (b) NOAA, climate.gov.]

FOCUSstudy 8.1 Climate Change
The Colorado River: A System Out of Balance

The Colorado River basin encompasses parts of seven states, all growing in population. (In 2015, Wyoming, Utah, Nevada, Colorado, and Arizona were ranked among the top 10 fastest-growing U.S. states.) The expanding urban areas of Las Vegas, Phoenix, Denver, San Diego, and Albuquerque all depend on Colorado River water, which supplies nearly 40 million people.

Allocating the Colorado's Water

As settlement of the U.S. West increased in the late 1800s, irrigation and water storage became important issues in lands where precipitation was not enough to meet water demand. Common thought was that water *reclamation*, the name given to irrigation projects at that time, would

"reclaim" the arid lands of the West, making them suitable for human settlement. In 1902, the government established the U.S. Reclamation Service, today known as the Bureau of Reclamation, to develop water projects on federal lands in the West. Because the Colorado River is the region's major water source, allocating its water among users was critical for development.

In 1923, six states signed the Colorado River Compact, which divided water allocations in the Colorado River basin between the upper basin and the lower basin (**Figure 8.1.1**). (The seventh basin state, Arizona, signed the compact 21 years later.)

In 1928, Congress authorized Hoover Dam as the basin's first major reclamation project. This dam would store water, divert

water for irrigation, provide flood control downstream, and generate hydroelectric power. This project included construction of a canal to carry water for irrigation into the Imperial Valley of California as well as construction of the Imperial Dam. Subsequent projects carried Colorado River water 390 km (240 mi) to Los Angeles. The most recent effort to redistribute Colorado River water was the Central Arizona Project, which carries water to the cities of Phoenix and Tucson.

Today, the Colorado River flows through a series of dams and reservoirs downstream from its confluence with the Green River, its largest tributary (Figure 8.1.1).

- Glen Canyon Dam, forming the major reservoir of Lake Powell

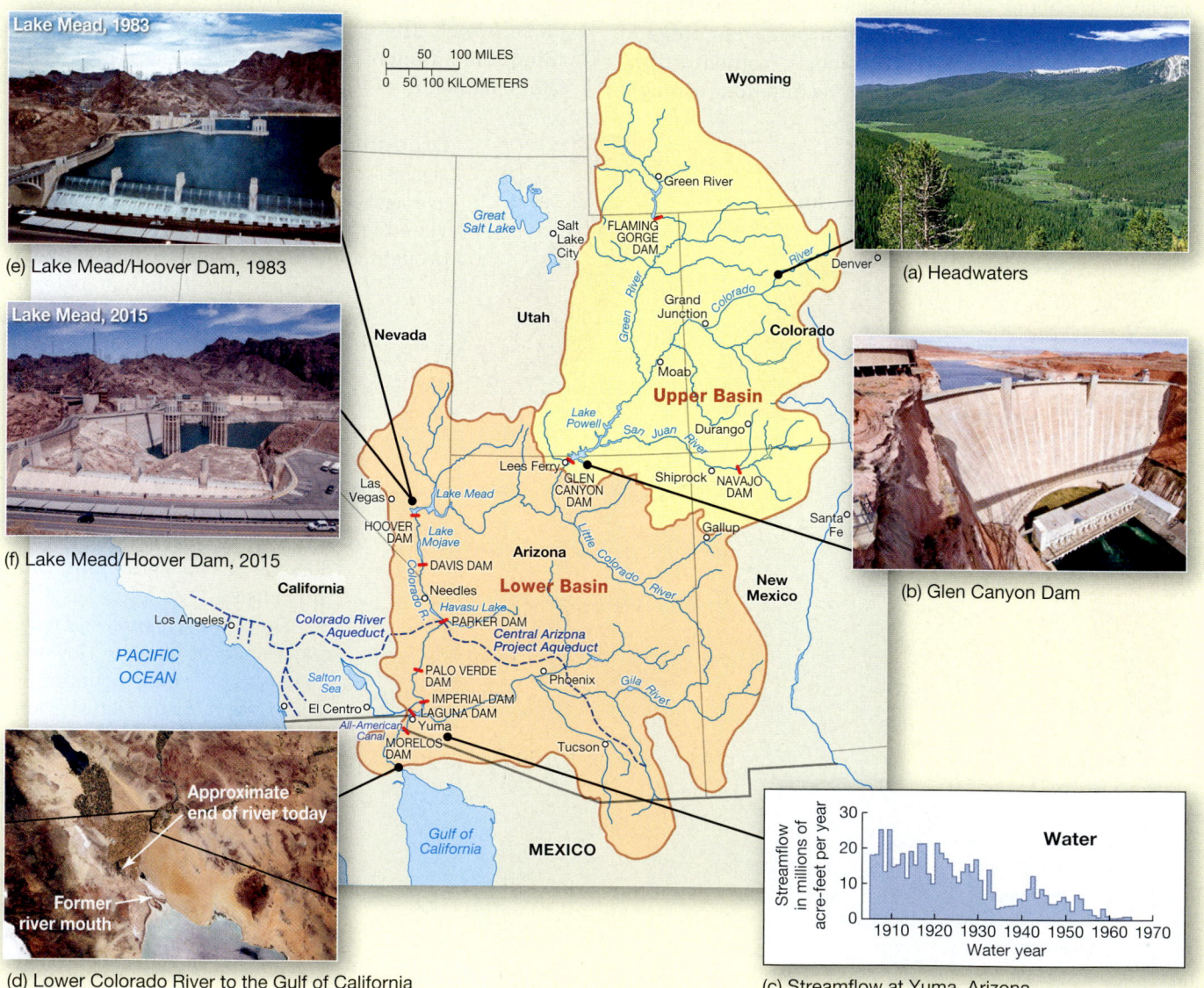

(e) Lake Mead/Hoover Dam, 1983

(f) Lake Mead/Hoover Dam, 2015

(a) Headwaters

(b) Glen Canyon Dam

(d) Lower Colorado River to the Gulf of California

(c) Streamflow at Yuma, Arizona

▲**Figure 8.1.1 The Colorado River drainage basin.** [(a–b), (f) Bobbé Christopherson. (e) Robert Christopherson. (c) Data from USGS, *National Water Summary 1984*, Water Supply Paper 2275, p. 55. (d) *Terra* image, NASA/GSFC.]

- Hoover Dam, forming the largest U.S. reservoir, Lake Mead
- Davis Dam, built to control the releases from Hoover Dam
- Parker Dam, forming Lake Havasu, the water source for water transfers to southern California and Arizona
- Palo Verde, Imperial, and Laguna dams, built to divert water for irrigation
- Morelos Dam at the Mexican border

In the 1960s, after completion of Glen Canyon Dam, the river's annual streamflow at Yuma, Arizona, fell to nearly zero (Figure 8.1.1c). At Morelos Dam, Mexico diverts the remaining flow for irrigation so the river now ends short of its former mouth in the Gulf of California (Figure 8.1.1d).

Problems with Water Allocations

The most notable flaw in long-range planning and water distribution in the Colorado River system relates to the river's highly variable flows, typical of a river that rises in a wet region, but flows mostly through drylands. The government based the terms of the Colorado River Compact on the river's average annual flows from 1914 up to the compact signing in 1923—an exceptionally high 18.8 million acre-feet (maf). That amount was perceived as more than enough to supply the upper and lower basins with 7.5 maf each and, later, to allow Mexico to receive 1.5 maf.

Scientific studies now reveal the problems in long-term planning based on data from such a short time period. Climate reconstructions for about the past 1000 years suggest that the only other time Colorado River flows were at the high 1914–1923 level was between 1606 and 1625. Since 1923, average annual river flows have varied from a high of 24.5 maf in 1984 to lows near 5.0 maf in 1934, 1977, and 2002. Thus, planners overestimated river flows, a situation that creates shortfalls when water demand exceeds water supply.

As Lake Powell filled from 1963 to 1983, planners discovered other water-budget problems. At full capacity, the reservoir loses an estimated 1 to 2 maf of water every year as water is absorbed by the porous sandstone forming the reservoir's boundary and evaporates from the water surface and streamside vegetation. These losses are additional water demands. In sum, the seven states want rights to Colorado River water that amount to more than

the river contains most years.

Drought and Water Management

Higher temperatures and evaporation rates, as well as reduced mountain snowpack and earlier spring melt, have caused drought in the Colorado River basin since 2000. The period from 2000 to 2010 marked the lowest 10-year-average total flow of the Colorado River in the 103-year record, with 2002 dropping to an all-time record low. Water inflow to Lake Powell is now less than one-third of long-term averages (in the lowest year, 2002, it ran at just 25%). According to regional tree-ring records, nine droughts have affected the American Southwest since 1226 C.E., with four of those lasting more than 20 years. However, the present drought is the first to occur with increasing demand for water as population grows throughout the region.

The effects of ongoing drought are evident in declining reservoir levels throughout the Colorado River system (Figure 8.1.1e and Figure 8.1.1f). This is the water reserve intended to offset variable river flows, especially during periods of drought. The largest reservoirs—Lake Mead and Lake Powell—account for over 80% of total system storage. In mid-2016, the level of Lake Mead behind Hoover Dam dropped to 328 m (1076 ft), far below the 375-m (1229-ft) full capacity reached in July 1983.

Lake Mead may soon drop to the critical 305-m (1000-ft) level below which water cannot enter the first two intake pipelines for transfers to Las Vegas or to CAP canals. Low reservoir levels also degrade hydropower capability because the efficiency of electrical output depends on the height of the reservoir—higher water means more water pressure, supplying more

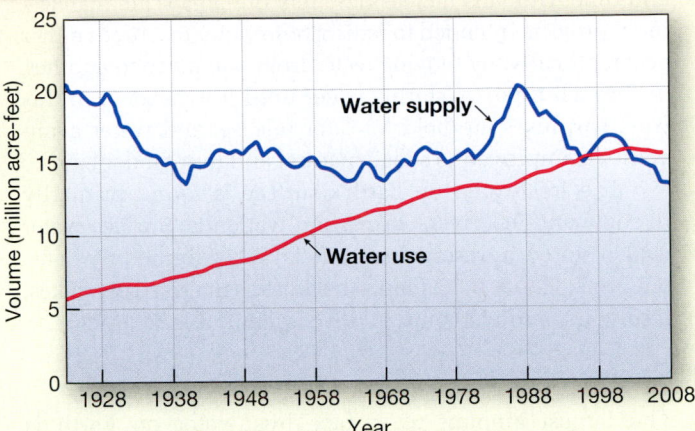

▲**Figure 8.1.2 Colorado River basin: Historical water supply and use, 1923–2008.** Plots for supply and use are 10-year running averages. Use includes Mexico's allotment and water losses to evaporation and vegetation. [U.S. Department of Interior, Bureau of Reclamation, 2012, Colorado River Basin Water Supply and Demand Study, Executive Summary, Fig. 2, page 10. See http://www.usbr.gov/lc/region/programs/crbstudy/finalreport/index.html.]

energy to turn the turbines. Scientists agree that the overall trend of declining precipitation is likely to continue. Increasing evaporation associated with rising temperatures across the Southwest and increasing human water use will make drought recovery slower than in the past.

Although the Colorado River continues to meet its water allotments, future projections show that the supply cannot continue to meet demand (**Figure 8.1.2**). As discussed in Geosystems Now, water users in parts of the Colorado River basin have initiated water-management practices to reduce the tremendous demand for water. Lowering water demand, rather than focusing solely on water supply, is the best solution to balance the Colorado River water budget. For more information, see https://www.doi.gov/water/owdi.cr.drought/en/index.html.

1. For what purposes has the Colorado River been dammed and diverted? Which major cities receive Colorado River water?

2. Will Colorado River flows be adequate to meet future demands in the region? Why or why not?

APPLYconcepts Classify these system components of the Colorado River basin as Inputs, Actions, or Outputs: drought, evaporation, snowfall, human uses of water, melting, reduced stream flow, higher temperatures

Inputs	
Actions	
Outputs	

Surface Water Resources

Water distribution over Earth's surface is uneven over space and time. Humans increasingly rely on large-scale management projects intended to redistribute water resources either geographically, by moving water from one place to another, or through time, by storing water until it is needed. In this way, surpluses are held for later release, and water availability is improved to satisfy natural and human demands.

The freshwater on Earth's surface is found primarily in snow and ice, rivers, lakes, and wetlands. Surface water is also stored in reservoirs, artificial lakes formed by dams on rivers. **Figure 8.15** shows the world's major rivers, lakes, reservoirs, and wetlands, all discussed in this section.

Snow and Ice

The largest amount of surface freshwater on Earth is stored in glaciers, permafrost, and polar ice (review Figure 8.4). Seasonal melting from glaciers and the annual snowpack in temperate regions feeds streamflow, contributing to water supplies. Snowpack melting captured in reservoirs behind dams is a primary water source for humans in many parts of the world.

Glaciers provide a form of water storage, although rising temperatures associated with recent climate change are causing accelerated rates of glacial melting. The residence time of water in glaciers can range between decades and centuries, and the relatively small, but continuous meltwater from glaciers can sustain streamflow throughout the year (Chapter 17 discusses glaciers and ice sheets).

On Asia's Tibetan Plateau, the world's largest and highest plateau at 3350 km (11,000 ft) elevation, climate change is causing mountain glaciers to recede at rates faster than anywhere else in the world (**Figure 8.16**). More than 1000 lakes store water on this plateau, forming the headwaters for several of the world's longest rivers. Almost half the world's population lives within the watersheds of these rivers; the Yangtze and Yellow Rivers (both flowing eastward through China) alone supply water to approximately 520 million people in China.

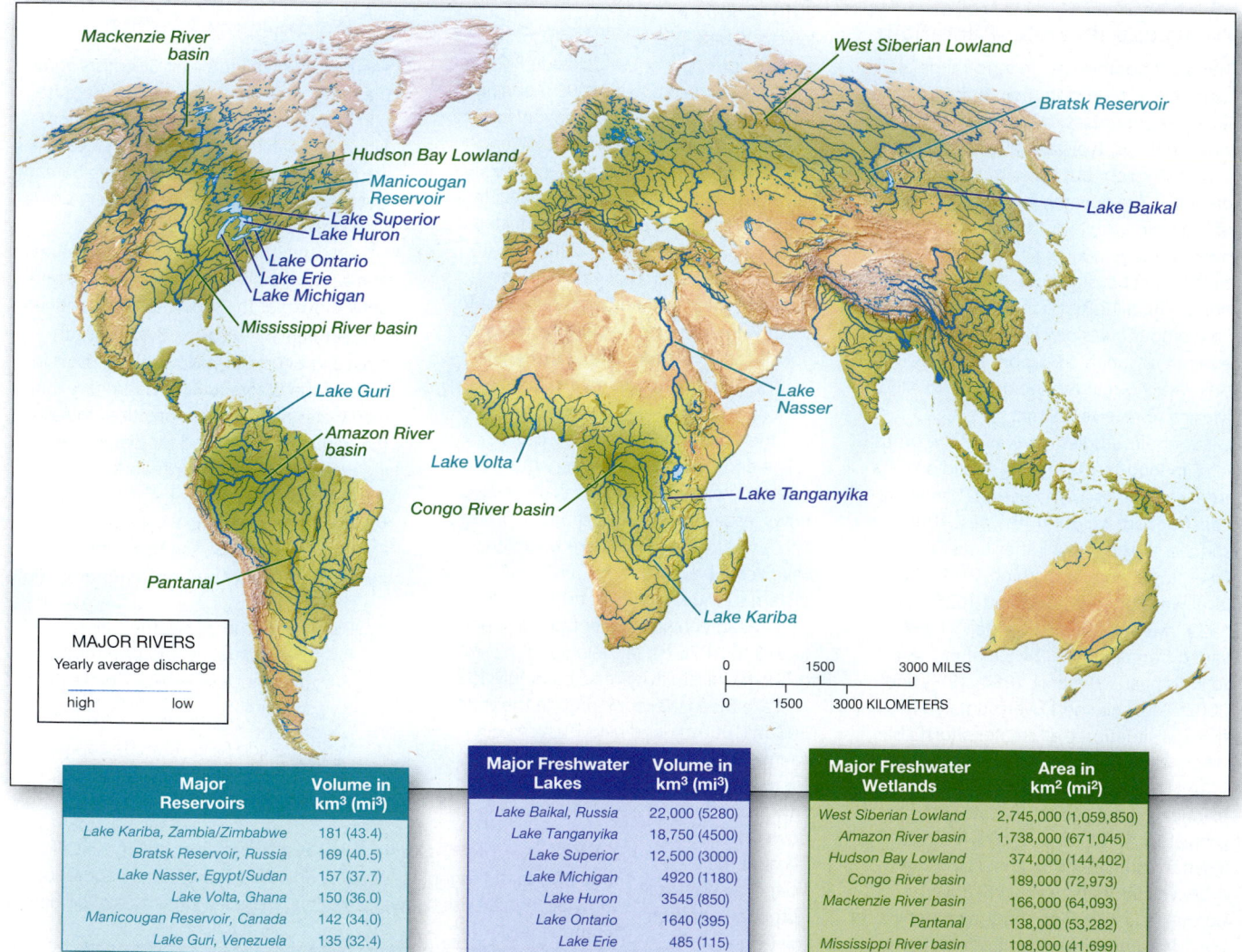

Major Reservoirs	Volume in km³ (mi³)
Lake Kariba, Zambia/Zimbabwe	181 (43.4)
Bratsk Reservoir, Russia	169 (40.5)
Lake Nasser, Egypt/Sudan	157 (37.7)
Lake Volta, Ghana	150 (36.0)
Manicougan Reservoir, Canada	142 (34.0)
Lake Guri, Venezuela	135 (32.4)

Major Freshwater Lakes	Volume in km³ (mi³)
Lake Baikal, Russia	22,000 (5280)
Lake Tanganyika	18,750 (4500)
Lake Superior	12,500 (3000)
Lake Michigan	4920 (1180)
Lake Huron	3545 (850)
Lake Ontario	1640 (395)
Lake Erie	485 (115)

Major Freshwater Wetlands	Area in km² (mi²)
West Siberian Lowland	2,745,000 (1,059,850)
Amazon River basin	1,738,000 (671,045)
Hudson Bay Lowland	374,000 (144,402)
Congo River basin	189,000 (72,973)
Mackenzie River basin	166,000 (64,093)
Pantanal	138,000 (53,282)
Mississippi River basin	108,000 (41,699)

▲**Figure 8.15 The world's major rivers, lakes, and wetlands.** Earth's largest streamflow volumes occur within and just adjacent to the tropics, reflecting the continual rainfall associated with the Intertropical Convergence Zone (ITCZ). Regions of lower streamflow coincide with Earth's subtropical deserts, rain-shadow areas, and continental interiors, particularly in Asia. [Adapted from William E. McNulty, National Geographic Society, based on data from USGS; World Wildlife Fund; State Hydrological Institute, Russia; University of Kassel Center for Environmental Systems Research, Germany.]

◄Figure 8.16 The Himalayas, southern Tibet. Warmer temperatures are causing glaciers to melt in this high-elevation region. At 8027 m (26,335 ft), Shishapangma in southern Tibet, pictured here, is the eighth highest mountain in the world. [Elena Belozorova/Alamy.]

Rivers and Lakes

Surface runoff and base flow from groundwater move across Earth's surface in rivers and streams, forming vast networks that drain the continents. Freshwater lakes are fed by precipitation, streamflow, and groundwater and store about 0.33% of the freshwater on Earth's surface. About 80% of this volume is in just 40 of the largest lakes, and about 50% is contained in just seven lakes.

The greatest single volume of lake water resides in Lake Baikal in south-central Siberia. This lake contains almost as much water as all five North American Great Lakes combined. Africa's Lake Tanganyika contains the next largest volume, followed by the five Great Lakes. About one-fourth of global freshwater lake storage is in small lakes. More than 3 million lakes exist in Alaska alone. Canada has at least that many in number and has more total surface area of lakes than any other country in the world.

Lakes Warm with Climate Change Increasing air temperatures are affecting lakes throughout the world. A recent study of 235 lakes on six continents revealed that lake temperatures are rising on average 0.34 C° (0.61 F°) per decade, with the greatest warming occurring at higher latitudes (http://www.nasa.gov/press-release/study-shows-climate-change-rapidly-warming-world-s-lakes). Some lake levels are rising in response to the melting of glacial ice; others are falling as a result of drought and high evaporation rates. In some regions, lakes are shrinking owing to warming temperatures in combination with poor water-management practices (**Figure 8.17**).

In East Africa, Lake Tanganyika is surrounded by an estimated 10 million people, with most depending on its fish stocks, especially freshwater sardines, for food. Present water temperatures have risen to 26°C (79°F), the highest in a 1500-year climate record revealed by lake-sediment cores. As warming temperatures affect nutrient availability, scientists fear that fish stocks will continue to decline.

▼Figure 8.17 Evaporation of Bolivia's second largest lake. Rising temperatures, drought, and water diversions caused the entirety of Lake Poopó to evaporate in 2016. At 3700 m (over 12,000 ft) elevation on the Bolivian Altiplano, the lake is an important fishing resource for local communities, and it has dried up in the past. However, scientists warn that recovery is unlikely as drought becomes more frequent and intense throughout the region. [NASA/USGS.]

Hydroelectric Power Human-made lakes, often formed by dams, are generally called *reservoirs*, although the term *lake* often appears in their name. The largest reservoir in the world by volume is Lake Kariba in Africa, impounded by the Kariba Dam on the Zambezi River (Figure 8.15). The largest U.S. reservoir is Lake Mead on the Colorado River, discussed in Focus Study 8.1.

Although flood control and water-supply storage are two primary purposes for dam construction, an associated benefit is power production. Hydroelectric power, or **hydropower**, is electricity generated using the power of moving water. Currently, hydropower supplies almost one-fifth of the world's electricity and is the most widely used source of renewable energy. However, because it depends on precipitation, hydropower is highly variable from month to month and year to year.

China is the world's leading hydropower producer. The Three Gorges Dam on the Yangtze River in China is the largest dam in the world (**Figure 8.18**). Over 1.2 million people were relocated to make room for the reservoir upstream from the dam. The immense scale of environmental, historical, and cultural losses associated with the project was the subject of great controversy. Benefits from the project include flood control, water storage, and electrical power production.

In the United States in 2015, hydropower accounted for 6% of total electricity production, down from past years owing to drought and declining hydropower production in the Pacific Northwest. The Grand Coulee Dam, on the Columbia River, is the world's fifth largest hydropower plant and the largest in the United States. In the U.S. Southeast, the Tennessee Valley Authority operates 29 dams and hydroelectric facilities in the Tennessee Valley. In the Southwest, dams on the Colorado River provide hydroelectric power to eight western states.

In the United States, dams have already been built on the best multipurpose dam sites, with numerous detrimental consequences for river environments. Many of the largest hydropower projects are old, and overall production of hydropower is declining. In 2015, solar, wind, and other renewable energy sources together exceeded hydropower generation, part of an ongoing trend. Chapter 14 examines the environmental effects of dams and reservoirs on river ecosystems and reports on recent dam removals. Worldwide,

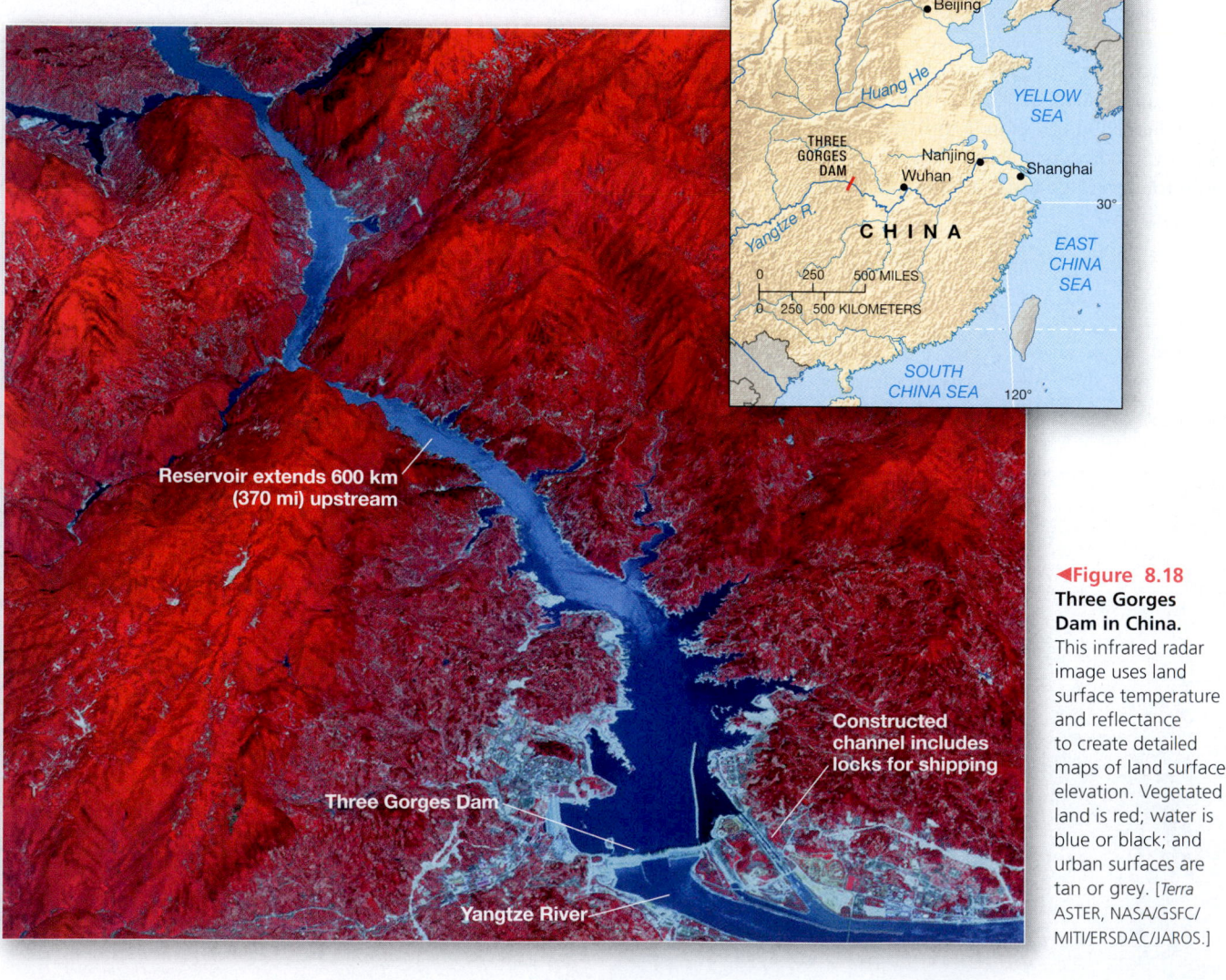

Reservoir extends 600 km (370 mi) upstream

Three Gorges Dam

Constructed channel includes locks for shipping

Yangtze River

◄**Figure 8.18 Three Gorges Dam in China.** This infrared radar image uses land surface temperature and reflectance to create detailed maps of land surface elevation. Vegetated land is red; water is blue or black; and urban surfaces are tan or grey. [*Terra* ASTER, NASA/GSFC/ MITI/ERSDAC/JAROS.]

(a) Much of southern California's water arrives via canal from central California, the Sierra Nevada, and the Colorado River.

(b) The 1207-km-long (750-mi-long) California Aqueduct, shown here near Victorville.

▲Figure 8.19 **Three aqueducts transfer water to southern California.** [Lucy Nicholson/Reuters.]

however, hydropower is increasing; several large projects are proposed and under construction in Brazil alone.

Water Transfer Projects The transfer of water over long distances in pipelines and aqueducts is especially important in dry regions where the most dependable water resources are far away from population centers. The California State Water Project (SWP) is the nation's most extensive water storage and delivery system, including dams, reservoirs, canals, pumping stations, and power plants that provide water for over 25 million people and 750,000 acres of farmland. Water distribution over time is altered by holding back winter runoff for release in summer, and water distribution over space is altered by pumping water from the northern to the southern parts of the state. Completed in 1971, California Aqueduct is a "river" flowing from the Sacramento River delta to the Los Angeles region, servicing irrigated agriculture in the San Joaquin Valley along the way (**Figure 8.19**).

Wetlands

A **wetland** is an area that is permanently or seasonally saturated with water and characterized by vegetation adapted to *hydric* soils (soils saturated long enough to develop anaerobic, or "oxygen-free," conditions). Marshes, swamps, bogs, and peatlands (bog areas composed of peat, or partly decayed vegetation) are types of freshwater wetlands that occur worldwide along river channels and lakeshores, in surface depressions such as the prairie potholes of the U.S Great Plains, and in the cool, lowland, high-latitude regions of Canada, Alaska, and Siberia. Figure 8.15 shows the global distribution of some major wetlands.

Large wetlands are important sources of freshwater and recharge groundwater supplies. When rivers flow

over their banks, wetlands absorb and spread out the floodwaters. For example, the Pantanal in Brazil and Paraguay occupies a vast natural depression in Earth's crust that collects surface runoff during the wet season (**Figure 8.20**). Throughout the dry season, the wetlands release water to the Paraguay River. In this manner, wetland storage mitigates wet-season flooding and adds to dry-season base flow. Wetlands are also significant for improving water quality by trapping sediment and removing nutrients and pollutants. In fact, constructed wetlands are increasingly used globally for water purification. (See Chapter 19 for more on freshwater wetlands.)

▼Figure 8.20 **Tropical wetlands of the Pantanal.** Wetlands near the confluence of the Paraguay and Cuiabá Rivers in the Pantanal, Brazil. [Nat Photos/Getty Images.]

Groundwater Resources

Although **groundwater** lies beneath the surface, beyond the soil-moisture zone and the reach of most plant roots, it is an important part of the hydrologic cycle. Groundwater is not an independent source of water; it is tied to surface supplies for recharge through pores in soil and rock. Because groundwater accumulated over millions of years, care must be taken not to deplete this long-term buildup with excessive short-term water demands.

Groundwater provides about 80% of the world's irrigation water for agriculture and nearly half the world's drinking water. Major aquifers occur on every continent except Antarctica (**Figure 8.21**). Groundwater is generally free of sediment, color, and disease organisms, although pollutants can cause contamination so that it becomes unfit for human use. Overconsumption can deplete groundwater volume in quantities beyond natural replenishment rates.

About 50% of the U.S. population derives a portion of its freshwater from groundwater sources. In some states, such as Nebraska, groundwater supplies 85% of water needs, with that figure as high as 100% in rural areas. Between 1950 and 2000, annual groundwater withdrawal in the United States and Canada increased more than 150%. For the latest research on U.S. groundwater resources, go to http://water.usgs.gov/ogw/gwrp/; for maps and data, see http://groundwaterwatch.usgs.gov/.

The Groundwater Environment

Geosystems in Action 8 brings together many groundwater concepts in a single illustration. Follow its 13 numbers as you read about each part of the groundwater environment.

Precipitation is the main source of groundwater, percolating downward as gravitational water from the soil-moisture zone. This water moves through the **zone of aeration**, where soil and rock are less than saturated (some pore spaces contain air), an area also known as the *unsaturated zone*.

Eventually, gravitational water accumulates in the **zone of saturation**, where soil pore spaces are completely filled with water. Like a hard sponge made of sand, gravel, and rock, the zone of saturation stores water in its countless pores and voids. It is bounded at the bottom by an impermeable layer of rock that obstructs further downward movement of water. The upper limit of the zone of saturation is the **water table** (note the white dashed lines across **Figure GIA 8.1**). The slope of the water table, which generally follows the contours of the land surface, drives groundwater movement toward areas of lower elevation and lower pressure.

Aquifers and Wells As discussed earlier, permeable rock or materials conduct water readily, while impermeable rock obstructs water flow. An **aquifer** is a subsurface layer of permeable rock or unconsolidated materials (silt, sand, or gravels) through which groundwater can

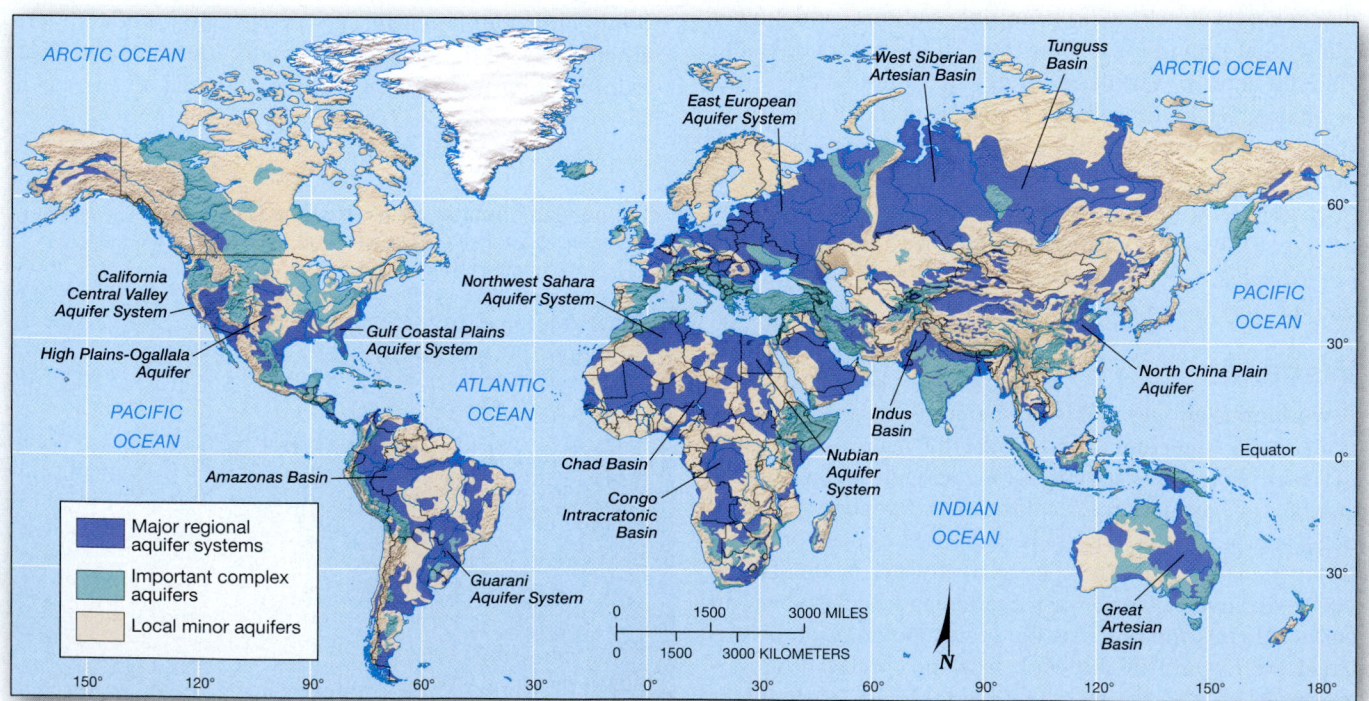

▲**Figure 8.21 Generalized map of global groundwater resources and important regional aquifer systems.** [Adapted from Taylor et al., 2013, *Groundwater and climate change, Nature Climate Change* 3: 322–329. Simplified map based on Struckmeier, W. et al., 2008, *Groundwater Resources of the World* (1:25,000,000), BGR & UNESCO World-wide Hydrogeological Mapping and Assessment Programme.]

flow in amounts adequate for wells and springs. An **unconfined aquifer** has a permeable layer above, which allows water to pass through, and an impermeable one beneath. A **confined aquifer** is bounded above and below by impermeable layers of rock or unconsolidated materials. The solid, impermeable layer that forms such a boundary is known as an *aquiclude*. An *aquitard* is a layer that has low permeability, but cannot conduct water in usable amounts. The zone of saturation may include the saturated portion of the aquifer and a part of the underlying aquiclude.

Humans commonly extract groundwater using wells that are drilled downward into the ground until they penetrate the water table. Shallow drilling results in a "dry well"; drilling too deeply will punch through the aquifer and into the impermeable layer below, also yielding little water. The water in a well drilled into an unconfined aquifer is not under pressure and so must be pumped to rise above the water table. In contrast, the water in a confined aquifer is under the pressure of its own weight, creating a pressure level called the **potentiometric surface** to which the water can rise on its own.

The potentiometric surface can be above ground level (as shown in Figure GIA 8.1, right side). Under this condition, **artesian water**, or groundwater confined under pressure, may rise in a well and even flow at the surface without pumping if the top of the well is lower than the potentiometric surface. (These wells are called *artesian* for the Artois area in France, where they are common.) In other wells, however, pressure may be inadequate, and the artesian water must be pumped the remaining distance to the surface.

The size of the *aquifer recharge area*, where surface water accumulates and percolates downward, differs for unconfined and confined aquifers. For an unconfined aquifer, the recharge area generally extends above the entire aquifer; the water simply percolates down to the water table. But in a confined aquifer, the recharge area is far more restricted. Pollution of this limited area causes groundwater contamination (see Figure GIA 8.1, right side).

Groundwater at the Surface Where the water table intersects the ground surface, water flows outward in the form of springs, streams, lakes, and wetlands (**Figure 8.22**). Springs are common in limestone environments, in which water dissolves rock by chemical processes and flows underground until it finds a surface outlet. Hot springs are common in volcanic environments where water is heated underground before emerging under pressure at the surface.

Groundwater interacts with streamflow to provide base flow during dry periods when runoff does not occur. Conversely, streamflow supplements groundwater during periods of water surplus (**Figure GIA 8.2**). In humid climates, the water table is higher in elevation than the stream channel and generally supplies a continuous base flow to a stream. In this environment, the stream is *effluent* because it receives the water flowing out from the surrounding ground. The Mississippi River is a classic example, among many other humid-region streams. In drier climates, the water table is lower than the stream, causing *influent* conditions in which streamflow feeds groundwater, sustaining deep-rooted vegetation along the stream. Parts of the Colorado River and Rio Grande of the American West are examples of influent streams.

Overuse of Groundwater

As water is pumped from a well, the surrounding water table within an unconfined aquifer may become lowered if the pumping rate exceeds the replenishment flow of water around the well. The resultant lowering of the water table around the well is a **cone of depression** (Figure GIA 8.1, left-hand side).

An additional problem arises when aquifers are overpumped near the ocean or seacoast. Along a coastline, the meeting of fresh groundwater and salty seawater establishes a natural interface in which the less-dense freshwater flows on top. But excessive withdrawal of freshwater can cause this interface to migrate inland. As a result, wells near the shore become contaminated with saltwater, and the aquifer becomes useless as a freshwater source. Pumping freshwater back into the aquifer may halt seawater intrusion, but once contaminated, the aquifer is difficult to reclaim.

▼**Figure 8.22 Thunder Springs, Grand Canyon, Arizona.** Groundwater emerges from a limestone layer to form Thunder River, a tributary of Tapeats Creek. [Whit Richardson/Alamy.]

Groundwater forms when rainfall and snowmelt seep down through the soil and accumulate in the pore spaces in fractured bedrock or sediment. GIA 8.1 shows the structure of groundwater deposits, called *aquifers*, and threats to this resource from pollution and overuse. GIA 8.2 shows how groundwater helps to maintain streamflow.

An artesian spring in Manitoba, Canada

8.1 THE WATER TABLE AND AQUIFERS

The water table is a boundary between the zones of aeration and saturation. Beneath the zone of saturation, an impermeable layer of rock blocks further downward movement of water. An aquifer contains groundwater stored in the zone of saturation.

(1) Zone of aeration
In this layer, some pore spaces contain air.

(2) Zone of saturation
In this layer, water fills the spaces between particles of sand, gravel, and rock.

(3) Slope and flow
The water table follows the slope of the land surface above it. The water in an aquifer flows toward areas of lower elevation and lower pressure. A plume of water pollution from septic systems or landfills can flow through an aquifer, contaminating wells.

(4) Unconfined aquifer
*An **unconfined aquifer** has a permeable layer above and an impermeable layer beneath.*

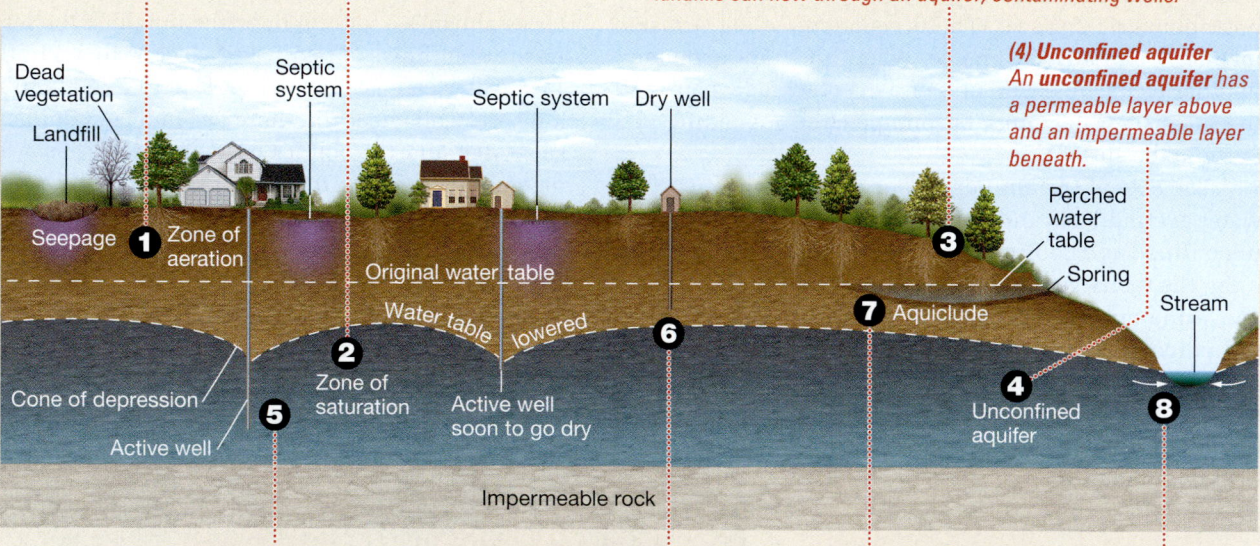

(5) Wells in an unconfined aquifer
The water in an unconfined aquifer is not under pressure and must be pumped to the surface.

(6) Dry wells and aquifer overuse
Wells pump groundwater to the surface, lowering the water table. Overuse, or groundwater mining, occurs when drawdown exceeds an aquifer's recharge capacity. A dry well results if a well is not drilled deep enough or if the water table falls below the depth of the well.

(7) Aquicludes and springs
*An **aquiclude** is a layer of impermeable rock or unconsolidated material that prevents water from seeping farther down. **Springs** form where the perched water table intersects the surface.*

(8) Water table at the surface
Streams, lakes, and wetlands form where the water table intersects the surface.

Animation MG
The Water Table

https://goo.gl/vesNqO

MasteringGeography™

Visit the Study Area in MasteringGeography™ to explore groundwater.

Visualize: Study a geoscience animation of groundwater, the water table, and aquifers.

Assess: Demonstrate understanding of groundwater (if assigned by instructor).

8.2 GROUNDWATER INTERACTION WITH STREAMFLOW

Runoff and groundwater together supply the water to keep streams flowing. Groundwater can maintain streamflow when runoff does not occur. The diagrams show the relationship of the water table and streamflow in humid and dry climates.

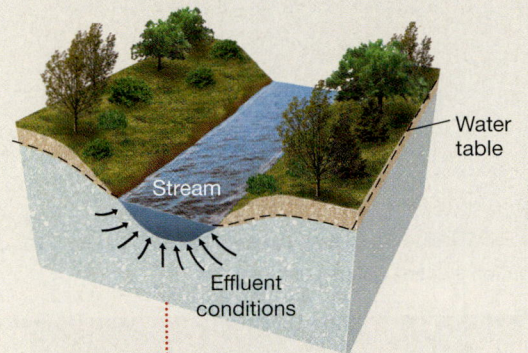

Dry river channel, influent conditions

Humid climate– effluent conditions
The water table is higher than the stream channel, so water flows out from the surrounding ground into the stream.

Dry climate– influent conditions
The water table is lower than the stream channel, so the stream's water flows into groundwater.

(9) Confined aquifer
A **confined aquifer** is bounded above and below by impermeable layers (aquicludes)

(10) Potentiometric surface
The **potentiometric surface** is the level to which groundwater under pressure can rise on its own, and can be above ground level.

(11) Artesian wells
Artesian water is groundwater in a sloping, confined aquifer where groundwater is under pressure. If the top of a well is lower than the potentiometric surface, artesian water may rise in the well and flow at the surface without pumping.

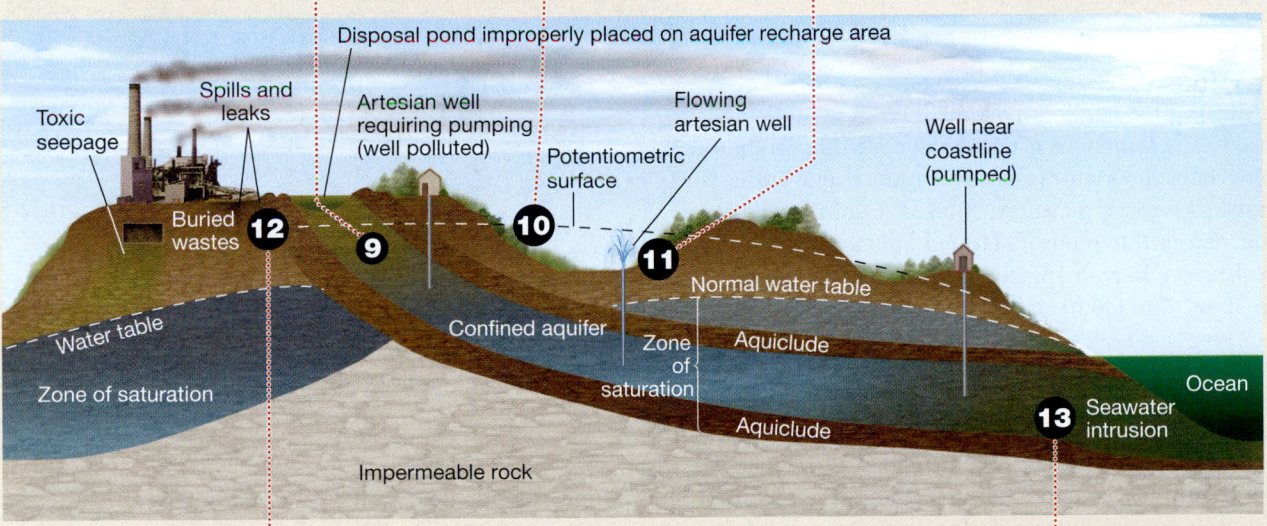

Disposal pond improperly placed on aquifer recharge area

(12) Pollution of aquifer
In industrial areas, spills, leaks, and improper disposal of wastes can pollute groundwater. Notice the improper placement of a disposal pond in the aquifer recharge area.

(13) Seawater intrusion
In coastal areas, overuse of groundwater can cause salty seawater to move inland, contaminating a freshwater aquifer. A rise in sea level can force seawater intrusion, forcing the local water table upward to the surface, with resulting flooding.

GEOquiz

1. **Apply Concepts:** Where in Figure GIA 8.1 could you drill a well that was free of pollutants and saltwater contamination? Explain.

2. **Infer:** In which direction does the water flow in the largest aquifer in Figure GIA 8.1? How can you tell?

3. **Predict:** What would happen to a stream with influent conditions if runoff were greatly reduced?

4. **Explain:** Suggest steps to prevent groundwater pollution from seawater intrusion.

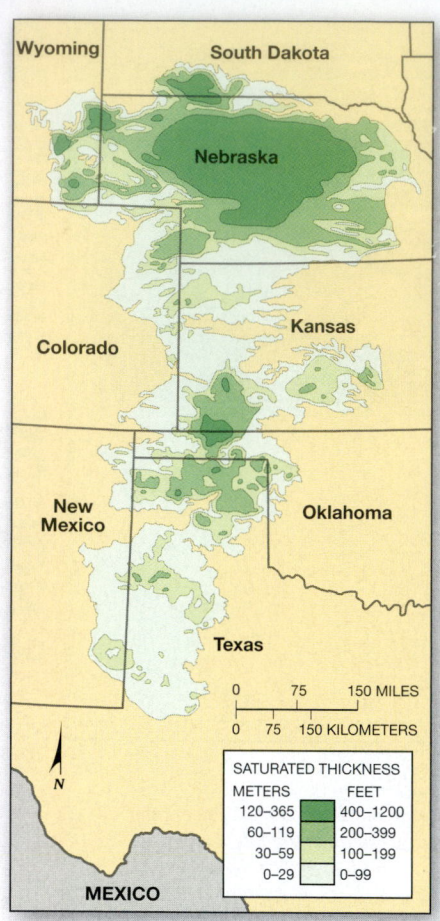

◀Figure 8.23 **Average saturated thickness of the High Plains Aquifer.** [After D. E. Kromm and S. E. White, 1987, Interstate groundwater management preference differences: The High Plains region, *Journal of Geography* 86(1):5.]

SATURATED THICKNESS

METERS	FEET
120–365	400–1200
60–119	200–399
30–59	100–199
0–29	0–99

(a) Center-pivot irrigation system waters a wheat field.

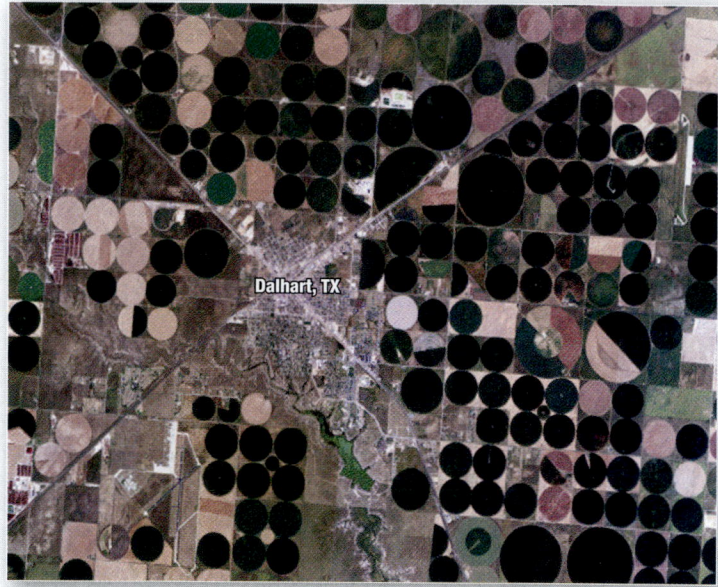

Dalhart, TX

(b) A pattern of quarter-section circular fields results from center-pivot irrigation systems near Dalhart, Texas. In each field, a sprinkler arm pivots around a center, delivering about 3 cm (1.18 in.) of High Plains Aquifer water per revolution.

▲**Figure 8.24** **Center-pivot irrigation.** [(a) Gene Alexander, USDA/NRCS. (b) USDA National Agricultural Imagery Program, 2010.]

The utilization of aquifers beyond their flow and recharge capacities is known as **groundwater mining**. In the United States, chronic groundwater overdrafts occur in the Midwest, lower Mississippi Valley, Florida, Central Valley of California, and in the intensely farmed Palouse region of eastern Washington. In many places, the water table has declined more than 12 m (40 ft) since 1950.

Groundwater Mining of the High Plains Aquifer

The High Plains Aquifer, North America's largest known aquifer system, underlies a vast area shared by eight states, extending from southern South Dakota to Texas. The Ogallala Aquifer, named for the principal geologic unit forming the aquifer system, is the largest aquifer in the High Plains Aquifer system. The average thickness of the saturated parts of the aquifer system is highest in Nebraska, southwestern Kansas, and the Oklahoma Panhandle (**Figure 8.23**). Throughout the region, groundwater flows generally from west to east through mainly sand and gravel, discharging at the surface into streams and springs. Precipitation, which varies widely over the region, is the main source of recharge. Drought conditions have prevailed throughout the region since 2000.

Heavy mining of High Plains groundwater for irrigation intensified after World War II with the introduction of center-pivot irrigation, in which large, circular devices provide water for wheat, sorghum, cotton, corn, and about 40% of the grain fed to cattle in the United States (**Figure 8.24**). The High Plains Aquifer now irrigates about one-fifth of all U.S. cropland from more than 160,000 wells. The aquifer also supplies drinking water for nearly 2 million people. Between 1950 and 1980, the annual rate of water pumped from the aquifer increased 300%. By 2000, withdrawals had decreased slightly due to declining well yields and increasing pumping costs, which led to the abandonment of thousands of wells.

The overall effect of groundwater withdrawals has been a drop in the water table of more than 30 m (100 ft) in most of the region. During the period from about 1950 to 2011, the level of the water table declined more than 45 m (150 ft) in parts of northern Texas, where the saturated thickness of the aquifer is least, and in

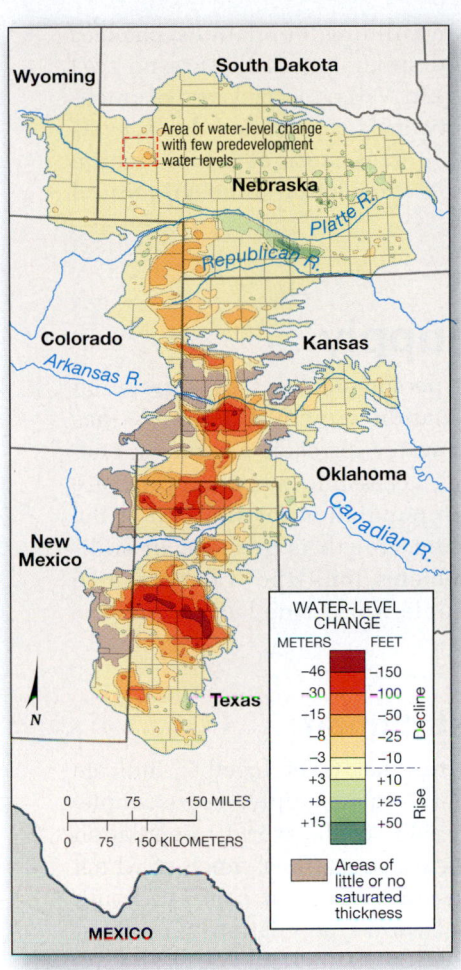

◄**Figure 8.25**
Water-level changes in the High Plains Aquifer, 1950 to 2011. The color scale indicates widespread declines and a few areas of water-level rise. [Adapted from V. L. McGuire, 2013, Water-level and storage changes in the High Plains aquifer, predevelopment to 2011 and 2009–2011, *USGS Scientific Investigations Report 2012–5291*, Fig. 1; available at http://ne .water.usgs.gov/ogw/ hpwlms/.]

Plains. Present irrigation practices, if continued, will deplete 69% of the High Plains Aquifer by 2060. Eventually, farmers will be forced to switch to nonirrigated crops, such as sorghum, and these are more vulnerable to drought conditions (and will also yield smaller economic returns). In addition, rising temperatures with climate change could cause a 10% loss of soil moisture due to increased evapotranspiration demand. Numerous federal and state agencies are working with land owners toward sustainable water practices in light of these challenging regional water issues.

Global Groundwater Decline Satellite measurements indicate that groundwater is declining in many regions of the world (**Figure 8.26**). The decrease in total groundwater storage is attributed to groundwater overuse. For example, measurements for parts of India indicate a fall in the water table as large as 33 cm (1 ft) between 2002 and 2008. These changes appear to be almost entirely caused by human use, which is depleting the resource more quickly than it can recharge. In Saudi Arabia, groundwater resources accumulated over tens of thousands of years. These reserves are known as "fossil aquifers" because they receive little or no recharge in the desert climate that exists in the region today. Thus, increasing withdrawals at present in Saudi Arabia and other parts of the Middle East are not being naturally recharged—in essence, groundwater has become a nonrenewable resource.

western Kansas (**Figure 8.25**). During that same period, rising water levels have occurred in Nebraska and in small areas of Texas due to recharge from surface irrigation, a short period of years with above-normal precipitation, and downward percolation from canals and reservoirs.

Water accumulation in the High Plains Aquifer occurred over millions of years, and recharge today is extremely slow. The USGS estimates that recovery of the aquifer would take at least 1000 years if groundwater mining stopped today. Obviously, billions of dollars of agricultural activity cannot be abruptly halted, but neither can extravagant water mining continue. Scientists now suggest that irrigated agriculture is unsustainable on the southern High

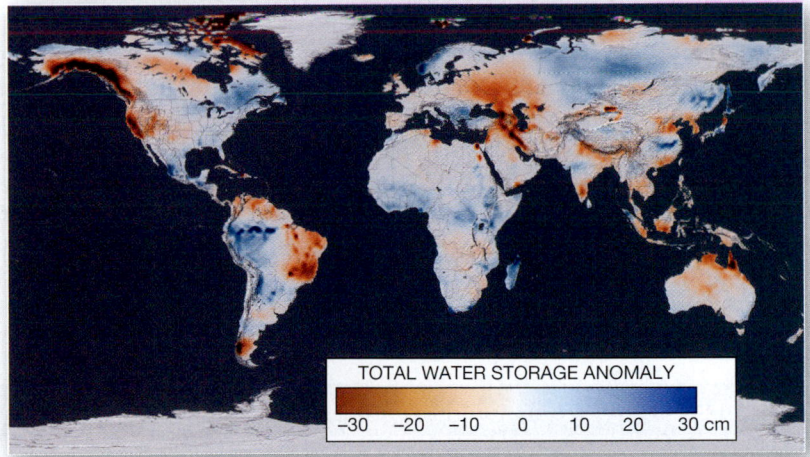

▲**Figure 8.26 Global water storage as measured by NASA's *GRACE* satellite.** Map represents the total water storage anomaly in April 2015, relative to the average water storage from 2002–2015. Reddish-brown shows areas with groundwater decreases; blue shows areas with groundwater increases. [NASA SVS.]

🌐 **GEOreport 8.1** Satellite *GRACE* enables groundwater measurements

Groundwater is difficult to study and measure because it lies hidden beneath Earth's surface. Scientists are now using NASA's Gravity Recovery and Climate Experiment (*GRACE*) satellites to study changes in groundwater storage using measurements of Earth's gravity field (see the map in Figure 8.26). *GRACE* has given scientists a "scale in the sky" that may prove critical for initiating action on water conservation in these regions.

visible result is cracks in building foundations, changes in surface drainage, and sinkholes. In the Fresno area of California's San Joaquin Valley, after years of intensive pumping of groundwater for irrigation, land levels dropped almost 10 m (33 ft) because of a combination of water removal and soil compaction from agricultural activity (**Figure 8.27**).

Our Water Supply

Water availability per person declines as population increases. World population growth since 1970 has reduced the supply of water for each person by one-third. On a global level, accessible water supplies are not well correlated with population distribution or the regions where population growth is greatest. In addition, water quality problems limit the water-resource base. Over 1 billion people worldwide lack safe drinking water.

Global Water Distribution

Table 8.1 provides statistics that, taken together, indicate the unevenness of Earth's water supply. For example, Asia has approximately 60% of the world's population but only 34% of the world's streamflow, much of which arrives during the monsoon season. In contrast, South America has 8% of the world's population with about 27% of its streamflow.

The adequacy of Earth's water supply is tied to climatic variability and to water demand. Water demand and actual usage is, in turn, tied to level of development and affluence. On an individual level, people in developed countries use more water than people in developing countries.

Water shortages can lead to water vulnerability, water stress, and water scarcity (**Figure 8.28**). For example, in Africa, 56 countries draw from a varied

▲**Figure 8.27 Land subsidence from groundwater withdrawal in California's Central Valley.** A USGS hydrologist holds a measuring stick showing land subsidence from 1988 to 2013 at the Santa Rita Bridge in Merced County. Note the greatest subsidence is from 2008 to 2013. [Justin Brandt/USGS.]

Mobile Field Trip (MG)
Moving Water Across California

https://goo.gl/hn5FDo

Aquifer Compaction and Collapse Because aquifers are layers of rock or unconsolidated material, a possible effect of removing water from an aquifer is that the ground will lose internal support and collapse as a result. Water in the pore spaces is not compressible, so it adds structural strength to the rock or other material. If the water is removed through overpumping, air infiltrates the pores. Air is readily compressible, and the tremendous weight of overlying rock may compact or crush the aquifer. The result is *land subsidence*, a settling or sinking of earth materials on the surface. The

TABLE 8.1 Regional Comparison of Factors Influencing Global Water Supply				
Region	2015 Population (in millions)	Share of Global Population	Share of Global Land Area	Share of Global Annual Streamflow
Africa	1171	16%	23%	11%
Asia	4397	60%	33%	34%
Australia–Oceania	40	0.5%	6%	5%
Europe	742	10%	7%	8%
North America*	484	6%	16%	15%
Central and South America†	630	8%	13%	27%
Global (excluding Antarctica)	7336	—	—	—

* Includes Canada, Mexico, and the United States. Population data from the *2015 World Population Data Sheet* (Washington, DC: Population Reference Bureau, 2015).
† Includes the Caribbean region.

water-resource base of rivers, lakes, and groundwater. Water demand is increasing with population growth and the need for increased irrigation during periods of drought. Conditions of water *stress* (where people have less than 1700 m³ of water per person per year) presently occur in 12 African countries; water *scarcity* (less than 1000 m³ per person per year) occurs in 14 African countries. Ongoing drought in some areas of the continent mean that both surface and groundwater reserves are being quickly depleted.

According to UN–Water, the United Nations committee on freshwater (see http://www.unwater.org/about/en/), by the year 2025, 1.8 billion people will be living in countries or regions with water scarcity. In addition, by 2025, two-thirds of the world's population could be living under conditions of water stress.

Water Supply in the United States

The precipitation input to the U.S. water supply (excluding Alaska and Hawai'i) is based on average annual precipitation of 76 cm (30 in.) divided among the 48 contiguous states. However, this precipitation is unevenly distributed over space (across the country) and time (throughout the year). For example, New England's water supply is so abundant that only about 1% of available water is consumed each year. In contrast, Arizona's surface water supply meets only 20% of demand. To compensate, the state gets 80% of its water from groundwater extraction and transfers of Colorado River water as part of the Central Arizona Project. Of the precipitation inputs, some is lost to the atmosphere, and some becomes surplus water for human use.

Surplus Water Use We can broadly categorize water use as nonconsumptive or consumptive. **Nonconsumptive use** refers to the removal or diversion of water, followed by the subsequent return of that water to the same supply. An example is water used for hydropower production. **Consumptive use** refers to the permanent removal of water from the immediate water environment. This water is not returned and so is not available for a second or third use. Examples of consumptive use include water consumed by humans or livestock and used in manufacturing.

In the United States, we use surplus water in one of two ways. About two-thirds of the total surplus goes to **instream use**, which refers to uses of streamflow while it remains in the channel, without being removed. Examples include water for transportation, waste dilution, hydroelectric power production, fishing, recreation, and ecosystem maintenance, such as sustaining wildlife. About one-third of the total surplus goes to **water withdrawal**, sometimes referred to as *off-stream use*. Examples include water use by industry, agriculture, and municipalities and for steam-electric power generation. A portion of water withdrawals may be returned to the water supply, and a portion may be consumed.

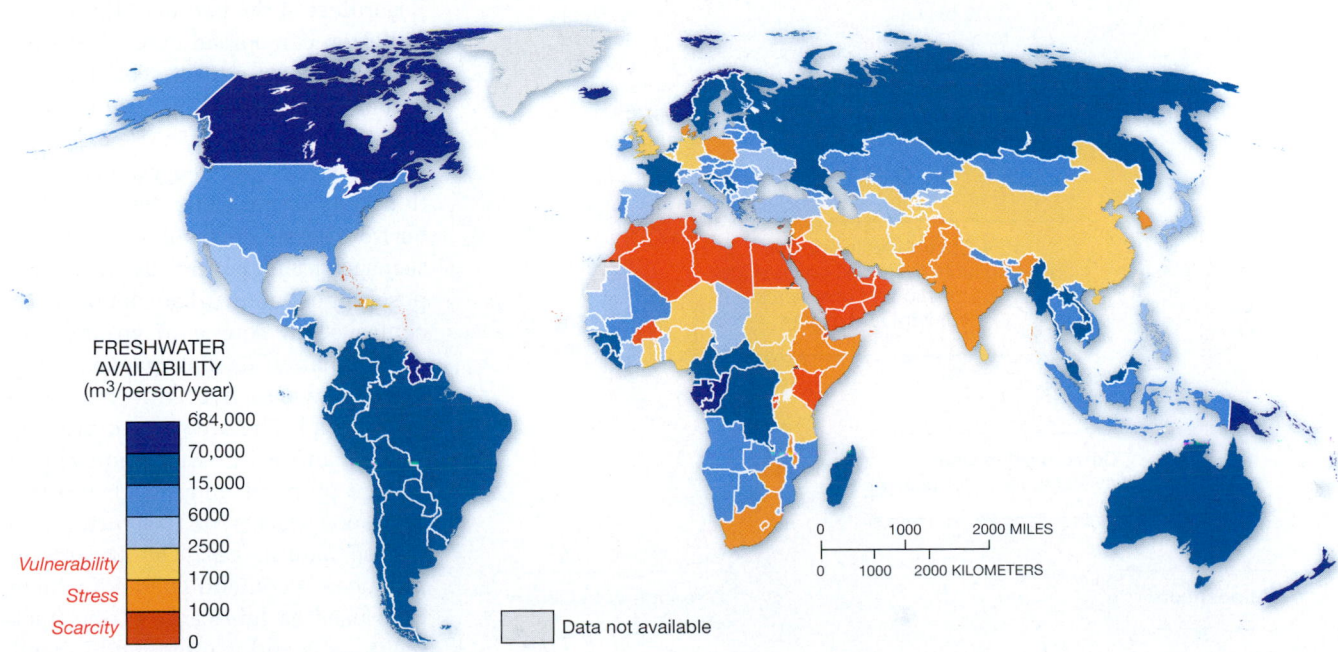

▲Figure 8.28 **Global freshwater availability.** Note degrees of water vulnerability (blue), water stress (yellow), and water scarcity (dark yellow/orange) by country. [UNEP, 2008.]

U.S. Water Budget Viewed daily, the U.S. national water budget has two general outputs: 70% actual evapotranspiration and 30% surplus (**Figure 8.29**). The 70% actual evapotranspiration is from agricultural crops and pastures, forests, and natural vegetation used by wildlife. The remaining 30% surplus feeds surface water, recharges groundwater, and provides the water that we directly use.

Surplus water is split unevenly between instream use and water withdrawal. In 2010, U.S water withdrawals were for steam-electric power, irrigation, livestock, aquaculture, domestic and commercial use, industry, and mining. Water withdrawal provides the opportunity to extend the water resource through reuse. However, when water returns to rivers and streams, its quality is sometimes altered—contaminated chemically with pollutants or waste or contaminated thermally with heat energy. Regardless of quality, returned water becomes a part of all water systems downstream as streamflow moves into oceans.

The estimated U.S. withdrawal of water for 2010 was 13% lower than in 2005, and down considerably from peak use in 1985. Increased water prices helped produce the recent downward trend. For studies of water use in the United States, see http://water.usgs.gov/public/watuse/.

WORKITOUT 8.3
Calculate Your Water Footprint

Just as you calculated your carbon footprint in Chapter 1, Critical Thinking 1.1, you can calculate your water footprint. Go to http://www.gracelinks.org/1408/water-footprint-calculator and "Get started."

1. How many gallons of water do you (or your household) use per day? How does your daily use compare to the U.S. average?
2. How can you lower the amount of "virtual" water used for the food you eat? Scroll down to "diet" and click on "Tips."
3. Read the tips for saving water in the kitchen. Which uses less water: using a dishwasher or doing dishes by hand?

Water Pollution

Protecting the integrity of our surface and subsurface water is critical to meet present and future water needs. Access to safe drinking water, known as *potable* water, is critical for human health, yet lacking in many countries. In addition, potable water sources can become polluted.

As we learned earlier, if surface water becomes polluted, it will eventually contaminate groundwater during recharge.

Pollution Sources Surface water pollution comes from *point sources*, such as a pipes, ships, or factories, and *nonpoint sources*, including fertilizers in agricultural runoff or oil and other chemicals in urban runoff. Regardless of the nature of the source, pollution can spread over a great distance as water moves over the landscape, and eventually into rivers, lakes, and wetlands (**Figure 8.30**).

As shown in Geosystems in Action 8, pollution can enter groundwater from numerous sources, including seepage from hazardous-waste disposal sites and urban landfills. A controversial source of groundwater contamination is shale gas extraction (also known as hydraulic fracturing, or fracking). The process requires that large quantities of water and chemicals be pumped under high pressure into subsurface rock, fracturing it to release natural gas. The wastewater produced is contaminated with chemicals used as lubricants in the fracking process and is often held in wells or containment ponds. Leaks or spills can send toxic wastewater into surface water supplies and groundwater. (We discuss shale gas in Chapter 11.)

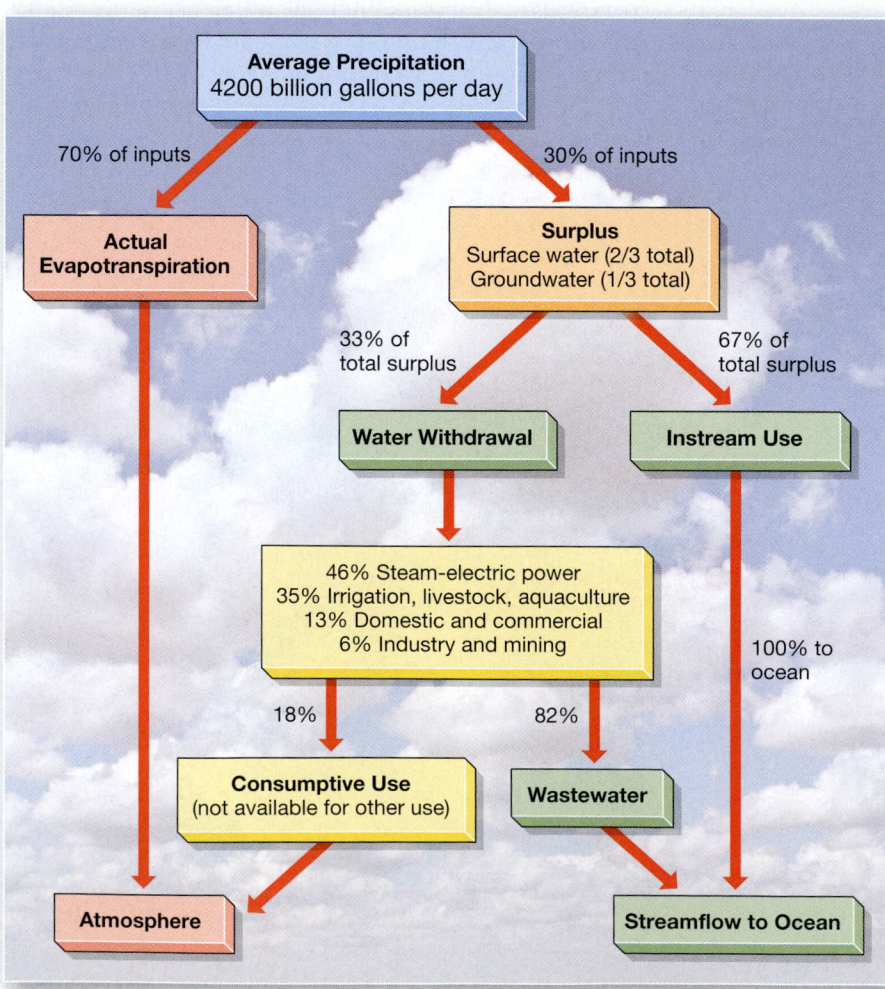

▲**Figure 8.29 Daily water budget for the contiguous 48 U.S. states.** [Data from M. Maupin, J. Kenny, S. Hutson, J. Lovelace, N. Barber, and K. Linsey, 2010, *Estimated Use of Water in the United States in 2010*, USGS Circular 1405.]

The U.S. Clean Water Act The Federal Water Pollution Control Act of 1948 was the first set of U.S. laws to address water pollution. Amended and renamed the Clean Water Act (CWA) in 1972, these laws make it illegal to discharge pollutants from a point source, such as factories and wastewater treatment plants, into surface waters without a permit. The act also set new standards for industrial wastewater contamination and provided funding for sewage treatment plant construction. The CWA also addressed wetland protection, making it illegal to dredge, drain, or fill a wetland without a permit. The CWA was amended in 1977 and 1987 and is today widely regarded as one of the most successful environmental laws in U.S. history.

Water Strategies for the Future

When we examine water supply and demand in terms of water budgets, the limits of the water resource become apparent. How can we satisfy the growing demand for water?

(a) In August 2015, pollution from a spill at the abandoned Gold King Mine in southwest Colorado contaminated the Animas River near Durango as it moved downstream into the San Juan River. Although mine drainage is generally classified as nonpoint source pollution, this accidental release of over 3 million gallons was from a point source.

Desalination Seawater desalination is an increasingly important method for obtaining freshwater. **Desalination** is the process that removes organic compounds, debris, and salinity from seawater, brackish (slightly saline) water found along coastlines, and saline groundwater, yielding potable water for domestic uses. In Saudi Arabia, 30 desalination plants currently supply 70% of the country's drinking water needs, providing an alternative to further groundwater mining and problems with saltwater intrusion.

In the United States, especially in Florida and along the coast of southern California, desalination use is slowly increasing. The Carlsbad Desalination Project, near San Diego, California, is the largest in the United States. One of the drawbacks to desalination is that concentrated salts must be disposed of in a manner that does not contaminate freshwater supplies. In addition, the desalination process is energy-intensive and expensive.

International Cooperation Water is a resource shared by all people on Earth. Over 260 lakes and river drainage basins throughout the world cross international boundaries, and more than 100 countries share a river basin with at least one other country. Over the last 1200 years of human history, over 3000 treaties have addressed international water resources, the earliest focusing on boundary demarcation and navigation and the most recent negotiating issues pertaining to water use, development, protection, and conservation. During this century, international cooperation will be critical as population growth, development, and climate change put more pressure on global water resources.

Water Efficiency and Conservation Water efficiency (more effective use of water) and water conservation (use of less water) can work together to reduce water demand. Simple strategies such as installing low-flow faucets and dual-flush toilets and replacing lawns with drought-tolerant landscaping are already proving effective. For example, in the city of San Antonio, Texas, conservation measures led to a 42% decrease in water consumption over the past few decades, despite a growing population. In California, water restrictions resulted in a statewide 24% decrease in consumption from June 2015 to March 2016.

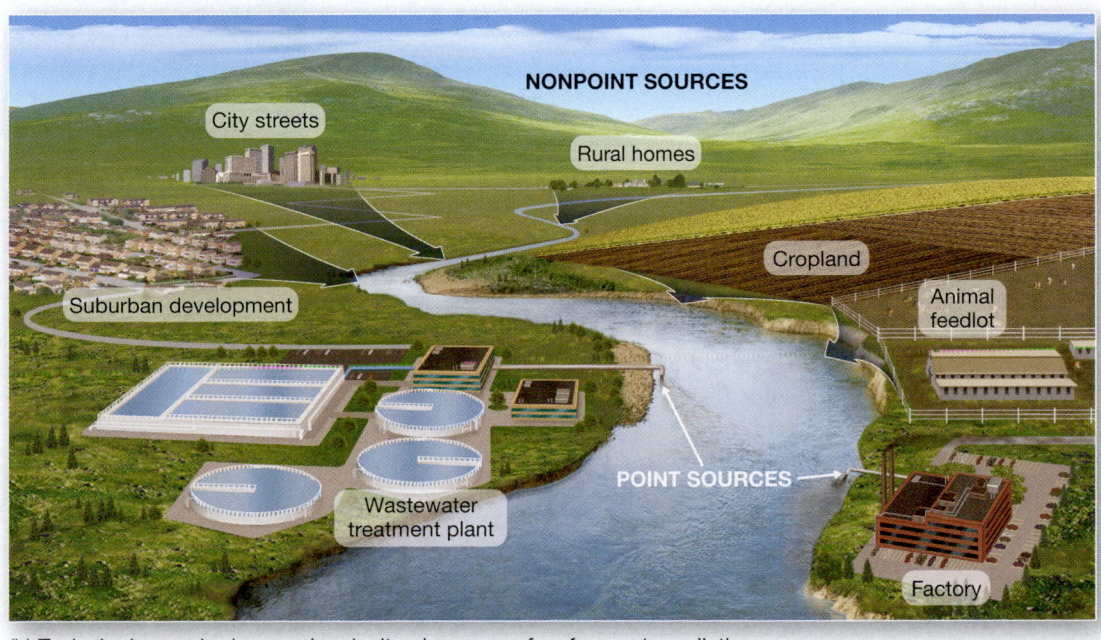

(b) Typical urban, suburban, and agricultural sources of surface water pollution.

▲**Figure 8.30 Water pollution from point and nonpoint sources.** [(a) Whit Richardson/Alamy.]

WATER RESOURCES IMPACT HUMANS

• What are the most important freshwater sources for human society and life on Earth?
• Drought is a water deficit. What are some effects of drought on human societies?

8a Desalination is an important supplement to water supplies in regions with large variations in rainfall throughout the year and declining groundwater reserves. This plant in Barcelona, Spain, uses the process of reverse osmosis to remove salts and impurities. [Jeronimo Alba/Alamy.]

HUMANS IMPACT WATER RESOURCES

• Climate change affects lake depth, thermal structure, and associated organisms.
• Water projects (dams and diversions) redistribute water over space and time.
• Groundwater overuse and pollution depletes and degrades the resource, with side effects such as collapsed aquifers and saltwater contamination.

8b The third largest reservoir in the world, Lake Nasser is formed by the Aswan High Dam on the Nile River in Egypt. Its water is used for agricultural, industrial, and domestic purposes, as well as for hydropower. [WitR/Shutterstock.]

Blue Marble–Next Generation image shows December land surface topography and bathymetry. [NASA]

8d

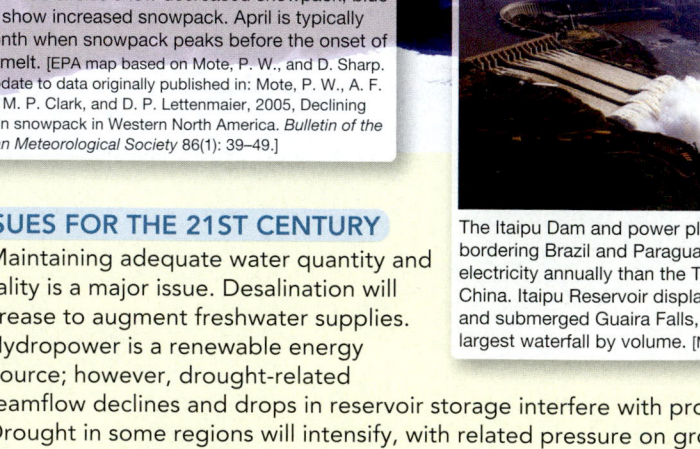

Trends in April snowpack in the western United States, measured in terms of snow water equivalent, show the effects of drought related to climate change. Red circles show decreased snowpack; blue circles show increased snowpack. April is typically the month when snowpack peaks before the onset of spring melt. [EPA map based on Mote, P. W., and D. Sharp. 2015 update to data originally published in: Mote, P. W., A. F. Hamlet, M. P. Clark, and D. P. Lettenmaier, 2005, Declining mountain snowpack in Western North America. *Bulletin of the American Meteorological Society* 86(1): 39–49.]

APRIL SNOWPACK, 1955–2015

Increase   Decrease
- Over 80%
- 40–60%
- 0–20%

8c

The Itaipu Dam and power plant on the Paraná River bordering Brazil and Paraguay produces more electricity annually than the Three Gorges Dam in China. Itaipu Reservoir displaced over 10,000 people and submerged Guaira Falls, formerly the world's largest waterfall by volume. [Mike Goldwater/Alamy.]

ISSUES FOR THE 21ST CENTURY

• Maintaining adequate water quantity and quality is a major issue. Desalination will increase to augment freshwater supplies.
• Hydropower is a renewable energy resource; however, drought-related streamflow declines and drops in reservoir storage interfere with production.
• Drought in some regions will intensify, with related pressure on groundwater and surface water supplies.

QUESTIONS TO CONSIDER

1. As a water resource planner in a western state, how would you plan for future use based on the recent snowpack trends shown in 8d?
2. What is the relationship between mountain snowpack and groundwater resources? Explain.

KEY**LEARNING**concepts**review**

The science of water at and below Earth's surface, including its global circulation, distribution, and properties, is **hydrology** (p. 218).

Describe the origin of Earth's waters and *list* the locations of Earth's freshwater supply.

Water molecules came from within Earth over a period of billions of years in the **outgassing** (p. 218) process.

Earth's hydrosphere is in steady-state equilibrium. **Eustasy** (p. 219) refers to worldwide changes in sea level and relates to changes in volume of water in the oceans. Water covers about 71% of Earth. Approximately 97% of it is saline seawater, and the remaining 3% is freshwater—most of it frozen.

1. Describe the locations of Earth's water, both oceanic and fresh. What is the largest repository of freshwater at this time? In what ways is this distribution of water significant to modern society?

Illustrate the hydrologic cycle with a simple sketch that labels each water pathway.

The **hydrologic cycle** (p. 220) is a model of Earth's water system, which has operated for billions of years from the lower atmosphere to several kilometers beneath Earth's surface. **Evaporation** (p. 220) is the net movement of free water molecules away from a wet surface into air. **Transpiration** (p. 220) is the movement of water through plants and back into the atmosphere. Evaporation and transpiration are combined into one term— **evapotranspiration** (p. 220).

Interception (p. 221) occurs when precipitation strikes vegetation or other ground cover. Water soaks into the subsurface through **infiltration** (p. 221), or penetration of the soil surface. Water may puddle on the surface or flow across the surface toward stream channels. This **overland flow** (p. 221), also called **surface runoff** (p. 221), may become *streamflow* as it moves into channels on the surface.

Surface water becomes groundwater when it permeates soil or rock through vertical downward movement called **percolation** (p. 221). The volume of subsurface water stored in the soil that is accessible to plant roots is contained in the **soil-moisture zone** (p. 221). The portion of streamflow that discharges naturally at the surface from groundwater is the **base flow** (p. 221).

2. What are the possible routes that a raindrop may take on its way to and into the soil surface?

Construct the water-budget equation and *explain* each of the components.

A **water budget** (p. 222) can be established for any area of Earth's surface by measuring the precipitation input and the output of various water demands in the area considered. If demands are met and extra water remains, a **surplus** (p. 222) occurs. If demand exceeds supply, a **deficit** (p. 222), or water shortage, results. Precipitation is the moisture supply to Earth's surface. The moisture demand at a given location is evapotranspiration, an actual expenditure of water to the atmosphere called **actual evapotranspiration** (p. 222). The ultimate demand for moisture is **potential evapotranspiration** (p. 222), the amount of water that would evaporate and transpire under optimum moisture conditions (adequate precipitation and adequate soil moisture).

The volume of water stored in the soil that is accessible to plant roots is the **soil-moisture storage** (p. 224). When soil is saturated after a precipitation event, surplus water in the soil becomes **gravitational water** (p. 224) and percolates to groundwater. **Capillary water** (p. 224) is generally accessible to plant roots because it is held in the soil by surface tension and hydrogen bonding between water and soil. After water drains from the larger pore spaces, the available water remaining for plants is termed **field capacity** (p. 225), or storage capacity. **Hygroscopic water** (p. 225) is inaccessible to plants because it is a molecule-thin layer that is tightly bound to each soil particle by hydrogen bonding. As available water is utilized, soil reaches the **wilting point**, p. 225 (all that remains is unextractable water). **Soil-moisture utilization** (p. 225) removes soil water, whereas **soil-moisture recharge** (p. 225) is the rate at which needed moisture enters the soil. The texture and the structure of the soil dictate available pore spaces, or **porosity** (p. 225). The soil's **permeability** (p. 225) is the degree to which water can flow through it, and depends on particle sizes and the shape and packing of soil grains.

Drought (p. 226) can be simply defined as an extended period of dry conditions caused by lower precipitation and higher temperatures than normal. However, the term has slightly different meanings depending on whether it is used for meteorological, agricultural, or hydrological applications.

3. What is potential evapotranspiration? How do we go about estimating this potential rate?
4. What is the difference between soil-moisture utilization and soil-moisture recharge? Explain these concepts in terms of capillary water, field capacity, and wilting point.

Discuss water storage in lakes, reservoirs, and wetlands and *describe* the nature of hydroelectric power production.

Surface water is transferred in canals and pipelines for redistribution over space and stored in reservoirs for redistribution over time to meet water demand. Hydroelectric power, or **hydropower** (p. 232), provides 20% of the world's electricity, and many large projects have changed river systems and affected human populations. Lakes and wetlands are important freshwater storage areas. A **wetland** (p. 233) is an area that is permanently or seasonally saturated with water and that is characterized by vegetation adapted to *hydric* soils (soils saturated for a long enough period to develop anaerobic, or "oxygen-free," conditions).

5. What changes occur along rivers as a result of the construction of large hydropower facilities?
6. In what ways are Earth's lakes affected by climate change?

List and *describe* the elements of the groundwater environment.

Groundwater (p. 234) lies beneath the surface beyond the soil-moisture root zone, and its replenishment is tied to surface surpluses. Excess surface water moves through the **zone of aeration** (p. 234), where soil and rock are less than saturated. Eventually, the water reaches the **zone of saturation** (p. 234), where the pores are completely filled with water. The upper limit of the water that collects in the zone of saturation is the **water table** (p. 234), forming the contact surface between the zones of saturation and aeration.

The permeability of subsurface rocks depends on whether they conduct water readily (higher permeability) or tend to obstruct its flow (lower permeability). They can even be impermeable. An **aquifer** (p. 234) is a rock layer that is permeable to groundwater flow in usable amounts. An **unconfined aquifer** (p. 235) has a permeable layer on top and an impermeable one beneath. A **confined aquifer** (p. 235) is bounded above and below by impermeable layers of rock or unconsolidated material. Water in a confined aquifer is under the pressure of its own weight, creating a pressure level to which the water can rise on its own. This **potentiometric surface** (p. 235) can be above ground level. Groundwater confined under pressure is

artesian water (p. 235); it may rise up in wells and even flow out at the surface without pumping if the head of the well is below the potentiometric surface.

As water is pumped from a well, the surrounding water table within an unconfined aquifer will become lower if the rate of pumping exceeds the horizontal flow of water in the aquifer around the well. This excessive pumping causes a **cone of depression** (p. 235). Aquifers frequently are pumped beyond their flow and recharge capacities, a condition known as **groundwater mining** (p. 238). **Desalination** (p. 243) of seawater and saline groundwater involves the removal of organics, debris, and salinity through distillation or reverse osmosis to yield potable water.

7. What is the relationship between groundwater resources and surface water supplies? Are they interrelated?
8. At what point does groundwater utilization become groundwater mining? Use the High Plains Aquifer example to explain your answer.
9. How does groundwater become polluted? Can contaminated groundwater be cleaned up easily?

Identify critical aspects of present freshwater supplies, and *discuss* the U.S. water budget.

The world's water supply is distributed unevenly over Earth's surface. In the United States, water surpluses are used in several ways. **Nonconsumptive use** (p. 241) refers to the removal or diversion of water, followed by the subsequent return of that water to the same supply. **Consumptive use** (p. 241) refers to the permanent removal of water from the immediate water environment. About two-thirds of the total surplus goes to **instream use** (p. 241), which refers to uses of streamflow while it remains in the channel, without being removed. About one-third of the total surplus goes to **water withdrawal** (p. 241), or *offstream use*. A portion of water withdrawals are consumed; the other portion is wastewater.

10. What is the difference between nonconsumptive and consumptive use of water resources? Give an example of each.
11. What are some strategies for meeting the future water needs of an expanding world population?

MasteringGeography™

Looking for additional review and test prep materials? Visit the Study Area in MasteringGeography™ to enhance your geographic literacy, spatial reasoning skills, and understanding of this chapter's content by accessing a variety of resources, including MapMaster™ interactive maps, videos, *Mobile Field Trips*, *Project Condor* Quadcopter Videos, *In the News* RSS feeds, flashcards, web links, self-study quizzes, and an eText version of *Geosystems*.

GEO**SPATIAL** ANALYSIS

Water Resources Near and Far

Across the United States we monitor water resources to find long-term trends and help communities plan for the future.

Activities

Go to the USGS National Water Information System: Mapper at http://maps.waterdata.usgs.gov/mapper/index.html. *The default map shows surface water measurement sites.*

1. Compare the locations of surface-water sites in the United States to the Annual Precipitation map (Figure 8.8.) What is the relationship between annual precipitation amount and the location of surface-water sites?

Click on "Surface-Water Sites" and uncheck the "Active Sites" box. Click on "Groundwater Sites" and check the "Active Sites" box.

2. Which state has the highest density of groundwater sites across the majority of the state? Which state has the second highest density across the state? You may need to zoom in and explore the map.

3. Compare the locations of groundwater sites to the High Plains Aquifer map (Figure 8.25.) Which portion of the High Plains Aquifer is most obvious on the groundwater sites map? How have water levels changed in this portion of the High Plains Aquifer?

4. What are some concerns with the number of wells on this aquifer?

Check the "Active Sites" box for Surface-water, Groundwater and Springs. Click on "Search" and enter your street address. Click the green arrow to zoom in to your location.

5. Zoom out to find the closest water resource. What is the distance to the nearest water resource? What type of resource is this?

6. Click on the nearest surface-water site. Click "Access Data," then click "Current/Historical Observations." If there are no Current/Historical Observations then choose a different site. How do recent discharge levels compare to the multi-year "median daily statistics" for discharge?

Examine the U.S. Drought Monitor map at http://droughtmonitor.unl.edu/.

7. Explore discharge rates for a few surface-water sites in extreme/exceptional, moderate/severe, and non-drought regions. What relationship do you see between drought status and stream discharge rates?

VISUAL ANALYSIS 8 DRYLAND AGRICULTURE

This false-color image shows irrigated fields in Saudi Arabia; new vegetation is bright green, dry vegetation and fallow fields are dark orange, barren desert surfaces are pink and yellow. [NASA image by Robert Simmon and Jesse Allen using Landsat data from USGS.]

1. What is the source of water used to irrigate the fields? Is this source renewable?

2. Describe the irrigation systems used in these fields. What is the evidence for your answer?

3. In your opinion, is irrigated agriculture in this region sustainable?

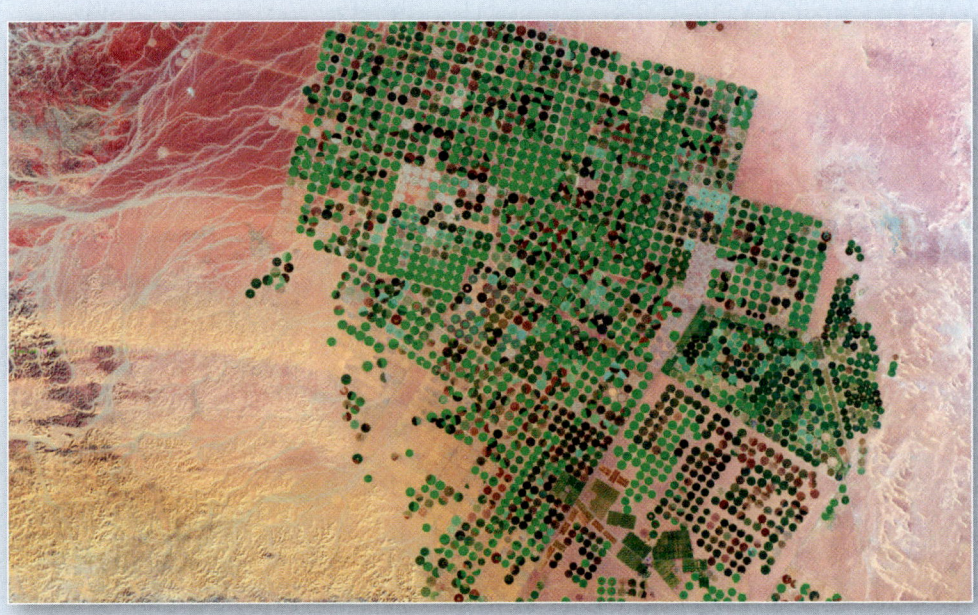

9 Earth's Climatic Regions

South Tirol, Italy

Cold winters and warm summers are typical of the continental climate in Val di Funes, Italy, at the foot of the Dolomites, part of the Alps mountain system. [Peter Adams/Getty Images.]

KEY**LEARNING**concepts

After reading the chapter, you should be able to:

- **Define** climate and climatology and **review** the principal components of Earth's climate system.

- **List** the main categories of world climates and **locate** the regions characterized by each climate type on a world map.

- **Discuss** the subcategories of the six world climate groups, including their causal factors.

- **Explain** the precipitation and moisture criteria used to classify the dry climates.

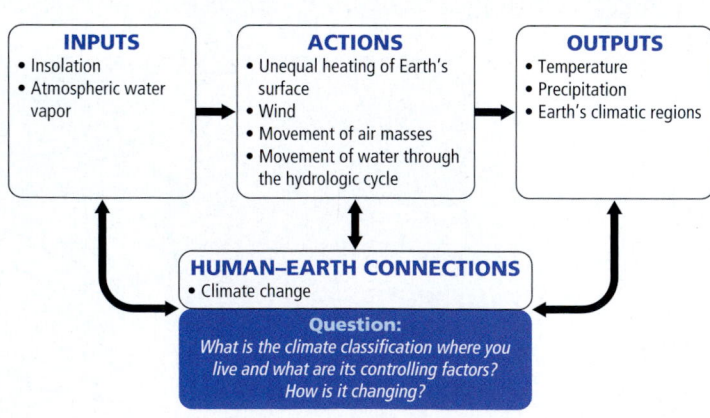

INPUTS
- Insolation
- Atmospheric water vapor

ACTIONS
- Unequal heating of Earth's surface
- Wind
- Movement of air masses
- Movement of water through the hydrologic cycle

OUTPUTS
- Temperature
- Precipitation
- Earth's climatic regions

HUMAN–EARTH CONNECTIONS
- Climate change

Question:
What is the climate classification where you live and what are its controlling factors? How is it changing?

A Close-up Look at New Zealand's Climate

New Zealand's two main islands, known as the North and South Islands, are located in the southwest Pacific Ocean about 2250 km (1400 mi) southeast of Australia. The country stretches over 1500 km (932 mi) from northeast to southwest, extending from 34° S to 47° S latitude. New Zealand's climate—its characteristic weather pattern over many years—is generally categorized as temperate, featuring mild winters and cool summers characteristic of marine west coast climates.

The small-scale world climate map in Figure 9.3 on pages 252–253, which identifies New Zealand's climate as warm and temperate (mesothermal), shows generalized climate information over broad areas. However, when we "zoom in" to examine specific regions of New Zealand using relatively large-scale precipitation and temperature maps (**Figure GN 9.1**), we see much more variation, including many localized climate types produced by differences in latitude, elevation, and position relative to the windward and leeward sides of the country's mountain ranges.

Several factors interact to determine New Zealand's climate zones. The ocean moderates temperatures throughout much of the country—an example of the marine effect discussed in Chapter 4. South of the 40th parallel, the country receives the westerly winds of the "roaring forties" latitudes, which blow from southwest to northeast in the Southern Hemisphere. Mountain ranges run north to south on both islands: On the South Island, the Southern Alps rise to 3754 m (12,316 ft); on the North Island, a series of smaller ranges, rarely higher than 1500 m (4920 ft), extend from Wellington north to the East Cape. These ranges form topographic barriers, adding an orographic component to the climate patterns. At higher elevations within these ranges, temperatures are colder, and snow is often present for much of the year.

New Zealand's windward western slopes intercept moisture brought by the westerlies. On the South Island, the West Coast region is the country's wettest, receiving 200 to 1000 cm (79 to 394 in.) of precipitation annually. In contrast, the leeward slopes and coastal plain 100 km (62 mi) to the east, in the rain shadow of the Southern Alps, register the lowest precipitation totals. A similar rainfall pattern occurs on the southern part of the North Island.

Precipitation and temperature combine to produce several climate zones. Subtropical climates (moist all year with a hot summer) occur on the North Island at latitudes lower than about 40° S, where climate is influenced by the trade winds. Temperate climates (with mild winters and cool summers) occur on both islands. Cold winters occur at high elevation in the mountain ranges (classified as highland climates) and in the rain shadow of the Southern Alps on the South Island. As we examine the global distribution of Earth's climates in this chapter, remember the local variation that occurs when we "zoom in" using a larger map scale.

1. How do latitude, elevation, and global wind patterns affect the climates of New Zealand?

2. What factors explain the distribution of precipitation on the South Island?

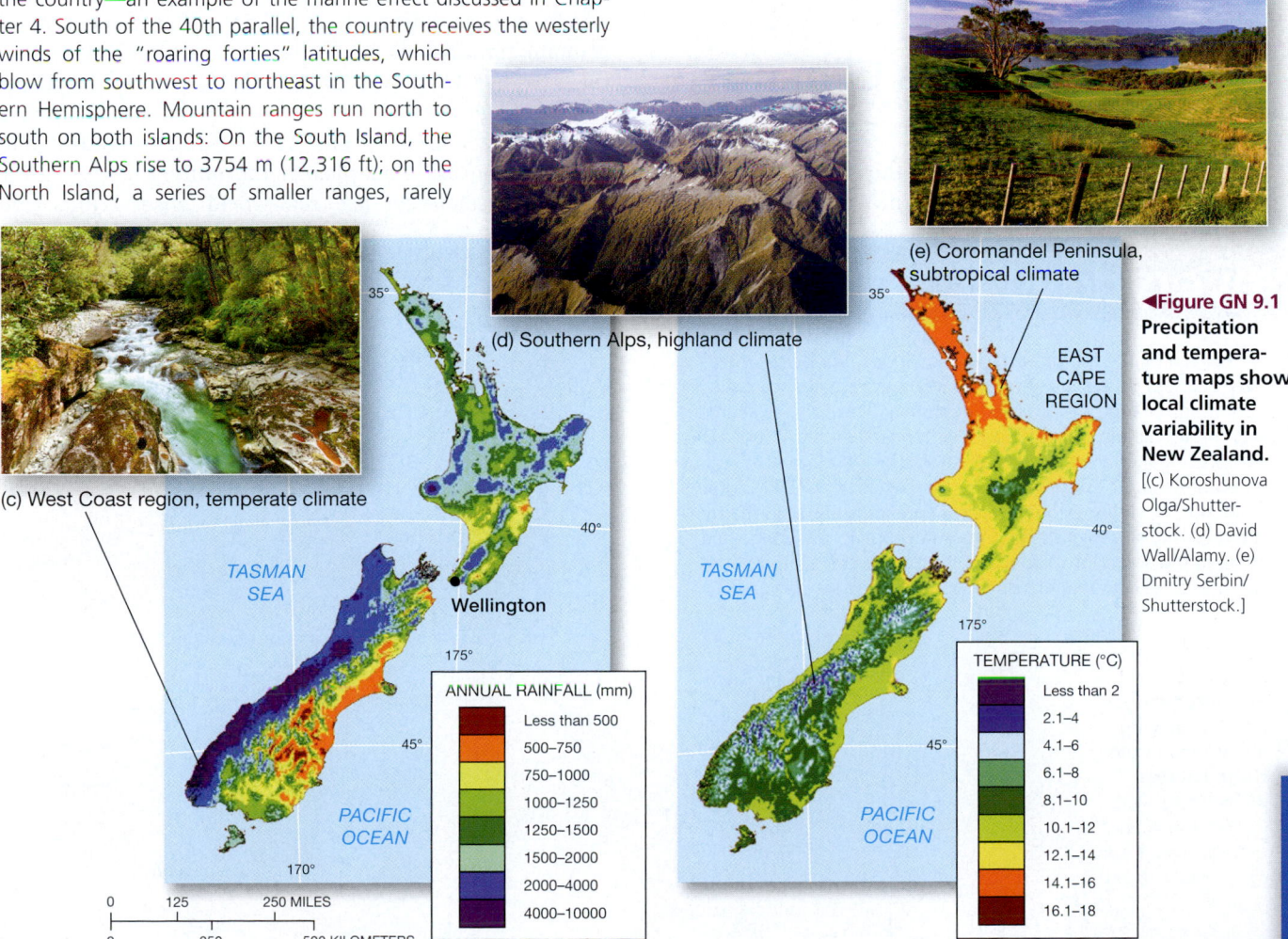

(e) Coromandel Peninsula, subtropical climate

(d) Southern Alps, highland climate

(c) West Coast region, temperate climate

EAST CAPE REGION

TASMAN SEA

Wellington

PACIFIC OCEAN

ANNUAL RAINFALL (mm)

	Less than 500
	500–750
	750–1000
	1000–1250
	1250–1500
	1500–2000
	2000–4000
	4000–10000

0   125   250 MILES
0   250   500 KILOMETERS

(a) Average annual precipitation

TASMAN SEA

PACIFIC OCEAN

TEMPERATURE (°C)

	Less than 2
	2.1–4
	4.1–6
	6.1–8
	8.1–10
	10.1–12
	12.1–14
	14.1–16
	16.1–18

(b) Average annual temperature

◄**Figure GN 9.1 Precipitation and temperature maps show local climate variability in New Zealand.** [(c) Koroshunova Olga/Shutterstock. (d) David Wall/Alamy. (e) Dmitry Serbin/Shutterstock.]

The climate where you live may be humid with distinct seasons, or dry with consistent warmth, or moist and cool—almost any combination is possible. **Climate** is the collective pattern of weather over many years. As we have seen, Earth experiences an almost infinite variety of *weather* at any given time or place. But if we consider a longer time scale, and the variability and extremes of weather over such a time scale, a pattern emerges that constitutes climate. For a given region, this pattern is dynamic rather than static; that is, climate changes over time (we examine this in Chapter 10).

Climatology is the study of climate and its variability, including long-term weather patterns over time (at least 30 years) and space and the controls (causal factors) that produce Earth's diverse climatic conditions. No two places on Earth's surface experience exactly the same climatic conditions; in fact, Earth is a vast collection of microclimates. However, broad similarities among local climates permit their grouping into **climatic regions**, which are areas with similarity in weather statistics. Today, the climate designations we study in this chapter are shifting as temperatures rise over the globe, with far-ranging effects on human societies and natural ecosystems (**Figure 9.1**).

Review of Earth's Climate System

Several important components of the energy–atmosphere system work together to determine climatic conditions on Earth. Simply combining the two principal climatic components—temperature and precipitation—reveals general climate types, sometimes called *climate regimes*, such as tropical deserts (hot and dry), polar ice sheets (cold and dry), and equatorial rain forests (hot and wet).

Figure 9.2 maps the worldwide distribution of precipitation. These patterns reflect the interplay of numerous factors that should now be familiar to you, including temperature and pressure distributions; air mass types; convergent, convectional, orographic, and frontal lifting mechanisms; and the general energy availability that decreases toward the poles. The principal components of Earth's climate system are summarized in Geosystems in Action 9.

Classifying Earth's Climates

Classification is the ordering or grouping of data or phenomena into categories of varying generality. Such generalizations are important organizational tools in science and are especially useful for the spatial analysis of climatic regions. Observed patterns confined to specific regions are at the core of climate classification. When using classifications, we must remember that the boundaries of these regions are *transition zones*, or areas of gradual change. The placement of climate boundaries depends on overall climate patterns rather than precise locations where classifications change.

Climate classifications based on temperature and precipitation are examples of the *empirical approach*, in which scientists use real-world observations and

everyday GEOSYSTEMS

Carried by the *Aedes aegypti* and *Aedes albopcitus* mosquitoes, viruses are spreading into new areas as climatic conditions change. Transmitted by both species, the Zika virus has spread rapidly through South America, Central America, the Caribbean, and into the United States. The estimated U.S. ranges of both mosquito species indicate the potential for Zika to spread to all but 10 states. Dengue fever is spreading through the movement of *Aedes aegypti* mosquitoes into previously unaffected parts of India and into Nepal and Bhutan. In the United States, dengue is still uncommon, but reported cases are rising.

Aedes aegypti

▶**Figure 9.1**
Estimated ranges of Zika-carrying mosquitos in the United States, 2016. [Photo: Nigel Caitlin/Alamy; Map: CDC Vital Signs, www. cdc.gov/vitalsigns/zika.]

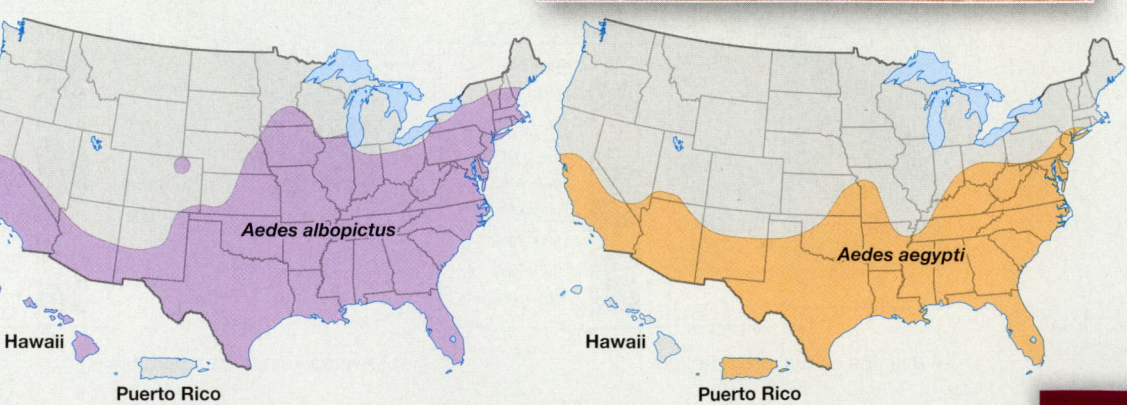

Aedes albopictus

Hawaii

Puerto Rico

Aedes aegypti

Hawaii

Puerto Rico

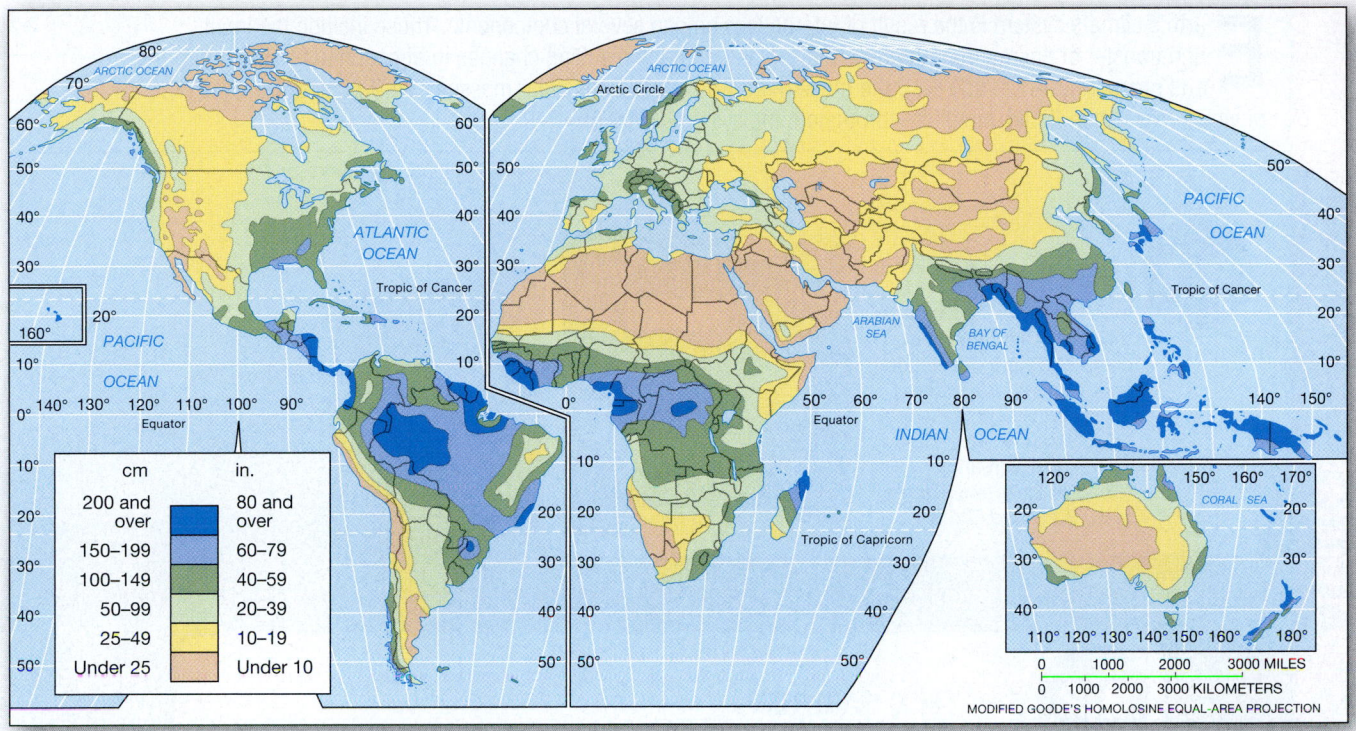

▲**Figure 9.2 Worldwide average annual precipitation.** Worldwide precipitation patterns reflect the interplay of the components of Earth's climate system (shown in GIA 9), and in part determine climate regions.

Animation ⓂⒼ
Global Patterns of Precipitation

https://goo.gl/90QMbl

measurement within the scientific method. An important empirical classification system is the widely recognized Köppen climate classification, designed by Wladimir Köppen (pronounced KUR-pen; 1846–1940), a German climatologist and botanist. Köppen introduced his map showing world climates, coauthored with his student Rudolph Geiger, in 1928, and it was soon widely adopted. Köppen continued to refine it until his death. Appendix B includes a description of his system and the detailed criteria he used to distinguish climatic regions and their boundaries.

The classification system used in *Geosystems* focuses on empirical data—temperature and precipitation measurements (and for the desert areas, moisture deficits). It also examines *causative factors* that produce climate regions, such as interactions between air masses. World climates are grouped into six primary categories. Four of these climate classifications are based mainly on temperature characteristics:

- Tropical climates: tropical latitudes, winterless
- Mesothermal climates: midlatitudes, mild winters
- Microthermal climates: midlatitudes and high latitudes, cold winters
- Polar and highland climates (high latitudes and polar regions, and high elevations at all latitudes)

Only one primary climate classification is based on both moisture and temperature characteristics:

- Dry climates: permanent moisture deficits at all latitudes

Each of these climates is divided into subcategories, all of which are presented on the world climate map in **Figure 9.3** and described in the following sections. The upcoming discussions include at least one **climograph** for each climate subcategory, showing monthly temperature and precipitation for a representative weather station at a selected city. Listed along the top of each climograph are the dominant weather features that influence that climate's characteristics. A location map and selected statistics—including location coordinates, average annual temperature, total annual precipitation, and elevation—complete the information for each station. For each main climate category, a text box introduces the climate characteristics and causal elements and includes a world map showing the general distribution of the climate subtypes.

Climates greatly influence *ecosystems*, the self-regulating communities formed by plants and animals in their nonliving environment. On land, the basic climatic regions determine to a large extent the location of the world's major ecosystems. These broad regions, with their associated soil, plant, and animal communities, are called *biomes*; examples include forest, grassland, savanna, tundra, and desert. We discuss the major terrestrial biomes that fully integrate these global climate patterns in Chapter 20.

Earth's climate system is the result of interactions among several components. These include the input and transfer of energy from the Sun (GIA 9.1 and 9.2); the resulting changes in atmospheric temperature and pressure (GIA 9.3 and 9.4); the movements and interactions of air masses (GIA 9.5); and the transfer of water—as vapor, liquid, or solid—throughout the system (GIA 9.6).

9.1 INSOLATION

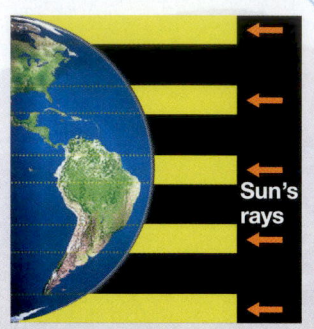

Incoming solar radiation is the energy input for the climate system. Insolation varies by latitude, as well as on a daily and seasonal basis with changing day length and Sun angle. (*Chapter 2; review Figures 2.10, 2.11, and GIA 2*)

Sun's rays

9.2 EARTH'S ENERGY BALANCE

The imbalance created by energy surpluses at the equator and energy deficits at the poles causes the global circulation patterns of winds and ocean currents that drive weather systems. (*Chapter 4; review Figure 4.13*)

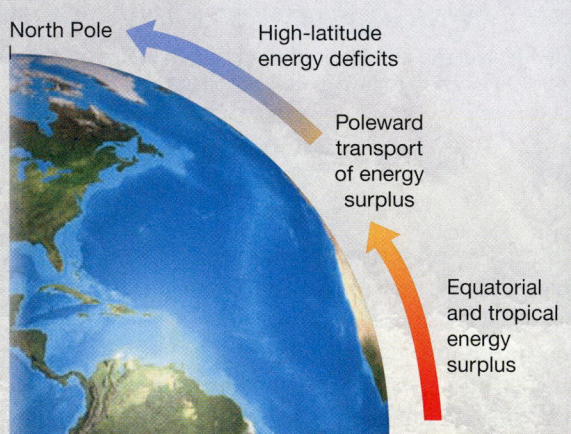

North Pole

High-latitude energy deficits

Poleward transport of energy surplus

Equatorial and tropical energy surplus

9.3 TEMPERATURE

Primary temperature controls are latitude, elevation, cloud cover, and land–water heating differences. The pattern of world temperatures is affected by global winds, ocean currents, and air masses. (*Chapter 4; review Figures 4.29 through 4.32*)

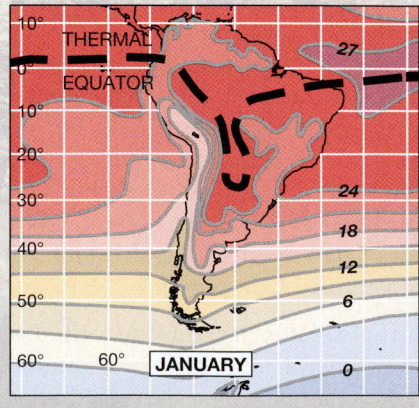

THERMAL EQUATOR

JANUARY

MasteringGeography™

Visit the Study Area in MasteringGeography™ to explore Earth's climate system.

Visualize: Study a NASA video of modeling Earth's climate.

Assess: Demonstrate understanding of Earth's climate system (if assigned by instructor).

9.4 AIR PRESSURE

Winds flow from areas of high pressure to areas of low pressure. The equatorial low creates a belt of wet climates. Subtropical highs create areas of dry climates. Pressure patterns influence atmospheric circulation and movement of air masses. Oceanic circulation and multiyear oscillations in pressure and temperature patterns over the oceans also affect weather and climate. (*Chapter 5; review Figures 5.12 and GIA 5*)

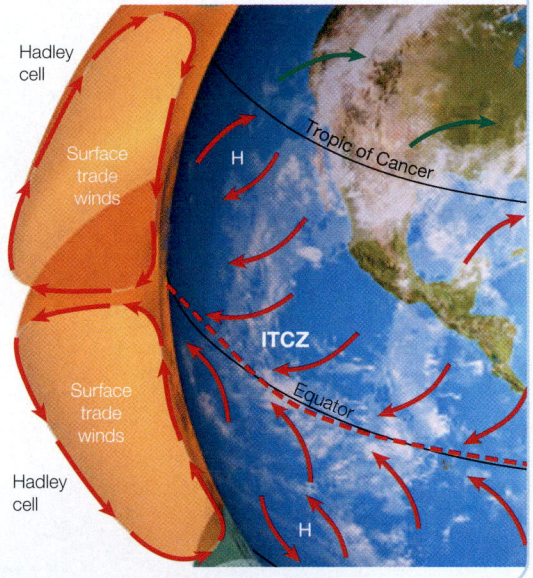

9.5 AIR MASSES

Vast bodies of homogeneous air form over oceanic and continental source regions, taking on the characteristics of their source region. As these air masses migrate, they carry their temperature and moisture conditions to new regions. (*Chapter 7; review Figure 7.2*)

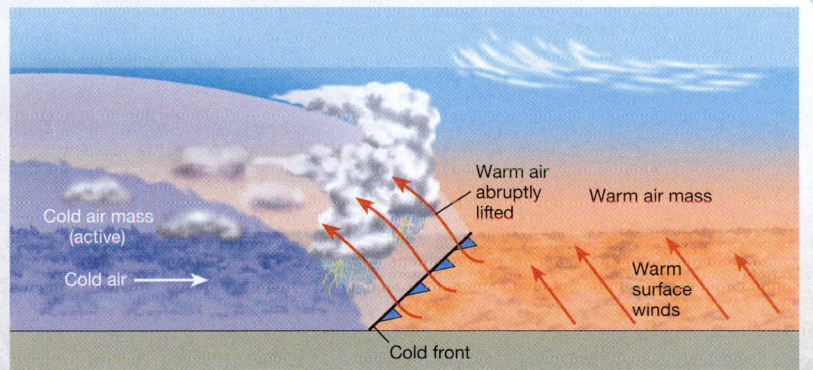

9.6 ATMOSPHERIC MOISTURE

The movement of water through the hydrologic cycle—including the processes of evaporation, transpiration, condensation, and precipitation—affects weather and ultimately determines Earth's climates. (*Chapters 6 and 8; review Figure 8.5*)

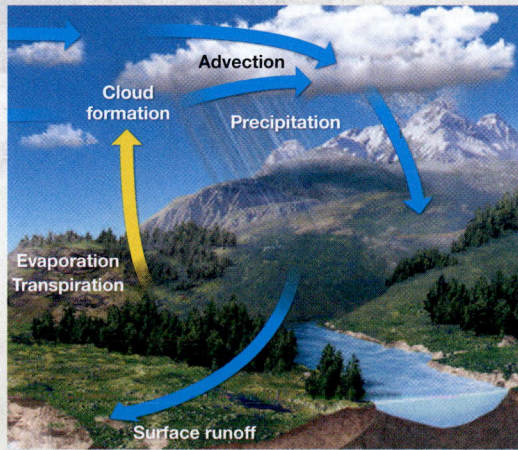

GEOquiz

1. Analyze: How do these six components of Earth's climate system interact to produce the world climates in Figure 9.3?

2. Explain: Where are the trade winds on the view of the globe in GIA 9.4 above? Explain and locate areas of warm, wet climates and hot, dry climates in relation to the Hadley cells.

3. Infer: What is the general pattern of energy flow in the atmosphere? Explain your answer.

4. Discuss: Describe the role that each component of the climate system plays in causing precipitation patterns on Earth.

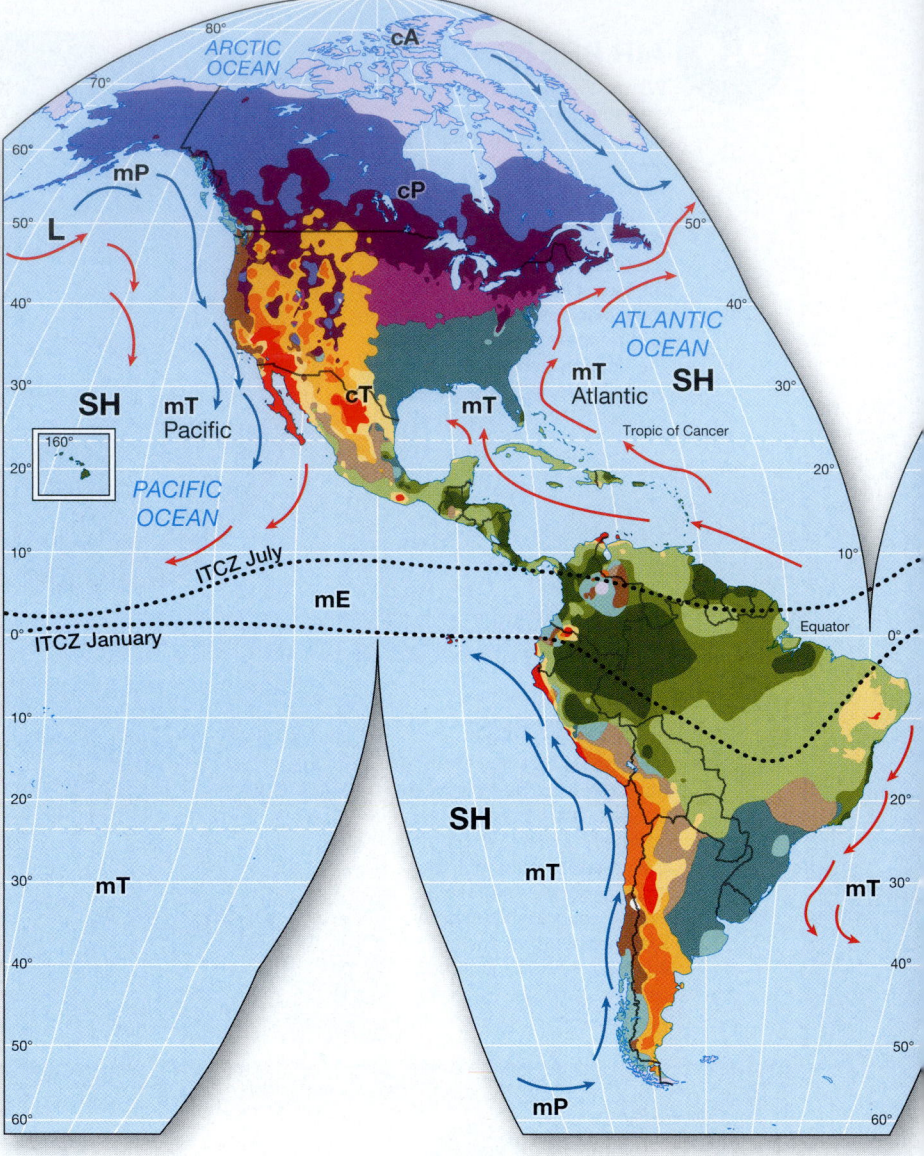

▲Figure 9.3 World climate classification. Annotated on this map are selected air masses, nearshore ocean currents, pressure systems, and the January and July locations of the ITCZ. Use the colors in the legend to locate various climate types. [Climate categories based on M. C. Peel, B. L. Finlayson, and T. A. McMahon et al., "Updated world map of the Köppen–Geiger climate classification," *Hydrology and Earth System Sciences* 11 (2007): 1633–1644.]

OCEAN CURRENTS (Fig. 5.21)

→ Warm current

→ Cool current

INTERTROPICAL CONVERGENCE ZONE
(Fig. 5.12, GIA 5)

•••• ITCZ July or January

AIR PRESSURE SYSTEMS (Fig. 5.12)

SH Subtropical high

L Aleutian Low, Icelandic Low

AIR MASSES (Fig. 7.2)

mP Maritime polar
(cool, humid)

cP Continental polar
(cool, cold, dry)

mT Maritime tropical
(warm, humid)

cA Continental arctic
(very cold, dry)

cT Continental tropical
(hot, dry summer only)

mE Maritime equatorial
(warm, wet)

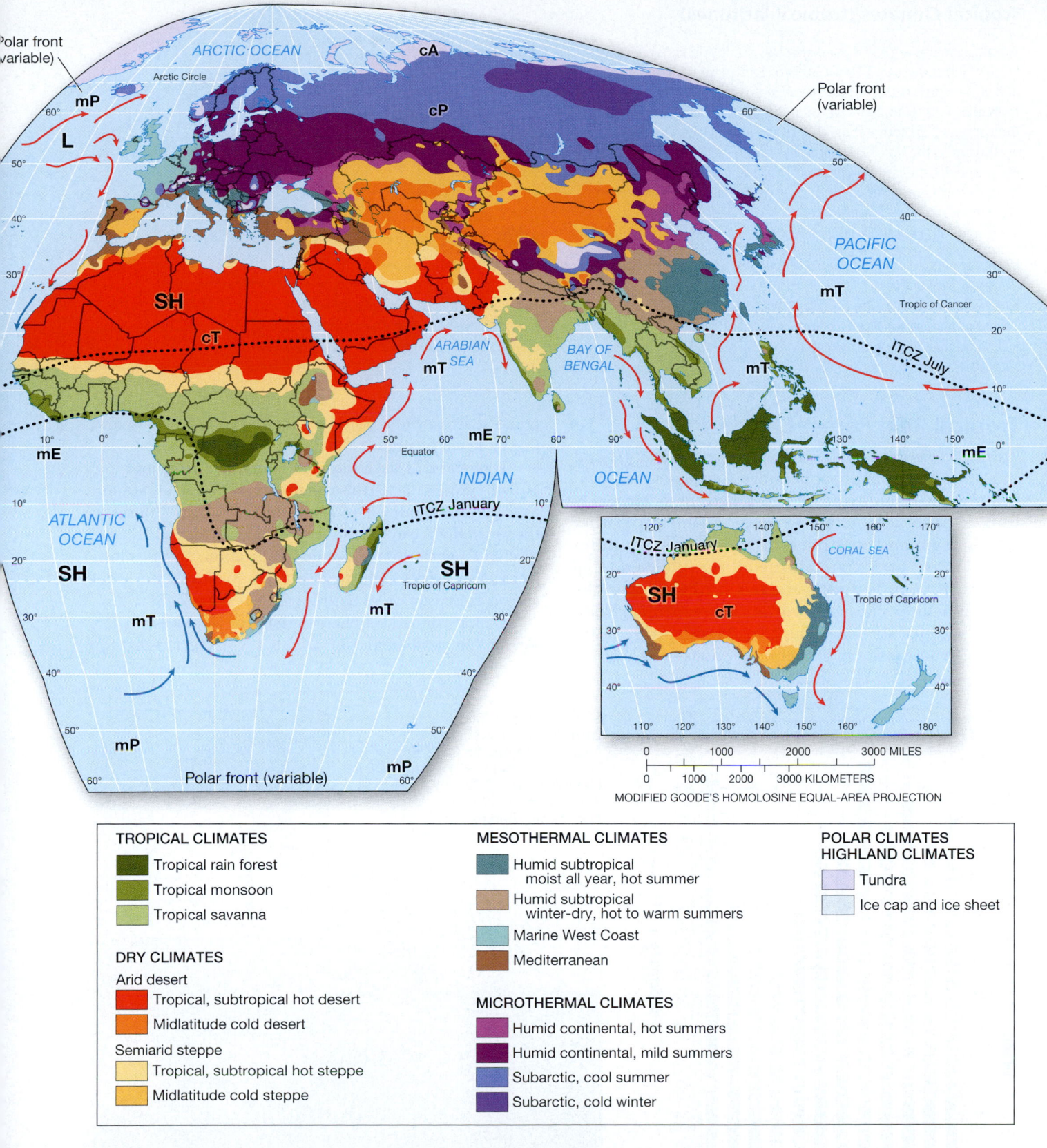

TROPICAL CLIMATES

- Tropical rain forest
- Tropical monsoon
- Tropical savanna

DRY CLIMATES

Arid desert
- Tropical, subtropical hot desert
- Midlatitude cold desert

Semiarid steppe
- Tropical, subtropical hot steppe
- Midlatitude cold steppe

MESOTHERMAL CLIMATES

- Humid subtropical
  moist all year, hot summer
- Humid subtropical
  winter-dry, hot to warm summers
- Marine West Coast
- Mediterranean

MICROTHERMAL CLIMATES

- Humid continental, hot summers
- Humid continental, mild summers
- Subarctic, cool summer
- Subarctic, cold winter

POLAR CLIMATES
HIGHLAND CLIMATES

- Tundra
- Ice cap and ice sheet

Tropical Climates (tropical latitudes)

Tropical climates are the most extensive, occupying about 19% of Earth's land surface and about 36% of Earth's total surface (land and water combined). The tropical climates straddle the equator from about 20° N to 20° S latitude, roughly between the Tropics of Cancer and Capricorn—thus, the name. Tropical climates stretch northward to the tip of Florida and to south-central Mexico, central India, and Southeast Asia and southward to northern Australia, Madagascar, central Africa, and southern Brazil. These climates truly are winterless.

Important causal elements include:

- Consistent daylength and insolation, which produce consistently warm temperatures;
- Effects of the intertropical convergence zone (ITCZ), which brings rains as it shifts seasonally with the high Sun;
- Warm ocean temperatures and unstable maritime air masses.

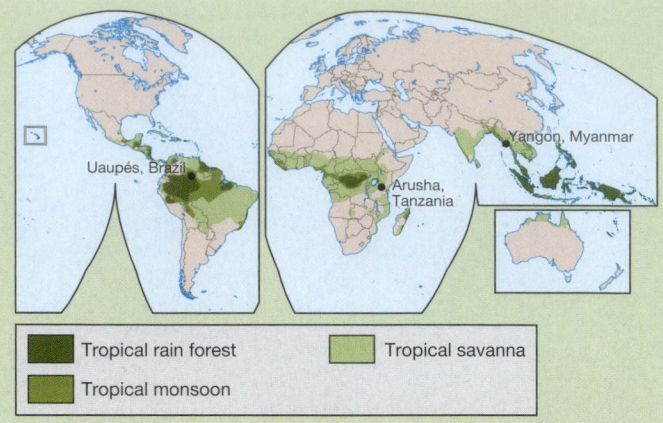

Tropical climates have three distinct regimes: *tropical rain forest* (ITCZ present all year), *tropical monsoon* (ITCZ present 6 to 12 months annually), and *tropical savanna* (ITCZ present less than 6 months).

Tropical Rain Forest Climates

Tropical rain forest climates are constantly moist and warm. Convectional thunderstorms, triggered by local heating and trade-wind convergence, peak each day from midafternoon to late evening inland and earlier in the day along coastlines, where the marine influence is strong. Precipitation follows the migrating ITCZ, which shifts northward and southward with the Sun throughout the year, but influences tropical rain forest regions all year long. Not surprisingly, water surpluses in these regions are enormous—the world's greatest streamflow volumes occur in the Amazon and Congo River basins.

High rainfall sustains lush evergreen broadleaf tree growth, producing Earth's equatorial and tropical rain forests. The leaf canopy is so dense that little light diffuses to the forest floor, leaving the ground surface dim and sparse in plant cover. Dense surface vegetation occurs along riverbanks, where light is abundant. (We examine widespread deforestation of Earth's rain forest in Chapter 20.)

Uaupés, Brazil, is characteristic of tropical rain forest. On the climograph in **Figure 9.4**, you can see that the

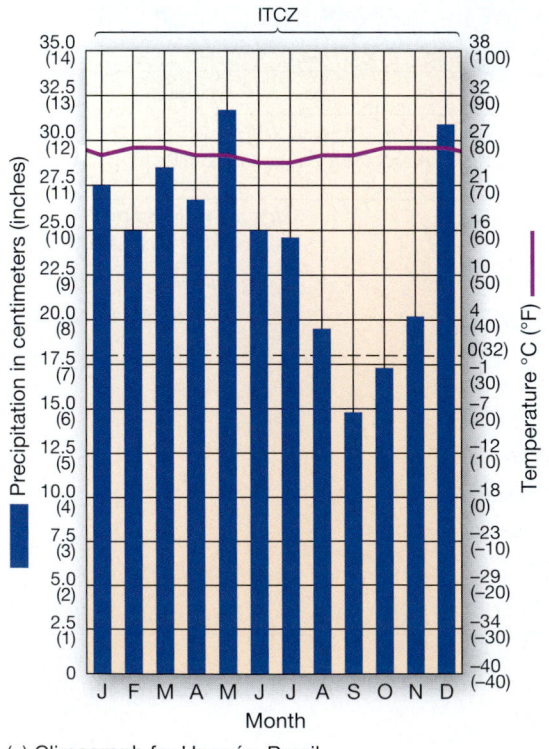

(a) Climograph for Uaupés, Brazil.

▲**Figure 9.4 Tropical rain forest climate.** [(b) Sue Cunnigham Photographic/Alamy.]

Station: Uaupés, Brazil
Lat/long: 0° 06′ S 67° 02′ W
Avg. Ann. Temp.: 25°C (77°F)
Total Ann. Precip.: 291.7 cm (114.8 in.)
Elevation: 86 m (282.2 ft)
Population: 10,000
Ann. Temp. Range: 2 C° (3.6 F°)
Ann. Hr of Sunshine: 2018

(b) The rain forest along a tributary of the Rio Negro, Amazonas state, Brazil.

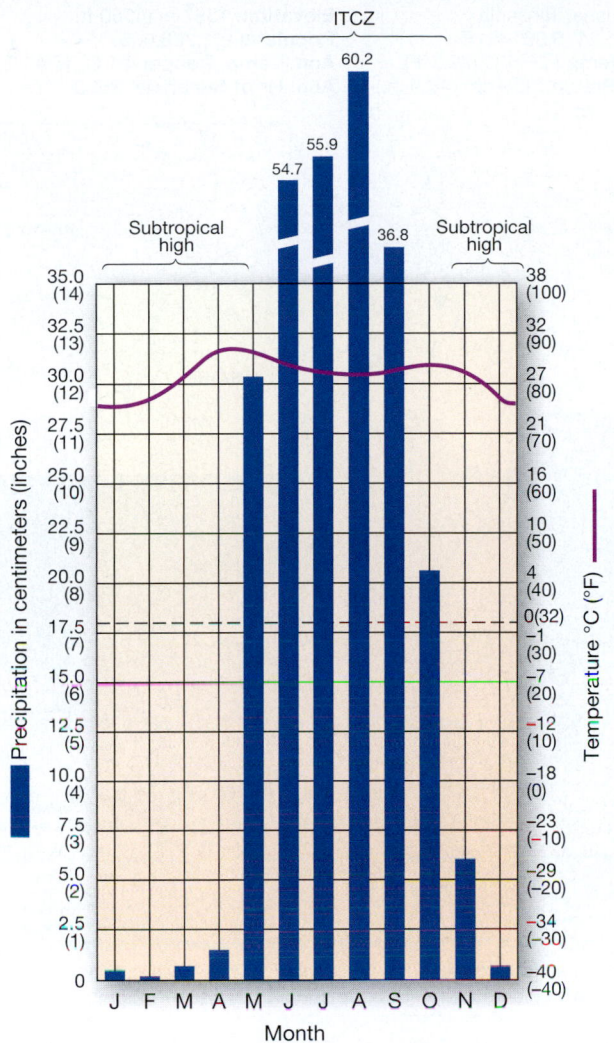

▼**Figure 9.5** **Tropical monsoon climate.** [(b) Shaileshnanal/
Shuttershock.]

Station: Yangon, Myanmar*
Lat/long: 16° 47' N 96° 10' E
Avg. Ann. Temp.: 27.3°C (81.1°F)
Total Ann. Precip.: 268.8 cm
(105.8 in.)
Elevation: 23 m (76 ft)
Population: 6,000,000
Ann. Temp. Range: 5.5 C° (9.9 F°)
*(Formerly Rangoon, Burma)

(a) Climograph for Yangon, Myanmar (formerly Rangoon, Burma); city of Sittwe also noted on map.

(b) Mixed monsoonal forest and scrub characteristic of the region in eastern India.

month of lowest precipitation receives nearly 15 cm (6 in.) and the annual temperature range is barely 2 C° (3.6 F°). In all such climates, the diurnal (day-to-night) temperature range exceeds the annual average minimum–maximum (coolest to warmest) range: Day–night differences can range more than 11 C° (20 F°), more than five times the annual monthly average range.

The only interruption in the distribution of tropical rain forest climates across the equatorial region is in the highlands of the South American Andes and in East Africa (see Figure 9.3). There, higher elevations produce lower temperatures; Mount Kilimanjaro is less than 4° south of the equator, but at 5895 m (19,340 ft), it has permanent glacial ice on its summit (although this ice has now nearly disappeared due to increasing air temperatures). Such mountainous sites fall within the *highland* climate category.

Tropical Monsoon Climates

Tropical monsoon climates feature a dry season that lasts 1 or more months. Rainfall brought by the ITCZ falls in these areas for 6 or more months each year (whereas

in the tropical rain forest regions, the ITCZ brings rain throughout the year). The dry season occurs when the ITCZ has moved away so that the convergence effects are not present. Yangon, Myanmar (formerly Rangoon, Burma), is an example of this climate type (**Figure 9.5**). Mountains prevent cold air masses from central Asia from moving over Yangon, resulting in its high average annual temperatures.

About 480 km (300 mi) north in another coastal city, Sittwe (Akyab), Myanmar, on the Bay of Bengal, annual precipitation rises to 515 cm (203 in.), considerably higher than Yangon's 269 cm (106 in.). Therefore, Yangon is a drier area than that farther north along the coast, but it still exceeds the 250-cm annual precipitation criterion in use for the tropical monsoon classification.

Tropical monsoon climates lie principally along coastal areas within the tropical rain forest climatic realm and experience seasonal variations of wind and precipitation. Vegetation in this climate type typically consists of evergreen trees grading into thorn forests on the drier margins near the adjoining tropical savanna climates.

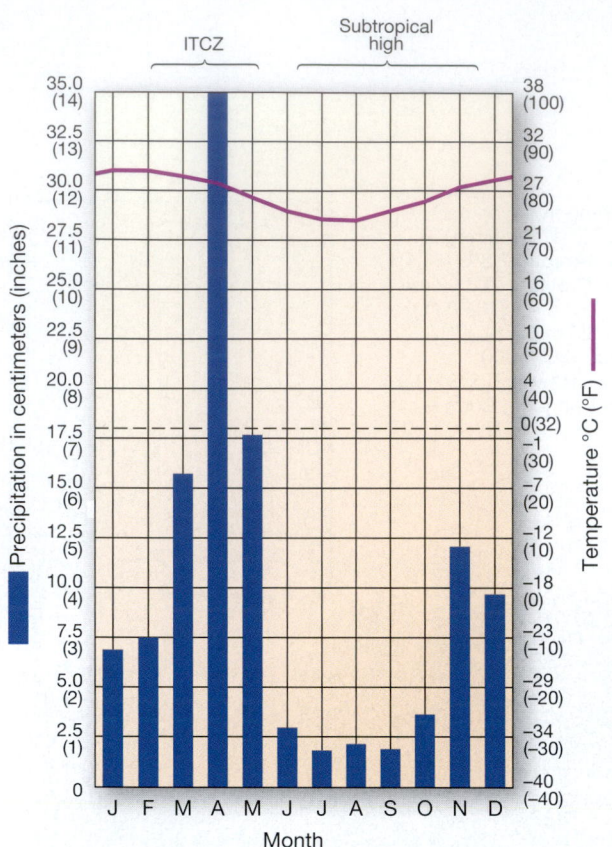

Station: Arusha, Tanzania
Lat/long: 3° 24′ S 36° 42′ E
Avg. Ann. Temp.: 26.5°C (79.7°F)
Total Ann. Precip.: 119 cm (46.9 in.)

Elevation: 1387 m (4550 ft)
Population: 1,368,000
Ann. Temp. Range: 4.1 C° (7.4 F°)
Ann. Hr of Sunshine: 2600

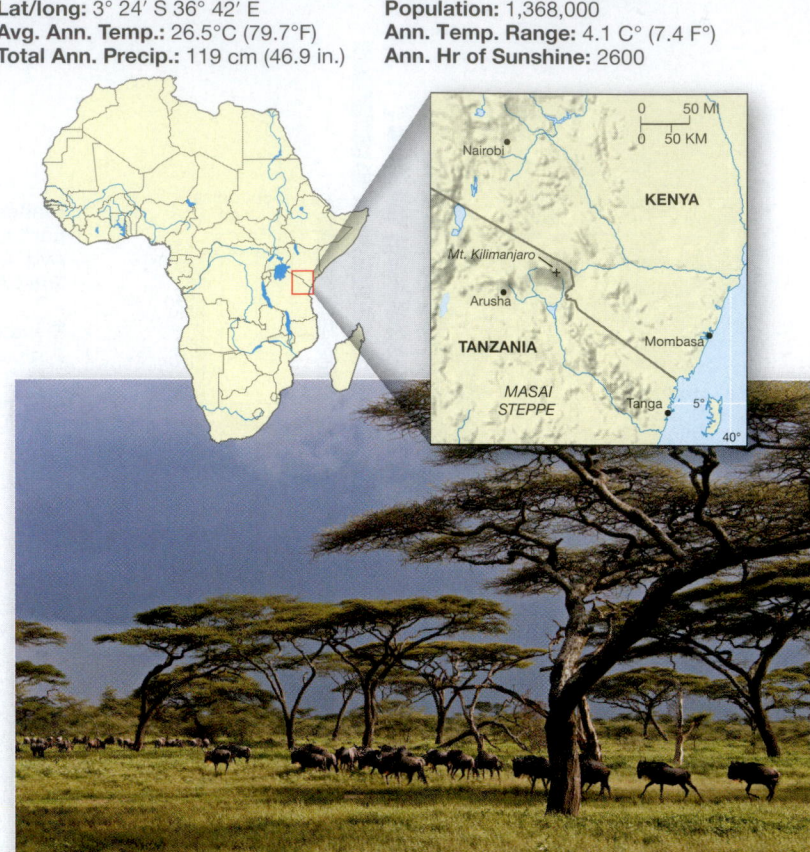

(a) Climograph for Arusha, Tanzania; note the intense dry period.

(b) Characteristic landscape in the Ngorongoro Conservation Area, Tanzania, near Arusha with plants adapted to seasonally dry water budgets.

▲**Figure 9.6 Tropical savanna climate.** [(b) Michele Burgess/Alamy.]

Tropical Savanna Climates

Tropical savanna climates exist poleward of the tropical rain forest climates. The ITCZ reaches these climate regions for about 6 months or less of the year as it migrates with the summer Sun. Summers are wetter than winters because convectional rains accompany the shifting ITCZ when it is overhead. In contrast, when the ITCZ is farthest away and high pressure dominates, conditions are notably dry. Thus, the moisture demand exceeds the moisture supply in winter, causing water-budget deficits.

Temperatures vary more in tropical savanna climates than in tropical rain forest regions. The tropical savanna regime can have two temperature maximums during the year because the Sun's direct rays are overhead twice—before and after the summer solstice in each hemisphere

as the Sun moves between the equator and the tropics. Grasslands with scattered trees, drought resistant to cope with the highly variable precipitation, dominate the tropical savanna regions.

The climate of Arusha, Tanzania, represents tropical savanna conditions (**Figure 9.6**). This metropolitan area is near the grassy plains of the Serengeti, a heavily visited national park that hosts one of the largest annual mammal migrations in the world. Temperatures are consistent with tropical climates, despite the elevation (1387 m, or 4550 ft) of the station. On the climograph, note the marked dryness from June to October, which indicates changing dominant pressure systems rather than annual changes in temperature. This region is near the transition to the drier *desert hot steppe* climates to the northeast (discussed later in the chapter).

GEOreport **9.1**   Tropical climate zones advance to higher latitudes

The belt of tropical climates that straddles the equator is getting wider. Recent research suggests that this zone has widened by more than 2° of latitude since 1979, with an overall advance of 0.7° of latitude per decade. As the tropical climates move poleward, the dry subtropical regions are becoming drier, with more frequent droughts.

Mesothermal Climates (midlatitudes, mild winters)

Mesothermal, meaning "middle temperature," describes these warm and temperate climates, where true seasonality begins. More than half the world's population resides in mesothermal climates, which occupy about 13% of Earth's land surface. The mesothermal climates, and nearby portions of the microthermal climates (cold winters), are regions of great weather variability, for these are the latitudes of greatest air mass interaction.

Causal elements include:

- Latitudinal effects on insolation and temperature, as summers transition from hot to warm to cool moving poleward from the tropics;
- Shifting maritime and continental air masses guided by upper-air westerly winds;
- Migrating cyclonic (low-pressure) and anticyclonic (high-pressure) systems, bringing changeable weather conditions and air mass conflicts;
- Effects of sea-surface temperatures on air mass strength; cooler temperatures along west coasts weaken air masses, and warmer temperatures along east coasts strengthen air masses.

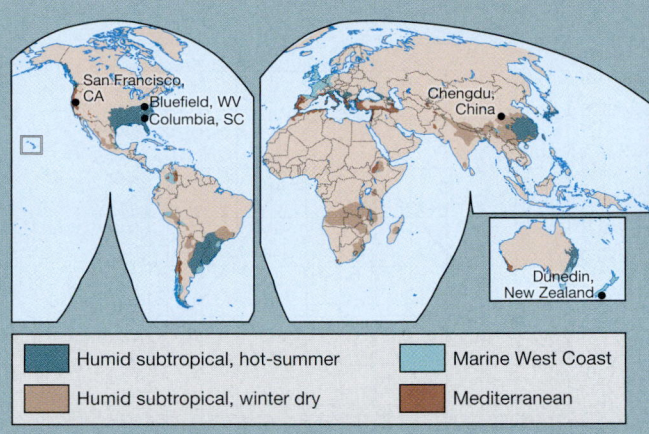

Mesothermal climates are humid, except where subtropical high pressure produces dry-summer conditions. Their four distinct regimes, based on precipitation variability, are *humid subtropical hot-summer* (moist all year), *humid subtropical winter-dry* (hot to warm summers, in Asia), *marine west coast* (warm to cool summers, moist all year), and *Mediterranean dry-summer* (warm to hot summers).

Humid Subtropical Hot-Summer Climates

Humid subtropical climates either have hot summers and are moist all year or have hot to warm summers and a pronounced winter-dry period, as occurs in eastern and southern Asia. *Humid subtropical hot-summer* climates are influenced during summer by maritime tropical air masses generated over warm waters off eastern coasts. This warm, moist, unstable air produces convectional showers over land. In fall, winter, and spring, maritime tropical and continental polar air masses interact, generating frontal activity and frequent midlatitude cyclonic storms. These two mechanisms produce year-round precipitation, which averages 100–200 cm (40–80 in.) a year.

In North America, humid subtropical hot-summer climates are found across the southeastern United States. Columbia, South Carolina, is a representative station (**Figure 9.7**), with characteristic winter precipitation from cyclonic storm activity (other examples are Atlanta, Memphis, and New Orleans). Nagasaki, Japan, is characteristic of an Asian humid subtropical hot-summer station (**Figure 9.8**), where winter precipitation is less because of the effects of the East Asian monsoon. However, the lower precipitation of winter is not quite dry enough to change the climate category to *humid subtropical winter-dry*. Nagasaki receives more overall annual precipitation (196 cm, 77 in.) than similar climates in the United States, owing to the monsoonal flow pattern.

Humid Subtropical Winter-Dry Climates

Humid subtropical winter-dry climates are related to the winter-dry, seasonal pulse of the monsoons. They extend poleward from tropical savanna climates and have a summer month that receives 10 times more precipitation than their driest winter month. Chengdu, China, is a representative station in Asia. **Figure 9.9** demonstrates the strong correlation between precipitation and the high summer Sun.

Large numbers of people live in the humid subtropical hot-summer and humid subtropical winter-dry climates, demonstrated by the large populations of north-central India, southeastern China, and the southeastern United States. Although these climates are relatively habitable for humans, natural hazards exist; for example, the intense summer rains of the Asian monsoon cause flooding in India and Bangladesh that affects millions of people. In the U.S. Southeast, dramatic thunderstorms are common, often spawning tornadoes, and rainfall associated with hurricanes can cause seasonal flooding events.

Marine West Coast Climates

Marine west coast climates, featuring mild winters and cool summers, are characteristic of Europe and other middle- to high-latitude west coasts (see Figure 9.3 and refer back to Geosystems Now). In the United States, these climates, with their cooler summers, are in contrast to the humid subtropical hot-summer climate of the Southeast.

Maritime polar air masses—cool, moist, unstable—dominate marine west coast climates. Weather systems forming along the polar front and maritime polar air masses move into these regions throughout the year, making weather quite unpredictable. Coastal fog, annually totaling 30 to 60 days, is a part of the moderating marine influence. Frosts are possible and tend to shorten the growing season.

Marine west coast climates are unusually mild for their latitude. They extend along the coastal margins of the Aleutian Islands in the North Pacific, cover the southern third of Iceland in the North Atlantic and coastal Scandinavia, and dominate the British Isles. Even at these high-latitude locations, average monthly temperatures are above freezing throughout the year. Unlike

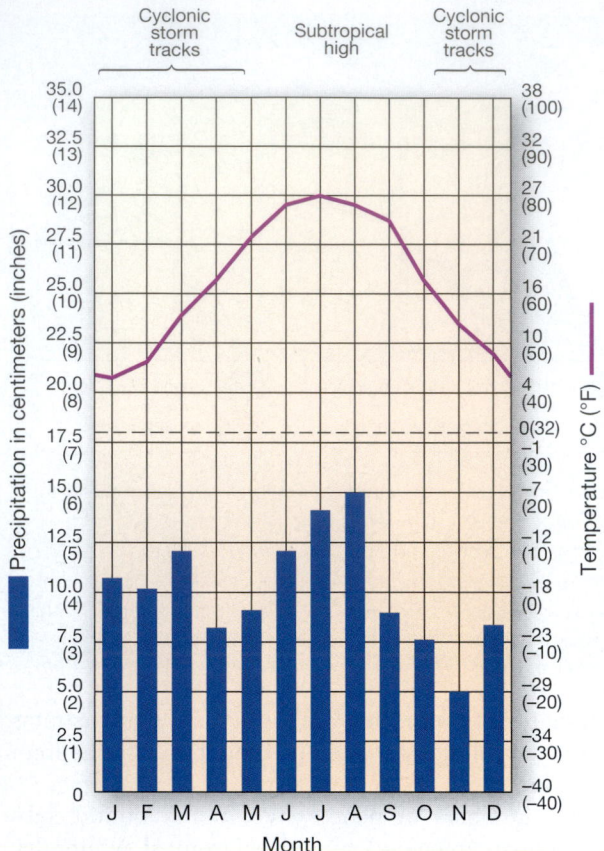

(a) Climograph for Columbia, South Carolina.

Station: Columbia, South Carolina
Lat/long: 34° N 81° W
Avg. Ann. Temp.: 17.3°C (63.1°F)
Total Ann. Precip.: 126.5 cm (49.8 in.)
Elevation: 96 m (315 ft)
Population: 116,000
Ann. Temp. Range: 20.7 C°
      (37.3 F°)
Ann. Hr of Sunshine: 2800

(b) Water lilies and mixed evergreen forest of cypress and pine in southern Georgia.

▲**Figure 9.7 Humid subtropical hot-summer climate.** [(b) Bobbé Christopherson.]

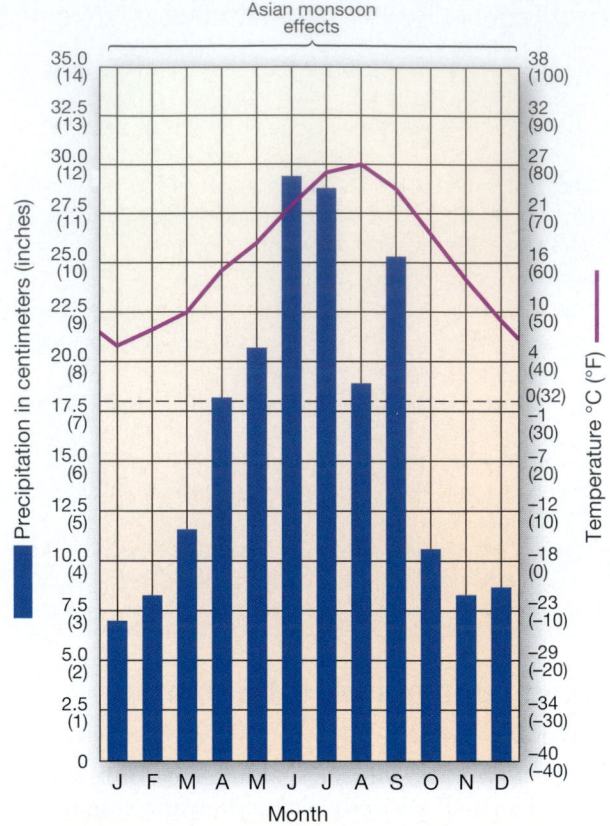

(a) Climograph for Nagasaki, Japan.

Station: Nagasaki, Japan
Lat/long: 32° 44′ N 129° 52′ E
Avg. Ann. Temp.: 16°C (60.8°F)
Total Ann. Precip.: 195.7 cm (77 in.)
Elevation: 27 m (88.6 ft)
Population: 1,585,000
Ann. Temp. Range: 21 C° (37.8 F°)
Ann. Hr of Sunshine: 2131

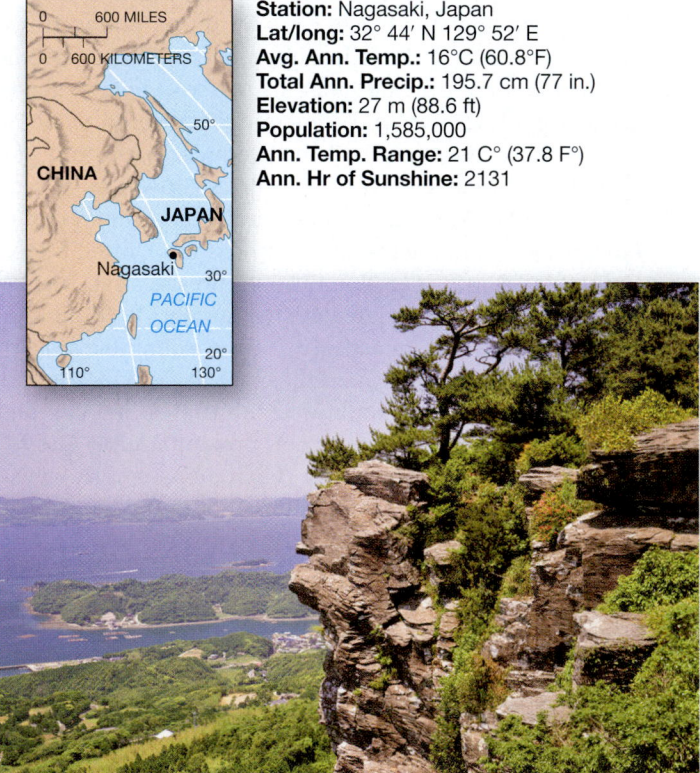

(b) Landscape on Kitakyujukuri Island, near Nagasaki and Sasebo, Japan, in spring season.

▲**Figure 9.8 Humid subtropical hot-summer climate, Asian region.** [(b) JTB Photo/photolibrary.com.]

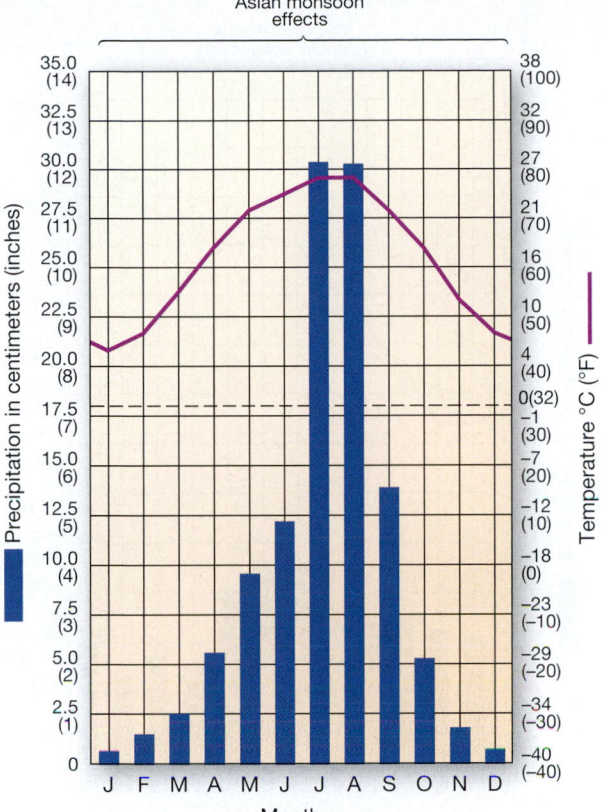

Asian monsoon effects

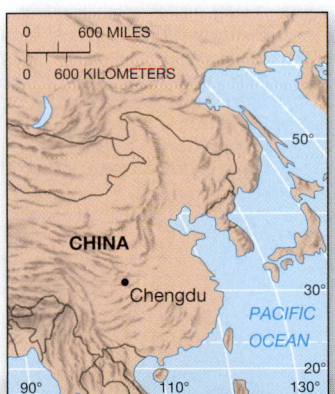

(a) Climograph for Chengdu, China. Note the summer-wet monsoonal precipitation.

Station: Chengdu, China
Lat/long: 30° 40′ N 104° 04′ E
Avg. Ann. Temp.: 17°C (62.6°F)
Total Ann. Precip.:
    114.6 cm (45.1 in.)
Elevation: 498 m (1633.9 ft)
Population: 2,500,000
Ann. Temp. Range:
    20 C° (36 F°)
Ann. Hr of Sunshine: 1058

(b) Agricultural fields near Chengdu, Sichuaun, China.

▲**Figure 9.9 Humid subtropical winter-dry climate.** [(b) TAO Images Limited/Alamy.]

Europe, where the marine west coast regions extend quite far inland, mountains in Canada, Alaska, Chile, and Australia restrict this climate to a relatively narrow coastal region. In the Southern Hemisphere, the marine west coast climate extends across New Zealand (see the maps in this chapter's *Geosystems Now*). The climograph for Dunedin, New Zealand, demonstrates the moderate temperature patterns and the annual temperature range for this climate type (**Figure 9.10**).

An interesting anomaly occurs in the eastern United States. In portions of the Appalachian highlands, which are in the humid subtropical hot-summer climate region of the continent, increased elevation affects temperatures, producing a cooler summer and an isolated area of marine west coast climate. The climograph for Bluefield, West Virginia (**Figure 9.11**), reveals marine west coast temperature and precipitation patterns, despite its continental location in the East. Vegetation similarities between the Appalachians and the Pacific Northwest attracted many emigrants from the East to settle in these climatically familiar environments in the Northwest.

Mediterranean Dry-Summer Climates

The *Mediterranean dry-summer* climate designation specifies that at least 70% of annual precipitation occurs during the winter months. This is in contrast to climates in most of the rest of the world, which exhibit summer-maximum precipitation. Across narrow bands of the planet during summer months, shifting cells of subtropical high pressure block moisture-bearing winds from adjacent regions. This shifting of stable, warm to hot, dry air over an area in summer and away from that area in winter creates a pronounced dry-summer and wet-winter pattern. For example, in summer the continental tropical air mass over the Sahara in Africa shifts northward over the Mediterranean region and blocks marine air masses and movement of cyclonic storms.

Worldwide, cool offshore ocean currents (the California Current, Canary Current, Peru Current, Benguela Current, and West Australian Current, shown in Figure 5.21) produce stability in overlying air masses along west coasts at higher latitude than the subtropical high pressure. The world climate map in Figure 9.3 shows Mediterranean dry-summer climates along the western margins of North America, central Chile, and the southwestern tip of Africa as well as across southern Australia and the Mediterranean Basin—the climate's namesake region. Examine the offshore currents along each of these regions on the map.

As discussed in Chapter 4, marine effects moderate the Mediterranean climate of San Francisco, California, producing a cool summer (**Figure 9.12**). The transition to a hot summer occurs no more than 24–32 km (15–20 mi) inland from the coast.

The Mediterranean dry-summer climate brings summer water-balance deficits. Winter precipitation recharges soil moisture, but water use usually

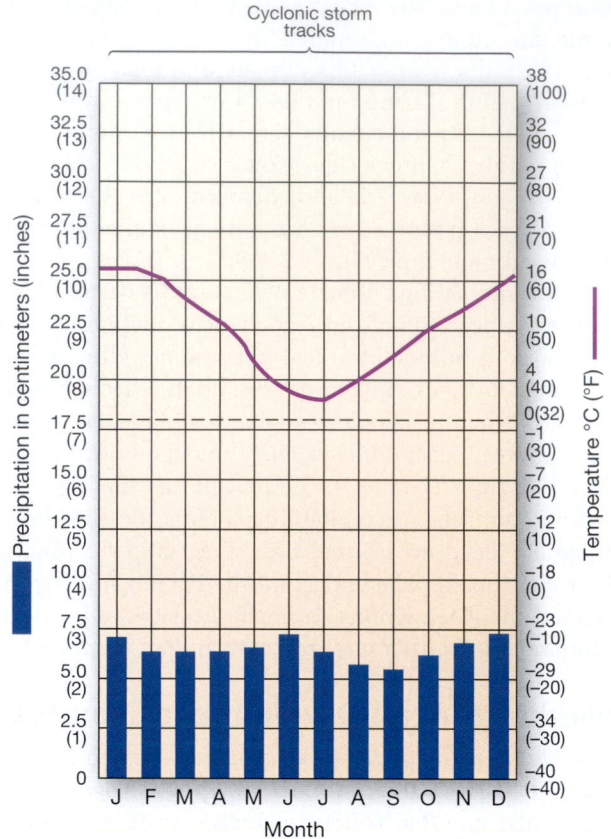

Cyclonic storm tracks

(a) Climograph for Dunedin, New Zealand.

Station: Dunedin, New Zealand
Lat/long: 45° 54′ S 170° 31′ E
Avg. Ann. Temp.: 10.2°C (50.3°F)
Total Ann. Precip.: 78.7 cm (31.0 in.)
Elevation: 1.5 m (5 ft)
Population: 120,000
Ann. Temp. Range: 14.2 C° (25.5 F°)

(b) Meadow, forest, and mountains, South Island, New Zealand.

▲**Figure 9.10 A Southern Hemisphere marine west coast climate.** [(b) David Wall/Alamy.]

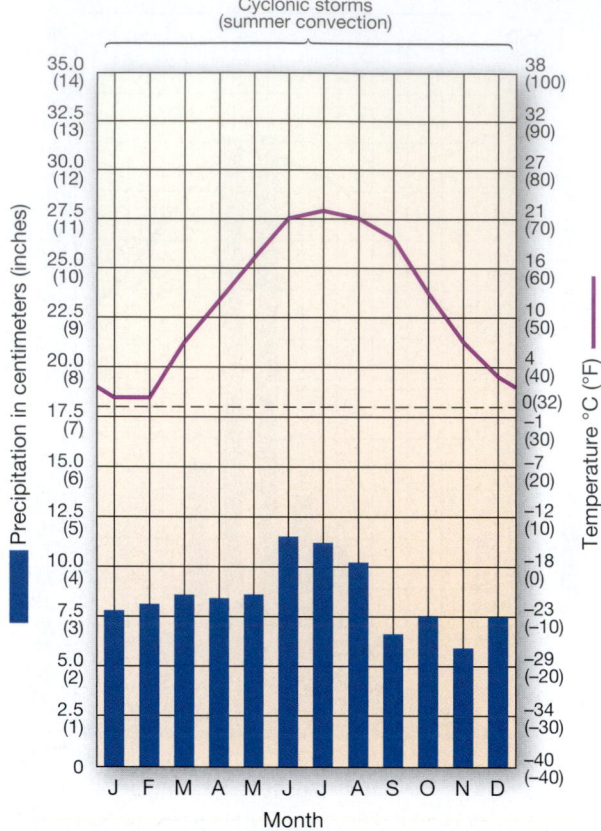

Cyclonic storms (summer convection)

(a) Climograph for Bluefield, West Virginia.

Station: Bluefield, West Virginia
Lat/long: 37° 16′ N 81° 13′ W
Avg. Ann. Temp.: 12°C (53.6°F)
Total Ann. Precip.: 101.9 cm (40.1 in.)
Elevation: 780 m (2559 ft)
Population: 11,000
Ann. Temp. Range: 21 C° (37.8 F°)

(b) Characteristic mixed forest in Pocahontas County, West Virginia.

▲**Figure 9.11 Marine west coast climate in the Appalachians of the eastern United States.** [(b) Thomas R. Fletcher/Alamy.]

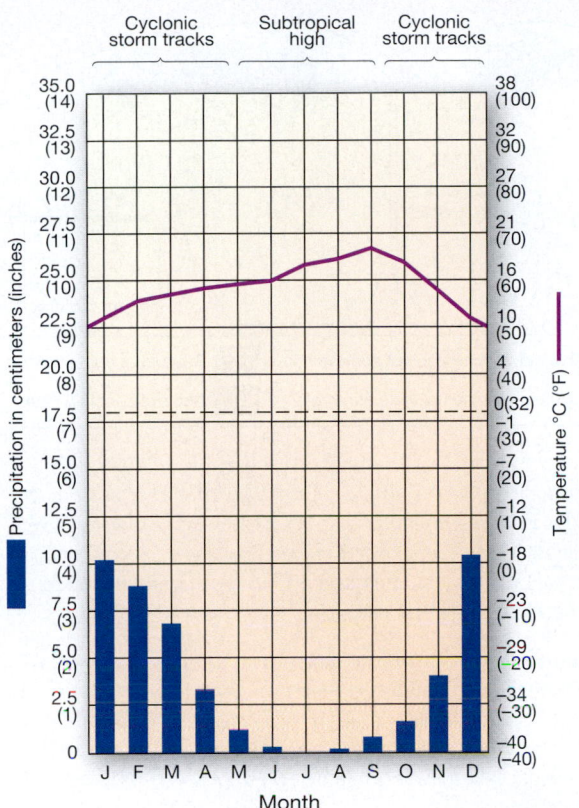

Cyclonic storm tracks | Subtropical high | Cyclonic storm tracks

(a) Climograph for San Francisco, California, with its cooler dry summer.

Station: San Francisco, California
Lat/long: 37° 37′ N 122° 23′ W
Avg. Ann. Temp.:
    14.6°C (57.2°F)
Total Ann. Precip.:
    56.6 cm (22.3 in.)
Elevation: 5 m (16.4 ft)
Population: 777,000
Ann. Temp. Range:
    11.4 C° (20.5 F°)
Ann. Hr of Sunshine:
    2975

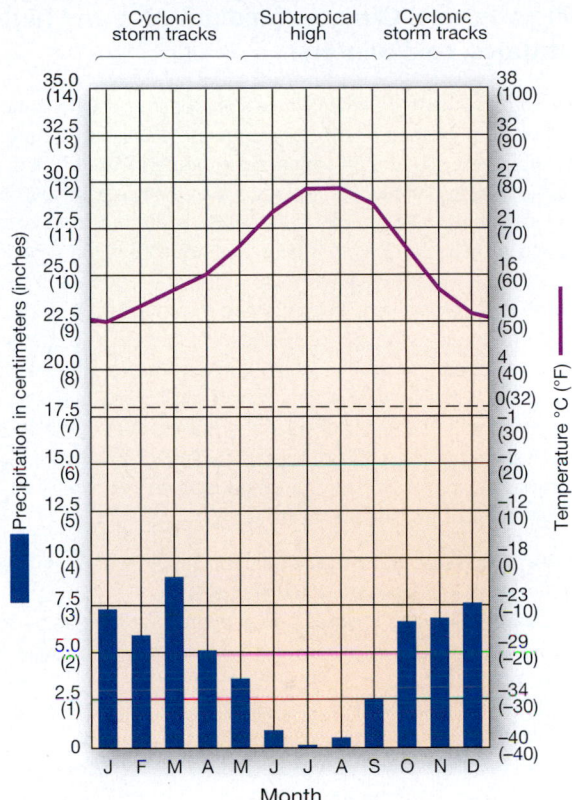

Cyclonic storm tracks | Subtropical high | Cyclonic storm tracks

(b) Climograph for Sevilla, Spain with its hotter dry summer.

Station: Sevilla, Spain
Lat/long: 37° 22′ N 6° W
Avg. Ann. Temp.:
    18°C (64.4°F)
Total Ann. Precip.:
    55.9 cm (22 in.)
Elevation: 13 m (42.6 ft)
Population: 1,764,000
Ann. Temp. Range:
    16 C° (28.8 F°)
Ann. Hr of Sunshine:
    2862

(c) Central California Mediterranean landscape of oak savanna.

(d) Sevilla, Spain, the El Peñon Mountains in the distance.

▲**Figure 9.12 Mediterranean climates, California and Spain.**
[(c) Bobbé Christopherson. (d) Design Pics Inc/Alamy.]

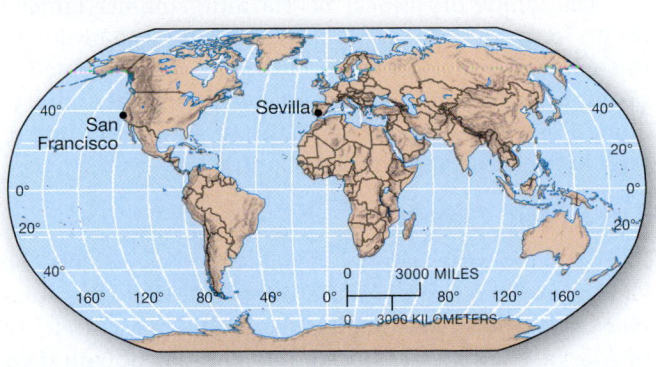

exhausts soil moisture by late spring. Large-scale agriculture in this climate requires irrigation, although some subtropical fruits, nuts, and vegetables are uniquely suited to these conditions. Hard-leafed, drought-resistant vegetation, known locally as *chaparral* in the western United States, is common. (Chapter 20 discusses this type of vegetation in other parts of the world.)

Microthermal Climates (midlatitudes and high latitudes, cold winters)

Humid microthermal climates have a winter season with some summer warmth. Here, the term *microthermal* means cool temperate to cold. These climates influence approximately 25% of Earth's land surface. These climates occur poleward of the mesothermal climates and experience great temperature ranges related to continentality and air mass conflicts. Temperatures decrease with increasing latitude and toward the interior of continental landmasses and result in intensely cold winters. In contrast to moist-all-year regions (the northern tier across the United States, the lower part of Canada, and eastern Europe through the Ural Mountains) is the winter-dry pattern associated with the Asian dry monsoon and cold air masses. In Figure 9.3, note the absence of microthermal climates in the Southern Hemisphere. Because the Southern Hemisphere lacks substantial landmasses, microthermal climates develop only in highlands.
    Important causal elements include:

- Increasing seasonality (daylength and Sun altitude) and greater temperature ranges (daily and annually);
- Latitudinal effects on insolation and temperature: summers become cool moving northward, with winters becoming cold to very cold;
- Upper-air westerly winds and undulating Rossby waves, which bring warmer air northward and colder air southward for cyclonic activity, and convectional thunderstorms from maritime tropical air masses in summer;

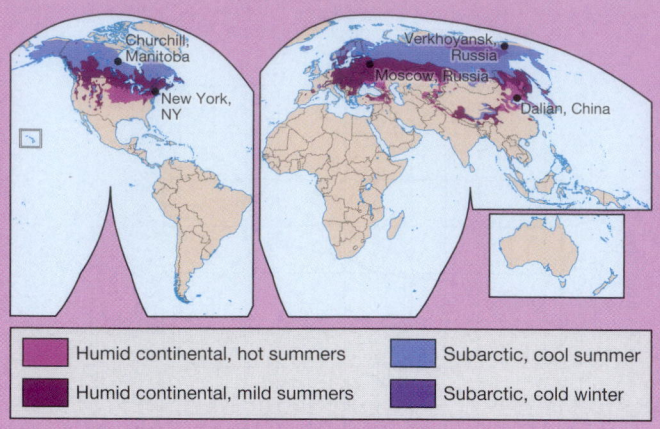

- Humid continental, hot summers
- Humid continental, mild summers
- Subarctic, cool summer
- Subarctic, cold winter

- Continental interiors serving as source regions for intense continental polar air masses that dominate winter, blocking cyclonic storms;
- Continental high-pressure and related air masses, increasing from the Ural Mountains eastward to the Pacific Ocean, producing the Asian winter-dry pattern.

Microthermal climates have four distinct regimes based on increasing cold with latitude and precipitation variability: *humid continental hot-summer* (Chicago, New York); *humid continental mild-summer* (Duluth, Toronto, Moscow); *subarctic cool-summer* (Churchill); and the formidable extremes of *subarctic cold-winter* (Verkhoyansk and northern Siberia).

Humid Continental Hot-Summer Climates

Humid continental hot-summer climates have the warmest summer temperatures of the microthermal category. In the summer, maritime tropical air masses influence precipitation, which may be consistent throughout the year or may have a distinct winter-dry period. In North America, conflicting air masses—maritime tropical and continental polar—often affect weather, especially in winter. New York City and Dalian, China (**Figure 9.13**), exemplify the two types of hot-summer microthermal climates—*moist-all-year* and *winter-dry*. The Dalian climograph demonstrates a winter-dry tendency caused by the intruding cold continental airflow that forces dry monsoon conditions.

    In the United States today, the humid continental hot-summer region extends westward to about the 98th meridian (98° W, in central Kansas) and is the location of corn, soybean, hog, feed crop, dairy, and cattle production. To the west, this climate type transitions into the dry climates discussed later in the chapter.

Humid Continental Mild-Summer Climates

Located farther toward the poles, *humid continental mild-summer* climates are slightly cooler. **Figure 9.14** presents a climograph for Moscow, Russia, which is at 55° N, or about the same latitude as the southern shore of Hudson Bay, in Canada. In the United States, this mild-summer climate occurs across the northern plains into the northeast region, from North Dakota to Maine (Figure 9.14c).

    Agricultural activity remains important in the cooler microthermal climates and includes dairy, poultry, flax, sunflower, sugar beet, wheat, and potato production. Frost-free periods range from fewer than 90 days in the northern portions of these regions to as many as 225 days in the southern parts. Overall, precipitation is less than in the hot-summer regions to the south; however, snowfall is notably heavier, and its melting is important to soil-moisture recharge. Among various strategies for capturing this snow is the use of fences and tall stubble left standing in fields to create snowdrifts and thus more moisture retention in the soil.

    The winter-dry aspect of the mild-summer climate occurs only in Asia, in a far-eastern area poleward of the winter-dry mesothermal climates. A representative of this type of humid continental mild-summer climate along Russia's east coast is Vladivostok, usually one of only two ice-free ports in that country.

Subarctic Climates

Farther poleward, seasonal change becomes greater. The short growing season is more intense during long summer days. The *subarctic* climates include vast stretches of Alaska, Canada, and northern Scandinavia, with their

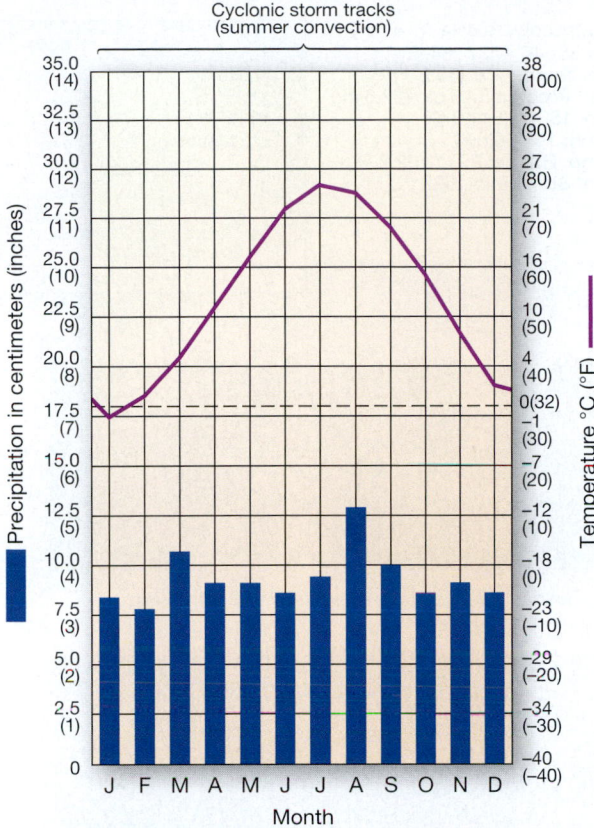

Cyclonic storm tracks
(summer convection)

(a) Climograph for New York City (humid continental hot-summer, moist all year).

Station: New York, New York
Lat/long: 40° 46′ N 74° 01′ W
Avg. Ann. Temp.:
    13°C (55.4°F)
Total Ann. Precip.:
    112.3 cm (44.2 in.)

Elevation: 16 m (52.5 ft)
Population: 8,092,000
Ann. Temp. Range:
    24 C° (43.2 F°)
Ann. Hr of Sunshine:
    2564

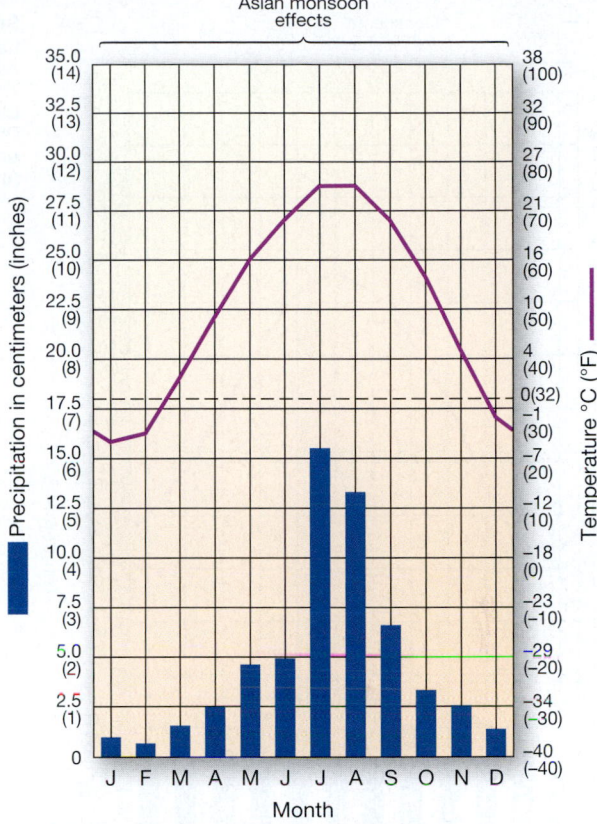

Asian monsoon
effects

(b) Climograph for Dalian, China (humid continental hot-summer, winter-dry).

Station: Dalian, China
Lat/long: 38° 54′ N 121° 54′ E
Avg. Ann. Temp.:
    10°C (50°F)
Total Ann. Precip.:
    57.8 cm (22.8 in.)

Elevation: 96 m (314.9 ft)
Population: 5,550,000
Ann. Temp. Range:
    29 C° (52.2 F°)
Ann. Hr of Sunshine:
    2762

(c) Autumn in New York's Central Park.

(d) Dalian, China, cityscape and park in summer.

▲**Figure 9.13 Humid continental hot-summer climates, New York and China.** [(c) Gavin Hellier/Alamy. (d) Henry Westheim Photography/Alamy.]

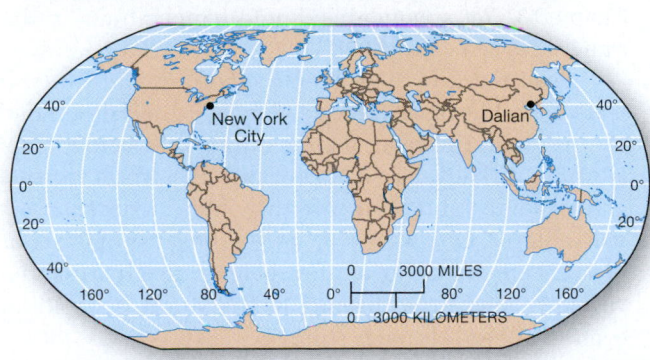

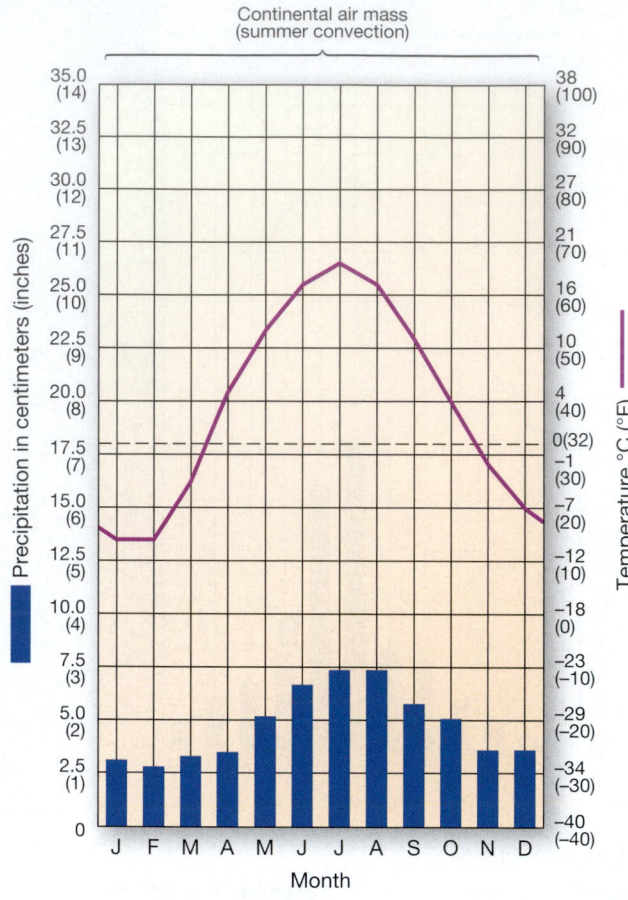

Station: Moscow, Russia
Lat/long: 55° 45′ N 37° 34′ E
Avg. Ann. Temp.: 4°C (39.2°F)
Total Ann. Precip.: 57.5 cm (22.6 in.)
Elevation: 156 m (511.8 ft)
Population: 11,460,000
Ann. Temp. Range: 29 C° (52.2 F°)
Ann. Hr of Sunshine: 1597

(a) Climograph for Moscow, Russia.

(b) Landscape between Moscow and St. Petersburg along the Volga River.

▲**Figure 9.14 Humid continental mild-summer climate.** [(b) David G. Hauser/Getty Images. (c) Bobbé Christopherson.]

(c) Winter scene of mixed forest near Brunswick, Maine, in the North American region with this climate type.

cool summers, and Siberian Russia, with its very cold winters.

Areas that receive 25 cm (10 in.) or more of precipitation a year on the northern continental margins and are covered by the so-called snow forests of fir, spruce, larch, and birch are the *boreal forests* of Canada and the *taiga* of Russia. These forests are in transition to the more open northern woodlands and to the tundra region of the far north. Forests thin out to the north wherever the warmest month drops below an average temperature of 10°C (50°F). Climate models and forecasts suggest that, during the decades ahead, the boreal forests will shift northward into the tundra in response to higher temperatures.

Precipitation is low, but so is potential evapotranspiration, so soils are generally moist and either partially or totally frozen beneath the surface, a phenomenon known as *permafrost* (discussed in Chapter 17). The Churchill, Manitoba, climograph (**Figure 9.15**) shows average monthly temperatures below freezing for 7 months of the year, during which time light snow cover and frozen ground persist. High pressure dominates Churchill

during its cold winter—this is the source region for the continental polar air mass. Churchill is representative of the *subarctic cool-summer* climate, with an annual temperature range of 40 C° (72 F°) and low precipitation of 44.3 cm (17.4 in.).

The subarctic climates that feature a dry and very cold winter occur only within Russia. The intense cold of Siberia and north-central and eastern Asia is difficult to comprehend, for these areas experience an average temperature lower than freezing for 7 months and minimum temperatures of below −68°C (−90°F), as described in Chapter 3. Yet summer-maximum temperatures in these same areas can exceed 37°C (98°F).

An example of this extreme *subarctic cold-winter* climate is Verkhoyansk, Siberia (**Figure 9.16**). For 4 months of the year, average temperatures fall below −34°C (−30°F). Verkhoyansk has probably the world's greatest annual temperature range from winter to summer: a remarkable 63 C° (113.4 F°). In Verkhoyansk, metals and plastics are brittle in winter; people install triple-thick windowpanes to withstand temperatures so cold that even antifreeze becomes solid.

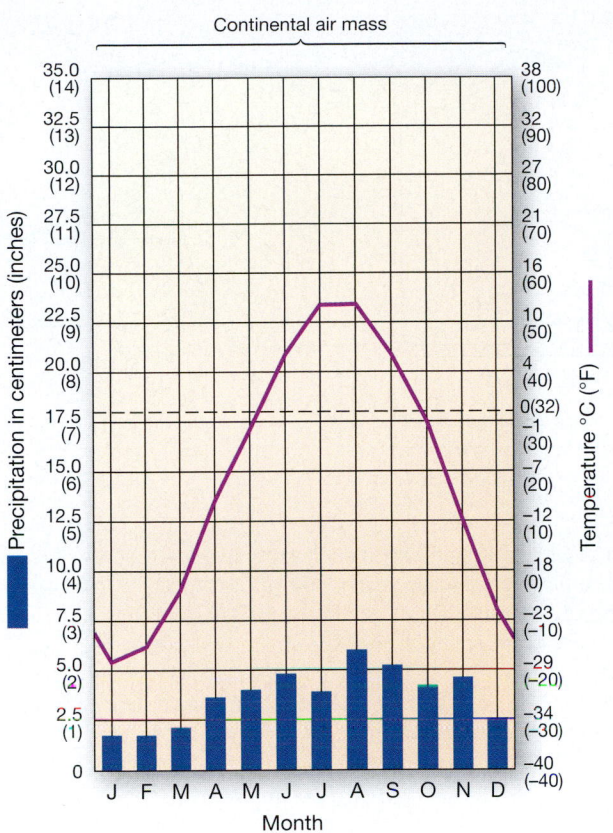

Continental air mass

(a) Climograph for Churchill, Manitoba.

Station: Churchill, Manitoba
Lat/long: 58° 45′ N 94° 04′ W
Avg. Ann. Temp.: −7°C (19.4°F)
Total Ann. Precip.: 44.3 cm (17.4 in.)
Elevation: 35 m (114.8 ft)
Population: 1400
Ann. Temp. Range: 40 C° (72 F°)
Ann. Hr of Sunshine: 1732

(b) Churchill and other port facilities on Hudson Bay may expand with renewed interest in mineral and petroleum reserves in subarctic regions.

▲**Figure 9.15 Subarctic cool-summer climate.** [(b) Bobbé Christopherson.]

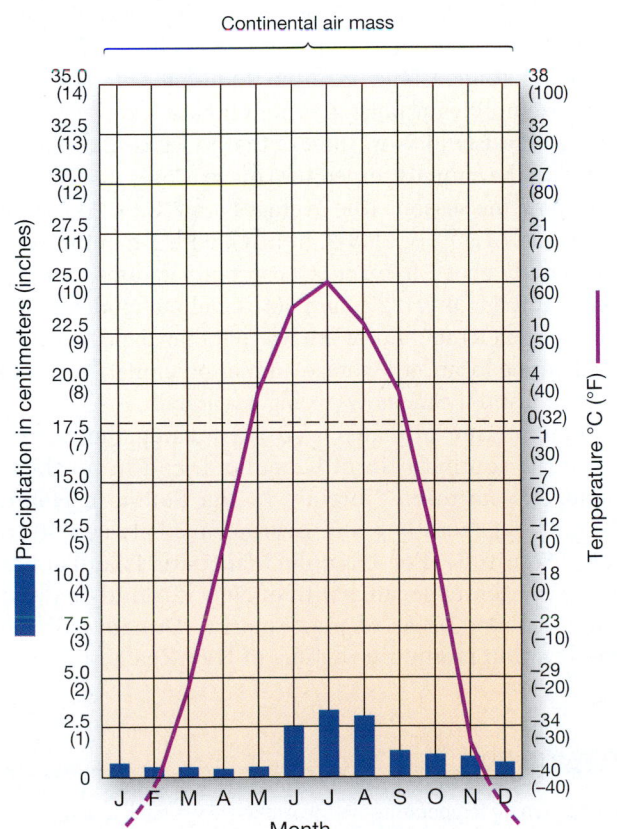

Continental air mass

(a) Climograph for Verkhoyansk, Russia.

Station: Verkhoyansk, Russia
Lat/long: 67° 35′ N 133° 27′ E
Avg. Ann. Temp.: −15°C (5°F)
Total Ann. Precip.: 15.5 cm (6.1 in.)

Elevation: 137 m (449.5 ft)
Population: 1500
Ann. Temp. Range: 63 C° (113.4 F°)

(b) A summer scene shows one of many ponds created by thawing permafrost.

▲**Figure 9.16 Extreme subarctic cold-winter climate.** [(b) Dean Conger/Getty Images.]

Polar and Highland Climates

The polar climates occupy about 13% of Earth's land and have no true summer like that in lower latitudes. The South Pole lies near the middle of the ice-covered continent of Antarctica, surrounded by the Southern Ocean, whereas the North Pole lies near the middle of the Arctic Ocean, surrounded by the continents of North America and Eurasia. Poleward of the Arctic and Antarctic Circles, daylength increases in summer until daylight becomes continuous, yet average monthly temperatures never rise above 10°C (50°F). These temperature conditions do not allow tree growth.

Important causal elements of polar climates include:

- Low Sun altitude even during the long summer days, which is the principal climatic factor;
- Extremes of daylength between winter and summer, which determine the amount of insolation received;
- Extremely low humidity, producing low precipitation amounts—these regions are Earth's frozen deserts;
- Surface albedo impacts, as light-colored surfaces of ice and snow reflect substantial energy away from the ground, thus reducing net radiation.

Polar climates have two primary regimes: *tundra* (at high latitude or high elevation)—including *polar marine* (with an oceanic

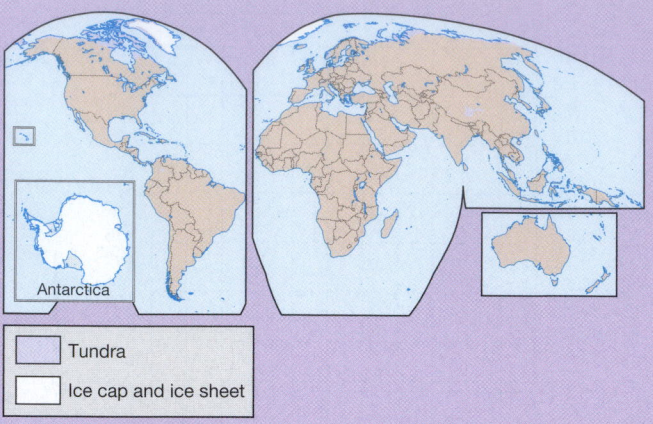

association and slight moderation of extreme cold)—and *ice cap* and *ice sheet* (perpetually frozen). Also in this climate category are *highland* climates, in which tundra and ice-cap conditions occur at nonpolar latitudes because of the effects of elevation. Highland climates occur on Earth's highest mountains (see Geosystems Now, Figure GN 9.1b). Glaciers on some tropical mountain summits attest to the cooling effects of altitude.

Tundra Climates

The term *tundra* refers to the characteristic vegetation of high latitudes and high elevations, where plant growth is restricted by cold temperatures and a short growing season. In *tundra* climates, land is under some snow cover for 8–10 months, with the warmest month above 0°C (32°F), yet never warming above 10°C (50°F). These climates occur only in the Northern Hemisphere, except for elevated mountain locations in the Southern Hemisphere and a portion of the Antarctic Peninsula. Because of its elevation, the summit of Mount Washington in New Hampshire (1914 m, or 6280 ft) statistically qualifies as a highland tundra climate despite its limited areal extent. In contrast, the area of tundra and rock in Greenland is about the size of California.

In spring when the snow melts, numerous plants appear—stunted sedges, mosses, dwarf shrubs, flowering plants, and lichens—and persist through the short summer (**Figure 9.17a**). Some of the dwarf willows (7.5 cm, or 3 in., tall) can exceed 300 years in age. Much of the area experiences permafrost and ground ice conditions; these are Earth's periglacial regions, discussed in Chapter 17.

Within the tundra climates, some areas have a strong marine influence. In 1964, geographer James Shear proposed a separate designation for *polar marine* climates, applying to areas with smaller annual temperature ranges and more moderate winter temperatures than other polar climates, with no month below −7°C (20°F). Overall, polar marine climates are not as warm as tundra climates.

South Georgia Island, near the tip of the Antarctic peninsula, exemplifies a polar marine climate (**Figure 9.17b**). Although the island is in the Southern Ocean and part of Antarctica, the annual temperature range is only 8.5 C° (15.3 F°) between the seasons (the averages are 7°C, or 44.6°F, in January and −1.5°C, or 29.3°F, in July), with 7 months averaging slightly above freezing. Ocean temperatures, ranging between 0°C and 4°C (32°F and 39°F), help to moderate the climate so that temperatures are warmer than expected at its 54°-S-latitude location. Average annual precipitation is 150 cm (59 in.), and it can snow during any month.

Polar marine climates also exist along the Bering Sea, on the southern tip of Greenland, and in northern Iceland and northern Norway. In the Southern Hemisphere, they generally occur over oceans between 50° S and 60° S latitude. For example, Macquarie Island at 54° S in the Southern Ocean, south of New Zealand, is polar marine. Isolated areas of polar marine climate exist in high-elevation mountain regions of New Zealand.

GEOreport 9.2   Tundra climates respond to warming

Global warming is bringing dramatic changes to the tundra climate regions, where temperatures in the Arctic are warming at a rate twice that of the global average increase. In parts of Canada and Alaska, near-record temperatures as much as 5 to 10 C° (9 to 18 F°) above average are a regular occurrence. As organic peat deposits in the tundra thaw, vast stores of carbon and methane are released to the atmosphere, further adding to the greenhouse gas problem (more discussion is in Chapters 10 and 17).

(a) Late September in East Greenland, with fall colors and musk oxen.

(b) An abandoned whaling station at Grytviken, South Georgia, last used in 1964.

◀**Figure 9.17** **Tundra climates.** [(a) Bobbé Christopherson. (b) Michael Nolan/Robert Harding.]

Ice-Cap and Ice-Sheet Climates

An *ice sheet* is a continuous layer of ice covering an extensive continental region. Earth's two ice sheets cover the Antarctic continent and most of the island of Greenland (**Figure 9.18**). An *ice cap* is smaller in extent, roughly less than 50,000 km² (19,300 mi²), but it completely buries the landscape like an ice sheet.

Most of Antarctica and central Greenland fall within the *ice-cap and ice-sheet* climate category, as does the North Pole, with all months averaging below freezing (the area of the North Pole is actually a sea covered by ice rather than a continental landmass). These regions are dominated by dry, frigid air masses, with vast expanses that never warm above freezing. In fact, minimum temperatures during central Antarctica's winter (July) frequently drop below the temperature of solid carbon dioxide, or "dry ice" (−78°C, or −109°F). Antarctica is constantly snow-covered, but receives less than 8 cm (3 in.) of precipitation each year. However, Antarctic ice has accumulated to several kilometers deep and is the largest repository of freshwater on Earth.

(a) The northern Antarctic Peninsula as seen from a NASA Operation Icebridge aircraft in October 2012.

(b) The eastern coast of Greenland as seen from an airplane at 12,200 m (40,000 ft) in March 2016.

▲**Figure 9.18** **Earth's ice sheets—Antarctica and Greenland.** [(a) Maria-Jose Vinas/NASA. (b) NASA.]

Dry Climates (permanent moisture deficits)

The dry climates occupy about 30% of Earth's land area, making it the most extensive climate type. To understand Earth's dry regions, with their sparse vegetation, we must consider moisture along with temperature. Overall, water demand exceeds the precipitation water supply, creating permanent water deficits. The extent of these deficits distinguishes two types of dry climatic regions: *arid deserts*, where the precipitation supply is roughly less than one-half of the natural moisture demand, and *semiarid steppes*, where the precipitation supply is roughly more than one-half of the natural moisture demand. (Review temperature controls in Chapter 4 and pressure systems in Chapter 5. We discuss desert environments in Chapter 15.)

Important causal elements in these dry lands include:

- The dominant presence of dry, subsiding air in subtropical high-pressure systems;
- Location in the rain shadow (or on the leeward side) of mountains, where dry air subsides after moisture is intercepted on the windward slopes;
- Location in continental interiors, particularly central Asia, which are far from moisture-bearing air masses;
- Location along western continental margins with cool, stabilizing ocean currents;

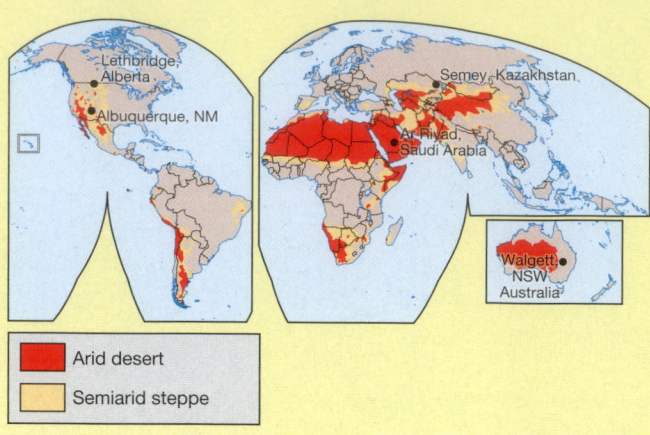

Arid desert
Semiarid steppe

- Shifting subtropical high-pressure systems, which produce semiarid steppes around the periphery of arid deserts.

Dry climates fall into four distinct regimes, according to latitude and the amount of moisture deficit: Arid climates include the *tropical, subtropical hot desert*, and *midlatitude cold desert* regimes, and semiarid climates include the *tropical, subtropical hot steppe*, and *midlatitude cold steppe* regimes.

Characteristics of Dry Climates

Dry climates are subdivided into deserts and steppes according to moisture—deserts have greater moisture deficits than do steppes, but both have permanent water shortages. **Steppe** is a regional term referring to the vast semiarid grassland biome of eastern Europe and Asia (the equivalent biome in North America is shortgrass prairie and in Africa, the savanna; see Chapter 20). In this chapter, we use steppe in a climatic context; a *steppe climate* is considered too dry to support forest, but too moist to be a desert.

Earth's dry climates cover broad regions between 15° and 30° latitude in the Northern and Southern Hemispheres under subtropical high-pressure cells with subsiding, stable air and low relative humidity. Under generally cloudless skies, these subtropical deserts extend to western continental margins, where cool, ocean currents flow offshore, enhancing the formation of summer advection fog. However, dry regions also extend into higher latitudes. Deserts and steppes occur as a result of orographic lifting over mountain ranges, which intercept moisture-bearing weather systems to create rain shadows, especially in North and South America. The isolated interior of Asia, distant from any moisture-bearing air masses, also falls within the dry climate classification. The lower-latitude deserts and steppes tend to be hotter with less seasonal change than the midlatitude deserts and steppes, where mean annual temperatures are below 18°C (64.4°F) and freezing winter temperatures are possible.

Tropical, Subtropical Hot Desert Climates

Tropical, subtropical hot desert climates are Earth's true tropical and subtropical deserts and feature annual average temperatures above 18°C (64.4°F). They generally are found on the western sides of continents, although Egypt, Somalia, and Saudi Arabia also fall within this classification. Rainfall is from local summer convectional showers. Some regions receive almost no rainfall, whereas others may receive up to 35 cm (14 in.) of precipitation a year. A representative subtropical hot desert city is Riyadh, Saudi Arabia (**Figure 9.19**).

Along the Sahara Desert's southern margin in Africa is a drought-prone region called the Sahel, where human populations suffer great hardship as desert conditions gradually expand over their homelands. In Chapter 15, we discuss the process of desertification (expanding desert conditions), an ongoing problem in many dry regions of the world.

Death Valley, in California, holds the record for highest temperature ever recorded, 57°C (134°F), during July 1913. Extremely hot summer temperatures occur in other hot desert climates, such as around Baghdad, Iraq, where air temperatures regularly reach 50°C (122°F) and higher in the city.

Midlatitude Cold Desert Climates

Midlatitude cold desert climates cover only a small area: the countries along the southern border of Russia, the Taklamakan Desert, and Mongolia in Asia; the central third of Nevada and areas of the American Southwest, particularly at high elevations; and Patagonia in Argentina. Because of lower temperature and lower moisture-demand criteria, rainfall must be low—in the realm of 15 cm (6 in.)—for a station to qualify as a midlatitude cold desert climate.

A representative station is Albuquerque, New Mexico, with 20.7 cm (8.1 in.) of precipitation and an annual average temperature of 14°C (57.2°F) (**Figure 9.20**). Note the precipitation increase from summer convectional

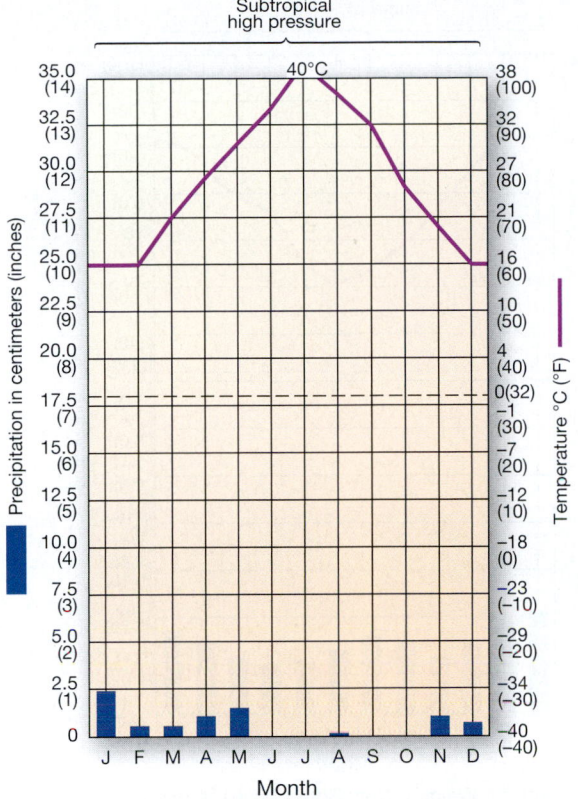

Subtropical
high pressure

40°C

(a) Climograph for Riyadh, Saudi Arabia.

Station: Riyadh, Saudi Arabia
Lat/long: 24° 42′ N 46° 43′ E
Avg. Ann. Temp.: 26°C (78.8°F)
Total Ann. Precip.: 8.2 cm (3.2 in.)
Elevation: 609 m (1998 ft)
Population: 5,024,000
Ann. Temp. Range: 24 C° (43.2 F°)

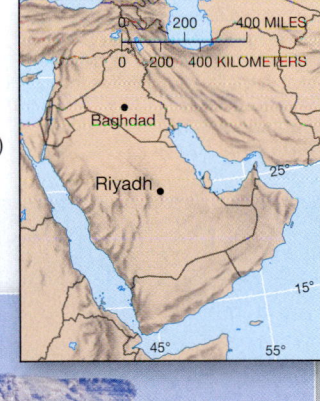

(b) The Arabian desert landscape of Red Sands near Riyadh.

▲Figure 9.19 **Tropical, subtropical hot desert climate.** [(b) Andreas Wolf/agefotostock.]

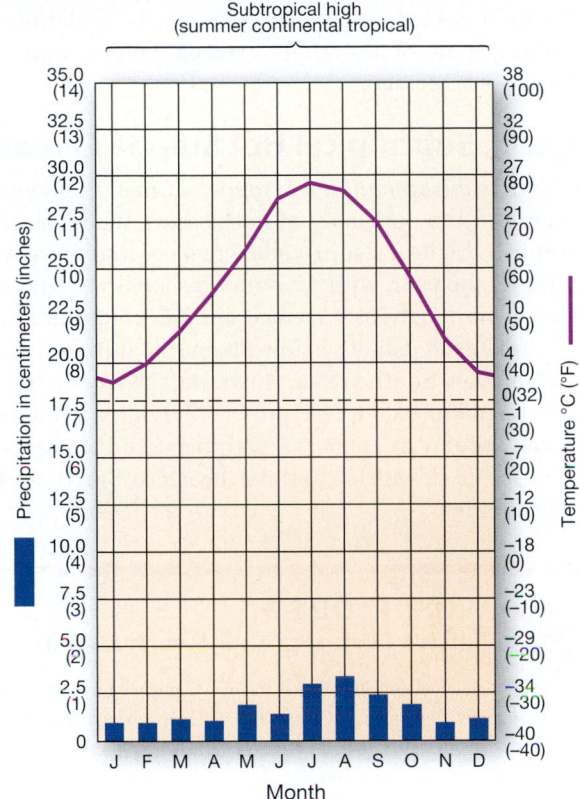

Subtropical high
(summer continental tropical)

(a) Climograph for Albuquerque, New Mexico.

Station: Albuquerque, New Mexico
Lat/long: 35° 03′ N 106° 37′ W
Avg. Ann. Temp.: 14°C (57.2°F)
Total Ann. Precip.: 20.7 cm (8.1 in.)
Elevation: 1620 m (5315 ft)
Population: 522,000
Ann. Temp. Range: 24 C° (43.2 F°)
Ann. Hr of Sunshine: 3420

(b) Late spring snow covers the Organ Mountains in south-central New Mexico.

▲Figure 9.20 **Midlatitude cold desert climate.** [(b) BLM.]

showers on the climograph. This characteristic expanse of midlatitude cold desert stretches across central Nevada, over the region of the Utah–Arizona border, and into northern New Mexico.

Tropical, Subtropical Hot Steppe Climates

Tropical, subtropical hot steppe climates generally exist around the periphery of hot deserts, where shifting subtropical high-pressure cells create variable rainfall throughout the year, with a distinct seasonal wet–dry pattern in some locations. Average annual precipitation in these climates is usually below 60 cm (23.6 in.). Walgett, in interior New South Wales, Australia, provides a Southern Hemisphere example (**Figure 9.21**). This climate is also seen around the Sahara's periphery, in Pakistan and parts of India, in Mexico and northeastern Brazil, and in southern Africa.

WORK**IT**OUT 9.1
Earth's Climates: An Interactive Map

Go to the map of world climate zones at http://oceanservice .noaa.gov/education/pd/oceans_weather_climate/media /climate_zones.swf. Use this map to review some of the climates discussed in this chapter.

1. Click on the light brown region in the U.S. West or inland from Sydney, Australia. What three characteristics differentiate an arid desert climate from a semiarid steppe climate?
2. Click on the green region of the Amazon rain forest. Do temperatures drop below freezing in tropical wet climates?
3. Click on the yellow region near Moscow, Russia. What climate type is this? Describe the characteristics and distribution of precipitation throughout the year.

Midlatitude Cold Steppe Climates

The *midlatitude cold steppe* climates occur poleward of about 30° latitude and of the *midlatitude cold desert* climates. As with other dry climate regions, rainfall in the steppes is widely variable and undependable, ranging from 20 to 40 cm (7.9 to 15.7 in.). Not all rainfall is convectional, for cyclonic storm tracks penetrate the continents; however, most storms produce little precipitation. Midlatitude steppes occur in the Southern Hemisphere in the Patagonia region of South America and across southern Australia. In the Northern Hemisphere, the western Great Plains of North America have a midlatitude steppe climate. In Asia, cold steppe climates occur across portions of Kazakhstan, Russia, and Mongolia.

Figure 9.22 presents a comparison between Asian and North American midlatitude cold steppe climates. Semey, Kazakhstan, has more even precipitation throughout the year, with only a slight summer precipitation maximum. Lethbridge, Alberta, in the rain shadow of the Rocky Mountains, has summer-maximum convectional precipitation and is dry in winter. Note the differences

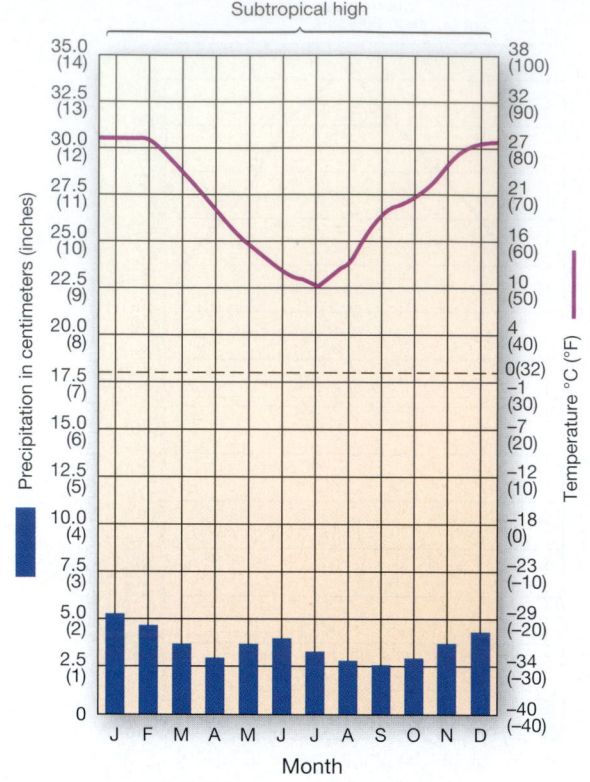

(a) Climograph for Walgett, New South Wales, Australia.

Station: Walgett, New South Wales, Australia
Lat/long: 30° S 148° 07′ E
Avg. Ann. Temp.: 20°C (68°F)
Total Ann. Precip.: 45.0 cm (17.7 in.)
Elevation: 133 m (436 ft)
Population: 8200
Ann. Temp. Range: 17 C° (31 F°)

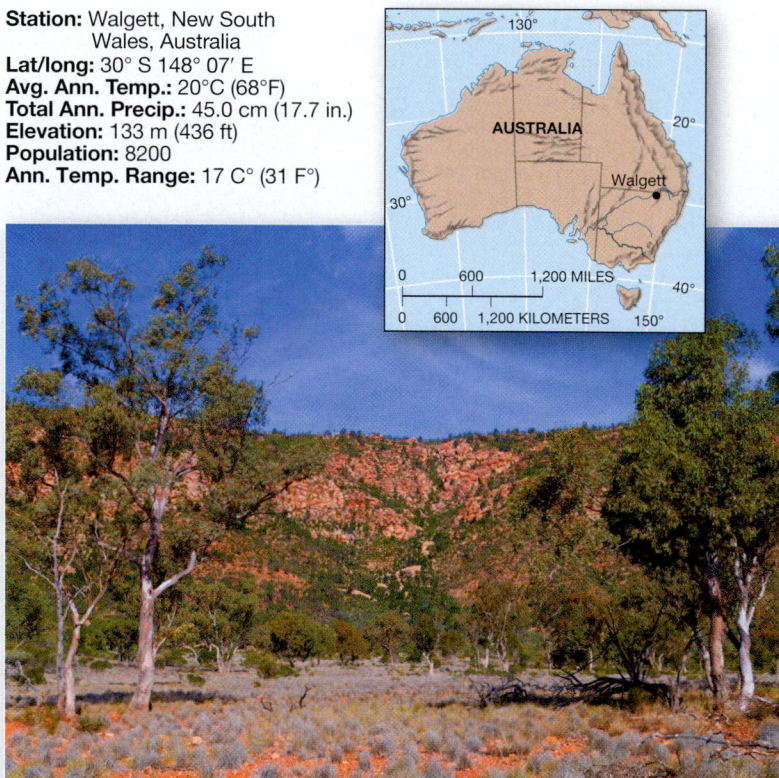

(b) Gundabooka National Park near Walgett in northwest New South Wales.

▲**Figure 9.21 Tropical, subtropical hot steppe climate.** [(b) Ashley Whitworth/Shutterstock.]

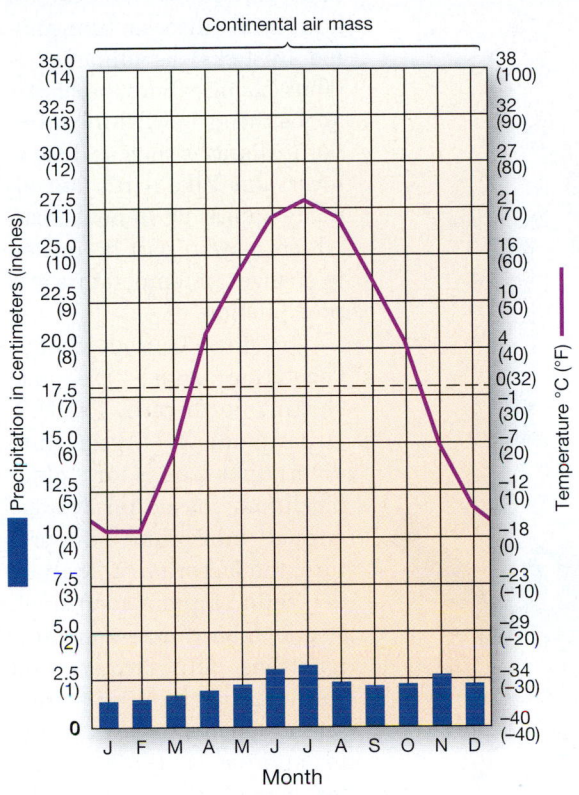

(a) Climograph for Semey (Semipalatinsk), Kazakhstan.

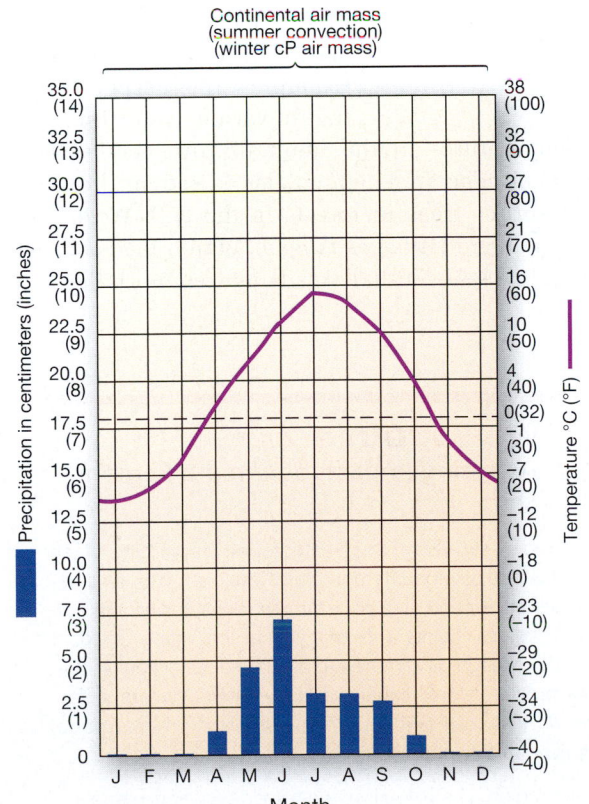

(c) Climograph for Lethbridge, Alberta.

Station: Semey, Kazakhstan
Lat/long: 50° 21′ N 80° 15′ E
Avg. Ann. Temp.: 3°C (37.4°F)
Total Ann. Precip.:
            26.4 cm (10.4 in.)

Elevation: 206 m (675.9 ft)
Population: 270,500
Ann. Temp. Range:
            39 C° (70.2 F°)

(b) Summer on the cold steppe of eastern Kazakhstan.

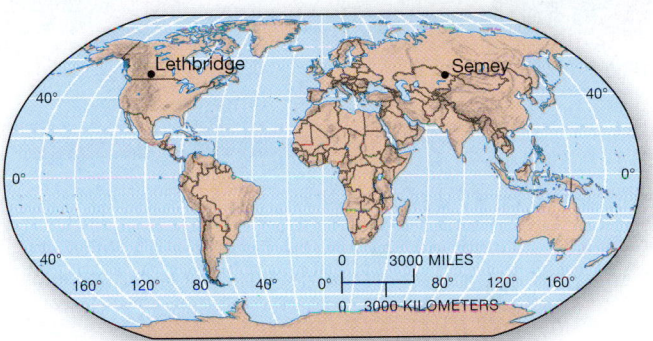

Station: Lethbridge, Alberta
Lat/long: 49° 42′ N 110° 50′ W
Avg. Ann. Temp.: 2.9°C (37.3°F)
Total Ann. Precip.: 25.8 cm (10.2 in.)

Elevation: 910 m (2985 ft)
Population: 73,000
Ann. Temp. Range: 24.3 C° (43.7 F°)

(d) Summer landscape along the Milk River near Lethbridge.

▲**Figure 9.22 Midlatitude cold steppe climates, Kazakhstan and Canada.** [(b) Nadezhda Bolotina/Shutterstock. (d) Bill Brooks/Alamy.]

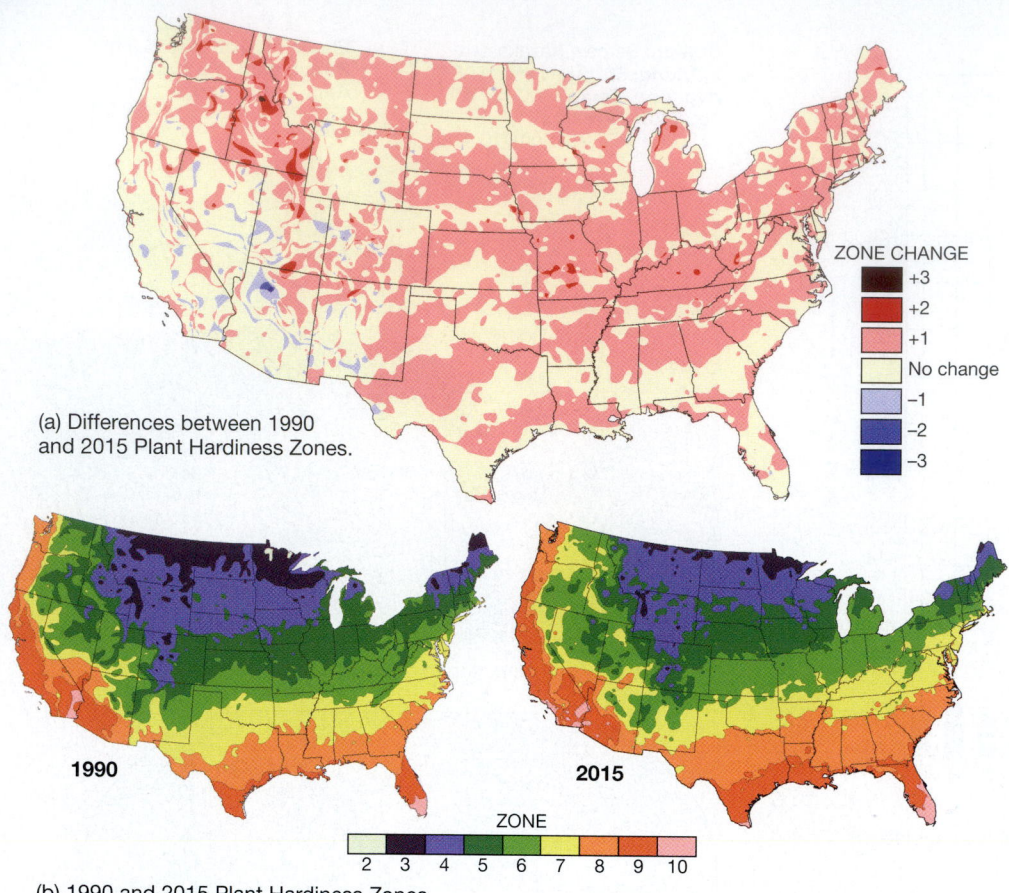

(a) Differences between 1990 and 2015 Plant Hardiness Zones.

ZONE CHANGE
+3
+2
+1
No change
−1
−2
−3

1990   **2015**

ZONE

2 3 4 5 6 7 8 9 10

(b) 1990 and 2015 Plant Hardiness Zones.

▲Figure 9.23 **Changes in U.S. Plant Hardiness Zones, 1990 to 2015.** [(a) Arborday.org. (b) USDA Miscellaneous Publication No. 1475, January 1990; Arborday map published 2015.]

in grassland characteristics, due in part to the timing of precipitation through the year, but also in part to soils and other ecological factors.

Climate Regions and Climate Change

The boundaries of climate regions are changing worldwide. The current expansion of tropical climates to higher latitudes means that subtropical high-pressure areas and dry conditions are also moving to higher latitudes. In addition, warming temperatures are making these areas more prone to drought. At the same time, storm systems are being pushed farther into the midlatitudes. In many cases, the evidence for shifting climate regions comes from changes in associated ecosystems—for example, the growth of trees in tundra climate regions or the expanding range of animals to higher latitudes or higher elevations on mountains. (More discussion of ecosystems, ranges, and biomes is in Chapters 19 and 20.)

Climate-related changes in the ranges of disease-carrying insects such as ticks and mosquitoes affect human populations. According to the 2016 U.S. Global Change Research Program report, *The Impacts of Climate Change on Human Health in the United States*, climate change will affect the seasonality and distribution of these insects, expanding the geographic area of West Nile virus

(also carried by mosquitoes) and Lyme disease (transmitted by ticks) as climatic regions change (https://health2016.globalchange.gov/). Mosquito-borne diseases such as dengue fever and Zika virus are already appearing in new areas, which may in part be related to changes in temperature and precipitation.

In the United States, vegetation zones are also shifting northward. The U.S. Department of Agriculture determines zones of "plant hardiness" based on average annual minimum temperature, the factor most likely to determine a plant's survival. Regional hardiness zone designations help farmers and gardeners determine which plant species are expected to survive a typical winter. **Figure 9.23** shows the northward shift of U.S. plant hardiness zones from 1990 to 2015. Pests and diseases that affect vegetation are also shifting in distribution. Examples of insects thriving in warmer nighttime and winter temperatures are the mountain pine beetle (*Dendroctonus ponderosae*), which has killed millions of pine and spruce trees in forests in the U.S. West, and the wooly adelgid (*Adelges tsugae*), which feeds on the sap of hemlocks—eventually causing tree mortality—in the U.S. East.

WORKITOUT 9.2
Assessing Impacts as Climate Regions Shift

Recent studies suggest that climate zones are shifting at an accelerated rate as global temperatures rise. As frost areas decrease, deserts expand, and cool-summer climates become hot-summer climates, plants and animals are struggling to adapt or shift their range as climate region boundaries change. Survey the article "More global warming speeds climate shifts" at http://www.scientificamerican.com/article/more-global-warming-speeds-climate-shifts/.

1. In the region where you live, what species or agricultural practices are at risk as climate zones shift?
2. Have you noticed climatic changes where you live? How will shifting climate affect your daily life?

CLIMATES IMPACT HUMANS

• Climate affects many facets of human society, including health, agriculture, water availability, and natural hazards such as floods.

A 2015 study revealed that the area covered by polar climate types is shrinking as air temperatures rise. In parts of Greenland, ice breakup has increased summer tourism, stimulating the economy, but has made hunting difficult for locals as animals shift their seasonal distribution. [Robert Harding Picture Library Ltd./Alamy.]

HUMANS IMPACT CLIMATES

• Anthropogenic climate change is altering Earth systems that affect temperature and moisture, and therefore climate.

In the Eurasian Arctic tundra, 30 years of warming temperatures have allowed willow and alder shrubs to grow into small trees. This trend may lead to changes in regional albedo as trees darken the landscape and cause more sunlight to be absorbed. [Alx Yago/Shutterstock.]

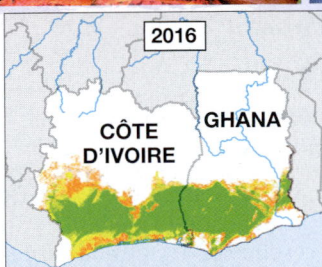

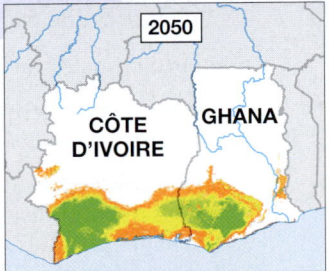

SUITABILITY FOR COCOA PRODUCTION
- Marginal
- Good
- Very good
- Excellent

Chocolate is made from seeds of the small evergreen cacao, or cocoa, tree (*Theobroma cacao*), which requires both the heat and humidity of a tropical rainforest climate. Ghana and Ivory Coast in West Africa are global leaders for cacao production. To maintain optimal growing conditions as global temperatures rise, cacao cultivation will need to move uphill into more limited terrain (see maps). In South America, growers are selectively breeding cacao plants for drought resistance and providing shade to decrease evapotranspiration. [Yai/Shutterstock. NOAA, www.climate.gov based on P. Läderach, A. Martinez-Valle, G. Schroth, N. Castro, 2013, Predicting the future climatic suitability for cocoa farming of the world's leading producer countries, Ghana and Côte d'Ivoire. *Climatic Change* 119: 841–854.]

As the tropics expand poleward, storm systems shift toward the midlatitudes, and the subtropics become drier. In East Africa, the 2015–2016 El Niño worsened ongoing drought related to climate change. In early 2016, failed crops in Ethiopia—shown here—led to 10 million people in need of international food aid and treatment for malnutrition. [Mulugeta Ayene/AP Photo.]

ISSUES FOR THE 21ST CENTURY

• Human-caused global warming is driving a poleward shift in the boundaries of climate regions.

QUESTIONS TO CONSIDER

1. What are West African cacao growers doing to maintain the world's supply of chocolate as climates warm?

2. How has climate change affected agriculture in East Africa? Explain in your own words.

275

KEY**LEARNING**concepts**review**

Define climate and climatology and **review** the principal components of Earth's climate system.

Climate (p. 250) is a synthesis of weather phenomena at many scales, from planetary to local, in contrast to weather, which is the condition of the atmosphere at any given time and place. **Climatology** (p. 250) is the study of climate and attempts to discern similar weather statistics and identify **climatic regions** (p. 250). The principal factors that influence climates on Earth include insolation, energy imbalances between the equator and the poles, temperature, air pressure, air masses, and atmospheric moisture (including humidity and precipitation).

1. Define climate and compare it with weather.

List the main categories of world climates and **locate** the regions characterized by each climate type on a world map.

Classification (p. 250) is the ordering or grouping of data or phenomena into categories. *Geosystems* uses a climate classification based on a combination of empirical data and causative factors. Temperature and precipitation data are measurable aspects of climate and are plotted on **climographs** (p. 251) to display the basic characteristics that determine climate regions. We group world climates into six primary categories—five based mainly on temperature characteristics and one based on moisture and temperature characteristics:

- Tropical (tropical latitudes)
- Mesothermal (midlatitudes, mild winters)
- Microthermal (midlatitudes and high latitudes, cold winters)
- Polar (high latitudes and polar regions)
- Highland (high elevations at all latitudes)
- Dry (permanent moisture deficits)

2. What is a climograph, and how is it used to display climatic information?
3. Which of the major climate types occupies the most land area on Earth?

Discuss the subcategories of the six world climate groups, including their causal factors.

Tropical climates include

- *tropical rain forest* (rainy all year),
- *tropical monsoon* (6 to 12 months rainy), and
- *tropical savanna* (less than 6 months rainy).

The shifting ITCZ is a major causal factor for seasonal moisture in these climates. Mesothermal climates include

- *humid subtropical* (hot to warm summers),
- *marine west coast* (warm to cool summers), and
- *Mediterranean* (dry summers).

These warm, temperate climates are humid, except where high pressure produces dry-summer conditions. Microthermal climates have cold winters, the severity of which depends on latitude; subcategories include

- *humid continental* (hot or mild summers) and
- *subarctic* (cool summers to very cold winters).

Polar climates have no true summer and include

- *tundra* (high latitude or high elevation) and
- *ice-cap and ice-sheet* (perpetually frozen) climates.

4. Using Africa's tropical climates as an example, characterize the climates produced by the seasonal shifting of the ITCZ with the high Sun.
5. Explain the distribution of the humid subtropical hot-summer and Mediterranean dry-summer climates at similar latitudes and the difference in precipitation patterns between the two types.

Explain the precipitation and moisture criteria used to classify the dry climates.

The dry climates of the tropics and midlatitudes consist of arid deserts, where precipitation (the natural water supply) is less than one-half of the natural water demand, and semiarid steppes, where precipitation, though insufficient, is more than one-half of the natural water demand. A **steppe** (p. 270) is a regional term referring to the vast semiarid grassland biome of eastern Europe and Asia. Arid climates include

- *tropical, subtropical hot deserts and*
- *midlatitude cold deserts.*

Semiarid climates include

- *tropical, subtropical hot steppes and*
- *midlatitude cold steppes.*

6. How are moisture and temperature used to differentiate the four desert climate subtypes?
7. What explains the presence of dry climates in Northern Africa? What factors contribute to the presence of deserts along the west coast of South America?

GEO**SPATIAL** ANALYSIS

Climate Classification and Climate Change

As climate changes the world climate classification boundaries also are changing. Predictions of how climate zones shift vary depending on several climate change scenarios.

Activities

Go to the Observed and Projected Climate Shifts page at http://koeppen-geiger.vu-wien.ac.at/shifts.htm. Compare the 1976–2000 map to the A1FI 2076–2100 map by opening each map in a separate window. The A1FI climate change scenario includes rapid economic growth and intense use of fossil fuels. Zoom in to the United States.

1. Based upon the Köppen-Geiger climate classification system, what are the principle classification categories?

2. What is the Köppen-Geiger climate classification in your approximate location according to the 1976–2000 map? Express using its name and using its classification symbol. Use the information on the map to describe your climate.

3. What is the Köppen-Geiger climate classification name and symbol for your approximate location according to the 2076–2100 map? Describe the changes you see in this transition.

4. In what direction do climate zones shift in the Eastern United States? In the western United States?

5. Compare the 2076–2100 map to the map in Figure 9.3. Examining the Great Lakes region, how do the climate categories

changed over this time span? Discuss both precipitation and temperature in your answer.

A shift in growing season has already been observed in the United States. Go to the article, "Planting your spring garden?" at https://www.climate.gov/news-features/featured-images/planting-your-spring-garden-consider-climate%E2%80%99s-%E2%80%98new-normal%E2%80%99.

6. What is plotted on the map?

7. What data are used to determine the "Normals"? And the "New Normals"?

8. When was the planting zone map updated?

9. What are the implications of the new climate normal for gardeners and landscapers?

10. Compare the "Updated Normals" and the "Previous Normals" maps. What is your previous climate-related planting zone? What is your updated zone?

11. According to the Zone Changes map, how have climate zones shifted in the Eastern United States? Western United States?

12. Compare this analysis to the maps in Figure 9.23, p. 274, that show Plant Hardiness Zones, 1990 and 2015, and a map plotting differences over those 25 years. Describe the changes you see for Zone #3, Zone #6, Zone #7, Zone #8, and Zone #9.

Mastering Geography™

Looking for additional review and test prep materials? Visit the Study Area in MasteringGeography™ to enhance your geographic literacy, spatial reasoning skills, and understanding of this chapter's content by accessing a variety of resources, including MapMaster™ interactive maps, videos, *Mobile Field Trips, Project Condor* Quadcopter Videos, *In the News* RSS feeds, flashcards, web links, self-study quizzes, and an eText version of *Geosystems*.

10 Climate Change

Malé, Maldives

The densely populated city of Malé, capital of the Maldives, is at risk of inundation during this century as sea level rises with climate change. Over 80% of Male is lower than 1 m (3.3 ft) above sea level, and the entire island is lower than 3 m (9.9 ft). The government is buying land in Australia to relocate its people as the seas rise. [Mohamed Sharif/Getty Images.]

KEY**LEARNING**concepts

After reading the chapter, you should be able to:

- **Describe** scientific tools used to study paleoclimatology.

- **Discuss** several natural factors that influence Earth's climate and **describe** climate feedbacks, using examples.

- **List** the key lines of evidence for present global climate change.

- **Summarize** the scientific evidence for anthropogenic forcing of climate and **list** some climate projections for the 21st century.

- **Describe** several mitigation measures to slow rates of climate change.

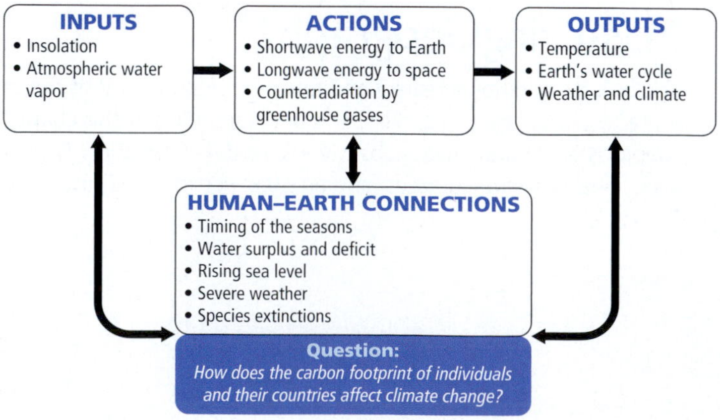

INPUTS
- Insolation
- Atmospheric water vapor

ACTIONS
- Shortwave energy to Earth
- Longwave energy to space
- Counterradiation by greenhouse gases

OUTPUTS
- Temperature
- Earth's water cycle
- Weather and climate

HUMAN–EARTH CONNECTIONS
- Timing of the seasons
- Water surplus and deficit
- Rising sea level
- Severe weather
- Species extinctions

Question:
How does the carbon footprint of individuals and their countries affect climate change?

GEOSYSTEMSnow

Rising Atmospheric CO₂ Affects Oceans and Marine Ecosystems

When was the last time you ate shellfish such as oysters, clams, scallops, or mussels? Depending on where you live, these may be a staple of your diet or be part of local and regional economies in your area. The U.S. shellfish industry along the Pacific, Atlantic, and Gulf Coasts is valued at over $700 million per year. As atmospheric carbon dioxide (CO_2) levels increase, seawater is absorbing CO_2 and becoming more acidic. In addition, as air temperatures rise, oceans are taking up some of the excess atmospheric thermal energy. In the cold coastal waters of the U.S. Northeast and Northwest, shellfish face an uncertain future unless they can adapt to warmer, more acidic seawater.

Oceans Absorb Atmospheric CO₂ As part of an ongoing natural cycling of carbon through Earth systems, the oceans absorb about one-quarter of the CO_2 emitted into the atmosphere. As atmospheric CO_2 increases, the oceans naturally offset the increase by taking up more CO_2. This triggers the process of *ocean acidification*, in which dissolved CO_2 mixes with seawater to form carbonic acid (H_2CO_3). Ocean acidification is now occurring across the globe.

Earth System Effects The movement of CO_2 from the atmosphere to the oceans has system-wide effects. The good news is that the oceanic uptake of CO_2 slows the warming of the atmosphere. The bad news is that increasingly acidic seawater threatens organisms that are vital to the health of ocean ecosystems, including some types of plankton—tiny organisms that are the base of the marine food web. The increased acidity changes seawater chemistry and harms marine organisms, especially those that build shells and other external structures from calcium carbonate (**Figure GN 10.1**).

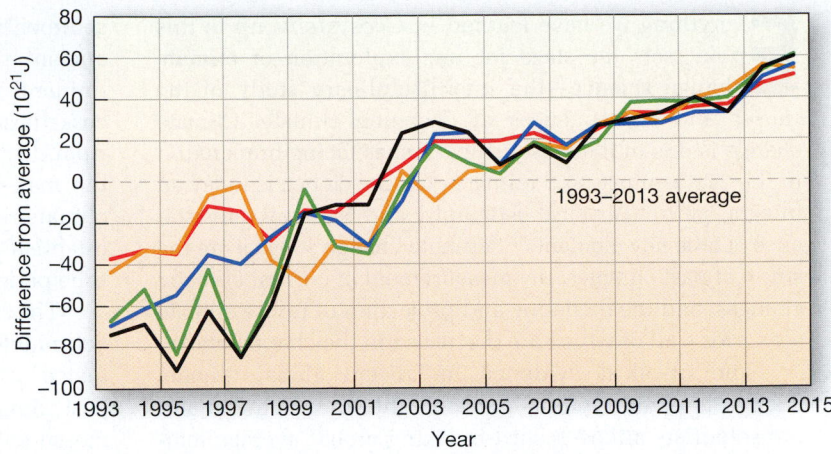

▲**Figure GN 10.2 Recent increases in upper ocean heat content.** Five different data sources show an upward trend in ocean heat content at depths from 0 to 700 m (2300 ft), represented on the vertical axis as the differences from the 1993–2013 average (dashed line). [NOAA climate.gov.]

The effects of ocean acidification are already in evidence, especially with regard to bivalve mollusks (oysters, mussels, clams, scallops) that have a two-part, hinged shell. In the U.S. Pacific Northwest, oyster larvae are dying in hatcheries exposed to corrosive seawater that prevents the young animals from developing shells. Between 2005 and 2009, oyster seed production declined up to 80%, costing the shellfish industry some $110 million and thousands of jobs. Along the Atlantic coast in Maine, mussels face the same problems in waters where acidification is augmented by acid deposition on the landscape, discussed in Chapter 3. Large storm events rinse acids from the land into rivers and eventually into coastal waters.

Oceans Also Absorb Thermal Energy As the oceans acidify, they are also absorbing excess thermal energy from the warming atmosphere. Data from buoys and satellites show significant increases in the heat content of the upper ocean (the region above 700 m, or 2300 ft) over the past 2 decades (**Figure GN 10.2**). Even deep-ocean currents that flow in cycles lasting thousands of years are showing a decisive warming trend.

Oceanic warming affects shellfish in different ways. For example, warming in the Gulf of Maine has allowed green crabs to move in, where they devour juvenile clams and mussels and destroy eelgrass that provides a protected nursery for shellfish and other species. Since 2012, squid, black sea bass, and Atlantic blue crabs have also invaded the Gulf, with unknown effects on shellfish and the marine ecosystem.

As atmospheric CO_2 continues to increase, ocean acidification and warming are changing marine ecosystems. These changes ultimately affect food resources for many of the world's people.

1. Describe the process of ocean acidification and explain how it is affecting shellfish in coastal waters of the Pacific Northwest.

2. How are increasing ocean temperatures affecting marine ecosystems?

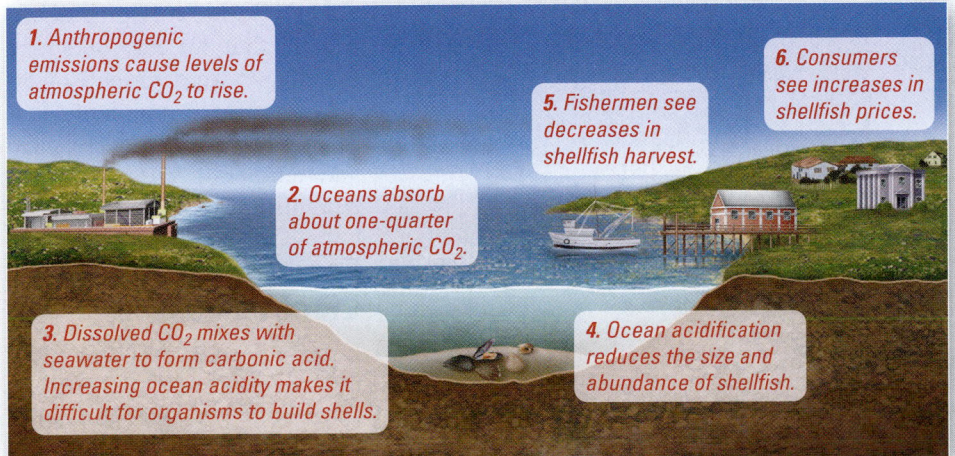

1. *Anthropogenic emissions cause levels of atmospheric CO₂ to rise.*

2. *Oceans absorb about one-quarter of atmospheric CO₂.*

3. *Dissolved CO₂ mixes with seawater to form carbonic acid. Increasing ocean acidity makes it difficult for organisms to build shells.*

4. *Ocean acidification reduces the size and abundance of shellfish.*

5. *Fishermen see decreases in shellfish harvest.*

6. *Consumers see increases in shellfish prices.*

▲**Figure GN 10.1 Effects of ocean acidification on the U.S. shellfish industry.** Increasing acidification affects shell-building organisms, leading to decreased harvest and rising prices for consumers.

Everything we have learned in *Geosystems* up to this point sets the stage for our exploration of **climate change science**—the interdisciplinary study of the causes and consequences of changing climate. Climate change is one of the most critical issues facing humankind in the 21st century, and climate change science is today an integral part of physical geography and Earth systems science. Three key elements of climate change science are the study of past climates, the measurement of current climatic changes, and the modeling and projection of future climate scenarios—all of which are discussed in the chapter ahead.

The physical evidence for recent global climate change is extensive and is observable by scientists and nonscientists alike—record-breaking global average temperatures for air, land surfaces, lakes, and oceans; ice losses from mountain glaciers and from the Greenland and Antarctic Ice Sheets; increasing intensity of precipitation events; changing distributions of plants and animals; and rising global sea level, which threatens coastal populations and development worldwide. Climate change science must address these and many other related issues so that we can adapt to and possibly mitigate the environmental changes ahead.

Deciphering Past Climates

To understand present climatic changes, we begin with a discussion of the climates of the past—specifically, how scientists reconstruct climates that occurred before human record-keeping began. Clues to past climates are stored in a variety of environments on Earth. Among these climatic indicators are fossil plankton in ocean-bottom sediments, gas bubbles in glacial ice, fossil pollen from ancient plants, and growth rings in trees, speleothems (mineral formations in caves), and corals. Scientists access these environmental indicators by extracting cores from deep within the various sources and then analyzing the materials by various methods to determine age and climate-related characteristics. In this way, scientists can establish a chronology of environmental conditions over time periods of thousands or millions of years.

The study of Earth's past climates is the science of **paleoclimatology**, which tells us that Earth's climate has fluctuated over hundreds of millions of years. To learn about past climates, scientists use **proxy methods** instead of direct measurements. A *climate proxy* is a piece of information from the natural environment that can be used to reconstruct climates that extend back further than our present instrumentation allows. For example, the widths of tree rings indicate climatic conditions that occurred thousands of years before temperature record-keeping began. By analyzing evidence from proxy sources, scientists are able to reconstruct climate in ways not possible using the record of firsthand scientific measurements over the past 140 years or so.

The study of rocks and fossils has provided paleoclimatologists with tools for understanding and reconstructing past climates over time spans on the order of hundreds of millions of years. (The geologic time scale, which shows Earth's 4.6-billion-year history, is in Chapter 11, Figure 11.2.) Geologists study past environments using techniques ranging from simple field observations of the characteristics and composition of rock deposits (for example, whether they are made up of dust, sand, or ancient coal deposits) to complex and costly laboratory analyses of rock samples (for example, using mass spectrometry to analyze the chemical makeup of rock or other materials). Fossils of animal and plant material preserved within rock layers also provide important climate clues; for example, fossils of tropical plants indicate warmer climate conditions, and fossils of ocean-dwelling creatures indicate ancient marine environments (**Figure 10.1**). The beds of coal that we rely on today for energy were formed of organic matter from plants that grew in warm, wet, tropical and temperate climates about 325 million years ago.

(a) Fossil palm frond found in 2008 near Castle Rock, Colorado, suggests a warmer climate 64 million years ago.

(b) This 1.8 m-long (6 ft-long) fossil palm frond from southwest Wyoming indicates a frost-free climate 52 million years ago.

▼**Figure 10.1** **Plant fossils indicate ancient climates.** [(a) Colorado Department of Transportation. (b) Photo/NPS. (c) Richard Maschmeyer/Alamy Stock Photo.]

(c) Petrified wood in Arizona reveals the presence of subtropical forests 225 million years ago.

Earth's Distant Climatic Past

Using fossils, sedimentary rock layers, and deep-ocean sediments, paleoclimatologists have determined that Earth's past climate generally was warmer than at present. Over the past 2.5 billion years, Earth has experienced *hothouse climates*, periods with relatively warmer temperatures, punctuated by *icehouse climates*, periods of cold temperatures during which glaciers covered Earth's surface. During this time, plate motions rearranged continents and the first life forms emerged. An interactive model of Earth's early climate and plate movement is at http://www.smithsonianmag.com/science-nature /travel-through-deep-time-interactive-earth-180952886/?no-ist.

One of the most extreme icehouse climates occurred from 600 to 700 million years ago, an expanse of time called "Snowball Earth." Glacial debris found in the tropics suggests that ice sheets extended during this time from the poles to the equator. Scientists hypothesize that during this time greenhouse gases, especially carbon dioxide, were not present to moderate Earth's temperature. As carbon dioxide began to accumulate in the atmosphere, Earth warmed. Deposits of carbonate sedimentary rock that formed in warm ocean environments are evidence of the change from icehouse to hothouse climate. Another well-documented icehouse climate occurred around 300 million years ago (shown ahead in Figure 10.18).

Methods for Long-Term Climate Reconstruction

Core samples drilled into ocean-bottom sediments or into the thickest ice sheets on Earth yield records that span 65 million years of Earth's climatic history. Once extracted, these cores reveal layers containing fossils, air bubbles, particulates, and other materials that provide paleoclimatic information.

The basis for long-term climate reconstruction is **isotope analysis**, a technique that uses the atomic structure of chemical elements—specifically, the relative amounts of their isotopes—to identify the chemical composition of past oceans and ice masses. Using this knowledge, scientists can reconstruct temperature conditions. Remember that the nuclei of atoms of a given chemical element, such as oxygen, always contain the same number of protons but can differ in the number of neutrons. Each number of neutrons found in the nucleus represents a different *isotope* of that element. Different isotopes have slightly different masses and therefore slightly different physical properties.

Oxygen Isotope Analysis Oxygen is an element with several isotopes, two of which are important to paleoclimatology. The most common oxygen isotope found in nature is oxygen-16, or ^{16}O ("light" oxygen), which makes up 99.76% of all oxygen atoms. Oxygen-18, or ^{18}O ("heavy" oxygen), comprises only about 0.20% of all oxygen atoms.

Both the ^{16}O and ^{18}O isotopes occur in water molecules. If the water contains "light" oxygen (^{16}O), it evaporates more easily but condenses less easily. The opposite is true for water containing "heavy" oxygen (^{18}O), which evaporates less easily but condenses more easily. These property differences affect where each of the isotopes is more likely to accumulate within Earth's vast water cycle. As a result, the relative amount, or *ratio*, of heavy to light oxygen isotopes ($^{18}O/^{16}O$) in water varies with climate—in particular, with temperature. By comparing the isotope ratio with an accepted standard, scientists can determine to what degree the water is enriched or depleted in ^{18}O relative to ^{16}O.

Since ^{16}O evaporates more easily, over time the atmosphere becomes relatively rich in "light" oxygen. Eventually, this water vapor condenses and falls to the ground. At higher latitudes, it falls as snow, accumulating in glaciers and ice sheets. At the same time, the oceans become relatively rich in ^{18}O—partly as a result of ^{16}O evaporating at a greater rate and partly from ^{18}O condensing and precipitating at a greater rate once it enters the atmosphere.

During periods of colder temperatures, when "light" oxygen is locked up in snow and ice in the polar regions, "heavy" oxygen concentrations are highest in the oceans (**Figure 10.2a**). Thus, a higher ratio of $^{18}O/^{16}O$ in ocean water indicates a colder climate. During warmer periods, when snow and ice melt returns ^{16}O to the oceans, the concentration of ^{18}O in the oceans becomes relatively less—the isotope ratio is essentially in balance (**Figure 10.2b**).

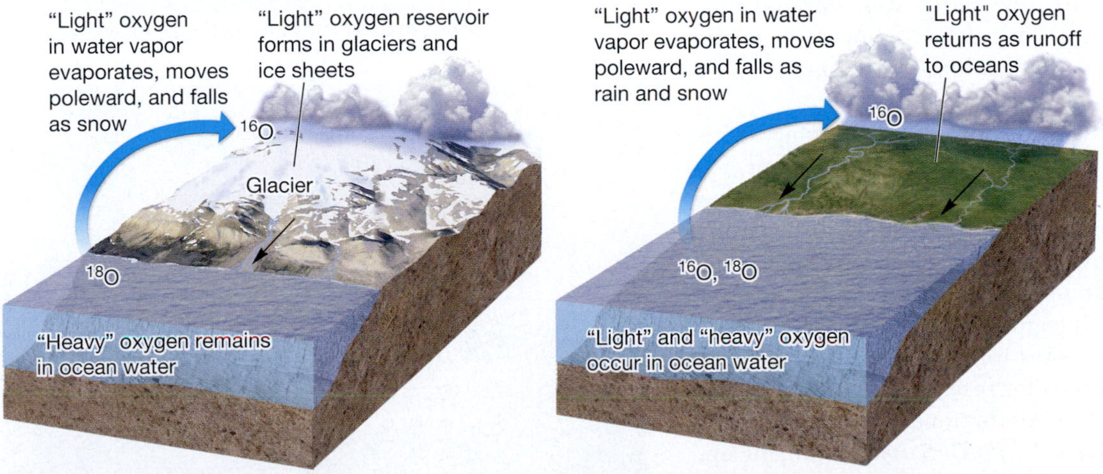

"Light" oxygen in water vapor evaporates, moves poleward, and falls as snow

"Light" oxygen reservoir forms in glaciers and ice sheets

^{16}O

Glacier

^{18}O

"Heavy" oxygen remains in ocean water

(a) In a cold (glacial) climate with a high volume of polar ice, seawater has an increased proportion of ^{18}O (higher $^{18}O/^{16}O$ ratio).

"Light" oxygen in water vapor evaporates, moves poleward, and falls as rain and snow

"Light" oxygen returns as runoff to oceans

^{16}O

$^{16}O, ^{18}O$

"Light" and "heavy" oxygen occur in ocean water

(b) In a warm (interglacial) climate with a low volume of polar ice, seawater has a decreased proportion of ^{18}O relative to ^{16}O (lower $^{18}O/^{16}O$ ratio).

▲Figure 10.2 **Relative oceanic concentrations of ^{18}O and ^{16}O during (a) colder (glacial) and (b) warmer (interglacial) periods.** [Based on *Analysis of Vostok Ice Core Data*, Global Change, available at http://www.globalchange.umich.edu/ globalchange1/current/labs/Lab10_Vostok/Vostok.htm.]

(a) Fossil foraminifera, as seen using a scanning electron microscope (magnification × 130).

(b) Deep-water foraminifera specimens.

▲**Figure 10.3 Examples of marine foraminifera.** These marine organisms live in a variety of ocean environments worldwide. The fossil foraminifera is from beach sand in the Maldives in the Indian Ocean. The living specimens are from the deepest part of the Pacific Ocean near the Mariana Trench. [(a) Science Photo Library/Alamy. (b) Scenics and Science/Alamy.]

techniques and the quality of ocean-core samples led to improved resolution of climate records for the past 70 million years.

Ice Cores In the cold regions of the world, snow accumulates seasonally in layers, and in regions where snow is permanent on the landscape, these layers of snow eventually form glacial ice (**Figure 10.5**). The world's largest accumulations of glacial ice occur in Greenland and Antarctica.

Ocean Sediment Cores Oxygen isotopes are found not only in water molecules, but also in calcium carbonate ($CaCO_3$), the primary component of the shells of marine microorganisms called *foraminifera* (**Figure 10.3**). These are some of the world's most abundant shelled marine organisms, living in a variety of environments from the equator to the poles. Upon the death of these organisms, their shells accumulate on the ocean bottom and build up in layers of sediment. By extracting a core of these ocean-floor sediments and comparing the ratio of oxygen isotopes in the $CaCO_3$ shells, scientists can determine the isotope ratio of seawater at the time the shells were formed. Foraminifera shells with a high $^{18}O/^{16}O$ ratio were formed during cold periods; those with low ratios were formed during warm periods. In an ocean sediment core, shells accumulate in layers that reflect these temperature conditions.

Specialized drilling ships have powerful rotary drills able to bore into ocean-bottom rock and sediment, extracting a cylinder of material—a *core sample*—within a hollow metal pipe. Such a core may contain dust, minerals, and fossils that have accumulated in layers over long periods of time on the ocean floor (**Figure 10.4a**). Over the past 50 years, the Integrated Ocean Drilling Program completed about 2000 cores in the ocean floor, yielding more than 35,000 samples for researchers (see http://iodp.tamu.edu/index.html). The international program includes two drilling ships: the U.S. *JOIDES Resolution*, in operation since 1985 (**Figure 10.4b**), and Japan's *Chikyu*, operating since 2007. The *Chikyu* set a new record in 2012 for the deepest hole drilled into the ocean floor—2466 m (8090 ft)—and is capable of drilling 10,000 m (32,800 ft) below sea level and yielding undisturbed core samples. Recent improvements in both isotope analysis

(a) Core samples of ocean sediments are split open for analysis.

(b) The U.S. *JOIDES Resolution* drilling ship.

▲**Figure 10.4 Ocean-bottom core sample and ocean drilling ship.** [(a) International Ocean Discovery Program. (b) William Crawford/International Ocean Discovery Program.]

▲**Figure 10.5 Layers of snow and ice, Greenland.** A scientist studies layers revealing individual snowfall events in a snow pit in 2013. [Joe Readle/Getty Images.]

the Dome C ice core, completed in 2004, reached a depth of 3270 m (10,729 ft), producing the longest ice-core record at that time: 800,000 years of Earth's past climate history. This record was correlated with a core record of 400,000 years from the nearby Vostok Station and matched with ocean sediment core records to provide scientists with a well-substantiated reconstruction of climate changes throughout this time period. In 2011, American scientists extracted an ice core from the West Antarctic Ice Sheet (WAIS) that is revealing 30,000 years of annual climate history and 68,000 years at resolutions from annual to decadal—a higher time resolution than previous coring projects. (For more information, see the WAIS Divide Ice Core site at http://www .waisdivide.unh.edu/news/.)

Scientists have extracted cores drilled thousands of meters deep into the thickest part of these ice sheets to reconstruct climate. These ice cores provide a climate record for the past 800,000 years, a shorter, but more detailed climatic record than in ocean sediment cores.

Extracted from areas where the ice is undisturbed, ice cores are about 13 cm (5 in.) in diameter and are composed of distinct layers of younger ice at the top and less-defined layering of older ice beneath. At the bottom of the core, the oldest layers are deformed from the weight of ice above. In this part of the core, layers can be defined based on horizons of dust and volcanic ash that landed on the ice surface and mark specific time periods (**Figure 10.6a**).

Within a core, any given year's accumulation consists of a layer of winter ice and a layer of summer ice, each differing in chemistry and texture. Scientists use oxygen isotope ratios to correlate these layers with environmental temperature conditions. However, oxygen isotope ratios in ice have a different relationship to climate than oxygen isotopes in ocean water.

In ice cores, a *lower* $^{18}O/^{16}O$ ratio (less "heavy" oxygen in the ice) suggests colder climates, with more ^{18}O tied up in the oceans and more light oxygen locked into glaciers and ice sheets. Conversely, a *higher* $^{18}O/^{16}O$ ratio (more "heavy" oxygen in the ice) indicates a warmer climate during which more ^{18}O evaporates and precipitates onto ice-sheet surfaces. Therefore, the oxygen isotopes in ice cores are a proxy for air temperature.

Ice cores also reveal information about past atmospheric composition. Within the ice layers, trapped air bubbles reveal concentrations of gases—mainly carbon dioxide and methane—indicative of environmental conditions at the time the bubbles were sealed into the ice (**Figure 10.6b**).

Several ice-core projects in Greenland produced data spanning more than 250,000 years. In Antarctica,

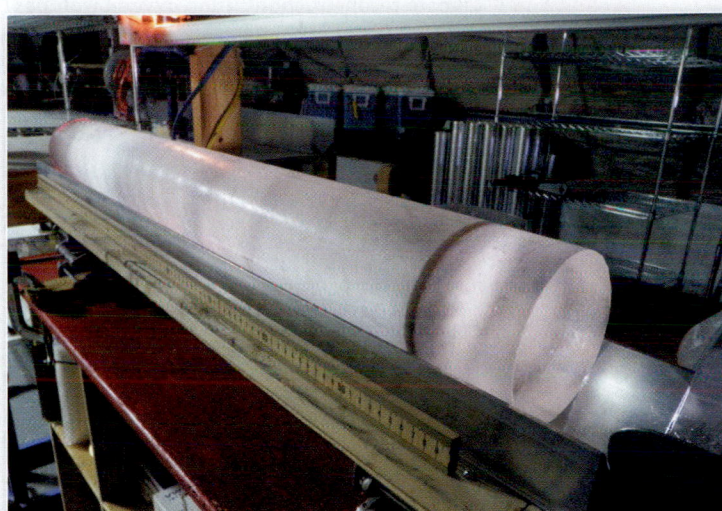

(a) A core from the West Antarctic Ice Sheet Divide project shows a dark band representing a layer of volcanic ash that settled on the ice sheet approximately 21,000 years ago.

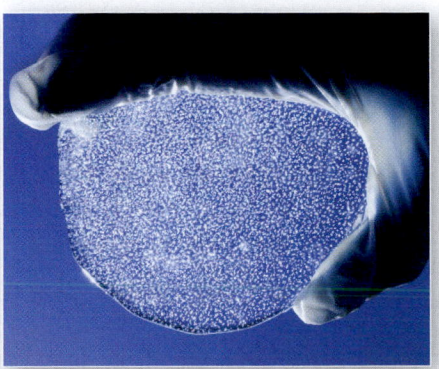

(b) Light shines through a thin section from the ice core, revealing air bubbles trapped within the ice.

▲**Figure 10.6 Antarctic Ice cores reveal information about past climates.** [(a) Heidi Roop/NSF. (b) British Antarctic Survey, https://www.bas .ac.uk/.]

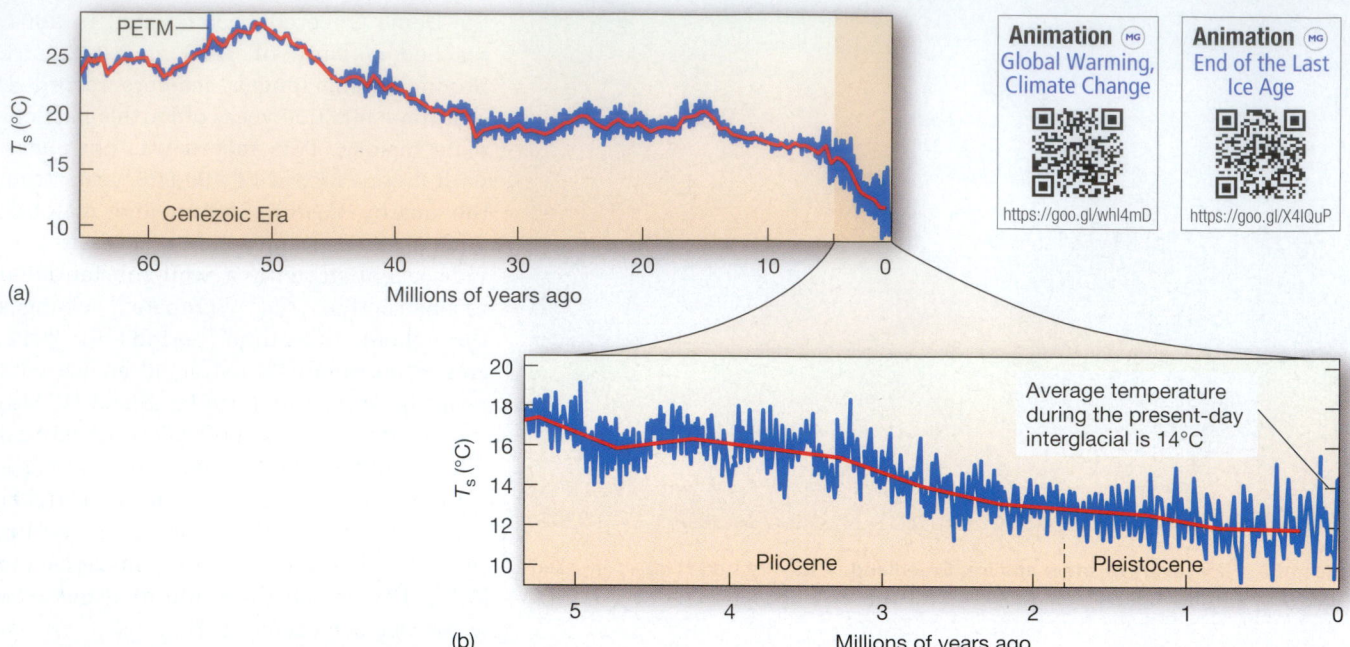

Animation (MG)
Global Warming,
Climate Change
https://goo.gl/whl4mD

Animation (MG)
End of the Last
Ice Age
https://goo.gl/X4lQuP

▲**Figure 10.7** **Climate reconstructions using oxygen isotopes (^{18}O) over two timescales.** The vertical axis (y-axis) shows the temperature change (a) over the past 70 million years and (b) over the past 5 million years. The average temperature from 1961 to 1990 was 14°C. Note the brief, distinct rise in temperature about 56 million years ago during the Paleocene–Eocene Thermal Maximum (PETM). The bottom graph shows alternating periods of warmer and colder temperatures within the 5-million-year time span. [After J. Hansen, M. Sato, G. Russell, and P. Kharecha, 2013, Climate Sensitivity, Sea Level, and Atmospheric Carbon Dioxide. *Philosophical Transactions of the Royal Society* 371 (2001), http://rsta.royalsocietypublishing.org/content/371/2001/20120294.]

Earth's Long-Term Climate History

Climatic reconstructions using fossils and deep-ocean sediment cores are shown on two different time scales in **Figure 10.7**. Over the span of 65 million years, we see that Earth's climate was much warmer in the distant past, during which time tropical conditions extended to higher latitudes than today. Since the warmer times of about 50 million years ago, climate has generally cooled.

A distinct short period of rapid warming occurred about 56 million years ago (known as the Paleocene–Eocene Thermal Maximum, or PETM). Scientists think that this temperature maximum was caused by a sudden increase in atmospheric carbon, the cause of which is still uncertain. One prominent hypothesis is that a massive carbon release in the form of methane occurred from the melting of gas hydrates (ice-like chemical compounds that are stable when frozen) in ocean-floor sediments near the margins of continents. If a sudden warming event caused a large amount of hydrates to melt, the release of potent greenhouse gases could drastically alter Earth's temperature.

During the PETM, the rise in atmospheric carbon probably happened over a period of about 20,000 years or less—a "sudden" increase in terms of the vast scale of geologic time. Today's accelerating concentrations of atmospheric CO_2 are building at a more rapid pace. Scientists estimate that the amount of carbon that entered the atmosphere during the PETM is similar to the amount of carbon that human activity would release to the atmosphere with the burning of all Earth's fossil-fuel reserves.

Over the span of the last 5 million years, high-resolution climatic reconstructions using deep-ocean sediment cores reveal a series of cooler and warmer periods (Figure 10.7b). These ocean-core data are correlated with ice-core records, which show nearly identical trends.

The period from about 2.5 million years ago to about 11,700 years ago is the Pleistocene Epoch. This was Earth's most recent period of repeated glaciation. The Pleistocene was a time of generally cold climate that included one or more *glacials* (glacial periods, characterized by glacial advance) interrupted by brief warm periods known as *interglacials*. The Holocene Epoch, which began after the Pleistocene, is the interglacial ongoing to the present day.

Air bubbles trapped in an ice core provide data on atmospheric composition—specifically, on concentrations of CO_2 and methane. **Figure 10.8** shows the changing concentrations of those two greenhouse gases, as well as changing temperature, during the last 650,000 years. Note the close correlation between the two gas concentrations and between the gases and temperature on the graphs. Analyses have shown that the changes in greenhouse gas concentrations lag behind the temperature changes, but scientists are not sure as to the amount of lag time and whether it could be a by-product of the methods of analyses.

The last time temperatures were similar to the present-day interglacial period was during the Eemian

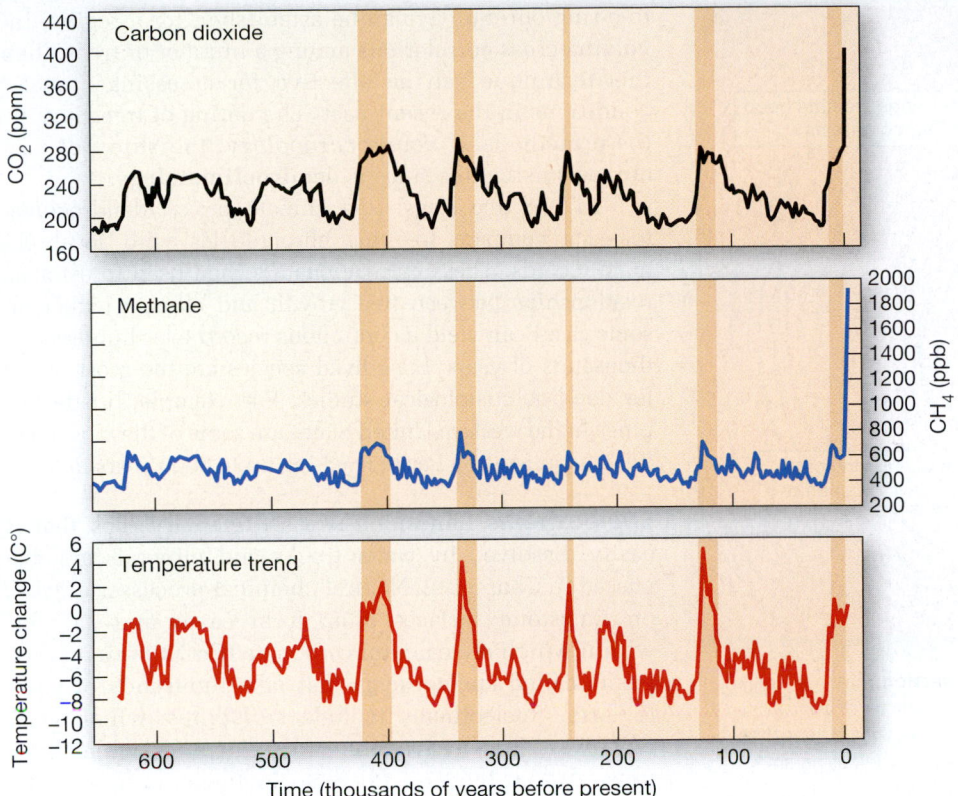

▲**Figure 10.8** **The 650,000-year record for carbon dioxide (CO₂), methane (CH₄), and temperature from ice-core data and recent atmospheric measurements.** Temperature trends are based on deuterium concentrations in Antarctic ice-core data. The shaded bands are interglacials, periods of elevated temperature and greenhouse gas concentrations. [Adapted from IPCC Fourth Assessment Report, *Climate Change 2007: The Physical Science Basis*, Working Group I, Figure TS-1; available at http://www.ipcc.ch/publications_and_data/ar4/wg1/en/tssts-2-1-1.html.]

interglacial about 125,000 years ago, during which time temperatures were warmer than at present. The cause for this warm period could relate to variations in solar output, although research is incomplete.

Methods for Short-Term Climate Reconstruction

Based on the paleoclimatic evidence just discussed, scientists know that Earth has undergone long-term climate cycles that have included conditions that were warmer and colder than today. Using a different set of indicators, they have also determined and verified climatic trends on shorter timescales, on the order of hundreds or thousands of years. The tools for short-term climate analysis consist mainly of radiocarbon dating and the analysis of growth rings of trees, speleothems, and corals.

Carbon Isotope Analysis Carbon is an element with two naturally occurring stable isotopes. Scientists use ^{12}C (carbon-12) and ^{13}C (carbon-13) to decipher past environmental conditions by analyzing the $^{13}C/^{12}C$ ratio in a manner similar to oxygen isotope analysis. In converting light energy from the Sun to food energy for growth, different plants use different types of photosynthesis, each of which

produces a different carbon isotope ratio in the plant products. Thus, scientists can use the carbon isotope ratio of dead plant material to determine past vegetation assemblages and their associated rainfall and temperature conditions.

Up to this point, we have discussed "stable" isotopes of oxygen and carbon, in which protons and neutrons remain together in an atom's nucleus. However, certain isotopes are "unstable" because the number of neutrons compared to protons is large enough to cause the isotope to decay, or lose energy by emitting radiation. This process often causes the isotope to break down into a different element. This type of unstable isotope is a **radioactive isotope**.

Atmospheric carbon includes the unstable isotope ^{14}C (carbon-14). The additional neutrons compared to protons in this isotope cause it to decay into a different atom, ^{14}N (nitrogen-14). The rate of decay is constant and is measured as a *half-life*, or the time it takes for half of a sample to decay (**Figure 10.9**). The half-life of ^{14}C is 5730 years. This decay rate can be used to date plant material, a technique known as *radiocarbon dating*.

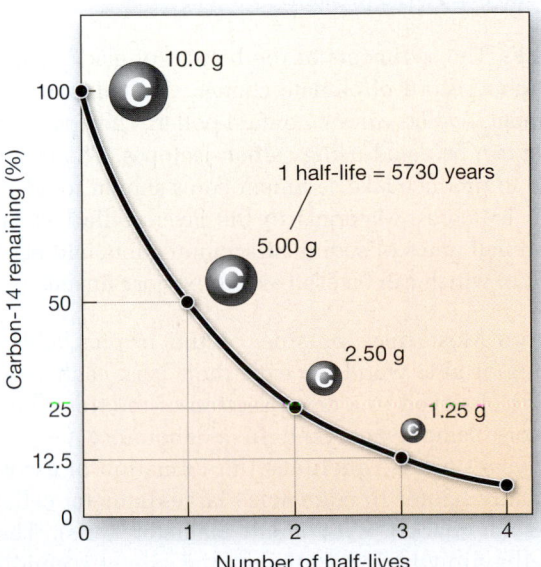

▲**Figure 10.9** **Decay rate of ^{14}C (carbon-14) as measured in half lives.** Carbon-14 has a half-life of 5730 years, meaning that half a sample decays to ^{14}N (nitrogen-14) over a period of 5730 years.

▲**Figure 10.10 Tree rings in trunk cross section.** Trees generally add one growth ring each year. The size and character of annual growth rings indicate growing conditions. Scientists can also analyze rings in a core sample extracted from a living tree trunk using an increment borer. [Dietrich Rose/Image Bank/Getty Images.]

Wider rings indicate good growing conditions

Narrower rings indicate harsh growing conditions

As an example, pollen is a plant material found in ice and lake sediments and is often dated using radiocarbon dating techniques. Since land plants use carbon from the air (specifically, carbon dioxide in photosynthesis), they contain ^{14}C in some amount, as does their pollen. As time passes, this radioactive carbon decays: After 5730 years, half of it will be gone, and, eventually, all of it will be gone. The amount of ^{14}C in the pollen can tell scientists how long ago it was alive. Radioactive isotopes are useful for dating organic material with ages up to about 50,000 years before the present.

Lake Cores The sediments at the bottom of glacial lakes also provide a record of climate change. Annual layers of lake sediments, called *varves*, contain pollen, charcoal, and fossils that can be dated using carbon isotopes. The layers are drilled to produce lake sediment cores similar to deep-ocean and ice cores. Materials in the layers reflect variations in rainfall, rates of sediment accumulation, and algal growth, all of which can be used as a proxy for climate.

Tree Rings Most trees outside of the tropics add a growth ring of new wood beneath their bark each year. This ring is observed in a cross section of the tree trunk or in a core sample analyzed in a laboratory (**Figure 10.10**). A year's growth includes the formation of early-wood (usually lighter in color with large-diameter cells) and latewood (darker with small-diameter cells). The width of the growth ring indicates the climatic conditions: Wider rings suggest favorable growth conditions, and narrower rings suggest harsher conditions or stress to the tree (often related to moisture or temperature). If a

tree-ring chronology can be established for a region, involving cross correlations among a number of trees, then this technique can be effective for assessing climatic conditions in the recent past. The dating of tree rings by these methods is *dendrochronology*; the study of past climates using tree rings is **dendroclimatology**.

To use tree rings as a climate proxy, dendroclimatologists compare tree-ring chronologies with local climate records. These correlations are then used to estimate relationships between tree growth and climate, which in some cases can yield a continuous record over hundreds or thousands of years. Long-lived species are the most useful for dendroclimatological studies. For example, bristlecone pines in the western United States are some of the most long-lived organisms on Earth, reaching up to 5000 years in age.

Speleothems Limestone is a sedimentary rock that is easily dissolved by water (rocks and minerals are discussed in Chapter 9). Natural chemical processes at work on limestone surfaces often form caves and caverns, within which are calcium carbonate ($CaCO_3$) mineral deposits called **speleothems** that take thousands of years to form. Speleothems include *stalactites*, which grow downward from a cave roof, and *stalagmites*, which grow upward from the cave floor. Speleothems form as water drips or seeps from the rock and subsequently evaporates, leaving behind a residue of $CaCO_3$ that builds up over time (**Figure 10.11**).

The rate of growth of speleothems depends on several environmental factors, including the amount of rainwater percolating through the rocks that form the cave, its acidity, and the temperature and humidity conditions in the cave. Like trees, speleothems have growth rings whose size and properties reflect the environmental conditions present when they formed and that can be dated using uranium isotopes. These growth rings also contain isotopes of

(a) Speleothems in Ngigli Cave, Australia.

(b) Growth bands in a speleothem cross section.

▲**Figure 10.11 Speleothems in a cavern and in cross section.**
[(a) robertharding/Alamy. (b) Robbie Shone / Alamy Stock Photo.]

oxygen and carbon, whose ratios indicate temperature and the amount of rainfall.

Scientists have correlated speleothem ring chronologies with temperature patterns in New Zealand and Russia (especially in Siberia) and with temperature and precipitation in the U.S. Southwest, among many other places. Some speleothem chronologies date to 350,000 years ago and are often combined with other paleoclimatic data to corroborate evidence of climate change.

Corals Corals are marine invertebrates with a body called a *polyp* that extracts calcium carbonate from seawater and then excretes it to form a calcium carbonate exoskeleton (like the shells found in ocean sediment cores). These skeletons accumulate over time in warm, tropical oceans, forming coral reefs. X-rays of core samples extracted from coral reefs reveal seasonal growth bands similar to those of trees, yielding information as to the water chemistry at the time the exoskeletons were formed (**Figure 10.12**). Scientists can

(a) A scientist drills into a coral head in Dry Tortugas National Park, located 112 km (70 mi) west of Key West in the Florida Keys archipelago.

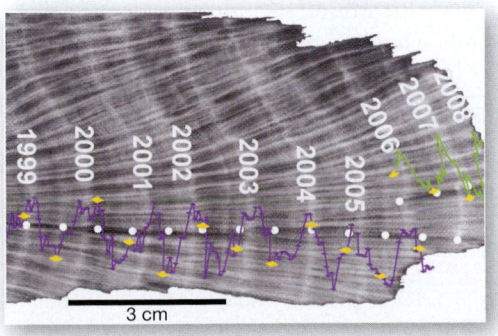

(b) X-ray of core cross section shows banding; each light/dark band indicates one year of growth.

▲**Figure 10.12 Extraction and cross section of coral core sample.** [(a) Hickey, D., Reich, C.D., DeLong, K.L., Poore, R.Z., Brock, J.C., 2013. Holocene core logs and site methods for modern reef and head-coral cores: Dry Tortugas National Park, Florida. Dept. of the Interior, U.S. Geological Survey, Washington DC, p. 27. (b) USGS.]

use these methods to identify the climatic conditions during which the coral grew and date samples to an exact year and season. Although the process damages polyps living at the surface of the drill site, it does not damage the reef, and drill holes are recolonized by polyps within a few years.

Earth's Short-Term Climate History

The Pleistocene Epoch, Earth's most recent period of repeated glaciations, began 2.5 million years ago. The last glacial period lasted from about 110,000 years ago to about 11,700 years ago. The *last glacial maximum* (LGM), the time when ice extent in the last glacial period was greatest, occurred about 20,000 years ago. Chapter 17 discusses changes to Earth's landscapes during this time, and Figure 17.XX shows the extent of glaciation during this prolonged cold period. The climate record for the past 20,000 years reveals the period of cold temperatures that occurred from the LGM to about 15,000 years ago (**Figure 10.13**).

About 14,500 years ago, average temperatures abruptly increased and then dropped again about 12,900 years ago in the Northern Hemisphere, leading into a colder period, known as the *Younger Dryas* (named for a flower that thrived in the cold conditions of this time). The Younger Dryas ended with abrupt warming about 11,700 years ago. This warming also marked the end of the Pleistocene Epoch.

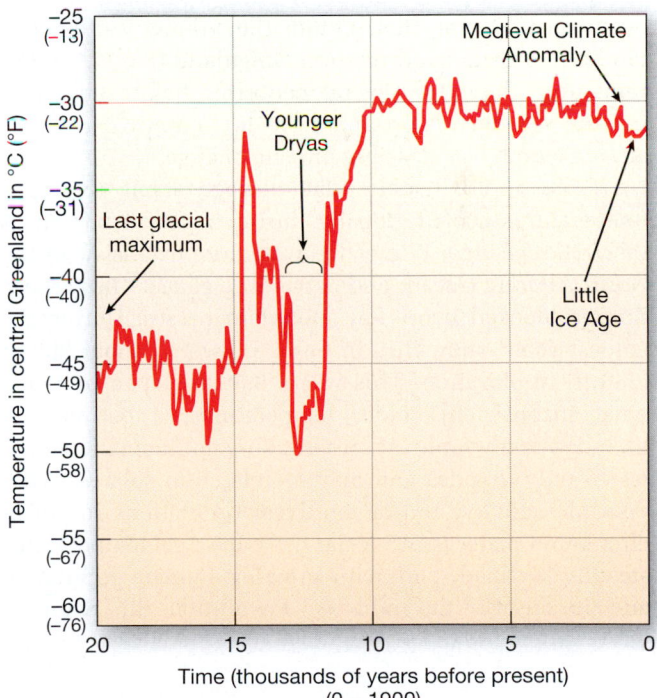

▲**Figure 10.13 The past 20,000 years of Greenland temperature.** Evidence from Greenland ice cores shows an abrupt temperature rise occurring about 14,000 years ago, followed by a cooler period known as the Younger Dryas, followed by another temperature rise about 11,700 years ago. The warmer temperatures of the brief Medieval Climate Anomaly and the cooler temperatures of the Little Ice Age are also visible on the temperature line. Although this graph uses ice-core data, these temperature trends correlate with other climate proxy records. [From R. B. Alley, 2000, "The Younger Dryas Cold Interval as Viewed from Central Greenland," *Quaternary Science Reviews* 19: 213–226; available at http://www.ncdc.noaa.gov/paleo/pubs/alley2000/alley2000.html.]

▲**Figure 10.14** **The remains of a Viking settlement in southwest Greenland.** During the Medieval Climate Anomaly, milder climates corresponded with the spread of the seafaring Vikings to Greenland and North America. Abandonment of the Greenland settlements corresponded with climatic cooling, but the exact cause is unknown.

From 800 to 1200 C.E., a number of climate proxies (tree rings, corals, and ice cores) show a mild climatic episode, now known as the *Medieval Climate Anomaly*. During this time, warmer temperatures—as warm as or warmer than today—occurred in some regions, whereas cooling occurred in other regions. The warmth over the North Atlantic region allowed a variety of crops to grow at higher latitudes in Europe, shifting settlement patterns northward. During this period, the Vikings settled Iceland and coastal southwestern Greenland (**Figure 10.14**), remaining there for several centuries before abandoning the settlements around 1400 for unknown reasons, among which was possibly climate change.

From approximately 1250 through about 1850 C.E., temperatures cooled globally during a period known as the *Little Ice Age*. Winter ice was more extensive in the North Atlantic Ocean, and expanding glaciers in western Europe blocked many key mountain passes. During the coldest years, snowlines in Europe lowered about 200 m (650 ft) in elevation. This was a 600-year span of somewhat inconsistent colder temperatures, a period that included many rapid, short-term climate fluctuations that lasted only decades and may be related to solar activity, volcanic activity, and/or multiyear oscillations in global circulation patterns. After the Little Ice Age, temperatures steadily warmed, and with growing human population and the onset of the Industrial Revolution, this warming has continued to the present day.

Mechanisms of Natural Climate Fluctuation

In reviewing climate records on various scales, we see that Earth's climate cycles between warmer and colder periods. When temperature is viewed over certain timescales, such as over periods of about 650,000 years (illustrated in Figure 10.8), cyclical patterns are apparent. Scientists have evaluated a number of natural mechanisms that affect Earth's climate and might cause these long-term cyclical climate variations.

Solar Variability

The Sun's output of energy toward Earth, known as *solar irradiance*, varies over several timescales, and these natural variations can affect climate. Over billions of years, solar output has generally increased by about one-third since the formation of the solar system. Over recent decades, scientists have used satellite data to determine slight variations in the amount of radiation received at the top of the atmosphere, and have correlated these variations to sunspot activity.

As discussed in Chapter 2, the number of sunspots varies over an 11-year solar cycle. When sunspot abundance is high, a slight increase occurs in solar activity and output. When sunspot abundance is low, solar output decreases slightly. Research shows that these relationships relate to climatic indicators such as temperature. For example, the record of sunspot occurrences shows a prolonged solar minimum (little sunspot activity) from about 1645 to 1715, known as the **Maunder Minimum** (**Figure 10.15**). This 70-year period corresponds with one of the coldest periods of the Little Ice Age, suggesting to some scientists that decreased sunspot abundance caused cooling in the North Atlantic region. However, the sunspot number since 1700 shows a fairly stable average, with no trend of increasing solar activity since 1950. Thus, scientists agree that solar irradiance is not a driver of global warming trends over the past century.

Earth's Orbital Cycles

Earth–Sun relationships affect energy receipts and seasonality on Earth and are another possible factor in climate change. These relationships include Earth's distance from the Sun, which varies within its orbital path, and Earth's orientation to the Sun, which varies as a result of the "wobble" of Earth on its axis and Earth's varying axial tilt (review Chapter 2, where we discussed Earth–Sun relations and the seasons).

Milutin Milankovitch (1879–1958), a Serbian astronomer, studied the irregularities in Earth's rotation on its axis, its axial tilt, and its orbit around the Sun and identified regular cycles that relate to climatic patterns (**Figure 10.16a**).

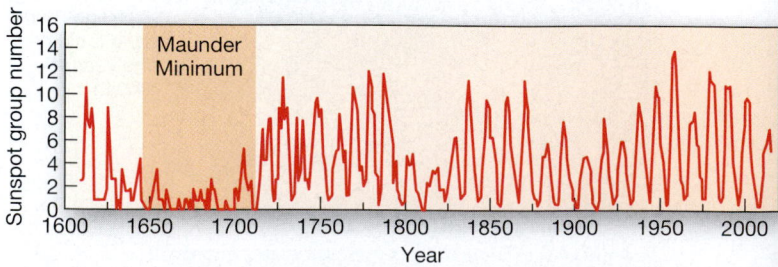

▲**Figure 10.15** **Newly calibrated sunspot number over the past 400 years.** The 2015 recalibration of sunspot occurrences, renamed Sunspot Number Version 2.0, shows no increase in solar activity as temperatures have warmed since the Industrial Revolution. [World Data Center–Sunspot Index and Long-term Solar Observations; http://www.sidc.be/silso/home.]

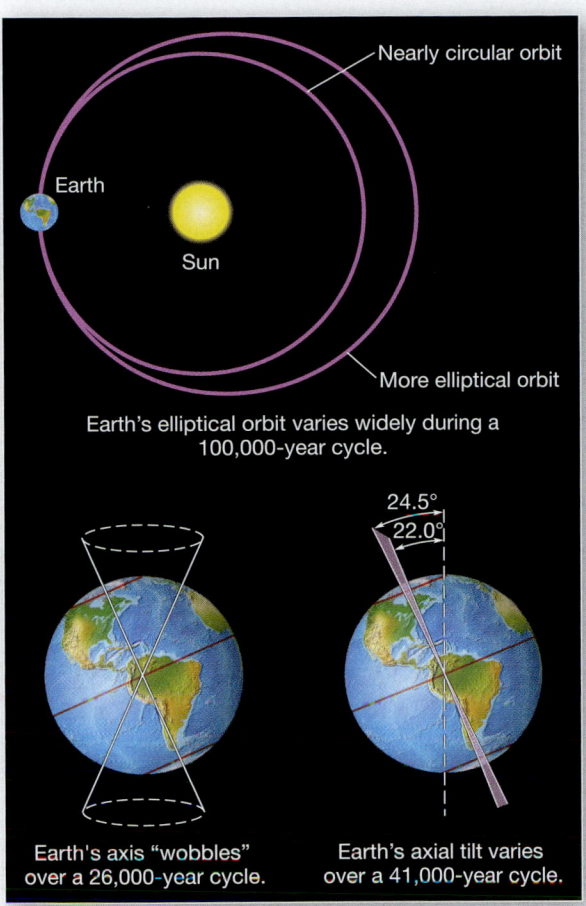

▲Figure 10.16 Astronomical factors that may affect broad climatic cycles. Drawings are an exaggeration of actual orbital paths, axis wobble, and axial tilt.

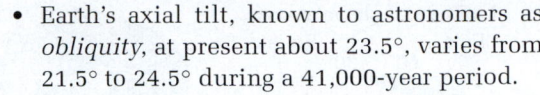

- Earth's axial tilt, known to astronomers as *obliquity*, at present about 23.5°, varies from 21.5° to 24.5° during a 41,000-year period.

These consistent orbital cycles, now called **Milankovitch cycles**, are today accepted as influencing Earth's climate system, though their exact role is still being investigated. Scientific evidence in ice cores from Greenland and Antarctica and in the accumulated sediments of Lake Baikal in Russia has confirmed a roughly 100,000-year climatic cycle; other evidence supports the effect on climate of shorter-term cycles of roughly 40,000 and 20,000 years. Milankovitch cycles appear to be an important cause of glacial–interglacial cycles, although other factors probably amplify the effects (such as changes in the North Atlantic Ocean, albedo effects from gains or losses of Arctic sea ice, and variations in greenhouse gas concentrations, discussed later in the chapter).

Atmospheric Gases and Aerosols

Natural processes can release gases and aerosols into Earth's atmosphere with varying impacts on climate. The primary natural source of atmospheric CO_2 is outgassing from Earth's interior through volcanoes and vents in the ocean floor. In addition to outgassing, volcanic eruptions produce aerosols that scientists have definitively linked to climatic cooling. Accumulations of aerosols ejected into the stratosphere can create a layer of particulates that increases albedo, so that more insolation is reflected and less solar energy reaches Earth's surface. Studies of 20th-century eruptions have shown that sulfur aerosol accumulations affect temperatures on timescales of months to years (**Figure 10.17**). For example, the aerosol cloud from the 1982 El Chichón eruption in Mexico lowered temperatures worldwide for several months, and the 1991 Mount Pinatubo eruption lowered temperatures for 2 years. Scientific evidence also suggests that a series of large volcanic eruptions may have initiated the colder temperatures of the Little Ice Age in the second half of the 13th century.

- Earth's elliptical orbit about the Sun, known as *orbital eccentricity*, is not constant and changes in cycles over several timescales. The most prominent is a 100,000-year cycle in which the shape of the ellipse varies by more than 17.7 million kilometers (11 million miles), from a shape that is nearly circular to one that is more elliptical.
- Earth's axis "wobbles" through a 26,000-year cycle, in a movement much like that of a spinning top winding down. Earth's wobble, known as *precession*, changes the orientation of hemispheres and landmasses to the Sun.

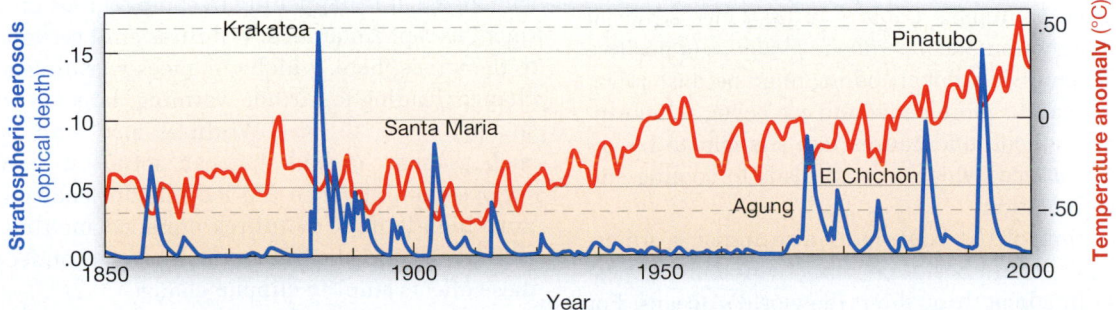

▲Figure 10.17 Temperature impacts of aerosols from volcanic eruptions. Satellite measurements of aerosols are based on optical thickness, or depth, determined by the way in which atmospheric particles change the reflection and absorption of light. An optical depth of 0.1 indicates a clear sky and maximum visibility; an optical depth of 1.0 indicates haze and reduced visibility. From 1850 to 2000, five volcanic eruptions lowered global temperatures for several years. [NASA.]

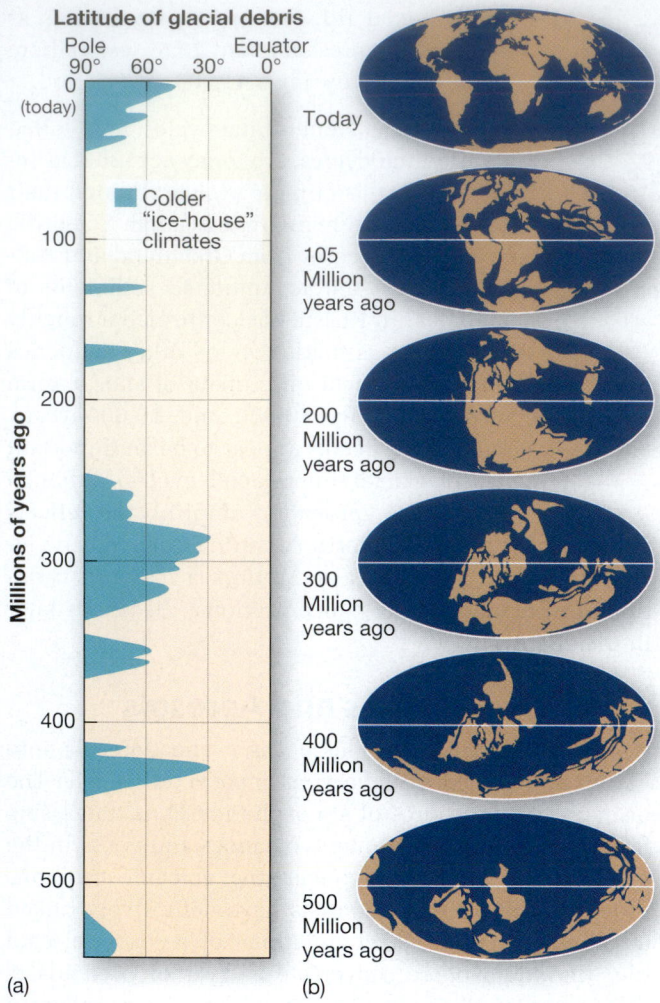

Latitude of glacial debris

Today

105 Million years ago

200 Million years ago

300 Million years ago

400 Million years ago

500 Million years ago

Colder "ice-house" climates

(a)   (b)

▲**Figure 10.18 Glaciation and the position of the continents.**
Periods of colder climates occurred when the continents were positioned
near the poles, for example about 300 million years ago. [Source: NPS.
Paleogeography maps modified from Ronald Blakey, Northern Arizona University
Department of Geology.]

Continental Landmasses

Because Earth's lithosphere is composed of moving plates,
continental rearrangement has occurred throughout geologic history. Some scientists suggest that having continental landmasses positioned in the polar regions is a factor
in starting a glacial cycle. Research shows that major glaciations over Earth's history correspond with the polar positioning of the continents (**Figure 10.18**). Once a glacial
period is set in motion, the *ice–albedo feedback* (a positive
feedback) can amplify a global cooling trend because lower
temperatures lead to more snow and ice cover, which increases Earth's albedo and causes less sunlight to be absorbed at the surface, which in turn leads to cooling and
more ice accumulation.

The position of the continents also impacts atmospheric circulation and ocean currents, which are critical
for redistributing heat throughout the world's oceans. For
example, the closing of the land bridge connecting North
and South America about 10 to 15 million years ago
redirected oceans currents, forming the Gulf Stream that
today affects climatic conditions in Europe.

Climate Feedbacks and the Carbon Budget

Several climate feedbacks influence Earth's global climate
system. Positive feedback amplifies system changes and
tends to destabilize the system; negative feedback inhibits
system changes and tends to stabilize the system. **Climate
feedbacks** are processes that either amplify or reduce climatic trends. For example, in a warming climate a positive
feedback will enhance warming and a negative feedback
will offset, or reduce, the warming trend. These feedback
mechanisms also affect the movement of carbon through
Earth systems—either in the short term (over years or hundreds of years) or in the long term (over millions of years).

Climate Feedback Examples

The *ice–albedo feedback* mentioned previously is a
positive climate feedback. Other examples of both positive and negative feedback relate to water vapor, frozen
ground, wildfire, and the weathering of rocks.

Water-Vapor Feedback Water vapor is the most abundant
natural greenhouse gas in the Earth–atmosphere system. The
water-vapor feedback occurs as air temperature rises and
evaporation increases because the capacity to absorb water
vapor is greater for warm air than for cooler air. Thus, more
water enters the atmosphere from land and ocean surfaces,
humidity increases, greenhouse warming accelerates, and
the positive feedback continues (**Figure 10.19a**).

Permafrost–Carbon Feedback Scientists hypothesize
that warming temperatures trigger the release of greenhouse gases (mainly CO_2 and methane), which then act as
a positive feedback mechanism: Initial warming leads to
increases in gas concentrations, which amplify warming,
and so on. This type of carbon–climate feedback occurs
in the Arctic, in areas of frozen ground known as *permafrost*. Focus Study 10.1 discusses the *permafrost–carbon
feedback*, which occurs as thawing permafrost leads to increased microbial activity in soils and releases more carbon to the atmosphere.

Wildfire–Carbon Feedback Another carbon–climate
feedback occurs as wildfires increase in size and intensity—
a change that is happening in some regions on every continent except Antarctica. Wildfires emit greenhouse gases
to the atmosphere, which enhances warming and climate
change, leading to further warming, larger wildfires, and
so on (**Figure 10.19b**). Wildfires also emit particulates
such as black carbon that can settle on snow and ice
surfaces and enhance the ice–albedo feedback. In addition, high-latitude wildfires enhance melting of frozen
ground, accelerating the permafrost–carbon feedback. All
these effects amplify climate change.

Earth's Carbon Budget

The carbon on Earth cycles through atmospheric, oceanic,
terrestrial, and living systems in a biogeochemical cycle

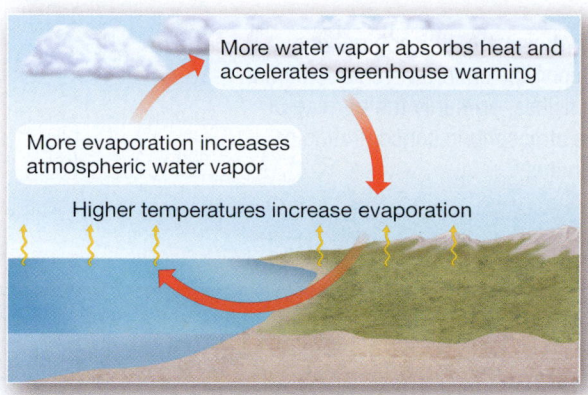

(a) The water-vapor climate feedback occurs as warming temperatures increase evaporation, which leads to increased water vapor in the atmosphere, which increases the greenhouse gas concentrations that cause warming.

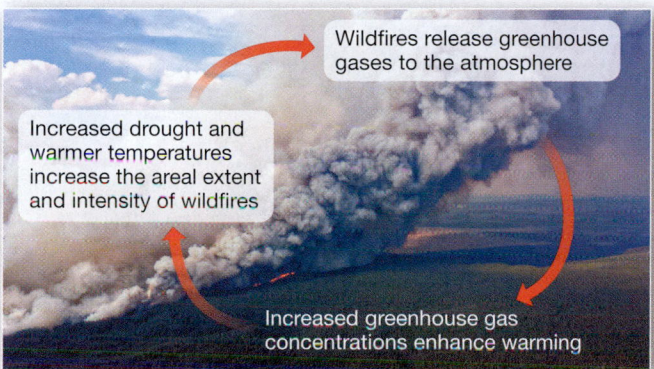

(b) The wildfire climate feedback occurs as warming temperatures and drought lead to increased wildfires, which increases greenhouse gases, especially CO_2 and methane. This enhances warming, leading to larger and more intense wildfires.

▲Figure 10.19 **Positive climate feedbacks: water vapor and wildfire.** [(b) NPS/Alamy.]

known as the *carbon cycle*. Areas of carbon release are carbon sources; areas of carbon storage are called **carbon sinks**, or carbon reservoirs. The overall exchange of carbon between the different systems on Earth is the **global carbon budget**, which should naturally remain balanced as carbon moves between sources and sinks. Geosystems in Action10 illustrates the components, both natural and anthropogenic, of Earth's carbon budget and the areas on Earth that are important carbon sinks.

Earth's largest carbon sink are the oceans. However, as the oceans increase in temperature, their ability to dissolve CO_2 is lessened. Thus, as global air and ocean temperatures warm, more CO_2 will likely remain in the atmosphere, with related impacts on Earth's climate.

Earth's terrestrial environment is also a carbon sink, as plants remove carbon from the atmosphere by photosynthesis. However, many human practices—for example, overgrazing, poor agricultural practices that lead to soil erosion, and removal of forests for wood products—reduce the capacity of the terrestrial carbon sink.

Earth's lithosphere takes up carbon over longer time scales than the movement of carbon between the atmosphere, ocean, and biosphere (**Figure 10.20**). Carbon dioxide in the atmosphere dissolves in rainwater to form a weak acid that decomposes rocks. The calcium ions released as rocks weather and erode eventually enter the oceans, where they become part of shelled marine organisms that die and lithify (are cemented together) to form limestone. The carbon in limestone is stored for hundreds of thousands to hundreds of millions of years, effectively removing CO_2 from the atmosphere into long-term storage in the ocean carbon sink.

CO_2–Weathering Feedback

The process of chemical weathering that transfers CO_2 from the atmosphere to the lithosphere and hydrosphere also acts as a long-term negative climate feedback, slowing a warming or cooling trend. This so-called *CO_2–weathering feedback* provides a natural buffer to climatic change over long time scales. For example, increasing CO_2 stored in the atmosphere increases global warming, which increases the amount of water vapor present in the atmosphere. Greater atmospheric moisture in a warmer climate generally leads to greater precipitation. With increasing rainfall comes an increase in the breakdown of exposed rock on Earth's surface by chemical weathering processes, thereby removing CO_2 from the atmosphere and transferring it to the oceans. In contrast, global cooling reduces precipitation and chemical weathering, thereby leaving more CO_2 in the atmosphere, where it works to increase temperatures. Throughout Earth's history, this natural buffer has helped prevent Earth's climate from becoming too warm or too cold. The present accelerating warming trend is clearly overpowering these natural buffers.

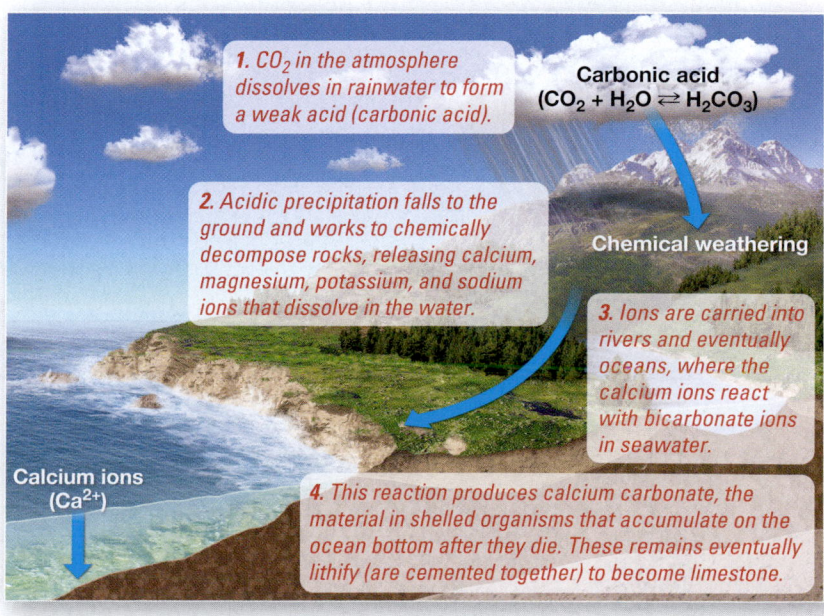

1. CO_2 in the atmosphere dissolves in rainwater to form a weak acid (carbonic acid).

Carbonic acid $(CO_2 + H_2O \rightleftarrows H_2CO_3)$

2. Acidic precipitation falls to the ground and works to chemically decompose rocks, releasing calcium, magnesium, potassium, and sodium ions that dissolve in the water.

Chemical weathering

3. Ions are carried into rivers and eventually oceans, where the calcium ions react with bicarbonate ions in seawater.

Calcium ions (Ca^{2+})

4. This reaction produces calcium carbonate, the material in shelled organisms that accumulate on the ocean bottom after they die. These remains eventually lithify (are cemented together) to become limestone.

▲Figure 10.20 **Earth's lithosphere takes up carbon over long timescales.**

Several processes transfer carbon between the atmosphere, hydrosphere, lithosphere, and biosphere (GIA 10.1). Over time, the distribution of carbon among the spheres—Earth's carbon budget—has remained roughly in balance. Today, human activities, primarily the burning of fossil fuels (GIA 10.2) and the removal of forests, are increasing the atmospheric concentration of carbon dioxide, altering the carbon budget and affecting Earth's climate.

10.1 COMPONENTS OF CARBON BUDGET

Numbers are in Gt (gigatonnes, or billions of tons) of carbon per year. White numbers represent natural carbon flows; white boxes indicate carbon reservoirs, or areas of carbon storage. Red numbers indicate changes in carbon exchange after the onset of the Industrial Era (about 1750).

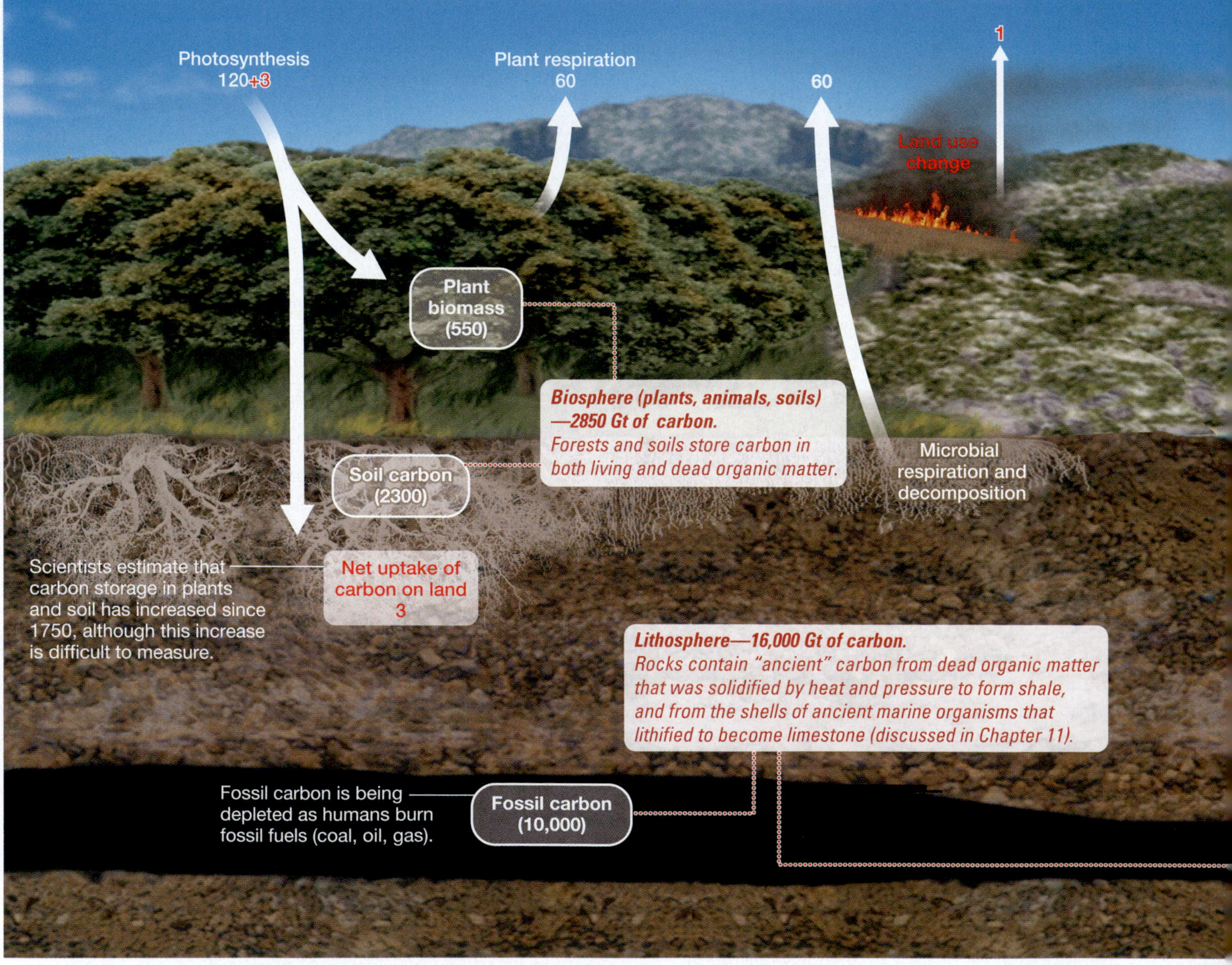

Photosynthesis
120 +3

Plant respiration
60

60

1

Land use change

Plant biomass (550)

Biosphere (plants, animals, soils) —2850 Gt of carbon.
Forests and soils store carbon in both living and dead organic matter.

Soil carbon (2300)

Microbial respiration and decomposition

Scientists estimate that carbon storage in plants and soil has increased since 1750, although this increase is difficult to measure.

Net uptake of carbon on land 3

Lithosphere—16,000 Gt of carbon.
Rocks contain "ancient" carbon from dead organic matter that was solidified by heat and pressure to form shale, and from the shells of ancient marine organisms that lithified to become limestone (discussed in Chapter 11).

Fossil carbon is being depleted as humans burn fossil fuels (coal, oil, gas).

Fossil carbon (10,000)

Video (MG)
Supercomputing the Climate

https://goo.gl/G1aNnu

MasteringGeography™

Visit the Study Area in MasteringGeography™ to explore the carbon budget.

Visualize: Study videos of the carbon cycle and climate modeling.

Assess: Demonstrate understanding of the carbon budget (if assigned by instructor).

Animation (MG)
Carbonate Buffering System

https://goo.gl/0hKkzt

10.2 CARBON EMISSIONS FROM FOSSIL-FUEL BURNING

This coal-fired power plant at Barentsburg, Svalbard, lacks scrubbers to reduce stack emissions.

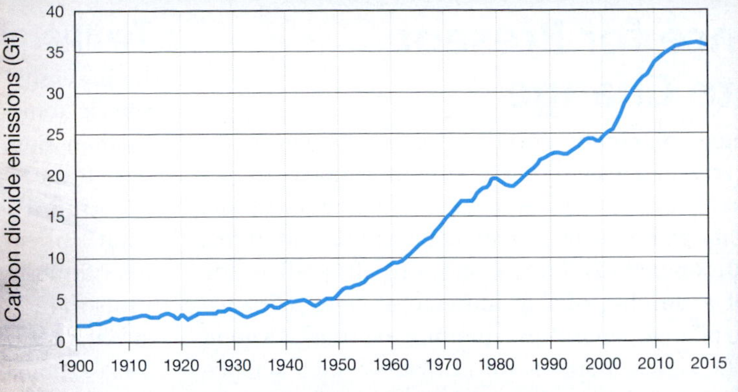

World carbon dioxide emissions, 1900–2015

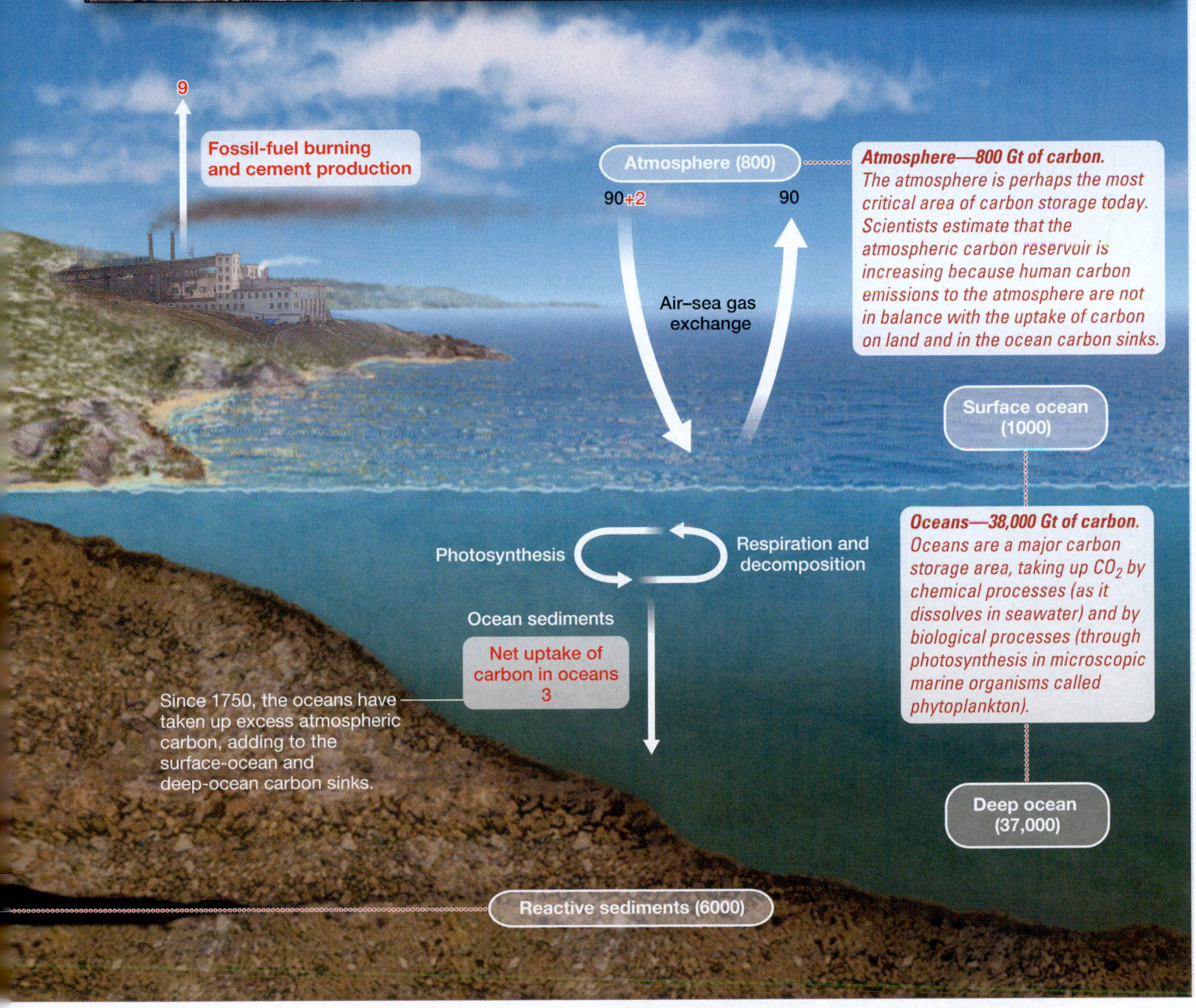

(Graph: Carbon dioxide emissions (Gt) vs. years 1900–2015, rising from about 2 Gt in 1900 to about 35 Gt by 2015)

9
Fossil-fuel burning and cement production

Atmosphere (800)
90 +2   90

Air–sea gas exchange

Atmosphere—800 Gt of carbon.
The atmosphere is perhaps the most critical area of carbon storage today. Scientists estimate that the atmospheric carbon reservoir is increasing because human carbon emissions to the atmosphere are not in balance with the uptake of carbon on land and in the ocean carbon sinks.

Surface ocean (1000)

Photosynthesis   Respiration and decomposition

Ocean sediments

Net uptake of carbon in oceans
3

Since 1750, the oceans have taken up excess atmospheric carbon, adding to the surface-ocean and deep-ocean carbon sinks.

Oceans—38,000 Gt of carbon.
Oceans are a major carbon storage area, taking up CO₂ by chemical processes (as it dissolves in seawater) and by biological processes (through photosynthesis in microscopic marine organisms called phytoplankton).

Deep ocean (37,000)

Reactive sediments (6000)

Video (MG)
Taking Earth's Temperature

https://goo.gl/f0aFue

GEOquiz

1. Infer: Some of the 10 Gt of carbon from fossil-fuel burning, cement production, and land-use change is taken up by plants and some is dissolved in the oceans. How much is left to increase CO₂ levels in the atmosphere?

2. Analyze: How much carbon leaves the atmosphere each year through natural and anthropogenic processes on land?

3. Calculate: How many times more carbon emissions do humans produce annually today than in 1950?

Video (MG)
Keeping Up with Carbon

https://goo.gl/87suSd

Evidence for Present Climate Change

The evidence for contemporary climate change comes from a variety of measurements showing global trends over the past century—and especially over the past three decades. Data gathered from weather stations, satellites, weather balloons, ships, buoys, and aircraft confirm the presence of a number of key indicators. New evidence and climate change reports are emerging regularly; a good source for the latest updates on climate change science is the U.S. Global Change Research Program (http://www.globalchange.gov/). International climate-change science is coordinated by the Intergovernmental Panel on Climate Change (IPCC), which issued its Fifth Assessment Report in 2013–2014 (see the summary at http://www.ipcc.ch/).

Figure 10.21 illustrates the measurable indicators that unequivocally show climatic warming. In this section, we discuss each of the main indicators.

Temperature

In previous chapters, we discussed the rise in atmospheric temperatures during this century. In Chapter 4, Human Denominator 4 presents an important graph of data from four independent surface-temperature records showing a warming trend since 1880. These records, each collected and analyzed using slightly different techniques, show remarkable agreement. Figure 10.22 plots the NASA temperature data of global mean annual surface air temperature anomalies (as compared to the 1951–1980 temperature-average baseline) and 5-year mean temperatures from 1880 through 2015. (Remember from Chapter 4 that temperature anomalies are the variations from the mean temperature during some period of record.)

The temperature data unmistakably show a warming trend. Since 1880, in the Northern Hemisphere the period from 2000 to 2010 was the warmest decade. The years with the warmest land-surface temperatures were 2015,

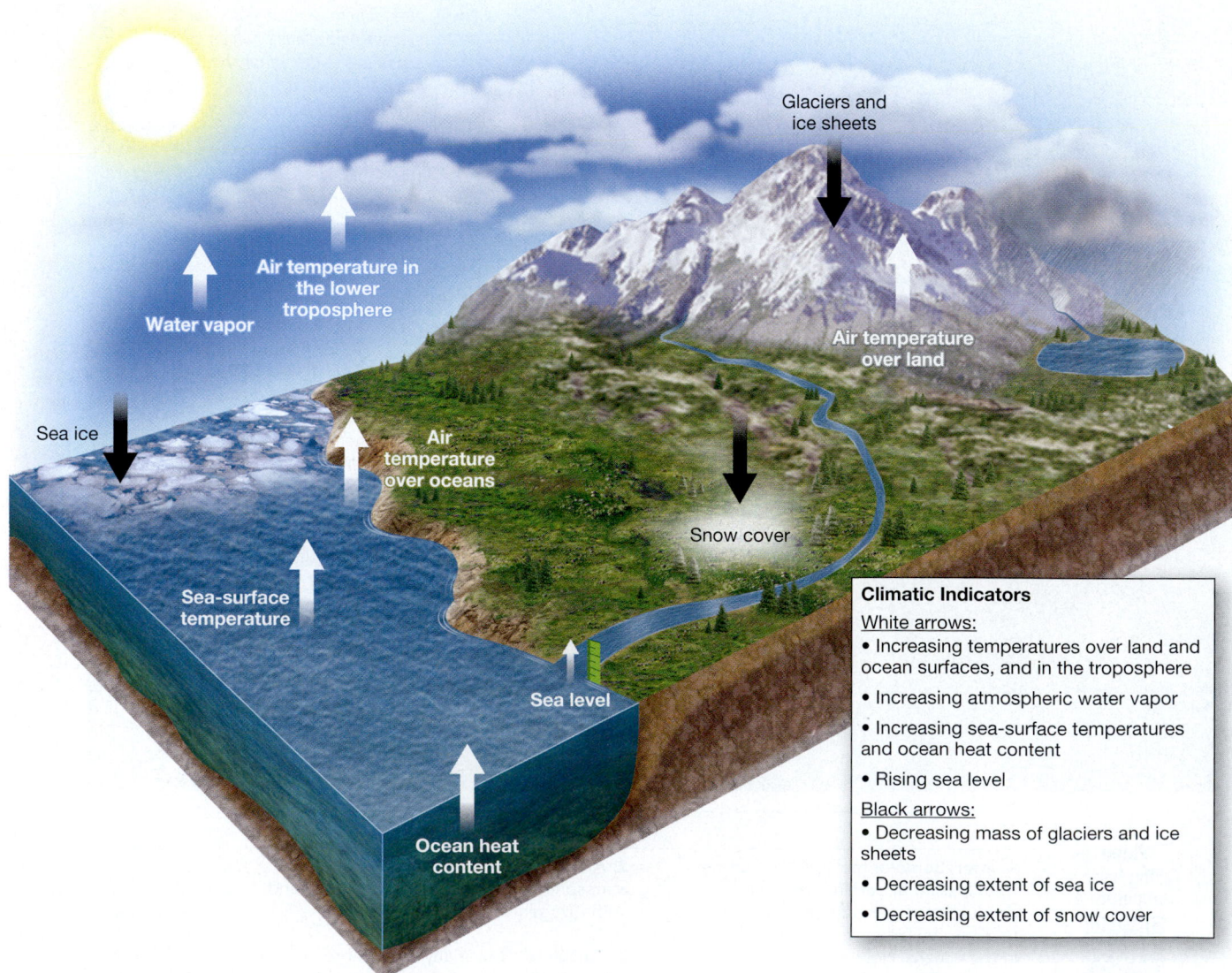

▲Figure 10.21 Key indicators of climatic warming. [Adapted from IPCC Fifth Assessment Report, *Climate Change 2013: The Physical Science Basis*, Working Group I, FAQ 2.1, Figure 1, p. 198.]

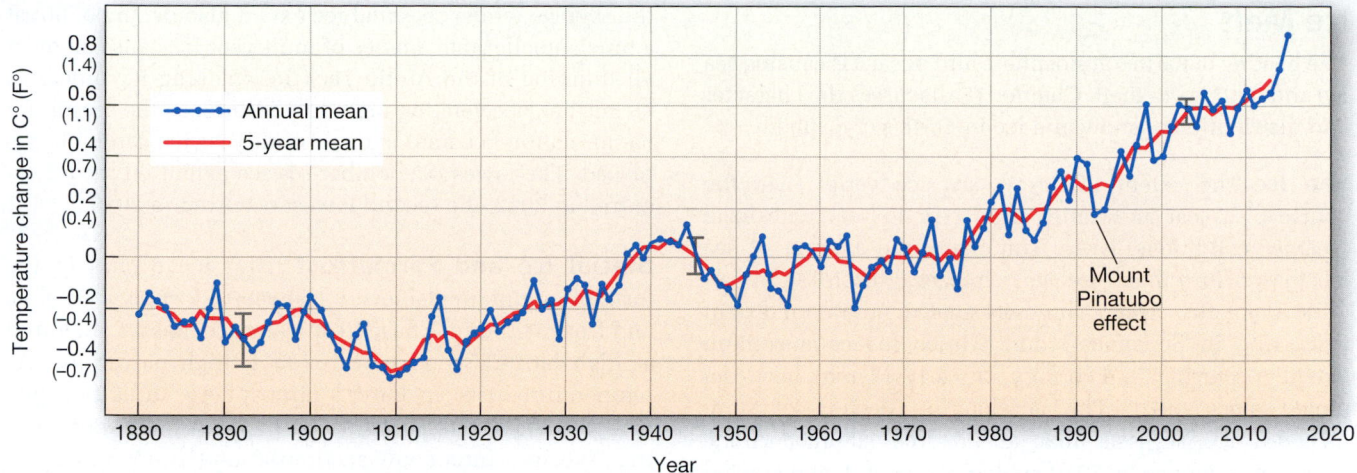

▲Figure 10.22 **Global land–ocean temperature trends, 1880–2015.** The graph shows change in global surface temperatures relative to the 1951–1980 global average. The gray bars represent uncertainty in the measurements. Note the inclusion of both annual average temperature anomalies and 5-year mean temperature anomalies; together, they give a sense of overall trends. [Based on data from NASA/GISS; available at http://climate.nasa.gov/vital-signs/global-temperature/.]

2014, and 2010. Global temperature in 2015 was 0.87°C warmer than the 1951–1980 average (**Figure 10.23**). The data from long-term climate reconstructions of temperature point to the present time as the warmest in the last 120,000 years. These reconstructions also suggest that the increase in temperature during the 20th century is *extremely likely* (having a greater than 95% probability of occurrence) to be the largest to occur in any century over the past 1000 years.

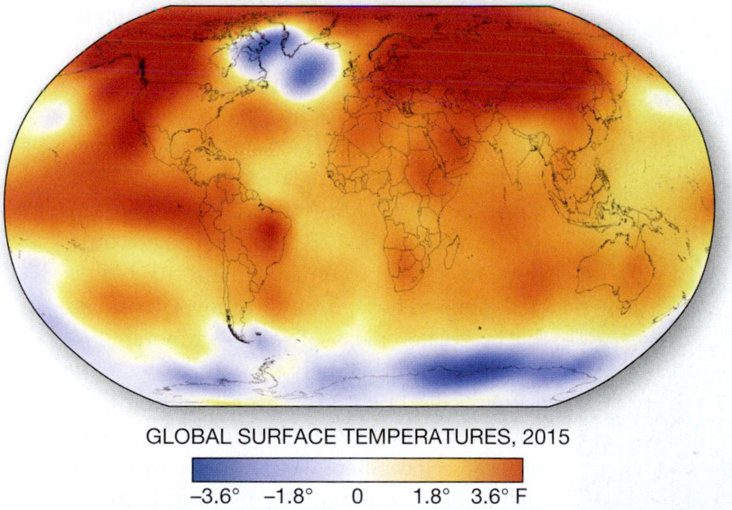

Record-setting summer daytime temperatures are being recorded in many countries. For example, in August 2013 temperatures in western Japan reached 41°C (106°F), the highest ever recorded in that country. Summer 2013 also brought a new high-temperature mark—40.8°C (105.4°F) in China. Summer 2015 brought record high temperatures in several countries on three continents. In May 2016, India recorded its highest temperature, a sweltering 51°C (123.8°F). In the United States, the number of unusually hot summer days has been rising since 1990. In addition, the number of unusually hot summer nights shows an even greater recent increase (see https://www3.epa.gov/climatechange/science/indicators/weather-climate/high-low-temps.html).

Ocean temperatures are also rising. As discussed in Chapter 5, sea-surface temperatures increased at an average rate of 0.07 C° (0.13 F°) per decade from 1901 to 2014 as oceans absorbed atmospheric heat. Measurements of the heat content in the upper 700 m (2296 ft) of the ocean show a steady increase since 1990. Measurements since 2005 of the upper 2000 m (6562 ft) of ocean indicate that this region is warming faster than the region closer to the surface (http://public.wmo.int/en/resources/library/wmo-statement-status-of-global-climate-2015). This increasing heat content is consistent with observed sea-level rise resulting from the thermal expansion of seawater (discussed ahead).

GLOBAL SURFACE TEMPERATURES, 2015

−3.6° −1.8° 0 1.8° 3.6° F

▲Figure 10.23 **Global land–ocean temperature trends, 2015.** Image shows change in global surface temperatures relative to the 1951–1980 global average. Note the areas where temperatures were colder than average. GeoReport 10.1 discusses the North Atlantic "cold blob." [NASA/GISS/NOAA.]

GEOreport **10.1** What explains the 2015 "cold blob" in the North Atlantic?

The temperature anomaly map in Figure 10.23 shows cooler than average temperatures over part of the North Atlantic Ocean. This "cold blob" concerns scientists because it suggests a slowing of the global deep-ocean circulation, including the northward movement of the warm Gulf Stream. As the freshwater of the Greenland Ice Sheet melts, the ocean becomes less salty—a change that slows the sinking of dense, salty water in the North Atlantic and the movement of currents to replace it. Slowing of the Gulf Stream would alter the climate of Northern Europe, and eventually affect climates on a global scale.

Ice Melt

The heating of Earth's atmosphere and oceans is causing sea ice and land ice to melt. Chapter 17 discusses the character and distribution of snow and ice in Earth's cryosphere.

Sea Ice The extent of Arctic sea ice varies over the course of a year and varies from year to year with local weather conditions. Every summer some amount of sea ice thaws. In winter, the ice refreezes. According to satellite data, the Arctic summer sea-ice minimum extent (occurring in September) and winter sea-ice maximum extent (occurring in February or early March) have declined since 1979. The accelerating decline of summer sea ice suggests that an ice-free summer Arctic Ocean may happen by 2040, which is sooner than predicted by most models.

As evidence of accelerating losses of Arctic sea ice, scientists have noted a decline in *multiyear ice*, the oldest and thickest ice, having survived through two or more summers. Younger, thinner, *seasonal ice* forms over one winter and typically melts rapidly the following summer. The Arctic multiyear ice extent declined from 1980 to 2012 (**Figure 10.24**). During that time,

Animation Arctic Sea Ice Decline

https://goo.gl/YEvVIe

▼**Figure 10.24 Comparison of Arctic winter sea ice in 1980 and 2012, showing multiyear and seasonal ice.** [NASA.]

the average winter seasonal ice extent also declined, but at a much smaller rate. Losses of multiyear ice cause an overall thinning of the Arctic pack ice, making it vulnerable for further, accelerating melt. In addition, as the season for ice formation becomes shorter, multiyear ice cannot be replaced. The lowest September sea ice extent on record occurred in 2012; the second lowest occurred in 2016.

Glacial Ice and Permafrost Land ice occurs in the form of mountain glaciers, ice sheets, ice caps, ice fields, and frozen ground. These freshwater ice masses are found at high latitudes and worldwide at high elevations. As temperatures rise in Earth's atmosphere, mountain glaciers are losing mass, shrinking in size as summer melting exceeds winter snow accumulation (**Figure 10.25**).

Earth's two largest ice sheets, in Greenland and Antarctica, contain 99% of Earth's freshwater locked up as ice. Satellite data show that these ice sheets are losing mass (**Figure 10.26**). Melting on these ice sheets appears to be accelerating and may cause faster sea-level rise than scientists have projected.

On the Greenland Ice Sheet, summer melt increased 30% from 1979 to 2006, with about half the surface area of the ice sheet experiencing some melting on average during the summer months. In July 2012, satellite data showed that 97% of the ice sheet's surface was covered by meltwater, the greatest extent in the 30-year record of satellite measurements. In May 2016, more than one-tenth of Greenland ice was melting, the earliest thaw on record.

Recent studies of the topography of the southern Greenland coastline beneath the ice sheet found deep canyons, extending to depths below sea level and reaching inland up to 96 km (60 mi). Scientists earlier predicted that recent melting would slow as glaciers retreat inland to higher elevations. These recent discoveries mean that a greater mass of ice is vulnerable to melting than previously thought.

In Antarctica, the rate of melting doubled from 2003 to 2014. Portions of the West Antarctic Ice Sheet (WAIS) are thinning, losing mass, and flowing more quickly toward the sea. Scientists think that the Amundsen Sea portion of the WAIS, which includes six glaciers, could melt in the next 100 to 200 years, an event that would raise sea level as much as 1.2 m (4 ft). If this destabilizes other areas of the ice sheet, the overall sea-level rise could be much greater.

Permafrost is perennially frozen ground found in the Arctic region. These permafrost reserves took tens of thousands of years to form and are now thawing at an accelerating rate. Focus Study 10.1 discusses the processes and climate feedbacks related to Arctic permafrost melt.

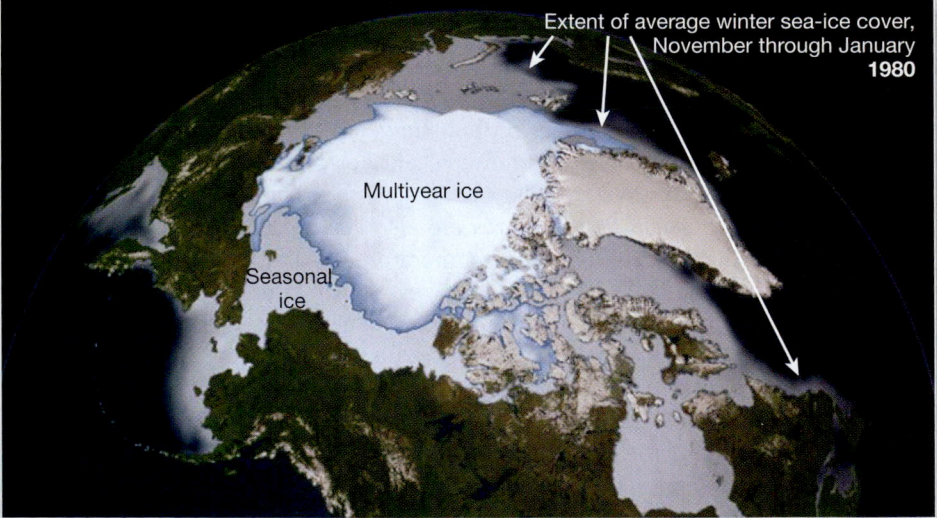

Extent of average winter sea-ice cover, November through January **1980**

Multiyear ice

Seasonal ice

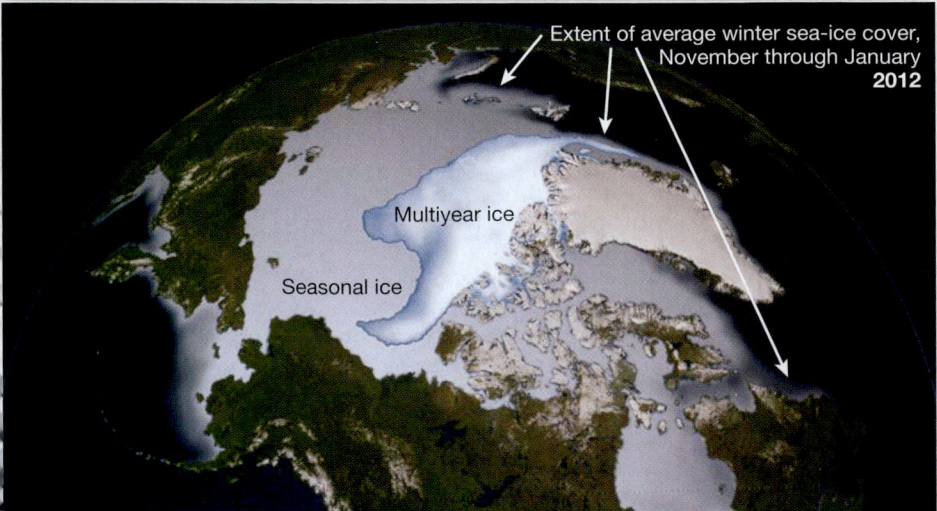

Extent of average winter sea-ice cover, November through January **2012**

Multiyear ice

Seasonal ice

(a) Alaska's Muir Glacier, August 13, 1941.

(b) Muir Glacier, August 31, 2004.

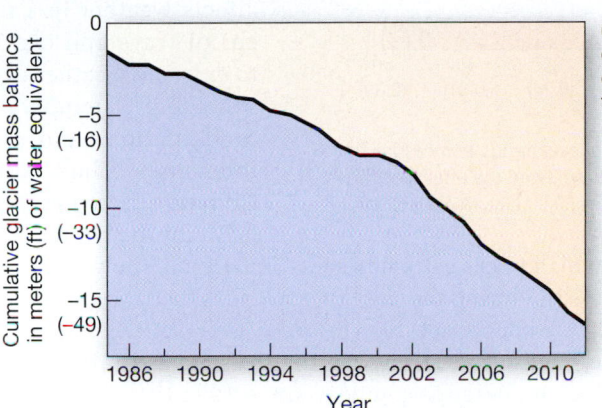

(c) Black line shows the negative cumulative annual mass balance of glaciers worldwide from 1980 to 2012.

▲Figure 10.25 **Worldwide annual glacial mass balance (the gain of snow minus the melt loss) and Muir Glacier show a net loss of glacial ice.** Glaciers grow when annual winter snowfall exceeds annual summer melt; when snowfall and melting are equal, glacial mass balance is zero (see the discussion in Chapter 17). [(a) NOAA graph adapted from *State of the Climate in 2012*, Bulletin of the American Meteorological Society. (b) and (c) USGS.]

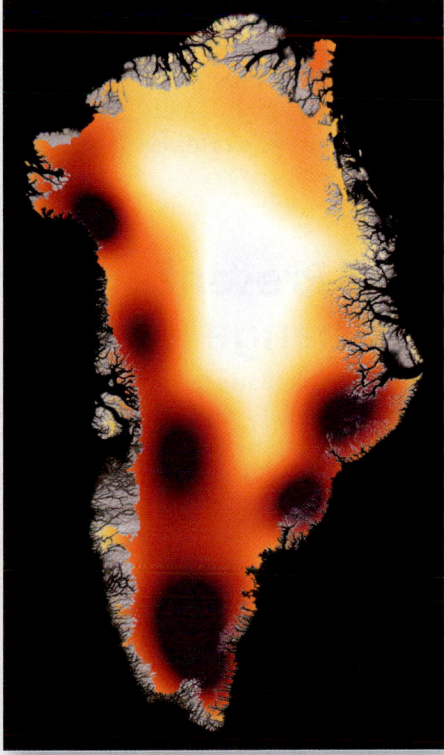

◄Figure 10.26 **Changes in mass of Greenland and Antarctic Ice Sheets, 2003–2013, as measured by *GRACE* satellites.** Orange and red show mass losses; light blue shows mass gains. White areas show no change. [NASA/GSFC. (a) http://svs.gsfc.nasa.gov/30478. (b) http://svs.gsfc.nasa.gov/30492.]

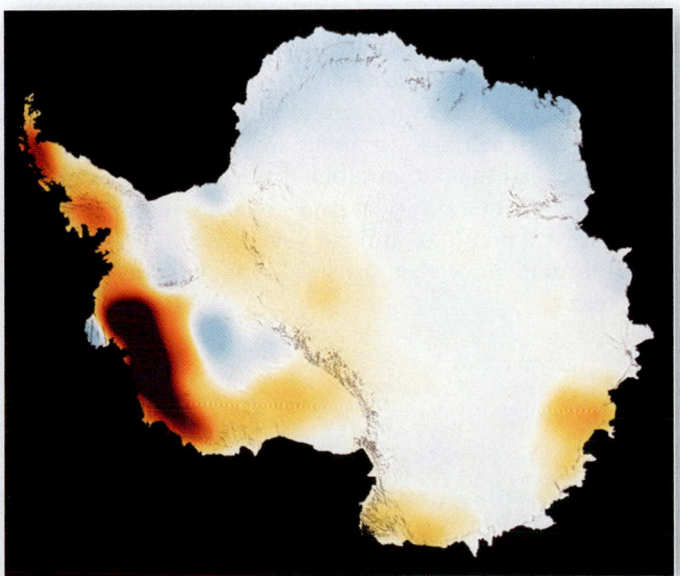

CHANGE IN ICE MASS 2003–2013
Equivalent water height in m (ft)

−3.0 (−9.8)   −2.0 (−6.7)   −1.0 (−3.3)   0   0.5 (1.6)

CHANGE IN ICE MASS 2003–2013
Equivalent water height in m (ft)

−2.0 (−6.7)   −1.0 (−3.3)   0   0.5 (1.6)

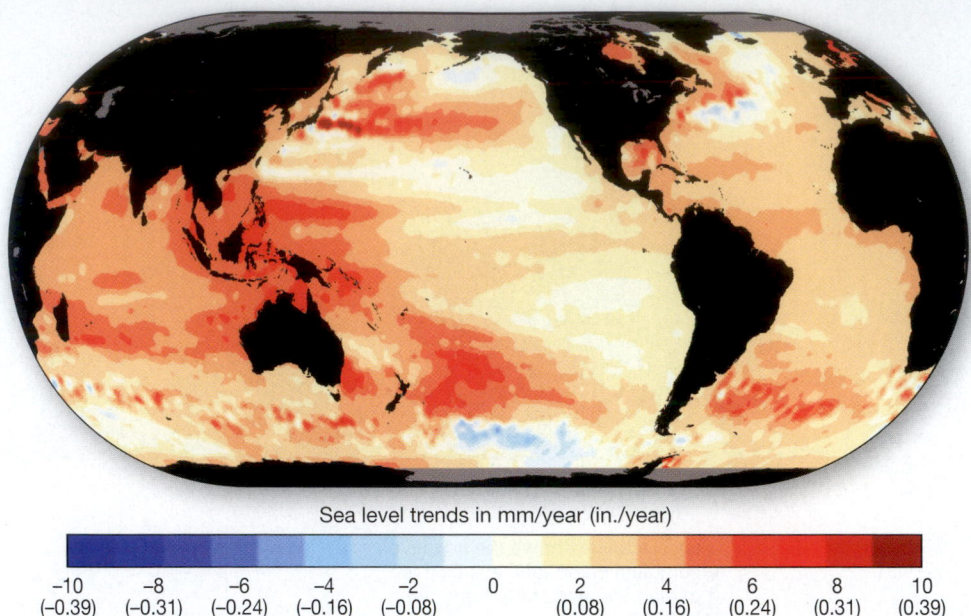

Sea level trends in mm/year (in./year)

| −10 | −8 | −6 | −4 | −2 | 0 | 2 | 4 | 6 | 8 | 10 |
| (−0.39) | (−0.31) | (−0.24) | (−0.16) | (−0.08) | | (0.08) | (0.16) | (0.24) | (0.31) | (0.39) |

▲Figure 10.27 **Rate of global mean sea-level change, 1992–2016.** Sea-level trends as measured by *TOPEX/Poseidon*, *Jason-1*, and *Jason-2* satellites vary with geographic location. Note the effects of the western intensification in the tropical Pacific, discussed in Chapter 5. [Laboratory for Satellite Altimetry/NOAA.]

Sea-Level Rise

Two primary factors are presently contributing to sea-level rise. Roughly two-thirds of the rise comes from the melting of land ice in the form of glaciers and ice sheets. The other third comes from the thermal expansion of seawater that occurs as oceans absorb heat from the atmosphere and expand in volume. The present sea-level rise is uneven over the globe. For example, the rate of rise along the coast of Argentina is greater than the rate along the coast of France, and the rate of rise along the U.S. East Coast is greater than the rate along the U.S. West Coast (**Figure 10.27**).

Sea level is now rising more quickly than predicted by most climate models, and the rate appears to be accelerating. During the last century, sea level rose 17–21 cm (6.7–8.3 in.), a greater rise in some areas (such as the U.S. Atlantic coast) than at any time during the past 3000 years. From 1901 to 2010, tidal gauge records show that sea level rose 1.7 mm (0.07 in.) per year. From 1993 to 2013, satellite data show that sea level rose 3.4 mm (0.13 in.) per year.

Atmospheric Water Vapor and Extreme Events

Since 1973, global average specific humidity has increased by about 0.1 g of water vapor per kilogram of air per decade. This change is consistent with rising air temperatures because warm air has a greater capacity to absorb water vapor. A greater amount of water vapor in the atmosphere affects weather in a number of ways and can lead to extreme weather events involving temperature, precipitation, and storm intensity. The Annual Climate Extremes Index (CEI) for the United States, which tracks extreme events since 1900, shows such an increase during the past four decades (see the data at http://www.ncdc.noaa.gov/extremes/cei/graph/cei/01-12). Since 1959, precipitation falling during the heaviest rainfall events has increased, especially since 1991 (**Figure 10.28**).

According to the World Meteorological Organization, the decade from 2001 to 2010 showed evidence of a worldwide increase in extreme events—notably, heat waves, increased precipitation, and floods. In 2015, one of the strongest ENSO events on record combined with climate change to intensify droughts, floods, and tropical cyclone activity in several world regions.

Causes of Present Climate Change

We have seen that fluctuations in the concentration of atmospheric CO_2 correlate with fluctuations in Earth's average surface temperature. Over long time scales, higher levels of greenhouse gases generally correlate

GEOreport10.2 Citizen science at the North Pole

Citizen scientists aboard Arctic expedition cruise ships are providing critical scientific data regarding sea-ice cover. In June 2016, as their ship approached the North Pole, citizen scientists conducted an "ice watch" in which they used scientific protocols to observe and record ice concentration, ice thickness, surface melting, topography, and meteorological conditions. When the ship moored at the North Pole, citizen scientists walked on the ice, measuring melt pond characteristics, snow depth, and ice surface properties. This citizen science effort not only advances scientific databases, but also creates a personal connection between expedition members and their environment, making them "ambassadors" for polar region protection.

◀Figure **10.28** **Floods in Louisiana, 2016, and Texas, 2015.** In Texas, 2015 was the wettest year since measurements began in the late 1800s. [(a) Max Becherer/AP Photo. (b) Cody Duty/Houston Chronicle via AP.]

(a) Flooded homes in Hammond, Louisiana, on August 13, 2016. Some parts of the state received over 79 cm (31 in.) of rain in a period of 3 days.

(b) Cars line the side of I-45 in Houston, Texas, on May 26, 2015, after one of several storms during the wettest month ever in the state's history.

with warmer interglacials and lower levels correlate with colder glacials. Scientists agree that rising concentrations of greenhouse gases in the atmosphere are the primary cause of recent worldwide temperature increases.

As discussed in earlier chapters, carbon dioxide (CO_2) produced from human activities is amplifying Earth's natural greenhouse effect. Natural sources—outgassing, microbial respiration—have contributed to atmospheric CO_2 for over a billion years, unaffected by the presence of humans. In recent times, however, the growing human population on Earth has produced significant quantities of atmospheric CO_2. The primary anthropogenic source (caused by human activity) is the burning of fossil fuels (coal, oil, and natural gas), which has increased dramatically in the last few centuries and added to greenhouse gas concentrations. To illustrate the increase, Figure 10.8 shows CO_2 levels for the last 650,000 years, including the steadily rising CO_2 trend since the Industrial Revolution began in the 1800s.

In 1958, Charles David Keeling of the Scripps Institute of Oceanography began collecting detailed measurements of atmospheric CO_2 in Hawai'i, producing what is considered by many scientists to be the single most important environmental data set of the 20th century. **Figure 10.29** shows the *Keeling Curve*, a graph of monthly average CO_2 concentrations from 1958 to 2016 as recorded at the Mauna Loa Observatory on the Big Island. The graph shows a steadily increasing trend for atmospheric CO_2.

In May 2016, atmospheric CO_2 at Mauna Loa reached 408 ppm, and continues to rise at an accelerating rate (see http://www.esrl.noaa.gov/gmd/ccgg/trends/global .html). The present CO_2 levels are unprecedented in the last 800,000 years, and perhaps 1.5 million years. In June 2016, CO_2 rose above 400 ppm at the South Pole, the last place on Earth to register the effects of human activities on the atmosphere.

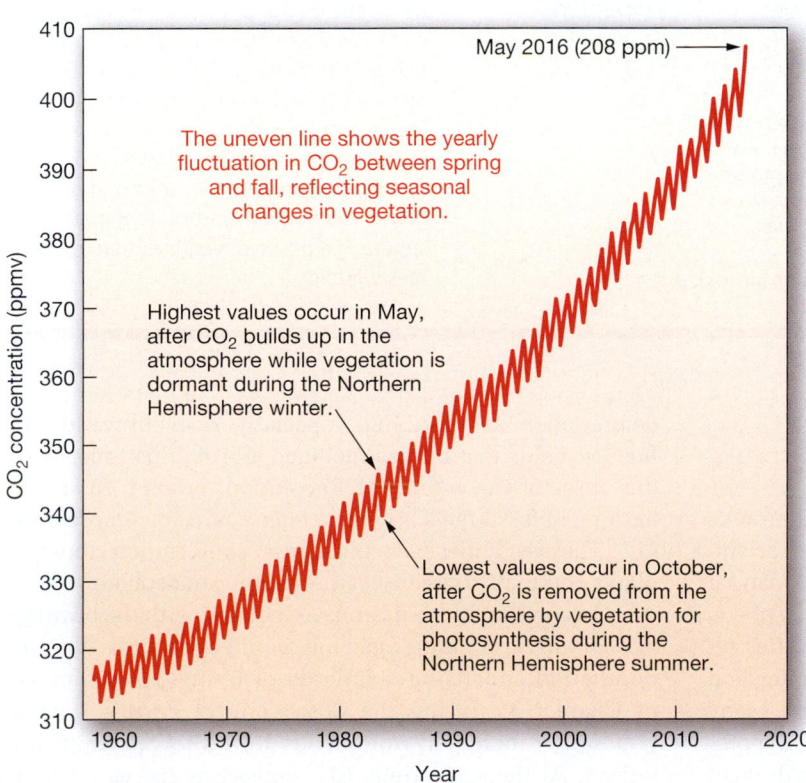

The uneven line shows the yearly fluctuation in CO_2 between spring and fall, reflecting seasonal changes in vegetation.

May 2016 (208 ppm)

Highest values occur in May, after CO_2 builds up in the atmosphere while vegetation is dormant during the Northern Hemisphere winter.

Lowest values occur in October, after CO_2 is removed from the atmosphere by vegetation for photosynthesis during the Northern Hemisphere summer.

◀Figure **10.29** **The Keeling Curve.** The graph shows rising monthly average CO_2 concentrations measured at the Mauna Loa Observatory, Hawai'i. The station's remote setting at 3397 m (11,141 ft) elevation minimizes pollution and is above the atmospheric inversion layer. The uneven line on the graph shows fluctuations in CO_2 that occur throughout the year, with May and October usually being the highest and lowest months, respectively, for CO_2 readings. [Data from NOAA posted at http://www.esrl.noaa.gov/gmd/ccgg/trends/.]

FOCUSstudy 10.1 Climate Change
Melting Permafrost Releases Greenhouse Gases in the Arctic

Rising global temperatures at high latitudes are affecting frozen ground. In Chapter 4, we discussed arctic amplification, the tendency for polar latitudes to experience enhanced warming relative to the rest of the planet. With Arctic air temperatures currently rising at a rate more than two times that of the midlatitudes, ground temperatures are increasing, causing permafrost to thaw.

Carbon in Permafrost

By definition, permafrost is soil and sediment that remain frozen for two or more consecutive years. It lies under a thin "active layer" of seasonally frozen ground that thaws every summer to provide a growing medium for seasonal grasses and other plants that absorb CO_2 from the atmosphere. In winter, the active layer freezes, trapping plant and animal material before it can decompose completely. Over hundreds of

thousands of years, this carbon-rich material has become incorporated into permafrost and now makes up roughly half of all the organic matter stored in Earth's soils—twice the amount of carbon that is stored in the atmosphere. Permafrost covers about 24% of land in subarctic and tundra climate regions of the Northern Hemisphere (**Figure 10.1.1**).

A Positive Feedback Loop As summers become warmer in the Arctic, heat radiating through the ground thaws the permafrost layers. Microbial activity in these layers increases, enhancing the breakdown of organic matter and releasing CO_2 into the atmosphere in a process known as *microbial respiration*. In anaerobic (oxygen-free) environments, such as lakes and wetlands, the process releases methane (CH_4). Studies show that thousands of methane seeps can develop under a single lake. When

▲Figure 10.1.2 Methane under Arctic lakebeds. Methane, although invisible, is highly flammable. Here, a scientist assesses methane stored under the ice, emitted from thawing permafrost under the lakebed. [Luis Sinco/Los Angeles Times via Getty Images.]

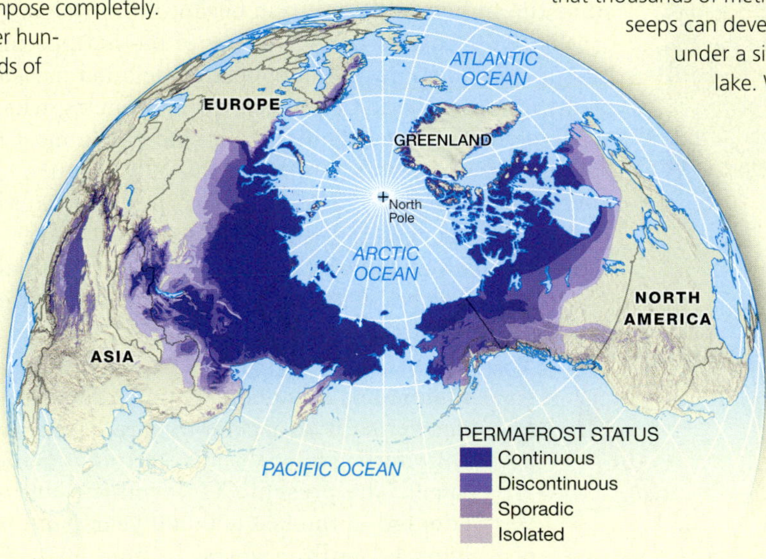

multiplied by hundreds of thousands of lakes across the northern latitudes, this process releases a huge amount of CH_4 to the atmosphere (**Figure 10.1.2**).

The *permafrost–carbon feedback* is a positive feedback loop now underway in the Arctic (**Figure 10.1.3**). This process occurs as warming temperatures lead to permafrost thaw, which increases microbial activity and releases more carbon to the atmosphere. Rising atmospheric CO_2 leads to increased plant growth and more abundant microbes, thus releasing even greater amounts of carbon to the atmosphere in a positive feedback that accelerates warming.

PERMAFROST STATUS
- Continuous
- Discontinuous
- Sporadic
- Isolated

ATLANTIC OCEAN
EUROPE
GREENLAND
+ North Pole
ARCTIC OCEAN
NORTH AMERICA
ASIA
PACIFIC OCEAN

▲Figure 10.1.1 Distribution of Northern Hemisphere permafrost. [NASA.]

Population Growth and Increasing Atmospheric Carbon

Humans have impacted Earth's carbon budget for thousands of years, beginning with the clearing of forests for agriculture, which reduces the areal extent of one of Earth's natural carbon sinks (forests) and transfers carbon to the atmosphere. Beginning about 8,000 years ago, agricultural societies replaced hunting and gathering as a way of life, initiating land use changes that released carbon into the atmosphere. Many scientists now support the "early Anthropocene hypothesis" that humans began influencing Earth's climate through

deforestation and farming, especially rice cultivation in flooded fields that release methane, during this time. With the onset of the Industrial Revolution, around 1850, the burning of fossil fuels became a large source of atmospheric CO_2. These activities have transferred solid carbon stored in plants and rock to gaseous carbon in the atmosphere.

Carbon dioxide emissions associated with the burning of coal, oil, and natural gas have increased with growing population and rising standards of living. As discussed in Chapter 1, during the 20th century Earth's human population increased from about 1.6 billion to about 6.1 billion. At the same time, CO_2 emissions increased by a

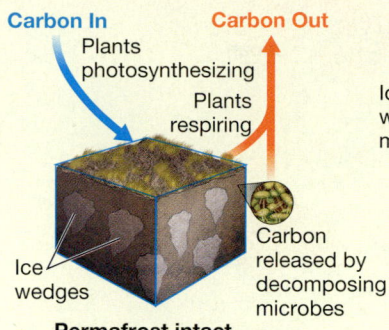

Carbon In   Carbon Out
Plants
photosynthesizing
Plants
respiring

Carbon
released by
decomposing
microbes

Ice
wedges

Permafrost intact
Neutral carbon balance
(a) Arctic vegetation absorbs
carbon through photosynthesis
during the warm summer months.
At the same time, vegetation and
microbial activity release carbon
to the atmosphere by respiration.

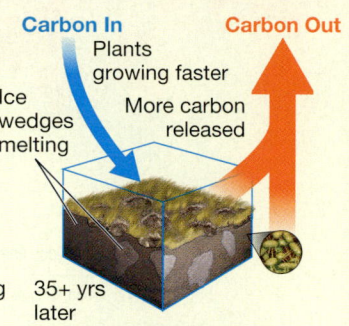

Carbon In   Carbon Out
Plants
growing faster
Ice
wedges
melting
More carbon
released

35+ yrs
later

Permafrost thawing
More carbon out than in
(b) Thawing of permafrost and
soil allows microbes to flourish
and decompose more organic
material, thus releasing large
amounts of carbon.

▲**Figure 10.1.3 The permafrost–carbon balance.** Warming Arctic
temperatures thaw permafrost and lead to an increase in carbon emissions.
This imbalance leads to a positive feedback between rising air temperature,
thawing permafrost, and rising atmospheric carbon concentrations. [After
Zina Deretsky, NSF, based on research by Ted Schuur, University of Florida.]

▲**Figure 10.1.4 Effects of thawing
ground on Arctic forests.** Thawing permafrost and ground ice makes land surfaces unstable, creating "drunken forests"
with trees leaning at various angles. [Ashley
Cooper/Alamy.]

Mobile MG
Field Trip
Climate Change
in the Arctic

https://goo.gl/5YMT2m

Effects of Permafrost Thaw

In addition to frozen soil and sediment,
permafrost contains ground ice, which
melts as the permafrost thaws. When the
supporting structure provided by the ice is
removed, land surfaces collapse and slump,
damaging buildings, forests, and coastlines
(**Figure 10.1.4**). When land sinks and
slumps, subsurface soils are then exposed
to sunlight, which speeds up microbial processes and associated carbon output to the
atmosphere.

Recently, large wildfires have accelerated
permafrost thaw, most notably in the tundra
region of northern Alaska. With continued
warming and associated forest and tundra
wildfires, scientists now estimate that between one- and two-thirds of Arctic permafrost will thaw over the next 200 years, if
not sooner.

APPLYconcepts The chart at right lists, in scrambled order, steps in the positive feedback involved in thawing permafrost. Renumber the steps in a logical sequence. The first
step is numbered for you.

Step in Feedback Process	Correct Sequence
Release of methane	
More microbial activity	
Thawing of permafrost layers	1.
More thawing	
Microbes break down organic matter	

1. What is causing permafrost to thaw and
   how can the process be explained as a
   positive feedback loop?

2. How does permafrost thaw affect other
   Earth systems?

factor of 10 or more. The burning of fossil fuels as an energy source has contributed to most of this increase, with
secondary effects from the clearing and burning of land
for development and agriculture. The rate of population
growth increased dramatically after 1950, and this trend
correlates with a dramatic rise in atmospheric CO_2 since
that time. At present, the more-developed countries produce the most carbon dioxide emissions from fossil fuels.

Sources of Atmospheric CO_2

How can scientists be sure that the primary source
of atmospheric CO_2 over the past 150 years is human
activities rather than natural factors? Scientists track
the amount of carbon burned by humans over periods of years or decades by estimating the amount of
CO_2 released by different activities. For example, the
amount of CO_2 emitted at a particular facility can be
computed by estimating the amount of fuel burned
multiplied by the amount of carbon in the fuel. Although some large power plants now have devices on
smoke stacks to measure exact emission rates, estima-
tion is the more common practice and is now standardized worldwide.

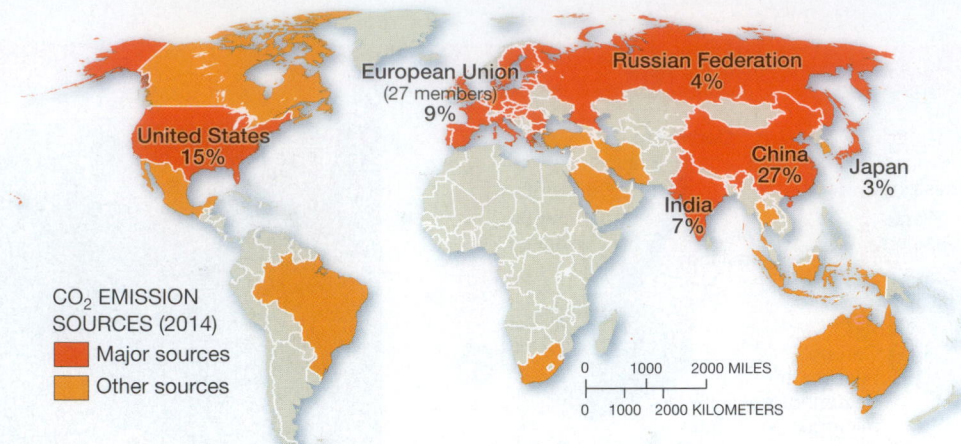

CO₂ EMISSION
SOURCES (2014)
- Major sources
- Other sources

▲**Figure 10.30** **Carbon dioxide emissions from fossil-fuel burning in 2014: The top 20 countries.** [Based on data from the Global Carbon Atlas, available at http://www.globalcarbonatlas.org/?q=en/content/welcome-carbon-atlas.]

Recently, scientists have used carbon isotopes to more accurately determine the atmospheric CO_2 emitted from fossil fuels. The basis for this method is the knowledge that fossil carbon—formed millions of years ago from organic matter that now lies deeply buried within layers of rock—contains low amounts of the carbon isotope ^{13}C (carbon-13) and none of the radioactive isotope ^{14}C (carbon-14). This means that as the concentration of CO_2 produced from fossil fuels rises, the proportions of ^{13}C and ^{14}C drop measurably. Scientists first discovered the decreasing proportion of ^{14}C within atmospheric CO_2 in the 1950s; regular measurement of this carbon isotope began in 2003. These data show that most of the CO_2 increase comes from the burning of fossil fuels.

In 2014, China led the world in CO_2 emissions (27%) with the United States second (15%) and the European Union third (9%; **Figure 10.30**). The countries with the highest per capita (per person) CO_2 output in 2014 were Saudi Arabia, the United States, Canada, and Australia. Overall, world CO_2 emissions for 2015 dropped slightly from 2014 (see Figure GIA 10.2).

WORK**IT**OUT 10.1
Tracking Global Carbon Dioxide Emissions Since 1750

Go to the Carbon Dioxide Information Analysis Center (CDIAC) website, http://cdiac.ornl.gov/CO2_Emission/gridded, to view a visualization of estimated global CO_2 emissions since the 1700s.

1. On which continent did CO_2 emissions first climb into the "red zone" of over 5 million metric tons of carbon per year? In what decade and in which country did that occur?
2. During which decade did CO_2 emissions enter the "red zone" in the United States?
3. In which Asian country did CO_2 emissions first reach the "red zone" and in what decade did that occur?
4. Notice the "bounce" of emissions in Europe during the middle of the 20th century. What event(s) might account for those fluctuations?

Contributions of Greenhouse Gases

We discussed in Chapter 4 the effect of greenhouse gases on Earth's energy balance. Increasing concentrations of greenhouse gases absorb longwave radiation and result in a warming trend in the lower atmosphere that drives shifts in climate. Today, CO_2 levels far exceed the natural range that has been the norm for hundreds of thousands of years.

The contribution of each greenhouse gas toward warming the atmosphere depends on which wavelengths of energy the gas absorbs and on the gas's *residence time*, the length of time that it resides in the atmosphere. The primary greenhouse gases in Earth's atmosphere are water vapor (H_2O), carbon dioxide (CO_2), methane (CH_4), nitrous oxide (N_2O), and halogenated gases. Of these, water vapor is the most abundant. However, water vapor has a short residence time in the atmosphere (about 9 days) and is subject to phase changes at certain temperatures. Carbon dioxide, in contrast, has a longer residence time in the atmosphere—50 to 200 years—and remains in a gaseous state at a wider range of temperatures.

Carbon Dioxide The primary anthropogenic sources of atmospheric CO_2 are fossil-fuel combustion, biomass burning (such as the burning of solid waste for fuel), the removal of forests, industrial agriculture, and cement production. Cement is used to make concrete, which is used globally for construction, accounting for about 5% of total CO_2 emissions. Fossil-fuel burning for electricity, transportation, and heating accounts for over 70% of the total.

Carbon dioxide has a residence time of 50 to 200 years in the atmosphere; however, the rates of CO_2 removal from the atmosphere vary for different processes. For example, the uptake of atmospheric CO_2 into the short-term oceanic carbon sink occurs over days, years, and hundreds of years, whereas the uptake of CO_2 into long-term carbon sinks such as marine sediments can take tens of thousands of years.

Methane After CO_2, methane is the second most prevalent greenhouse gas with concentrations increasing from human activities (**Figure 10.31a**). About two-thirds of total atmospheric methane comes from anthropogenic sources, including livestock (from waste and from bacterial activity in the animals' intestinal tracts); the mining of coal, oil, and natural gas; anaerobic ("without oxygen") processes in flooded agricultural fields; and the burning of vegetation in fires. Natural sources of methane include wetlands—some of which occur in areas of melting permafrost—and bacterial activity in the digestive systems of animals and termites.

Methane has a residence time of about 12 years in the atmosphere, much shorter than that of CO_2. After this time, methane oxidizes to form water vapor and CO_2 in the atmosphere. However, methane is more efficient at trapping longwave radiation. Over a 100-year timescale, methane is 25 times more effective at trapping atmospheric heat than CO_2, making its global warming potential higher. On a shorter timescale of 20 years, methane is 72 times more effective than CO_2 as a greenhouse gas. At present, atmospheric methane concentrations are much smaller than CO_2; note that the units for methane are parts per billion, in contrast to parts per million for CO_2.

Nitrous Oxide The third most important greenhouse gas produced by human activity is nitrous oxide (N_2O), which increased 21% in atmospheric concentration since 1750 and is now higher than at any time in at least the past 10,000 years. Nitrous oxide has a lifetime in the atmosphere of about 120 years—giving it a high global warming potential.

Although nitrous oxide is produced naturally as part of Earth's nitrogen cycle, human activities—primarily the use of fertilizer in agriculture, but also wastewater management, fossil-fuel burning, and some industrial practices—also release it to the atmosphere. Scientists attribute the recent rise in atmospheric concentrations mainly to emissions associated with agricultural activities (**Figure 10.31b**).

Halogenated Gases Containing fluorine, chlorine, or bromine, halogenated gases are produced only by human activities. These gases have high global warming potential; even small quantities can accelerate greenhouse warming. The most important of these are chlorofluorocarbons (CFCs), especially CFC-12 and CFC-11, and hydrochlorofluorocarbons (HCFCs), especially HCFC-22. Atmospheric concentrations of CFC-12 and CFC-11 have decreased in recent years owing to regulations in the Montreal Protocol (**Figure 10.31c**; also see the discussion of stratospheric ozone in Chapter 3). However, hydrofluorocarbons (HFCs), fluorinated gases that are used as substitutes for CFCs and other ozone-depleting substances, have increased since the early 1990s. In general, fluorinated gases are the most potent greenhouse gases with the longest atmospheric residence times.

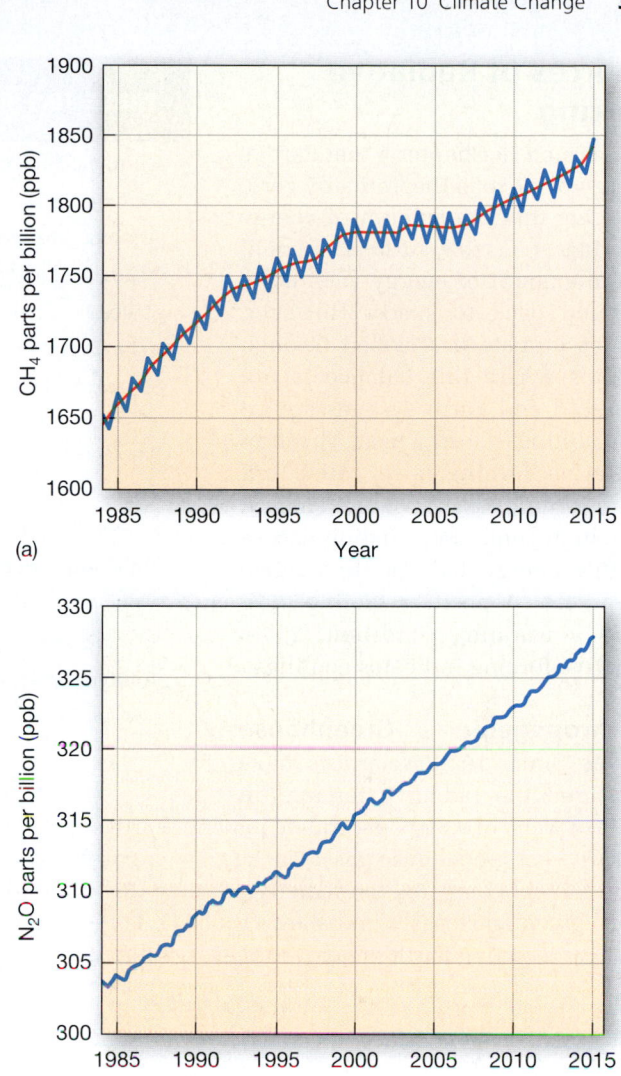

(a)

(b)

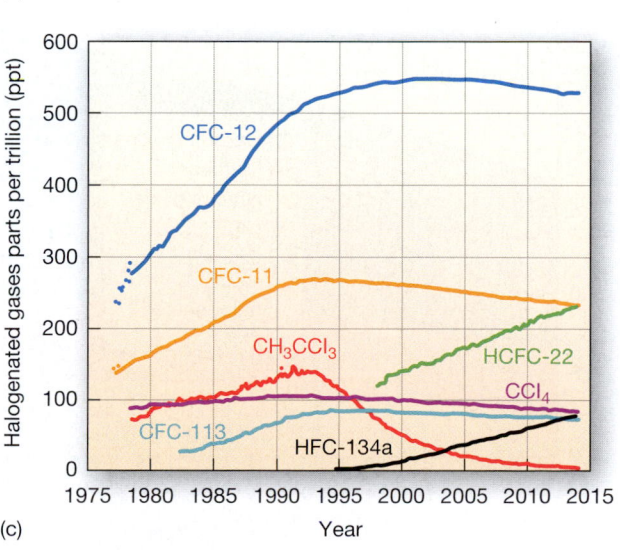

(c)

▲**Figure 10.31 Concentrations of methane, nitrous oxide, and halogenated gases since 1985.** Gas concentrations are in parts per billion (ppb) or parts per trillion (ppt), indicating the number of molecules of each gas per billion or trillion molecules of air. [From World Meteorological Organization, 2016, *WMO Statement on the Status of the Global Climate in 2015*, WMO–NO. 1167; data available at http://ds.data.jma.go.jp/gmd/wdcgg/pub/global/globalmean.html.]

Sources of Radiative Forcing

We learned in Chapter 4 that Earth's energy balance is theoretically zero, meaning that the amount of energy arriving at Earth's surface is equal to the amount of energy eventually radiated back to space. However, Earth's climate has cycled through periods where this balance is not achieved and Earth systems are either gaining or losing heat. The term **radiative forcing**, also called *climate forcing*, describes the amount by which some perturbation causes Earth's energy balance to deviate from zero. A positive forcing indicates a warming condition and a negative forcing indicates cooling.

Anthropogenic Greenhouse Gases

Since 1979, scientists have measured the radiative forcing—in units of watts of energy per square meter of Earth's surface (W/m²) —of greenhouse gases on Earth's energy budget. **Figure 10.32** compares the radiative forcing (RF) exerted by 20 greenhouse gases and shows that CO_2 is the dominant gas affecting Earth's energy budget. On the right side of the figure is the Annual Greenhouse Gas Index (AGGI), which reached 1.37 in 2015. This indicator converts the total radiative forcing for each gas into an index by using the ratio of the RF for a particular year compared to the RF in 1990 (the baseline year). The graph shows that RF has increased steadily for all gases, with the proportion attributed to CO_2 increasing the most.

Comparison of RF Factors

In its Fifth Assessment Report, the IPCC estimated the amount of radiative forcing of climate between the years 1750 and 2011 for a number of natural and anthropogenic factors (**Table 10.1**). This analysis revealed that by far the highest positive radiative forcing, causing atmospheric warming, is from greenhouse gases, with carbon dioxide responsible for about 60% of the total. The second most important positive forcing factor is tropospheric ozone (in contrast to stratospheric ozone, which has a negative forcing, or cooling, effect on climate). Other factors causing positive

TABLE 10.1 Radiative Forcing Factors for Climate, 1750–2011*

Climatic Factor	Global Average Radiative Forcing (W/m²)	
Anthropogenic	Positive	Negative
Anthropogenic greenhouse gases	2.83	
Tropospheric ozone	0.40	
Stratospheric water vapor	0.07	
Contrails and contrail cirrus clouds	0.05	
Surface albedo of black carbon aerosols on ice	0.04	
Stratospheric ozone		−0.05
Aerosols: Radiation/cloud interactions		−0.90
Surface albedo from land use		−0.15
Total anthropogenic forcing	**2.30**	
Natural		
Solar irradiance	0.05	
Total natural forcing	**0.05**	

* Data from IPCC Fifth Assessment Report, *Climate Change 2013: The Physical Science Basis*, Working Group I, Table 8.6, p. 696.

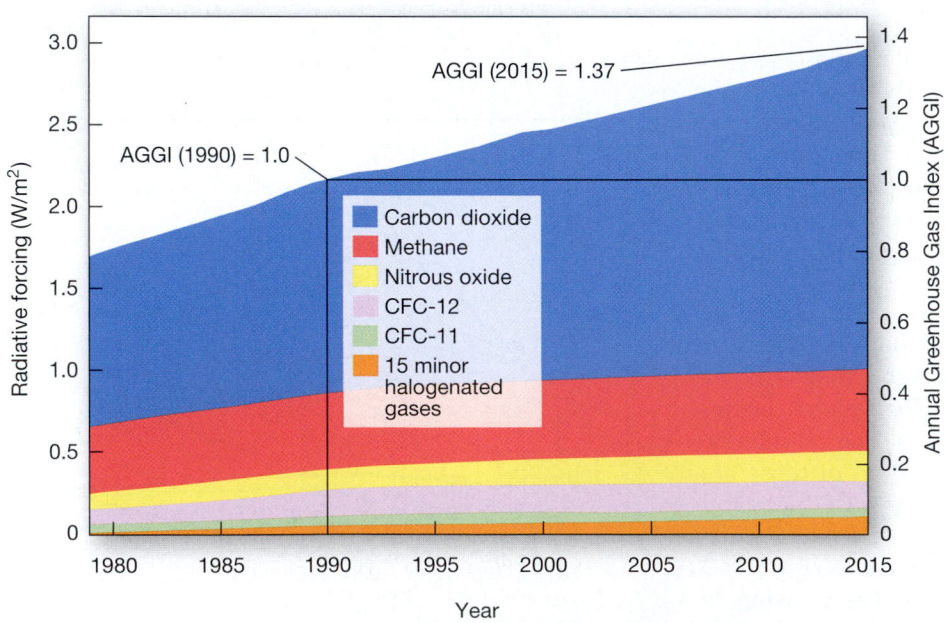

▲Figure 10.32 **Greenhouse gases: Relative percentages of radiative forcing.** The colored areas indicate the amount of radiative forcing accounted for by each gas, based on the concentrations present in Earth's atmosphere. The right side of the graph shows radiative forcing converted to the AGGI, set at a value of 1.0 in 1990. In 2015, the AGGI was 1.37, an increase of 37% in 25 years. [Based on *The NOAA Annual Greenhouse Gas Index (AGGI)*, NOAA, updated summer 2016.]

forcing are stratospheric water vapor, contrail cirrus clouds, and black carbon on snow. The highest negative forcing of climate is from aerosols.

The IPCC analysis included one important natural forcing factor for climate—solar irradiance (the output of energy from the Sun). The overall effect of solar irradiance was a positive forcing of 0.05 W/m², a small amount compared to the overall 2.3 W/m² of forcing caused by the combined anthropogenic factors in the analysis.

Climate Models and Radiative Forcing

Scientists use computer models of climate to assess past trends, determine causes, and forecast future changes. A **general circulation model (GCM)**, also known as a global climate model, is a mathematical representation of the processes and interacting factors that make up Earth's climate systems, including the atmosphere, the oceans, and all land and ice. GCMs can be programmed to model the effects of linkages between specific climatic components over different time frames and at various scales. The most sophisticated models couple atmosphere and ocean submodels and are known as *Atmosphere–Ocean General Circulation Models* (AOGCMs). At least a dozen established GCMs are now in operation around the world.

Scientists can use GCMs to determine the relative effects of various climate forcings on temperature. In Figure 10.32, we saw that greenhouse gases caused the strongest radiative forcing of climate since 1750 and that the

estimated positive net radiative forcing of anthropogenic factors was far greater than the positive forcing from solar irradiance. But what is the role of other natural factors, such as volcanic eruptions, on the radiative forcing of temperature?

Figure 10.33 shows the results from two sets of climate simulations as compared to observed global average temperatures (land and ocean) from 1906 to 2010. The first simulation compared natural forcing, modeled from solar variability and volcanic output alone (shaded blue area), to the observed temperatures (black line). The second simulation compared both natural and anthropogenic forcings (shaded pink area) to the observed temperatures. In the graph, you can see that the model using both natural and anthropogenic forcings (including greenhouse gas concentrations) was the one that produced the closer match to the actual observed temperature averages. Simulations based on natural forcings alone do not match the increasing temperature trend.

Scientific Consensus

The world's climate scientists have reached overwhelming consensus that human activities are causing recent climate change. A 2009 survey found that 97 to 98% of actively publishing climate scientists support the conclusion that ongoing climate change is anthropogenic (see http://www.pnas.org/content/early/2010/06/04/1003187107). Numerous policy statements and position papers from professional organizations (for example, the Association of American Geographers, the American Meteorological Society, the Geological Society of America, and the American Geophysical Union) also support this consensus. This consensus is confirmed throughout the scientific community as well as the international community. In April 2016, 165 countries signed the Paris Climate Agreement to reduce greenhouse gas emissions that cause climate change.

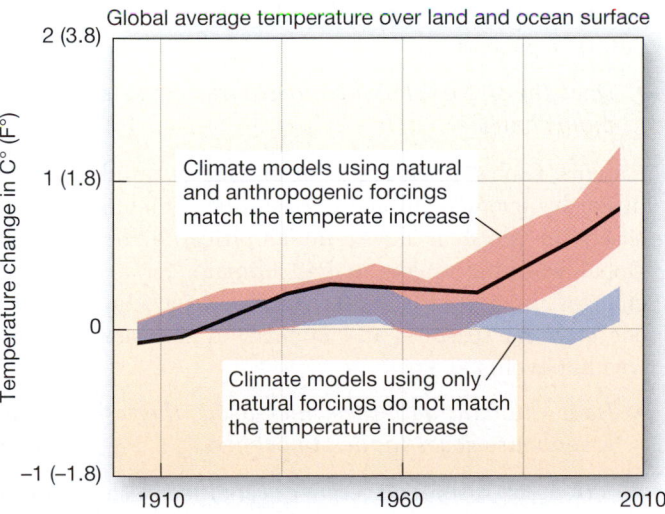

▲Figure 10.33 **Climate model showing the relative effects of natural and anthropogenic forcing.** This computer model tracks the agreement of observed temperature anomalies (black line) with two forcing scenarios: combined natural and anthropogenic forcings (pink shading) and natural forcing only (blue shading). The natural forcing factors include solar activity and volcanic activity, which alone do not explain the temperature increases. [IPCC Fifth Assessment Report, *Climate Change 2013: The Physical Science Basis*, Working Group I, Figure SPM-6, p. 32.]

✔ **WORKITOUT 10.2**
Consider Your Carbon Footprint

In Chapters 1 and 8, you assessed your "footprint" in terms of your impact on Earth systems. To assess your carbon emissions, you can calculate your "carbon footprint" online (an example is at http://www.nature.org/greenliving/carboncalculator/).

1. In what sector is your carbon footprint highest (for example, home energy, transportation, or recycling and waste)?
2. Are you above or below the U.S. average?
3. In what three ways can you reduce your carbon footprint?

TABLE 10.2 Summary Points for the Working Groups of the IPCC Fifth Assessment Report*

Working Group I: The Physical Science Basis	Working Group II: Impacts, Adaptation, Vulnerability	Working Group III: Mitigation of Climate Change
Warming of the climate system is unequivocal and it is extremely likely that humans are the dominant cause (95–100% certainty). Many observed changes since the 1950s (warming atmosphere and oceans, melting snow and ice, rising sea level, rising greenhouse gas concentrations) are unprecedented over decades to millennia.	Human interference with the climate system is occurring, and climate change poses risks for human and natural systems. Increasing magnitudes of warming increase the likelihood of severe, pervasive, and irreversible impacts on species, ecosystems, crop yields, human health, natural hazards, and food security.	Effective mitigation of climate change requires collective action at the global scale, because most greenhouse gases (GHGs) accumulate over time and mix globally. International cooperation is needed to effectively mitigate GHG emissions and address other climate change issues.

*The free Summary for Policy Makers for each AR5 Working Group is available at https://www.ipcc.ch/report/ar5/.

The IPCC, formed in 1988 and operating under sponsorship of the United Nations Environment Programme and the World Meteorological Organization, is a global collaboration of scientists and policy experts that coordinate climate change research, climate forecasts, and policy formulation. Bringing together leading scientists from an array of disciplines, the IPCC is the world's foremost scientific entity reporting on climate change. Its reports represent peer-reviewed, consensus opinions among experts in the scientific community concerning the causes of climate change as well as the uncertainties and areas where further research is needed. The 2013–2014 IPCC Fifth Assessment Report describes as 95–100% certain that human activities are the primary cause of the observed global temperature increase from 1951 to 2010. Table 10.2 briefly summarizes some important findings.

Taking a Position on Climate Change

Despite the consensus among scientists, some controversy still surrounds the topic of climate change among the public at large in the United States. The disagreement focuses on first, whether climate change is occurring, and, second, whether its cause is anthropogenic. The fuel for the continuing "debate" on this topic appears to come in part from media coverage that may be biased or factually incorrect. In other cases, errors come from simple misinterpretation of the facts, sometimes as reported by blogs and other social media that present results not yet evaluated by scientific peer review. The bottom line is that having an informed position on climate change requires an understanding of Earth's physical laws and an awareness of the scientific evidence.

In Chapter 1, we discussed the scientific process, which encourages peer evaluation, criticism, and cautious skepticism through the scientific method. Many would argue that skepticism concerning climate change is simply part of this process. As new information about Earth's climate system becomes available, scientists will constantly need to reevaluate evidence and formulate new hypotheses. However, the case for anthropogenic climate change has become more convincing with continued scientific research.

When considering the facts behind climate change, several key questions can help guide you to an informed position:

- *Does increasing atmospheric carbon dioxide in the atmosphere cause warming temperatures?*

Yes. Scientists know that CO_2 acts as a greenhouse gas and that increased concentrations produce warming in the lower atmosphere. Scientists have understood the physical processes related to atmospheric CO_2 for almost 100 years, since well before the effects of global warming became apparent to the scientific community or to the public in general.

- *Does the rise of global temperatures cause global climate change?*

Yes. Global warming is an unusually rapid increase in Earth's average surface temperature. Scientists know, based on physical laws and empirical evidence, that global warming affects overall climate; for example, it changes precipitation patterns, causes ice melt, lengthens growing seasons, and appears to increase extreme weather events.

- *Have human activities increased the amount of greenhouse gases in the atmosphere?*

Yes. As discussed earlier, scientists use radioactive carbon isotopes to measure the amount of atmospheric CO_2 that originates from fossil-fuel burning and other human activities. They now know that human sources account for all of the increasing atmospheric CO_2 concentrations.

- *If climate change on Earth has occurred in the past, then why are the present conditions problematic?*

Carbon dioxide concentrations are today rising more quickly than is seen throughout most of the

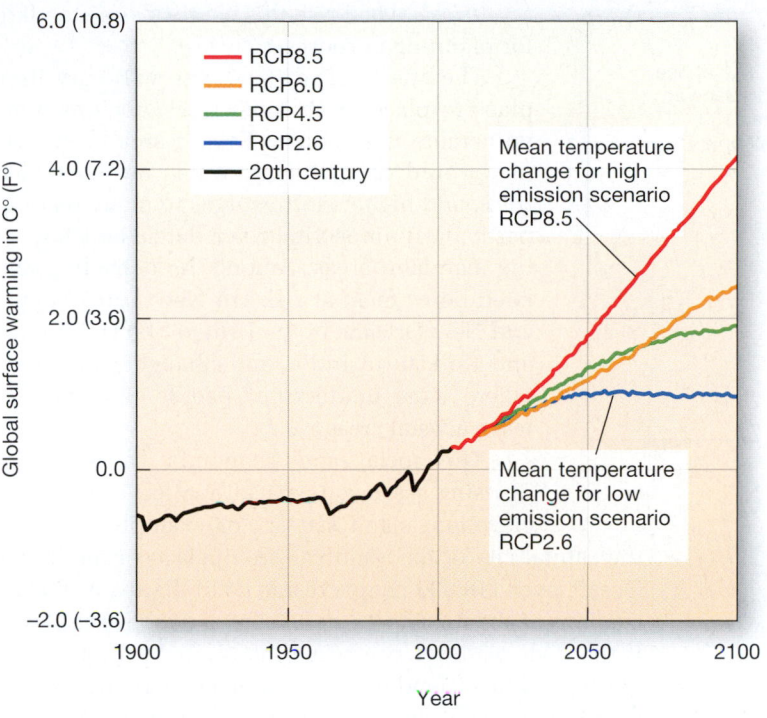

(a) Models suggest that the smallest amount of warming corresponds to the lowest CO_2 emissions scenario (RCP2.6). Warming is greatest under the RCP8.5 scenario, with the highest CO_2 emissions and strongest positive radiative forcing of temperature.

(b) Possible temperature responses in 2081–2100 to high-emission scenario RCP8.5

(c) Possible temperature responses in 2081–2100 to low-emission scenario RCP2.6

▲Figure 10.34 **AOGCM scenarios for surface warming during this century.** Temperature change is relative to the 1986–2005 average temperature. [IPCC Fifth Assessment Report, *Climate Change 2013: The Physical Science Basis*, Working Group I, FAQ 12.1, Figure 1, p. 1037.]

long-term climate record. This rate of change puts Earth systems in uncharted territory for assessing impacts at a time when Earth's human population exceeds 7.3 billion.

- *Can scientists definitively attribute the changes we are seeing in climate (including extreme events and weather anomalies) to anthropogenic causes alone?*

Yes. With nearly 100% statistical certainty, ongoing research supports human-forced climate change. Several issues still need further study. One example is the effect of multiyear oscillations in global circulation patterns (such as ENSO) on short- and long-term climate.

Climate Change and the Future

GCMs and AOGCMs are mainly physical models, incorporating atmospheric processes, sea ice and land ice, ocean circulation, and land hydrology. Scientists also use *Earth Systems Models* (ESMs) to study climate change and forecast future climate scenarios. An ESM incorporates the physical factors of an AOGCM with additional biogeochemical elements—focusing on the movement of carbon throughout all Earth systems—and factors such as land-use changes, plant biomass, and marine ecology.

Future Temperature Scenarios

Climate models do not predict specific temperatures, but they do offer various scenarios of future global warming. GCM-generated maps correlate well with the observed global warming patterns experienced since 1990, and various AOGCM and ESM forecast scenarios are now used to predict temperature change during this century.

Figure 10.34a depicts four temperature scenarios presented in the IPCC Fifth Assessment Report, each with different conditions of radiative forcing. Each Representative Concentration Pathway, or RCP, is identified by the approximate radiative forcing it predicts for the year 2100 as compared to 1750; for example, RCP2.6 denotes 2.6 W/m² of forcing. Each RCP correlates with certain levels of greenhouse gas emissions, land use, and air pollutants that combine to produce the forcing value. For RCP2.6—the lowest level—forcing peaks and declines before 2100. This scenario could occur with major reductions in CO_2 emissions and actions to remove CO_2 from the atmosphere. RCP4.5 represents stabilization of forcing by the year 2100. For RCP6.0 and RCP8.5, high-emission scenarios of continued heavy fossil-fuel use, radiative forcing does not peak by the year 2100. According to these models, continued CO_2 emissions and other human activities that enhance radiative forcing is the scenario that would cause the greatest amount of warming over the 21st century.

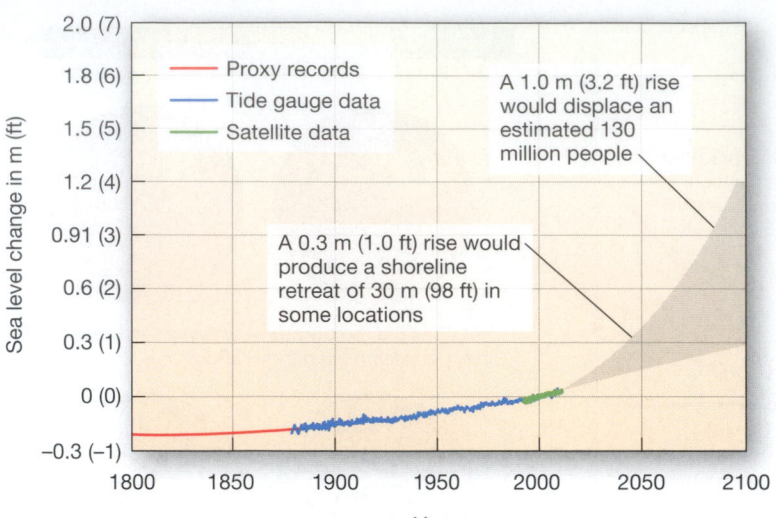

▲Figure 10.35 **Past and projected global sea level.** Estimated, measured, and possible future changes in sea-level from 1800 to 2100 show an overall rise. Proxy data are in red (pink band shows uncertainty). Tidal gauge data are in blue (1880–2009) and satellite observations are in green (1993–2012). Future scenarios range from 0.20 m (0.66 ft) to 2.0 m (6.6 ft) in 2100. [U.S. Global Change Research Program, 2014 National Climate Assessment. http://nca2014.globalchange.gov/.]

Sea-Level Projections

In 2012, NOAA scientists developed scenarios for sea-level rise based on present ice-sheet losses coupled with losses from mountain glaciers and ice caps worldwide (**Figure 10.35**). These models project a rise of 0.3 m (1.0 ft) at the low end of the range, under the lowest emission scenarios. On the high end, 1.2 m (4.0 ft) is plausible, with up to 2.0 m (6.6 ft) as the extreme.

In the United States, sea level is rising more quickly on the East Coast than on the West Coast. **Figure 10.36** shows the area that would potentially be affected by a range of sea-level increases along the U.S. East and Gulf Coasts. The largest areas of inundation at a rise of only 1 m are around the low-elevation cities of Miami and New Orleans. Many states, including California, presently use a 1.4-m sea-level rise this century as a standard for planning purposes.

The effects of sea-level rise will vary from place to place, with some world regions more vulnerable than others. Even a small sea-level rise would bring higher water levels, higher tides, and higher storm surges to many regions, particularly impacting river deltas and low-lying mainland areas. Among the densely populated cities most at risk are New York, Miami, and New Orleans in the United States, Mumbai and Kolkata in India, and Shanghai in China, where large numbers of people will have to leave coastal areas.

The social and economic consequences of rising sea level especially affect small, low-elevation island states. For example, in Malé, the capital city of the Maldives archipelago in the Indian Ocean, over 110,000 people reside behind a sea wall at elevations of about 2.0 to 2.4 m (6.7 to 8.0 ft) above sea level. If the high sea-level rise scenarios occur by 2100, major portions of this island will be inundated. National and international migration—a flood of environmental refugees driven by climate change—would be expected to continue for decades (look back to the chapter-opening photo). Sea-level increases will continue beyond 2100, even if greenhouse gas concentrations were to be stabilized today.

Possible Climate Futures

The IPCC Fifth Assessment Report includes a number of projections for Earth's climate in the later 21st century. These projections come with a range of statistical probabilities, from exceptionally unlikely (0–1% probability of occurrence) to virtually certain (99–100% probability of occurrence). **Figure 10.37** reviews some of the projections that are *virtually certain* or *very likely* to occur. Taken together, these elements of Earth's changing climate present challenges to human societies, especially with regard to water resources, food production, and related effects on human health.

▲Figure 10.36 **Coastal inundation caused by a 1-m (3.28-ft) rise in sea level along three portions of U.S. coastline.** [Maps prepared by Weiss and Overpeck, Environmental Studies Laboratory, Department of Geosciences, University of Arizona. Used by permission.]

Virtually certain (99–100% probability of occurrence)

Cold days and nights will be warmer and less frequent over most land areas.

Hot days and nights will be warmer and more frequent over most land areas.

The extent of permafrost will decline.

Ocean acidification will increase as the atmosphere accumulates CO_2.

Global mean sea level will rise and continue to do so for many centuries.

Extremely likely (90–100% probability of occurrence)

Arctic sea ice cover will continue to shrink and thin; Northern Hemisphere spring snow cover will decrease.

The frequency of warm spells and heat waves will increase.

The frequency of heavy precipitation events will increase.

The ocean's conveyer-belt circulation will weaken.

Extreme high sea-level events will increase, as will ocean wave heights of midlatitude storms

◄**Figure 10.37 IPCC climate projections for the late 21st century.** The Fifth Assessment Report projects a number of climatic changes with greater than 90% certainty. [Tomasz Zajda/fotolia; Gabriele Maltinti/fotolia; U.S. Geological Survey; yossarian6/fotolia; arkady_z/fotolia; Vladimir Melnik/fotolia; Elena Belyaeva/fotolia; Kevin Griffin/123rf; zsv3207/fotolia; underworld/Fotolia]

Japan, 84 countries signed the *Kyoto Protocol*, a legally binding international agreement that set specific targets to reduce emissions of greenhouse gases. The United States was among the signatory countries; however, it never ratified the treaty.

In 2015, at COP 21 in Paris, France, 196 countries agreed to reduce greenhouse gas emissions, with the goal to cap global warming at less than 2.0°C (3.6°F)—relative to preindustrial levels—during this century. After 55 countries (representing 55% of greenhouse gas emissions) sign and ratify the agreement, it becomes legally binding. Although COP 21 was considered a success, many scientists have stated that the agreement falls far short of the aggressive action needed to curb climate change.

Taking Action on Climate Change

Given this scientific knowledge base, taking action on climate change must focus on lowering atmospheric CO_2. As emphasized in numerous scientific and economic assessments pertaining to climate change, opportunities to reduce carbon dioxide emissions are readily available, have additional *co-benefits* that go beyond slowing climate change, and can be accomplished with little cost to society. For example, a co-benefit from reducing greenhouse gas emissions is improved air quality, with related benefits to human health.

International Agreements

In 1995, the first United Nations international conference on climate change met in Berlin, Germany. Each year since then, under the United Nations Framework Convention on Climate Change, a formal meeting, known as a conference of the parties (COP) occurs to address greenhouse gas emissions and climate change. In 1997, at COP 3 in Kyoto,

Reducing Greenhouse Gas Emissions

Worldwide, many large urban areas are working to reduce greenhouse gas emissions. According to the nonprofit Carbon Disclosure Project (CDP), 110 cities reported in 2013 that actions to mitigate climate change have co-benefits that save money, attract new businesses, and improve the health of residents. In 2015, the CDP reported that cities are increasingly taking action to move away from a fossil-fuel economy and that business opportunities are increasing with the transition to renewable and sustainable energy development.

Planning for Impacts Both governments and businesses are now planning for climate change impacts. For example, in New York City—in response to the damage from Hurricane Sandy in 2012—over $1 billion is being spent on upgrades to raise flood walls, bury equipment, and assess other changes needed to prevent future damage from extreme weather events.

On a national and regional level, human society must strive to mitigate and adapt to climate change. For example, land managers can change land-use practices to preserve forests and other vegetation. Farmers can use methods that retain more carbon in the soil and plant crop varieties bred to withstand drought or flood inundation. In coastal areas, landowners can utilize natural shoreline protection, such as sand dunes, and allow for shifting of natural features during storms. All societies can promote efficient water use, especially in areas prone to drought. These are only a few examples among many for mitigating and adapting to climate change.

What Can You Do?

On an individual level, what can you do to address climate change? The principal way to slow the pace of climate change—not only as individuals, but also as an international community—is to reduce carbon emissions, especially the burning of fossil fuels. One way to begin this process is to examine the sustainability of your daily practices and take action to reduce your carbon footprint. Scientists suggest that reducing atmospheric concentrations of CO_2 to 350 ppm will slow the rate of climate change and stabilize Earth systems (**Figure 10.38**). Consider these ideas and statistics related to achieving the 350 ppm goal:

- Driving a vehicle that gets 30 miles per gallon saves 2.9 tons of CO_2 annually over one that gets 20 miles per gallon.

- Replacing incandescent light bulbs with compact fluorescent (CFL) bulbs saves 100 pounds of carbon over the life of each bulb. Using LED bulbs more than doubles this savings.
- Planting trees removes CO_2 and ground-level ozone from the atmosphere, and can reduce your heating and cooling bill by 20–50% each year.

All of your actions and decisions have positive and negative consequences for Earth's environment and for our changing climate. Remember that actions taken on an individual level by millions of people can be effective in slowing climate change for present and future generations. Given that atmospheric CO_2 concentrations are already above 400 ppm, can our global society still achieve the 350 ppm goal? Yes. The 2015 COP 21 agreement in Paris establishes realistic methods to reduce emissions and meet this goal.

Present greenhouse gas concentrations will remain in the atmosphere for many decades to come, but the time for action is now. Scientists describe 450 ppm as a possible climatic threshold at which Earth systems become destabilized, transitioning into a chaotic mode. With accelerating CO_2 emissions, this tipping point could occur in the decade of the 2020s. Avoiding this threshold will delay the worst consequences of our current path, and allow time for adaptation to climate change and mitigation of its effects. The information presented in this chapter is offered in the hope of providing understanding, motivation, and empowerment—personally, locally, regionally, nationally, and globally.

Website (MG)
Carbon Footprint Calculator
https://goo.gl/CLmH32

Reduce; reuse; recycle
Savings: Every 2 glass bottles recycled saves 2 lbs of carbon

Landscape wisely; plant trees
Plant trees to shade your house. Savings: 200 to 2000 lbs of carbon over the tree's lifetime

Use renewable energy
Purchase renewable energy for your house, or generate your own power using solar or wind

Drive less; walk and bike more
Savings: One lb of carbon for every mile

Goal:
350 ppm CO_2 in atmosphere

Use energy wisely
Turn down heat and turn up air conditioning settings when you leave the house; insulate your home

Use Energy Star products
Look for the Energy Star label on appliances, electronics, light bulbs, and heating and cooling equipment

Think globally: act locally
Buy local produce and other food; reduce meat consumption

▲**Figure 10.38 Individual actions to reduce atmospheric CO_2 to 350 ppm.** [(center) NASA. (clockwise from top) William Perugini/Shutterstock; Jordan Tan/Shutterstock; Hgalina/Fotolia; Aerogondo/Fotolia; Esbobeldijk/Shutterstock; Martin Shields/Alamy; Steve Cukrov/Shutterstock.]

CLIMATE CHANGE IMPACTS HUMANS

• Climate change affects all Earth systems.
• Climate change drives weather and extreme events, such as drought, heat waves, storm surge, and sea-level encroachment, which cause human hardship and fatalities.

HUMANS IMPACT CLIMATE CHANGE

• Anthropogenic activities produce greenhouse gases that alter Earth's radiation balance and drive climate change.

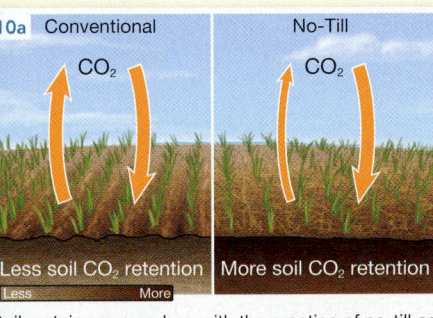

10a Conventional No-Till
CO_2 CO_2
Less soil CO_2 retention More soil CO_2 retention
Less More

Soils retain more carbon with the practice of no-till agriculture, in which farmers do not plow fields after a harvest but instead leave crop residue on the fields. (See discussion in Chapter 18.) In the photo, a farmer uses no-till agricultural practices in New York by planting corn into a cover crop of barley. [After U.S. Department of Energy Pacific Northwest National Laboratory. NRCS.]

10b
Nations Unies
Conférence sur les Changements Climatiques 2015
COP21/CMP11
Paris France

In November 2015 at the United Nations Climate Change Conference, 195 countries agreed to reduce greenhouse gas emissions, with the overall goal to limit global warming to less than 2.0°C (3.6°F) during this century. [Arnaud BOUISSOU/COP21/Anadolu Agency/Getty Images.]

10d Through the International Small Group and Tree Planting Program, subsistence farmers are planting trees to reverse deforestation and combat climate change. For each tree planted, farmers earn greenhouse gas credits that translate into small cash stipends. Planting trees is one of the simplest and most effective ways to combat climate change. [Charles Sturge/Alamy.]

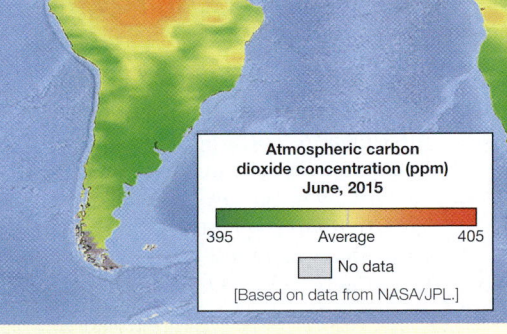

Atmospheric carbon dioxide concentration (ppm) June, 2015
395 Average 405
No data
[Based on data from NASA/JPL.]

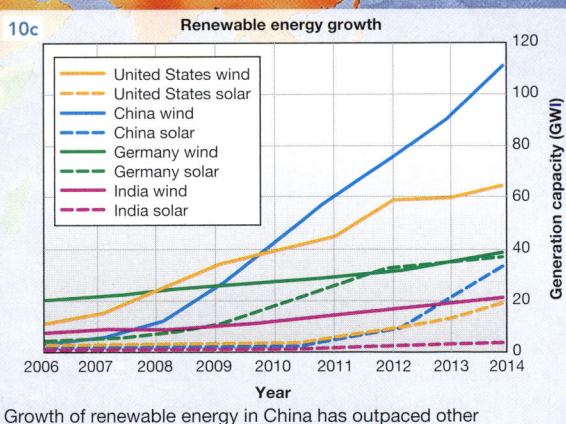

10c **Renewable energy growth**
— United States wind
---- United States solar
— China wind
---- China solar
— Germany wind
---- Germany solar
— India wind
---- India solar

Generation capacity (GWi)
120
100
80
60
40
20
0
2006 2007 2008 2009 2010 2011 2012 2013 2014
Year

Growth of renewable energy in China has outpaced other developed countries in recent years. In 2014, China invested $90 billion in low-carbon energy; wind power is the sector of greatest growth. [Source: Bloomberg New Energy Finance and World Resources Institute.]

ISSUES FOR THE 21ST CENTURY

How will human society curb greenhouse gas emissions and mitigate change effects? Some examples:
• Using agricultural practices that help soils retain carbon.
• Planting trees to help sequester carbon in terrestrial ecosystems.
• Supporting renewable energy, and changing lifestyles to use fewer resources.
• Protecting and restoring natural ecosystems that are carbon reservoirs.

QUESTIONS TO CONSIDER

1. Why is planting trees a helpful strategy to mitigate climate change?
2. Review the benefits of solar and wind power over coal-burning power plants discussed in earlier chapters. Why do you think China's recent investment in renewable energy is greater than that of the United States and Germany?

KEY**LEARNING**concepts**review**

Describe scientific tools used to study paleoclimatology.

The study of the causes of changing climate and the consequences for Earth systems is **climate change science** (p. 280). The study of natural climatic variability over the span of Earth's history is the science of **paleoclimatology** (p. 280). Since scientists do not have direct measurements for past climates, they use **proxy methods** (p. 280), or *climate proxies*—sources of climate data from preserved natural archives that can be used to estimate past climatic conditions. One tool for long-term climatic reconstruction is **isotope analysis** (p. 281), a technique that uses relative amounts of the isotopes of chemical elements to identify the composition of past oceans and ice masses. **Radioactive isotopes** (p. 285), such as ^{14}C (carbon-14), are unstable and decay at a constant rate measured as a *half-life* (the time it takes half the sample to break down). The science of using tree growth rings to study past climates is **dendroclimatology** (p. 286). Analysis of mineral deposits in caves that form **speleothems** (p. 286) and the growth rings of ocean corals can also identify past environmental conditions.

1. Describe an example of a climate proxy used in the study of paleoclimatology.
2. Explain how oxygen isotopes can identify glacials and interglacials.
3. What climatic data do scientists obtain from ice cores? Where on Earth have scientists drilled the longest ice cores?

Discuss several natural factors that influence Earth's climate and describe climate feedbacks, using examples.

Several natural mechanisms can potentially cause climatic fluctuations. The Sun's output varies over time, but this variation has not been definitely linked to climate change. The **Maunder Minimum** (p. 288), a solar minimum from about 1645 to 1715, corresponded with one of the coldest periods of the Little Ice Age. However, other solar minimums do not correlate with colder periods. Earth's orbital cycles and Earth–Sun relationships, called **Milankovitch cycles** (p. 289), appear to affect Earth's climate—especially glacial and interglacial cycles—although their role is still under study. Continental position and atmospheric aerosols, such as those produced by volcanic eruptions, are other natural factors that affect climate.

Climate feedbacks (p. 290) are processes that either amplify or reduce climatic trends toward warming or cooling. Many climate feedbacks involve the movement of carbon through Earth systems between carbon sources, areas where carbon is released, and **carbon sinks** (p. 291), areas where carbon is stored (carbon reservoirs)—the overall exchange between sources and sinks is the **global carbon budget** (p. 291).

4. What is the connection between sunspots and solar output? What happened to sunspot activity during the Maunder Minimum?
5. Describe the effect of volcanic aerosols on climate.

List the key lines of evidence for present global climate change.

Several indicators provide strong evidence of climate warming: increasing air temperatures over land and oceans, increasing sea-surface temperatures and ocean heat content, melting glacial ice and sea ice, rising global sea level, and increasing water vapor.

6. Describe recent changes in land ice—glaciers, ice sheets, and permafrost—and sea ice extent.
7. How do rising air temperatures relate to changes in atmospheric water vapor? Explain the connection.

Summarize the scientific evidence for anthropogenic forcing of climate and list some climate projections for the 21st century.

The scientific consensus is that present climate change is caused primarily by increased concentrations of atmospheric greenhouse gases resulting from human activities. The primary greenhouse gases produced by human activities are carbon dioxide, methane, nitrous oxide, and halogenated gases, such as chlorofluorocarbons (CFCs) and hydrofluorocarbons (HFCs). The increasing presence of these gases is causing a positive **radiative forcing** (or climate forcing), p. 304, the amount by which some perturbation causes the Earth–atmosphere energy balance to deviate from zero. Studies show that CO_2 has the largest radiative forcing among greenhouse gases and that this forcing surpasses other natural and anthropogenic factors that force climate.

A **general circulation model (GCM)**, p. 305, is a complex computerized climate model used to assess past climatic trends and their causes and to project future changes in climate. The most sophisticated atmosphere and ocean submodels are known as *Atmosphere–Ocean General Circulation Models (AOGCMs)*. Climate models show that positive radiative forcing is caused by anthropogenic greenhouse gases rather than natural factors.

8. What are the main sources of atmospheric carbon dioxide and methane? Why is methane considered to be a potent greenhouse gas as compared to CO_2?
9. According to the IPCC, what was the most important radiative forcing factor for climate from 1750 to 2011?
10. Describe projected rates of sea-level rise, and potential effects in low-elevation regions of the world.

Describe several mitigation measures to slow rates of climate change.

Actions taken on an individual level by millions of people can slow the pace of climate change for us and for future generations. The principal way we can do this—as individuals, as a country, and as an international community—is to reduce carbon emissions, especially in our burning of fossil fuels.

11. What are the international actions being taken at present to delay the effects of global climate change?
12. Describe several personal, local, or regional mitigation actions to reduce climate-change impacts.

GEO**SPATIAL** ANALYSIS

Tides and Sea Level Rise

Tides account for daily changes in coastal sea levels. Long-term changes in sea level also are observed as a result of increased ocean temperatures, reduction of polar sea-ice extent, and the melting of glaciers, ice caps, and ice sheets—all forced by ongoing climate change.

Activities

Go to the NOAA Tides and Currents page at http://tidesandcurrents .noaa.gov/. Click on "Tides and Currents Map" and click on the station at Miami, FL. Use "Help" to learn how to use this map. Before you begin, read about tides in Chapter 16, pages 470–471.

1. What time is the next high and the next low tide?

2. What is the height (in feet) for each of these tides?

3. What is the local time for the two most recent flood tides? And, Ebb tides?

4. What is the tidal range currently in Miami?

Examine high tide for stations in the New Jersey, Delaware, and Maryland region.

5. Notice that the time of high tide changes by location. What factors control the time of high tide?

Click a station on the East Coast that allows you to "Jump to:" "Sea Level Trends."

6. How many years are shown on the graph? How long is the actual data record for this station?

7. Using the "Linear Mean Sea Level Trend" line, what is the total sea level change over the data record for this station?

Go back to the NOAA Tides and Currents page. Click on "Sea Level Trends" and zoom out to see the entire world.

8. 8. In general, which regions are experiencing higher sea levels? Lower sea levels?

Go to the Sea Level Rise and Coastal Flooding Impacts site at https://coast.noaa.gov/slr/. Zoom in to a state along the East Coast. Use the "Sea Level Rise" slider to raise the sea level.

9. What is the effect of rising sea level? What percentage of the coastline is affected?

Click on several "Visualization Locations" and use the slider to see the effect of rising sea level in each location.

10. Which locations did you visualize in your selections, and what effects do you see?

VISUAL ANALYSIS 10   WILDFIRE, CLOUDS, CLIMATIC REGIONS, AND CLIMATE CHANGE

The King Fire in the central Sierra Nevada of California scorched more than 98,000 acres in September and October 2014, and formed a *pyrocumulus cloud* in which the rising thermal plume is fed by heat from the fire. [Bobbé Christopherson.]

1. What two forms of clouds do you see in the photo? Describe the processes that formed each type.

2. What characteristics of the Mediterranean climate make it prone to the occurrence of wildfire?

3. Given what you have learned about the current state of global temperatures, heat waves, and drought in the first two parts of this textbook, would you expect wildfire occurrence and severity to be increasing, decreasing, or remaining the same as climate changes? See Chapters 19 and 20 for more discussion of wildfire as it relates to ecological processes, climate regions, and climate change.

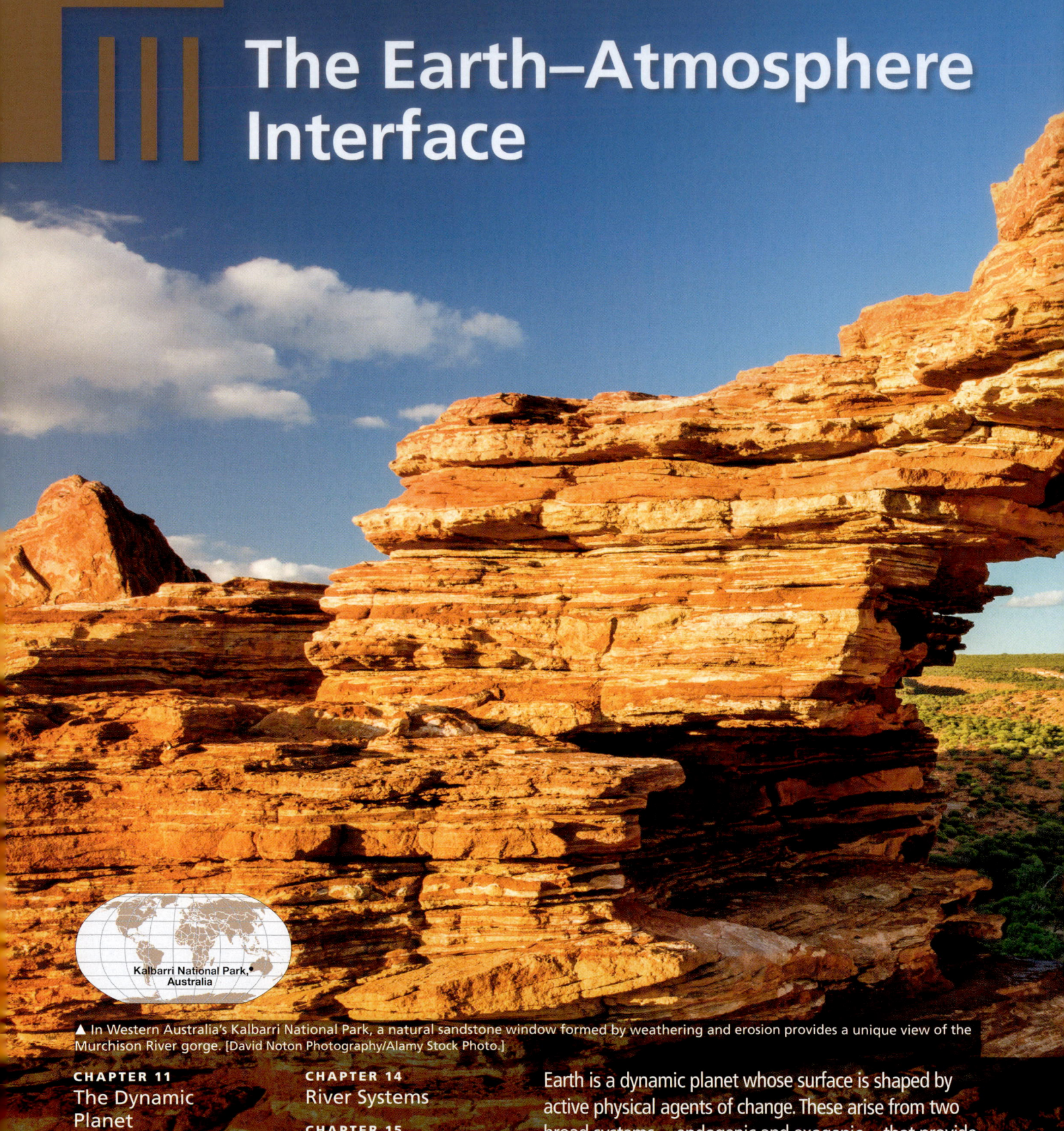

The Earth–Atmosphere Interface

▲ In Western Australia's Kalbarri National Park, a natural sandstone window formed by weathering and erosion provides a unique view of the Murchison River gorge. [David Noton Photography/Alamy Stock Photo.]

Kalbarri National Park, Australia

Earth is a dynamic planet whose surface is shaped by active physical agents of change. These arise from two broad systems—endogenic and exogenic—that provide a framework for the organization of Part 3. The *endogenic system* (Chapters 11 and 12) encompasses internal processes that produce flows of heat and material from deep below Earth's crust. Radioactive decay is the principal source of power for these processes. The materials

INPUTS
- Heat from within Earth
- Solar energy to Earth
- Precipitation
- Wind

ACTIONS
- Rock formation
- Tectonic processes
- Crustal deformation
- Weathering and erosion

OUTPUTS
- Folded and faulted landscapes
- Mountain chains
- Landforms related to water, wind, waves, ice

HUMAN–EARTH CONNECTIONS
- Geothermal energy
- Earthquakes and volcanism
- Landslides
- Floodplain management
- Desertification

Question:
What is the composition and structure of Earth's surface crust within a 100-km radius of your home town?

Atmosphere

Lithosphere

Biosphere

Hydrosphere

constitute the solid realm of Earth. Earth's surface responds by moving, warping, and breaking, sometimes in dramatic episodes of earthquakes and volcanic eruptions, constructing the crust.

The *exogenic system* (Chapters 13 through 17) consists of external processes at Earth's surface that set into motion air, water, and ice, all powered by solar energy. These agents carve, shape, and wear down the landscape.

One such process, *weathering*, breaks up and dissolves the crust. *Erosion* picks up these materials; transports them in rivers, coastal waves, winds, and flowing glaciers; and deposits them in new locations. Thus, Earth's surface is the interface between two vast open systems: one that builds the landscape and creates topographic relief and one that tears the landscape down into relatively low-elevation plains of sedimentary deposits.

11 The Dynamic Planet

Cotopaxi
Province,
Ecuador

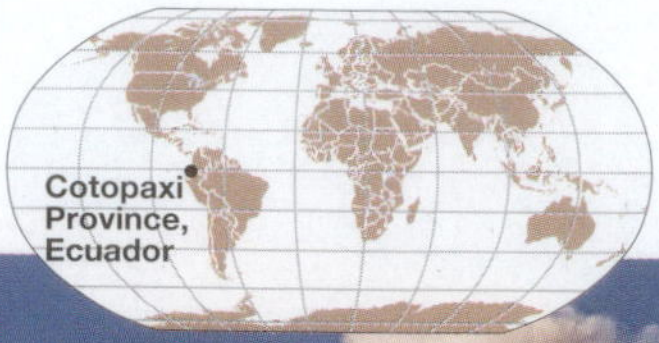

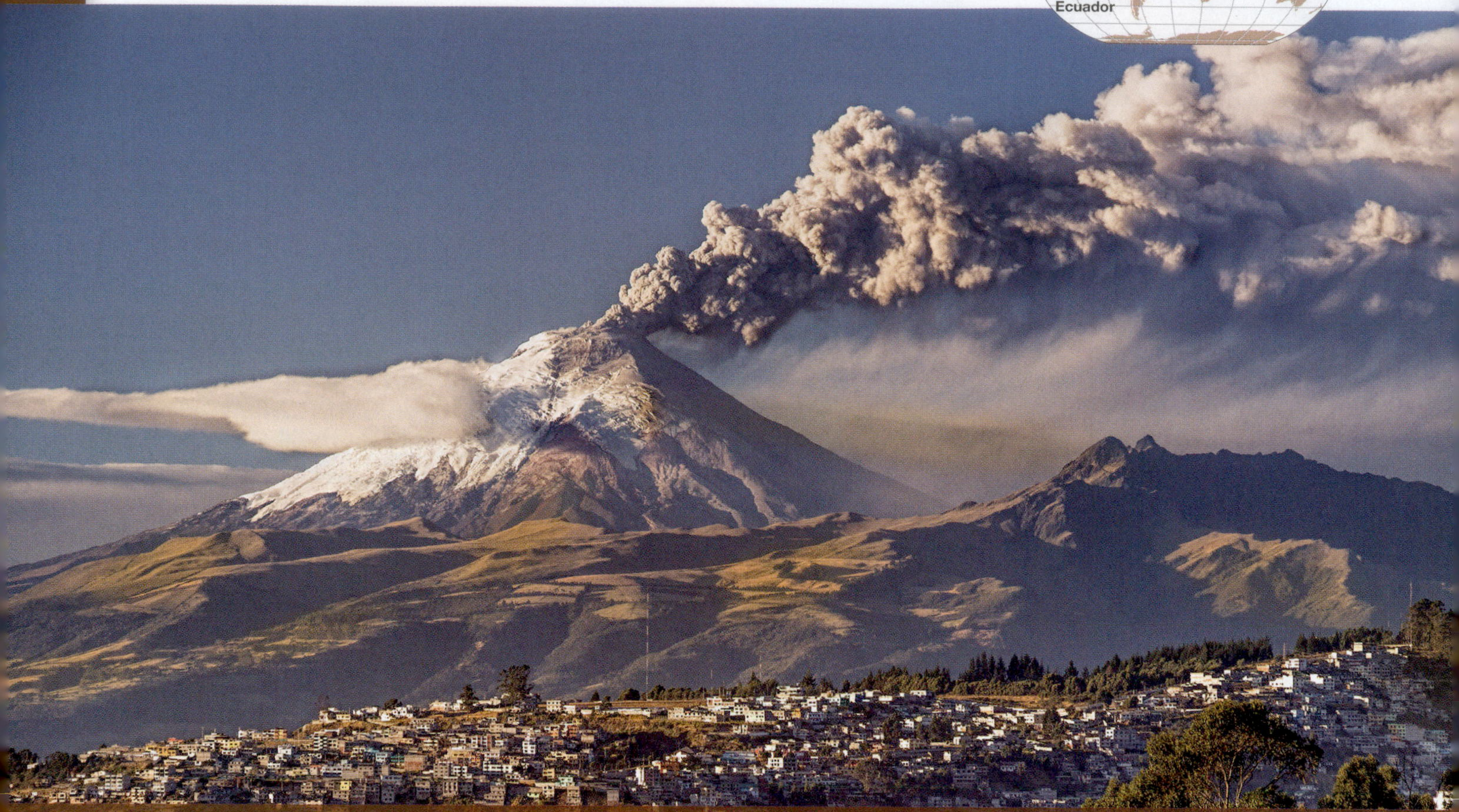

Cotopaxi in the Andes Mountains of Ecuador erupted in 2015, part of an intermittent series of eruptions since 1738. The upper slopes, reaching 5897 m (19,347 ft) in elevation, are covered by one of the few equatorial glaciers on Earth. [Henri Leduc/Moment/Getty Images.]

KEY**LEARNING**concepts

After reading the chapter, you should be able to:

- ***Discuss*** the time spans into which Earth's geologic history is divided and ***explain*** the principle of uniformitarianism.
- ***Depict*** Earth's interior in cross section and ***describe*** each distinct layer.
- ***Describe*** the three main groups of rock and ***diagram*** the rock cycle.
- ***Describe*** Pangaea and its breakup and ***explain*** the physical evidence that crustal drifting is continuing today.
- ***Draw*** the pattern of Earth's major plates on a world map and ***relate*** this pattern to the occurrence of earthquakes, volcanic activity, and hot spots.

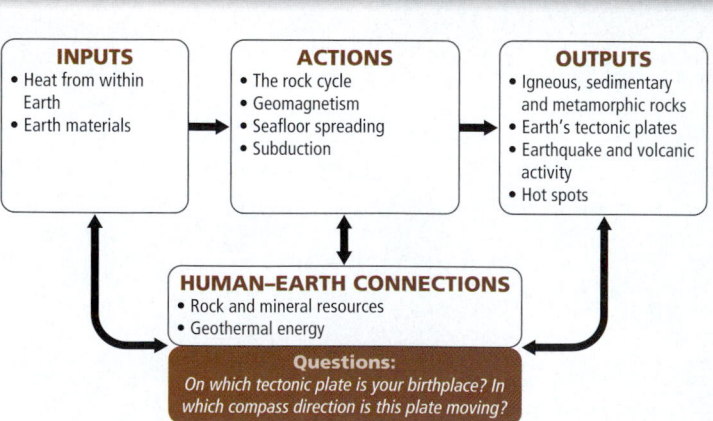

INPUTS
• Heat from within Earth
• Earth materials
ACTIONS
• The rock cycle
• Geomagnetism
• Seafloor spreading
• Subduction
OUTPUTS
• Igneous, sedimentary and metamorphic rocks
• Earth's tectonic plates
• Earthquake and volcanic activity
• Hot spots
HUMAN–EARTH CONNECTIONS
• Rock and mineral resources
• Geothermal energy
Questions:
On which tectonic plate is your birthplace? In which compass direction is this plate moving?

Fracking for Shale Gas: An Energy Resource for the Future?

In recent decades, a new method for mining natural gas has evoked controversy. *Fracking*, the nickname for hydraulic fracturing, is a technique used to extract natural gas from deeply buried sedimentary rock layers. Fracking proponents praise the technique as an economical way to tap abundant U.S. natural gas resources. However, fracking opponents condemn the technique, pointing out potential environmental hazards, such as groundwater contamination and wastewater injections that can induce earthquakes, including two 2016 quakes that damaged buildings in several Oklahoma towns.

Shale Gas Essentials The term *shale gas* refers to the natural gas trapped within shale, a type of sedimentary rock. Formed over millions of years from a mixture of silt and clay that resembles mud, shale is a fine-grained rock commonly called "mudstone." Many shale formations contain organic matter from plant and animal remains, and this organic matter can break down under certain processes to yield oil and natural gas.

The largest area of U.S. shale gas production is the Marcellus Shale, which stretches from Ohio to western New York (**Figure GN 11.1**). Scientists suggest that this ancient rock layer, underlying 60% of Pennsylvania, may be one of the most significant reservoirs of natural gas in the world (**Figure GN 11.2**). Pennsylvania alone is dotted with nearly 6000 shale gas wells. Methane, a potent greenhouse gas, is the primary constituent of natural gas. In the United States, the natural gas industry makes up the largest percentage of total methane emissions.

The Fracking Process To release methane trapped within shale layers, the rock must be broken up so that gas diffuses into the cracks and flows upward. Advances in horizontal drilling techniques, combined with the process of fracking, have recently opened access to large amounts of natural gas previously deemed too expensive or difficult to tap. A typical shale gas well descends vertically 2.4 km (1.5 mi), turns, and then extends horizontally into the rock strata. Horizontal drilling exposes a greater area of the rock, allowing more of it to be broken up and more gas to be released (**Figure GN 11.3**).

Hydraulic fracturing is the process of injecting a pressurized fluid to fracture the shale so that gas flows up the well to be collected at the surface. This fluid is a mixture of water, sand or glass beads that prop open the fissures, and chemical additives that act as lubricants. The specific chemicals used are still undisclosed by the industry, and some may be toxic.

▲Figure GN 11.1 Shale deposits and areas of exploration for natural gas extraction, United States and Canada. [U.S. Energy Information Administration.]

◀Figure GN 11.2 Marcellus shale outcrop, New York, and close-up of shale. [John Cancalosi/Alamy.]

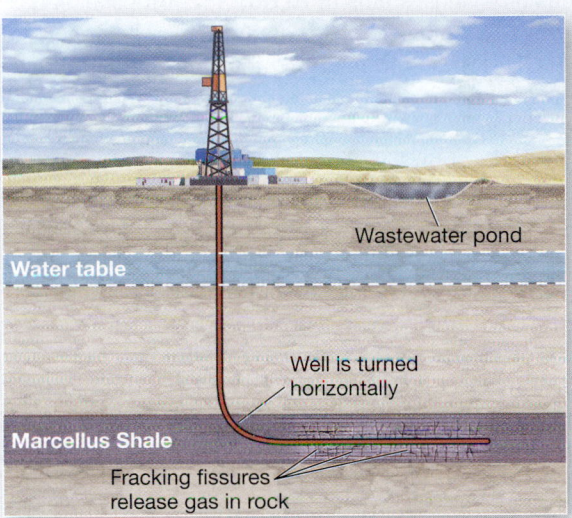

▲Figure GN 11.3 Horizontal drilling for hydraulic fracturing (fracking) and shale gas extraction.

Environmental Effects As with other resource-extraction techniques, fracking disturbs landscapes and leaves hazardous by-products. The fracking process uses massive quantities of water, which can deplete natural water sources, affecting stream or lake ecosystems. Fracking also produces large amounts of toxic wastewater, often held in wells or containment ponds. Scientific evidence has linked wastewater injection wells to earthquake activity in several U.S. states. In addition, methane adds to air pollution and the accumulation of greenhouse gases that cause climate change.

In 2007, fracking for shale gas began a multiyear boom, greatest in Pennsylvania, North Dakota, Colorado, Oklahoma, and Texas. In 2011, the U.S. Energy Information Administration (EIA) projected that U.S. shale gas production would rise to over 50% of all natural gas production by 2040. But in 2015, amid falling oil and natural gas prices, the boom went bust, making the future of shale gas uncertain. Should the United States and other countries expand shale gas as an energy resource for the future? Do the benefits outweigh the costs?

1. How does the fracking process release natural gas from shale?

2. List three environmental effects of fracking for shale gas.

The Earth–atmosphere interface is the meeting place of internal and external processes that build up and wear away landscapes. In this chapter, we begin our study of the solid portion of Earth, broadly called the lithosphere. (However, you will see that the lithosphere also has a more specific definition in relationship to the Earth's crust.) Another term for the solid sphere of Earth is the *geosphere*.

We begin with Earth's **endogenic system**—the processes operating in Earth's interior, driven by heat from deep within the planet. These internal processes cause the building of mountains and the dramatic volcanic eruptions that bring molten materials to Earth's surface. In later chapters, we look at Earth's **exogenic system**, the processes that wear away Earth's surface. These external processes produce many of the iconic landscapes of weathering and erosion that humans visit and admire—for example, Niagara Falls, the Grand Canyon, and Mount St. Helens (see Geosystems in Action 11.2 on page 344).

Geology is the science that studies all aspects of Earth—its history, composition and internal structure, surface features, and the processes acting on them. In this chapter, we focus on some essentials of geology including the types of rocks on Earth and their formation processes and the theory of plate tectonics. These essentials provide a conceptual framework for the study of processes occurring at Earth's surface, which are important to physical geography and the geospatial sciences.

The branch of physical geography that examines the Earth–atmosphere interface is **geomorphology**, the study of Earth's surface landforms—specifically, their origin, evolution, form, and spatial distribution. Geomorphology is a subfield of both geology and physical geography.

In Chapter 10, we discussed some of the climatic changes over the vast time scale of Earth's history. We also looked at the relatively recent effects of human activities on our atmosphere. The Anthropocene (from *anthropo*, meaning human, and *cene*, meaning new) is the name now commonly used for the most recent years of geologic history, during which time the influence of humans has become the overriding force of change for Earth systems. Forest destruction, land conversion for agriculture, dams and reservoirs on rivers, open-pit mines, and the global effects of climate change are products of the Anthropocene (**Figure 11.1**). For the first time in Earth's history, one species is affecting the entire face of the planet and is aware of the global changes underway.

Geologic Time and Change

The full scope of Earth's history can be represented in a summary timeline known as the **geologic time scale** (**Figure 11.2**). The scale breaks the past 4.6 billion years down into several time spans. *Eons* are the largest time span, although some refer to the Precambrian as a *supereon*. The increasingly shorter time spans within eons are *eras*, *periods*, and *epochs*. Major events in Earth's history determine the boundaries between these intervals, which are not equal in length. Examples are the six major extinctions of life forms in Earth history, labeled in Figure 11.2. The timing of these events ranges from 440 million years ago (m.y.a.) to the ongoing present-day extinction episode caused by modern civilization.

The most recent epoch in the geologic time scale is the *Holocene*, consisting of the 11,700 years since the last glacial period. As the impacts of humans on Earth systems increase, numerous scientists agree that we are in a new epoch, the Anthropocene.

everyday GEOSYSTEMS

How do humans impact landscapes?

Most of Earth's surface is today altered from human activity. Open-pit mining extracts gold, copper, and other resources by rearranging rock, sediment, and soils, leaving scars on the landscape. When the resource is depleted, the mine is abandoned, leaving waste rock and toxic materials that can move through the environment. Open-pit mines, discussed in Chapter 13, are one example of the human impacts that define the Anthropocene.

▶ **Figure 11.1 Landscapes of the Anthropocene.** Scars on the landscape from an open-pit gold mine in South Dakota's Black Hills. Note the Terry Peak ski area in the background, another example of anthropogenic landscape change. [Charles Wollertz/Alamy.]

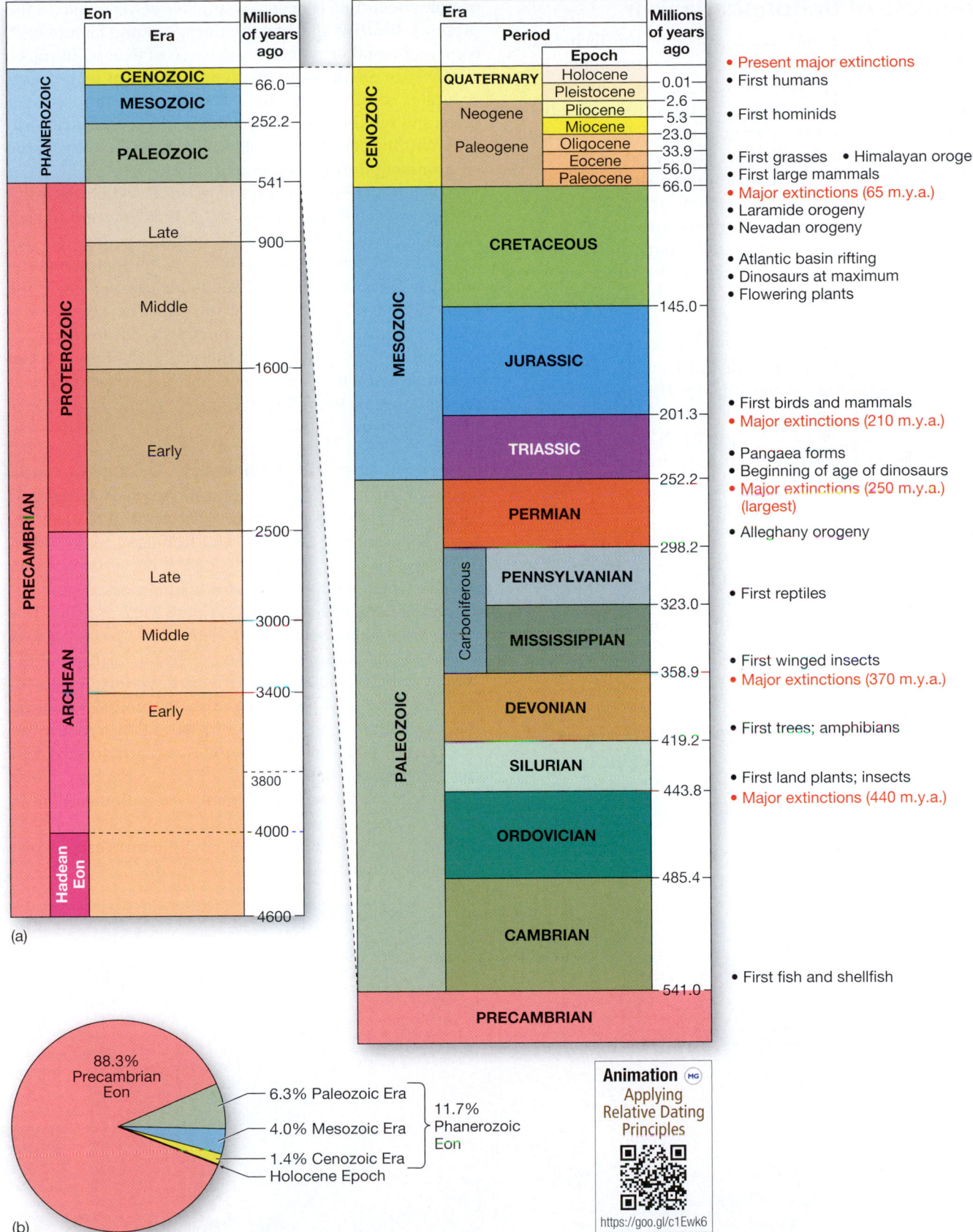

▲Figure 11.2 Geologic time scale showing highlights of Earth's history. (a) Dates appear in m.y.a. (millions of years ago). The scale uses currently accepted names of time intervals, except for the Hadean Eon, the proposed, but as yet unofficial, name for the period before the Archean. The six major extinctions or depletions of life forms are shown in red. (b) The chart shows the relative percentages of Earth's history during the Precambrian and Phanerozoic Eons. [Data from Nature 429 (May 13, 2004): 124–125 and the International Commission on Stratigraphy, 2015 International Chronostratigraphic Chart, v 2015/01.]

Priniciple of Uniformitarianism

In Chapter 10, we discussed paleoclimatic techniques that establish chronologies of past environments, enabling scientists to reconstruct the age and character of past climates. An assumption of these reconstructions is that the movements, systems, and cycles that occur today also operated in the past. This guiding principle of Earth science, called **uniformitarianism**, presupposes that the same physical processes now active in the environment were operating throughout Earth's history. The phrase "the present is the key to the past" describes the principle. For example, the processes by which streams carve valleys at present are assumed to be the same as those that carved valleys 500 million years ago. Evidence from the geologic record, preserved in layers of rock that formed over millennia, supports this concept, which was first hypothesized by geologist James Hutton in the 18th century and later amplified by Charles Lyell in his influential book *Principles of Geology* (1830).

Although the principle of uniformitarianism applies mainly to the gradual processes of geologic change, it also includes sudden, catastrophic events such as massive landslides, earthquakes, volcanic eruptions, and asteroid impacts. These events have geological importance and may occur as small interruptions in the generally uniform processes that shape the slowly evolving landscape. Thus, uniformitarianism means that the natural laws that govern geologic processes have not changed throughout geologic time even though the rate at which these processes operate is variable.

Relative Age and the Principle of Superposition

Geologists assign ages to events or specific rocks, structures, or landscapes using the geologic time scale, based on either relative time (what happened in what order) or numerical time (the actual number of years before the present). *Relative age* refers to the age of one feature with respect to another within a sequence of events. In rocks, relative age refers to the relative positions of rock layers, or strata, within a sequence. The scientific study of the order and relative position of rock sequences is **stratigraphy**. Within rock strata, clues such as fossils indicate the environment during rock formation.

Determinations of relative age are based on the principle of *superposition*, which states that rock and unconsolidated particles are deposited with the youngest layers "superposed" toward the top of a rock formation and the oldest at the base. This principle holds true as long as the materials have remained undisturbed. The horizontally arranged rock layers of the Grand Canyon are a classic example of superposition, as the youngest rock is at the top, underlying the canyon rim, and the oldest rock is at the bottom, exposed along the inner canyon of the Colorado River (**Figure 11.3**).

Numerical Age and Radiometric Dating *Numerical age* (sometimes called absolute age) is today determined using isotopic dating techniques (discussed in Chapter 10) and other scientific methods. The technique of *radiometric dating*, for example, uses the rate of decay for different unstable isotopes to provide a steady time clock to pinpoint the ages of Earth materials. Precise knowledge of radioactive decay rates allows scientists to determine the date a rock formed by comparing the amount of original isotope in the sample with the amount of decayed end product in the sample. Numerical ages permit scientists to refine the geologic scale and improve the accuracy of relative dating sequences.

The oldest known surface rocks on Earth formed during the Archean Eon, about 4 billion years ago. These rocks are today found in Greenland (3.8 billion years old), northwestern Canada (about 4 billion years old), northern Quebec, Canada (4.3 billion years old), and Western Australia (4.4 billion years old; **Figure 11.4**).

Rock layer
(age in millions of years)

Kaibab Limestone
(270)

Toroweap Formation
(273)

Coconino Sandstone
(275)

Hermit Shale
(280)

Supai Group
(285–315)

Redwall Limestone
(340)

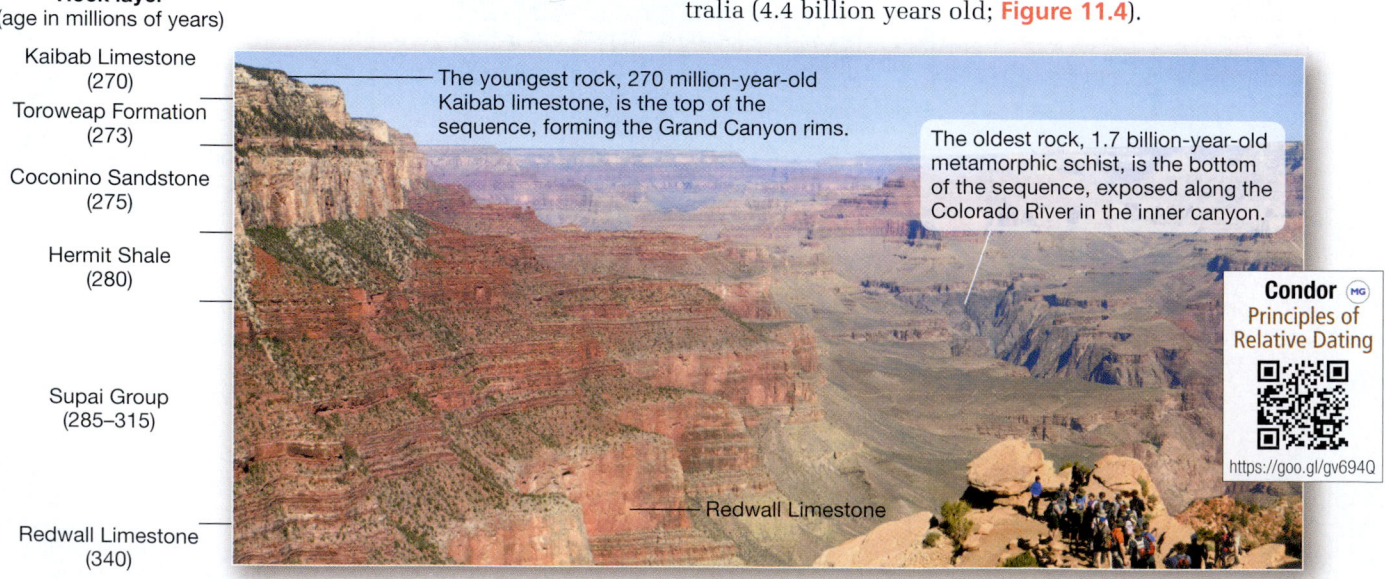

The youngest rock, 270 million-year-old Kaibab limestone, is the top of the sequence, forming the Grand Canyon rims.

The oldest rock, 1.7 billion-year-old metamorphic schist, is the bottom of the sequence, exposed along the Colorado River in the inner canyon.

Redwall Limestone

Condor MG
Principles of Relative Dating
https://goo.gl/gv694Q

▲**Figure 11.3 The principle of superposition.** The Grand Canyon, viewed here from Cedar Ridge on the South Rim, exposes 1524 m (5000 ft) of rock strata with the youngest layers at the top of the sequence. [M. Quinn/NPS.]

Earth's Interior

The processes that formed the structure of Earth's interior began about 4.6 billion years ago, as Earth condensed and congealed from a nebula of dust, gas, and icy comets (discussed in Chapter 2). As Earth solidified, gravity sorted materials by density. Heavier, denser substances such as iron gravitated slowly to its center, and lighter, less-dense elements such as silica slowly welled upward to the surface and became concentrated in the outer shell. Consequently, Earth's interior consists of roughly concentric layers, each distinct in either composition or temperature.

Earth's Structure and Temperature

Scientists have direct evidence of Earth's internal structure down to about 12.2 km (7.6 mi) from cores drilled into Earth's surface layer. Below this region, scientific knowledge of Earth's internal layers is acquired entirely through indirect evidence. In the late 19th century, scientists discovered that the shock waves created by earthquakes were useful for identifying Earth's internal materials. Earthquakes are the surface vibrations felt when rocks near the surface suddenly fracture, or break (discussed in Chapter 12). These fractures generate **seismic waves**, or shock waves, that travel throughout the planet. The speed of the waves varies as they pass through different materials—cooler, more rigid areas transmit seismic waves at a higher velocity than do the hotter, more deformable or fluid areas. *Plastic*, or deformable, layers do not transmit some seismic waves; they absorb them. Waves may also be refracted (bent) or reflected, depending on the density of the material. Thus, scientists are now able to identify the boundaries between different layers within Earth by measuring the depths of changes in seismic wave velocity and direction (**Figure 11.5**).

The temperature of Earth's interior increases with depth so that the hottest temperatures are found deep within Earth's core. At Earth's center, temperatures are 6000°C (10,800°F), as hot as the surface of the Sun. The internal heat that fuels processes beneath Earth's surface comes from residual heat left over from the planet's formation and from the decay of radioactive elements (specifically, from isotopes of potassium, uranium, and thorium). Heat energy migrates outward from the core by conduction in the solid layers as well as by convection in the plastic layers. This internal heat produces fiery volcanic explosions and powers the convection currents upon which Earth's lithospheric plates move and collide.

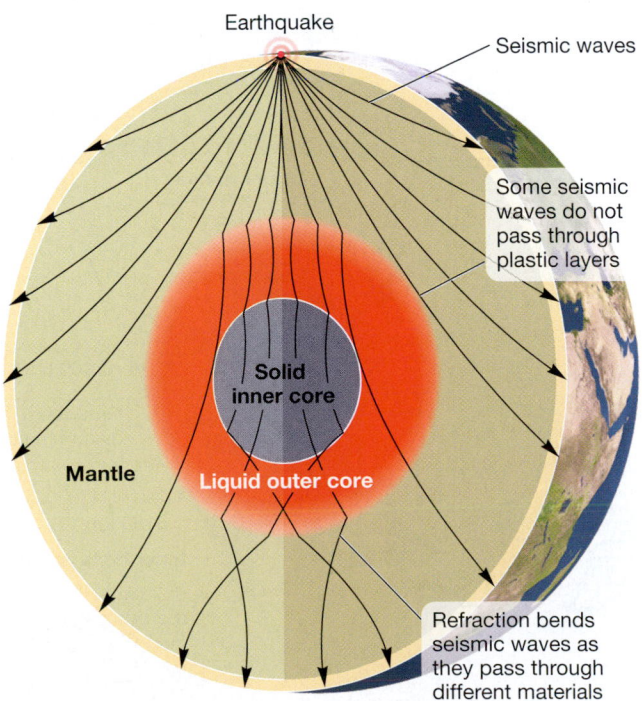

▲**Figure 11.5** **Seismic waves.** Earthquake waves help scientists "see" Earth's interior because they change velocity and direction when they pass through different materials.

Earth's Core and Mantle

A third of Earth's entire mass, but only a sixth of its volume, lies in its dense core (**Figure 11.6a**). The **core** is differentiated into two regions—*inner core* and *outer core*—divided by a transition zone several hundred kilometers wide (**Figure 11.6b**). Scientists think that the inner core formed before the outer core, shortly after Earth condensed. The inner core is solid iron that is well above the melting temperature of iron at the surface but remains solid because of tremendous pressure. The iron is not pure, but probably is combined with silicon and possibly oxygen and sulfur. The outer core is molten, metallic iron with lighter densities than the inner core. The high temperatures keep the outer core in a liquid state, and the flow of this material generates Earth's magnetic field.

Earth's outer core is separated from the mantle by a transition zone several hundred kilometers wide. This zone is a *discontinuity*, or a place where physical differences occur between adjoining regions in Earth's interior. By studying the seismic waves of more than 25,000 earthquakes, scientists determined that this transition area, the *Gutenberg discontinuity*, is uneven, with ragged peak-and-valley-like formations.

Together, the lower and upper mantles represent about 80% of Earth's total volume. The **mantle** is rich in iron and magnesium oxides and in silicates, which are dense and tightly packed at depth, grading to lesser densities toward the surface. Temperatures are highest at depth and decrease toward the surface; materials are thicker at depth, with higher viscosity, due to increased pressure. A broad transition zone of several hundred kilometers, centered between 410 and 660 km (255 and 410 mi) below the surface, separates the lower mantle from the upper mantle. Rocks in the lower mantle are at high enough temperature that they become soft and are able to flow slowly, deforming over millions of years.

The boundary between the uppermost mantle and the crust above is another discontinuity, known as the **Mohorovičić discontinuity**, or **Moho** (**Figure 11.6c**). Croatian seismologist Andrija Mohorovičić identified this discontinuity using seismic waves, which change at this depth due to sharp contrasts in material composition and density.

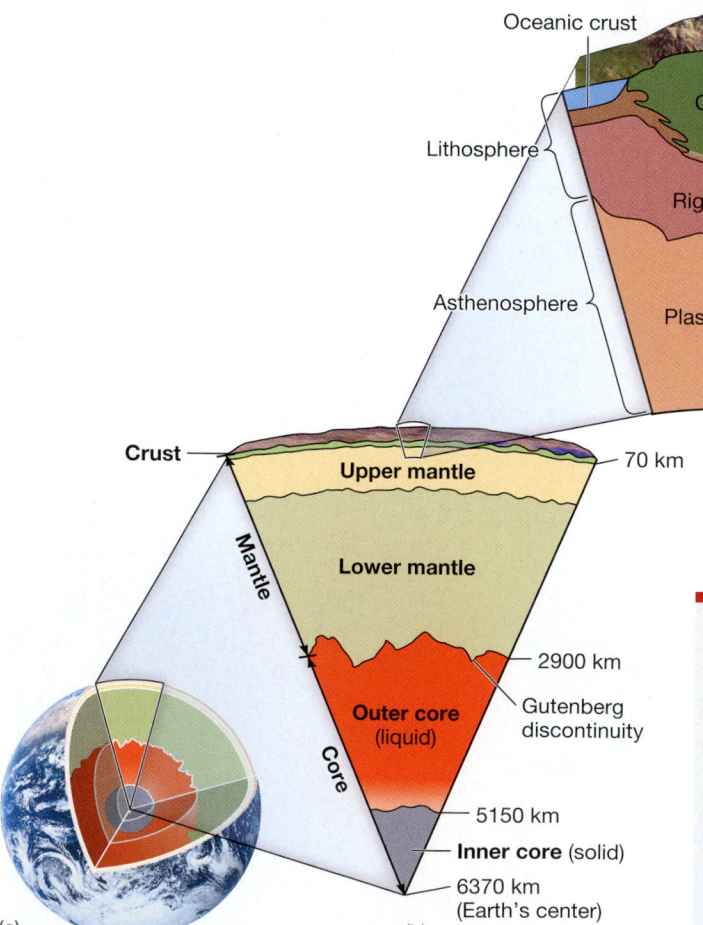

Oceanic crust
Continental crust
Lithosphere
Moho
Rigid mantle
Depth varies up to 200 km
Asthenosphere
Plastic mantle
(c) Depth varies up to 700 km

Crust
Upper mantle
70 km
Mantle
Lower mantle
2900 km
Outer core (liquid)
Gutenberg discontinuity
Core
5150 km
Inner core (solid)
6370 km (Earth's center)

(a)   (b)

▲**Figure 11.6 Earth in cross section.** (a) Cutaway showing Earth's interior. (b) Earth's interior in cross section, from the inner core to the crust. (c) Detail of the structure of the lithosphere and its relation to the asthenosphere.

WORK**IT**OUT 11.1
Digging a Hole Through Earth

Suppose you could drill a hole straight down through the center of Earth to the other side? What conditions would you encounter?

1. Would your drilling project pass through solid rock or molten magma or both? Describe the order of solid or plastic materials you would encounter.
2. At what point would you encounter the highest temperatures? The highest pressure?
3. If you jumped into the hole, would you fly out the other end at maximum velocity? What force would control your speed?

Go to  http://indianapublicmedia.org/amomentofscience/hole-in-the-earth/ for answers and more information.

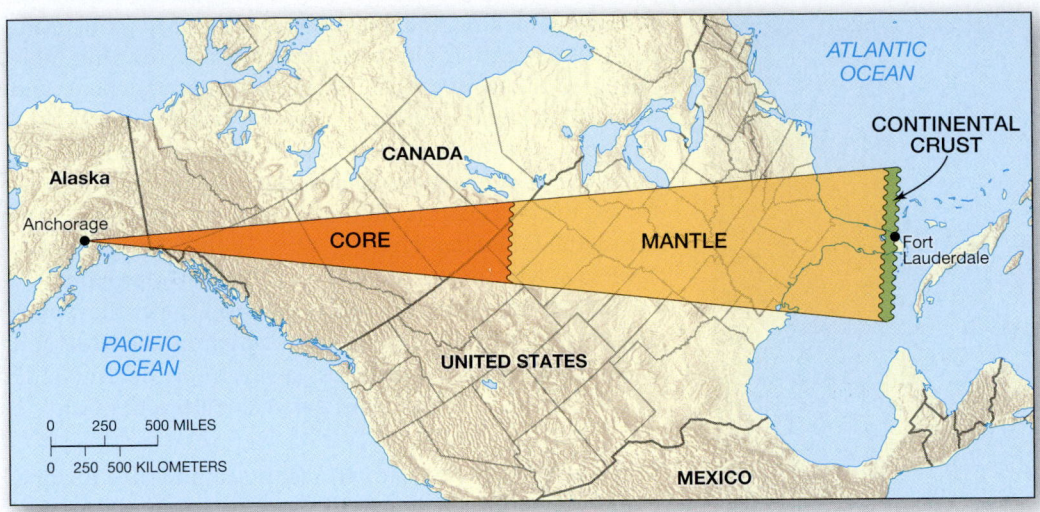

◄**Figure 11.7 Distances from core to crust.** The distance from Anchorage, Alaska, to Fort Lauderdale, Florida, is the same as the distance from Earth's center to its outer crust. The distance from Boca Raton, Florida, to Fort Lauderdale (30 km, or 18.6 mi) represents the thickness of the continental crust.

Earth's Crust

Above the Moho is Earth's outer layer, the **crust**, which makes up only a fraction of Earth's overall mass and only a small portion of the overall distance from Earth's center to its surface (**Figure 11.7**). The thickness of Earth's crust varies over the extent of the planet. Crustal areas beneath mountain masses are thicker, extending to about 70 km (43 mi), whereas the crust beneath continental interiors averages about 30 km (19 mi) in thickness. Oceanic crust averages only 5 km (3 mi) in thickness.

Just eight natural elements make up over 98% of Earth's crust by weight, and just two of these—oxygen and silicon—together account for 74.3% (**Figure 11.8**).

Oxygen is the most reactive gas in the lower atmosphere, readily combining with other elements. For this reason, the percentage of oxygen is higher in the crust (at 46%) than in the atmosphere, where it makes up 21%. As a result of the internal differentiation process, less-dense elements are nearer the surface, which explains the relatively large percentages of elements such as silicon and aluminum in the crust.

Continental crust is relatively low in density and sometimes called *sial*, shorthand for the dominant elements of *si*lica and *al*uminum. Oceanic crust is denser than continental crust and is sometimes called *sima*, short for the dominant elements of *si*lica and *ma*gnesium.

The Asthenosphere and Lithosphere

The interior layers of core, mantle, and crust are differentiated by chemical composition. Another way to distinguish layers within the Earth is by their rigid or plastic character. A rigid layer will not flow when a force acts on it; instead, it will bend or break. A plastic layer will slowly deform and flow when a force is present. Using this criterion, scientists divide the outer part of Earth into two layers: the **lithosphere**, or rigid layer (from the Greek *lithos*, or "rocky"), and the **asthenosphere**, or plastic layer (from the Greek *asthenos*, meaning "weak").

The lithosphere includes the crust and the uppermost mantle, to about 200 km (125 mi) in depth, and forms the rigid, cooler layer at Earth's surface (Figure 11.6c). Note that the terms *lithosphere* and *crust* are not the same; the crust makes up the upper portion of the lithosphere to about 70 km (43 mi) in depth.

The asthenosphere lies within the mantle from about 70 km to 250 km (43 mi to 155 mi) in depth. About 10% of the asthenosphere is molten in uneven patterns. The movement of convection currents in this zone in part causes the shifting of lithospheric plates, discussed later in the chapter.

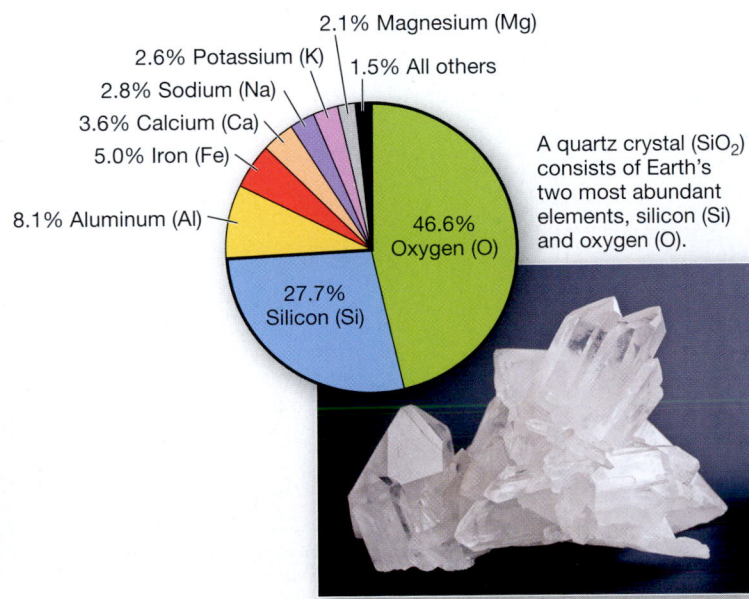

2.1% Magnesium (Mg)
2.6% Potassium (K) 1.5% All others
2.8% Sodium (Na)
3.6% Calcium (Ca)
5.0% Iron (Fe)
8.1% Aluminum (Al)
46.6% Oxygen (O)
27.7% Silicon (Si)

A quartz crystal (SiO_2) consists of Earth's two most abundant elements, silicon (Si) and oxygen (O).

▲**Figure 11.8 Common elements of Earth's crust.** [Quartz: Stefano Cavoretto/Shutterstock.]

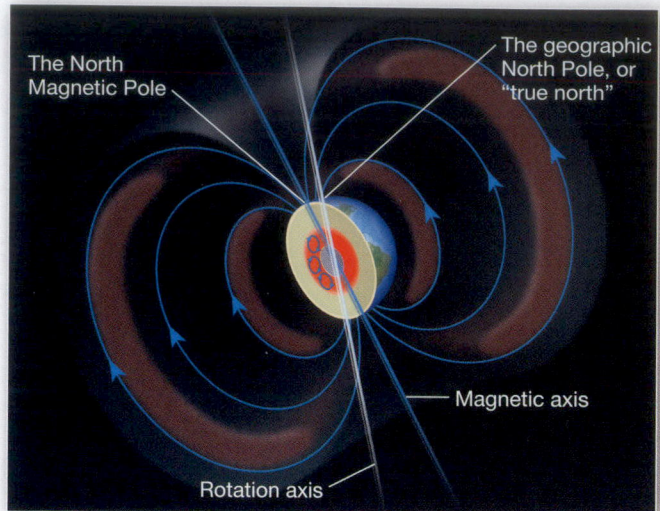

▲**Figure 11.9** **Earth's magnetic field.** Motion of the fluid outer core generates the magnetic field. Note that the geographic and magnetic poles are in different locations. Earth's magnetosphere in reality is elongated into a tear-drop shape distorted by pressure from the solar wind.

Earth's Magnetism

The fluid material of Earth's outer core generates most (at least 90%) of Earth's magnetic field. This is the magnetosphere—discussed in Chapter 2—that surrounds and protects Earth from solar wind and cosmic radiation. Like a bar magnet, the magnetic field has poles with opposite charges. This produces the north and south magnetic poles, located where the magnetic field enters and leaves the planet along Earth's magnetic axis (**Figure 11.9**).

Remember from Chapter 1 that the *north geographic pole* lies along Earth's axis of rotation where the meridians of longitude converge. This is *true north* and is a fixed point. In contrast, the *North Magnetic Pole* (NMP) is the pole toward which a compass needle points and is not a fixed point. The movement of the north and south magnetic poles results from changes in Earth's magnetic field. (We discuss in later chapters the effects of the magnetic field on animal migration, notably birds and sea turtles.)

Movement of the Magnetic Poles

Before the Global Positioning System (GPS) was in widespread use, people relied on the compass to find direction, making the location of the NMP pole critical for navigation. Because the location of this pole changes, the NMP must be periodically detected and pinpointed by magnetic surveys. NOAA tracks the location and movement of the magnetic poles (see http://www.ngdc.noaa.gov/geomag/GeomagneticPoles.shtml). During the past century, the NMP moved 1100 km (685 mi) across the Canadian Arctic (**Figure 11.10a**). Presently, the NMP is moving northwest toward Siberia at approximately 60 km (37 mi) per year. Earth's opposite pole, the *South Magnetic Pole* (SMP), moves separately from the NMP and is presently headed northwest away from the Antarctic coastline at just 5 km (3.1 mi) per year (**Figure 11.10b**).

Magnetic Reversals At various times in Earth's history, the magnetic field has faded to zero and then returned to full strength with the polarity reversed (meaning that the North Magnetic Pole then lies near the south geographic pole, so that a compass needle would point south). In the process, the field does not blink on and off, but instead diminishes slowly to low intensity, perhaps 25% strength, and then rapidly regains full power. This **geomagnetic reversal** has taken place nine times during the past 4 million years and hundreds of times over Earth's history. During the transition interval of low strength, Earth's surface receives higher levels of cosmic radiation and solar particles, but not to such an extent as to cause species extinctions. Life on Earth has weathered many of these transitions. Although the cause and timing of these reversals are unknown, they have become a key tool in understanding the movements of the continents, discussed later in the chapter.

(a) Movement of the North Magnetic Pole, 1831 to 2015.

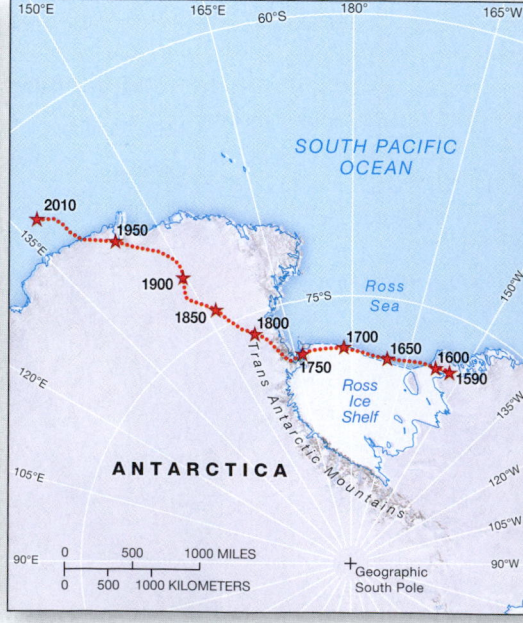

(b) Movement of the South Magnetic Pole, 1590 to 2010.

▲**Figure 11.10** **Movement of the magnetic poles during the last several centuries.** [(a) Data from NOAA NCEI/NGDC. (b) Based on Magnetic Field Models, NOAA NGDC.]

Earth Materials and the Rock Cycle

To understand and classify rocks, we must begin with minerals, which are the building blocks of rocks. A **mineral** is an inorganic, or nonliving, natural solid compound having a specific chemical formula and usually possessing a crystalline structure. Each mineral has its own characteristic color, texture, crystal shape, and density, among other unique properties. For example, the common mineral *quartz* is silicon dioxide, SiO_2, and has a distinctive six-sided crystal (see Figure 11.8). Ice fits the definition of a mineral, although water does not.

Mineralogy is the study of the composition, properties, and classification of minerals. Of the more than 5300 minerals known, about 30 are the most common components of rocks. *Silicates* make up roughly 95% of Earth's crust and are one of the most widespread mineral families—not surprising, considering the percentages of silicon and oxygen on Earth and their readiness to combine with each other and with other elements. This mineral family includes quartz, feldspar, clay minerals, and numerous gemstones. *Carbonates* are another common group of minerals that feature carbon in combination with oxygen and other elements such as calcium, magnesium, and potassium. Calcium carbonate, which makes up the shells of many marine organisms, in its mineral form *calcite* is an essential part of sedimentary rocks such as limestone. Other important mineral groups are *oxides*, in which oxygen combines with metallic elements to form minerals, and *sulfides* and *sulfates*, in which sulfur compounds combine with metallic elements to form minerals.

A **rock** is an assemblage of minerals bound together—such as granite, a rock containing three minerals. A rock can also be a mass composed of a single mineral (such as rock salt), of undifferentiated material (such as the noncrystalline glassy obsidian), or even of solid organic material (such as coal). Scientists have identified thousands of different rocks, all of which can be sorted according to three types that depend on the processes that formed them: *igneous* (formed from molten material), *sedimentary* (formed from compaction or chemical processes), and *metamorphic* (altered by heat and pressure). The movement of material through these processes is the *rock cycle*, summarized at the end of this section.

Igneous Processes

An **igneous rock** is one that solidifies and crystallizes from a molten state (*igneous* means "fire-formed" in Latin). Igneous rocks form from **magma**, which is molten rock beneath Earth's surface. When magma emerges at the surface, it is **lava**, although it retains its molten characteristics. Overall, igneous rocks make up approximately 90% of Earth's crust, although sedimentary rocks, soil, or oceans frequently cover them.

Igneous Environments Magma is fluid, highly gaseous, and under tremendous pressure. The result is that it either *intrudes* into crustal rocks, cooling and hardening below the surface to form **intrusive igneous rock**, or it *extrudes* onto the surface as lava and cools to form **extrusive igneous rock**. Extrusive igneous rocks result from volcanic eruptions and flows, processes discussed in Chapter 12.

The location and rate of cooling determine the crystalline texture of a rock, that is, whether it is made of coarser (larger) or finer (smaller) materials. Thus, the texture indicates the environment in which the rock formed. The slower cooling of magma beneath the surface allows more time for crystals to form, resulting in coarse-grained rocks such as **granite**. Even though this rock cooled below Earth's surface, subsequent uplift of the landscape has exposed granitic rocks (**Figure 11.11a**), some of which are famous cliff faces (such as Mount Rushmore) and rock-climbing destinations—El Capitan and Half Dome in Yosemite Valley, California, and the Great Trango Tower in Pakistan are examples (see the Human Denominator 11 on

(a) In Acadia National Park, Maine, granite outcrops occur along the Atlantic shoreline. In the U.S. East, exposed granitic rocks are also found in upstate New York, Vermont, New Hampshire, and across the southern Appalachian Mountains from north Georgia to Virginia.

(b) Basalt underlies more of Earth's surface than any other rock type. Shown here are basalt formations along the Fjollum River in northern Iceland, a country known for its active volcanoes and basalt landscapes.

▲**Figure 11.11** **Examples of intrusive granite and extrusive basalt.** [(a) Terry Donnelley/Alamy. (b) Gareth McCormack/Alamy.]

TABLE 11.1 Classification of Igneous Rocks

	Felsic ⟷		Mafic (Ultramafic)
Silica content of magma	High	Medium	Low
Chemical composition	High in potassium and sodium		High in magnesium and iron
Mineral content	Quartz Feldspars	Mica Amphibole	Pyroxine (Olivine)
Coloration	Lighter ⟷		Darker
Melting temperature	Lower ⟷		Higher
Resistance to weathering	Higher ⟷		Lower

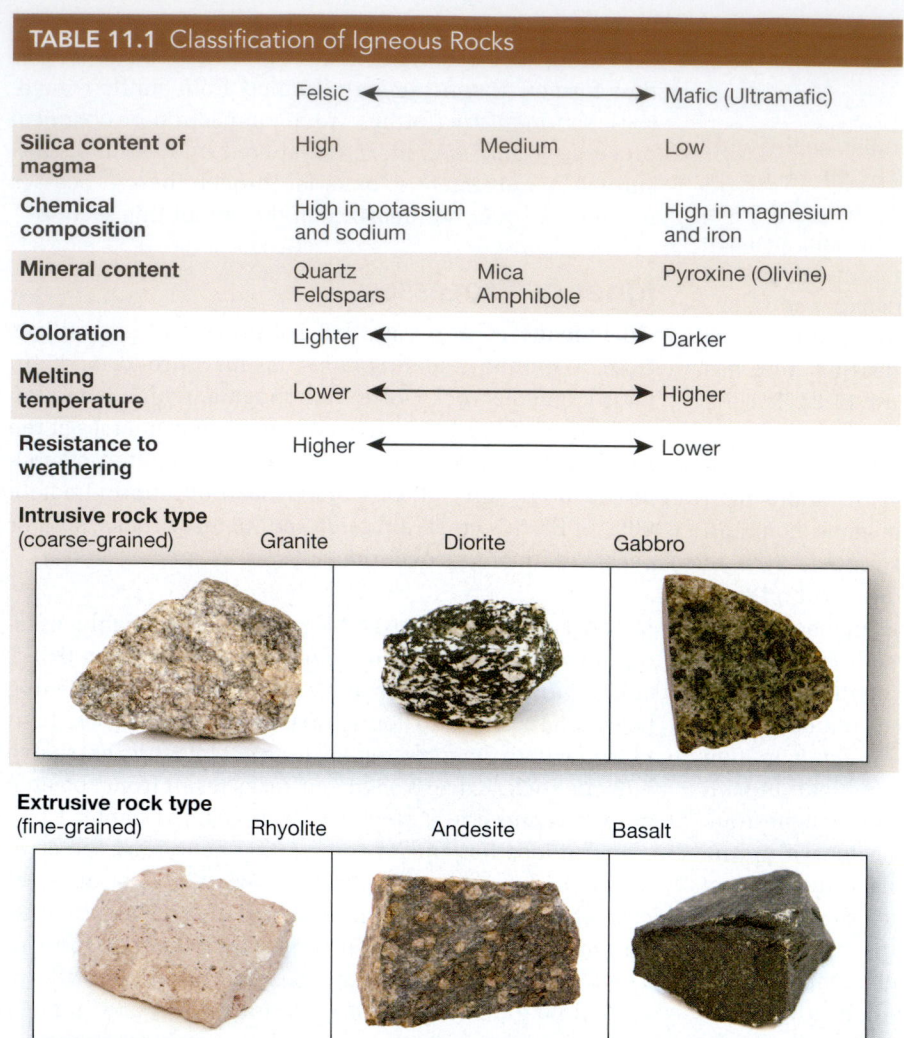

Intrusive rock type (coarse-grained): Granite, Diorite, Gabbro

Extrusive rock type (fine-grained): Rhyolite, Andesite, Basalt

[Granite: Givaga/Shutterstock. Diorite and basalt: Tyler Boyes/Shutterstock. Gabbro: Slim Sepp/Shutterstock. Rhyolite: Tyler Boyes. Shutterstock. Andesite: Siim Sepp/Alamy.]

page 343). The faster cooling of lava at the surface forms finer-grained rocks, such as **basalt**, the most common extrusive igneous rock (**Figure 11.11b**). As discussed later in the chapter, basalt makes up the bulk of the ocean floor, accounting for 71% of Earth's surface.

If cooling is so rapid that crystals cannot form, the result is a glassy rock such as *obsidian*, or volcanic glass. *Pumice* is another glassy rock (one that does not have a crystal structure) that forms when bubbles from escaping gases create a frothy texture in lava. Pumice is full of small holes, is light in weight, and is low enough in density to float in water.

Igneous Rock Classification Scientists classify the many types of igneous rocks according to their texture and composition (**Table 11.1**). The same magma that produces coarse-grained granite when it cools beneath the surface can form fine-grained basalt when it cools above the surface. The mineral composition of a rock, especially the relative amount of silica (SiO_2), provides information about the source of the magma that formed it and affects its physical characteristics. *Felsic* igneous rocks, such as

granite, are high in silicate minerals, such as feldspar and quartz (pure silica), and have low melting points. The category name is derived from *feld*spar and *sil*ica. Rocks formed from felsic minerals generally are lighter in color and less dense than those from mafic minerals.

Mafic igneous rocks, such as basalt, are derived from magnesium and iron (the Latin word for iron is *ferrum*). Mafic rocks are lower in silica and higher in magnesium and iron and have high melting points. Rocks formed from mafic minerals are darker in color and of greater density than those from felsic minerals. Ultramafic rocks have the lowest silica content; an example is peridotite (less than 45% silica).

Intrusive Igneous Landforms

Intrusive igneous rock that cools slowly in the crust forms a **pluton**, the general term for any intrusive igneous body, regardless of size or shape. (The Roman god of the underworld, Pluto, is the namesake.) If plutons or other igneous intrusions are uplifted by internal processes, the work of air, water, and ice then sculpts them into unique landforms.

The largest plutonic form is a **batholith**, usually made up of multiple plutons (**Figure 11.12**). When exposed by weathering and erosion, a batholith often has a surface greater than 100 km² (40 mi²). Batholiths form the mass of many large mountain ranges—for example, the Sierra Nevada batholith in California and the Coast Range batholith of British Columbia and Washington State.

Smaller plutons include the magma conduits of ancient volcanoes that have cooled and hardened (**Figure 11.13**).

- A *laccolith* is a lens-shaped body of igneous rock formed as magma intruded between rock layers and forced the overlying strata upward in the shape of a dome. A laccolith that is exposed by erosion forms a small, dome-shaped mountain (Figure 11.13a).
- A *volcanic neck* is a solidified column of magma that formed in a volcanic vent (Figure 11.13b).
- *Sills* are parallel to the layers of rock that they intrude into (Figure 11.13c).
- *Dikes* cross the layers of rock that they intrude into, indicating that they are younger in age (Figure 11.13d).

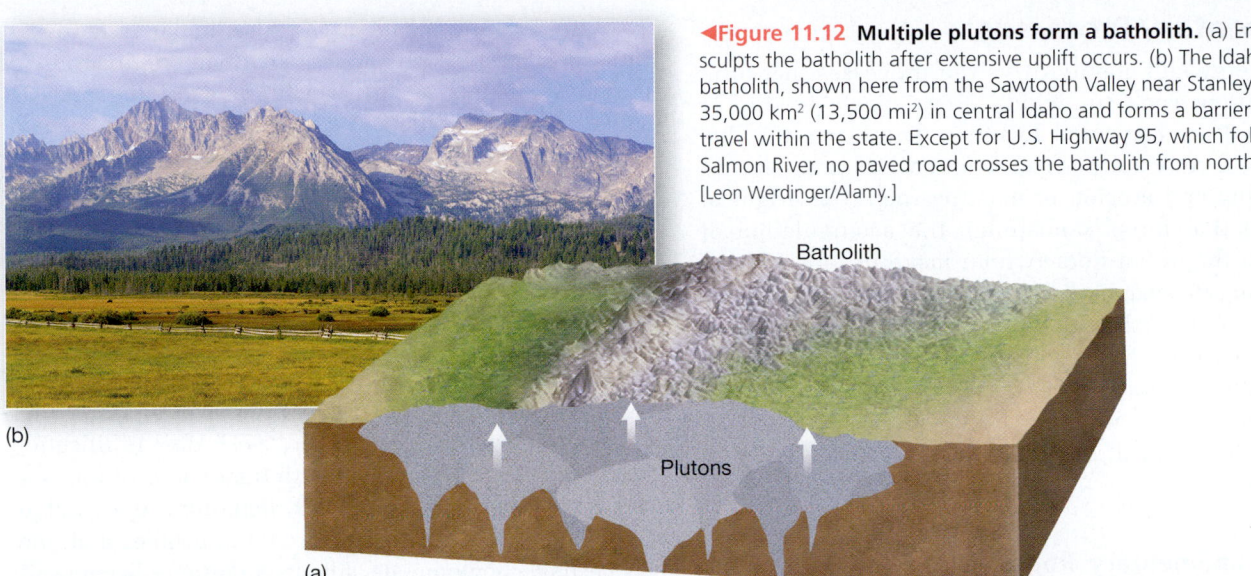

◀**Figure 11.12** **Multiple plutons form a batholith.** (a) Erosion sculpts the batholith after extensive uplift occurs. (b) The Idaho batholith, shown here from the Sawtooth Valley near Stanley, covers 35,000 km² (13,500 mi²) in central Idaho and forms a barrier to travel within the state. Except for U.S. Highway 95, which follows the Salmon River, no paved road crosses the batholith from north to south. [Leon Werdinger/Alamy.]

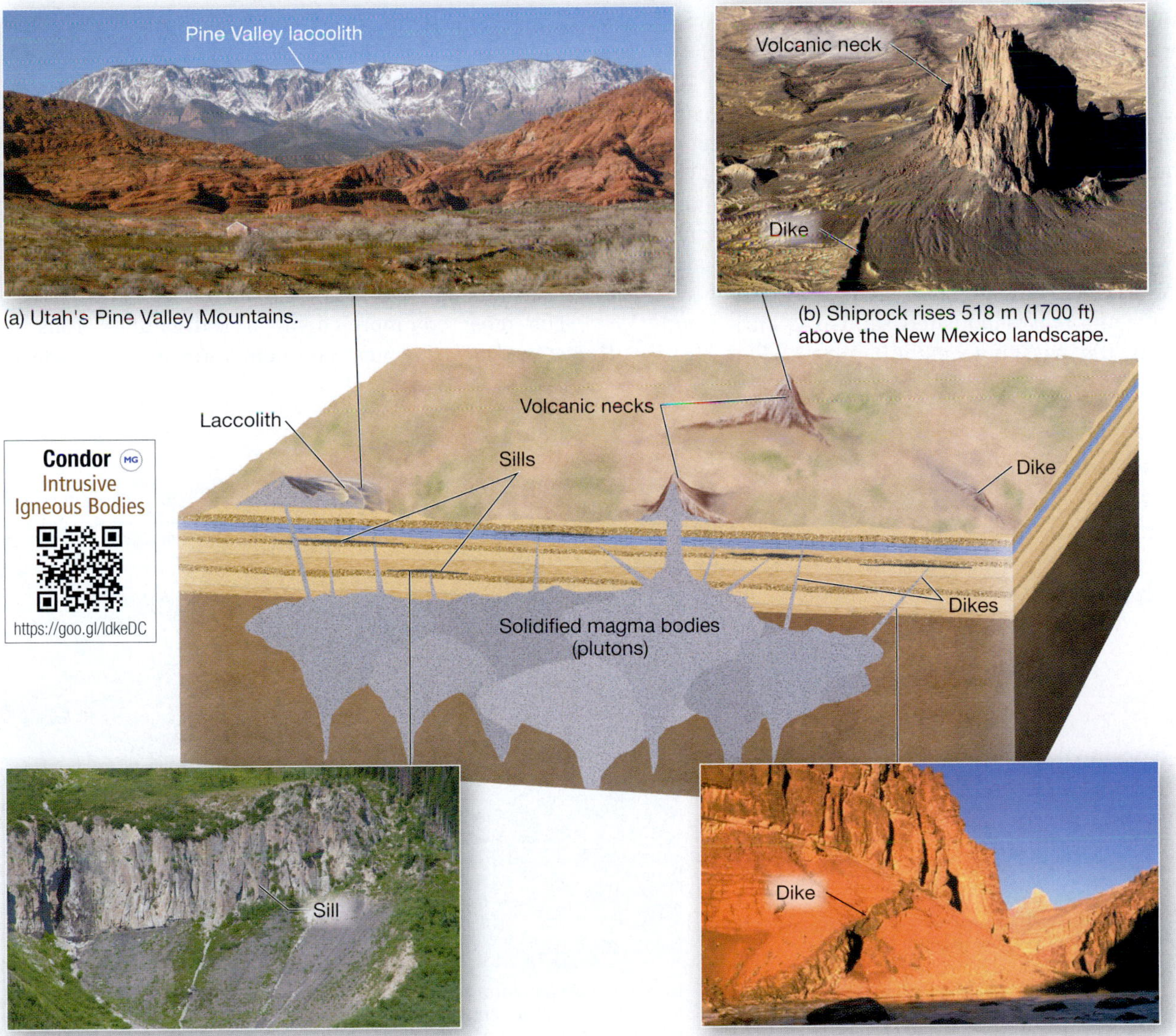

(b)

Batholith

Plutons

(a)

Pine Valley laccolith

(a) Utah's Pine Valley Mountains.

Volcanic neck

Dike

(b) Shiprock rises 518 m (1700 ft) above the New Mexico landscape.

Condor Ⓜ
Intrusive
Igneous Bodies

https://goo.gl/ldkeDC

Laccolith

Volcanic necks

Sills

Dike

Solidified magma bodies (plutons)

Dikes

Sill

(d) Sill in between shale layers, Colorado.

Dike

(c) Dike cuts through reddish shale, Arizona.

▲**Figure 11.13** **Examples of igneous intrusions and associated landforms after erosion.** [(a) Dixie National Forest, USFS. (b) Blend Images/Alamy. (c) National Park Service. (d) Arizona Geological Survey.]

Sedimentary Processes

Solar energy and gravity drive the processes that form **sedimentary rock**, in which loose *clasts* (grains or fragments) are cemented together. The clasts that become solid rock are derived from several sources: the weathering and erosion of existing rock (the origin of the sand that forms sandstone), the accumulation of shells on the ocean floor (which make up one form of limestone), the accumulation of organic matter from ancient plants (which forms coal), and the precipitation of minerals from water solution (the origin of the calcium carbonate, $CaCO_3$, that forms chemical limestone). Sedimentary rocks are divided into several categories—clastic, biochemical, organic, and chemical—based on their origin.

Clastic Sedimentary Rocks The formation of clastic sedimentary rock involves several processes. *Weathering* disintegrates and dissolves existing rock into clasts. *Erosion* by gravity, water, wind, and ice then carries these rock particles across landscapes—at this point, the moving material is called **sediment**. Transport occurs from "higher-energy" sites, where the carrying medium has the energy to pick up and move the material, to "lower-energy" sites, where the sediment is deposited. *Deposition* is the process whereby sediment settles out of the transporting medium and results in material dropped along river channels, on beaches, and on ocean bottoms, where it is eventually buried. Sandstone is an example of a clastic sedimentary rock, formed in environments where wind- and wave-deposited sand was buried and compacted by the overlying weight (**Figure 11.14a**).

Lithification occurs as loose sediment is hardened into solid rock. This process involves *compaction* of buried sediments as the weight of overlying material squeezes out the water and air between clasts and *cementation* as minerals fill any remaining spaces and fuse the clasts—principally quartz, feldspar, and clay minerals—into a coherent mass. The type of cement varies with different environments. Calcium carbonate ($CaCO_3$) is the most common cement, followed by iron oxides and silica. Drying (dehydration) and heating can also unite particles.

The different sediments that make up sedimentary rock range in size from boulders to gravel to sand to microscopic clay particles (**Table 11.2**). After lithification, these size classes, combined with their composition, sorting, and cement characteristics, determine the common sedimentary rock types. For example, pebbles and gravels become conglomerate, silt-sized particles become siltstone or mudstone, and clay-sized particles become shale.

Chemical Sedimentary Rocks Some sedimentary rocks are formed not from pieces of broken rock, but instead from the shells of organisms that contain calcium carbonate (a biochemical process) or from dissolved minerals that precipitate out of water solutions (a chemical process) and build up to form rock. *Chemical precipitation* is the formation of a separate solid substance from a solution, such as when water evaporates and leaves behind a residue of salts. These processes are important in oceanic environments, as well as in areas of karst topography (discussed in Chapter 13).

The most common chemical sedimentary rock is **limestone**, and the most common form of limestone is

(a) Sandstone in Valley of Fire State Park, Nevada.

(b) Chemical limestone in south-central Indiana. Inset photo shows close-up of biochemical limestone, with shells and clasts cemented together.

▲**Figure 11.14** **Sedimentary rocks: sandstone and limestone.** [(a) Joseph S. Giacalone/Alamy. (b) and (c) Bobbé Christopherson.]

TABLE 11.2 Clast Sizes and Related Sedimentary Rocks

Clast Size	Sediment Type	Rock Type
80 mm (very coarse)	Boulders, cobbles	Conglomerate (breccia, if pieces are angular)
>2 mm (coarse)	Pebbles, gravel	Conglomerate
0.5–2.0 mm (medium to coarse)	Sand	Sandstone
0.062–0.5 mm (fine to medium)	Sand	Sandstone
0.004–0.062 mm (fine)	Silt	Siltstone (mudstone)
<0.004 mm (very fine)	Clay	Shale (mudstone)

Conglomerate

Sandstone

Cobbles

Gravel

Coarse sand

Fine sand

Silt

[Conglomerate by John Cancalosi/Alamy. Sandstone by Siim Sepp/Alamy. Cobbles by Paul Heinrich/Alamy. Gravel by FLPA/Alamy. Coarse sand by Solomonjee/Alamy. Fine sand by ImageBroker/Alamy. Silt by Fabio Lamanna/Alamy.]

biochemical limestone from marine organic origins. As discussed in Chapter 10, many organisms extract dissolved $CaCO_3$ from seawater to construct solid shells. When these organisms die, the solid shell material builds up on the ocean floor where it eventually lithifies to become limestone (**Figure 11.14b**).

Limestone is also formed from a chemical process in which $CaCO_3$ in solution is chemically precipitated out of groundwater that has seeped to the surface. This process forms *travertine*, a mineral deposit that commonly forms terraces or mounds near springs (**Figure 11.15a**). The precipitation of carbonates from the water of these natural springs is driven in part by "degassing": Carbon dioxide bubbles out of solution at the surface, making the remaining solutes more likely to precipitate. Cave features such as speleothems, discussed in Chapter 10, are another type of travertine deposit.

Salt and other mineral deposits that precipitate when water evaporates can build up to form *evaporites*, another type of chemical sedimentary rock. Examples of evaporites are found in Utah on the Bonneville Salt Flats, created when an ancient salt lake evaporated, and across the dry landscapes of the American Southwest (**Figure 11.15b**).

(a) Travertine is a chemical limestone composed of calcium carbonate, shown here at the natural hot springs of Pamukkale in southwestern Turkey.

(b) Evaporites are crystallized mineral deposits left behind after evaporation occurs. Shown here are salt deposits on a dry lake bed in Death Valley, California.

▲**Figure 11.15 Chemical sedimentary rock.** [(a) Funkyfood London/Paul Williams/Alamy. (b) Flaherty Dennis/Getty Images]

Metamorphic Processes

Any igneous or sedimentary rock may be transformed into a **metamorphic rock** by going through profound physical or chemical changes under pressure and increased temperature (*metamorphic* comes from the Greek "to change form"). Metamorphic rocks generally are more compact than the original rock and therefore are harder and more resistant to weathering and erosion (**Figure 11.16**).

The four processes that can cause metamorphism are heating, pressure, heating and pressure together, and compression and shear. When heat is applied to rock, the atoms within the minerals may break their chemical bonds, move, and form new bonds, leading to new mineral assemblages that develop into solid rock. When pressure is applied to rock, mineral structure may change as atoms become packed more closely. When rock is subject to both heat and pressure at depth, the original mineral assemblage becomes unstable and changes. Finally, rocks may be compressed by overlying weight and subject to shear when one part of the mass moves sideways relative to another part. These processes change the shape of the rock, leading to changes in the mineral alignments within.

Processes occurring at the boundaries of lithospheric plates can subject the rock of Earth's crust to heating, pressure, compression, and shear. Metamorphic rock may form from igneous rocks as plates shift, especially when one plate is thrust beneath another (discussed with plate tectonics, just ahead). *Contact metamorphism* occurs when magma rising within the crust "cooks" adjacent rock; this type of metamorphism occurs adjacent to igneous intrusions and results from heat alone (**Figure 11.17a**). *Regional metamorphism* occurs when a large areal extent of rock is subject to metamorphism (**Figure 11.17b**). This can occur as lithospheric plates collide and mountain building adds weight to the crust. Regional metamorphism also occurs when sediments collect in broad depressions in Earth's crust and, because of their own weight, create enough pressure on the bottommost layers to transform the sediments into metamorphic rock.

▼**Figure 11.16** **Metamorphic rock along the Colorado River in the Grand Canyon.** The metamorphic Vishnu Schist exposed at the bottom of the Grand Canyon in the inner gorge is harder and more resistant to erosion than the softer sedimentary rocks above. Note the pink granitic intrusions in the schist on both sides of the river. [Zack Holmes/Alamy.]

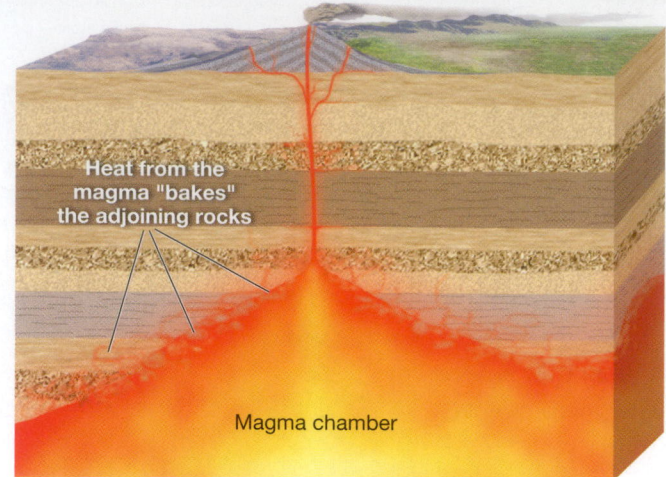

(a) Contact metamorphism occurs in the upper crust where heat from a magma body is intense.

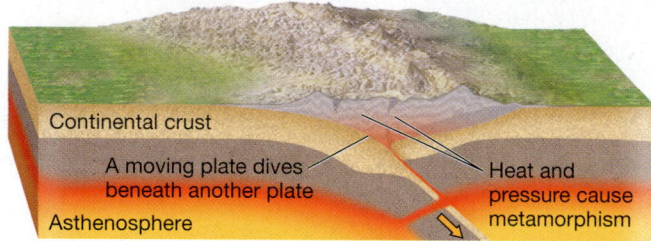

(b) Regional metamorphism occurs deep beneath a mountain belt or vast sedimentary plain, under conditions of extreme heat and pressure.

▲**Figure 11.17** **Metamorphic processes.** Metamorphic rock forms under extreme heat and pressure, which can occur by contact metamorphism and regional metamorphism.

Animation (MG)
Foliation of Metamorphic Rock
https://goo.gl/NbwUFI

Metamorphic rocks have textures that are foliated or nonfoliated, depending on the arrangement of minerals after metamorphism (**Table 11.3**). *Foliated* rock has a banded or layered appearance, demonstrating the alignment of minerals, which may appear as wavy striations (streaks or lines) in the rock. *Nonfoliated* rocks do not exhibit this alignment.

The Rock Cycle

Although rocks appear stable and unchanging, they are not. The **rock cycle** is the name for the continuous alteration of Earth materials from one rock type to another (**Figure 11.18**). For example, igneous rock formed from magma may break down into sediment by weathering and erosion and then lithify into sedimentary rock. This rock may subsequently become buried and exposed to pressure and heat deep within Earth, forming metamorphic rock. This may, in turn, break down and become sedimentary rock. Igneous rock may also take a shortcut through that cycle by directly becoming metamorphic rock. As the arrows indicate, there are many pathways through the rock cycle.

Two cyclic systems drive the rock cycle. At and above Earth's surface, the hydrologic cycle, fueled by solar energy, drives the exogenic processes. Below Earth's surface and within the crust, the tectonic cycle, powered by internal heat, drives the endogenic processes. We now discuss plate tectonics theory and the tectonic cycle.

TABLE 11.3 Metamorphic Rocks

Parent Rock	Metamorphic Equivalent	Texture
Shale (clay minerals)	Slate	Foliated
Granite, slate, shale	Gneiss	Foliated
Basalt, shale, peridotite	Schist	Foliated
Limestone, dolomite	Marble	Nonfoliated
Sandstone	Quartzite	Nonfoliated

Slate   Gneiss   Marble

[Slate and gneiss by Siim Sepp/Alamy. Marble by www.sandatlas.org/Shutterstock. Chimney Rock by John Elk III/Alamy.]

Henderson Gneiss, Chimney Rock, North Carolina

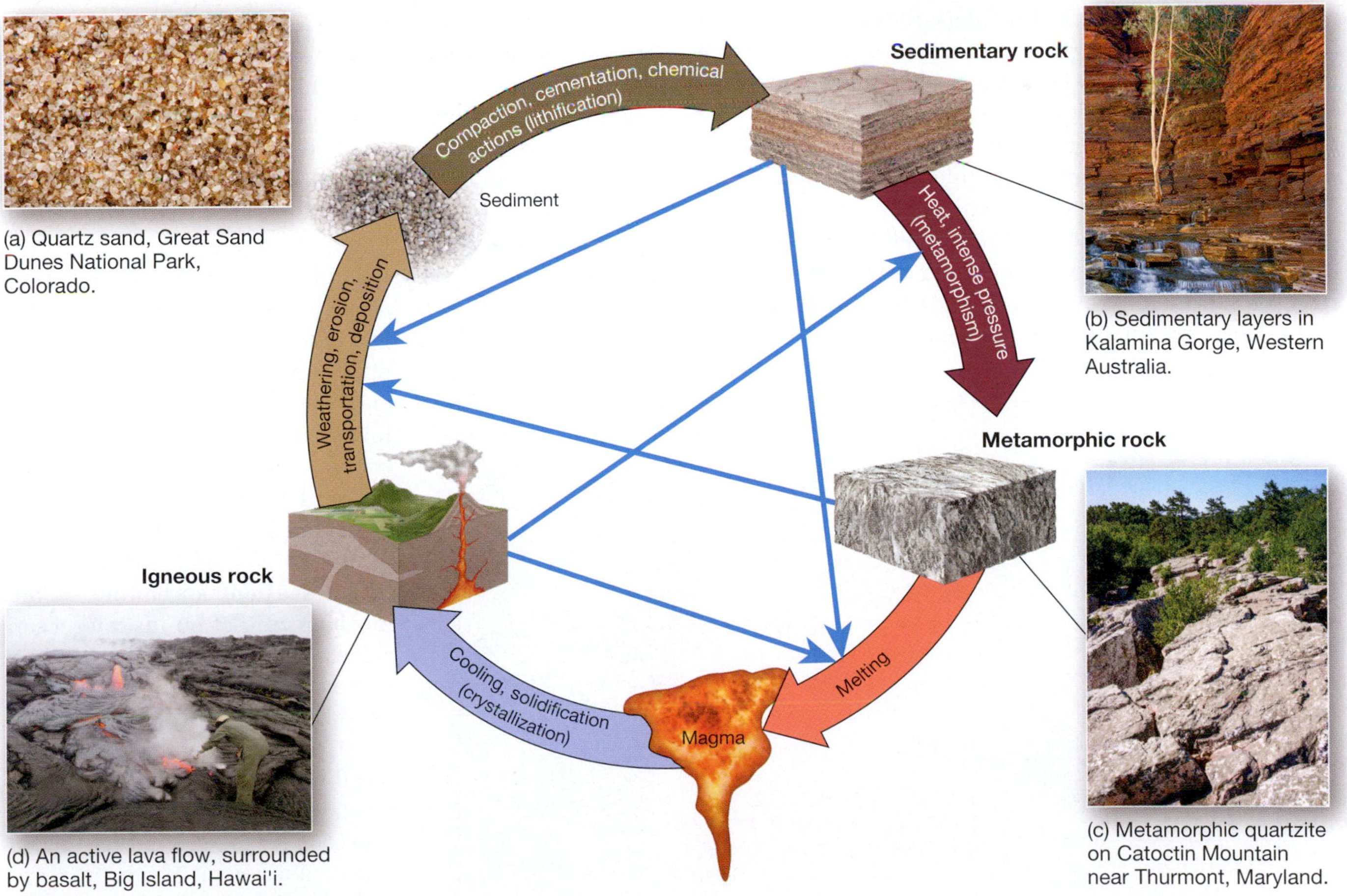

(a) Quartz sand, Great Sand Dunes National Park, Colorado.

Compaction, cementation, chemical actions (lithification)

Sediment

Weathering, erosion, transportation, deposition

Sedimentary rock

(b) Sedimentary layers in Kalamina Gorge, Western Australia.

Heat, intense pressure (metamorphism)

Metamorphic rock

Igneous rock

Cooling, solidification (crystallization)

Magma

Melting

(d) An active lava flow, surrounded by basalt, Big Island, Hawai'i.

(c) Metamorphic quartzite on Catoctin Mountain near Thurmont, Maryland.

▲Figure 11.18 **The rock cycle.** In this schematic of the relations among igneous, sedimentary, and metamorphic processes, the thin blue arrows indicate "shortcuts"—such as when igneous rock is melted and becomes metamorphic rock without first going through a sedimentary stage. [(a) Marek Uliasz/Alamy. (b) Sailer/Blickwinkel/Alamy. (c) Zack Frank/Shutterstock. (d) USGS Hawaiian Volcano Observatory.]

Plate Tectonics

Have you ever looked at a world map and noticed that a few of the continental landmasses appear to have matching shapes like pieces of a jigsaw puzzle—particularly South America and Africa? The reality is that the continental pieces once did fit together. Continental landmasses migrated to their present locations, and are continuing to move today at speeds up to 6 cm (2.4 in.) per year. We say that the continents are *adrift* because convection currents in the asthenosphere and upper mantle provide upwelling and downwelling forces that push and pull portions of the lithosphere. Thus, the arrangement of continents and oceans we see today is not permanent, but is in a continuing state of change.

Continental Drift

German geophysicist and meteorologist Alfred Wegener first presented the idea of continental drift in 1912, and 3 years later published his book *Origin of the Continents and Oceans.* After studying the geologic record represented in the rock strata, Wegener found evidence that the rock assemblages on the east coast of South America were the same as those on the west coast of Africa, suggesting that the continents were at one time connected. The fossil record provided further evidence, as did the climatic record found in sedimentary rocks (**Figure 11.19**). Wegener hypothesized that the coal deposits found today in the midlatitudes exist because these regions were at one time nearer the equator and were covered by lush vegetation that later became the lithified organic material that forms coal. Wegener concluded that all landmasses migrate and that they once formed one supercontinent, which he named **Pangaea**, meaning "all Earth."

Today, scientists regard Wegener as the father of plate tectonics, which evolved out of his idea of continental drift. However, scientists at the time were unreceptive to Wegener's revolutionary proposal. A great debate began that lasted almost 50 years. As modern scientific capabilities led to discoveries that built the case for continental drift, the 1950s and 1960s saw a revival of interest in Wegener's concepts and, finally, confirmation. Although his initial model kept the landmasses together too long and his proposal included an incorrect driving mechanism for the moving continents, Wegener's arrangement of Pangaea and its breakup was correct. **Figure 11.20** shows the changing arrangement of the continents, beginning with the Pangaea configuration of 225 m.y.a. and ending with the arrangement of the continents today.

The word *tectonic*, from the Greek *tektonikùs*, meaning "building" or "construction," refers to changes in the configuration of Earth's crust as a result of internal forces. **Plate tectonics** is the theory that the lithosphere is divided into a number of plates that float independently over the mantle. Along the boundaries of these plates occur the formation of new crust, the building of mountains, and the seismic activity that causes earthquakes. Plate tectonics theory although at first controversial, now provides the underlying foundation for much of Earth systems science.

Seafloor Spreading

The key to establishing the theory of continental drift was a better understanding of the seafloor crust. As scientists acquired information about the bathymetry (depth variations) of the ocean floor, they discovered an interconnected worldwide mountain chain, forming a ridge some 64,000 km (40,000 mi) in extent and averaging more than 1000 km (600 mi) in width. The underwater mountain systems that form this chain are termed **mid-ocean ridges**.

In the early 1960s, geophysicist Harry H. Hess proposed that these mid-ocean ridges are new ocean floor formed by upwelling flows of magma from hot areas in the upper mantle and asthenosphere and perhaps from the deeper lower mantle. While upwelling occurs, the new seafloor moves outward from the ridge as plates pull apart and new crust is formed (**Figure 11.21**). This process, now called **seafloor spreading**, is the mechanism that builds mid-ocean ridges, also known as spreading centers, and drives continental movement.

Hess and other geologists then faced a new problem: If seafloor spreading and the creation of new crust are ongoing, then old ocean crust must somewhere be consumed; otherwise, Earth would be expanding. Hess and another geologist, Robert S. Dietz, proposed

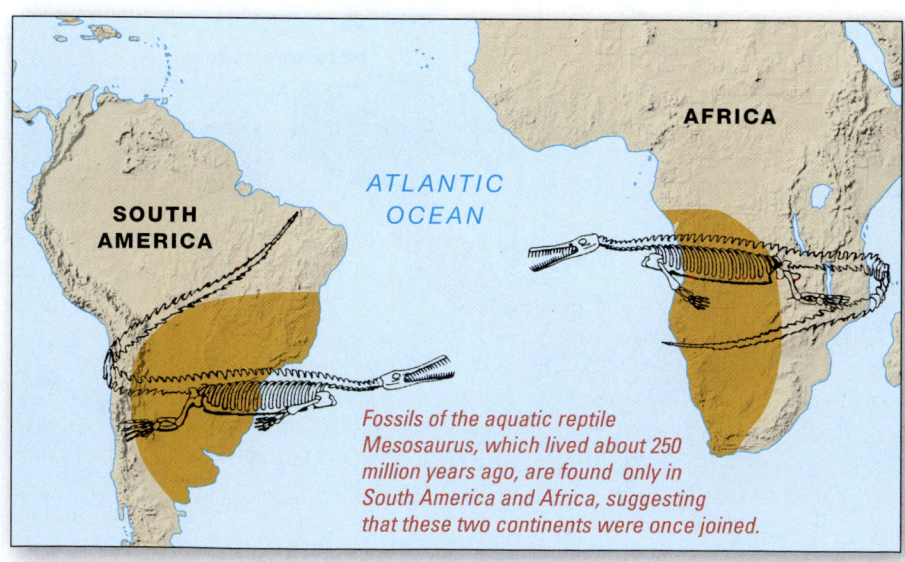

AFRICA

SOUTH AMERICA

ATLANTIC OCEAN

Fossils of the aquatic reptile Mesosaurus, which lived about 250 million years ago, are found only in South America and Africa, suggesting that these two continents were once joined.

▲Figure 11.19 **Fossil evidence for continental drift.**

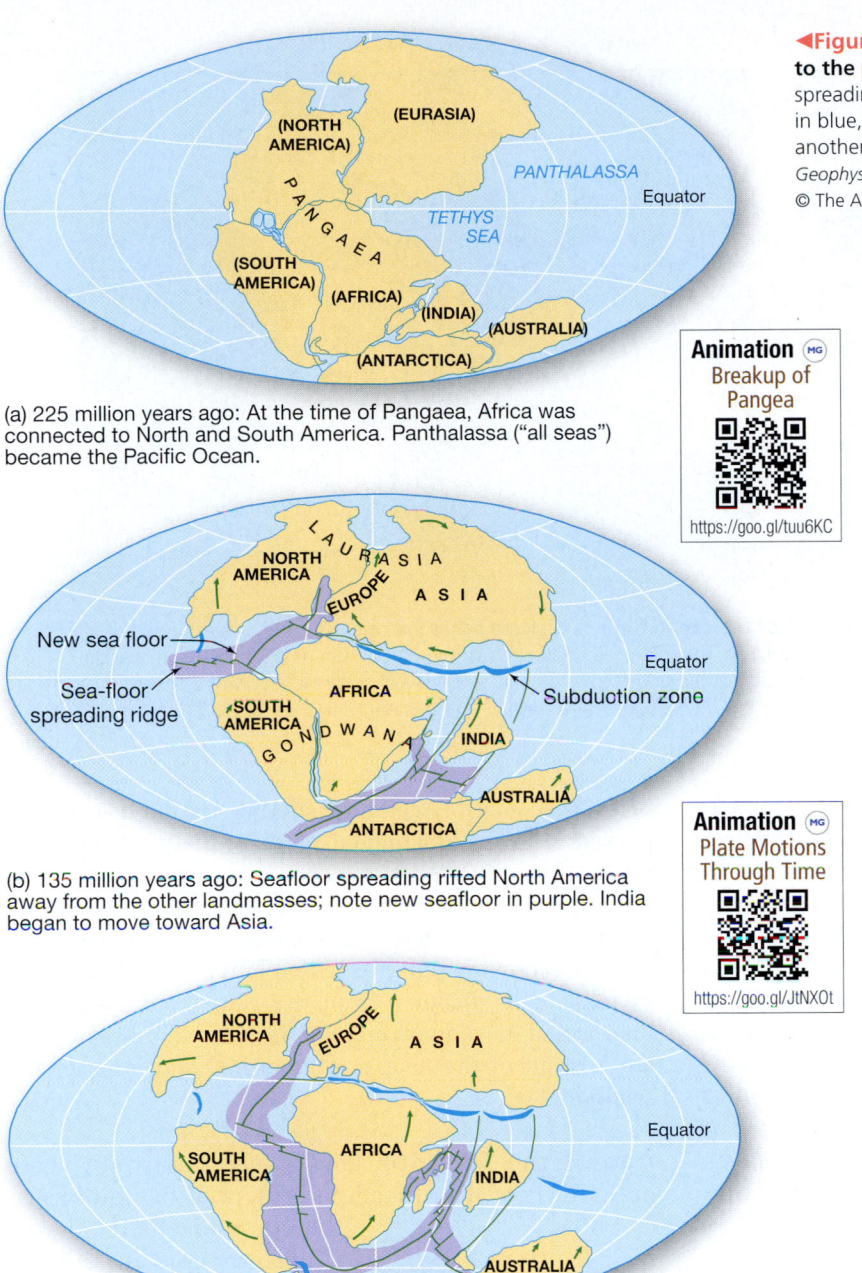

◄**Figure 11.20 Continents adrift, from 225 m.y.a. to the present.** New seafloor is in purple and seafloor spreading ridges are in green. Subduction zones, marked in blue, occur where plates collide and one dives beneath another. [(a) From R. S. Dietz and J. C. Holden, *Journal of Geophysical Research 75*, no. 26 (September 10, 1970): 4939–4956, © The American Geophysical Union.]

(a) 225 million years ago: At the time of Pangaea, Africa was connected to North and South America. Panthalassa ("all seas") became the Pacific Ocean.

Animation (MG)
Breakup of Pangea

https://goo.gl/tuu6KC

(b) 135 million years ago: Seafloor spreading rifted North America away from the other landmasses; note new seafloor in purple. India began to move toward Asia.

Animation (MG)
Plate Motions Through Time

https://goo.gl/JtNXOt

(c) 65 million years ago: Seafloor spreading rifted South America away from Africa. India continued drifting toward Asia.

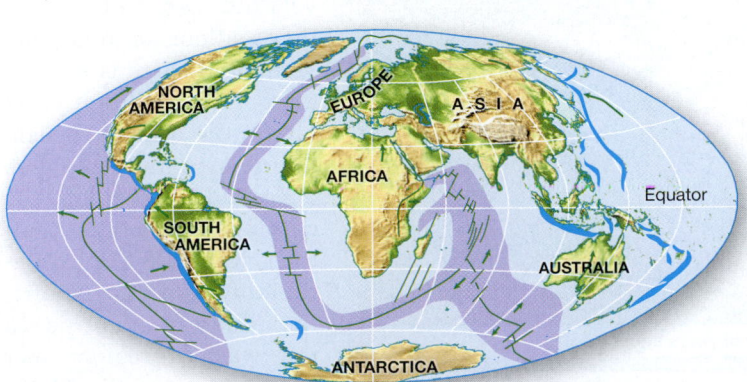

(d) Today: From 65 m.y.a. to the present, seafloor spreading renewed more than half the ocean floor. India subducted beneath Asia, forming the Himalayas.

that old seafloor sinks back into the Earth's mantle at deep-ocean trenches and in subduction zones where plates collide.

These hypotheses formed the basis for our current understanding of sea-floor spreading. However, scientists now think that the upward movement of material beneath an ocean ridge is a consequence of seafloor spreading rather than the cause. As the plates continue to move apart, more magma rises from below to fill the gaps, accumulating in magma chambers beneath the centerline of the ridge. Some of the magma rises and erupts through fractures and small volcanoes along the ridge, forming new oceanic crust. In the areas of ocean basins farthest from the mid-ocean ridges, the oldest sections of oceanic lithosphere are slowly plunging beneath continental lithosphere along Earth's deep-ocean trenches.

Magnetic Reversals Earlier we discussed the history of reversals in Earth's magnetic field. As rocks cool and solidify from molten material (lava) at Earth's surface, the small magnetic particles (usually iron) in the material align according to the orientation

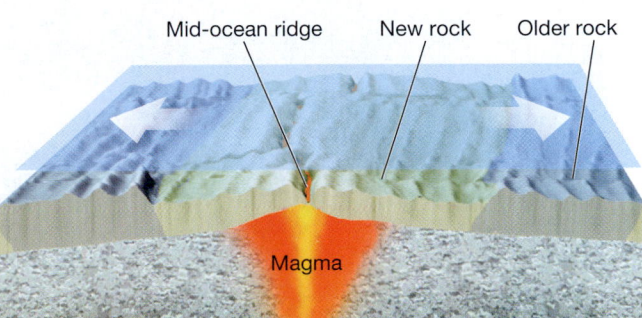

▲**Figure 11.21 Seafloor spreading.** Along Earth's underwater mid-ocean ridge system, upwelling magma emerges along the spreading center and cools to form new oceanic lithosphere.

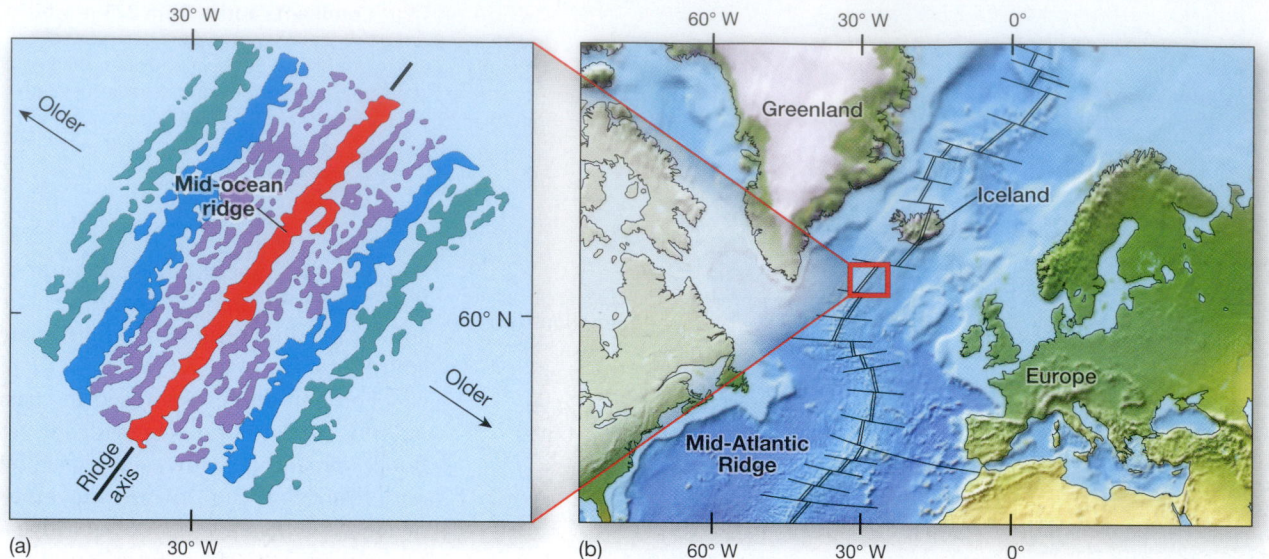

▲**Figure 11.22** **Magnetic reversals recorded in a portion of the ocean floor.** (a) Colored bands indicate magnetic stripes on the seafloor with reversed polarity, while the areas between have normal polarity. The mid-ocean ridge (red stripe) is a section of the Mid-Atlantic Ridge south of Iceland, located in (b). Similar colored bands on either side of the ridge indicate symmetrical seafloor spreading, with oldest rock bands farthest from the ridge. [Adapted from J. R. Heirtzler, S. Le Pichon, and J. G. Baron, *Deep-Sea Research 13*, © 1966, Pergamon Press, p. 247.]

of the magnetic poles at that time, and this alignment locks in place. Thus, rocks of the same age bear identical particle alignments, illustrating global patterns of changing magnetism. The average period of a magnetic reversal is about 500,000 years, with a range from as short as 20,000 years to as long as 50 million years.

As seafloor spreading occurs and magma emerges at the surface, magnetic particles in the lava orient with the magnetic field in force at the time it cools and hardens. The particles become locked in this alignment as part of the new seafloor, creating an ongoing magnetic record of Earth's polarity. Using isotopic dating methods, scientists have established the actual years in which the polarity

reversal occurred. Ages for materials on the ocean floor proved to be a fundamental piece of the plate tectonics puzzle.

Figure 11.22 shows a record from the Mid-Atlantic Ridge, illustrating the magnetic stripes preserved in the minerals showing polarity. The relative ages of the rocks increase with distance from the ridge, and the mirror images that develop on either side of the mid-ocean ridge are a result of the nearly symmetrical spreading of the seafloor.

Age of the Seafloor The youngest crust anywhere on Earth is at the spreading centers of the mid-ocean ridges, and with increasing distance from these centers, the crust gets steadily older (**Figure 11.23**). Compared to the 4.6-billion-year-old age of Earth, the seafloor is relatively young; nowhere is it more than 280 million years old. In the Atlantic Ocean, the oldest large-scale area of seafloor is along the continental margins, farthest from the Mid-Atlantic Ridge. In the Pacific, the oldest seafloor is in the western region near Japan. Parts of the Mediterranean Sea contain the oldest seafloor remnants,

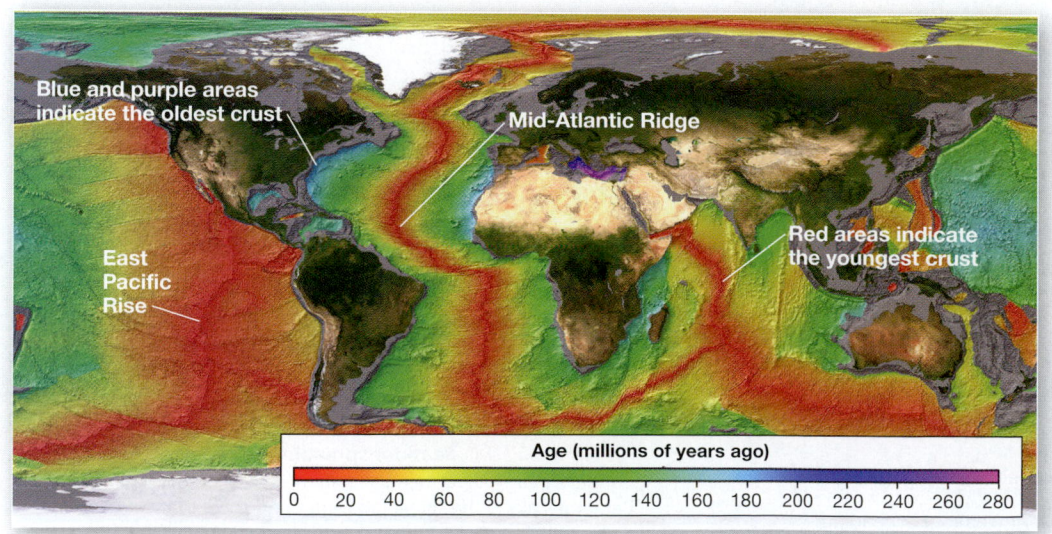

▲**Figure 11.23** **Relative ages of oceanic crust.** Reds and oranges indicate younger crust; purples and blues indicate older crust. [Image by Elliot Lim, CIRES.]

which may have been part of the Tethys Sea, which existed before the breakup of Pangaea (see Figure 11.20).

Subduction and Plate Motion

When lithospheric plates meet, and one descends beneath another and dives downward into the mantle, the process is called *subduction*, and the area is a **subduction zone**. As discussed earlier in the chapter, continental crust differs greatly from oceanic crust in composition, texture, and density, and the difference affects subduction. Continental crust is relatively low in density, averaging 2.7 g/cm³ (or 2700 kg/m³), and is composed mainly of *granite*, a crystalline intrusive igneous rock. Oceanic crust is denser than continental crust, averaging 3.0 g/cm³

(or 3000 kg/m³), and is composed of *basalt*, a fine-grained extrusive igneous rock. When continental crust and oceanic crust slowly collide, the denser ocean floor will dive beneath the lighter continental crust, thus forming a subduction zone (**Figure 11.24**).

The world's deep-ocean trenches coincide with these subduction zones and are the lowest features on Earth's surface. The Mariana Trench near Guam is the deepest, descending below sea level to −11,030 m (−36,198 ft). For comparison, in the Atlantic Ocean, the Puerto Rico Trench drops to −8605 m (−28,224 ft), and in the Indian Ocean, the Java Trench drops to −7125 m (−23,376 ft).

Plate motion results in part from mantle convection, mentioned earlier, in which heated material rises from deep within Earth's mantle and cooler material nearer the surface sinks to replace it. Subduction and seafloor spreading also drive plate motion through the processes of ridge push and slab pull. *Ridge push* occurs as upwelling magma forms elevated mid-ocean ridges and gravity pushes material downhill, away from the spreading center. *Slab pull* occurs as the diverging plate cools, increases in density, and sinks, exerting a gravitational pull on the rest of the plate. The subducted portion travels down into the asthenosphere, where it remelts and eventually is recycled as magma, rising again toward the surface through deep fissures and cracks in crustal rock. Rising plumes of magma form volcanic mountains inland of these subduction zones; examples are the Andes in South America and the Cascade Range running from northern California to the Canadian border.

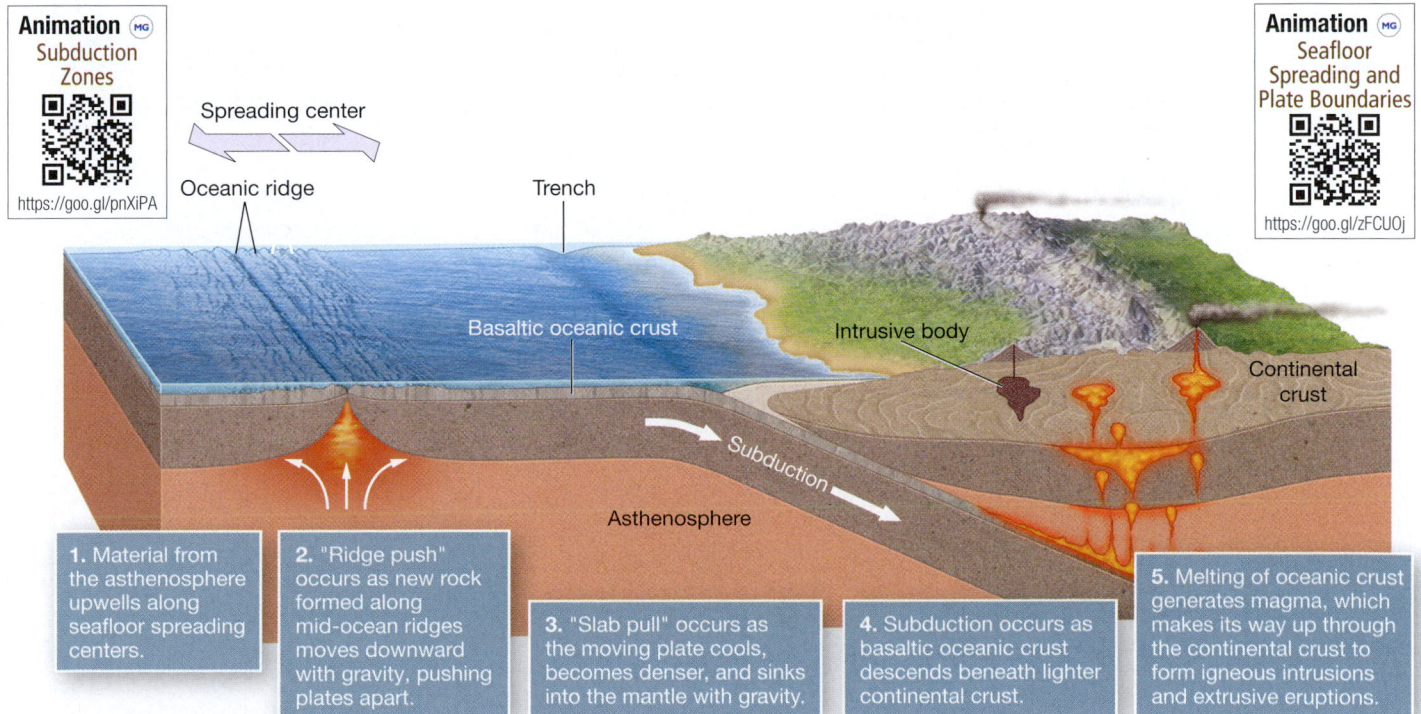

▲Figure 11.24 **Subduction and mechanisms of plate motion.** Upwelling magma, seafloor spreading, and subduction, shown in cross section. Arrows indicate the direction of plate movement.

Plate Boundaries

Earth's present crust is divided into at least 14 plates, of which about half are major and half are minor in terms of area (**Figure 11.25**). Hundreds of smaller pieces and perhaps dozens of microplates migrating together make up these broad, moving plates.

The boundaries where plates meet are dynamic places when considered over geologic time scales, although they are slow moving within human time frames. The block diagrams in Figure 11.25 show the three general types of boundaries and the interacting movements of plates at those locations.

- *Convergent boundaries* occur in areas of crustal collision and subduction. As discussed earlier, where areas of continental and oceanic lithosphere meet, crust is compressed and lost through subduction as it moves downward into the mantle. Convergent boundaries form subduction zones, such as off the west coast of South and Central America, along the Aleutian Island trenches, and along the east coast of Japan. Convergent boundaries also occur where plates of continental crust collide, such as the collision zone between India and Asia, and where oceanic plates collide, such as along the deep trenches in the western Pacific Ocean.

- *Divergent boundaries* occur in areas of seafloor spreading, where lithospheric plates spread apart and upwelling material from the mantle forms new seafloor. An example is the divergent boundary along the East Pacific Rise, which gives birth to the Nazca

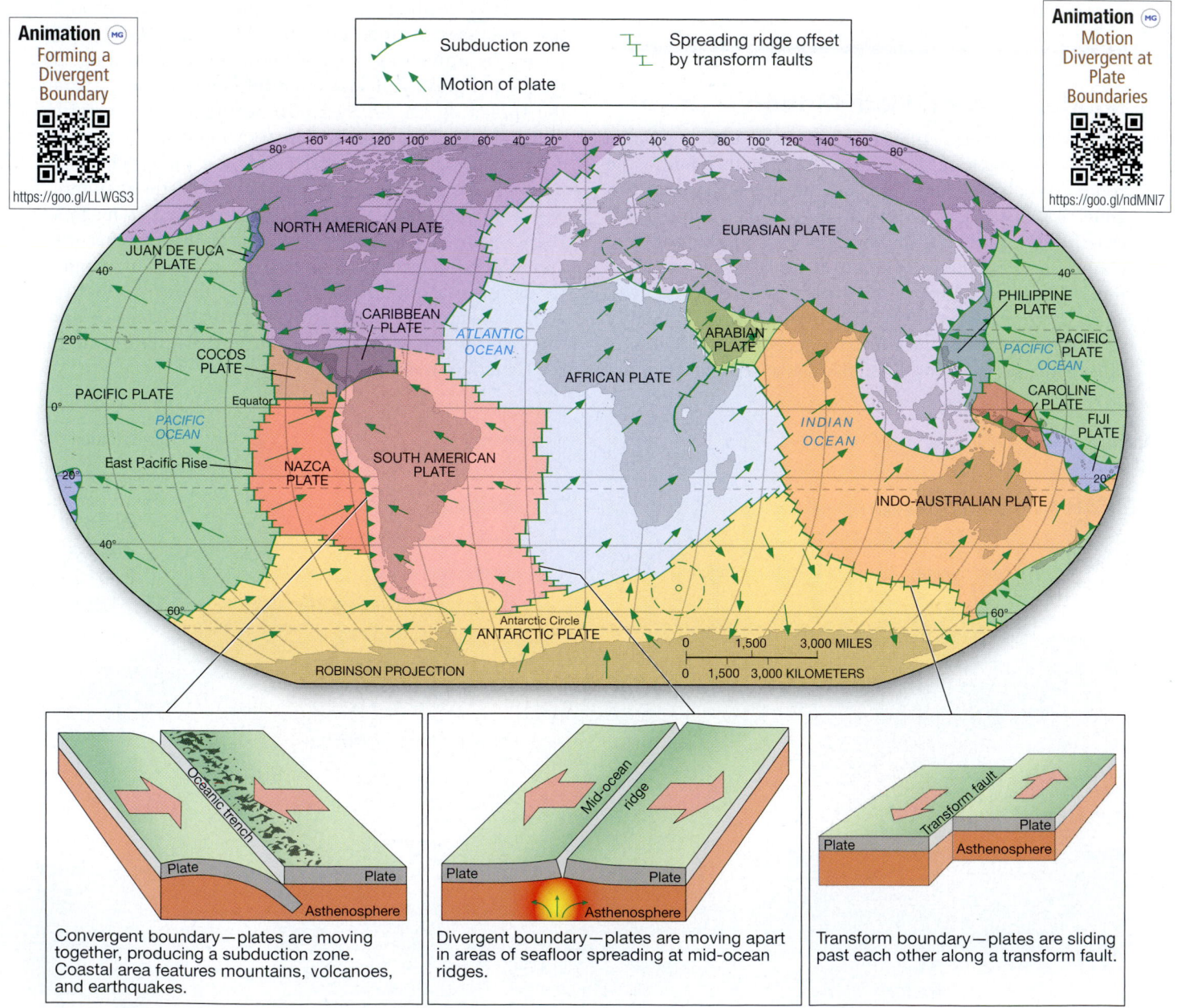

▲**Figure 11.25 Earth's major lithospheric plates and their movements.** Arrows indicate the direction of present plate movement; arrow length suggests the relative rate of movement during the past 20 million years. For example, longer arrows indicate that the Pacific and Nazca plates are moving more rapidly than the Atlantic plates. [Adapted from U.S. Geodynamics Committee, National Academy of Sciences and National Academy of Engineering.]

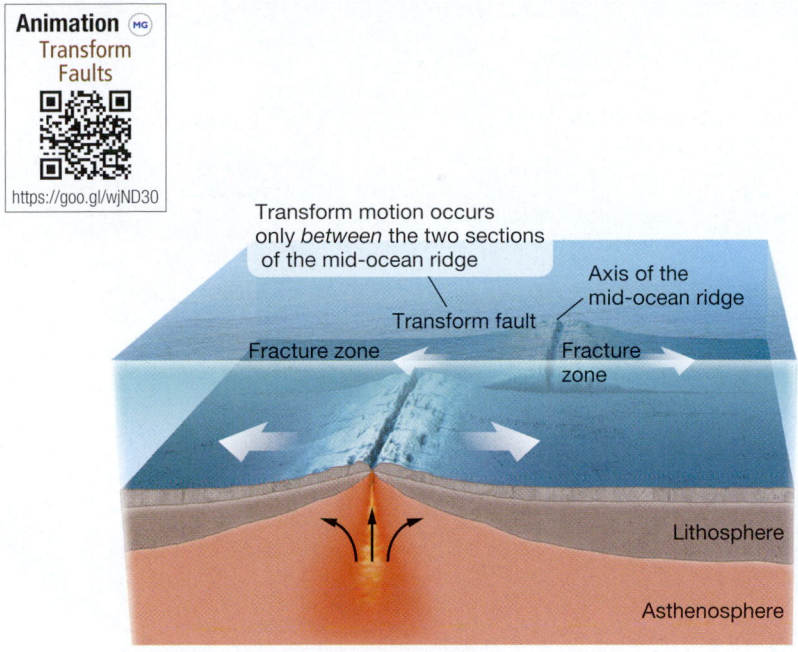

Transform motion occurs only *between* the two sections of the mid-ocean ridge

Axis of the mid-ocean ridge

Transform fault

Fracture zone

Fracture zone

Lithosphere

Asthenosphere

(a) Transform faults and fracture zones.

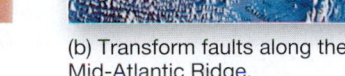

Greenland Iceland

Eurasian plate

Mid-Atlantic ridge

North American plate

Transform faults

Inactive fracture zones

(b) Transform faults along the Mid-Atlantic Ridge.

▲**Figure 11.26 Transform faults and fracture zones.** Along mid-ocean ridges at transform plate boundaries, spreading plates form a fracture zone that includes a transform fault. At a transform fault, plates move past each other in the opposite direction. Along the fracture zone outside of the active fault, plates move in the same direction [(b) Office of Naval Research].

plate (moving eastward) and the Pacific plate (moving northwestward). Whereas most divergent boundaries occur at mid-ocean ridges, a few occur within continents themselves. An example is the Great Rift Valley of East Africa, where continental crust is rifting apart.

- *Transform boundaries* occur where plates slide past one another, usually at right angles to a seafloor spreading center. These are the fractures stretching across the mid-ocean ridge system worldwide, first described in 1965 by University of Toronto geophysicist Tuzo Wilson. As plates move past each other horizontally, they form a type of *fault*, or fracture, in Earth's crust—a *transform fault*.

Along these fracture zones that intersect ridges, a transform fault occurs only along the fault section that lies *between* two segments of the fragmented mid-ocean ridge (**Figure 11.26**). Along the fracture zone outside of the transform fault, the crust moves in the same direction (away from the mid-ocean ridge) as the spreading plates. The movement along transform faults is that of horizontal displacement—no new crust is formed or old crust subducted.

These features are *transform* because of the apparent transformation in the direction of fault movement—these faults can be distinguished from other horizontal faults (discussed in Chapter 12) because the movement along one side of the fault line is opposite to the movement along the other side. This unique movement results from the creation of new material as the seafloor spreads.

All the seafloor spreading centers on Earth feature these fractures, which are perpendicular to the mid-ocean ridges. Some are a few hundred kilometers long; others, such as those along the East Pacific Rise (shown in Figure 11.25), stretch out 1000 km or more (over 600 mi).

Transform boundaries are associated with earthquake activity, especially where they cut across portions of continental crust, such as along the San Andreas fault in California, where the Pacific and North American plates meet, and along the Alpine fault in New Zealand, the boundary between the Indo-Australian and Pacific plates. The San Andreas, running through several metropolitan areas of California, is perhaps the most famous transform fault in the world (see the discussion in Chapter 12).

GEOreport 11.1 Spreading along the East Pacific Rise

The fastest rate of seafloor spreading on Earth occurs along the East Pacific Rise, which runs roughly north–south along the eastern edge of the Pacific plate from near Antarctica to North America (see Figure 11.25). Spreading is occurring at a rate of 6 to 16 cm/yr (2.4 to 6.3 in./yr), depending on location. For perspective, human fingernails grow at a rate of about 4 cm/yr (1.6 in./yr).

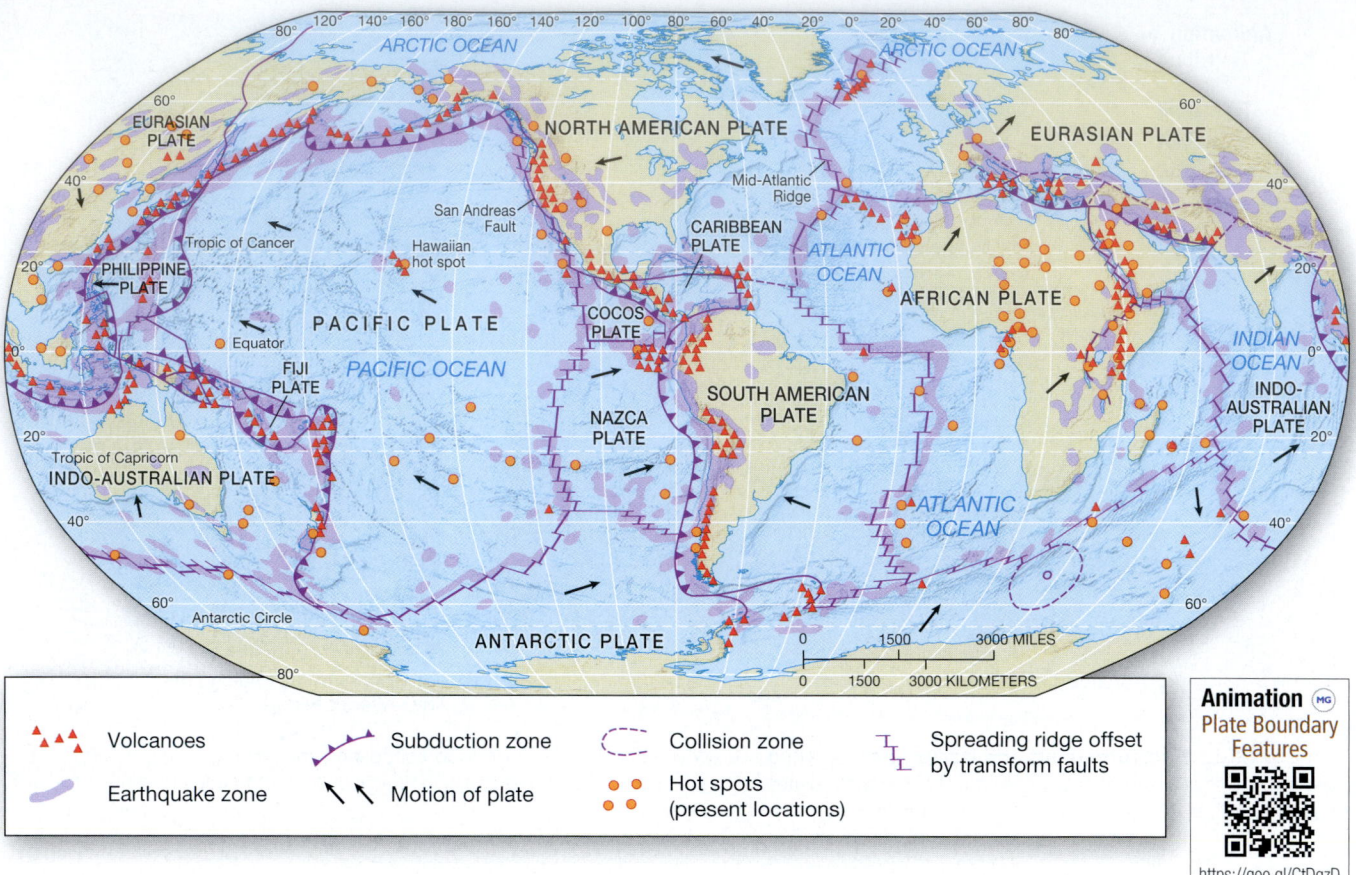

▲**Figure 11.27** **Locations of earthquake and volcanic activity in relation to major tectonic plate boundaries and principal hot spots.** [Earthquake, volcano, and hot-spot data adapted from U.S. Geological Survey.]

Earthquake and Volcanic Activity

Plate boundaries are the primary locations of earthquake and volcanic activity, and the correlation of these phenomena is an important aspect of plate tectonics (**Figure 11.27**). The area surrounding the Pacific Ocean basin, known as the Pacific Rim, is often referred to as the *circum-Pacific belt* or, more popularly, the **Pacific Ring of Fire**, named for the frequent incidence of volcanoes along its margin. The features that form this "ring" are caused by the subducting edge of the Pacific plate as it thrusts deep into the crust and mantle and produces molten material that makes its way back toward the surface. The upwelling magma forms active volcanoes along the Pacific Rim. Such processes occur at similar subduction zones throughout the world. Chapter 12 discusses earthquakes and volcanic activity in more detail.

Hot Spots

As mentioned, volcanic activity is often associated with plate boundaries. However, scientists have found an estimated 50 to 100 active sites of upwelling material that exist independent of plate boundaries. Plumes of magma rise from the mantle at these locations, producing **hot spots** (or hot-spot volcanoes) of volcanic activity and crustal uplift at the surface.

Hot spots occur beneath both oceanic and continental crust. Some hot spots are anchored deep in the lower mantle, tending to remain fixed relative to migrating plates; others appear to be above plumes that move by themselves or shift with plate motion. In the case of a fixed hot spot, the area of a plate that passes above it is locally heated for the brief geologic time it remains above that spot (a few hundred thousand or million years), sometimes producing a hot-spot island chain of volcanic features.

Hot-Spot Island Chains A hot spot in the Pacific Ocean produced, and continues to form, the Hawaiian–Emperor Islands chain, including numerous *seamounts*, submarine mountains that do not reach the surface (**Figure 11.28**). The Pacific plate moved across this hot, upward-erupting plume over the last 80 million years, creating a string of volcanic islands and seamounts with ages increasing northwestward away from the hot spot. The oldest island in the Hawaiian part of the chain is Kaua'i, approximately 5 million years old; today, it is weathered and eroded into deep canyons and valleys.

To the northwest of Hawai'i, the Midway Islands rise as a part of the same system. From there, the Emperor seamounts spread northwestward and are progressively older until they reach about 40 million years in age. At that point, this linear island chain shifts direction northward. This bend in the chain results from a change in the movement of the Pacific plate combined with the slow movement of the hot spot itself, a revision of past thinking that all hot-spot mantle plumes remain

Animation (MG)
Hot-Spot
Volcano Tracks

https://goo.gl/sOHRDv

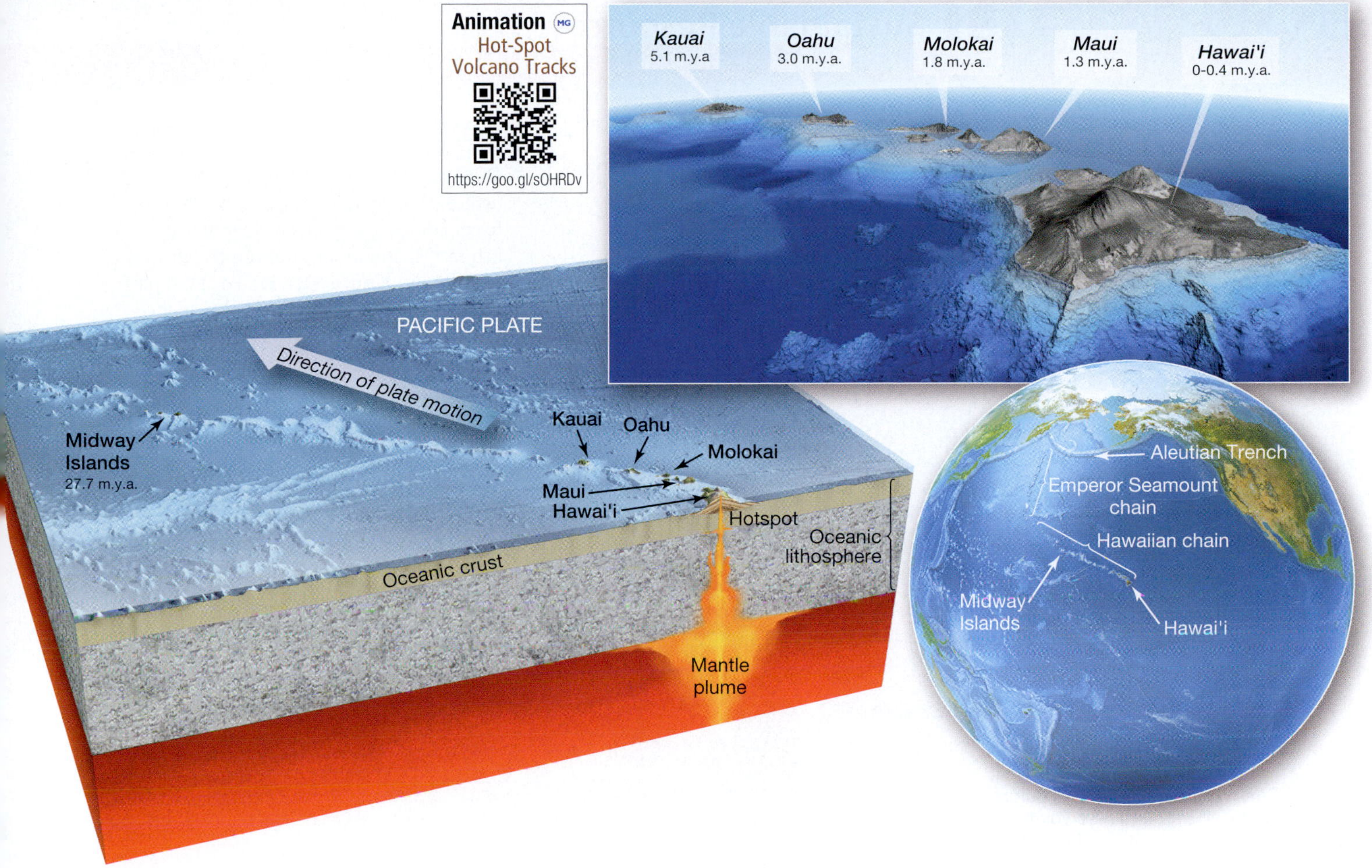

Kauai
5.1 m.y.a

Oahu
3.0 m.y.a.

Molokai
1.8 m.y.a.

Maui
1.3 m.y.a.

Hawai'i
0–0.4 m.y.a.

PACIFIC PLATE

Direction of plate motion

Midway
Islands
27.7 m.y.a.

Kauai Oahu

Molokai

Maui
Hawai'i

Hotspot

Oceanic crust

Oceanic
lithosphere

Mantle
plume

Aleutian Trench

Emperor Seamount
chain

Hawaiian chain

Midway
Islands

Hawai'i

▲Figure 11.28 **Island and seamount chain formed by a hot-spot magma plume.** The Hawaiian Islands–Emperor Seamount chain in the north Pacific Ocean extends from the Big Island of Hawai'i to the Aleutian Trench off Alaska. This series of volcanic islands and seamounts are progressively younger toward the southeast, reflecting the movement of the Pacific plate over the Hawaiian hot spot. The Midway Islands are 27.7 million years old, meaning that the islands were over the plume 27.7 m.y.a., as determined by radiometric dating.

fixed relative to the migrating plate. At the northernmost extreme, the seamounts that formed about 80 m.y.a. are now approaching the Aleutian Trench, where they eventually will be subducted beneath the Eurasian plate. At the southernmost extreme lies the new addition to the Hawaiian chain, Lo'ihi, which is still a seamount 975 m (3200 ft) beneath the ocean surface.

The big island of Hawai'i, the youngest in the island chain, actually took less than 1 million years to build to its present stature. The island is a huge mound of lava, formed from magma from several seafloor fissures and volcanoes. The island's total height, from the seafloor to the top of its highest peak, Mauna Kea, is almost 10,000 m (32,800 ft), making it the highest mountain on Earth if measured from the ocean floor.

WORK**IT**OUT 11.3
The Hawaiian Hot Spot

Based on Figure 11.28, answer these questions regarding the islands and seamounts of the Hawaiian–Emperor chain.

1. What causes the sharp bend where the Hawaiian chain meets the Emperor Seamount chain?
2. Approximately how many years ago were the Midway Islands located over the mantle plume?
3. Which of the five main Hawaiian Islands was first located at the Hawaiian hot spot? Which island is closest to the hot spot today?
4. Why is the island of Kaua'i more weathered and eroded than the Big Island of Hawai'i?

GEOreport 11.2   The largest volcano on Earth

In 2013, scientists confirmed that the Tamu Massif, located in the Pacific Ocean about 1600 km (1000 mi) east of Japan, is the largest volcano on Earth and one of the biggest in the solar system. Part of the Shatsky Rise, a massive undersea volcanic plateau similar in size to California, the Tamu Massif covers an area far larger than Mauna Kea on Hawai'i. This feature formed some 145 m.y.a. above a hot spot that coincides with the boundaries of three tectonic plates.

FOCUSstudy 11.1　Sustainable Resources
Heat from Earth—Geothermal Energy

At almost any location on Earth, the nearly consistent ground temperatures just a few feet below Earth's surface can provide heating and cooling for buildings using ground-source pumps for air circulation. However, in areas with naturally occurring geothermal activity along plate boundaries or near hot-spot magma plumes, Earth's interior generates a tremendous amount of heat, and this geothermal energy can be harnessed for heating and power production.

Direct Geothermal Heating

The process of pumping hot water at varying depths and temperatures from underground reservoirs to the surface is *direct geothermal heating*. This technology uses water at moderate temperatures (20°C to 150°C, or 68°F to 302°F) in heat-exchange systems that provide heat for buildings, commercial greenhouses, fish farms, and other locations (**Figure 11.1.1a** and **Figure 11.1.1b**). For example, the state capitol building in Boise, Idaho, located near the Yellowstone hot-spot

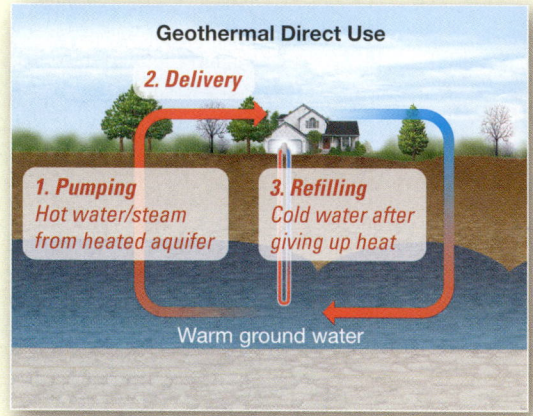

(a) Direct geothermal heating pumps hot water from an underground reservoir to the surface and later returns used water to the aquifer.

(b) A greenhouse uses direct geothermal heating at Chena Hot Springs Resort near Fairbanks, Alaska.

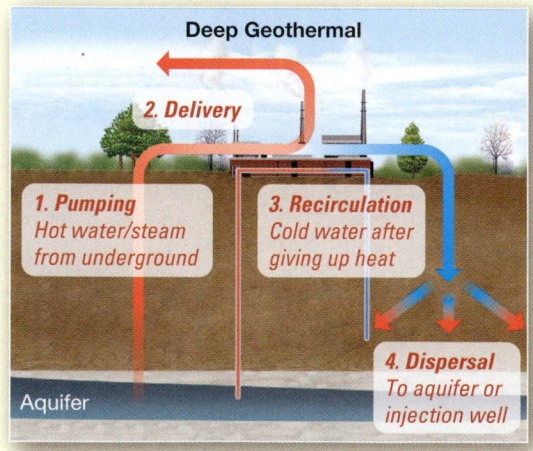

(c) Geothermal power requires water at high temperature to drive turbines that generate electricity.

(d) Svartsengi geothermal power plant on the Reykjavík Peninsula, Iceland, produces electricity and provides hot water for homes and businesses. Nearby is the Blue Lagoon Spa, filled with warm geothermal waters.

▲**Figure 11.1.1 Geothermal technologies for direct heating and power production.** [(a) and (c) based on EPA. (b) Design Pics Inc./Alamy. (d) Eco Images/Universal Images Group/Getty Images.]

Hot-Spot Hydrothermal Features Hot spots may evidence hydrothermal features related to the heating of groundwater within the crust. Some of these sites produce enough heat from Earth's interior, or **geothermal energy**, to be developed for human uses, as discussed in Focus Study 11.1.

Iceland, another island formed by an active hot spot, this one sitting along a mid-ocean ridge, produces more geothermal power for human use than any other country on Earth. It is an excellent example of a segment of mid-ocean ridge rising above sea level. This hot spot continues to generate eruptions from deep in track, uses direct geothermal heating and returns the used water to underground wells. In Reykjavík, Iceland, a volcanically active island located on the Mid-Atlantic Ridge, more than 85% of space heating systems are geothermal. Overall, these systems are inexpensive and provide clean energy.

Geothermal Power Production

Power plants produce *geothermal electricity* using hot water and steam from a natural underground reservoir to drive a turbine that powers a generator (**Figure 11.1.1c**). Groundwater for this purpose ideally has a temperature of from 180°C to 350°C (355°F to 600°F) and flows through rock of high porosity and permeability, allowing the water to move freely through connecting pore spaces. The Geysers Geothermal Field in northern California (so named despite the absence of any geysers in the area) is the largest geothermal power production plant using this method in the world. Because the steam comes directly from Earth's interior

(with no burning of fuel to produce it), geothermal electricity is a relatively clean energy.

In the United States, geothermal power production is increasing, with stations operating in the numerous Western states, Alaska, and Hawai'i. In Iceland, the world authority on geothermal use, geothermal energy accounts for 25% of total electrical production (**Figure 11.1.1d**).

The newest geothermal technology seeks to create conditions for power production at locations where underground rock temperatures are high, but where water or permeability is lacking. In an *enhanced geothermal system* (EGS), cold water is pumped underground into hot rock, causing the rock to fracture and become permeable to water flow; the cold water, in turn, is heated to steam as it flows through the high-temperature rock. The potential for EGS, as with other geothermal technologies, is highest in the U.S. West and in areas of the world along active plate boundaries **(Figure 11.1.2)**. In 2013, the Nevada Desert Peak station became the first U.S. enhanced

geothermal facility to supply electricity to the power grid.

Geothermal as a Resource

Geothermal power production has many advantages, including only minimal production of carbon dioxide. Geothermal power can be produced 24 hours a day, an advantage when compared with solar or wind energy, in which the timing of production is linked to daylight or other natural variations in the resource.

Although geothermal is billed as renewable and self-sustaining, research shows that some geothermal fields are being depleted as the extraction rate exceeds the rate of recharge. In addition, the drilling of wells and the injection or removal of water in connection with geothermal energy projects can produce seismic activity in the form of minor earthquakes. Research is ongoing to address and mitigate the seismicity issues. If these problems are solved, geothermal is a promising source of clean energy for the future.

1. In terms of plate tectonics, what regions of Earth are most likely to have geothermal energy resources?

2. What are the characteristics and applications of direct, deep, and enhanced geothermal systems?

APPLYconcepts *Part 1:* List advantages and disadvantages of geothermal energy.

Advantages	Disadvantages
a. _____	a. _____
b. _____	_____
c. _____	b. _____
d. _____	_____

Part 2: Is geothermal energy a renewable or nonrenewable resource? Explain.

_____
_____

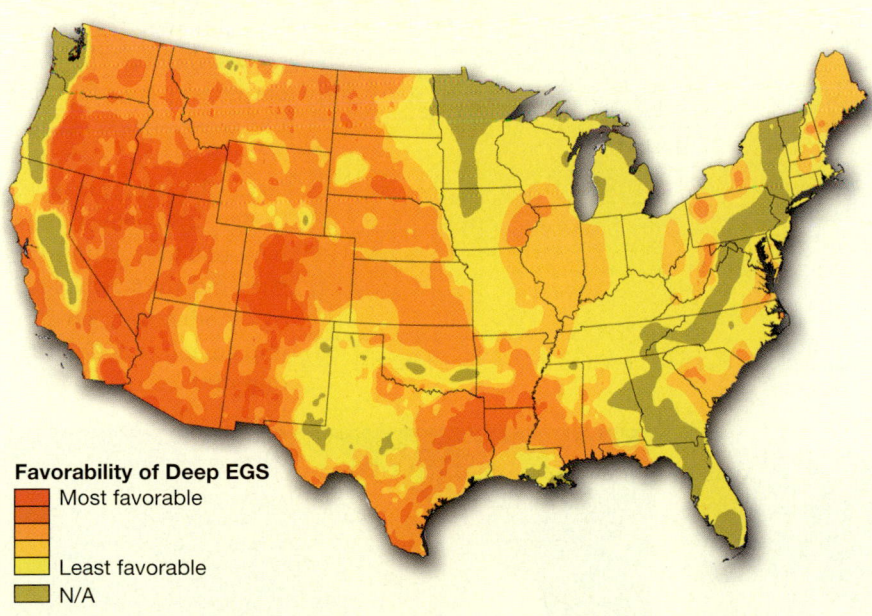

Favorability of Deep EGS
- Most favorable
- Least favorable
- N/A

▲**Figure 11.1.2 Potential for development of enhanced geothermal systems.** Favorability ranges from red (most favorable) to yellow (least favorable). [Source: NREL.]

the mantle so that Iceland is still growing in area and volume.

Yellowstone National Park in Montana and Wyoming is another region known for geothermal energy and hydrothermal features. A hot spot that is today below Yellowstone

was the source for isolated areas of volcanism in Oregon, Nevada, Idaho, and Wyoming. As the North American plate moved westward over the mantle plume, hot-spot volcanism occurred from southwest Oregon to northwest Wyoming along a path parallel to plate movement (**Figure 11.29a**).

Recent and ongoing volcanic activity around Yellowstone produces several types of hydrothermal features, including hot springs, geysers, mud pots, and fumaroles. Pockets of magma and other hot portions of the crust heat groundwater, which may emerge as a hot spring or erupt explosively from the ground as a *geyser*—a spring characterized by intermittent discharge of water and steam (**Figure 11.29b** and **11.29c**). Mud pots are bubbling pools that are highly acidic with limited water supply, and thus produce mainly gases. Microorganisms break down the gases to release sulfuric acid, which in turn breaks down rock into clays that form mud. As gases escape through the mud, they produce the bubbling action that makes these features distinct. Fumaroles are steam vents that emit gases that may contain sulfur dioxide, hydrogen chloride, or hydrogen sulfide—some areas of Yellowstone are known for the characteristic odor of "rotten eggs" caused by hydrogen sulfide gas.

The Geologic Cycle

Earth's crust is in an ongoing state of change, being formed, deformed, moved, and broken down by physical and chemical processes. While the planet's endogenic (internal) system is at work building landforms, the exogenic (external) system is busily wearing them down. This vast give-and-take at the Earth–atmosphere–ocean interface is summarized in the **geologic cycle**. It is fueled from two sources—Earth's internal heat and solar energy from space—while being influenced by the ever-present leveling force of gravity (see Geosystems in Action 11, pp. 344–345).

The geologic cycle is itself composed of three principal cycles—the hydrologic cycle, summarized in Chapter 8, and the rock and tectonic cycles covered in this chapter. The hydrologic cycle works on Earth's surface through the exogenic processes of weathering, erosion, and deposition driven by the energy–atmosphere and water–weather systems and represented by the physical action of water, ice, and wind. The rock cycle produces the three basic rock types found in the crust—igneous, metamorphic, and sedimentary. The tectonic cycle brings heat energy and new material to the surface and then recycles it by subduction, creating movement and deformation of the crust.

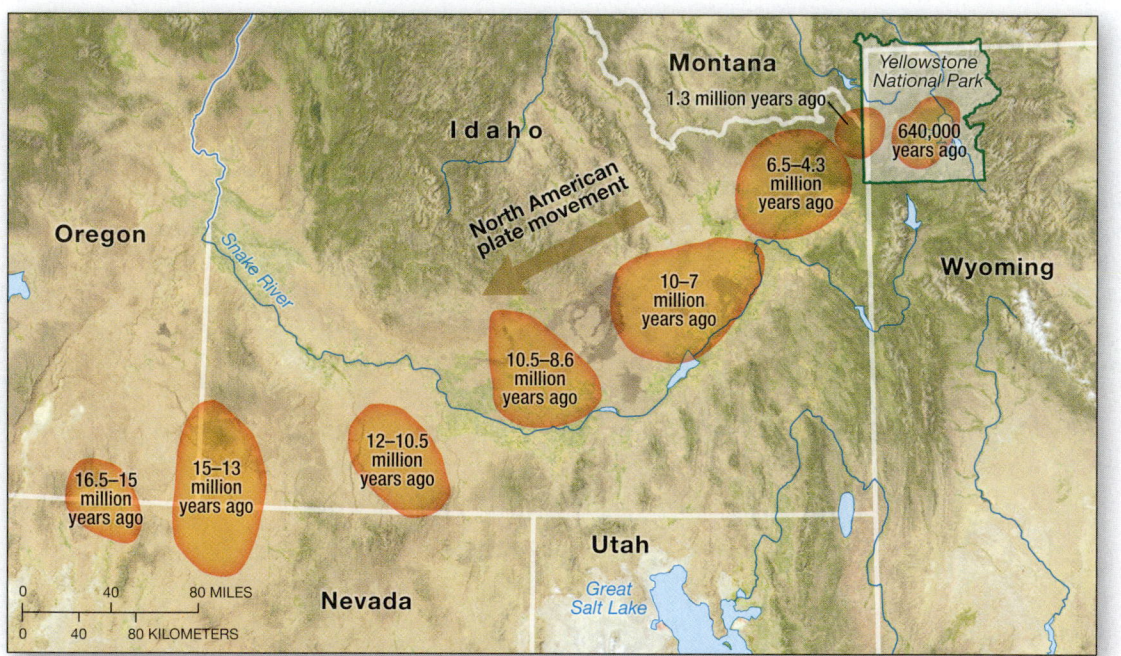

(a) Volcanic activity above the stationary hot spot magma plume that now underlies Yellowstone National Park began about 16 million years ago in southwest Oregon.

(b) Yellowstone is known for its hydrothermal features. Grand Prismatic Spring is the largest U.S. hot spring, and the third largest in the world. Masses of microbes living around the edges of the mineral-rich water produce the vivid colors. The deep blue at the center results from scattering of blue light by particles in the water.

(c) Old Faithful geyser, named for its predictability, erupts every 35 to 210 minutes, shooting boiling water to heights of 32 to 56 m (106 to 185 ft) and lasting for 1.5 to 5 minutes.

▲Figure 11.29 **Yellowstone hot-spot track and hydrothermal features.** [(a) Source: National Park Service. (b) Oscity/Shutterstock. (c) Lee Prince/Shutterstock.]

EARTH'S INTERNAL PROCESSES IMPACT HUMANS

- Endogenic processes cause natural hazards such as earthquakes and volcanic events that affect humans and ecosystems.
- Rocks provide resources for human use.
- Geothermal power may be a promising clean energy resource.

HUMANS IMPACT EARTH'S INTERNAL PROCESSES

- Wells drilled into Earth's crust in association with oil and gas drilling and enhanced geothermal systems may cause earthquakes.

11a

Visited by more than 3 million people annually, Mount Rushmore is carved into an 18-meter (60-foot) face of a granite batholith in the Black Hills of South Dakota. Depicted in the sculpture are U.S. presidents Washington, Jefferson, Roosevelt, and Lincoln. [Jesse Kraft/Alamy.]

11b

The White Cliffs of Dover lie along the south England coastline on the Strait of Dover, the narrowest part of the English Channel. The cliff material is fine-grained white chalk, the remains of algae whose calcium carbonate skeletons sank to the bottom of a shallow sea during the Cretaceous period about 70 million years ago. The cliffs are easily seen from France on a clear day. [Irlmeier/Blickwinkel/Alamy.]

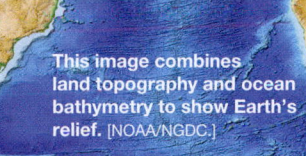

This image combines land topography and ocean bathymetry to show Earth's relief. [NOAA/NGDC.]

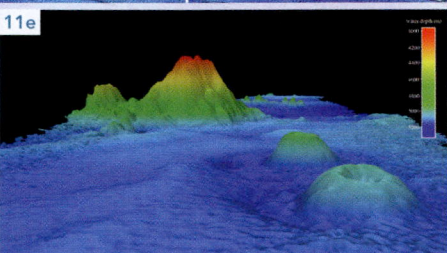

11e

This three-dimensional view of the Pacific Ocean floor shows two volcanoes (foreground) and a seamount discovered in 2014 (background). Occurring along plate boundaries and above hot spots, seamounts are habitat for diverse communities of marine life (crabs, sponges, anemones), commercially important fish, and deep-sea corals. [James V. Gardner, University of New Hampshire.]

11d

The granite of the Trango Tower region in the Karakorum Range, Pakistan, is a premier destination for big wall climbers. Near the eastern end of the Himalayas, Kangchen-junga in Nepal is the world's tallest granite mountain at 8586 m (28,169 ft) elevation and the third highest overall. (Mount Everest, the world's tallest mountain, is composed of limestone.) [Bill Hatcher/National Geographic/Getty.]

11c

Built between 1631 and 1648, the Taj Mahal in Agra, India, is a mausoleum of pure white marble universally admired as a masterpiece of Muslim heritage. The metamorphic marble was transported 400 km (250 mi) from the mines of Makrana, Rajasthan, the only marble deposit in India. [aravind chandramohanahan/Alamy.]

ISSUES FOR THE 21ST CENTURY

- Human will deplete some rock and mineral resources with ongoing population growth and lifestyle demands.
- Geothermal capacity will continue to be explored as an alternative energy source to fossil fuels.

QUESTIONS TO CONSIDER

1. What characteristic makes granite suitable for an enduring monument such as Mount Rushmore (11a) and for rock climbing (11d)? (*Hint:* Refer to Table 11.1.)

2. Based on the description of how the White Cliffs of Dover (11b) formed, how would you classify chalk as a sedimentary rock? Explain.

The geologic cycle is a model made up of the hydrologic, rock, and tectonic cycles (GIA 11.1). Earth's exogenic (external) and endogenic (internal) systems, driven by solar energy and Earth's internal heat, interact within the geologic cycle (GIA 11.2). The processes of the geologic cycle create distinctive landscapes (GIA 11.3).

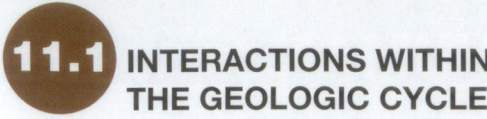

11.1 INTERACTIONS WITHIN THE GEOLOGIC CYCLE

The cycles that make up the geologic cycle influence each other. For example, over millions of years, the tectonic cycle slowly leads to the building of mountains, which affects global precipitation patterns, one aspect of the hydrologic cycle.

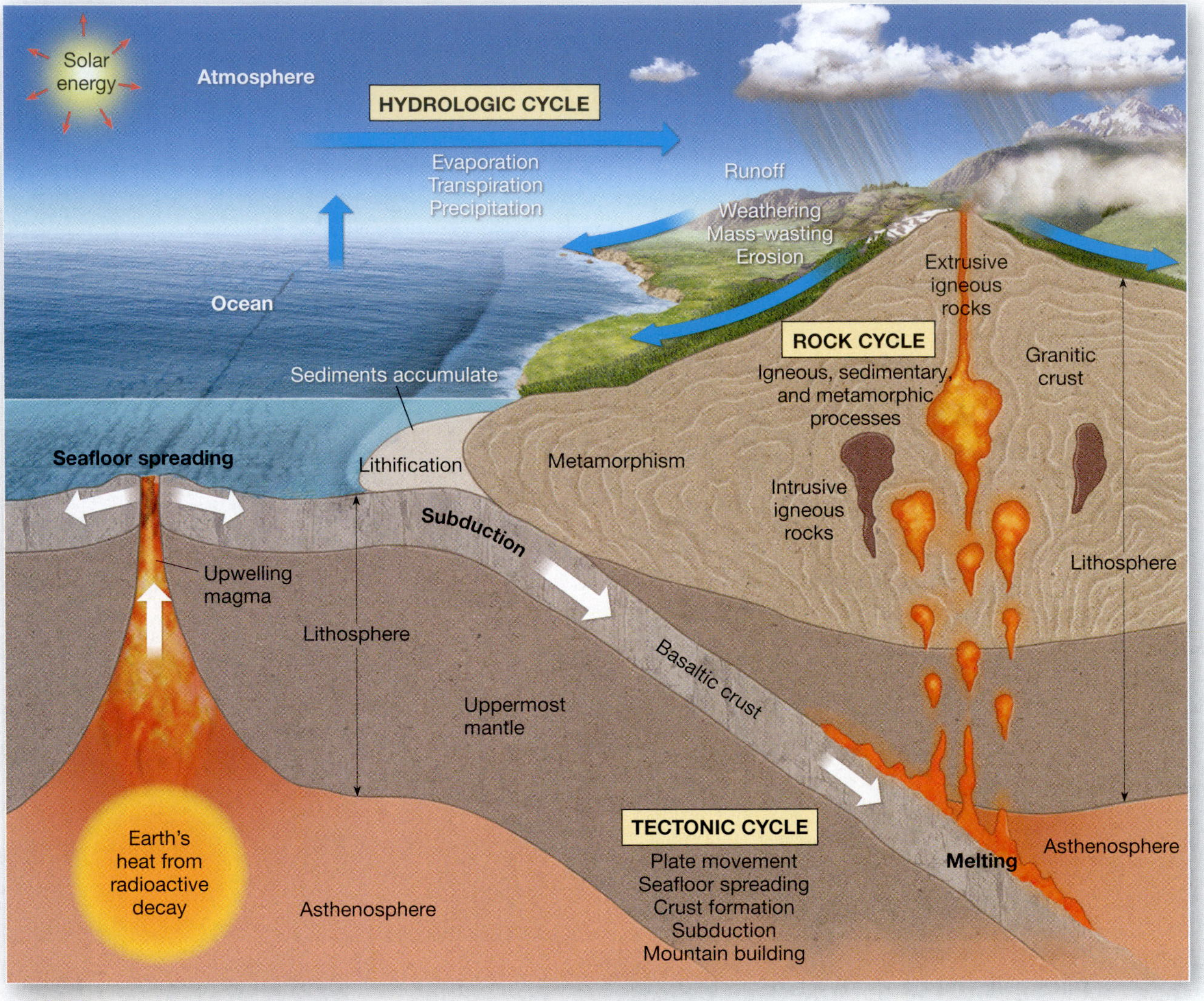

Solar energy

Atmosphere

HYDROLOGIC CYCLE

Evaporation
Transpiration
Precipitation

Runoff

Weathering
Mass-wasting
Erosion

Ocean

Extrusive igneous rocks

ROCK CYCLE

Igneous, sedimentary, and metamorphic processes

Granitic crust

Sediments accumulate

Lithification

Metamorphism

Intrusive igneous rocks

Seafloor spreading

Subduction

Lithosphere

Upwelling magma

Lithosphere

Basaltic crust

Uppermost mantle

Earth's heat from radioactive decay

Asthenosphere

TECTONIC CYCLE

Plate movement
Seafloor spreading
Crust formation
Subduction
Mountain building

Melting

Asthenosphere

11.2 ROLE OF EXOGENIC AND ENDOGENIC SYSTEMS

Exogenic processes drive the hydrologic cycle; both endogenic and exogenic processes contribute to the rock cycle; and endogenic processes drive the tectonic cycle.

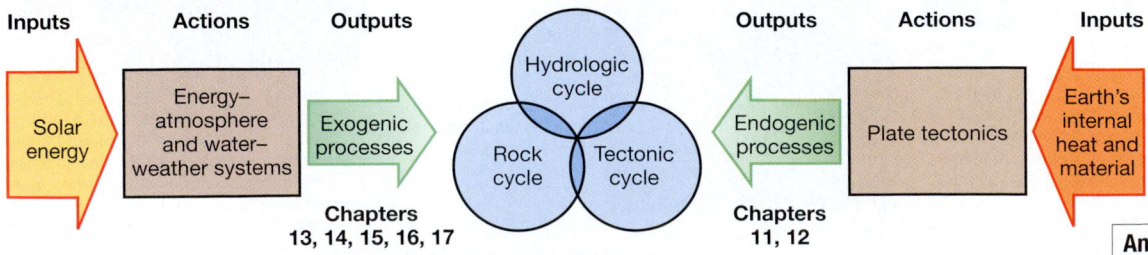

Inputs   Actions   Outputs   Outputs   Actions   Inputs

Solar energy → Energy–atmosphere and water–weather systems → Exogenic processes → Hydrologic cycle / Rock cycle / Tectonic cycle ← Endogenic processes ← Plate tectonics ← Earth's internal heat and material

Chapters 13, 14, 15, 16, 17   Chapters 11, 12

Animation (MG)
Convection within the Mantle

https://goo.gl/5DqKqc

MasteringGeography™

Visit the Study Area in MasteringGeography™ to explore the geologic cycle.

Visualize: Study a geosciences animation of convection and plate tectonics.

Assess: Demonstrate understanding of the geologic cycle (if assigned by instructor).

11.3 PROCESSES AND LANDSCAPES OF THE GEOLOGIC CYCLE

Hydrologic Cycle

11.3a Earth's water cycles continuously among the atmosphere, hydrosphere, lithosphere, and biosphere.

Sources of Energy:
• Solar energy provides the heat necessary for water to evaporate.
• Gravity causes precipitation to fall.

During the monsoon in India, atmospheric moisture flows inland from the Indian Ocean and falls as heavy rains.

Example of systems interaction:
Water in the hydrologic cycle weathers, erodes, and deposits sediments—processes that are part of the rock cycle.

Example of systems interaction:
Volcanic activity in the tectonic cycle releases gases and particles that change the atmosphere and thus affect the hydrologic cycle.

Tectonic processes produced Indonesia's many active volcanoes, including these in Bromo National Park, on the island of Java.

These layers of sandstone in Canyonlands National Park, Utah, formed from particles of other rock, pressed and cemented together.

Example of systems interaction:
Igneous rock in the rock cycle forms from the cooling and hardening of molten rock, a process that is part of the tectonic cycle.

Rock Cycle

11.3b The processes that form igneous, sedimentary, and metamorphic rocks operate so that each rock can enter the cycle and be transformed into other rock types.

Sources of Energy:
• Solar energy drives the processes involved in weathering, eroding, and transporting sediment.
• Gravity causes sediment deposition and compaction.
• Earth's internal heat causes melting of rock.

Tectonic Cycle

11.3c Earth's plates diverge, collide, subduct, and slide past each other, changing the continents and ocean basins and causing earthquakes, volcanoes, and mountain building.

Sources of Energy:
• Earth's internal heat provides energy that powers plate motions and melts rock to form magma.
• Gravity drives the subduction of lithospheric plates.

GEOquiz

1. Infer: How could mountain building (tectonic cycle) affect weather and climate (hydrologic cycle)?

2. Apply concepts: Describe the role of exogenic and endogenic processes in the rock cycle.

3. Give examples: List two additional examples of ways in which the cycles within the geologic cycle could affect each other.

4. Explain: How could processes in the tectonic cycle contribute to the formation of metamorphic rock in the rock cycle?

KEY**LEARNING**concepts**review**

The Earth–atmosphere interface is where the **endogenic system** (p. 318), powered by heat energy from within the planet, interacts with the **exogenic system** (p. 318), powered by insolation and influenced by gravity. **Geomorphology** (p. 318) is the subfield within physical geography that studies the development and spatial distribution of landforms.

Discuss the time spans into which Earth's geologic history is divided and *explain* the principle of uniformitarianism.

The most fundamental principle of Earth science is **uniformitarianism** (p. 320), which assumes that the same physical processes active in the environment today have been operating throughout geologic time. Dramatic, catastrophic events such as massive landslides or volcanic eruptions can interrupt the long-term processes that slowly shape Earth's surface. Scientists use the **geologic time scale** (p. 318) to organize the vast span of geologic time. **Stratigraphy** (p. 320) is the study of layered rock strata, including their sequence (superposition), thickness, and spatial distribution, which yield clues to the age and origin of the rocks.

1. What is the difference between relative age and numerical age in geology? How do scientists assign these ages?
2. What era, period, and epoch of the geologic time scale are we living in today? What is the meaning of the term "Anthropocene?"

Depict Earth's interior in cross section and *describe* each distinct layer.

We have learned about Earth's interior indirectly, from the way its various layers transmit **seismic waves** (p. 321). The **core** (p. 322) is differentiated into an inner core and an outer core, divided by a transition zone. Above Earth's core lies the **mantle** (p. 322), differentiated into lower mantle and upper mantle. The boundary between the uppermost mantle and the crust is the **Mohorovičić discontinuity**, or **Moho** (p. 322). The outer layer is the **crust** (p. 323). The uppermost mantle, along with the crust, makes up the **lithosphere** (p. 323). Below the lithosphere is the **asthenosphere** (p. 323), or plastic layer. It contains pockets of increased heat from radioactive decay and is susceptible to slow convective currents in these hotter materials.

Earth's magnetic field is generated almost entirely within Earth's outer core. Polarity reversals in Earth's magnetism are recorded in cooling magma that contains iron minerals. The patterns of **geomagnetic reversal**, (p. 324), (reversal of Earth's polarity) in rock help scientists piece together the history of Earth's crustal movement.

3. Describe the asthenosphere. Why is it also known as the plastic layer? What are the consequences of its convection currents?
4. How does Earth generate its magnetic field? Is the magnetic field constant, or does it change?

Describe the three main groups of rock and *diagram* the rock cycle.

A **mineral** (p. 325) is an inorganic natural compound having a specific chemical formula and possessing a crystalline structure. A **rock** (p. 325) is an assemblage of minerals bound together (such as granite, a rock containing three minerals), or a mass of a single mineral (such as rock salt).

Igneous rock (p. 325) forms from **magma** (p. 325), which is molten rock beneath the surface. **Lava** (p. 325) is the name for magma once it has emerged onto the surface. Magma either intrudes into crustal rocks, cools, and hardens, forming **intrusive igneous rock** (p. 325), or extrudes onto the surface, forming **extrusive igneous rock** (p. 325). The crystalline texture of igneous rock is related to the rate of cooling. **Granite** (p. 325) is a coarse-grained intrusive igneous rock; it is crystalline and high in silica, aluminum, potassium, calcium, and sodium. **Basalt** (p. 326) is a fine-grained extrusive igneous rock; it is granular and high in silica, magnesium, and iron. Intrusive igneous rock that cools slowly in the crust forms a **pluton** (p. 326). The largest pluton form is a **batholith** (p. 326).

Sedimentary rock (p. 328) is formed when loose *clasts* (grains or fragments) derived from several sources are compacted and cemented together in the process of **lithification** (p. 328). Clastic sedimentary rocks are derived from the fragments of weathered and eroded rocks and the material that is transported and deposited as **sediment** (p. 328). Chemical sedimentary rocks are formed either by biochemical processes or from the chemical dissolution of minerals into solution; the most common is **limestone** (p. 328), which is lithified calcium carbonate, $CaCO_3$. Any igneous or sedimentary rock may be transformed into **metamorphic rock** (p. 330) by going through profound physical or chemical changes under pressure and increased temperature. The **rock cycle** (p. 330) describes the three principal rock-forming processes and the rocks they produce.

5. Describe igneous processes. What is the difference between intrusive and extrusive types of igneous rocks?
6. What is lithification, and how does it form sedimentary rock? Describe the particle sizes of conglomerate and compare to that of shale.
7. Describe two processes that form metamorphic rocks.

Describe Pangaea and its breakup and *explain* the physical evidence that crustal drifting is continuing today.

The present configuration of the ocean basins and continents is the result of tectonic processes involving Earth's interior dynamics and crust. **Pangaea** (p. 332) was the name Alfred Wegener gave to a single assemblage of continental crust existing some 225 m.y.a. that subsequently broke apart. Wegener coined the phrase *continental drift* to describe his idea that the crust is moved by vast forces within the planet. The theory of **plate tectonics** (p. 332) is that Earth's lithosphere is fractured into huge slabs or plates, each moving in response to gravitational pull and to flowing currents in the mantle that create frictional drag on the plate. Geomagnetic reversals along **mid-ocean ridges** (p. 332) on the ocean floor provide evidence of **seafloor spreading** (p. 332), which accompanies the movement of plates toward the continental margins of ocean basins. At some plate boundaries, denser oceanic crust dives beneath lighter continental crust along **subduction zones** (p. 335).

8. Briefly review the history of the theory of plate tectonics, including the concepts of continental drift and seafloor spreading. What was Alfred Wegener's role?

9. Describe the process of upwelling as it refers to magma under the ocean floor.

10. What is a subduction zone, and how does it occur?

Draw the pattern of Earth's major plates on a world map and *relate* this pattern to the occurrence of earthquakes, volcanic activity, and hot spots.

Earth's lithosphere is made up of 14 large plates, and many smaller ones, that move and interact to form three types of plate boundaries: divergent, convergent, and transform. Along the offset portions of mid-ocean ridges, horizontal motions produce *transform faults*. The area surrounding the Pacific Ocean basin is the *circum-Pacific belt* or **Pacific Ring of Fire** (p. 338), named for the numerous volcanoes along its margin.

As many as 50 to 100 **hot spots** (p. 338) exist across Earth's surface, where plumes of magma—some anchored in the lower mantle, others originating from shallow sources in the upper mantle—generate an upward flow. Some hot spots produce **geothermal energy** (p. 340), or heat from Earth's interior, which may be used for direct geothermal heating or geothermal power. The **geologic cycle** (p. 342) is a model of the internal and external interactions that shape the crust—including the hydrologic, rock, and tectonic cycles.

11. Characterize the three types of plate boundaries and the actions associated with each type.

GEO**SPATIAL** ANALYSIS

Measuring the Movement of Land

As tectonic plates shift Earth's crust deforms along fault lines. By measuring these movements scientists investigate the physical processes responsible for fault movement and develop earthquake risk forecast models.

Activities

Go to the USGS Earthquake Hazards Program at http://earthquake.usgs.gov/. *Click on "Monitoring," choose "Crustal Deformation Monitoring" and select "Fault Creep, Borehole Strain, and Tiltmeter Monitoring Measurements."*

1. Which instruments are used to measure land movement? Click on "Monitoring Instruments" and briefly describe each instrument.

Go to the Real-Time PPP Displacements page at http://escweb.wr.usgs.gov/highrate-gps/realtime-ppp/. *Hover over each region to see its name. Click on the "Pacific Northwest" region. Each triangle represents a data collection location. Click on a location with recent data (less than 30 seconds old) in northwestern Washington and select "View processed GPS data."*

2. What are the latitude and longitude coordinates for this location? Over what range of years are data available?

3. Using the North American Fixed graphs, what is the total northward movement of this location on the North American Plate from the beginning to the end of the data record? Eastward movement? (It may help to use the trend line showing the average motion). How does this compare to the movement indicated in Figure 11.25? Why might they be different?

4. What is the range (upward plus downward) of upward motions experienced by this location? What is the average (using the trend line) upward motion?

5. Using the table below the graph, what is the magnitude of the horizontal velocity for this location (in mm/yr)?

6. Repeat 2–5 for a station in the regions Northern California and Southern California.

Go back to the "Real-time GPS Data" and click on "GPS Velocities."

7. Examine the velocities in the Pacific Northwest, Northern California and Southern California. Do most or all of the stations move in the way you determined above? What are the overall directions of movement for these regions?

8. Examine the Northern Rockies region. How is this land moving?

Mastering Geography™

Looking for additional review and test prep materials? Visit the Study Area in MasteringGeography™ to enhance your geographic literacy, spatial reasoning skills, and understanding of this chapter's content by accessing a variety of resources, including MapMaster™ interactive maps, videos, *Mobile Field Trips*, *Project Condor* Quadcopter Videos, *In the News* RSS feeds, flashcards, web links, self-study quizzes, and an eText version of *Geosystems*.

12 Tectonics, Earthquakes, and Volcanism

Mt. Everest North Base Camp, Tibet, China

Mount Everest, the world's tallest peak as measured from sea level, moves toward the northeast about 4 cm (1.6 in.) each year and grows upward in height about 0.3 cm (0.1 in.) each year as the Indian plate grinds beneath the Eurasian plate. The April 2015 earthquake in Nepal shifted the mountain about 3.0 cm (1.2 inches) southwest but did not change the height. [Ratnakorn Piyasirisorost/Moment Open/Getty Images.]

KEY**LEARNING**concepts

After reading the chapter, you should be able to:

- *Describe* the formation of continental crust and *define* displaced terranes.

- *Explain* the process of folding and *describe* the principal types of faults and their characteristic landforms.

- *List* the three types of plate collisions associated with mountain building and *identify* specific examples of each.

- *Explain* earthquake characteristics and measurement and *describe* earthquake fault mechanics.

- *Describe* volcanic landforms and *distinguish* between an effusive and an explosive volcanic eruption.

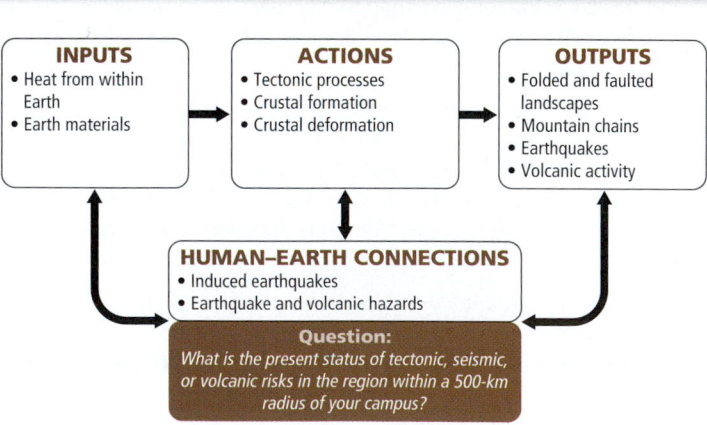

INPUTS
- Heat from within Earth
- Earth materials

ACTIONS
- Tectonic processes
- Crustal formation
- Crustal deformation

OUTPUTS
- Folded and faulted landscapes
- Mountain chains
- Earthquakes
- Volcanic activity

HUMAN–EARTH CONNECTIONS
- Induced earthquakes
- Earthquake and volcanic hazards

Question:
What is the present status of tectonic, seismic, or volcanic risks in the region within a 500-km radius of your campus?

The U.S. Pacific Northwest Earthquake Hazard

Just offshore from the North American continent stretching from northern California to Vancouver Island, Canada, lies the Juan de Fuca tectonic plate. About 230,000 km² (90,000 mi²) in size, this small plate is moving toward and diving beneath the North American plate, forming the Cascadia subduction zone (**Figure GN 12.1**).

The Cascadia plate convergence creates the Cascade Range, a volcanic mountain chain about 160 km (100 mi) inland. The subduction zone is part of the Pacific Ring of Fire, home to numerous active volcanoes and the world's strongest earthquakes (**Figure GN 12.2**).

As in other subduction zones, the plate convergence is not a smooth and seamless process. Friction at the plate boundary builds pressure and strain, causing the crust to bulge and shorten as it deforms. Eventually, the plate boundary snaps, releasing energy in the form of seismic waves that produce an earthquake. The last major quake along the Cascadia subduction zone happened in 1700 C.E., giving rise to tsunami—huge seismic sea waves—that hit the Pacific Northwest coast and Japan. Scientists estimate that the odds of another Cascadia full rupture are growing with each passing year as the plates remain "locked" in position, accumulating strain.

How Big? Scientists estimate that the 1700 Cascadia earthquake was an M 9.0 on the moment magnitude "M" scale, discussed in this chapter. Scientists use this scale to classify the energy of large earthquakes—an M 3.0 earthquake is barely felt, an M 7.0 quake can cause extensive damage and fatalities, and an M 9.0 is catastrophic.

If the entire length of the Cascadia subduction zone snaps at once, known as a "full-margin rupture," scientists estimate an earthquake between M 8.7 and M 9.2. Then, as the edge of the North American continent drops in elevation and subsequently rebounds to the west, the displacement of the ocean floor will cause the tsunami. The first wave will reach the coasts of California, Oregon, and Washington 10 to 30 minutes after the quake occurs.

How Much Damage? Scientists classify earthquake intensity based on structural damage from ground shaking, which can range from not felt or barely perceptible to violent shaking that causes total destruction. The shaking from a Cascadia full rupture would be violent and could cause nearly total damage. This translates into houses sliding off their foundations, building collapse, ruptured gas lines, and failed electrical grids.

The destruction from the tsunami could surpass that of the earthquake itself. Wave heights could vary between about 6 m (20 ft) and 30 m (100 ft), depending on the shape of the coastline. To escape impact, people must completely evacuate all low-lying coastal areas in the few minutes before the first wave arrives.

When? Think Earthquake Probability Sediment cores extracted from the Pacific Ocean floor show evidence of ancient submarine landslides corresponding with major earthquakes. Using these data, scientists suggest that 43 major quakes have occurred along the Cascadia subduction zone in the last 10,000 years. Throughout this period, the events occurred as close together as 100 years and as far apart as 1,000 years.

Based on this history, scientists estimate that a major quake (M 8.0 or higher) has a 14–20% chance of occurrence in the next 50 years. The percent probability for Northern Oregon, home to the city of Portland, is at the high end of that range.

Throughout the Cascadia region, over 70,000 people live in the tsunami inundation zone. In Oregon, an estimated 75% of structures are not designed to withstand a major earthquake. Other than Portland, cities in the area of impact include Seattle, Tacoma, Olympia, Salem, and Eugene—about 7 million people in total. As the hazard awareness increases, the region's residents can begin now to take action toward disaster planning. But the question remains whether they will do so.

1. What tectonic processes create the earthquake hazard in the Pacific Northwest?

2. Describe the two main ways in which earthquakes in this region can cause severe damage.

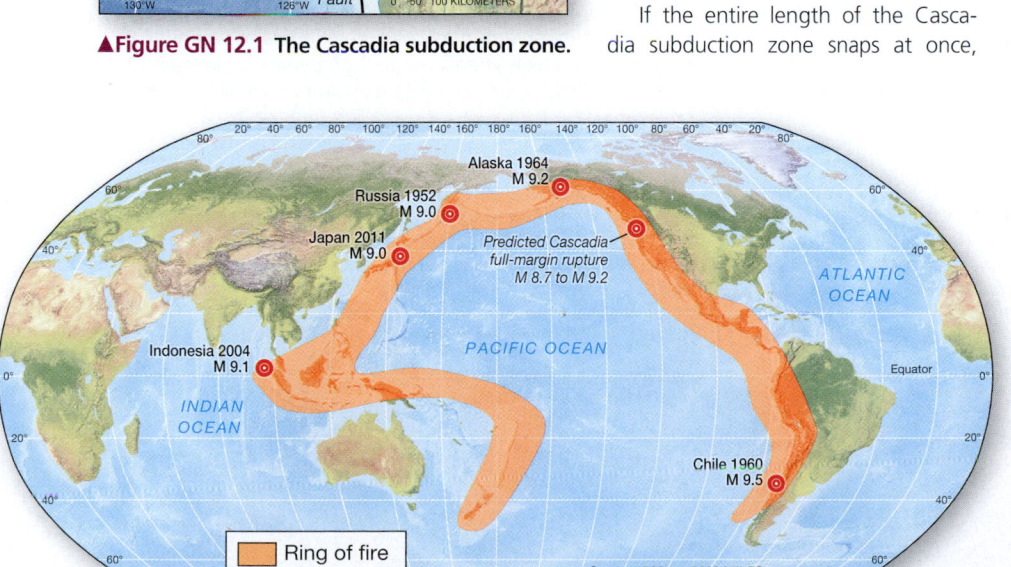

▲Figure GN 12.1 The Cascadia subduction zone.

▲Figure GN 12.2 Locations of the five largest earthquakes on record, all located along the Pacific Ring of Fire. Also shown is the location and potential magnitude of a Cascadia subduction zone quake. [USGS/National Earthquake Information Center; http://earthquake.usgs.gov/earthquakes/world/10_largest_world.php.]

The arrangement of continents and oceans, the uplift and erosion of mountain ranges, and global patterns of earthquake and volcanic activity are all evidence of dynamic forces shaping the planet. Earth's endogenic systems send flows of heat and material toward the surface. These ongoing processes alter continental landscapes, sometimes in dramatic events that make headline news.

Natural hazards such as earthquakes and volcanic eruptions near population centers pose threats to lives and property. The world was riveted to images of massive earthquakes in Japan in 2011 and again in 2016, Nepal in 2015, and Ecuador in 2016 as unstable plate boundaries snapped into new positions. Volcanic activity continued in Indonesia, Central and South America, and Alaska in 2016—during one 24-hour period in May, six volcanoes erupted worldwide (in Mexico, Costa Rica, Colombia, two in Indonesia, and on Bristol Island in the South Atlantic Ocean). Earth systems science is now providing analysis of seismic and volcanic activity that is helping to develop early warning systems aimed at reducing injury and lives lost during these events (Figure 12.1).

Crustal Formation

Tectonic activity generally is slow, taking place over millions of years. Earth's internal processes result in gradual uplift and new landforms, with major mountain building occurring along plate boundaries. The uplifted crustal regions are quite varied, but they can be grouped into three general categories:

- Residual mountains and stable continental cratons, consisting of inactive remnants of ancient tectonic activity
- Tectonic mountains and landforms, produced by active folding, faulting, and crustal movements
- Volcanic landforms, formed by the surface accumulation of molten rock from eruptions of subsurface materials

The various processes mentioned in these descriptions operate in concert to produce the continental crust we see around us.

Continental Shields

All continents have a nucleus, called a *craton*, consisting of ancient crystalline rock on which the continent "grows" through the addition of crustal fragments and sediments. Cratons are generally old and stable masses of continental crust that have eroded to a low elevation and relief. Most date to the Precambrian Eon and can be more than 2 billion years old. The lack of basaltic components in these cratons offers a clue to their stability. The lithosphere underlying a craton is often thicker than the lithosphere underlying younger portions of continents and oceanic crust.

everyday GEOSYSTEMS

How does an earthquake early warning system work?

A 2015 study showed that nearly half of all Americans live in an earthquake-prone area (see the map in Figure 12.23). The ShakeAlert early warning system, presently in development, is designed to alert people via phone and computer that earthquake shaking is about to occur. Even a minute of warning can help shut down transportation systems, prepare emergency responders, and enable people to move to safe locations. ShakeAlert begins when early earthquake waves hit instrument sensors. A message then transmits instantly to an app that gives the minutes or seconds to take action before shaking begins. Although currently planned for use on the U.S. West Coast, the system could ultimately work in all vulnerable areas.

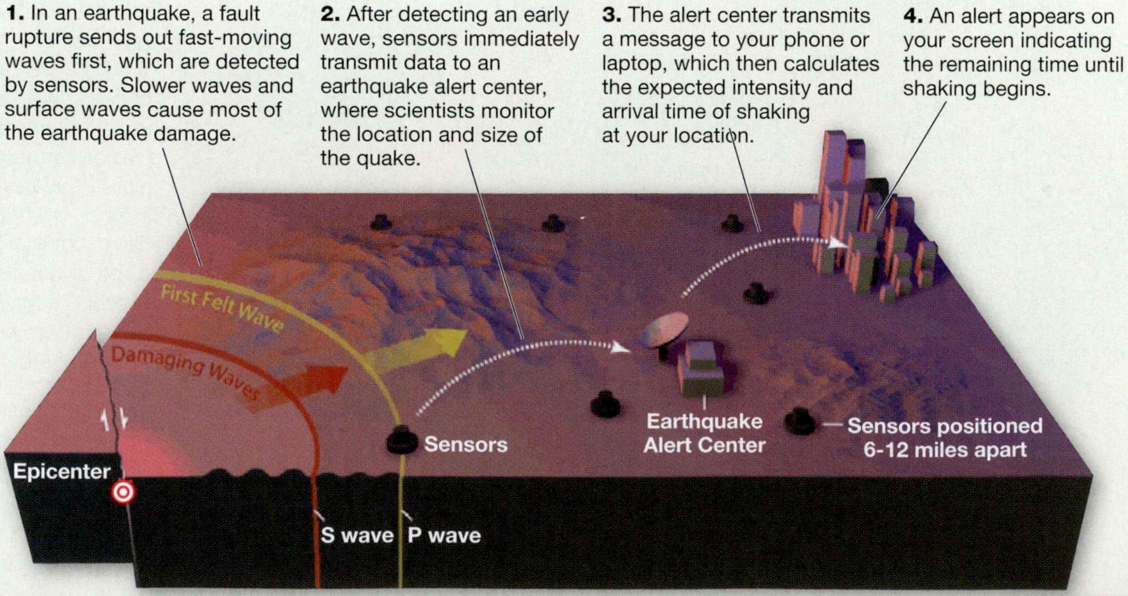

1. In an earthquake, a fault rupture sends out fast-moving waves first, which are detected by sensors. Slower waves and surface waves cause most of the earthquake damage.

2. After detecting an early wave, sensors immediately transmit data to an earthquake alert center, where scientists monitor the location and size of the quake.

3. The alert center transmits a message to your phone or laptop, which then calculates the expected intensity and arrival time of shaking at your location.

4. An alert appears on your screen indicating the remaining time until shaking begins.

▶Figure 12.1 U.S. earthquake early warning system in development. The ShakeAlert system (a) sends instantaneous data to your phone (b) when an earthquake begins (see http://www .shakealert.org/). [USGS.]

First Felt Wave
Damaging Waves
Epicenter
Sensors
Earthquake Alert Center
Sensors positioned 6–12 miles apart
S wave P wave

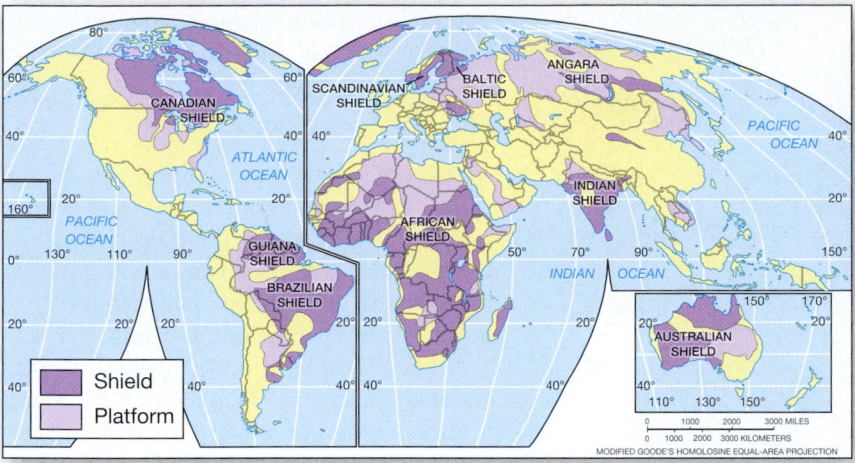

(a) Earth's major continental shields exposed by erosion. Continental platforms are the adjacent portions of these shields that remain covered by younger sedimentary layers.

(b) Aerial view of the Canadian shield landscape in northern Québec.

◀**Figure 12.2** **Continental shields.** [(a) Adapted from USGS Geologic Provinces map, available at http://earthquake.usgs.gov/data/crust/maps.php. (b) Bobbé Christopherson.]

A **continental shield** is a large region where a craton is exposed at the surface (**Figure 12.2**). Layers of younger sedimentary rock—called continental platforms—surround these shields and appear quite stable over time. Examples of such stable platforms include the region from east of the Rockies to the Appalachians and northward into central and eastern Canada, a large portion of China, eastern Europe to the Ural Mountains, and portions of Siberia.

Building Continental Crust

The formation of continental crust is complex and takes hundreds of millions of years. It involves the entire sequence of seafloor spreading and formation of oceanic crust, eventual subduction and remelting of that oceanic crust, and the subsequent rise of remelted material as new magma (**Figure 12.3**). In this process of crustal formation, you can follow the cycling of materials through the tectonic cycle.

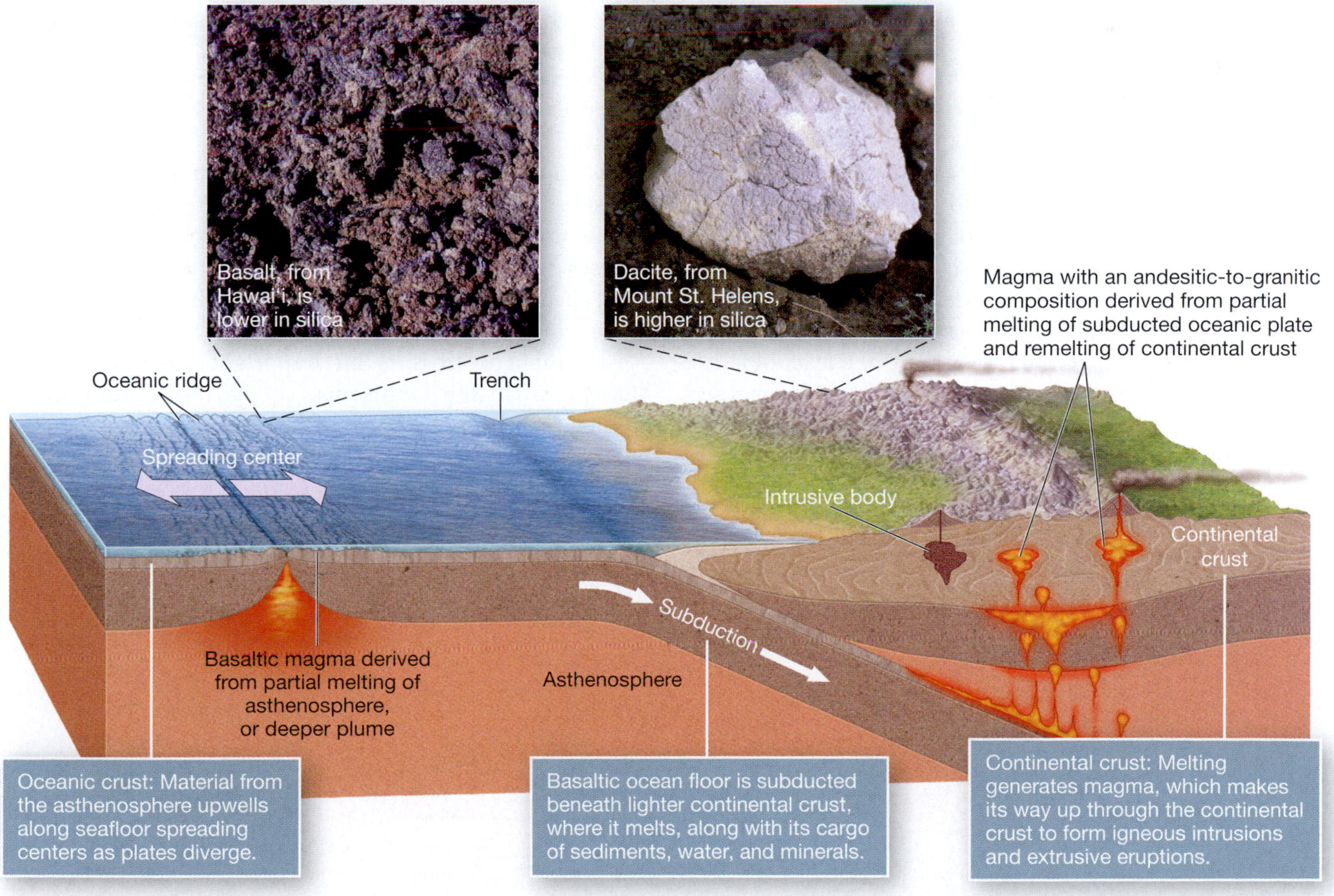

Basalt, from Hawai'i, is lower in silica

Dacite, from Mount St. Helens, is higher in silica

Magma with an andesitic-to-granitic composition derived from partial melting of subducted oceanic plate and remelting of continental crust

Oceanic ridge

Trench

Intrusive body

Continental crust

Spreading center

Subduction

Basaltic magma derived from partial melting of asthenosphere, or deeper plume

Asthenosphere

Oceanic crust: Material from beneath the asthenosphere upwells along seafloor spreading centers as plates diverge.

Basaltic ocean floor is subducted beneath lighter continental crust, where it melts, along with its cargo of sediments, water, and minerals.

Continental crust: Melting generates magma, which makes its way up through the continental crust to form igneous intrusions and extrusive eruptions.

▲**Figure 12.3** **Crustal formation processes, with examples of extrusive igneous rock types.** [Bobbé Christopherson.]

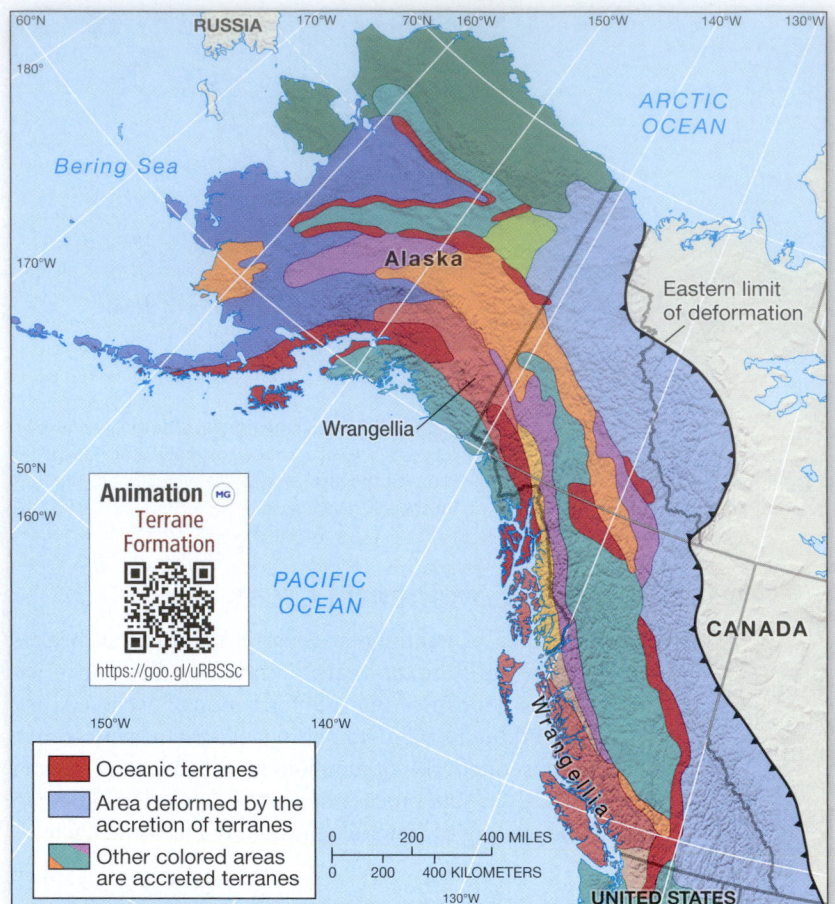

◀**Figure 12.4 North American terranes.**
Originating thousands of kilometers south of their present location, numerous terranes have migrated and accreted to western Canada and Alaska over the past 200 million years. [USGS.]

In the regions surrounding the Pacific Ocean, accreted terranes are particularly prevalent. At least 25% of the growth of western North America can be attributed to the accretion of more than 50 terranes since the early Jurassic Period (190 million years ago). For example, the *Wrangellia terranes* migrated approximately 10,000 km (6200 mi) to form mountains along the western margin of the continent in Canada and Alaska (**Figure 12.4**). The Wrangellia terranes were originally a volcanic island arc and associated marine sediments from near the equator.

The Appalachian Mountains, extending from Alabama to the Maritime Provinces of Canada, possess bits of land once attached to ancient Europe, Africa, South America, Antarctica, and various oceanic islands. The discovery of terranes, which occurred as recently as the 1980s, revealed one of the ways continents are assembled.

Accretion of Terranes

Each of Earth's major lithospheric plates actually is a collage of many crustal pieces brought together by plate motions. Over time, slowly migrating fragments of ocean floor, curving chains (or arcs) of volcanic islands, and pieces of crust from other continents all have been forced against the edges of continental shields and platforms. These varied crustal pieces that are now attached, or accreted, to the plates are **terranes** (not to be confused with *terrain*, which refers to the topography of a tract of land). Such displaced terranes, also known as *exotic terranes*, have histories different from those of the continents that capture them. They are usually framed by fault-zone fractures and differ in rock composition and structure from their new continental homes.

Crustal Deformation

Rocks, whether igneous, sedimentary, or metamorphic, are subjected to powerful stress by tectonic forces, gravity, and the weight of overlying rocks. *Stress* is any force that affects an object, measured as force per unit area; note that these units are the same as for pressure. Three types of stress are important for crustal deformation: *tension*, which causes stretching; *compression*, which causes shortening; and *shear*, which causes twisting or tearing as objects slide parallel to one another (**Figure 12.5**).

Although stress is an important force in shaping Earth's crust, the landforms we see result from strain, which is how rocks respond to stress. *Strain* is a measure of the stretching, shortening, and twisting of rock that result from stress. Rocks respond to strain by *folding* (bending) or *faulting* (breaking). Whether a rock bends or

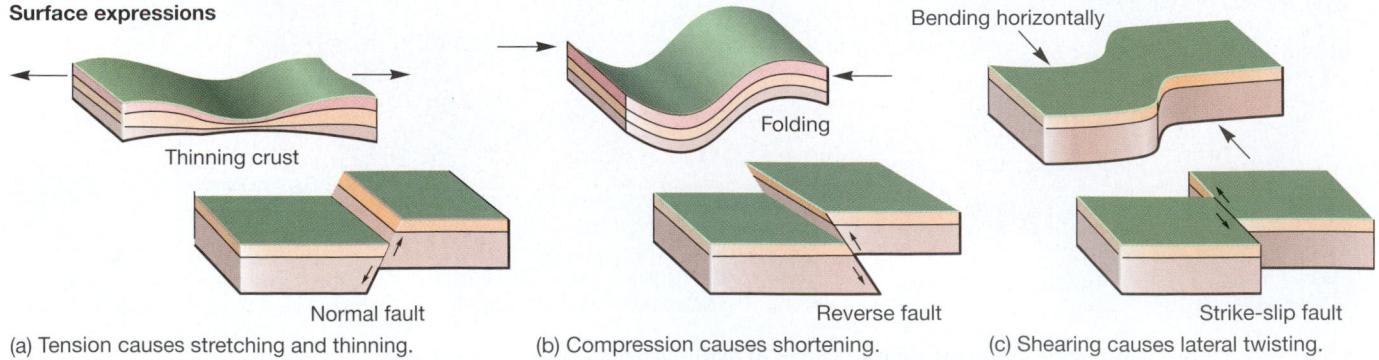

Surface expressions

(a) Tension causes stretching and thinning.

Thinning crust

Normal fault

(b) Compression causes shortening.

Folding

Reverse fault

Bending horizontally

Strike-slip fault

(c) Shearing causes lateral twisting.

▲**Figure 12.5 Three kinds of stress and strain and the resulting surface expressions on Earth's crust.**

▲**Figure 12.6** **Folds on Mount Kidd, Alberta, Canada.** Compression of limestone and other sedimentary strata associated with the formation of the Rocky Mountains caused the folded structure of this 2958 m (9705 ft) peak in the Canadian Rockies. [All Canada Photos/Alamy.]

breaks depends on several factors, including its composition and the amount of pressure it is undergoing.

Folding and Broad Warping

When rock strata are subjected to compressional forces, they become deformed (**Figure 12.6**). **Folding** occurs when rocks are deformed as a result of compressional stress and shortening. We can visualize this process by stacking sections of thick fabric on a table and slowly pushing on opposite ends of the stack. The cloth layers will bend and rumple into folds similar to those shown in the landscape, with some folds forming arches (upward folds) and some folds forming troughs (downward folds).

Anticlines, Synclines, and Monoclines An arch-shaped upward fold is an **anticline**, in which the rock strata slope downward away from an imaginary center axis that divides the fold into two parts (**Figure 12.7a**). A trough-shaped downward fold is a **syncline**, in which

the strata slope upward away from the center axis. The erosion of a syncline may form a *synclinal ridge*, produced when the different rock strata offer different degrees of resistance to weathering processes (**Figure 12.7b**).

Several features are associated with the folded landscapes shown in Figure 12.7a. The *hinge* is the horizontal line that defines the part of the fold with the sharpest curvature. If the hinge is not horizontal, meaning that it is not "level" (parallel with Earth's surface), the fold is *plunging*, or dipped down (inclined) at an angle. If the *axial plane* of the fold, an imaginary surface that parallels the hinge but descends downward through each layer, is inclined from vertical, the resulting configuration is an *overturned anticline*, in which folds have compressed so much that they overturn upon their own strata.

Further stress eventually fractures the rock strata along distinct lines, a process that forms a thrust fault. Some overturned folds are thrust upward, causing a considerable shortening of the original strata.

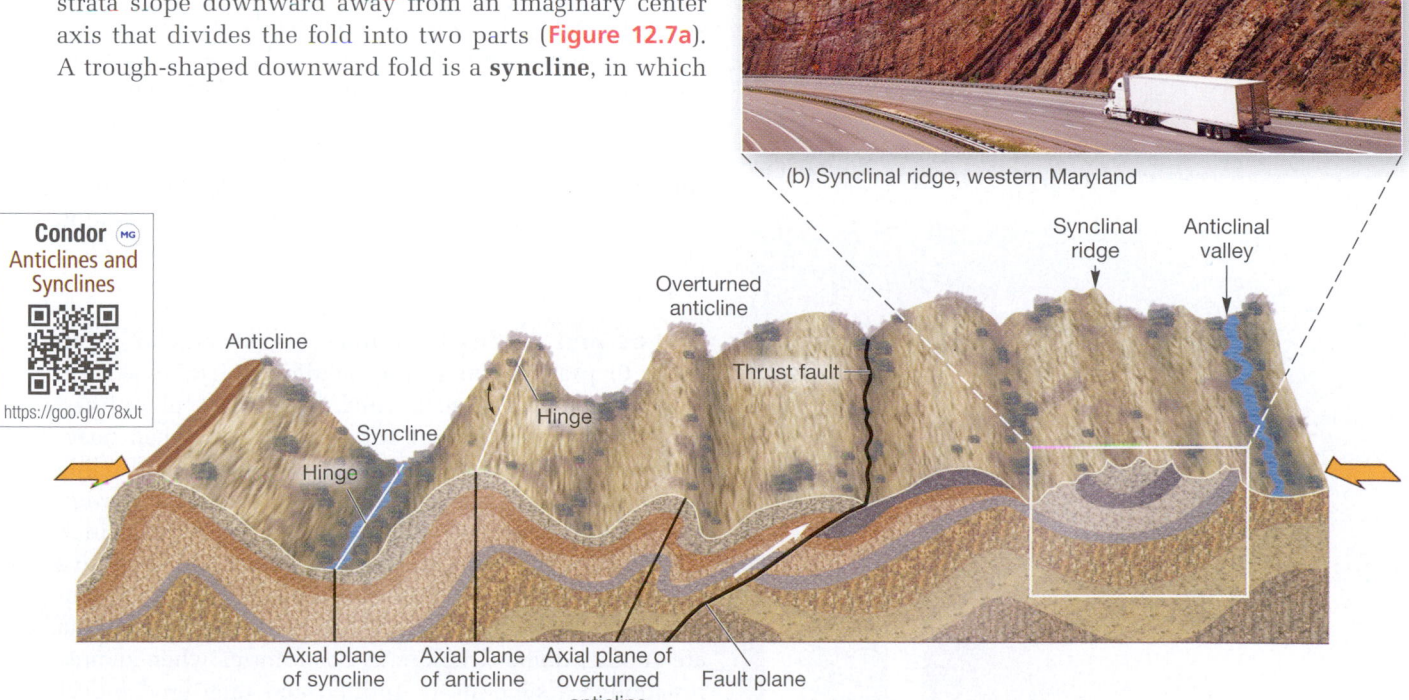

(b) Synclinal ridge, western Maryland

(a) Types of folds and their features.

▲**Figure 12.7** **Types of folds and their features.** [(b) Squirlgirl/Fotolia.]

A *monocline* is a large fold that resembles a carpet overlaid on a stair step. In the U.S. Southwest, numerous monoclines have formed in response to faulting deep below the surface. As the basement rocks break in a fault, the relatively softer sedimentary strata on the surface bend to form a fold. As the forces of weathering and erosion wear away a monocline, resistant strata are sometimes left standing at steep angles, such as along the Waterpocket Fold in south central Utah (**Figure 12.8**).

Knowledge of folding and stratigraphy are important for the petroleum industry. For

▼**Figure 12.8 Utah's Waterpocket Fold, a monocline.** The Waterpocket Fold is the longest exposed monocline in North America, running over 145 km (90 mi) in length. The west side of the monocline was uplifted about 2134 m (7000 ft) above the east side during the mountain-building event that formed the Rockies 40 to 80 million years ago. [(b) Niebrugge Images/Alamy.]

(a) The monocline consists of sedimentary strata that bent in response to faulting in the bedrock below.

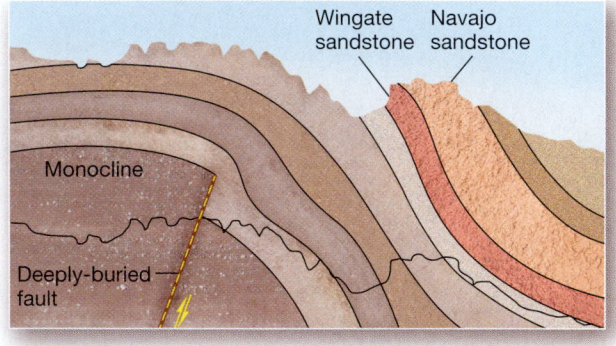

(b) Over time, erosion exposed the folded strata, wearing away the less-resistant shales and creating steep, inclined ridges of resistant sandstone.

Condor (MG)
Monoclines of the Colorado Plateau

https://goo.gl/KBUlp7

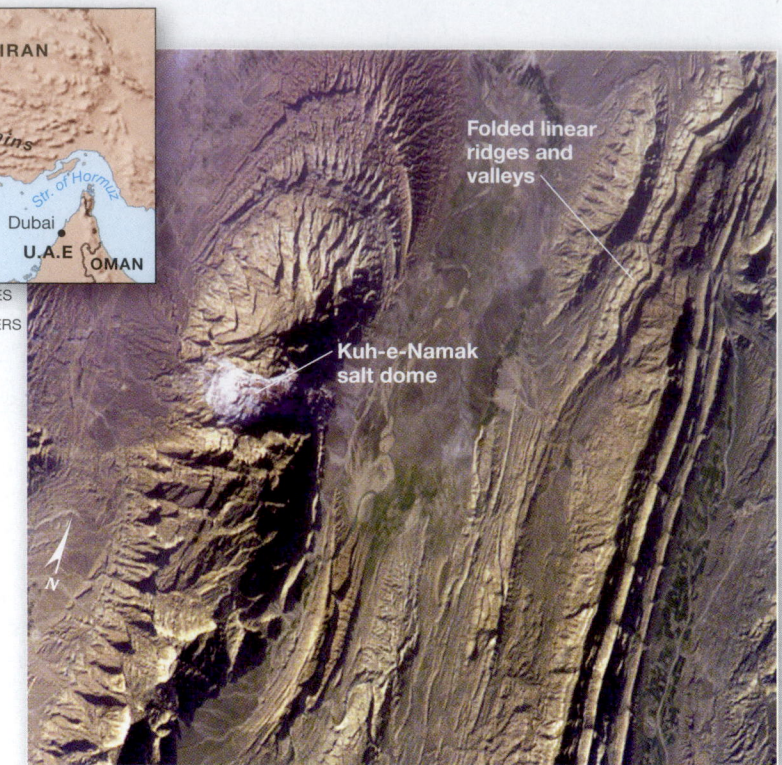

▲**Figure 12.9 Folded mountains at the edge of the Zagros Crush Zone, Iran.** The collision of the Eurasian and Arabian plates formed the ridge and valley folded structure of these mountains. Also shown is a salt dome, formed as buried layers of lower-density salt slowly flow upward in response to accumulating pressure from rock layers above. Eventually the salt bends the overlying layers, forming a dome-like structure. [Astronaut photograph ISS012-E-18774/NASA.]

example, petroleum geologists know that oil and natural gas collect in the upper portions of anticlinal folds in permeable rock layers such as sandstone. For example, the folded Zagros Mountains of Iran are an important oil-producing region of the Middle East. The area north of the Persian Gulf in the Zagros Mountains was an exotic terrane that separated from the Eurasian plate. However, the northward push of the Arabian plate is now shoving this terrane back into Eurasia and forming an active plate margin known as the Zagros Crush Zone (**Figure 12.9**).

Domes and Basins Over time, folded structures can erode to produce interesting landforms (**Figure 12.10**). An example is a *dome*, which is an area of uplifted rock strata resembling an anticline that has been heavily eroded over time (Figure 12.10a). Since an anticline is a fold that is convex in an upward direction, erosion exposes the oldest rocks in the center of a dome, which often have a circular pattern that resembles a bull's eye when viewed from the air—the Richat Structure in Mauritania is an example. The Black Hills of South Dakota are another dome structure. A *basin* forms when an area resembling a syncline is uplifted and then erodes over time. In a basin, the oldest rock strata are at the outside

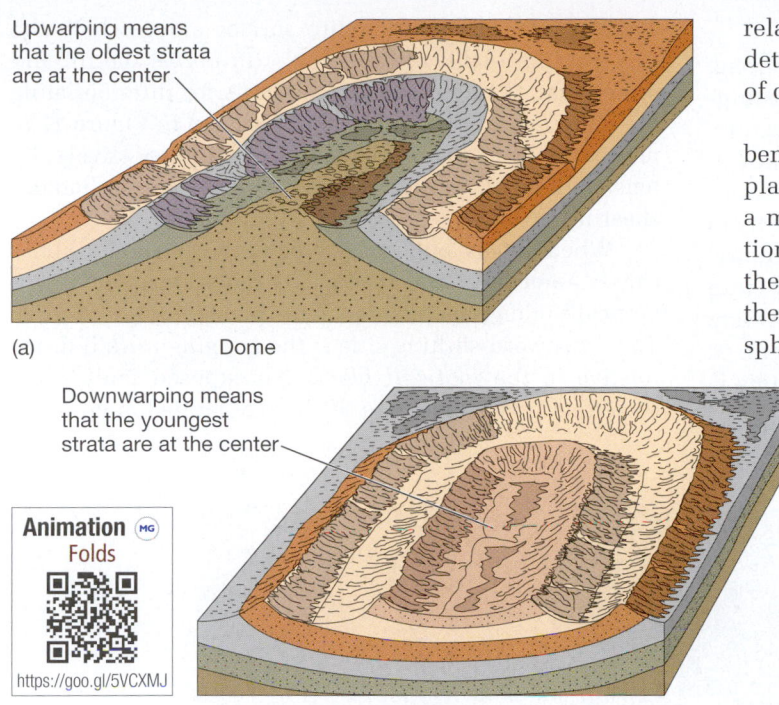

Upwarting means that the oldest strata are at the center

(a) Dome

Downwarping means that the youngest strata are at the center

Animation MG
Folds

https://goo.gl/5VCXMJ

(b) Basin

▲Figure 12.10 **Domes and basins.**

of the circular structure (Figure 12.10b). Since a syncline is concave when considered from above, erosion exposes the youngest rocks in the center of the structure.

WORK**IT**OUT 12.1
Dome and Basin Structures

Use Figures 12.9, 12.10, and the accompanying text to think through these questions.

1. In which roughly circular, eroded structure are the oldest strata in the center—a dome or a basin?
2. Which structure—a dome or a basin—is synclinal in nature? Are the youngest rocks exposed at the edges or in the center?
3. Is the salt dome in Figure 12.9 the same type of structure as the dome illustrated in Figure 12.10a? Explain your answer.

Warping Processes and Isostasy In addition to the types of folding discussed above, broad warping actions are another cause of bending in continental crust. Warping produces bends that are far greater in extent than the folds produced by compression. Forces responsible for such large-scale warping include the upwelling of magma associated with a hot spot and the uplift or sinking of the lithosphere in response to weight at the surface, a process known as *isostatic adjustment* of the crust.

Remember from our discussion of air parcels in Chapter 6 that *buoyancy* is the principle that something less dense, such as wood, floats in something more dense, such as water. The forces of buoyancy and gravity also relate to vertical movements of Earth's crust, which determine the elevations of continents and the depths of ocean floors.

Earth's lithosphere floats on the denser layers beneath, much as a boat floats on water. If a load is placed on the surface, such as the weight of a glacier, a mountain range, or an area of sediment accumulation, the lithosphere tends to sink, or ride lower in the asthenosphere (**Figure 12.11**). When this happens, the rigid lithosphere bends, and the plastic asthenosphere flows out of the way. If the load is removed, such as when a glacier melts or a mountain range erodes, the crust lifts gradually to ride higher, and the asthenosphere flows back toward the region of uplifting lithosphere. The equilibrium between Earth's crust and mantle as determined by the forces of the buoyancy and gravity is **isostasy**. The entire crust is in a constant state of isostatic adjustment, slowly rising and sinking in response to changes in weight at the surface. These movements can cause warping of broad areas of Earth's crust.

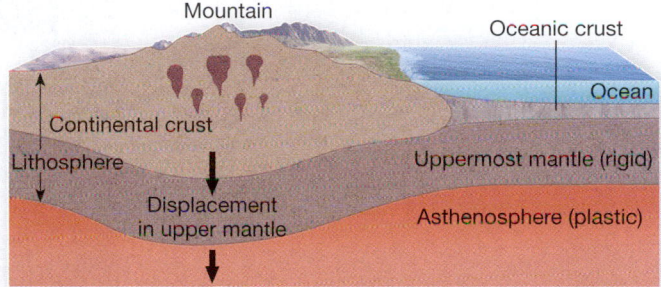

(a) The mountain mass slowly sinks, displacing mantle material.

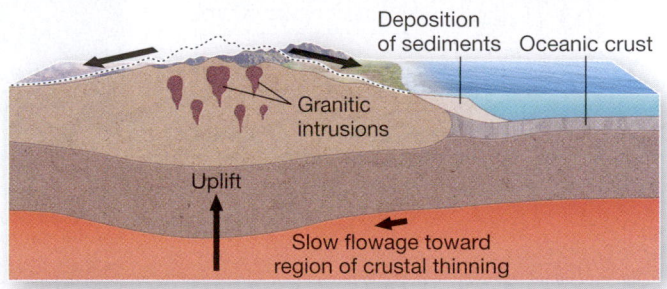

(b) Weathering and erosion transport sediment from land into oceans; as land loses mass, the crust isostatically adjusts upward.

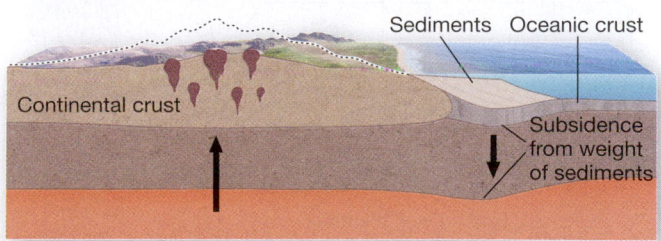

(c) As the continental crust erodes, the heavy sediment load offshore deforms the lithosphere beneath the ocean.

▲Figure 12.11 **Isostatic adjustment of the crust produces broad warping.**

Faulting

A freshly poured concrete sidewalk is smooth and strong. Adding stress to the sidewalk by driving heavy equipment over it may result in strain that causes a fracture. Pieces on either side of the fracture may move up, down, or horizontally, depending on the direction of stress. Similarly, when rock strata are stressed beyond their ability to remain a solid unit, they express the strain as a fracture. **Faulting** occurs when rocks on either side of the fracture shift relative to the other side. *Fault zones* are areas where fractures in the rock demonstrate crustal movement. A displacement of the ground surface caused by faulting is commonly called a *fault scarp*, or *escarpment*.

Types of Faults The fracture surface along which the two sides of a fault move is the *fault plane*; the tilt and orientation of this plane are the basis for differentiating the three main types of faults introduced in Figure 12.5: normal, reverse, and strike-slip, caused, respectively, by tensional stress, by compressional stress, and by lateral-shearing stress.

When forces pull rocks apart, the tensional stress causes a **normal fault**, in which rock on one side moves vertically along an inclined fault plane (**Figure 12.12a**). The downward-shifting side is the *hanging wall*; it drops relative to the *footwall block*. An exposed fault plane sometimes is visible along the base of faulted mountains,

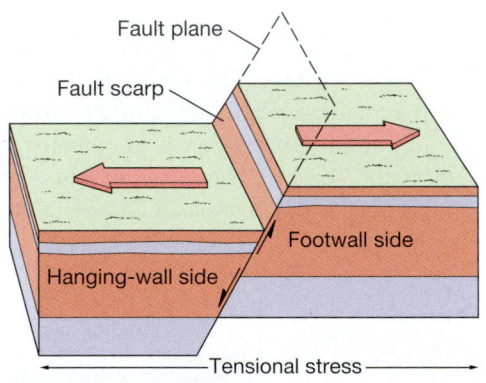

(a) Normal fault (tension)

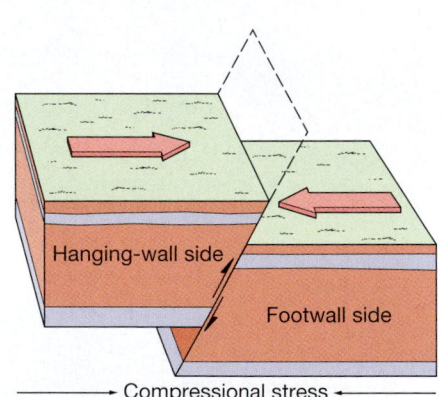

(b) Thrust or reverse fault (compression)

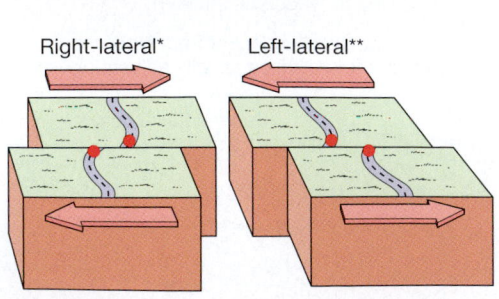

(c) Strike-slip fault (lateral shearing)

* Viewed from either dot on each road, movement of opposite side is *to the right.*
** Viewed from either dot on each road, movement of opposite side is *to the left.*

(a) A normal fault visible along the edge of mountain ranges in California and Utah.

(b) A thrust fault near Las Vegas, Nevada, has pushed older, Cambrian-aged limestone (dark color) above younger Jurrassic sandstone (pink color).

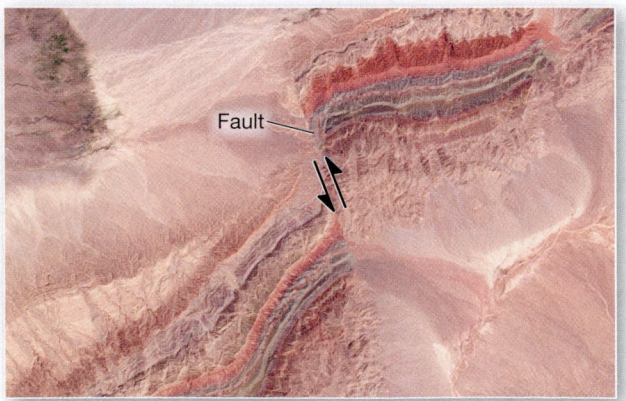

(c) Satellite view of a strike-slip fault cutting through sedimentary ridges near the Tien Shan mountains of China.

▲Figure 12.12 **Types of faults.** [(a) Bobbé Christopherson. (b) Marli Bryant Miller. (c) NASA/USGS.]

Condor ᴹᴳ
Faults versus Joints

https://goo.gl/76COSo

Animation ᴹᴳ
Transform Faults

https://goo.gl/wjND30

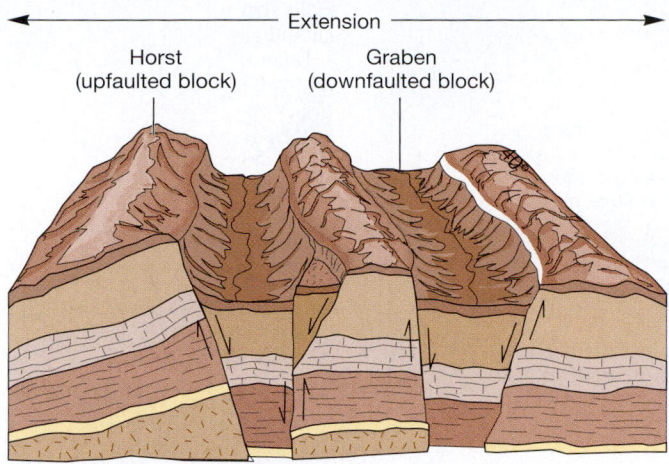

(a) Pairs of faults produce a horst-and-graben landscape.

(b) Horst-and-graben landscape of the Gregory Rift in Tanzania, part of the eastern branch of Africa's Great Rift Valley. Lake Manyara occupies part of the graben.

▲**Figure 12.13 Normal faults in an extensional landscape.** [(b) Nigel Pavitt/AWL Image/Getty Images.]

where the movements of the fault have cut into individual ridges so that they end in triangular facets.

When forces push rocks together, such as when plates converge, the compression causes a **reverse fault**, in which rocks move upward along the fault plane (**Figure 12.12b**). On the surface, it appears similar to a normal fault, although more collapse and landslides may occur from the hanging-wall component. In England, when miners worked along a reverse fault, they would stand on the lower side (footwall) and hang their lanterns on the upper side (hanging wall), giving rise to these terms.

A **thrust fault**, or *overthrust fault*, is a type of reverse fault that occurs when the fault plane forms a low angle relative to the horizontal, so that the overlying block has shifted far over the underlying block (see Figure 12.7). Place your hands palms down on your desk, with fingertips together, and slide one hand up over the other—this is the motion of a low-angle thrust fault, with one side pushing over the other.

In the Alps, several such overthrust faults have resulted from compressional forces of the ongoing collision between the African and Eurasian plates. Beneath the Los Angeles Basin, overthrust faults caused numerous earthquakes in the twentieth century, including the 1994 Northridge earthquake. Many of the faults beneath the Los Angeles region are "blind thrust faults," meaning that no evidence of rupture exists at the surface. Such faults are essentially buried under the crust, but remain a major earthquake threat.

When lateral shear causes horizontal movement along a fault plane, such as produced along a transform plate boundary and the associated transform faults, the fault is called a **strike-slip fault** (**Figure 12.12c**). The movement is right lateral or left lateral, depending on the direction of motion an observer on one side of the fault sees occurring on the other side. Even though the primary movement is horizontal, strike-slip faults can produce vertical ground displacement evidenced by a fault scarp on the landscape.

Faults and Extensional Landscapes Across extensional tectonic landscapes, where plates are diverging, pairs of normal faults act in concert to form distinctive terrain. The term **horst** applies to upward-faulted blocks; **graben** refers to downward-faulted blocks (**Figure 12.13a**). The Great Rift Valley of East Africa, associated with crustal spreading, is an example of such a horst-and-graben landscape (**Figure 12.13b**). This rift extends northward to the Red Sea, which fills the rift formed by parallel normal faults. The arid landscapes of Nevada and Utah also have a characteristic horst-and-graben landscape, caused by the westward movement of the North American plate (discussed in Chapter 15).

The San Andreas Fault System A famous example of both a transform and a strike-slip fault is the San Andreas fault system. Recall from Chapter 11 that transform faults occur along transform plate boundaries; most are found in the ocean basins along mid-ocean ridges, but some are overridden by continental crust that becomes faulted. The crust on either side of a transform fault moves parallel to the fault itself. Thus, transform faults are a type of strike-slip fault. However, since some strike-slip faults occur at locations away from plate boundaries, not all strike-slip faults are transform.

Along the western margin of North America, plate boundaries take several forms (**Figure 12.14a**). The San Andreas transform fault is the product of a continental plate (the North American plate) overriding an oceanic transform plate boundary. At its northern end, the San Andreas fault meets a seafloor spreading center and a subduction zone at the Mendocino Triple Junction (a *triple junction* is where three plates intersect).

Strike-slip faults often create linear valleys, or rifts, along the fracture zone, such as those along the San Andreas (**Figure 12.14b**). Offset streams are another landform associated with strike-slip faults, characterized by an abrupt bend in the course of the stream as it crosses the fault.

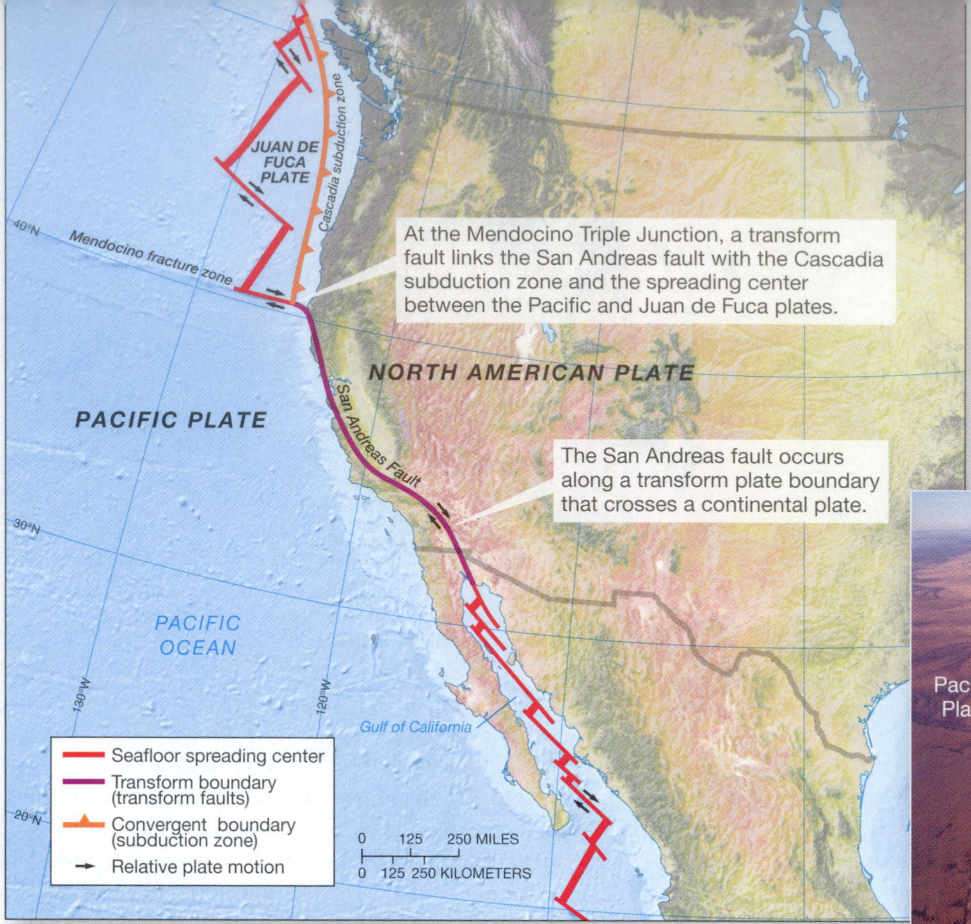

At the Mendocino Triple Junction, a transform fault links the San Andreas fault with the Cascadia subduction zone and the spreading center between the Pacific and Juan de Fuca plates.

NORTH AMERICAN PLATE

The San Andreas fault occurs along a transform plate boundary that crosses a continental plate.

PACIFIC PLATE

JUAN DE FUCA PLATE

PACIFIC OCEAN

Gulf of California

Legend:
— Seafloor spreading center
— Transform boundary (transform faults)
— Convergent boundary (subduction zone)
→ Relative plate motion

0 125 250 MILES
0 125 250 KILOMETERS

(a) The western margin of North America is the meeting point of three plates with different types of boundaries. Between the Juan de Fuca and Pacific plates is a spreading center with transform faults linking mid-ocean ridges. Between the Juan de Fuca and North American plates is the Cascadia subduction zone. The San Andreas transform fault separates the Pacific and North American plates. The meeting point of three plates is a "triple junction."

▲Figure 12.14 Plate boundaries of western North America and the San Andreas fault.
[(a) Communications and Education Division/NOAA. (b) Kevin Schafer/Alamy.]

Mobile (MG)
Field Trip
San Andreas Fault

https://goo.gl/OmZL3a

(b) Aerial view looking northwest along the San Andreas fault in the Carrizo Plain, San Luis Obispo County, California.

Pacific Plate
North American Plate

WORKITOUT 12.2
Faulting and Fault Types

In 2010, the El Major–Cucapah earthquake resulted from movement along northern Mexico's Laguna Salada Fault, an extension of California's Elsinore Fault, one of hundreds of faults in the San Andreas system. During the earthquake, the land surface shifted as much as 3.0 m (9.8 ft) in some areas, as shown in **Figure WIO 12.2.1**.

1. What type of fault produced this movement? Did the movement involve tectonic plates, and if so, which plates?
2. What is the name for the fault-related landform marked A?

▶Figure WIO 12.2.1 Land surface shift caused by the El Major–Cucapah quake. [John Fletcher, CICESE/NASA.]

A

GEOreport 12.1 Movement along California's San Andreas fault

   In 2016, scientists confirmed significant vertical movement along the San Andreas fault, a strike-slip fault known for its horizontal displacement. Evidence from an array of GPS receivers in California shows that several 100-kilometer-long "lobes" along the fault line are shifting vertically about 2 mm/year (0.1 in./year). The crust is both rising and subsiding within the "lobes" as strain builds along the plate boundaries. Although scientists suspected that such movements were occurring, this is the first direct documentation of the hypothesis. Improved understanding of these vertical shifts help scientists understand fault behavior, especially in areas where rupture has not occurred for decades or centuries, as is the case along the San Andreas.

Mountain Building

The geologic term for mountain building is **orogenesis**, literally meaning the birth of mountains (*oros* comes from the Greek for "mountain"). An *orogeny* is a mountain-building episode, occurring over millions of years, usually caused by large-scale deformation and uplift of the crust. An orogeny may begin with the capture of migrating terranes and their accretion to the continental margins or with the intrusion of granitic magmas to form plutons. The net result of this accumulating material is a thickening of the crust. The next event in the orogenic cycle is uplift, which is followed by the work of weathering and erosion, exposing granite plutons and creating rugged mountain topography. Geosystems in Action 12.1 presents the major mountain ranges and the latest related orogenies that caused them (also review Figure 11.2 for orogeny dates within the context of the geologic time scale).

Mountain Building at Plate Boundaries

Three types of tectonic activity cause mountain building along convergent plate margins, each illustrated in Geosystems in Action 12.2.

- An *oceanic plate–continental plate collision* produces a subduction zone as the denser oceanic plate dives beneath the continental plate (**Figure GIA 12.2a**). This convergence creates magma that is forced upward to become igneous intrusions and sometimes volcanic activity at the surface. Compressional forces cause the crust to uplift and buckle. This type of convergence is now occurring along the Cordilleran mountain system that follows the Pacific coast of the Americas and has formed the Rockies, the Sierra Madre of Central America, and the Andes.

- An *oceanic plate–oceanic plate collision* can produce curving belts of mountains called *island arcs* that rise from the ocean floor. When oceanic plates collide, the older seafloor will subduct beneath the younger seafloor, creating an oceanic trench. Magma forms at depth and rises upward, erupting as it reaches the seafloor and beginning the construction of a volcanic island. As the process continues along the trench, the eruptions and accumulation of volcanic material form a volcanic island arc (**Figure GIA 12.2b**). These processes formed island arcs and volcanoes from the southwestern Pacific to the Philippines and on through portions of the Aleutians near Alaska. Indonesia and Japan are complex arcs that exhibit surface rock deformation and metamorphism.

- A *continental plate–continental plate collision* produces orogenesis by mechanical processes, as large masses of continental crust are subjected to intense folding, overthrusting, faulting, and uplifting (**Figure GIA 12.2c**). The converging plates crush and deform both marine sediments and basaltic oceanic crust. The European Alps are a result of such compression

forces and exhibit considerable crustal shortening in conjunction with great overturned folds, called *nappes*.

The collision of India with the Eurasian landmass, producing the Himalayas, is estimated to have shortened the overall continental crust by as much as 1000 km (about 600 mi) and to have produced sequences of thrust faults at depths of 40 km (25 mi). The Himalayas feature the tallest above-sea-level mountains on Earth, and many of Earth's highest peaks.

The Tetons and the Sierra Nevada

Mountain landscapes can be altered when a normal fault along one side of a range produces a tilted linear landscape with dramatic relief known as a *tilted-fault-block* mountain range. The Tetons of Wyoming and the Sierra Nevada of California are recent examples of this stage of mountain building. In both these ranges, mountain building first began hundreds of millions of years ago with magma intrusions that cooled to form granitic cores of coarsely crystalline rock. Tectonic uplift followed, with subsequent faulting and tilting occurring less than 10 m.y.a. The removal of overlying material through weathering, erosion, and transport then exposed the granitic masses, leaving the rugged topography and steep vertical relief we see today (**Figure 12.15**).

(a) The east face of the Tetons, with 2130 m (7000 ft) of vertical relief between the valley of Jackson Hole and the mountain summits.

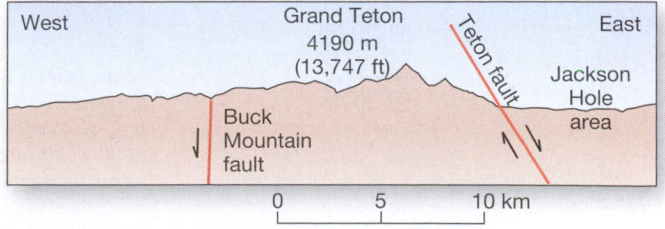

(b) Erosion of the upthrown footwall side of the 70-km-long (44-mi-long) Teton fault (a normal fault) causes the rugged topography and vertical relief of the Teton range.

▲**Figure 12.15 The Tetons of Wyoming, a tilted-fault-block mountain range.** [Robert Christopherson.]

Orogenesis, or mountain building, is the result of plate interactions and related processes that thicken and uplift the crust, such as folding, faulting, and volcanism. Combined with weathering, erosion, and isostatic adjustment, these processes produce the striking landscapes of Earth's mountain ranges (GIA 12.1). Collisions of Earth's plates produce three distinct kinds of orogenesis (GIA 12.2).

12.1 MAJOR MOUNTAIN RANGES AND OROGENIES

The mountain ranges we see today have roots deep in geologic time—some, such as the Appalachians, have repeatedly been formed, eroded away, and uplifted again as Earth's plates interacted over hundreds of millions of years.

12.1a — Mount Katahdin, Maine

12.1f — Three Sisters, Canadian Rockies, Alberta

12.1b — French Alps

Rocky Mountains:
Formed mainly during the **Laramide orogeny***, 40–80 m.y.a., but also during several earlier orogenies, beginning 170 m.y.a. (including the* **Sevier orogeny***).*

Appalachian Mountains:
Formed during the **Alleghany orogeny***, 250–300 million years ago (m.y.a.), when Africa and North America collided. Includes folded Ridge and Valley Province of the eastern United States and extends into Canada's Maritime Provinces.*

Alps:
Formed during the **Alpine orogeny***, 2–66 m.y.a., and continuing to the present across southern Europe and the Mediterranean.*

12.1e — Klamath Mountains, Oregon

Sierra Nevada and Klamath Mountains:
Formed during the **Nevadan orogeny***, with faulting 29–35 m.y.a. (older batholithic intrusions date to 80–180 m.y.a.).*

Animation (MG)
Subduction Zones

https://goo.gl/pnXiPA

12.1d — Chimborazo, Ecuador

Andes:
Formed during the **Andean orogeny** *over the past 65 million years, the Andes are the South American segment of a vast north–south belt of mountains running along the western margin of the Americas.*

12.1c — Himalayas, Pakistan

Himalayas:
Formed during the **Himalayan orogeny***, 45–54 m.y.a., beginning with the collision of the Indian and Eurasian plates and continuing to the present.*

Animation (MG)
Plate Boundary Features

https://goo.gl/CtDgzD

MasteringGeography™

Visit the Study Area in MasteringGeography™ to explore mountain building.

Visualize: Study geosciences animations of subduction zones and plate boundaries.

Assess: Demonstrate understanding of mountain building (if assigned by instructor).

12.2 MOUNTAIN BUILDING AT CONVERGENT BOUNDARIES

Three different types of lithospheric plate collisions result in mountain building: (a) oceanic plate–continental plate, (b) oceanic plate–oceanic plate, (c) continental plate–continental plate. Each plate interaction leads to a different kind of orogenesis.

Oceanic plate–continental plate
Where a dense oceanic plate collides with a less-dense continental plate, a subduction zone forms. As magma erupts to the surface, volcanic mountains form. Magma may also harden beneath the surface, forming batholiths.

Example: *The Andes of South America formed as Nazca plate subducts beneath the South American plate.*

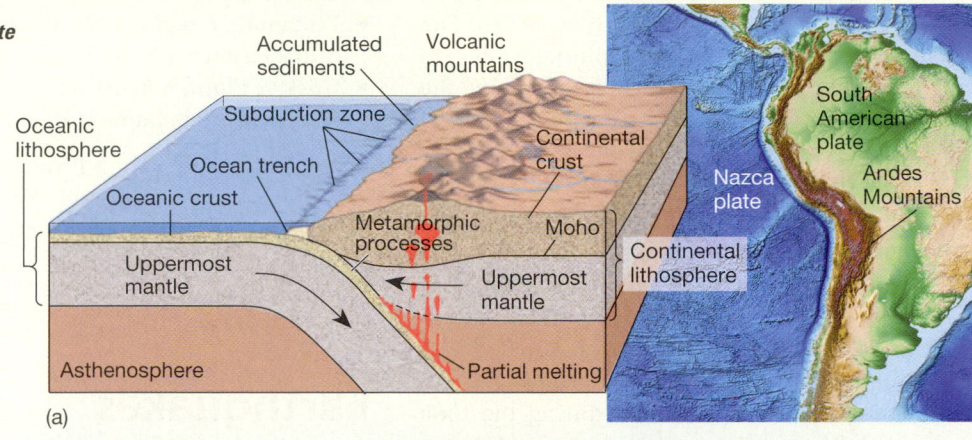

Oceanic plate–oceanic plate
Where two oceanic plates collide, one plate is subducted beneath the other. Magma reaching the surface gives rise to a volcanic island arc.

Example: *As part of the "Ring of Fire," volcanic island arcs extend from the southwestern Pacific (shown here) through Indonesia, the Philippines, and Japan to the Aleutians.*

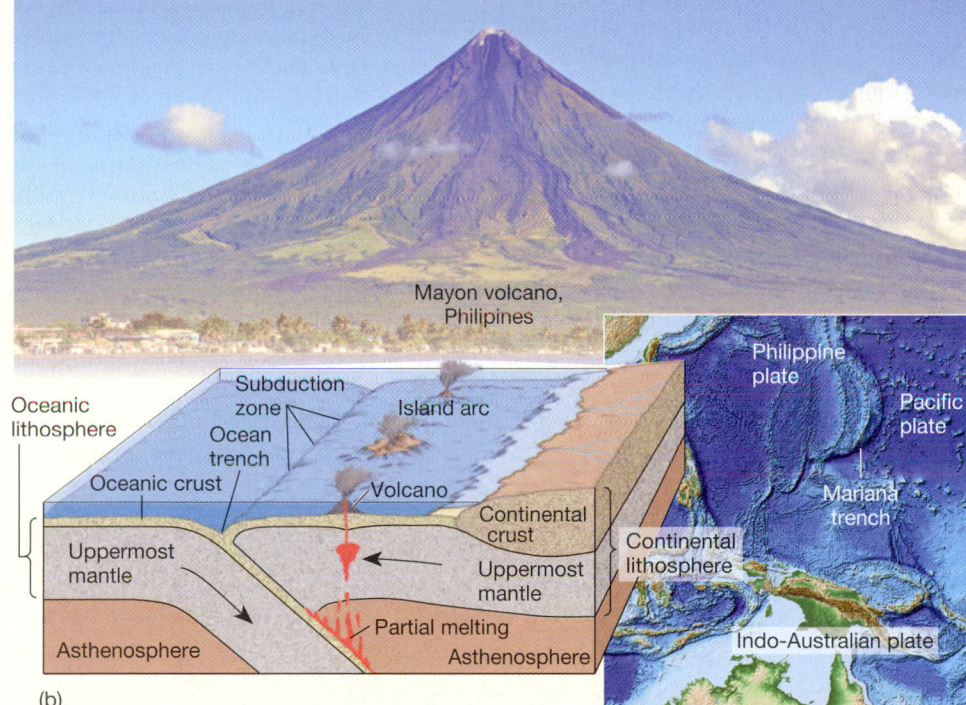

Continental plate–continental plate
Where two continental plates collide, neither plate is subducted. Instead, the collision subjects the plates to powerful compression forces that fold, fault, and uplift the crust, pushing up huge mountain ranges.

Example: *The Himalayas formed as a result of the ongoing collision of the Indian and Eurasian plates.*

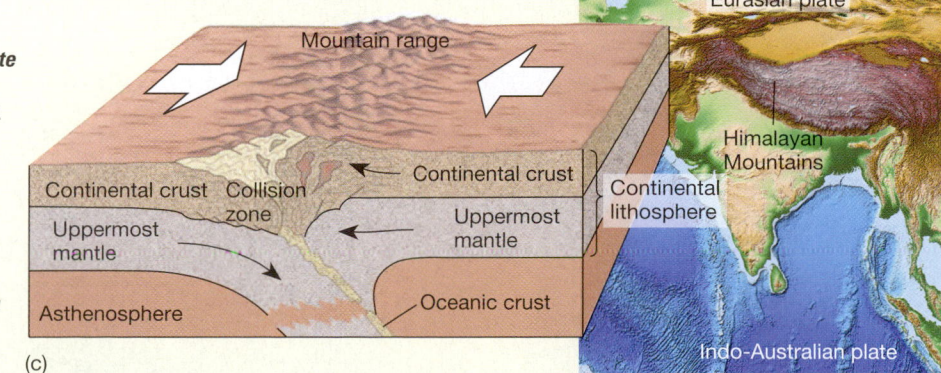

GEOquiz

1. Predict: Will the Himalayas keep growing higher and higher indefinitely? Explain your answer.

2. Compare: In terms of orogenesis and plate tectonics, how are the Alps and the Andes similar? How are they different?

3. Identify: What geologic event triggered the Alleghany orogeny, which formed the Appalachians?

4. Infer: Why doesn't subduction occur when two continental plates collide?

Recent research in the Sierra Nevada disclosed that some of the uplift in this range was isostatic, in response to the erosion of overlying material and the melting of ice following the last ice age some 18,000 years ago. The accumulation of sediments in the adjoining valley to the west depressed the crust there, further enhancing the topographic relief.

The Appalachian Mountains

The origin of the Appalachian Mountains of the eastern United States and southeastern Canada dates to the formation of Pangaea and the collision of Africa with North America (250–300 m.y.a.). The complexity of the *Alleghany orogeny* derives from at least two earlier orogenic cycles of uplift and the accretion of several terranes.

Mountain ranges that were linked during the time of Pangaea, but that are now separated by the Atlantic Ocean, are similar in both structure and composition. Such similarities indicate that the Lesser (or Anti-) Atlas Mountains of Mauritania and northwestern Africa were connected to the Appalachians in the past. Subsequent plate movement created active plate boundaries and several orogenic periods that gave rise to the mountains of today, stretching from Newfoundland, Canada, to central Alabama in the United States.

The central Appalachian Mountain region includes several landscape subregions (**Figure 12.16**):

- Appalachian Plateau, consisting of eroded sedimentary rock on the western edge;
- Ridge and Valley Province, made up of elongated sequences of folded sedimentary strata;

- Blue Ridge Mountains, an area principally of crystalline rock, highest where North Carolina, Virginia, and Tennessee converge;
- Piedmont, a region of hilly to gentle terrain along most of the eastern and southern margins of the mountains
- Coastal Plain, consisting of gentle hills descending to flat plains that extend to the Atlantic coast.

In the Ridge and Valley Province, folded anticlines and synclines form prominent linear ridges. Rivers such as the Susquehanna flow across these ridges, forming water gaps that were vital for human settlement and transportation.

Earthquakes

Crustal plates do not glide smoothly past one another. Instead, tremendous friction exists along plate boundaries. The stress, or force, of plate motion builds strain, or deformation, in the rocks until friction is overcome and the sides along plate boundaries or fault lines suddenly break loose. The sharp release of energy that occurs at the moment of fracture, producing seismic waves, is an **earthquake**, or *quake*. The two sides of the fault plane then lurch into new positions, moving distances ranging from centimeters to several meters, and release enormous amounts of seismic energy into the surrounding crust. This energy radiates throughout the planet, diminishing with distance.

Most earthquakes occur along the faults associated with tectonic plate boundaries. **Megathrust earthquakes**

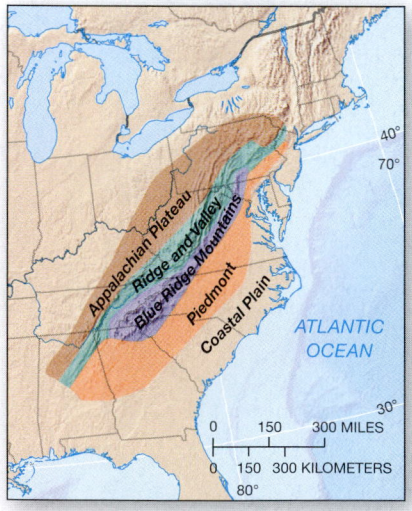

(a) Landscape subregions of the central Appalachian Mountains. The folded Ridge and Valley Province extends from Pennsylvania south through Maryland, Virginia, and West Virginia.

▲**Figure 12.16 The folded Ridge and Valley Province of the Appalachian Mountains.** [(a) USGS. (b) *ISS* Crew Earth Observations Experiment and Image Science & Analysis Laboratory/Johnson Space Center/NASA. (c) *Landsat-7*, NASA.]

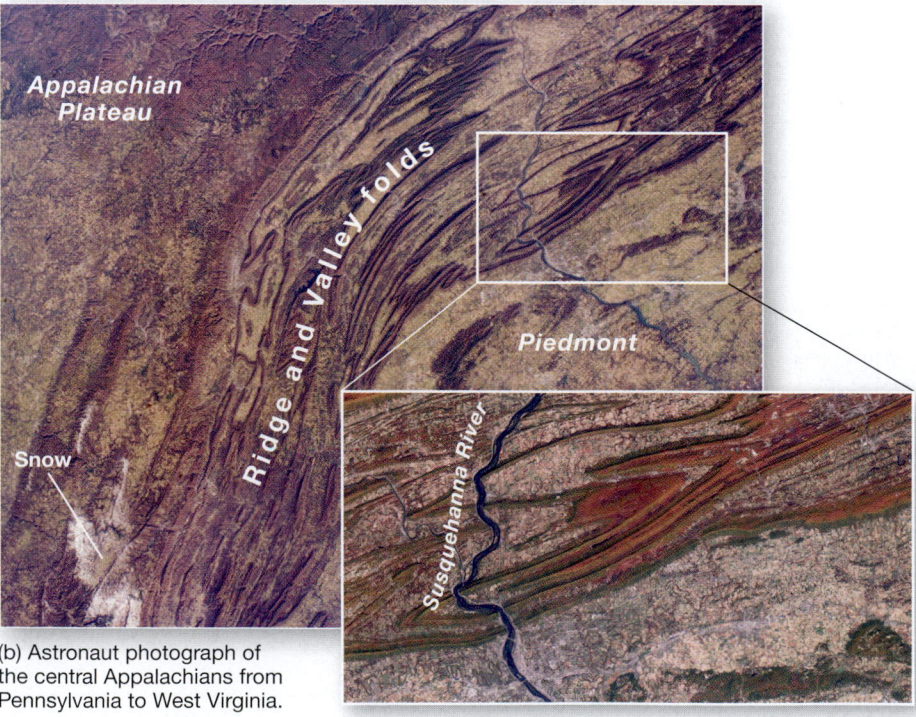

(b) Astronaut photograph of the central Appalachians from Pennsylvania to West Virginia.

(c) The Susquehanna River flows across the ridge and valley structure.

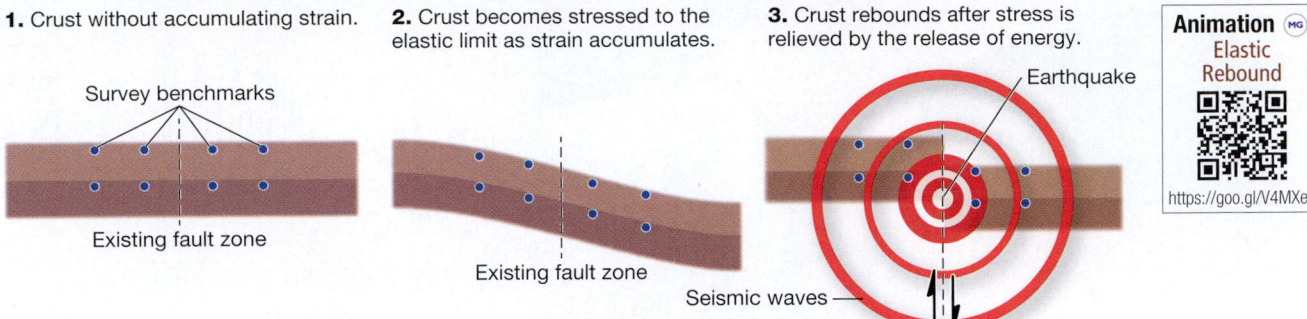

1. Crust without accumulating strain.

2. Crust becomes stressed to the elastic limit as strain accumulates.

3. Crust rebounds after stress is relieved by the release of energy.

Survey benchmarks

Existing fault zone

Existing fault zone

Earthquake

Seismic waves

Animation

Elastic Rebound

https://goo.gl/V4MXeY

▲**Figure 12.17** **Elastic-rebound theory.** According to the theory, strain accumulates until the rock breaks, abruptly releasing elastic energy. Viewed from above the fault zone, you see in part 3 that both sides of the fault then rebound, returning to a condition of less strain.

occur along subduction zones, producing the most powerful earthquakes on Earth. These quakes often deform the ocean floor, producing tsunami (seismic sea waves) that travel long distances across oceans (discussed in Chapter 16). However, earthquakes also occur along faults that are distant from plate boundaries, as well as in association with volcanic activity. Recent research suggests that the injection of wastewater from oil and gas drilling into subsurface areas is another cause, leading to *induced earthquakes* (discussed at the end of this section).

Fault Mechanics and Earthquake Anatomy

In the early 1900s, after studying the 1906 San Francisco earthquake, geologist Henry Reid proposed the **elastic-rebound theory** to describe the basic process of how rocks break along a fault during an earthquake. Rocks, like numerous other solids, are elastic. Under pressure, they can bend and deform, and then spring back to their initial shape when the pressure is released. However, if pressure continues and even increases, rocks will break, as when you bend a tree branch until it snaps. Rocks can also permanently deform, like a piece of Silly Putty, as happens in the process of folding described earlier in the chapter.

When two sides along a slowly moving fault become locked by friction, they resist any movement despite the forces acting on them. This ongoing stress builds strain along the fault, deforming the rock. When the building strain finally exceeds the strength of the frictional lock, both sides of the fault abruptly move, releasing a burst of mechanical energy. The rocks then rebound back to their original shape (**Figure 12.17**).

The location below the surface where an earthquake starts is the **focus**, or hypocenter. This is where the motion of seismic waves initiates along the fault plane (**Figure 12.18**). The area at the surface directly above the focus is the **epicenter**. Shock waves produced by an earthquake radiate outward through the crust from the focus and epicenter.

A *foreshock* is a smaller quake that precedes the main shock. An *aftershock* occurs after the main shock,

sharing the same general area of the epicenter. Some aftershocks rival the main tremor in size and intensity. For instance, on the South Island of New Zealand an M 7.1 quake struck in September 2010 with an epicenter 45 km (30 mi) from Christchurch, causing about USD$3 billion in damage and no deaths. Seventeen days later, an M 6.3 aftershock with an epicenter just 6 km (3 mi) from the city produced building collapses, 350 deaths, and more than USD$15 billion in damage. These events also show that the distance from the epicenter is an important factor in determining overall earthquake effects on urban areas.

Earthquake Intensity and Magnitude

A **seismometer**, or seismograph, is an instrument used to detect and record the ground motion that occurs during an earthquake. This instrument records motion in only a single direction, so scientists use a combination of vertical-motion and horizontal-motion seismometers to determine the source and strength of seismic waves. The instrument detects body waves (traveling through Earth's interior) first,

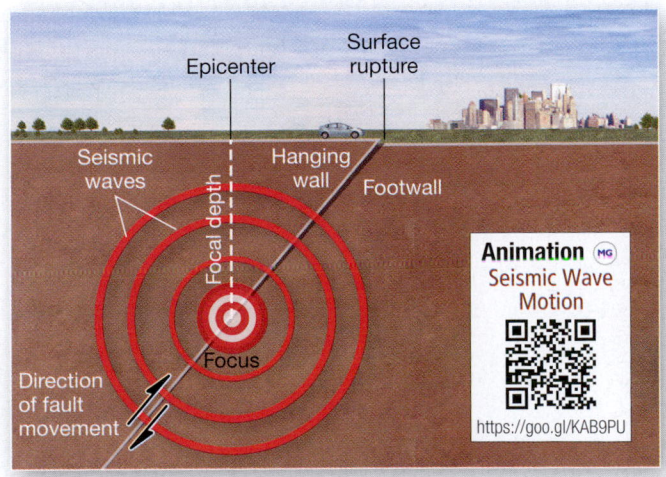

Epicenter

Surface rupture

Seismic waves

Focal depth

Hanging wall

Footwall

Direction of fault movement

Focus

Animation

Seismic Wave Motion

https://goo.gl/KAB9PU

▲**Figure 12.18** **Earthquake anatomy.** The focus is the zone at depth where the initial displacement occurs. The epicenter is at the surface above the focus.

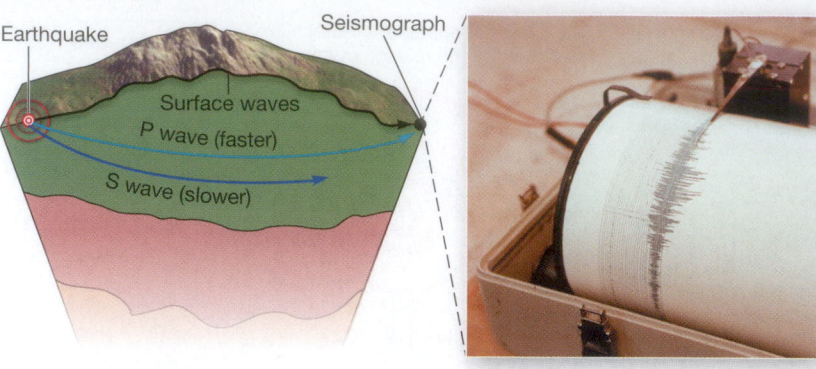

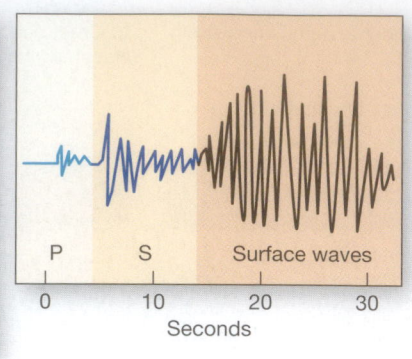

▲**Figure 12.19 Seismic waves and seismograph.** The first waves are faster P waves (or primary waves), followed by slower S waves (or secondary waves), and then by the surface waves that cause the most ground shaking. [Zephyr/Science Source.]

followed by surface waves, recording both on a *seismogram* in the form of a graph (**Figure 12.19**). Scientists use a worldwide network of more than 4000 seismometers to sense earthquakes, and these quakes are then classified on the basis of either damage intensity or the magnitude of energy released.

Intensity and Ground Shaking One way to assess earthquakes is by rating the intensity in terms of observed effects on Earth's surface, such as damage to structures and severity of shaking. Developed in 1931, the *Modified Mercalli Intensity (MMI) scale* is a Roman numeral scale from I to XII that rates earthquakes from those that are "barely felt" (lower numbers) to those that cause "catastrophic total destruction" (higher numbers; see **Table 12.1**). This scale is useful for non-scientists because it assesses the actual effects experienced at the exact time and location of the quake. The USGS routinely uses online reports from the public to produce "Shake Maps" such as the one in **Figure 12.20a**, using the Mercalli scale.

Ground shaking during an earthquake can liquefy soils, enhancing the collapse of structures. **Liquefaction** is the process whereby ground shaking disrupts and loosens the structure of the soil, causing it to flow. This typically occurs in sandy soils, which cannot retain their structure as the pressure from the shaking overcomes the friction between particles. Liquefaction affects building foundations and can cause highway collapse, such as occurred during California's 1989 Loma Prieta earthquake.

The Loma Prieta quake struck south of San Francisco on an October afternoon just before the third game of the World Series at Candlestick Park. The quake killed 63 people, displaced 14,000, and caused $8 billion in damage. Because of the extent of landfill in the San Francisco Bay area, liquefaction added to the damage (Figure 12.20).

Earthquake Energy Earthquake *magnitude* is a measure of the energy released and provides a way to compare earthquake size. In 1935, Charles Richter designed a system to estimate earthquake magnitude based on measurement of maximum wave amplitude on a seismometer. *Amplitude* is the height of a seismic wave and is directly related to the amount of ground movement. The size and timing of maximum seismic wave height can be plotted on a chart called the **Richter scale**, which provided a number for earthquake magnitude in relation to a station located more than 100 km (62 mi) from the epicenter of the quake.

The Richter scale is logarithmic: Each whole number on it represents a 10-fold increase in the measured wave amplitude. Translated into energy, each whole number signifies a 31.5-fold increase in energy released. Thus, a magnitude of 3.0 on the Richter scale represents 31.5 times more energy than a 2.0 and 992 times more energy than a 1.0. Although useful for measuring shallow earthquakes, the Richter scale does not properly measure or differentiate between quakes of high intensity.

TABLE 12.1 Earthquake Intensity According to the Modified Mercalli Scale

Intensity	Perceived Shaking	Effects on Populated Areas
I	Not felt	Instrumental. Not felt, but recorded.
II–III	Weak	Slight. Felt by some, especially on upper floors of buildings.
IV–V	Light to moderate	Moderate. Felt by some to felt by many; some disturbance and vibration.
VI–VII	Strong to very strong	Strong. Felt by all, with slight building damage.
VIII–IX	Severe to violent	Destructive. Slight to considerable damage, depending on building design; buildings shifted off their foundations.
X–XI	Extreme	Disastrous. Major damage; bridges destroyed, most structures partially collapsed; railroad tracks bent.
XII	Extreme	Catastrophic. Damage nearly total.

Source: USGS Earthquake Hazards Program.

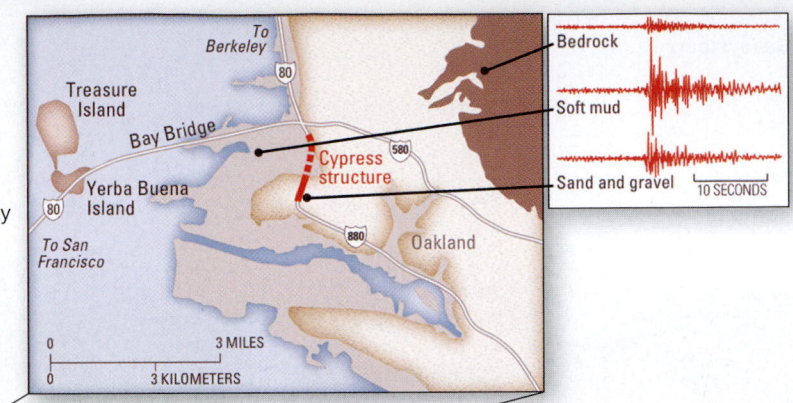

(b) The collapse of the Cypress Freeway structure resulted from the soft mud (dashed red line) on which it was built. Adjacent parts of the structure built on firmer ground (solid red line) remained standing. Seismographs recorded the more severe shaking in the soft mud versus other materials.

(c) Repair crews examine damage to the Cypress Freeway structure after the 1989 quake.

▲Figure 12.20 Ground shaking and liquefaction, Loma Prieta, California, earthquake. [(a) and (b) USGS. (c) Dave Bartruff/Getty Images.]

PERCEIVED SHAKING	Not tell	Weak	Light	Moderate	Strong	Very strong	Severe	Violent	Extreme
POTENTIAL DAMAGE	None	None	None	Very light	Light	Moderate	Moderate/Heavy	Heavy	Very Heavy
INSTRUMENTAL INTENSITY	I	II–III	IV	V	VI	VII	VIII	IX	X+

(a) This Loma Prieta shake map was created many years after the quake based on actual 1989 data. Nearly 70% of damage and fatalities were caused by strong ground shaking.

The **moment magnitude (M) scale** replaced the Richter scale in 1993. Moment magnitude considers the amount of fault slippage produced by the earthquake, the size of the surface (or subsurface) area that ruptured, and the nature of the materials that faulted, including how resistant they were to failure. This scale considers extreme ground acceleration (movement upward), which the Richter amplitude magnitude method underestimates.

In an average year, hundreds of thousands of earthquakes occur, most of them small in magnitude (Table 12.2). As magnitude increases, the expected frequency decreases. The strongest earthquake in recorded history was the 1960 M 9.5 earthquake in Chile, which produce Mercalli XII damage.

TABLE 12.2 Earthquake Magnitude and Expected Frequency

Magnitude (M)	Annual Average (Expected)*
2.0–2.9	1,300,000
3.0–3.9	130,000
4.0–4.9	13,000
5.0–5.9	1319
6.0–6.9	134
7.0–7.9	15
8.0 and higher	1

*Based on observations from 1900 to 2012. Source: USGS.

▼**Figure 12.21** The 2011 Japan earthquake and tsunami.
[(a) Kyodo News/Reuters. (b) AP Photo/Kydo News.]

(a) Honshu Island, Japan, after the quake and tsunami. The epicenter was on a convergent plate boundary between the Pacific and North American plates.

(b) Tsunami moves ashore, Iwanuma, Japan. Iwanuma is 20 km (12.4 mi) south of Sendai, the city closest to the epicenter.

Japan Earthquake and Tsunami, 2011

When an earthquake occurs offshore, the displacement of the ocean floor can cause a set of huge seismic sea waves known as a *tsunami*. Two devastating tsunami occurred during this century as a result of megathrust earthquakes: the 2004 Indian Ocean tsunami resulting from the M 9.0 quake in Sumatra, Indonesia, and the 2011 Japan tsunami resulting from the M 9.0 Tohoku quake off the coast of Honshu Island.

Even in Japan, a country with strict and extensive earthquake preparedness standards, the damage and human cost associated with an earthquake and tsunami can be enormous (**Figure 12.21a**). The quake occurred when an area of ocean floor some 340 km (N–S) by 150 km (210 mi by 90 mi) snapped, shifting 50 m (160 ft) to the southeast. The seafloor lifted some 7 m (23 ft), displacing the ocean above it. This disturbance caused the tsunami, in which the largest wave averaged 10 m (33 ft) along the coast near Iwanuma (**Figure 12.21b**). Where it entered narrow harbors and embayments, wave height reached nearly 30 m (98 ft). Although Japan's tsunami warning system sent out immediate alerts, the time window before the tsunami hit was too short for evacuation.

Haiti and Nepal Earthquakes, 2010 and 2015

The 2010 Haiti earthquake hit an impoverished country where little of the infrastructure was built to withstand earthquakes. Over 2 million people live in the capital city of Port-au-Prince, which has experienced earthquake destruction several times, mostly notably in 1751 and 1770. The total damage from the 2010 magnitude 7.0 quake exceeded the country's $14 billion gross domestic product (GDP). In developing countries such as Haiti, inadequate construction, lack of enforced building codes, and the difficulties of getting food, water, and medical help to those in need worsen earthquake damage (**Figure 12.22a**).

The Maule, Chile, M 8.8 earthquake, which occurred just 6 weeks later in 2010, caused only minimal damage, in large part due to the fact that the country enacted strict building codes in 1985. The result was a fraction of the human cost compared to the Haiti earthquake.

The tragic scenario of earthquake destruction in a developing country played out again in Nepal in 2015. The plate collision in which India is moving northeastward toward the Asian landmass causes frequent earthquakes in the region. As evidence of the ongoing strain, the April 2015 quake in Nepal occurred along the fault zone that marks the meeting of the Indo-Australian and Eurasian plates. The M 7.8 earthquake killed more than 8000 people as an estimated 25,000 buildings collapsed, some of them dating back to the Middle Ages (**Figure 12.22b**).

Earthquake Forecasting and Warning Systems

Although scientists are not able to predict earthquake occurrences, they are able to use scientific data to forecast earthquake probabilities, which vary with location. In the United States, regions having a particularly high risk include California and the Yellowstone area of Wyoming, Idaho, and Montana (**Figure 12.23**). Scientists estimate that over the next 30 years the probability of an M 7.0 earthquake occurring along the San Andreas fault in California is 75–76%.

The science of *paleoseismology* studies the history of plate boundaries and the frequency of past earthquakes. Paleoseismologists construct maps that estimate expected earthquake activity based on past performance.

(a) Destruction in Port-au-Prince, Haiti, in 2010. The quake epicenter was along multiple surface faults and a previously unknown subsurface thrust fault.

(b) Destruction in Bhaktapur, Nepal, in the Kathmandu Valley, home to over 2.5 million people. More than 100 aftershocks followed the M 7.8 quake.

▲**Figure 12.22 Earthquakes in Haiti in 2010 and Nepal in 2015.** [(a) Julie Jacobson/AP Images. (b) Nepal Photos/Alamy.]

The science behind the forecasting of a major earthquake along the Cascadia subduction zone discussed in Geosystems Now relies on these types of data.

Several countries have successfully implemented earthquake warning systems using electronic communications, which travel faster than seismic waves. A Mexico City warning system provides 70-second notice of arriving seismic waves. The system was effective in March 2012, when a senate hearing at the capitol was interrupted by the sirens indicating an imminent earthquake. Shaking began about a minute later. Japan is the only nation with a comprehensive, nationwide alert system. During the 2011 Tohoku earthquake, the system sent alerts to televisions and cell phones and automatically shut down some transportation services. (We discuss the Pacific Ocean tsunami warning system in Chapter 16.) In Vancouver, British Columbia, an early warning system is in place to protect the George Massey Tunnel that runs underwater, connecting the north and south banks of the Fraser River. If sensors detect seismic waves, electronic signs turn on at the tunnel entrances, warning drivers to avoid entering. As previously discussed, a U.S. earthquake early warning system is still in development.

Human-Induced Earthquakes

Recently, human activities have altered the natural processes occurring along faults, causing *induced seismicity*, or human-induced earthquakes. For example, if the pressure on the pores and fractures in rocks is increased by the addition of fluids through fluid injection in deep wells, then earthquake activity may accelerate. The extraction of fluids, especially at a rapid rate, can also induce seismicity by causing subsidence of the ground and enhancing slippage along faults.

Both fluid injection and fluid extraction are common activities associated with oil and natural gas drilling and with geothermal energy production. Hydraulic fracturing, or fracking, associated with shale gas extraction injects large quantities of fluid to break up subsurface rock, making this process a probable cause for induced earthquakes, discussed in Focus Study 12.1. Enhanced geothermal systems, discussed in Chapter 11, also use hydraulic fracturing, which has resulted in seismic activity at several locations, including The Geysers Geothermal Field in California.

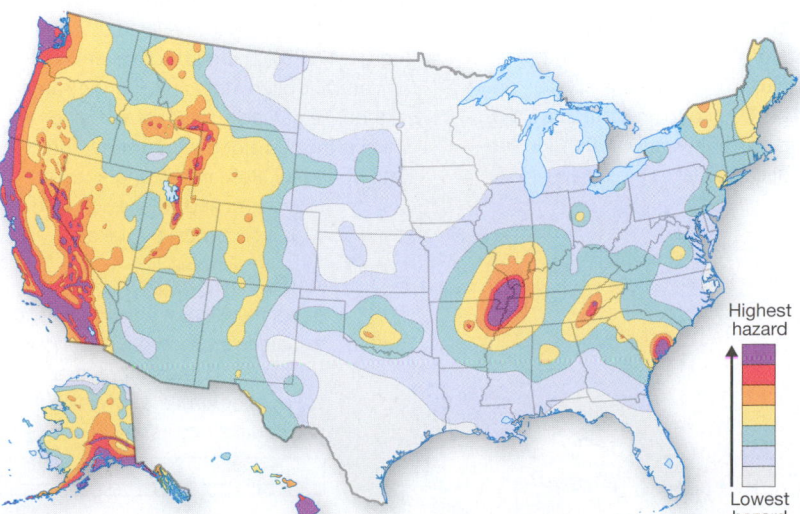

▲**Figure 12.23 Earthquake hazard map for the United States.** Colors on the map indicate the probability of ground motion, with red being the highest. Active seismic regions include the West Coast, the Wasatch Front of Utah northward into Canada, the central Mississippi Valley, the southern Appalachians, and portions of South Carolina, upstate New York, and Ontario. [USGS; see http://earthquake.usgs.gov/hazards/products/.]

Highest hazard

Lowest hazard

FOCUS STUDY 12.1 Natural Hazards
Human-caused Earthquakes on the Increase

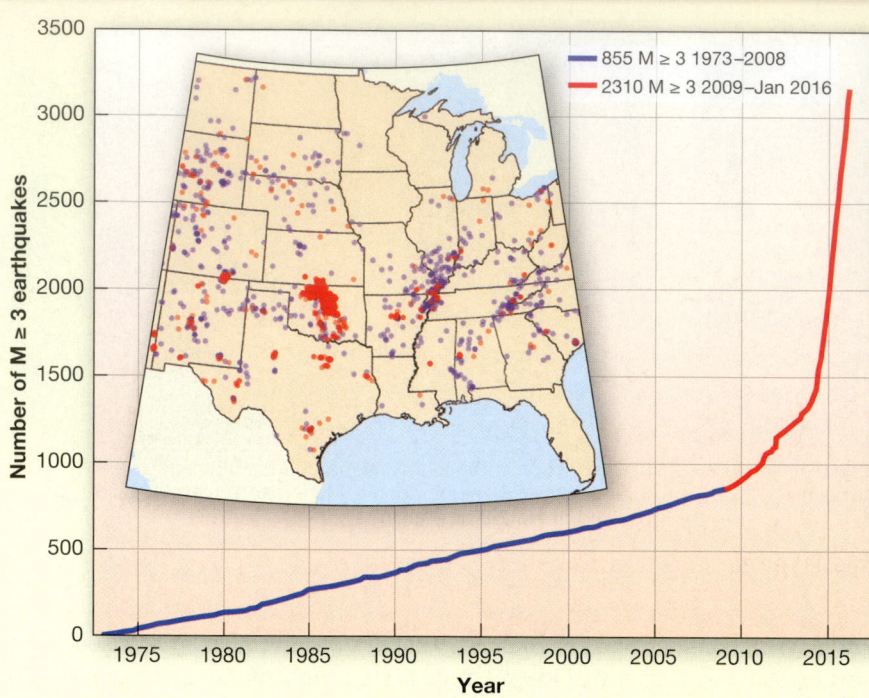

Figure 12.1.1 Number of earthquakes with magnitude 3.0 or greater from 1970–2016. The blue line shows earthquakes occurring from 1973 to 2008. The red line shows earthquakes from 2009 through 2015. The inset map shows the locations of earthquakes colored blue or red to correspond to the dates on the graph. [USGS.]

Graph legend:
- 855 M ≥ 3 1973–2008
- 2310 M ≥ 3 2009–Jan 2016

Figure 12.1.2 Induced-earthquake damage, Oklahoma. Sandstone bricks from the historic Pawnee County Bank litter the sidewalk after an M 5.8 earthquake in 2016. [Paul Hellstern /The Okahoman/AP Photo.]

Since 2009, scientists have recorded a dramatic increase in the number of earthquakes in the central United States. This rise is concentrated in a few areas, most notably central Oklahoma (**Figure 12.1.1**). Mounting evidence indicates that the recent earthquakes are human-induced, caused by the deep injection of wastewater from oil and gas production.

Some 40,000 deep wells drilled below drinking water aquifers now hold the wastewater from the extraction of shale gas and oil from underground rock. Some of the wastewater is a by-product of hydraulic fracturing, or fracking. In the fracking process, fluids are pumped under pressure into shale to fracture the rock, creating pathways for gas and oil collection and removal. After fracking is done, water and fracking fluids are injected back into the ground, into deep wells, for long-term disposal.

A mixture of saltwater and chemicals, the wastewater is injected at high pressure into the rock. When the wastewater enters into fractures, or faults, in rock at depth, it counteracts the forces of friction holding the fault blocks together. The fluid essentially pries apart the fault line, leading to an earthquake slip.

The process of hydraulic fracturing produces small earthquakes (less than M 2.0) as the fluids break up the rock to produce oil and gas. However, the recent rise in frequency of larger earthquakes is not attributed to this part of the process. Earthquakes related to wastewater injection are far larger—for example, an injection well in Oklahoma is thought to have caused an M 5.8 quake in 2016, the largest quake on record at that time (**Figure 12.1.2**). Scientists recently confirmed that the increased pressure at injection wells can migrate away from the site, causing earthquakes to occur several kilometers away in both a horizontal and vertical direction.

In 2016, the USGS released a 1-year map forecasting the potential for natural and induced quakes in the United States (**Figure 12.1.3**). The map shows areas of the central United States having the same earthquake damage potential as California, which is located along an active tectonic plate boundary. Research is ongoing into the causes and risks associated with induced earthquakes.

APPLYconcepts Use your understanding of earthquakes to explain in your own words how fracking and related practices change the process by which an earthquake occurs.

1. _____

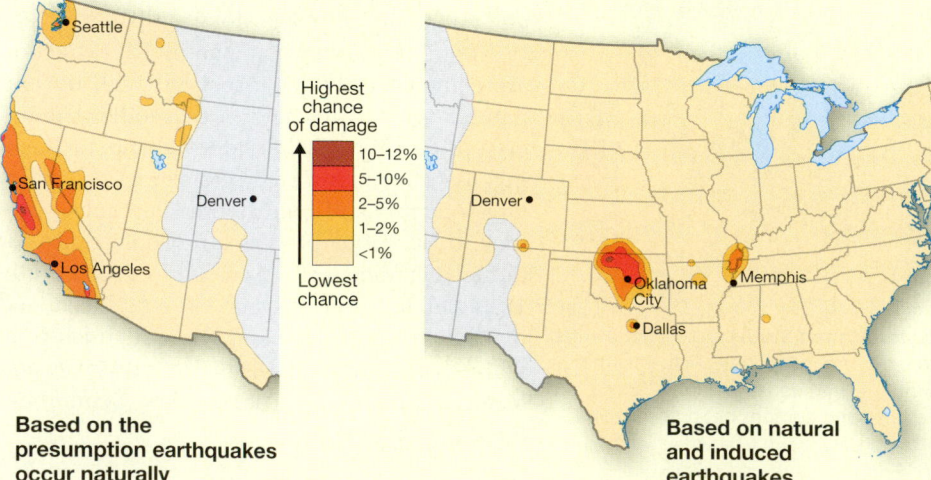

Based on the presumption earthquakes occur naturally

Based on natural and induced earthquakes

Map legend: Highest chance of damage
- 10–12%
- 5–10%
- 2–5%
- 1–2%
- <1%
- Lowest chance

Figure 12.1.3 Potential for natural- or induced-earthquake damage in 2016. Map at left shows potential for natural earthquakes. Map at right shows potential for both natural and induced earthquakes. Damage potential ranges from 1% to 12%. [USGS.]

Volcanism

Volcanic eruptions across the globe remind us of Earth's tremendous internal energy and of the dynamic forces shaping the planet's surface. The distribution of ongoing volcanic activity matches the distribution of plate boundaries, as shown on the map in Figure 11.27, as well as indicating the location of hot spots. Over 1300 identifiable volcanic cones and mountains exist on Earth, although fewer than 600 are active.

An *active* volcano is defined as one that has erupted at least once in recorded history. In an average year, about 50 volcanoes erupt worldwide, varying from small-scale venting of lava or fumes to major explosions. North America has about 70 volcanoes (mostly inactive) along the western margin of the continent. The Global Volcanism Program lists information for more than 8500 eruptions at http://www.volcano.si.edu/, and the USGS provides extensive information about current volcanic activity at http://volcanoes.usgs.gov/.

Eruptions in remote locations and at depths on the seafloor go largely unnoticed, but the occasional eruption of great magnitude near a population center makes headlines. Even a distant eruption has global atmospheric effects. For example, in April 2010, the eruption of the Eyjafjallajökull volcano in southern Iceland garnered world attention for its effects on air transportation, as did the 2016 eruption of Pavlof in Alaska (see Chapter 3, Figure 3.10).

Settings for Volcanic Activity

Volcanic activity occurs in three settings, listed below with representative examples and illustrated in **Figure 12.24**:

- Along *subduction zones* at continental plate–oceanic plate convergence (for example, Mount St. Helens) or oceanic plate–oceanic plate convergence (Mount Pinatubo in the Philippines)
- Along *continental rift zones* created by plate divergence (for example, the rift zone in East Africa)
- Along *seafloor spreading centers* on the ocean floor (for example, Iceland, on the Mid-Atlantic Ridge)
- At *hot spots*, where individual plumes of magma rise to the crust (for example, Hawai'i and Yellowstone National Park, discussed in Chapter 11)

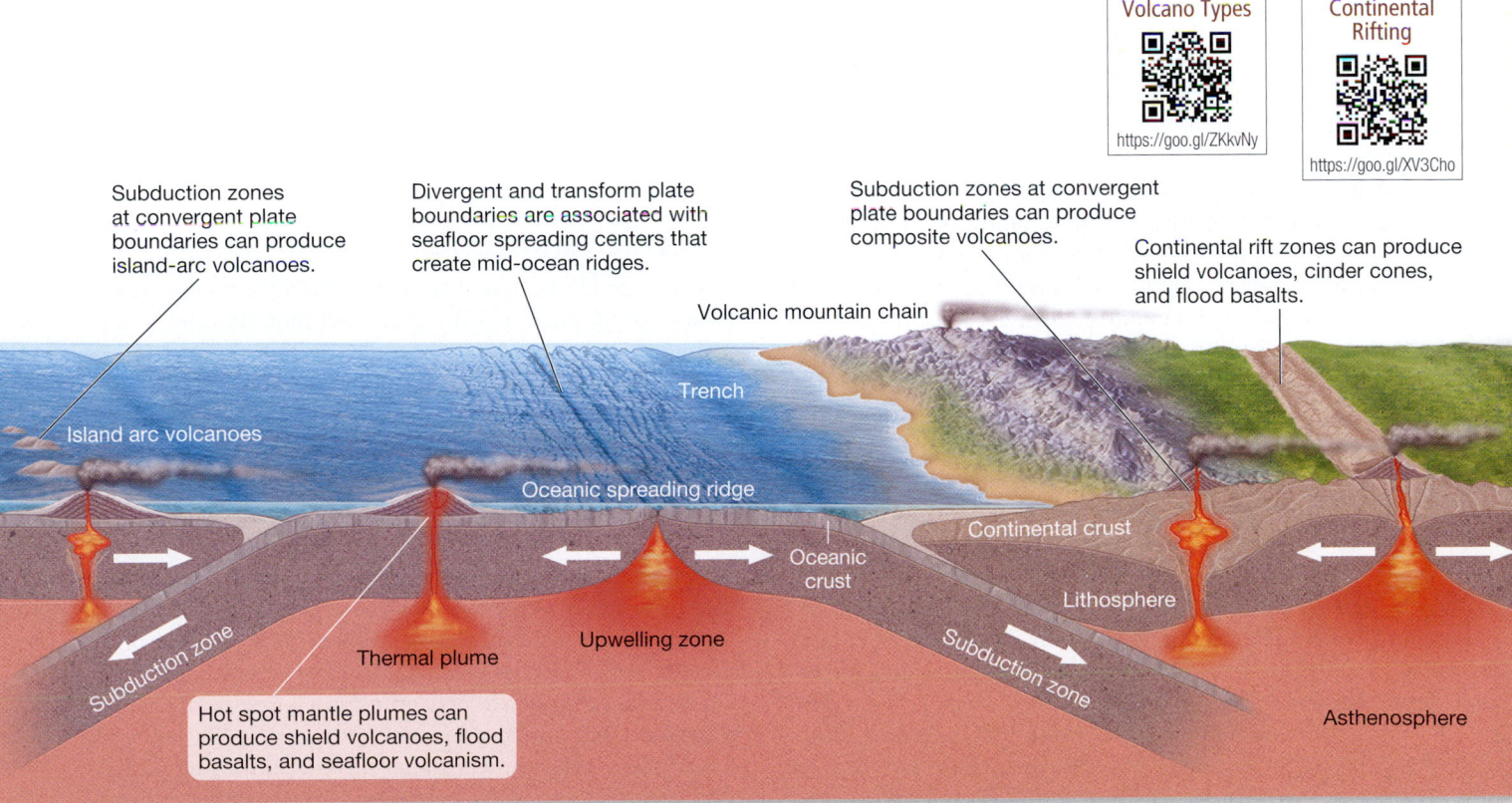

Animation (MG)
Volcano Types
https://goo.gl/ZKkvNy

Condor (MG)
Continental Rifting
https://goo.gl/XV3Cho

Subduction zones at convergent plate boundaries can produce island-arc volcanoes.

Divergent and transform plate boundaries are associated with seafloor spreading centers that create mid-ocean ridges.

Subduction zones at convergent plate boundaries can produce composite volcanoes.

Continental rift zones can produce shield volcanoes, cinder cones, and flood basalts.

Volcanic mountain chain

Trench

Island arc volcanoes

Oceanic spreading ridge

Continental crust

Oceanic crust

Lithosphere

Subduction zone

Thermal plume

Upwelling zone

Subduction zone

Hot spot mantle plumes can produce shield volcanoes, flood basalts, and seafloor volcanism.

Asthenosphere

▲Figure 12.24 **Tectonic settings of volcanic activity.** Magma rises and lava erupts from rifts, through crust above subduction zones, and where thermal plumes at hot spots break through the crust. [Adapted from USGS.]

(a) Aa is a rough, sharp-edged lava said to get its name from the sounds people make if they attempt to walk on it.

(b) Pahoehoe forms ropy cords in twisted folds.

▲**Figure 12.25 Two types of basaltic lava in Hawai'i.** [USGS.]

Volcanic Materials

A **volcano** is the structure in the Earth's crust containing an opening at the end of a central vent or pipe through which magma rises from the asthenosphere and upper mantle. Magma rises and collects in a magma chamber deep below the volcano until conditions are right for an eruption. This subsurface magma emits tremendous heat; in some areas, it boils groundwater, as seen in the thermal springs and geysers of Yellowstone National Park and at other locations with surface expressions of geothermal energy.

Various materials pass through the central vent to the surface to build volcanic landforms, including lava (magma that has cooled to form rock), gases, and **pyroclastics**—pulverized rock and clastic materials of various sizes ejected violently during an eruption (also called *tephra*). These materials may emerge explosively, or they may emerge effusively (flowing gently) from the vent (eruption types are discussed ahead).

As discussed in Chapter 11, solidified magma forms igneous rock. When magma emerges at the surface, it is *lava*. The chemistry of lava determines its behavior (whether it is thin and liquid or is thick and forms a plug).

Geologists classify lava depending on its chemical composition. Basaltic lava, which is low in silica and high in magnesium and iron, has two principal forms, both known by Hawaiian names (**Figure 12.25**). The composition of both these forms of lava is the same; the texture difference results from the manner in which the lava flows while it cools. Rough and jagged basalt with sharp edges is **aa**; it forms as a thick skin over the surface of a slowing lava flow, cracking and breaking as it cools and solidifies. Shiny and smooth basalt that resembles coiled, twisted rope is **pahoehoe**; it forms as a thin crust that develops folds as the lava

cools. Both forms can come from the same eruption, and sometimes pahoehoe becomes aa as the flow progresses. Other types of basaltic magma are described later in this section.

During a single eruption, a volcano may behave in several different ways, which depend primarily on the chemistry and gas content of the lava. These factors determine the lava's *viscosity*, or resistance to flow. Viscosity can range from low (very fluid) to high (thick and flowing slowly). For example, pahoehoe has lower viscosity than aa.

Volcanic Landforms

Volcanic eruptions result in structures that range among several forms, such as hill, cone, and mountain. In a volcanic mountain, a *crater*, or circular surface depression, is usually found at or near the summit.

A **cinder cone** is a small, cone-shaped hill usually less than 450 m (1500 ft) high, with a truncated top formed from cinders that accumulate during moderately explosive eruptions. Cinder cones are made of pyroclastic material and *scoria* (cindery rock, full of air bubbles). Several notable cinder cones are located on the San Francisco volcanic field of northern Arizona. Ascension Island, at about 8° S latitude in the Atlantic Ocean, has over 100 cinder cones and craters to mark its volcanic history (**Figure 12.26**).

A **caldera** (Spanish for "kettle") is a large, basin-shaped depression that forms when summit material on a volcanic mountain collapses inward after an eruption or other loss of magma (**Figure 12.27**). In contrast to a smaller volcanic crater, a caldera has a diameter of 1 km (0.6 mi) or larger. A caldera may fill with rainwater to form a lake, such as Crater Lake in southern Oregon, Mount Pinatubo Lake in the Philippines, and numerous lakes in the Andes Mountains of South America (**Figure 12.28**).

◄**Figure 12.26 Sunset Crater, a cinder cone.** Located in northern Arizona, the Sunset Crater cinder cone formed about 1100 c.e. during a series of eruptions that forced the temporary abandonment of the area by the local Sinagua people. The Sinagua left the region around 1400 c.e. for unknown reasons. [Tim Roberts Photography/Shutterstock.]

Effusive Eruptions

Effusive eruptions are outpourings of low-viscosity magma that produce enormous volumes of lava annually on the seafloor and in places such as Hawai'i and Iceland. These eruptions flow directly from the asthenosphere and upper mantle, releasing fluid magma that cools to form a dark, basaltic rock low in silica (less than 50%) and rich in iron and magnesium. Gases readily escape from this magma because of its low viscosity. Effusive eruptions pour out on the surface with relatively small explosions and few pyroclastics. However, dramatic fountains of basaltic lava sometimes shoot upward, powered by jets of rapidly expanding gases.

An effusive eruption may come from a single vent or from the flank of a volcano through a side vent. If such vent openings are linear in form, they are *fissures*, which sometimes erupt in a dramatic "curtain of fire" as sheets of molten rock spray into the air.

On the island of Hawai'i, the continuing Kīlauea eruption is the longest in recorded history—active since January 3, 1983. Although this eruption is located on the slopes of the massive Mauna Loa volcano, scientists have determined that Kīlauea has its own magma system extending down some 60 km (37 mi) into Earth. To date, the active crater on Kīlauea (called Pu'u O'o) has produced more lava than any other in recorded history—some 3.0 km³ (0.7 mi³).

Prior to 2011, massive flows of basaltic lava from the Kilauea volcano moved southward toward the ocean. In 2011, lava flows changed course as new eruptions began west of the Pu'u O'o crater. In the summer of 2014, new active flows moved northeastward into the town of Pāhoa, Hawai'i (**Figure 12.29**).

A typical mountain landform built from effusive eruptions is gently sloped, gradually rising from the surrounding landscape to a summit crater. The shape is similar in outline to a shield of armor lying face up on the ground and therefore is called a **shield volcano**. Mauna Loa is one of five shield volcanoes that make up the island of Hawai'i. The height of the Mauna Loa shield is

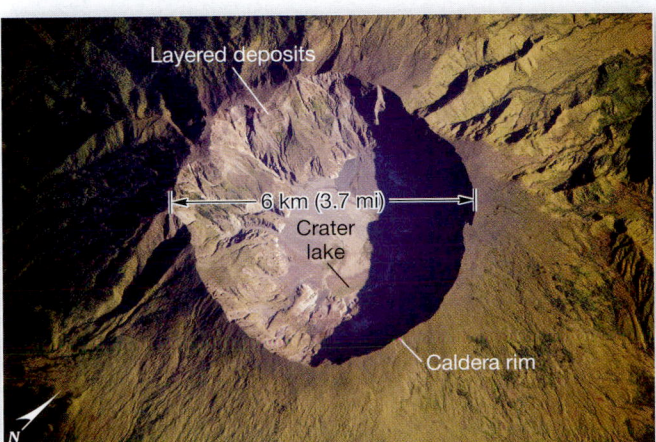

▲**Figure 12.27 Tambora caldera, Sumbawa Island, Indonesia.** The 1815 Tambora eruption was the largest in recorded history. The caldera, formed during the eruption, is 6 km (3.7 mi) in diameter and 1100 m (0.7 mi) deep. [2009 astronaut photograph ISS020-E-6563, *ISS Crew Earth Observations Experiment and Image Science & Analysis Laboratory*, Johnson Space Center, NASA.]

▲**Figure 12.28 Quilitoa caldera and lake, Ecuador.** The caldera is about 3.0 km (1.9 mi) wide and 250 m (820 ft) deep and formed when the top of the volcano collapsed during a catastrophic eruption about 1280 c.e. [Kalypso World Photography/Alamy.]

the result of successive eruptions, flowing one on top of another. At least 1 million years were needed to accumulate this shield volcano, forming one of the most massive single mountains on Earth (although Mauna Kea, also located on Hawai'i, is slightly taller). The shield shape and size of Mauna Loa are distinctive when compared with Mount Rainier in Washington, which is a different type of volcano and the largest in the Cascade Range (**Figure 12.30**).

In volcanic settings above hot spots and in continental rift valleys, effusive eruptions send material out through elongated fissures, forming extensive sheets of basaltic lava on the surface, known as **flood basalts**. The Columbia Plateau of the northwestern United States is made up of flood basalts, which form volcanic strata some 2–3 km thick (1.2–1.8 mi), now exposed by rivers throughout the region (**Figure 12.31a**).

Flood basalts make up several of Earth's large igneous provinces, vast areas where magma reached Earth's surface by processes unrelated to standard seafloor spreading and subduction processes (**Figure 12.31b**). Many large igneous provinces are linked to regional uplift and continental rifting and include continental and ocean basin flood basalts and oceanic plateaus. The Deccan Traps is an igneous province in west-central India that is more than double the size of the Columbia Plateau. *Trap* is Dutch for "staircase," referring to the typical steplike form of the eroded flood basalts. The Siberian Traps flood basalts are more than twice the area of the Deccan Traps and are exceeded in size only by the Ontong Java Plateau, which covers

▲**Figure 12.29** **Kīlauea lava flow, 2014.** Active flows began in June 2014 and reached private property near the town of Pāhoa, Hawai'i, in late October. Flows reached the ocean in 2016. [USGS.]

an extensive area of the seafloor in the Pacific. None of the presently active sites forming flood basalts (such as on Mauna Loa) come close in size to the largest of the extinct igneous provinces, some of which formed more than 200 million years ago.

Explosive Eruptions

Violent explosions of magma, gas, and pyroclastics driven by the buildup of pressure in a magma conduit form **explosive eruptions**. This buildup occurs because magma produced by the melting of subducted oceanic plate and

(a) Mauna Loa is a gently sloping shield volcano on the Big Island of Hawai'i.

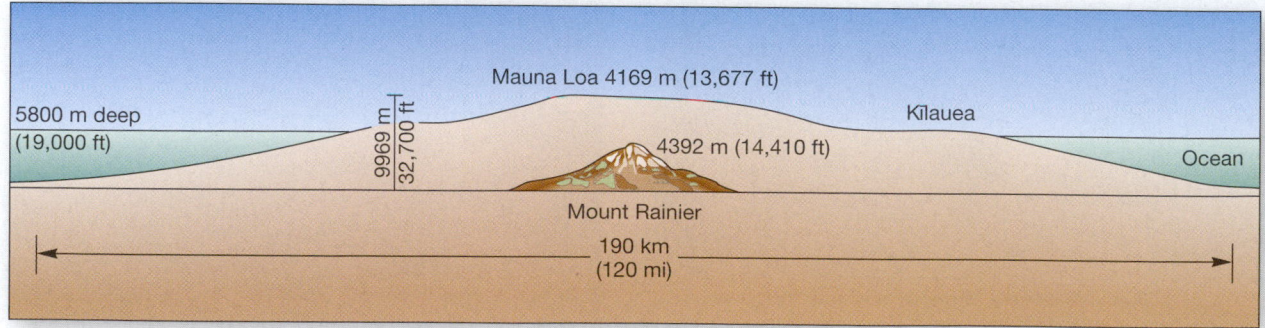

(b) Comparison of Mauna Loa and Mount Rainier in Washington State, a composite volcano. Their strikingly different profiles reveal their different tectonic origins.

▲**Figure 12.30** **Shield and composite volcanoes compared.** [(a) Alvis Uptis/Getty Images. (b) After USGS, *Eruption of Hawaiian Volcanoes*, 1986.]

(a) Flood basalt formed by effusive eruptions is exposed by erosion along the Columbia River, Washington.

(b) Large igneous provinces are vast accumulations of igneous rocks that erupted during a relatively short time interval (less than a few million years).

▲**Figure 12.31 Flood basalts and Earth's large igneous provinces.** [(a) Spring Images/Alamy. (b) After M. F. Coffin and O. Eldholm, "Large igneous provinces," *Scientific American* (October 1993): 42–43. © Scientific American, Inc.]

other materials is thicker (more viscous) than magma that forms effusive volcanoes. Consequently, it tends to block the magma conduit by forming a plug near the surface. The blockage traps and compresses gases (so much so that they remain liquefied) until their pressure is great enough to cause an explosive eruption.

Such an explosion is equivalent to megatons of TNT blasting the top and sides off the mountain. This type of eruption produces much less lava than effusive eruptions, but larger amounts of pyroclastics, which include volcanic ash (<2 mm, or <0.08 in., in diameter), dust, cinders, scoria (dark-colored, cindery rock with holes from gas bubbles), pumice (lighter-colored, less-dense rock

with holes from gas bubbles), and *aerial bombs* (explosively ejected blobs of incandescent lava). A *nuée ardente*, French for "glowing cloud," is an incandescent, hot, turbulent cloud of gas, ash, and pyroclastic that can jet across the landscape in these kinds of eruptions (**Figure 12.32**).

A mountain produced by a series of explosive eruptions is a **composite volcano**, formed by multiple layers of lava, ash, rock, and pyroclastics. These landforms are sometimes called *stratovolcanoes* to describe the alternating layers of ash, rock, and lava, but shield volcanoes also can exhibit a stratified structure, so composite is the preferred term. Composite volcanoes tend to have steep

GEOreport 12.2 Living with active volcanoes in Ecuador

Cotopaxi volcano near Quito, Ecuador, is the most closely monitored volcano in South America since it became active in 2015 (see the Chapter 11 opening photo). Many nearby towns are well-prepared for an eruption. In Sangolquí, for example, a 10-siren alarm system will allow about 45 minutes for people to evacuate their homes. Residents will grab pre-packed emergency kits and follow green lines painted in the streets to emergency shelters. Schools and families practice the evacuation scenario regularly, especially when the warning level is high, in hopes of saving lives when Cotopaxi erupts.

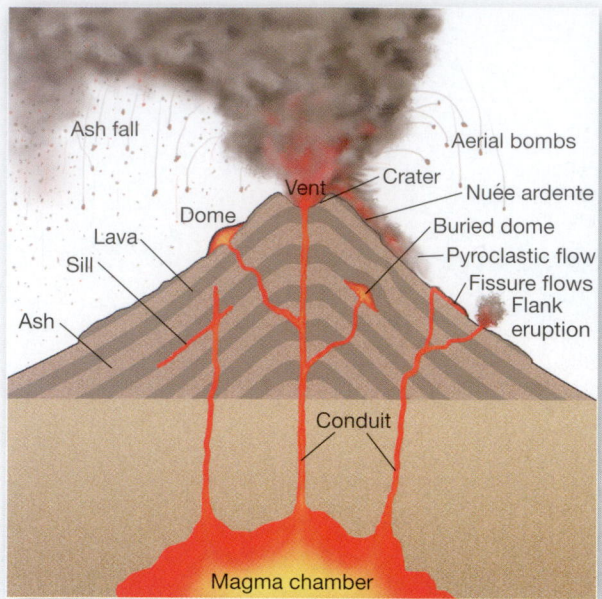

(a) A typical composite volcano with its cone-shaped form in an explosive eruption.

(b) Mount Redoubt, Alaska, erupts in 2009.

▲Figure 12.32 **A composite volcano.** [(b) Game McGimsey, USGS.]

sides and a distinct conical shape and therefore are also known as *composite cones*. If a single summit vent erupts repeatedly, a remarkable symmetry may develop as the mountain grows in size.

Mount Ontake, Japan On September 27, 2014, in central Japan, as hundreds of people hiked toward the 3067 m (10,062 ft) summit, Mount Ontake erupted. The surprise eruption triggered a pyroclastic flow—a fast-moving, billowing mixture of hot steam, gases, and ash—that killed more than 50 people (**Figure 12.33**). Although the Japan Meteorological Association detected harmonic (volcanic) tremors on the mountain early in September, scientists did not raise the volcano alert level, nor did they detect rising subsurface magma. Mount Ontake's shallow steam eruption was mainly water, gases, and heat emerging through surface vents, pulverizing rock in the process. Scientists cannot accurately predict steam eruptions. Mount Ontake's last steam eruption was in 2007; the volcano's last explosive eruption was in 1979.

Mount St. Helens Probably the most studied and photographed composite volcano on Earth is Mount St. Helens, the youngest and most active of the Cascade Range of volcanoes, which extend from Mount Lassen in California to Mount Meager in British Columbia. The Cascade Range is the product of the subduction zone between the Juan de Fuca and North American plates (see **Figure GN 12.1**). Today, more than 1 million tourists visit the Mount St. Helens Volcanic National Monument each year.

In 1980, after 123 years of dormancy, Mount St. Helens erupted. As the contents of the mountain exploded, a surge of hot gas (about 300°C, or 570°F), steam-filled ash, pyroclastics, and a nuée ardente moved northward, hugging the ground and traveling at speeds up to 400 kmph

WORK**IT**OUT 12.3
Pumice, A Volcanic Rock

Pumice is used in skin products, soaps, pencil erasers, and as a conditioner for "stone-washed" denim products. A volcanic rock, pumice is light-colored and usually has a vesicular (containing pores or vesicles) texture. The small holes, or vesicles, form as gas bubbles escape during rapid cooling. Some samples of pumice are so light that they float in water (**Figure WIO 12.3.1**).

▲Figure WIO 12.3.1 **Pumice floats in water.** [© 2005 Chip Clark, Fundamental Photographs, NYC]

1. Would you classify pumice as an intrusive or extrusive igneous rock? Why?
2. Based on its characteristics, would you expect to find pumice in landscapes associated with shield volcanoes or composite volcanoes? Why?
3. What characteristics make some pumice light enough to float in water? Explain your answer.

▲**Figure 12.33** **The 2014 eruption of Mount Ontake, Japan.**
Mount Ontake erupted shortly before noon on Saturday, September 28, 2014, covering its slopes and the surrounding area in ash.
[AP Photo/Kyodo News.]

(250 mph) for a distance of 28 km (17 mi). A series of photographs, taken at 10-second intervals from the east looking west, records the sequence of the eruption, which continued with intensity for 9 hours and then blasted new material intermittently for days (**Figure 12.34a–c**).

The slumping that occurred along the north face of the mountain produced the greatest landslide witnessed in recorded history; about 2.75 km³ (0.67 mi³) of rock, ice, and trapped air, all fluidized with steam, surged at speeds approaching 250 kmph (155 mph). Landslide materials traveled for 21 km (13 mi) into the valley, blanketing the forest, covering a lake, and filling the rivers below.

As destructive as such eruptions are, they also are constructive, for this is the way in which a volcano eventually builds its height. Before the eruption, Mount St. Helens was 2950 m (9677 ft) tall; the eruption blew away 418 m (1370 ft). Today, Mount St. Helens is building a lava dome within its crater (see the post-eruption photo in **Figure 12.34d**). The thick lava rapidly and repeatedly plugs and breaks in a series of lesser dome eruptions that may continue for several decades. The buildup of the lava dome is now more than 300 m (1000 ft) high, so a new mountain is being born from the eruption of the old.

Mount Pinatubo The 1991 eruption of Mount Pinatubo in the Philippines was the second largest of that century (the largest was Novarupta on the Katmai Peninsula in Alaska in 1912) and the largest to affect a densely populated area. The eruption produced 15 to 20 million tons of ash and 12 km³ (3.0 mi³) of magma, ash, and pyroclastics—about 12 times the volume of material produced by Mount St. Helens. The loss of this vast amount of material caused the summit of the volcano to collapse, forming a caldera 2.5 km (1.6 mi) in diameter. The eruption killed 800 people and devastated many surrounding villages. However, accurate prediction of this event saved many lives, as approximately 60,000 evacuated their homes prior to the eruption.

Animation (MG)
The Eruption of Mount Saint Helens

https://goo.gl/jWkj3o

(a)

Landslide area

(b)

(c)

(d) After the eruption, the scorched earth and tree blow-down area covered some 38,950 hectares (96,000 acres).

▲**Figure 12.34** **Photo series recording the Mount St. Helens eruption on May 18, 1980, and the post-eruption mountain and landscape.** Photos (a) through (c) were taken at 10-second intervals.
[(a–c) sequence by Keith B. Ronnholm. All rights reserved. (d) Images & Volcans/Science Source.]

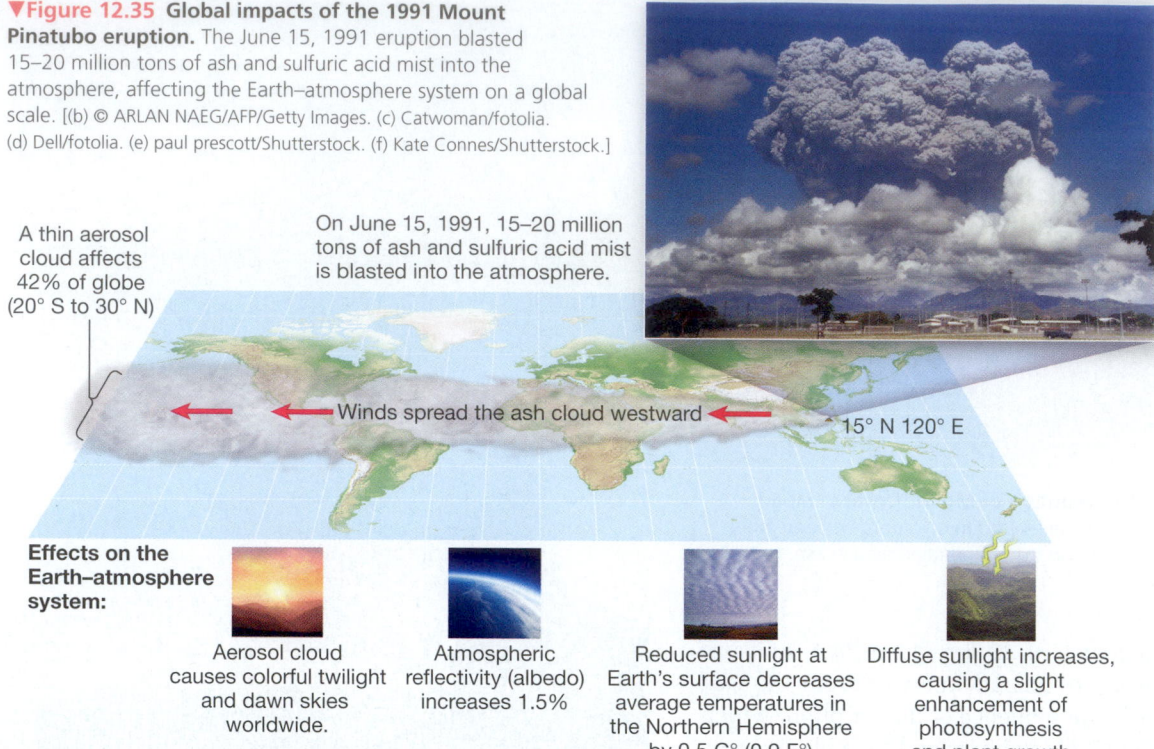

▼**Figure 12.35 Global impacts of the 1991 Mount Pinatubo eruption.** The June 15, 1991 eruption blasted 15–20 million tons of ash and sulfuric acid mist into the atmosphere, affecting the Earth–atmosphere system on a global scale. [(b) © ARLAN NAEG/AFP/Getty Images. (c) Catwoman/fotolia. (d) Dell/fotolia. (e) paul prescott/Shutterstock. (f) Kate Connes/Shutterstock.]

A thin aerosol cloud affects 42% of globe (20° S to 30° N)

On June 15, 1991, 15–20 million tons of ash and sulfuric acid mist is blasted into the atmosphere.

Winds spread the ash cloud westward

15° N 120° E

Effects on the Earth–atmosphere system:

Aerosol cloud causes colorful twilight and dawn skies worldwide.

Atmospheric reflectivity (albedo) increases 1.5%

Reduced sunlight at Earth's surface decreases average temperatures in the Northern Hemisphere by 0.5 C° (0.9 F°)

Diffuse sunlight increases, causing a slight enhancement of photosynthesis and plant growth

Although volcanoes are local events, they have global effects (**Figure 12.35**). As discussed in Chapter 5, the Mount Pinatubo eruption affected Earth's climate, releasing an aerosol cloud that changed atmospheric albedo, impacted atmospheric absorption of insolation, and altered net radiation at Earth's surface.

Volcano Forecasting and Planning

After 23,000 people died in the 1985 eruption of Nevado del Ruiz in Colombia, the USGS and the Office of Foreign Disaster Assistance established the Volcano Disaster Assistance Program (VDAP; see http://vulcan.wr.usgs.gov/Vdap/). In the United States, VDAP helps local scientists forecast eruptions by setting up mobile volcano-monitoring systems at sites with activity or with vulnerable populations. A number of "volcano cams" are positioned around the world for 24-hour surveillance (go to https://volcanoes.usgs.gov/vhp/multimedia.html).

At Mount St. Helens, a dozen survey benchmarks and several tiltmeters have been placed within the crater to monitor the building lava dome. The monitoring, accompanied by intensive scientific research, has paid off, as every eruption since 1980 was successfully forecasted from days to as long as 3 weeks in advance (with the exception of one small eruption in 1984). Swarms of minor earthquakes along the north flank of the mountain occurred in 2001, and dome eruptions of varying intensities occurred through 2007.

Early warning systems for volcanic activity are now possible through integrated seismographic networks and monitoring (**Figure 12.36**). In addition, satellite remote sensing allows scientists to monitor eruption cloud dynamics and the climatic effects of volcano emissions and to estimate volcanic hazard potential. In 2005, the USGS identified 57 priority volcanoes in the United States in need of improved monitoring as part of the National Volcano Early Warning System.

Remote sensing

Ground deformation

Gas

Geophysical measurements

Seismicity

Hydrology

(a)

Mobile Field Trip
Kilauea Volcano

https://goo.gl/gKPZ8Y

▲**Figure 12.36 Monitoring volcanic activity.** Scientists use a variety of instruments to monitor seismic activity, ground deformation, gas levels, and other indications of volcanic activity. [USGS.]

(b)

EARTHQUAKES AND VOLCANOES IMPACT HUMANS

• Earthquakes cause damage and human casualties; destruction is amplified in developing countries, such as Nepal.
• Volcanic eruptions can devastate human population centers, disrupt human transportation, and affect global climate.

HUMANS IMPACT EARTHQUAKES AND VOLCANOES

• Human activity such as subsurface fluid injections associated with gas drilling can cause earthquakes.

12a

A photo and thermal image show a scientist at the Hawaiian Volcano Observatory taking a sample from an active lava flow at Kīlauea. Chemical analyses of lava samples provide information about the magma system feeding the eruption. [USGS.]

Thermal temperature °C

<200.0   862.2

12b

Rescuers search for survivors amid collapsed buildings in Amatrice, central Italy, after an M 6.2 earthquake in August 2016. The quake occurred along a normal fault in the tectonically complex Apennines mountain belt, causing extensive damage in several towns and over 240 fatalities. [Italian Firefighters Vigili del Fuoco/AP Photo.]

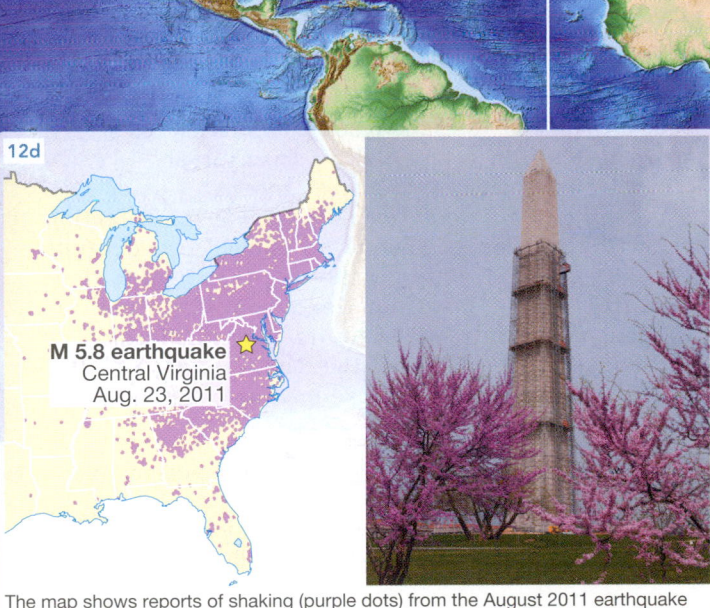

12d

M 5.8 earthquake
Central Virginia
Aug. 23, 2011

The map shows reports of shaking (purple dots) from the August 2011 earthquake with epicenter (yellow star) northwest of Richmond, Virginia. Scientists attribute the huge area affected to the older, more rigid bedrock throughout the region. Shaking caused damage to the Washington Monument in Washington, D.C., shown here undergoing repair in 2013. The monument reopened to the public in 2014. [YT HARYONO/Anadolu Agency/Getty Images.]

12c

Residents leave a village near Mount Sinabung on the island of Sumatra in Indonesia as it erupts in February 2016. The volcano erupted again in May 2016, part of an ongoing series of eruptions since 2010. [YT HARYONO/Anadolu Agency/Getty Images.]

ISSUES FOR THE 21ST CENTURY

• Growing human population centers in regions prone to seismic activity and near active volcanoes will increase the hazard.
• Scientific research is needed for earthquake prediction and volcano forecasting.

QUESTIONS TO CONSIDER

1. Compare the shaking reports from the 2011 Virginia earthquake in HD 12d to the Loma Prieta shake map in Figure 12.20a. Which quake had a larger affected area? Why?
2. What type of eruption occurred at Indonesia's Sinabung volcano in HD 12c? What type of volcanic materials can you see in the photo?

KEY**LEARNING**concepts**review**

Describe the formation of continental crust and **define** displaced terranes.

A continent has a nucleus of ancient crystalline rock called a *craton*. A region where a craton is exposed is a **continental shield** (p. 351). Continental platforms are layers of younger sedimentary rock that surround these shields and appear stable over time. As continental crust forms, it is enlarged through accretion of dispersed **terranes** (p. 352), crustal pieces that have become attached to tectonic plates.

1. What is a craton? Describe the relationship of cratons to continental shields and platforms, and describe these regions in North America.
2. How do dispersed terranes add to the formation of continental landmasses?

Explain the process of folding and **describe** the principal types of faults and their characteristic landforms.

Folding, broad warping, and faulting deform the crust and produce characteristic landforms. Compression causes rocks to deform in a process known as **folding** (p. 353), during which rock strata bend and may overturn. Along the ridge of a fold, layers slope downward away from the axis, forming an **anticline** (p. 353). In the trough of a fold, however, layers slope downward toward the axis; this is a **syncline** (p. 353).

When rock strata are stressed beyond their ability to remain a solid unit, they express the strain as a fracture. Rocks on either side of the fracture are displaced relative to the other side in a process known as **faulting** (p. 356). Thus, fault zones are areas where fractures in the rock demonstrate crustal movement. When forces pull rocks apart, the tension causes a **normal fault** (p. 356), sometimes visible on the landscape as a scarp, or escarpment. Compressional forces associated with converging plates force rocks to move upward, producing a **reverse fault** (p. 357). A type of low-angle reverse fault is a **thrust fault** (p. 357). Horizontal movement along a fault plane, often producing a linear rift valley, is a **strike-slip fault** (p. 357). The term **horst** (p. 357) is applied to upward-faulted blocks; **graben** (p. 357) refers to downward-faulted blocks.

3. Diagram a simple folded landscape in cross section and identify some features created by the folded strata.
4. Define four basic types of faults. How are faults related to earthquakes and seismic activity?

List the three types of plate collisions associated with mountain building and **identify** specific examples of each.

Orogenesis (p. 359) is the birth of mountains. An *orogeny* is a mountain-building episode, occurring over millions of years, that thickens continental crust. It can occur through large-scale deformation and uplift of the crust. It also may include the capture and cementation of migrating terranes to the continental margins and the intrusion of granitic magmas to form plutons.

Three types of tectonic activity cause mountain building along convergent plate margins. *Oceanic plate–continental plate collisions* are now occurring along the Pacific coast of the Americas, forming the Andes, the Rockies, and other western mountains. *Oceanic plate–oceanic plate collisions* produce volcanic island arcs such as Japan, the Philippines, and portions of the Aleutians. In a *continental plate–continental plate collision*, large masses of continental crust, such as the Himalayan Range, are subjected to intense folding, overthrusting, faulting, and uplifting.

5. Describe how different types of plate boundaries produce differing episodes of mountain building.

Explain earthquake characteristics and measurement and **describe** earthquake fault mechanics.

An **earthquake** (p. 362) is the release of energy that occurs at the moment of fracture along a fault in the crust, producing seismic waves. **Megathrust earthquakes** (p. 362) occur along subduction zones, producing the most powerful earthquakes on Earth. The **elastic-rebound theory** (p. 363) describes the basic process of how a fault breaks. When the elastic energy is released abruptly as the rock breaks, both sides of the fault return to a condition of less strain. The subsurface area where the motion of seismic waves is initiated along a fault plane is the **focus** (p. 363). The area at the surface directly above the focus is the **epicenter** (p. 363). Seismic motions are measured with a **seismometer** (p. 363), also called a seismograph.

Scientists rate earthquake *intensity* using the *Modified Mercalli Intensity (MMI) scale*. **Liquefaction** (p. 364) is the process whereby ground shaking disrupts and loosens the structure of the soil, causing it to flow. Scientists measure earthquake magnitude using the **moment magnitude (M) scale** (p. 365), a more precise and quantitative scale than the **Richter scale** (p. 364), which was mainly an effective measure for small-magnitude quakes.

6. What is the relationship between the epicenter and focus of an earthquake?
7. Differentiate among the Mercalli scale and moment magnitude (M) scale as used to describe an earthquake.

Describe volcanic landforms and **distinguish** between an effusive and an explosive volcanic eruption.

A **volcano** (p. 370) forms at the end of a central vent or pipe that rises from the asthenosphere through the crust. Eruptions produce lava (molten rock), gases, and **pyroclastics** (p. 370), pulverized rock and clastic materials ejected violently during an eruption, that pass through the vent to openings and fissures at the surface and build volcanic landforms. Basaltic lava flows occur in two principal textures: **aa** (p. 370), rough and sharp-edged lava, and pahoehoe (p. 370), smooth, ropy folds of lava. Landforms produced by volcanic activity include **cinder cones** (p. 370), which are small conical-shaped hills, and **calderas** (p. 370), large basin-shaped depressions caused by the collapse of a volcano's summit.

Volcanoes are of two general types, based on the chemistry and gas content of the magma involved. An **effusive eruption** (p. 371) produces a **shield volcano** (p. 371), such as Mauna Loa on Hawai'i. **Flood basalts** (p. 372) are extensive deposits of igneous rock produced by effusive eruptions. **Explosive eruptions** (p. 372) produce a **composite volcano** (p. 373), such as Mount Pinatubo in the Philippines.

8. Describe several tectonic settings for volcanic activity.
9. How are effusive and explosive eruptions different? What distinct landforms are produced by each type?

GEOSPATIAL ANALYSIS

Recent Volcanic Activity

The Smithsonian Institution Global Volcanism Program and the USGS report new and changing volcanic activity worldwide. NOAA issues Volcanic Ash Advisories to alert aircraft downwind from volcanic eruptions.

Activities

Go to the Weekly Volcanic Activity Report page at http://volcano.si.edu/reports_weekly.cfm.

1. Where is volcanic activity occurring according to the map?

2. Click on "Criteria and Disclaimers." Why are some volcanoes not displayed on the map?

3. Click on "Weekly Report." List the new volcanic activity locations and list at least 3 locations of ongoing activity.

Click on a volcano under "New Activity Highlights."

1. List the city, country, volcanic region, latitude and longitude, and dates of recent volcanic activity.

2. What are the key features for this type of volcano?

3. Is this volcano located near a tectonic plate boundary or hot spot? Explain.

4. Click on "Archive." Click on this volcano, and summarize its eruptive history.

Go to the Volcanic Ash Advisory Center (VAAC) page at: http://www.ssd.noaa.gov/VAAC/washington.html .

1. List the 9 VAAC locations.

2. Click on "Current Volcanic Ash Advisories." According to the list for the present year, what is the most active VAAC region? What is the name of the volcano with the most ash advisories?

MasteringGeography™

Looking for additional review and test prep materials? Visit the Study Area in MasteringGeography™ to enhance your geographic literacy, spatial reasoning skills, and understanding of this chapter's content by accessing a variety of resources, including MapMaster™ interactive maps, videos, *Mobile Field Trips*, *Project Condor* Quadcopter videos, *In the News* RSS feeds, flashcards, web links, self-study quizzes, and an eText version of *Geosystems*.

13 Weathering, Karst Landscapes, and Mass Movement

Capitol Reef National Park, Utah, USA

Weathering, hillslope processes, and erosion shape the landscape of central Utah, from the Henry Mountains to the cliffs and canyons of Capitol Reef National Park. [Scott Smith/Getty Images.]

KEY**LEARNING**concepts

After reading the chapter, you should be able to:

- **Describe** the dynamic equilibrium approach to the study of landforms and *illustrate* the forces at work on materials residing on a slope.

- **Define** weathering and *explain* the factors that influence weathering processes.

- **Describe** the physical weathering processes of frost wedging, salt-crystal growth, and pressure-release jointing.

- **Explain** the chemical weathering processes of hydration, hydrolysis, oxidation, carbonation, and dissolution.

- **Review** the processes and features associated with karst topography.

- **Categorize** the various types of mass movements and *identify* examples of each.

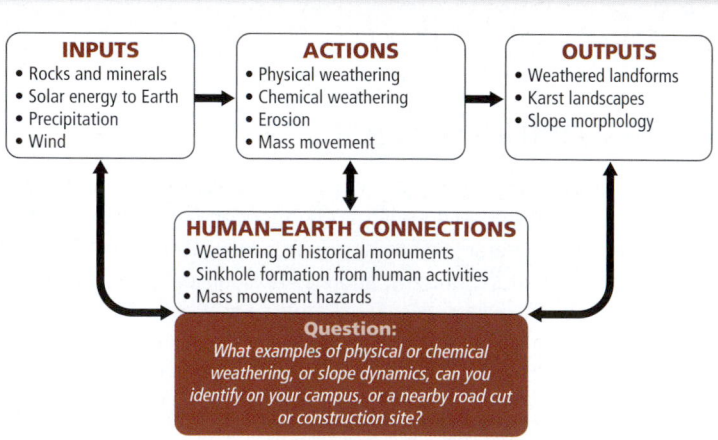

INPUTS
- Rocks and minerals
- Solar energy to Earth
- Precipitation
- Wind

ACTIONS
- Physical weathering
- Chemical weathering
- Erosion
- Mass movement

OUTPUTS
- Weathered landforms
- Karst landscapes
- Slope morphology

HUMAN–EARTH CONNECTIONS
- Weathering of historical monuments
- Sinkhole formation from human activities
- Mass movement hazards

Question:
What examples of physical or chemical weathering, or slope dynamics, can you identify on your campus, or a nearby road cut or construction site?

The Oso, Washington, Landslide

On the morning of March 22, 2014, residents in a riverside neighborhood just east of Oso, Washington, about 80 km (50 mi) northeast of Seattle, went about their usual weekend activities. Around 11 A.M., with no warning to those in the homes below, the mountainside above the North Fork of the Stillaguamish River gave way, unleashing an estimated 18 million tons of material—enough to cover 600 football fields 10 feet deep. The block of earth slid rapidly down to the valley floor, breaking into pieces and picking up debris as it fell, and then flowed 1.1 km (0.7 mi) across the valley, damming the river channel and burying a portion of Oso and State Route 530 with mud, rock, trees, and other wreckage. The slide—ultimately covering 2.6 km² (1 mi²) of the valley floor—destroyed more than 35 houses and caused 41 fatalities (**Figure GN 13.1**).

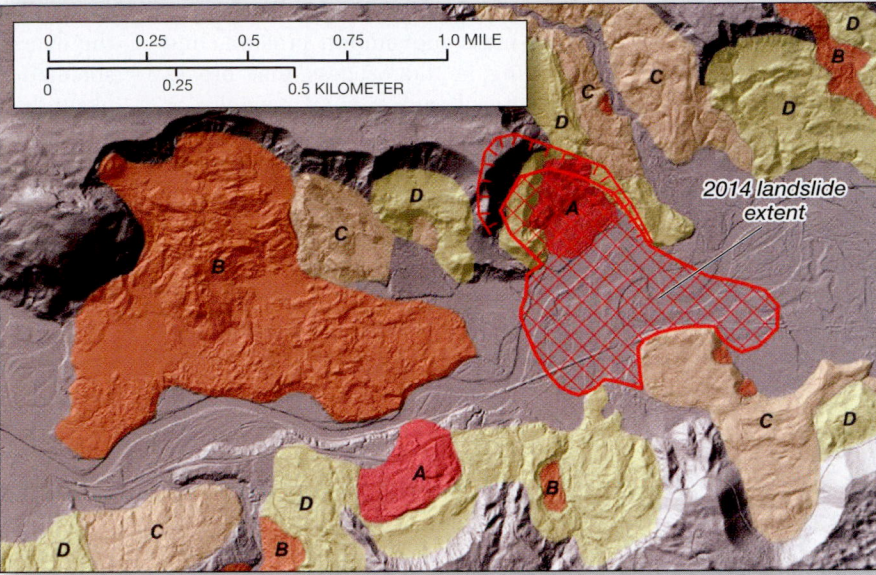

▲**Figure GN 13.2 Map of landslide deposits near Oso.** Shaded relief image from a 2013 LiDAR survey shows older landslide deposits (colored areas) ranging from youngest (A) to oldest (D). Red cross-hatching marks the extent of the 2014 event; the red line with tick marks shows the approximate headscarp. [Ralph Haugerud, 2014, Preliminary Interpretation of Pre-2014 Landslide Deposits in the Vicinity of Oso, Washington; USGS Open File Report 2014–1065, page 4.]

Conditions for Mass Movement Landslides are a type of mass movement, a process in which large bodies of earth materials move downslope with gravity. On the western slopes of the Cascade Range in Washington, the winter of 2013–2014 was wetter than normal, with precipitation in February and March at 150 to 200% of the long-term average. In this region of steep slopes and heavy rainfall, landslides are not uncommon. In fact, the slope above Oso, known as the Hazel landslide, had a well-known history of significant mass-movement events, including episodes in 1951, 1961, 1988, and, most recently, 2006 (**Figure GN 13.2**).

A 1999 scientific report warned of the potential for a "large, catastrophic" slope failure, with large amounts of rainfall or high streamflows that could erode the base of the slope increasing the hazard. Tree removal associated with logging on mountain slopes could also increase the landslide risk. Past logging around the Hazel slide area may have helped trigger the 2014 event.

Over the years, despite the history of mass-movement activity, people built houses closer to the toe of the slope. Prior to and just after the 2006 slide, the state spent millions of dollars on reinforcements to the riverbanks and slope toe, all of which created a false sense of security for residents in the slide path.

Anatomy of the Landslide The Oso event involved a complex series of sliding and flowing movements that scientists classify as a "debris-avalanche flow." At the headscarp—the top of the slide, where the material initially broke loose—rotational slumping occurred as the sliding block of earth broke loose and turned on its side. This action resulted in the stepped appearance of the new mountainside. The slide then accelerated, becoming a high-speed debris avalanche. At the toe, after crossing the river, the slurry of mud, rock, and sediment became a debris flow, a fluidized mass that can move long distances and pick up materials the size of large boulders. This particular landslide was unusual in its extensive path across the valley.

Over 600 people took part in the rescue effort, which took place in mud and debris up to 6 m (20 ft) deep. The question remains whether many of the consequences of this disaster might have been avoided if officials and residents had heeded earlier warnings of the landslide hazard.

▲**Figure GN 13.1 The Oso landslide and North Fork of the Stillaguamish River valley.** Note the landslide scarp on the right side and the blue water (in the foreground) of the temporary lake formed by the slide debris. Two main factors contribute to ongoing slope instability: erosion by the Stillaguamish River, which causes oversteepening of the toe of the slope, and water saturation of the unconsolidated slope materials, which can cause the material to flow. [Ted S. Warren/AP Images.]

1. What were two possible causes of the Oso landslide?

2. Describe the characteristics of the landslide from scarp to toe.

The exogenic processes at work on Earth's landscapes include weathering, mass movement, erosion, and deposition. *Weathering* is the process that breaks down rock by disintegrating it into mineral particles or dissolving it into water. Weathering produces an overall weakening of surface rock, which makes it more susceptible to erosion. While weathering is the breakdown of materials, *erosion* includes the transport of weathered materials to different locations. *Mass movement* is the downslope movement of a mass of rock, soil, or sediment under the force of gravity. All of these processes contribute to landscape **denudation**, the rearranging and wearing away of landforms over time.

Basic Concepts for Landform Study

Geomorphology is the science of the origin, development, and spatial distribution of landforms. The concept of dynamic equilibrium, the relationship between event magnitude and frequency, and the concept of force and resistance are important concepts in geomorphology.

Landforms and Dynamic Equilibrium

A landscape is an open system, with highly variable inputs of energy and materials. As the forces acting on a landscape change, the surface constantly responds in search of equilibrium. Every change produces compensating actions and reactions. The idea of landscape formation as a balancing act between tectonic uplift and reduction by weathering and erosion is the **dynamic equilibrium model**. Landscapes in a dynamic equilibrium show small variations over time as they are constantly adapting to the ever-changing conditions of force and resistance associated with local relief, rock structure, and climate. For example, a mountain range will maintain a constant average slope if the rates of uplift and erosion remain stable over time, even if local events throw off the balance on short time scales.

In Chapter 1, we described a *steady-state equilibrium* as one in which conditions fluctuate around a stable average (**Figure 13.1b**). An example is a river that maintains its form even as inputs of sediment and water vary over time. When a system in steady-state equilibrium demonstrates a changing trend over time, the condition is known as dynamic equilibrium (**Figure 13.1c**). A river may tend toward channel widening as it adjusts to greater inputs of sediment over some time scale, but the overall system will adjust to this new widening condition as part of the dynamic equilibrium condition.

Abrupt or catastrophic changes—for example, a massive landslide or flood, abrupt faulting, or a huge wildfire—may destabilize the relationships between elements within a landscape, sending it to a **geomorphic threshold**, or tipping point. At this point, the system lurches to a new operational level (**Figure 13.1d**). A geomorphic system reaches this threshold when the sudden change takes it to a new system state—such as when a flood establishes a new river channel or a landslide reshapes the angle and form of hillslope (**Figure 13.1a**). After crossing this threshold, the system establishes a new set of equilibrium relationships. The dynamic equilibrium model encompasses the entire sequence over time: an equilibrium condition, followed by a destabilizing event, followed by a period of adjustment, followed by a new and different equilibrium condition.

(a) Part of a house hangs over an eroding cliff in Pacifica, California on January 27, 2016. Storms and powerful waves related to El Niño eroded coastal bluffs until they reached a geomorphic threshold as the bluffs collapsed.

▼Figure 13.1 **Steady-state and dynamic equilibrium concepts as applied to landforms.** [(a) Josh Edelson/AFP/Getty Images.]

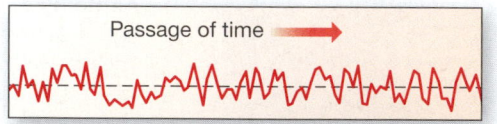

Passage of time

(b) Steady-state equilibrium: Over time, the system fluctuates around a stable average.

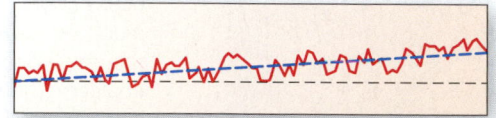

(c) Dynamic equilibrium: Over time, the system fluctuates around an average with a long-term trend.

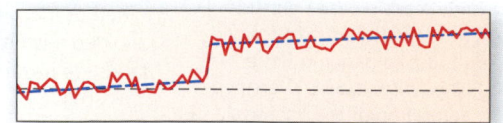

(d) Dynamic equilibrium with threshold: The long-term trend is interrupted by a threshold, or tipping point.

Magnitude and Frequency

In addition to the hazards related to large-magnitude endogenic events such as earthquakes, many large-magnitude events related to Earth's exogenic processes affect human life: for example, landslides in the Himalayas and mudflows in California. All of these events alter Earth's surface on a wide range of scales, from a massive volcanic eruption depositing layers of ash and debris across a landscape to a tree falling over in a forest, disturbing the soil. The magnitude (size or extent) and frequency

Small-magnitude events are common (occurring with high frequency, once every year or decade). Their collective effect can shape landforms over time.

(b) Large floods, such as on the Big Thompson River, Colorado, in 2013, may occur only once in our lifetimes.

Large-magnitude events are rare (occurring with low frequency, once every hundred or thousand years). These single, sometimes catastrophic, events can greatly alter landforms and landscapes.

(a) High flows that barely overtop the banks occur every year or two on most streams.

Frequency of event — High / Low

Magnitude of event — Low / High

◄**Figure 13.2 Magnitude and frequency of geomorphic events.** The magnitude-frequency relationship in geomorphology is an inverse relationship in which small magnitude events occur with greater frequency and vice versa. Frequent, small events can shape landforms over long time scales. Rare, large events can also shape landforms in a single episode. [(a) Pete Ryan/Alamy. (b) DOD Photo/Alamy.]

For example, the angle of repose for dry sand is about 35° and for wet sand is about 45°, illustrating that higher water content can increase shear strength and allow for a steeper slope angle (**Figure 13.3**).

(the rate of occurrence over a period of time) of geomorphic events tends to have a predictable relationship, as shown in **Figure 13.2** (further discussion is in Chapter 14).

Force and Resistance on Slopes

Slopes, or *hillslopes*, are curved, inclined surfaces that form the boundaries of landforms such as valleys and plateaus. Slopes are open systems whose form reflects an equilibrium angle that balances the driving forces and resisting forces, as illustrated in Geosystems in Action 13. When any condition in the balance is altered, all forces on the slope adjust and compensate as part of the equilibrium condition.

For material to move downslope, the forces of erosion must overcome the other forces of inertia (the natural tendency of matter at rest to remain at rest unless an external force is applied), cohesion among particles, and internal friction. If the angle is steep enough for gravity to overcome frictional forces or if the impact of raindrops, moving animals, or wind dislodges material, then erosion of particles and deposition in a new location downslope can occur.

Downslope movement occurs on slopes under the driving force of gravity, which creates *shear stress*. Gravity includes a parallel component that makes material move down the slope and a perpendicular component that holds material against the slope. The driving force is countered by the resisting force created by the *shear strength* of the slope materials. Shear strength is determined mainly by cohesion (the ability of the particles to attract and hold together) and internal friction (the friction between particles).

The angle at which a slope is inclined and beyond which downslope movement (slope failure) will occur is called the **angle of repose**. This angle is the limit of steepness on a slope and depends on the size and texture of the particles (**Figure GIA 13.1**), as well as the water content.

everyday GEO**SYSTEMS**

What causes a sand castle to hold its shape?

If you have built a sand castle at the beach, you know that using wet, but not saturated, sand produces the most stable structure. The castle holds its shape from the molecular attractions of water in the pore spaces between the sand grains. Building with dry sand will cause instability and slope failure because the dry particles are less cohesive. However, too much water in the sand will also cause instability and slope failure. On hillslopes, these same principles apply: Heavy rainfall can fill the pore spaces on a hillslope and cause slope failure.

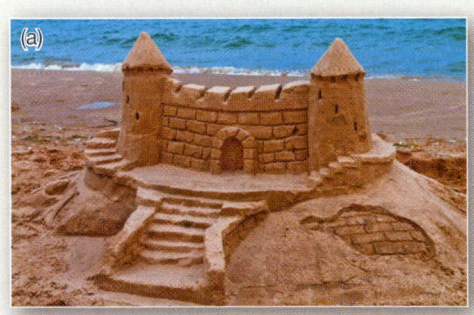

◄**Figure 13.3 A sand castle illustrates the cohesiveness of damp sand.** [Kris Wiktor/Shutterstock.]

More cohesive ———————→ Less cohesive

Damp sand — **Dry sand** — **Water-saturated sand**

(b)

(i) Wet or damp sand particles are more cohesive, bound together by molecular attractions that cause surface tension.

(ii) Dry sand particles are less cohesive, bound together only by their shape, size, and the force of internal friction.

(iii) Saturated sand particles are the least cohesive because the spaces between particles are filled with water, which acts as a lubricant.

A slope is an open system that tends toward dynamic equilibrium. A slope remains stable if it does not exceed the angle of repose (GIA 13.1). On a stable slope, the forces acting on slope materials—shown in GIA 13.2—are balanced. If the forces become unbalanced, the slope changes until a new equilibrium is reached. Over time, this equilibrium-seeking process gives slopes a characteristic structure, or "anatomy" (GIA 13.3).

13.1 ANGLE OF REPOSE

The angle of repose is the maximum slope angle, measured in degrees from horizontal, at which material will remain in place. If this angle is exceeded, slope failure will occur. The angle of repose for dry sand is about 35° and for dry, angular gravel is about 45°. This difference occurs because the smaller, smoother sand grains are not as cohesive as the larger, rougher gravels, which can form a steeper slope.

Angle of repose

35°

Fine sand

45°

Angular pebbles

13.2 FORCES ON A SLOPE

Directional forces (noted by arrows) act on materials along an inclined slope. If the force promoting motion (gravity, the driving force) exceeds the forces opposing the motion (the resisting force), the slope is destabilized and material moves downhill. A variety of events can destabilize a slope, including heavy rain, a wildfire that destroys protective plant cover, or an earthquake.

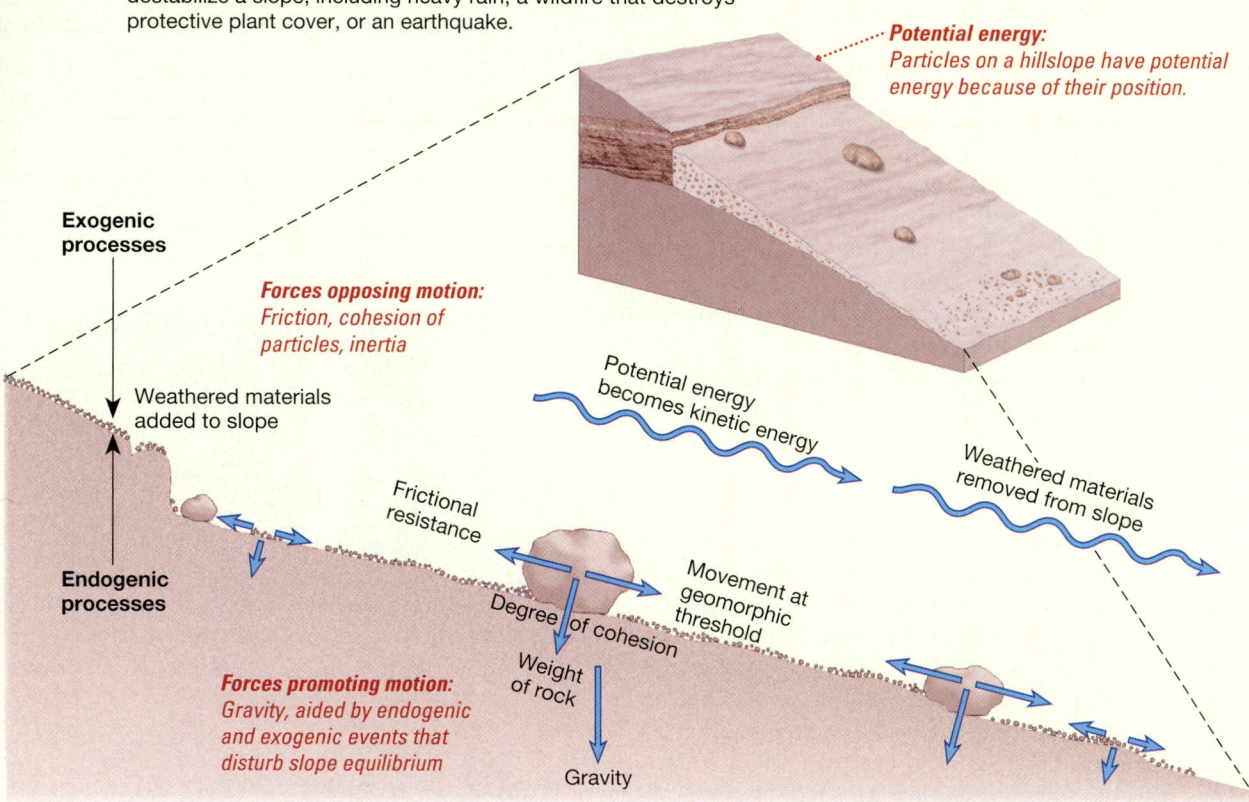

Potential energy:
Particles on a hillslope have potential energy because of their position.

Exogenic processes

Forces opposing motion:
Friction, cohesion of particles, inertia

Weathered materials added to slope

Potential energy becomes kinetic energy

Weathered materials removed from slope

Endogenic processes

Frictional resistance

Movement at geomorphic threshold

Degree of cohesion

Weight of rock

Forces promoting motion:
Gravity, aided by endogenic and exogenic events that disturb slope equilibrium

Gravity

MasteringGeography™

Visit the Study Area in MasteringGeography™ to explore slopes and the dynamic equilibrium model.

Visualize: Study a geosciences animation of mass movement.

Assess: Demonstrate understanding of slopes and the dynamic equilibrium model (if assigned by instructor).

Animation (MG)
Mass Movements

https://goo.gl/sxcsbg

13.3 ANATOMY OF A SLOPE

Hillslopes typically develop a structure made up of several elements: a convex *waxing* slope, rock outcrop, debris slope, and concave *waning* slope. One main process predominates on each part of a hillslope: physical and chemical weathering on the upper slope, transportation on the debris slope, and deposition on the lower, waning slope.

Rock outcrop (free face):
The rock outcrop interrupts the slope.
Frost wedging loosens rock fragments
from the outcrop to form the debris slope.

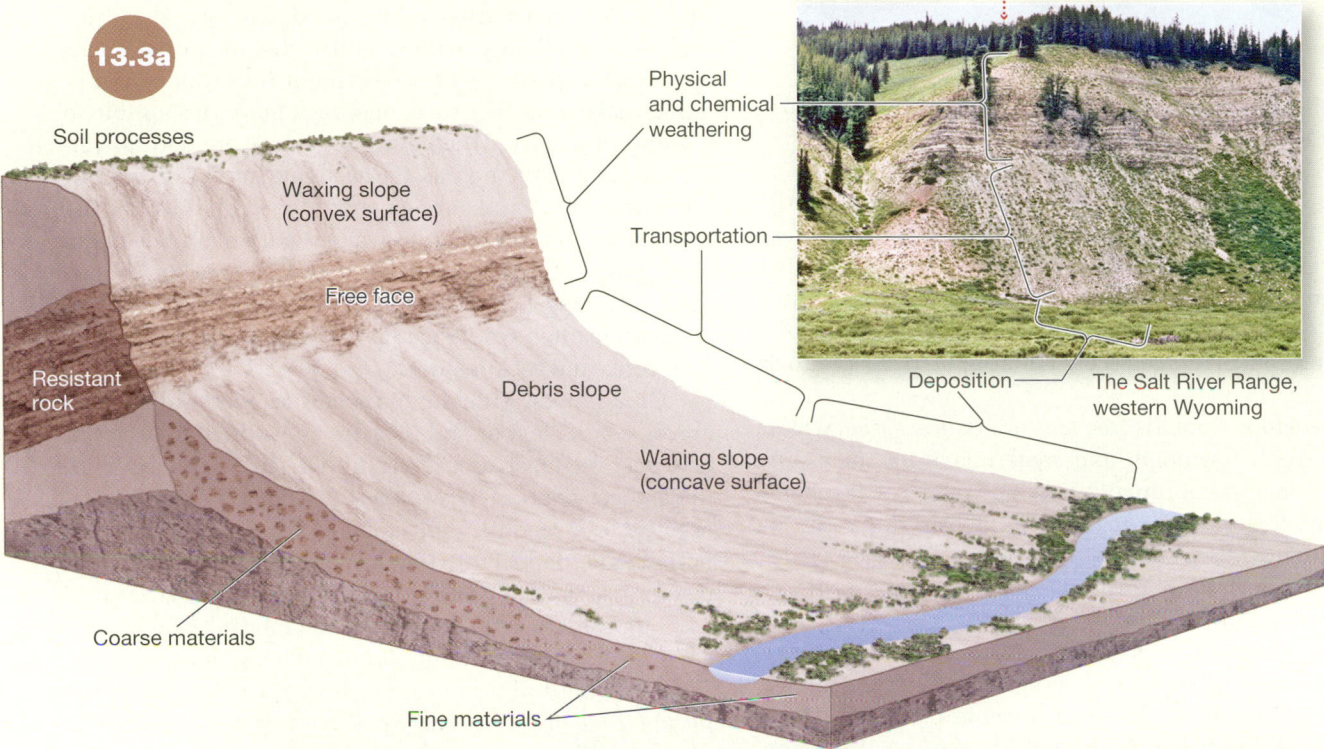

13.3a

Soil processes

Waxing slope (convex surface)

Free face

Resistant rock

Coarse materials

Physical and chemical weathering

Transportation

Debris slope

Waning slope (concave surface)

Deposition

The Salt River Range, western Wyoming

Fine materials

13.3b

Many slope elements are visible in the Gros Ventre Range near Jackson Hole Airport, Jackson, Wyoming. Locate some of the named features in the illustration above.

GEOquiz

1. Explain: Explain how an exogenic event results in a rock particle's movement down a hillslope. Refer to the forces and energy types shown in GIA 13.2 in your answer.

2. Infer: What events or processes could reduce the degree of cohesion of particles on a slope?

3. Apply concepts: Is the slope in GIA 13.3 at its angle of equilibrium? Explain your answer, referring to specific parts of the slope and the processes that affect them.

4. Predict: What will eventually happen to the coarse materials on the debris slope?

Increase in surface area

▲**Figure 13.4 Physical weathering increases surface area.** As rock breaks down into smaller pieces, the overall surface area available for weathering processes increases.

The basic components of a slope vary with conditions of rock structure and climate. Slopes generally feature an upper *waxing slope* near the top (*waxing* means increasing). This convex surface curves downward and may grade into a *free face* below, a steep scarp or cliff whose presence indicates an outcrop of resistant rock (**Figure GIA 13.3**).

Downslope from the free face is a *debris slope*, which receives rock fragments and materials from above. In humid climates, continually moving water carries material away, lowering the angle of the debris slope. But in arid climates, debris slopes accumulate material. A debris slope grades into a *waning slope*, a concave surface along the base of the slope.

In summary, the shape of a slope results from the delicate balance between driving and resisting forces. A slope is *stable* if the shear strength of its materials exceeds shear stress, the driving forces of erosion and mass movement. A slope is *unstable* if the shear

(a) A cross section of a typical hillside.

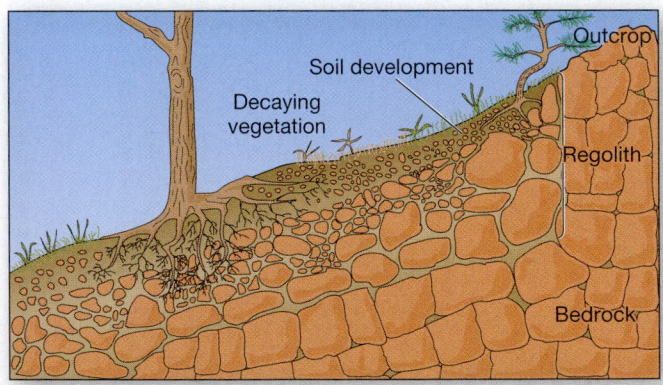

(c) The sands of Coral Pink Sand Dunes State Park in Utah derive their color from the sandstone parent rock in the background.

strength of its materials is weaker than these driving forces.

Weathering Processes

The process of **weathering** breaks down rock at Earth's surface and slightly below, either disintegrating rocks into mineral particles or dissolving it into water. Weathering weakens surface rock, making it more susceptible to the pull of gravity. Weathering processes are both physical (mechanical), such as the wedging action of frost in the cracks of a rock surface, and chemical, such as the dissolution of minerals into water. Often the mechanical breakdown of rock increases the surface area for chemical weathering (**Figure 13.4**). These two broad types of weathering often work together, producing Earth's unique landforms and rock features.

On a typical hillside, loose surface material such as gravel, sand, clay, or soil overlies consolidated, or solid, **bedrock**. In most areas, the upper surface of bedrock undergoes continual weathering, creating broken-up **regolith**. As regolith continues to weather, or is transported and deposited, the loose surface material that results becomes the basis for soil development (**Figure 13.5**). In some areas, regolith may be missing or undeveloped, exposing an outcrop of unweathered bedrock.

As a result of this process, bedrock is known as the *parent rock* from which weathered regolith and soils develop. Wherever a soil is relatively young, its parent rock is traceable through similarities in composition. For example, in the canyon country of the U.S. Southwest, sediments derive their color and character from the surrounding sedimentary parent rock (Figure 13.5c). **Parent material** is the consolidated or unconsolidated material from which soils develop, ranging from bedrock to unconsolidated sediments and weathered rock.

◀**Figure 13.5 Soil, regolith, and parent materials.** [(b) Derek Adams/Alamy. (c) Michele Falzone/Alamy.]

(b) A cliff exposes hillslope components.

Mobile Field Trip

The Critical Zone at Boulder Creek

https://goo.gl/4qw4nB

Factors Influencing Weathering Processes

A number of factors affect the rate of weathering and the type of weathering that occurs.

- **Rock composition and structure (jointing).** The character of the bedrock (hard or soft, soluble or insoluble, broken or unbroken) and its mineral composition (different minerals weather at different rates) influence the rate of weathering. **Joints** are fractures or separations in rock that occur without displacement of the rock on either side (in contrast with faulting). Jointing increases the surface area of rock exposed to both physical and chemical weathering (**Figure 13.6**).

- **Climate (precipitation and temperature).** Wetter, warmer environments speed up chemical weathering processes; colder environments have freeze–thaw cycles that cause physical weathering. Rocks that weather rapidly in warm, humid climates may be resistant to weathering in dry climates (an example is limestone).

- **Slope orientation.** Whether a slope faces north, south, east, or west controls the slope's exposure to Sun, wind, and precipitation. Slopes facing away from the Sun's rays tend to be cooler, moister, and more vegetated than are slopes in direct sunlight. This effect of orientation is especially noticeable in the middle and higher latitudes.

- **Subsurface water.** The position of the water table and water movement within soil and rock structures influence weathering.

- **Vegetation.** Although vegetative cover can protect rock by shielding it from raindrop impact and providing roots to stabilize soil, it also produces organic acids, from the partial decay of organic matter, that contribute to chemical weathering. Moreover, plant roots can enter crevices and mechanically break up a rock, exerting enough pressure to force rock segments apart,

▲**Figure 13.7 Physical weathering by tree roots.** The fracturing of rocks by plant roots is known as "root wedging." [Dennis Frates/Alamy.]

thereby exposing greater surface area to other weathering processes (**Figure 13.7**). You may have observed how tree roots can heave the sections of a sidewalk or driveway sufficiently to raise and crack concrete.

Weathering processes occur on micro- as well as macroscopic scales. In particular, research at *microscale* levels reveals a more complex relationship between climate and weathering than previously thought. At the local scale of actual reaction sites on the rock surface, both physical and chemical weathering processes can occur over a wide range of climate types. At this scale, soil moisture activates chemical weathering processes even in the driest landscape. Similarly, the role of bacteria in weathering is important, with these organisms potentially affecting physical processes as they colonize rock surfaces and chemical processes as they metabolize certain minerals and secrete acids.

Keep in mind that, in the complexity of nature, all these factors influencing weathering rates are operating in concert and that physical and chemical weathering processes usually operate together. *Time* is the final critical factor affecting weathering, for these processes require long periods. Usually, the longer the duration of exposure for a particular surface, the more it will be weathered.

▼**Figure 13.6 Joints in sandstone, Australia.** Joints are common in most rock types, occurring singly or as extensive joint systems. Shown here are vertical joints and horizontal bedding planes undergoing weathering in Kings Canyon, Watarrka National Park, in the Northern Territory. [Nigel Pavitt/Getty Images.]

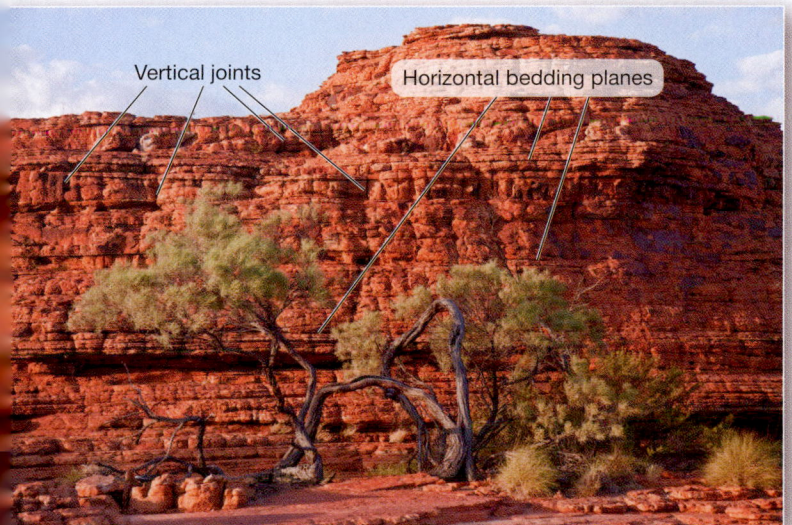

Vertical joints

Horizontal bedding planes

Physical Weathering Processes

The disintegration of rock without any chemical alteration is **physical weathering**, also called *mechanical weathering*. By breaking up rock, physical weathering produces more surface area on which all weathering may operate. For example, breaking a single stone into eight pieces exposes double the surface area susceptible to weathering processes (Figure 13.4). Physical weathering occurs primarily by frost wedging, thermal expansion, salt-crystal growth, and exfoliation.

Frost Wedging When water freezes, its volume expands as much as 9% (see Chapter 5). This expansion produces a powerful mechanical force that can overcome the tensional strength of rock. Repeated freezing (expanding) and thawing (contracting) of water is *frost action*, or *freeze–thaw*, which breaks rocks apart in the process of **frost wedging** (Figure 13.8).

The work of ice begins in small openings along existing joints and fractures, gradually expanding them and cracking or splitting the rock in varied shapes, depending on the rock structure. Sometimes frost wedging results in blocks of rock, or *joint-block separation* (Figure 13.9).

Frost wedging is an important weathering process in the humid microthermal climates (*humid continental* and *subarctic*) and the polar climates and in

▲Figure 13.9 **Frost wedging along joints.** Joint-block separation in slate on Spitsbergen Island in the Arctic Ocean. [Bobbé Christopherson.]

the highland climates at high elevations in mountains worldwide.

Thermal Expansion Physical weathering related to daily and seasonal temperature changes can also occur in the absence of water. *Thermal expansion* occurs as rock surfaces heated by the Sun during the day expand slightly, and then contract with nighttime cooling. Over time, these volume changes cause the outer layer of rock to loosen and peel away in small fragments or in massive slabs.

As winter ends and temperatures warm in mountainous terrain, the falling of rocks from cliff faces occurs more frequently. Recently, a team of researchers investigated the role of thermal expansion as a cause of rockfall in Yosemite National Park, California (discussed in Focus Study 13.1 on p. 400).

Salt-Crystal Growth (Salt Weathering) Especially in arid climates where heating is intense, evaporation draws moisture to the surface of rocks, leaving behind previously dissolved minerals, especially salts, in the form of crystals (the process of crystallization). Salt crystals can change in volume from 1% to 5% with changes in temperature of the rock surface. Over time, as salt crystals accumulate, they exert a force great enough to separate the grains making up the rock and begin breaking the rock to pieces, a process known as *salt-crystal growth*, or *salt weathering*. This process is common in coastal regions, and results in pitted rock surfaces known as *tafoni*, or honeycomb weathering (Figure 13.10).

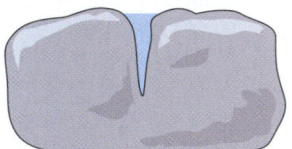  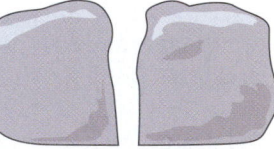

Water enters joints and fractures in rock.　　Water freezes and expands in volume, wedging apart the rock.　　Repeated cycles of freeze–thaw break the rock into pieces.

(a) The process of frost wedging.

(b) Ice expansion breaks up marble, a metamorphic rock.

Animation (MG)
Physical Weathering

https://goo.gl/kMLLJU

(c) Freeze–thaw action causes joints to expand in granite.

▲Figure 13.8 **Physical weathering by frost wedging.** [(b) Bobbé Christopherson. (c) Walt Anderson/Getty Images.]

Exfoliation The process whereby rock peels or slips off in sheets instead of breaking up into grains is **exfoliation**, a term that generally refers to the removal or shedding of an outer layer. This process, also known as *sheeting*, occurs commonly in high-silica intrusive igneous rocks and is rare in other rock types. Exfoliation creates arch-shaped and dome-shaped features on the exposed landscape. These *exfoliation domes* are probably the largest weathering features, in areal extent, on Earth (**Figure 13.11**).

Exfoliation occurs as pressure is released from the removal of overlying rock. Recall from Chapter 11 how magma that rises into the crust and then remains deeply buried under high pressure forms intrusive igneous rocks called plutons. These plutons cool slowly into coarse-grained, crystalline, granitic rocks that may then be uplifted and subjected to weathering and erosion. As the tremendous weight of overlying material is removed from a granite pluton, the pressure of deep burial is relieved. Over millions of years, the granite slowly responds with an enormous physical heave, initiating a process known as *pressure-release jointing*, in which the rock cracks into joints. Exfoliation is the mechanical weathering that separates the joints into layers resembling curved slabs or plates, often thinner at the top of the rock structure and thicker at the sides. Recent research suggests that exfoliation may also result from the force of gravity working a curved surface, creating tension beneath a dome that augments pressure-release processes.

▲**Figure 13.10** **Tafoni, or honeycomb weathering, in sandstone along the Pacific Coast in Salt Point State Park, California.**
[ABN Images/Alamy.]

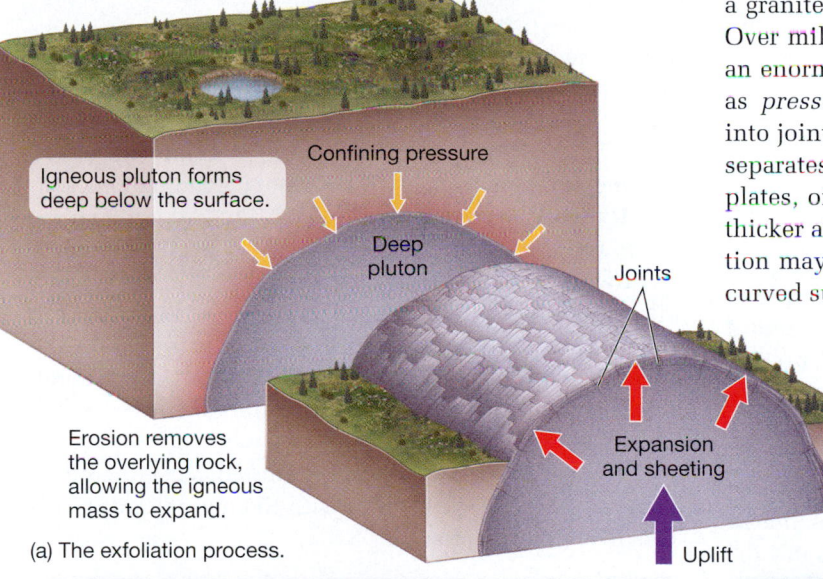

Igneous pluton forms deep below the surface.

Confining pressure

Deep pluton

Joints

Erosion removes the overlying rock, allowing the igneous mass to expand.

Expansion and sheeting

Uplift

(a) The exfoliation process.

▼**Figure 13.11** **Exfoliation in granite.**
Exfoliation loosens slabs of rock, freeing them for further weathering and downslope movement. [(b) Bobbé Christopherson. (c) Robert Christopherson.]

(b) Exfoliated granite, White Mountains, New Hampshire.

(c) Exfoliation forms characteristic granite domes such as Half Dome in Yosemite, California.

(a) The Devil's Marbles in Australia's Northern Territory are a collection of granite boulders rounded by spheroidal weathering processes.

(b) Note the thin layer peeling from the rock surface on this boulder.

▲Figure 13.12 Spheroidal weathering, a chemical process. Over time, chemical weathering dissolves minerals in the rock, causing thin layers to peel away from the rock surface, thus gradually rounding the rock. [(a) Krzysztof Dydynski/Lonely Planet Images/Getty. (b) imageBROKER/Alamy.]

Chemical Weathering Processes

The chemical breakdown, always in the presence of water, of the constituent minerals in rock is **chemical weathering**. The chemical decomposition and decay become more intense as both temperature and precipitation increase. Although individual minerals vary in susceptibility, all rock-forming minerals are responsive to some degree of chemical weathering. An example of chemical weathering is the eating away of cathedral façades and the etching of tombstones by acid precipitation. In Europe, where increasingly acidic rains resulted from the burning of coal, chemical weathering processes are visible on many buildings.

Spheroidal weathering is chemical weathering that softens and rounds the sharp edges and corners of jointed rock (thus the name *spheroidal*) as water penetrates the joints and dissolves weaker minerals or cementing materials (**Figure 13.12**). As weathering progresses, the rock sheds spherical shells of decayed rock like the layers of an onion. Spheroidal weathering of rock resembles exfoliation, but it does not result from pressure-release jointing.

Hydration and Hydrolysis Chemical decomposition of rock by water can result from the simple combination of water with a mineral, in the process of *hydration*, and from the chemical reaction of water with a mineral, in the process of *hydrolysis*. **Hydration**, meaning "combination with water," involves little chemical change (it does not form new chemical compounds) but does involve a change in structure. Water becomes part of the chemical composition of the mineral, forming a hydrate. One such hydrate is gypsum, which is hydrous calcium sulfate ($CaSO_4 \cdot 2H_2O$).

When some minerals undergo hydration, they expand, creating a strong mechanical wedging effect that stresses the rock, forcing grains apart in a physical weathering process. A cycle of hydration and dehydration can lead to granular disintegration and further susceptibility of the rock to chemical weathering. Hydration also works with other processes to convert feldspar, a common mineral in many rocks, into clay minerals.

Hydrolysis is the decomposition of a chemical compound by reaction with water. In geomorphology, hydrolysis is of interest as a process that breaks down silicate minerals in rocks. In contrast with hydration, in which water merely combines with minerals in the rock, hydrolysis chemically breaks down a mineral, thereby producing a different mineral through the chemical reaction.

For example, the weathering of feldspar minerals in granite can occur by reaction with the normal mild acids dissolved in precipitation:

feldspar (K, Al, Si, O) + carbonic acid and water $\longrightarrow$ residual clays + dissolved minerals + silica

The products of chemical weathering of feldspar in granite include clay (such as kaolinite) and silica. The particles of quartz (silica, or SiO_2) formed in this process are resistant to further chemical breakdown and may wash downstream, eventually becoming sand on some distant beach. Clay minerals become a major component in soil and in shale, a common sedimentary rock.

When minerals in rock are changed by hydration and hydrolysis, the interlocking crystal network consolidating the rock breaks down, and *granular disintegration* takes place. Such disintegration in granite may make the rock appear corroded and even crumbly (**Figure 13.13**).

Oxidation Another type of chemical weathering occurs when certain metallic elements combine with oxygen to form oxides. This process is known as **oxidation**. Perhaps

▲Figure 13.13 **Close up of granular disintegration in granite.** Hydrolysis produces the coarse, crumbly texture of the granite surface under the rock hammer. [Dr. Marli Miller/Visuals Unlimited/Getty Images.]

▲Figure 13.15 **Oxidation processes in soil.** Oxidation of iron minerals produces the reddish colors in the tropical rain forest soils of eastern Puerto Rico. [Bobbé Christopherson.]

the most familiar oxidation is the "rusting" of iron to produce iron oxide (Fe_2O_3). You see the result of this oxidation after leaving a tool or nails outside, only to find them, weeks later, coated with a crumbly reddish-brown substance. This rusty color is visible on the surfaces of rock in which oxidation reactions have removed iron (**Figure 13.14**). It is also visible in heavily oxidized soils such as those in the humid southeastern United States, the arid U.S. Southwest, and the tropics (**Figure 13.15**). Here is a simple oxidation reaction in iron:

$$\text{iron (Fe)} + \text{oxygen (O}_2) \longrightarrow \text{iron oxide (hematite; Fe}_2\text{O}_3)$$

When oxidation removes iron from the minerals in a rock, the disruption of the crystal structures makes the rock more susceptible to further chemical weathering and disintegration.

Dissolution of Carbonates Chemical weathering also occurs when a mineral dissolves into solution—for example, when sodium chloride (common table salt) dissolves in water. Remember, water is called the universal solvent because it is capable of dissolving at least 57 of the natural elements and many of their compounds.

Water vapor in the atmosphere readily dissolves carbon dioxide, thereby yielding precipitation containing carbonic acid (H_2CO_3). This acid is strong enough to dissolve many minerals, especially limestone, by a **carbonation** reaction. This type of chemical weathering breaks down minerals that contain calcium, magnesium, potassium, or sodium. When rainwater attacks formations of limestone (mainly calcium carbonate, $CaCO_3$), the constituent minerals dissolve and wash away with the mildly acidic rainwater:

$$\text{calcium carbonate} + \text{carbonic acid and water} \longrightarrow \text{calcium bicarbonate (Ca}_2{}^{2+}\text{CO}_2\text{H}_2\text{O})$$

The dissolution of marble, a metamorphic form of limestone, is apparent on tombstones in many cemeteries and on statues (**Figure 13.16**). In environments where adequate water is available for dissolution, weathered limestone and marble take on a pitted and worn appearance. Acid precipitation also enhances carbonation processes, as discussed in Focus Study 3.1.

Differential Weathering

Various weathering processes sometimes work in combination with the differing resistances of rocks to produce dramatic landforms. **Differential weathering** is the process

(a) Iron oxidation in rock across from Fungus Lake located near Wawa, Ontario, Canada.

(b) The Aboriginal people of Australia mined and traded ochre, a natural red, yellow, or brown pigment containing iron oxide. Shown here is a wall of red ochre in the Flinders Range, South Australia, one of the foremost regions for ochre mining.

▲Figure 13.14 **Iron oxides in rock outcrops, Canada and Australia.** The chemical process of oxidation makes rock more susceptible to disintegration. [(a) All Canada Photos/Alamy. (b) Age fotostock/Alamy.]

◀**Figure 13.16 Dissolution of limestone.** A marble tombstone is chemically weathered beyond recognition in a Scottish churchyard. Marble is a metamorphic form of limestone. Readable dates on surrounding tombstones suggest that this one is about 228 years old. [Bobbé Christopherson.]

whereby rock strata with different characteristics erode differently even though exposed to the same environmental conditions. The stepped appearance of the Grand Canyon in alternating cliffs and slopes is a result of this process—the cliffs represent rock that weathers relatively slowly (is more resistant) and the slopes represent rock that weathers relatively quickly (is less resistant). The buttes and mesas of the U.S. Southwest result from the removal of less resistant sedimentary strata. Differential weathering also produces landforms—arches, bridges, hoodoos, and delicately balanced rocks—in which a more resistant cap rock protects supporting strata below (**Figure 13.17**).

▼**Figure 13.17 Differential weathering and arch formation in Arches National Park, Utah.** [(a) Source: National Park Service. (b) Don Geyer/Alamy. (c) Gabbro/Alamy.]

Precipitation aided by wind causes physical and chemical weathering in joints, which break apart to form fins.

Water accumulates above the less porous strata below; frost wedging pries rock apart, forming an alcove.

The weight of the overlying rock compacts and strengthens sand grains in the pillars, making them resistant to weathering and erosion.

Less porous sandstone strata (mixed sand and clay)

Porous sandstone strata

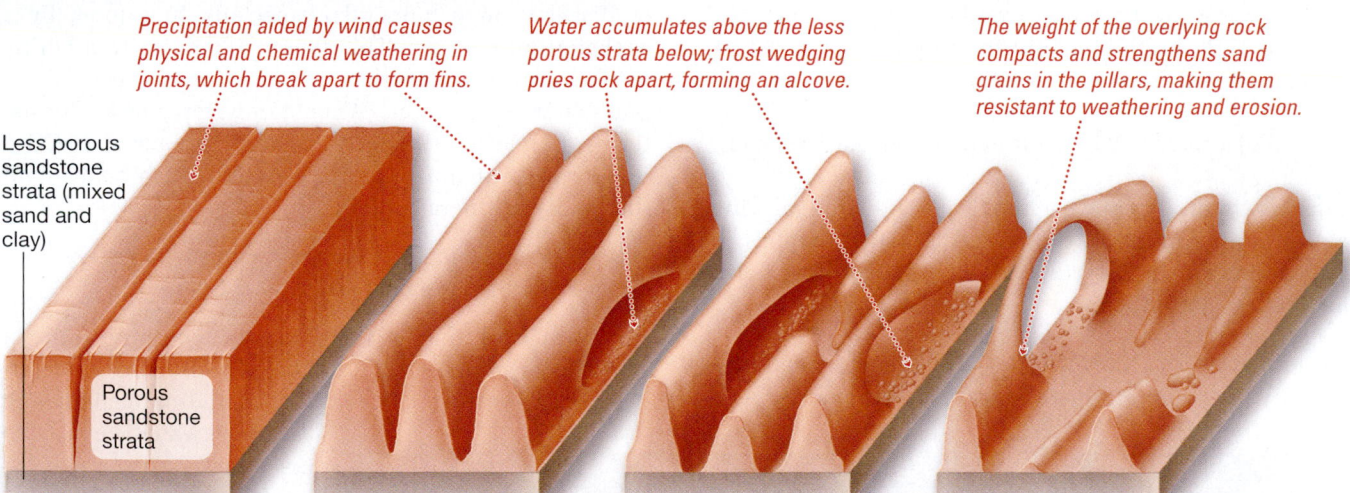

(a) Stages in the formation of sandstone arches. Note that a natural arch differs from a natural bridge, which forms over a flowing stream.

(b) Double O Arch. Note the second smaller arch at bottom left center.

(c) Delicate Arch, probably the most well-known and photographed arch in the park.

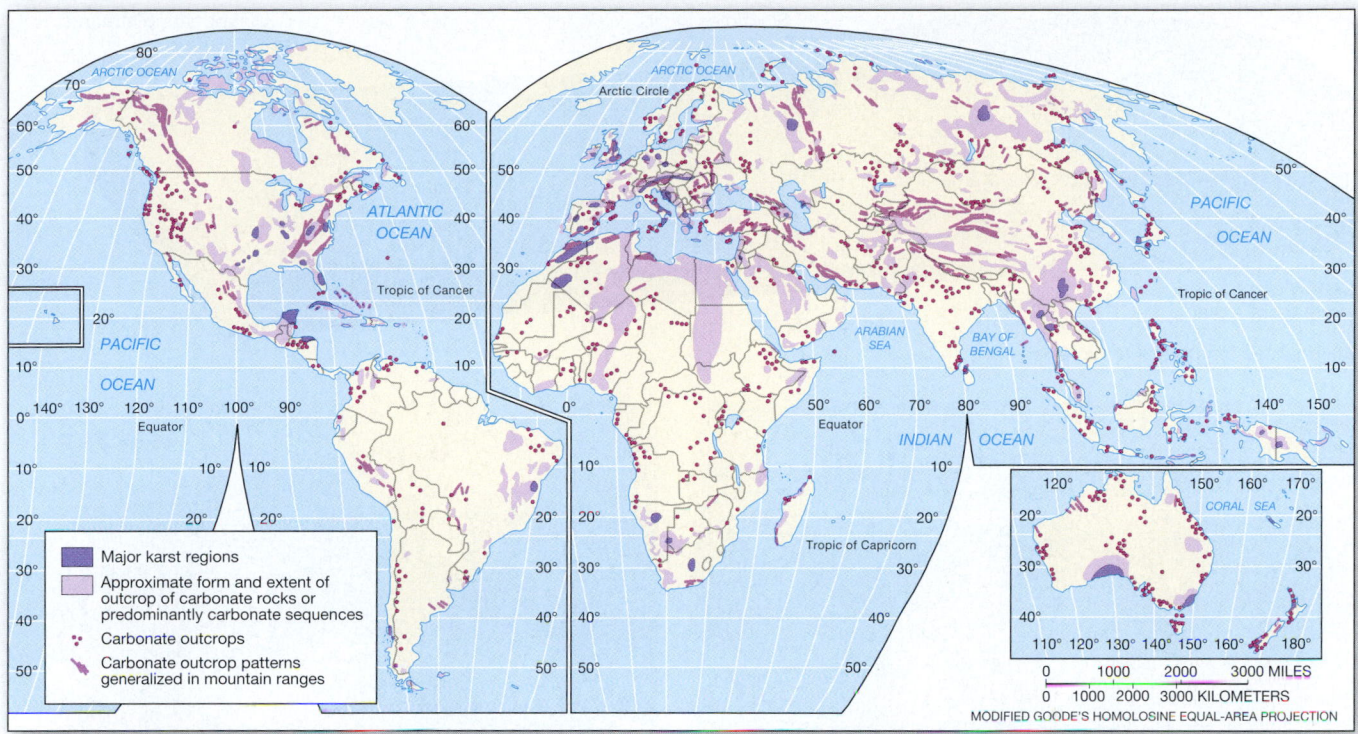

▲**Figure 13.18 Karst landscapes and limestone regions.** Major karst regions exist on every continent except Antarctica. The outcrops of carbonate rocks or predominantly carbonate sequences are limestone and dolomite (calcium magnesium carbonate), but they may contain other carbonate rocks. [Map adapted by Pam Schaus, after USGS sources, and D. C. Ford and P. Williams, *Karst Geomorphology and Hydrology*, p. 601. © 1989 by Kluwer Academic Publishers. Adapted by permission.]

Karst Topography

In certain areas of the world with extensive limestone formations, chemical weathering involving dissolution of carbonates dominates entire landscapes (**Figure 13.18**). These areas are characterized by pitted, bumpy surface topography and well-developed *solution channels* (dissolved openings and conduits) underground. In landscapes of this type, weathering and erosion caused by groundwater may result in remarkable mazes of underworld caverns. Approximately 15% of Earth's land area has some karst features, with outstanding examples found in southern China, the United Kingdom, Puerto Rico, Jamaica, the Yucatán of Mexico, Kentucky, Indiana, New Mexico, and Florida.

Formation of Karst

The distinct features and landforms of karst landscapes are collectively known as **karst topography**, named for the Krš Plateau in Slovenia (formerly Yugoslavia), where karst processes were first studied. For a limestone landscape to develop into karst topography, several conditions are necessary:

- The limestone formation must contain 80% or more calcium carbonate for dissolution processes to proceed effectively.
- Complex patterns of joints in the otherwise impermeable limestone are needed for water to form routes to subsurface drainage channels (**Figure 13.19**).
- An aerated (air-containing) zone must exist between the ground surface and the water table.
- Vegetation cover is needed to supply varying amounts of organic acids that enhance the dissolution process.

The role of climate in providing optimum conditions for karst processes remains under debate, although the amount and distribution of rainfall appear important. The karst features found today in arid regions were formed during past climatic conditions of greater humidity. Karst is rare in the Arctic and Antarctic regions because subsurface water, although present there, is generally frozen.

As with all weathering processes, time is an important factor. Early in the 20th century, scientists proposed that karst landscapes progress through identifiable stages of development, from youth to old age. Evidence has not supported this idea, and today karst landscapes are thought to be locally unique, a result of site-specific conditions. Nonetheless, mature karst landscapes display certain characteristic forms.

▼**Figure 13.19 Joints in a limestone pavement in the Burren, Ireland.** Limestone pavement is a special type of karst landform consisting of a flat limestone surface in which weathering of joints has formed blocks that resemble human-made paving stones. [Joan Gravell/Alamy.]

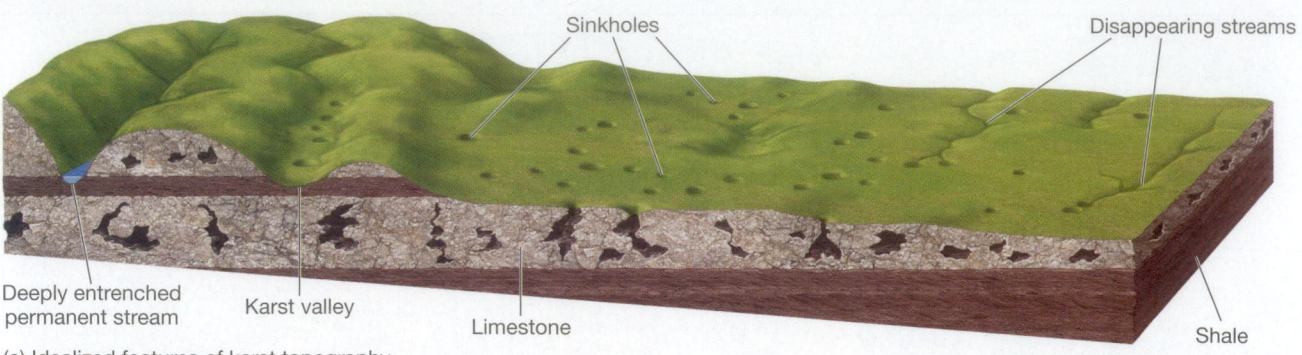

(a) Idealized features of karst topography.

Sinkholes

Disappearing streams

Deeply entrenched permanent stream

Karst valley

Limestone

Shale

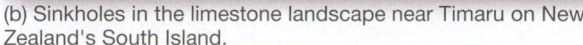

(b) Sinkholes in the limestone landscape near Timaru on New Zealand's South Island.

(c) The Wadi Baatara, a surface stream, flows into the Baatara Gorge sinkhole in Lebanon, forming a dramatic waterfall.

▲**Figure 13.20 Features of karst topography.** Sinkholes and disappearing streams are common features associated with karst topography.
[(b) David Wall/Alamy. (c) dkaranouh/Getty Images.]

Karst Landforms

Several landforms and other features are typical of karst topography. Each form results to some extent from the interaction among surface weathering processes, underground water movement, and processes occurring in subterranean cave networks.

Sinkholes The weathering by dissolution of limestone landscapes creates **sinkholes**, or *dolines*, which are circular depressions in the ground surface that may reach 600 m (2000 ft) in depth (**Figure 13.20**). Two types of sinkholes are most prominent in karst terrain. A *solution sinkhole* forms by the slow subsidence of surface materials along joints or at an intersection between joints. These sinkholes typically have depths of 2–100 m (7–330 ft) and diameters of 10–1000 m (33–3300 ft) (Figure 13.20b). A *collapse sinkhole* develops over a period of hours or days and forms when a solution sinkhole collapses through the roof of an underground cavern. Many such sinkholes occur in western Florida where sandy soils with little clay (which helps hold the soil together) overlay limestone. When

groundwater dissolves underground limestone, the overlying soil cannot support its own weight, leading to sinkhole collapse. Human activities can cause sinkhole subsidence events, as described in GeoReport 13.1. Through continuing dissolution and collapse, sinkholes may coalesce to form a *karst valley*—an elongated depression up to several kilometers long enclosing several sinkholes.

Karst topography commonly features bogs or ponds in sinkhole depressions and unusual drainage patterns. Surface streams may dive underground to join and recharge the subterranean water flow typical of karst landscapes. These "disappearing" streams may join subsurface flows by way of joints or "swallow holes" linking to cavern systems or may flow directly into caves (Figure 13.20c).

The carbonate rock underlying Mexico's Yucatán Peninsula forms an extensive karst landscape with thousands of sinkholes, known as cenotes. Named by the ancient Maya civilization, a *cenote* is a collapse sinkhole whose bottom intersects the water table so that groundwater is present (**Figure 13.21**). Some of these cenotes, especially those along the Caribbean Sea coastline, are

GEOreport **13.1** Recent natural and human-caused sinkholes

In 2015, heavy rains caused a large sinkhole collapse on a Branson, Missouri, golf course. Instead of filling the hole, the owner initiated further sinkhole excavation, still ongoing, in hopes of finding a connection to a nearby underground cave system. In Stockertown, Pennsylvania, along Bushkill Creek downstream from the Hercules mining quarry enterprise, several dozen sinkholes have collapsed since 2000, taking down a bridge from State Route 33 and threatening neighborhoods. Sinkhole development correlated with groundwater pumping at the nearby quarry, which lowered water tables.

(a) Cenote Cristalino, near Playa del Carmen on the Carribbean coast, is shallow and connects to an underground system of caves and caverns.

(b) Cenote Ik Kil is about 60 m (200 ft) in diameter with the water surface about 26 m (85 ft) below ground level.

▲**Figure 13.21 Cenotes on the Yucatán Peninsula, Mexico.** Cenotes Cristalino and Ik Kil are two of some 7000 sinkholes on the Yucatán's karst landscape. [(a) Frederica Grassi/Moment Open/Getty Images. (b) age fotostock/Alamy.]

linked to an expansive network of underground caves and caverns. These sites are popular swimming holes and also attract cavers and cliff divers.

Cones, Cockpits, and Towers In tropical climates, karst topography includes two characteristic landforms—cockpits and cones—with prominent examples found in the Caribbean region (Puerto Rico, Jamaica) and southeast Asia (China, Vietnam, and the Philippines). Weathering in these wet climates, where thick beds of limestone are deeply jointed (exposing a large surface area for dissolution processes), forms a complex topography called *cockpit karst*, resembling the shape of an egg-carton (**Figure 13.22**). The "cockpits" are steep-sided, star-shaped hollows in the landscape with water draining by percolation from the bottom of the cockpit to the underground water flow. Sinkholes may form in the cockpit bottoms,

and according to some hypotheses, solution sinkhole collapse is an important cause of cockpit karst topography.

Dissolution weathering in the tropics also leaves isolated resistant limestone blocks that form cones known as *tower karst*. These resistant limestone towers are most remarkable in several areas of China, where towers up to 200 m (660 ft) high interrupt an otherwise flat, low-elevation plain (**Figure 13.23**).

Caves and Caverns

Caves are defined as natural underground areas large enough for humans to enter. Caves form in limestone because it is so easily dissolved by carbonation; any large cave formed by chemical processes is a *cavern*. The largest limestone caverns in the United States are Mammoth Cave in Kentucky (also the longest surveyed cave in the world with 560 km, or 350 mi, of passages), Carlsbad Caverns in New Mexico, and Lehman Cave in Nevada.

▼**Figure 13.22 Cockpit karst landscape, Philippines.**
[Jeremy Vilasis/Moment/Getty Images.]

▼**Figure 13.23 Tower karst, Li River valley, China.**
[Keren Su/Getty Images.]

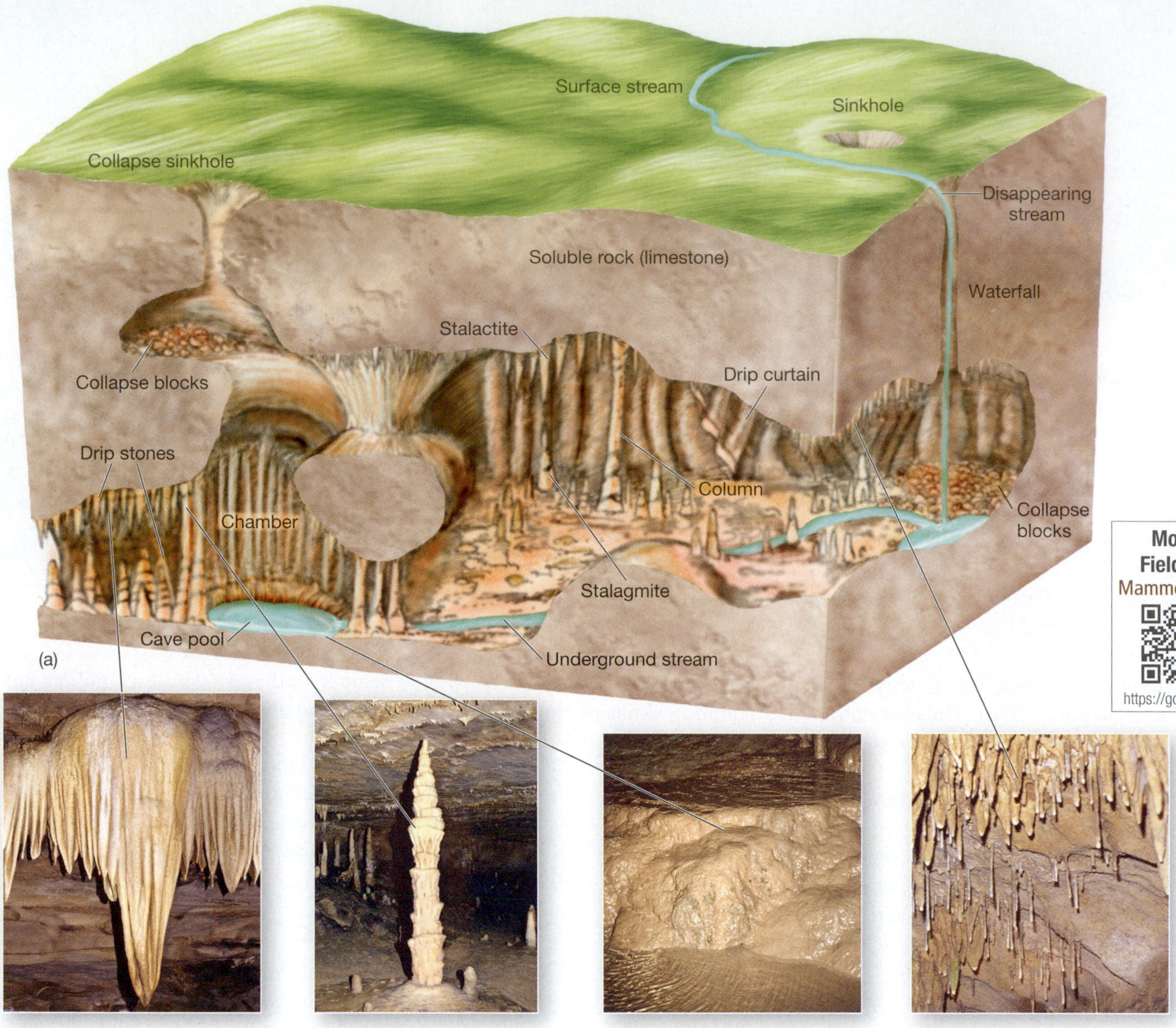

(a)

(b) Dripstone drapery

(c) Near column

(d) Flowstone and pool

(e) Soda straws

▲**Figure 13.24 An underground cavern and related forms in limestone.** A column is created when stalactites from the ceiling and stalagmites from the floor connect. All cave photos from Marengo Caves, Indiana. For more on caves and related formations, see http://cavern.com. [Bobbé Christopherson.]

Cave Features Caves generally form just beneath the water table, where later lowering of the water level exposes them to further development (**Figure 13.24**). As discussed in Chapter 10, speleothems are formations consisting of mineral deposits inside caves and occur in various characteristic shapes. *Dripstones* are speleothems formed as water containing dissolved minerals slowly drips from the cave ceiling. Calcium carbonate precipitates out of the evaporating solution, literally one molecular layer at a time, and accumulates on a spot below on the cave floor.

Thus dripstones are depositional features—*stalactites* growing from the ceiling and *stalagmites* building from the floor. Sometimes a stalactite and stalagmite grow until they connect and form a continuous *column* (Figure 13.24b and Figure 13.24c). Soda straws are a type of thin, long stalactite (Figure 13.24e). *Flowstones* are sheet-like

formations of calcium carbonate on cave floors and walls (Figure 13.24d).

Cave Science and Discoveries *Speleology* is the exploration and scientific study of caves. Scientists and explorers estimate that some 90% of caves worldwide still lie undiscovered. Local residents and amateur cavers— "spelunkers"—have made many important cave discoveries, a fact that adds to the popularity of this sport. For example, in the early 1940s near Bedford, Indiana, a man awoke to find his farm pond at the bottom of a deep collapsed sinkhole. This sinkhole became the entrance to the extensive Marengo cave system, shown in Figure 13.24. In 1991 in Viet Nam, a local farmer reported the entrance to a large, previously unknown cave in the remote jungle. In 2009, this farmer led a joint British–Vietnamese expedition into what is now believed to be the largest single cave passage in the world.

Mass-Movement Processes

The downslope movement of a body of material made up of soil, sediment, or rock propelled by the force of gravity is **mass movement**, also called **mass wasting**. Mass movements can occur on land, or they can occur beneath the ocean as submarine landslides. (For current information on landslide activity, go to http://blogs.agu.org/landslideblog/.)

Mass movement involves either saturated or unsaturated materials that fail simultaneously, often with no warning. Landslides kill 8000 people on average every year worldwide, with about 12 fatalities each year in the United States. The element of surprise increases the hazard, and the prediction of landslides remains an imprecise science. Scientists are using the Global Positioning System (GPS) to monitor landslide movement, measuring slight land shifts as clues to the impending danger.

Mass-Movement Mechanics

All mass movements occur on slopes under the influence of gravitational stress. As discussed earlier, the driving force in mass movement is the shear stress created by gravity, which works in conjunction with the weight, size, and shape of the surface material. The greater the slope angle, the more susceptible the surface material is to mass-wasting processes. The resisting force for mass movement is the shear strength of the slope material—that is, its cohesiveness and internal friction, which work against gravity. If force overcomes resistance, slope failure occurs.

Conditions for Slope Failure Several conditions can lead to slope failure and mass movement.

- A slope becomes saturated by prolonged heavy rainfall or an intense heavy rainfall event, such as a tropical cyclone.

- A slope becomes oversteepened (meaning that it exceeds the angle of repose), such as when river or ocean waves erode the base.
- A volcanic eruption melts snow and ice and carries the fluid debris downslope and into a river channel.
- An earthquake shakes debris loose or fractures the rock that stabilizes an oversteepened slope.

Water content (either frozen or fluid) is an important factor for slope stability. An increase in water content may cause rock or regolith to begin to flow. Clay surfaces are highly susceptible to hydration (physical swelling in response to the presence of water). When clay surfaces are wet, they deform slowly in the direction of movement; when saturated, they form a viscous fluid that fails easily with overlying weight. When ice is present in soils or sediments, as in high-latitude or high-elevation regions, the gradual movement, or "creep," of materials downslope occurs by frost-heaving action and from saturation of seasonally thawed permafrost.

Classes of Mass Movements

In any mass movement, gravity pulls on a mass of material until it reaches a geomorphic threshold. The material then can *fall*, *slide*, or *flow*—the main classes of mass movement. The amount of material moving in each type ranges in volume from small to massive. These classes also range in their moisture content (dry to wet) and rate of movement (rapid free-falling rock to slow-moving soil creep), summarized in **Figure 13.25**.

Note that today's media often uses the term **landslide**—any sudden rapid movement of a cohesive mass of soil, regolith, or bedrock—as a catch-all term for material that falls, slides, or flows. Because many forms

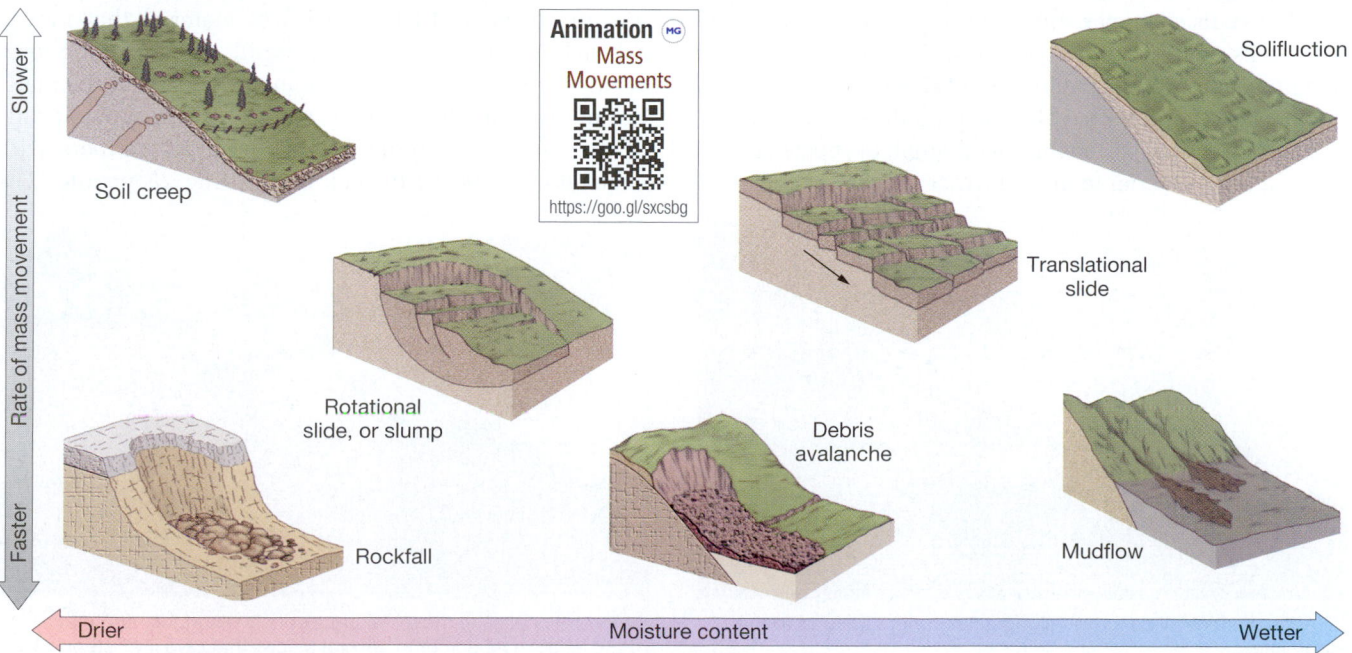

Animation _{MG}
Mass Movements
https://goo.gl/sxcsbg

Slower → Faster (Rate of mass movement)

Soil creep

Rotational slide, or slump

Rockfall

Translational slide

Debris avalanche

Solifluction

Mudflow

Drier ← Moisture content → Wetter

▲**Figure 13.25** **Mass-movement classification.** Principal types of mass movement produced by variations in water content and rates of movement.

▲**Figure 13.26 Talus slopes.** Rockfall, talus deposits, and talus cones at the base of cliffs above Bow Lake in Banff National Park, Alberta, Canada. [Richard Wong/Alamy.]

of mass wasting involve multiple trigger mechanisms and types of movement, exact classification is sometimes difficult and the generalized term "landslide" is applicable.

Falls Rockfalls are a type of mass movement that occur at faster rates and in materials that usually have little or no water content. A **rockfall** is the detachment and rapid downward movement of a volume of rock by gravity. Such falls are abrupt, usually consist of rocks and boulders (rather than soil or sediment), and result from detachment of geologic materials from steep slopes or cliffs. When a rockfall hits the surface below, it breaks up into pieces of various sizes. Focus Study 13.1 discusses weathering and rockfall in California's Yosemite Valley.

Rockfalls characteristically form piles of irregular broken rocks called *talus*. These cone-shaped piles, known as talus cones, often coalesce in a **talus slope**, also called a *scree slope*, at the base of a steep incline (**Figure 13.26**). If the talus slope exceeds its steep angle of repose, it will fail, causing material to move further downslope.

Slides Slides are a type of mass movement in which material moves as a unit along a zone of weakness that separates the slide material from more stable underlying material. Slides tend to be intermediate in both rate of movement and water content. The Oso, Washington, mass movement described in Geosystems Now had characteristics of a slide in its upper reaches. Near the top of the hillslope, the remaining materials show evidence of a slide that broke free as a single unit. However, at the toe of the slope, the landscape shows the signs of a debris flow—a fast-moving slurry of water, mud, soil, and rock (discussed ahead).

Slides usually take one of two forms: translational or rotational (**Figure 13.27**).

- *Translational slides* involve movement along a planar (flat) surface roughly parallel to the angle of the slope, with no rotation. In this type of slide, the landslide mass may consist of a single unit or a few closely related units that move downslope as a relatively coherent mass. Flow and creep patterns (discussed ahead) also are considered translational in nature.

- *Rotational slides*, also called *slumps*, occur when surface material moves along a concave surface. Frequently, underlying clay presents an impervious barrier to percolating water. As a result, water flows along the clay's surface, lubricating the overlying block. The overlying material may rotate as a single unit, or it may acquire a stepped appearance.

Landslides can move huge amounts of material down hillslopes and into river valleys, creating landslide dams. In August 1959, an M 7.5 earthquake triggered a slide in the Madison River Canyon near West Yellowstone, Montana (**Figure 13.28**), releasing 32 million m³ (1.13 billion ft³) of material that moved downslope at 95 kmph (60 mph), causing gale-force winds through the canyon. Momentum carried the material more than 120 m (about 400 ft) up the opposite side of the canyon, trapping several hundred campers with about 80 m (260 ft) of rock and killing 28 people. The

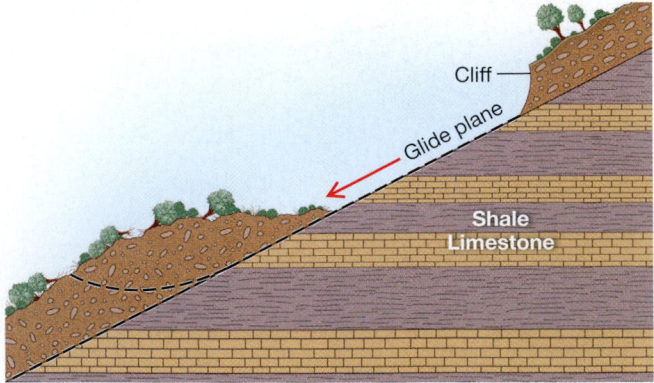

(a) A translational slide moves along a flat surface parallel to the slope angle.

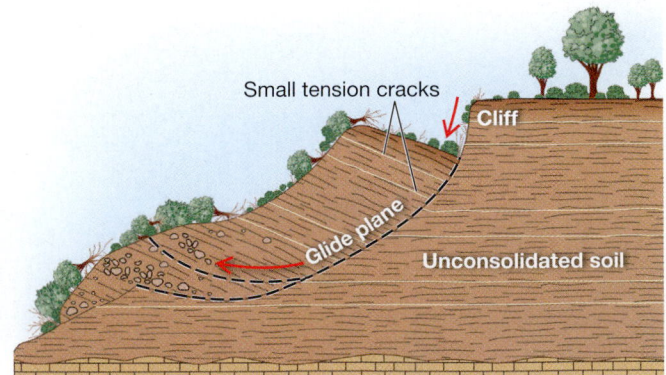

(b) A rotational slide moves along a concave surface, and may rotate as a single unit or in several pieces that give it a "stepped" appearance.

▲**Figure 13.27 Two types of slides: translational and rotational.**

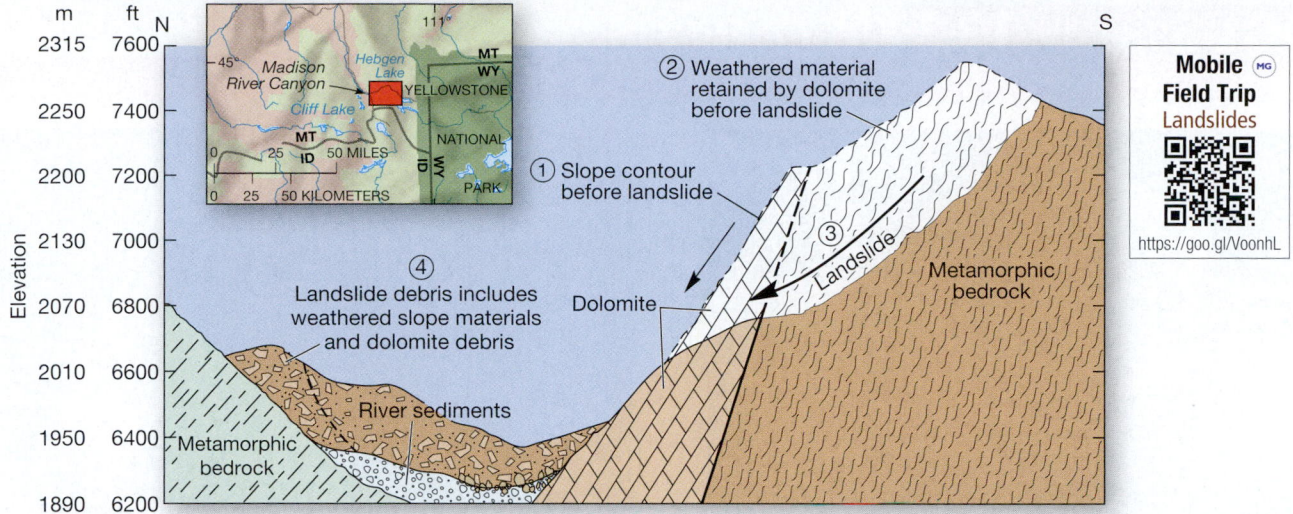

(a) Cross section of the Madison River canyon shows the geologic structure. Numbers indicate (1) pre-landslide topography; (2) area of weathered rock that moved during the slide; (3) direction of landslide; and (4) location and type of debris that dammed the Madison River.

(b) Aerial view of the landslide scar and debris dam across the Madison River, forming Quake Lake.

▲**Figure 13.28 The 1959 Madison River Canyon landslide near Yellowstone National Park, Montana.** This aerial view shows the landslide scar and debris 42 years after the slide. [(a) Source: USGS 1959, USGS Professional Paper 435-K. (b) Larry Mayer/Billings Gazette/AP.]

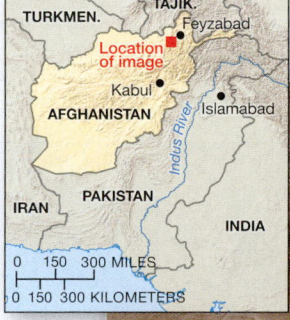

causing hundreds of fatalities (**Figure 13.29**). The cause of the slide, which also had characteristics of a mudflow, was prolonged heavy rainfall occurring on fine-grained soils that are prone to failure when saturated.

> ✓ **WORKITOUT 13.1**
> ## Compare Two Mass-Movement Events
>
> Compare the Figure GN 13.1 photo of the 2014 Oso landslide with the photo of the 2014 Afghanistan landslide in Figure 13.29, and review the descriptions of each mass-movement event.
>
> 1. What factors contributed to instability on each slope?
> 2. How are these landslides similar? How are they different?

▼**Figure 13.29 Landslide in northeast Afghanistan, May 2014.** The landslide occurred after prolonged heavy rainfall saturated the fine-grained soils typical of this region. [Rahmat Gul/AP.]

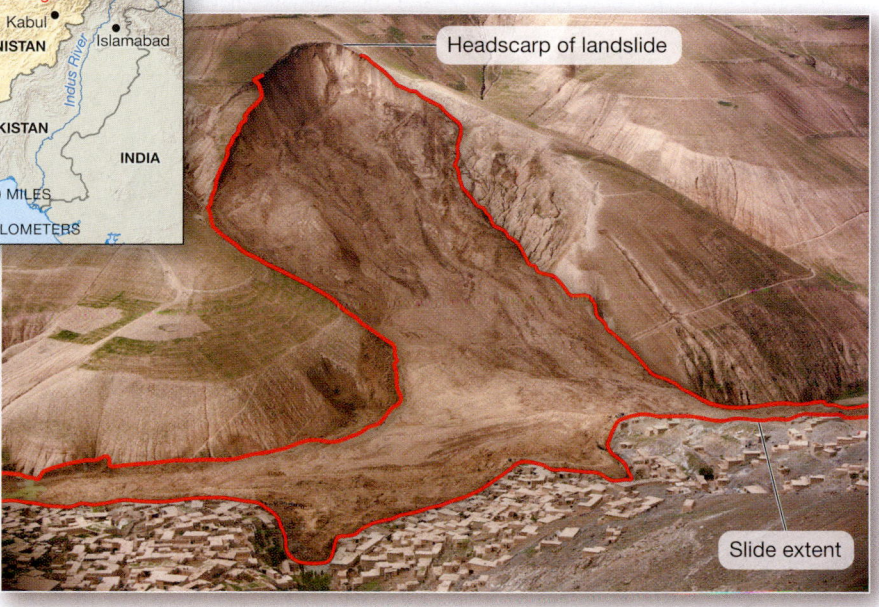

mass of material dammed the Madison River, creating a new lake, dubbed Quake Lake. To prevent overflow and associated erosion and flooding downstream, the U.S. Army Corps of Engineers excavated a channel through which the lake could drain.

On May 5, 2014, a large landslide in northeastern Afghanistan buried 700 homes in the village of Abi Barak,

FOCUSstudy 13.1   Natural Hazards
Is Summer Heat a Trigger for Yosemite Rockfalls?

▲**Figure 13.1.1 Rockfall damage to a cabin in Curry Village, Yosemite Valley.** A rockfall from Glacier Point on October 8, 2008, caused this boulder to come to rest against a tree and a cabin roof. Older, darker colored rockfall boulders are in the background. Buildings in this region were permanently closed following the rock fall. [USGS.]

▲**Figure 13.1.2 Yosemite Valley rockfall, 2010.** [Tom Evans.]

The granite cliffs of Yosemite Valley in California's Yosemite National Park are one of the world's premier rock-climbing destinations. Although the valley's sheer walls appear quiet most of the time, they are dynamic landforms prone to unpredictable and dangerous rock falls (**Figures 13.1.1** and **13.1.2**). Such events threaten human structures and roads. In 2009 a rockfall prompted the evacuation of one of the Park hotels. Then, in 2012, the Park Service closed numerous cabins and several campgrounds near the base of cliffs in areas of rockfall hazard.

Yosemite Rockfall Events

Scientists have tracked the timing and location of rockfalls in Yosemite Valley using historical data (photos, written records, and oral accounts) as well as modern observations and reports (**Figure 13.1.3**). Over the past 150 years, more than 1000 rockfalls have occurred, ranging in size and sometimes having

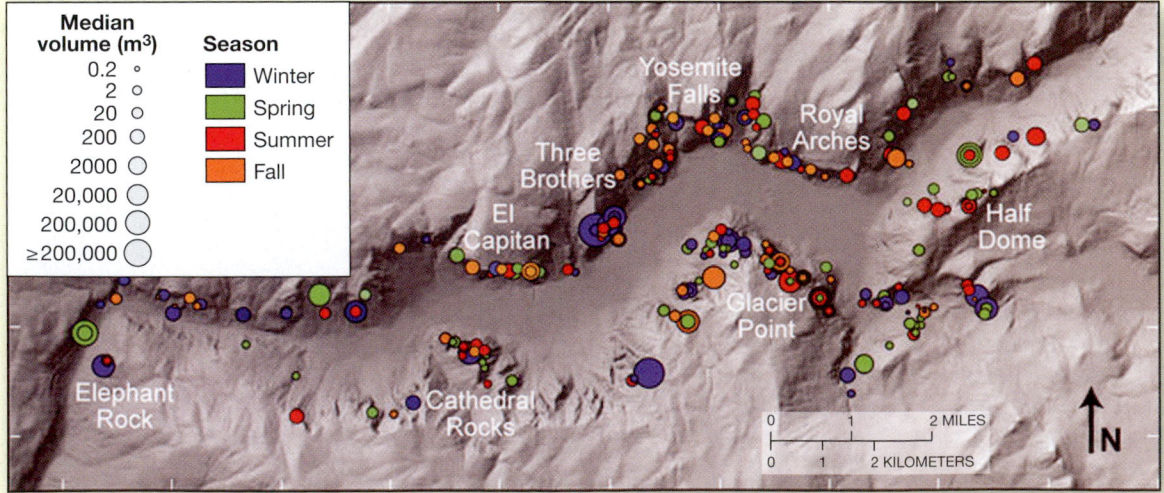

◀**Figure 13.1.3 Document Yosemite Valley rockfalls, 1857–2011, for which size (volume) and season of occurrence are known.** [NPS, see http://www.nps.gov/yose/naturescience/rockfall.htm.]

Median volume (m³)
- 0.2
- 2
- 20
- 200
- 2000
- 20,000
- 200,000
- ≥200,000

Season
- Winter
- Spring
- Summer
- Fall

Map labels: Yosemite Falls, Royal Arches, Three Brothers, El Capitan, Half Dome, Glacier Point, Elephant Rock, Cathedral Rocks

0   1   2 MILES
0   1   2 KILOMETERS
N

dramatic effects on the valley floor. For example, in July 1996, a 162,000-ton granite slab dropped 670 m at 260 kmph (2200 ft at 160 mph), felling more than 500 trees before pulverizing into a light dust that covered 50 acres.

The rockfall record helps scientists and park managers identify zones of instability and hazard. But rockfalls cannot readily be predicted without a full understanding of their causes. Although scientists understand the general trigger mechanisms, the exact cause of a particular event is often uncertain. In Yosemite, the detachment of exfoliating granite slabs can occur from shaking related to seismic activity, by the frost wedging action of water after it collects in cracks and freezes, or by the prying force of vegetation roots as they grow in rock joints. The rockfall database includes many events with too little data to determine a cause. Even for about 200 well-documented events, the exact trigger remains unclear. These unknowns prompted two scientist climbers to take a closer look at the causes of Yosemite rockfalls.

Thermal Stress—A Rockfall Trigger?

In 2011, a Yosemite Park geologist and a U.S. Geological Survey engineer analyzed the Yosemite rockfall records and calculated that 15% of the rockfalls with no identifiable cause occurred in the warmest summer months—July, August, and September—during the hottest time of day—between 1 P.M. and 6 P.M. Meanwhile, climbers that frequent Yosemite's sheer granite faces had reported for years that their hardware—metal protection placed in a crack to secure a rope—shifted in position throughout the day. Specifically, they said that protection placed in granite "flakes" during the heat of the day was difficult to remove in the cooler evening temperatures. The database analysis combined with the climbers' reports led the scientists to hypothesize that thermal stress, the force associated with the volume expansion of rock under changing temperatures, might be an important trigger for Yosemite rockfalls.

To test their hypothesis, the scientists devised an instrument they called a "crackometer," which uses sensors to measure changes in crack width over time. They placed multiple crackometers behind a 19-meter-tall and 4-meter-wide granite flake that was partially detached from the wall. Then they monitored the crack for 3.5 years, assessing movement throughout the day and through each season (**Figure 13.1.4**).

▲**Figure 13.1.4 Data download on the face of the granite cliff.** Scientists retrieve data from instruments measuring movement of the granite flake with daily temperature variations. [Valerie Zimmer/NPS.]

The resulting data showed three trends:

- The granite flake moved toward and away from the wall about 1 cm (0.4 in.) per day, with the rate of movement greatest in summer.
- The flake's movement away from the wall was cumulative, with each summer season's movement building on the summer before.
- The flake itself was deforming in the heat, bowing outward at the center as the rock surface heats and the interior remains cool.

These results led the scientists to tentatively conclude that the stress resulting from these movements aids the process of exfoliation, causing rock cracks to grow and ultimately break apart from the cliff, producing a rockfall.

Although the study sheds light on the processes and causes of weathering and rockfall, it does not aid prediction of the timing of these events. Scientists still cannot estimate when a flake undergoing thermal stress might pass the tipping point at which detachment from the cliff occurs. The results bring up many more questions, and research is ongoing to expand on this study.

1. What specific weathering processes loosen the granite slabs that make up Yosemite's cliffs?

2. In your own words, state the scientists' hypothesis about rockfalls in Yosemite. Did their results support the hypothesis? Explain.

APPLYconcepts Referring to Figure 13.1.3, determine the largest rockfall that has occurred in each season, and check the appropriate box in the table. Then, taking into consideration the rockfall data and the factors that influence mass movements, write a hypothesis that might explain the seasonal distribution of rockfalls in Yosemite.

Volume of Rockfall	Winter	Spring	Summer	Fall
200,000 m³ or above				
Between 20,000 m³ and 200,000 m³				
20,000 m³ or below				

▲**Figure 13.30** **Debris flow in Macedonia.** A destroyed car sits among debris and mud near Tetovo in northwestern Macedonia in August 2015, after a debris flow swept through the village.
[Zoran Andonov/AP Images.]

▲**Figure 13.31** **Mudslide in southern California.** A mudflow trapped more than 180 vehicles—including passenger cars, tractor-trailers, and tour buses—on California Highway 58 in Mojave, California, on October 16, 2015, after torrential rains in the area.
[Mark Ralston/AFP/Getty Images.]

Flows When unconsolidated moving material forms a slurry containing water, scientists classify it as a flow. A **debris flow** is a mixture of water and sediment that is mainly gravels, boulders, and other rock fragments coarser than sand, but also includes mud, silt, and sand (**Figure 13.30**). Debris flow material is loosely consolidated and capable of flow, as opposed to the fairly cohesive blocks that make up a slide. Debris flows can be fast-moving or gradual, and both characteristics can be found within the same flow as it moves from steeper into more gentle terrain. A **mudflow** is composed of water and finer materials (smaller than sand), forming a more fluidized flow with greater speed (**Figure 13.31**).

A type of debris flow associated with volcanic activity is a *lahar*, an Indonesian word referring to a mudflow of volcanic origin. A lahar is a mixture of volcanic ash and liquefied mud that develops as a hot eruption melts ice near the top of a composite volcano. As it moves downslope, a lahar may enter a river channel, which concentrates the flow and enhances the destruction.

Lahars can cause extreme damage and fatalities, as happened in 1985 on Nevado del Ruiz in Colombia, South America. At 11:00 P.M. on November 13, a violent eruption triggered a flow that ran downslope and into the Lagunilla River, forming a wall of mud at least 40 m (130 ft) high as it neared villages and the city Armero, with a population of 25,000. The lahar buried the city, killing 23,000 and leaving 60,000 people homeless across the region. A lahar also occurred on the slopes of Mount St. Helens after the 1980 eruption.

A **debris avalanche**, or *rock avalanche*, is a high-speed flow of rock and debris, sometimes fluidized by ice in steep mountain regions. Often a debris avalanche will become a debris flow as it moves downslope or across a valley, as happened in the Oso landslide discussed in *Geosystems Now*. The danger of a debris avalanche

reaching a populated area results from its tremendous speed. One of the most destructive mass movement events on record was the 1970 debris avalanche on the west face of Nevado Huascarán, the highest peak in the Peruvian Andes. Initiated by an earthquake, the debris avalanche traveled at about 300 kmph (185 mph) and buried the city of Yungay, killing 18,000 people.

Recently, scientists began using satellite images and seismographic data to detect debris avalanches and other landslides that occur in remote high-mountain regions. In 2007 and again in 2015, massive debris avalanches tumbled down the sides of Canada's Mount Steele and then moved across the surface of the Steele Glacier (**Figure 13.32**). Located in the uninhabited Saint Elias Mountains in southwestern Yukon, Mount Steele is Canada's fifth highest mountain. Scientists detected the 2015 event from seismic data on October 11 and confirmed the debris avalanche 2 days later using satellite imagery. Considered large for a debris avalanche, the event moved about 45 megatons of material—a mass of rock and ice equivalent to the weight of 700 aircraft carriers. The largest events, observed in India's Kashmir region and in Tibet, have moved up to 550 megatons of debris.

Creep: The Slowest Type of Flow The persistent, gradual mass movement of surface soil is **soil creep**. In creep, individual soil particles are lifted and disturbed, whether by the expansion of soil moisture as it freezes, by cycles of moistness and dryness, by diurnal temperature variations, or by grazing livestock or digging animals.

In the freeze–thaw cycle, expansion of ice lifts soil particles at right angles to the slope (**Figure 13.33**).

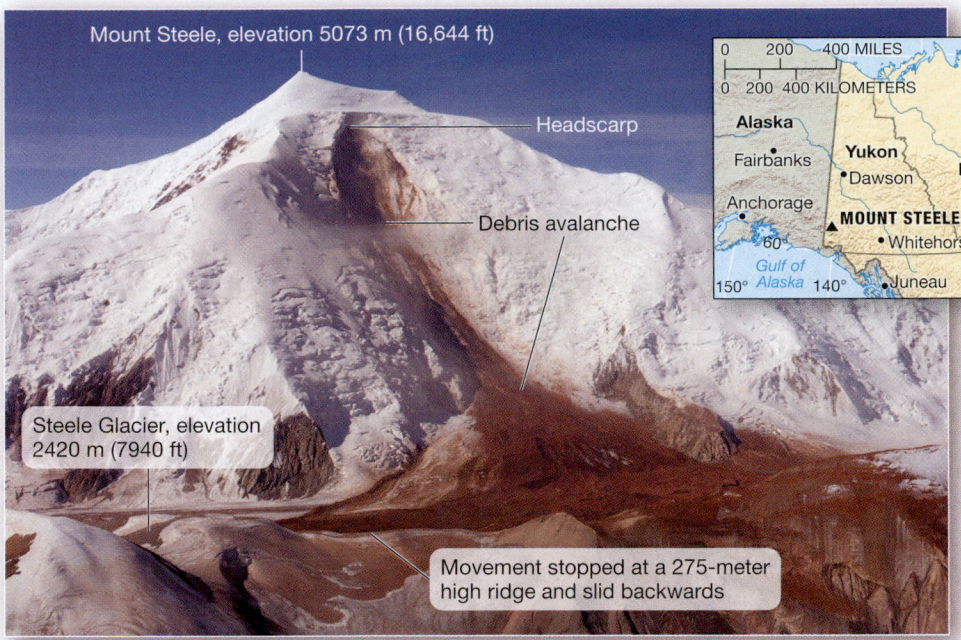

Mount Steele, elevation 5073 m (16,644 ft)

Headscarp

Debris avalanche

Steele Glacier, elevation 2420 m (7940 ft)

Movement stopped at a 275-meter high ridge and slid backwards

(a) A drone photograph of the 2007 event.

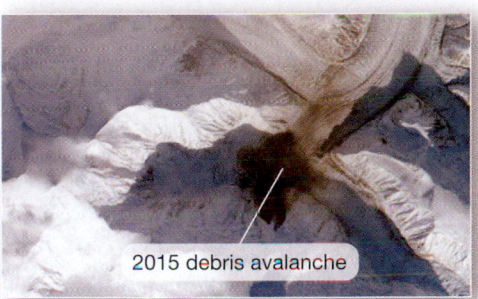

2015 debris avalanche

(b) Satellite image shows the 2015 event, indicated by the brown area on the slopes and extending onto the Steele Glacier (the dark areas are shadows). Material flowed about 2 km (1.2 mi) across the glacier, an unusually long runout enhanced by low friction on the ice.

▲ **Figure 13.32 Debris avalanches on Mount Steele, Yukon, Canada.** [(a) Peter von Gaza; www.petervongaza.com. (b) *Landsat-8* image by Jesse Allen/NASA.]

When the ice melts, however, the particles fall straight downward in response to gravity. As the process repeats, the surface soil gradually creeps downslope.

The overall wasting of a creeping slope may cover a wide area and may cause fence posts, utility poles, and even trees to lean downslope. Various strategies are used to arrest the mass movement of slope material—grading the terrain, building terraces and retaining walls, planting ground cover—but the persistence of creep often renders these strategies ineffective.

In polar regions and at high elevations, freeze–thaw processes are a key factor in mass wasting. During the summer when the upper layers of soil thaw and become saturated, slow downslope movement occurs, called **solifluction** (discussed in Chapter 17).

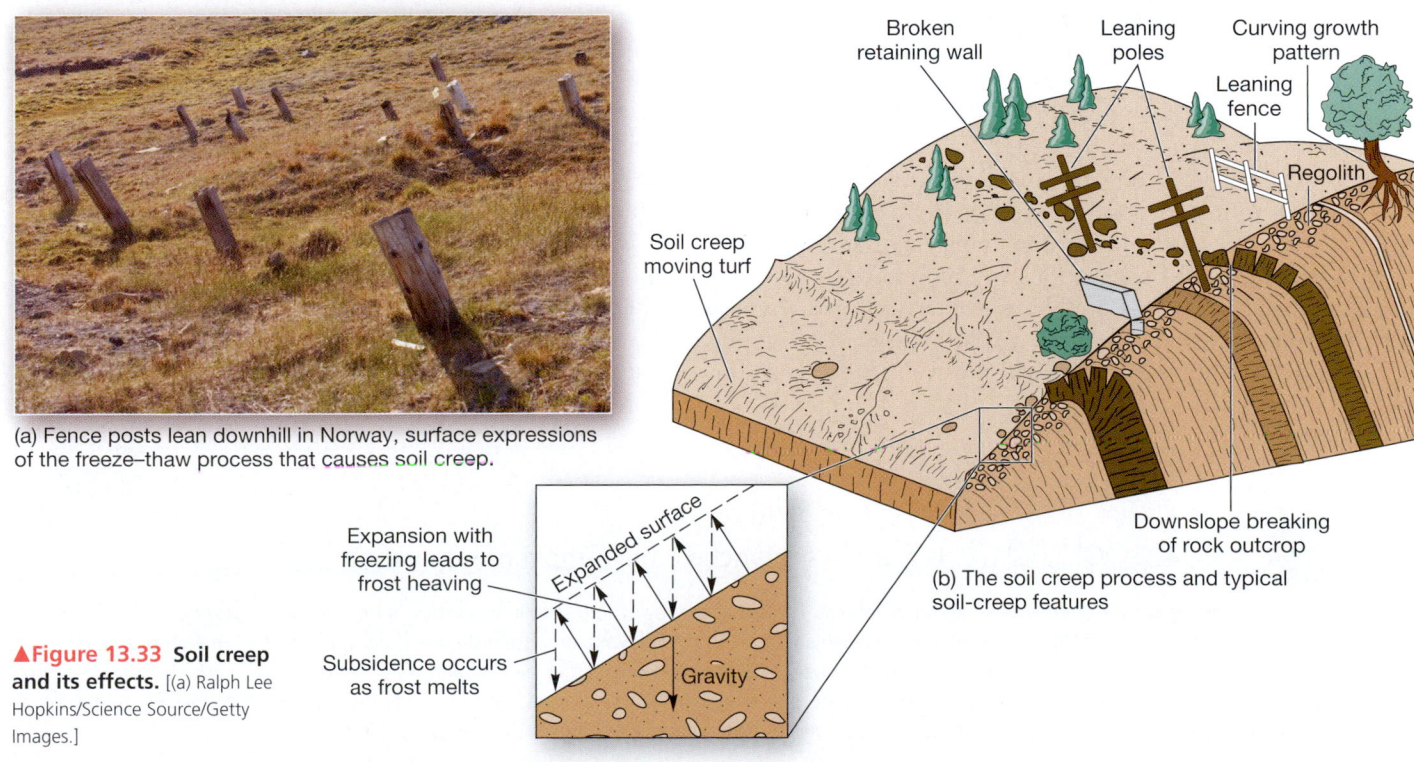

(a) Fence posts lean downhill in Norway, surface expressions of the freeze–thaw process that causes soil creep.

Broken retaining wall — Leaning poles — Curving growth pattern — Leaning fence — Regolith

Soil creep moving turf

Downslope breaking of rock outcrop

(b) The soil creep process and typical soil-creep features

Expansion with freezing leads to frost heaving — Expanded surface

Subsidence occurs as frost melts — Gravity

▲**Figure 13.33 Soil creep and its effects.** [(a) Ralph Lee Hopkins/Science Source/Getty Images.]

▲**Figure 13.34** **The Bingham Canyon Mine outside Salt Lake City, Utah, 2014.** Also known as the Kennecott Copper Mine, this is the world's largest and deepest excavated hole. In 2013, a large landslide occurred on an unstable slope within the open pit. No fatalities occurred [DEA/PUBBLI AER FOTO/Getty Images.]

▲**Figure 13.35** **Mountaintop removal from coal mining on Kayford Mountain, West Virginia.** [Debbie Hill/UPI/Newscom.]

Human-Induced Mass Movement

Any human disturbance of a slope—highway road cutting, surface mining, or construction of a shopping mall, housing development, or home—can hasten mass wasting. Large open-pit surface mines, such as the Bingham Canyon Copper Mine west of Salt Lake City and the abandoned Berkeley Pit in Butte, Montana, are examples of human impacts that move sediment, soil, and rock material. At the Bingham Canyon Copper Mine, a mountain literally was removed since mining began in 1906, forming a pit 4 km wide and 1.2 km deep, or 2.5 mi wide and 0.75 mi deep. This is easily the largest human-made excavation on Earth (**Figure 13.34**).

The disposal of tailings (mined ore of little value) and waste material is a significant problem at any mine and adds to the geomorphic impacts of mining practices. Such large excavations produce tailing piles that are unstable and susceptible to further weathering, mass wasting, or wind dispersal. Additionally, the leaching of toxic materials from tailings and waste piles poses an ever-increasing problem for streams, aquifers, and public health across the country.

Where underground mining is common, particularly for coal in the Appalachians, land subsidence and collapse may produce mass movement on hillslopes that affects homes, highways, streams, wells, and property values. A controversial form of mining called *mountaintop removal* is done by removing the materials that form ridges and summits, thereby exposing the coal seams for mining. Material and debris (known as mine tailings) are usually dumped into stream valleys, where they bury the stream channel. Mountaintop removal on Kayford Mountain, West Virginia, and elsewhere in the region has flattened more than 500 mountaintops, removing an estimated 1.2 million acres and filling some 2000 km (1245 mi) of streams with tailings (**Figure 13.35**). These valley fills affect downstream water quality, increasing concentrations of potentially toxic nickel, lead, cadmium, iron, and selenium to levels that generally exceed government standards.

Research suggests that humans are a significant geomorphic agent, on the order of 10 times more active in shaping the landscape than are natural processes such as river erosion and wave action along coastlines.

Mobile MG
Field Trip
Tar Sands

https://goo.gl/fbq6SV

🌍 **GEO**report **13.2** Is a snow avalanche a mass-movement event?

We define mass movement as the downslope movement of a body of soil, sediment, or rock under the pull of gravity. Does a snow avalanche—the sudden release and movement of massive amounts of snow down a mountain slope—qualify as a type of mass movement? Snow avalanches are related to mass wasting because snow moves with gravity and may pick up and transport other materials, such as trees and houses. However, the primary material in a snow avalanche is snow rather than soil or rock, and scientists study snow avalanches by examining snow characteristics. We discuss snow avalanches within the context of the cryosphere in Chapter 17.

GEOMORPHIC PROCESSES IMPACT HUMANS

• Chemical weathering processes break down carvings made by humans in rock, such as tombstones, cathedral facades, and bridges.
• Sudden sinkhole formation in populated areas can cause damage and human casualties.
• Mass movements cause fatalities and sometimes catastrophic damage, burying cities, damming rivers, and sending flood waves downstream.

HUMANS IMPACT GEOMORPHIC PROCESSES

• Mining causes scarification, often moving contaminated sediments into surface water systems and groundwater.
• Removal of vegetation on hillslopes may lead to slope failure, destabilizing streams and associated ecosystems.
• Lowering of water tables from groundwater pumping causes sinkhole collapse in population centers.

13a Blue holes are typical karst sinkholes located in what are now offshore areas but that formed during times when sea level was lower. The Great Blue Hole near Belize is part of the Belize Barrier Reef Reserve System designated as a World Heritage site by the United Nations. [Schafer and Hill/Getty Images.]

13b The 71-m-tall (233-ft-tall) Grand Buddha at Leshan in the Sichuan province of southern China is an example of chemical weathering accelerated by air pollution. Carved over 1000 years ago, the statue is now being corroded by acid rain from nearby industrial development. [Bennet Dean/Corbis.]

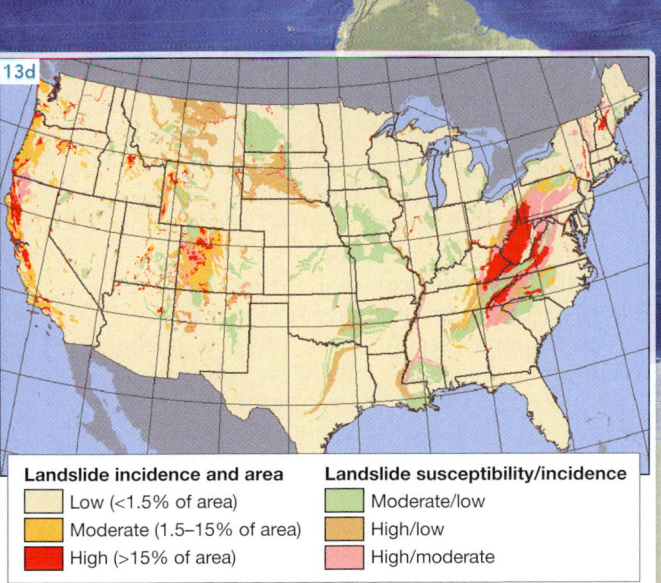

13d

Landslide incidence and area
- ☐ Low (<1.5% of area)
- ☐ Moderate (1.5–15% of area)
- ☐ High (>15% of area)

Landslide susceptibility/incidence
- ☐ Moderate/low
- ☐ High/low
- ☐ High/moderate

The map shows relative landslide incidence (actual occurrence) and susceptibility (the likelihood of occurrence based on local terrain) across the continental United States. Red and pink areas have the highest incidence and susceptibility. [USGS.]

13c In 2016, a landslide occurred at a hot spring resort in Minamiaso, a village of 12,000 in southern Japan, following a series of earthquakes and aftershocks. Over 40 people were killed in the region as a result of the quakes and associated mass-movement events. [Kyodo News via AP.]

ISSUES FOR THE 21ST CENTURY

• Global climate change could affect forest health; declining forests (from disease or drought) will increase slope instability and mass-movement events.
• Open-pit mining worldwide will continue to move massive amounts of Earth materials, with associated impacts on ecosystems and water quality.

QUESTIONS TO CONSIDER

1. Which two main regions have the highest landslide incidence and susceptibility in the continental United States?
2. What factors contribute to slope failure in these regions?

KEY**LEARNING**concepts**review**

Describe the dynamic equilibrium approach to the study of landforms and *illustrate* the forces at work on materials residing on a slope.

Geomorphology is the science that analyzes and describes the origin, evolution, form, and spatial distribution of landforms. Earth's exogenic system, powered by solar energy and gravity, tears down the landscape through processes of landmass **denudation** (p. 382) involving weathering, mass movement, erosion, transportation, and deposition.

Agents of change include moving air, water, waves, and ice. Since the 1960s, research and understanding of the processes of denudation have moved toward the **dynamic equilibrium model** (p. 382), which considers slope and landform stability to be consequences of the resistance of rock materials to the attack of denudation processes. When a destabilizing event occurs, a landform or landform system may reach a **geomorphic threshold** (p. 382), where force overcomes resistance and the system moves to a new level and toward a new equilibrium state.

Slopes (p. 383) are shaped by the relation between the rate of weathering and breakup of slope materials and the rate of mass movement and erosion of those materials. Slopes that form the boundaries of landforms have several general components: *waxing slope*, *free face*, *debris slope*, and *waning slope*. The **angle of repose** (p. 383) of loose sediment grains represents a balance of driving and resisting forces on a slope.

1. Define landmass denudation. What processes are included in the concept?
2. Describe conditions on a hillslope that is right at the geomorphic threshold. What factors might push the slope beyond this point?

Define weathering and *explain* the factors that influence weathering processes.

Weathering (p. 386) processes disintegrate both surface and subsurface rock into mineral particles or dissolve them in water. On a typical hillside, loose surface material overlies consolidated, or solid, rock called **bedrock** (p. 386). In most areas, the upper surface of bedrock undergoes continual weathering, creating broken-up rock called **regolith** (p. 386). The unconsolidated, fragmented material that is carried across landscapes by erosion, transportation, and deposition is sediment, which along with weathered rock forms the **parent material** (p. 386) from which soil evolves.

Important in weathering processes are **joints** (p. 387), the fractures and separations in the rock that open up additional surfaces on which weathering processes operate. Factors that influence weathering include the character of the bedrock (hard or soft, soluble or insoluble, broken or unbroken), climatic elements (temperature, precipitation, freeze–thaw cycles), position of the water table, slope orientation, surface vegetation and its subsurface roots, and time.

3. What is the relationship between parent rock, parent material, regolith, and soil?

Describe the physical weathering processes of frost wedging, thermal expansion, salt-crystal growth, and pressure-release jointing.

Physical weathering (p. 388), or mechanical weathering, refers to the breakup of rock into smaller pieces with no alteration of mineral identity. The physical action of water when it freezes (expands) and thaws (contracts) causes rock to break apart in the process of **frost wedging** (p. 388). Working in joints, expanded ice can produce *joint-block separation* through this process. *Thermal expansion* occurs as rock surfaces heated by the Sun expand and then contract with nighttime cooling. Another physical weathering process is *salt-crystal growth* (*salt weathering*); as crystals in rock grow and enlarge over time by crystallization, they force apart mineral grains and break up rock. Removal of overburden from a granitic batholith relieves the pressure of deep burial, producing joints. **Exfoliation** (p. 389), or *sheeting*, occurs as mechanical forces enlarge the joints, separating the rock into layers of curved slabs or plates (rather than granular disintegration that occurs with many weathering processes).

4. Why is freezing water such an effective physical weathering agent?
5. What weathering processes produce a granite dome? Describe the sequence of events.

Explain the chemical weathering processes of hydration, hydrolysis, oxidation, carbonation, and dissolution.

Chemical weathering (p. 390) is the chemical decomposition of minerals in rock. It can cause **spheroidal weathering** (p. 390), in which chemical weathering that occurs in cracks in the rock removes cementing and binding materials so that the sharp edges and corners of rock disintegrate and become rounded. **Hydration** (p. 390) occurs when a mineral absorbs water and expands, thus changing the mineral structure. This process also creates a strong mechanical (physical weathering) force that stresses rocks. **Hydrolysis** (p. 390) breaks down silicate minerals in rock through reaction with water, as in the chemical weathering of feldspar into clays and silica. **Oxidation** (p. 390) is a chemical weathering process in which oxygen reacts with certain metallic elements, the most familiar example being the rusting of iron to produce iron oxide. The *dissolution* of materials into solution is also considered chemical weathering. An important type of dissolution is **carbonation** (p. 391), resulting when carbonic acid in rainwater reacts to break down certain minerals, such as those containing calcium, magnesium, potassium, or sodium.

Different rocks offer differing resistance to physical and chemical weathering processes and produce a pattern on the landscape of **differential weathering** (p. 391).

6. What is the difference between physical and chemical weathering?
7. How does *spheroidal weathering* occur?
8. Iron minerals in rock are susceptible to which form of chemical weathering?

Review the processes and features associated with karst topography.

Karst topography (p. 393) refers to distinctively pitted and weathered limestone landscapes. **Sinkholes** (p. 394) are circular surface depressions that may be *solution sinkholes* formed by slow subsidence or *collapse sinkholes* formed in a sudden collapse through the roof of an underground cavern below. In tropical climates, karst landforms include *cockpit karst* and *tower karst*.

9. Describe the development of limestone topography. What is the name applied to such landscapes?
10. What are some of the characteristic erosional and depositional features you find in a limestone cavern?

Categorize the various types of mass movements and *identify* examples of each.

Any movement of a body of material, propelled and controlled by gravity, is **mass movement** (p. 397), or **mass wasting** (p. 397). **Landslide** (p. 397) is the general term for a large amount of soil, regolith, or bedrock that moves downslope. Mass movement of Earth's surface can be categorized into falls, slides, and flows. **Rockfalls**, (p. 398) (rock that becomes detached and falls to the surface below), can form a **talus slope** (p. 398) of loose rock along the base of the cliff. *Translational slides* and *rotational slides* include cohesive masses of material that slide along a plane of weakness. Flows are fluidized with water or ice. **Debris flows** (p. 402) include flowing rock, debris, and soil. **Mudflows** (p. 402) consist of flowing material of smaller size and higher water content than a debris flow. **Debris avalanches** (p. 402) are fast-moving flows in steep regions that include rock and debris fluidized by water or ice. Creep is the slowest type of flow. **Soil creep** (p. 402) is the gradual, persistent movement of individual soil particles that are lifted by the expansion of soil moisture as it freezes, by cycles of wetness and dryness, by temperature variations, or by the impact of grazing animals. **Solifluction** (p. 403) is soil creep that occurs in the summer months in the frozen soils in polar regions and at high elevations.

11. What are the classes of mass movement? Describe each briefly and differentiate among these classes.
12. Name and describe the type of mudflow associated with a volcanic eruption.

GEO**SPATIAL** ANALYSIS

Sinkholes

The U.S. Geological Survey (USGS) studies karst regions and monitors sinkhole activity across the United States. Sinkholes tend to form in regions where the underlying bedrock is water soluble, such as in areas of extensive limestone formations susceptible to chemical weathering.

Activities

Go to the Tennessee sinkholes map at http://tnlandforms.us/heatmap/3x3heat.html. Change the base map to terrain by clicking on "Map" and choosing "Terrain." Click "Change Radius" to see higher resolution data. Zoom out so you can see the entire state of Tennessee.

1. Which cities have the highest occurrence of sinkholes?
2. Do sinkholes occur in valleys or mountainous regions? If not, why not there?
3. What is the overall pattern of sinkhole distribution? What geographic feature does this directional trend follow?

Read The Science of Sinkholes article at https://www2.usgs.gov/blogs/features/usgs_top_story/the-science-of-sinkholes/.

4. What percentage of the United States is susceptible to sinkholes?
5. In which states, besides Tennessee, does the most damage from sinkholes occur?
6. How can you determine if there is a sinkhole on your property?
7. According to the article, how do sinkholes form in humid areas? How is this the basis for karst topography?

Examine the Areas of the United States with potential for karst features map at http://geology.er.usgs.gov/egpsc/graphics/06_karst_studies_weary.jpg.

8. Based on the location of soluble bedrock, does this correlate to your answer in question 5? Why or why not?
9. Name 9 additional states that are likely to have sinkholes.

MasteringGeography™

Looking for additional review and test prep materials? Visit the Study Area in MasteringGeography™ to enhance your geographic literacy, spatial reasoning skills, and understanding of this chapter's content by accessing a variety of resources, including MapMaster™ interactive maps, videos, *Mobile Field Trips*, *Project Condor* Quadcopter videos, *In the News* RSS feeds, flashcards, web links, self-study quizzes, and an eText version of *Geosystems*.

14 River Systems

Yellowstone
National Park,
Wyoming, USA

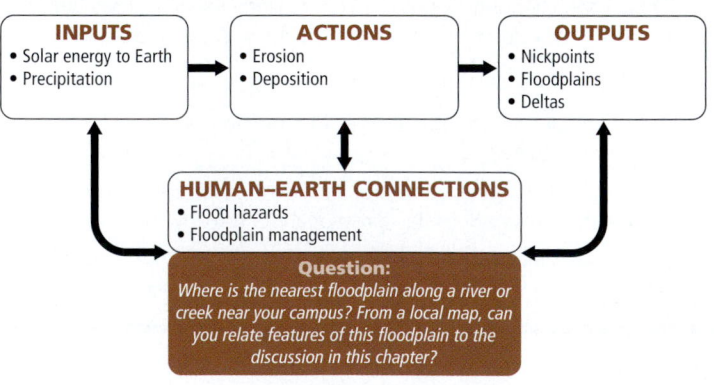

Yellowstone Falls and the Grand Canyon of the Yellowstone are near the headwaters of the Yellowstone River, the last major undammed river in the continental United States and considered one of the greatest trout streams in the world. [Matt Anderson Photography/Getty Images.]

KEY**LEARNING**concepts

After reading the chapter, you should be able to:

- *Sketch* a basic drainage basin model and *describe* different types of drainage patterns.
- *Explain* stream discharge calculation, measurement, and variation over space and time.
- *Describe* the processes involved in stream erosion and sediment transport.
- *Explain* stream gradient and *discuss* the processes by which streams adjust their gradient over time.
- *Describe* the depositional landforms associated with river systems.
- *Explain* flood probability estimates and *discuss* floodplain protection using artificial levees.

INPUTS	ACTIONS	OUTPUTS
• Solar energy to Earth • Precipitation	• Erosion • Deposition	• Nickpoints • Floodplains • Deltas

HUMAN–EARTH CONNECTIONS
- Flood hazards
- Floodplain management

Question:
Where is the nearest floodplain along a river or creek near your campus? From a local map, can you relate features of this floodplain to the discussion in this chapter?

Changes on the Mississippi River Delta

The immense Mississippi River basin drains 41% of the continental United States (**Figure GN 14.1**). From its headwaters in Lake Itasca, Minnesota, the Mississippi's main stem flows southward, collecting water and sediment over hundreds of miles. As the river nears the Gulf of Mexico, the flow energy diminishes and the river deposits its sediment load. This area of deposition forms the *delta*, the low-lying plain at the river's end.

Like most rivers, the Mississippi continuously changes its channel, seeking the shortest and most efficient course to the ocean. In southern Louisiana, the Mississippi's channel has—over thousands of years—shifted course across an area encompassing thousands of square miles. Throughout this time span, floods caused the river to abandon previous channels and carve new ones. The Mississippi River attained its present position about 500 years ago and began building the delta we see today (**Figure GN 14.2**).

Engineering the River Channel Since about 1950, engineers have worked to keep the Mississippi River in its present channel, a feat accomplished by dams, floodgates, and artificial levees (earthen embankments designed to prevent channel overflow). The U.S. Army Corps of Engineers built the Old River Control Structure in 1963 to block the Mississippi River from shifting westward toward the Atchafalaya River, which takes a steeper, shorter route to the Gulf of Mexico. Such a shift would cause the river to bypass two major U.S. ports, Baton Rouge and New Orleans, with negative economic consequences. Despite such measures, the Atchafalaya delta is growing even as the rest of the Mississippi's delta disappears.

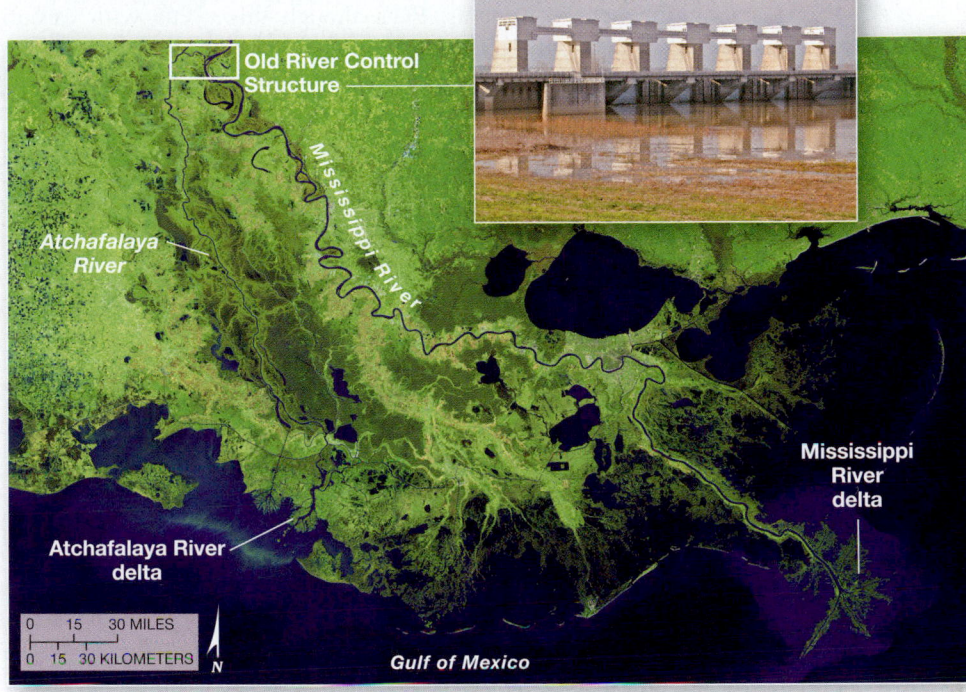

▲**Figure GN 14.2 Mississippi River landscape, southern Louisiana.** Inset photo shows the Old River Control Auxilliary Structure. NASA/USGS; Inset photo by Bobbé Christopherson.

The Disappearing Delta Before modern engineering of the channel, the Mississippi River carried over 400 million metric tons of sediment annually to its mouth. River deposits built from this sediment now underlie most of coastal Louisiana. Today, the flow carries less than half its previous sediment load. This decline, combined with land subsidence and sea-level rise, means that the delta region is shrinking in size each year.

The tremendous weight of sediment deposition at the Mississippi's mouth has caused the entire delta region to lower as sediments become compacted, a process that is worsened by human activities such as oil and gas extraction. In the past, additions of sediment balanced this subsidence, allowing the delta to build. With the onset of human activities such as upstream dam construction, the delta is now subsiding without sediment replenishment.

Compounding the problem is the maze of excavated canals through the delta for shipping and oil and gas exploration. As the land surface sinks, these canals allow seawater to flow inland, changing the salinity of inland waters. Freshwater wetlands whose roots help stabilize the land surface during floods are now declining. This makes the delta more vulnerable to flooding from hurricane storm surge, another factor hastening the delta's demise.

Finally, sea-level rise threatens coastal land and wetlands, most of which are less than 1 m (3.2 ft) above sea level. With continued local sea-level rise, lands not protected by levee embankments and other structures that prevent flooding will continue to submerge.

In this chapter, we examine the natural processes by which rivers erode, transport, and deposit sediment, forming landforms such as deltas.

1. Why are engineers trying to keep the Mississippi River in its present channel?

2. What three factors are causing the Mississippi delta to disappear?

▲**Figure GN 14.1 Map of the Mississippi River basin.**

Mobile (MG)
Field Trip
Mississippi River
Delta

https://goo.gl/bpcQAU

409

Earth's rivers and waterways form vast arterial networks that drain the continents. Even though this volume is only 0.003% of all freshwater, the work performed by this energetic flow makes it an important natural agent of landmass denudation. Rivers shape the landscape by removing the products of weathering, mass movement, and erosion and transporting them downstream.

Remember from Chapter 8 that *hydrology* is the science of water at and below Earth's surface. Processes that are related expressly to streams and rivers are termed **fluvial** (from the Latin *fluvius*, meaning "river"). The terms *river* and *stream* share some overlap in usage. Specifically, the term *river* is applied to the trunk or main stream of the network of tributaries forming a *river system*. *Stream* is a more general term for water flowing in a channel and is not necessarily related to size. Fluvial systems, like all natural systems, have characteristic processes and produce recognizable landforms.

The ongoing interaction between erosion, transportation, and deposition in a river system produces fluvial landscapes. **Erosion** in fluvial systems is the process by which water dislodges, dissolves, or removes weathered surface material. This material is then transported to new locations, where it is laid down in the process of **deposition**. Running water is an important erosional force; in fact, in desert landscapes it is the most significant agent of erosion even though precipitation events are infrequent. We discuss fluvial processes in arid landscapes in Chapter 15.

Rivers also serve society in many ways. They provide us with essential water supplies; dilute, and transport wastes; provide critical cooling water for industry; and form critical transportation networks. Throughout history, civilizations have settled along rivers to farm the fertile soils formed by river deposits. These areas continue to be important sites of human activity and settlement, placing lives and property at risk during floods (**Figure 14.1**).

Drainage Basins

Streams, which come together to form river systems, lie within drainage basins, the portions of landscape from which they receive their water. Every stream has its own **drainage basin**, or *watershed*, ranging in size from tiny to vast. A major drainage basin system is made up of many smaller drainage basins, each of which gathers and delivers its runoff and sediment to a larger basin, eventually concentrating the volume into the main stream. **Figure 14.2** illustrates the drainage basin of the Amazon River, from headwaters to the river's mouth (where the river meets the ocean). The Amazon carries millions of tons of sediment through the drainage basin, which is as large as the Australian continent.

Drainage Divides

In any drainage basin, water initially moves downslope as *overland flow*, which takes two forms: It can move as

everyday GEOSYSTEMS

What kind of damage occurs during a river flood?

A flooding river carries not only water but also sediment and debris. When a river overflows its banks into human developments, the flow can pick up vehicles and knock houses off their foundations. As the floodwaters recede, debris such as trees come to rest and sediment is deposited over most surfaces, including the interiors of houses. In June 2016, flooding in West Virginia caused extensive damage, 23 fatalities, and left residents cleaning up a landscape of mud.

◄**Figure 14.1** The aftermath of flooding along the Elk River, Clendenin, West Virginia, in June 2016.
[Ty Wright/Getty Images.]

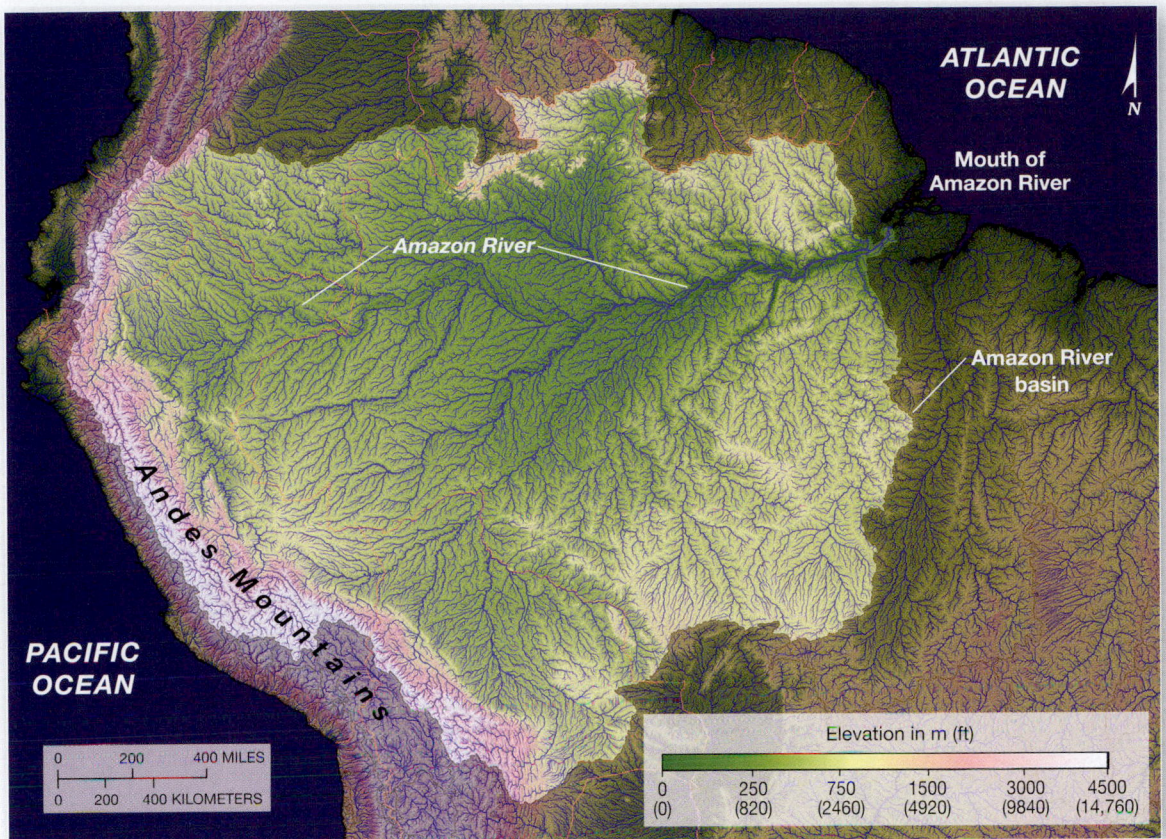

▲**Figure 14.2 Amazon River drainage basin and mouth.** [NASA SRTM image by Jesse Allen, University of Maryland, Global Land Cover Facility; stream data World Wildlife Fund, HydroSHEDS project (see http:// hydrosheds.cr.usgs.gov/).]

sheetflow, a thin film spread over the ground surface, and it can concentrate in *rills*, small-scale grooves in the landscape made by the downslope movement of water. Rills may develop into deeper *gullies* and then into stream channels leading to the valley floor.

The high ground that separates one valley from another and directs sheetflow is called an *interfluve* (**Figure 14.3**). Ridges act as *drainage divides* that define the *catchment*, or water-receiving, area of every drainage basin; such ridges are the dividing lines that control into which basin the surface runoff drains.

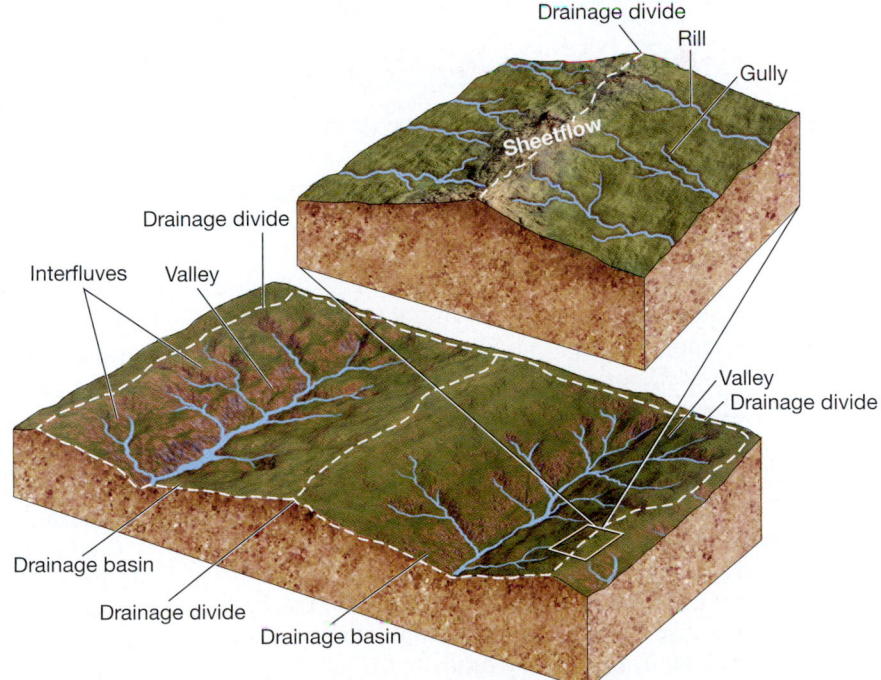

▶**Figure 14.3 Drainage divides.** A drainage divide separates drainage basins.

GEOreport 14.1   Locating the source of the Amazon

Over the past several centuries, scientists and explorers have designated at least six different sources as the true beginning of the Amazon River. In the 1970s, southwest Peru's Apurímac River was deemed the longest tributary stream, and in 2000, Lake Ticlla Cocha on the slopes of Mount Mismi was named as the Apurimac's source. Then in 2014, a team of kayakers used GPS tracking data and satellite images to determine that the Mantaro River, also in southwest Peru, is the longest upstream extension of the Amazon River. However, the new claim remains under debate.

(a) Loveland Pass, Colorado, lies along the continental divide between the Pacific and Gulf/Atlantic drainage basins.

(b) A backpacker approaches the continental divide at Cutbank Pass, Glacier National Park, Montana.

▲**Figure 14.4 The U.S. Continental Divide, Colorado and Montana.** [(a) Erika Nusser/Alamy. (b) Design Pics Inc./Alamy.]

rivers then join at Pittsburgh to form the Ohio River. The Ohio connects with the Mississippi River, which eventually flows to the Gulf of Mexico. Each contributing tributary, large or small, adds its discharge and sediment load to the larger river. In our example, sediment weathered and eroded in Pennsylvania is transported thousands of kilometers and accumulates on the floor of the Gulf of Mexico, where it forms the Mississippi River delta.

Internal Drainage

The ultimate outlet for most drainage basins is the ocean. In some regions, however, stream drainage does not reach the ocean. Instead, the water leaves the drainage basin by means of evaporation or subsurface gravitational flow. Such basins are described as having **internal drainage**. Regions of internal drainage occur in Asia, Africa, Australia, Mexico, and the western United States in Nevada and Utah (discussed in Chapter 15). An example within this region is the Humboldt River, which flows westward across Nevada and eventually disappears into the Humboldt Sink as a result of evaporation and seepage losses to groundwater. The area surrounding Utah's Great Salt Lake, outlet for many streams draining the Wasatch Mountains, also exemplifies internal drainage, since its only outlet is evaporation. Internal drainage is also a characteristic of the Dead Sea region in the Middle East and the region around the Aral Sea and Caspian Sea in Asia (**Figure 14.6**).

Drainage Basins as Open Systems

Drainage basins are open systems. Inputs include precipitation and the minerals and rocks of the regional geology. Energy and materials are redistributed as the stream constantly adjusts to its landscape. System outputs of water and sediment disperse through the mouth of the stream or river into a lake, another stream or river, or the ocean.

Change that occurs in any portion of a drainage basin can affect the entire system. For example, the building of a dam not only affects the immediate stream environment around the structure, but can also change the movement of water and sediment for hundreds of miles downstream. Natural processes such as floods can also push river systems to thresholds, where banks collapse or channels change course. Throughout changing conditions, a river system constantly strives for equilibrium among the interacting variables of discharge, channel steepness, channel shape, and sediment load, all of which are discussed in the chapter ahead.

A special class of drainage divides, **continental divides**, separate drainage basins that empty into different bodies of water surrounding a continent (**Figure 14.4**). For North America, these bodies are the Pacific Ocean, the Gulf of Mexico, the Atlantic Ocean, Hudson Bay, and the Arctic Ocean. These divides form water-resource regions and provide a spatial framework for water-management planning. In North America, the continental divide separating the Pacific and Gulf/Atlantic basins runs the length of the Rocky Mountains, reaching its highest point in Colorado at the summit of Gray's Peak at 4352 m (14,278 ft) elevation (**Figure 14.5**).

As discussed in Geosystems Now, the great Mississippi–Missouri–Ohio River system drains 41% of the continental United States. Within this basin, rainfall in northern Pennsylvania feeds hundreds of small streams that flow into the Allegheny River. At the same time, rainfall in western Pennsylvania feeds hundreds of streams that flow into the Monongahela River. The two

DRAINAGE BASIN DISCHARGE

CANADA:
millions m³ per year
(millions acre-feet per year)

Hudson Bay 682,000 (553)
Atlantic 670,000 (544)
Pacific 602,000 (488)
Arctic 440,000 (356)
Gulf of Mexico 105 (0.9)

UNITED STATES:
millions acre-feet per year
(millions m³ per year)

Gulf/Atlantic 718 (886,000)
Pacific 334 (412,000)
Atlantic 293 (361,000)

⎯⎯⎯ Continental divides

| 0 | 250 | 500 MILES |
| 0 | 250 | 500 KILOMETERS |

◀**Figure 14.5 Drainage basins and continental divides, North America.** Continental divides (red lines) separate the major drainage basins that empty through the United States into the Pacific Ocean, Atlantic Ocean, and Gulf of Mexico, and to the north, through Canada into Hudson Bay and the Arctic Ocean. Subdividing these major drainage basins are major river basins. [After U.S. Geological Survey; *The National Atlas of Canada*, 1985, "Energy, Mines, and Resources Canada"; and Environment Canada, *Currents of Change—Inquiry on Federal Water Policy—Final Report 1986*.]

◀**Figure 14.6 Utah's Great Salt Lake, part of an interior drainage system.** [Delphotos/Alamy.]

Drainage Patterns

A primary feature of any drainage basin is its **drainage density**, determined by dividing the total length of all stream channels in the basin by the area of the basin. The number and length of channels in a given area reflect the landscape's regional geology and topography. For example, landscapes with underlying materials that are easily erodible will have a higher drainage density than landscapes of more resistant rock.

The **drainage pattern** is the arrangement of channels in an area. Distinctive patterns can develop based on a combination of factors, including

- regional topography and slope inclination,
- variations in rock resistance,
- climate and hydrology, and
- structural controls imposed by the underlying rocks.

Consequently, the drainage pattern of any land area on Earth is a remarkable visual summary of every geologic and climatic characteristic of that region.

A familiar pattern is *dendritic* drainage (**Figure 14.7a**), a treelike pattern (from the Greek word *dendron*, meaning "tree") similar to that of many natural systems, such as capillaries in the human circulatory system or the veins in tree leaves. Energy expenditure in the moving of water and sediment through this drainage system is efficient because the total length of the branches is minimized. In landscapes with steep slopes, *parallel* drainage may occur (**Figure 14.7b**). In some landscapes, drainage patterns alter their characteristics abruptly in response to slope steepness or rock structure (**Figure 14.7c**).

Other drainage patterns are closely tied to geologic structure. Around a volcanic mountain or uplifted dome, a *radial* drainage pattern results when streams flow off a central large peak. New Zealand's Mount Ruapehu, an active volcano on the North Island, shows such a radial drainage pattern (**Figure 14.8**). In a faulted and

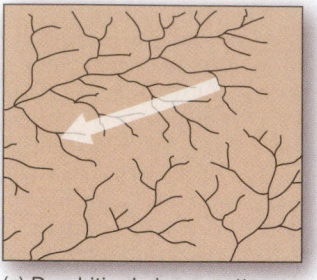

(a) Dendritic drainage pattern.

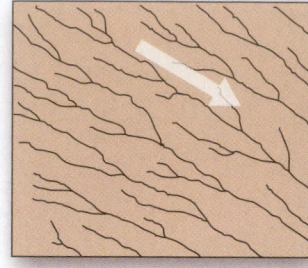

(b) Parallel drainage pattern.

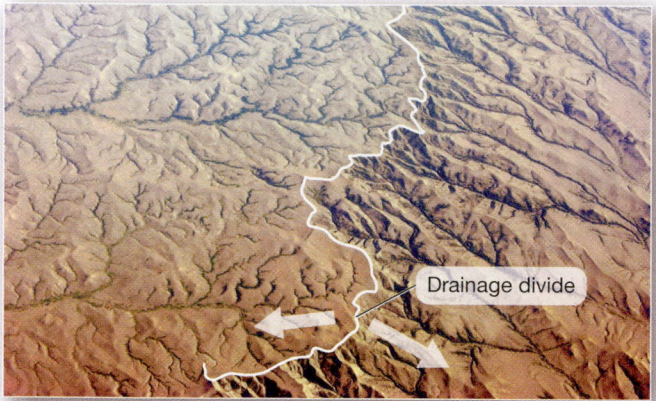

(c) Dendritic and parallel drainage in response to local geology and relief in central Montana.

▲**Figure 14.7 Dendritic and parallel drainage patterns.** [Bobbé Christopherson.]

◀**Figure 14.8 Radial drainage on Mount Ruapehu, North Island, New Zealand.** This false-color image of the composite vocano shows vegetation as red, the crater lake as light blue, and rocks as brown. [NASA.]

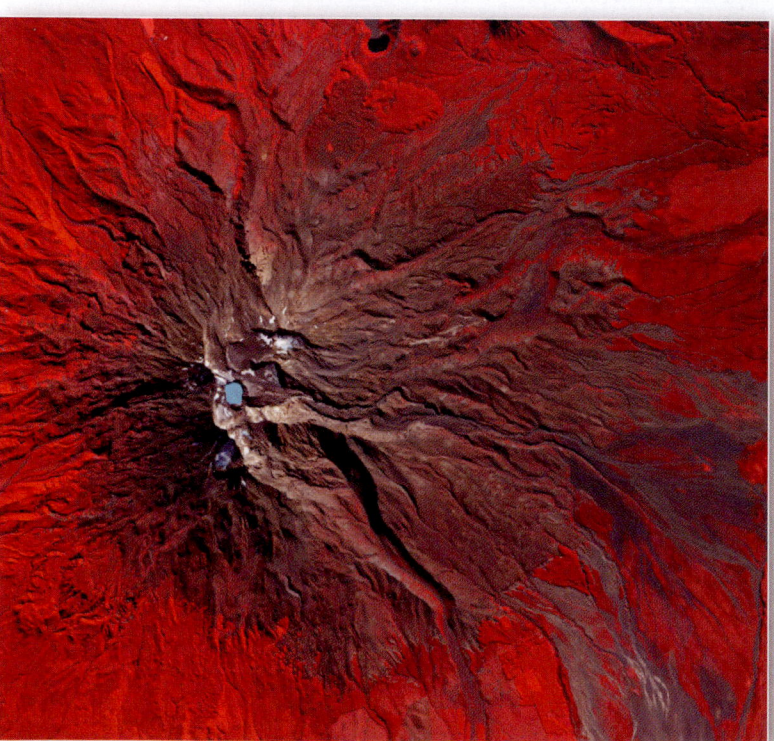

(a) Note the drainage channels flowing off the central peak of Mount Ruapehu, which last erupted in 2007.

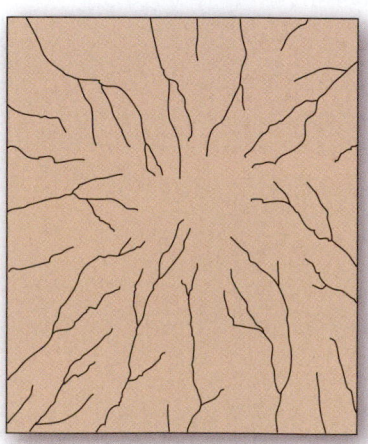

(b) Radial drainage pattern.

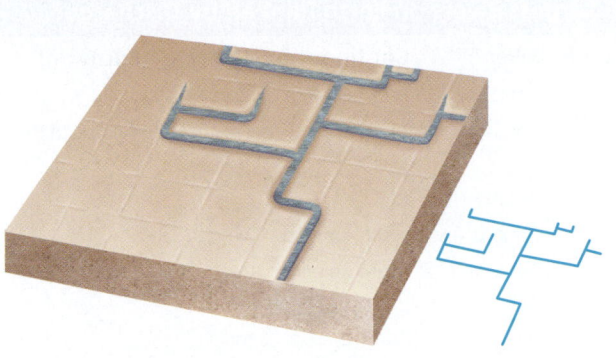

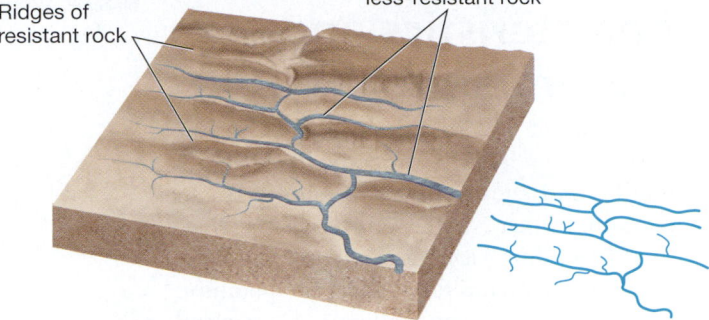

Ridges of
resistant rock

Valleys cut in
less-resistant rock

(a) A rectangular stream pattern develops in areas with jointed bedrock.

(b) A trellis stream pattern develops in areas where the geologic structure is a mix of weak and resistant bedrock (such as in folded landscapes).

▲**Figure 14.9** **Drainage patterns controlled by geologic structure: rectangular and trellis.**

jointed landscape, a *rectangular* pattern (**Figure 14.9a**) directs stream courses in patterns of right-angle turns. In dipping or folded topography, the *trellis* drainage pattern develops, influenced by folded rock structures that vary in resistance to erosion (**Figure 14.9b**). Parallel structures direct the principal streams, while smaller dendritic tributary streams are at work on nearby slopes, joining the main streams at right angles, as in a plant trellis. Such drainage is seen in the nearly parallel mountain folds of the Ridge and Valley Province

in the eastern United States and in the folded landscapes of south-central Utah. Some landscapes display a *deranged* pattern with no clear geometry and no true stream valley. Examples include the glaciated shield regions of Canada, northern Europe, and some parts of the U.S. upper Midwest.

Occasionally, drainage patterns occur that seem to be in conflict with the landscape through which they flow. For example, a stream may initially develop a channel in horizontal strata deposited on top of uplifted, folded structures. As the stream erodes into the older folded rock layers, it keeps the original course, downcutting into the rock in a pattern contrary to the structure of the older layers. Such a stream is a *superposed stream*, in which a preexisting channel pattern has been imposed upon older underlying rock structures (**Figure 14.10**). For example, Wills Creek, presently cutting a water gap through Haystack Mountain at Cumberland, Maryland, is a superposed stream. A *water gap* is a notch or opening cut by a river through a mountain range and is often an indication that the river is older than the landscape.

WORKITOUT 14.1
Stream Drainage Patterns

Choose among dendritic, parallel, radial, rectangular, trellis, and deranged drainage patterns to answer the following questions.

1. Which drainage pattern often occurs in a landscape with a central mountain peak?
2. Which pattern is prominent in the Amazon River basin in Figure 14.2?
3. Which pattern often occurs in landscapes of jointed bedrock?
4. Which pattern occurs in landscapes of folded rock, such as in southern Utah?
5. Which pattern might be found in the Canadian Shield landscape shown in Figure 12.2?

Susquehanna River

As erosion exposes underlying rock with a different structure, the river cuts through ridges of resistant rock rather than flowing around them.

Water gap

▲**Figure 14.10** **The Susquehanna River in Pennsylvania, a superposed stream.** The Susquehanna River established its course on relatively uniform rock strata that covered more complex geologic structure below. Over time, as the landscape eroded, the river "superposed" its course onto the older structure by cutting through the resistant strata. [*Landsat-7*, NASA.]

Streamflow Characteristics and Measurement

The volume of water flowing in a particular stream or river is strongly connected to precipitation and snowmelt in a drainage basin, which are, in turn, connected to weather patterns. Streamflow varies throughout the year, depending on precipitation and temperature. Most fluvial systems are made up of *perennial streams*, which flow all year, fed by snowmelt, rainfall, groundwater, or some combination of those sources. In regions with dry climates, streams may have ephemeral or intermittent flow. *Ephemeral streams* flow only after precipitation events and are not connected to groundwater systems. *Intermittent streams* flow for several weeks or months each year and may have some groundwater inputs. On any stream, high flows and floods can result from periods of prolonged rainfall over a broad region, from intense rainfall associated with short-lived thunderstorms, and from rapid melting of the snowpack.

Stream Discharge: The Volume of Flow

A stream's volume of flow per unit of time is its **discharge** and is calculated by multiplying three variables measured at a given cross section of the channel (**Figure 14.11**). It is summarized in the simple expression

$$Q = wdv$$

where Q = discharge, w = channel width, d = channel depth, and v = stream velocity. Discharge is expressed in either cubic meters per second (m^3/s or cms) or cubic feet per second (ft^3/s or cfs). According to this equation, as Q increases, one or more of the other variables—channel width, channel depth, and stream velocity—must also increase. How these variables interact depends on the climate and geology of the fluvial system.

TABLE 14.1 Largest Rivers on Earth Ranked by Discharge

Rank by Volume	River	Continent	Outflow (Location)
1	Amazon	South America	Brazil
2	Congo	Africa	Democratic Republic of the Congo
3	Yangtze	Asia	China
4	Orinoco	South America	Venezuela
5	Rio de la Plata	South America	Argentina
6	Ganges	Asia	India
7	Yenisey	Asia	Russia
8	Mississippi	North America	United States

Discharge Measurement Because streams vary in channel characteristics, a variety of methods can be used to measure discharge. In streams that are too deep and wide to walk across, current meters and Acoustic Doppler Current Profilers are common instruments for discharge measurement (**Figure 14.12**). Current meters are often used at stream-gaging stations; the U.S. Geological Survey maintains more than 8100 stations in the United States. Many of these stations automatically send telemetry data to satellites, from which information is retransmitted to regional centers to track changing flows.

Rivers Ranked by Discharge Of the world's rivers, those with the greatest *discharge* are the Amazon of South America and the Congo of Africa. In North America, the greatest discharges are from the Missouri–Ohio–Mississippi, Saint Lawrence, and Mackenzie River systems (**Table 14.1**).

WORKITOUT 14.2
The Interacting Variables of Stream Discharge

As shown in Figure 14.11 the value for stream discharge depends on the variables of width, depth, and velocity. If one variable in the discharge equation changes, then another variable must change. For example, if discharge remains the same along a stream, but the channel narrows and deepens, velocity must also change.

1. What is the discharge of a stream that is 3 m deep, 4 m wide, and has a velocity of 4 m/s?
2. What is the discharge of a stream that is 5 ft deep, 20 ft wide, and has a velocity of 3 ft/s?
3. For the stream in **2**, if discharge remains the same, what is the velocity of the stream when it deepens to 6 ft and narrows to 10 ft? (Hint: rearrange the discharge equation to solve for velocity.)
4. Is the velocity of the deeper, narrower stream in **3** higher or lower than the velocity of the stream in **2**? What other factor discussed in the text influences velocity in these two example channels?

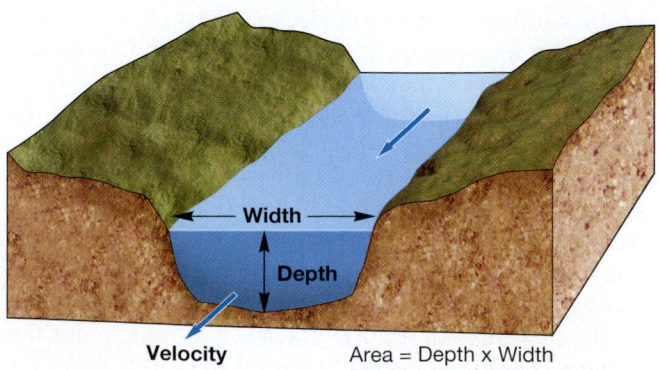

Area = Depth x Width
Discharge = Area x Velocity

▲**Figure 14.11 Stream discharge.** The volume of streamflow is discharge, measured at a stream cross section by multiplying channel area (width × depth) by the average velocity of the flow.

Velocity and Flow Characteristics As discharge increases, velocity usually increases. Stream velocity depends not only on the flow volume but also on the amount of friction along the channel bed and banks. Obstacles in the channel, such as boulders and tree trunks that alter the direction of flow, also create friction. In a section of channel, the greatest flow velocities are usually near the surface at the center, corresponding to the deepest part of the stream. Velocities decrease closer to the sides and bottom of the channel because of the frictional drag on the water flow.

Friction is highest in shallow streams with boulders and other obstacles that add roughness and slow the flow. In streams where friction is high (more contact with the bed and banks and/or obstacles in the channel), as in a section of rapids, *turbulent flow* occurs, and most of the stream's energy is expended in turbulent eddies (**Figure 14.13**). Friction is reduced in deep, lowland rivers where the flow has less contact with the bed and banks and the channel has fewer obstacles that create roughness (**Figure 14.14**).

(a) Measuring stream velocity using a current meter (a wheel with cups that rotate) suspended from the cable car at a stream-gaging station. Shown here is the Animas River in Colorado, polluted with mining wastewater that colored the river orange for several days in 2015 (see Figure 8.30).

(b) Measuring discharge using an Acoustic Doppler Current Profiler mounted in a small boat. The instrument measures velocity and depth using sound pulses.

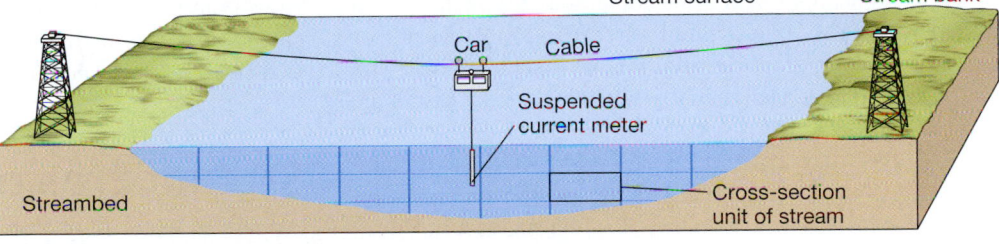

(c) Current meters measure discharge at numerous subsections of the channel, which are added together to determine total cross-section discharge.

▲**Figure 14.12 Measuring stream discharge.** [(a) USGS. (b) Jochen Tack/Alamy Stock Photo.]

▼**Figure 14.13 A turbulent stream.** Rapids on the St. Louis River in Jay Cooke State Park, Minnesota. [Vladimir Daragan/Shutterstock.]

▼**Figure 14.14 A river with high velocity and discharge.** The smooth, quiet surface of a large river can mask the high-velocity flow. Shown here is the Ocmulgee River near Jacksonville, Georgia. [Bobbé Christopherson.]

Changes in Discharge with Distance Downstream

In most drainage basins in humid regions, stream discharge increases from the headwaters to the mouth. The Mississippi River is typical, beginning as many small streams that merge successively with tributaries to form a large-volume river. However, this relationship may change along an *exotic stream*, one that originates in a humid region and subsequently flows through an arid region. High potential evapotranspiration rates in arid regions can cause discharge to decrease with distance downstream, a process that is often accelerated by water removal for irrigation.

The Nile River is an exotic stream that drains much of northeastern Africa. As it flows through the deserts of Sudan and Egypt, it loses water due to evaporation and withdrawal for agriculture. On the Colorado River in the U.S. West, discharge decreases with distance from its source so that the Colorado no longer reaches its mouth in the Gulf of California most years. After withdrawals for agriculture and other uses by the region's growing human population, only some agricultural runoff remains at its delta. Recently, prolonged drought has caused further discharge declines (review Focus Study 8.1).

Changes in Discharge over Time

At any given channel cross section, discharge changes over time. A graph of stream discharge over time for a specific location is a **hydrograph**. The time scale of a hydrograph can vary. For example, *annual hydrographs* show discharge over the course of an entire year, usually with the highest discharge occurring during the spring snowmelt season. *Storm hydrographs* may cover only a period of days, reflecting changes in discharge caused by specific precipitation events that lead to local flooding. The hydrograph in **Figure 14.15a** shows the relation between precipitation input (the bar graphs) and stream discharge (the curves). During dry periods, the low discharge is described as *base flow* (dark blue line) and is largely maintained by input from local groundwater (review the discussion in Chapter 8).

When rainfall occurs in some portion of the watershed, the runoff is concentrated in streams and tributaries in that area. The amount, location, and duration of the rainfall episode determine the *peak flow*, the highest discharge that occurs as a result of a precipitation event. The nature of the surface in a watershed, whether permeable or impermeable, affects peak flow and the timing of changes recorded in the hydrograph. In deserts, where surfaces have thin, impermeable soils and little vegetation, runoff can be high during rainstorms. A rare or large precipitation event in a desert can fill a stream channel with a torrent. This type of sudden local high flow, usually happening with no warning, is known as a **flash flood** and can occur in a number of different environments. In deserts, flash floods occur regularly and can fill channels in minutes during or just after a storm.

Human activities have enormous impact on patterns of discharge in a drainage basin. A disturbance such as a forest fire or urbanization of the watershed can cause peak flows to occur sooner during a precipitation event, altering the storm hydrograph. The effects of urbanization are quite dramatic, both increasing and hastening peak flow (Figure 14.15a). In fact, urban areas produce runoff patterns quite similar to those of deserts, since the sealed surfaces of the city drastically reduce infiltration and soil-moisture recharge (**Figure 14.15b**).

Stream Erosion

A mass of water in a stream has potential energy. As the water flows downslope, or downstream, under the influence of gravity, this energy becomes kinetic energy. The rate of this conversion from potential to kinetic energy

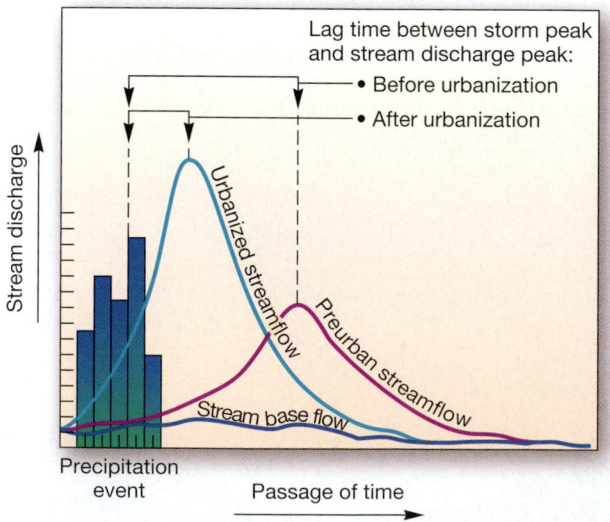

(a) Normal base flow is indicated with a dark blue line. The purple line indicates post-storm discharge prior to urbanization. Following urbanization, stream discharge dramatically increases, as shown by the light blue line.

(b) Increasing urbanization has worsened flooding in many parts of Asia, including Bangkok, Thailand, pictured here when flooding submerged part of the highway system in 2011.

▲**Figure 14.15 Effect of urbanization on a typical stream hydrograph.** Note the difference between discharge prior to an area's urbanization (purple curve) and discharge after urbanization has occurred (light blue curve). [(b) Apichart Weerawong/AP Images.]

determines the ability of the stream to dislodge channel material and transport it downstream.

The erosive work performed by a stream depends on the volume of water and the total amount of sediment in the flow. **Hydraulic action** is a type of erosion performed by flowing water alone that loosens, lifts, and breaks up rock in the channel bed and mechanically wears away bedrock along the sides. Hydraulic action is often at a maximum where the flow is turbulent. **Abrasion** is another type of erosion that occurs as boulders and gravels moving along the channel tumble into each other and break apart and as rocks and sediment grind and carve the streambed. Abrasion is at a maximum during a flood, when high flows pick up rocks of varying sizes, and in rivers that carry large amounts of sediment. The process of abrasion is responsible for the rounded rocks we see along most rivers.

Sediment Load

When stream energy is high and a supply of sediment is present, streamflow propels sand, pebbles, gravel, and boulders downstream in the process known as **sediment transport**. The material carried by a stream is its *sediment load*, and the sediment supply is determined by topographic relief, the nature of rock and soil through which the stream flows, climate, vegetation, and human activity in a drainage basin. Discharge is also closely linked to sediment transport—increased discharge moves a greater amount of sediment, often causing streams to change from clear to murky brown after a heavy or prolonged rainfall. Sediment is moved as dissolved load, suspended load, or bed load by four primary processes: solution, suspension, traction, and saltation (**Figure 14.16**).

The **dissolved load** of a stream is the material that travels in solution, especially the dissolved chemical compounds derived from minerals such as limestone or dolomite or from soluble salts. The main process contributing material in solution is chemical weathering. Along the San Juan and Little Colorado Rivers, which flow into the Colorado River near the Utah–Arizona border, the salt content of the dissolved load is so high that human use of the water is limited.

The **suspended load** consists of fine-grained clastic particles (bits and pieces of rock). They are held aloft in the stream until the stream velocity slows nearly to zero, at which point even the finest particles are deposited. Turbulence in the water, with random upward motion, is an important mechanical factor in holding a load of sediment in suspension.

Bed load refers to coarser materials that are moved by **traction**, which is the rolling or dragging of materials along the streambed, or by **saltation**, a term referring to the way particles may bounce along in short hops and jumps (from the Latin *saltim*, which means "by leaps or jumps"). Particles transported by saltation are too large to remain in suspension, but are not confined to the sliding and rolling motion of traction (see Figure 14.16). Stream velocity affects these processes, particularly the stream's ability to retain particles in suspension. With increased kinetic energy in a stream, parts of the bed load are rafted upward and become suspended load.

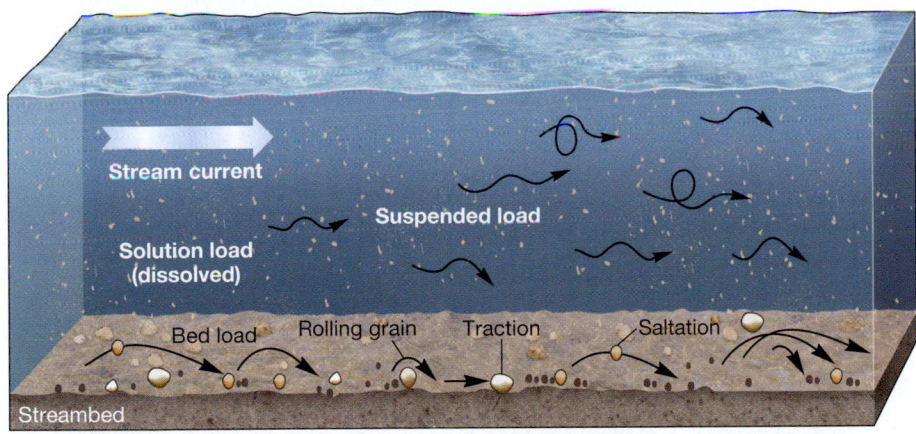

(a) Sediment and chemical compounds move downstream as dissolved load, suspended load, and bed load.

◀**Figure 14.16 Fluvial transport and sediment load.** [(b) Prisma Bidagentur/Alamy. (c) Gary Whitton/Alamy.]

(b) Bedload deposited in a mountain stream in Switzerland.

(c) Suspended load in the Paria River, northern Arizona.

Sediment Transport During a Flood During a flood (a high flow that overtops the channel banks), a river may carry an enormous sediment load, as larger material is picked up and carried by the flow. The *competence* of a stream is its ability to move particles of a specific size. Competence is a function of stream velocity and the energy available to move materials. As flood flows build, stream energy increases and the competence of the stream becomes high enough that sediment transport occurs. The *capacity* of a stream is the total possible sediment load that it can transport and is a function of discharge; thus, a large river has higher capacity than a small stream.

The erosion of a stream channel during sediment transport is known as **degradation**. With the return of flows to normal, stream energy is reduced, and the sediment transport slows or stops. If the load exceeds a stream's capacity, sediment accumulates in the stream bed, building up the channel through deposition; this is the process of **aggradation**. This type of channel adjustment is ongoing, as the system continuously works toward equilibrium, maintaining a balance between discharge, sediment load, and channel form.

Effects of Dams on Sediment Transport Dams disrupt natural river discharge and sediment regimes, usually with detrimental effects on river systems. For example, Glen Canyon Dam on the Colorado River near the Utah–Arizona border controls discharge and blocks sediment from flowing into the Grand Canyon downstream. Consequently, over the years, the river's sediment supply was cut off, the river's sandy beaches eroded, and fisheries declined.

Recent dam removals have allowed scientists to study post-dam sediment redistribution. Focus Study 14.1 discusses dam deconstruction and other stream restoration practices. See Figure 14.1.1 for a photo of the sediment outflow into the Strait of Juan de Fuca in Washington following removal of two dams on the Elwha River.

Stream Gradient

Within its drainage basin, every stream has a degree of inclination or gradient, which is also known as the channel slope. The **gradient** of a stream is defined as the drop in elevation per unit of distance, usually measured in meters per kilometer or feet per mile. Characteristically, a river has a steeper slope nearer the headwaters and a more gradual slope downstream (**Figure 14.17a**). A stream's gradient affects its energy and ability to move material.

WORKITOUT 14.3
Sediment Load and Pollutants

Consider a jar of stream water collected from a nearby stream channel.

1. What part of the sediment load will settle to the bottom of the sample container? What part of the sediment load will remain in the water? What part of the sediment load is probably not represented in your sample?

2. Some pollutants can attach to particles in the stream. What happens to these pollutants during a flood? Where do sediment and pollutants accumulate when a dam is built?

A *longitudinal profile* shows the changes in a river's gradient from its headwater to its mouth in a side view. The curve of a river's overall gradient is generally concave (**Figure 14.17b**). The causes of this shape are related to the energy available to the stream for transporting its sediment load.

Headward Erosion The work of fluvial erosion can cause streams to erode upstream, lengthening the channel in the process of *headward erosion*. This process occurs near the headwaters, as rills and gullies erode the channel in an upslope direction (**Figure 14.18**). Headward erosion toward a drainage divide can eventually cause an eroding rill in one stream system to break through the interfluve and *capture* part of the headwaters of another stream—a process known as *stream piracy*. This process can occur rapidly over a period of weeks or can take thousands of years, depending on local climate and landscape characteristics.

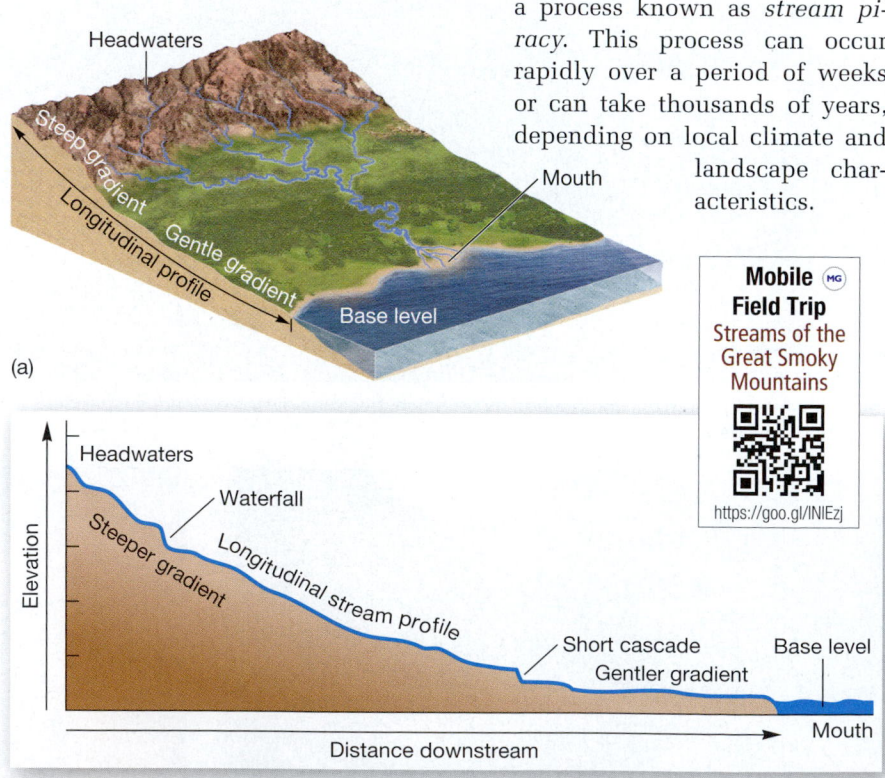

Mobile (MG) **Field Trip**
Streams of the Great Smoky Mountains

https://goo.gl/INIEzj

(a)

(b)

▲**Figure 14.17 A stream profile from headwaters to mouth.** The characteristic sloping profile of a stream from headwaters to mouth. Upstream segments of the profile have a steeper gradient; downstream the gradient is gentler. (b) A characteristic longitudinal profile shown by plotting elevation versus distance downstream.

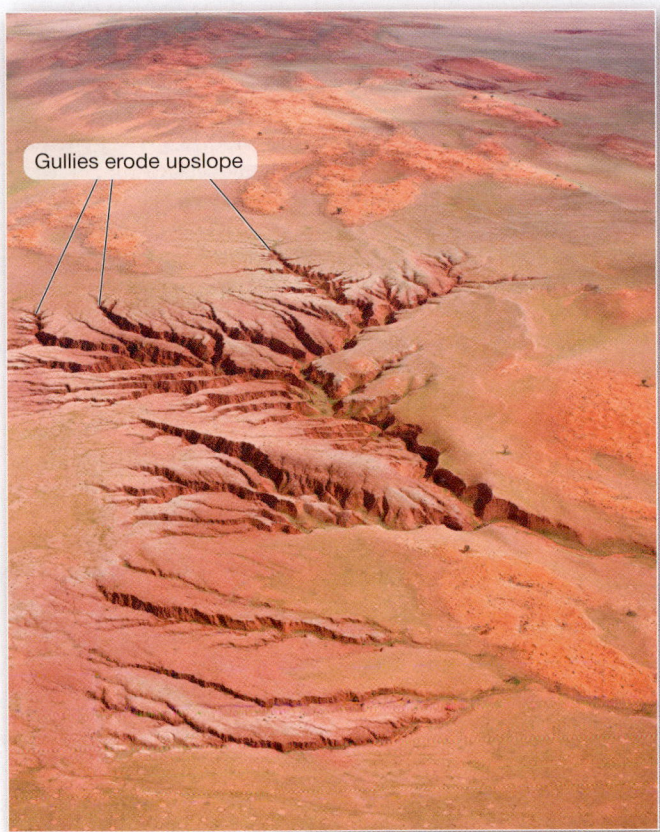

▲**Figure 14.18** **Headward erosion.** Gullies erode in an upslope direction toward a drainage divide. [robertharding/Alamy.]

Gullies erode upslope

Base Level The level below which a stream cannot erode its valley is **base level**. In general, the *ultimate base level* is sea level, the average level between high and low tides. Base level can be visualized as a surface extending inland from

sea level, inclined gently upward under the continents. In theory, this is the lowest practical level for all denudation processes (**Figure 14.19a**).

American geologist and explorer John Wesley Powell, leader of the first expedition on the Colorado River through the Grand Canyon, put forward the idea of base level in 1875. Powell recognized that not every landscape has degraded all the way to sea level; clearly, other intermediate base levels are in operation. A *local base level*, or temporary one, may determine the lower limit of local or regional stream erosion. A river or lake is a natural local base level; the reservoir behind a dam is a human-caused local base level (**Figure 14.19b**). In arid landscapes with internal drainage, valleys, plains, or other low points act as local base level.

The Graded Condition The tendency of natural systems, including streams, to move toward a state of equilibrium causes stream channels, over a period of years, to adjust their channel characteristics so that the flow is able to move the sediment supplied from the drainage basin. A **graded stream** is one in which the channel slope has adjusted, given the discharge and channel conditions, so that stream velocity is just enough to transport the sediment load.

A graded stream has the characteristic longitudinal profile illustrated in Figure 14.17. Any variation, or bump, in the profile, such as the steep drop of a waterfall, will be smoothed out over time as the stream adjusts toward a graded condition. Attainment of a graded condition does not mean that the stream is at its lowest gradient, but rather that it has achieved a state of *dynamic equilibrium* between its gradient and its sediment load. This balance depends on many factors that work together on the landscape and within the river system.

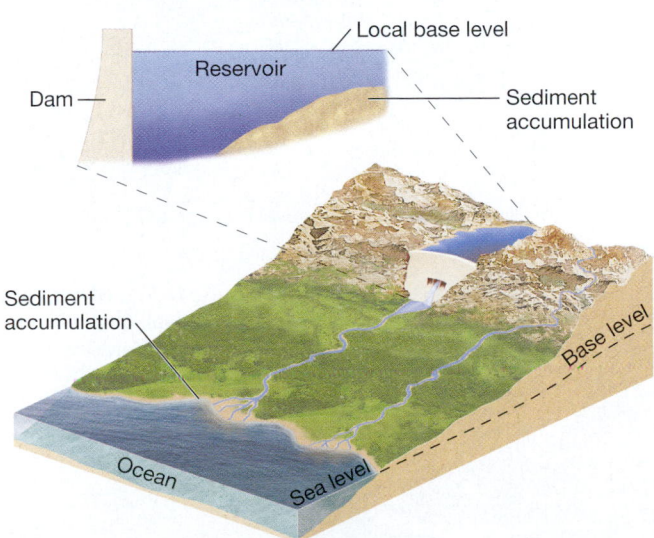

(a) The ultimate base level is sea level. Note how base level curves gently upward from the sea as it is traced inland; this is the theoretical limit for stream erosion. The reservoir behind a dam is a local base level.

(b) Grand Coulee Dam forms Roosevelt Lake, a temporary local base level on the Columbia River in northeast Washington.

▲**Figure 14.19** **Ultimate and local base levels.** [(b) U.S. Bureau of Reclamation.]

FOCUS Study 14.1 Environmental Restoration
Dam Removal and Stream Restoration

In 2013, the largest dam removal in U.S. history occurred with the deconstruction of the Elwha and Glines Canyon Dams in northwest Washington. The project restored fish passage and streamside ecosystems on the 72-km-long (45-mi-long) Elwha River (**Figure 14.1.1**). A free-flowing Elwha River enables the return of five species of Pacific salmon to the watershed, with fish numbers already rising and expected to increase dramatically over the next 30 years. Such species are *anadromous* (from the Greek *anadromos*, "running up"), meaning they migrate upstream from the sea into freshwater rivers to spawn.

A year after the Elwha dam removals began, scientists reported that native steelhead and salmon were already making their way into previously inaccessible stream reaches. Willow and cottonwood saplings were beginning to establish in the newly exposed, silt-laden river channel. In that first year, an estimated half million tons of sediment, previously trapped behind the dams, began moving downstream and exiting at the river's mouth.

Dam Removals

Over the past 30 years, many small dams have come up for relicensing by the Federal Energy Regulatory Commission (FERC). Many of these dams are now being dismantled, having been deemed unsafe or outdated, with an original purpose that is no longer valid. In 1999, Edwards Dam on the Kennebec River in Augusta, Maine, was torn down, marking the first U.S. dam removal for ecological reasons (in this case, primarily to restore passage between the river and sea for migratory fish). Since then other dams have come down, and many others are targeted for removal.

Stream Restoration Science

Dam removals are part of the emerging science of *stream restoration*, also called *river restoration*, the process that reestablishes the health of a fluvial ecosystem. Every stream restoration project has a particular focus, which varies with the problems and impacts on that particular stream. Common restoration goals are to reinstate instream flows, restore fish passage, prevent bank erosion, and reestablish vegetation along the channel or on the floodplain. Projects vary in scale from short local stretches of stream

to hundreds of kilometers of river to an entire watershed.

Stream restoration has become a lucrative business for hundreds of companies throughout the United States, with Americans spending an estimated $1 billion annually on stream projects. However, the science of stream restoration is still young.

Given the complexities of streams and their ecosystems, practitioners may use intuition mixed with scientific knowledge to design a stream channel, and not all reconstructed channels withstand the test of time. Furthermore, the intensive monitoring needed to evaluate a project's success or failure is often neglected due to lack of funds.

(b) A barge-mounted hydraulic hammer chips away at the top of the Glines Canyon Dam in 2012.

(a) Sites of former dams on the Elwha River.

(c) Glines Canyon Dam removal in progress, 2012.

(d) Sediment flows from the mouth of the Elwha River after dam removal.

▲**Figure 14.1.1** **Glines Canyon Dam removal, Elwha River.** [(a) NPS/USGS. (b) NPS. (c) Brian Cluer/NOAA. (d) Elaine Thompson/AP Photo.]

▲**Figure 14.1.2** **Excavators breach the Veazie Dam on the Penobscot River in Maine in preparation for dam removal.** [Gordon Chibroski/Portland Press Herald/Getty Images. Map source: Atlantic Salmon Federation.]

A Cooperative Process

Stream restoration involves the cooperation of numerous landowners and regulating agencies and must balance different water use needs within a drainage basin. In Maine's largest watershed, the Penobscot River restoration project restored fisheries, while at the same time maintained hydropower production. Project stakeholders included environmentalists, the Penobscot Indian Nation, state and federal entities, and hydropower companies. The project removed two dams, in 2012 and 2014, and built a fish bypass around a third dam, thereby restoring fish access along 1000 miles of streams (**Figure 14.1.2**). Completed in 2015, the project cost $60 million. River herring and shad are among the fish already reestablishing in the river since dam removal.

Smaller stream restoration projects may be part of larger restoration efforts involving estuaries, bays, and harbors. Near New Bedford Harbor, Massachusetts, state, federal, and local agencies implemented several small stream projects as part of a larger effort to clean up pollution and restore migratory fish passage. In 2007, restoration specialists partially breached the Sawmill Dam and constructed a passage structure, or "fishway," consisting of a stone step-pool system designed to mimic natural conditions (**Figure 14.1.3**). Over the next 4 years, river herring (alewives and blueback herring) increased over 1000% as fish passage around Sawmill and another nearby dam allowed access to prime spawning grounds.

Ongoing dam removals and continued societal and scientific emphasis on ecosystem health have made stream restoration science a growing field—and one to which geographers and other Earth systems scientists can contribute.

1. What are some reasons for recent dam removals? What are some goals of stream restoration?

2. What was the focus of the Penobscot River restoration?

APPLYconcepts Based on Figure 14.1.1, explain what is happening at the mouth of the Elwha River in terms of (a) the river's sediment load, (b) stream gradient, and (c) base level.

1a. _____

1b. _____

1c. _____

(a) Sawmill Dam, before it was partially breached during fishway construction.

(b) Step-pool fish passage structure.

▲**Figure 14.1.3** **Step-pool fishway construction on the Acushnet River, Massachusetts.** [Steve Block/NOAA.]

An individual stream can have both graded and ungraded portions, and it can have graded sections without having an overall graded slope. In fact, variations and interruptions are the rule rather than the exception. Disturbances in a drainage basin, such as mass wasting on hillslopes that carries material into stream channels or overgrazing of streamside vegetation that leads to bank erosion, can cause disruptions to this equilibrium condition. The concept of stream gradation is intimately tied to stream gradient; any change in the characteristic longitudinal profile of a river causes the system to respond, seeking a graded condition.

Nickpoints When the longitudinal profile of a stream contains an abrupt change in gradient, such as at a waterfall or an area of rapids, the point of interruption is a **nickpoint** (also spelled *knickpoint*). Nickpoints can result when a stream flows across a resistant rock layer or a recent fault line or area of surface deformation. Temporary blockage in a channel, caused by a landslide or a logjam, also could be considered a nickpoint; when the logjam breaks, the stream quickly readjusts its channel to its former grade. Thus, a nickpoint is a relatively temporary and mobile feature on the landscape.

Figure 14.20 shows two nickpoints—an area of rapids (with an increased gradient) and a waterfall (with an even steeper gradient). At a waterfall, the conversion of potential energy in the water at the lip of the falls to concentrated kinetic energy at the base works to eliminate the nickpoint interruption and smooth out the gradient. At the edge of a waterfall, a stream is freefalling, moving at high velocity under the acceleration of gravity, and causes abrasion and hydraulic action in the channel below. Over time, the increased erosive action slowly undercuts the waterfall in the process of

nickpoint retreat. Eventually, the rock ledge at the lip of the fall collapses, and the height of the waterfall is gradually reduced as debris accumulates at its base. Thus, a nickpoint migrates upstream, sometimes for kilometers, until it becomes a series of rapids and is eventually eliminated.

The evolution of Niagara Falls on the Ontario–New York border provides a spectacular example of nickpoint migration. In the region of the falls, glaciers advanced and then receded some 13,000 years ago. In doing so, they exposed resistant rock strata that are underlain by less-resistant shales. The resulting tilted formation is a *cuesta*, which is a ridge with a steep slope on one side (called an escarpment) and beds gently sloping away on the other side. The Niagara escarpment actually stretches across more than 700 km (435 mi) across Ontario, Canada, the Upper Peninsula of Michigan, and Wisconsin along the western shore of Lake Michigan. As the less-resistant material continues to weather, the overlying rock strata collapse, and Niagara Falls erodes upstream (**Figure 14.21**). Nickpoint retreat has moved the location of the falls more than 11 km (6.8 mi) upstream from the steep face of the Niagara escarpment.

Tectonic Uplift Lifting of the landscape changes the elevation of the stream relative to its base level, stimulating erosional activity. As tectonic uplift increases the stream gradient, a previously low-energy river flowing through the newly uplifted landscape becomes *rejuvenated*; that is, the river gains energy and actively returns to downcutting (**Figure 14.22a**). Stream rejuvenation can also result from a lowering of global sea level in the absence of tectonic uplifting of the land.

The process of downcutting whereby streams deepen their channel is known as *channel incision*. This process can eventually form *entrenched meanders* that are deeply incised in the landscape (**Figure 14.22b**). Entrenched meanders occur where a stream is superposed upon a landscape (discussed earlier), or along an *antecedent stream* (from the Greek *ante*, meaning "before"), which downcuts at the same rate at which tectonic uplift occurs in response to the increased gradient. Thus an antecedent stream maintains its course as uplift occurs; an example is the Virgin River canyon and famous Zion Narrows in southwest Utah.

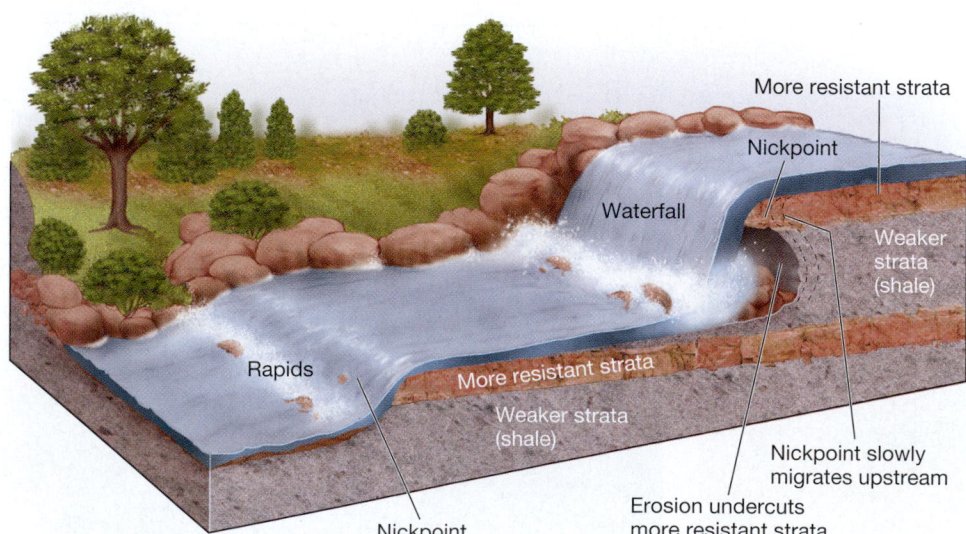

More resistant strata

Nickpoint

Waterfall

Weaker strata (shale)

Rapids

More resistant strata

Weaker strata (shale)

Nickpoint

Nickpoint slowly migrates upstream

Erosion undercuts more resistant strata

▲**Figure 14.20** **Nickpoints interrupting a stream profile.** Longitudinal profile of a stream section shows nickpoints produced by resistant rock strata. Stream energy is concentrated at the nickpoint, accelerating erosion, which will eventually eliminate the feature.

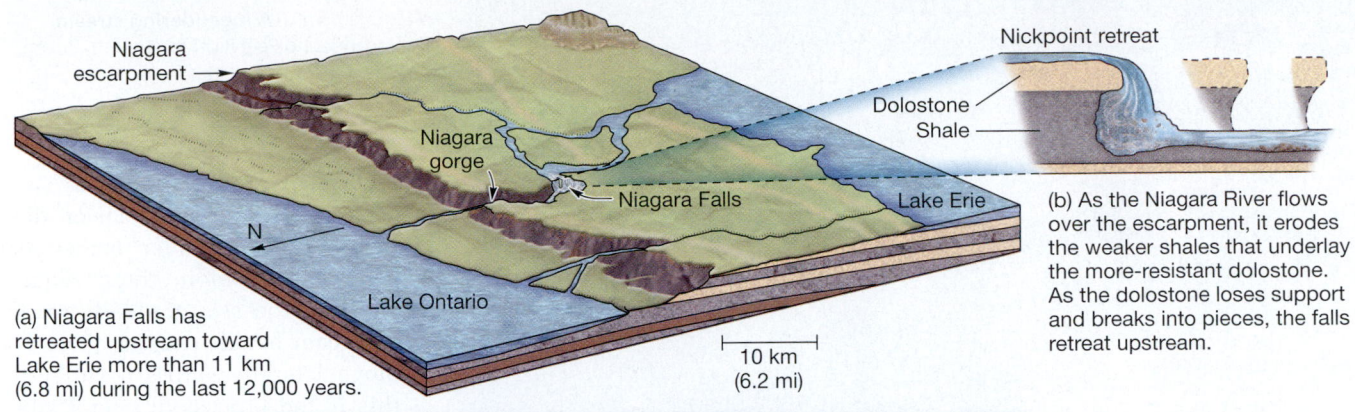

(a) Niagara Falls has retreated upstream toward Lake Erie more than 11 km (6.8 mi) during the last 12,000 years.

10 km (6.2 mi)

(b) As the Niagara River flows over the escarpment, it erodes the weaker shales that underlay the more-resistant dolostone. As the dolostone loses support and breaks into pieces, the falls retreat upstream.

(c) Niagara Falls includes Horseshoe Falls in Ontario, Canada, and American Falls and Bridal Veil Falls in New York.

◀**Figure 14.21 Nickpoint retreat at Niagara Falls.** The waterfalls on the Niagara River occur at nickpoints along the Niagara Escarpment at the U.S.– Canada border in Ontario and New York. [(c) SongQuan Deng/ Shutterstock.]

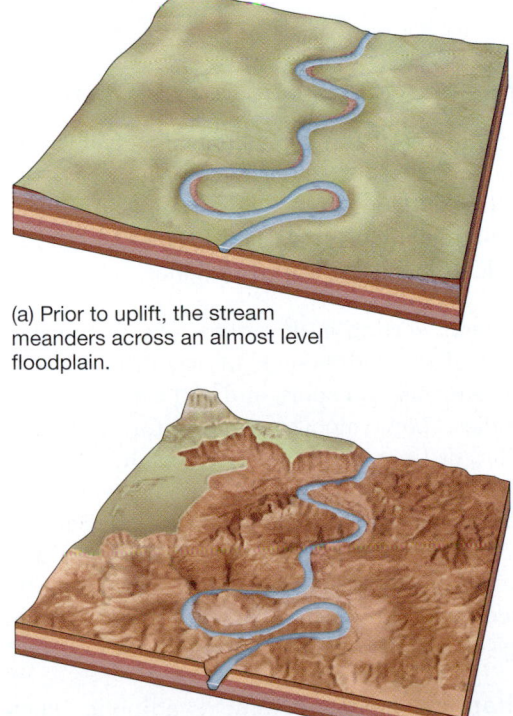

(a) Prior to uplift, the stream meanders across an almost level floodplain.

(b) During uplift, the increased gradient causes the stream to downcut, forming entrenched meanders.

(c) Entrenched meanders on the Colorado River in Canyonlands National Park, Utah.

◀**Figure 14.22 Entrenched meanders.** In response to uplift of the landscape, a stream becomes rejuvenated and actively downcuts in response to the steepened channel relative to base level, maintaining its channel pattern and over time forming entrenched meanders. [Hemis/Alamy.]

◀Figure 14.23 **A meandering stream.**
The meandering Peel River in autumn, Yukon,
Canada. [Peter Mather/Getty Images.]

that results in a **point bar**, an accumulation of sediment on the inside of a meander bend. As meanders develop, these scour-and-fill processes gradually work at stream banks, causing them to move laterally across a valley—this is the process of lateral erosion. As a result, the landscape near a meandering river bears marks called *meander scars* that are the residual deposits from previous river channels.

Actively meandering streams erode their outside banks as they migrate, often forming a narrow neck of land that eventually erodes through and forms a *cutoff*. A cutoff marks an abrupt change in the stream's lateral movements—the stream becomes straighter. After the former meander becomes isolated from the rest of the river, the resulting **oxbow lake** may gradually fill with organic debris and silt or may again become part of the river when it floods. The Mississippi River is many miles shorter today than it was in the 1830s because of artificial cutoffs that were dredged across meander necks to improve navigation and safety.

Stream Meandering and Channel Widening

Where channel slope is gradual, streams develop a sinuous (snakelike) form, weaving back and forth across the landscape in a **meandering stream** pattern (**Figure 14.23**). Meandering streams have distinctive flow and channel characteristics and vary in their sinuosity (their ability to form curving bends in the landscape). *Sinuosity* is the ratio between the distance between two points along the deepest part of the stream channel as it curves and the shortest, straight-line distance in the stream valley between the same two points.

Geosystems in Action 14 illustrates some of the processes associated with meandering streams. A cross-sectional view of a meandering stream channel shows the flow characteristics that produce the channel deposits typical of these streams. In a straight channel or section of channel, the greatest flow velocities are near the surface at the center, corresponding to the deepest part of the stream (Figure GIA 14.1a). Velocities decrease closer to the sides and bottom of the channel because of friction. As the stream flows around a meander curve, the maximum flow velocity shifts from the center of the stream to the outside of the curve. As the stream then straightens, the maximum velocity shifts back to the center, until the next bend, where it shifts to the outside of that meander curve. Thus, the portion of the stream flowing at maximum velocity moves diagonally across the stream from bend to bend.

Because the outer portion of each meandering curve is subject to the fastest water velocity, it undergoes the greatest scouring. This erosive action can form a steep **undercut bank**, or *cutbank* (Figure GIA 14.1b). In contrast, the inner portion of a meander experiences the slowest water velocity and thus is a zone of fill (or aggradation)

Stream Deposition

The general term for the unconsolidated gravel, sand, silt, and mineral fragments deposited by running water is **alluvium**. Stream deposition occurs when a stream deposits alluvium, thereby creating depositional landforms, such as bars, floodplains, terraces, and deltas.

Sorting Sediment sorting is the process by which particles drop out of the sediment load according to size. High-velocity streams transport and deposit larger, or coarser, particles. Low-velocity streams transport and deposit smaller, or finer, particles. As a result, alluvium accumulates in well-sorted deposits as stream velocity gradually slows with distance downstream—coarser particles generally settle out closer to the headwaters and finer particles generally settle out closer to the mouth. (Unsorted sediment deposition is typical of glacial action, discussed in Chapter 17.)

Braided Channels Under certain conditions, such as near the mouth of large rivers, streams form a complex pattern with multiple channels. A **braided stream** is a maze of interconnected channels formed on a river

with a high sediment load (**Figure 14.24**). Braiding often occurs when reduced discharge lowers a stream's transporting ability, such as after flooding, or when a landslide deposits sediment into a channel, or when sediment load increases in channels that have weak banks of sand or gravel. Braided rivers commonly occur in glacial environments, where coarse sediment is abundant and slopes are steep, as in New Zealand, Alaska, and Tibet. This pattern also occurs in wide, shallow channels with variable discharge, such as in the U.S. Southwest.

Floodplains The flat, low-lying area adjacent to a meandering channel and subjected to recurrent flooding is a **floodplain**. It is the area that is inundated when the river overflows its channel during times of high flow. When the water recedes, it leaves behind alluvial deposits that generally mask the underlying rock with their accumulating thickness. The present river channel is embedded in these alluvial deposits. As discussed earlier, stream meanders tend to migrate laterally across a valley. Over time, this process produces characteristic depositional landforms in the floodplain (**Figure 14.25**).

◄**Figure 14.25** **Floodplain landforms.** [(b) USDA NRCS. (c) Shirley Kilpatrick/Alamy]

(a) Typical floodplain landscape and related landscape features.

Labels: Meander scar, Floodplain, Oxbow lake, Meander scars, Cutoff, Point bar, Yazoo stream, Bluffs, Undercut bank, Alluvial deposits, Natural levees, Backswamp

Animation MG
Stream
Processes,
Floodplains
https://goo.gl/mlH2m7

Animation MG
Oxbow
Lake
Formation
https://goo.gl/A17lCx

(b) Floodplain wetlands, or backswamps, store floodwaters and provide habitat for wildlife. Humans filled many such wetlands for development during the 20th century; restoration is now a priority, since wetland water storage feeds streamflow during drought conditions.

(c) Point bars on the insides of meander bends, Stanislaus River, California.

Meandering channels curve from side to side in a snakelike pattern and usually occur where low-gradient streams flow through fine sediments. *Meanders* form because the portion of the stream with maximum velocity shifts from one side of the stream to the other as the stream bends, thus affecting erosion and deposition along the stream's banks (GIA 14.1). Through these "scour-and-fill" processes, a meandering stream moves position laterally across its valley and creates a distinctive landscape (GIA 14.2).

14.1a PROFILE OF A MEANDERING STREAM

The cross sections show how the location of maximum flow velocity shifts from the center along a straight stretch of the stream channel to the outside bend of a meander. The oblique view shows how the stream erodes, or "scours," an *undercut bank* on the outside of a bend, while depositing a *point bar* on the inside of the bend.

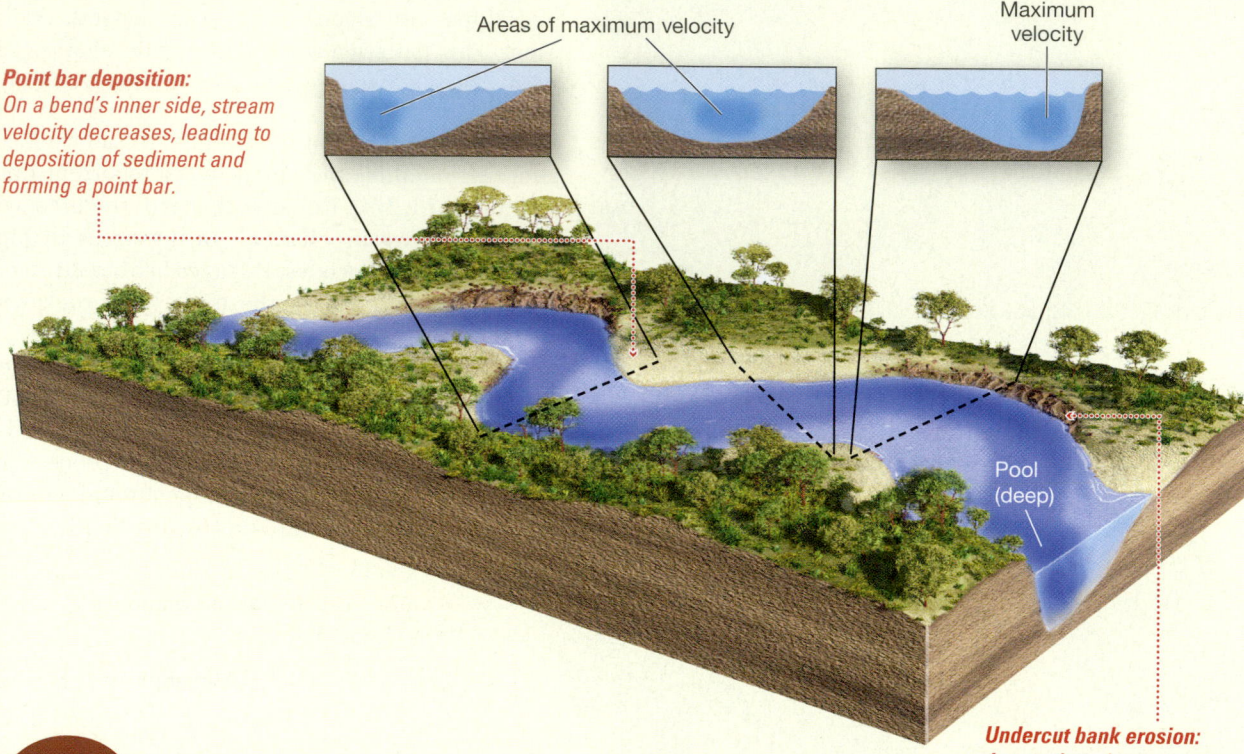

Areas of maximum velocity

Maximum velocity

Point bar deposition:
On a bend's inner side, stream velocity decreases, leading to deposition of sediment and forming a point bar.

Pool (deep)

Undercut bank erosion:
Areas of maximum stream velocity (darker blue) have more power to erode, so they undercut the stream's banks on the outside of a bend.

14.1b ACTIVE EROSION ALONG A MEANDER

Notice how this stream in Iowa has eroded a steep cutbank on the outside of a bend.

Cutbank

Condor (MG)
Meandering Rivers

https://goo.gl/xvnDxw

Animation (MG)
Meandering Streams

https://goo.gl/8Vzdnx

MasteringGeography™

Visit the Study Area in MasteringGeography™ to explore meander and oxbow lake formation.

Visualize: Study a geosciences animation of meander and oxbow lake formation.

Assess: Demonstrate understanding of meander and oxbow lake formation (if assigned by instructor).

14.2a STREAM MEANDERING PROCESS

Over time, stream meanders migrate laterally across a stream valley, eroding the outsides of bends and filling the insides of bends. Narrow areas between meanders are *necks*. When discharge increases, the stream may scour through the neck, forming a *cutoff*.

Stream valley landscape:
A neck has recently been eroded, forming a cutoff and straightening the stream channel. The bypassed portion of the stream may become a meander scar or an oxbow lake.

Direction of flow

Cutoff

Neck

A cutoff forms on the Itkillik River, north slope of the Brooks Range, Alaska.

14.2b FORMATION OF AN OXBOW LAKE

The diagrams below show the steps often involved in forming an oxbow lake; this photo corresponds to Step 3, the formation of a cutoff. As stream channels shift, these processes leave characteristic landforms on a floodplain.

Step 1:
A neck forms where a lengthening meander loops back on itself.

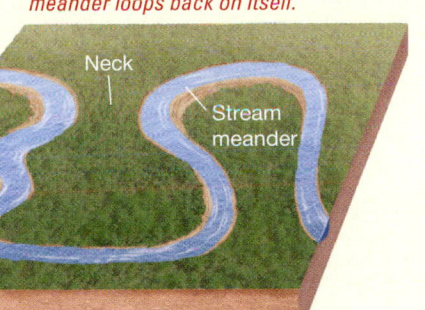

Neck

Stream meander

Step 2:
Over time, the neck narrows as erosion undercuts the banks.

Point bar

Undercut bank

Step 3:
Eventually, the stream erodes through the neck, forming a cutoff.

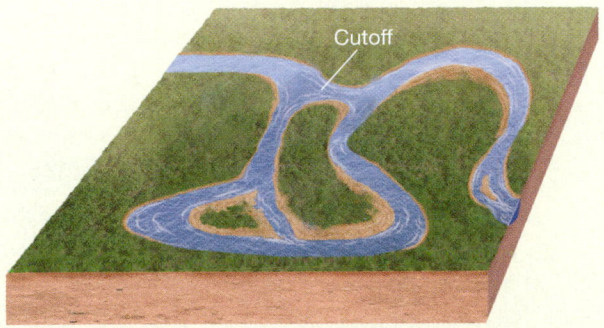

Cutoff

Step 4:
An oxbow lake forms as sediment fills the area between the new stream channel and its old meander.

Oxbow lake

GEOquiz

1. Explain: Explain the relationship between stream velocity, erosion, and deposition in the formation of a meander.

2. Explain: Explain the processes that cause a gentle bend along a stream to become a deeply looping meander.

3. Follow up: In your own words, describe the sequence of steps in the process that forms an oxbow lake.

4. Summarize: Summarize the process by which a stream, over time, could produce the landscape in the GIA14.2a photograph.

429

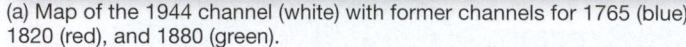

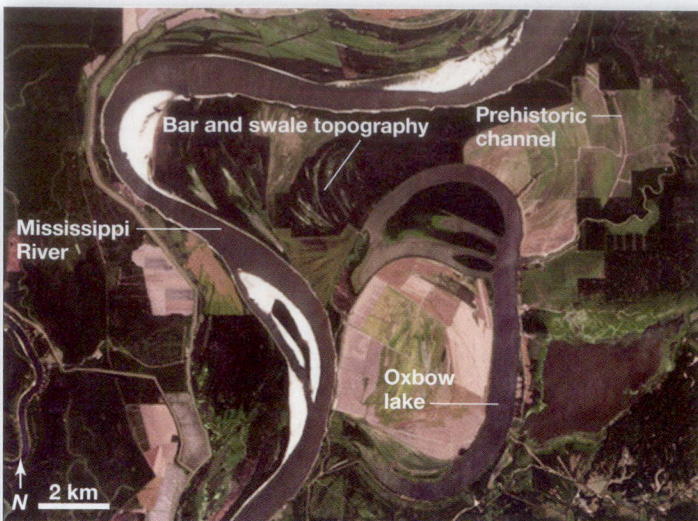

(a) Map of the 1944 channel (white) with former channels for 1765 (blue), 1820 (red), and 1880 (green).

(b) Image of the same portion of the river channel in 1999.

▲**Figure 14.26 Historical shifting of the Mississippi River.** The map and image show the portion of the river north of the Old River Control Structure (see Figure GN 14.2). [(a) Army Corps of Engineers, *Geological Investigation of the Alluvial Valley of the Lower Mississippi*, 1944. (b) *Landsat* image, NASA.]

On either bank of some rivers, low ridges of coarse sediment known as **natural levees** are formed as by-products of flooding. As discharge increases during a flood, the river overflows its banks, loses stream competence and capacity as it spreads out, and drops a portion of its sediment load. Coarser, sand-sized particles (or larger) are deposited first, forming the principal component of the natural levees; finer silts and clays are deposited farther from the river. Successive floods increase the height of the natural levees (*levée* is French for "raising").

On meandering river floodplains, wetlands (sometimes called backswamps) often form in the poorly drained fine sediments deposited by overbank flows (Figure 14.25b). Another floodplain feature is *yazoo streams*, also known as *yazoo tributaries*, which flow parallel to the main river but are blocked from joining it by the presence of natural levees. (These streams are named after the Yazoo River in the southern part of the Mississippi River floodplain.)

Low-lying ridges of alluvium that accumulate on the inside of meander bends as they migrate across a floodplain often form a landscape referred to as *bar and swale topography* (the bars form the higher areas, while swales are the low areas). The map and image in **Figure 14.26** illustrate the changing landforms over time along a portion of the meandering Mississippi River floodplain.

Stream Terraces As noted earlier, an uplifting of the landscape or a lowering of base level may rejuvenate stream energy so that a stream again scours downward with increased erosion. The resulting entrenchment of the river into its own floodplain can produce **alluvial terraces** on both sides of the valley, which look like topographic steps above the river. Alluvial terraces generally appear paired at similar elevations on the sides of the valley (**Figure 14.27**). If more than one set of paired terraces is present, the valley probably has undergone more than one episode of rejuvenation.

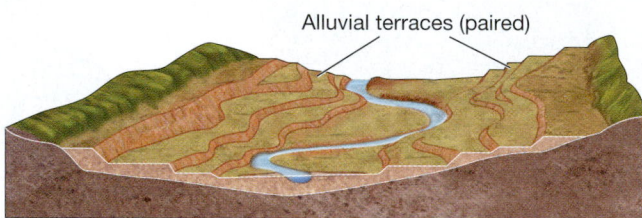

Animation (MG)
Stream Terrace Formation

https://goo.gl/90dVlF

(a) Alluvial terraces are formed as a stream cuts into a valley.

Condor (MG)
River Terraces and Base Level

https://goo.gl/7pY2z9

(b) Sunrise illuminates stream terraces along the Snake River near Jackson, Wyoming.

▲**Figure 14.27 Alluvial stream terraces.** [(a) After W. M. Davis, *Geographical Essays* (New York: Dover, 1964 [1909]), p. 515. (b) Henk Meijer/Alamy.]

▶**Figure 14.28 Distributaries on the Selenga River delta.** The Selenga River flows into Lake Baikal in Russia, Earth's largest lake by volume. Note the meandering channels in the alluvial floodplain and the numerous distributaries of the delta. [*Landsat* image, USGS/NASA.]

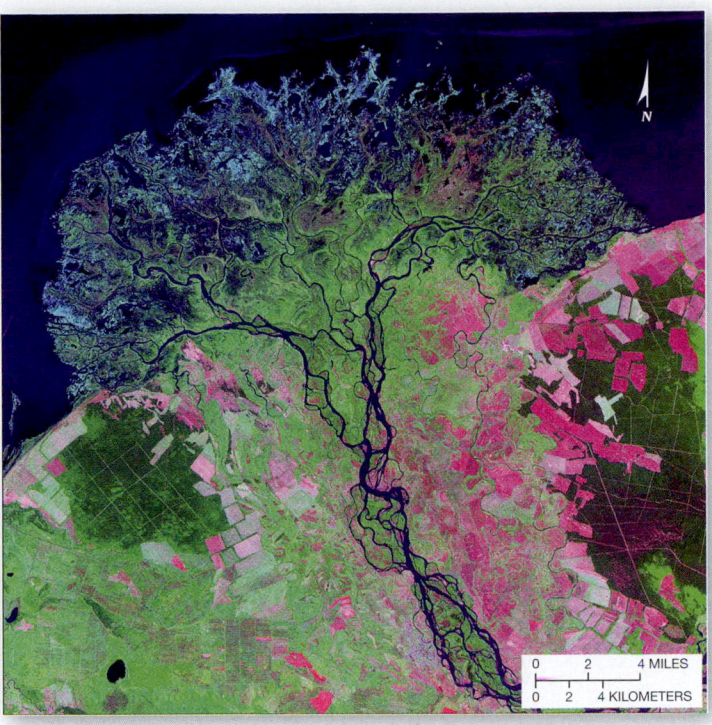

River Deltas The mouth of a river is where the river reaches a base level. There the river's velocity rapidly decelerates as it enters a larger, standing body of water. The reduced stream energy causes deposition of the sediment load. The level or nearly level depositional plain that forms at the mouth of a river is a **delta**, named for its characteristic triangular shape, after the Greek letter delta (Δ). The river deposits coarser materials first, closest to the river's mouth, and finer materials, such as silts and clays, beyond the river's mouth at the extreme end of the delta deposit. Some materials in the delta may be underwater even at low tide. Because of its position on the landscape, both fluvial processes and wave and tidal action influence the delta landform.

Each flood deposits a new layer of alluvium over portions of the delta, extending the delta outward.

Channels running through the delta divide into smaller courses known as *distributaries* that do not reconnect to the main channel (**Figure 14.28**). Distributaries in a river delta appear as a reverse of the dendritic drainage pattern discussed earlier (see Figure 14.7a).

Rivers can form several types of deltas:

* An *arcuate delta* has an intricate maze of distributaries in an arc-shaped pattern (**Figure 14.29a**).
* An *estuarine delta* is one that is in the process of filling an **estuary**, an enclosed body of water at a river's mouth where freshwater flow encounters seawater (**Figure 14.29b**). Estuaries are connected to the open sea at the transition zone between fluvial and marine environments.
* A *bird's-foot delta* has a few widely spaced distributary channels that extend a long distance into the ocean; the Mississippi River delta is a classic example (**Figure 14.29c**).

(a) The arcuate delta of the Horton River, Northwest Territories, Canada, extends into the Arctic Ocean's Beaufort Sea.

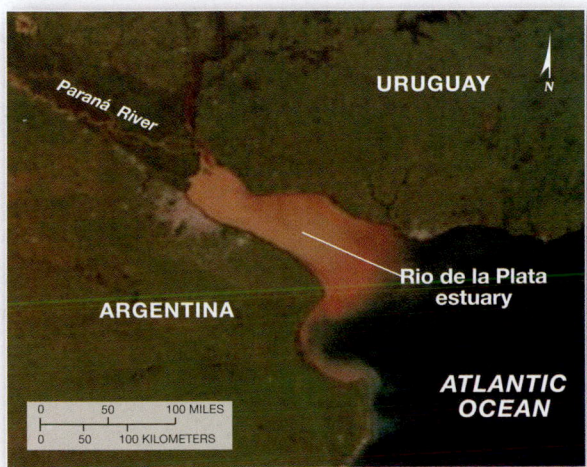

(b) The Paraná River, second longest in South America, has an estuarine delta. The Parana and the Uruguay Rivers together form the Rio de la Plata estuary, which is influenced by both fluvial and tidal processes.

(c) The bird's-foot shape of the Mississippi River extends into the Gulf of Mexico.

◀**Figure 14.29 Three river delta shapes— arcuate, estuarine, and bird foot.** [(a) NASA EO-1 Team. (b) NASA/GSFC/METI/ ERSDAC/JAROS, and U.S./Japan ASTER Science Team. (c) *Suomi NPP*, NOAA/NASA.]

▲Figure 14.30 The Nile River in Egypt and its delta in 2014.
Without nutrients supplied by seasonal flooding, productivity is declining along the Nile floodplain and on the delta. Even so, agricultural use remains intense. Population is rising throughout the region, putting even more pressure on the Nile as a water resource in this arid region. [*Terra* image, NASA/GSFC/JPL.]

The Nile River in Egypt forms an arcuate delta in the Mediterranean Sea, with a delta coastline that is receding at an alarming 50 to 100 m (165 ft to 330 ft) per year (**Figure 14.30**). In 1964, completion of the Aswân High Dam blocked sediment movement downstream, decreasing the sediment supply to the delta. Today, seawater is intruding inland into both surface water and groundwater. Rising sea level also threatens the delta, which provides the fertile soils that produce 60% of Egypt's food. A 1-m sea-level rise, considered likely during the next 100 years, would inundate one-third of the delta and displace about 8 million people.

As discussed in Geosystems Now, the history of the Mississippi River delta shows a dynamic system with inputs and outputs of sediment and shifting distributaries. Over the past 120 million years, the Mississippi River has transported alluvium throughout its vast basin into the Gulf of Mexico. During the past 5000 years, the river has formed a succession of seven distinct deltaic complexes along the Louisiana coast (**Figure 14.31**). Each new complex formed after the river changed course, probably during an episode of catastrophic flooding. The first of these deltas was located near the mouth of the Atchafalaya River. The seventh and current delta has been building for at least 500 years. The bird's-foot delta is caused in part by the meander cutoffs shown in Figure 14.26, which increase the channel slope, thereby increasing stream velocity and carrying sediments further into the Gulf.

Numerous rivers throughout the world lack a true delta. In fact, Earth's highest-discharge river, the Amazon, carries sediment far into the deep Atlantic offshore, but lacks a delta. Its mouth, 160 km (100 mi) wide, has formed an underwater deposit on a sloping continental shelf. As a result, the river ends by braiding into a broad maze of islands and channels. Deltaic formations are also absent on rivers that do not produce significant sediment or that discharge into strong erosive currents. The Columbia River of the U.S. Northwest lacks a delta

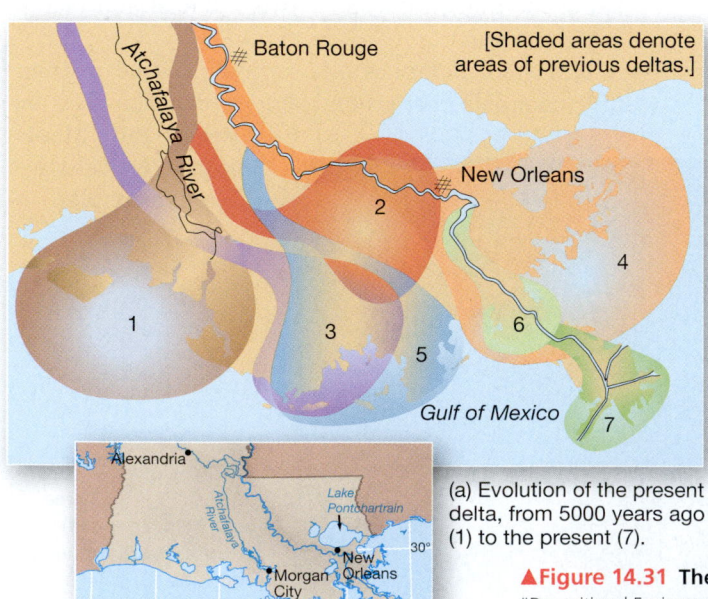

(a) Evolution of the present delta, from 5000 years ago (1) to the present (7).

(b) Sediment plumes at the mouth of the Atchafalaya River and at the present-day bird's-foot delta of the Mississippi.

▲Figure 14.31 The Mississippi River delta. [(a) Adapted from C. R. Kolb and J. R. Van Lopik, "Depositional Environments of the Mississippi River Deltaic Plain," in *Deltas in Their Geologic Framework* (Houston, TX: Houston Geological Society, 1966). (b) *Terra* image courtesy of Liam Gumley, Space Science and Engineering Center, University of Wisconsin, and NASA.]

TABLE 14.2 Recurrence Interval and Probability of Occurrence for Flood Discharges

Recurrence Interval, in Years	Probability of Occurrence in a Given Year	Percent Chance of Occurrence in a Given Year
10	1 in 10	10
50	1 in 50	2
100	1 in 100	1
500	1 in 500	0.20
1000	1 in 1000	0.10

▲ **Figure 14.32 Flooding from Hurricane Matthew in 2016.** Rising floodwater caused by heavy rainfall from Hurricane Matthew inundated portions of North Carolina in October 2016; shown here is the town of Rocky Mount, flooded by the Tar River. [Thomas Babb/The News & Observer via AP.]

because offshore currents remove sediment as quickly as it is deposited.

Floods

Despite our historical knowledge of flood events and their effects, floodplains continue to be important sites of human activity and settlement. These activities place lives and property at risk during floods, especially in less-developed regions of the world. Bangladesh is perhaps the most persistent example: It is one of the most densely populated countries on Earth, and more than three-fourths of its land area is a floodplain and delta complex—an area the size of Alabama. The historic floods of 1988 and 1998 inundated 60% and 75%, respectively, of the country's land area, causing extensive crop losses and thousands of fatalities.

A **flood** is defined as a high water flow that passes over the natural bank along any portion of a stream. As discussed earlier, floods in a drainage basin are strongly connected to precipitation and snowmelt, which are, in turn, connected to weather patterns (**Figure 14.32**). Floods can result from periods of prolonged rainfall over a broad region, from intense rainfall associated with short-lived thunderstorms, from rapid melting of the snowpack, or from rain-on-snow events that accelerate snowpack melting. Floods vary in magnitude and frequency, and their effects depend on many factors.

Flood Probability

Maintaining extensive historical records of discharge during precipitation events is critical for predicting the behavior of present streams under similar conditions. The U.S. Geological Survey has detailed records of stream discharge at stream-gaging stations since the 1900s, with the most consistent data collected since the 1940s. These relatively short-term historical data form the basis for flood probability estimates.

Recurrence Interval Scientists rate flood discharges statistically according to the recurrence interval (or return interval), the estimated time interval between peak discharges of similar size. For example, based on discharge data for a particular stream, a "100-year flood" on that stream has a recurrence interval of 100 years and a 1% chance of occurring in any given year (**Table 14.2**). The use of historical data works well where available; however, urbanization and dam construction can change the magnitude and frequency of flood events on a stream or in a watershed.

These statistical estimates are probabilities that events will occur randomly during a specified period; they do not mean that events will occur regularly during that time period. For example, several centuries might pass without a 100-year flood, or a 100-year level of flooding could occur twice in one century.

Annual Exceedance Probability Another method for describing floods and precipitation events uses the annual exceedance probability (AEP) to represent the statistical likelihood of occurrence. By this measure, a 100-year flood has a 1% AEP.

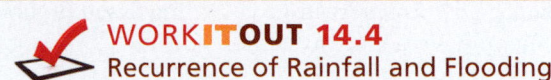

WORK**IT**OUT 14.4
Recurrence of Rainfall and Flooding

News reports about the 2016 West Virginia flooding pictured in Everyday Geosystems (Figure 14.1) described it as being caused by a "thousand-year precipitation event."

1. What is the percent chance of a rainfall event of this magnitude occurring in any given year?
2. Could a precipitation event of that magnitude occur again in your lifetime?
3. Does a 1000-year rain event produce a 1000-year flood event? Explain.

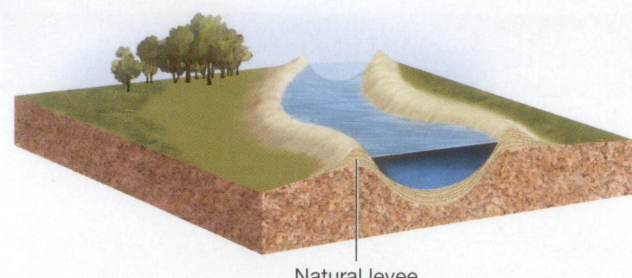

(a) A natural levee.

Natural levee

(b) Sheep graze on the slopes of an artificial levee along the Sacramento River in California. Note that the agricultural fields are lower in elevation than the river, caused by subsidence of the Sacramento River delta.

(c) The Mississippi River flows over part of an intentional breach in the Bird's Point levee in Missouri in 2011. During the winter floods of early 2016, 11 levees were breached nearby as the Mississippi crested to near-record levels in the U.S. Midwest.

▲Figure 14.33 **Natural and artificial levees.** [(b) California Department of Water Resources. (c) Scott Olsen/Getty Images News.]

Floodplain Risk

The flood recurrence interval is useful for floodplain management and hazard assessment. A 10-year flood indicates a moderate threat to a floodplain. A 50-year or 100-year flood is of greater consequence, but it is also less likely to occur in a given year.

Scientists and developers define and map floodplains using flood recurrence intervals, for example, by delineating the "100-year floodplain." Using these maps, scientists and engineers can develop the most effective flood-management strategy. Restrictive zoning using these floodplain designations helps determine degrees of risk across the floodplain and can help avoid potential flood damage. However, restrictive zoning based on flood hazard mapping is not always enforced.

Flood Protection

In the United States, floods cause an average of about $6 billion in annual losses. The catastrophic floods along the Mississippi River and its tributaries in 1993 and 2011 produced damage that exceeded $30 billion in each occurrence. Flood protection, when in place, generally takes the form of dams (discussed in Chapter 8) and artificial levee construction along river channels.

Usually, the term *levee* connotes an element of human construction, and these engineered features are common across the United States and throughout the world. **Artificial levees** are earthen embankments, often built on top of natural levees. They run parallel to the channel (rather than across it, like a dam) and increase the capacity in the channel by adding to the height of the banks (**Figure 14.33**). For efficient use of time and materials, channels are often straightened during levee construction. Levees are intended to hold floods within the channel, but not prevent them completely. Eventually, given severe enough conditions, an artificial levee will be overtopped or damaged in a flood. When overtopping (known as levee breaching) or levee failure occurs, extensive flood damage and erosion can result downstream.

GEOreport 14.2 America's levees

By several estimates, over 100,000 miles of artificial levees exist along rivers and streams in the United States, the vast majority of them privately owned. The U.S. population living in areas protected by levees is estimated to be in the tens of millions; some major urban areas with levee systems are New Orleans, Sacramento, Dallas–Fort Worth, St. Louis, and Washington, D.C. In fact, over 30 major cities in America are located on floodplains. Currently, no national policy exists concerning the safety of levees (see http://www.leveesafety.org/docs/NCLS-Recommendation-Report_012009_DRAFT.pdf).

RIVER SYSTEMS IMPACT HUMANS

- Humans use rivers for recreation and have farmed fertile floodplain soils for centuries.
- Flooding affects human settlements on floodplains and deltas.

In 2011, Americans spent $42 million on fishing-related activities. Streams in Montana, Missouri, Michigan, Utah, and Wisconsin are of high enough quality that they are designated "blue ribbon fisheries" based on sustainability criteria such as water quality and quantity, accessibility, and the specific species present. [Karl Weatherly/Getty Images.]

HUMANS IMPACT RIVER SYSTEMS

- Dams and diversions alter river flows and sediment loads, affecting river ecosystems and habitat. River restoration efforts include dam removal to restore ecosystems and threatened species.
- Urbanization, deforestation, and other human activities in watersheds alter runoff, peak flows, and sediment loads in streams.
- Levee construction affects floodplain ecosystems; levee failures cause destructive flooding.

After days of heavy rain, the Seine River reached its highest flood stage in over 30 years in Paris, France, in June 2016. High water closed rail lines, the Metro system, numerous tourist attractions, and all boat traffic through the city. [Joel Saget/AFP/Getty Images.]

A Texas Department of Safety boat patrols the U.S.–Mexico border along the Rio Grande in Texas for drug trafficking and human smuggling activities. The border follows the center of the river and was surveyed and permanently established to avoid disputes related to channel changes. [Polaris/Newscom.]

A proposed series of dams on the free-flowing Nu/Salween River system in Southeast Asia would relocate some 60,000 people in China. The dams would also block the movement of sediment that replenishes farmlands along the river's floodplain and delta. [Bradley Mayhew/Getty Images.]

ISSUES FOR THE 21ST CENTURY

- Increasing population will intensify human settlement on floodplains and deltas worldwide, especially in developing countries, making more people vulnerable to flood impacts.
- Stream restoration will continue, including dam decommissioning and removal, flow restoration, vegetation reestablishment, and restoration of stream geomorphology.
- Global climate change may intensify storm systems, including hurricanes, increasing runoff and flooding in affected regions. Rising sea level will make delta areas more vulnerable to flooding.

QUESTIONS TO CONSIDER

1. How do human activities affect river systems? Try to think of both negative and positive impacts.
2. What hazards will human populations on floodplains and deltas face during the 21st century?

KEY**LEARNING**concepts**review**

Fluvial (p. 410) processes are stream-related. In fluvial systems, water dislodges, dissolves, or removes surface material and moves it to new locations in the process of **erosion** (p. 410). Sediments are laid down by the process of **deposition** (p. 410).

Sketch a basic drainage basin model and *describe* different types of drainage patterns.

The basic fluvial system is a **drainage basin** (p. 410), or *watershed*, which is an open system. *Drainage divides* define the catchment (water-receiving) area of a drainage basin. In any drainage basin, water initially moves downslope in a thin film of **sheetflow** (p. 411), or *overland flow*. This surface runoff concentrates in *rills*, or small-scale downhill grooves, which may develop into deeper *gullies* and a stream course in a valley. High ground that separates one valley from another and directs sheetflow is an *interfluve*. Extensive mountain and highland regions act as **continental divides** (p. 412) that separate major drainage basins. Some regions have **internal drainage** (p. 412) that does not reach the ocean, the only outlets being evaporation and downward movement to groundwater.

Drainage density (p. 414) is determined by the number and length of channels in a given area and is an expression of a landscape's topographic surface appearance. **Drainage pattern** (p. 414) refers to the arrangement of channels in an area as determined by the steepness, variable rock resistance, variable climate, hydrology, relief of the land, and structural controls imposed by the landscape.

1. What is the basic organizational unit of a river system? How is it identified on the landscape?
2. Describe dendritic and radial drainage patterns.

Explain stream discharge calculation, measurement, and variation over space and time.

Discharge (p. 416), a stream's volume of flow per unit of time, is calculated by multiplying the velocity of the stream by its width and depth for a specific cross section of the channel. Streams may have *perennial*, *ephemeral*, or *intermittent* flow regimes.

A graph of stream discharge over time for a specific place is called a **hydrograph** (p. 418). Precipitation events in urban areas result in higher peak flows during floods. A torrent of water that fills a stream channel during or just after a rainstorm is a **flash flood** (p. 418).

3. How might a natural stream hydrograph differ from one in an urbanized area?

Describe the processes involved in stream erosion and sediment transport.

Hydraulic action (p. 419) is the erosive work of water caused by hydraulic squeeze-and-release action to loosen and lift rocks and sediment. As this debris moves along, it mechanically erodes the streambed further through a process of **abrasion** (p. 419).

When stream energy is high, particles move downstream in the process of **sediment transport** (p. 419). The sediment load of a stream can be divided into three primary types. The **dissolved load** (p. 419) travels in solution, especially the dissolved chemicals derived from minerals such as limestone or dolomite or from soluble salts. The **suspended load** (p. 419) consists of fine-grained, clastic particles held aloft in the stream. **Bed load** (p. 419) refers to coarser materials that are dragged and pushed and rolled along the streambed by **traction** (p. 419) or that bounce and hop along by **saltation** (p. 419). **Degradation** (p. 420) occurs when sediment is eroded and channel incision occurs. If the load in a stream exceeds its capacity, **aggradation** (p. 420) occurs as sediment accumulates on the bed of the stream channel.

4. What processes cause a stream to erode its channel?
5. Differentiate between three types of sediment load. How do larger particles move along the channel bed?

Explain stream gradient and *describe* the processes by which streams adjust their gradient over time.

The **gradient** (p. 420) of a stream is the slope, or the stream's drop in elevation per unit distance. The drop in elevation along a river from headwaters to mouth is usually represented in a side view called a *longitudinal profile*. **Base level** (p. 421) is the lowest-elevation limit of stream erosion in a region. A *local base level* occurs when something interrupts the stream's ability to achieve base level, such as a dam or a landslide that blocks a stream channel. A **graded stream** (p. 421) condition occurs when the slope is adjusted so that a channel has just enough energy to transport its sediment load; this represents a balance between slope, discharge, channel characteristics, and the load supplied from the drainage basin. An interruption in a stream's longitudinal profile is called a **nickpoint** (p. 424). This abrupt change in slope can occur as the stream flows across hard, resistant rock or after tectonic uplift episodes. Tectonic uplift may cause *stream rejuvenation* (a return to active downcutting); an example is the development of *entrenched meanders* as a stream carves the landscape during uplift.

Where the slope is gradual, stream channels develop a sinuous form called a **meandering stream** (p. 426). The outer portion of each meandering curve is subject to the fastest water velocity and can be the site of a steep **undercut bank** (p. 426). The inner portion of a meander experiences the slowest water velocity and forms a **point bar** (p. 426) deposit. When a meander neck is cut off as two undercut banks merge, the meander becomes isolated and forms an **oxbow lake** (p. 426).

6. Explain the base level concept. What happens to a stream's base level when a reservoir is constructed?
7. Are all streams graded streams? Why or why not?

Describe the depositional landforms associated with river systems.

Alluvium (p. 426) is the general term for the clay, silt, sand, gravel, or other unconsolidated rock and mineral fragments deposited by running water. With excess sediment, a stream may become a maze of interconnected channels that form a **braided stream** (p. 426) pattern. The flat, low-lying area adjacent to a stream channel that is subjected to recurrent flooding is a **floodplain** (p. 427). On either bank of some streams, **natural levees** (p. 430) develop as by-products of flooding. Entrenchment of a river into its own floodplain forms **alluvial terraces** (p. 430). A depositional plain formed at the mouth of a river is called a **delta** (p. 431). Deltas may be arcuate or bird's foot in shape or estuarine in nature. When the mouth of a river enters the sea and is inundated by seawater in a mix with freshwater, it is called an **estuary** (p. 431).

8. Describe the formation of a floodplain. How are natural levees, oxbow lakes, and yazoo tributaries produced?

Discuss floodplain protection using artificial levees and **explain** flood probability estimates.

Despite historical devastation by floods, floodplains and deltas are important sites of human activity and settlement. A **flood** (p. 433) occurs when high water overflows the natural bank along any portion of a stream. Floods are often described by their recurrence interval, the statistical probability rating for the expected time interval between peak discharges. Human-constructed **artificial levees** (p. 434) are common features along many rivers of the United States where flood protection is needed for developed floodplains.

9. What is a flood? What is a "100-year flood"?
10. How does an artificial levee differ from a natural levee?

GEO**SPATIAL** ANALYSIS

Streamflow Conditions Near You

Rivers are an important resource for communities, but they can cause dangerous flooding. River water levels are monitored across the United States to determine flow rates (discharge) and flood stage (the level at which water rises to hazard status.)

Activities

Go to http://waterwatch.usgs.gov/. Click on the Current Streamflow map.

1. Click on "Map" to see information about the map. What do the map dots display? For how long must data be recorded at a streamgage for the gage to appear on this map?

2. Why might some states have few data points in the winter? What are the effects of ice?

3. Click anywhere in the "Explanation – Percentile classes" table to bring up information about the classes. What do these percentile classes mean?

4. Based on the current streamflow map, which areas of the United States are experiencing higher than normal streamflow? Which areas are experiencing lower than normal streamflow?

5. Explore the different Water-Resources Regions in the drop-down menu. In which water-resource region do you live? Based on the number of stations in each percentile class, how would you describe the streamflow conditions in your region?

Click on a ranked (colored) stream gage near your current location that has "Hydrograph, Peak," and "Forecast" graphs. Be sure the Peak graph also shows the National Weather Service "Flood Stage" level. Click on each of these graphs to bring up a larger version.

6. Where is this streamflow site located?

7. What is the flood stage water height for this location? What is the current water height for this location?

8. What is the drainage area (in square miles)? How does this compare to nearby waterways?

9. What is the current discharge (in cubic feet per second)? How does this compare to nearby waterways?

10. Click on Hydrograph. Is the current discharge higher or lower than the median daily discharge?

11. Click on Peak. When was the most recent flood stage for this waterway? When was the largest flood stage?

MasteringGeography™

Looking for additional review and test prep materials? Visit the Study Area in MasteringGeography™ to enhance your geographic literacy, spatial reasoning skills, and understanding of this chapter's content by accessing a variety of resources, including MapMaster™ interactive maps, videos, *Mobile Field Trips*, *Project Condor* Quadcopter videos, *In the News* RSS feeds, flashcards, web links, self-study quizzes, and an eText version of *Geosystems*.

15 Eolian Processes and Arid Landscapes

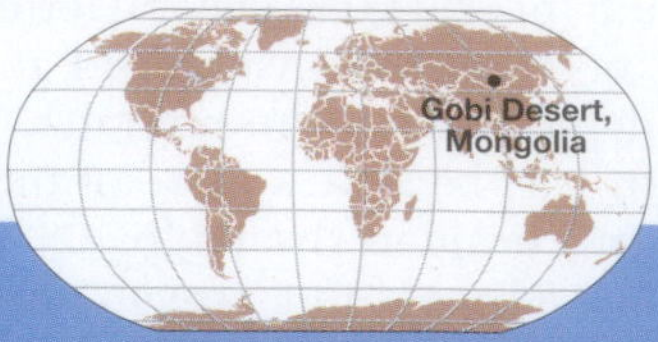

Gobi Desert, Mongolia

At the foot of the Gurvan Saikhan Mountains in the Gobi Desert of southern Mongolia lie the Khongoryn Els sand dunes, known as the "singing sands" for the sound made by moving sand grains. Bactrian camels, which inhabit the steppes of central Asia, graze nearby. [Tuul and Bruno Morandi/Getty Images.]

KEY**LEARNING**concepts

After reading the chapter, you should be able to:

- **Describe** eolian transport of dust and sand.
- **Discuss** eolian erosion and the resultant landforms.
- **Explain** the formation of sand dunes and *describe* loess deposits and their origins.
- **Discuss** the causes and human impacts of desertification.
- **List** some landforms unique to arid regions and *explain* their formation.

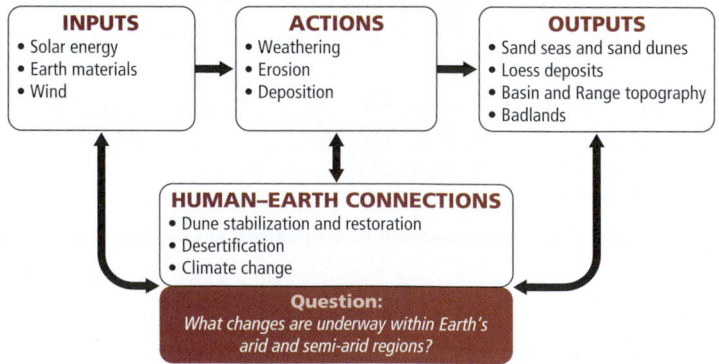

INPUTS
- Solar energy
- Earth materials
- Wind

ACTIONS
- Weathering
- Erosion
- Deposition

OUTPUTS
- Sand seas and sand dunes
- Loess deposits
- Basin and Range topography
- Badlands

HUMAN–EARTH CONNECTIONS
- Dune stabilization and restoration
- Desertification
- Climate change

Question:
What changes are underway within Earth's arid and semi-arid regions?

GEOSYSTEMSnow

Sliding Rocks on Death Valley's Racetrack Playa

In a remote, low-elevation basin between mountain ranges in southern California and Nevada, rocks are moving with no obvious cause. From year to year, unseen by humans, the rocks shift position along a flat, hard-surfaced playa, a dry lakebed. The rocks leave trails behind them, furrows in the silty lakebed sediments, as proof of their movement (**Figure GN 15.1**). The tracks are hundreds of meters in length, and some of the rocks weigh hundreds of kilograms. The movement is episodic and unpredictable—years, even decades, can pass between movement events.

Possible Causes for Movement The rock trails on Racetrack Playa suggest that movement happens when the playa is wet from infrequent rains and the sediments form a soft mud. If animals or humans were moving the rocks, they would leave tracks on the playa's surface. If gravity were moving the rocks, a slope would be present, but the playa surface is nearly flat. If streams were moving the rocks, a channel would be present, as well as other alluvial material. Eliminating these factors leaves two possibilities: the forces of wind and ice.

For years, scientists sought an explanation for the sliding rocks. The dominant hypothesis was that strong winds were the force for rock movement. The prevailing winds on Racetrack Playa blow from the southwest, parallel to most of the rock tracks. However, some of the heaviest sliding rocks were embedded several centimeters into the playa sediments. Could strong winds alone be enough to force their movement?

On Racetrack Playa, winter rains sometimes produce a shallow lake that lasts for weeks or months. Every few years, conditions are such that a shallow lake forms and then freezes so that a thin layer of ice on the surface covers the water below. During the day, the ice breaks up and melts, and then at night it refreezes. If the rocks become embedded in the ice layer, could wind work together with ice to move the rocks over the wet, slippery surface?

▲Figure GN 15.1 **A sliding rock at rest on Racetrack Playa, Death Valley National Park, California.** When in motion, the rocks slide over the wet playa at slow speeds for brief periods of time, sometimes only for seconds. [Daniel Osterkamp/Getty Images.]

Solving the Mystery In 2011, researchers set up a weather station and time lapse cameras on Racetrack Playa to test this hypothesis. On the playa surface, they placed rocks with GPS trackers designed to record position and speed at the onset of movement. Then they waited, and in December 2013, rock movement occurred.

Measurements and observations in 2013 and 2014 showed that the rocks slide across the wet surface of the playa on sunny days that follow nights with subfreezing temperatures. At night, the shallow water on the playa freezes to form a thin layer of ice at the surface (**Figure GN 15.2**). During the late morning, as the sun warms the basin, the ice breaks up into thin panes. Then wind—both light breezes and strong gusts—moves the ice panels, effectively "bulldozing" the rocks across the saturated, muddy surface of the playa.

The conditions necessary for rock movement occur infrequently at Racetrack Playa. A shallow lake must be present at the same time that nighttime temperatures dip below freezing to initiate surface freeze. The winters of 2010–2011 and 2011–2012 included infrequent snow and rain events but not enough moisture to form a lake. Once formed, a lake that persists over weeks or months in combination with temperature conditions that promote nighttime freezing and daytime ice breakup can have numerous rock sliding events. (For more information, see http://journals .plos.org/plosone/article?id=10.1371/journal. pone.0105948.)

1. What conditions did scientists observe at the playa surface when rock movement occurred?

2. Why do the rocks on Racetrack Playa move in some years and not in others?

---

1. Rain creates a shallow water layer on the dry lakebed.

2. Water freezes overnight. In the morning, ice breaks into thin sheets.

3. The floating ice panels, driven by wind and flowing water, push rocks across the playa surface.

◄Figure GN 15.2 **The observed process for rock movement on Racetrack Playa.** [Based on R.D. Norris et al., 2014, Sliding Rocks on Racetrack Playa, Death Valley National Park: First Observation of Rocks in Motion. *PLoS ONE* 9(8): e105948.]

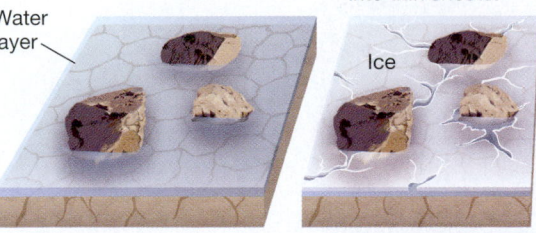

Water layer

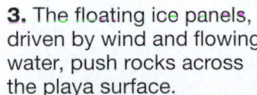

Ice

Light wind

Ice

Wind is a significant agent of geomorphic change in many environments. Winds contribute to soil formation and even spread organisms. In Earth's arid and semiarid regions, wind rearranges vast seas of sand and erodes landscapes to form fascinating landforms. In the polar-region deserts of Antarctica, cold katabatic winds, drainage winds that flow downslope from high elevations, carry sand and other particles that scour rock and shape the landscape.

Arid and semiarid climates cover about one-third of Earth's surface. Over the past several decades, land degradation in these dry regions has caused *desertification*, the expansion of deserts. This worldwide phenomenon along the margins of arid and semiarid lands is caused mainly by poor agricultural practices combined with worsening drought, and usually results in losses of topsoil and declines in food production. Desertification now affects over a billion people worldwide.

Wind Processes

Like water, moving air is a fluid, and like moving water, it transports materials such as dust, sand, and snow. Wind-blown dust and sand affect air quality in arid and semiarid regions worldwide (**Figure 15.1**). Wind transported materials also create erosional and depositional

landforms. The work of wind is **eolian** (also spelled *aeolian*, for Aeolus, ruler of the winds in Greek mythology).

Since the viscosity and density of air are much lower than those of other transporting agents such as water and ice, the ability of wind to move materials is correspondingly weaker. Yet, over time, wind accomplishes enormous work. Consistent local wind can prune and shape vegetation, form massive deposits of sand in dunes, and erode bedrock.

How Wind Moves Dust and Sand

Just like water in a stream picking up sediment, wind exerts a drag, or frictional pull, on surface particles until they become airborne. Grain size, or particle size, is important in wind erosion. Intermediate-sized grains move most easily, whereas movement of the largest and the smallest sand particles requires the strongest winds. Stronger wind is needed for the large particles because they are heavier and for the smaller particles because they are mutually cohesive. Eolian processes work only on dry surface materials because wet soils and sediments are too cohesive for movement to occur.

The mechanisms for wind transport include suspension, saltation, and surface creep (**Figure 15.2**). The distance that wind is capable of transporting particles in *suspension* varies with particle size (for comparison,

everyday GEOSYSTEMS

How does wind-blown dust and sand affect urban areas?

Dust storms can occur in cities in dry climates or in regions subject to drought. Large quantities of dust and fine sand particles moving in suspension reduce visibility, aggravate asthma and other human respiratory illnesses, and enter ventilation systems in buildings, causing damage to computers and other sensitive electronics.

◄**Figure 15.1 Dust storm in Dubai, United Arab Emirates, in April 2015.** Travelers wear medical masks amid a severe storm of dust and sand that engulfed the city, disrupting one of the world's busiest airports and closing local schools. [MARWAN NAAMANI/AFP/Getty Images.]

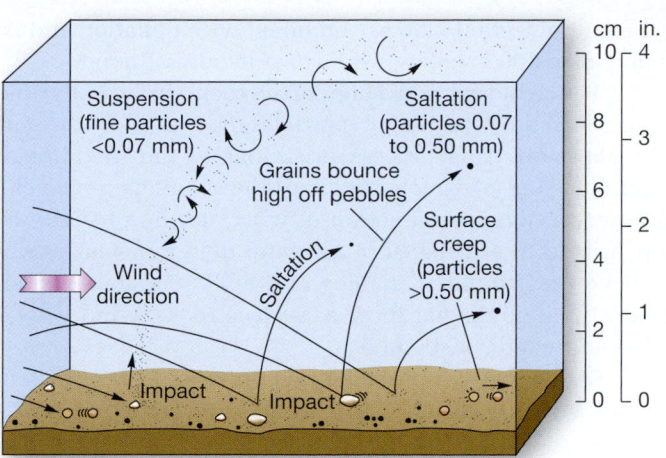

(a) Eolian suspension, saltation, and surface creep are transportation mechanisms.

▲**Figure 15.2   How the wind moves sand.** [(b) Robert Christopherson.]

(b) Sand grains saltating along the surface in the Stovepipe Wells dune field, Death Valley, California.

Animation
How Wind
Moves Sand

https://goo.gl/R9gvEw

Figure 14.16 shows the transport of stream sediment in suspension, a similar process). In a dust storm, fine materials are lifted higher and travel farther, a condition known as long-term suspension. In a sandstorm, slightly larger sand particles remain lower to the ground in short-term suspension.

As discussed in previous chapters, atmospheric circulation can transport fine material, such as volcanic debris, fire soot and smoke, and dust, worldwide within days. In some arid and semiarid regions, downburst winds associated with thunderstorms can cause dramatic dust storms known as *haboobs* (**Figure 15.3**). Such storms consist of fine particles that infiltrate even the smallest cracks of homes and businesses.

Eolian processes transport sand between 0.07 and 0.50 mm (0.0027 and 0.02 in.) in size along the ground by *saltation*, the bouncing and skipping action of particles that

accounts for about 80% of sediment transport by wind. Particles larger than about 0.50 mm (0.02 in.) slide and roll along the ground surface, a type of movement called **surface creep**. Saltating particles may collide with sliding and rolling particles, knocking them loose and forward in this process, which affects about 20% of the material transported by wind. In a desert or along a beach, sometimes you can hear a slight hissing sound, almost like steam escaping, produced by the myriad saltating grains of sand as they bounce along and collide with surface particles. Once particles are set in motion, the wind velocity need not be as high to keep them moving.

British Army Major Ralph Bagnold, an engineering officer stationed in Egypt in 1925, pioneered studies of wind transport and authored a classic work in geomorphology, *The Physics of Blown Sand and Desert Dunes,*

(a) Ground view of a massive dust storm moving through Phoenix, Arizona, in August 2013.

(b) Aerial view of a thunderhead and dust storm sweeping over Phoenix, Arizona, in 2016. The thunderhead causes downbursts that pick up dust on the ground, forming a wall of blowing material that affects transportation and downs power lines.

▲**Figure 15.3   Dust storms engulf Phoenix, Arizona, in 2013 (ground view) and 2016 (aerial view).** Also known as haboobs, these storms occur in the U.S. Southwest mainly during the North American monsoon season from about June 15 to September 15. The dust storm results when downdraft winds (downbursts, or microbursts) kick up areas of dense blowing dust that can reach 160 km (100 mi) in width. [(a) Christian Petersen/ Getty Images Sport. (b) © Ryan Vermillion]

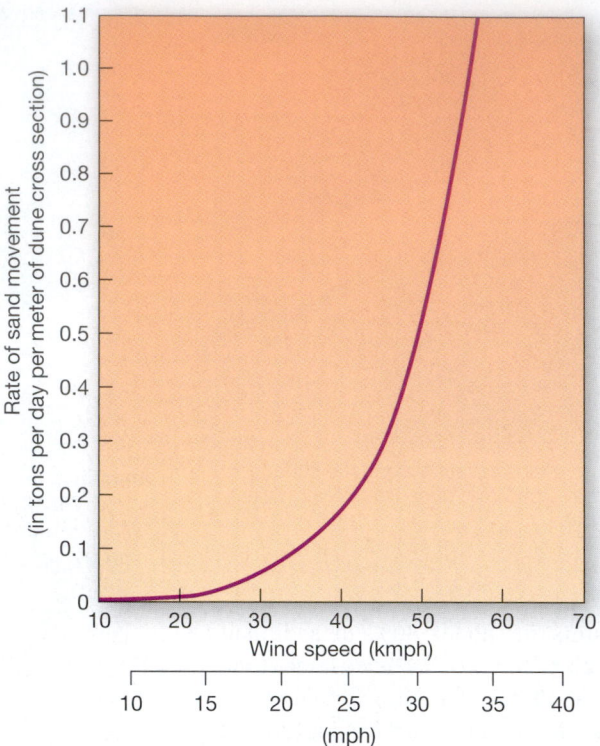

▲**Figure 15.4 Sand movement and wind velocity.** Sand movement relative to wind velocity, as measured over a meter cross section of ground surface. [Created from data in *The Physics of Blown Sand and Desert Dunes*, by R.A. Bagnold, © 1941, 1954 (Methuen and Co., 1954).]

published in 1941. Bagnold's studies of wind transport over the surface of a sand dune showed that at lower wind speeds, sand moves only in small amounts; however, beyond a wind speed of about 30 kmph (19 mph), the amount of sand moved increases rapidly (**Figure 15.4**). A steady wind of 50 kmph (30 mph) can move approximately one-half ton of sand per day over a 1-m-wide section of dune.

Eolian Erosion and Related Landforms

Erosion of the ground surface resulting from the lifting and removal of individual particles by wind is **deflation**. Wherever wind encounters loose sediment, deflation may remove enough material to form depressions in the landscape ranging in size from small indentations less than a meter wide up to areas hundreds of meters wide and many meters deep. The smallest of these are known as *deflation hollows*, or *blowouts*. They commonly occur in dune environments, where winds remove sand from specific areas, often in conjunction with the removal of stabilizing vegetation (possibly by fire, by grazing, or from drought).

Large depressions in the Sahara Desert are at least partially formed by deflation but are also affected by large-scale tectonic processes. For example, the enormous Munkhafad el Qattâra (Qattâra Depression), which covers 18,000 km² (6950 mi²) in western Egypt, formed as a result of tectonic forces combined with deflation and is now over 100 m below sea level at its lowest point.

The grinding and shaping of rock surfaces by the "sandblasting" action of particles captured in the air is **abrasion**. This process is similar to the intentional sandblasting of streets and buildings for maintenance. However, the natural action of wind abrasion usually is restricted to a distance of no more than a meter or two above the ground. Variables that affect eolian abrasion rates include the hardness of surface rocks, wind velocity, and wind constancy.

Rocks that are pitted, fluted (grooved), or polished from eolian erosion are called **ventifacts** (literally, "artifacts of the wind," shown in **Figure 15.5**). They usually become aerodynamically shaped in a direction determined by the consistent flow of airborne particles in prevailing winds. On a larger scale, deflation and abrasion together are capable of streamlining multiple rock structures in a landscape in alignments parallel to the most effective wind direction, thus producing distinctive, elongated formations called **yardangs**. Abrasion is concentrated on the windward end of each yardang, with deflation operating on the leeward portions. These wind-sculpted features can range from meters to kilometers in length and up to many meters in height (**Figure 15.6**).

On Earth, some yardangs are large enough to be detected on satellite imagery. The Ica Valley of southern Peru contains yardangs reaching 100 m (330 ft) in height and several kilometers in length. The Sphinx in Egypt was perhaps partially formed as a yardang, whose natural shape suggested a head and body.

Desert Pavement

The work of wind deflation is important for the formation of **desert pavement**, a hard, stony surface—as opposed

▲**Figure 15.5 A ventifact.** One of the wind-eroded rocks in the Dry Valleys area of Antarctica, a snow-free polar desert with winds reaching speeds of 320 kmph (200 mph). [Scott Darsney/Lonely Planet Images/Getty.]

▲Figure 15.6 **A field of yardangs.** Abrasion from consistent, unidirectional winds shaped these yardangs in the Sahara Desert, Egypt. [Mike P. Shepard/Alamy.]

(a) A typical desert pavement.

to the usual sand—that commonly occurs in arid regions (**Figure 15.7a**). Scientists have put forth several explanations for the formation of desert pavement. One explanation is that deflation literally blows away loose or noncohesive sediment, eroding fine dust, clay, and sand and leaving behind a compacted concentration of pebbles and gravel (**15.7b**).

Another hypothesis that better explains some desert pavement surfaces states that deposition of windblown sediments, not removal, is the formative process. Windblown particles settle between and below coarse rocks and pebbles that are gradually displaced upward. Rainwater plays a part, as wetting and drying episodes swell and shrink clay-sized particles. The gravel fragments are gradually lifted to surface positions to form the pavement (**15.7c**).

Desert pavements are so common that many provincial names are used for them—for example, *gibber plain* in Australia; *gobi* in China; and in Africa, *lag gravels* or *serir*, or *reg* desert if some fine particles remain. Most desert pavements are strong enough to support human weight, and some can support motor vehicles, but in general, these surfaces are fragile. They are also of critical importance, since they protect underlying sediment from further deflation and water erosion.

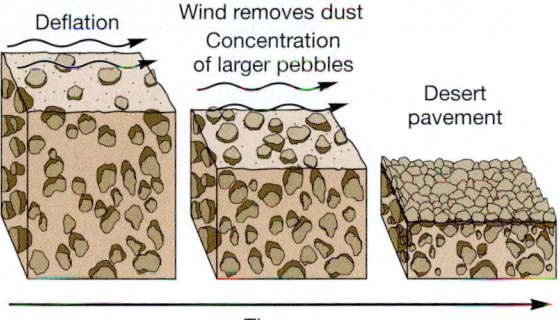

(b) The deflation hypothesis: Wind removes fine particles, leaving larger pebbles, gravels, and rocks, which become consolidated into desert pavement.

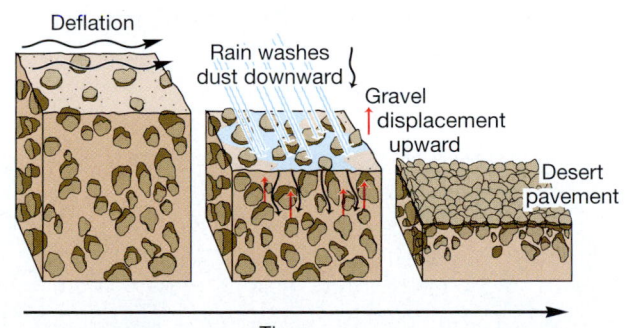

(c) The sediment-accumulation hypothesis: Wind delivers fine particles that settle and wash downward as cycles of swelling and shrinking cause gravels to migrate upward, forming desert pavement.

▲Figure 15.7 **Desert pavement.** [(a) Bobbé Christopherson.]

🌐 **GEOreport 15.1**   Human activities disturb eolian landforms

   Recreational off-road vehicles (ORVs) and all-terrain vehicles (ATVs), which currently number more than 15 million in the United States, erode desert dunes and disrupt desert pavement. Military activities such as the movement of heavy vehicles also destroy desert pavement, as in the Middle East, where the breakdown of thousands of square kilometers of stable desert pavement has sent dust and sand into nearby cities and onto farmland. In the Registan Desert of southern Afghanistan, military activities have combined with drought conditions to cause enough erosion that wind transport for fine particles has covered more than 100 villages with dust and sand.

Landforms of Eolian Deposition

The smallest features shaped by the movement of wind-blown sand are ripples, which form in crests and troughs, positioned transversely (at a right angle) to the direction of the wind. Larger deposits of sand grains form **dunes**, defined as wind-sculpted, transient ridges or hills of sand.

An extensive area of windblown sand (usually larger than 125 km², or 48 mi²) is an **erg** (after the Arabic word for "dune field"), also called a *sand sea*. The Grand Erg Oriental in the hot desert of the central Sahara, active for more than 1.3 million years, exceeds 1200 m (4000 ft) in depth and covers an area comparable to the state of Nebraska (**Figure 15.8**). The world's largest erg is the Rub'al Khālī, or Empty Quarter, in the Arabian Desert of Saudi Arabia, Oman, the United Arab Emirates, and Yemen. Extensive dune fields characterize ergs, which are also present in semiarid regions such as the Great Plains of the United States. Active ergs have constantly shifting sand, while inactive ergs may be stabilized by vegetation growth, as has occurred in Nebraska's Sand Hills.

Dune Formation and Movement When saltating sand grains encounter small patches of sand, their kinetic energy (motion) is dissipated and they accumulate. Once the height of such accumulations increases above 30 cm (12 in.), a *slipface* and characteristic dune features form. Geosystems in Action 15 illustrates a dune profile and various dune forms.

A dune usually is asymmetrical in one or more directions. Winds characteristically create a gently sloping *windward side*, with a more steeply sloped slipface on the *leeward side* (Figure GIA 15.1). The angle of a slipface is the steepest angle at which loose material is stable—its *angle of repose*. Thus, the constant flow of new material makes a slipface a type of avalanche slope: Sand builds up as it moves over the crest of the dune to the brink; then it avalanches, falling and cascading as the slipface continually adjusts, seeking its angle of repose (usually 30° to 34°). In this way, a dune migrates downwind, in the direction in which winds are blowing and transporting sand (see the successive dune profiles in Figure GIA 15.1). Even more effective for dune migration than prevailing winds are stronger seasonal winds or winds from a passing storm.

Active sand dunes cover about 10% of Earth's deserts. Dune fields are also present in humid climates, such as along coastal Oregon, the south shore of Lake Michigan, and the U.S. Gulf and Atlantic coastlines.

Desert Dune Classification Dunes have many wind-produced shapes that make classification difficult. Scientists generally classify dunes according to three general shapes—*crescentic* (crescent, curved shape), *linear* (straight form), and massive *star dunes*. Figure GIA 15.2 shows six types of dunes that fall within these classes or are a complex mix of these general shapes.

- The crescentic class includes *barchan*, *transverse*, *parabolic*, and *barchanoid ridge* dunes. **Barchan dunes** form with their tips pointing downwind, usually in areas with limited sand supply and little or no vegetation (**Figure 15.9**). The tips of the dune are symmetrical when the wind direction is consistent; in areas where the wind direction shifts slightly, one tip will be elongated compared to the other. Parabolic dunes are essentially the reverse of a barchan, forming with their tips pointed upwind, usually in vegetated dune landscapes. These dunes often begin with a blowout, after which sand deposits along the curved rim and vegetation anchors the tips in place.

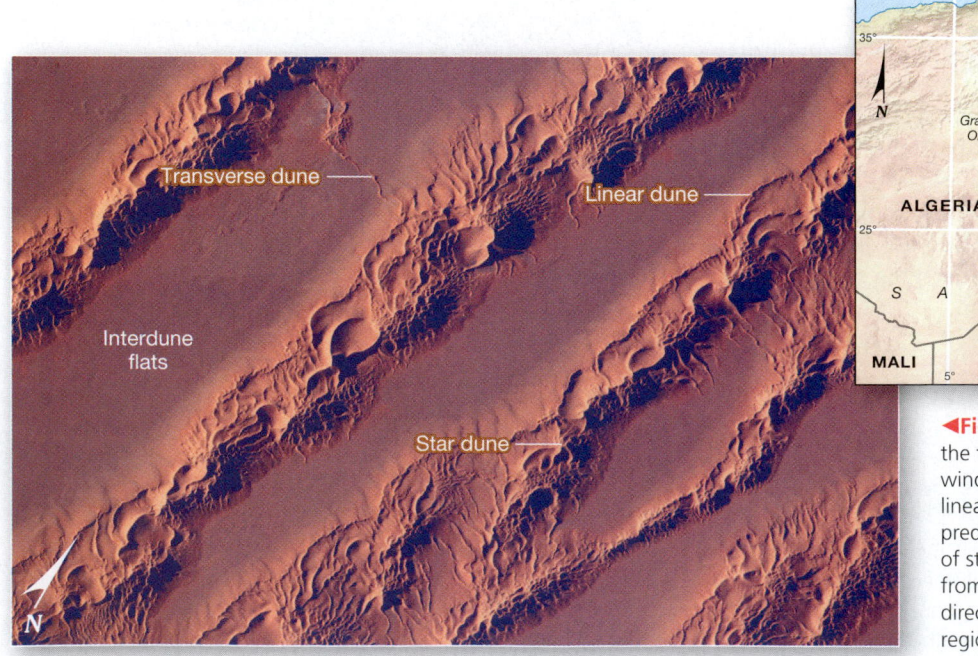

◀Figure 15.8 **A sand sea, or erg.** In the the Sahara Desert's Grand Erg Oriental, wind has organized vast sand seas into linear chains of dunes formed parallel to the predominate wind direction. The presence of star dunes, formed when winds blow from several directions, suggests that wind direction has changed over time in this region. [ISS astronaut photo, NASA/GSFC.]

▲**Figure 15.9** **Barchan dune, Namib Desert, Africa.** Wind direction is from right to left. [Thierry Grun-Aero/Alamy.]

▲**Figure 15.11** **Cross bedding in eolian sandstone.** The pattern of cross stratification indicates the changing angles of the dune before lithification occurred. [Corbin 17/Alamy.]

- The linear class includes *longitudinal* dunes, also called *seif* dunes after the Arabic word for "sword." These dunes form parallel to the prevailing wind, and can extend for hundreds of kilometers in length.
- **Star dunes** are the largest in size, with multiple slipfaces produced by winds from varying directions (**Figure 15.10**). They are pinwheel-shaped, with several radiating arms rising and joining to form a common central peak that can approach 200 m (650 ft) in height.

Reversing dunes can form in regions where winds reverse direction. For example, large reversing dunes form in central Colorado's San Luis Valley as the prevailing

westerly winds reverse direction during summer storms (see Figure GIA 15.2).

Ancient sand dunes can be lithified into sedimentary rock that carries patterns of cross bedding, or *cross stratification*. As the ancient dune was accumulating, the sand that cascaded down its slipface established distinct bedding planes (layers) that remained as the dune lithified. These layers are now visible as cross bedding, so named because they form at an angle to the horizontal layers of the main strata (**Figure 15.11**). Ripple marks, animal tracks, and fossils also are found preserved in these desert sandstones.

▶**Figure 15.10** **Star dune, Namibia.** Star dunes form in regions with shifting wind direction, such as the Namib Desert, in Namib-Naukluft National Park, Namibia. [Felix Lipov/Alamy.]

The dramatic, sculptural shapes of dunes occur in a variety of settings: along shorelines, in sandy parts of deserts, and in semiarid regions. Wherever there is a sufficient supply of loose, dry sand or other fine particles unprotected by plant cover, wind erosion and deposition can build dunes (GIA 15.1). Prevailing winds, along with other factors, create dunes of many sizes and shapes (GIA 15.2).

15.1 DUNE PROFILE

Wind erosion and deposition work together to build a dune's characteristic profile. A dune grows as wind-borne particles accumulate on the gentler, windward slope, then cascade down the steep slipface of the leeward slope.

Angle of repose:
The loose particles on the slipface tend to slip and slide downhill until the slope stabilizes at its angle of repose—about 30°–34°—the steepest angle at which the particles are stable.

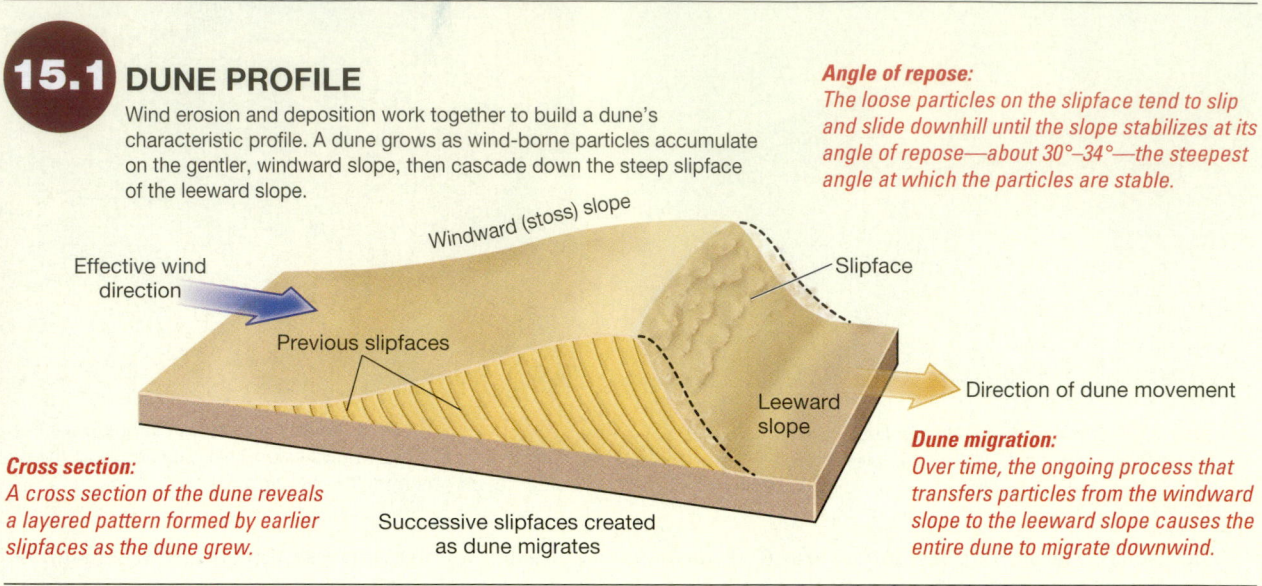

Effective wind direction

Windward (stoss) slope

Slipface

Previous slipfaces

Leeward slope

Direction of dune movement

Cross section:
A cross section of the dune reveals a layered pattern formed by earlier slipfaces as the dune grew.

Successive slipfaces created as dune migrates

Dune migration:
Over time, the ongoing process that transfers particles from the windward slope to the leeward slope causes the entire dune to migrate downwind.

15.2 DUNE FORMS

The different types of sand dunes vary in shape and size depending on several factors including:
- directional variability and strength (or "effectiveness") of the wind
- whether the sand supply is limited or abundant
- presence or absence of vegetation

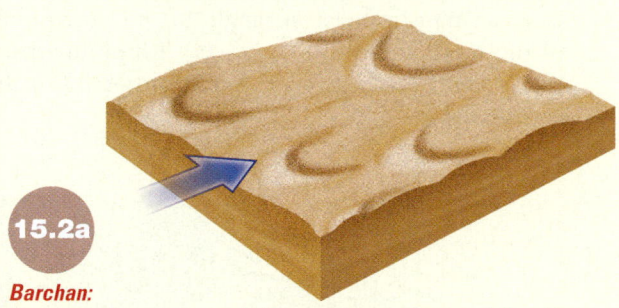

15.2a

Barchan:
Crescent-shaped dune with horns pointed downwind; found in areas with constant winds and little directional variability, and where limited sand is available.

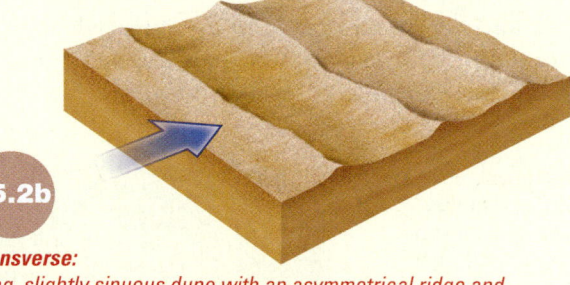

15.2b

Transverse:
Long, slightly sinuous dune with an asymmetrical ridge and only one slipface, aligned transverse (or perpendicular) to wind direction; results from relatively ineffective wind and abundant sand supply.

15.2c

Parabolic:
Crescent-shaped dune with opening end facing upwind; U-shaped "blowout" and arms anchored by vegetation, which stabilizes dune form.

15.2d

Barchanoid ridge:
Wavy, asymmetrical, dune formed from coalesced barchans with ridges aligned transverse to effective winds; resembles connected crescents in row with open areas between.

Animation (MG)
Dune Formation and Cross-Bedding

https://goo.gl/Bvl9g1

15.2 DUNE FORMS (continued)

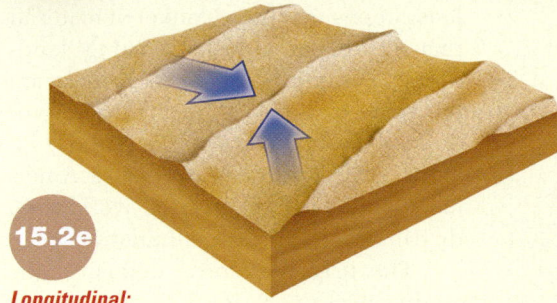

15.2e

Longitudinal:
Linear, slightly sinuous, ridge-shaped dune, aligned parallel with the wind direction. Averages 100 m (328 ft) high and 100 km (63 mi) long but can reach to 400 m (1312 ft) high.

Longitudinal dunes in Australia's Simpson Desert result from bidirectional winds and a low sand supply.

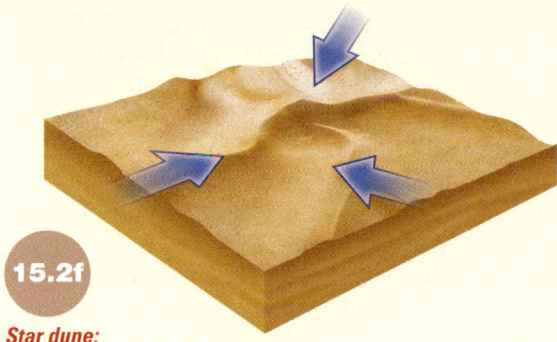

15.2f

Star dune:
Pyramidal-shaped structure with three or more sinuous, radiating arms extending outward from a central peak; results from effective winds shifting in all directions.

Star dunes in Namibia reflect the region's multidirectional wind patterns.

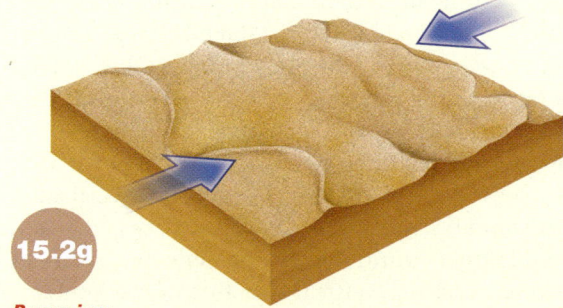

15.2g

Reversing:
Dune with asymmetrical ridge, intermediate between star dune and transverse dune; wind variability can alter shape between these forms.

Reversing dunes, shown here covered in snow, are common in Colorado's Great Sand Dunes National Park, where winds reverse direction in late summer. Reversing dunes grow in height instead of moving across the landscape.

GEOquiz

1. Summarize: Describe the growth, structure, and migration of a sand dune beginning with a small obstacle that intercepts sand particles and assuming a relatively constant wind direction.

2. Explain: Why do sand dunes migrate across the land surface?

3. Infer: Give one reason that star dunes and longitudinal dunes are often higher than other types of dunes.

4. Compare: How are barchan and parabolic dunes similar? How are they different?

▲**Figure 15.12 Preventing sand transport in coastal environments.** Fences are effective for slowing the movement of sand, which accumulates until the fence is buried, shown here at Assateague Island National Seashore, Maryland. [D. Trozzo/Alamy.]

Preventing Sand Transport Dunes in both deserts and coastal regions are often subject to erosion from human foot traffic, off-road vehicles, and animals. Several techniques can slow both human and natural sand erosion from a dune or beach (**Figure 15.12**). Vegetation stabilizes soil and sediments, but planting needs to be followed by adequate watering and protection from disturbance as the plants establish. Fences are also effective at slowing wind velocity in the immediate vicinity. Often fences and vegetation—native shrubs, grasses, and trees—are used together for the most effective dune stabilization. These methods and others are helping slow dune movement in China and other locations where deserts are encroaching on villages and cities, discussed later in the chapter.

Loess Deposits

Windblown dust that accumulates into homogeneous (evenly mixed) deposits is known as **loess** (pronounced "luss"), originally named by peasants working along the Rhine River Valley in Germany. Loess deposits are composed of fined-grained sediment, such as clay, silt, and fine sand, often cemented together with calcium carbonate. In some regions, loess deposits form a blanket of material that covers previously existing landforms. The soils derived from loess are the basis for some of Earth's most productive farming regions, especially in North America, Asia, and South America. **Figure 15.13** shows the worldwide distribution of loess accumulations.

The origin of loess deposits varies by location. Some loess is derived from the sediments left behind by glacial activity. About 15,000 years ago, near the end of the Pleistocene, melting glaciers in many parts of the world deposited fine-grained sediments formed as glacial movement ground up the underlying rock. Wind later transported these sediments long distances, redepositing them into thick unstratified deposits. Loess is also derived from desert sediments and volcanic ash that are redeposited by wind.

The loess deposits in Europe and North America are thought to be derived mainly from glacial and periglacial sources. In the United States, significant loess accumulations with glacial origins occur in the Palouse region of Washington and throughout the Mississippi and Missouri River Valleys, forming continuous deposits 15–30 m (50–100 ft) thick. The Loess Hills of Iowa reach heights of about 61 m (200 ft) above the nearby prairie farmlands and run north–south for more than 322 km (200 mi).

The vast deposits of loess in China, covering more than 300,000 km^2 (116,000 mi^2), are derived from windblown desert sediment. Accumulations in the Loess Plateau of China are more than 300 m (1000 ft) thick, forming a complex topography of deeply eroded gullies mixed with good agricultural land (**Figure 15.14**). Because of its binding strength and internal coherence, loess weathers and erodes into steep bluffs, or vertical faces. When a bank is cut into a loess deposit, it generally will stand vertically, although it can fail if saturated. On China's loess plateau, as in several other world regions, people have carved dwellings into the strong vertical structure of loess cliffs.

GEOreport 15.2 Living in caves on China's Loess Plateau

In the Shaanxi province of China on the Loess Plateau (shown in Figure 15.14), over 20 million people today live comfortably in caves dug into loess cliffs. As living quarters, the caves are cool in the summer, warm in the winter, quiet, and traditional. In fact, many cave dwellings are handed down through generations. Some are updated and modernized with electricity and running water. In 2012 in the city of Yan'an, the market price for a three-room cave with a bathroom was US$46,000. But not many caves come up for sale. Cave living, one of the earliest forms of human architecture, is now praised by architects as sustainable and practical for a simple lifestyle.

(b) Glacial loess underlies the fertile Palouse region of eastern Washington.

(c) Homes built into the loess bluffs in southern Spain near Granada.

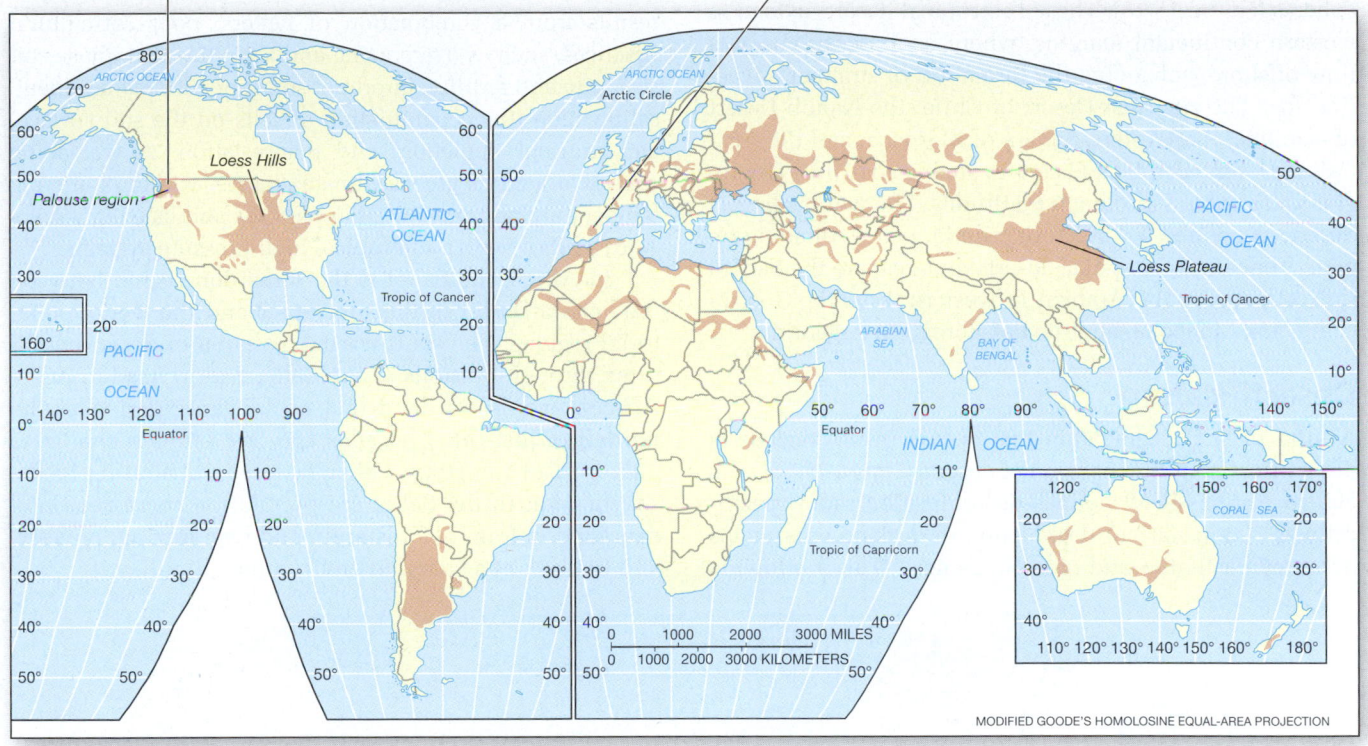

(a) Global distribution of loess deposits.

▲Figure 15.13 **Global major loess deposits, with examples from the United States and Spain.** [(a) Adapted from NRCS, FAO, and USGS data. (b) Edmund Lowe Photography/Shutterstock. (c) Christa Knijff/Alamy.]

▼Figure 15.14 **The Loess Plateau, China.** The loess bluffs exposed by erosion are structurally strong. Pictured here is the area near Yulin, Shaanxi Province. [Jim Richardson/Getty Images.]

Arid Landscapes

As discussed in Chapter 9, dry climates occupy about 30% of Earth's land surface. The spatial distribution of these *drylands* (regions defined by a scarcity of water) relates primarily to three causal elements.

- The presence of dry, subsiding air within subtropical high-pressure systems.
- Location in the rain shadow of mountain ranges, where dry air subsides after moisture is intercepted on the windward slopes.
- Location in continental interiors, far from moisture-bearing air masses.

Earth's dry climates cover broad regions between 15° and 30° latitude in the Northern and Southern Hemispheres (**Figure 15.15**). These subtropical deserts extend to western continental margins, where cool, ocean currents flow offshore, enhancing the formation of summer advection fog. The Atacama Desert of Chile, the Namib Desert of Namibia, the Western Sahara of Morocco, and the Australian Desert each lie adjacent to such a coastline. Dry regions also extend into higher latitudes. The world's largest desert, as defined by moisture criteria, is the Antarctic region. The largest nonpolar deserts, by area, are the Sahara in North Africa, the Arabian in western Asia, the Gobi in China and Mongolia, and the Patagonian in Argentina.

Desertification

A form of land degradation that occurs in dry regions is **desertification**, the expansion of deserts (**Figure 15.16**). The United Nations (UN) defines desertification more specifically as "the persistent degradation of dryland ecosystems by human activities and climate change." This worldwide

WORK**IT**OUT 15.1
Test Your Knowledge about Eolian Processes

1. Given what you know about the transport of dust, silt, and sand, why is wind a more effective agent of erosion in dry climates than in humid climates?
2. What does the existence of sand dunes on Mars tell you about weather and conditions at the Martian surface?
3. If you compare an area of stream-deposited sediment with an equivalent area of wind-deposited sediment, which would have the more uniform particle size? Why?

phenomenon along the margins of semiarid and arid lands results from a combination of factors: poor agricultural practices, such as overgrazing and activities that abuse soil structure and fertility; improper soil-moisture management; salinization (the accumulation of salts on the soil surface) and nutrient depletion; and deforestation. A worsening causative force is global climate change, which is altering temperature and precipitation patterns and causing a poleward shift of Earth's subtropical high-pressure systems.

In Africa, the Sahel is the transition region between the Sahara Desert in the subtropics and the wetter equatorial regions. The southward expansion of desert conditions through portions of the Sahel region has left many African peoples on land that no longer experiences the rainfall of just three decades ago. Yet climate change is only part of the story: Other factors contributing to desertification in the Sahel are population increases, land degradation from deforestation and overgrazing, poverty, and the lack of a coherent environmental policy.

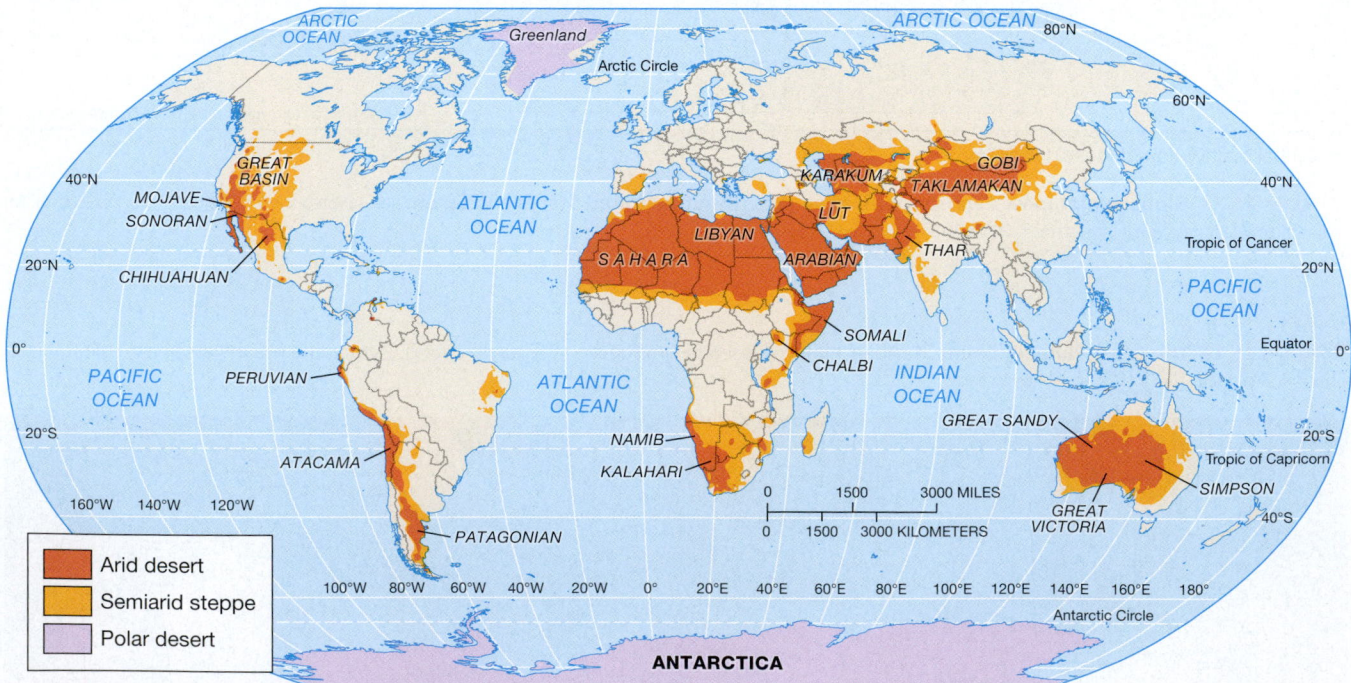

▲**Figure 15.15 Global distribution of arid and semiarid climate regions.** Also labeled on the map are the world's major deserts and steppes. The lower-latitude deserts and steppes tend to be hotter with less seasonal change than the midlatitude deserts and steppes, where freezing winter temperatures are common.

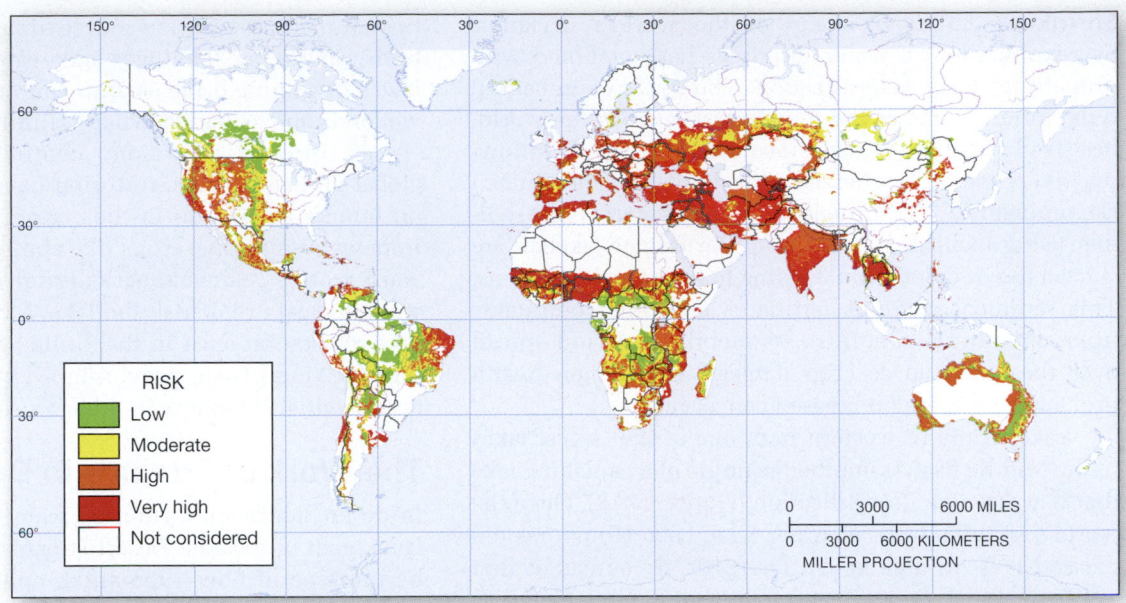

►Figure 15.16
Areas at risk of desertification.
The UN estimates that degraded lands worldwide cover some 1.9 billion hectares (4.7 billion acres) and affect 1.5 billion people, with additional land added each year. [Map prepared by USDA–NRCS, Soil Survey Division; includes consideration of population densities provided by the National Center for Geographic Information Analysis at the University of California, Santa Barbara.]

RISK
Low
Moderate
High
Very high
Not considered

Globally, overgrazing is an important cause of desertification. Overgrazing occurs when the number of grazing animals is greater than the productive capacity of the land. The resulting reduction in plant leaf area weakens plants and leads to deterioration of vegetation and soils. In southern Argentina, sheep ranching is the primary economic activity in the expansive steppe grasslands, once home to only one native grazing mammal: the guanaco, a relative of the llama. Although sheep numbers have declined since the 1950s, overgrazing over the past century has led to widespread desertification. Sustainable grazing practices are becoming a priority as this region seeks to preserve its economic base of wool and meat production and reverse the desertification trend.

Dune Migration The edge of the Gobi Desert in the Inner Mongolia Autonomous Province of China is an area plagued by desertification. In a region devastated by sandstorms and deteriorating land, forest restoration is underway to combat dune migration (**Figure 15.17**). Several private organizations as well as the Chinese government are supporting volunteer efforts to plant trees, monitor water availability for tree growth, and educate communities about the importance of trees for preventing erosion, producing oxygen, and storing carbon dioxide. However, drought conditions make these efforts more difficult. To the west, in the Taklamakan Desert of central Asia, many trees are declining with ongoing drought.

In China, desertification has lessened in some areas but worsened in others. Although government policies have restricted grazing for several decades, overgrazing remains a significant cause of desertification throughout northwest China. In this region, the main causes of desertification are related to socioeconomic factors, as land-use practices that yield short-term gains related to crops and livestock cause long-term deterioration of the land. Climate change is another important cause of desertification in China as temperatures rise and drought becomes more intense.

▼Figure 15.17 **Vegetation and straw grids combat desertification in China.** [(a) TAO Images Limited/Alamy. (b) Lucas Schifres/Getty Images.]

(a) Shrubs stabilize soils at the southern edge of the Gobi Desert near the border of Gansu and Inner Mongolia.

(b) In the Ningxia Hui Autonomous Region, just south of Inner Mongolia, straw grids prevent sand transport and provide protection for seedlings.

Shrinking Lakes In many of the world's drylands, overexploitation of water resources has combined with drought to cause desertification. The Aral Sea in central Asia, formerly one of the four largest lakes in the world, has steadily shrunk in size since the 1960s, when inflowing rivers were diverted for irrigation (see The Human Denominator 15 at the end of this chapter). Fine sediment and alkali dust blanketing the former lakebed are subject to wind deflation, leading to massive dust storms. This sediment contains fertilizers and other pollutants from agricultural runoff, so its mobilization and spread over the land causes crop damage and human health problems, including increased cancer rates.

Lake Urmia in western Iran, one of the largest lakes in the Middle East, is another example of a vanishing lake that is worsening desertification (**Figure 15.18**). Once the world's sixth largest salt water lake, Lake Urmia has decreased 88% in area since the 1970s. Scientists at first attributed this change to drought, but satellite imagery shows that the lake is shrinking even during years with adequate precipitation. These data indicate that water withdrawals for agriculture and development are the main cause of the lake's decreasing size. Over 50 dams on rivers in Lake Urmia's basin divert water for human use. In addition, groundwater pumping from wells affects the overall water level of the lake.

As Lake Urmia becomes shallower, evaporation along the margins leaves the former shoreline covered in salt deposits that are vulnerable to eolian erosion. Evaporation also increases the salinity of the remaining lake water, making it unsuitable for brine shrimp. These tiny animals are the food source for a variety of migratory birds, including flamingos and egrets. At present, the lake's remaining brine shrimp can only survive in a few wetlands and estuaries, where salinity is lower.

As drought conditions continue or worsen with global climate change, restoring Lake Irmia will depend on human adaptation in the region. Transitioning away from water-intensive crops like apples and sugar beets toward more sustainable agricultural practices will allow water to again replenish the lake. Models for this type of lake restoration exist in the United States, such as California's Mono Lake, providing a blueprint for planners and scientists to follow in other world regions.

The Work of Streams in Drylands

In desert landscapes, running water is the most significant agent of erosion. Desert streams are often described by the type of flow—perennial, ephemeral, or intermittent. As discussed in Chapter 14, *perennial streams* flow all year, *intermittent streams* flow for several weeks or months each year, and *ephemeral streams* flow only after precipitation events. In some arid regions, years may pass between flow events in ephemeral stream channels.

Many deserts are landscapes of interior drainage, where streams and rivers do not flow to the ocean. The Basin and Range Province of the U.S. West, discussed ahead, is an example. Water in this dry region flows into basins and then evaporates or seeps downward into subsurface groundwater.

Desert Floods Precipitation events in some deserts are infrequent, even a year or two apart. In response to a short-lived, intense rainfall event, an ephemeral channel can quickly fill with water to form a flash flood. Depending on the region, such an ephemeral channel is known as a *wash*, an *arroyo* (in the U.S. Southwest and Latin America), or a *wadi* (in certain Arabic countries). In response to a long, steady rainfall event, material on slopes may become saturated, giving rise to a debris flow (discussed in Chapter 13). Debris flows can travel at high speed down desert washes and canyons, carrying a mixture of mud, sand, debris, and larger particles such as cobbles and boulders.

Flash floods and debris flows are a hazard in deserts, causing both damage and fatalities. For

▲**Figure 15.18 Drying Lake Urmia in western Iran.** Lake Urmia lost most of its volume from the 1980s (upper right false-color image) to 2014 (large natural-color image) as a result of human water use. Rivers are narrow green lines and deltas are green agricultural fields. The United Nations designated the lake and its wetlands a Biosphere Reserve in 1976. [*ISS* astronaut photograph/NASA.]

▲**Figure 15.19 Flash flood aftermath, Utah.** Mangled cars sit in the channel of Short Creek near Hilldale, Utah, after they were swept downstream when heavy rains caused a flash flood in September 2015. [George Frey/Getty Images.]

▲**Figure 15.20 Badwater alluvial fan, Death Valley, California.** [USGS.]

Condor (MG)
Characteristics of Alluvial Fans

https://goo.gl/YjqXQT

example, flash floods along the Utah–Arizona border in 2015 killed 20 people. The sudden flooding in Short Creek swept away several cars in Hilldale, Utah (**Figure 15.19**). In nearby Zion National Park, seven hikers perished in a narrow bedrock canyon as the flood swept through.

Alluvial Fans In arid and semiarid climates, stream sediments at the mouth of canyons form prominent cone-shaped, or fan-shaped, deposits called **alluvial fans**. They commonly occur at the mouth of a canyon where an ephemeral stream channel exits the mountains into a flatter valley (**Figure 15.20**). Alluvial fans form when flowing water (such as a flash flood) abruptly loses velocity as it leaves the constricted channel of a canyon. At this point, the stream drops layer upon layer of sediment along the base of the mountain block. Water then flows over the surface of the fan and produces a braided drainage pattern, sometimes shifting from channel to channel. A continuous apron, or **bajada** (Spanish for "slope"), may form if individual alluvial fans coalesce into one sloping surface. Alluvial fans also can occur in humid climates along mountain fronts, such as in Japan, Nepal, and Venezuela.

The sediment composing alluvial fans is naturally sorted by size. The coarsest materials (gravels) are deposited near the mouth of the canyon at the apex of the fan, grading slowly to pebbles and finer gravels, and then to sands and silts, with the finest clays and dissolved salts carried in suspension and solution all the way to the valley floor. This intermittently wet and dry lowest area of a closed drainage basin is the site of an *ephemeral lake* when water is present. When the water evaporates to form a dry lakebed, the area is a **playa**. As water evaporates, salt crusts may be left behind on the desert floor, forming a salt crust made up of *evaporites*—a chemical sedimentary rock formed as salt deposits precipitate when water evaporates.

Well-developed alluvial fans also can be a major source of groundwater. Some cities—San Bernardino, California, for example—are built on alluvial fans and extract their municipal water supplies from them. In other parts of the world, such water-bearing alluvial fans and water channels are known as *qanat* (Iran), *karex* (Pakistan), or *foggara* (western Sahara).

Badlands In arid and semiarid regions, intense rainfall can generate overland flow that wears away shales and siltstones to form **badlands**, a rugged terrain of slopes dissected by rills and gullies. These landscapes usually lack developed soils and vegetation cover. The name "badlands" refers to the difficulty of crossing the steep, complex topography of these regions and their lack of value as farmlands. Badlands occur throughout the U.S. West, with perhaps the most famous in Badlands National Park, South Dakota (**Figure 15.21**).

▼**Figure 15.21 Badlands National Park, South Dakota.** Erosion began in the badlands of western South Dakota about 500,000 years ago and may continue for only another 500,000 years, until they are completely eroded away. The shales are rich in fossils of early mammals (from about 30 to 50 m.y.a) and marine life (about 75 m.y.a.). [Richard Green/Alamy.]

(a) The Basin and Range Province extends from Oregon and Idaho southward into Mexico.

(b) Looking across Badwater Basin in Death Valley, at elevation below sea level, to the top of Telescope Peak, at over 3360 m (11,000 ft). Note the bajada on the far side of the basin, and the playa marked by salt deposits on the basin floor.

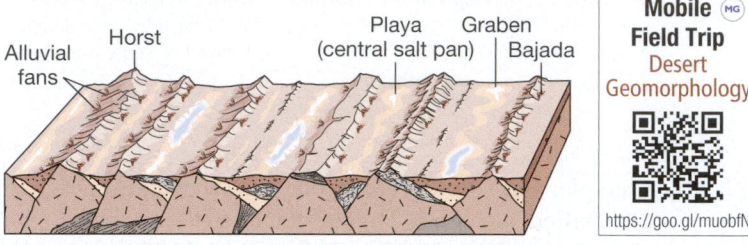

(c) Parallel faults produce a series of ranges and basins. Infrequent precipitation events leave alluvial fan deposits at the mouths of canyons; coalesced alluvial fans join to form a bajada.

▲Figure 15.22 The Basin and Range Province. [(b) Corbin 17/Alamy.]

Mobile Field Trip MG
Desert Geomorphology

https://goo.gl/muobfN

Basin and Range Topography

A large region that is identified by several geologic or topographic traits is known as a *physiographic province*. In the semiarid U.S. West, the **Basin and Range Province** is a physiographic province recognized for its north-and-south-trending basins and mountains—the basins are low-elevation areas that dip downward toward the center; the ranges are interconnected mountains of varying elevations above the basins. These roughly parallel mountains and valleys (known as *basin-and-range topography*) are aligned pairs of normal faults, an example of a horst-and-graben landscape (**Figure 15.22**).

The Basin and Range Province formed as a result of tectonic processes. The driving force is the westward movement of the North American plate, which causes tension that leads to thinning of the crust, uplifting and stretching it so that it fractures. Basin-and-range relief is abrupt, and its rock structures are angular and rugged. As the ranges erode, transported materials accumulate to great depths in the basins, gradually producing extensive plains. Basin elevations average roughly 1200–1500 m (4000–5000 ft) above sea level, with mountain crests rising higher by another 900–1500 m (3000–5000 ft).

Death Valley, California, is the lowest of these basins, with an elevation of −86 m (−282 ft). Directly to the west,

✔ **WORKITOUT 15.2**
Basin and Range Landforms

California's Eureka Dunes are a small dune field roughly 8 km² (3 mi²) in size, containing dunes that reach over 200 m (650 ft) in height—some of the tallest dunes in North America (**Figure WIO 15.2.1**).

1. What two types of dunes can you identify in the sandy region marked by A? (Hint: Review Geosystems in Action 15, considering dune shape and height.)
2. What landform is marked by the letter B? What agent of erosion created this landform?
3. What accounts for the different colors of the materials in A versus those in B? Do they come from the same source?

▲Figure WIO 15.2.1 Eureka Dunes, California. [David Clapp /Getty Images.]

(a) Desert varnish on a sandstone cliff in Long Canyon, Grand Staircase-Escalante National Monument, Utah.

(b) Petroglyphs carved in desert varnish, Indian Creek Canyon, Utah.

▲Figure 15.23 **Desert varnish formed by biochemical processes.** [(a) Bob Gibbons/Alamy. (b) TMI/Alamy.]

the Panamint Range rises to 3368 m (11,050 ft) at Telescope Peak, producing almost 3.5 vertical kilometers (2.2 mi) of relief from the desert valley to the mountain peak (Figure 15.22b). Racetrack Playa, discussed in Geosystems Now, occupies another basin within this province.

Weathering in Arid Landscapes

Although physical and chemical weathering processes (discussed in Chapter 13) occur in arid regions, physical weathering plays a more important role. Because chemical weathering processes rely on both water and the presence of vegetation, such processes work slowly in dry climates. However, some chemical weathering occurs in many deserts. An example is the formation of *desert varnish*, or *rock varnish* (**Figure 15.23**). This thin, dark coating is composed of clay particles and iron and manganese that is taken up and metabolized by microbes to form oxide minerals. Thus, it is formed by a combination of chemical and biological processes in dry environments. Ancient peoples have carved figures and symbols called *petroglyphs* into desert varnish by scratching through the black coating to reveal the lighter rock surface below.

Alcoves and Cliff Dwellings In the U.S. Southwest, ancient peoples took advantage of the alcoves formed by weathering processes by building dwellings under the natural overhangs. The alcoves form as slightly saline groundwater moves through the porous sandstone until meeting an impermeable layer, such as shale. As the water seeps slowly from the rock to the surface, freeze–thaw processes pry apart joints in the rock. As water evaporates, it leaves salt crystals, which expand and contract with temperature changes, loosening the sand grains within the overlying rock. Subsequent erosion by water and wind complete the sculpting process, forming alcoves at the base of sandstone cliffs. More than 1000 years ago, Native Americans built entire villages in these weathered niches, as in Mesa Verde in Colorado and Arizona's Canyon de Chelly (**Figure 15.24**).

In other regions of the world, humans used natural sandstone features for dwellings and even built cities in part hewn into bedrock. In the Middle East, in present-day Jordan, Arab peoples built the city of Petra about 2000 years ago. Focus Study 15.1 discusses the human history of Petra and the modern challenge of preserving its archaeological heritage in the face of natural weathering processes and increasing tourism.

(a) Over 600 cliff dwellings are built in alcoves in the Cliff House sandstone at Mesa Verde in southwest Colorado.

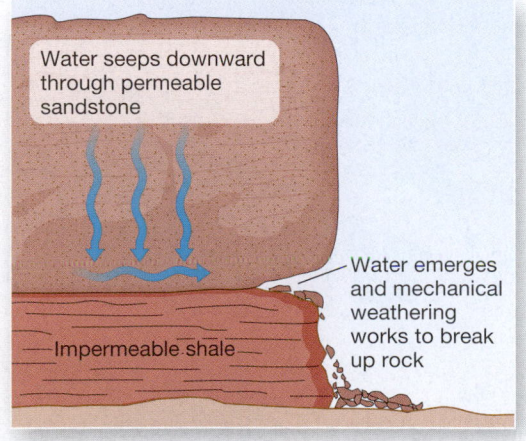

Water seeps downward through permeable sandstone

Water emerges and mechanical weathering works to break up rock

Impermeable shale

(b) Alcoves form as surface water and groundwater move through porous sandstone until meeting an impermeable layer, where the water flows laterally to the surface. Frost wedging and salt-crystal growth then break up the rock to form an alcove.

▲Figure 15.24 **Weathering of sandstone alcoves used for ancient cliff dwellings.** [(a) Zachary Frank/Alamy.]

FOCUS study 15.1
Petra, Jordan—Human Impacts on an Ancient City in an Arid Land
By Tom Paradise, University of Arkansas

Most major cities in the ancient world developed near rivers. Petra, Jordan, in the Middle East is an exception. Petra lies at the western edge of Jordan's Great Southern Desert. Set in a crescent-shaped valley bounded by high cliffs and active faults, the city is known for its ancient tombs, buildings, and monuments carved directly into sandstone cliffs. The regional climate varies between hot desert and hot steppe, with hot and dry conditions in the summer and a slight peak in precipitation in winter. Occupied by the Nabateans between about 400 b.c.e. and 100 c.e., Petra was the capital city of the Nabatean Kingdom, which numbered an estimated 50,000 people at its peak 2000 years ago (**Figure 15.1.1**). Petra is today a major tourist destination, where increasing human impacts are affecting the ancient sandstone structures.

From Trade to Tourism

At its peak, Petra was a major urban center that linked the north–south caravan routes of nomadic traders with the east–west Silk Routes that connected Asia to the Mediterranean seaports. Petra prospered at the crossroads of these trade routes. In 106 c.e., the Roman Empire annexed the Nabatean Kingdom, but Petra continued to thrive with expanded trade. Millennia later, in 1985, the United Nations designated Petra a World Heritage site, and the city garnered new attention as a tourist destination.

Water Resources at Petra

A large population center in an arid climate can only prosper through innovative and widespread water resource management. In a region that receives roughly 100–150 mm (4–6 in.) of rainfall each year, precipitation arrives in infrequent torrents throughout the wet months from November to March. The Nabataeans, and later the Romans, harnessed overland flow using an elaborately engineered water diversion network that included 36 dams and more than 125 miles of water pipes and channels. Recent mapping of this water storage and delivery system showed that it extended throughout Petra's valley.

Sandstone Weathering and Tourism Impacts

Over time, earthquakes and floods have damaged Petra's structures, eroding stone columns and causing structural collapse. Weathering has worn away the original sandstone façades (the exterior front of the buildings) and other surfaces, mainly through mechanical processes such as thermal expansion (the expansion and contraction of rock surfaces throughout the day).

Today, human impacts are accelerating these natural weathering processes. Since the 1989 blockbuster film, *Indiana Jones and the Last Crusade*, which included scenes filmed at Petra, the number of tourists viewing the city's ancient architecture has increased to more than 500,000 each year. This increase led to environmental changes and further degradation of rock building façades. Research in the 1990s indicated that visitor foot traffic caused the hewn sandstone steps of Petra's Theater to recede, crack, flake, and break (**Figure 15.1.2**). In parts of the Theater, the deterioration from human impacts during the 20th century was greater than from natural processes over the past 2000 years.

The rise in tourism—up to 4000 visitors daily during the peak seasons of spring and fall—also increased humidity within the interiors of the sandstone tombs. This change in humidity increases the cycles of wetting and drying, which accelerates rock weathering. Throughout the day, 20 to 30 people may be waiting to enter the two most popular tombs—the Khazneh, or Treasury, and the Urn Tomb. On these busy days, interior humidity increases 20%–40% due to human respiration and perspiration. Studies show that in the Khazneh, tour groups exceeding 30–40 visitors at a time increased the relative humidity by roughly 30% (**Figure 15.1.3**).

◀**Figure 15.1.1 Petra's 2000-year-old city center.** This view looks east from the Colonnade Road toward Petra's Royal Tombs. [Tom Paradise.]

Architectural Preservation

Scientific research led to tourism management strategies designed to preserve Petra's stone architecture. For example, weathering research prompted the Jordanian government to prohibit walking across the benches and steps of the Theater. The government also now prohibits visitors from entering the Khazneh (with a smaller interior volume of 2000 m²), although visitation is still allowed inside the Urn Tomb (with the larger chamber volume of 3600 m²).

1. How has natural weathering affected Petra's ancient stone architecture?

2. How has the growth in tourism affected Petra's structures, and what is being done to preserve them?

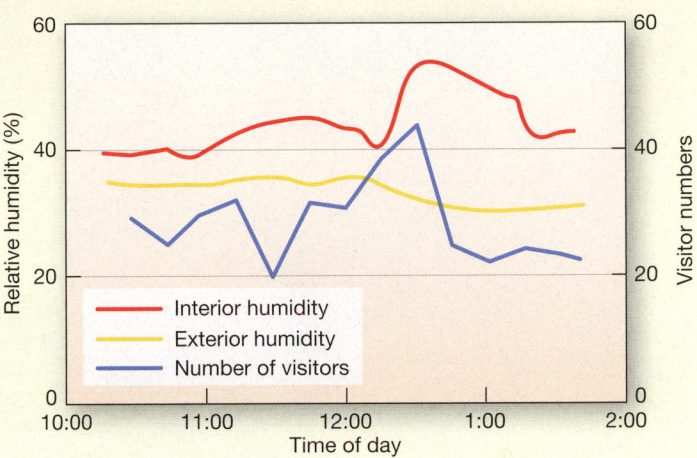

(a) Graph shows the changes in relative humidity in relation to the number of visitors during the day inside the chambers of the Khazneh.

◄**Figure 15.1.3**
Changes in relative humidity and numbers of visitors inside Al Khazneh (the Treasury) at Petra. [Tom Paradise.]

▲**Figure 15.1.2 The Theater at Petra.** Hewn directly from the sandstone, the Theater could accommodate 6000–8000 people. Note the fault scarp visible in the right-hand side of the theater seats. [Tom Paradise.]

(b) Entering the Khazneh chambers is now prohibited due to the effects of increased humidity on sandstone weathering within the tomb.

APPLYconcepts The graph in Figure 15.1.3a shows the relationship between three variables that affect weathering inside monuments at Petra.

Describe the daily pattern of change in each variable:	a. _____	b. _____	c. _____
If the number of visitors to the monuments is reduced, how will the other two variables change?			
The text describes another variable, not shown on the graph, that affects weathering inside the monuments. Identify the variable and explain why it is important.			

▲**Figure 15.25 Mesa and buttes, Arizona.** At the base of a butte, talus accumulates on the gentle slopes of less resistant shale. [Fred Bahurlet/EyeEm/Getty Images.]

weathering by frost action and other processes involving water plays a larger role than wind.

On the Colorado Plateau in the U.S. Southwest, where sedimentary rock strata were uplifted hundreds of millions of years ago, the work of streams and weathering subsequently removed less resistant strata, carving the landscape into canyons, and eventually, mesas and buttes. This differential erosion produced **mesas**—flat-topped landforms with steep slopes on all sides that are elevated above the surrounding landscape—and **buttes**—smaller steep-sided landforms that form from the weathering and mass wasting of mesas. Together, these features form mesa-and-butte topography; a spectacular example is Arizona's Monument Valley (**Figure 15.25**).

Mesas and Buttes As discussed in Chapter 13, differential weathering refers to the process whereby more resistant rock strata erode differently from less resistant strata. The horizontally layered strata of the Grand Canyon are an example; the cliffs represent rock that weathers relatively slowly (is more resistant) and the slopes represent rock that weathers relatively quickly (is less resistant).

In drylands, differential weathering often produces landforms, such as delicately balanced rocks, in which a more resistant cap rock protects supporting strata below (shown in Human Denominator 15b). In hot deserts with little rainfall, wind is the main agent of such erosion. However, in cold deserts and semiarid steppes,

Inselbergs An **inselberg** is an isolated remnant formed of resistant rock, a product of long-term weathering and erosion. Most inselbergs are composed of intrusive igneous granite, although they also form in sedimentary rock. Australia's best-known landmark is Uluru, also known as Ayers Rock, a sandstone inselberg (**Figure 15.26**). Inselbergs rise abruptly from a flat landscape and tend to be rounded, in contrast to the angular rock faces of many other isolated rock features formed by differential weathering processes. Inselbergs occur in the Basin and Range Province, rising above the alluvial sediments of a basin floor, as well as in many other desert locations (even in humid regions).

▲**Figure 15.26 An inselberg.** Uluru, also known as Ayer's Rock, in central Australia is a steep-sided sandstone inselberg—about 3.5 km long and 1.9 km (1.2 mi) wide—that has cultural significance for the Aboriginal peoples. [Thierry Grun- Aero/Alamy.]

EOLIAN PROCESSES AND DESERTS IMPACT HUMANS

- Dust storms create hazards in developed areas.
- Dune migration affects human developments and agriculture.

HUMANS IMPACT EOLIAN PROCESSES AND DESERTS

- Poor land-use practices are combining with changing climate to cause desertification.
- Humans accelerate weathering processes on stone monuments.
- Human development and water diversions combine with natural processes to cause shrinking of desert lakes.

15a

Adventure travel is a growing industry in the deserts of some developing countries, as shown here in the Merzouga sand dunes of the western Sahara Desert in Morocco. Camel rides, hot air balloon trips, rock climbing, and jeep tours are just a few of the activities now offered to vising tourists. [Arco Images GmbH/Alamy.]

15b

In the eastern Sahara desert, visitors tour areas that feature the stark and fascinating landforms of eolian erosion, such as this pedestal rock. The pedestal was formed by eolian erosion of the softer strata below leaving the more resistant caprock above. [Mike P. Shepard/Alamy.]

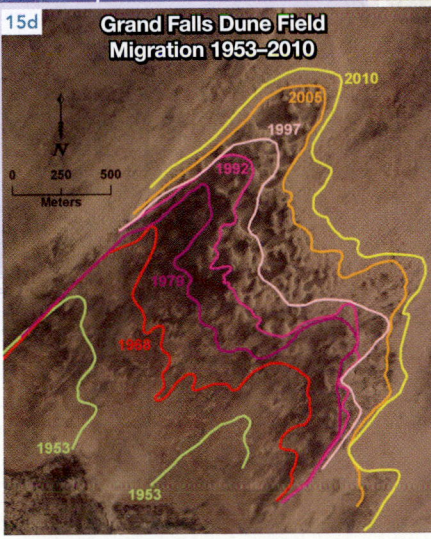

15d

Grand Falls Dune Field Migration 1953–2010

On Navajo Nation lands in the U.S Southwest, dune migration is threatening houses and transportation, and affecting human health. A recent USGS study revealed that the Grand Falls dune field in northeast Arizona increased 70% in areal extent from 1997 to 2007. The increasingly dry climate of this region has caused accelerated dune migration and reactivation of inactive dunes. See http://sgst.wr.usgs.gov/dunes/dune-migration-measures/.

15c

Dessication of the Aral Sea began when rivers were diverted to irrigate cotton fields. The shrinking lake has accelerated desertification in the Aral basin of Kazakhstan and Uzbekistan and affected local climate, now hotter in summer without the water's moderating influence. [NASA.]

ISSUES FOR THE 21ST CENTURY

- Efforts to curb desertification are needed to prevent declines in agricultural production on the margins of arid and semiarid lands.

QUESTIONS TO CONSIDER

1. What are some causes and effects of the recent shrinking of the Aral Sea?
2. What are three ways in which dune migration has adversely impacted the Navajo Nation?

KEY**Learning**concepts**review**

Describe eolian transport of dust and sand.

Wind, or **eolian** (p. 440), processes transport dust, silt, and sand by suspension, saltation, and surface creep. Wind exerts a drag or frictional pull on surface particles until they become airborne. The finer material suspended in a dust storm is lifted much higher than are the coarser particles of a sandstorm; only the finest dust particles travel significant distances. Saltating particles crash into other particles, knocking them both loose and forward. The motion of **surface creep** (p. 440) slides and rolls particles too large for saltation.

1. Explain the concept of surface creep.
2. What is the difference between eolian saltation and fluvial saltation?

Discuss eolian erosion and the resultant landforms.

Erosion of the ground surface from the lifting and removal of particles by wind is **deflation** (p. 441). Wherever wind encounters loose sediment, deflation may remove enough material to form depressions called *deflation hollows*, or *blowouts*, ranging in size from small indentations less than a meter wide up to areas hundreds of meters wide and many meters deep. **Abrasion** (p. 442) is the "sandblasting" of rock surfaces with particles captured in the air. Rocks that bear evidence of eolian abrasion are **ventifacts** (p. 442). On a larger scale, deflation and abrasion are capable of streamlining rock structures, leaving behind distinctive rock formations or elongated ridges called **yardangs** (p. 442). **Desert pavement** (p. 442) is the name for the hard, stony surface that forms in some deserts and protects underlying sediment from erosion.

3. What is deflation and what role does it have in the formation of desert pavement?
4. How are ventifacts and yardangs formed by wind processes?

Explain the formation of sand dunes and describe loess deposits and their origins.

Dunes (p. 444) are wind-sculpted accumulations of sand that form in arid and semiarid climates and along some coastlines where sand is available. An extensive area of dunes, such as that found in North Africa, is an **erg** (p. 444), or *sand sea*. When saltating sand grains encounter small patches of sand, kinetic energy is dissipated, and the grains start to build into a dune. As the height of the sand pile increases above 30 cm (12 in.), a steeply sloping *slip-face* on the lee side and characteristic dune features are formed. Dune forms are broadly classified as *crescentic*, *linear*, and *star*. **Barchan dunes** (p. 444) form with their tips pointing downwind, usually in areas with limited sand supply and little or no vegetation. **Star dunes** (p. 445) are the largest dunes, formed in areas with shifting wind directions.

Windblown **loess** (p. 448) consists of fine-grained clays and silts that are moved long distances by wind and are redeposited as an unstratified, homogeneous blanket of material. These windblown deposits occur worldwide and can develop into good agricultural soils.

5. Where does the sediment that forms the loess deposits of China come from? What is the origin of loess in the Palouse?

Discuss the causes and consequences of desertification.

The ongoing degradation of drylands caused by human activities and climate change is **desertification** (p. 450), a process that currently affects some 1.5 billion people. In some drylands, overgrazing is a primary cause, often in combination with socioeconomic factors. In other regions, overexploitation of water resources has combined with drought to cause desertification. With water diversions for agriculture and development, lakes are shrinking, leaving salt and dust that is moved by wind across the landscape.

6. What world regions are affected by desertification? What are the main causes and consequences of this problem?
7. Describe and explain the recent changes at Lake Urmia in Iran.

List some landforms unique to arid regions and explain their formation.

Along mountain fronts in drylands, **alluvial fans** (p. 453) develop where ephemeral stream channels exit from canyons into the valley below. A **bajada** (p. 453) may form where individual alluvial fans coalesce along a mountain block. Runoff may flow all the way to the valley floor, where it forms a **playa** (p. 453), a low, intermittently wet area in a region of internal drainage. **Badlands** (p. 453) are a rugged terrain of slopes dissected by rills and gullies, another example of the erosive work of water in arid and semiarid regions.

In the U.S. interior west, the **Basin and Range Province** (p. 454) is known for its north-and-south-trending basins and mountains—the basins are low-elevation areas that dip downward toward the center; the ranges are interconnected mountains of varying elevations above the basins. This region is an example of aligned pairs of normal faults and a distinctive horst-and-graben landscape.

Differential erosion can produce **mesas** (p. 458)—flat landforms with steep slopes on all sides that are elevated above the surrounding landscape—and **buttes** (p. 458)—smaller, steep-sided landforms that form from the weathering and mass wasting of mesas. Together, these features form the mesa-and-butte topography seen in parts of Arizona and Utah. An **inselberg** (p. 458) is an isolated remnant formed of resistant rock, a product of weathering and erosion.

8. What processes are involved in the formation of an alluvial fan? What is the arrangement, or sorting, of alluvial material on the fan?
9. Describe two landforms associated with basin and range topography.
10. What is the role of chemical weathering processes in arid environments?

GEO**SPATIAL** ANALYSIS

The Aral Sea

The Aral Sea was once the fourth largest lake in the world. Over the last several decades, the lake decreased in size by more than 80% and the Southern (larger) Aral Sea disappeared altogether. This disappearance had devastating effects on communities in the region.

Activities

Go to NASA's Earth Observatory site at http://earthobservatory .nasa.gov/, select the "World of Change" under Special Collections and select "Shrinking Aral Sea." As you step forward in time you see dramatic changes in the aerial extent of the Aral Sea.

1. When did the Aral Sea begin to shrink? What caused the Aral Sea to shrink?

2. How has the shrinking lake affected the quality of the water and farmland in the region?

3. How has the lake's loss affected local summer and winter temperatures?

Step forward in time to see changes in the Aral Sea. The green region is the lake and the white region around the lake is the result of salt deposits. You may also click on "Google Earth" to step through time using the slider and use the measuring tool to answer some of these questions.

4. What was the distance between the eastern edge of the Aral Sea in 1960 and the western edge of the Southern Aral Sea in 2000? Compared to 2005? Compared to the distance in 2010? And, in 2015?

5. What was the distance change between 2000 and 2005? Between 2005 and 2010? And, between 2005 and 2015? Does the rate of loss appear to be accelerating?

6. What is the average rate at which the Aral Sea has been shrinking since 2000? (Remember that rate of change is the distance change divided by the number of years.)

Examine the image of a dust storm at http://eoimages.gsfc.nasa. gov/images/imagerecords/19000/19853/aral_amo_2008120_lrg.jpg.

7. Compare this image to the Aral Sea images from NASA's Earth Observatory. Approximately when was the dust storm image taken (A range of a couple of years is fine)?

8. The winds in the image are blowing from which direction?

VISUAL ANALYSIS 15 PROCESSES ON AN ALLUVIAL FAN

1. Which process, wind or flowing water, is more important in shaping this landform?

2. Are the coarser (larger) materials on the alluvial fan deposited at the apex, near the mountain front, or in the middle and outer edges, known as the apron?

3. What is the source of the water used to irrigate the fields?

▶ This 2013 *Landsat-8* image shows an alluvial fan partially covered in agricultural fields in the Karakum Desert of Kazakhstan in Central Asia. [NASA/USGS.]

Mastering Geography™

Looking for additional review and test prep materials? Visit the Study Area in MasteringGeography™ to enhance your geographic literacy, spatial reasoning skills, and understanding of this chapter's content by accessing a variety of resources, including MapMaster™ interactive maps, videos, *Mobile Field Trips*, *Project Condor* Quadcopter Videos, *In the News* RSS feeds, flashcards, web links, self-study quizzes, and an eText version of *Geosystems*.

16 Oceans and Coastal Systems

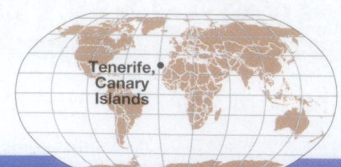

Waves break along the rugged Taganana coast near the village of Almáciga on the island of Tenerife, Canary Islands. Tenerife, the largest of the Canary Islands, is home to Teide volcano, Spain's highest mountain at 3718 m (12,198 ft) elevation as well as several black sand beaches. [Prisma Bildagentur AG/Alamy.]

KEY**LEARNING**concepts

After reading the chapter, you should be able to:

- **Describe** the chemical composition and physical structure of the ocean.

- **Identify** the components of the coastal environment and *explain* the actions of tides.

- **Describe** wave motion at sea and near shore and *explain* coastal straightening and coastal landforms.

- **Describe** barrier beaches and islands and their hazards as they relate to human settlement.

- **Describe** the nature of coral reefs and coastal wetlands and *assess* human impacts on these living systems.

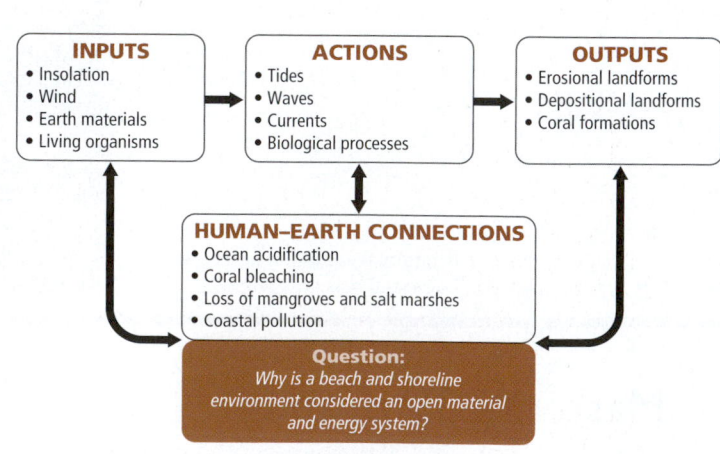

INPUTS
- Insolation
- Wind
- Earth materials
- Living organisms

ACTIONS
- Tides
- Waves
- Currents
- Biological processes

OUTPUTS
- Erosional landforms
- Depositional landforms
- Coral formations

HUMAN–EARTH CONNECTIONS
- Ocean acidification
- Coral bleaching
- Loss of mangroves and salt marshes
- Coastal pollution

Question:
Why is a beach and shoreline environment considered an open material and energy system?

GEOSYSTEMSnow

Coral Reefs in Decline

Threatened by climate change and other human activities, the health of Earth's coral reefs is declining. What is the problem, and how can we save these ecosystems?

What Are Corals, Exactly? Corals are simple marine animals (related to jellyfish and anemones) with a body consisting of a stomach with a single mouth opening surrounded by stinging tentacles. Each coral individual is a *polyp*, and most polyps live in groups of hundreds to hundreds of thousands of individuals that form a colony. Corals can be classified as "soft" corals or "hard" corals, and the latter are the corals that build reefs (**Figure GN 16.1**).

Hard corals secrete calcium carbonate ($CaCO_3$) from the lower half of their bodies, forming a hard, calcified external skeleton. Coral colonies can build enormous structures formed by the accumulation of these skeletons. Coral reefs form through many generations, with live corals near the ocean's surface building on the foundation of older coral skeletons below.

Reef-building corals are found in both warm and cold ocean environments. Cold-water corals occupy deep-ocean habitats, do not need sunlight for survival, and are widely distributed. Warm-water, or tropical, corals live in shallow water at temperatures from about 18°C to 29°C (64°F to 85°F) and are globally distributed from about 30° N to 30° S latitude. Tropical corals require clear, sediment-free water conditions and exist only at depths where sunlight is available.

Survival with an Essential Partner The secret of tropical coral survival is linked to *zooxanthellae*, tiny, plant-like, single-celled organisms that live within the coral tissues. Because warm-water corals cannot photosynthesize, they act as host for the photosynthesizing zooxanthellae, which provide the corals with up to 90% of their nutrition as well as their color. In return, corals provide zooxanthellae with shelter and certain nutrients.

This mutually beneficial relationship works successfully until corals become stressed, say, from a change in ocean temperature. Heat stress disrupts zooxanthellae function, causing toxins to enter the coral's tissue. The corals then destroy and expel the zooxanthellae, which ultimately causes corals to turn stark white in the process of *coral bleaching* (**Figure GN 16.2**). Without their partners, corals begin to starve. If the stress is short-lived (a few weeks), corals can reacquire zooxanthellae and recover. If the stress is prolonged, the corals die.

Tropical Corals: Importance and Threats Although they occupy less than 1% of the global ocean floor, coral reefs are habitat for more than 25% of marine life. They protect shorelines from the waves of tropical storms, provide food for millions of people, and are a focus of tourism, generating over $11 billion annually for nations with reef-formed coasts.

As sea-surface temperatures rise with climate change, corals are increasingly at risk of mass bleaching events, the bleaching of entire reef systems. The first global

▲**Figure GN 16.1** **Close-up view of hard coral and polyps, Uepi, Solomon Islands.** [cbpix/Alamy.]

mass bleaching event on record occurred in 1998, affecting about 30% of the world's reefs. A second occurred in 2010, and a third began in 2015, corresponding to increased sea-surface temperatures related to El Niño, and is ongoing. Corals can recover from mass bleaching, but only if conditions return to normal, and even then recovery can take decades or longer.

Rising ocean temperatures are not the only problem. Ocean acidification related to climate change threatens corals because lowered seawater pH inhibits the formation of calcium carbonate skeletons. Decreased sunlight affects tropical corals, and can occur when sea level rises or when sediment inputs increase (such as from coastal storms or agricultural runoff). Overfishing also impacts corals, damaging habitat and depleting species.

What can you do to slow coral reef decline? Lower your carbon footprint, reduce your use of garden and lawn chemicals, eat sustainable seafood, and volunteer for beach and waterway clean-up efforts.

1. What environmental conditions do tropical corals require to remain healthy?

2. How are human activities affecting tropical corals?

(a) Healthy reef, Fiji, 2011.

(b) Bleached reef, Maldives, 2016.

▲**Figure GN 16.2** **Healthy and bleached coral reefs.** [(a) Reinhard Dirscherl/Alamy. (b) The Ocean Agency/XL Catlin Seaview Survey.]

Earth's vast oceanic, atmospheric, and lithospheric systems reach a meeting point along seacoasts. At times, the ocean attacks the coast in a stormy rage of erosive power; at other times, the moist sea breeze, salty mist, and repetitive motion of the water are gentle and calming. Coastlines are areas of dynamic change and beauty.

Commerce and access to sea routes, fishing, and tourism prompt many people to settle near the ocean. In fact, about 40% of Earth's population lives within 100 km (62 mi) of an ocean coast. In the United States, about 53% of the people live in areas designated as *coastal* (this includes the Great Lakes). Globally, over 630 million people live in low-elevation coastal areas that are less than 30 m (98 ft) above sea level. This means that 1 in 10 people on Earth live in a zone that is highly vulnerable to tropical storm damage, flooding, and rising sea level (**Figure 16.1**). Given this population distribution, an understanding of coastal processes and landforms is important for planning and development.

Global Oceans and Seas

The oceans are one of Earth's last great scientific frontiers. Remote sensing from orbiting spacecraft and satellites, aircraft, surface vessels, and submersibles now provides a wealth of data and a new capability for understanding oceanic systems. Earlier chapters have touched on a number of topics related to oceans. We discussed sea-surface temperatures in Chapter 4 and ocean currents, both surface and deep, in Chapter 5. The National Ocean Service coordinates many scientific activities related to oceans; information is available at http://www.nos.noaa.gov/.

A *sea* is smaller than an ocean and tends to be associated with a landmass. **Figure 16.2** shows the world's principal oceans and seas. The term *sea* may also refer to a large, inland, salty body of water, such as the Black Sea in Europe. A *gulf* is a portion of an ocean or sea that is partially enclosed by land, such as the Gulf of Mexico and the Gulf of Alaska. A *strait* is a narrow waterway that connects two seas or other large water bodies; for example, the Strait of Magellan connects the Atlantic and Pacific Oceans at the tip of South America.

Properties of Seawater

As mentioned in Chapter 6, water dissolves many elements found in nature and is known as the "universal solvent." In fact, most natural elements and the compounds they form are found in the world's oceans and seas as dissolved solids, or *solutes*. Thus, seawater is a solution, and the concentration of dissolved solids in that solution

everyday GEO SYSTEMS

What are the visible effects of rising sea level?

The effects of rising sea level from climate change have become readily observable along U.S. coastlines. As high tides increase, nuisance flooding, also known as "sunny-day flooding," now occurs regularly in some regions, causing public inconvenience. In many communities along the Atlantic coastline, nuisance flooding inundates roads, swamps basements, and disrupts storm drainage systems. In Miami Beach, where nuisance flooding increased 400% from 2006 to 2016, city officials have implemented programs to install storm water pumps and raise road elevations, at a cost of $400 to $500 million.

◀**Figure 16.1 Nuisance flooding, Florida.** A street floods in Miami Beach in 2015 at high tide, an example of nuisance flooding from rising sea level along the U.S. East Coast. [Joe Raedle/Getty Images.]

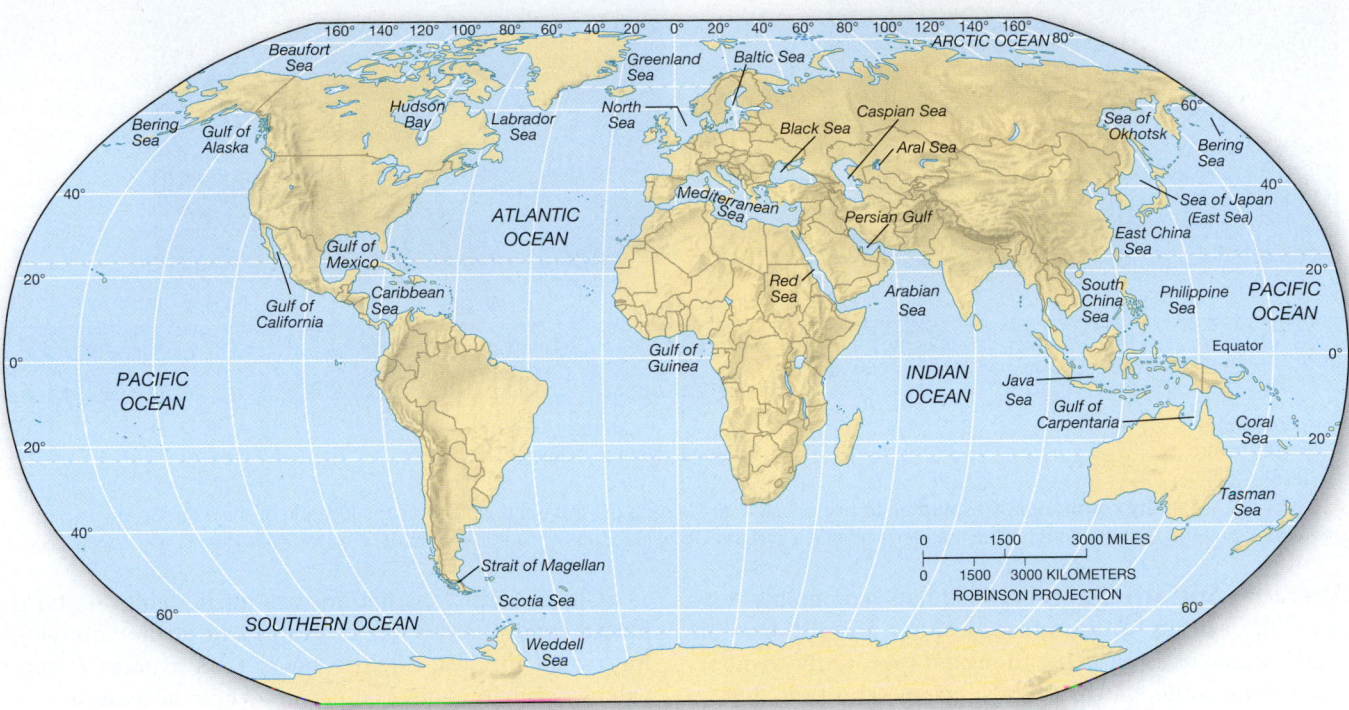

▲**Figure 16.2 Principal oceans and seas of the world.**

is known as **salinity**, commonly expressed as dissolved solids per volume. Although water moves continuously through the hydrologic cycle, driven by energy from the Sun, the dissolved solids remain in the ocean, left behind as water evaporates.

Chemical Composition Seawater has a mostly uniform chemical composition—the ratio of individual salts does not change, despite minor fluctuations in overall salinity. The atmosphere, minerals, bottom sediments, and living organisms affect the chemical composition of seawater. For example, the flows of mineral-rich water from hydrothermal (hot water) vents in

the ocean floor alter ocean chemistry in that area. However, the continuous mixing among the interconnected ocean basins keeps the overall chemical composition mostly uniform. Slight chemical variations in seawater have occurred over time. The variations are consistent with changes in seafloor spreading rates, volcanic activity, and sea level.

Six elements account for more than 99% of the dissolved solids in seawater (**Figure 16.3**). In solution, they take their ionic form. Seawater also contains dissolved gases (such as carbon dioxide, nitrogen, and oxygen), suspended and dissolved organic matter, and a multitude of trace elements.

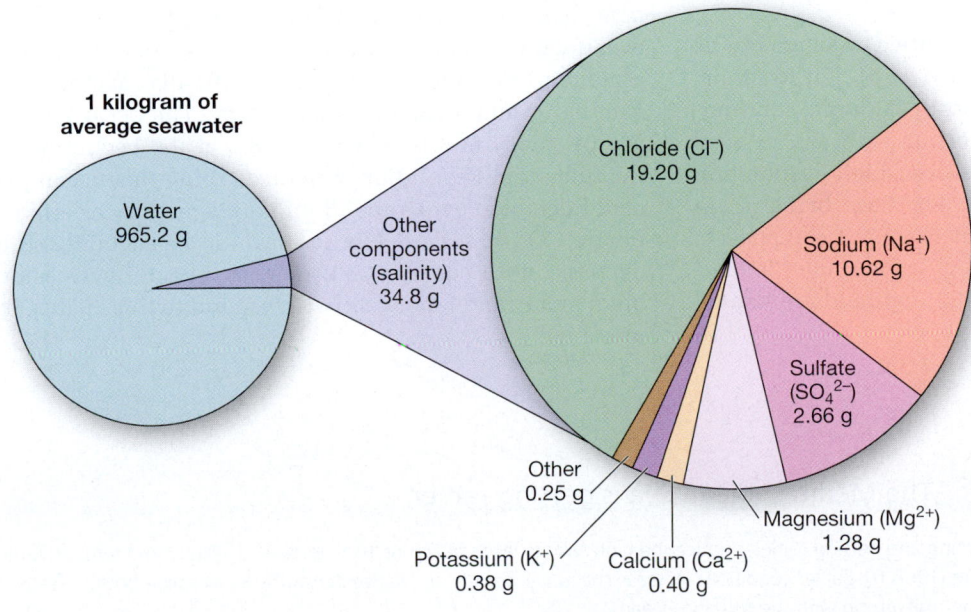

◄**Figure 16.3 Major dissolved components of seawater.** The major constituents in one kilogram of seawater with average salinity of 34.8 grams (35 ppt). The constituents are listed in grams/kilogram, which is equivalent to parts per thousand (ppt).

1 kilogram of average seawater

Water 965.2 g

Other components (salinity) 34.8 g

Chloride (Cl⁻) 19.20 g

Sodium (Na⁺) 10.62 g

Sulfate (SO₄²⁻) 2.66 g

Other 0.25 g

Potassium (K⁺) 0.38 g

Calcium (Ca²⁺) 0.40 g

Magnesium (Mg²⁺) 1.28 g

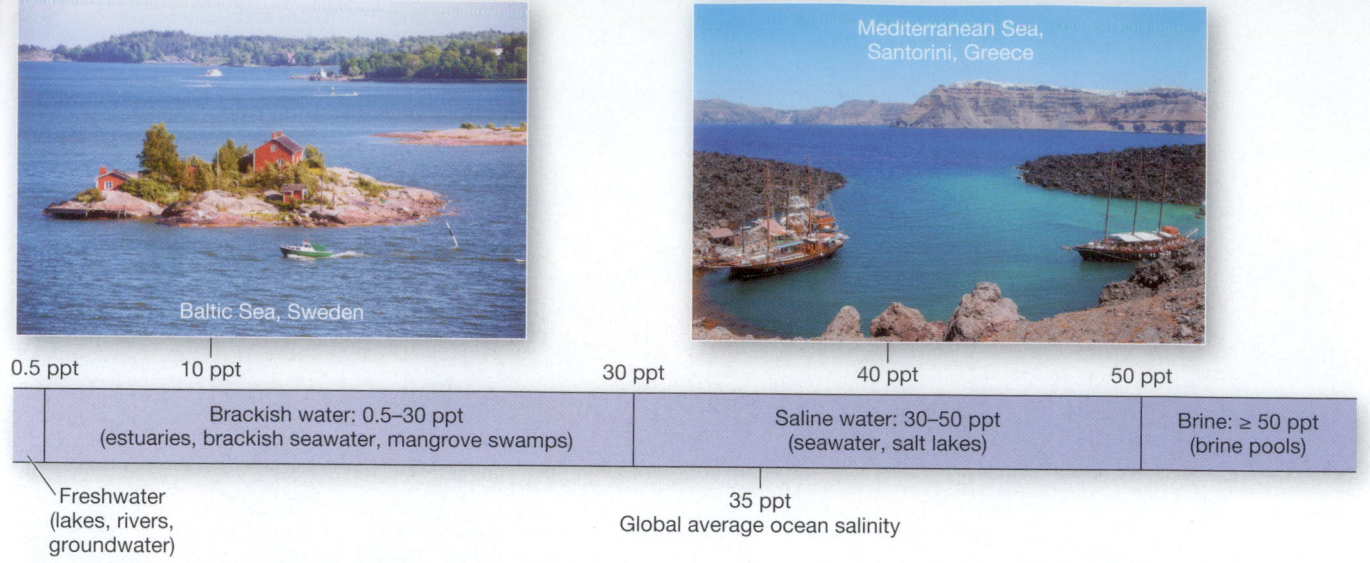

▲**Figure 16.4 Salinity continuum, freshwater to brine.** Values are in parts per thousand (ppt). Note the location of the Baltic Sea in Figure 16.2 and the salinity values for the Mediterranean Sea in Figure 16.5. [Sweden: Veronika Galkina/Fotolia. Greece: Mark and Anna Wison/Shutterstock.]

Average Surface Salinity Scientists commonly express the salinity of seawater as either a percentage of total volume or as parts per thousand (ppt, or the symbol ‰). For example, global average ocean salinity is 3.5%, meaning that seawater, on average, is 3.5% dissolved solids and 96.5% pure water. Alternatively, we can say that seawater has a salinity of 35 ppt (or 35‰). The advantage of using parts per thousand is that the value converts directly to grams per kilogram (g/km). Therefore, the global average ocean salinity of 35 ppt has 35 grams of salt for every kilogram of seawater (see Figure 16.3).

Globally, most seawater ranges in salinity between 30 and 40 ppt; however, the overall pattern of salinity is variable and includes values beyond this range. In general, oceans are lower in salinity near landmasses because of freshwater inputs. The term **brackish** applies to water that is less than 30 ppt salts (**Figure 16.4**). The Baltic Sea north of Poland and Germany is an extreme example, with an average salinity of about 10 ppt. This brackish water results from heavy freshwater runoff and low evaporation rates.

A number of regions in the Atlantic Ocean are on the high end of the global range (**Figure 16.5**). For example, the Sargasso Sea, within the North Atlantic subtropical gyre, averages 38 ppt. The Persian Gulf has an even higher salinity of 40 ppt as a result of high evaporation rates in a nearly enclosed basin. The term **brine** is applied to water that exceeds 50 ppt salinity. Deep pockets of water along the floor of the Red Sea and the Mediterranean Sea register up to a salty 225 ppt and are known as "brine pools" or "brine lakes."

Global salinity variations are attributable to atmospheric conditions above the water and to the volume of freshwater inflows. Slightly lower than average salinity values occur in equatorial oceans where annual precipitation is high (note the lower values in the Pacific Ocean along the Intertropical Convergence Zone in Figure 16.5). Slightly higher than average salinity values occur in subtropical oceans where high evaporation rates relate to the influence of hot, dry subtropical high-pressure cells. In these regions, salinity is presently increasing as rising temperatures lead to increased evaporation rates. Thus, salinity depends in part on temperature, which also varies with latitude over Earth's surface (**Figure 16.6**).

Ocean Acidification As discussed in Chapter 10, the oceans absorb excess carbon dioxide from the atmosphere as part of the global carbon cycle. As atmospheric CO_2 levels increase from human activities, excess CO_2 dissolves in the oceans, where it undergoes carbonation, forming carbonic acid. This is the process of *ocean acidification*—a lowering of the ocean pH. A more acid ocean causes certain marine organisms such as corals, plankton, and shellfish to have difficulty maintaining external calcium carbonate structures. The ocean's average pH today is 8.1, down from 8.2 at the beginning of the Industrial Revolution. Scientists think that ocean pH could decrease by 0.4 to 0.5 units this century as atmospheric CO_2 increases. The pH scale is logarithmic, so a decrease of 0.1 equals a 30% increase in acidity. Oceanic biodiversity and food webs will respond to this change in unknown ways.

GEOreport 16.1 The Mediterranean Sea is getting saltier

The Mediterranean Sea is warming and getting saltier—notice the high salinity levels in Figure 16.5. Increased salinity and temperatures are found in the deep layers, below 600 m (1968 ft). Saltier conditions increase the water density and cause net outflows of saline bottom water past the Strait of Gibraltar, thus limiting natural mixing with the Atlantic Ocean.

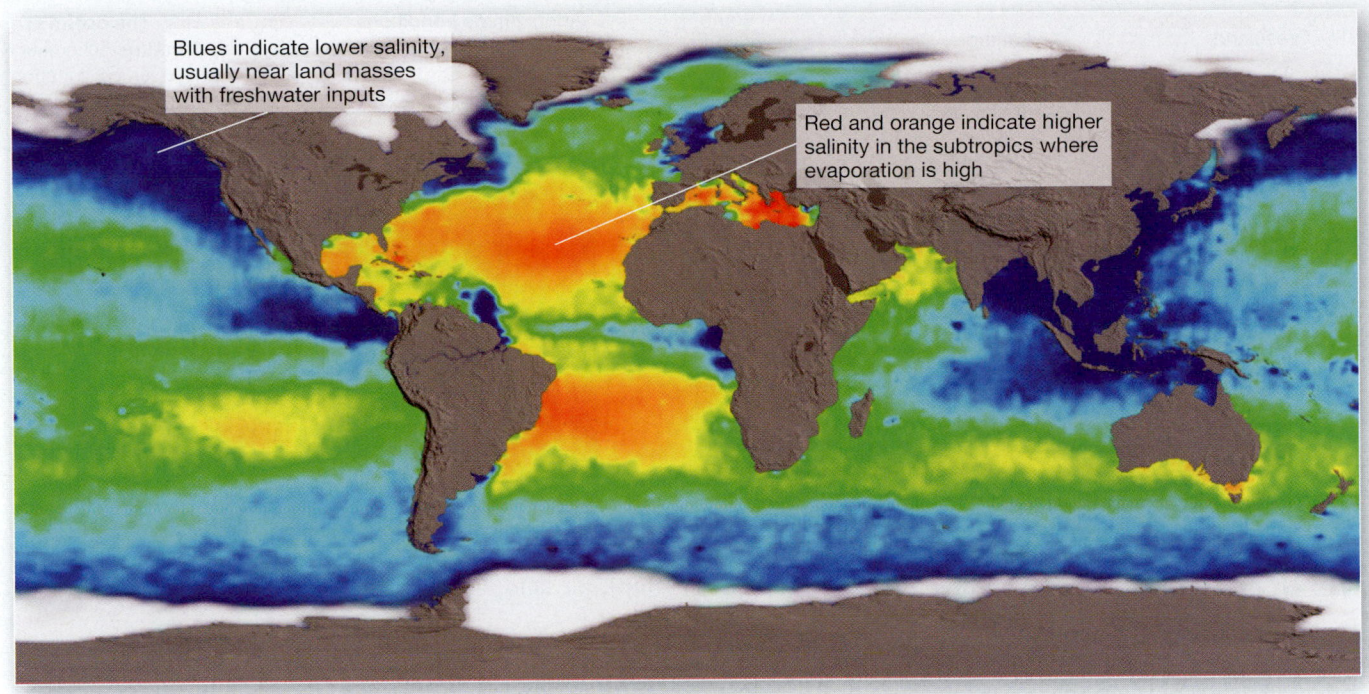

Blues indicate lower salinity, usually near land masses with freshwater inputs

Red and orange indicate higher salinity in the subtropics where evaporation is high

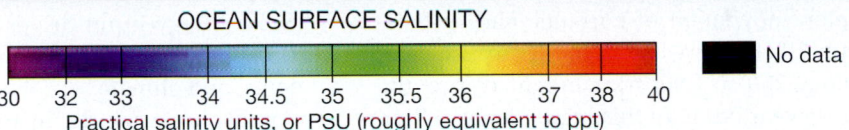

OCEAN SURFACE SALINITY

No data

30   32   33   34   34.5   35   35.5   36   37   38   40

Practical salinity units, or PSU (roughly equivalent to ppt)

▲**Figure 16.5 Ocean surface salinity.** Composite image of global ocean surface salinity from September 2011 to September 2014 using data from the *Aquarius* satellite (see http://aquarius.nasa.gov/). Scientists measure ocean salinity as PSU, practical salinity units, which are equivalent to grams per kilogram and ppt. [NASA.]

The presence of large amounts of runoff from land in far northern latitudes causes salinity to be lower there compared to equivalent latitudes in the Southern Hemisphere.

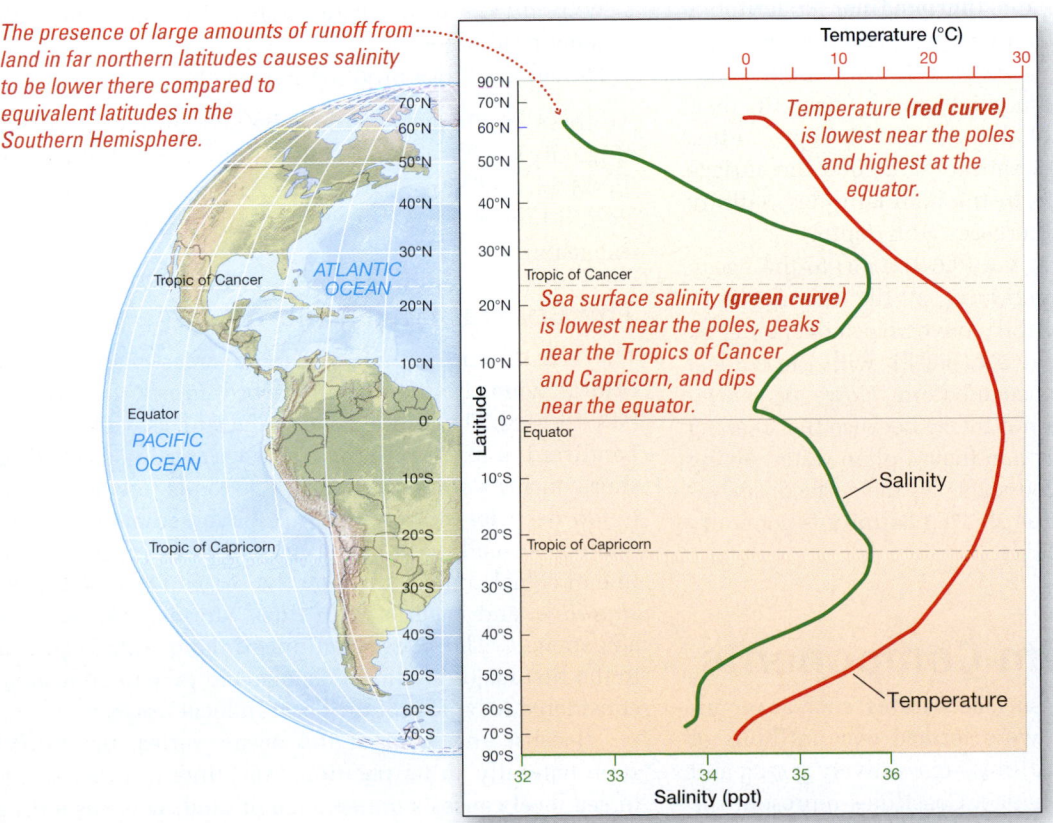

◄**Figure 16.6 Latitudinal variation of surface salinity and temperature.** Note the surface salinity is highest near the Tropics of Cancer and Capricorn. Temperature is highest in the equatorial region.

Temperature (°C)

0   10   20   30

*Temperature (**red curve**) is lowest near the poles and highest at the equator.*

Tropic of Cancer

*Sea surface salinity (**green curve**) is lowest near the poles, peaks near the Tropics of Cancer and Capricorn, and dips near the equator.*

Equator

Salinity

Tropic of Capricorn

Temperature

32   33   34   35   36

Salinity (ppt)

ATLANTIC OCEAN

Tropic of Cancer

Equator

PACIFIC OCEAN

Tropic of Capricorn

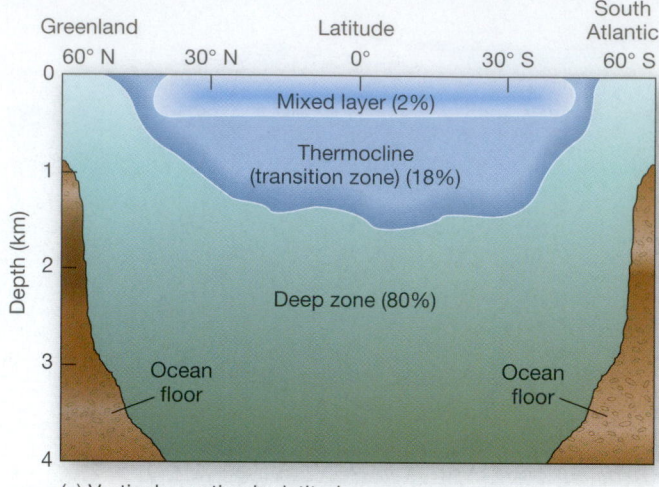

Greenland   Latitude   South Atlantic
60° N   30° N   0°   30° S   60° S

Mixed layer (2%)

Thermocline (transition zone) (18%)

Deep zone (80%)

Ocean floor   Ocean floor

(a) Vertical zonation by latitude.

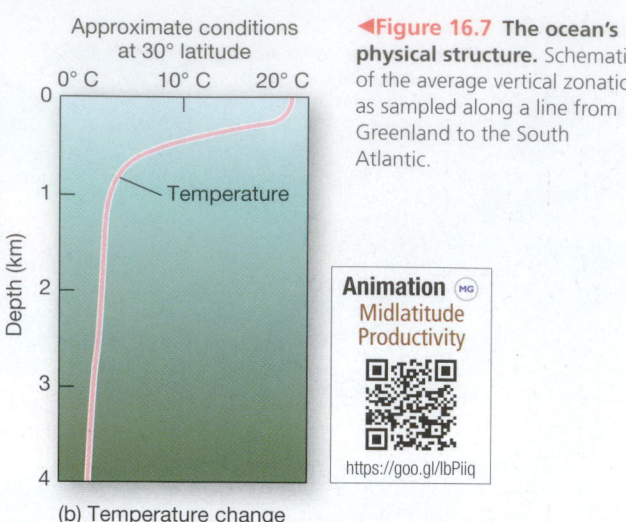

▲Figure 16.7 The ocean's physical structure. Schematic of the average vertical zonation as sampled along a line from Greenland to the South Atlantic.

Approximate conditions at 30° latitude
0° C   10° C   20° C

Temperature

Animation MG
Midlatitude Productivity

https://goo.gl/lbPiiq

(b) Temperature change with depth at 30° latitude.

Vertical Zonation

From the surface to the ocean floor, Earth's oceans vary in temperature, salinity, and density. The basic vertical zonation consists of three horizontal layers that affect mixing of seawater, movement of currents, and the distribution of marine life (**Figure 16.7a**). In the surface layer to a depth of about 300 m (984 ft), sunlight warms the water and winds drive mixing. In this *mixed layer*, which represents only 2% of the oceanic mass, water at different temperatures constantly mixes with solutes.

Below the mixed layer, to a depth of about 1000 m (3300 ft), is a zone that lacks the motion of the surface. Temperature changes rapidly with depth in this transitional layer, known as the **thermocline**. At latitudes lower than about 50° N and S, temperatures decrease along the thermocline (**Figure 16.7b**), but at higher latitudes, where sea-surface temperatures are lower, the thermocline is absent. Salinity also varies with depth in this layer. In the low latitudes, salinity is high at the surface and decreases with depth. In the high latitudes, salinity is low at the surface and increases with depth.

From a depth of 1–1.5 km (0.6–0.9 mi) to the ocean floor, colder water temperatures at the thermocline's lower margin tend to inhibit convective movements so that this *deep zone* is near 0°C (32°F), with the coldest water generally along the ocean bottom. However, seawater in the deep zone does not freeze because the freezing point of seawater is lower than that of plain water, owing to the presence of dissolved salts. (At the surface, seawater freezes at about −2°C, or 28.4°F.) Salinity is generally uniform throughout this layer.

Coastal System Components

Although many of Earth's surface features, such as mountains and crustal plates, were formed over millions of years, most of Earth's coastlines are relatively young and undergoing continuous change. Coastlines represent the interaction of processes in the atmosphere (driven by the Sun), on land, and in the oceans (driven by waves and tides).

Inputs to the coastal environment include many elements discussed in previous chapters:

- Solar energy input drives the atmosphere and the hydrosphere, including prevailing winds, weather systems, and climate.
- Atmospheric winds, in turn, generate ocean currents and waves, key inputs to the coastal environment.
- Climatic regimes, which result from insolation and moisture, strongly influence coastal geomorphic processes.
- Local rock types and coastal geomorphology combine with climate to determine rates of erosion and sediment production.
- Human activities produce coastal change.

All these inputs occur within the ever-present influence of gravity's pull—exerted not only by Earth, but also by the Moon and Sun—that produces the tides. A dynamic equilibrium among all these components produces coastline features.

The Coastal Environment

The coastal and shallow offshore areas make up the **littoral zone**, from the Latin word *litoris*, for "shore" (**Figure 16.8**). The littoral zone spans land as well as water. Landward, it extends to the highest waterline reached on shore during a storm. Seaward, it extends to where water is too deep for storm waves to move sediments on the seafloor—usually around 60 m, or 200 ft, in depth. The line of actual contact between the sea and the land is the *shoreline*, and it shifts with tides, storms, and sea-level adjustments. The *coast* continues inland from high tide to the first major landform change and may include areas considered to be part of the coast in local usage.

Because the level of the ocean varies, the littoral zone naturally shifts position from time to time. A rise in sea level causes submergence of land, whereas a drop in sea level exposes new coastal areas. In addition, uplift

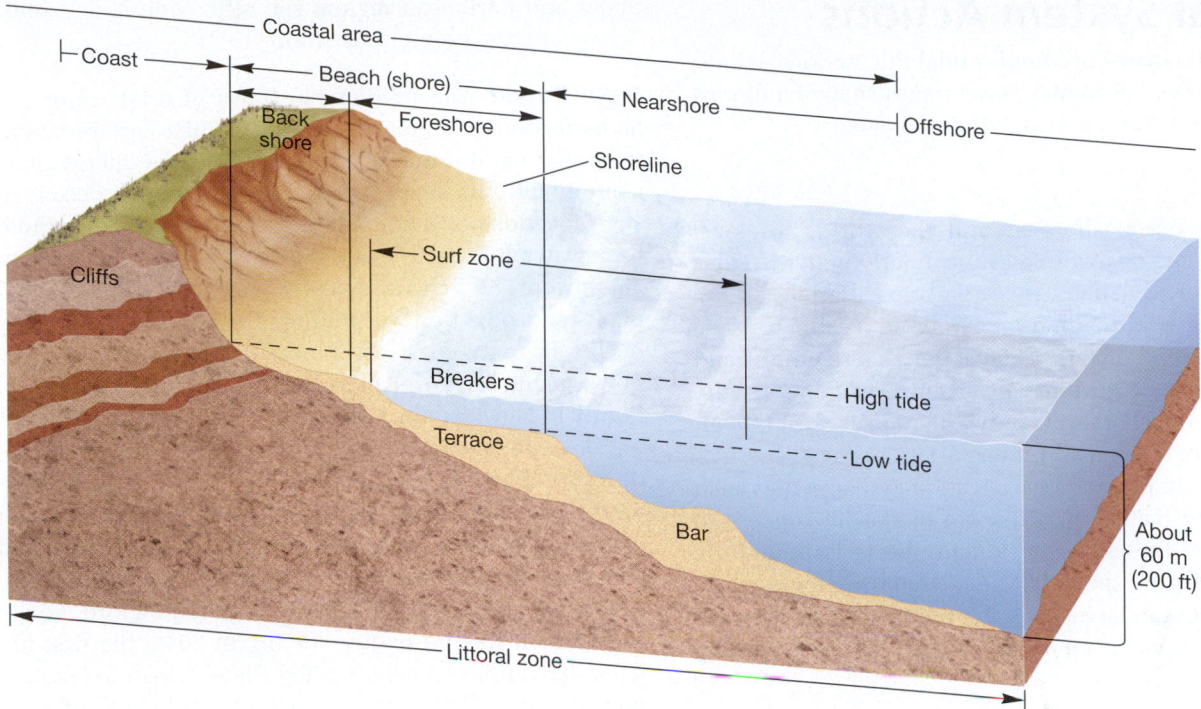

▲Figure 16.8 **The littoral zone.** The littoral zone spans the coast, beach, nearshore, and part of the offshore environment.

and subsidence of the land itself initiate changes in the littoral zone.

Sea Level

As discussed in Chapter 10, elevation on Earth is referenced to **mean sea level (MSL)**, a value based on average tidal levels recorded hourly at a given site over many years. At present, the overall U.S. MSL is calculated at approximately 40 locations along the coastal margins of the continent. At a given instant, sea level varies along the full extent of North American shorelines, as measured by the height of the water relative to a specific point on land. The lowest MSL in North America is along Florida's east coast. MSL along North America's Pacific coast averages about 66 cm (26 in.) higher than the Atlantic coast.

Changes in sea level occur naturally over a range of time scales, from hours (tides) to thousands or millions of years (tectonic activity and glaciation). In Chapter 8, we discussed *eustasy*, global sea level change caused by changes in the volume of water in the oceans. Long-term, climate-related changes in the amount of water bound up in glacial ice can cause eustatic changes in sea level, with sea level lower during cold climates and higher during warm climates.

Changes in sea level can also occur from human activities. Sea level is today rising as air and ocean temperatures rise with human-forced climate change. Both melting glacial ice and thermal expansion of seawater (volume expansion as seawater warms) are causing the current sea-level increase. This climate-related change is occurring over decades and centuries.

Sea level can also change due to land surface uplift or subsidence, which causes a relative change rather than an actual increase in ocean water amount. In southern Louisiana and other areas along the Atlantic Seaboard, the land surface is dropping owing to human activities, mainly the extraction of groundwater and fossil fuels and land compaction associated with agriculture and wetland drainage (**Figure 16.9**). For information and updates, see https://sealevel.nasa.gov/news-features/sea-level-news.

▲Figure 16.9 **Subsidence in southern Louisiana.** Seawater partially inundates a cemetery in Leeville in 2012, as subsidence worsens regional sea level rise. The cemetery's bricks and concrete date to the late 1800s and are now only accessible by boat. Storm surge from hurricanes make this region even more vulnerable. [Dave Martin/AP Photo.]

Coastal System Actions

The coast is the scene of complex tidal fluctuations, winds, waves, and ocean currents. These forces shape landforms and at the same time sustain living ecosystems.

Tides

Along every ocean shore around the world, sea level changes to some degree in a cyclical daily pattern. **Tides** are the complex, usually twice-daily oscillations in sea level, ranging worldwide from barely noticeable to a rise and fall of several meters. Tidal action is a relentless and energetic agent of geomorphic change, causing a daily migration of the shoreline landward and seaward that affects sediment erosion and transportation.

Tides are important for navigation and activities such as fishing and recreation. They are of special concern to ships because the entrance to many ports is limited by shallow water, and thus high tide is required for passage. Tides also occur in large lakes, but the tidal range is small. Lake Superior, for instance, has a tidal variation of only about 5 cm (2 in.).

Causes of Tides

The gravitational pull of both the Sun and the Moon produces tides, as illustrated in Geosystems in Action 16. *Gravity* is the force of attraction between two bodies, and the strength of this force depends on distance. The Sun's gravitational pull is only about half that of the Moon's because of the Sun's greater distance from Earth. Thus, *lunar tides* are stronger than *solar tides*. The result of these gravitational forces is a slight elongation or stretching, called a *tidal bulge*, of Earth's oceans. The elongation occurs on the side of the Earth facing the Moon due to the gravitational force, and on the opposite side of Earth due to the counterbalancing force of inertia (the tendency of moving objects to keep moving in a straight line). Earth's surface rotates into and out of the relatively "fixed" tidal bulges. Every 24 hours and 50 minutes, any given point on Earth rotates through two bulges. Thus, every day, most coastal locations experience two rising tides, known as **flood tides**, that reach a maximum height at **high tide**, and two falling tides, known as **ebb tides**, that reach a minimum height at **low tide**. The difference between consecutive high and low tides is the *tidal range*.

Geosystems in Action 16 illustrates tidal bulges as Earth changes position in relation to the Sun and Moon. The highest tidal ranges are *spring tides*, when the Earth, Sun, and Moon are aligned. The lowest tidal ranges are neap tides, which occur when the Earth–Moon alignment is at a 90° angle from the Earth–Sun alignment (Figure GIA 16.1).

Additional factors influencing tides—such as ocean-basin characteristics (size, depth, and topography), latitude, and shoreline shape—cause a great variety of tidal ranges. Some locations may experience almost no difference between high and low tides. The highest tides occur when open water is forced into partially enclosed gulfs or bays. The Bay of Fundy in Nova Scotia records the greatest tidal range on Earth, a difference of 16 m (52.5 ft; see Figure GIA 16.2). For tide predictions in the United States and Caribbean region, see http://tidesandcurrents.noaa.gov/tide_predictions.shtml.

Tidal Power

The predictable flows of tidal water can be harnessed to generate electricity under certain conditions. Bays and estuaries tend to focus tidal energy, concentrating it in a smaller area than in the open ocean. At such locations, a dam, called a *tidal barrage*, can hold back water at flood tide and release it at ebb tide to generate power. The first tidal power plant using this method of power production was built on the Rance River estuary on the Brittany coast of France in 1967. The first tidal power plant in North America, built in 1984 in the Bay of Fundy in Nova Scotia, Canada, also uses a tidal barrage.

A more sustainable method for tidal power generation that does not involve building a dam in a tidal estuary is the use of *tidal stream generators*, underwater turbines that are powered by the movement of flood and ebb tides to produce electricity. The first tidal stream generator was completed in 2007 at Strangford Lough in Northern Ireland (**Figure 16.10**). In 2013, the first underwater turbines in the United States began generating power near Eastport, Maine, at the mouth of the Bay of Fundy. The main limitation of tidal power is the tidal energy required; only about 30 locations in the world have the tidal energy needed to turn the turbines. However, this energy resource has huge potential in some regions.

Animation MG
Tidal Forces
https://goo.gl/d3LlhS

Animation MG
Monthly Tidal Cycles
https://goo.gl/40KFnP

▲**Figure 16.10** **Tidal power generation.** A turbine harnesses power from tidal currents at Strangford Lough, Northern Ireland. [Robert Harding/Alamy.]

T ides are the usually twice-daily oscillations in sea level that affect coastlines and human activities. Gravitational relations of the Sun, Moon, and Earth combine to produce the tidal range, consisting of spring tides and neap tides.

16.1ab SPRING TIDES

The average tidal range on Earth is slightly greater two times each month, just after a new moon and just after a full moon. These *spring tides* occur when the Earth, Sun, and Moon are in alignment (shown in GIA 16.1a and b). As coastal locations move through the elongated tidal bulges, they experience a maximum range between high and low tide—the highest high tide and the lowest low tide. (Used here, *spring* refers to the tide "springing forth.")

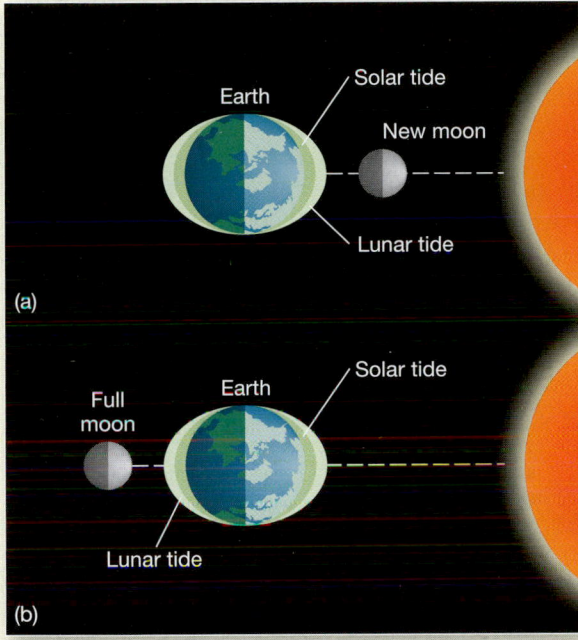

16.1cd NEAP TIDES

The tidal range on Earth is slightly less when the Moon is at first quarter or at third quarter, producing *neap tides*. (Neap means "without the power of advancing.") These tides occur when the Moon and Sun are not aligned, but are instead offset by about 90° (shown in GIA 16.1c and d). In this position, the gravitational influences of the Sun and Moon counteract each other, producing a minimum tidal range.

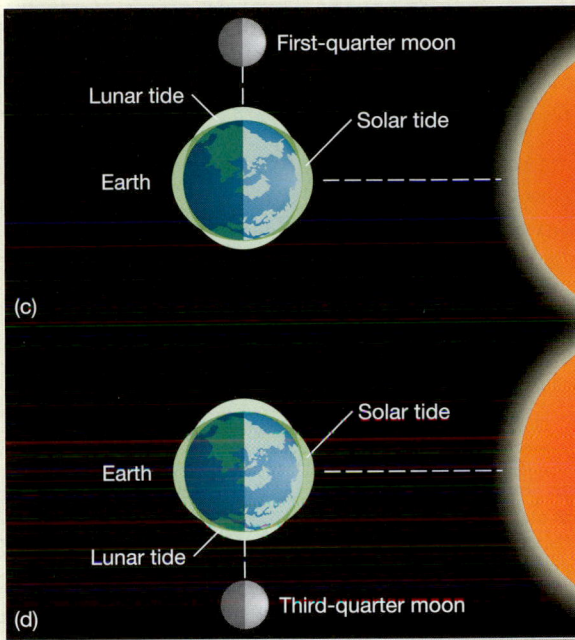

(Note that the tidal bulges are greatly exaggerated for illustration.)

16.2 TIDAL RANGE

Within the twice daily cycle, the maximum tide height is high tide (left) and the minimum tide height is low tide (right), shown here at Hall's Harbor, Nova Scotia, Canada, near the Bay of Fundy.

High tide

Low tide

MasteringGeography™

Visit the Study Area in MasteringGeography™ to explore tides.

Visualize: Study a geosciences animation of tides.

Assess: Demonstrate understanding of tides (if assigned by instructor).

GEOquiz

1. Identify: What is the force that causes tides?

2. Describe: Referring to the appropriate parts of GIA 16.1, state why there are two high tides per day.

3. Explain: Why are spring tides higher than neap tides?

4. Analyze: Viewed from a global perspective, does the tide rise because ocean water moves toward a coastline? Explain your answer.

Waves

Friction between moving air (wind) and the ocean surface generates undulations of water in **waves**, which travel in groups known as *wave trains*. Waves vary widely in scale: On a small scale, a moving boat creates a wake of small waves; at a larger scale, storms generate large wave trains. A stormy area at sea can be a generating region for large wave trains, which radiate outward in all directions.

Regular patterns of smooth, rounded waves, often in the open ocean, are **swells**. As these swells, and the energy they contain, leave the generating region, they can range from small ripples to very large, flat-crested waves. A wave leaving a deep-water generating region tends to extend its wavelength horizontally for many meters (wavelength is the distance between corresponding points on any two successive waves).

Wave Energy Wave movement in open water suggests to an observer that the water is migrating in the direction of wave travel, but only a slight amount of water is actually advancing. The wave energy moving through the flexible medium of water produces the appearance of movement. The water within a wave in the open ocean is transferring energy from molecule to molecule in simple cyclic undulations known as *waves of transition* (**Figure 16.11**). Individual water particles move forward only slightly, in a vertical pattern of circles.

As a deep-ocean wave approaches the shoreline and enters shallower water (10–20 m, or 30–65 ft), the orbiting water particles are vertically restricted, causing elliptical, flattened orbits of water particles to form near the bottom. This change from circular to elliptical orbits slows the entire wave, although more waves keep arriving. The result is closer-spaced waves, growing in height and steepness, with sharper wave crests. As the crest of each wave rises, its height exceeds its vertical stability at a certain point and the wave falls into a characteristic **breaker**, crashing onto the beach (Figure 16.11b).

In a breaker, the orbital motion of transition gives way to elliptical *waves of translation*, in which both energy and water move toward shore. The slope of the shore determines wave type. Plunging breakers indicate a steep bottom profile, whereas spilling breakers indicate a gentle, shallow bottom profile.

Animation MG
Wave Motion, Wave Refraction

https://goo.gl/RyROKB

▼**Figure 16.11 Wave formation and breakers.**
[(b) and (c) Bobbé Christopherson.]

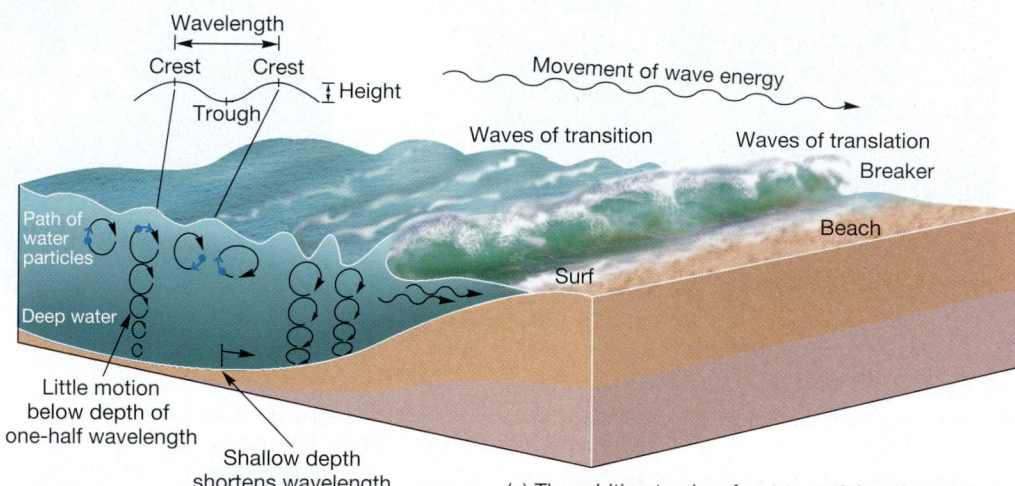

(a) The orbiting tracks of water particles change from circular motions and swells in deep water (waves of transition) to more eliptical orbits near the bottom in shallow water (waves of translation).

(b) Breakers along the coast of Baja California, Mexico.

(c) A dangerous rip current interrupts approaching breakers. Note the churned-up water where the rip current enters the surf.

(b) Headland

(c) Cove

(d) Lighthouse on headland bluff on Farne Island, England.

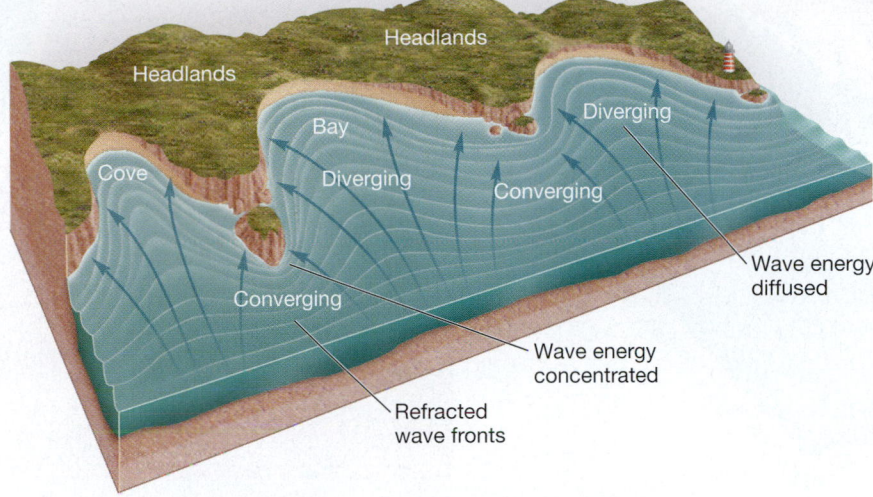

Headlands

Headlands

Cove

Bay

Diverging

Diverging

Converging

Converging

Wave energy diffused

Wave energy concentrated

Refracted wave fronts

(a) Wave energy is concentrated as it converges on headlands and is diffused as it diverges in coves and bays.

◀Figure 16.12 **Wave refraction and coastal straightening.** [(b)–(d) Bobbé Christopherson.]

Rip Currents A potential danger along shorelines is the *rip current* created when the backwash of water produced by breakers flows to the ocean from the beach in a concentrated column, usually at a right angle to the line of breakers (Figure 16.11c). A person caught in one of these can be swept offshore, but usually only a short distance. However, drownings in rip currents are a continuing threat; in Australia, rip currents were a factor in an average 21 deaths per year from 2004 to 2011, with 59% of these occurring on beaches patrolled by lifeguards. In the United States, rip currents played a role in 678 fatalities between 2002 and 2015 (see http://www.ripcurrents.noaa.gov/fatalities.shtml).

Rogue Waves As various wave trains move along in the open sea, they interact by *interference*. When these interfering waves are in alignment, or in phase, so that the crests and troughs from one wave train are in phase with those of another, the height of the waves becomes amplified, sometimes dramatically. For example, in 1933 a U.S. Navy tanker reported a wave in the north Pacific higher than its mainmast, at about 34 m (112 ft). Such amplified waves, called "killer," "sleeper," "rogue," or "sneaker" waves, have caused fatalities in several incidents. For example, on March 3, 2010, a large cruise ship in the western Mediterranean Sea, off the coast of Marseilles, France, was struck by three surprise waves about 7.9 m (26 ft) in height. Two passengers were killed and many injured as windows shattered and water flooded parts of the ship's interior.

Wave Refraction In general, wave action tends to straighten a coastline. Where waves approach an irregular coast, the submarine topography refracts, or bends, approaching waves around headlands, which are protruding landforms generally composed of resistant rocks (**Figure 16.12**). The refracted energy becomes focused around the headlands and dissipates in coves, bays, and the submerged coastal valleys between headlands. Thus, headlands receive the brunt of wave attack along a coastline. The result of **wave refraction** is a redistribution of wave energy, so that different sections of the coastline vary in erosion potential, with the long-term effect of straightening the coast.

GEOreport 16.2 Rogue waves overtake unsuspecting victims

Signs along portions of the California, Oregon, Washington, and British Columbia coastline warn beachgoers to watch for rogue waves. In November 2012 in northern California, three people were drowned in an incident that began when a family dog was carried away by a sleeper wave. A little over a month later, another person and her dog perished in Shelter Cove, California, victims of the same wave phenomenon. On Vancouver Island, British Columbia, an estimated 20 people have been killed by rogue waves since 1985.

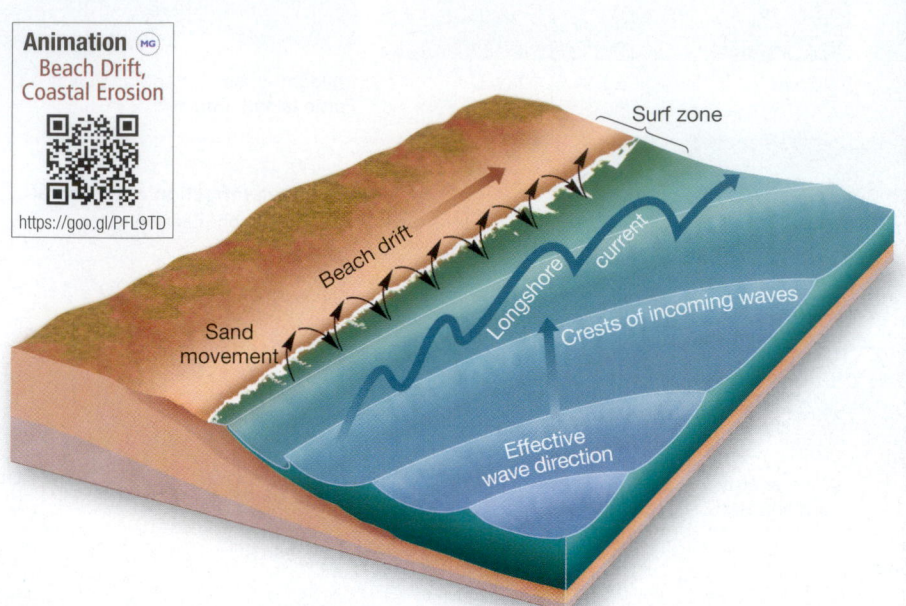

(a) Longshore currents are produced as waves approach the surf zone and shallower water. Beach drift results as substantial volumes of material are moved along the shore.

(b) Processes at work along Point Reyes Beach, Point Reyes National Seashore, California (aerial view to the south).

▲**Figure 16.13 Longshore current and beach drift.** [(b) Bobbé Christopherson.]

Waves usually approach the coast at a slight angle (**Figure 16.13**). In consequence, as the shoreline end of the wave enters shallow water and slows down, the portion of the wave in deeper water continues to move at a faster speed. The velocity difference refracts the wave, producing a current that flows parallel to the coast, zigzagging in the prevalent direction of the incoming waves. This **longshore current**, or *littoral current*, depends on wind direction and the resultant wave direction. A longshore current is generated only in the surf zone and works in combination with wave action to transport large amounts of sand, gravel, sediment, and debris along the shore. This process, called **beach drift**, moves particles along a beach with the longshore current by shifting them back and forth between water and land with each *swash* and *backwash* of surf. **Littoral drift** is the term for the combined actions of the longshore current and beach drift. The particles dislodged and transported by littoral drift can represent a significant volume of sediment that is eventually deposited in coves, inlets, and other low-energy areas along the coast.

Tsunami A series of waves generated by a large undersea disturbance is known as a **tsunami**, Japanese for "harbor wave" and named for the large size and devastating effects of the waves when their energy is focused in harbors. Often, tsunami are reported incorrectly as "tidal waves," but they have no relation to the tides. Sudden, sharp motions in the seafloor, caused by earthquakes, submarine landslides, eruptions of undersea volcanoes, or meteorite impacts in the ocean, produce tsunami. They are also known as *seismic sea waves* because about 80% of tsunami occur in the tectonically active region associated with the Pacific Ring of Fire. However, tsunami can also be caused by nonseismic events. Often, the first wave of a tsunami is the largest, fostering the misconception that a tsunami is a single wave. However, successive waves may be larger than the first wave, and tsunami danger may last for hours after the first wave's arrival.

Tsunami generally exceed 100 km (60 mi) in wavelength (crest to crest), but are only a meter (3 ft) or so in height. They travel at great speeds in deep-ocean water—velocities of 600–800 kmph (375–500 mph) are not uncommon—but often pass unnoticed on the open sea because their long wavelength makes the rise and fall of water hard to observe. As a tsunami approaches a coast, the increasingly shallow water forces the wavelength to shorten. As a result, the wave height may increase up to 15 m (50 ft) or more, potentially devastating a coastal area far beyond the tidal zone.

For Hawai'i and nations surrounding the Pacific, the Pacific Tsunami Warning Center (PTWC) issues tsunami warnings. Alaska and the U.S. West Coast rely on the West Coast/Alaska Tsunami Warning Center. These warning centers, and others throughout the world, use a network of 39 stations in the Pacific, Indian, and

Atlantic Oceans, part of the Deep-Ocean Assessment and Reporting of Tsunamis (DART) system. DART monitors tsunami wave heights as part of a global tsunami warning system developed by NOAA in the United States. The tsunami warning process begins when ocean-bottom sensors register a change in pressure associated with an ocean disturbance. Data then relays to surface buoys and then to regional warning centers, which issue bulletins to areas likely to be affected. The effectiveness of these warnings varies; for those closest to the undersea disturbance, even the most accurate warning cannot help when there are only minutes to reach safety.

The 2004 Indian Ocean Tsunami On December 26, 2004, the M 9.3 Sumatra–Andaman earthquake struck off the west coast of northern Sumatra along the subduc-

tion zone formed where the Indo-Australian plate moves beneath the Burma plate along the Sunda Trench. The earthquake caused the island of Sumatra to spring up about 13.7 m (45 ft) from its original elevation, triggering a massive tsunami that traveled across the Indian Ocean (**Figure 16.14**). Energy from the tsunami waves traveled around the world several times through the global ocean basins before dissipating.

The total human loss from the Indonesian quake and tsunami exceeded 150,000 people. This event prompted the United Nations to expand its tsunami warning system into the Indian Ocean and prompted the addition of 32 ocean stations as part of the DART system. (For NOAA's tsunami research program, see http://nctr.pmel.noaa.gov/.)

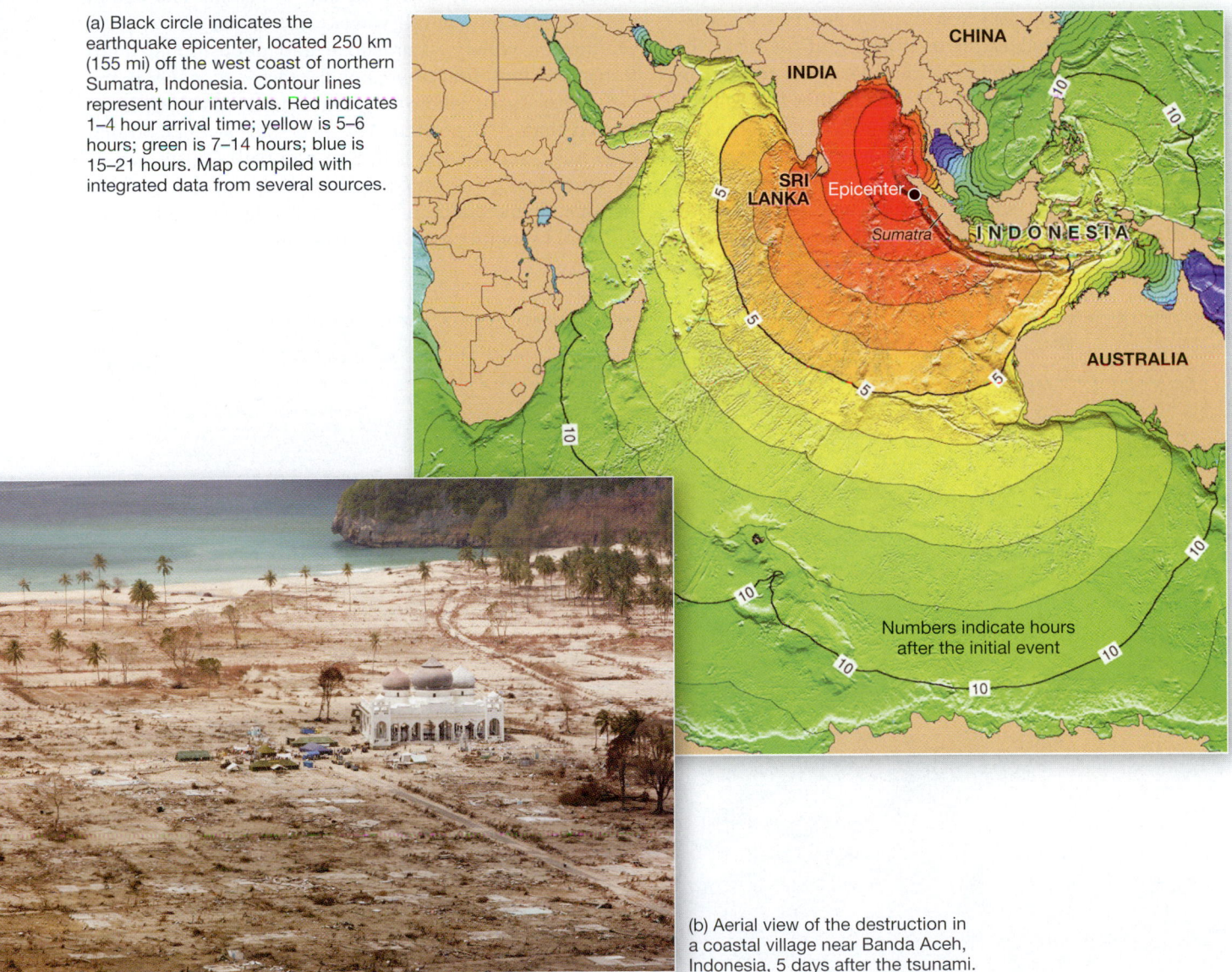

(a) Black circle indicates the earthquake epicenter, located 250 km (155 mi) off the west coast of northern Sumatra, Indonesia. Contour lines represent hour intervals. Red indicates 1–4 hour arrival time; yellow is 5–6 hours; green is 7–14 hours; blue is 15–21 hours. Map compiled with integrated data from several sources.

Numbers indicate hours after the initial event

(b) Aerial view of the destruction in a coastal village near Banda Aceh, Indonesia, 5 days after the tsunami.

▲**Figure 16.14 Travel times for and damage from the 2004 Indian Ocean tsunami.** [(a) NOAA. (b) Greg Baker/AP Photo.]

The 2011 Japan Tsunami On March 11, 2011, the Tohoku earthquake in Japan triggered a tsunami that killed over 15,000 people. The first tsunami wave hit the northeastern coast of Honshu, the closest shoreline to the earthquake epicenter, 8 to 10 minutes after the quake. Tsunami wave heights averaged 10 m (33 ft) in some areas and reached 30 m (98 ft) in narrow harbors. At Ofunato, the tsunami traveled 3 km (1.8 miles) inland; in other areas, waves reached 10 km (6.2 miles) inland. Although seawalls and breakwaters designed for typhoon and tsunami waves guard about 40% of Japan's coastline, the deep coastal embayments worked to magnify the tsunami energy to the point that the walls offered little protection (**Figure 16.15**). In Kamaishi, the $1.5 billion tsunami seawall, anchored to the seafloor and extending 2 km (1.2 mi) in length, was breached by a 6.8-m (22-ft) wave, submerging the city center.

Japan's tsunami early warning system uses the seismic signals measured during the first minute of the earthquake as input for computer models designed to estimate the size of the tsunami wave. Moments after the Tohoku quake, the Japan Meteorological Agency (JMA) issued a tsunami warning that we now know was an underestimation of the actual wave size. The quake continued for over 2 minutes after the tsunami model calculations began, and during this time, the tsunami energy increased. JMA issued a corrected warning, but not until 20 minutes after the quake and too late for evacuation.

Nine minutes after the initial earthquake, the Pacific Tsunami Warning Center (PTWC) issued tsunami warnings to the Pacific islands and continents around the Pacific basin. Over the next hour, tsunami forecasts and warnings continued for the Pacific region as the tsunami moved across the ocean, its energy guided and deflected by seafloor topography. Nearly 12 hours after the Tohoku quake, waves 2.1 m (7 ft) high reached the northern and central California shorelines, causing several million dollars in damage to harbors, boats, and piers.

Coastal System Outputs

Coastlines are active, energetic places, with sediment being continuously delivered and removed. The action of tides, currents, wind, waves, and changing sea level produces a variety of erosional and depositional landforms. We look first at erosional coastlines, such as the U.S. West Coast, where in general more sediment is removed than is deposited. We then look at depositional coastlines, such as the U.S. East and Gulf Coasts, where in general more sediment is deposited, primarily from streams, than eroded. In this era of rising sea level, coastlines are becoming even more dynamic.

▲**Figure 16.15 Tsunami wave breaks over a seawall, Miyako, Japan.** A tsunami wave, triggered by the M 9.0 Tohoku earthquake of March 11, 2011, breaks over a protective wall onto the streets of Miyako, Iwate Prefecture, in northeastern Japan. Buildings, cars, houses, and victims were carried far inland. Miyako is about 120 km (75 mi) north of the quake epicenter. [Mainichi Shimbun/Reuters.]

Erosional Coasts

Areas where the land is typically rising in relation to sea level produce **erosional coastlines**, also called *emergent coastlines*, that are rugged, of high relief, and tectonically active (**Figure 16.16**). Uplift of these regions can result from tectonic plate movement or from changes in sea level related to glacial ice melt. The active margin of the Pacific Ocean along North and South America is a typical erosional coastline. Some of the landforms within this setting may be formed from depositional processes, despite the erosional nature of the overall landscape.

Sea cliffs are formed by the undercutting action of the sea. As indentations slowly grow at water level, a sea cliff becomes notched and eventually will collapse and retreat (Figure 16.16d). Other erosional forms that evolve along cliff-dominated coastlines include *sea caves* and *sea arches* (Figure 16.16a). As erosion continues, arches may collapse, leaving isolated *sea stacks* in the water (Figure 16.16c).

Wave action can cut a horizontal bench in the tidal zone, extending from the foot of a sea cliff out into the sea. Such a structure is a **wave-cut platform**, or *wave-cut terrace*. In places where the elevation of the land relative to sea level has changed over time, multiple platforms or terraces may rise like stair steps back from the coast; some terraces may be more than 370 m (1200 ft) above sea level. A tectonically active region, such as the California coast, has many examples of multiple wave-cut platforms, which at times can be unstable and prone to mass wasting (Figures 16.16b and e).

(a) Arch, Ascension Island, Atlantic Ocean.

(b) Wave-cut platform, Monterey County, California.

Former sea cliffs

Terrace

Wave-cut platform (terrace)

Sea arch

Sea cave

Sea cliff

Landslides

Notched cliff

Sea stack

(c) Stacks and headland, Gough Island, South Atlantic Ocean.

(d) Notched cliff, Bear Island, Barents Sea.

(e) Collapsing cliffs, California.

▲**Figure 16.16 Erosional coastal landforms.** [(a)–(e) Bobbé Christopherson.]

Depositional Coasts

The characteristic landforms of deposition, such as beaches and other sand deposits, generally occur along coastlines where relief is gentle and lots of sediment is available from river systems. **Depositional coastlines**, also known as *submergent coastlines*, occur in regions where the land is subsiding because of tectonic plate movement and long-term changes in sea level. Such is the case with the Atlantic and Gulf coastal plains of the United States, as well as along portions of the U.S. Pacific coast. Although the landforms are generally classified as depositional along such coastlines, erosional processes are also at work, especially during storms.

Figure 16.17 illustrates characteristic landforms deposited by waves and currents. **Barrier spits** consist of material deposited in a long ridge extending out from a coast, sometimes partially crossing and blocking the mouth of a bay. A classic barrier spit is Sandy Hook, New Jersey (south of New York City). Such barrier spit formations are also found at Point Reyes (Figure 16.19a) and Morro Bay (Figure 16.17b) in California.

If a spit grows to completely cut off the bay from the ocean, it becomes a **bay barrier**, or *baymouth bar*. Spits and barriers are made up of materials transported by littoral drift. For sediment to accumulate, offshore currents must be weak, since strong currents carry material away before it can be deposited. Bay barriers often surround an inland **lagoon**,

(a) The Limantour barrier spit nearly blocks the entrance to Drakes Estero, along Point Reyes.

(b) A barrier spit forms Morro Bay, with the sound opening to the sea near 178-m (584-ft) Morro Rock, a volcanic plug.

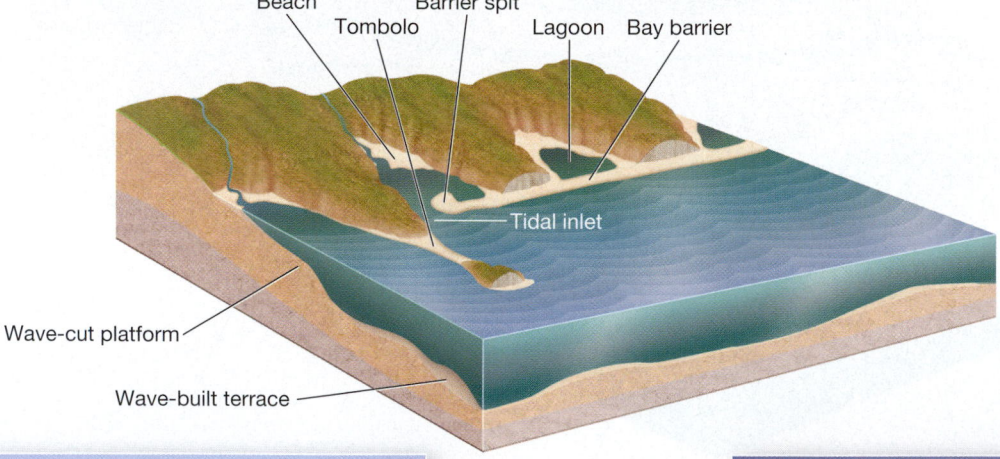

(c) A tombolo at Point Sur along the central California coast, where sediment deposits connect the shore with an island.

(d) A shell beach along the U.S. Atlantic coast.

▲**Figure 16.17** **Depositional coastal landforms: barrier spits, lagoons, tombolos, and beaches.** [(a)–(d) Bobbé Christopherson.]

a shallow saltwater body that is cut off from the ocean. A **tombolo** occurs when sediment deposits connect the shoreline with an offshore island or sea stack by accumulating on an underwater wave-built terrace (Figure 16.17c).

WORK**IT**OUT 16.1
Erosional and Depositional Coasts

Compare Figures 16.16 and 16.17 and the associated text as you answer the following questions.

1. What is the primary difference between an erosional coastline and a depositional coastline?
2. Along which type of coast would you expect to find a bay barrier? How does this feature form?
3. Along which coast would you expect to find cliffs?
4. Why does California's emergent coastline also feature bars and beaches in some areas?

Beaches Of all the depositional landforms along coastlines, beaches probably are the most familiar. Technically, a **beach** is the relatively narrow strip along a coast where sediment is reworked and deposited by waves and currents. The size and location of the beach zone varies greatly along individual shorelines. Sediment temporarily resides on the beach while in active transit along the shore. Beaches vary in type and permanence, especially along coastlines dominated by wave action.

Beaches occur along seacoasts, lakeshores, and rivers. Worldwide, quartz (SiO_2) dominates beach sands because it resists weathering and therefore remains after other minerals are removed. In volcanic areas, beaches are derived from wave-processed lava. Hawai'i and Iceland, for example, feature some black sand beaches. Beaches can also be made of *shingles* (beach gravel) and shells, among other materials (Figure 16.17d). Gravels reflect the contribution of stream sediments into coastal areas; shells reflect the contribution of materials from oceanic sources. Many beaches, such as those in southern France and western Italy, lack sand and are composed of pebbles and cobbles—a type of *shingle beach*. Some shores have no beaches at all, but are lined with boulders and cliffs. The coasts of Maine and portions of Canada's Atlantic Provinces are examples of rugged coasts composed of resistant granite rock with few beaches.

A beach acts to stabilize a shoreline by absorbing wave energy. Some beaches are stable; others have seasonal cycles of deposition, erosion, and redeposition. Many beaches accumulate during the summer; are moved offshore by winter storm waves, forming a submerged bar; and are redeposited onshore the following summer. Protected areas along a coastline tend to accumulate sediment, which can lead to large coastal sand dunes. Prevailing winds and storms often drag such coastal dunes inland, sometimes burying trees, highways, and housing developments.

Beach Protection Because changes in coastal sediment transport can disrupt human activities, people use various strategies to interrupt littoral drift (**Figure 16.18**). The goal is either to halt sand accumulation or to force a more desirable type of accumulation through construction of engineered structures, or "hard" shoreline protection. Common approaches include the building of *groins* to slow drift action along the coast, *jetties* to block material from harbor entrances, and *breakwaters* to create zones of still water near the coastline. However, interrupting the littoral drift disrupts the natural beach replenishment process and may lead to unwanted changes in sediment distribution in areas nearby. Careful planning and impact assessment should be part of any strategy for preserving or altering a beach.

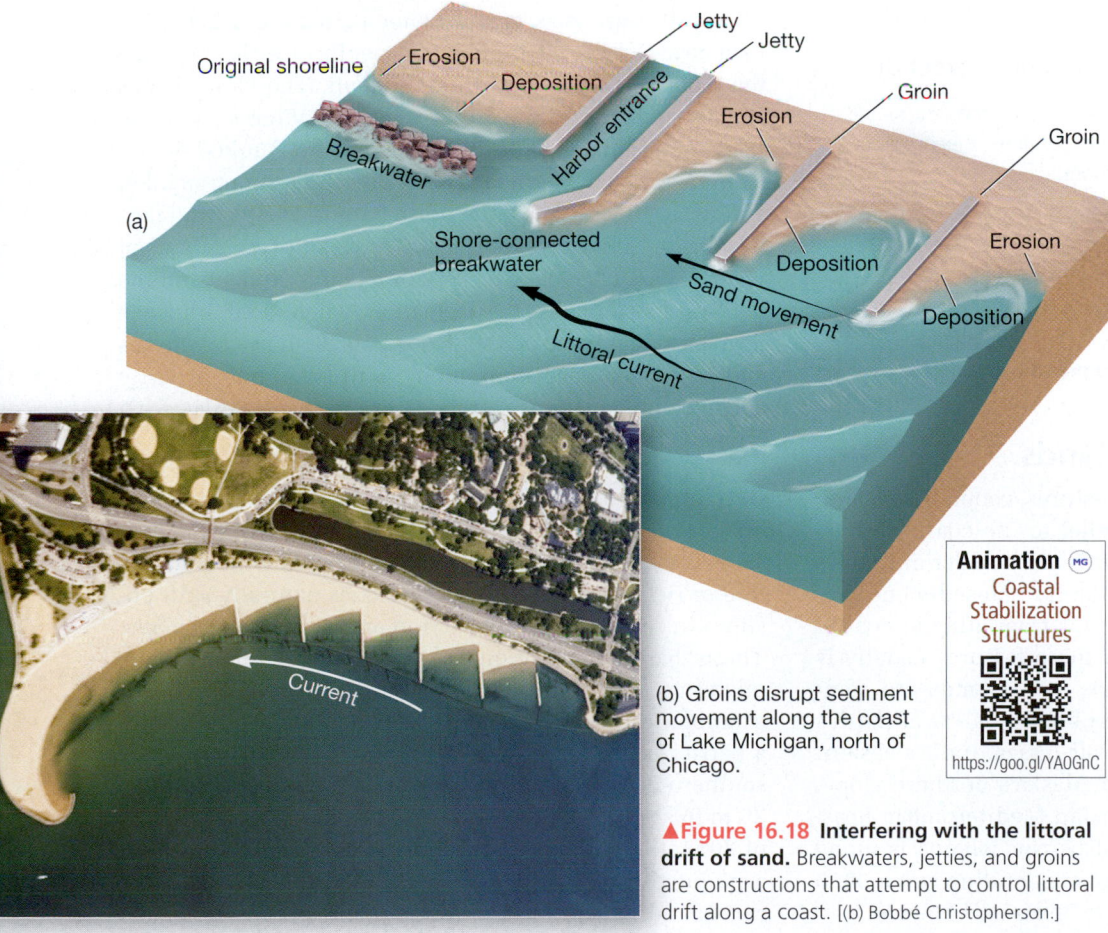

(a)

Animation (MG)
Coastal Stabilization Structures

https://goo.gl/YA0GnC

(b) Groins disrupt sediment movement along the coast of Lake Michigan, north of Chicago.

▲**Figure 16.18 Interfering with the littoral drift of sand.** Breakwaters, jetties, and groins are constructions that attempt to control littoral drift along a coast. [(b) Bobbé Christopherson.]

In contrast to "hard" protection, the hauling of sand to replenish a beach is considered "soft" shoreline protection, a category that includes nonstructural stabilization methods. *Beach nourishment* refers to the artificial replacement of sand along a beach. Theoretically, through such efforts, a beach that normally experiences a net loss of sediment will be fortified with new sand. However, years of human effort and expense to build beaches can be erased by a single storm. In addition, disruption of marine and littoral zone ecosystems may occur if the new sand does not physically and chemically match the existing sand.

In Florida, local, state, and federal agencies spend over $100 million annually on replenishment projects and manage over 200 miles of restored beaches. Until recently, sand was pumped from offshore onto the beach. However, over 30 years of dredging for sand has depleted offshore sand supplies, and now sand must be brought in from faraway source areas. In Virginia Beach, Virginia, a $9 million beach replenishment project in 2013 rebuilt a strip of sand for the 49th time since 1951. The Army Corps of Engineers, which typically executes such projects on the U.S. East Coast, states that beach replenishment saves money in the long run by preventing damage to coastal development. Others, including scientists and politicians, disagree. At present, the federal government pays for about 65% of all beach replenishment projects, with the remaining cost picked up by state and local communities.

▲**Figure 16.19 Barrier island chain along North Carolina coast.** The Outer Banks of North Carolina are presently designated as one of 10 national seashore reserves supervised by the National Park Service. [*Terra* MODIS, NASA/GSFC.]

WORK**IT**OUT 16.2
Hard versus Soft Shoreline Protection

Consider "hard" (structural, such as sea walls and jetties) and "soft" (nonstructural, such as organic plantings or beach nourishment) shoreline stabilization methods.

1. In what type of coastal environment is hard protection appropriate?
2. Which method requires more long-term maintenance?
3. What are some drawbacks and benefits of hard versus soft shoreline stabilization?

Barrier Beaches and Islands

The long, narrow depositional features, generally of sand, that form offshore roughly parallel to the coast are **barrier beaches**. When these features are broader and more extensive, they form **barrier islands**. The sediment supplied to these beaches often comes from alluvial coastal plains, and tidal variation near these features usually is moderate to low. Barrier beaches and islands are common worldwide, lying offshore of nearly 10% of Earth's coastlines. Examples are found off Africa, India's eastern coast, Sri Lanka, Australia, and Alaska's northern slope, as well as offshore in the Baltic and Mediterranean Seas. Earth's most extensive chain of barrier islands is along the U.S. Atlantic and Gulf Coasts, extending some 5000 km (3100 mi) from Long Island to Texas and Mexico.

North Carolina's famed Outer Banks are a 200-mile-long string of barrier islands and peninsulas that separate the Atlantic Ocean from the mainland. The Outer Banks stretch southward from Virginia Beach, Virginia, to Cape Lookout, separated from the mainland by Pamlico Sound (*sound* is a general term for a body of water forming an inlet) and two other sounds to the north (**Figure 16.19**). Mud flats (also called tidal flats) and salt marshes (a type of coastal wetland) are characteristic low-relief environments on the landward side of a barrier formation, where tidal influence is greater than wave action. **Figure 16.20** shows landforms and associated vegetation, along with basic human usage and recommendations from a planning perspective, for a typical barrier island along the U.S. East Coast.

Barrier Island Processes Barrier islands may begin as offshore bars or low ridges of submerged sediment near shore and then gradually migrate landward with wave action or rising sea level. Barrier beaches naturally shift position in response to wave action and longshore currents. These "barrier" formations take the brunt of storm energy, migrating over time with erosion and redeposition. For example, during Hurricane Sandy in 2012, Fire Island, a barrier island and popular summer destination off the southern coast of Long Island, New York, expanded 19 to 25 m (65 to 85 ft) toward the mainland (**Figure 16.21**). As of 2013, the new inlet had allowed seawater to flush out a polluted section of Great South Bay; however, the barrier island breach makes the mainland more vulnerable

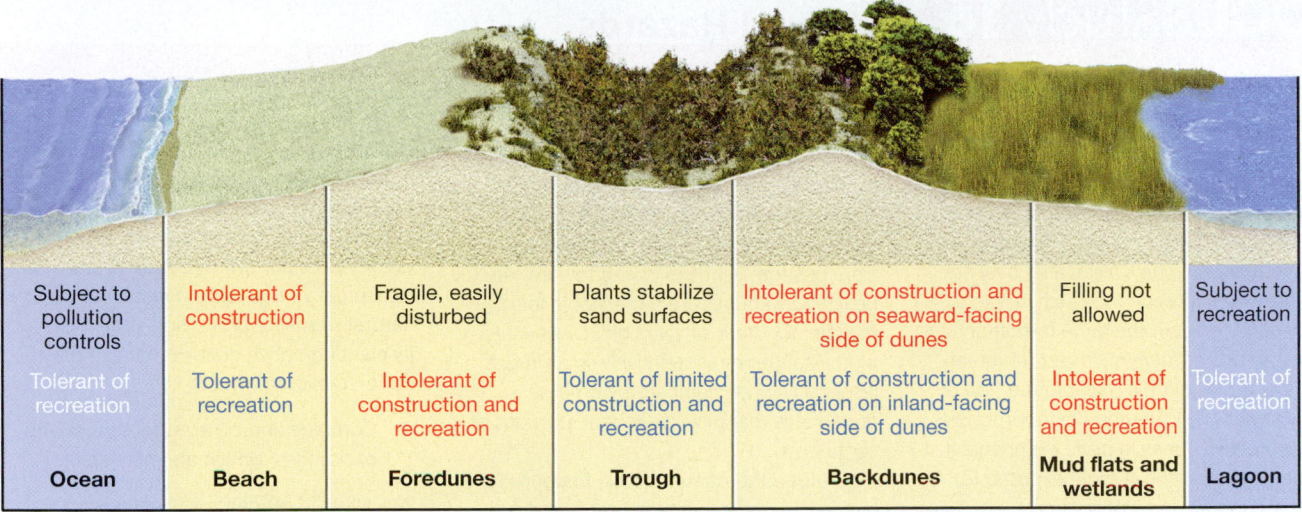

▲**Figure 16.20** **Barrier island landforms and ecosystems, with planning guidelines based on the New Jersey coastal environment.**
[Planning content after Ian McHarg, *Design with Nature*, Copyright © 1969.]

to the effects of future storms. The processes at work at Fire Island were typical of the effects of storms on barrier islands: erosion on the beach and foredune, deposition in the backdune area and in the lagoon, formation of new inlets, and a general shifting of the barrier formation toward shore in response to waves and storm surge.

Development on Barrier Islands Human-built structures on barrier islands are vulnerable to rearrangement

of coastal sediments by tropical storms and rising sea level. Hurricanes have altered barrier island geomorphology along the U.S. Gulf and Atlantic coastlines. The effects of hurricanes have also inflicted tremendous economic losses, human hardship, and fatalities on barrier islands, as proven again in the aftermath of Superstorm Sandy in 2012. Focus Study 16.1 examines one strategy for protecting shorelines from erosion and structural damage during large storm events.

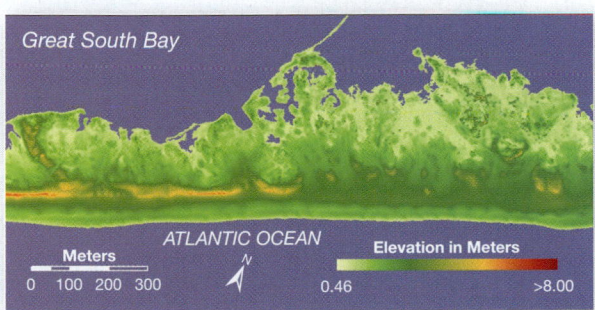

(a) Pre-Sandy LiDAR elevations along a narrow portion of the island.

(b) Post-Sandy LiDAR elevations, showing beach erosion through 4-m-high sand dunes, forming a new inlet.

(c) Changes in elevation related to Sandy. Red-orange colors indicate loss of sand; blue-green colors indicate sand accumulation caused by waves and surge.

Animation (MG)
Movement of a Barrier Island in Response to Rising Sea Level

https://goo.gl/FfuHs5

Video (MG)
Making of a Superstorm

https://goo.gl/BGHqL9

▲**Figure 16.21** **Coastal change at Fire Island National Seashore, New York, after Hurricane Sandy.** [(a)–(c) USGS.]

FOCUSStudy 16.1 Natural Hazards
Sand Dunes Protect Coastlines during Superstorm Sandy

During the winter of 2013, several months after Superstorm Sandy, many residents along New Jersey's coastline added their discarded Christmas trees to carefully stacked lines of trees acting as "seeds" for new sand dune formation along several area beaches. The trees were intended to catch wind-blown sand to begin the dune formation process in one of many such restoration efforts along the Atlantic coast. In the face of Sandy's winds, houses and neighborhoods with protective dunes in place experienced less damage than those more exposed to the ocean waves and storm surge.

Dune Protection versus Ocean Views

During Superstorm Sandy, local residents easily observed the effectiveness of dune systems as protection from wave erosion and storm surge. However, the fostering of large and sometimes obtrusive sand dunes near the shoreline is controversial in coastal communities with million-dollar homes. For such dunes to function as barriers to erosion, they must sit between oceanfront property and the sea, thus blocking ocean views and decreasing property values (**Figure 16.1.1**). For many landowners, establishing dunes for storm protection means financial loss in the short term, even if long-term protection is the result.

Coastal Dune Geomorphology

Coastal sand dunes consist of sediment supplied by the work of ocean waves and by fluvial processes that move sediment onto deltas and estuaries. Once sand is deposited on shore, wind processes rework the sand into the shape of dunes. Dunes along seacoasts are either *foredunes*, where sand is pushed up the seaward-facing slope, or *backdunes*, which form farther away from the beach and are protected from onshore winds (blowing toward the beach); backdunes are more stable and may be hundreds of years old. Most areas of coastal dunes are relatively small in size (especially when compared with desert dune fields that may cover large portions of continents).

Along the Atlantic coast, foredunes are moving inland as sea level rises and storm energy increases with climate change. In developed areas, this landward retreat of foredunes impinges on human development. When storms occur, dune movement intensifies, and either dune erosion or sand deposition, or both, occurs within the developed area of the coast (**Figure 16.1.2**).

Dune Restoration Efforts

The establishment of new foredunes replenishes the sand supply and protects structures and infrastructure, making this a worthwhile investment of money and effort for communities along the New Jersey shoreline. Many experts point out that dunes are *not* a guarantee of storm protection and that Sandy's winds and storm surge were strong enough to erode some large natural dune systems along the Atlantic Seaboard. However, in Bradley Beach, New Jersey, where the storm eroded several miles of restored dunes about 4.6 m (15 ft)

in height, the community still escaped excessive damage, since the dunes absorbed much of the storm's impact.

Today, many local communities and national organizations support dune restoration, as evidenced by the 2013 Christmas tree initiative and current initiatives using natural shoreline protection strategies, such as planting native grasses that can have dune-stabilizing effects.

1. Compare and contrast foredunes and backdunes. Which are more stable?

2. Why did residents of New Jersey's coastal communities stack Christmas trees along beaches during the winter following Superstorm Sandy?

APPLYconcepts Summarize the advantages and disadvantages of building new foredunes to reduce coastal erosion and property damage during storms.

| 1. Advantages: _____ |
| 2. Disadvantages: _____ |

▼Figure 16.1.1 **Constructed dunes.** Restored sand dunes shield homes in Mantoloking, New Jersey, from an incoming nor'easter a few weeks after Hurricane Sandy. [Sharon Karr/FEMA.]

May 21, 2009

November 5, 2012

▲Figure 16.1.2 **Coastal damage from Sandy in Mantoloking, New Jersey.** View looking west before and after Hurricane Sandy. The yellow arrow points to the same feature in each image. [USGS.]

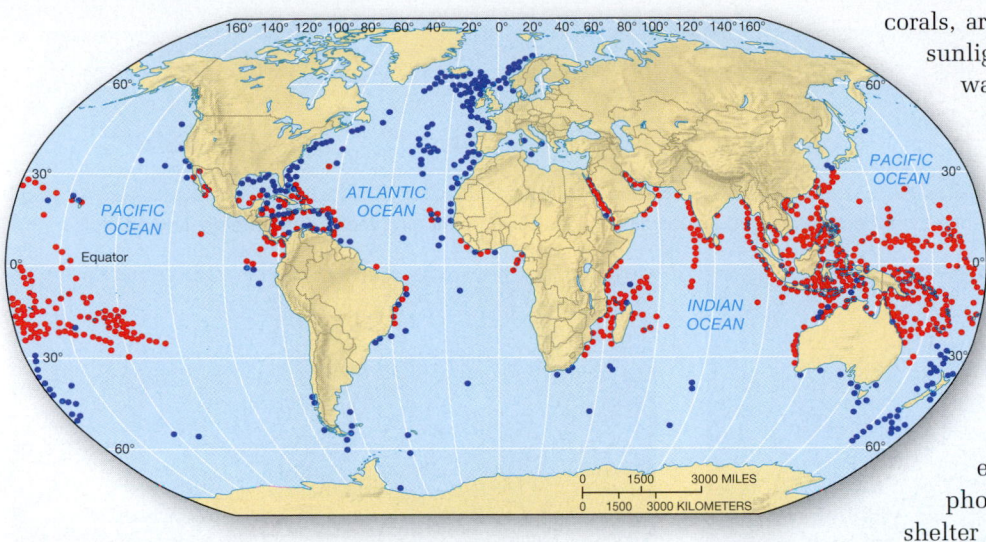

▲Figure 16.22 Worldwide distribution of warm-water and cold-water coral reefs. The red dots represent major warm-water coral reefs, which occur from about 30° N to 30° S latitude. Blue dots represent cold-water coral reefs and structures. [NOS/NOAA and UNEP.]

Coral Coasts

Not all coastlines form by purely physical processes. Some form as the result of biological processes, such as coral growth. As discussed in Geosystems Now, a **coral** is a simple marine invertebrate with a cylindrical, saclike body that includes a stomach with a single mouth opening.

Coral Types and Distribution Corals are either hard or soft, and live in either warm-water or cold-water environments. As discussed in Geosystems Now, *hard corals*, also called *stony corals*, are reef-building corals that secrete calcium carbonate ($CaCO_3$), forming a hard, calcified external skeleton. *Soft corals*, including sea fans and sea whips, have a woody core that supports their structure, but they do not generate a rock-like calcareous skeleton. Warm-water corals require temperatures between from about 18°C to 29°C (64°F to 85°F) and are distributed throughout tropical waters but not in areas with cold ocean currents (**Figure 16.22**). Cold-water corals, also called deep-sea

corals, are reef-building but do not need sunlight for survival. They can live in water temperatures as cold as 4°C (39°F) and at depths to 2000 m (6562 ft).

Warm-water, or tropical, corals live together with single-celled zooxanthellae in a *symbiotic relationship*, an overlapping arrangement in which each depends on the other for survival. Zooxanthellae provide corals with nutrition by converting solar energy to chemical energy during photosynthesis, and corals provide shelter and some nutrients in return. Changes in environmental conditions can cause corals to expel their symbiotic partners and turn white in the process of **coral bleaching**.

Threats to Coral Structures Climate change and other human activities threaten both warm-water and cold-water corals and their structures. Bleaching and reef deterioration can occur from local pollution, disease, sedimentation, changes in ocean salinity, and increasing oceanic acidity. Warm-water corals are most susceptible to warming of sea-surface temperatures, which is a greater threat than local pollution or other environmental problems. Cold-water corals are most susceptible to deep-sea trawling and ocean acidification from climate change, which has its greatest impacts at higher latitudes.

The 2015 El Niño in the Pacific combined with rising air and sea-surface temperatures from climate change to trigger a global mass bleaching event (**Figure 16.23**). Along Australia's Great Barrier Reef (GBR), the largest single living marine structure on Earth, bleaching has devastated corals, especially in the pristine northern region of the reef. In May 2016, Australians scientists estimated that 80% of coral in the northern GBR was bleached or dead. In the United States in 2016, an estimated 72% of reefs were in warm enough water to cause extreme stress. For more information, see http://coralreef.noaa.gov/.

POTENTIAL STRESS LEVEL: Watch   Warning   Alert Level 1   Alert Level 2

▲Figure 16.23 Potential for thermal stress that leads to coral bleaching. This NOAA outlook for early 2016 shows areas with 60% probability of thermal stress that causes bleaching. Alert Level 1 indicates that bleaching is likely; Alert Level 2 indicates that coral mortality is likely. [NOAA.]

(a) Common coral formations in a sequence of reef growth around a subsiding volcanic island: fringing reefs, barrier reefs, and an atoll.

(b) Barrier reef surrounds Bora Bora, Tahiti.

(c) Tikehau atoll, French Polynesia.

Animation (MG)
Seamounts &
Coral Reefs

https://goo.gl/cy1kiS

▲**Figure 16.24 Coral formations.** [(a) After D. R. Stoddart, *The Geographical Magazine* 63 (1971): 610. (b) Chad Ehlers/Getty Images. (c) Jacques Gillardi/Getty Images.]

Reef Formation and Types A **coral reef** is a ridge or mound of marine rock that forms over long time periods from the deposition of calcium carbonate by living organisms, mainly corals, but also other organisms such as algae and shellfish. Over time, the accumulated calcium carbonate skeletons become lithified into rock. *Coral reefs* form through many generations, with live corals near the ocean's surface building on the foundation of older coral skeletons that may rest on a feature built up from the ocean floor (such as a seamount). Thus, a coral reef is a biologically derived sedimentary rock that can assume one of several distinctive shapes.

In 1842, Charles Darwin proposed a hypothesis for reef formation. He suggested that, as reefs develop around a volcanic island and the island itself gradually subsides, equilibrium is maintained between the subsidence of the island and the upward growth of the corals (to keep the living corals at their optimum depth, not too far below the surface). This idea, generally accepted today, is portrayed in **Figure 16.24**. Note the specific examples of each reef stage: *fringing reefs* (platforms of surrounding coral rock), *barrier reefs* (reefs that enclose lagoons), and *atolls* (circular, ring-shaped reefs).

Earth's most extensive fringing reef is the Bahama Platform in the western Atlantic, covering some 96,000 km² (37,000 mi²). The Bahama archipelago is made up of two carbonate platforms consisting of shallow-water

limestone formations (**Figure 16.25**). The largest barrier reef, the Great Barrier Reef along the shore of the state of Queensland, Australia, exceeds 2025 km (1260 mi) in length, is 16–145 km (10–90 mi) wide, and includes at least 700 coral-formed islands and keys (coral islets or barrier islands).

▲**Figure 16.25 The Bahama Platform.** The Bahama archipelago is made up of two carbonate platforms consisting of shallow-water limestone formations (light blue colors). The slopes of the platforms reach depths of 4000 m (13,100 ft; darker blue colors). [*Terra* image, NASA/GSFC.]

▲**Figure 16.26 Mangrove forest, Thailand.** Corals, sponges, anemones, fish, and invertebrates live among the roots of some mangrove forests. Development and aquaculture such as shrimp farming are two of many threats to mangrove ecosystems. [Nature Capture Realfoto/Shutterstock.]

Coastal Wetlands

In some coastal areas, sediments are rich in organic matter, leading to lush plant growth and spawning grounds for fish, shellfish, and other organisms. A coastal marsh environment of this type provides optimal habitat for varied wildlife. Unfortunately, these wetland ecosystems are quite fragile and are threatened by human development.

As discussed in Chapter 8, wetlands are permanently or seasonally saturated with water, and as such, they have hydric soils (with anaerobic, or oxygen-free, conditions) and support *hydrophytic vegetation* (plants that grow in water or wet soil). Coastal wetlands are of two general types—mangrove swamps (occurring between 30° N and 30° S latitude) and salt marshes (occurring at latitudes of 30° and higher). This distribution is dictated by temperature—specifically, the occurrence of freezing conditions.

In tropical regions, sediment accumulation on coastlines provides sites for mangroves, the name for the trees, shrubs, palms, and ferns that grow in these intertidal areas as well as for the habitat, which is known as a **mangrove swamp** (**Figure 16.26**). These ecosystems have a high diversity of species that are tolerant of saltwater inundation, but generally intolerant of freezing temperatures (especially as seedlings). Mangrove roots are typically visible above the waterline, but the root portions that reach below the water surface provide a habitat for a

multitude of specialized life forms. The root systems maintain water quality by trapping sediment and taking up excess nutrients and prevent erosion by stabilizing accumulated sediments.

Humans have removed mangroves over the years in part from falsely conceived fears that they harbor disease or pestilence. Other threats to mangrove ecosystems from human activities include:

- Overharvesting, especially in developing countries that use mangroves for firewood
- Pollution, especially from agricultural runoff
- Storm surges, especially in areas where protective barrier islands and coral reefs have disappeared
- Climate change, since mangroves require a stable sea level for long-term survival.

According to the Food and Agriculture Organization of the United Nations, 20% of the world's mangroves were lost from 1980 to 2005. A 2011 study using satellite data reported that the remaining extent of global mangroves is 12% less than previously thought. Loss of these ecosystems also affects climate, since mangroves store carbon in greater amounts than other tropical forests.

Salt marshes consist mainly of *halophytic plants*, which are salt tolerant, primarily grasses. Salt marshes usually form in estuaries and in the tidal mud flats behind barrier beaches and spits (**Figure 16.27**). These marshes occur in the intertidal zone and are often characterized by sinuous, branching water channels produced as tidal waters flood into and ebb from the marsh. Marsh vegetation traps and filters sediment, spreads out floodwaters, and buffers coastlines from storm surges associated with hurricanes. However, in many regions pollution from human activities and the effects of climate change, especially rising sea level, threaten these coastal wetlands.

▼**Figure 16.27 Coastal salt marsh.** Note the tidal creek and fall colors at Massacre Marsh, Rye, New Hampshire. [Danita Delimont/Alamy.]

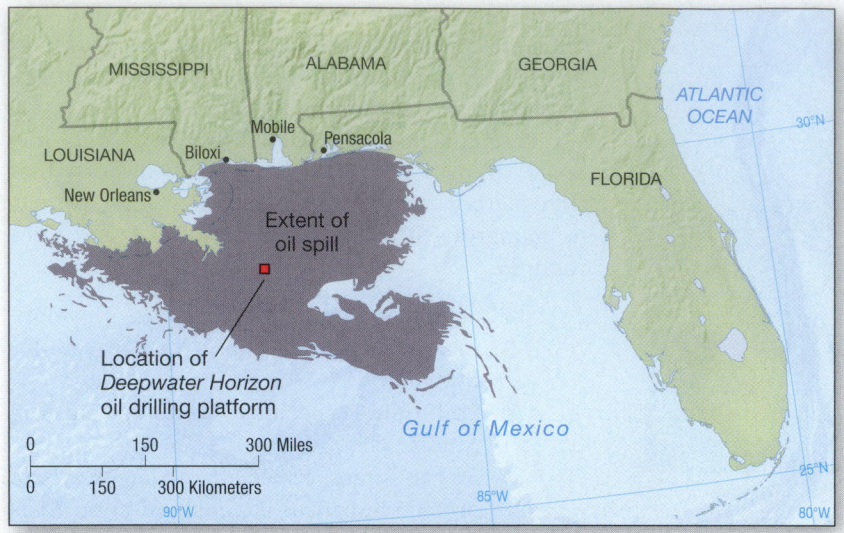

(a) The extent of spreading oil in the Gulf of Mexico on May 24, 2010, just over a month after the *Deepwater Horizon* spill.

(b) Oil within a Louisiana coastal wetland after the Gulf spill.

◄**Figure 16.28 The 2010 oil spill in the Gulf of Mexico.** [(a) and (b) NOAA. (c) Bobby Haven/ Brunswick News/AP Photo.]

(c) Workers release brown pelicans that were rescued during the spill. Volunteers cleaned oil from thousands of birds throughout the Gulf region in the months after the spill.

Mobile Field Trip
Gulf Coast Processes

https://goo.gl/LZ55qr

Coastal Louisiana includes about 40% of the coastal marshes in the United States. However, human activities have profoundly altered and disrupted most of the region through dam and levee construction, flow alterations, oil and gas exploration and pumping, pipelines, and dredging for navigation and industrial needs. Wetlands in the Mississippi delta are disappearing at the rate of 65 km² (25 mi²) per year.

Oil Spills and Coastal Ecosystems

The largest oil spill in U.S. history occurred in 2010 in the Gulf of Mexico (**Figure 16.28**). Somewhere between 50,000 and 95,000 barrels of oil a day, for 86 days, exploded from a broken wellhead on the seafloor—between 2.1 and 4.0 million gallons a day. The *Deepwater Horizon* well, at an ocean depth of 1.6 km (1 mi), was one of the deepest drilling attempts ever made, and much of the technology of the operation remains untested or unknown. Scientists are analyzing many aspects of the tragedy to determine the extent of the biological effects on the open water, beaches, wetlands, and wildlife of the Gulf.

When oil spills into seawater, it first spreads out on the surface, forming an oil slick that may be cohesive or may be broken up by rough seas. The slick may drift over large areas of open ocean, affecting marine habitat, or toward shorelines, impacting coastal wetlands and associated wildlife. The oil may partially evaporate, making the remaining slick denser; it may partially dissolve into the water; or it may combine with particulate matter and sink to the bottom. Over the long term, some of the oil breaks down through processes driven by sunlight and through decomposition by microorganisms—the rate of this deterioration depends on temperature and the availability of oxygen and nutrients. Along a coastline, oil spreads over beach sediments and drifts into coastal wetlands, contaminating and poisoning aquatic organisms and wildlife and disrupting human activities such as fishing and recreation.

Coastal restoration in the Gulf is ongoing, even though the most immediate and dramatic effects of the 2010 oil spill subsided within the first year. Oil has the potential to persist in the environment for decades, coating sandy beach sediments and sinking into the muddy bottoms of salt marshes. In May 2013, almost 3 years after the initial Gulf spill, the long-term restoration of Gulf ecosystems and economies was still in the planning stages, with an emphasis on future protection and revitalization. By 2016, the Gulf Coast Ecosystem Restoration Council was using funds from the settlement with Transcean Deepwater, Inc., for ongoing ecosystem restoration projects (more information is at https://www.restorethegulf.gov/).

COASTAL SYSTEMS IMPACT HUMANS

- Rising sea level has potential to inundate coastal communities.
- Tsunamis cause damage and loss of life along vulnerable coastlines.
- Coastal erosion changes coastal landscapes, affecting developed areas; human development on depositional features such as barrier island chains is at risk from storms, especially hurricanes.

HUMANS IMPACT COASTAL SYSTEMS

- Rising ocean temperatures, pollution, and ocean acidification impact corals and reef ecosystems.
- Human development drains and fills coastal wetlands and mangrove swamps, removing their ability to buffer storms.

16a Residents look at road damage from the storm surge associated with Hurricane Hermine in September 2016 at Alligator Point, Florida. [Mark Wallheiser/Getty Images.]

16b Dredgers pump sand through a hose to replenish beaches on Spain's Mediterranean coast, a popular tourist destination. Near Barcelona, pictured here, storms frequently erode sand that is not replenished naturally because structures block longshore currents. [Imagebroker.net/Superstock.]

16c In Arkan, Myanmar, locals plant mangroves in an effort to help protect coral reefs, restore habitat for marine and terrestrial animals, and protect against tsunami damage. [Pacific Press/Alamy.]

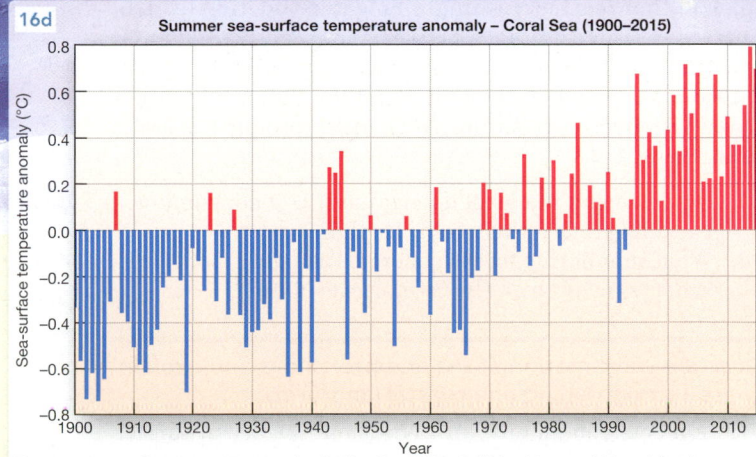

16d
Summer sea-surface temperature anomaly – Coral Sea (1900–2015)

Recent sea-surface temperature rise in the Coral Sea is linked to coral bleaching in Australia's Great Barrier Reef [Source: Climate Council of Australia and Bureau of Meteorology, 2016, Australian climate variability and change, time series graphs, http://www.bom.gov.au/climate/change/index.shtml.]

ISSUES FOR THE 21ST CENTURY

- Coastal development and climate change threaten coastal ecosystems—corals, mangroves, and salt marshes. Restoration, awareness, and a focus on sustainability can help preserve these ecosystems.
- Continued building on vulnerable coastal landforms will necessitate expensive recovery efforts, especially if storm systems become more intense with climate change.

QUESTIONS TO CONSIDER

1. What are some of the services that coral reefs, coastal salt marshes, and mangroves provide for humans?
2. How do coastal erosion and deposition affect barrier islands?

KEY**LEARNING**concepts**review**

Describe the chemical composition and physical structure of the ocean.

Because water is the "universal solvent," dissolving at least 57 of the 92 elements found in nature, seawater is a solution, and the concentration of dissolved solids is its **salinity** (p. 465). **Brackish** (p. 466) water has less than 30 ppt (parts per thousand) salinity; **brine** (p. 466) exceeds 50 ppt. The ocean is divided by depth into the narrow mixed layer at the surface, the transitional **thermocline** (p. 468), and the deep zone.

1. Describe the salinity and composition of seawater, including its constituent solutes.
2. Why is salinity less along the equator and greater in the subtropics?

Identify the components of the coastal environment and **explain** the actions of tides.

The coastal environment is the **littoral zone** (p. 468) and exists where the tide-driven, wave-driven sea confronts the land. System inputs to the coastal environment include solar energy, wind and weather, climatic variation, coastal geomorphology, and human activities. Elevation on Earth is referenced to **mean sea level (MSL)**, p. 469, a value based on average tidal levels recorded hourly at a given site over many years. MSL varies over space and is rising worldwide in response to global warming of the atmosphere and oceans.

Tides (p. 470) are complex daily oscillations in sea level, ranging worldwide from barely noticeable to many meters. Tides are produced by the gravitational pull of both the Moon and the Sun. Most coastal locations experience two rising **flood tides** (p. 470) that reach a maximum height at **high tide** (p. 470) and two falling **ebb tides** (p. 470) that reach a minimum height at **low tide** (p. 470) every day. The difference between consecutive high and low tides is the *tidal range*. *Spring tides* exhibit the greatest tidal range, when the Moon and the Sun are in either conjunction or opposition. *Neap tides* produce a lesser tidal range.

3. How is mean sea level determined? Is it constant or variable around the world? Explain.
4. What interacting forces generate the pattern of tides? What is meant by a flood tide? An ebb tide?

Describe wave motion at sea and near shore and **explain** coastal straightening and coastal landforms.

Friction between moving air (wind) and the ocean surface generates undulations of water that we call **waves** (p. 472). Wave energy in the open sea travels through water, but the water itself stays in place. Regular patterns of smooth, rounded waves—the mature undulations of the open ocean—are **swells** (p. 472). Near shore, the restricted depth of water slows the wave, forming *waves of translation*, in which both energy and water move forward toward shore.

As the crest of each wave rises, the wave falls into a characteristic **breaker** (p. 472).

Wave refraction (p. 473) redistributes wave energy along a coastline. Headlands are eroded, whereas coves and bays are areas of deposition, with the long-term effect of these differences being a straightening of the coast. As waves approach a shore at an angle, refraction produces a **longshore current** (p. 474) of water moving parallel to the shore. Particles move along the beach as **beach drift** (p. 474), shifting back and forth between water and land. The combined action of these processes produces the **littoral drift** (p. 474) of sand, sediment, gravel, and assorted materials along the shore. A **tsunami** (p. 474) is a seismic sea wave triggered by an undersea landslide or earthquake. It travels at great speeds in the open sea and gains height as it comes ashore, posing a coastal hazard.

An **erosional coastline** (p. 477) features wave action that cuts a horizontal bench in the tidal zone, extending from a sea cliff out into the sea. Such a structure is a **wave-cut platform** (p. 477), or *wave-cut terrace*. In contrast, **depositional coastlines** (p. 478) generally are located along land of gentle relief, where depositional sediments are available from many sources. Characteristic landforms deposited by waves and currents are the **barrier spit**, p. 478 (material deposited in a long ridge extending out from a coast); the **bay barrier** (p. 478), or *baymouth bar* (a spit that cuts the bay off from the ocean and forms an inland **lagoon** (p. 478); the **tombolo**, p. 479 (where sediment deposits connect the shoreline with an offshore island or sea stack); and the **beach**, p. 479 (land along the shore where sediment is in motion, deposited by waves and currents).

5. Describe the refraction process that occurs when waves reach an irregular coastline. Why is the coastline straightened?
6. Explain how a tsunami occurs and why it is so destructive.
7. How do people attempt to modify littoral drift? What strategies do they use?

Describe barrier beaches and islands and their hazards as they relate to human settlement.

Barrier chains are long, narrow depositional features, generally of sand, that form offshore roughly parallel to the coast. Common forms are **barrier beaches** (p. 480) and the broader, more extensive **barrier islands** (p. 480). Barrier formations are transient coastal features, constantly on the move, and they are a poor, but common, choice for development.

8. What types of impacts did Hurricane Sandy have on barrier beaches and islands along the Atlantic coast?
9. On the basis of the information in the text and any other sources at your disposal, do you think barrier islands and beaches should be used for

development? If so, under what conditions? If not, why not?

Describe the nature of coral reefs and coastal wetlands and ***assess*** human impacts on these living systems.

A **coral** (p. 483) is a simple marine invertebrate that forms a hard, calcified, external skeleton. Over generations, corals accumulate in large structures known as **coral reefs** (p. 484). Corals live in a *symbiotic* (mutually helpful) relationship with algae; each is dependent on the other for survival. Changes in environmental conditions can cause

corals to expel their symbiotic partners and turn white in the process of **coral bleaching** (p. 483).

Wetlands are lands saturated with water that support specific plants adapted to wet conditions. Coastal wetlands form as **mangrove swamps** (p. 485) equatorward of the 30th parallel in each hemisphere and as **salt marshes** (p. 485) poleward of these parallels.

10. How are corals able to construct reefs and islands?
11. Describe the differences between coastal wetlands that are poleward of 30° N and S latitude and those that are equatorward.

GEO**SPATIAL** ANALYSIS

Chlorophyll Concentrations in the Ocean

Phytoplankton are tiny floating plants that underpin most marine food chains. The MODIS (Moderate Resolution Imaging Spectroradiometer) sensor on NASA's Aqua satellite measures phytoplankton abundance by monitoring the concentration of chlorophyll, a green pigment that is essential for photosynthesis. We discuss phytoplankton, food chains, and photosynthesis in Chapter 19.

Activities

Go to the NASA Earth Observations at http://neo.sci.gsfc.nasa.gov/. Click on "Ocean" and choose "Chlorophyll Concentration." Read both the "Basic" and "Intermediate" versions of the "About this dataset" description.

1. How is the chlorophyll concentration determined?

2. Why do scientists measure the chlorophyll concentration in the ocean?

3. Why is chlorophyll important to Earth's climate system?

Be sure that "1 mo" (1 month) is selected under "View by date" and select the most recent year that has twelve months of data. The availability of sunlight and nutrients control phytoplankton population distribution.

4. Examine each month's map to see trends in chlorophyll concentration for the Northern Hemisphere in the Atlantic Ocean. How does the location of the peak chlorophyll change throughout the course of the year? Why does chlorophyll change in this way?

5. Examine the Southern Hemisphere seasonal trend in chlorophyll concentration (Southern Ocean, and South Pacific and South Atlantic Oceans). During which months would you predict a large phytoplankton population?

6. Chlorophyll concentrations are relatively high near the Equatorial region for every month. What does this imply about nutrient availability in the Equatorial region?

Under "Downloads" click on "3600 x 1800" to display a 0.1 degree resolution map for February. The image will open in a new window.

7. Notice that there are often high chlorophyll concentrations near coastlines. What is one plausible explanation for this occurrence?

MasteringGeography™

Looking for additional review and test prep materials? Visit the Study Area in MasteringGeography™ to enhance your geographic literacy, spatial reasoning skills, and understanding of this chapter's content by accessing a variety of resources, including MapMaster™ interactive maps, videos, *Mobile Field Trips*, *Project Condor* Quadcopter videos, *In the News* RSS feeds, flashcards, web links, self-study quizzes, and an eText version of *Geosystems*.

17 Glacial Landscapes and the Cryosphere

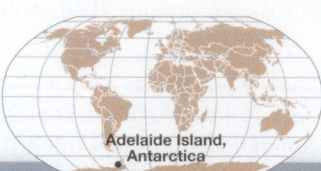

Adelaide Island, Antarctica

Icebergs and ice floes fill the channel separating Adelaide Island from the Antarctic Peninsula, one of the fastest-warming places on Earth during the latter half of the 20th century. [Danita Delimont/Getty Images.]

KEY**LEARNING**concepts

After reading the chapter, you should be able to:

- *Explain* the process by which snow becomes glacial ice.
- *Differentiate* between alpine glaciers and continental ice sheets.
- *Illustrate* the mechanics of glacial movement.
- *Describe* characteristic erosional and depositional land-forms created by glaciation.
- *Discuss* the distribution of permafrost and *explain* several periglacial processes.
- *Describe* landscapes of the Pleistocene Epoch and *list* changes occurring today in the polar regions.

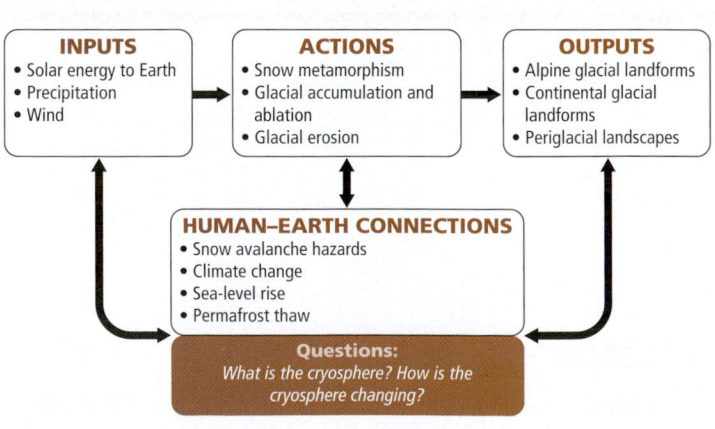

INPUTS
- Solar energy to Earth
- Precipitation
- Wind

ACTIONS
- Snow metamorphism
- Glacial accumulation and ablation
- Glacial erosion

OUTPUTS
- Alpine glacial landforms
- Continental glacial landforms
- Periglacial landscapes

HUMAN–EARTH CONNECTIONS
- Snow avalanche hazards
- Climate change
- Sea-level rise
- Permafrost thaw

Questions:
What is the cryosphere? How is the cryosphere changing?

GEOSYSTEMSnow

Surface Melting Changes Earth's Ice Sheets

Warming air and ocean temperatures are causing changes to snow and ice features across the globe, and these changes are perhaps most visible in Greenland. A continuous mass of glacial ice—the Greenland Ice Sheet—covers nearly 80% of Greenland's land mass (**Figure GN 17.1**). As temperatures in the Arctic rise, research shows that this ice sheet is now melting at a rate three times faster than in the 1990s. One of several indicators is an increase in summer meltwater on the surface of the ice. This water appears as turquoise-blue ponds, lakes, and river networks, all draining to the base of the glacier and eventually to the sea (**Figure GN 17.2**).

Meltwater Characteristics As water melts on the ice-sheet surface during the summer months, it collects in ponds, flows in channels, and seeps through cracks into the ice below. Meltwater lakes, known as *supraglacial lakes*, occur where meltwater pools over a large area. As on ice-free land surfaces, streams and rivers of meltwater often flow together to feed these lakes. Also present are features known as *moulins*, openings in the ice that resemble sinkholes. Moulins are roughly circular, vertical or almost-vertical shafts on the ice surface into which water flows and then drains downward (**Figure GN 17.3**). Some meltwater stream channels flow into moulins,

which then act as vertical conduits carrying water to the base of the ice sheet hundreds or thousands of meters below.

Vanishing Supraglacial Lakes For several years, scientists witnessed supraglacial lakes on the ice-sheet surface abruptly vanish in a matter of hours, apparently draining into some unknown reservoir within the ice sheet. Research later revealed an interesting process for these events. As a moulin near a glacial lake drains meltwater to the base of the

▲Figure GN 17.2 **River network and meltwater lake, west Greenland.** [Maria-José Viñas, NASA Earth Science News Team.]

(a) A supraglacial stream flows across the ice sheet.

(b) Meltwater flows into a moulin.

▲Figure GN 17.3 **Meltwater stream and moulin, Greenland.** [(a) Global Warming Images / Alamy Stock Photo. (b) JPL/NASA.]

ice mass, it causes the surrounding portion of the ice sheet to float. As more water accumulates at the ice-sheet bed, the surface ice bows upward, including the area beneath the nearby lake. When the surface stress builds to a high enough level, the ice below the lake fractures, creating a large opening through which the entire lake drains rapidly. Scientists estimate that this drainage can occur at flow rates comparable to the water moving over Niagara Falls.

As the large volume of water arrives suddenly at the base of the glacier, friction

between the ice and bedrock decreases, and ice flow accelerates toward the ocean. At the same time, meltwater flows directly to the ocean through subglacial channels. These rivers can carve subglacial canyons through the ice as they flow to the sea.

Similar Trends in Antarctica Supraglacial lakes also occur on the Antarctic Ice Sheet, most frequently in West Antarctica where rising temperatures have caused outlet glaciers and ice shelves to shed massive icebergs over the past several decades. In 2016, scientists reported supraglacial lakes in East Antarctica, the colder, higher, more stable region of the ice sheet. These new lakes are a concern given that Antarctic ice represents about 60% of all the freshwater on Earth. Melting glacial ice contributes to rising sea level, and scientists now suggest that the runoff from surface melt also alters ocean currents, with far-reaching effects on Earth's climate.

1. How does summer melting affect the surface and interior structure of the Greenland ice sheet?

2. Describe changes in the Antarctic ice sheet resulting from warming air and sea temperatures.

▼Figure GN 17.1 **The upper Midgard Glacier system in southeast Greenland in May 2016.** Note the blue areas showing surface melting. [Operation IceBridge/NASA.]

About three-quarters of Earth's freshwater is frozen. The bulk of that snow and ice sits in just two places—Greenland and Antarctica—forming vast ice sheets on a continental scale. The remaining snow and ice covers other near-polar regions and various mountains and alpine valleys (**Figure 17.1**). These glaciers, large masses of ice resting on land or floating in the sea attached to a landmass, are constantly moving, either under the pressure of their own weight or with the pull of gravity toward the sea.

Earth's **cryosphere** consists of the portions of the hydrosphere and lithosphere that are perennially frozen, including the freshwater making up snow, ice, glaciers, and frozen ground and the frozen saltwater in sea ice. These cold regions are generally found at high latitudes and, worldwide, at high elevations on mountains. The extent of the cryosphere changes on a seasonal basis, given that more snow accumulates and more soil and freshwater freeze during the winter. With rising air temperatures causing worldwide glacial and polar ice melt, the cryosphere today is in a state of dramatic change.

▼**Figure 17.1** **Two satellite views of southeast Alaska's Malaspina Glacier.** Malaspina Glacier is the world's largest piedmont glacier, a type of glacier that flows down a valley and then spills out onto a flat plain, often forming lobes as shown here. [(a) SRTM team, NASA/JPL/NIMA. (b) *Landsat-8* image, USGS/NASA.]

(a) Perspective view combining a *Landsat* image with a digital elevation model generated by NASA's Shuttle Radar Topography Mission. The color composite image combines visible and infrared light to show glacial ice in light blue, snow in white, vegetation in green, bare rock in grays and tans, and the ocean (foreground) in dark blue.

(b) The true color image showing the Malaspina Glacier and its tributaries in 2014.

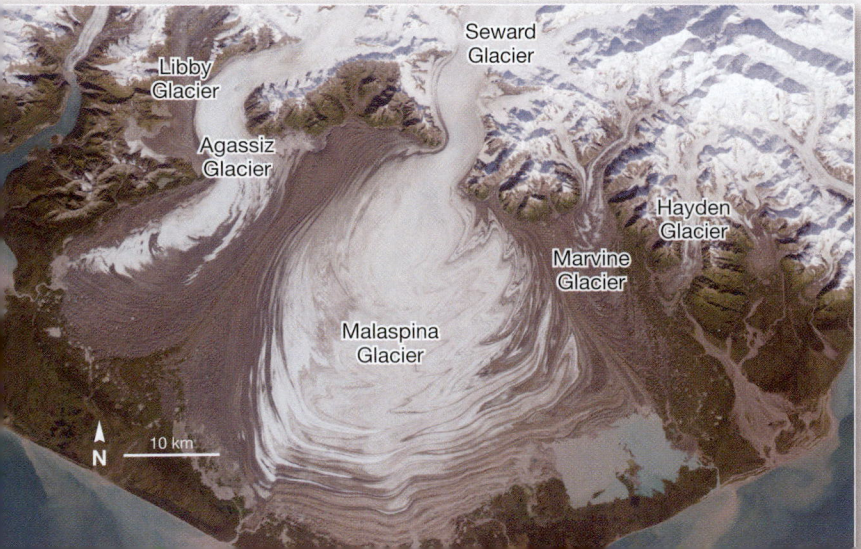

Libby Glacier

Seward Glacier

Agassiz Glacier

Hayden Glacier

Marvine Glacier

Malaspina Glacier

N   10 km

Snow into Ice—The Basis of Glaciers

In previous chapters, we discussed some of the important aspects of seasonal and permanent snow cover on Earth. Water stored as snow is released gradually during the summer months, feeding streams and rivers and the resources they provide (discussed in Chapter 8). For example, many states of the U.S. West rely heavily on snowmelt for their municipal water supplies. Another important role of Earth's snow and ice cover is that it increases Earth's albedo, or reflectivity, affecting the Earth–atmosphere energy balance (discussed in Chapter 4). As temperatures increase with climate change, ice cover decreases, creating a positive feedback loop in which decreasing snow and ice lowers the global albedo, leading to more warming and, in turn, further decreasing the snow and ice cover.

Properties of Snow

When conditions are cold enough, precipitation falls to the ground as snow. As discussed in Chapter 6, all ice crystals have a six-sided preference owing to the molecular structure of water. Snowflakes, which are made up of ice crystals, also have six sides, yet each snowflake is unique because its growth is dictated by the temperature and humidity conditions in the cloud in which it forms. As snowflakes fall through layers of clouds, their growth follows different patterns, resulting in the intricate shapes that arrive at Earth. Because the temperature at which snowflakes exist is very near their melting point, the flakes can change rapidly once they are on the ground, in a process known as *snow metamorphism*.

When snow falls to Earth, it either accumulates or melts. During the winter in high latitudes or at upper elevations, cold temperatures allow the snow to accumulate seasonally. Each storm is unique, so the snowpack is deposited in distinguishable layers, much like the layered sedimentary rock strata of the Grand Canyon (**Figure 17.2**). In mountain regions, the properties of each snow layer and the relationship between them determine the susceptibility of a slope to snow avalanches, a significant natural hazard in mountain environments.

Snow Avalanches

A *snow avalanche* is the sudden release and movement of massive amounts of snow down a mountain slope, a process that can leave visible

everyday GEO SYSTEMS

How do we assess snow layers within the snowpack?

The most effective way to understand snowpack is to dig a snow pit, a trench with a flat, vertical face that extends from the snow surface to the ground. The layers of snow exposed in a snow pit have characteristics that reflect the winter's weather history, with storms and periods of warm, sunny weather recorded within the snow sequence as it becomes compacted. Snow scientists and snow professionals, such a ski patrollers and snow rangers, use snow pits to examine snow metamorphism and assess the stability of the snowpack in relation to avalanches. Snow pits help hydrologists understand the depth of water in the snowpack, which is important for assessing water supply.

►**Figure 17.2 Scientists examine snow layers in a snow pit on Sperry Glacier in Glacier National Park, Montana.** [NPS/Alamy.]

evidence in mountain landscapes (**Figure 17.3a**). Snow avalanches move with forces equal to or exceeding those in tornadoes and hurricanes, and they can destroy entire towns. For example, an enormous avalanche destroyed the town of Alta, Utah, in 1874, killing more than 60 people. Although often mischaracterized as a type of mass wasting, snow avalanches result from different processes and have a different medium than mass-movement events. Of the main causes of mass wasting discussed in Chapter 13 (saturated slope materials, oversteepened slopes, volcanic eruptions, earthquakes, freeze–thaw cycles in soils), none are involved in triggering a snow avalanche. Because the moving material is snow rather than soil or rock, avalanche scientists study snow avalanches by examining snow characteristics.

Snow avalanches happen in steep terrain, often but not always on unforested slopes, under specific conditions related to snowpack characteristics and weather. On these slopes the mountain snowpack accumulates in layers that reflect differences in the atmospheric conditions, temperature, and wind conditions associated with each storm. Once deposited, these different layers change constantly with snow metamorphism. The snowpack normally consists of both stronger and weaker layers; when a stronger layer, called a slab, overlies a weaker layer, avalanches are possible.

Weather, especially new snowfall, is important because the weight of new snow adds stress to the snowpack, increasing the probability of avalanches. Wind is also conducive to dangerous avalanche conditions because it is

(a) In the Madison Range of southwest Montana, snow avalanches occur repeatedly, so that avalanche paths are visible features of the landscape. On forested slopes, trees are sometimes completely cleared from these paths; continued avalanche activity prevents new trees from establishing.

(b) An avalanche triggered using explosives descends down Snow Gulch Creek along Thane Road during avalanche control by the Department of Transportation in Juneau, Alaska.

▲**Figure 17.3 Avalanche paths and avalanche control work.** [(a) Karl Birkeland. (b) Michael Penn/The Juneau Empire/AP Photo.]

capable of transporting huge volumes of snow from the windward sides of ridges and gullies onto the lee slopes, where the added weight increases the avalanche danger.

Snow avalanches claim about 30 lives each year in the United States, most often skiers, snowboarders, snowmobilers, and climbers. To lower avalanche risk, workers in some areas can induce avalanches that remove unstable snow before it becomes a hazard. Avalanche control by highway workers on mountain passes and by ski patrollers at ski areas is done using hand-thrown explosives and, in some cases, military artillery to trigger avalanches so these areas can be safely opened to the public (**Figure 17.3b**). See http://www.avalanche.org/ for more information.

Formation of Glacial Ice

Glaciers form in the regions on Earth—both at high latitudes and at high elevations at any latitude—where snow is permanent on the landscape. As discussed in Chapter 4, a **snowline** is the lowest elevation where snow remains year-round. More specifically, it is the lowest line where winter snow accumulation persists throughout the summer. On equatorial mountains, the snowline is around 5000 m (16,400 ft) above sea level; on midlatitude mountains, such as the European Alps, snowlines average 2700 m (8850 ft); and in southern Greenland, snowlines are as low as 600 m (1970 ft).

Glaciers form by the continual accumulation of snow that recrystallizes under its own weight into an ice mass. Ice, in turn, is both a mineral (an inorganic natural compound of specific chemical makeup and crystalline structure) and a rock (a mass of one or more minerals). As mentioned earlier, the accumulation of snow in layered deposits is similar to the layering in sedimentary rock. To give birth to a glacier, snow and ice are transformed under pressure, recrystallizing into a type of metamorphic rock.

As snow accumulates during the winter, the increasing thickness results in increased weight and pressure on the underlying layers. The increasing pressure compresses air spaces between ice crystals as the snow consolidates and recrystallizes as it packs to a greater density. In summer, rain and snowmelt contribute water, which stimulates further melting, and this meltwater seeps down into the snowfield and refreezes. Through this process, snow that survives the summer and is still present the following winter begins a slow transformation into glacial ice. In a transition step, the snow becomes **firn**, a granular, partly compacted snow that is intermediate between snow and ice.

Dense **glacial ice** is produced over a period of many years as this process continues. In Antarctica, glacial ice formation may take 1000 years because of the dryness of the climate and minimal snowfall, whereas in wet climates, the time is reduced to several years because of frequent heavy snowfall.

Types of Glaciers

A **glacier** is defined as a large mass of ice resting on land, formed from the accumulation and recrystallization of snow. Glaciers are not stationary; they move under the pressure of their own great weight and the pull of gravity. In fact, they move in stream-like patterns, merging as tributaries into large rivers of ice that slowly flow outward toward the ocean (**Figure 17.4**). For an inventory of world glaciers, go to http://glims .colorado.edu/glacierdata/db_summary_stats.php.

Although glaciers are as varied as the landscape itself, they fall within two general groups based on their form, size, and flow characteristics: alpine glaciers and continental ice sheets (also called continental glaciers), both of which we describe below. Today, alpine glaciers and ice sheets cover about 10% of Earth's land area, ranging from the polar regions to midlatitude mountain ranges to some of the high mountains along the equator, such as in the Andes Mountains of South America and on Mount Kilimanjaro in Africa. During colder climate episodes in the past, glacial ice covered as much as 30% of continental land.

Alpine Glaciers

With few exceptions, a glacier in a mountain range is an **alpine glacier**, or *mountain glacier*. The name comes from the Alps of central Europe, where such glaciers abound. Alpine glaciers have several subtypes. *Valley glaciers* are masses of ice confined within a valley that originally was formed by stream action. These glaciers range in length from as little as 100 m (325 ft) to more than 100 km (60 mi). **Figure 17.5** shows a valley glacier in the Tien Shan in

▲**Figure 17.4 Alpine glaciers merge into a river of ice, Ellesmere Island, Canadian Arctic.** How many valley glaciers do you see joining the main glacier in this image? [*Terra* MODIS, NASA.]

▲Figure 17.5 **Aerial view of alpine glaciers in Glacier Bay National Park, Alaska.** Note the cirque glaciers and valley glaciers. [Wildlife GmbH/Alamy.]

central Asia, one of the largest continuous mountain ranges in the world. The two highest peaks in the central part of this range, both shown in the photo, are Xuelian Feng at 6527 m (21,414 ft) and Peak 6231, aptly named at 6231 m (20,443 ft) above sea level.

A glacier that forms within the snow filling a **cirque**, or bowl-shaped recess at the head of a valley, is a *cirque glacier*. Several cirque glaciers may jointly feed a valley glacier (Figure 17.4). A *piedmont glacier* is formed wherever several valley glaciers pour out of their confining valleys and coalesce at the base of a mountain range. A piedmont glacier spreads freely over the lowlands; an example is the Malaspina Glacier, which flows into Yakutat Bay, Alaska (see Figure 17.1).

As a valley glacier flows slowly downhill, it erodes the mountains, canyons, and river valleys beneath its mass, transporting material within or along its base. A portion of the transported debris may also be carried on its icy surface, visible as dark streaks and bands. This surface debris originates either from rockfalls and other gravity-driven processes that carry material downward from above or from processes that float material upward from the glacier's bed.

A *tidewater glacier*, or *tidal glacier*, ends in the sea. Such glaciers are characterized by **calving**, a process in which pieces of ice break free to form floating ice masses known as *icebergs*, which are usually found wherever glaciers meet an ocean, bay, or fjord (**Figure 17.6**).

Icebergs are inherently unstable, as their center of gravity shifts with melting and further breakup.

Continental Ice Sheets

An **ice sheet** is an extensive, continuous mass of ice that may occur on a continental scale. Most of Earth's glacial ice exists in the ice sheets that blanket 81% of Greenland—1,756,000 km² (678,000 mi²) of ice—and 90% of Antarctica—14.2 million km² (5.48 million mi²) of ice. Antarctica alone contains 92% of all the glacial ice on the planet.

The ice sheets of Antarctica and Greenland have such enormous mass that large portions of each landmass beneath the ice are isostatically depressed (pressed down by weight) below sea level. Each ice sheet reaches thicknesses of more than 3000 m (9800 ft), with average thickness around 2000 m (6500 ft), burying all but the highest peaks of land.

Where a continental ice sheet meets the coast, the ice may extend out over the sea as an *ice shelf*. These shelves are often found in protected inlets and bays, cover thousands of square kilometers, and reach thicknesses of 1000 m (3280 ft).

Ice caps and ice fields are two additional types of glaciers with continuous ice cover, on a slightly smaller scale than an ice sheet. An **ice cap** is roughly circular and, by definition, covers an area of less than 50,000 km² (19,300 mi²), completely burying the underlying landscape.

▲Figure 17.6 **Glacial calving.** A huge piece of ice calves from the Hubbard Glacier into Disappointment Bay, Alaska, in 2015. [Don Menning/Alamy.]

▲**Figure 17.7** **Ice caps.** Vatnajökull in southeastern Iceland is the largest of four ice caps on the island (*jökull* means "ice cap" in Danish). Note the ash on the ice cap from the 2004 Grímsvötn eruption [NASA/GSFC.]

text, glacial processes are linked to the concept of equilibrium. A glacier at equilibrium maintains its size because the incoming snow is approximately equal to the melt rate. In a state of disequilibrium, the glacier either expands (causing its terminus to move downslope) or retreats (causing its terminus to move upslope).

Glacial Mass Balance

A glacier is an open system, with *inputs* of snow and *outputs* of ice, meltwater, and water vapor, as illustrated in Geosystems in Action 17. Glaciers acquire snow in their accumulation zone, a snowfield at the highest elevation of an ice sheet or ice cap or at the head of a valley glacier, usually in a cirque (**Figure GIA 17.1**). Snow avalanches from surrounding steep mountain slopes can add to the snowfield depth. The accumulation zone ends at the **firn line**, which marks the elevation above which the winter snow and ice remained intact throughout the summer melting season, but below which melting occurs. At the lower end of the glacier, far below the firn line, the glacier undergoes wasting (reduction) through several processes: melting on the surface, internally, and at the base; sublimation (the phase change of solid ice directly into water vapor), evaporation, and calving of ice blocks at the glacier's terminus. Collectively, these processes cause losses to the glacier's mass, known as **ablation**.

These gains (accumulation) and losses (ablation) of glacial ice determine the glacier's *mass balance*, the property

The volcanic island of Iceland features several ice caps; an example is Vatnajökull, shown in **Figure 17.7**. Volcanoes lie beneath these icy surfaces. Iceland's Grímsvötn Volcano erupted in 1996 and 2004, producing large quantities of melted glacial water in a sudden flood called a *jökulhlaup*, an Icelandic term that is now widely used to describe a glacial outburst flood. The most recent eruption in 2011 was the largest in a century, but did not produce an outburst flood.

An **ice field** extends in a characteristic elongated pattern over a mountainous region and is not large enough to form the dome of an ice cap. The Patagonian ice field of Argentina and Chile is one of Earth's largest. It is only 90 km (56 mi) wide, but stretches 360 km (224 mi), from 46° to 51° S latitude (**Figure 17.8**).

Ice sheets and ice caps may be drained by rapidly moving *ice streams*, made up of solid ice that flows at a faster rate than the main ice mass toward lowland areas or the sea. For example, a number of ice streams flow through the periphery of Greenland and Antarctica. An *outlet glacier* is a stream of ice flowing out from an ice sheet or ice cap, usually constrained on each side by the bedrock of a mountain valley.

▼**Figure 17.8** The Patagonian ice fields and major glacial lakes of Argentina and Chile. [NASA/GSFC.]

Glacial Processes

A glacier is a dynamic body, moving relentlessly downslope at rates that vary within its mass, shaping the landscape through which it flows. Like so many of the systems described in this that decides whether the glacier will advance (grow larger) or retreat (grow smaller). During cold periods with adequate precipitation, a glacier has a *positive net mass balance* and advances. In warmer times, a glacier has a *negative net mass balance* and retreats. Internally, gravity continues to move a glacier forward even though its lower terminus might be in retreat owing to ablation. Within the glacier is a zone where accumulation balances ablation; this is known as the *equilibrium line* (**Figure GIA 17.2**), and it generally coincides with the firn line.

Scientists are using repeat photography to assess changes in glacial mass balance in North America since the late 1800s (see https://www2.usgs.gov/climate_landuse /glaciers/repeat_photography.asp or https://www.usgs.gov /centers/norock/science-topics/repeat-photography). The overall trend toward a negative mass balance in North America matches that for other glaciers in the world, showing that temperature changes are causing widespread reductions in middle- and lower-elevation glacial ice (**Figure GIA 17.3**).

Glacial Movement

Glacial ice is quite different from the small, brittle cubes of ice we find in our freezer. In particular, glacial ice behaves in a plastic (pliable) manner; it distorts and flows in its underlying portions in response to the weight and pressure of overlying snow and the degree of slope below. In contrast, the glacier's upper-surface portions are quite brittle. Rates of flow range from almost no movement to a kilometer or two of movement per year on a steep slope. The rate of accumulation of snow in the glacier's formation area is critical to the speed of forward motion.

Glaciers, then, are not rigid blocks that simply slide downhill. The greatest movement within a valley glacier occurs *internally*, below the rigid surface layer, which fractures as the underlying plastic zone moves forward (**Figure 17.9a**). At the same time, the base creeps and slides along, varying its speed with temperature and the presence of any lubricating water beneath the ice. This *basal slip* usually is much less rapid than the internal plastic flow of the glacier, so the upper portion of the glacier flows ahead of the lower portion.

Unevenness in the landscape beneath the ice may cause the pressure to vary, melting some of the basal ice by compression at one moment, only to have it refreeze later. This process is *ice regelation*, meaning to refreeze, or re-gel. Such melting/refreezing action incorporates rock debris into the glacier. Consequently, the basal ice layer, which can extend tens of meters above the base of the glacier, has a much higher debris content than the ice above.

A flowing alpine glacier or ice stream can develop vertical cracks known as **crevasses** (**Figure 17.9b**). Crevasses result from friction with valley walls, from tension due to stretching as the glacier passes over convex slopes, or from compression as the glacier passes over concave slopes. Traversing a glacier, whether an alpine glacier or an ice sheet, is dangerous because a thin veneer of snow sometimes masks the presence of a crevasse.

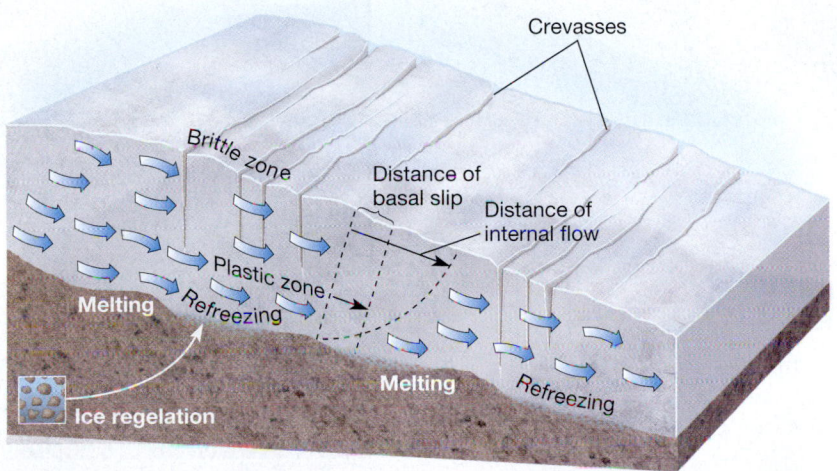

(a) Cross section of a glacier, showing its forward motion, brittle cracking at the surface, and flow along its basal layer.

(b) Surface crevasses are evidence of forward movement on the Fox Glacier, South Island, New Zealand.

▲**Figure 17.9 Glacial movement.** [(b) David Wall/Alamy.]

As an open system, a glacier is in equilibrium if it is neither advancing nor retreating. But if inputs of snow are greater than losses through melting, evaporation, sublimation, and calving, the glacier will expand. If ice losses exceed inputs, the glacier will retreat (GIA 17.1). Whether a glacier is in equilibrium can be determined from its mass balance (GIA 17.2). Today, many alpine glaciers worldwide are retreating as they melt because of warming related to climate change (GIA 17.3).

17.1 CROSS SECTION OF A TYPICAL RETREATING ALPINE GLACIER

The diagram shows the relationship between the zone of accumulation, the equilibrium line, and the zone of ablation. In a retreating glacier, ice continues to slide downhill as the glacier's terminus retreats upslope, depositing terminal and recessional moraines. Additional inputs of ice can come from tributary glaciers as glaciers merge.

At least four tributary glaciers flowing into a valley glacier, Greenland

Merging glaciers, Nordaustlandet Island

Terminal moraine, Nordaustlandet Island, Arctic Ocean

Accumulation zone:
Snow and firn build up in this zone, are compressed by their own weight, and change to glacial ice as the glacier increases in thickness.

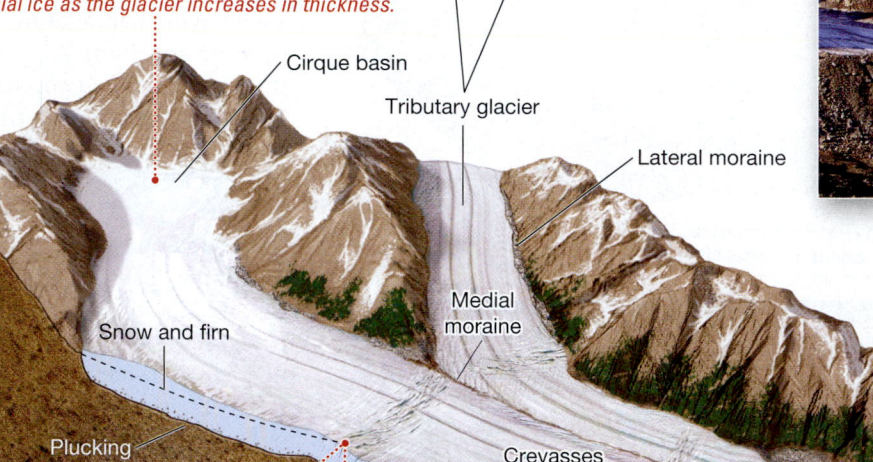

Cirque basin

Tributary glacier

Lateral moraine

Snow and firn

Medial moraine

Plucking

Abrasion

Crevasses

Recessional moraine

Melting and evaporation

Terminal moraine

Glacial ice

Bedrock

Till

Meltwater stream

Outwash plain

Firn line:
The accumulation zone ends; summer melting occurs below this line.

Equilibrium line:
Accumulation and ablation are in balance; generally matches the firn line.

Ablation zone:
In this zone the glacier loses mass through melting and other processes.

Animation (MG)
Glacial Processes

https://goo.gl/PLBaFC

MasteringGeography™

Visit the Study Area in MasteringGeography™ to explore glacial mass balance.

Visualize: Study a geosciences animation of glacial processes.

Assess: Demonstrate understanding of a glacier's mass balance (if assigned by instructor).

Video (MG)
A Tour of the Cryosphere

https://goo.gl/v5Pwme

17.2 GLACIAL MASS BALANCE

The diagram shows the annual mass balance of a glacial system, which determines the location of the equilibrium line. Generally, a glacier with a positive mass balance will advance, while a glacier with a negative mass balance will retreat.

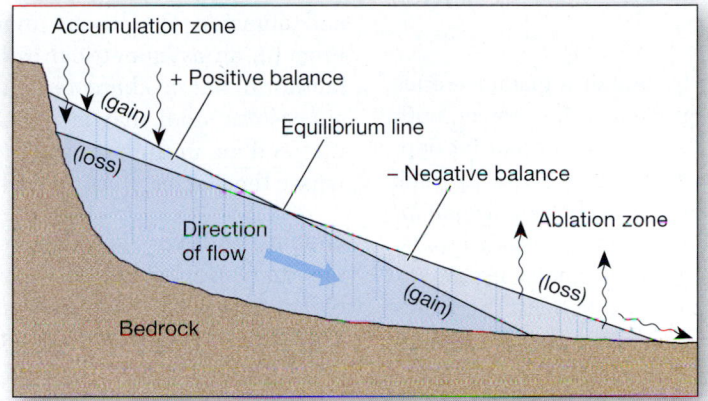

Video (MG)
Operation Ice Bridge

https://goo.gl/4j1zH2

Accumulation zone

+ Positive balance
(gain)
(loss)
Equilibrium line
− Negative balance
Direction of flow
Ablation zone
(gain)
(loss)
Bedrock

Animation (MG)
Flow of Ice Within a Glacier

https://goo.gl/n79lTN

17.3 PORTRAIT OF A RETREATING GLACIER, 1979–2010

Photographs and ground measurements reveal that the South Cascade Glacier in Washington is retreating and that its mass balance is declining. This glacier is one of several being intensively monitored by USGS scientists to assess the effects of climate change.

1979

2010

GEOquiz

1. Predict: How would the position of the firn line change if a glacier receives more snowfall at higher elevations for several years in a row? Explain.

2. Explain: Thinking of a glacier as a system, explain how changes to inputs and outputs result in a glacier's having a positive or negative mass balance.

3. Infer: Based on what you can see in the photos, outline the largest area formerly occupied by South Cascade Glacier. What evidence helped you arrive at this conclusion?

4. Compare: How are the accumulation zone and the ablation zone similar? How are they different?

Glacier Surges Although glaciers flow plastically and predictably most of the time, some will advance rapidly at speeds much faster than normal, in a **glacier surge**. A surge is not quite as abrupt as it sounds; in glacial terms, a surge can be tens of meters per day. The Jakobshavn Glacier on the western Greenland coast, for example, is one of the fastest moving, at between 7 and 12 km (4.3 and 7.5 mi) a year.

Scientists are investigating the exact causes of glacier surges. Some surge events result from a buildup of water pressure under the glacier—sometimes enough to actually float the glacier slightly, detaching it from its bed during the surge. Another cause of glacier surges is the presence of a water-saturated layer of sediment, a *soft bed*, beneath the glacier. This is a deformable layer that cannot resist the tremendous shear stress produced by the moving ice of the glacier.

Glacial Erosion The process by which a glacier erodes the landscape is similar to a large excavation project, with the glacier hauling debris from one site to another for deposition. The passing glacier mechanically picks up rock material and carries it away in a process known as *glacial plucking*. Debris is carried on its surface and is also transported internally, embedded within the glacier itself.

When a glacier retreats, it can leave behind cobbles or boulders (sometimes house-sized) that are "foreign" in composition and origin to the ground on which they are deposited. These *glacial erratics*, lying in strange locations with no obvious sign of how they got there, were an early clue to the glacial plucking that occurred during times when blankets of ice covered the land (pictured ahead in Figure 17.13).

The rock pieces frozen to the basal layers of the glacier enable the ice mass to scour the landscape like sandpaper as it moves. This process of **abrasion** produces a smooth surface on exposed rock, which shines with *glacial polish* when the glacier retreats (**Figure 17.10**). Larger rocks in the glacier act much like chisels, gouging the underlying surface and producing glacial striations parallel to the flow direction.

Glacial Landforms

Glacial erosion and deposition produce distinctive landforms that differ greatly from those existing before the ice came and went. Alpine glaciers and continental ice sheets each produce characteristic landscapes, although some landforms exist in either type of glacial environment.

Erosional Landforms

A landscape feature produced by both glacial plucking and abrasion is a **roche moutonnée** ("sheep rock" in French), an asymmetrical hill of exposed bedrock. This landform has a characteristic gently sloping upstream side (stoss side) that is polished smooth by glacial action and an abrupt and steep downstream side (lee side) where the glacier plucked rock pieces (**Figure 17.11**).

Glacial Valleys The effects of alpine glaciation created the dramatic landforms of the Canadian Rockies, the Swiss Alps, and the Himalayan peaks. Geomorphologist William Morris Davis depicted the stages of a valley glacier in drawings published in 1906 and redrawn here in **Figures 17.12** and **17.13**. Study of these figures reveals the handiwork of ice as sculptor in mountain environments.

Figure 17.12a shows the **V** shape of a typical stream-cut valley as it existed before glaciation. Figure 17.12b shows the same landscape during subsequent glaciation. Glacial erosion actively removes much of the regolith (weathered bedrock) and the soils that covered the stream-valley landscape. When glaciers erode parallel valleys, a thin, sharp ridge forms between them, known as an **arête** ("knife-edge" in French). Arêtes can also form between adjacent cirques as they erode in a headward direction. Two eroding cirques may reduce an arête to a saddlelike depression or pass, forming a **col**. A **horn**, or pyramidal peak, results when several cirque glaciers gouge an individual mountain summit from all sides. Most famous is the Matterhorn in the Swiss Alps, but many others occur worldwide. A **bergschrund** is a crevasse, or wide crack, that separates flowing ice from stagnant ice in the upper reaches of a glacier or in a cirque. Bergschrunds are often covered in snow in winter but become apparent in summer when this snow cover melts.

▲**Figure 17.10 Glacial sandpapering of rock.** Glacial polish and striations are examples of glacial abrasion and erosion, shown here on limestone at Kelleys Island State Park in Ohio. [Joel Zatz/Alamy.]

(a) Lembert Dome in the Tuolumne Meadows area of Yosemite National Park, California.

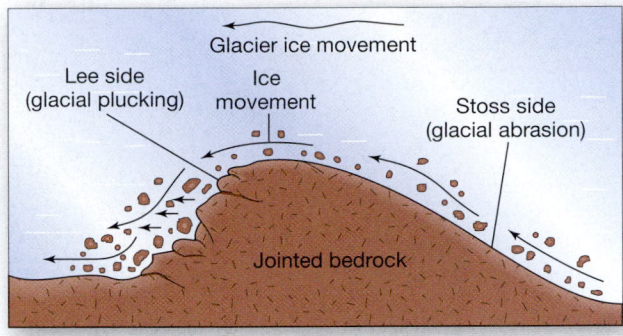

(b) Glacial processes that formed Lembert Dome (the bluish/whitish color represents glacial ice).

▲**Figure 17.11 Roche moutonnée.** Glacial plucking and abrasion work together to erode bedrock into an asymmetrical hill with a gentle sloping stoss side and a steep lee side. [(a) Robert Christopherson.]

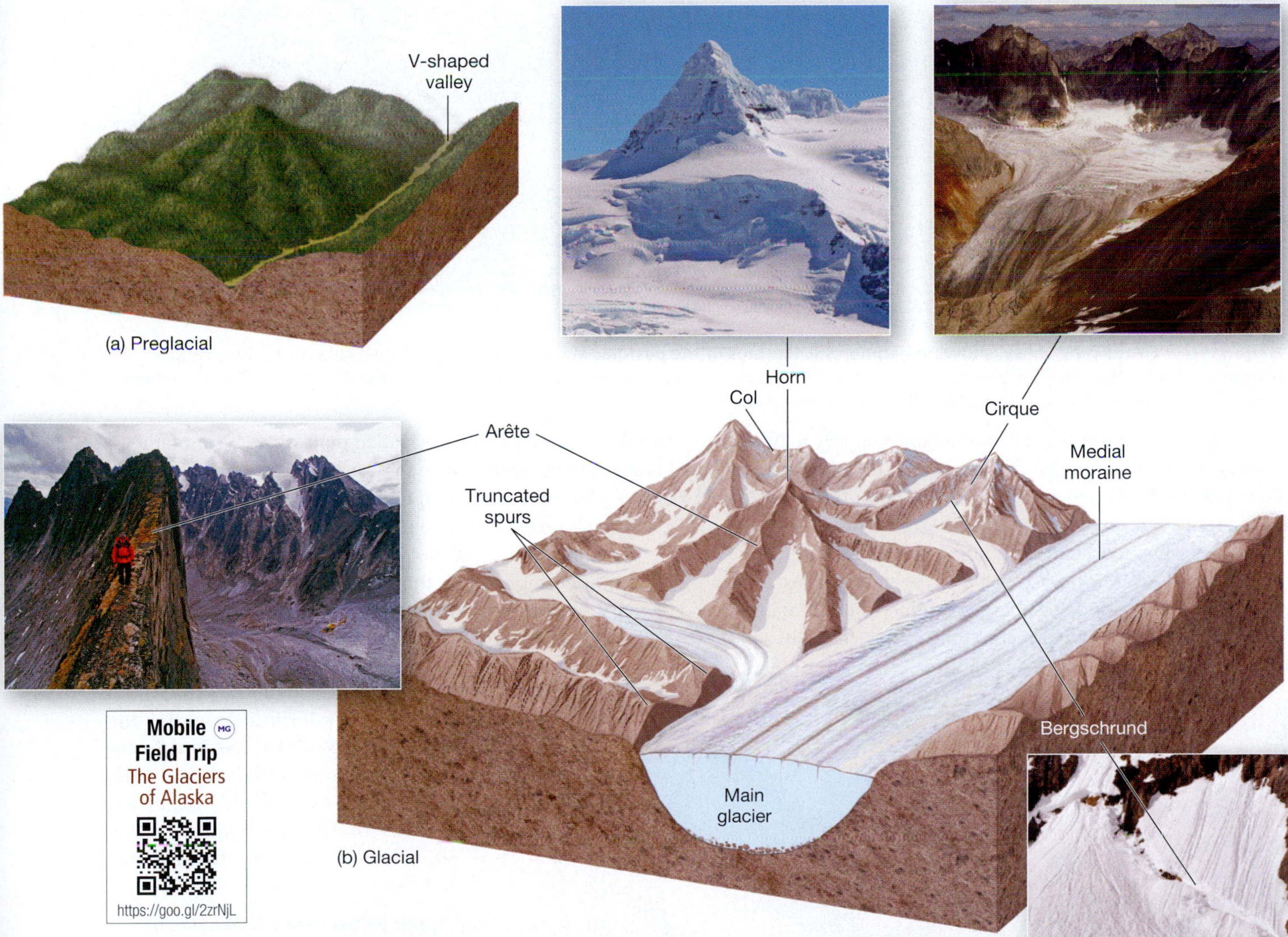

Mobile Field Trip MG
The Glaciers of Alaska

https://goo.gl/2zrNjL

▲**Figure 17.12 An alpine valley, showing preglacial and glacial landscape.** Inset photos are of an arête in Canada, a horn in Antarctica, a cirque in Nepal, and a bergschrund in Spitsbergen. [Arêtes by National Geographic Creative/Alamy. Cirque by Peter Mather/Getty Images. Horn and bergschrund by Bobbé Christopherson.]

Glacial erratics

Arête

Col

Horn

Paternoster lakes

Hanging valley

Cirques

U-shaped glacial trough

Hanging waterfall

Postglacial

U-shaped valley

Tarn

U-shaped valley, aerial

Hanging waterfall

Tarn

U-shaped valley

Mobile (MG)
Field Trip
Yosemite

https://goo.gl/pij5SY

▲**Figure 17.13** **An alpine valley, showing geomorphic features of the postglacial landscape.** Glacial retreat reveals a new landscape. U-shaped valley aerial and surface photos are views in Norway. Erratic and waterfall are in Sierra Nevada, California. Tarn is in the Rockies. [Erratics, valleys, and tarn by Bobbé Christopherson. Waterfall by Robert Christopherson.]

Figure 17.13 shows the same landscape at a time of warmer climate, when the ice retreated. The glaciated valleys now are U-shaped, greatly changed from their previous stream-cut V form. Physical weathering from the freeze–thaw cycle has loosened rock along the steep cliffs, and it has fallen to form *talus slopes* along the valley sides. In the cirques where the valley glaciers originated, small mountain lakes called **tarns** have formed. Some cirques contain small,

circular, stair-stepped lakes, called **paternoster** ("our father") **lakes** for their resemblance to rosary (religious) beads. Paternoster lakes may form from the differing resistance of rock to glacial processes or from damming by glacial deposits.

In some cases, valleys carved by tributary glaciers are left stranded high above the main valley floor because the primary glacier eroded the main valley so deeply. These *hanging valleys* are the sites of spectacular waterfalls.

Fjords Where a glacial trough encounters the ocean, the glacier can continue to erode the landscape, even below sea level. As the glacier retreats, the trough floods and forms a deep **fjord** in which the sea extends inland, filling the lower reaches of the steep-sided valley (**Figure 17.14**). The fjord may be flooded fur-

HPS 19

Penguin Glacier

Fjord

Fjord

N

◄**Figure 17.14** **Fjords on the Pacific Ocean side of the South Patagonian Ice Field, Chile.** As ice from the Penguin Glacier and HPS 19 flows into fjords, it calves and forms icebergs. (HPS stands for Hielo Patagónico Sur, or South Patagonian Ice Field, in the numbering system for glaciers with no geographic name.) The largest iceberg in the image is about 2 km (1.2 mi) wide. [NASA *ISS* astronaut photo.]

▲**Figure WIO 17.1 Erosional features of alpine glaciation.**
[P.A. Lawrence, LLC/Alamy.]

ther by rising sea level or by changes in the elevation of the coastal region. All along the glaciated coast of Alaska, retreating alpine glaciers are opening many new fjords that previously were blocked by ice. Coastlines with notable fjords include those of Norway (**Figure 17.15**), Chile, the South Island of New Zealand, Alaska, and British Columbia.

Fjords also occur along the edges of Earth's ice sheets. In Greenland, rising water temperatures in some of the longest fjord systems in the world appear to be accelerating melt rates where the glaciers meet the sea. In Antarctica, recent use of ice-penetrating radar identified numerous fjords beneath the Antarctic ice sheet, indicating that the present ice sheet was smaller in areal extent in the past.

Depositional Landforms

Glaciers transport materials upon and within the ice, producing unsorted sediment deposits, as well as by the actions of meltwater streams at the glacier's downstream end, producing sorted deposits. The general term for all glacial deposits, both unsorted and sorted, is **glacial drift**.

Moraines As mentioned earlier, as a glacier flows to a lower elevation, a wide assortment of rock fragments become *entrained* (carried along) on its surface or embedded within its mass or in its base. As the glacier melts, this unsorted and unstratified debris is deposited

on the ground as **till**, usually marking the glacier's former margins (**Figure 17.16**).

The deposition of glacial sediment also produces a class of landform called a **moraine**, which may take several forms. In areas that have undergone alpine glaciations, **lateral moraines** are lengthy ridges of till along each side of a glacier. If two glaciers with lateral moraines join, a **medial moraine** may form (see Figure GIA 17.1). In areas that were formerly covered by single, large ice sheets, lateral moraines and medial moraines are lacking.

End moraines accumulate at the glacier's *terminus*, or endpoint, and are associated with both alpine and continental-scale glaciation. Eroded debris that is dropped at the glacier's farthest extent is a **terminal moraine** (Figure GIA 17.1). *Recessional moraines* may also be present, having formed at other points where a glacier paused after reaching a new equilibrium between accumulation and ablation.

▶**Figure 17.15 Norwegian fjord.** Sediment carried in runoff is visible in this fjord, which fills a U-shaped, glacially carved valley. [Bobbé Christopherson.]

▲**Figure 17.16 Terminal moraine.** A terminal moraine of unsorted till, Russell Glacier, Greenland. [Jason Edwards/National Geographic/Getty Images.]

Till Plains When the ice sheets retreated from their maximum extent, about 18,000 years ago, during the most recent glaciation in North America and Europe (portrayed later in Figure 17.27), they left distinct landscapes that we see today. A **till plain**, also called a *ground moraine*, is a deposition of till that forms behind a terminal moraine as the glacier retreats. The till in such cases (as in parts of the U.S. Midwest) is generally spread widely across the ground surface, usually hiding the former landscape and creating irregular topography, but not the characteristic ridges of other moraines. **Figure 17.17** illustrates common depositional features associated with the retreat of a continental ice sheet.

▼**Figure 17.17 Landforms associated with ice sheets.** [(b) Bobbé Christopherson.]

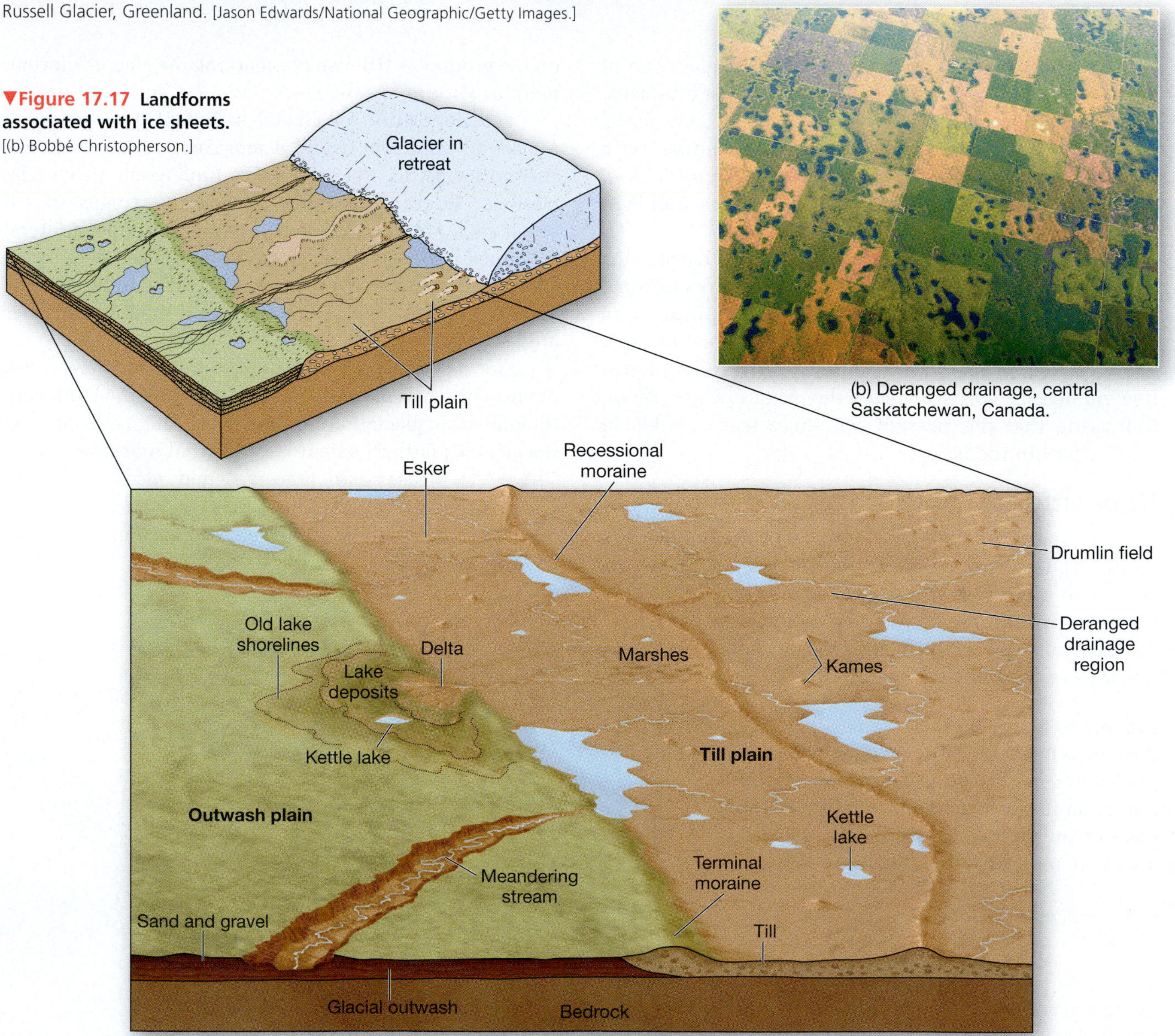

Glacier in retreat

Till plain

(b) Deranged drainage, central Saskatchewan, Canada.

Esker

Recessional moraine

Drumlin field

Deranged drainage region

Old lake shorelines

Delta

Marshes

Kames

Lake deposits

Kettle lake

Till plain

Outwash plain

Kettle lake

Meandering stream

Terminal moraine

Till

Sand and gravel

Glacial outwash

Bedrock

(a) Common depositional landforms produced by continental glaciation.

▲**Figure 17.18** **A drumlin.** This elongated hill, a drumlin, is in the glaciated landscape near Dunmore, County Galway, Ireland. [Paul Heinrich/Alamy.]

Till plains are composed of coarse till, with low and rolling relief, and a deranged drainage pattern that includes scattered wetlands (Figure 17.17b). Common features of till plains are **drumlins**, hills of deposited till that are streamlined in the direction of ice-sheet movement, with blunt end upstream and tapered end downstream (**Figure 17.18**). The shape of a drumlin sometimes resembles an elongated teaspoon bowl, lying face down. Multiple drumlins, known as *drumlin swarms*, occur across the landscape in portions of New York and Wisconsin, among other areas.

Drumlins may attain lengths of 100–5000 m (330 ft–3.1 mi) and heights up to 200 m (650 ft). Although similar in shape to an erosional roche moutonnée, a drumlin is a depositional feature with tapered end downstream.

Glacial Outwash Beyond the glacial terminus, meltwater flows downstream and is typically milky in color owing to the sediment load of fine-grained materials, known as "rock flour." This meltwater flow occurs when a glacier is retreating or during any period of ablation; flow volumes are highest during the warm summer months.

Sediments deposited by glacial meltwater are sorted by size, becoming **stratified drift**. The sorting comes from the combined effect of *glaciofluvial* (glacial and fluvial) processes—flowing water sorts sediments according to size, often with the largest particles dropped out of the sediment load closest to the glacial terminus (forming an alluvial fan) and the smaller particles carried farthest downstream. These glaciofluvial sediments are also stratified, with sediments laid down in layers.

The area of sediment deposition beyond the glacial terminus can form an extensive **outwash plain**. Outwash plains feature braided stream channels, which typically form when streams carry a large sediment load.

A typical landform that is composed of glacial outwash, but located on a till plain, is a sinuously curving, narrow ridge of coarse sand and gravel called an **esker**. Eskers form along the channel of a meltwater stream that flows beneath a glacier, in an ice tunnel, or between ice walls. The esker forms while the glacier is stagnant; then as the glacier contracts in volume, the steep-sided esker is left behind in a pattern roughly parallel to the path of the glacier (**Figure 17.19**). The ridge may not be continuous and in places may even appear to be branched, following the path set by the subglacial watercourse. Commercially valuable deposits of sand and gravel are quarried from some eskers.

Another landform composed of glaciofluvial deposits is a **kame**, a small hill, knob, or mound of sorted sand and gravel that is deposited by water on the surface of a glacier (for example, after having collected in a crevasse) and then is left on the land surface after the glacier retreats. Kames also can be made of material originally deposited as deltas at the edges of glacial lakes—and in terraces along valley walls.

▼**Figure 17.19** **An esker.** This esker near Whitefish Lake in Canada's Northwest Territories was formed along the channel of a meltwater stream flowing beneath a glacier. [All Canada Photos/Alamy.]

▲**Figure 17.20 Kettle lake, Massachusetts.** Walden Pond, made famous by American essayist and poet Henry David Thoreau, is a glacial kettle left when glaciers retreated at the end of the Pleistocene Epoch. [Steve Dunwell/Getty Images.]

Periglacial Landscapes

In 1909, Polish geologist Walery von Lozinski coined the term **periglacial** to describe processes of frost action weathering and freeze–thaw rock shattering in the Carpathian Mountains. The term now is used to describe places where geomorphic processes related to freezing water occur. These periglacial regions occupy over 20% of Earth's land surfaces. At high latitudes, they have a near-permanent ice cover; at high elevation in lower latitudes, they are seasonally snow-free. Periglacial landscapes occur in the *subarctic* and *polar* climate zones, especially in *tundra* climate regions either at high latitude or at high elevation in lower-latitude mountains (review climate types in Chapter 9).

Permafrost and Its Distribution

When soil, sediment, or rock temperatures remain below 0°C (32°F) for at least 2 years, **permafrost** (perennially frozen ground) develops. An area of permafrost that is not covered by glaciers is considered periglacial; the largest extent of such lands is in Russia (**Figure 17.21**). Approximately 80% of Alaska has permafrost beneath its surface, as do parts of Canada, China, Scandinavia, Greenland, and Antarctica, in addition to alpine mountain regions of the world. Note that the criterion for a permafrost designation is based solely on *temperature* and has nothing to do with how much or how little water is present. Two factors other than temperature also contribute to permafrost conditions and occurrence: the presence of fossil permafrost from previous ice-age conditions and the insulating effect of snow cover or vegetation that inhibits heat loss.

Sometimes an isolated block of ice, perhaps more than a kilometer across, remains on a ground moraine, on an outwash plain, or on a valley floor after a glacier has retreated. As much as 20 to 30 years is required for it to melt. In the interim, material continues to accumulate around the melting ice block. When the block finally melts, it leaves behind a steep-sided hole that then frequently fills with water, forming a **kettle**, also known as a *kettle lake* (**Figure 17.20**).

▶**Figure 17.21 Permafrost distribution in the Northern Hemisphere.** Alpine permafrost is noted except for small occurrences in Hawai'i, Mexico, Europe, and Japan. Subsea permafrost occurs in the ground beneath the Arctic Ocean along the margins of the continents, as shown. Note the towns of Resolute and Kugluktuk in Nunavut and Hotchkiss in Alberta. A cross section of the permafrost beneath these towns is shown in Figure 17.22. [Adapted from USGS, 2007, *Circumpolar permafrost extent*, based on J. Brown et al., 1997, *Circum-Arctic Map of Permafrost and Ground Ice Conditions*, NSIDC; http://nsidc.org/data/ggd318.]

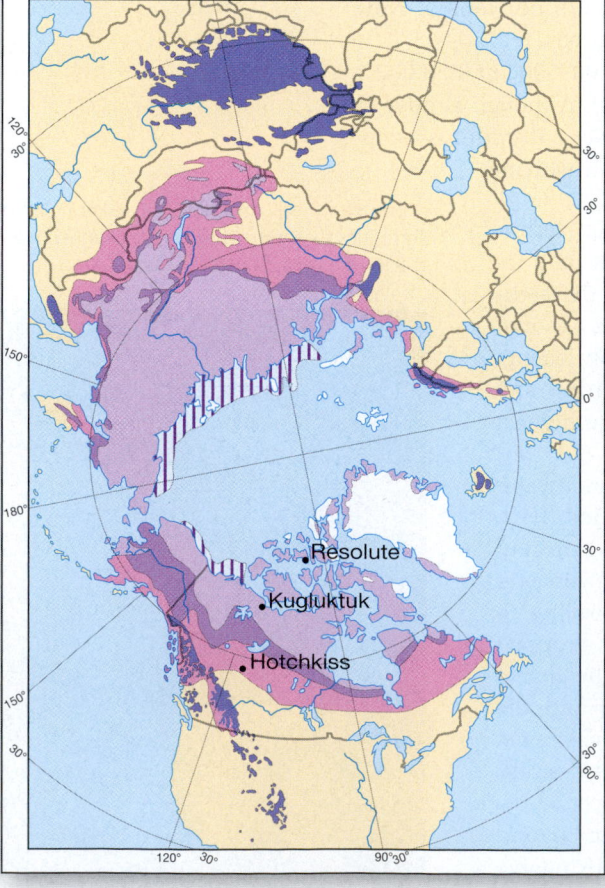

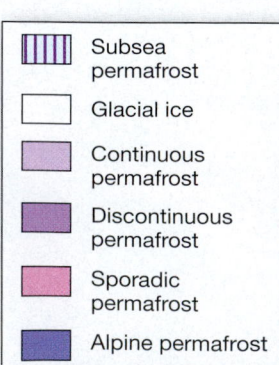

Subsea permafrost	
Glacial ice	
Continuous permafrost	
Discontinuous permafrost	
Sporadic permafrost	
Alpine permafrost	

Continuous and Discontinuous Zones Permafrost regions are divided into two general categories, continuous and discontinuous, which merge along a general transition zone. *Continuous permafrost* occurs in the region of severest cold and is perennial, roughly poleward of the −7°C (19°F) mean annual temperature isotherm (white area in Figure 17.21). Continuous permafrost affects all surfaces except those beneath deep lakes or rivers. The depth of continuous permafrost averages approximately 400 m (1300 ft) and may exceed 1000 m (3300 ft).

Unconnected patches of *discontinuous permafrost* gradually coalesce poleward of the −1°C (30.2°F) mean annual temperature isotherm (light purple area in Figure 17.21), toward the continuous zone. In contrast, equatorward of this isotherm, permafrost becomes scattered or sporadic until it gradually disappears. In the discontinuous zone of the Northern Hemisphere, permafrost is absent on sun-exposed south-facing slopes, in areas of warm soil, and in areas insulated by snow. In the Southern Hemisphere, north-facing slopes experience increased warmth.

Discontinuous permafrost zones are the most susceptible to thawing with climate change. Their peat-rich soils, discussed in Chapter 18, contain large amounts of carbon, and as they thaw, the release of carbon dioxide creates a powerful positive feedback that accelerates warming (review Focus Study 10.1).

Permafrost Behavior Figure 17.22 shows a cross section of a periglacial region in northern Canada, extending

from approximately 75° N to 55° N latitude through the three sites located on the map in Figure 17.21. The zone of seasonally frozen ground that exists between the subsurface permafrost layer and the ground surface is called the **active layer** and is subjected to consistent daily and seasonal freeze–thaw cycles. This zone ranges in depth by latitude (thinner at higher latitude, slightly thicker at lower latitude) and also occurs in alpine permafrost, such as in the Colorado Rockies.

Permafrost actively adjusts to changing climatic conditions: Higher temperatures reduce permafrost thickness and increase the thickness of the active layer; lower temperatures gradually increase permafrost thickness and reduce active-layer thickness. Although somewhat sluggish in response, the active layer is a dynamic, open system driven by energy gains and losses in the subsurface environment.

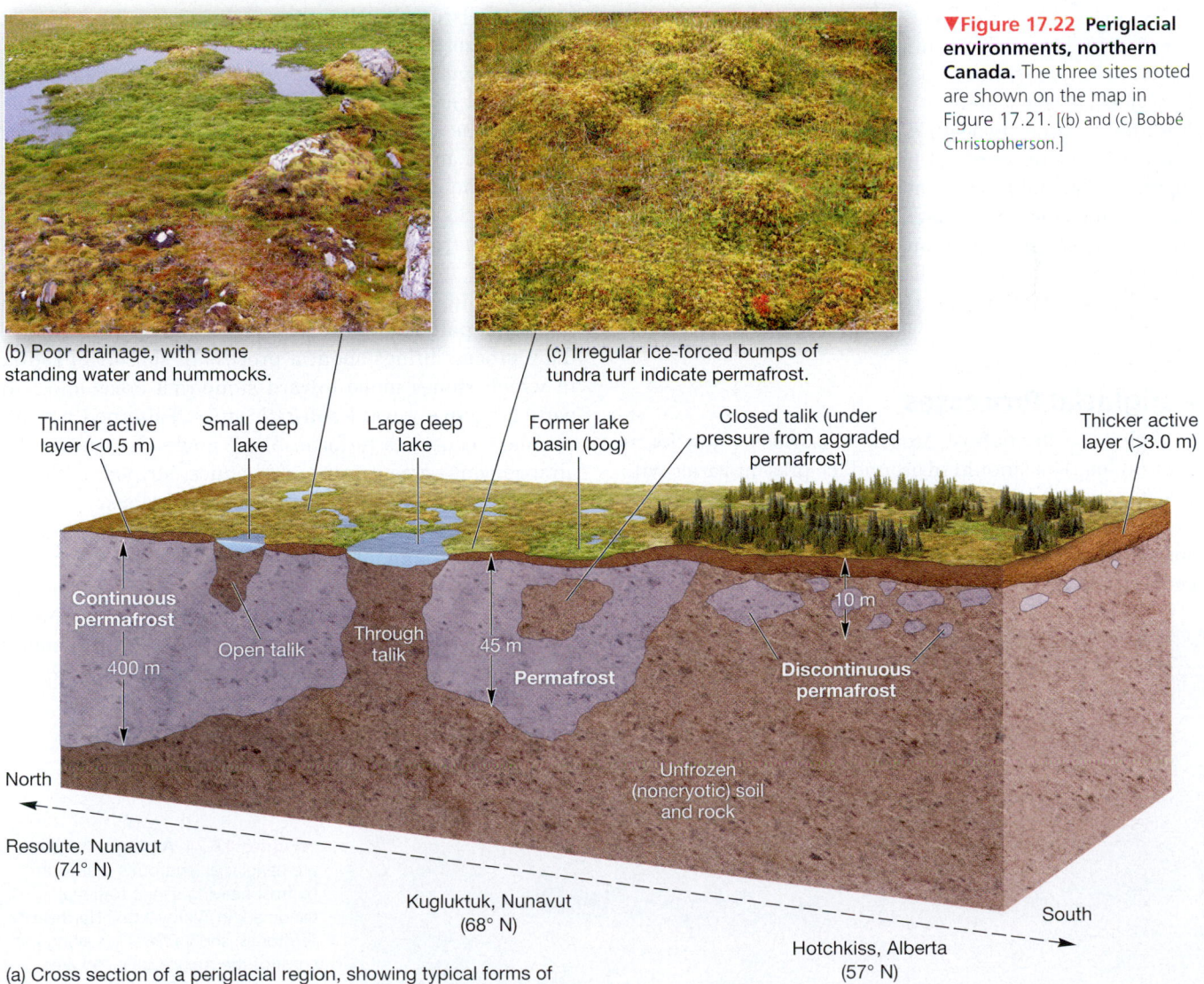

▼**Figure 17.22 Periglacial environments, northern Canada.** The three sites noted are shown on the map in Figure 17.21. [(b) and (c) Bobbé Christopherson.]

(b) Poor drainage, with some standing water and hummocks.

(c) Irregular ice-forced bumps of tundra turf indicate permafrost.

Thinner active layer (<0.5 m)

Small deep lake

Large deep lake

Former lake basin (bog)

Closed talik (under pressure from aggraded permafrost)

Thicker active layer (>3.0 m)

Continuous permafrost

Open talik

Through talik

400 m

45 m

Permafrost

10 m

Discontinuous permafrost

Unfrozen (noncryotic) soil and rock

North

Resolute, Nunavut (74° N)

Kugluktuk, Nunavut (68° N)

Hotchkiss, Alberta (57° N)

South

(a) Cross section of a periglacial region, showing typical forms of permafrost in relation to the active layer, talik, and surface features.

(b) Polygons and circles (about a meter across) in a stone-dominant area, Nordaustlandet Island, Arctic Ocean. The stone-centered polygons indicate higher stone concentrations.

(c) Polygons and circles in a soil-dominant area, Spitsbergen Island, northern Norway. The soil-centered polygons indicate higher soil-particle concentrations with lesser availability of stones.

▲Figure 17.23 **Patterned-ground phenomena.** [(a) Courtesy of Joan Myers. (b) and (c) Bobbé Christopherson.]

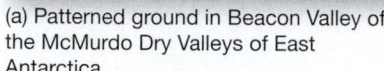

(a) Patterned ground in Beacon Valley of the McMurdo Dry Valleys of East Antarctica.

A *talik* is an area of unfrozen ground that may occur above, below, or within a body of discontinuous permafrost or beneath a water body in regions of continuous permafrost. Taliks occur beneath deep lakes and may extend to bedrock and unfrozen soil beneath large, deep lakes (see Figure 17.22). Taliks in areas of discontinuous permafrost form connections between the active layer and groundwater, whereas in continuous permafrost, groundwater is essentially cut off from surface water. In this way, permafrost disrupts aquifers and taliks, leading to water-supply problems.

Periglacial Processes

In regions of permafrost, frozen subsurface water forms **ground ice**. The amount of ground ice present varies with moisture content, ranging from only a small percentage in drier regions to almost 100% in regions with saturated soils. The presence of frozen water in the soil initiates geomorphic processes associated with *frost action*.

Frost Action Processes The 9% expansion of water as it freezes produces strong mechanical forces that fracture rock and disrupt soil at or below the surface. If sufficient water freezes, the saturated soil and rocks are subjected to *frost heaving* (vertical movement) and *frost thrusting* (horizontal movement). Boulders and rock slabs may be thrust to the surface. Layers of soil may be disrupted by frost action and appear to be stirred or churned. Frost action also can produce contractions in soil and rock, opening up cracks in which ice wedges can form.

In some periglacial regions, the expansion and contraction of frost action result in the movement of soil particles, stones, and small boulders into distinct shapes known as **patterned ground** (**Figure 17.23**). This freeze–thaw process brings about a process of self-organization in which stones move toward stone-rich areas and soil particles move toward soil-rich areas. Patterned ground may take centuries to form. Slope angle also affects the arrangement—greater slopes produce striped patterns, whereas lesser slopes result in sorted polygons.

A distinct periglacial landform that results from the heaving of ground ice within permafrost is a *pingo*, a large mound of earth-covered ice (**Figure 17.24**). Some of the largest pingos in the Arctic are 600 m (2000 ft) in diameter and up to 70 m (230 ft) tall.

◀Figure 17.24 **A pingo.** Pingos are periglacial landforms that form by frost heaving. Pingo National Landmark in Tuktoyaktuk, Northwest Territories, shown here, lies along the coast of the Arctic Ocean, an area that includes about one-quarter of the world's pingos. [Timothy Epp/Alamy.]

▲Figure 17.25 **Solifluction lobes, Breiddalfjellet mountain, Troms, Norway.** [blickwinkel/Alamy.]

Hillslope Processes: Gelifluction and Solifluction

Soil drainage is poor in areas of permafrost and ground ice. The active layer of soil and regolith is saturated with soil moisture during the thaw cycle (summer), and the whole layer commences to flow from higher to lower elevation if the landscape is even slightly inclined. This flow of soil is generally called *solifluction*. In the presence of ground ice or permafrost, the more specific term *gelifluction* is applied. In this ice-bound type of soil flow, movement up to 5 cm (2 in.) per year can occur on slopes as gentle as a degree or two.

The cumulative effect of this flow can be an overall flattening of a rolling landscape, combined with visibly sagging surfaces and scalloped and lobed patterns in the downslope soil movements (**Figure 17.25**). Other types of periglacial mass movement include failure in the active layer, producing translational and rotational slides and rapid flows associated with melting ground ice. Periglacial mass-movement processes are related to slope dynamics and processes discussed in Chapter 13

Human Structures and Permafrost In areas of permafrost, people face certain problems related to periglacial landforms and phenomena. Because thawed ground above the permafrost zone frequently shifts, highways and rail lines may warp or twist, and utility lines are disrupted. In addition, any building placed directly on frozen ground will "melt" (subside) into the defrosting soil (**Figure 17.26**).

In periglacial regions, structures must be suspended slightly above the ground to allow air circulation beneath. The airflow permits the ground to cycle through its normal annual temperature pattern. Utilities such as water and sewer lines must be enclosed aboveground to protect them from freezing and thawing ground. The trans-Alaska oil pipeline was constructed aboveground on racks to avoid thawing the frozen ground and causing shifting that could rupture the line (see Figure HD 17a).

(a)

(b)

▲Figure 17.26 **Permafrost thawing and structure collapse.** (a) An improperly constructed building conducts heat to the ground and causes permafrost thaw. (b) A cabin sinks and eventually collapses as permafrost thaws south of Fairbanks, Alaska. [Photo by Steve McCutcheon/Anchorage Museum; based on U.S. Geological Survey pamphlet "Permafrost" by L. L. Ray.]

GEOreport **17.1** Frozen debris lobes approach highways in Alaska

Along interior northern Alaska's main highway, giant slabs of slowly moving ice, soil, and sediment known as frozen debris lobes, or FDLs, are threating to overrun everything in their path—including portions of the road and the trans-Alaska oil pipeline. FDLs are slow-moving landslides that occur in permafrost, and many are located on the southern slopes of Alaska's Brooks Range. As of October 2016, the lobe dubbed "FDL-A" was about 34 m (112 ft) away from the Dalton Highway, approaching at a rate of 1.5 cm/day. See http://fdlalaska.org/ for videos and more information.

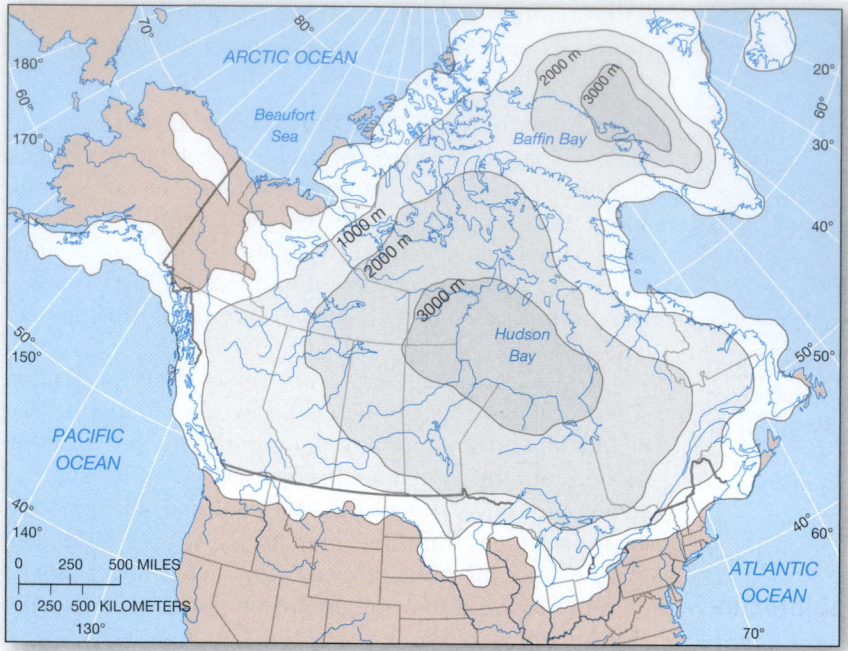

(a) Ice-sheet extent 18,000 years ago over North America, with ice sheet thickness (in meters).

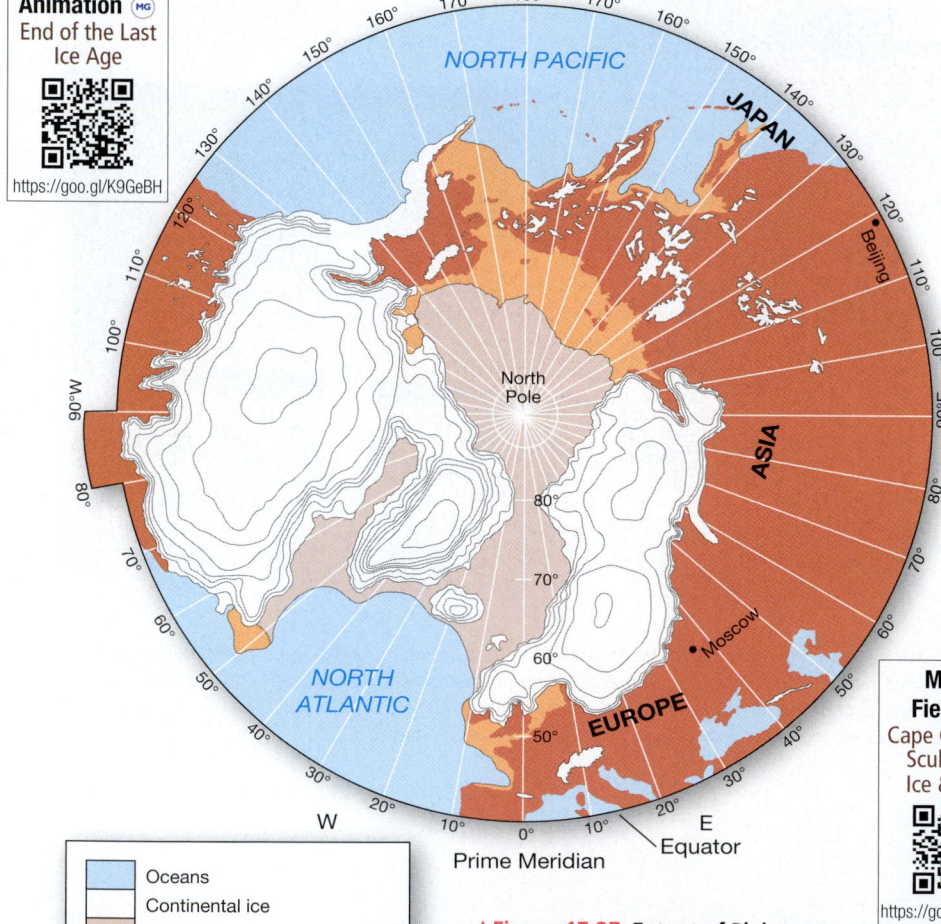

Animation MG
End of the Last Ice Age

https://goo.gl/K9GeBH

Mobile MG
Field Trip
Cape Cod: Land Sculpted by Ice & Storm

https://goo.gl/mQquM6

Legend:
- Oceans
- Continental ice
- Sea ice
- Continents
- Ice extent at glacial maximum (about 20,000 years ago)

(b) Polar perspective, 18,000 years ago.

▲Figure 17.27 **Extent of Pleistocene glaciation.** Earlier episodes produced ice sheets of slightly greater extent. [From A. McIntyre, *CLIMAP* (Climate: Long-Range Investigation, Mapping, and Prediction) Project, Lamont–Doherty Earth Observatory. © 1981 by the GSA. Adapted by permission.]

The Pleistocene Epoch

Imagine almost a third of Earth's land surface buried beneath ice sheets and glaciers—most of Canada, the northern Midwest, England, and northern Europe, with many mountain ranges beneath thousands of meters of ice. This occurred at the height of the Pleistocene Epoch of the late Cenozoic Era (see Chapter 11, Figure 11.2). During this time, periglacial regions along the margins of the ice covered about twice the areal extent of periglacial regions today.

The Pleistocene Epoch, thought to have begun about 2.6 million years ago, was one of the more prolonged cold periods in Earth's history. The term **ice age**, or *glacial age*, is applied to any extended period of cold (not a single brief cold spell), in some cases lasting several million years. An ice age includes one or more *glacials*, characterized by glacial advance, interrupted by brief warm spells known as *interglacials*. The Pleistocene featured not just one glacial advance and retreat, but at least 18 expansions of ice over Europe and North America. Glaciation can take about 100,000 years, whereas deglaciation is rapid, requiring less than about 10,000 years for the ice accumulation to melt away.

Pleistocene Landscapes

Extensive continental ice sheets covered portions of Canada, the United States, Europe, and Asia about 18,000 years ago (**Figure 17.27**). These ice sheets ranged in thickness to more than 3 km (1.9 mi). In North America, the Ohio and Missouri River systems mark the southern terminus of continuous ice at its greatest extent during the Pleistocene Epoch. The ice sheet disappeared by 7000 years ago.

Continental glaciation occurred several times over the region we know as the Great Lakes (**Figure 17.28**). The ice enlarged and deepened stream valleys to form the basins of the future lakes. This complex history produced five lakes that hold some 18% of all the lake water on Earth. Figure 17.28 shows the final sequence in the formation of today's Great Lakes, which involved two advancing and two retreating stages—between 13,200 and 10,000 years before the present. During the final retreat, tremendous quantities of glacial meltwater flowed into the isostatically depressed basins—that is, basins that were lowered by the weight of the ice. Drainage at first was to the Mississippi River via the Illinois River, to the St. Lawrence River via the Ottawa River, and to the Hudson River in the east. Today, drainage is solely through the St. Lawrence system.

As the Pleistocene glaciers retreated, they exposed a drastically altered landscape: the rocky soils of New England, the polished and scarred surfaces of Canada's Atlantic Provinces, the sharp crests of the Sawtooth Range in Idaho, the scenery of the Canadian Rockies and the Sierra Nevada, the Matterhorn of Switzerland, and much more. In the Southern Hemisphere, evidence of this ice age exists in the form of fjords and sculpted mountains in New Zealand and Chile.

Sea levels 18,000 years ago were approximately 100 m (330 ft) lower than they are today because so much of Earth's water was frozen in glaciers. Imagine the coastline of New York being 100 km farther east, Alaska and Russia connected by land across the Bering Strait, and England and France joined by a land bridge.

Paleolakes

From 12,000 to 30,000 years ago, the American West was dotted with large, ancient lakes—**paleolakes**, or *pluvial lakes* (**Figure 17.29**). The term *pluvial* (from the Latin word for "rain") describes any extended period of wet conditions, such as occurred during the Pleistocene Epoch. During pluvial periods in arid regions, lake levels increase in closed basins with internal drainage. During these wet periods, **lacustrine deposits** of lake sediments form terraces, or benches, along shorelines. Then, during the drier periods between pluvials, called *interpluvials*, these deposits are exposed on the landscape. Except for the Great Salt Lake in Utah (a remnant of the former Lake Bonneville; Figure 17.29a) and a few smaller lakes, only dry basins, ancient shorelines, and lake sediments remain today.

Recent evidence suggests that the occurrence of paleolakes in North America was related to specific changes in the polar jet stream that steered storm tracks across the region, creating pluvial conditions. The continental ice sheet evidently influenced changes in the position of the jet stream.

Paleolakes existed in North and South America, Africa, Asia, and Australia. Today, ancient shorelines about 80 m (265 ft) above the present level of the Caspian Sea in Kazakhstan and southern Russia indicate the extent of this paleolake. In North America, the two largest late Pleistocene paleolakes were Lake Bonneville and Lake Lahontan, located in the Basin and Range Province in the western United States. These two lakes were much larger than their present-day remnants.

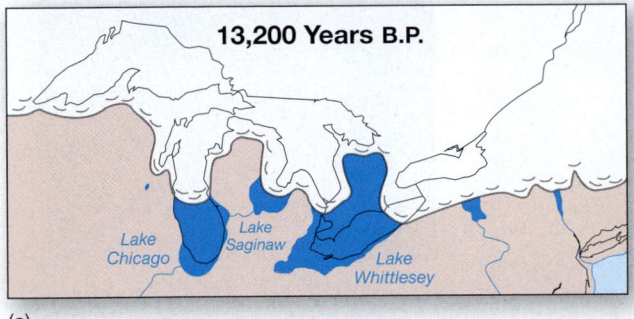
(a)

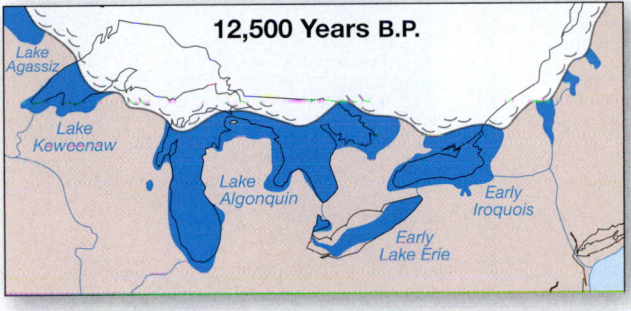
(b)

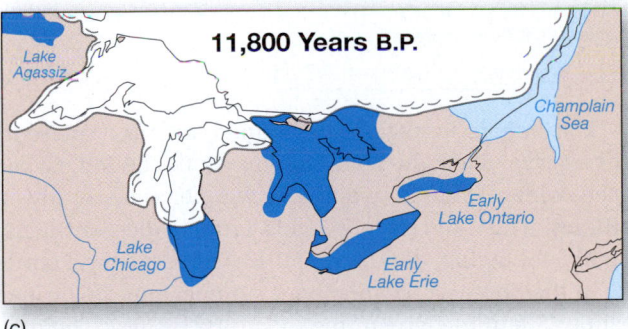
(c)

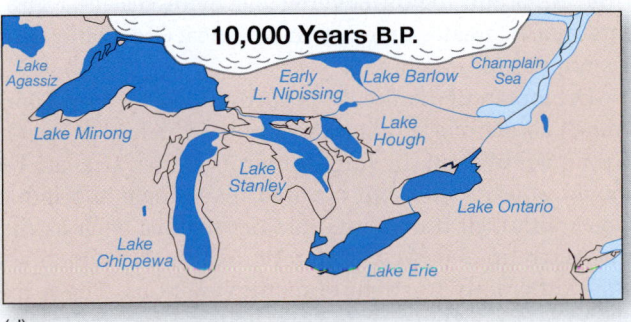
(d)

▲**Figure 17.28 Late stages of Great Lakes formation.** Four "snapshots" illustrate the evolution of the Great Lakes during the most recent glacial retreat. Note the change in stream drainage between (b) and (d). Time is in years before the present (B.P.). [*After The Great Lakes— An Environmental Atlas and Resource Book*, Environment Canada, U.S. EPA, Brock University, and Northwestern University, 1987.]

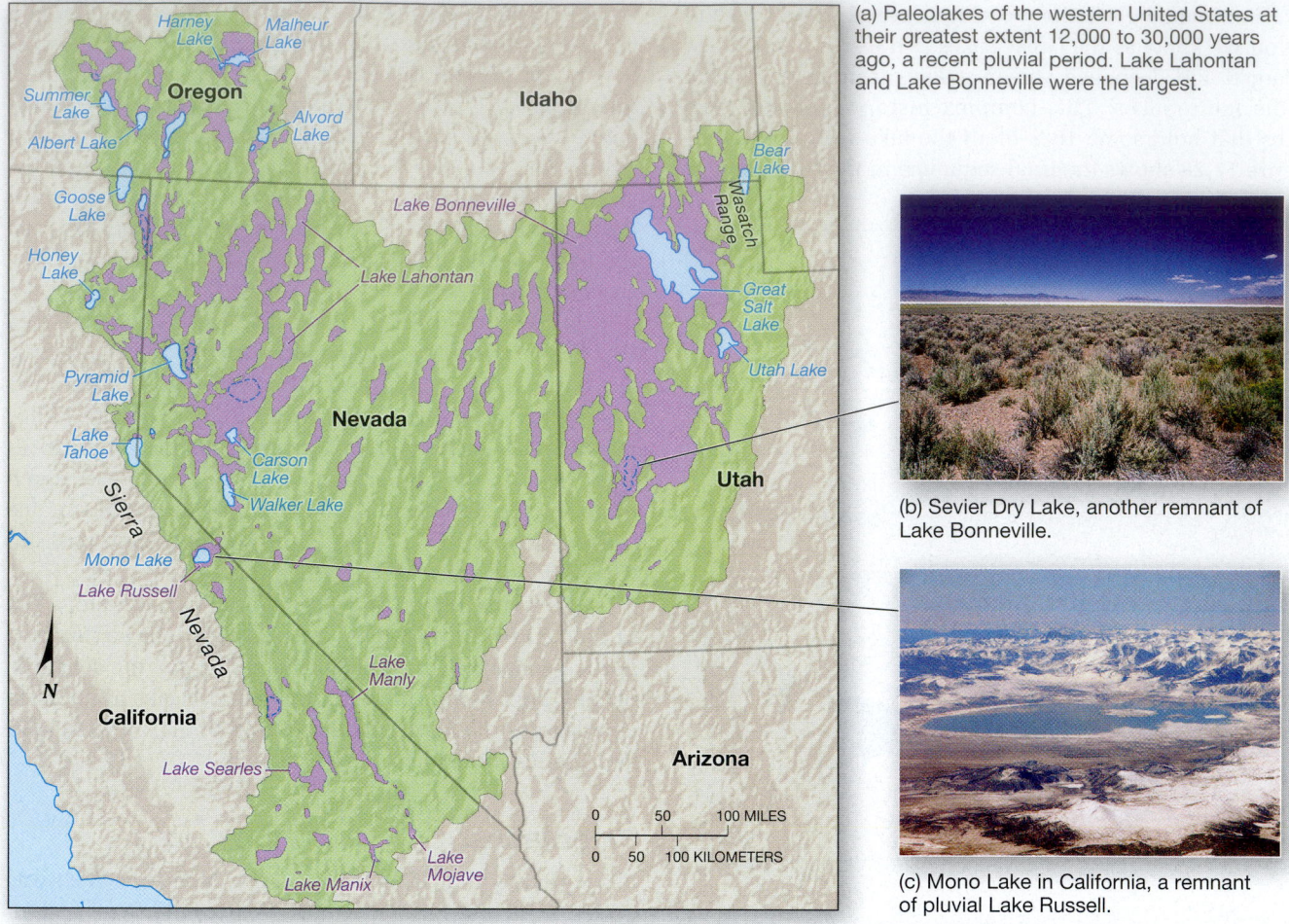

(a) Paleolakes of the western United States at their greatest extent 12,000 to 30,000 years ago, a recent pluvial period. Lake Lahontan and Lake Bonneville were the largest.

(b) Sevier Dry Lake, another remnant of Lake Bonneville.

(c) Mono Lake in California, a remnant of pluvial Lake Russell.

▲Figure 17.29 Paleolakes in the western United States. [(a) After USGS. (b) and (c) Bobbé Christopherson.]

The Great Salt Lake, near Salt Lake City, Utah, and the Bonneville Salt Flats in western Utah are remnants of Lake Bonneville. The Great Salt Lake is today the fourth largest saline lake in the world. At its greatest extent, this paleolake covered more than 50,000 km² (19,500 mi²) and reached depths of 300 m (1000 ft), spilling over into the Snake River drainage to the north. Now, it is a closed-basin terminal lake with no drainage except an artificial outlet to the west, where excess water from the Great Salt Lake can be pumped during rare floods. Lake levels continue to decline in response to climate change to drier conditions.

Arctic and Antarctic Regions

Climatologists use environmental criteria to designate the Arctic and the Antarctic regions. The 10°C (50°F) isotherm for July defines the Arctic region (green line on the map in **Figure 17.30a**). This line coincides on land with the visible tree line—the boundary between the northern forests and tundra. On the sea, the Arctic region is characterized by the presence of *pack ice* (masses of drifting ice, unattached to shore), which occurs as two general types: *floating sea ice* (frozen seawater) and *glacier ice* (frozen freshwater). This pack ice thins in the summer months and sometimes breaks up.

The Antarctic region is defined by the Antarctic convergence, a narrow zone that marks the boundary between colder Antarctic water and warmer water at lower latitudes. This boundary extends around the continent, roughly following the 10°C (50°F) isotherm for February, in the Southern Hemisphere summer, and is located near 60° S latitude (green line in **Figure 17.30b**). The part of the Antarctic region covered just with sea ice represents an area greater than North America, Greenland, and Western Europe combined.

The Antarctic landmass is surrounded by ocean and is much colder overall than the Arctic, which is an ocean surrounded by land. In simplest terms, Antarctica can be thought of as a continent covered by a single enormous glacier, although it contains distinct regions such as the East Antarctic and West Antarctic Ice Sheets, which respond differently to slight climatic variations. These ice sheets are in constant motion.

Recent Polar Region Changes

As discussed in Geosystems Now, the polar regions are changing as air and ocean temperatures warm, and many of these changes are part of feedback loops that accelerate melting. In this section, we discuss declining sea ice, ice-sheet darkening, and the recent breakup of outlet glaciers and ice shelves in Greenland and Antarctica.

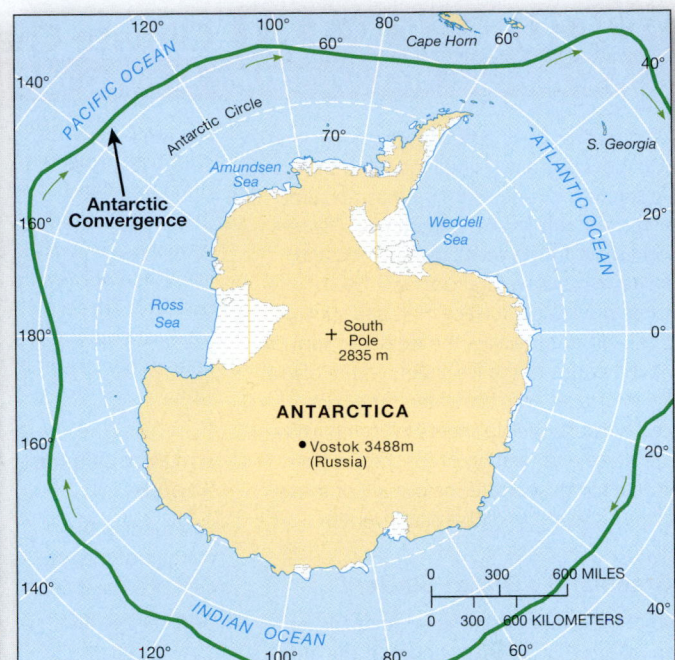

(a) Note the 10°C (50°F) isotherm in midsummer, which designates the Arctic region.

(b) The Antarctic convergence, which varies seasonally in latitude, designates the Antarctic region.

▲**Figure 17.30 The Arctic and Antarctic regions.**

Sea Ice Since satellite measurements began in 1979, the annual sea-ice volume in the Arctic region has decreased by nearly half due to warming throughout the region. Every year, the frozen seawater floating on top of the Arctic Ocean and its connected seas melts during the spring and summer, reaching its lowest yearly extent in September. The ice then reforms in the fall and winter months, reaching its maximum yearly extent between February and April. The smallest summer sea-ice minimum extent on record occurred in the year 2012; the second smallest summer extent was in 2007 and 2016. Because the region is now ice-free for a portion of the summer, cruise ships and container ships today travel the northern passages across the Arctic Ocean. Winter ice

is also declining. The smallest winter sea-ice maximum extent on record occurred in March 2016 (**Figure 17.31a**). These changes affect surface albedo, with impacts on global climate (review the Chapter 4 Geosystems Now).

In the Antarctic region, sea ice has increased since 1979—a trend opposite that which is occurring in the Arctic. Scientists attribute the increase to winds, ocean currents, and pressure systems, all of which influence ice formation. Antarctic annual winter sea ice extent reached a record high in 2014 (**Figure 17.31b**), before returning to average in 2015. When the Arctic and Antarctic trends are taken together, research shows that the decrease in Arctic ice exceeds the increase in Antarctic ice, for an overall trend toward global losses of sea-ice volume.

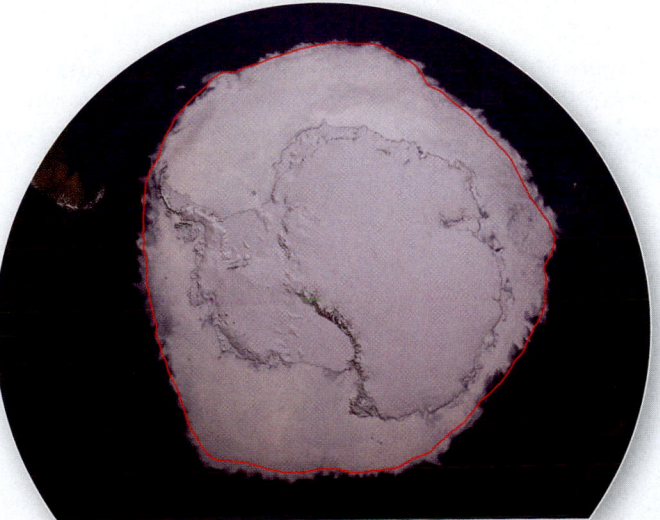

(a) Arctic maximum winter sea-ice extent was at a record low in March 2016.

(b) Antarctic maximum winter sea-ice extent was at a record high in September 2014.

▲**Figure 17.31 Arctic and Antarctic winter sea-ice extent.** The red line in (b) shows the 1979-2014 average. [NASA.]

FOCUSstudy 17.1 Climate Change
Greenland and Antarctica: Melting at the Edges of the Continental Ice

As discussed in Chapter 10, the Greenland Ice Sheet is today losing mass, and the Antarctic Ice Sheet is losing mass in some areas, notably in West Antarctica. Glaciers gain mass from snow accumulation and lose mass by several processes. Two of these processes, surface melt and sublimation, can occur across the ice-sheet surface. At the edges of the ice sheet, where glacial ice interfaces with seawater, other processes cause the ice sheets to shrink: calving of ice and melting of ice shelves from contact with seawater below. All of these changes relate to global sea-level rise.

Greenland's Outlet Glaciers

Outlet glaciers along the edge of the ice sheet are thinner than the ice at the interior and move more rapidly than the ice sheet itself. These outlet glaciers terminate either on land or at the sea (forming a tidewater glacier). With warmer air melting ice from above and higher sea temperatures melting ice from below, calving from these tidewater glaciers continues to increase.

In northwest Greenland in August 2010, an island of ice measuring 251 km² (97 mi²) broke loose from the Petermann Glacier, forming the largest iceberg in the Arctic in a half century. Then in July 2012, another large iceberg broke off the tongue of the glacier near the 2010 event (**Figure 17.1.1**). The rate of melting in Greenland—both surface melt and the rapid flow and breakup of glaciers into the ocean—continues to accelerate so that scientists cannot accurately forecast the effects of freshwater melt on sea level. In 2013, scientists projected that Greenland melt rates would produce a 23 cm (9 in.) rise in sea level by 2100. These forecasts now appear to be conservative.

Antarctica's Ice Shelves

Surrounding the margins of the Antarctic Ice Sheet and constituting about

(a) Scientists use GPS and tiltmeters to measure the effect of ocean tides on the Nansen Ice Shelf in 2016.

(b) Scientists photographed a large crack extending across almost the entire width of the ice shelf in December 2015.

▲**Figure 17.1.2 Breakup of the Nansen Ice Shelf, Antarctica.** The Nansen Ice Shelf is near the Ross Ice Shelf in West Antarctica. [NASA.]

11% of its surface area are *ice shelves*—thick, floating platforms of ice that extend over the sea while still attached to continental ice.

Although ice shelves constantly break up to produce icebergs, more large sections have broken free in the past two decades than expected. In March 2000, an iceberg tagged B-15, measuring twice the area of Delaware, broke off the Ross Ice Shelf. In 2002, the Larsen Ice shelf lost a large section, which collapsed into icebergs in only 35 days. In 2013, the Wilkins Ice Shelf underwent further disintegration after major breakup events in 2008 and 2009. Scientists hypothesize that the recent breakups made the remaining ice more vulnerable, especially in places where the shelf remnants are in direct contact with open water and the force of ocean waves. Research is ongoing (**Figure 17.1.2**).

▼**Figure 17.1.1 Greenland tidewater glacier breakup, 2012.** A large iceberg (black arrow) breaks off the Petermann Glacier in northwest Greenland. [*Aqua* MODIS, NASA.]

July 17, 2012

Petermann Glacier

10 km
N

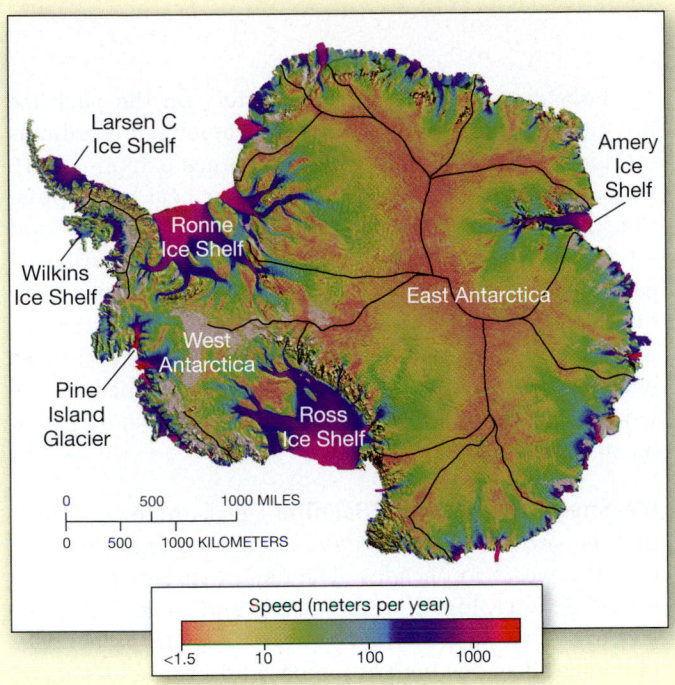

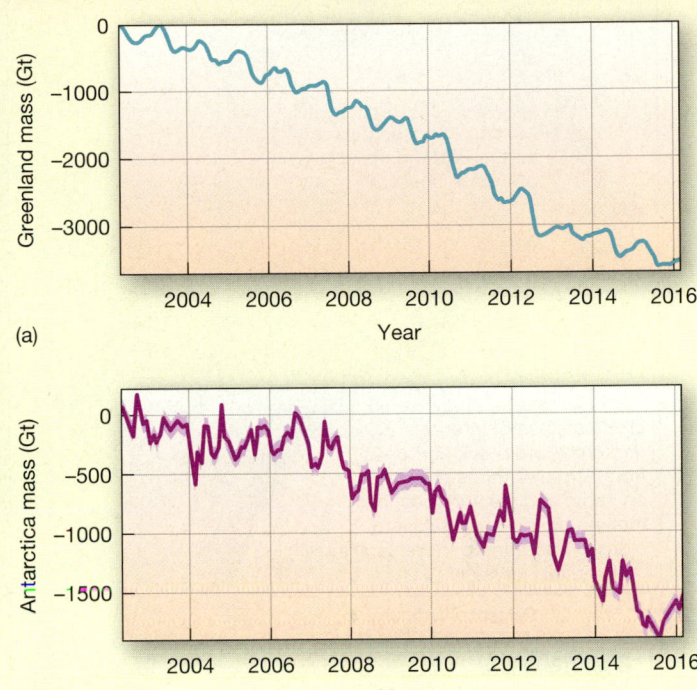

▲**Figure 17.1.3 First complete map of ice movement speed in Antarctica.** The black lines show ice divides, similar to drainage divides. Colors indicate the speed of ice movement; fastest movement is in red and purple. The tributaries shown in blue are moving faster than the ice sheet around them, but do not move as quickly as an ice stream. [*RADARSAT–SAR*, NASA/JPL.]

▲**Figure 17.1.4 Mass losses from the Greenland and Antarctic Ice Sheets from 2002 to 2016.** [Data from *GRACE* satellites, NASA; climate.nasa.gov.]

A map of ice movement speed on the Antarctic continent reveals that many of the tributaries around ice shelves extend surprisingly far inland (**Figure 17.1.3**). The tributaries are moving by basal slip (sliding on the ground) rather than slowly deforming under the weight of the ice (as happens on the ice-sheet interior). Identifying the areal extent of this type of motion on the ice sheet is important because a loss of ice at the coasts as ice shelves break up may open the tap for massive amounts of grounded ice to flow more quickly from the interior. As the ice shelves disappear, their buttressing effect is lost, allowing the outlet glaciers to flow more rapidly.

The breakup of an ice shelf does not directly influence sea level because the ice shelf mass has already displaced its own volume in seawater. However, as tributary glaciers reach the sea, the melting of grounded ice enhances sea-level rise. In 2014, scientists suggested that a large portion of the West Antarctic Ice Sheet could melt in the next 100 to 200 years, an event that would raise sea level as much as 1.2 m (4 ft).

In 2015, scientists reported that East Antarctica, which is higher in elevation and generally colder than the rest of the ice sheet, gained enough mass from snowfall to offset the losses of ice in West Antarctica. However, this temporary increase falls within an overall trend of ice mass decline on both the Antarctic and Greenland Ice Sheets (**Figure 17.1.4**).

1. Compare and contrast the effects of the melting of Greenland's outlet and tidewater glaciers with the melting of ice shelves around Antarctica.

2. Assuming that the amounts of ice involved are the same, which would contribute more to sea-level rise: the melting of an outlet glacier in Greenland or the melting of part of an ice shelf in Antarctica? Explain.

APPLYconcepts Use the map in Figure 17.1.3 to answer the questions about Antarctica's ice sheet.

1. Where are Antarctica's largest ice shelves?	1. _____
2. In which region are the tributary glaciers around ice shelves extending farthest inland?	2. _____
3. What is the approximate speed of the tributary glaciers?	3. _____
4. In what part of Antarctica is ice movement speed slowest?	4. _____
5. State one generalization about the spatial distribution of melting in Antarctica based on patterns you see in the map.	5. _____

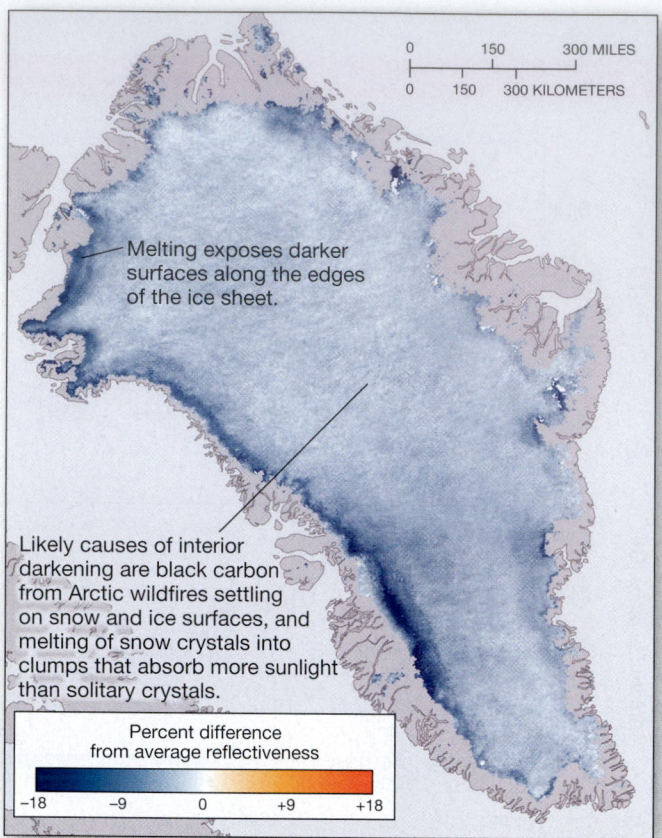

Melting exposes darker surfaces along the edges of the ice sheet.

Likely causes of interior darkening are black carbon from Arctic wildfires settling on snow and ice surfaces, and melting of snow crystals into clumps that absorb more sunlight than solitary crystals.

Percent difference from average reflectiveness

−18   −9   0   +9   +18

(a) Data from this 2011 image indicate that some areas of the ice sheet reflect 20% less sunlight than just a decade ago.

▲**Figure 17.32** **Darkening of Greenland ice surfaces and recent ice-sheet melting.** [(a) *Terra/Aqua* MODIS, NASA. (b) Data courtesy NSIDC/ Thomas Mote, University of Georgia.]

Polar bears (*Ursus maritimus*) rely on the pack ice for hunting and breeding, and are among the animals most affected by changes in Arctic sea-ice extent. A 2016 study found that, across 17 of 19 polar bear subpopulations, days with sea-ice cover declined between 7 and 19 days per decade from 1979 to 2014. These areas saw earlier ice breakup in the spring and later freeze-up in the fall. Although the bears can exist on land, the sea ice is where they feed on seals, their main prey. If these animals lose their sea-ice habitat, some two-thirds of the world's 23,000 polar bears will be seriously endangered by 2050 or earlier.

Ice-Sheet Darkening Satellite measurements show that the surface of the Greenland Ice Sheet has darkened over the past two decades. The darker surface decreases the reflectivity, lowering the albedo and causing the surface to absorb more thermal energy. Along the outer edges of the ice sheet, ice melt has exposed darker land, vegetation, and water surfaces. On the interior, ice melt has exposed older, "dirtier" ice surfaces, with accumulations of materials such as dust and black carbon from wildfires in Asia and North America (**Figure 17.32**). Another factor contributing to overall darkening may be related to basic processes of snow metamorphism: As temperatures rise, snow crystals clump together in the snow pack, reflecting less light than the smaller, faceted individual crystals. The overall effect is that the ice sheet now absorbs more sunlight, which speeds up melting and causes a positive feedback that accelerates warming.

In July 2012, a record 97% of the Greenland Ice Sheet was covered with meltwater (Figure 17.32b). In 2016, the melt started early in the spring but was closer to average overall. During the 2012 melt, the number of melt streams and *supraglacial lakes* (meltwater collections on the ice surface) increased. As discussed in Geosystems Now, these meltwater features drain through the ice sheet through *moulins*, nearly vertical conduits through the ice that carry water from the surface to the base of the ice sheet.

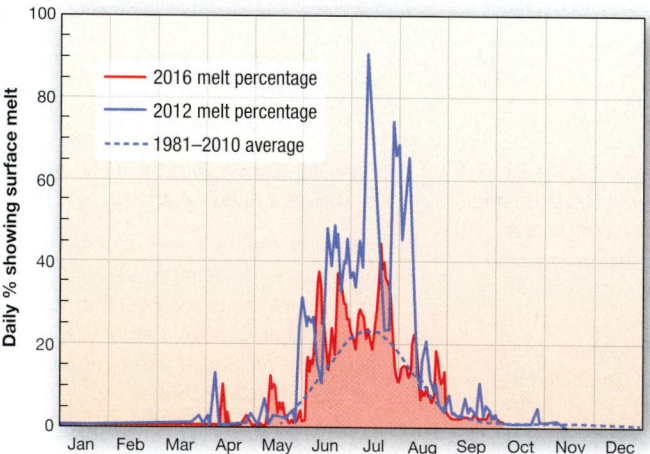

(b) Surface melt on the Greenland Ice Sheet in 2012 reached its greatest extent in the satellite record since 1979. Melt during 2016 was above the average (dotted line).

GEOreport 17.2   A luxury cruise ship crosses the Northern Passage

On August 16, 2016, the *Crystal Serenity* cruise ship with 1700 passengers aboard set out from Seward, Alaska, bound for New York City by way of the Northwest Passage through the Arctic Ocean. Recently open to boat traffic for only about a decade, the Northwest Passage was historically blocked by ice even during the summer months. With ongoing climate change, the sea route is now open to boat traffic for several months a year. Hailed on one hand as "a pioneering journey" and on the other hand as "an abomination" for the ship's use of fossil fuels and emissions of soot into the atmosphere, the 2016 voyage evoked media controversy. For better or worse, the once-pristine Alaskan and Canadian Arctic—abundant with wildlife and noted for its isolation—is now open for the business of high-end tourism.

GLACIAL ENVIRONMENTS IMPACT HUMANS

• Glacial ice is a freshwater resource; ice masses affect sea level, which is linked to human population centers along coastlines.
• Snow avalanches are a natural hazard in mountain environments.
• Permafrost soils are a carbon sink; thawing permafrost releases carbon to the atmosphere.

HUMANS IMPACT GLACIAL ENVIRONMENTS

• Rising temperatures with climate changes are accelerating ice-sheet losses and glacial melting, and hastening permafrost thaw.
• Particulates in the air from natural and human sources darken snow and ice surfaces, which accelerates melting.

17a A 675-km (420-mi) section of the trans-Alaska oil pipeline was constructed above the ground to prevent permafrost thaw. The pipeline is 1.2 m (4 ft) in diameter, and throughout this distance is supported on racks that average 1.5 to 3.0 m (5 to 10 ft) high. [Rough Guides/Zumapress/Newscom.]

17b A USGS scientist photographs Grinnell Glacier in Glacier National Park, Montana, as part of a repeat photography project to document the effects of climate change on glacial retreat. [USGS/Lisa McKeon, Northern Rocky Mountain Science Center.]

17d Argentina's Perito Moreno Glacier on the South Patagonian Ice Field in Los Glaciares National Park is a premier tourist destination. Recent research found that glaciers in this region are thinning at a rate of about 1.8 m (5.9 ft) per year. These freshwater losses will impact regional water supplies. [elnavegante/Shutterstock.]

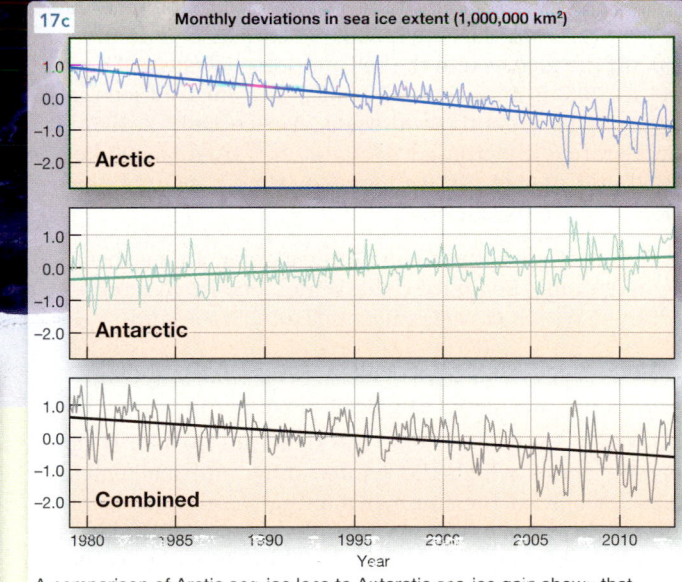

17c Monthly deviations in sea ice extent (1,000,000 km²)

Arctic

Antarctic

Combined

A comparison of Arctic sea-ice loss to Antarctic sea-ice gain shows that, overall, Earth has steadily lost sea ice since 1979. Despite the small Antarctic gains, each year an area of sea ice larger than the state of Maryland disappears. [Joshua Stevens and Jesse Allen/NASA.]

ISSUES FOR THE 21ST CENTURY

• Melting of glaciers and ice sheets will continue to raise sea level, with potentially devastating consequences to low-lying island nations and coastal communities.
• Permafrost thaw will release carbon to the atmosphere and affect tundra ecosystems.

QUESTIONS TO CONSIDER

1. In your own words, write a sentence based on Figure HD17c summing up the contributions of both polar regions to recent global changes in sea-ice extent.
2. What process associated with glacial melting are the tourists aboard the boat in Figure HD17d likely to observe as they cruise past the Perito Moreno glacier?

KEY**LEARNING**concepts**review**

Explain the process by which snow becomes glacial ice.

More than 77% of Earth's freshwater is frozen, and ice covers about 11% of Earth's surface. Earth's **cryosphere** (p. 492) is the portion of the hydrosphere and ground that is perennially frozen, generally at high latitudes and elevations.

A **snowline** (p. 494) is the lowest elevation where snow occurs year-round, and this elevation varies by latitude—higher near the equator, lower poleward. Snow becomes glacial ice through stages of accumulation, increasing thickness, pressure on underlying layers, and recrystallization. Snow progresses through transitional steps from compact, granular **firn** (p. 494), to a denser **glacial ice** (p. 494) after many years.

1. Locate and describe the cryosphere.
2. Trace the evolution of glacial ice from fresh fallen snow.

Differentiate between alpine glaciers and continental ice sheets.

A **glacier** (p. 494) is a mass of ice sitting on land or floating as an ice shelf in the ocean next to land. Glaciers form in areas of permanent snow. A glacier in a mountain range is an **alpine glacier** (p. 494). If confined within a valley, it is termed a *valley glacier*. The area of origin is a snowfield, usually in a bowl-shaped erosional landform called a **cirque** (p. 495). Where alpine glaciers flow down to the sea, the process of **calving** (p. 495) occurs as masses of ice break off the glacier into the sea and form *icebergs*. An **ice sheet** (p. 495) is an extensive, continuous mass of ice that may occur on a continental scale. An **ice cap** (p. 495) is a smaller, roughly circular ice mass, less than 50,000 km² (19,300 mi²) in size. An ice mass covering a mountainous region is an **ice field** (p. 496).

3. Differentiate between an alpine glacier, an ice sheet, an ice cap, and an ice field. Which occurs in mountains? Which covers Antarctica and Greenland?

Illustrate the mechanics of glacial movement.

A glacier is an open system. The **firn line** (p. 496) is the elevation above which the winter snow and ice remain intact throughout the summer melting season, but below which melting occurs. A glacier is fed by snowfall and is wasted by **ablation** (p. 496), the combined processes that cause ice losses from a glacier'sl surface, base, or margins. Accumulation and ablation achieve a mass balance in each glacier.

As a glacier moves downhill, vertical **crevasses** (p. 497) may develop. Sometimes a glacier will move rapidly, an event known as a **glacier surge** (p. 500). The presence of water along the basal layer appears to be important in glacial movements. As a glacier moves, it plucks rock pieces and debris, incorporating them into the ice, and this debris scours and sandpapers underlying rock through **abrasion** (p. 500).

4. What is meant by glacial mass balance? What are the basic inputs and outputs?
5. What is meant by a glacier surge? What do scientists think produces surging episodes?

Describe characteristic erosional and depositional land-forms created by glaciation.

A **roche moutonnée** (p. 500) is an erosional landform produced by plucking and abrasion. It is an asymmetrical hill of exposed bedrock, gently sloping on the upstream end and abruptly sloping on the downstream end.

Extensive valley glaciers have profoundly reshaped mountains worldwide, transforming **V**-shaped stream valleys into **U**-shaped glaciated valleys and producing many other distinctive erosional and depositional landforms. As cirque walls erode away, sharp **arêtes**, p. 500 (sawtooth, or serrated, ridges) form, dividing adjacent cirque basins. Two eroding cirques may reduce an arête to a saddlelike **col** (p. 500). A **horn** (p. 500) results when several cirque glaciers gouge an individual mountain summit from all sides, forming a pyramidal peak. A **bergschrund** (p. 500) is a crevasse, or wide crack, that separates flowing ice from stagnant ice in the upper reaches of a glacier or in a cirque. An ice-carved rock basin left as a glacier retreats may fill with water to form a **tarn** (p. 502); tarns in a string separated by moraines are **paternoster lakes** (p. 502). Where a glacial trough joins the ocean and the glacier retreats, the sea extends inland to form a **fjord** (p. 502).

All glacial deposits, whether ice-borne or meltwater-borne, constitute **glacial drift** (p. 503). Direct deposits from ice consist of unstratified and unsorted **till** (p. 503). Specific landforms produced by the deposition of till at glacial margins are **moraines** (p. 503). A **lateral moraine** (p. 503) forms along each side of a glacier. Lateral moraines of converging glaciers can merge to form a **medial moraine** (p. 503). Eroded debris dropped at the farthest extent of a glacier's terminus is a **terminal moraine** (p. 503). Recessional moraines mark temporary endpoints as the glacier advances and retreats over time.

A **till plain** (p. 504), which forms behind a terminal moraine, features unstratified coarse till, low and rolling relief, and deranged drainage. **Drumlins** (p. 505) are elongated hills of deposited till, streamlined in the direction of continental ice movement (blunt end upstream and tapered end downstream).

Glacial meltwater deposits are sorted and stratified and called **stratified drift** (p. 505), forming **outwash plains** (p. 505) featuring braided stream channels that carry a heavy sediment load. An **esker** (p. 505) is a sinuously curving, narrow ridge of coarse sand and gravel that forms along the channel of a meltwater stream beneath a glacier. A **kame** (p. 505) is a small hill, knob, or mound of poorly sorted sand and gravel that is deposited directly on top of glacial ice and then deposited on the ground when the glacier melts. An isolated block of ice left by a retreating glacier becomes surrounded by debris; when the block finally melts, it leaves a steep-sided depression called a **kettle** (p. 506) that, when filled with water, forms a *kettle lake*.

6. Describe the transformation of a **V**-shaped stream valley into a **U**-shaped glaciated valley. What features are visible after the glacier retreats?

7. What is a morainal deposit? What specific moraines are created by alpine glaciers?

Discuss the distribution of permafrost and **explain** several periglacial processes.

The term **periglacial** (p. 506) describes cold-climate processes, landforms, and topographic features that exist along the margins of glaciers, past and present. When soil or rock temperatures remain below 0°C (32°F) for at least 2 years, **permafrost**, p. 506 (perennially frozen ground), develops. The **active layer** (p. 507) is the zone of seasonally frozen ground that exists between the subsurface permafrost layer and the ground surface. In regions of permafrost, frozen subsurface water forms **ground ice** (p. 508). **Patterned ground** (p. 508) forms in the periglacial environment where freezing and thawing of the ground create polygonal forms of circles, polygons, stripes, and nets.

8. Define two types of permafrost. What are the characteristics of each, and where does each occur on Earth?

9. Explain some of the specific problems humans encounter in building on periglacial landscapes.

Describe landscapes of the Pleistocene Epoch and **list** changes occurring today in the polar regions.

An **ice age** (p. 510) is any extended period of cold. The late Cenozoic Era featured pronounced ice-age conditions during the Pleistocene. In regions not covered with ice, **paleolakes** (p. 511) formed because of wetter conditions. **Lacustrine deposits** (p. 511) are lake sediments that form terraces along former shorelines.

The 10°C (50°F) isotherm for July, coinciding with the visible tree line separating northern forests and tundra, defines the Arctic region. The Antarctic convergence located near 60° S latitude defines the Antarctic region. Warming temperatures are causing the collapse of ice shelves, the breakup of tidewater glaciers, and surface melting on Earth's ice sheets.

10. Explain the criteria defining the Arctic and Antarctic regions.

GEO**SPATIAL** ANALYSIS

Columbia Glacier

Columbia Glacier flows directly into the sea and is one of the most rapidly changing glaciers in the world. The Columbia Glacier began retreating unevenly in 1986.

Activities

Go to NASA's Earth Observatory page at http://earthobservatory.nasa.gov/. Click on "World of Change" in the Browse Topics list, select "Columbia Glacier, Alaska," and read the text that accompanies the satellite images.

1. What does the color cyan represent on the map? Green? Brown? Dark blue?

2. Why did this glacier's retreat slow between 2000 and 2006?

3. What role does the underwater terminal moraine play in ice accumulation downstream of the terminus?

4. Why is there no accumulation of ice downstream of the terminus in some years?

5. Is the glacier expected to continue to retreat? Why or why not?

Examine the changes in the glacier's extent from 1986 to 2016 to answer the following questions. You can also click on the "Google Earth" button and open this map in Google Earth (use the show historical imagery and tools.)

6. What is the distance (in km) between the north shore of Heather Island and the terminus in 1985? 1990? 1995? 2000? 2005? 2010? 2015? In 2010 and 2015 you will have to measure the distance in segments. Measure to the Main Branch.

7. During which 5-year period did the glacier retreat the fastest? How much did the glacier retreat during this 5-year period?

8. What is the average rate of decrease per 5-year period?

9. In what year did the medial moraine disappear? (The medial moraine marks the zone where the Main Branch and West Branch meet.)

Mastering Geography™

Looking for additional review and test prep materials? Visit the Study Area in MasteringGeography™ to enhance your geographic literacy, spatial reasoning skills, and understanding of this chapter's content by accessing a variety of resources, including MapMaster™ interactive maps, videos, *Mobile Field Trips*, *Project Condor* Quadcopter videos, *In the News* RSS feeds, flashcards, web links, self-study quizzes, and an eText version of *Geosystems*.

IV Soils, Ecosystems, and Biomes

Soufrière, Saint Lucia

▲ On the Caribbean island of Saint Lucia, tropical rain forest surrounds a coastal bay near the town of Soufrière, with the volcanic Pitons in the distance. [Paul Baggaley/Getty Images.]

Earth is the home of the Solar System's only known biosphere—a uniquely complex system of interacting abiotic (nonliving) and biotic (living) components working together to sustain a tremendous diversity of life. Energy enters the biosphere through conversion of solar energy by photosynthesis in the leaves of plants. Energy then moves through a feeding hierarchy from producers to consumers, ending with decomposers. Together, these

INPUTS
- Insolation
- Precipitation
- Earth materials
- Biotic interactions

ACTIONS
- Weathering/erosion
- Photosynthesis/respiration
- Biogeochemical cycling
- Evolution
- Disturbance and succession

OUTPUTS
- Soil types
- Species distributions
- Biodiversity
- Earth's biomes

HUMAN–EARTH CONNECTIONS
- Soil erosion
- Biodiversity losses
- Invasive species
- Ecosystem restoration

Question:
How is present climate change impacting PART IV inputs, actions, and outputs, which form the biosphere?

varied organisms, in concert with the Earth's abiotic components, produce aquatic and terrestrial ecosystems, generally organized into various biomes. Soil is the essential link connecting the living world to the lithosphere and the rest of Earth's physical systems. Thus, soil is the appropriate bridge between Part 3 and Part 4 of this text.

Today, we face the crucial issue of how to preserve the diversity of life in the biosphere with increasing human population and a changing global climate, including shifts in patterns of land and ocean temperatures, precipitation, and extreme weather phenomena, all of which impact Earth's living systems. The resilience of the biosphere as we know it is being tested in a real-time, one-time experiment. We consider these important issues of biogeography in Part 4.

18 The Geography of Soils

Bali, Indonesia

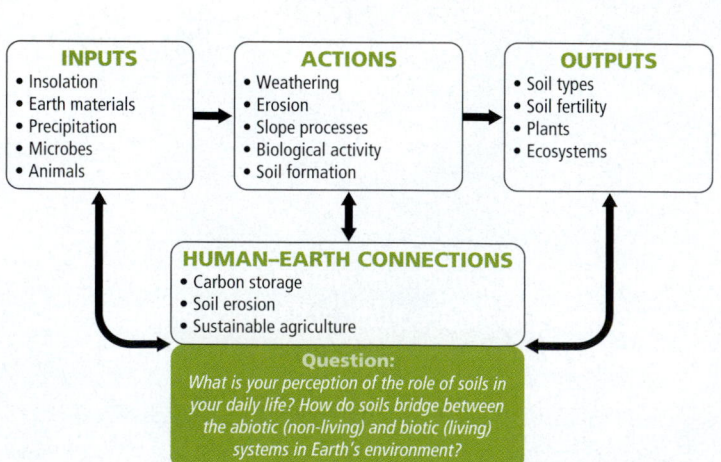

Rice, shown here growing in terraced fields in Bali, Indonesia, is a staple food worldwide. Depletion of soil nutrients and drought associated with El Niño and climate change threaten production of this water-intensive crop. [Edmund Lowe Photography/Getty Images.]

KEY**LEARNING**concepts

After reading the chapter, you should be able to:

- **Define** soil and soil science and **list** four components of soil.

- **Describe** the principal soil-formation factors and the horizons of a typical soil profile.

- **Describe** the physical properties used to classify soils: color, texture, structure, consistence, porosity, and soil moisture.

- **Explain** basic soil chemistry, including cation-exchange capacity, and **relate** these concepts to soil fertility.

- **Describe** the 12 soil orders of the Soil Taxonomy classification system and **explain** their general distribution across Earth.

INPUTS	ACTIONS	OUTPUTS
• Insolation • Earth materials • Precipitation • Microbes • Animals	• Weathering • Erosion • Slope processes • Biological activity • Soil formation	• Soil types • Soil fertility • Plants • Ecosystems

HUMAN–EARTH CONNECTIONS
- Carbon storage
- Soil erosion
- Sustainable agriculture

Question:
What is your perception of the role of soils in your daily life? How do soils bridge between the abiotic (non-living) and biotic (living) systems in Earth's environment?

Soils, a Critical Resource at Risk

Soil covers almost all land surfaces on Earth. Soils develop from rock and sediment and are the medium through which the diversity of life on land has evolved. In fact, the organisms—microbes, fungi, insects, earthworms—that live in soil represent a large part of Earth's biodiversity. Soils also store vast amounts of carbon and thus help regulate climate.

The Critical Zone Soils are an essential part of the region known as the Critical Zone, the area of Earth's surface extending from the top of the tree canopy to the bottom of groundwater (**Figure GN 18.1**). In this region, water circulates, soils form, and nutrients cycle. All of the interactions between rock, soil, water, and biota (living organisms)

in the Critical Zone combine to provide the growing medium for plants, an essential resource that sustains life. The layered nature of soils reflects processes related to all of Earth's spheres: Climate and biota interact to form the surface layers, while the accumulation of weathered and decayed materials leached by water form the layers below.

Soils Vary Across the Globe Climate, geology, and living organisms have a huge influence on the type of soil that develops in an area. Because these three factors differ widely across Earth's surface, soil types have great spatial variability. Some soils are highly productive for agriculture, and some are less fertile. Some soils are easily disturbed by human activities, and some are more resilient. Throughout history and the rise of agriculture, humans have increasingly modified the world's soils, causing a loss of natural variability and an overall decline in soil productivity.

Soil Erosion Once a soil system is altered by poor cultivation, deforestation, or overgrazing, soils are prone to erosion. Worldwide, about one-third of potentially farmable land has been lost to erosion, much of that in the past 40 years. What happens when soils erode? The topsoil is either washed away by water or blown away by wind (**Figure GN 18.2**). Water erosion carries soils into lakes and rivers, causing sedimentation. Wind erosion impacts human health and accelerates desertification, as discussed in Chapter 15. Soil forms slowly and is now being lost at a much faster rate than soil development occurs.

Soils—A Carbon Sink As discussed in Chapter 10, soils store carbon, making them a carbon sink. Soils store nearly 80% of terrestrial carbon (plants and animals store the other 20%), and the amount of carbon in soil is about three times larger than the carbon in the atmosphere.

As humans alter natural landscapes—as when they convert natural grasslands into cultivated fields—soils

▲**Figure GN 18.2 Soil erosion.** In the West African country of Mali, deforestation and overgrazing cause ongoing soil erosion. Improper agricultural practices, a common problem in Africa and worldwide, also degrade soils and lead to erosion. [Bert de Ruiter/Alamy.]

▲**Figure GN 18.3 Local solutions to control soil erosion.** Discarded tires help control soil erosion along a roadcut in Petrópolis, near Rio de Janeiro, Brazil. [AlessandraRCstock/Alamy.]

are exposed to the air and microbial activity releases soil carbon to the atmosphere as carbon dioxide. Carbon is returned to the soil through plants and decaying organic matter. However, current rates of land conversion and soil erosion are far outpacing natural replenishment of the soil carbon sink.

Soils and the Future Many opportunities and challenges exist for maintaining soils and their vital role in food security, climate change, and preserving functioning ecosystems on Earth. Soil management at local, regional, and global scales must focus on reducing erosion and preventing carbon losses (**Figure GN 18.3**). Sustainable agriculture and other practices geared toward passing a habitable landscape to future generations are key to preserving this essential part of Earth's Critical Zone.

1. Why do soils vary in nature over Earth's surface?

2. How do soils affect Earth's climate system?

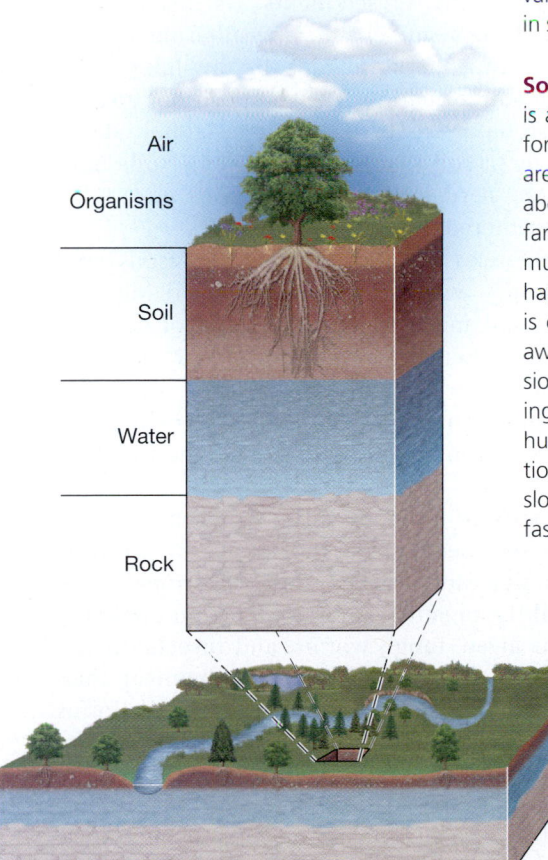

Air

Organisms

Soil

Water

Rock

▲**Figure GN 18.1 The Critical Zone.** This region of Earth's surface provides essential resources, such as food and water. [National Science Foundation, see http://criticalzone.org/national/research/the-critical-zone-1national/.]

Earth's landscape generally is covered with **soil**, a dynamic natural material at or near the surface composed of water, air, and fine particles—both mineral fragments (sands, silts, clays) and organic matter (**Figure 18.1**). Soil is the substrate for plant growth and the basis for functioning ecosystems. Soil retains and filters water; provides habitat for a host of microbial organisms, many of which produce antibiotics that fight human diseases; serves as a source of slow-release nutrients; and stores carbon dioxide and other greenhouse gases.

Soils develop over long periods of time; in fact, many soils bear the legacy of climates and geological processes during the last 15,000 years or more. Soils do not reproduce, nor can they be re-created—they are a nonrenewable natural resource. This fact means that human use and abuse of soils is happening at rates much faster than those at which soils form or can be replaced.

Soil is a complex substance whose characteristics vary from kilometer to kilometer—and even centimeter to centimeter. Physical geographers are interested in the spatial distributions of soil types and the physical factors that interact to produce them. **Soil science**, the interdisciplinary study of soil as a natural resource on Earth's surface, draws on aspects of physics, chemistry, biology, mineralogy, hydrology, climatology, and cartography. *Pedology* deals with the origin, classification, distribution, and description of soils (*ped* is from the Greek *pedon*, meaning "soil" or "earth"). Soil is sometimes called the edaphosphere, as *edaphos* means "soil" or "ground."

Soil Development and Soil Profiles

The soil of a given area is an open system with physical inputs of insolation, water, rock and sediment, and microorganisms and outputs of plant ecosystems that sustain animals and human societies. Soil scientists recognize five primary natural soil-forming factors: parent material, climate, organisms, topography and relief, and time. Human activities, especially those related to agriculture and livestock grazing, also affect soil development.

Natural Soil-Formation Factors

Soils develop at the interface between processes in the atmosphere, lithosphere, and biosphere.

- The *parent material* for a soil is the underlying geologic material from which the soil forms, usually bedrock, rock fragments, or sediments. As discussed in Chapter 13, physical and chemical weathering of rocks in the upper lithosphere provides the raw mineral ingredients for soil formation. The composition, texture, and chemical nature of the parent material help determine the type of soil that forms, and some soils have more than one parent material. Clay minerals are the principal weathered by-products in soil.

- *Climate* influences soil development, and soil types correlate closely with climate types worldwide. The temperature and moisture characteristics of climates determine the chemical reactions, organic activity, and movement of water within soils. The present-day climate is important, but many soils also exhibit the imprint of past climates, sometimes over thousands of years.

- *Biological activity* is an essential factor in soil development (see Geosystems in Action 18 on page 529). Vegetation and the activities of animals and bacteria—all the organisms living in, on, and over the soil, such as algae, fungi, worms, and insects—determine the organic content of soil. The chemical characteristics of the vegetation and many other life forms contribute to the acidity or alkalinity of the soil solution. For example, broadleaf trees tend to increase alkalinity, whereas needleleaf trees tend to produce higher acidity. When humans move into new areas and alter natural vegetation by logging or plowing, the affected soils are likewise altered, often permanently.

- *Relief and topography* also affect soil formation (**Figure 18.2**). Slopes that are too steep cannot have full soil development because gravity and erosional processes

25% air

45% mineral matter

25% water

5% organic matter

▲**Figure 18.1 The composition of soil.** [Danylo Samiylenko/Shutterstock.]

▲Figure 18.2 **Topography and soil development, Blue Mountains, Oregon.**
[Kevin Ebi/Alamy.]

Thicker soils develop on plateaus and in valleys

Thinner soils develop on steep slopes

Soils on north-facing slopes hold more moisture

Soils on south-facing slopes are drier

remove materials. Lands that are level or nearly level tend to develop thicker soils but may be subject to soil drainage issues such as waterlogging. The orientation of slopes relative to the Sun is also important because it controls exposure to sunlight. In the Northern Hemisphere, south-facing slopes are warmer overall through the year because they receive higher-angle direct sunlight. North-facing slopes are colder, causing slower snowmelt and a lower evaporation rate, thus providing more moisture for plants than is available on south-facing slopes, which tend to dry out faster.

- All of the identified natural factors in soil development require *time* to operate. The rate of soil development is closely tied to the nature of the parent material (soils

develop more quickly from sediments than from bedrock) and to climate (soils develop at a faster rate in warm, humid climates). Over geologic time, plate tectonics has redistributed landscapes and thus subjected soil-forming processes to diverse conditions.

Once fully developed, soils are the substrate for natural vegetation and agriculture that produces human food supplies. Soils develop from a variety of parent materials, ranging from those that have remained in place to transported materials, such as the sediments carried by glaciers, rivers, gravity, or wind. For example, in Chapter 15 we discussed *loess*, the fine-grained sediment transported by wind and redeposited into homogeneous (evenly mixed) accumulations. Loess acts as the parent material for soils that develop over time in certain climates. The soils derived from loess are the basis for some of Earth's most productive farming regions (**Figure 18.3**).

Soil Horizons

Scientists evaluate soils using a **soil profile**, a vertical section of soil that extends from the surface to the deepest extent of plant roots or to the point where regolith or bedrock is encountered (as discussed in Chapter 13, *regolith* is the partially weathered rock overlying bedrock). Soil profiles may be exposed by human activities, such as at a construction site or along a highway road cut. When soil is not exposed by natural processes or human activity, scientists dig soil pits to expose a soil profile for analysis.

(a) Agricultural fields in the Loess Hills of western Iowa. Terraces provide flat surfaces for planting crops.

(b) Terraced farming near the Yellow River on the Loess Plateau in northern China.

▲Figure 18.3 **Loess soils and agriculture, North America and China.** Loess deposits form some of the world's most fertile soils, shown here planted in terraces to reduce soil erosion. [(a) Clint Farlinger/Alamy. (b) Lu Jian/Featurechina/Newscom.]

Soil pedon

Soil horizons

Solum

O
A
E
B

C

R

Soil profile

(a) An idealized soil profile within a pedon.

Soil horizons

O and A

E

B

C

(b) Profile of a well-drained soil with till as parental material (a Mollisol) in southeastern South Dakota. Carbonate nodules are visible in the lower B and upper C horizons.

▲**Figure 18.4** **A typical soil profile within a pedon, and example.** [(b) Marbut Collection, Soil Science Society of America, Inc.]

For soil classification, pedologists use a three-dimensional representation of the soil profile, known as a *pedon* (**Figure 18.4**). A soil pedon is the smallest unit of soil that displays all the characteristics and properties used for classification. A soil profile represents one side of a pedon (shown in Figure 18.4a).

Within a soil profile, soils are generally organized into distinct horizontal layers known as **soil horizons**. These horizons are roughly parallel to the land surface, and each has characteristics recognizably different from those of horizons directly above or below. The four "master" horizons in most agricultural soils are known as the O, A, B, and C horizons (Figure 18.4). The boundary between horizons usually is distinguishable when viewed in profile, owing to differences in one or more physical soil characteristics.

O Horizon At the top of the soil profile is the *O horizon*, named for its *o*rganic composition, derived from plant and animal litter that was deposited on the surface and transformed into **humus**, a mixture of decomposed and synthesized organic materials that is usually dark in color. Microorganisms work busily on this organic debris, performing a portion of the *humification* (humus-making) process. The O horizon is 20%−30% or more organic matter, which is important because of its ability to retain water and nutrients and because of the way its behavior complements that of clay minerals.

The A, E, B, and C horizons extend below the O horizon to the lower portion of the profile at the R horizon. These middle layers are composed of sand, silt, clay, and other weathered by-products.

A Horizon Commonly known as topsoil, the *A horizon* usually is richer in organic content, and hence darker,

than lower horizons. Human disruption through plowing, pasturing, and other activities takes place in the A horizon. In the A horizon, humus and clay particles provide essential chemical connections between soil nutrients and plants.

E Horizon The A horizon grades downward into the lighter-colored *E horizon*, which is made up mainly of coarse sand, silt, and leaching-resistant minerals. As water percolates through the soil, it removes silicate clays and oxides of aluminum and iron and carries them to lower horizons. In soils, the action of draining away chemicals and minerals by rainwater is known as leaching. In the E horizon, leaching specifically removes fine particles and minerals, leaving behind sand and silt in the process of **eluviation**—thus, the E designation for this horizon. As precipitation increases, so does the rate of eluviation.

B Horizon In contrast to the A and E horizons, *B horizons* accumulate clays, aluminum, and iron. In B horizons, the process of **illuviation** dominates as materials leached by water from one layer enter and accumulate in another. In both eluviation and illuviation, water moves material (such as nutrients, salts, and clays) downward in the soil. To clarify, eluviation is the downward or sideways movement of dissolved or suspended material in rainwater and illuviation is the accumulation of material and water-soluble compounds leached from an overlying soil layer.

B horizons may exhibit reddish, yellowish, or white hues because of the presence of illuviated minerals (silicate clays, iron and aluminum, carbonates, and gypsum) and organic oxides. Some materials occurring in the B horizon may have formed in place from weathering processes, especially in the humid tropics.

Together, the A, E, and B horizons are designated the **solum**, considered the true definable soil of the profile (and labeled in Figure 18.4a). The horizons of the solum experience active soil processes.

C Horizon Below the solum is the *C horizon*, made up of weathered bedrock or weathered parent material. This zone is identified as regolith (although the term sometimes is used to include the solum as well). Plant roots and soil microorganisms are rare in the C horizon, which lies outside the biological influences experienced in the shallower horizons.

R Horizon At the bottom of the soil profile is the *R* (rock) *horizon*, consisting of either unconsolidated (loose) material or consolidated bedrock. When bedrock physically and chemically weathers into regolith, it may or may not contribute to overlying soil horizons.

Soil Characteristics

A number of physical and chemical characteristics differentiate soils and affect their fertility and resistance to erosion. **Soil fertility** is the ability of soil to sustain plants, and fertile soil conditions are critical for agriculture. Here, we discuss the most widely applicable properties for describing and classifying soils; however, other properties exist and may be of value depending on the particular site.

Physical Properties

The physical properties that distinguish soils and can be observed in soil profiles are color, texture, structure, consistence (meaning soil consistency or cohesiveness), porosity, and moisture. These and other soil properties, discussed next, all affect soil function.

Soil Texture The mixture and proportions of different particle sizes is *soil texture*, one of soil's most permanent attributes. Soil texture is classified according to the relative amounts of different-sized particles smaller in diameter than 2 mm (0.08 in.), ranging from coarse sand to clay. Sands are graded from coarse to medium to fine, down to 0.05 mm; silt is finer, to 0.002 mm; and clay is finer still, at less than 0.002 mm.

A *soil texture triangle* shows the relation of sand, silt, and clay concentrations in soils (**Figure 18.5**). Each corner of the triangle represents a soil consisting solely of the particle size noted (although rarely are true soils composed of a single range of particle sizes). Every soil on Earth is defined somewhere in this triangle.

To see how the soil texture triangle works, consider *Miami silt loam*, a soil type that is common in Indiana. Samples from this soil type are plotted on the soil texture triangle in Figure 18.5 and summarized in the table and pie diagrams (at right). Note that silt dominates the surface, clay the B horizon, and sand the C horizon.

Loam is the common designation for the balanced mixture of sand, silt, and clay that is beneficial to plant growth. Farmers consider a sandy loam with clay content below 20% (lower left in Figure 18.5) as the ideal soil because of its water-holding characteristics and ease of cultivation. Soil texture is important in determining water-retention and water-transmission traits.

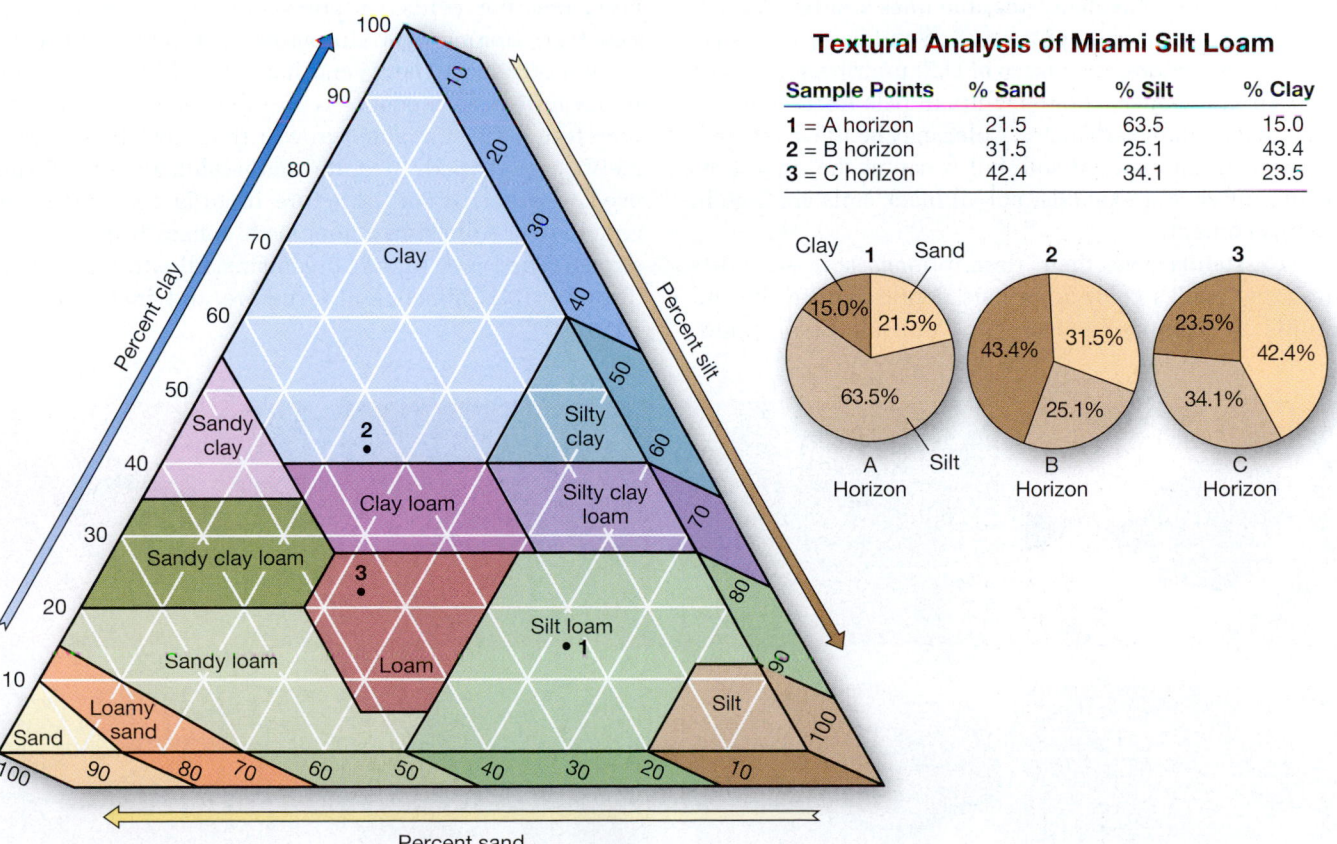

Textural Analysis of Miami Silt Loam

Sample Points	% Sand	% Silt	% Clay
1 = A horizon	21.5	63.5	15.0
2 = B horizon	31.5	25.1	43.4
3 = C horizon	42.4	34.1	23.5

▲**Figure 18.5 Soil texture triangle.** The ratio of clay, silt, and sand determines soil texture. As an example, points 1 (horizon A), 2 (horizon B), and 3 (horizon C) designate samples taken from three different horizons in the Miami silt loam in Indiana. Note the ratios of sand to silt to clay shown in the three pie diagrams and table. [After USDA–NRCS, *Soil Survey Manual*, Agricultural Handbook No. 18, p. 138 (1993).]

▲Figure 18.6 The Munsell Soil Color Chart. A soil sample is viewed through the holes in the page to match it with a color on the chart. The Munsell system assesses several color characteristics, including hue, value, and chroma. [Zuma Press/Newcom.]

developed by artist and teacher Albert Munsell in 1913. These charts display 175 colors, each identified by a number, so that soil scientists can make worldwide comparisons of soil color (**Figure 18.6**).

Soil Structure Soil texture describes the size of soil particles, but *soil structure* refers to the size and shape of the aggregates of particles in the soil. Structure can partially modify the effects of soil texture. The smallest natural lump or cluster of particles is a *ped*. The shape of soil peds determines which of the structural types the soil exhibits: crumb or granular, platy, blocky, or prismatic or columnar (**Figure 18.7**).

Soil Color The property of soil color is important because it suggests the composition and chemical makeup of a soil. Among the many possible hues are the reds and yellows found in soils of the U.S. Southeast, which are high in iron oxides; the blacks of U.S. prairie soils, which are rich in organics; and the white to pale hues, found in soils that contain carbonates. Color may be the most obvious trait in an exposed soil, but it can at the same time be deceptive. For example, not all black soils are high in humus content.

To standardize their descriptions, soil scientists describe a soil's color at various depths within the soil profile by comparing it with a *Munsell Color Chart*,

Peds separate from each other along zones of weakness, creating voids, or pores, that are important for moisture storage and drainage. Rounded peds have more pore space between them, resulting in greater permeability than occurs with other shapes. They are therefore better for plant growth than are blocky, prismatic, or platy peds, despite comparable fertility. Terms used to describe soil structure include *fine*, *medium*, and *coarse*. Adhesion among peds ranges from weak to strong. The work of soil organisms, illustrated in Figure GIA 18.1, affects soil structure and increases soil fertility.

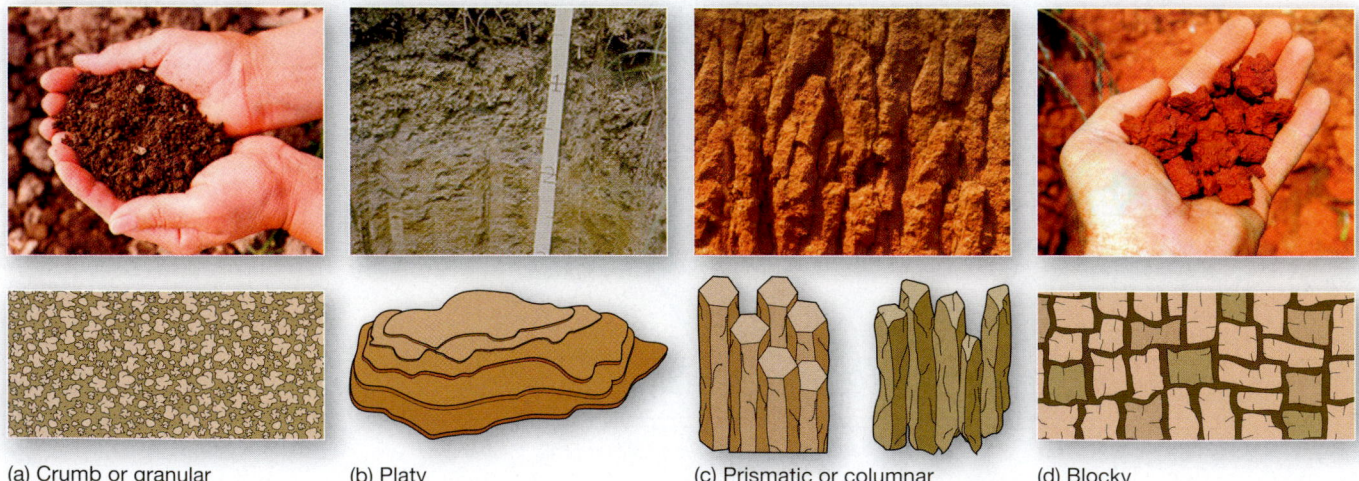

(a) Crumb or granular   (b) Platy   (c) Prismatic or columnar   (d) Blocky

▲Figure 18.7 Types of soil structure. Structure is important because it controls drainage, rooting of plants, and how well the soil delivers nutrients to plants. The shape of individual peds, shown here, controls a soil's structure. [(a) Boyan Dimitrov/123RF. (b) USDA National Soil Survey Center. (c) John Kelley/USDA NRCS. (d) USDA/NRCS.]

A diverse collection of organisms inhabits soil environments. Organisms play a vital role in soil-forming processes, helping to weather rock both mechanically and chemically, breaking up and mixing soil particles, and enriching soil with organic matter from their remains and wastes.

Moles can cause extensive soil disturbances.

18.1 SOIL ORGANISMS

Soil organisms range in size from land mammals that burrow into the ground, such as badgers, prairie dogs, and voles; to earthworms that ingest and secrete soil; to microscopic organisms that break down organic matter. The actions of these living organisms help maintain soil fertility.

Mammals:
*Mammals cause mechanical disturbances that mix soil, a process known as **bioturbation**.*

Earthworms:
Earthworms increase soil porosity, breaking up organic matter and then recycling soil aggregates to new locations (upward or downward in the soil column) by ingesting and secreting soil material.

Plant litter:
The remains of plants, from leaves and stems to tree trunks, accumulate on the surface, and as they decay gradually add organic matter to the soil.

Insects and other invertebrates:
A wide range of insects, including ants and beetles, inhabit soil, along with spiders, mites, and many other invertebrates. All contribute to soil-forming processes.

Plant roots:
Plant roots provide channels for water and air movement within the soil; these channels remain intact even after the root decomposes. The area around plant roots is biologically active and contains nutrients from root secretions and sloughed-off root cells.

Fungi:
Fungi have threadlike extensions (called mycelia) that extend beneath the soil surface and that bind soil particles together.

Root nodes

Nematodes

Some bacteria live on root nodes, where they "fix" nitrogen so that it can be taken up by plants.

Microorganisms:
Soil bacteria and other microorganisms such as protozoa (single-celled organisms) and nematodes (nonsegmented roundworms) help to break down the remains of organisms in the soil or release wastes other organisms can use.

MasteringGeography™

Visit the Study Area in MasteringGeography™ to explore biological activity in soil.

Visualize: Study a video of NASA's Soil Moisture (SMAP) Mission.

Assess: Demonstrate understanding of biological activity in soil (if assigned by instructor).

GEOquiz

1. Compare: How are the effects of mammals and plant roots on soil similar? How are they different?

2. Explain: Explain three ways in which organisms improve soil fertility.

3. Describe: How do earthworms affect soil?

529

Soil Consistence In soil science, the term *consistence* is used to describe the consistency of a soil or cohesion of its particles. Consistence is a product of texture (the mix of particle sizes) and structure (the shape of peds). Consistence reflects a soil's resistance to breaking and manipulation under varying moisture conditions:

- A *wet soil* is sticky between the thumb and forefinger, ranging from a little adherence to either finger, to sticking to both fingers, to stretching when the fingers are moved apart. Wet soils are also moldable and will form a thin strand when rolled between fingers and thumb.
- A *moist soil* is filled to about half of field capacity (the usable water capacity of soil), and its consistence grades from loose (noncoherent) to *friable* (easily pulverized) to firm (not crushable between the thumb and forefinger).
- A *dry soil* is typically brittle and rigid, with consistence ranging from loose to soft to hard to extremely hard.

Soil Porosity *Porosity* refers to the available air spaces within a material; **soil porosity** denotes the part of a volume of soil that is filled with air, gases, or water (as opposed to soil particles or organic matter). We discussed soil porosity, permeability, and moisture storage in Chapter 8.

Pores in the soil horizon control the movement of water—its intake, flow, and drainage—and air ventilation. Important porosity factors are pore *size*, pore *continuity* (whether pores are interconnected), pore *shape* (whether pores are spherical, irregular, or tubular), pore *orientation* (whether pore spaces are vertical, horizontal, or random), and pore *location* (whether pores are within or between soil peds).

Porosity is improved by the presence of plant roots; by animal activity, such as the tunneling actions of gophers or worms (see Geosystems in Action 18); and by human actions, such as supplementing the soil with humus or sand or planting soil-building crops. Much of the soil-preparation work done by farmers before they plant—and by home gardeners as well—is toward improving soil porosity.

Soil Moisture As discussed in Chapter 8, plants operate most efficiently when the soil is at *field capacity*, which is the maximum water available for plant roots after large pore spaces have drained of water. Soil type determines field capacity. If soil moisture is below field capacity, plant roots may be unable to access available water, and the plant will eventually reach the wilting point. Beyond this point, plants are unable to extract the water they need, and they die. More than any other factor, soil moisture regimes shape the biotic and abiotic properties of the soil.

Chemical Properties

Recall that soil pores may be filled with air, water, or a mixture of the two. Consequently, soil chemistry involves both air and water. The atmosphere within soil pores is mostly nitrogen, oxygen, and carbon dioxide. Nitrogen concentrations in soil pores are about the same as in the atmosphere, but oxygen is less and carbon dioxide is greater because of ongoing respiration processes in the ground.

Water present in soil pores is called the *soil solution* and is the medium for chemical reactions in soil. This solution is a critical source of nutrients for plants, providing the foundation of soil fertility. Carbon dioxide combines with the water to produce carbonic acid, and various organic materials combine with the water to produce organic acids. These acids are then active participants in soil processes, as are dissolved alkalis and salts.

A brief review of chemistry basics helps us understand how the soil solution behaves. An *ion* is an atom or group of atoms that carries an electrical charge (examples: Na^+, Cl^-, HCO_3^-). An ion has either a positive charge or a negative charge. For example, when NaCl (sodium chloride) dissolves in solution, it separates into two ions: Na^+, which is a *cation* (positively charged ion), and Cl^-, which is an *anion* (negatively charged ion). Some ions in soil carry single charges, whereas others carry double or even triple charges (e.g., sulfate, SO_4^{2-}, and aluminum, Al^{3+}).

Soil Colloids and Mineral Ions The tiny particles of clay or organic material (humus) suspended in the soil solution are **soil colloids**. Because they carry a negative electrical charge, they attract any positively charged ions in the soil (**Figure 18.8**). The positive ions, many metallic, are critical to plant growth. If it were not for the negatively charged soil colloids, the positive ions would be leached away in the soil solution and thus would be unavailable to plant roots.

Individual clay colloids are thin and platelike, with parallel surfaces that are negatively charged. They are more chemically active than silt and sand particles, but less active than organic colloids. Metallic cations attach

---

GEOreport 18.1 Soil compaction—causes and effects

Soil compaction is the physical consolidation of the soil that destroys soil structure and reduces porosity. The increasing weight of today's heavy agricultural machinery, in addition to earlier planting and the conventional arrangement of row crops, tends to increase soil compaction and can result in a 50% reduction in crop yields owing to restricted root growth, poor aeration of the root zone, and poor drainage. Scientists now suggest that no-till agricultural practices (in which plowing does not occur), combined with maintaining a continuous cover of actively growing plants, is the best way to reduce soil compaction, since roots increase porosity and water availability, preserve organic matter content, and reduce surface erosion.

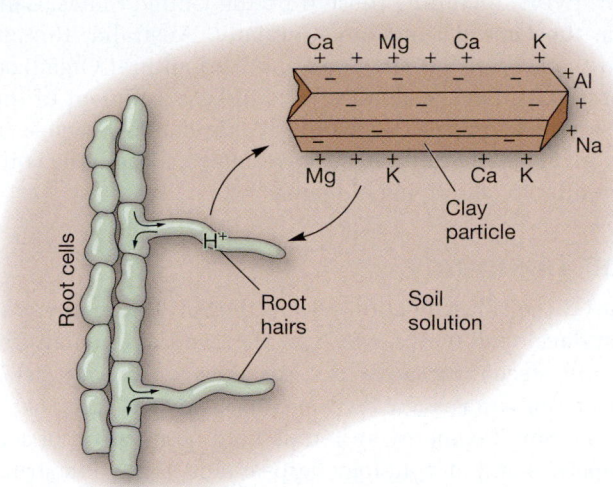

▲**Figure 18.8 Soil colloids and cation-exchange capacity (CEC).**
A soil colloid, such as this clay particle, retains mineral ions by
adsorption to its surface (opposite charges attract). This process holds
the ions until they are absorbed by root hairs.

▲**Figure 18.10 Soil degradation.** An example of soil loss through
sheet and gully erosion on a northwest Iowa farm. One millimeter of
soil lost from an acre weighs about 5 tons. [USDA–NRCS, National Soil
Survey Center.]

to the surfaces of the colloids by *adsorption* (not *absorption*, which means "to enter"). **Cation-exchange capacity
(CEC)** is the total number of cations that the soil is capable of adsorbing and exchanging. A high CEC means
that the soil colloids can store or exchange a relatively
large amount of cations from the soil solution. These
cations then become available to plants through their
roots. Thus, a high CEC indicates good soil fertility (unless a complicating factor exists, such as a soil that is too
acidic). Soil is fertile when it contains organic substances
and clay minerals that *absorb* water and *adsorb* certain
elements needed by plants.

Soil Acidity and Alkalinity A soil solution may contain a significant amount of hydrogen ions (H^+), the cations that stimulate acid formation. The result is a soil
rich in hydrogen ions, or an *acid soil*. A soil high in base
cations (calcium, magnesium, potassium, and sodium)
is a *basic* or *alkaline soil*. Such acidity or alkalinity is
expressed on the pH scale (**Figure 18.9**). Acidity usually is regarded as strong at 5.0 or lower on the pH scale,
whereas 10.0 or above is considered strongly alkaline.

As discussed in Chapter 3, acid deposition contributes to soil acidity in many world regions, including the U.S. Northeast. Increased acidity in the soil
solution reduces the CEC (H^+ ions attach to colloids,
pushing other cations into the soil solution) and can accelerate the chemical weathering of minerals, either of
which can reduce soil fertility. Because most crops are
sensitive to specific pH levels, acid soils below pH 6.0
require treatment to raise the pH. This soil treatment is
accomplished by the addition of bases in the form of
minerals that are rich in base cations, usually lime (calcium carbonate, $CaCO_3$).

Human Impacts on Soils

Unlike living species, soils do not propagate themselves. Furthermore, owing to their complexity and
long developmental histories, all soils are unique and
cannot be duplicated. A few centimeters' thickness of
prime farmland soil may require 500 years to mature.
Yet this same thickness is being
lost annually through soil erosion that occurs when humans
remove vegetation and plow the
land, whether on a mountainside or on a valley floor (**Figure
18.10**). As a result of human intervention and unsustainable agricultural practices, some 35%
of farmlands are losing soil faster
than it can form. The impact on
society is potentially disastrous
as population and food demands
increase.

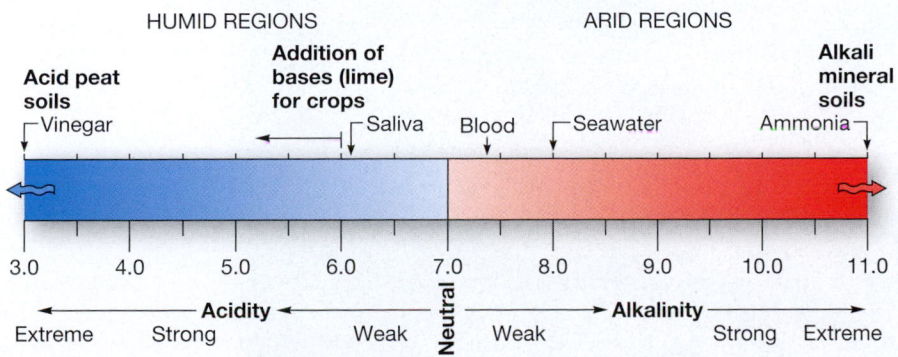

▲**Figure 18.9 pH scale.** The pH scale measures acidity (lower pH) and alkalinity (higher pH). (The
complete pH scale ranges between 0 and 14.)

Soil Erosion

Overcultivation and excessive plowing, overgrazing, and the clearing of forested slopes are some of the main human activities that make soils more prone to erosion by wind and water. In the 1930s, a catastrophic soil erosion event known as the Dust Bowl occurred in the United States, centered on the southern Great Plains but also extending into southern Canada and northern Mexico. Focus Study 18.1 examines this time of drought and intensive wind erosion, characterized by topsoil losses and massive dust storms.

Soil erosion removes topsoil, the layer that is richest in organic matter and nutrients. In order to curb soil erosion, farmers have throughout history in most cultures planted slopes "on the contour," sowing seeds in rows or mounds that run around a slope at the same elevation rather than vertically up and down the slope. Planting on the contour, still practiced today, prevents water from flowing straight down the slope and thus reduces soil erosion (**Figure 18.11**). In steep mountains, farmers use *terracing*, the cutting of level platforms into steep terrain, to prevent erosion. An expanding practice for slowing soil erosion is *no-till agriculture* (also called no-till farming; see GeoReport 18.1). In this approach, farmers no longer till, or plow, the soil after a harvest. Instead, they leave crop residue on the field between plantings, which helps prevent soil erosion by wind and water.

Soil Classification

Soil classification is complicated by the variety of interactions that create thousands of distinct soils—well over 15,000 soil types in the United States and Canada alone. A number of different classification systems are in use worldwide, including those from the United States, Canada, the United Kingdom, Germany, Australia, Russia, and the United Nations Food and Agricultural Organization (FAO). Each system reflects the environment of the country or countries in which it originated. Because of the involvement of interacting variables, classifying soils is similar to classifying climates.

Soil Taxonomy

The U.S. soil classification system, the **Soil Taxonomy**, was first developed by the NRCS in 1975 and is updated frequently (see http://www.nrcs.usda.gov/wps/portal/nrcs/detail/national/nedc/training/soil/?cid=nrcs142p2_053580. The basis for the Soil Taxonomy system is field observation of soil properties and morphology (appearance, form, and structure). The smallest unit of soil used in soil surveys is a **pedon**, a hexagonal column measuring 1 to 10 m² in top surface area (see Figure 18.4a). A pedon is considered a soil individual, and a soil profile within it is used to evaluate its soil horizons. In the Soil Taxonomy, pedons with similar characteristics are grouped together to form a *soil series*, the lowest and most precise level of the classification system. Sequentially higher-level categories are *soil families*, *soil subgroups*, *soil great groups*, *soil suborders*, and finally, the 12 *soil orders* discussed in this section.

Diagnostic Soil Horizons Soil scientists use diagnostic soil horizons to group soils into each soil series. A *diagnostic horizon* has distinctive physical properties (color, texture, structure, consistence, porosity, and moisture) or a dominant soil process (discussed ahead). A diagnostic horizon can occur at the surface or just below it, or it can occur below the soil surface at varying depths, in which case it is a *diagnostic subsurface horizon*.

◄**Figure 18.11**
Contour planting. Farmers help prevent soil erosion by planting alternating bands of corn and alfalfa in a field on the Iowa–Minnesota border. [Tim McCabe/NRCS.]

FOCUSstudy 18.1
The 1930s Dust Bowl: Regional-Scale Soil Erosion

◀**Figure 18.1.1 Black blizzard hits Elkhart, Kansas, in May 1937.** By 1933, dust storms had reduced the wheat crop near Elkhart to 37% of its pre-Dust Bowl size. [Photo Researchers, Inc./ Alamy.]

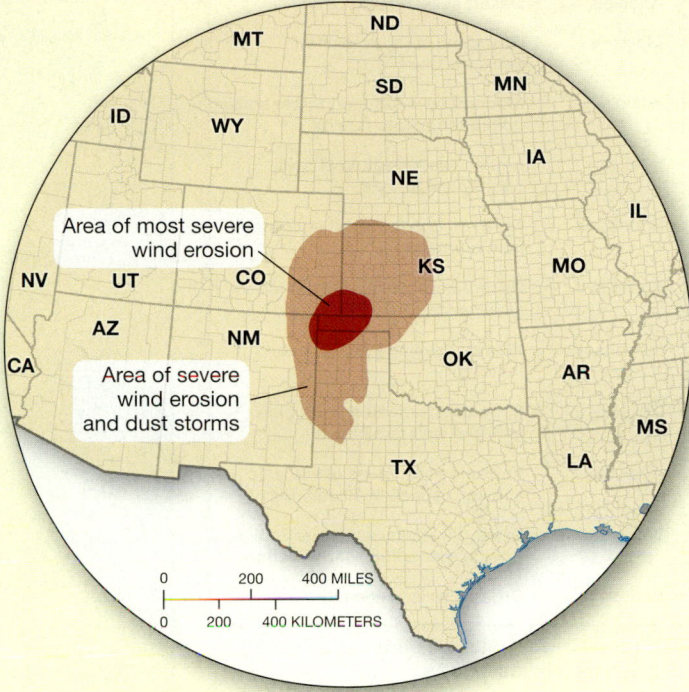

▲**Figure 18.1.3 Regions of severe wind erosion from 1935 to 1938 during the Dust Bowl.** [NRCS.]

During the late 1800s and early 1900s, farmers moved into the Great Plains, removing native vegetation and converting natural landscapes to cultivation. Over the next few decades, amid a series of unusually wet years, intensive agriculture and overgrazing degraded soils. In the 1930s, reduced precipitation and above-normal temperatures triggered a multiyear period of severe wind erosion and loss of farmlands known as the Dust Bowl (**Figure 18.1.1**).

Without the roots of native grasses to anchor the soils in place, winds picked up topsoil and transported it in clouds of dust nicknamed "black blizzards." The transported dust darkened the skies of Midwestern towns, making it difficult to see or breathe during the height of a storm. In the storm aftermath, dust and soil drifted over farmland, accumulating in depths that covered failing crops (**Figure 18.1.2**). Several dust storms traveled all the way to the U.S. East Coast, darkening the skies over Washington, DC, and other cities on their way to the Atlantic Ocean.

During the Dust Bowl, the deflation of soil—in some places as much as 10 cm (4 in.) over several years—occurred mainly in southern Nebraska, Kansas, Oklahoma, Texas, and eastern Colorado, but also extended into southern Canada and northern Mexico (**Figure 18.1.3**). By 1940, more than 2.5 million people had moved out of the Plains states—the largest migration in American history (see http://www.pbs.org/wgbh/americanexperience/films/dustbowl/ for more information).

In 1935, the federal government established the Soil Conservation Service to monitor soil erosion problems and work toward soil sustainability. The Dust Bowl ended in the 1940s, when regional weather conditions returned to normal. When the next drought arrived in the 1950s, farmers tapped groundwater—the vast High Plains Aquifer system—to irrigate fields and prevent erosion. In 1994, the SCS was renamed the Natural Resources Conservation Service (NRCS), tasked with protecting and improving soils, water, and natural resources on private lands.

1. Explain how natural conditions and human activities combined to cause the Dust Bowl.

2. Describe the effects of the Dust Bowl in terms of erosion and deposition of sediment.

▲**Figure 18.1.2 Aftermath of a Dust Bowl storm.** Machinery lies buried by dust and sand in Dallas, South Dakota, after a dust storm in the 1930s. The Dust Bowl was caused in part by poor farming practices that degraded soils throughout the region, making them susceptible to wind erosion during the multiyear drought. [Omikron/ Getty Images.]

APPLYconcepts

List two changes that reduced the chances of another Dust Bowl on the Great Plains after the 1930s.	a. _____	b. _____
What factors regarding climate, water availability, and agricultural practices make the Great Plains states vulnerable to another Dust Bowl? Explain your answer. (*Hint*: Compare Figure 18.1.3 with Figure 8.23.)	_____ _____ _____ _____ _____	

SOIL ORDER	DESCRIPTION/LOCATION
Oxisols	Tropical soils; hot, humid areas
Aridisols	Desert soils; hot, dry areas
Mollisols	Grassland soils; subhumid, semiarid lands
Alfisols	Moderately weathered forest soils; humid temperate forests
Ultisols	Highly weathered forest soils; subtropical forests
Spodosols	Northern conifer forest soils; cool, humid forests
Entisols	Recent soils; profile undeveloped, all climates
Inceptisols	Weakly developed soils; humid regions
Gelisols	Permafrost-affected soils; high latitudes and mountains
Andisols	Volcanic soils; areas of volcanic activity, especially Pacific Rim
Vertisols	Expandable clay soils; subtropics, tropics with sufficient dry period
Histosols	Organic soils; wetlands

(b) See Table 18.1 on page 546 for a summary of soil order characteristics.

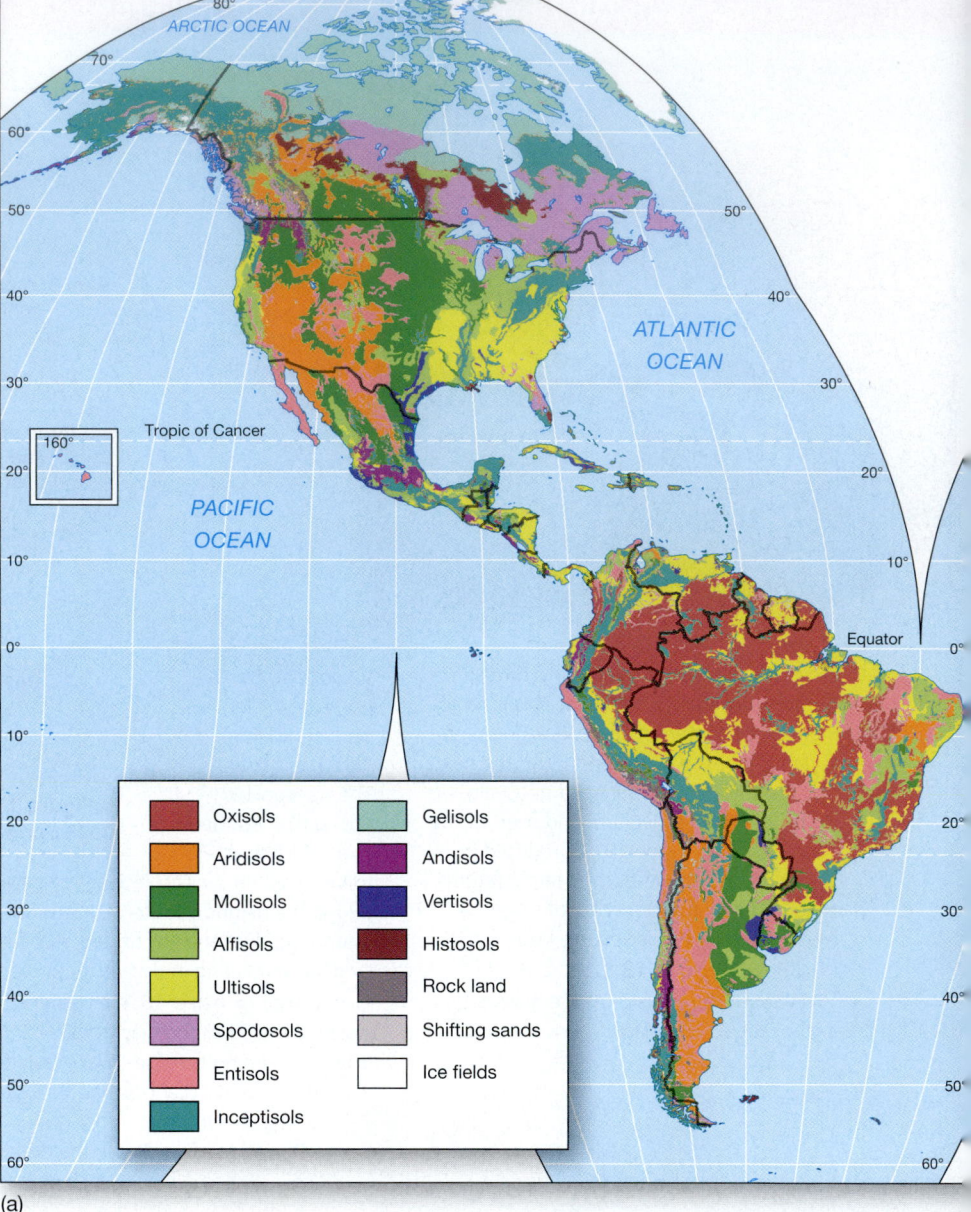

(a)

▶**Figure 18.12 Soil Taxonomy.** Worldwide distribution of the Soil Taxonomy's 12 soil orders, with each order listed and briefly described at left. [Adapted from NRCS maps, 1999, 2006.]

Pedogenic Regimes Prior to the U.S. Soil Taxonomy system, scientists used **pedogenic regimes** to describe soils. These regimes attach specific soil-forming processes to climatic regions. Although such climate-based regimes are convenient for relating climate and soil processes, the use of climatic variables as the sole basis of soil classification leads to uncertainty and inconsistency. In this chapter, we discuss each pedogenic regime with the soil order in which it most commonly occurs, even though each pedogenic process may be active in several soil orders and in different climates.

The five pedogenic regimes are:

- **Laterization**—a process that leaches most cations and silica (SiO_2) in humid and warm climates (discussed with Oxisols and shown in Figure 18.15)

- **Calcification**—a process that produces an illuviated accumulation of calcium carbonates in arid and semi-arid deserts and grasslands (discussed with Aridisols and shown in Figure 18.17)
- **Salinization**—a process that concentrates salts in soils in climates with high potential evapotranspiration (PE) rates (discussed with Aridisols)
- **Podzolization**—a process of eluviation–illuviation of iron and aluminum oxides in an acid regime, associated with forest soils in cool climates (discussed with Spodosols and shown in Figure 18.23)
- **Gleization**—a process that results in an accumulation of humus and a thick, water-saturated gray layer of clay beneath, associated with poor drainage conditions, usually in cold, wet climates

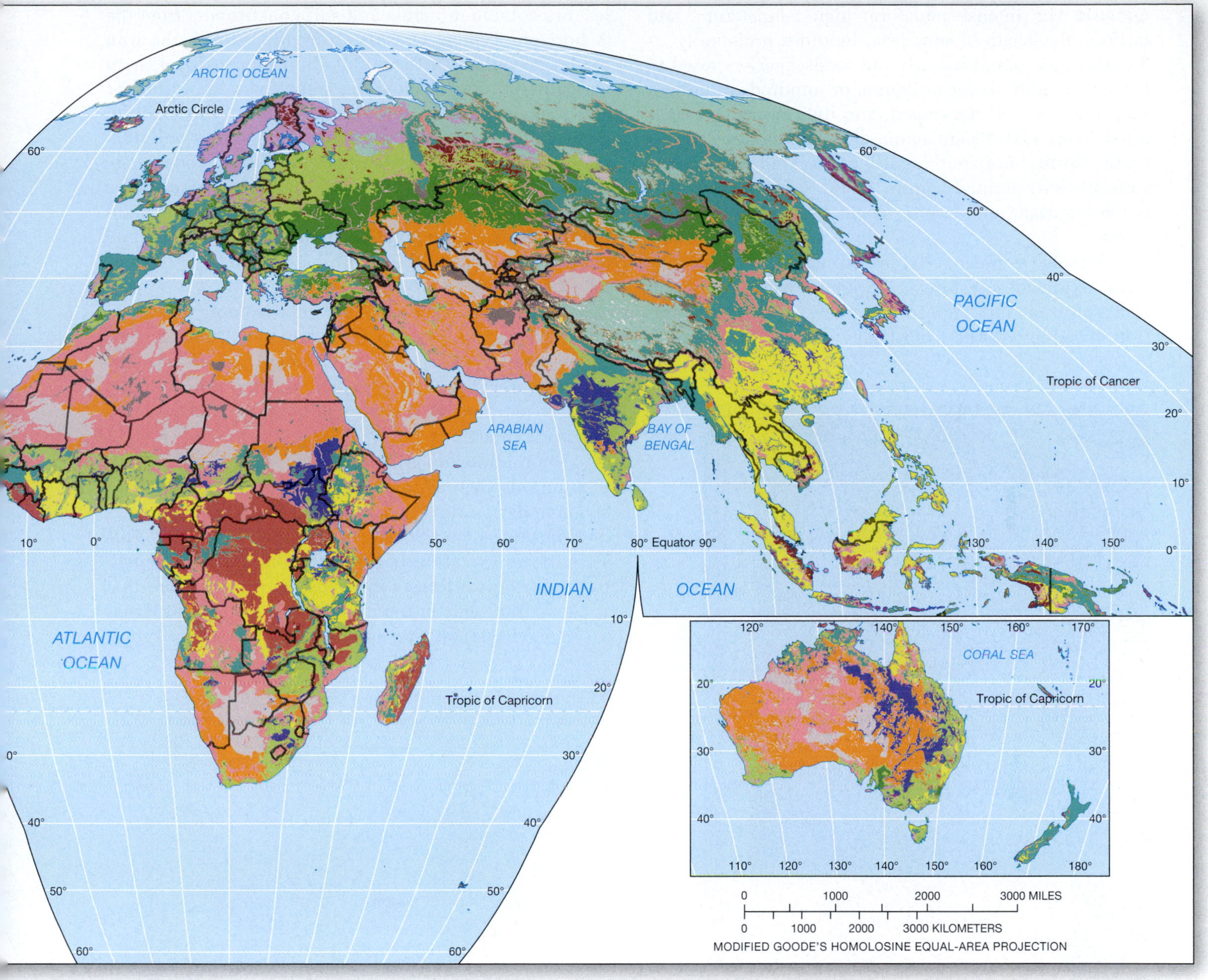

Soil Orders of the Soil Taxonomy

The Soil Taxonomy includes 12 general soil orders. Their worldwide distribution is shown in **Figure 18.12** and in individual maps provided with the soil discussions that follow (further information on each soil order is at http://soils.ag.uidaho.edu/soilorders/.) Because the Soil Taxonomy evaluates each soil order on the basis of its particular characteristics, the classification has no priority. However, we use a progression arranged loosely by latitude, beginning along the equator. At the end of the chapter, Table 18.1 presents a summary of the soil orders with brief descriptions.

WORKITOUT 18.1
Soil Distributions

Use the map and table in Figure 18.12 to answer these questions.

1. On which continents are Gelisols found, and what is their main characteristic?
2. Which soil type is most common in the U.S. Great Plains? Which other soil orders are extensive across the contiguous 48 U.S. states?
3. Describe two soil orders found in Europe.

Oxisols The intense moisture, high temperature, and uniform daylength of equatorial latitudes profoundly affect soils. In these generally old landscapes, exposed to tropical conditions for millennia or hundreds of millennia, soils are well developed, and their minerals are altered. Thus, Oxisols are among the most mature soils on Earth. Distinct horizons usually are lacking where these soils are well drained (**Figure 18.13**). Related vegetation is the luxuriant and diverse tropical and equatorial rain forest.

Oxisols (tropical soils) are so named because they have oxidized subsurface horizons with accumulations of iron and aluminum oxides. The concentration of oxides results from heavy precipitation, which leaches soluble minerals and soil constituents from the A horizon. Typical Oxisols are reddish (from the iron oxide) or yellowish (from the aluminum oxides), with a weathered claylike texture, sometimes in a granular soil structure that is easily broken apart. The high degree of eluviation removes basic cations and colloidal material to lower illuviated horizons. Thus, Oxisols are usually low in CEC and fertility. In short, Oxisols have a diagnostic subsurface horizon that is highly weathered, contains iron and aluminum oxides, is at least 30 cm (12 in.) thick, and lies within 2 m (6.5 ft) of the surface (see Figure 18.13).

Even though these soils are poor in inorganic nutrients, Oxisols are home to the world's lush rain forests. These forest systems rely on the recycling of nutrients from soil organic matter to sustain fertility. However, this nutrient-recycling ability is quickly lost when the ecosystem is disturbed.

The traditional agricultural practice of shifting cultivation, also known as *slash-and-burn agriculture* or *swidden agriculture*, is common in the Oxisols in parts of Asia, Africa, and South America (**Figure 18.14**). This style of crop rotation begins with the cutting of small tracts of tropical forests into *slash* (cut vegetation) that is then dried and burned. The resultant ash provides a soil environment that is rich in nutrients for crops,

(a) Highly weathered Oxisol profile in central Puerto Rico.

▼**Figure 18.13 Oxisols.** [(a) Marbut Collection, Soil Science Society of America, Inc. (c) imageBROKER/Alamy Stock Photo. (d) Bobbé Christopherson.]

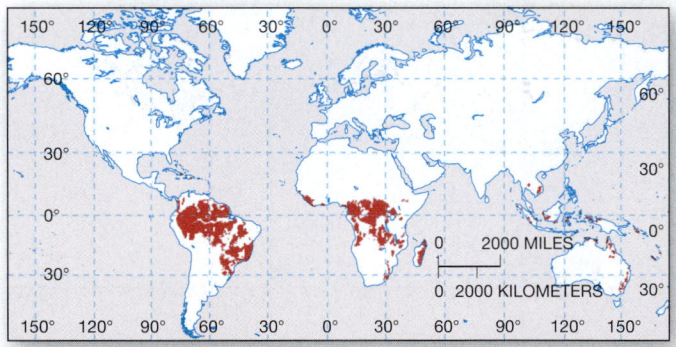

(b) Worldwide Oxisol distribution.

(d) Close-up view of oxisols in the tropical rain forest of the Sierra de Luquillo mountains, Puerto Rico.

(c) Oxisols underlie the tropical rain forests of South America. Note the lack of distinct soil horizons.

▲**Figure 18.14** **Swidden agriculture in the Amazon basin.** Crops grow in this recently cleared and burned tract of rain forest in Peru in 2013. [National Geographic Creative/Alamy Stock Photo.]

usually maize, beans, and squash. However, after 3 to 5 years, soil fertility declines through leaching by intense rainfall, causing farmers to shift cultivation to another tract, where the process is repeated. After a period of recovery, a previously used tract can again be cut and burned as the cycle repeats.

Today, the orderly land rotation essential to the success of swidden agriculture, in place for thousands of years, is disrupted by the conversion of forested land to pasture, soybean and palm oil plantations, and local development. Erosion is now a major problem on permanent tracts of cleared land taken out of the former rotation mode. When Oxisols are disturbed, soil loss can exceed 1000 tons per square kilometer per year. In addition, rain forest destruction and soil depletion threaten native plant and animal species. The regions dominated by the Oxisols and rain forests continue to garner worldwide environmental attention.

Figure 18.15 illustrates *laterization*, the leaching process that operates in well-drained soils in warm, humid tropical and subtropical climates. If the soils are

subjected to repeated wetting and drying, a *hardpan* (a hardened soil layer)—in this case, an iron-rich and humus-poor clay with quartz and other minerals—develops in the lower A or in the B horizon. This process forms *plinthite* (from the Greek *plinthos*, meaning "brick"), which can be quarried in blocks and used as a building material.

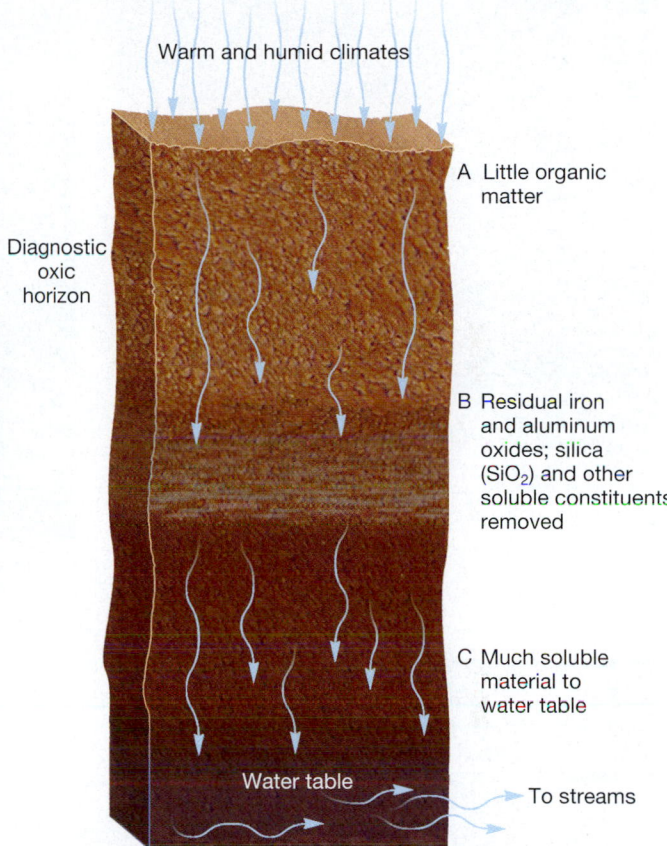

(a) Laterization is characteristic of moist tropical and subtropical climate regions.

(b) Laterization produces soils with high iron oxide content, many of which are used as a building material for roads and structures, as here in the village of Sovakimby, Madagascar.

▲**Figure 18.15** **A soil undergoing laterization.** Leaching occurs as water moves downward through the soil. [(b) robertharding/Alamy.]

(a) Aridisol profile in central Arizona.

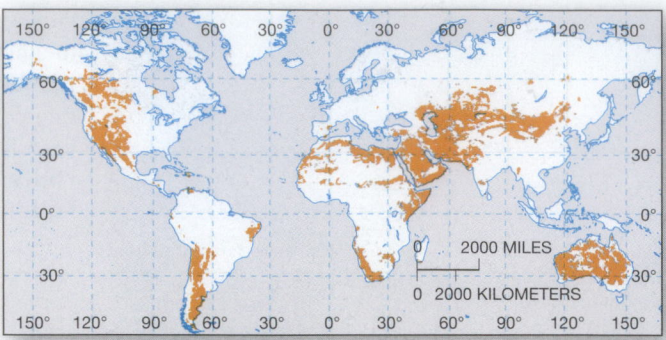

(b) Worldwide Aridisol distribution.

(c) Irrigated cropland and surrounding desert, Imperial Valley, southern California.

▲**Figure 18.16 Aridisols.** [(a) Marbut Collection, Soil Science Society of America, Inc. (c) Bobbé Christopherson. (d) Eduardo Pucheta/Alamy.]

(d) Salinization in an irrigated vineyard, San Juan, Argentina.

Aridisols The largest single soil order occurs in the world's dry regions. **Aridisols** (desert soils) occupy approximately 19% of Earth's land surface. A pale, light soil color near the surface is diagnostic (**Figure 18.16**).

Regions of Aridisols are characterized by generally inadequate soil moisture for plant growth. High potential evapotranspiration and low precipitation produce very shallow soil horizons. Usually, these soils have adequate moisture for only several months a year, have little vegetation, and are low in organic matter. Low precipitation means infrequent leaching.

In dry climates, calcium carbonate ($CaCO_3$) commonly forms the cementing material that causes hardening of the B layer. *Calcification* is a soil process characteristic of Aridisols and some Mollisols (discussed

ahead) in which calcium carbonate or magnesium carbonate accumulates in the B and C horizons. This process forms a diagnostic calcic subsurface horizon (**Figure 18.17**).

Aridisols can be made productive for agriculture using irrigation. Two related problems common in irrigated lands are salinization and waterlogging. *Salinization* occurs as salts dissolved in soil water migrate to surface horizons and are deposited as the water evaporates. These deposits appear as subsurface salty horizons, which will damage or kill plants if the horizons occur near the root zone. Salinization is common in Aridisols and results from the excessive potential evapotranspiration rates in arid and semiarid regions. Waterlogging (saturation of the soil that interferes with plant growth) occurs with the introduction of irrigation water for farming, especially in soils that are poorly drained.

Irrigated agriculture has increased greatly since 1800, when only 8 million hectares (about 20 million acres) were irrigated worldwide. Today, approximately 255 million hectares (about 630 million acres) are irrigated, many of them Aridisols, and this figure is on the increase in some parts of the world. However, in many of these areas, crop production has decreased and even ended because of salt buildup in the soils. Examples include areas along the Tigris and Euphrates Rivers in Iraq, the Indus

Potential evapotranspiration ≥ precipitation

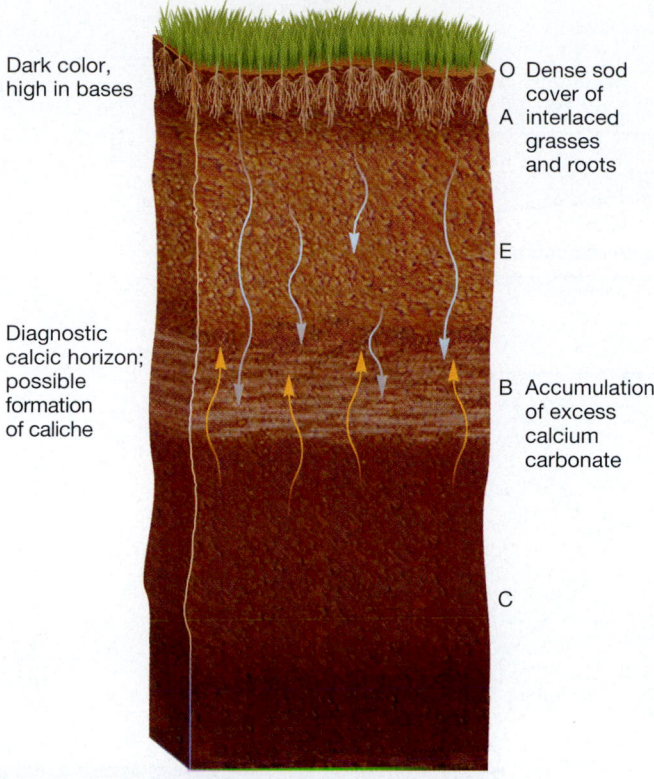

Dark color, high in bases

O Dense sod cover of
A interlaced grasses and roots

E

Diagnostic calcic horizon; possible formation of caliche

B Accumulation of excess calcium carbonate

C

▲**Figure 18.17** **A soil undergoing calcification.** This process occurs in desert and grassland soils in climatic regimes that have potential evapotranspiration equal to or greater than precipitation.

River Valley in Pakistan, sections of South America and Africa, and the western United States.

Mollisols Some of Earth's most significant agricultural soils are **Mollisols** (grassland soils). This group includes seven recognized suborders that vary in fertility. The dominant diagnostic horizon is a dark, organic surface layer some 25 cm (10 in.) thick (**Figure 18.18**). As the Latin origin of the name implies (*mollis*, meaning "soft," is the root of *mollify* and *emollient*), Mollisols are soft, even when dry. They have granular or crumbly peds, loosely arranged when dry. These humus-rich soils are high in basic cations (calcium, magnesium, and potassium) and have a high CEC and therefore high fertility. In soil moisture, these soils are intermediate between humid and arid. The B horizon can have clay accumulation and can be enriched in calcium carbonate in drier climates. The carbonate-enriched B horizon is thickest along the boundary between dry and humid climates (**Figure 18.19**).

Mollisols include soils of the steppes and prairies—the North American Great Plains, the Palouse of Washington State, the Pampas of Argentina, and the region stretching from Manchuria in China to Europe. Agriculture in these areas ranges from large-scale commercial grain farming to grazing along the drier portions. With fertilization or soil-building practices, high crop yields are common. The "fertile triangle" of Ukraine, Russia, and western portions of the former Soviet Union is of this soil type.

(a) Mollisol profile in eastern Idaho, from loess that is high in calcium carbonate, related to the soils of the Palouse agricultural region.

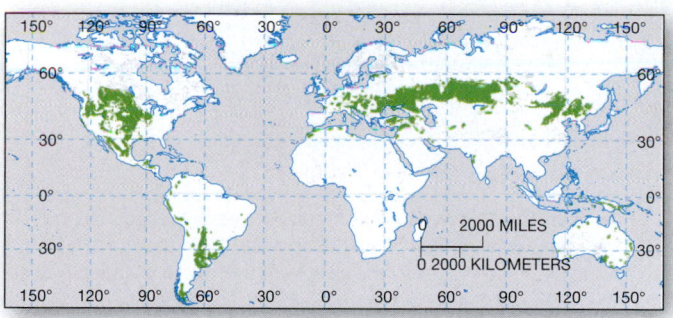

(b) Worldwide Mollisol distribution.

(c) Wheat flourishes in the fertile Palouse of eastern Washington.

▲**Figure 18.18** **Mollisols.** [(a) Marbut Collection, Soil Science Society of America, Inc. (c) Bobbé Christopherson.]

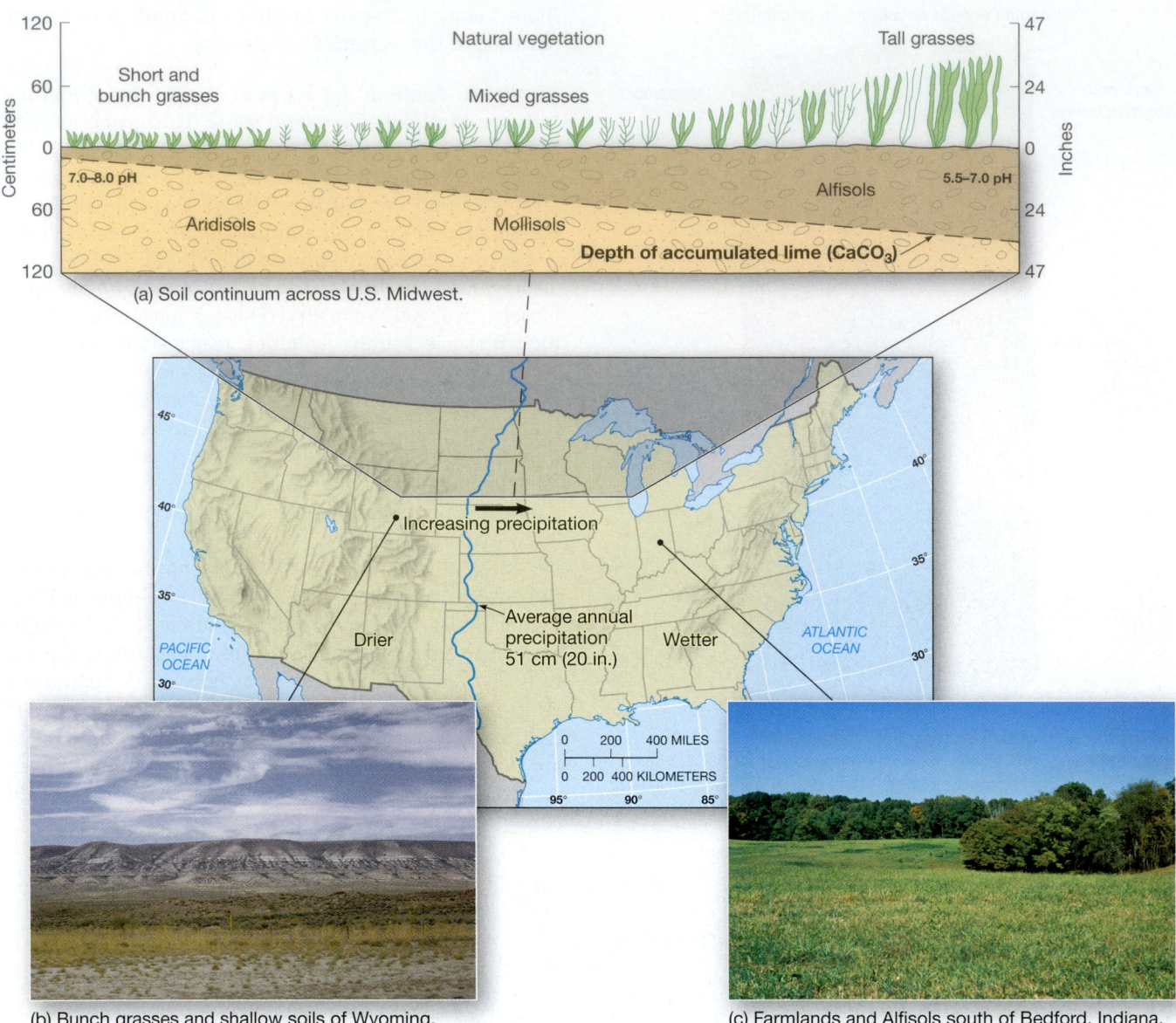

(a) Soil continuum across U.S. Midwest.

(b) Bunch grasses and shallow soils of Wyoming.

(c) Farmlands and Alfisols south of Bedford, Indiana.

▲Figure 18.19 **Soils of the Midwest.** Aridisols (to the west), Mollisols (central), and Alfisols (to the east) are part of a soil continuum in the north-central United States and southern Canadian prairies. Note the line of 51-cm annual precipitation on the map, roughly along the 98th meridian—drier to the west and wetter to the east, with associated changes in soil pH and depth of accumulated calcium carbonate. [(a) Illustration adapted from N. C. Brady, *The Nature and Properties of Soils*, 10th ed., © 1990 by Macmillan Publishing Company, adapted by permission. (b) Robert Christopherson. (c) Bobbé Christopherson.]

In North America, the Great Plains straddle the 98th meridian, which is coincident with a line equivalent to about 51 cm (20 in.) of annual precipitation. On the east side of this line, higher precipitation leads to wetter soil conditions; on the west side, conditions are drier. This line marks the historic division between the short- and tall-grass prairies (Figure 18.18).

Alfisols Spatially, **Alfisols** (moderately weathered forest soils) are the most widespread of the soil orders, extending in five suborders from near the equator to high latitudes. Representative Alfisol areas include parts of interior western Africa; Fort Nelson, British Columbia; the states near the Great Lakes; and the valleys of central California. Most Alfisols are grayish brown to reddish and

are considered moist versions of the Mollisol soil group. Moderate eluviation is present as well as a subsurface horizon of illuviated clays and clay formation because of a pattern of increased precipitation (**Figure 18.20**).

Alfisols have moderate to high reserves of basic cations and are fertile. However, productivity depends on moisture and temperature. Alfisols usually are supplemented by a moderate application of lime and fertilizer in areas of active agriculture.

Some of the best U.S. farmland occurs in the humid continental, hot summer climates surrounding the Great Lakes. Alfisols in this region produce grains, hay, and dairy products. The moist winter, dry summer pattern of the Mediterranean climate also produces Alfisols. These naturally productive soils are farmed intensively for subtropical

(a) Alfisol profile in northern Idaho loess.

▲**Figure 18.20 Alfisols.** [(a) Marbut Collection, Soil Science Society of America, Inc. (c) Bobbé Christopherson.]

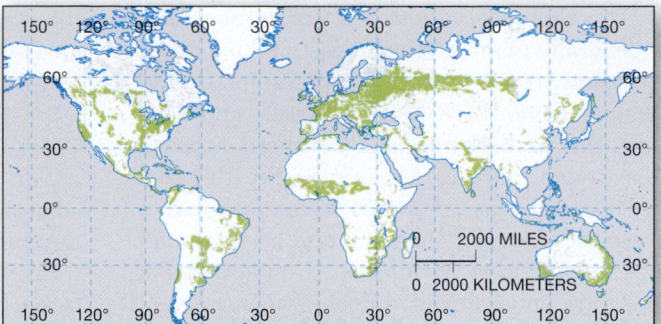

(b) Worldwide Alfisol distribution.

(c) An olive orchard in northern California, where virtually all U.S. olive production occurs.

fruits, nuts, and special crops that grow in only a few locales worldwide—for example, California olives, grapes, citrus, artichokes, almonds, and figs (Figure 18.19c).

Ultisols Farther south in the United States are the **Ultisols** (highly weathered forest soils). An Alfisol might evolve into an Ultisol, given time and exposure to increased weathering under moist conditions. These soils tend to be reddish because of residual iron and aluminum oxides in the A horizon (**Figure 18.21**).

The relatively high precipitation in Ultisol regions causes greater mineral alteration and more eluvial leaching than in other soils. Therefore, the level of basic cations is lower, and the soil fertility is lower. Fertility is further reduced by certain agricultural practices and the effect of soil-damaging crops such as cotton and tobacco, which deplete nitrogen and expose soil to erosion. These soils respond well to good management—for example, crop rotation restores nitrogen, and certain cultivation practices prevent the washing action of rain that leads to soil erosion. Peanut plantings assist in nitrogen restoration.

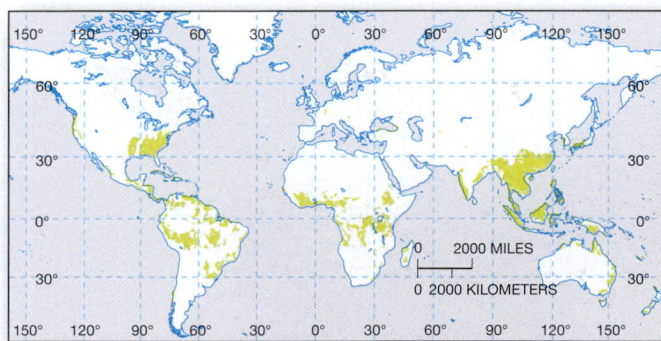

(a) Worldwide Ultisol distribution.

▲**Figure 18.21 Ultisols.** [(b) Bobbé Christopherson.]

(b) Ultisols planted with rows of peanuts in west-central Georgia have the characteristic reddish color.

Spodosols The **Spodosols** (northern coniferous forest soils) occur generally to the north and east of the Alfisols, mainly in forested areas in the humid continental mild-summer climates of northern North America and Eurasia, Denmark, the Netherlands, and southern England. Because comparable climates are rare in the Southern Hemisphere, this soil type is rare there. Spodosols form from sandy parent materials, shaded under evergreen forests of spruce, fir, and pine. Spodosols with more moderate properties form under mixed or deciduous forests. An ashen-gray color is common in these subarctic forest soils (**Figure 18.22**). Agricultural use of Spodosols may require

the addition of a soil amendment such as limestone to increase crop production by raising the pH of these acidic soils.

The colors of a Spodosol profile display the eluvial–illuvial relationship in soils produced by *podzolization*. These soils commonly have an O horizon, and some have an A horizon below the O. Beneath that is the light-colored E horizon, characterized by eluviated iron and aluminum oxides and bases leached downward through the soil profile (**Figure 18.23**). Beneath is the B horizon containing illuviated organic matter and iron and aluminum oxides. Podzolization is most prominent in sandy parent materials and in the low-pH soil solution produced by the decomposition of base-poor, acid-rich evergreen tree litter.

Entisols The **Entisols** (recent, undeveloped soils) lack vertical development of their horizons and occur in many climates worldwide. Entisols are true soils, but they have not had sufficient time to generate the usual horizons.

Entisols generally are poor agricultural soils. The same conditions that inhibit complete development—too much or too little water, poor structure, and insufficient accumulation of weathered nutrients—also prevent adequate fertility. The exception is Entisols formed from river silt deposits, which are quite fertile. Entisols are characteristically found on active slopes, floodplain

(a) Spodosol profile from northern New York.

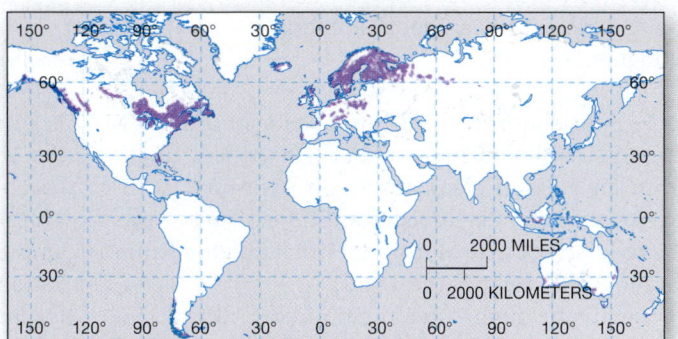

(b) Worldwide Spodosol distribution.

(c) Characteristic temperate forest and Spodosols in the cool, moist climate of central Vancouver Island.

(d) Freshly plowed Spodosols (Podzolic soils, in the Canadian System) near Lakeville, Nova Scotia. The soils are formed beneath mixed and deciduous forest before the land is cleared for agriculture.

▲**Figure 18.22 Spodosols.** [(a) Marbut Collection, Soil Science Society of America, Inc. (c) and (d) Bobbé Christopherson.]

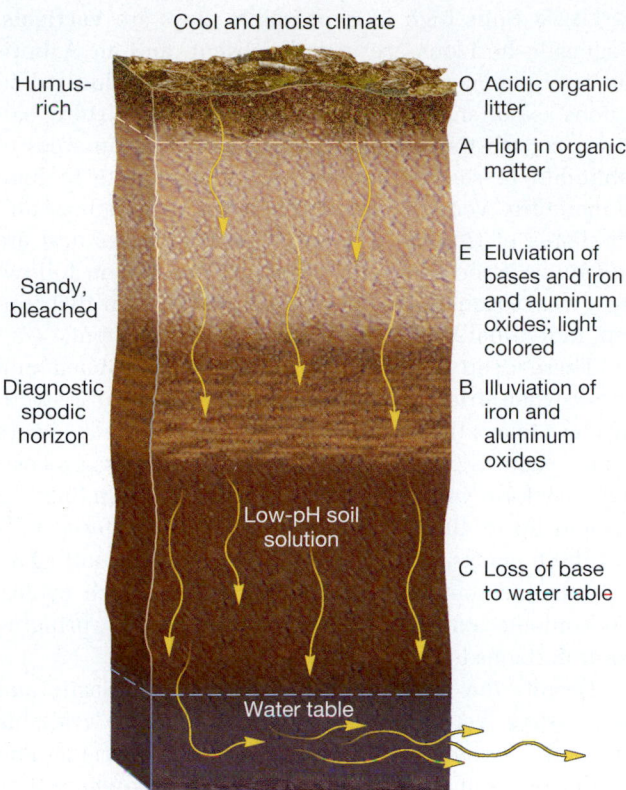

Cool and moist climate

Humus-rich

Sandy, bleached

Diagnostic spodic horizon

Low-pH soil solution

Water table

O Acidic organic litter

A High in organic matter

E Eluviation of bases and iron and aluminum oxides; light colored

B Illuviation of iron and aluminum oxides

C Loss of base to water table

▲Figure 18.23 **A soil undergoing podzolization.** This process is typical in cool and moist climatic regimes and Spodosols.

▲Figure 18.24 **Entisols.** A landscape showing Entisols—undeveloped soils forming in the shales of the Anza–Borrego Desert, California. [Bobbé Christopherson.]

alluvium, poorly drained tundra, tidal mudflats, dune sands and ergs, and plains of glacial outwash. **Figure 18.24** shows a landscape of Entisols in a desert climate where shales formed the parent material.

Inceptisols Although more developed than the Entisols, **Inceptisols** (weakly developed soils) are young, infertile soils. This order includes a wide variety of different soils, all having in common a lack of maturity and most showing only the beginning stages of weathering.

Inceptisols are associated with moist soil regimes and are regarded as eluvial because they demonstrate a loss of soil constituents throughout their profile; however, they do retain some weatherable minerals. This soil group has no distinct illuvial horizons. Most of the glacially derived till and outwash materials from New York down through the Appalachians are Inceptisols, as is the alluvium on the Mekong and Ganges floodplains.

Gelisols The **Gelisols** (cold and frozen soils) contain permafrost within 2 m (6.5 ft) of the surface and are found at high latitudes (Canada, Alaska, Russia, Arctic Ocean islands, and the Antarctic Peninsula) and high elevations (mountains). Temperatures in these regions are at or below 0°C (32°F), making soil development a slow process and disturbances of the soil long-lasting. Cold temperatures slow the decomposition of materials in the soil, so Gelisols can store large amounts of organic matter; thick O horizons are common (**Figure 18.25**). Only Histosols (discussed ahead) have a content of organic matter as high as Gelisols.

Gelisols store large quantities of organic carbon, an estimated 1.7 trillion tons worldwide. When permafrost within these soils thaws, the process releases greenhouse gases into the atmosphere (as discussed in Chapter 10). Warming in the higher latitudes begins the process, as Gelisols can quickly become wet and soggy with only a slight shift in their thermal balance. As thawing progresses, the poorly decomposed organic content in the soil begins to decay, and its decomposition releases enormous quantities of carbon dioxide and methane into the atmosphere through increased respiration.

GEOreport **18.2** Biological soil crusts

In arid and semiarid regions, where vegetation is sparse or absent, soil surfaces are host to a community of organisms that glue soil particles together, forming a crust several centimeters thick. Such a biological soil crust, also known as a cryptobiotic crust, helps stabilize soils and prevent wind and water erosion. The organisms in these crusts include cyanobacteria, algae, lichens, mosses, fungi, and other bacteria, all of which grow on the soil surfaces between vascular plants. Such crusts trap and store water, nutrients, and organic matter for vegetation growth, but are easily disturbed by humans and animals. For photos and more information, see http://www.nps.gov/cany/naturescience/soils.htm.

Gelisols are subject to *cryoturbation* (frost churning and mixing) in the freeze–thaw cycle in the active layer (described in Chapter 17). This process disrupts soil horizons, pulling organic material to lower layers and drawing rocky C-horizon material to the surface, a process that often forms patterned ground.

Andisols Areas of volcanic activity feature **Andisols** (soils formed from volcanic parent materials). Andisols are derived from volcanic ash and glass and frequently bury previous soil horizons with materials from repeated eruptions. Volcanic soils have high mineral content because they are recharged by eruptions.

Weathering and mineral transformations are important in this soil order. For example, volcanic glass weathers readily into a clay colloid and oxides of aluminum and iron. Andisols have a high CEC and high water-holding ability and develop moderate fertility, although phosphorus availability is an occasional problem. In Hawai'i, fields of Andisols produce coffee, pineapples, macadamia nuts, and small amounts of sugar cane as important cash crops. Andisol distribution is small in areal extent; however, such soils are locally important in regions associated with the volcanic Pacific Rim, discussed in Chapter 11 (**Figure 18.26**).

Vertisols Soils high in expandable clays are **Vertisols**. Diagnostic horizons are usually absent, and an A horizon is common (**Figure 18.27**). Vertisols are located in regions experiencing highly variable soil-moisture balances through the seasons. These soils occur in areas of subhumid to semiarid moisture and moderate to high temperature. Vertisols frequently form in savannas and grasslands of tropical and subtropical climates and are sometimes associated with a distinct dry season following a wet season. Although widespread in their distribution, individual Vertisol units are limited in extent.

These deep clay soils swell when moistened and shrink when dried. They contain more than 30% swelling clays (clays that swell significantly when they absorb water), such as *montmorillonite*. In the drying process, they may form vertical cracks as wide as 2–3 cm (0.8–1.2 in.) and up to 40 cm (16 in.) deep. Loose material falls into these cracks, only to disappear when the soil again expands and the cracks close. After many such cycles, soil contents tend to invert, or mix vertically, bringing lower horizons to the surface.

Despite the fact that clay soils become plastic and heavy when wet and leave little soil moisture available for plants, Vertisols are high in bases and nutrients and thus are some of the better farming soils where they occur. Vertisols often are planted with grain sorghums, corn, and cotton (Figure 18.26c).

Histosols Accumulations of thick organic matter can form **Histosols** (organic soils). In the midlatitudes, when conditions are right, beds of former lakes may

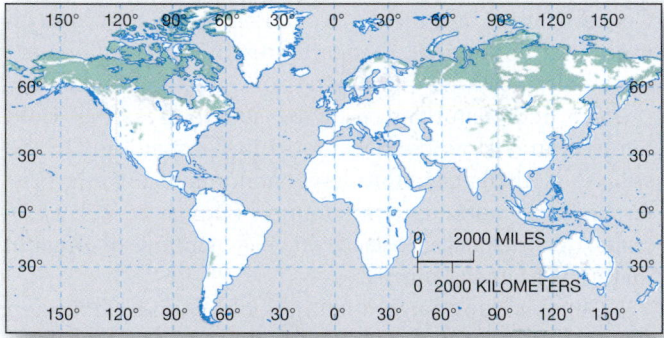

(a) Worldwide Gelisol distribution.

(b) The tundra is green in the brief summer season on Spitsbergen Island, northern Norway, as the active layer thaws.

(c) Fibrous organic content exposed on the underside of a soil clod, Spitsbergen.

▲**Figure 18.25 Gelisols.** [(b) and (c) Bobbé Christopherson.]

▲**Figure 18.26 Andisols in agricultural production.** An onion plantation in the Chiriquí Province on the west coast of Panama in Central America. [Alfredo Maiquez/Getty Images.]

turn into Histosols, with water gradually replaced by organic material to form a bog. Histosols also form in small, poorly drained depressions, where conditions can be ideal for significant deposits of sphagnum peat to form (**Figure 18.28**).

Peat beds, often more than 2 m (6.5 ft) thick, can be cut by hand with a spade into blocks, which are then dried, baled, and sold as a soil amendment (Figure 18.27a). Peat is the first stage in the natural formation of lignite, an intermediate step toward coal. The Histosols that formed in lush swamp environments in the Carboniferous Period (359 to 299 million years ago) eventually underwent coalification to become coal deposits.

Most Histosols are **hydric soils**, defined as soils that are saturated or flooded for long enough periods of time to develop anaerobic (oxygen-free) conditions during the growing season. The presence of hydric soils is the basis for the legal delineation of wetlands, which are protected from dredging, filling, and the discharge of pollutants under the U.S. Clean Water Act. Bogs are a type of wetland, and many Histosols develop in wetland environments (Figure 18.27c). Entisols are another soil order that frequently develops as hydric soils in large river valleys and along coastlines.

The 12 soil orders of the Soil Taxonomy are summarized in **Table 18.1**. As you review the soil orders and descriptions, try to generally locate each one on the world map in Figure 18.12.

(a) Vertisol profile in the Lajas Valley of Puerto Rico.

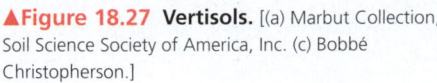

▲**Figure 18.27 Vertisols.** [(a) Marbut Collection, Soil Science Society of America, Inc. (c) Bobbé Christopherson.]

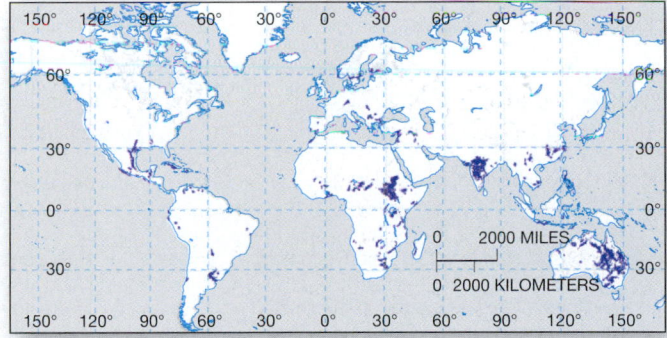

(b) Worldwide Vertisol distribution.

(c) Commercial sorghum crop planted in Vertisols on the Texas coastal plain, northeast of Palacios. Note the characteristic dark soil color.

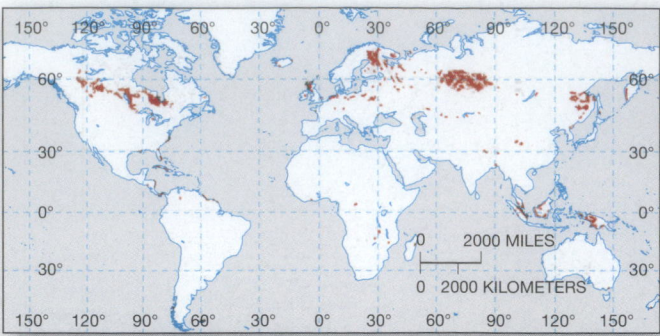

(b) Worldwide Histosol distribution.

(a) A Histosol profile on Mainland Island in the Orkneys, north of Scotland. The inset photo shows drying blocks of peat, used as fuel. Note the fibrous texture of the sphagnum moss growing on the surface and the darkening layers with depth in the soil profile as the peat is compressed and chemically altered.

(c) A bog in coastal Maine near Acadia National Park.

▲**Figure 18.28 Histosols.** [(a) Bobbé Christopherson. (c) Jorge Moro/Shutterstock.]

TABLE 18.1 Soil Orders

Order	Description/Climate/Location	Characteristics
Oxisols	Tropical soils; hot, humid areas	Maximum weathering of Fe and Al and eluviation; no clearly marked horizons.
Aridisols	Desert soils; hot, dry areas	Limited alteration of parent material; light color; low humus content; subsurface illuviation of carbonates.
Mollisols	Grassland soils; subhumid, semiarid lands	Noticeably dark with organic material; humus-rich; surface with well-structured horizons.
Alfisols	Moderately weathered forest soils; humid temperate climate	B horizon high in clays; no pronounced color change with depth.
Ultisols	Highly weathered forest soils; subtropical climate	Similar to Alfisols; B horizon high in clays; strong weathering in subsurface horizons.
Spodosols	Northern conifer forest soils; cool, humid climate	Illuvial B horizon of Fe/Al clays; partially cemented; highly leached; strongly acid.
Entisols	Recent soils; profile undeveloped; all climates	Limited development; inherited properties from parent material; pale color; low humus; hard and massive when dry.
Inceptisols	Weakly developed soils; humid regions	Young soils with few diagnostic features.
Gelisols	Permafrost-affected soils; tundra climate at high latitude and in mountain highlands	Permafrost within 100 cm of the soil surface; evidence of cryoturbation and/or an active layer.
Andisols	Soils formed from volcanic activity; especially common along the Pacific Rim	Volcanic parent materials; weathering and mineral transformation important; generally fertile.
Vertisols	Expandable clay soils; subtropics, tropics; sufficient dry period	Forms large cracks on drying; self-mixing action; contains >30% swelling clays; light color; low humus content.
Histosols	Organic soils; wetlands	Peat or bog; >20% organic matter; surface organic layers; no diagnostic horizons.

SOILS IMPACT HUMANS

• Soils are the foundation of basic ecosystem function and are a critical resource for agriculture.
• Soils store carbon dioxide and other greenhouse gases in soil organic matter.

HUMANS IMPACT SOILS

• Humans have modified soils through agricultural activities. Recently, fertilizer use, nutrient depletion, and salinization have increased soil degradation.
• Poor land-use practices are combining with changing climate to cause desertification, soil erosion, and loss of prime farmland.

Volunteers set logs known as waterbars across a trail near Mount Evans, Colorado, to prevent soil erosion, which is worsened by trampling of tundra vegetation in this mountain ecosystem. [Jim West/Alamy.]

Grapevines grow in the Andisols of Lanzarote in the Canary Islands, producing wines from the fertile black ash of some of the most isolated vineyards in the world. Stone walls protect plants from Atlantic Ocean winds. [Greg Balfour Evans/Alamy.]

Forest clearing in Brazil for development and agriculture exposes Oxisols, which have low fertility. Further disturbance of these tropical rainforest soils produces high rates of erosion. [BrazilPhotos.com/Alamy.]

A farmer opens the gate of a small irrigation canal that brings water from the Nile River to irrigate fields in northern Egypt. Increasing soil salinity is a major problem on the Nile delta. [Friedrich Stark/Alamy.]

ISSUES FOR THE 21ST CENTURY

• Increased use of sustainable agriculture is needed to keep productivity high as world population grows.
• Thawing frozen soils (Gelisols) will continue to emit carbon to the atmosphere, continuing the positive feedback loop that enhances global warming, unless humans curb their use of fossil fuels and slow climate change.

QUESTIONS TO CONSIDER

1. Why are Oxisols (tropical soils) less fertile than other soils?
2. What are some strategies to reduce soil erosion?

KEY**LEARNING**concepts**review**

Define soil and soil science and **list** four components of soil.

Soil (p. 524) is a dynamic natural mixture of fine materials, including both mineral and organic matter. **Soil science** (p. 524) is the interdisciplinary study of soils involving physics, chemistry, biology, mineralogy, hydrology, taxonomy, climatology, and cartography. Soil is composed of about 50% mineral and organic matter and 50% water and air contained in pore spaces between the soil particles.

1. Soils provide the foundation for animal and plant life and therefore are critical to Earth's ecosystems. Why is this true?

Describe the principal soil-formation factors and **describe** the horizons of a typical soil profile.

Environmental factors that affect soil formation include parent materials, climate, biological activity, topography, and time. To evaluate soils, scientists use a **soil profile** (p. 525), a vertical section of soil that runs from the surface to the deepest extent of plant roots or to the point where regolith or bedrock is encountered. Each discernible layer in a soil profile is a **soil horizon** (p. 526). O (horizon contains **humus** (p. 526), a complex mixture of decomposed and synthesized organic materials. The A horizon is darker and rich in humus and clay. The E horizon is the zone of **eluviation** (p. 526), the removal of fine particles and minerals by water. The B horizon is the zone of **illuviation** (p. 526), the deposition of clays and minerals translocated from elsewhere. The C horizon contains mainly *regolith*, weathered bedrock. The R horizon is bedrock. Soil horizons A, E, and B experience the most active soil processes and together are designated the **solum** (p. 526).

2. Briefly describe the contributions of the following factors and their effects on soil formation: parent material, climate, vegetation, landforms, time, and humans.
3. Characterize the principal aspects of each soil horizon. Where does the main accumulation of organic material occur? Where does humus form?
4. Explain the difference between the processes of eluviation and illuviation.

Describe the physical properties used to classify soils: color, texture, structure, consistence, porosity, and soil moisture.

We use several physical properties to assess **soil fertility** (p. 527), the ability of soil to sustain plants, and classify soils. Soil texture refers to the size of individual mineral particles and the ratios of different sizes. For example, **loam** (p. 527) is a balanced mixture of sand, silt, and clay. Soil color suggests composition and chemical makeup. Soil structure refers to the shape and size of the soil *ped*, which is the smallest natural cluster of particles in a given soil. The cohesion of soil particles to each other is called soil consistence. **Soil porosity** (p. 530) refers to the size, alignment, shape, and location of spaces in the soil that are filled with air, gases, or water. Soil moisture refers to water in the soil pores and its availability to plants.

5. How can soil color be an indication of soil qualities? Give a couple of examples.
6. What is the soil texture triangle? What is loam and why is it regarded so highly by agriculturists?

Explain basic soil chemistry, including cation-exchange capacity, and **relate** these concepts to soil fertility.

Particles of clay and organic material form negatively charged **soil colloids** (p. 530) that attract and retain positively charged mineral ions in the soil. The capacity to exchange ions between colloids and roots is called the **cation-exchange capacity (CEC)**, p. 531.

7. What are soil colloids? How are they related to cations and anions in the soil? Explain cation-exchange capacity.
8. What is meant by the concept of soil fertility, and how does soil chemistry affect fertility?

Describe the 12 soil orders of the Soil Taxonomy classification system and **explain** their general distribution across Earth.

The U.S. **Soil Taxonomy** (p. 532) classification system is built around an analysis of various diagnostic horizons and 12 soil orders, as actually seen in the field. The basic sampling unit used in soil surveys is the **pedon** (p. 532). To identify soils, the Soil Taxonomy system uses *diagnostic horizons*, either the surface soil or the soil layer below the surface (at various depths) having properties specific to the type of soil.

Specific soil-forming processes keyed to climatic regions (not a basis for classification) are called **pedogenic regimes** (p. 534). These include

- **laterization** (p. 534), leaching in warm and humid climates
- **calcification** (p. 534), accumulation of carbonates in the B and C horizons in drier continental climates
- **salinization** (p. 534), collection of salt residues in surface horizons in hot, dry climates
- **podzolization** (p. 534), soil acidification in forest soils in cool climates
- **gleization** (p. 534), humus and clay accumulation in cold, wet climates with poor drainage

The Soil Taxonomy system divides soils into six hierarchical categories, the largest of which are the soil orders. The 12 soil orders are

Oxisols (p. 536), tropical soils
Aridisols (p. 538), desert soils
Mollisols (p. 539), grassland soils
Alfisols (p. 540), moderately weathered, temperate forest soils
Ultisols, (p. 541), highly weathered, subtropical forest soils

Spodosols (p. 542), northern conifer forest soils
Entisols (p. 542), young, undeveloped soils
Inceptisols (p. 543), weakly developed, humid-region soils
Gelisols (p. 543), cold soils underlain by permafrost
Andisols (p. 544), soils formed from volcanic materials
Vertisols (p. 544), expandable clay soils
Histosols (p. 544), organic soils.

Soils saturated for long enough periods to develop anaerobic, or "oxygen-free," conditions are **hydric soils** (p. 545).

9. Describe the salinization process in arid and semi-arid soils. What associated soil horizons develop?
10. Which of the soil orders are associated with Earth's most productive agricultural areas?
11. Why is the 51-cm (20-in.) line of annual precipitation in the Midwest significant to plants? How do soil characteristics change on either side of this line.
12. Describe the location, nature, and formation processes of Gelisols. What is the linkage between these soils and climate change?

GEO**SPATIAL** ANALYSIS

Soil Types

Soil types are mapped across the United States. Farmers and planners use this information to determine optimum land use. Farmers need to know if soils are suitable for the crops they want to plant. Urban and regional planners working for real-estate developers or local governments take soils into account as they plan residential, commercial, and industrial developments and determine the environmental effects of land use changes.

Activities

Go to the USDA's Web Soil Survey at http://websoilsurvey.sc.egov.usda.gov. Click on the "Start WSS" button. Select "State and County" under "Quick Navigation"; enter your state and county and then click "View". Click on the "i" tool and then click on your location to display location information.

1. What is the latitude and longitude for the location you selected?

2. What is the date of the aerial photograph?

Create an Area of Interest (AOI) around your location by clicking the AOI rectangle tool, then drag the mouse to create a space around the location. This area should encompass at least a few streets. When a striped area appears, click on the "Soil Map" tab. Click on the Map Unit Legend to see soil types in your area and on Map Unit Name for details.

3. What type(s) of soil is (are) most abundant at your location?

4. Based on Figure 18.5 and soil texture, what is the percentage of sand, silt, and clay in these soils?

Clear the current AOI by clicking "Clear AOI." Choose "State and County" and select Fulton County, Illinois. Zoom in and create an AOI south of Cuba, IL. Click on the "Soil Data Explorer" tab and be sure "Suitabilities and Limitations for Use" is selected. Select Land Classification and choose Farmland Classification, then click "View Rating."

5. What information is displayed by clicking "View Description."

6. What is the dominant rating for this area? What other ratings are available in this area?

7. What percentage is prime farmland or farmland of statewide importance?

Select Land Management under Soil Classification and choose Erosion Hazard (Off-Road, Off-Trail), then click "View Rating."

8. What information is displayed by clicking "View Description."

9. What is the dominant rating for this area? What other ratings are available in your area?

10. In the aerial photographs, what are the characteristics of areas with the highest erosion ratings? Lowest ratings?

MasteringGeography™

Looking for additional review and test prep materials? Visit the Study Area in MasteringGeography™ to enhance your geographic literacy, spatial reasoning skills, and understanding of this chapter's content by accessing a variety of resources, including MapMaster™ interactive maps, videos, *Mobile Field Trips*, *Project Condor* Quadcopter Videos, *In the News* RSS feeds, flashcards, web links, self-study quizzes, and an eText version of *Geosystems*.

19 Ecosystem Essentials

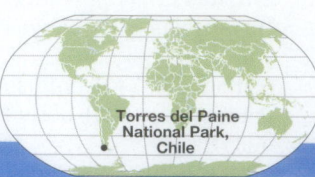

Torres del Paine
National Park,
Chile

A small herd of guanacos graze on the slopes of Torres del Paine National Park in southern Chile. Related to camels, guanacos inhabit the arid deserts and semiarid steppes and mountains of South America. [Blickwinkel/Alamy.]

KEY**LEARNING**concepts

After reading the chapter, you should be able to:

- **Define** ecology, biogeography, and ecosystem.
- **Explain** photosynthesis and respiration and **describe** the world pattern of net primary productivity.
- **Discuss** the oxygen, carbon, and nitrogen cycles and **explain** trophic relationships.
- **Describe** communities and ecological niches and **list** several limiting factors on species distributions.
- **Outline** the stages of ecological succession in both terrestrial and aquatic ecosystems.
- **Explain** how biological evolution led to the biodiversity of life on Earth.

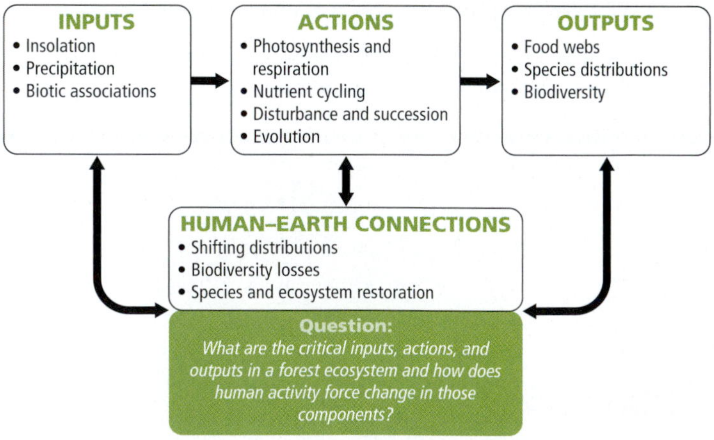

INPUTS
- Insolation
- Precipitation
- Biotic associations

ACTIONS
- Photosynthesis and respiration
- Nutrient cycling
- Disturbance and succession
- Evolution

OUTPUTS
- Food webs
- Species distributions
- Biodiversity

HUMAN–EARTH CONNECTIONS
- Shifting distributions
- Biodiversity losses
- Species and ecosystem restoration

Question:
What are the critical inputs, actions, and outputs in a forest ecosystem and how does human activity force change in those components?

Animals Shift Their Ranges with Climate Change

On the rocky slopes of mountains near treeline, you may have heard the pika's whistle, an unusually loud call coming from a creature so small. The American pika is a mammal, related to rabbits and hares, that lives on talus slopes in mountain ranges of the U.S. and Canadian West (**Figure GN 19.1**). Pikas spend their summers collecting food to store and eat during the winter months. They are sensitive to heat and stop foraging to take refuge under the rocks when midday temperatures rise higher than about 25.5°C (78°F). Pikas do not hibernate during the winter months and require adequate winter snow cover to provide insulation from freezing temperatures. Although not officially listed as a threatened or endangered species, pikas are today declining throughout some of their former range.

Changing Pika Distributions In 2016, scientists reported that pikas had disappeared from some of their former mountain habitats in the U.S. West, and in other places pika numbers were declining. Present in parts of southern Utah from the 1960s to about 2010, pikas were either gone or they were down to only several individuals in 2015. In the Great Basin mountain ranges of Nevada, scientists noted a 44% loss of pikas over dozens of

sites within the same time frame. In places where scientists found pikas in 2015, the animals had moved upslope from the earlier sightings, toward areas with cooler temperatures and higher snowfall. In California, pika sightings were down by about 25%, and the greatest declines occurred in isolated populations that have no suitable habitat nearby.

Tolerance Limits and Species Range Every plant or animal species in nature has a range of tolerance for variations in the physical characteristics of its environment, and this range of tolerance affects its geographical distribution (**Figure GN 19.2**). In particular, temperature and moisture requirements are often critical for determining a species' range. This is one reason global climate change can have a huge effect on animals. As environmental conditions shift (with temperatures becoming too high or too low and rainfall too much

or too little), species must adapt or expand their range, or become extinct.

Other Animals Move Higher Pikas are not the only animals disappearing or shifting their ranges in response to climate change. Over the past two decades, scientists have reported that other land species are shifting higher in altitude (toward the tops of mountains), as well as higher in latitude (toward the poles). A long-term study in Yosemite National Park, California, found that small-mammal communities shifted their distributions in response to rising temperatures throughout the 20th century. Half the species monitored showed substantial movement toward cooler temperatures at higher elevations. Animals formerly found at low elevations expanded their ranges higher, and high-elevation species contracted their ranges away from lower areas.

Some animals risk extinction as warming pushes the zone of optimum range beyond the reaches of mountain summits. In southern California, the endangered Inyo chipmunk has not been seen for more than 7 years in the Sierra Nevada. Throughout the U.S. West, species of voles and bats are also at risk as climates shift.

1. How has climate change affected the pika's distribution and abundance in the mountains of the western United States?

2. Which two factors are often critical for determining a species' range?

▲**Figure GN 19.2 Range of tolerance for an environmental factor.** Pika distributions are today shifting toward higher elevations in mountains to stay within their optimum range of tolerance.

(a)

(b)

▲**Figure GN 19.1 The American pika.** Pikas, which inhabit cold climates near mountain summits, have disappeared from some areas of Nevada and Utah in recent decades. [Imagebroker/SuperStock.]

The biosphere, the sphere of life and organic activity, extends from the ocean floor to an altitude of about 8 km (5 mi) into the atmosphere. It consists of a vast number of ecosystems, from simple to complex, each operating within general spatial boundaries.

An **ecosystem** is a self-sustaining association of living plants and animals and their nonliving physical environment. Earth's natural ecosystems are open systems with regard to both solar energy and matter, with almost all ecosystem boundaries functioning as transition zones rather than as sharp demarcations. Ecosystems vary in size from the scale of organisms, such as in a drop of pond water; to local scale, such as a city park, a mountaintop, or a beach; to regional scale, such as a forest or desert. Internally, every ecosystem is a complex of many interconnected variables, all functioning independently yet in concert, with complicated flows of energy and matter.

Ecology is the study of the relationships between organisms and their environment and among the various ecosystems in the biosphere. The word *ecology*, developed by German naturalist Ernst Haeckel in 1869, is derived from the Greek *oikos* ("household" or "place to live") and *logos* ("study of"). **Biogeography** is the study of the distribution of plants and animals, the diverse spatial patterns they create, and the physical and biological processes, past and present, that produce Earth's species richness.

The diversity of organisms on the living Earth is one of our planet's most impressive features. This diversity is a response to the interaction of the atmosphere, hydrosphere, and lithosphere, which produces a variety of conditions within which the biosphere exists. The diversity of life also results from the intricate interplay of living organisms themselves. Humans are Earth's most influential species. From the time humans first developed agriculture, tended livestock, and used fire, they have increasingly impacted Earth's physical systems. As we discuss in this chapter, humans are impacting biodiversity directly through harvesting and habitat destruction and indirectly through climate change (**Figure 19.1**).

everydayGEOSYSTEMS

Have you noticed fewer bees in your neighborhood?

Bees are some of the most important pollinators on Earth for crops and natural vegetation. Pesticides, disease, introduced species, and human development have caused declines in bee populations. Research now shows that climate change is causing bees to shift the southern limits of their ranges to the north. Because the northern end of their range has not changed, this shift means that their overall distribution is shrinking. Loss of these pollinators will affect both agriculture and natural ecosystems.

▲**Figure 19.1 A bumble bee collects pollen from a foxglove flower.** [Frederico Quevedo/Shutterstock.]

Energy Flows and Nutrient Cycles

By definition, an ecosystem includes both biotic and abiotic components. Chief among the abiotic components is the direct input of solar energy, on which nearly all ecosystems depend. A few ecosystems exist in dark caves or on the ocean floor, depending not on sunlight but instead on chemical reactions—chemosynthesis—for energy. Other abiotic processes that drive ecosystem function include the cycling of gases, water, and mineral matter.

Converting Energy to Biomass

The energy that powers the biosphere comes primarily from the Sun. Solar energy enters the ecosystem energy flow by way of **photosynthesis** (*photo-* refers to sunlight and *synthesis* describes the "manufacturing" of starches and sugars through chemical reactions within plant leaves). Heat energy is an output of the system, dissipated from the energy flow at many points.

Plants (in terrestrial ecosystems) and algae (in aquatic ecosystems) are the critical biotic link between solar energy and the biosphere. Organisms that are capable of using the Sun's energy directly to produce their own food (using carbon dioxide, CO_2, as their sole source of carbon) are **producers**. These include plants, algae, and cyanobacteria (a type of blue-green algae). Producers accomplish this transformation of light energy into chemical energy by the process of

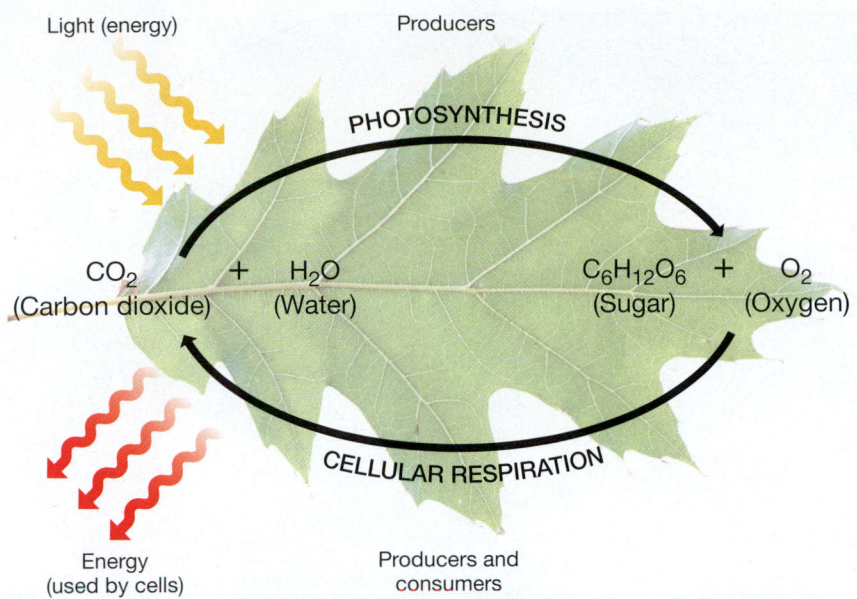

Light (energy) Producers

PHOTOSYNTHESIS

CO_2 + H_2O → $C_6H_{12}O_6$ + O_2
(Carbon dioxide) (Water) (Sugar) (Oxygen)

CELLULAR RESPIRATION

Energy
(used by cells)

Producers and
consumers

▲**Figure 19.2 Photosynthesis and respiration.** In the process of photosynthesis, plants consume light, carbon dioxide (CO_2), nutrients, and water (H_2O) and produce outputs of oxygen (O_2) and carbohydrates (sugars) as stored chemical energy. Cellular respiration, which occurs at night and during the day, approximately reverses this process. The balance between photosynthesis and respiration determines net photosynthesis and plant growth.

Photosynthesis and Cellular Respiration Powered by energy from certain wavelengths of visible light, photosynthesis unites CO_2 and hydrogen (hydrogen is derived from water in the plant) to produce energy-rich food for the plant and release oxygen (**Figure 19.2**). Photosynthesis occurs within the photosynthetic structures in leaf cells called *chloroplasts*, found just below the leaf surface. Each chloroplast contains a green, light-sensitive pigment called **chlorophyll**. Light stimulates the molecules of this pigment, producing a photochemical, or light-driven, reaction.

Only about one-quarter of the light energy arriving at the surface of a leaf is useful to the light-sensitive chlorophyll. Chlorophyll absorbs only the orange-red and violet-blue wavelengths for photochemical operations, and it reflects predominantly green hues; thus trees and other vegetation look green.

Photosynthesis in plants essentially follows this equation:

$$6CO_2 + 6H_2O + Light \rightarrow C_6H_{12}O_6 + 6O_2$$
(carbon dioxide) (water) (solar energy) (glucose, carbohydrate) (oxygen)

From the equation, you can see that photosynthesis removes carbon (in the form of CO_2) from Earth's atmosphere. The quantity of carbon involved in this process, called *carbon fixation*, is enormous: approximately 91 billion metric tons (100 billion tons) of CO_2 per year. Carbohydrates are the organic result of the photosynthetic process; an example is simple sugar *glucose* ($C_6H_{12}O_6$). Plants use glucose to build starches, which are more complex carbohydrates and the principal food stored in plants.

Plants store energy (in the bonds within carbohydrates) for later use. They consume this energy as needed through cellular respiration, which converts the carbohydrates to energy for their other operations. Thus, **cellular respiration** is essentially a reverse of the photosynthetic process:

$$C_6H_{12}O_6 + 6O_2 \rightarrow 6CO_2 + 6H_2O + Energy$$
(glucose, carbohydrate) (oxygen) (carbon dioxide) (water) (heat energy)

In respiration, plants oxidize carbohydrates (break them down through reaction with oxygen), releasing CO_2, water, and energy as heat. The difference between photosynthetic production of carbohydrates and respiration loss of carbohydrates is *net photosynthesis*. The overall growth of a plant depends on the amount of net photosynthesis, a surplus of carbohydrates beyond those lost through plant respiration.

photosynthesis. The biosphere depends on the success of these organisms and their ability to turn sunlight into food.

The first photosynthesizing bacteria appeared in oceans on Earth about 2.7 billion years ago. These *cyanobacteria*—microscopic, usually unicellular, blue-green algae that can form large colonies—were fundamental to the creation of Earth's modern atmosphere.

Vascular plants, which along with animals became common about 430 million years ago, are land plants that have conductive tissues and true roots for internal transport of fluid and nutrients. (*Vascular* is from a Latin word for "vessel-bearing," referring to the conducting cells.) In vascular plants, photochemical reactions take place in the leaves. Veins in the leaf bring in water and nutrient supplies and carry off the sugars (food) produced by photosynthesis. The veins in each leaf connect to the stems and branches of the plant and to the main circulation system.

Flows of CO_2, water, light, and oxygen enter and exit the surface of each leaf. Gases move into and out of a leaf through small pores, the **stomata** (singular: *stoma*), which usually are most numerous on the lower side of the leaf. Each stoma is surrounded by guard cells that open and close the pore, depending on the plant's changing needs. Water that moves through a plant exits the leaves through the stomata in the process of transpiration, thereby assisting the plant's temperature regulation. As water evaporates from the leaves, a pressure gradient is created that allows atmospheric pressure to push water up through the plant all the way from the roots, in the same manner that a soda straw works.

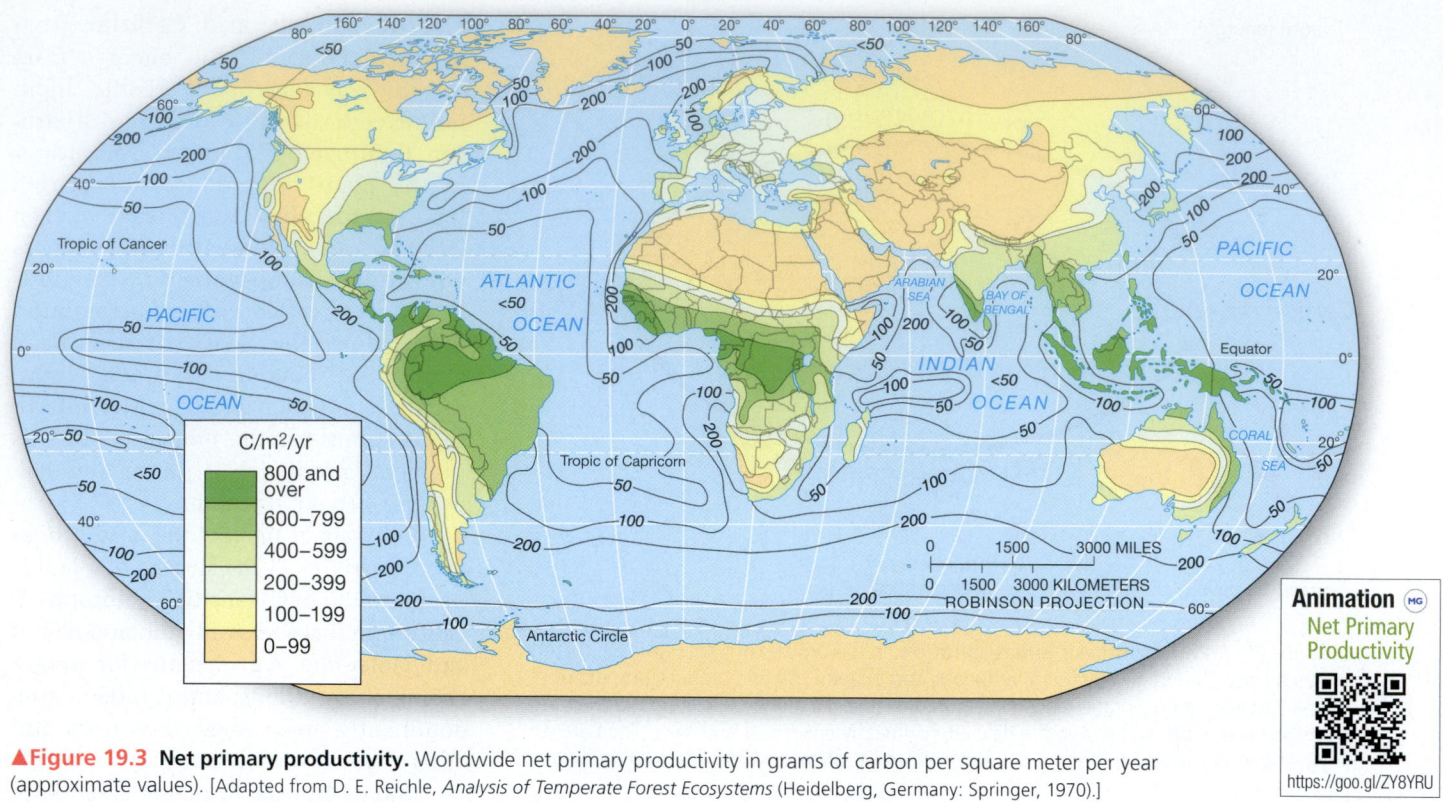

▲**Figure 19.3 Net primary productivity.** Worldwide net primary productivity in grams of carbon per square meter per year (approximate values). [Adapted from D. E. Reichle, *Analysis of Temperate Forest Ecosystems* (Heidelberg, Germany: Springer, 1970).]

Net Primary Productivity The net photosynthesis for an entire ecosystem is its **net primary productivity**. This is the amount of stored chemical energy that the ecosystem generates. The total organic matter (living and recently living, both animal and plant) in an ecosystem, with its associated chemical energy, is the ecosystem's **biomass** and is often measured as the net dry weight of all organic material. Net primary productivity is an important factor in any type of ecosystem because it determines the biomass available for consumption by **consumers**—organisms that feed on organic matter for energy. The distribution of productivity over Earth's surface is an important aspect of biogeography.

On land, net primary productivity tends to be highest between the Tropics of Cancer and Capricorn at sea level and decreases toward higher latitudes and elevations (**Figure 19.3**). Productivity levels are tied to both sunlight and precipitation, as evidenced by the correlations of abundant precipitation with high productivity adjacent to the equator and reduced precipitation with low productivity in the subtropical deserts. Even though deserts receive high amounts of solar radiation, water availability and other controlling factors, such as soil conditions, limit productivity.

In temperate and high latitudes, the rate at which carbon is fixed by vegetation varies seasonally. It increases in spring and summer as plants flourish with increasing solar input and, in some areas, with more available (nonfrozen) water, and it decreases in late fall and winter. In contrast, productivity rates in the tropics are high throughout the year, and turnover of carbon in the photosynthesis–respiration cycle is faster, exceeding by many times the rates experienced in a desert environment or in the far northern limits of the tundra. A lush hectare (2.5 acres) of sugarcane in the tropics might fix 45 metric tons (50 tons) of carbon in a year, whereas desert plants in an equivalent area might achieve only 1% of that amount.

In the oceans, differing nutrient levels control and limit productivity. Regions where upwelling brings cold, nutrient-rich waters to the surface off western coastlines generally are the most productive. Figure 19.3 shows that the tropical oceans and areas of subtropical high pressure are quite low in productivity.

Table 19.1 lists the net primary productivity of various ecosystems and provides an estimate of net total biomass worldwide. Note in the table how the productivity of cultivated land compares with that of natural communities.

Elemental Cycles

The cycling of nutrients and flow of energy between organisms determines the structure of an ecosystem. As energy cascades through the system, it is constantly replenished by the Sun. But nutrients and minerals cannot be replenished from an external source, so they constantly cycle within each ecosystem and through the biosphere.

The most abundant natural elements in living matter are hydrogen (H), oxygen (O), and carbon (C). Together, these elements make up more than 99% of Earth's biomass. In addition, nitrogen (N), calcium (Ca),

TABLE 19.1 Net Primary Productivity and Plant Biomass on Earth

Ecosystem	Area (10^6 km^2)[a]	Net Primary Productivity per Unit Area (g/m^2/yr)[b] Normal Range	Mean	Mean Biomass per Unit Area (kg/m^2)
Tropical rain forest	17.0	1000–3500	2200	44.00
Tropical seasonal forest	7.5	1000–2500	1600	36.00
Temperate evergreen forest	5.0	600–2500	1300	36.00
Temperate deciduous forest	7.0	600–2500	1200	30.00
Boreal forest	12.0	400–2000	800	20.00
Woodland and shrubland	8.5	250–1200	700	6.80
Savanna	15.0	200–2000	900	4.00
Temperate grassland	9.0	200–1500	600	1.60
Tundra and alpine region	8.0	10–400	140	0.67
Desert and semidesert scrub	18.0	10–250	90	0.67
Extreme desert, rock, sand, ice	24.0	0–10	3	0.02
Cultivated land	14.0	100–3500	650	1.10
Swamp and marsh	2.0	800–3500	2000	15.00
Lake and stream	2.0	100–1500	250	0.02
Total continental	**149.0**	—	**773**	**12.30**
Open ocean	332.0	2–400	125	0.003
Upwelling zones	0.4	400–1000	500	0.02
Continental shelf	26.6	200–600	360	0.01
Algal beds and coral reefs	0.6	500–4000	2500	2.00
Estuaries	1.4	200–3500	1500	1.00
Total marine	**361.0**	—	**152**	**0.01**
Grand total	**510.0**	—	**333**	**3.62**

Source: Whittaker, R.C., *Communities and Ecosystems*, 1975, p. 224.
[a]1 km^2 = 0.38 mi^2.
[b]1 g/m^2 = 8.92 lb/acre.

potassium (K), magnesium (Mg), sulfur (S), and phosphorus (P) are significant nutrients, elements necessary for the growth of a living organism.

These key elements flow through the natural world in various chemical cycles. Oxygen, carbon, and nitrogen each have *gaseous cycles*, parts of which take place in the atmosphere. The recycling of gases forms Earth's **biogeochemical cycles**, so called because they involve chemical reactions necessary for growth and development of living systems.

Oxygen and Carbon Cycles We consider the oxygen and carbon cycles together because they are so closely intertwined through photosynthesis and respiration (**Figure 19.4**). The atmosphere is the principal reservoir of available oxygen. Larger reserves of oxygen exist in Earth's crust, but they are unavailable, being chemically bound with other elements, especially in the silicate (SiO_2) and carbonate (CO_3) mineral families. Unoxidized reserves of fossil fuels and sediments also contain oxygen.

As discussed in Chapter 10, the oceans are enormous carbon sinks; however, all of this carbon is bound chemically in CO_2, calcium carbonate, and other compounds. The ocean initially absorbs CO_2 by means of the photosynthesis carried on by phytoplankton; it becomes part of the living organisms and through them is fixed in certain carbonate minerals, such as limestone ($CaCO_3$). The ocean water can also absorb CO_2 directly from the atmosphere, resulting in ocean acidification.

The atmosphere, which is the integrating link between photosynthesis (fixation) and respiration (release) in the carbon cycle, contains only about 800 billion metric tons of carbon (as CO_2) at any moment. This is far less carbon than is stored in fossil fuels and oil shales (as hydrocarbon molecules) or in living and dead organic matter (as carbohydrate molecules). In addition to being released into the atmosphere through the respiration of plants and animals, CO_2 is released through the burning of grasslands and forests, volcanic activity, land-use changes, and fossil-fuel combustion by industry and transportation (review Geosystems in Action 10 on pages 292–293).

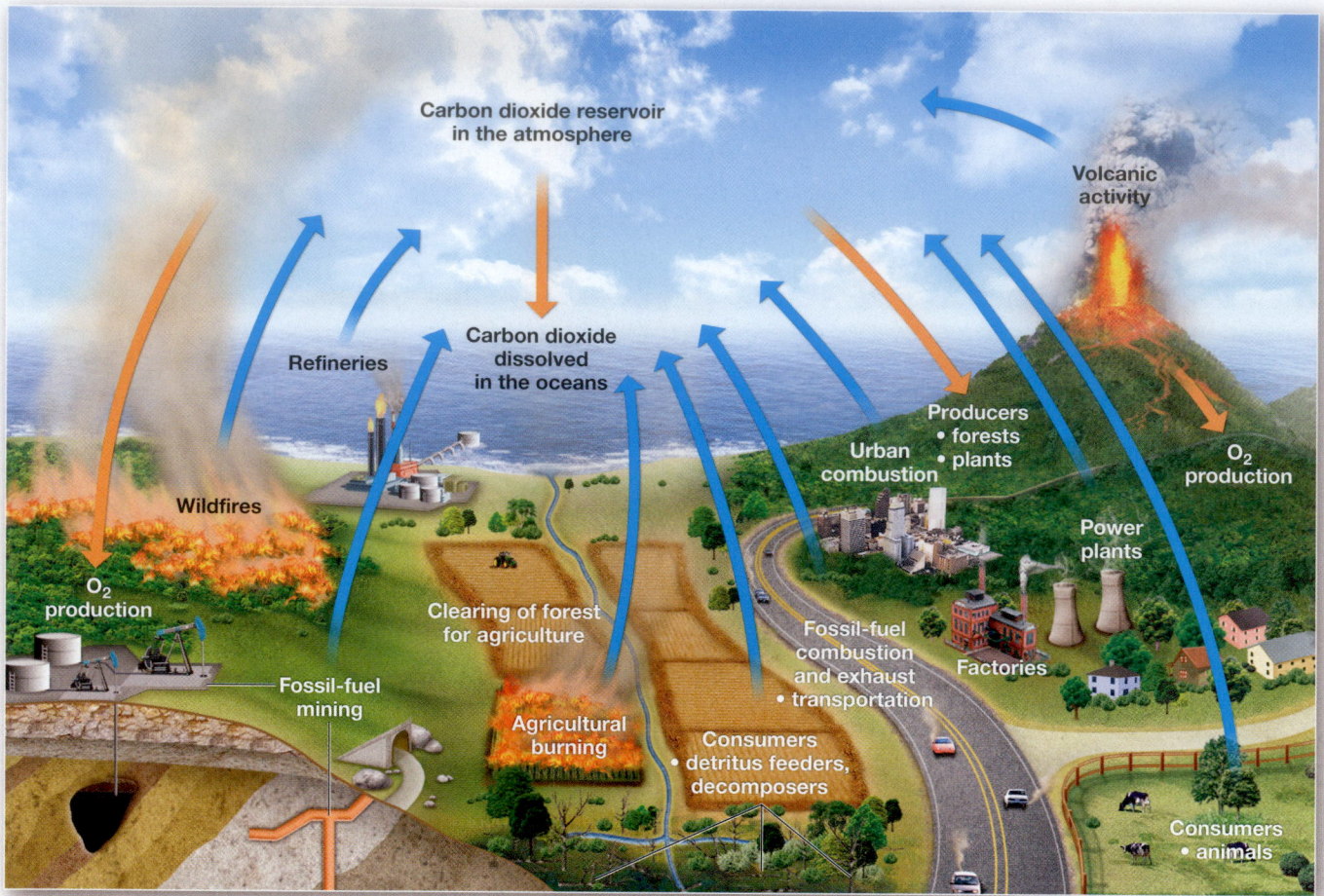

▲**Figure 19.4 The carbon and oxygen cycles.** Carbon is fixed (orange arrows) through photosynthesis, with oxygen as a by-product. Respiration by living organisms, the burning of forests and grasslands, and the combustion of fossil fuels release carbon to the atmosphere (blue arrows). These cycles are greatly influenced by human activities.

Nitrogen Cycle Nitrogen, which accounts for about 78% of each breath we take, is the major constituent of the atmosphere. Nitrogen also is important in the makeup of organic molecules, especially proteins, and therefore is essential to living processes.

Nitrogen-fixing bacteria, which live principally in the soil and are associated with the roots of certain plants, are critical for bringing atmospheric nitrogen into living organisms as part of the nitrogen cycle (**Figure 19.5**). Colonies of these bacteria reside in nodules on the roots of legumes (plants such as clover, alfalfa, soybeans, peas, beans, and peanuts) and chemically combine the nitrogen from the air into nitrates (NO_3) and ammonia (NH_3). Plants use the nitrogen from these molecules to produce their own organic matter. Anyone or anything feeding on the plants thus ingests the nitrogen. Finally, the nitrogen in the organic wastes of the consuming organisms is freed by denitrifying bacteria, which recycle it to the atmosphere.

To improve agricultural yields, many farmers enhance the available nitrogen in the soil by means of synthetic inorganic fertilizers as opposed to soil-building organic fertilizers (manure and compost). Inorganic fertilizers are chemically produced through artificial nitrogen fixation at factories.

This surplus of usable nitrogen accumulates in Earth's ecosystems. Some is present as excess nutrients, washed from soil into waterways and eventually to the ocean. This excess nitrogen load begins a water pollution process that feeds an excessive growth of algae and phytoplankton, increases biochemical oxygen demand, diminishes dissolved oxygen reserves, and eventually disrupts the aquatic ecosystem. In addition, excess nitrogen compounds in air pollution are a component in acid deposition, further altering the nitrogen cycle in soils and waterways.

Dead Zones Along coastlines and in lakes, especially where rivers carry outflows of sediment and nutrients from their watersheds, low-oxygen conditions can create **dead zones**, where dissolved oxygen is so low that marine life cannot survive. Coastal dead zones occur as the result of nutrient outflows from more than 400 river systems worldwide, affecting almost 250,000 km² (94,600 mi²) of offshore oceans and seas. Geosystems in Action19 examines the dead zones in the Gulf of Mexico

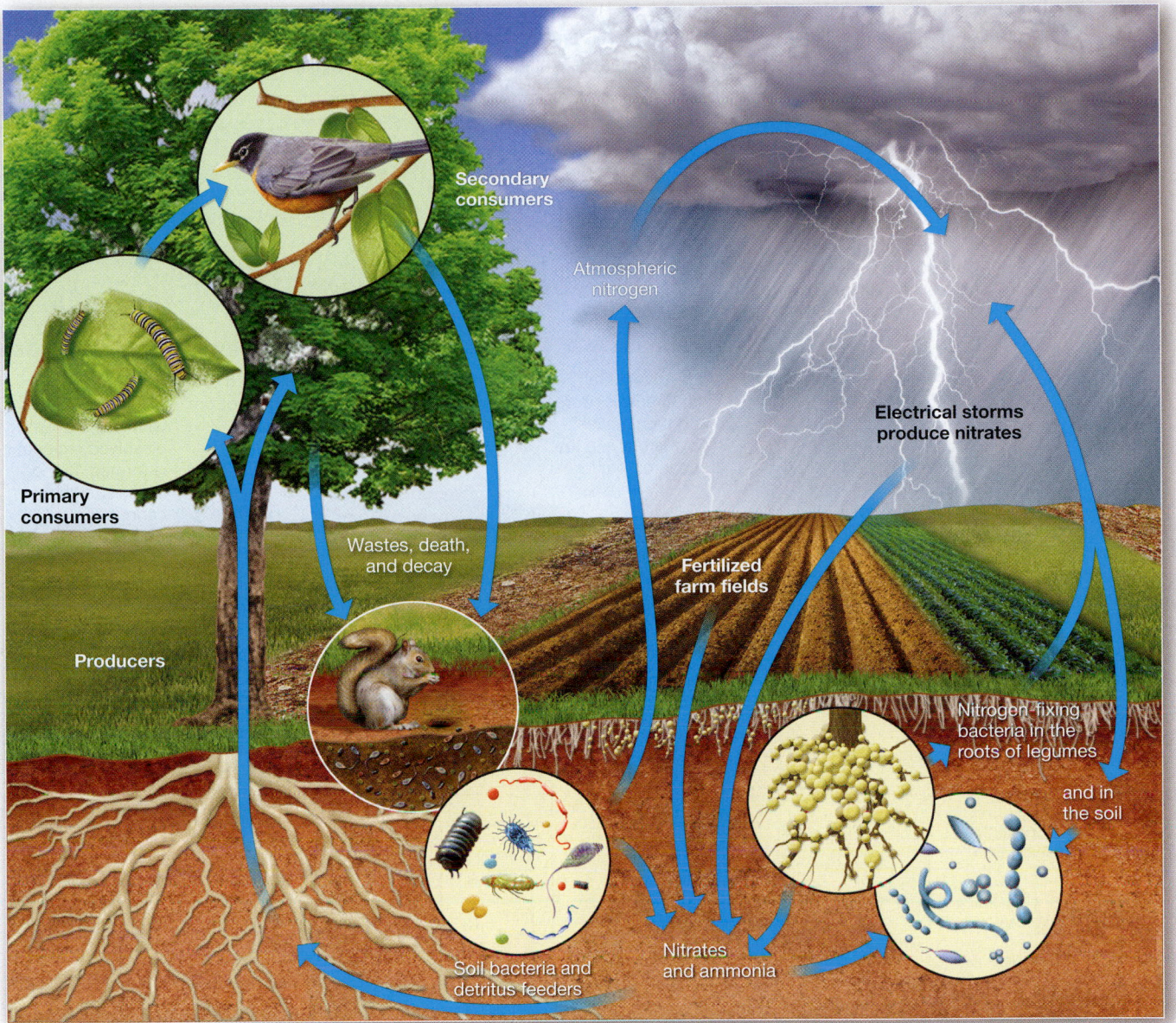

▲**Figure 19.5 The nitrogen cycle.** The atmosphere is the reservoir of gaseous nitrogen. Atmospheric nitrogen gas is chemically fixed by bacteria in producing ammonia. Lightning and forest fires produce nitrates, and fossil-fuel combustion forms nitrogen compounds that are washed from the atmosphere by precipitation. Plants absorb nitrogen compounds and incorporate the nitrogen into organic material.

and in Lake Erie, one of the U.S. Great Lakes. In 2011, the dead zone in Lake Erie reached its largest extent in recorded history, caused by fertilizers (mainly phosphorus) flowing into the lake combined with slower natural mixing attributed to climate change.

The Mississippi River receives runoff from 41% of the area of the continental United States. It carries agricultural fertilizers, farm sewage, and other nitrogen-rich wastes to the Gulf, causing huge spring blooms of phytoplankton: an explosion of primary productivity. By summer, the biological oxygen demand of bacteria feeding on the decay of the spring bloom exceeds the dissolved oxygen content of the water; hypoxia (oxygen depletion) develops, killing any fish that venture into the area. The

agricultural, feedlot, and fertilizer industries dispute the connection between their nutrient input and this extensive dead zone. The human-caused creation of dead zones in water bodies is cultural eutrophication, discussed later in the chapter.

In Sweden and Denmark, however, a concerted effort to reduce nutrient flows into rivers reversed hypoxic conditions in the Kattegat Strait (between the Baltic and North Seas). Also, fertilizer use has decreased more than 50% in the former Soviet Republics since the fall of state agriculture in 1990. The Black Sea no longer undergoes year-round hypoxia at river deltas, as the dead zones in those areas now disappear for several months each year.

Coastal ocean waters are often highly productive ecosystems teeming with marine life. Yet they can become dead zones where organisms die for lack of oxygen (GIA 19.1). The Gulf of Mexico dead zone, like others worldwide, results from a process that begins with agricultural runoff of fertilizers and farm-animal wastes (GIA 19.2 and 19.3). The size of dead zones can vary from year to year. Freshwater lakes are also subject to "blooms" of the algae that form dead zones (GIA 19.4).

19.1 FORMATION OF A DEAD ZONE

In the water's surface layer, agricultural runoff delivers nitrogen and phosphorus, nutrients that greatly boost the growth of algae, producing an algal bloom. When the algae die, they sink into the bottom layer. Bacteria feed on the dead algae and deplete the water of oxygen, forming a dead zone. Marine organisms that cannot leave the dead zone will die.

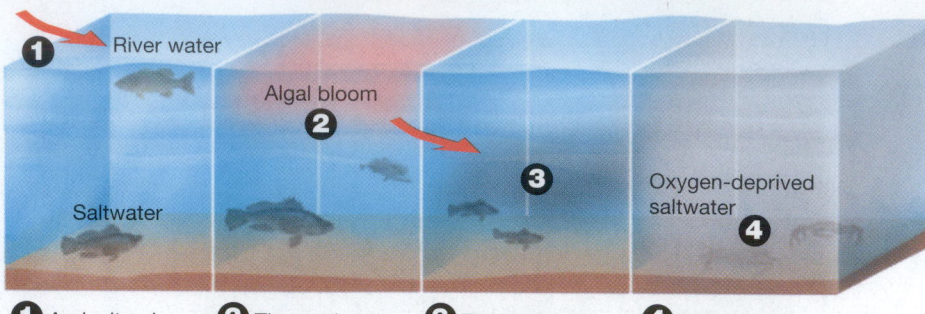

1 Agricultural runoff enters rivers, and then moves downstream to the ocean or to a lake.

2 The nutrients, mainly nitrogen and phosphorus, cause algal blooms.

3 The algae die, sink into the bottom layer, and are decomposed by bacteria, using up the oxygen in the water.

4 A dead zone (defined as water with less than 2 mg/L dissolved oxygen) is formed, killing organisms that cannot flee.

19.2 THE GULF OF MEXICO DEAD ZONE

Agricultural runoff from the Mississippi River watershed provides the nitrogen for the Gulf of Mexico dead zone (GIA 19.2a). In 2013, the dead zone extended along much of the Louisiana coast (GIA 19.2b).

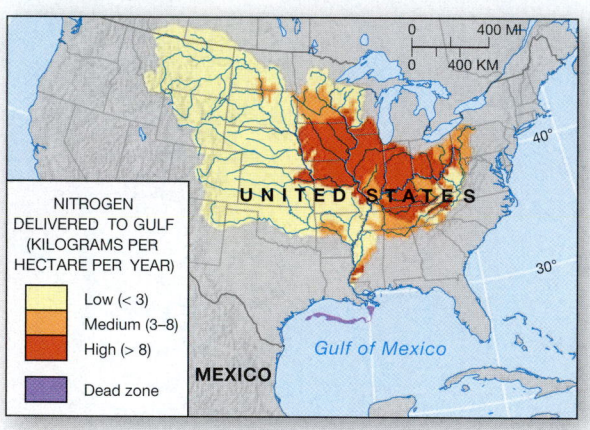

19.2a The map shows total nitrogen in the upstream portion of the Mississippi River watershed.

Bottom-water dissolved oxygen across the Louisiana shelf from July 28–August 3, 2015

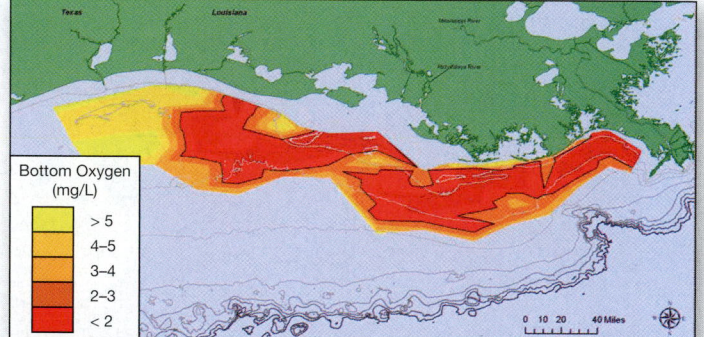

19.2b Nutrients from the Mississippi River enrich the offshore waters of the Gulf, causing huge algal blooms in early spring that later form the dead zone (red areas).

 **19.2c** **Gulf of Mexico algal bloom:** Channels in the Mississippi River's delta bring nutrients that fuel the green algal blooms seen in this image and help to form the Gulf's large, and expanding, dead zone.

MasteringGeography™

Visit the Study Area in MasteringGeography™ to explore dead zones.
Visualize: Study the video of phytoplankton.
Assess: Demonstrate understanding of dead zones (if assigned by instructor).

19.3 WORLDWIDE COASTAL DEAD ZONES

On the map, the amount of organic matter in the ocean surface layer is shown in shades of blue. Dead zones, which form where organic matter is high, are shown as red circles. Black dots show where dead zones have been observed, but their size is unknown.

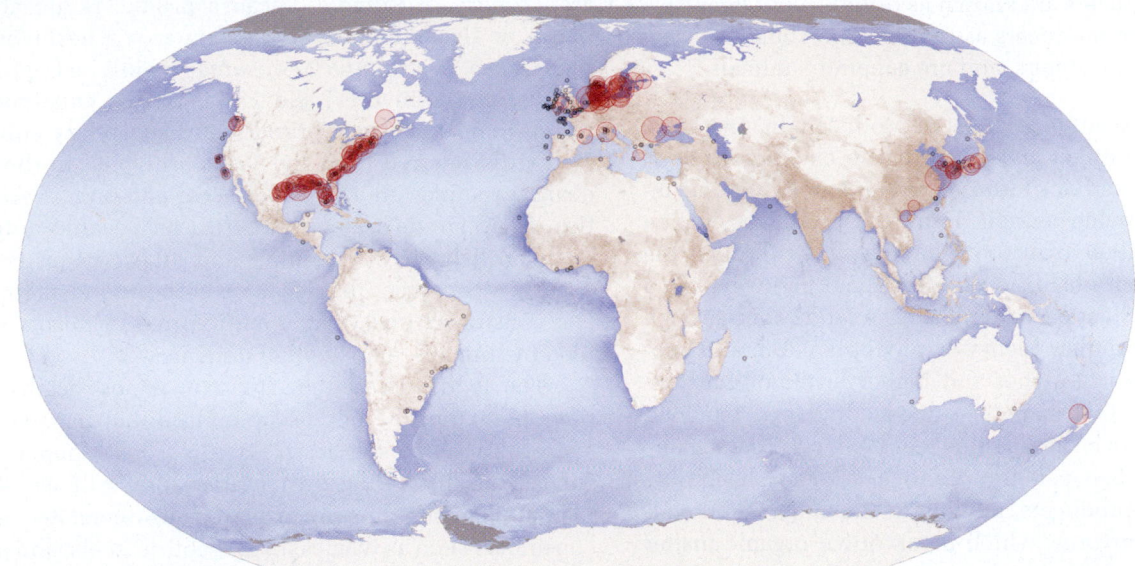

Particulate Organic Carbon (mg/m³)
10 20 50 100 200 500 1,000

Population Density (persons/km²)
1 10 100 1,000 10k 100k

Dead Zone Size (km²)
unknown 0.1 1 10 100 1k 10k

19.4 LAKE ERIE ALGAL BLOOM, 2011

The bright green areas in the lake are an algal bloom. The 2011 bloom was 2.5 times larger than any previously observed on Lake Erie.

19.4a

MICHIGAN
Detroit
Windsor
ONTARIO
Lake Erie
Toledo
Cleveland
OHIO
20 km

19.4b Algae deposits along the shore of Lake Erie during the 2011 bloom.

GEOquiz

1. Explain: How does the water in a dead zone become depleted of oxygen?

2. Interpret Maps: Look at the map in GIA 19.3. Why do you think the dead zones in the Southern Hemisphere are so much smaller and fewer in number than those in the Northern Hemisphere?

3. Solve Problems: Suppose you are a member of a commission charged with developing a plan to reduce the size of the Gulf of Mexico dead zone. Describe strategies you would suggest and the changes needed to achieve this goal.

4. Explain: What must happen to transform the phytoplankton bloom in the satellite image into a dead zone?

Energy Pathways The feeding relationships among organisms make up the energy pathways in an ecosystem. These *trophic relationships*, or feeding levels, consist of food chains and food webs that range from simple to complex. Producers are known as *autotrophs*. Organisms that depend on producers as their carbon source are *heterotrophs*, or consumers, and are generally animals.

Trophic Relationships Most of producers in an ecosystem capture sunlight and convert it to chemical energy, incorporating carbon, forming new plant tissue and biomass, and freeing oxygen. From the producers, which manufacture their own food, energy flows through the system along an idealized unidirectional pathway called a **food chain**. Solar energy enters each food chain through the producers, either plants or phytoplankton, and subsequently flows to higher and higher levels of consumers. Organisms that share the same feeding level in a food chain are said to be at the same *trophic level*. Food chains usually have between three and six levels, beginning with primary producers, moving to consumers, and ending with *detritivores*, which break down organic matter and are the final link in the theoretical chain.

The actual trophic relationships between species in an ecosystem are usually more complex than the simple food chain model might suggest. The more common arrangement of feeding relationships is a **food web**, a complex network of interconnected food

chains with multidirectional branches. In a food web, consumers often participate in several different food chains (**Figure 19.6a**).

In a food web, the organisms that feed on producers are *primary consumers*. Because producers are always plants or algae, the primary consumer is a **herbivore**, or plant eater. A *secondary consumer* mainly eats primary consumers (herbivores) and is therefore a **carnivore**. A *tertiary consumer* eats primary and secondary consumers and is referred to as the "top carnivore" in the food chain; examples are the leopard seal and orca in Antarctica. In Antarctic waters, the orca, an oceanic dolphin, feeds on fish, seals, penguins, and other whales (**Figure 19.6b**). A consumer that feeds on both producers (plants) and consumers (meat) is an **omnivore**—a category occupied by humans, among other animals.

The food web in the Antarctic region begins with phytoplankton, the microscopic algae that harvest solar energy in photosynthesis. Herbivorous zooplankton, such as the shrimplike crustaceans called krill, eat phytoplankton and are thus the primary consumers. Secondary consumers such as whales, fish, seabirds, seals, and squid eat krill, forming the next trophic level. Many Antarctic-dwelling seabirds depend on krill and on fish that eat krill. All of these organisms participate in other food chains, some as consumers and some being consumed.

Nutrient cycling is continuous within a food web, aided by **detritivores** (also known as detritus feeders),

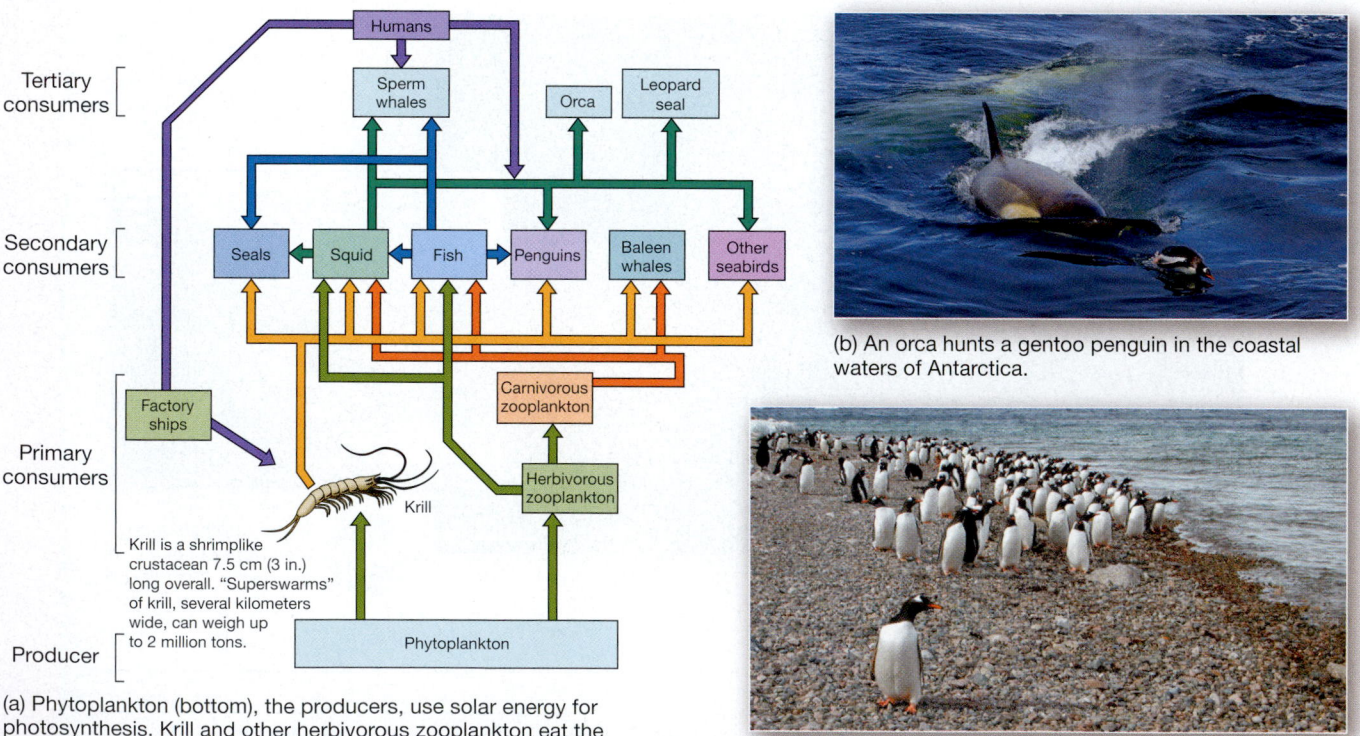

(a) Phytoplankton (bottom), the producers, use solar energy for photosynthesis. Krill and other herbivorous zooplankton eat the phytoplankton. Krill, in turn, are consumed by organisms at the next trophic level.

(b) An orca hunts a gentoo penguin in the coastal waters of Antarctica.

(c) Gentoo penguins (*Pygoscelis papua*) on a rocky shore in Antarctica watch the water for leopard seal predators.

▲**Figure 19.6 A simplified Antarctic Ocean food web.** Phytoplankton (bottom), the producers, use solar energy for photosynthesis. Krill and other zooplankton eat the phytoplankton and are then consumed by organisms at the next trophic level. [(b) Justin Hofman/Alamy. (c) Bobbé Christopherson.]

the organisms that feed on *detritus*—dead organic debris (dead bodies, fallen leaves, and waste products) produced by living organisms. Detritivores include worms, mites, termites, centipedes, snails, and slugs in terrestrial environments and bottom feeders in marine environments. These organisms renew the entire system by breaking down these organic materials and releasing simple inorganic compounds and nutrients. **Decomposers** are primarily bacteria and fungi that digest organic debris outside their bodies and absorb and release nutrients in the process. The metabolic work of microbial decomposers produces the "rotting" action that breaks down detritus. Detritus feeders and decomposers, although operating differently, have a similar function in an ecosystem. **Figure 19.7** shows part of a temperate forest food web, including detrivores and decomposers, in eastern North America.

WORKITOUT 19.1
Trophic Levels in a Forest Food Web

1. Using Figure 19.7, assign the animals to the appropriate trophic level.
2. What role do earthworms and bacteria play in the food web?

Energy Pyramids The overall amount of energy moving through trophic levels decreases from lower to higher levels, a pattern that can be illustrated in an *energy pyramid* in which horizontal bars represent each trophic level. (Ecological pyramids also include *biomass pyramids*, discussed ahead.)

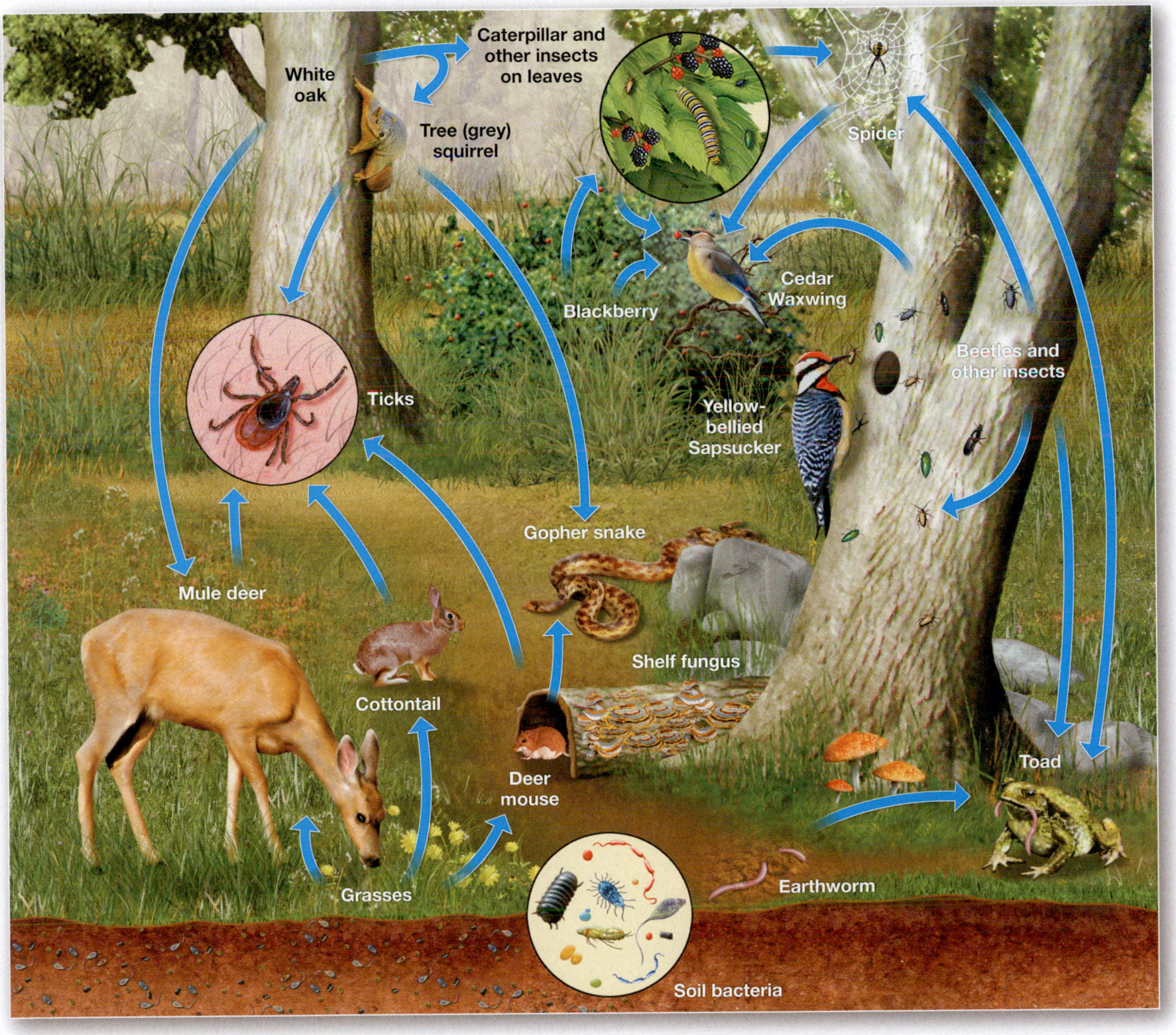

▲**Figure 19.7 Temperate forest food web.**

At the bottom of the pyramid are the producers, which have the most energy and usually (but not always) the highest biomass and numbers of organisms. The next level, primary consumers, represents less energy because energy is used up by metabolism and given off as heat as one organism eats another. Energy decreases again at the next level (secondary consumers), with each trophic level having (usually) less biomass and fewer organisms than the one beneath (**Figure 19.8a**). Although the pattern generally holds for numbers of organisms and biomass, exceptions exist, and pyramids can be inverted, such as when the number of large trees (producers) is less than the number of small insects (primary consumers) or when the biomass of phytoplankton (which have short life spans) is less than that of the zooplankton that eat them. Only energy consistently decreases between lower and higher trophic levels, maintaining the true pyramid shape.

Food Web Efficiency In terms of energy, only about 10% of the kilocalories (food calories, not heat calories) in plant matter are passed from primary producers to primary consumers. In turn, only about 10% of the energy for primary consumers is passed to secondary consumers, and so on. Thus, the most efficient consumption of resources happens at the bottom of the food chain, where plant biomass is higher and the energy input toward food production is lowest.

This concept applies to human eating habits and, on a broader scale, to world food resources. If humans take the role of herbivores, or primary consumers, they eat food with the highest energy available in the food chain. If humans take the role of carnivores, or secondary consumers, they eat food in which the available energy has been cut by 90% (the grain is fed first to cattle, and then the cattle are consumed by humans). In terms of biomass, 810 kg of grain is reduced to 81 kg of meat. In terms of the numbers of organisms, if 1000 people can be fed as primary consumers, only 100 people can be fed as secondary consumers. By the latter analysis, far more people can be fed from the same land area if it is producing grain than if it is producing meat (**Figure 19.8b**).

Today, approximately half of the cultivated acreage in the United States and Canada is planted for animal consumption—beef and dairy cattle, hogs, chickens, and turkeys. Much of U.S. grain production goes to livestock feed rather than to human consumption, perpetuating inefficiencies in terms of energy. In general, consumption of animal products requires much more energy for each calorie produced than consumption of plant products.

Biological Amplification When chemical pesticides are applied to an ecosystem of producers and consumers, the food web concentrates some of these chemicals. Many chemicals are degraded or diluted in air and water and thus are rendered relatively harmless. Other chemicals, however, are long-lived, stable, and soluble in the fatty tissues of consumers. They become increasingly concentrated at each higher trophic level. This is called *biological amplification*, or *biomagnification.* In the 1970s, scientists determined that the pesticide DDT was biomagnifying, especially in birds, building up in their fat tissues and causing a thinning of eggshells that caused hatchling mortality. The subsequent ban on DDT for agricultural use is now credited by many experts as saving the Brown Pelican and Peregrine Falcon from extinction.

Thus, pollution in a food web can efficiently poison the organism at the top. The polar bears of the Barents Sea near northern Europe have some of the highest levels of *persistent organic pollutants* (POPs) in any animal in the world, despite their remoteness from civilization. Many species are threatened in this manner. An example are the orcas of Puget Sound in Washington (**Figure 19.9**). Humans are at the top of many food chains and are therefore at risk of ingesting chemicals concentrated in this way.

Communities and Species Distributions

The levels of organization within ecology and biogeography range from the biosphere, at the top, encompassing all life on Earth, down to single living organisms at the bottom (**Figure 19.10**). The biosphere can be broadly divided into ecosystems (including biomes, discussed in Chapter 20), each of which can then be divided into **communities**, made up of interacting populations of living plants and animals in a particular place. A community

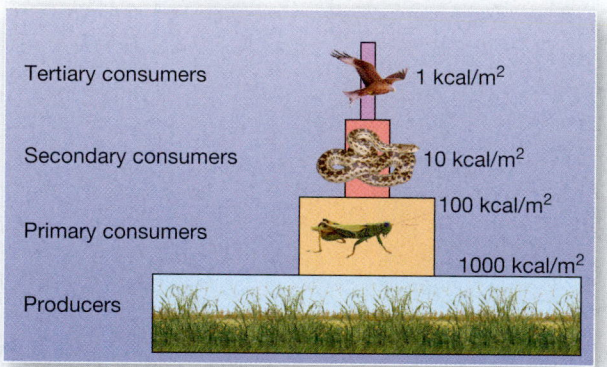

(a) A pyramid shape illustrates the decrease in energy between lower and higher trophic levels. Kilocalorie amounts are idealized to show the general trend of the energy decrease.

Tertiary consumers — 1 kcal/m²
Secondary consumers — 10 kcal/m²
100 kcal/m²
Primary consumers
1000 kcal/m²
Producers

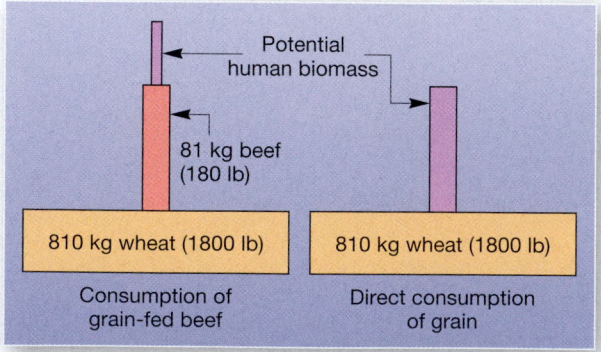

Potential human biomass

81 kg beef (180 lb)

810 kg wheat (1800 lb) — 810 kg wheat (1800 lb)

Consumption of grain-fed beef — Direct consumption of grain

(b) Biomass pyramids illustrate the difference in efficiency between direct and indirect consumption of grain.

▲**Figure 19.8** **Pyramids of energy and biomass.**

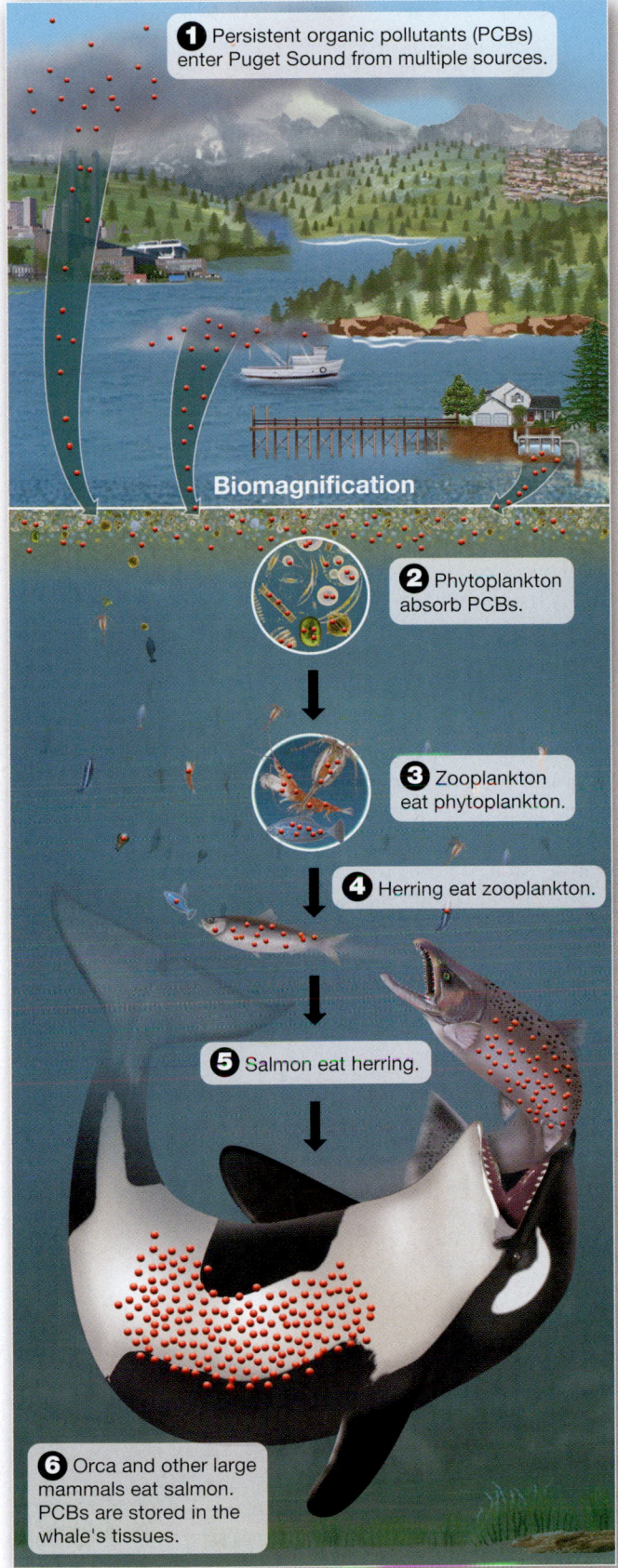

Biomagnification

1 Persistent organic pollutants (PCBs) enter Puget Sound from multiple sources.

2 Phytoplankton absorb PCBs.

3 Zooplankton eat phytoplankton.

4 Herring eat zooplankton.

5 Salmon eat herring.

6 Orca and other large mammals eat salmon. PCBs are stored in the whale's tissues.

◄Figure 19.9 **Biomagnification.** Orcas (*Orcinus orca*), also known as killer whales, are threatened by high levels of polychlorinated biphenyls (PCBs), as well as other contaminants, in Puget Sound, Washington. PCBs remain in fatty tissue of organisms and bioaccumulate in higher and higher concentrations through each trophic level. PCBs may be a primary cause for declining resident populations of these marine mammals in Puget Sound. [Source: Puget Sound Institute; https://www.eopugetsound.org/magazine/pcb-theory.]

Biosphere

Biome

Ecosystem

Community

Population

Individual

▲Figure 19.10 **Scales of analysis: Biosphere to individual.**
[Biosphere and biome: NASA. Ecosystem: Volodymr Burdiak/Alamy. Community: FLPA/Alamy. Population: Philip Mugridge. Individual: Ger Bosma/Alamy.]

▲**Figure 19.11** **Great Blue Heron with chicks in a treetop nest.**
[Wolf Mountain Images/Shutterstock.]

may be identified in several ways—by its physical appearance, by the species present and the abundance of each, or by the complex patterns of their interdependence, such as the trophic (feeding) structure.

For example, in a forest ecosystem, a specific community may exist on the forest floor, while another community may function in the canopy of leaves high above. Similarly, within a lake ecosystem, the plants and animals that flourish in the bottom sediments form one community, whereas those near the surface form another.

Whether viewed in terms of its ecosystem or in terms of its community within an ecosystem, each species has a **habitat**, defined as the environment in which an organism resides or is biologically adapted to live. A habitat includes both biotic and abiotic elements of the environment, and habitat size and character vary with each species' needs. For example, Great Blue Herons (*Ardea herodias*)* are large wading birds that occupy shoreline habitats (riverbanks, freshwater marshes, tidal flats) throughout North America. They frequently nest in the tops of trees near their preferred foraging areas, thereby keeping their young safe from terrestrial predators and humans (**Figure 19.11**).

The Niche Concept

An **ecological niche** (from the French word *nicher*, meaning "to nest") is the function, or occupation, of a life form within a given community. A niche is determined by the physical, chemical, and biological needs of the organism. This is not the same concept as habitat. Niche and habitat are different in that habitat is an environment that can be shared by many species, whereas niche is the specific, unique role that a species performs within that habitat.

* Scientists give animals, plants, and other organisms scientific names that usually consist of two parts: The first gives the genus (*Ardea*) and the second gives the species (*herodias*) to which the organism belongs (a third name, when present, denotes subspecies or varieties). These names are part of a larger, hierarchical system of biological classification. Each species has only one scientific name (although species can have several common names).

For example, the White-breasted Nuthatch (*Sitta carolinensis*) is a small bird that occurs throughout the United States and in parts of Canada and Mexico in forest habitats, especially in *deciduous forests* (those that drop their leaves in winter). Like other nuthatches, this species occupies a particular ecological niche by foraging for insects up and down tree trunks, probing into the bark with their sharp bills and often turning upside down and sideways as they move (**Figure 19.12**). This behavior enables them to find and extract insects that are overlooked by other birds. They have a rear-facing toe that enables them to hang on when moving downward. Another common bird occupying the same habitat is the Pileated Woodpecker (*Dryocopus pileatus*), a bird that forages only by climbing up the tree trunk, clinging with feet designed to move upward and cling (two toes forward and two toes back), and bracing itself with a long stiff tail. Although nuthatches and woodpeckers occupy a similar habitat, the nuthatch's distinctive foraging behavior causes it to occupy a specific niche that is different from a woodpecker's.

The *competitive exclusion principle* states that no two species can occupy the same niche (using the same food or space) because one species will always outcompete the other. Thus, closely related species are spatially separated either by distance or by species-specific strategies. In other words, each species operates to reduce competition and to maximize its own reproduction rate—because, literally, species survival depends on successful reproduction. This strategy, in turn, leads to greater diversity as species shift and adapt to fill different niches.

▼**Figure 19.12** **White-breasted Nuthatch and Pileated Woodpecker in their ecological niches.** [(a) Doug Lemke/Shutterstock. (b) William Leaman/Alamy.]

(a) White-breasted Nuthatch, southwestern Ohio.

(b) Pileated Woodpecker, near Cleveland, Ohio.

(a) Mutualism: Lichen growing on a tree trunk in Sweden is an example of mutualism, in which fungus joins with algae or cyanobacteria in a mutually beneficial relationship.

(c) Commensalism: Club mosses use a tree trunk for support in the temperate rain forest of Olympic National Park, Washington. These mosses are epiphytes, plants which grow harmlessly on other plants for support, an example of commensalism.

(b) Parasitism: Dwarf mistletoe are parasitic plants found on conifers (cone-bearing trees) throughout the U.S. West, shown here on a juniper in Utah. The host trees suffer reductions in growth and seed production and are prone to infectious diseases.

▲Figure 19.13 **Species interactions: Mutualism, parasitism, and commensalism.** [(a) blickwinkel/Alamy. (b) Bob Gibbons/Alamy. (c) Don Johnston/Alamy.]

Species Interactions

Within communities, some species are *symbiotic*—that is, have some type of overlapping relationship. One type of symbiosis, *mutualism*, occurs when each organism benefits and is sustained over an extended period by the relationship. For example, lichen (pronounced "liken") is made up of algae and fungi living together (**Figure 19.13a**).

The alga is the producer and food source for the fungus, and the fungus provides structure and physical support. Their mutualism allows the two to occupy a niche in which neither could survive alone. Lichen developed from an earlier parasitic relationship in which the fungi broke into the algal cells. Today, the two organisms have evolved into a supportive and harmonious symbiotic relationship. The partnership of corals and algae discussed in Chapter 16 is another example of mutualism in a symbiotic relationship.

Another form of symbiosis is *parasitism*, in which one species benefits and another is harmed by the association. Often this association involves a parasite living off a host organism, such as a flea living on a dog. A parasitic relationship may eventually kill the host—an example is parasitic mistletoe (*Phoradendron*), which lives on and can kill various kinds of trees (**Figure 19.13b**).

A third form of symbiosis is *commensalism*, in which one species benefits and the other experiences neither harm nor benefit. An example is the remora (a sucker fish) that lives attached to sharks and consumes the waste produced as the shark eats its prey. Epiphytic plants, such as club mosses and orchids, are another example; these "air plants" grow on the branches and trunks of trees, using them for physical support (**Figure 19.13c**).

A final symbiotic relationship is *amensalism*, in which one species harms another but is not affected itself. This typically occurs either when two organisms are in competition and one deprives the other of food or habitat or when a plant produces chemical toxins that damage or kill other plants. For example, black walnut trees excrete a chemical toxin through their root systems into the soil that inhibits the growth of other plants beneath them.

GEOreport **19.1** Will species adapt to climate change?

A 2013 study reveals that in order for vertebrate species to adapt to projected changes in climate by the year 2100, they will need to evolve their niche requirements 10,000 times faster than rates in the past. Using genetic data for over 500 species of terrestrial vertebrates, including frogs, snakes, birds, and mammals, the scientists examined how long each species took to shift its climatic niche under past environmental conditions. They found that over about a million years, species were able to adapt to a temperature difference of 1 C°. These results suggest that adaptation may not be an option for species survival in today's rapidly warming climate.

Vertical zonation
Increasing elevation from sea level

Ice and snow

Tundra

Needleleaf forest

Temperate
deciduous
forest

Tropical
rain forest

Treeline

(b) Treeline for a needleleaf forest in the
Canadian Rockies marks the point above
which trees cannot grow.

▲Figure 19.14 **Vertical and latitudinal
zonation of plant communities.** [Robert
Christopherson.]

Ice and snow

Tundra

Needleleaf forest

Temperate
deciduous forest

Tropical rain
forest

Latitudinal zonation
Increasing latitude from the equator

(a) Progression of plant community life zones with changing elevation or latitude.

Abiotic Influences

A number of abiotic environmental factors influence species distributions, interactions, and growth. For example, the distribution of some plants and animals depends on *photoperiod*, the duration of light and dark over a 24-hour period. Many plants require longer days for flowering and seed germination, such as ragweed (*Ambrosia*). Other plants require longer nights to stimulate seed production, such as the poinsettia (*Euphorbia pulcherrima*), which needs at least 2 months of 14-hour nights to start flowering. These species cannot survive in equatorial regions with little daylength variation. They are instead restricted to latitudes with appropriate photoperiods, although other factors may also affect their distribution.

Birds and bees can detect the abiotic influence of Earth's magnetic field and use it for finding direction. Small amounts of magnetically sensitive particles in the skull of the bird and the abdomen of the bee provide compass directions. Recently, scientists found that sea turtles can apparently detect magnetic fields, allowing them to navigate between certain locations on Earth. Loggerhead turtles (*Caretta caretta*) hatch in Florida, crawl into the water, and spend the next 70 years traveling between North America and Africa around the subtropical high-pressure gyre in the Atlantic Ocean. The females

return to where they were hatched to lay their eggs. In turn, magnetic data unique to their location imprints on the hatchlings at birth, determining their global sense of position as they live a life swimming across the ocean.

In terms of entire ecosystems, air and soil temperatures are important, since they determine the rates at which chemical reactions proceed. Precipitation and water availability are also critical, as is water quality—its mineral content, salinity, and levels of pollution and toxicity. All of these factors work together to determine the distributions of species and communities in a given location.

In the 1800s, geographer and explorer Alexander von Humboldt was one of the first scientists to study the effect of climatic factors on species distributions. After several years of study in the Andes Mountains of Peru, von Humboldt hypothesized that plants and animals occur in related groupings wherever similar climatic conditions occur. His ideas were the basis for the *life zone concept*, which describes this zonation of flora and fauna along an elevational transect (**Figure 19.14**). Each **life zone** possesses its own temperature and precipitation regime and therefore its own biotic communities. Ecologist C. Hart Merriam later mapped 12 life zones with distinct plant associations in the San Francisco Peaks in northern Arizona. Merriam also expanded the concept to include the changing zonation from the equator toward higher latitudes (discussed further in Chapter 20).

Limiting Factors

The term **limiting factor** refers to physical, chemical, or biological characteristics of the environment that determine species distributions and population size. For example, in some ecosystems, precipitation is a limiting factor on plant growth, through either its lack or its

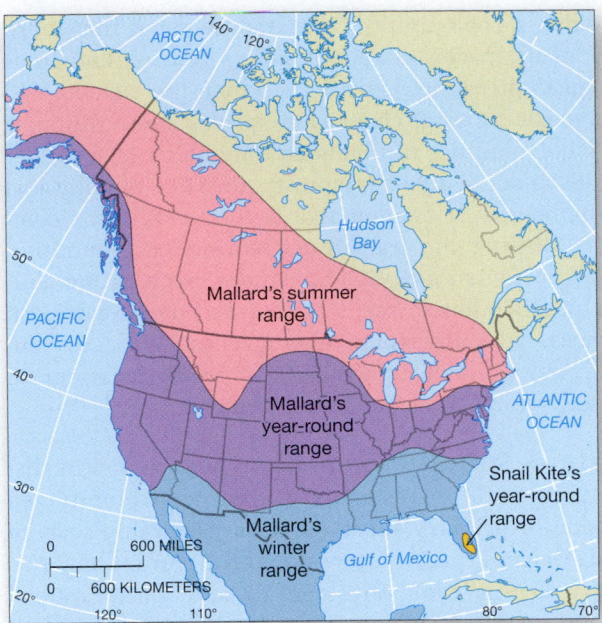

(b) A male Snail Kite in Florida.

(c) A male and female Mallard in Indiana.

(a) The Snail Kite's small range in North America depends on a single food source; the Mallard Duck is a generalist and feeds widely.

▲**Figure 19.15 Food resources as a limiting factor for species distributions.** [(b) Margery Maskell/Alamy. (c) Danial Dempster Photography/Alamy.]

excess. Temperature, light levels, and soil nutrients all affect vegetation patterns and abundance:

- Low temperatures limit plant growth at high elevations.
- Lack of water limits growth in a desert; excess water limits growth in a bog.
- Changes in salinity levels affect aquatic ecosystems.
- Low phosphorus content of soils limits plant growth.
- The general lack of active chlorophyll above 6100 m (20,000 ft) limits primary productivity.

For animal populations, limiting factors may be the number of predators, availability of suitable food and habitat, availability of breeding sites, and prevalence of disease. The Snail Kite (*Rostrhamus sociabilis*), a tropical raptor with a small U.S. population in the Florida Everglades, is a specialist that feeds on only one specific type of snail (**Figure 19.15a and b**). In contrast, the Mallard Duck (*Anas platyrhynchos*) is a generalist, feeds from a variety of widely diverse sources, is easily domesticated, and is found throughout most of North America (**Figure 19.15c**).

For some species, one critical limiting factor determines survival and growth; for other species, a combination of factors is at play, with no one single factor being dominant. When taken together, limiting factors determine the *environmental resistance*, which eventually stabilizes populations in an ecosystem.

Each organism possesses a *range of tolerance* for physical and chemical environmental characteristics. Within that range, species abundance is high; at the edges of the range, the species is found infrequently; and beyond the range limits, the species is absent. For example, the coast redwood (*Sequoia sempervirens*) is abundant within a narrow range along the California and Oregon coast where foggy conditions provide condensation to meet the tree's water needs (review the discussion in Focus Study 6.1). Redwoods at the limit of their range—for example, at higher elevations above the fog layer—are shorter, smaller, and less abundant. The red maple (*Acer rubrum*) has a wide tolerance range and is distributed over a large area with varying moisture and temperature conditions (**Figure 19.16**).

As discussed in this chapter's Geosystems Now, recent scientific studies show that climate change is causing animals to move their ranges to higher elevations with more suitable climates as established life zones shift. Evidence exists that some species have run out of space on mountains, as environmental conditions are pushing them to elevations beyond their mountains' reach, essentially taking them "out of bounds," forcing them either to move elsewhere or into extinction.

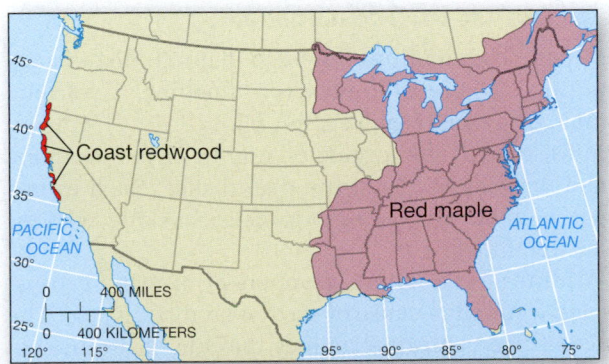

▲**Figure 19.16 Limiting factors and range of tolerance.** The presence of fog as a moisture source limits the distribution of coast redwood, discussed in Focus Study 6.1. Red maple tolerates a variety of environmental conditions.

(a) Damage from a debris flow in North Carolina, triggered by the rainfall associated with Hurricane Ivan in 2004.

(b) Thunderstorm winds damaged forests in eastern Minnesota and northwest Wisconsin in July 2011; wind speeds reached over 160 kmph (100 mph).

▲Figure 19.17 **Ecosystem disturbance, making way for new communities.** [NOAA.]

Disturbance and Succession

Over time, communities undergo natural disturbance events such as windstorms, severe flooding, a volcanic eruption, or an insect infestation (**Figure 19.17**). Human activities, such as the logging of a forest or the overgrazing of a rangeland, also create disturbance. Such events damage or remove existing organisms, making way for new communities.

Wildfires are a natural component of many ecosystems and a common cause of ecosystem disturbance. The science of **fire ecology** examines the role of fire in ecosystems, including the adaptations of individual plants to the effects of fire and the human management of fire-adapted ecosystems. Focus Study 19.1 takes a look at this important subject.

When a community is disturbed enough that most, or all, of its species are eliminated, a process known as **ecological succession** occurs, in which the cleared area undergoes a series of changes in species composition as newer communities of plants and animals replace older ones. Each successive community modifies the physical environment in a manner that favors a different community. During the transitions between communities, species having an adaptive advantage, such as the ability to produce lots of seeds or disperse them over great distances, will outcompete other species for space, light, water, and nutrients. Successional processes occur in both terrestrial and aquatic ecosystems.

Terrestrial Succession An area of bare rock or a disturbed site with no vestige of a former community can be a site for **primary succession**, the beginning stage of an ecosystem. Primary succession can occur on new surfaces created by mass movement of land, glacial retreat, volcanic eruptions, surface mining, clear-cut logging, or the movement of sand dunes. In terrestrial ecosystems, primary succession begins with the arrival of organisms that are well adapted for colonizing new substrates, forming a **pioneer community**. For example, a pioneer community of lichens, mosses, and ferns may establish on bare rock (**Figure 19.18**). These early inhabitants prepare the way for further succession: Lichens secrete acids that break down rock, which begins the process of soil formation, which enhances habitat for other organisms. As new organisms colonize soil surfaces, they bring nutrients that further change the habitat, eventually leading to the growth of grasses, shrubs, and trees.

More commonly encountered in nature is **secondary succession**, which occurs when some aspect of a previously functioning community is still present: for example, a disturbed area where the underlying soil remains intact. As secondary succession begins, new plants and animals having niches that differ from those of the previous community colonize the area; species assemblages may shift as soil develops, habitats change, and the community matures.

Most of the areas affected by the Mount St. Helens eruption and blast in 1980, which burned or blew down about 38,450 hectares (95,000 acres) of trees, underwent secondary succession (**Figure 19.19**). Some soils, young trees, and plants were protected under ash and snow, so community development began almost immediately after the event. The areas completely destroyed near the Mount St. Helens volcano and those buried beneath the massive landslide north of the mountain became candidates for primary succession.

For much of the 20th century, ecologists thought that communities of plants and animals passed through several successional stages, eventually reaching a mature state with a predictable *climax community*—a stable, self-sustaining assemblage of species that would remain until the next major disturbance. However, contemporary biogeography and ecology assume that disturbances constantly

◀Figure 19.18
Primary succession. Plants establishing on recently cooled lava flows from the Kīlauea volcano in Hawai'i illustrate primary succession. [Bobbé Christopherson.]

disrupt the sequence and that a community may never reach what would be considered a climax stage. Mature communities are in a state of constant adaptation—a dynamic equilibrium—sometimes with a lag time in their adjustment to environmental changes. Scientists now know that successional processes are driven by a dynamic set of interactions with sometimes unpredictable outcomes.

Disturbance often occurs in discrete spatial units across the landscape, creating habitats, or *patches*, at different successional stages. The concept of *patch dynamics* refers to the interactions between and within this mosaic of habitats, which add to complexity across the landscape. The overall biodiversity of an ecosystem is in part the result of such patch dynamics.

(a) Mount St. Helens, 2008.

(b) Repeat photography of post-eruption recovery at Meta Lake, 1983 and 1999.

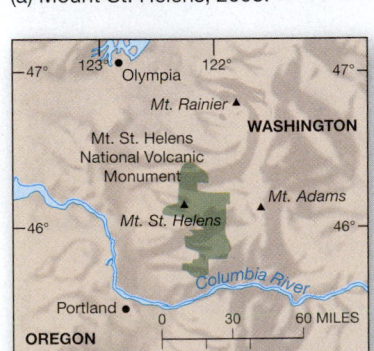

(c) Repeat photography showing secondary succession, 1983 and 1999.

▲**Figure 19.19 The pace of change in the region of Mount St. Helens.** [(a) *ISS* astronaut photo, NASA/GSFC; (b) and (c) 1983 photos by Robert Christopherson; 1999 photos by Bobbé Christopherson.]

FOCUS Study 19.1 Natural Hazards
Wildfire and Fire Ecology

Fire is one of Earth's significant natural hazards. In the United States, wildfires burned over 9 million acres in 2015, mainly in Alaska, Washington, and California (**Figure 19.1.1**). In Australia, the "Black Saturday" fires in 2009, the most destructive in the country's history, destroyed more than 2000 homes and claimed 173 lives. The cost of fighting wildfires in the United States topped $2 billion in 2012, and continues to rise. The science of *pyrogeography* examines the spatial distribution and ecological effects of fire across Earth. As fires intensify, the connections between fire, ecosystem processes, climate, and human health and property are gaining significance.

▶**Figure 19.1.1**
California wildfire. In 2016, the Blue Cut Fire burned homes and other structures near Wrightwood in southern California, fueled by hot weather, wind, and extreme drought. Shown here in the San Bernardino National Forest, the fire prompted mandatory evacuations of 80,000 people. [David McNew/Getty Images.]

▼**Figure 19.1.2 Two types of wildfire.** Ground fires burn surface fuels but do not reach the tree crowns. Crown fires occur when fuels accumulate on the forest floor, either through fire suppression or natural processes. [Adapted from USFS and Adam Cole/NPR.]

Tree crowns

Surface fuel

(a) Forest where fires are frequent.

1. Frequent ground fires burn surface fuels.

2. Even a large ground fire cannot reach the tree canopy.

3. The ground fire scorches bark but the tree crowns remain healthy.

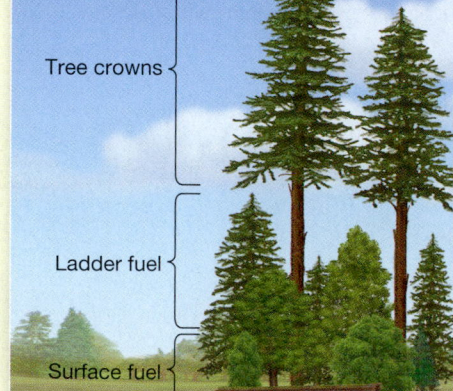

Tree crowns

Ladder fuel

Surface fuel

(b) Forest with history of fire suppression.

1. A ground fire spreads through accumulated surface fuels.

2. The fire moves upward by burning ladder fuels.

3. A crown fire burns the top of the tree canopy.

Mobile Ⓜ
Field Trip
Forest Fires in the West

https://goo.gl/vm6c9q

(a) New shoots emerge from the trunk of a paperbark (*Melaleuca*) tree in Australia after bushfires in January 2016.

(b) Lodgepole pine regrowth 8 years after a fire in Yellowstone National Park. Tree regrowth is slow in the short growing seasons on this high-elevation plateau.

◄**Figure 19.1.3 Fire adaptations and landscape recovery after wildfire.** [(a) Suzanne Long/Alamy. (b) Lee Foster/Alamy.]

from being released. California's giant sequoia trees readily colonize open, burned sites where seedlings can thrive without grasses or other vegetation competing for resources. Fire-disturbed areas quickly recover with stimulated seed production, protein-rich woody growth, and young plants that provide abundant food for animals (**Figure 19.1.3b**).

Wildfire Characteristics and Management

Lightning-caused wildfire is a natural disturbance in some ecosystems. In forests with frequent wildfires, *surface fuel*—the leaf litter, tree branches, and other ground debris—burns in small ground fires (sometimes called "cool fires" because they burn at a lower temperature). These *ground fires* keep the forest floor free of surface fuels, which prevents more destructive fires in the tree canopy (**Figure 19.1.2a**). Fire specialists worldwide today use "controlled" ground fires that are deliberately set to prevent undergrowth accumulation and maintain ecosystem health.

During the 20th century, before scientists understood some of these principles of fire ecology, forestry management in North America focused on fire prevention and fire suppression. This strategy led to a buildup of surface fuel so that by the end of the century many forests were ripe for large and destructive wildfires. In a fire-suppressed forest, a ground fire can feed off surface fuel and then spread upward into *ladder fuel*, the taller undergrowth of shrubs and tree branches. These fuels then allow the fire to move upward toward the forest canopy, leading to *crown fires*, "hot" fires that burn through the top layers of tree foliage and are extremely difficult to control (**Figure 19.1.2b**).

Effects of Fire on Ecosystems

Wildfires create a mosaic of habitats, ranging from totally burned to partially burned to unburned areas. This patchwork of habitats ultimately benefits biodiversity. Fire affects soils, making them more nutrient-rich after cooler ground fires or more susceptible to erosion after intensely hot crown fires. Fire also affects plants and animals, with some species adapted to, even dependent on, frequent fire occurrence.

A number of Earth's grasslands, forests, and scrublands (where the dominant vegetation is shrubs) have evolved through interaction with fire and are known as *fire-adapted ecosystems*. Plant species in such environments may have thick bark, which protects them from heat, or lack lower branches, which protects them from ground fires. Fire-adapted species, such as chaparral in California, typically resprout quickly after fire destroys their branches or trunks. Several tree species in Australia resprout from buds on burned tree trunks (**Figure 19.1.3a**).

Several North American tree species depend on fire for reproduction. For example, lodgepole pine and jack pine rely on fire to crack and open the resin that otherwise seals their cones and keeps seeds

The Human–Wildfire Interface

Wildfires are increasing in many regions of the world with rising temperatures and more frequent and lasting drought. In the U.S. West, earlier spring snowmelt has extended the length of the fire season. In addition, especially in North America, tree die-off from insect infestations (such as spruce beetle and pine beetle) has helped produce more fuel and feed larger fires.

In the United States, the devastation caused by wildfires is increasing as urban development encroaches on forests, putting homes at risk and threatening public safety. In 2016, wildfires devastated communities in southern California and in Alberta, Canada, where tens of thousands of people were evacuated from their homes.

1. What vegetation characteristics are present in fire-adapted ecosystems? Describe some fire adaptations of North American plant species.

2. Is fire suppression in forest ecosystems an effective strategy for forest management? Explain.

APPLYconcepts Compare and contrast the forest conditions that result from two types of wildfire management: fire suppression versus controlled burns.

Forest Characteristic	Forest Managed by Fire Suppression	Forest Managed by Controlled Burns
Surface fuel availability	1a. _____	1b. _____
Ladder fuel availability	2a. _____	2b. _____
Effect of fire on tree structure and canopy	3a. _____	3b. _____
Overall effect of fire on forest ecosystem	4a. _____	4b. _____

Aquatic Succession Aquatic ecosystems occur in lakes, estuaries, and wetlands and along shorelines, and the communities in these systems also undergo succession. For example, lakes and ponds exhibit successional stages as they fill with sediment and nutrients and as aquatic plants take root and grow. The plant growth captures more sediment and adds organic debris to the system (**Figure 19.20**). This gradual enrichment in water bodies is known as **eutrophication** (from the Greek *eutrophos*, meaning "well nourished").

In moist climates, a lake will develop a floating mat of vegetation that grows outward from the shore to form a bog. Cattails and other marsh plants become established, and partially decomposed organic material accumulates in the basin, with additional vegetation bordering the remaining lake surface. Vegetation and soil and a meadow may fill in as water is displaced; willow trees follow, and perhaps cottonwood trees; eventually, the lake may evolve into a forest community. Thus, when viewed across geologic time, a lake or pond is really a temporary feature on the landscape.

Even large bodies of water may have eutrophic areas along the shore. As humans dump sewage, agricultural runoff, and pollution into waterways, the nutrient load is enhanced beyond the cleansing ability of natural biological processes. This human-caused eutrophication, known as *cultural eutrophication*, hastens succession in aquatic systems.

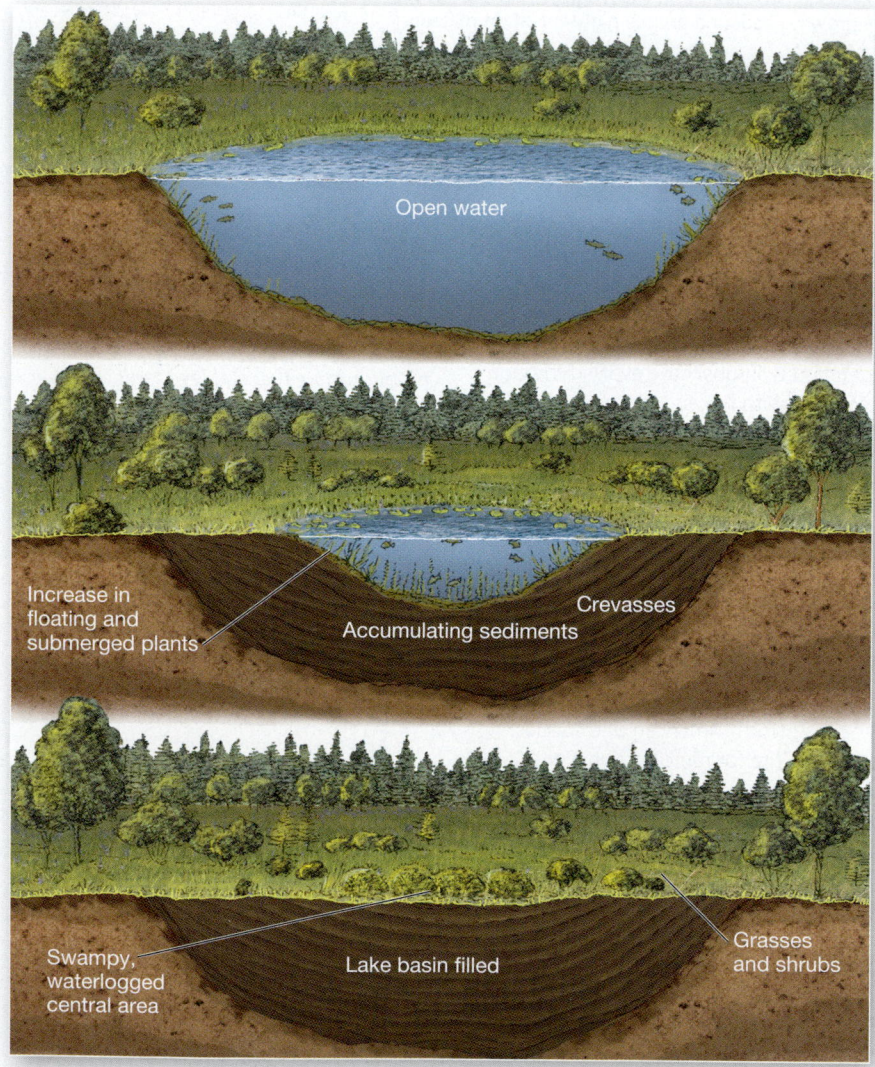

(a) A lake gradually fills with organic and inorganic sediments, shrinking the area of open water. A bog forms, then a marsh, and finally a meadow, the last of the successional stages.

(b) Spring Mill Lake, Indiana.

(c) Organic content increases as succession progresses in a mountain lake.

(d) Peat bog with acidic soils, Richmond Nature Park, near Vancouver, British Columbia.

▲**Figure 19.20 Idealized lake–bog–meadow succession in temperate conditions, with real-world examples.** [Bobbé Christopherson.]

Biodiversity and Evolution

Far from being static, Earth's ecosystems have been dynamic—vigorous, energetic, and ever-changing—from the beginning of life on the planet. Over time, communities of plants and animals have adapted and evolved to produce great diversity and, in turn, have shaped their environments. As we have seen, communities and ecosystems are constantly adjusting to changing conditions and disturbances.

The variety of life on Earth is **biodiversity**, defined as the variation of life (a combination of the terms *bio*logical and *diversity*). The concept of biodiversity encompasses species diversity, the number and variety of different species; genetic diversity, the amount of genetic variation within these species; and ecosystem diversity, the number and variety of ecosystems, habitats, and communities on a landscape scale.

Presently, about 270,000 species of plants are known to exist, with many more species yet to be identified. They represent a great untapped resource base. Only about 20 species of plants provide 90% of food for humans; just three—wheat, maize (corn), and rice—make up half of that supply. Plants are also a major source of new medicines and chemical compounds that benefit humanity.

Table 19.2 summarizes the numbers of known and estimated species on Earth. Scientists have classified only 1.75 million species of plants and animals. The wide range of estimates for the count of total species is between a low of 3.6 million and a high of 111.7 million. This figure represents an increase in what scientists

once thought to be the diversity of life on Earth. Estimates of annual species loss range between 1000 and 30,000 species, although this range might be conservative. The possibility exists that over half of Earth's present species could be extinct within the next 100 years.

Biological Evolution

The origin of Earth's biodiversity is laid out in the *theory of evolution*. **Evolution** is the process in which the first, single-celled organisms adapted, modified, and passed along inherited changes to descendants, eventually producing the world's diverse species of organisms, many of which are multicellular. A *species* is a population that can reproduce sexually and produce viable offspring. By this definition, each species is reproductively isolated from other species.

Natural Selection The genetic makeup of successive generations is shaped by environmental factors, physiological functions, and behaviors that lead to greater rates of survival and reproduction in some members of a population than in others. Traits that help a species survive and reproduce—especially the traits that are most successful at exploiting niches different from those of other species or that help the species adapt to environmental changes—are passed along to offspring and their descendants more frequently than those that do not. Such differential reproduction and adaptation is known as *natural selection* and is the basis of evolutionary change. The process continues

TABLE 19.2 Known and Estimated Species on Earth

Categories of Living Organisms	Number of Known Species	Estimated Number of Species		Working Estimate (x1000)	Accuracy
		High (x1000)	Low (x1000)		
Viruses	4000	1000	50	400	Very poor
Bacteria	4000	3000	50	1000	Very poor
Fungi	72,000	27,000	200	1500	Moderate
Protozoa	40,000	200	60	200	Very poor
Algae	40,000	1000	150	400	Very poor
Plants	270,000	500	300	320	Good
Nematodes	25,000	1000	100	400	Poor
Arthropods:					
Crustaceans	40,000	200	75	150	Moderate
Arachnids	75,000	1000	300	750	Moderate
Insects	950,000	100,000	2000	8000	Moderate
Mollusks	70,000	200	100	200	Moderate
Chordates	45,000	55	50	50	Good
Others	115,000	800	200	250	Moderate
Total	**1,750,000**	**111,655**	**3635**	**13,620**	**Very poor**

Source: United Nations Environment Programme, *Global Biodiversity Assessment* (Cambridge, England: Cambridge University Press, 1995), Tables 3.1–3.2, p. 118, used by permission.

generation after generation, tracing the passage of inherited characteristics that were successful—the failures pass into extinction. Thus, today's humans are the result of billions of years of natural selection.

Inherited traits are encoded by an array of genes, part of an organism's primary genetic material—*DNA* (deoxyribonucleic acid)—which resides in the nest of chromosomes in every cell nucleus. New genes in the *gene pool*, the collection of all genes possessed by individuals in a given population, result from *mutation*, a process in which a random occurrence, perhaps an error as the DNA reproduces, alters the genetic material. Mutation can introduce new traits to be selected for or against in the process of natural selection. As this genetic mutation is passed through generations, it becomes an *adaptation* that helps the organism survive in its environment. Adaptations can be structural, such as the thick stem and leaves of desert plants for water storage, or the long, thin beak of a hummingbird that enables it to reach deep into flowers for nectar (**Figure 19.21**). Adaptations can also be behavioral, such as the seasonal migration of whales and hibernation of bears and squirrels.

Biogeography and Speciation Geography also comes into play in natural selection, since spatial variation in physical environments affects survival and reproductive success. For example, a species may disperse through migration, such as across ice bridges or land connections at times of low sea level, to a different environment where new traits are favored. A species may also be separated from other species by a natural *vicariance* event (a fragmentation of the environment). An example is continental drift, which establishes natural barriers to species movement and results in *speciation*, the evolution of new species.

Evolutionary Change The physical and chemical evolution of Earth's systems is closely linked to the biological evolution of life. As conditions on Earth change over geologic time, species respond in several different ways. First, a species can change its geographic distribution to track optimal conditions. For instance, during ice ages, many species moved southward in latitude. Today, as global temperatures rise, species are moving northward in latitude and altitude (**Figure 19.22**). Second, a species can adapt to changing conditions and undergo evolutionary change. Finally, if a species is unable to shift its geographic range or does not have time to adapt, the species will become extinct. **Extinction** occurs when the last individual of a species dies. Extinctions have occurred naturally throughout Earth's history.

Biodiversity on the Decline

Human activities have great impact on global biodiversity; the present loss of species is irreversible and is accelerating. We are now facing a loss of genetic diversity that may be unparalleled in Earth's history, even compared with the major extinctions that punctuate the geologic record. According to a 2014 study, species are now disappearing at a rate 1000 times faster than natural, pre-human extinction rates.

The greatest threats to biodiversity are habitat loss, degradation, and fragmentation; pollution of air, water, and soils; harvesting of plants and animals at unsustainable levels; human-induced climate change; and the introduction of non-native plants and animals (discussed in Chapter 20).

Threatened Species—Examples Amphibians have a higher risk of extinction than mammals, fish, and birds because they are vulnerable to changes in both terrestrial and aquatic ecosystems such as habitat destruction, pollution, invasive species, and changing climate. Although amphibian declines can also be attributed to natural causes such as competition, predation, and disease, the bottom line is that these species are not evolving fast enough to keep up with the rate of environmental change.

Some animal species are captured, transported and traded and sold illegally, a practice known as wildlife

(a) The beak of the Red Crossbill (*Loxia curvirostra*) is adapted to pry apart the scales of evergreen conifer cones (such as spruce and pine) so that the bird can dislodge the seed with its tongue. Different forms of crossbills forage on different types of cones—large-billed birds feed on the largest cones.

(b) The marmot (genus *Marmota*), found in alpine areas near treeline, is one of the largest ground squirrels. The animals hibernate for up to 8 months each year, during which time their metabolism is suppressed and their core temperature drops.

▲**Figure 19.21 Structural and behavioral adaptations.** [(a) imagebroker/Alamy. (b) blickwinkel/Alamy.]

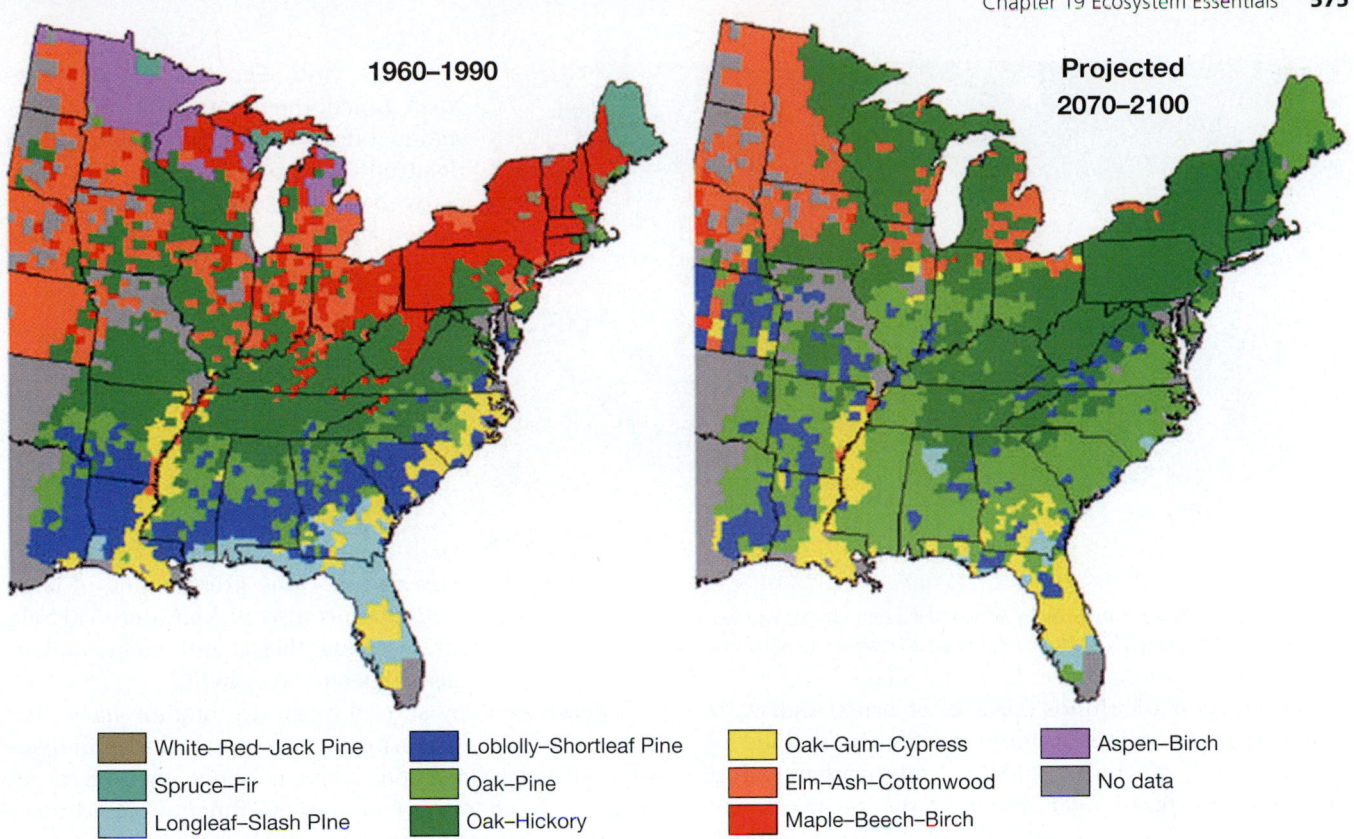

1960–1990

Projected 2070–2100

▮ White–Red–Jack Pine	▮ Loblolly–Shortleaf Pine	▮ Oak–Gum–Cypress	▮ Aspen–Birch
▮ Spruce–Fir	▮ Oak–Pine	▮ Elm–Ash–Cottonwood	▮ No data
▮ Longleaf–Slash Pine	▮ Oak–Hickory	▮ Maple–Beech–Birch	

▲**Figure 19.22 Shifting forests with climate change.** The maps show forest distribution from 1960 to 1990 as compared to the projected distributions of forest at the end of this century under a mid-range climate warming scenario. The maple–beech–birch forest type dominant in 1990 is projected to be completely displaced by other forest types in a warmer future. [U.S. Global Change Research Program, 2009, *Global Climate Change Impacts in the United States*; https://downloads.globalchange.gov/usimpacts/pdfs/climate-impacts-report.pdf.]

trafficking (or wildlife smuggling). The illegal wildlife trade focuses on exotic pets, food, and products for medicine, clothing, or jewelry. For example, traders and poachers kill elephants for their tusks, rhinos for their horns, and tigers for their bones and skins. The most widely trafficked animal on Earth is the pangolin, a scaled mammal that is native to parts of Asia and Africa (**Figure 19.23**). All eight species of pangolin are threatened, and two are critically endangered. Pangolin meat is considered a rare delicacy, now popular among wealthy urbanites in southeast Asia, and pangolin scales are valued for traditional medicine in Vietnam and China.

(a) Illegally smuggled, endangered pangolins (*Manis javanica*) in Sumatra await transport after being confiscated by Indonesia's Natural Resources Conservation Agency in 2016. These animals will be released back into their rain forest habitat.

(b) Pangolins are the only know mammals with protective scales. In southern China and Vietnam, pangolin scales are sold for traditional medicine.

▲**Figure 19.23 Pangolins, the animal most subjected to illegal trafficking.** [(a) Zuma Press/Alamy. (b) Reuters/Alamy.]

▲**Figure 19.24** **The rhinoceros in Africa.** White rhinoceros with young, from the southern population, Lake Nakuru National Park, Kenya. [Pal Taravagimov/Shutterstock.]

Species and Ecosystem Restoration Since the 1990s, species restoration efforts in North America have focused on returning predators such as wolves and condors to parts of the American West and, recently, jaguars to the Southwest. Other efforts have resulted in rising populations of black-footed ferrets and Whooping Cranes in the prairie regions and shortnose sturgeon along the Atlantic seaboard. These projects have reintroduced captive-bred animals or relocated wild animals into their former habitats, while at the same time limiting practices such as hunting that once caused species decline. The preservation of large habitats has also played a critical role in restoring these, and other, endangered species worldwide.

In Africa, black rhinos (*Diceros bicornis*) and white rhinos (*Ceratotherium simum*) exemplify species in jeopardy from declining habitat and overharvesting. Rhinos once grazed over much of the savannas and woodlands. Today, they survive only in protected districts in heavily guarded sanctuaries. Consider these statistics:

- Black rhinos: The population of 70,000 in 1960 dropped to 2599 in 1998—a decline of 96%. South Africa guards about 50% of the herd. Slow recovery is underway; numbers rose to 4880 in 2010. The western black rhino, a subspecies, is now considered extinct.

- White rhinos: The 11 northern white rhinos surviving in 1984 increased to over 25 by 1998 but then dropped as political unrest in the Congo slowed protection efforts. In 2015, only 4 were left in the Ol Pejeta Conservancy in Kenya. The southern white rhinos are on the increase; their population topped 20,000 in 2014 (**Figure 19.24**).

Rhinoceros horn sells for $29,000 per kilogram as an aphrodisiac (but in reality has no medicinal effect). These large land mammals are nearing extinction and will survive only as a dwindling zoo population. The limited genetic pool that remains complicates further reproduction.

Recent efforts at ecosystem restoration have had some success in restoring or preserving biodiversity, although questions remain about the effects of such work on overall ecosystem functioning. Numerous river restoration projects, such as the dam removals discussed in Chapter 14, are successfully restoring natural conditions for fisheries and riparian wetlands in the short term. In the Florida Everglades, a $9.5 billion restoration project began in 2000 and is ongoing. The goal is to return freshwater flow into the south Florida swamplands to revive the dying ecosystem. The Everglades restoration is the largest and most ambitious watershed restoration project in history (see http://evergladesrestoration.gov/).

The question of what is "natural" related to ecosystems restoration is important, especially considering the frequent involvement of human activity as a factor in ecosystem changes. Scientists and others have expanded the goal of returning ecosystems to the conditions that prevailed before human intervention to include the possibility of creating *novel ecosystems*, human-built or human-modified ecosystems that may have species and habitats that have never occurred together. These novel systems have no natural analogs on which to base scientific hypotheses or restoration strategies—and yet, to sustain biodiversity and ecosystem function in our changing world, humans may need to understand and manage such ecosystems.

GEOreport 19.2 Rising sea level causes the first mammal extinction

In 2016, scientists reported that the Bramble Cay melomys (*Melomys rubicola*), a small rodent that lives on a single island offshore of Australia's Cape York Peninsula, was extinct. Last seen in 2009, the melomys were absent throughout an extensive trapping effort in 2014. Bramble Cay is a 3.6-hectare (8.9-acre) low-elevation island in the Torres Strait at the northern end of the Great Barrier Reef, an area where sea level is rising at a rate far higher than the global average. Scientists estimate that the melomys lost 97% of their habitat on this small island in just 10 years, and are now the first modern species loss caused entirely by climate change.

ECOSYSTEM PROCESSES IMPACT HUMANS

• All life depends on healthy, functioning ecosystems, which provide the food and all other natural resources that humans use.

19a Hunted to near-extinction by the early 1900s, the Eurasian beaver (*Castor fiber*) was successfully reintroduced throughout most of its former range. The North American beaver (*Castor canadensis*) also declined but has now recovered in most regions. Beaver are large, semi-aquatic rodents whose dams create wetland habitat for many plants and other animals. [Danita Delimont/Getty Images.]

HUMANS IMPACT ECOSYSTEM PROCESSES

Human activities cause declining biodiversity. For example,
• Habitat loss occurs as natural areas are converted for agriculture and urban development.
• Pesticides and other pollutants poison organisms in food webs.
• Climate change affects plant and animal distributions and overall ecosystem function.
• Fertilizer use and industrial activities alter biogeochemical cycles, as when dead zones disrupt the nitrogen cycle.

19b Scientists outfit baby loggerhead sea turtles with satellite tracking tags that allow experts to follow migration routes throughout all life stages, providing critical information for sea turtle conservation. [NOAA.]

19d The rare Andean flamingo (*Phoenicoparrus andinus*) lives in high-altitude wetlands in the Andes Mountains of South America. The flamingo's curved beak is an adaptation to its wetland habitat, enabling it to filter out plankton, insects, and small fish from the water and mud. [Joe Blossom/Alamy.]

19c Elephants swim across the Chobe River in Botswana as tourists on safari take photos. A 2016 study showed that Africa's elephant population is declining rapidly from poaching, which has recently increased in Botswana and in other countries. [Tim Hester/Alamy.]

ISSUES FOR THE 21ST CENTURY

• Species and ecosystem conservation and restoration will be essential to save species from extinction.
• Fire ecology will become increasingly important as climate change leads to prolonged drought in some areas and as human populations spread farther into wildlands.
• Addressing and mitigating climate change may become essential to preserving a future for all species, including humans.

QUESTIONS TO CONSIDER

1. How do beavers change the environment and affect biodiversity in the areas where they live?
2. What abiotic factors discussed in this chapter affect sea turtle migration?

KEY**LEARNING**concepts**review**

Define ecology, biogeography, and ecosystem.

Earth's biosphere is made up of **ecosystems** (p. 552), self-sustaining associations of living plants and animals and their nonliving physical environment. **Ecology** (p. 552) is the study of the relationships between organisms and their environment and among the various ecosystems in the biosphere. **Biogeography** (p. 552) is the study of the distribution of plants and animals and the diverse spatial patterns they create.

1. Define ecosystem, and give some examples.
2. What does biogeography include? Describe its relationship to ecology.

Explain photosynthesis and respiration and describe the world pattern of net primary productivity.

Solar energy enters the ecosystem energy flow by way of **photosynthesis** (p. 552), the process whereby plants convert sunlight into starches and sugars through chemical reactions within plant leaves. **Producers** (p. 552), which fix the carbon they need from CO_2, are the plants, algae, and cyanobacteria (a type of blue-green algae). As plants evolved, the **vascular plants** (p. 553) developed conductive tissues. **Stomata** (p. 553) on the underside of leaves are the portals through which the plant interacts with the atmosphere and hydrosphere. Plants (primary producers) perform photosynthesis as sunlight stimulates a light-sensitive pigment called **chlorophyll** (p. 553). This process produces food sugars and oxygen to drive biological processes. **Respiration** (p. 553) is essentially the reverse of photosynthesis and is the way the plant derives energy by oxidizing carbohydrates. **Net primary productivity** (p. 554) is the net photosynthesis (photosynthesis minus respiration) of an entire community. **Biomass** (p. 554) is the total organic matter derived from all living and recently living organisms and is measured as the net dry weight of organic material. Net primary productivity produces the energy needed for **consumers** (p. 554)—generally animals (including zooplankton in aquatic ecosystems)—that depend on producers as their carbon source.

3. How do plants function to link the Sun's energy to living organisms? What is formed within the light-responsive cells of plants?
4. Briefly describe the global pattern of net primary productivity.

Discuss the oxygen, carbon, and nitrogen cycles and explain trophic relationships.

Life is sustained by **biogeochemical cycles** (p. 555), through which circulate the gases and nutrients necessary for growth and development of living organisms. Excessive nutrient inputs into oceans or lakes can create **dead zones** (p. 556) in the water, areas with low-oxygen conditions that limit underwater life.

Energy in an ecosystem flows through *trophic levels*, or feeding levels, which are the links that make up a **food chain** (p. 560), the linear energy flow from producers through various consumers. Producers, at the lowest trophic level, build sugars (using sunlight, carbon dioxide, and water) to use for energy and tissue components. Within ecosystems, the feeding relationships are arranged in a complex network of interconnected food chains called a **food web** (p. 560).

Herbivores (plant eaters), p. 560, are primary consumers. **Carnivores** (meat eaters), p. 560, are secondary consumers. A consumer that eats both producers and other consumers is an **omnivore** (p. 560)—a role occupied by humans. **Detritivores** (p. 560) are detritus feeders (including worms, mites, termites, and centipedes) that ingest dead organic material and waste products and release simple inorganic compounds and nutrients. **Decomposers** (p. 561) are the bacteria and fungi that process organic debris outside their bodies and absorb nutrients in the process, producing the rotting action that breaks down detritus. Energy and biomass pyramids illustrate the flow of energy between trophic levels; energy always decreases with movement from lower to higher feeding levels in an ecosystem.

5. What are biogeochemical cycles? Describe the nitrogen cycle.
6. What is an energy pyramid and how does it relate to the nature of trophic levels?

Describe communities and ecological niches and list several limiting factors on species distributions.

A **community** (p. 562) is formed by the interactions among populations of living animals and plants. Within a community, a **habitat** (p. 564) is the specific environment in which an organism resides, analogous to its address. An **ecological niche** (p. 564) is the function or operation of a life form within a given community—its occupation.

Light, temperature, water, and nutrients constitute the life-supporting abiotic components of ecosystems. The zonation of plants and animal communities with altitude underlies the **life zone** (p. 566) concept, based on visible differences between ecosystems at different elevations. Each species has a *range of tolerance* that determines distribution. Species populations are stabilized by **limiting factors** (p. 566), which may be physical, chemical, or biological characteristics of the environment.

7. Describe these four types of symbiotic relationships: mutualism, parasitism, commensalism, and amensalism.
8. Discuss several abiotic influences on the function and distribution of species and communities.
9. What is a limiting factor? How does it function to control populations of plant and animal species?

Outline the stages of ecological succession in both terrestrial and aquatic ecosystems.

Natural and anthropogenic disturbance are common in most ecosystems. Wildfire can have far-ranging effects on communities; the science of **fire ecology** (p. 568) examines the role of fire in ecosystem maintenance. **Ecological**

succession (p. 568) describes the process whereby communities of plants and animals change over time, often after an initial disturbance. An area of bare rock and soil with no trace of a former community can be a site for **primary succession** (p. 568). The species that first establish in a disturbed area make up the **pioneer community** (p. 568) that then alters the habitat such that different species arrive. **Secondary succession** (p. 568) begins in an area that has a vestige of a previously functioning community in place. Rather than progressing smoothly to a definable stable end point, ecosystems tend to operate in a dynamic condition, with intermittent disturbance that forms a mosaic of habitats at different successional stages. Aquatic ecosystems also undergo succession; **eutrophication** (p. 572) is the gradual enrichment of water bodies that occurs with nutrient inputs, either natural or human-caused.

10. How does ecological succession proceed? Describe the character of a pioneer community. What is the difference between primary and secondary succession?
11. Summarize the process of succession in a body of water. What is meant by eutrophication?

Explain how biological evolution led to the biodiversity of life on Earth.

Biodiversity (p. 573) refers to the number and variety of different species, the genetic diversity within species, and ecosystem and habitat diversity. The greater the biodiversity within an ecosystem, the more stable and resilient the system is and the more productive it will be.

Evolution (p. 573) states that the original, single-cell organisms adapted, modified, and passed along inherited changes that eventually led to the development of diverse multicellular organisms. The genetic makeup of successive generations is shaped by environmental factors, physiological functions, and behaviors that result in greater rates of survival and reproduction. This so-called *natural selection* determines the traits that are passed along to offspring and their descendants. **Extinction** (p. 574) occurs when the last individual of a species dies.

12. List some of the human activities that are causing declining biodiversity at present.
13. Describe two adaptations that animals have developed to help them survive in their particular environment.

GEO**SPATIAL** ANALYSIS

Mapping Wildfire Danger

Wildfire is an important component of most ecosystem processes, and fire ecology is an integral part of ecological science. Conditions of increased spring and summer temperatures, earlier spring snowmelt, drought, dry soil conditions, and drought-stressed forests, link wildfire occurrence and climate change.

Activities

Go to the Wildfire Assessment System page at http://www.wfas .net/ and examine the "Wildland Fire Assessment System" (WFAS) map. Spatial Preparedness Level (SPL) indicates fire potential, with SPL–I lowest and SPL–V highest.

1. What is the fire potential level in your area?

2. Do you see evidence in the area you identified that these conditions exist? Describe some indicators.

3. Click on the layers icon and (un)check the GeoMac Current Fires box to turn current fires on/off. What fraction of the current fires are located in regions with SPL–III or higher fire potential?

Weather plays a role in determining where fires occur. Use "Fire Potential Danger" and "Weather" links to answer the following question:

4. How do the weather factors you considered affect the risk of wildfires in the   southwestern United States?

Go to the U.S. Drought Monitor map at http://droughtmonitor.unl.edu/.

1. Compare the Fire Assessment map to the Drought map. Describe similarities and differences.

Go to the Active Fire Mapping Program's Current Large Incidents map at http://activefiremaps.fs.fed.us/.

1. How many large fires are there currently?

2. Where are the fires located in relation to drought regions and fire potential regions?

3. Click on a fire currently displayed on the map. Record this fire's location, fire potential region, burnt area, cause, and containment status.

MasteringGeography™

Looking for additional review and test prep materials? Visit the Study Area in MasteringGeography™ to enhance your geographic literacy, spatial reasoning skills, and understanding of this chapter's content by accessing a variety of resources, including MapMaster™ interactive maps, videos, *Mobile Field Trips*, *Project Condor* Quadcopter Videos, *In the News* RSS feeds, flashcards, web links, self-study quizzes, and an eText version of *Geosystems*.

20 Terrestrial Biomes

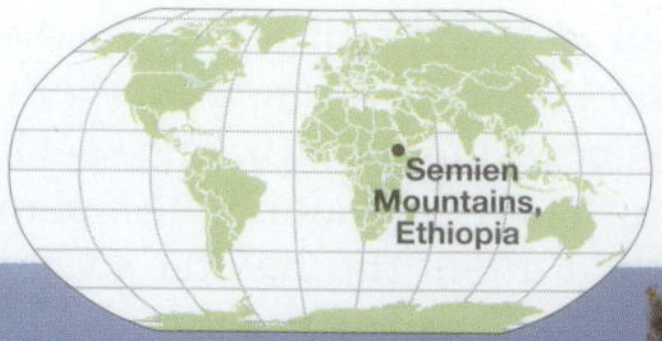

The Semien Mountains in the Ethiopian Highlands are one of the few locations in Africa with regular snowfall. Giant lobelia (*Lobelia deckenii*), pictured here in the foreground, are common in this region's tropical montane forests, adapted to the intense solar radiation and cold temperatures of this high-elevation environment. [Juan Carlos Muñoz/agefotostock.]

KEY**LEARNING**concepts

After reading the chapter, you should be able to:

- *Locate* the world's biogeographic realms and *discuss* the basis for their specification.
- *Explain* the basis for grouping plant communities into biomes and *list* the major terrestrial biomes on Earth.
- *Explain* the potential impact of non-native species on biotic communities, using several examples, and *discuss* strategies for biodiversity conservation based on principles of biogeography.
- *Summarize* the characteristics of Earth's 10 major terrestrial biomes and *locate* them on a world map.

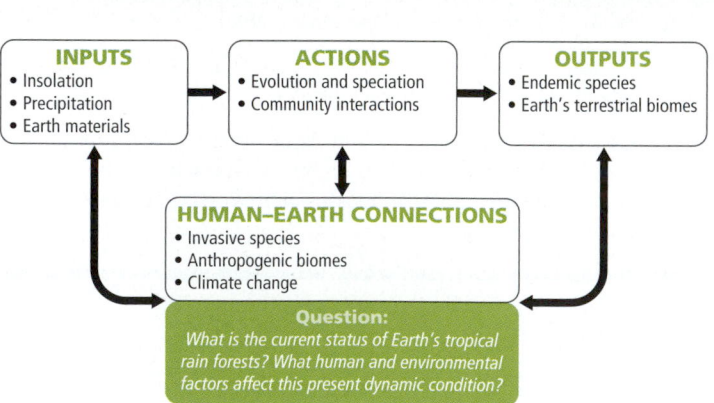

INPUTS
- Insolation
- Precipitation
- Earth materials

ACTIONS
- Evolution and speciation
- Community interactions

OUTPUTS
- Endemic species
- Earth's terrestrial biomes

HUMAN–EARTH CONNECTIONS
- Invasive species
- Anthropogenic biomes
- Climate change

Question:
What is the current status of Earth's tropical rain forests? What human and environmental factors affect this present dynamic condition?

GEOSYSTEMSnow

Ecological Corridors Connect Grizzly Bears

In the remote Cabinet Mountains of northwestern Montana, a population of about 30 grizzly bears lives in some of the last remaining truly wild country in the U.S. Lower 48. The surrounding landscapes, fragmented by roads, agriculture, and human development, isolate the bears in their rugged habitat, where they remain cut off from other ecosystems and grizzly populations. In recent years, the U.S. Fish and Wildlife Service has occasionally captured a sow from a different bear population and moved it to the Cabinet Mountains to add a breeding female and increase genetic diversity. Despite these efforts, the long-term survival of the Cabinet Mountain grizzlies depends on establishing ecological corridors—travel pathways that connect fragmented habitat—to link this bear population to a larger range.

Grizzlies in North America Western North America was once home to over 50,000 grizzlies, officially known as North American brown bears (*Ursus arctos*),

►Figure GN 20.2 **Grizzly sow and cubs, Greater Yellowstone Ecosystem.** The bears cross a road in Grand Teton National Park, Wyoming, at the southern end of the recovery area. [Zuma Press, Inc/Alamy.]

which ranged from the Arctic Ocean to Mexico (**Figure GN 20.1**). Today, the grizzly bear (*Ursus arctos horribilis*) occupies a much smaller range, with the highest densities in northern Canada and Alaska.

In the contiguous United States (the Lower 48), grizzlies declined with expanding human settlement until the 1920s, when only isolated populations remained. By the 1970s, grizzlies occupied 2% of their previous range, inhabiting only five ecosystems.

After the U.S. government listed grizzlies in the Lower 48 as an endangered species, their numbers rebounded from the edge of extinction. Today, the two largest Lower 48 populations are in the Northern Continental Divide Ecosystem and the Greater Yellowstone Ecosystem (**Figure GN 20.2** and **GN 20.3**). However, four of the five remaining populations remain isolated from healthy grizzly populations in Canada, a situation that weakens the gene pool and makes the bears vulnerable to inbreeding.

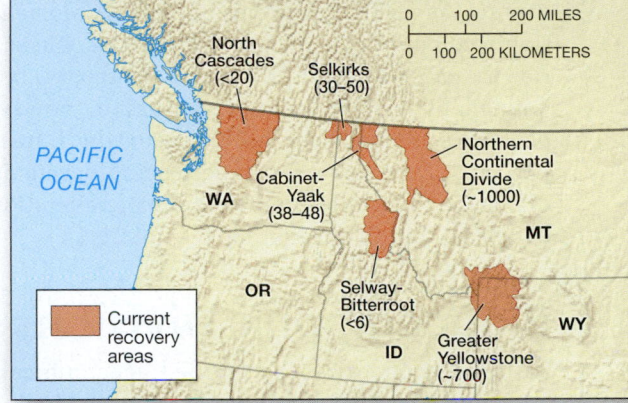

▲Figure GN 20.3 **Grizzly bear recovery ecosystems in the Lower 48.** Estimated bear numbers are in parentheses. [USFWS and the Center for Biological Diversity.]

Connecting "Island" Habitats

Habitat fragmentation results in isolated "islands" of biodiversity containing species that are disconnected from other ecosystems. The idea of linking such "island" habitats using ecological corridors resulted in part from the theory of island biogeography, proposed in the 1960s to explain species patterns on islands. The theory (discussed ahead in this chapter) recognizes that fewer species extinctions occur on larger islands, and that the probability of species extinction is lower on islands that are located close to one another. Decades later, scientists transferred the tenets of island biogeography to wildlife conservation, designing larger reserves to preserve more species. Further studies revealed that even the largest reserves would need connectivity for long-term species survival.

The Yellowstone to Yukon Corridor For grizzly bears and other animals that roam for hundreds of kilometers, ecological corridors must allow safe passage between habitat fragments over a large area. Effective corridors can range in size from kilometers-wide swaths of forest to narrow tunnels under interstate highways. One of the largest corridor projects in the world is the Yellowstone to Yukon Conservation Initiative, which seeks to establish corridors serving not only grizzly bears, but also black bears, wolves, lynx, wolverines, elk, and moose. The Yellowstone to Yukon (Y2Y) corridor (outlined in Figure GN 20.1) includes a network of protected lands to maintain connectivity between habitat patches.

In Montana, as part of the Y2Y project, wildlife managers are currently working to establish a corridor connecting the Cabinet Mountain grizzlies with the Selway–Bitterroot Wilderness to the south (**Figure GN 20.3**). Preserving key parcels of land will provide opportunities for safe travel, but the challenge remains how to help the bears take advantage of them.

1. What causes grizzly habitat to become fragmented, and how does this threaten grizzly populations?

2. How can ecological corridors help ensure grizzly recovery in the U.S. Lower 48?

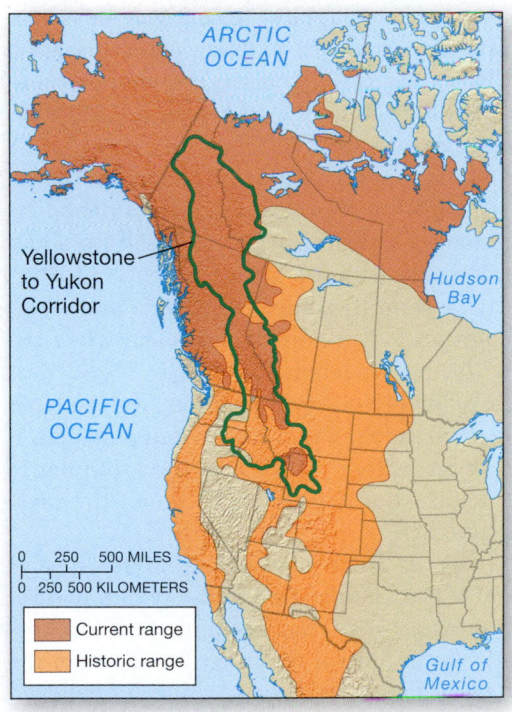

▲Figure GN 20.1 **Grizzly range, past and present.** The area outlined in green is the Yellowstone to Yukon corridor. [Adapted from Environment Canada and the Yellowstone to Yukon Conservation Initiative; https://y2y.net/.]

The patterns of species distributions on Earth are important subjects of biogeography. Earth's biodiversity is spread unevenly across the planet and is related to geology, climate, and the evolutionary history of particular species and species assemblages. The branch of biogeography that is concerned with the past and present distributions of animals is called *zoogeography*; the corresponding branch for plants is *phytogeography*.

Plant and animal communities are commonly grouped into *biomes*, also known as *ecoregions*, representing the major ecosystems of Earth. A biome is a large, stable community of plants and animals whose boundaries are closely linked to climate. In theory, biomes are defined by mature, natural vegetation; however, most of Earth's biomes have been affected by human activities, and many are now experiencing accelerated rates of change that could produce dramatic alterations in the biosphere within our lifetime (**Figure 20.1**).

Biogeographic Divisions

Earth's biosphere can be divided geographically based on assemblages of similar plant and animal communities. One class of geographic division—the biogeographic region, or realm—is determined by species distributions and their evolutionary history. Another class—the biome—is based on plant communities; it is determined mainly according to vegetation growth forms and community characteristics as they relate to climate and soils.

Biogeographic Realms

The recognition that distinct regions of broadly similar flora (plants) and fauna (animals) exist was the earliest beginning of *biogeography* as a discipline. (*Flora* and *fauna* are general terms for the typical collections of plants and animals throughout an ecosystem.) A **biogeographic realm** (sometimes called an *ecozone*) is a geographic region where a group of associated plant and animal species evolved. Alfred Wallace (1823–1913), the first scholar of zoogeography, developed a map delineating six zoogeographical regions in 1860, building on earlier work by others regarding bird distributions (**Figure 20.2a**). Wallace's realms correspond generally to the continental plates, although Wallace knew nothing of the theory of plate tectonics at the time. Today's biogeographic realms, originally defined on the basis of plant associations and modified over time, are similar to Wallace's realms, though more specific (**Figure 20.2b**).

Species interactions occurred as continents collided and accreted; species became separated when continents drifted apart. Consequently, the organisms within each realm are a product of plate tectonics and evolutionary processes. For example, the Australian realm is unique for over 400 species of *Eucalyptus* among its plants and for over 100 species of marsupials—animals, such as kangaroos, that carry their young in pouches, where gestation is completed (**Figure 20.3**). The presence of monotremes, egg-laying mammals such as the platypus, adds further distinctiveness to this realm.

Australia's unique native flora and fauna are the result of its early isolation from the other continents. As the supercontinent of Pangaea began to break up about 225 million years ago (discussed in Chapter 11), Australia drifted away from the other continents and never again was reconnected by a land bridge, even when sea level lowered during repeated glacial ages. New Zealand, although relatively close in location, was isolated from Australia, explaining why it has no native marsupials. However, other factors resulted in the grouping of New Zealand within the Australian realm in the most recent classification.

Wallace noted the stark contrast in animal species between several of the islands of present-day Indonesia—Borneo and Sulawesi, in particular—and those of Australia. This led him to draw a dividing line between the Oriental and Australian realms over which he believed species did not cross. A deep water barrier existed here even during the lower sea levels of the last glacial maximum, when land connections existed elsewhere in the Indonesian archipelago. His boundary is today known as "Wallace's line." Modern biogeographers have modified

▼**Figure 20.1 A freight train and wheat fields in western Minnesota.** As this landscape shows, little of the original midlatitude mixed forest remains today in many parts of the U.S. Midwest. [National Geographic Creative/Alamy.]

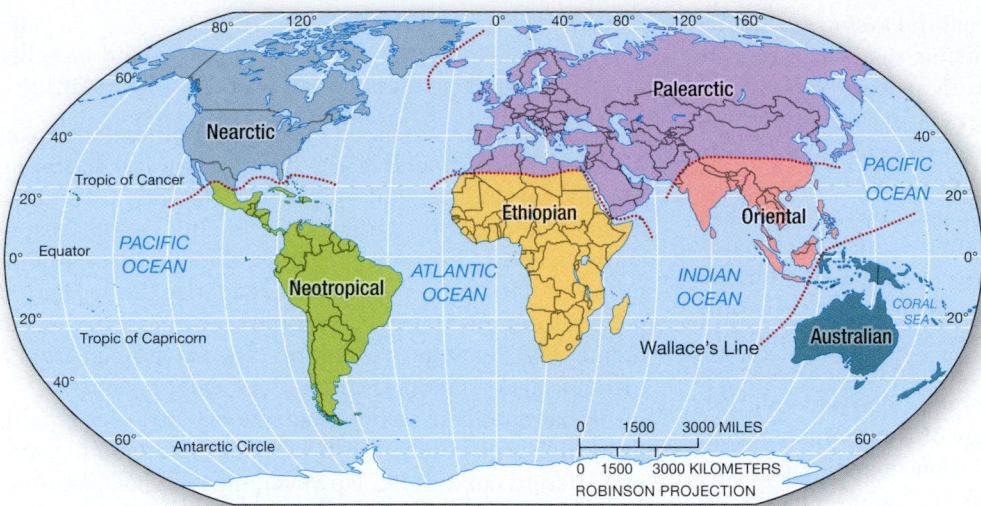

(a) The six animal realms as defined by biogeographer Alfred Wallace in 1860.

◀**Figure 20.2 Biogeographic realms.** [(b) After D. M. Olsen et al., "Terrestrial Ecoregions of the World: A New Map of Life on Earth," *Bioscience* 51 (2004): 933–938; modified by UNEP/WCMC, 2011.]

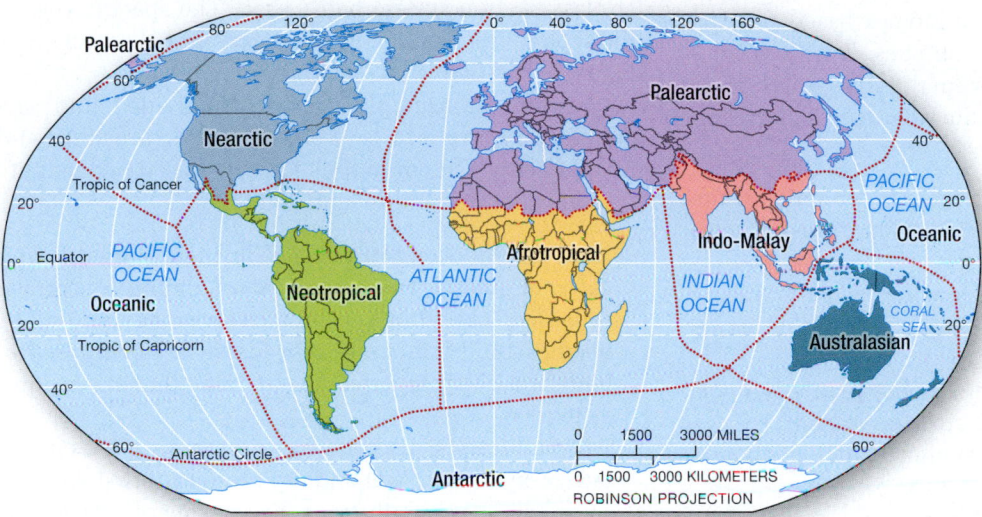

(b) The eight realms in use today, based on plant and animal associations and evolution.

identified on many biome maps reflects idealized potential mature vegetation, given the environmental characteristics in a region. For example, in the eastern United States, old-growth forested landscapes are today a mix of second-growth forests, farmlands, and altered landscapes (Figure 20.1). However, the forest biome designation for this region remains, based on idealized conditions before human impacts (discussed later in the chapter).

this line so that it now encircles the island region between Java and Papua New Guinea, an area that never had a land connection to the mainland and is now sometimes referred to as *Wallacea*.

Biomes

A **biome** is defined as a large, stable, terrestrial or aquatic ecosystem classified according to the predominant vegetation type and the adaptations of particular organisms to that environment. Although scientists identify and describe aquatic biomes (the largest of which are separated into freshwater and marine), biogeographers have applied the biome concept much more extensively to *terrestrial ecosystems*, associations of land-based plants and animals and their abiotic environment.

Biomes are defined by species that are native to a region, meaning that their occurrence is a result of natural processes. Today, few natural communities of plants and animals remain; most biomes have been greatly altered by human intervention. Thus, the "natural vegetation"

▲**Figure 20.3 Unique Australian fauna.** Australia's marsupials evolved in isolation; here Eastern grey kangaroos, some with young known as "joeys," stand in a meadow in New South Wales. [Westend61/Alamy.]

Ecotones Boundaries between natural systems, whether they separate biomes, ecosystems, or small habitats, are often zones of gradual transition in species composition rather than rigidly defined frontiers marked by abrupt change. A boundary zone between different, but adjoining, ecosystems at any scale is an **ecotone**.

Ecotones vary in width. For example, the climatic boundary between grasslands and forests can occupy many kilometers of land, while a boundary in the form of a river, a lakeshore, or a mountain ridge may occupy only a few meters. As human impacts cause ecosystem fragmentation, ecotones are becoming more numerous across the landscape (**Figure 20.4**). Ecotones often have high biodiversity resulting from the range of environmental conditions, as well as larger population densities of many organisms relative to the communities on either side.

Vegetation Types *Vegetation* refers to the entire flora of a region. Scientists determine biomes based on easily identifiable vegetation characteristics. Earth's vegetation types can be grouped according to the *growth form* (sometimes called *life form*) of the dominant plants. Examples of growth forms include:

- *Winter-deciduous trees*—large, woody, perennial plants that lose leaves during the cold season in response to temperature
- *Drought-deciduous shrubs*—smaller woody plants with stems branching at the ground that lose leaves during the dry season
- *Annual herbs*—small seed-producing plants without woody stems that live for one growing season
- *Bryophytes*—nonflowering, spore-producing plants, such as mosses (see GeoReport 20.1)

- *Lianas*—woody vines
- *Epiphytes*—plants growing above the ground on other plants and using them for support (see Figure 19.13)

Growth forms are based on size, woodiness, life span, leaf traits, and general plant morphology (for example, trees, shrubs, vines, and epiphytes). Vegetation can also be characterized by the structure of the canopy, especially in forested regions. Together, the dominant growth form and the canopy structure characterize the vegetation type; the dominant vegetation type then characterizes the biome. The dominant vegetation type extending across a region is also sometimes called the *formation class*.

Biogeographers often designate six major groups of terrestrial vegetation: forest, savanna, shrubland, grassland, desert, and tundra. However, most biome classifications are more specific, with the total number of biomes usually ranging from 10 to 16, depending on the particular classification system being used. The specific vegetation types of each biome have related animal associations that also help define its geographic area.

Forests, for example, can be subdivided into several biomes—rain forests, seasonal forests, broadleaf and mixed forests, and coniferous forests—based on moisture regime, canopy structure, and leaf type.

- *Rain forests* occur in areas with high rainfall; tropical rain forests are composed of mainly evergreen *broadleaf trees* (having broad leaves, as opposed to needles), and temperate rain forests are composed of both broadleaf and *needleleaf trees* (having needles as leaves).
- *Seasonal forests*, also known as dry forests, are characterized by distinct wet and dry seasons during the year, with trees that are mainly *deciduous* (shedding their leaves for some season of the year) during the dry season.
  - *Broadleaf mixed forests* occur in temperate regions and include broadleaf deciduous trees as well as needleleaf trees.
  - *Coniferous forests* are cone-bearing trees with needles or scaled evergreen leaves, such as pines, spruces, firs, and larches. *Needleleaf forests* are the coniferous forests of Earth's high-latitude and high-elevation mountain regions.

In their form and distribution, plants reflect all Earth's physical systems, including temperature and winds; precipitation quantity and seasonal timing; soils and nutrients; and chemical pathways. Biomes usually correspond directly to moisture and temperature regimes (**Figure 20.5**). In addition, plant communities reflect the growing influence of humans.

▲**Figure 20.4 Desert landscape modified by human activity in the Mohave Desert, California.** Plants and animals that thrive in the varied border zones where natural habitat adjoins human-modified lands are known as edge species. Such species exist in natural ecotones as well as those formed in anthropogenic landscapes. [Jim West/Alamy.]

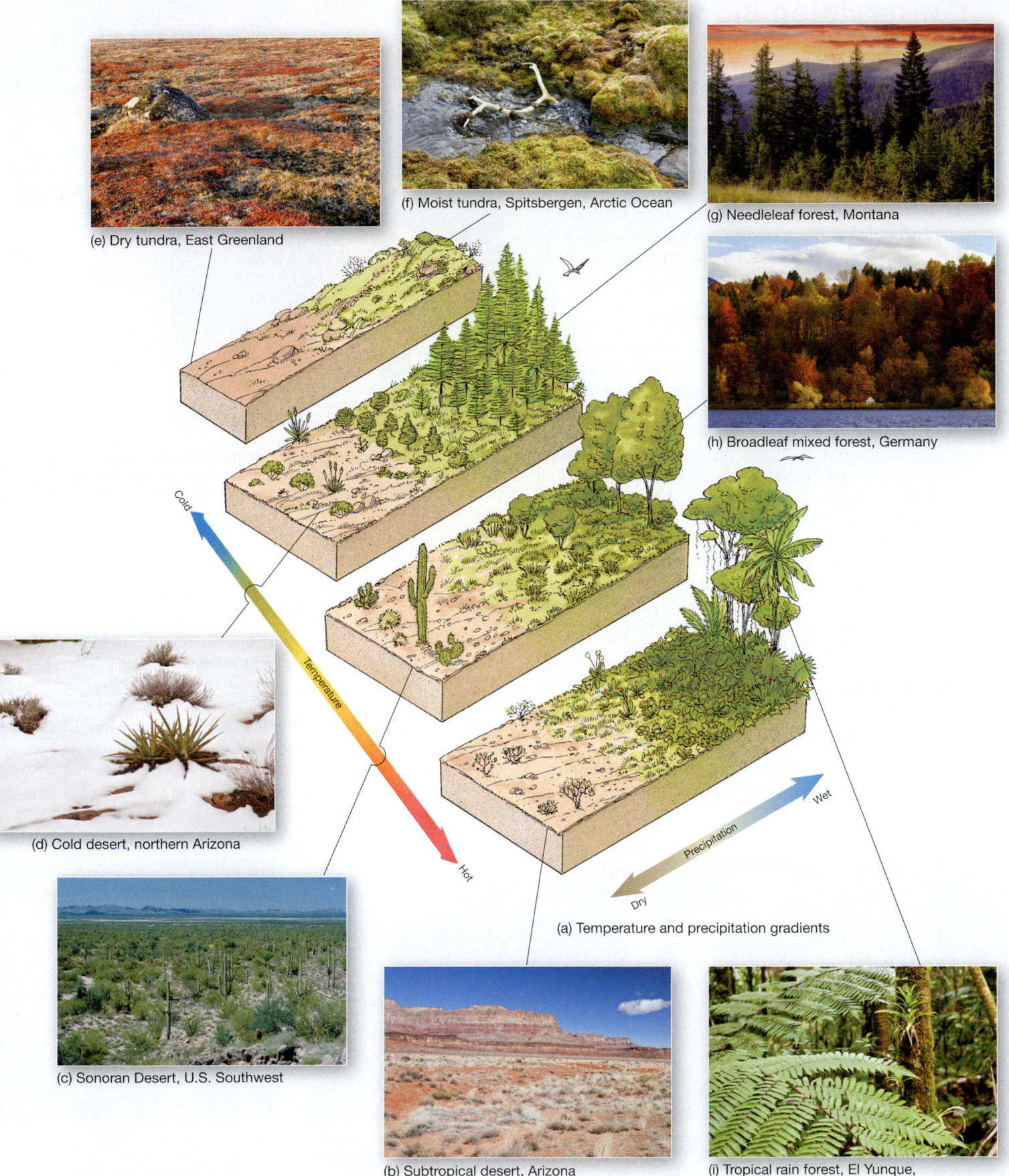

(e) Dry tundra, East Greenland

(f) Moist tundra, Spitsbergen, Arctic Ocean

(g) Needleleaf forest, Montana

(h) Broadleaf mixed forest, Germany

(d) Cold desert, northern Arizona

(c) Sonoran Desert, U.S. Southwest

(b) Subtropical desert, Arizona

(i) Tropical rain forest, El Yunque, Puerto Rico

Cold

Temperature

Hot

Wet

Precipitation

Dry

(a) Temperature and precipitation gradients

▲Figure 20.5 **Vegetation patterns in relationship to temperature and precipitation.** [(b), (d)–(f), and (i) Bobbé Christopherson. (c) Robert Christopherson. (g) Snehit/Shutterstock. (h) blickwinkel/Hartl/Alamy.]

Conservation Biogeography

With the increasing influence of human activity on natural species distributions, conservation has become a focus for scientists and the public. In the early 2000s, biogeographers defined the new, emerging scientific field of *conservation biogeography*. This subdiscipline applies biogeographic principles, theories, and analyses to solve problems in biodiversity conservation. Among the important research topics in this field are the impacts of rapid climate change on biodiversity (discussed in Chapter 19), the distribution and effects of invasive species, and the implementation of conservation planning and establishment of protected areas.

Endemic and Invasive Species

Native species are those that occur naturally in a particular biome as a consequence of the evolutionary and physical factors discussed previously in this chapter and in Chapter 19. Some, but not all, native species are also **endemic species**, meaning that they live in only one geographic location on Earth. An example is the lemur, a type of primate, found only in Madagascar (**Figure 20.6**). Over 100 species of lemurs exist on the island of Madagascar, all of which are today highly endangered. Although many endemic species occur on islands, such as Australia and Hawai'i, any type of geographic isolation can give rise to endemic species. The isolated mountaintops surrounded by desert in the Great Basin of the U.S. West support endemic animals and plants, some of which are now threatened by climate change.

Communities, ecosystems, and biomes can also be inhabited by species that are introduced from elsewhere by humans, either intentionally or accidentally. Such nonnative species are also known as *exotic species*, or *aliens*.

Invasive Species Examples After arriving from a different ecosystem, an estimated 90% of introduced non-

▲**Figure 20.6 Endemic primate, Madagascar.** The ring-tailed lemur, well known for its distinct tail, is one of over 100 lemur species endemic to Madagascar and is today an endangered species. [Gudkov Andrey/Shutterstock.]

native species fail to move into established niches in their new community or habitat. However, some species are able to do so, taking over niches already occupied by native species and thus becoming **invasive species**. The 10% that become invasive can alter community dynamics and lead to declines in native species. Prominent examples are Africanized "killer bees" in North and South America; brown tree snakes in Guam; zebra and quagga mussels in the Great Lakes (**Figure 20.7a**); kudzu in the U.S. Southeast (**Figure 20.7b**); and purple loosestrife,

(a) Zebra mussels, native to Russia, cover most hard surfaces in the Great lakes. They rapidly colonize any surface, even sand, in freshwater environments.

(b) Kudzu, imported from Asia as an ornamental and for erosion control, spread from Pennsylvania to Texas; here, it overruns pasture and forest in western Georgia.

(c) Purple loosestrife, shown here in southern Ontario, is a non-native species from Europe that has invaded wetland habitats throughout much of the United States and Canada.

▲**Figure 20.7 Invasive species.** [(a) Purestock/Alamy. (b) Bobbé Christopherson. (c) Gaertner/Alamy.]

▲**Figure 20.8 The threatened Hawaiian I'iwi, a Honeycreeper.** Once found throughout the Hawaiian Islands and prized for its striking plumage, the I'iwi is now extinct on Lana'i and extremely rare on O'ahu and Moloka'i. On the other islands, the bird is still relatively common above 1000 m (3280 ft), beyond the reach of mosquitos that transmit disease. [Chris Johns/National Geographic/Getty Images.]

which was introduced to North America from Europe as an ornamental plant with some medicinal applications (**Figure 20.7c**). For information on invasive species prevention and management, see https://www.doi.gov/invasivespecies.

Invasive Species in Hawai'i When the first European settlers landed on the islands of Hawai'i in the late 1700s, they encountered 71 endemic species and subspecies of birds. However, as these settlers introduced rabbits, goats, rats, and other non-native species into the island ecosystems, native species declined. Today, 23 of the original 71 endemic birds are extinct, and 30 of the remaining species and subspecies are listed as threatened or endangered. In most of Hawai'i, native birds no longer exist below elevations of 1220 m (4000 ft) because of an introduced avian virus (**Figure 20.8**). This is just one example of declining biodiversity on islands, which are particularly vulnerable to species losses because their unique ecosystems evolved in isolation from mainland species.

Island Biogeography for Species Preservation

A key conceptual model for understanding species distributions and the effects of fragmented habitat is Robert MacArthur and E. O. Wilson's theory of **island biogeography**, published as a book of the same name in 1967. The theory, based on scientific work on small, isolated mangrove islands in the Florida Keys, links the number of species (species richness) on an island to the island's size and distance from the mainland.

The theory summarized three patterns of species distributions on islands: (1) The number of species increases with island area (**Figure 20.9**), (2) the number of species decreases with island isolation (distance from the mainland), and (3) the number of species on an island represents an equilibrium between the rates of immigration and extinction. Larger islands have a wider variety of habitat and niches and thus lower extinction rates. This theory provided the foundation for understanding "islands" of fragmented habitat, inspired thousands of studies in biogeography and ecology, and increased awareness of the importance of landscape-scale thinking for species preservation. Although present research goes beyond the original theory, the basic conceptual ideas inform conservation science, especially with regard to proper formation of parks and reserves.

A common strategy for conservation of species is to focus on setting aside large habitats protected as national parks and wildlife refuges. Yet these protected areas are less effective for species preservation if they are surrounded by human development and disconnected from other natural habitat. As discussed in Geosystems Now, habitat fragmentation is problematic for species requiring a large range for survival. Wildlife managers now recognize the importance of *ecological corridors*, travel pathways for animals and dispersal pathways for plants that link habitat fragments. In southern Africa, for example, five nations are currently working to establish a vast transboundary conservation area in hopes of saving Africa's savanna elephant.

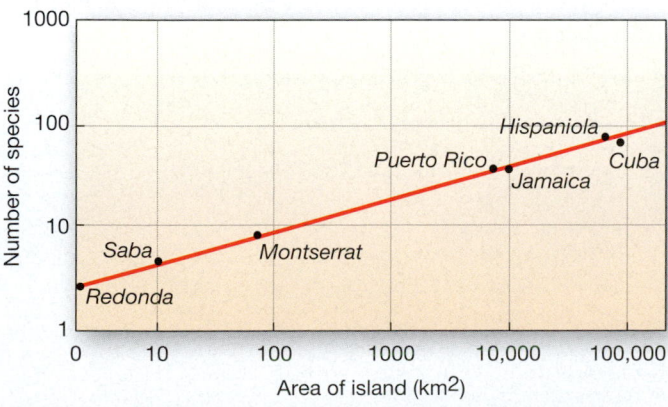

(a) Note that both axes are logarithmic. Species numbers represent data collected in the 1950s, so would be different today.

(b) The islands on the graph range in size from Cuba (the largest) to Saba and Redonda, both of which are too small to be seen on a map at this scale.

▲**Figure 20.9 Relationship between number of species and island area.** Larger islands in the Caribbean region support higher numbers of reptile and amphibian species than smaller islands. [After R.H. MacArthur and E.O. Wilson, 1967, *The Theory of Island Biogeography*, Princeton University Press.]

Earth's Terrestrial Biomes

Given that extensive transition zones separate many of Earth's biomes, the classification of biomes according to distinct vegetation associations is difficult and somewhat arbitrary. This results in a number of classification systems—similar in concept, but different in detail. Here, we describe 10 biomes that are common to most of these classification systems: tropical rain forest, tropical seasonal forest and scrub, tropical savanna, midlatitude broadleaf and mixed forest, boreal and montane forest, temperate rain forest, Mediterranean shrubland, midlatitude grassland, desert, and arctic and alpine tundra. The global distribution of these biomes is portrayed on the map in **Figure 20.10**.

The following pages provide descriptions of each biome, synthesizing information from previous chapters about the interactions of atmosphere, hydrosphere, lithosphere, and biosphere. Each biome discussion begins with a summary of global distribution, general vegetation characteristics, and the pertinent environmental factors related to climate, soils, and water availability. Because plant distributions respond to environmental conditions and reflect variations in climate and soil, the world climate map in Chapter 9, Figure 9.2, is a helpful reference for this discussion.

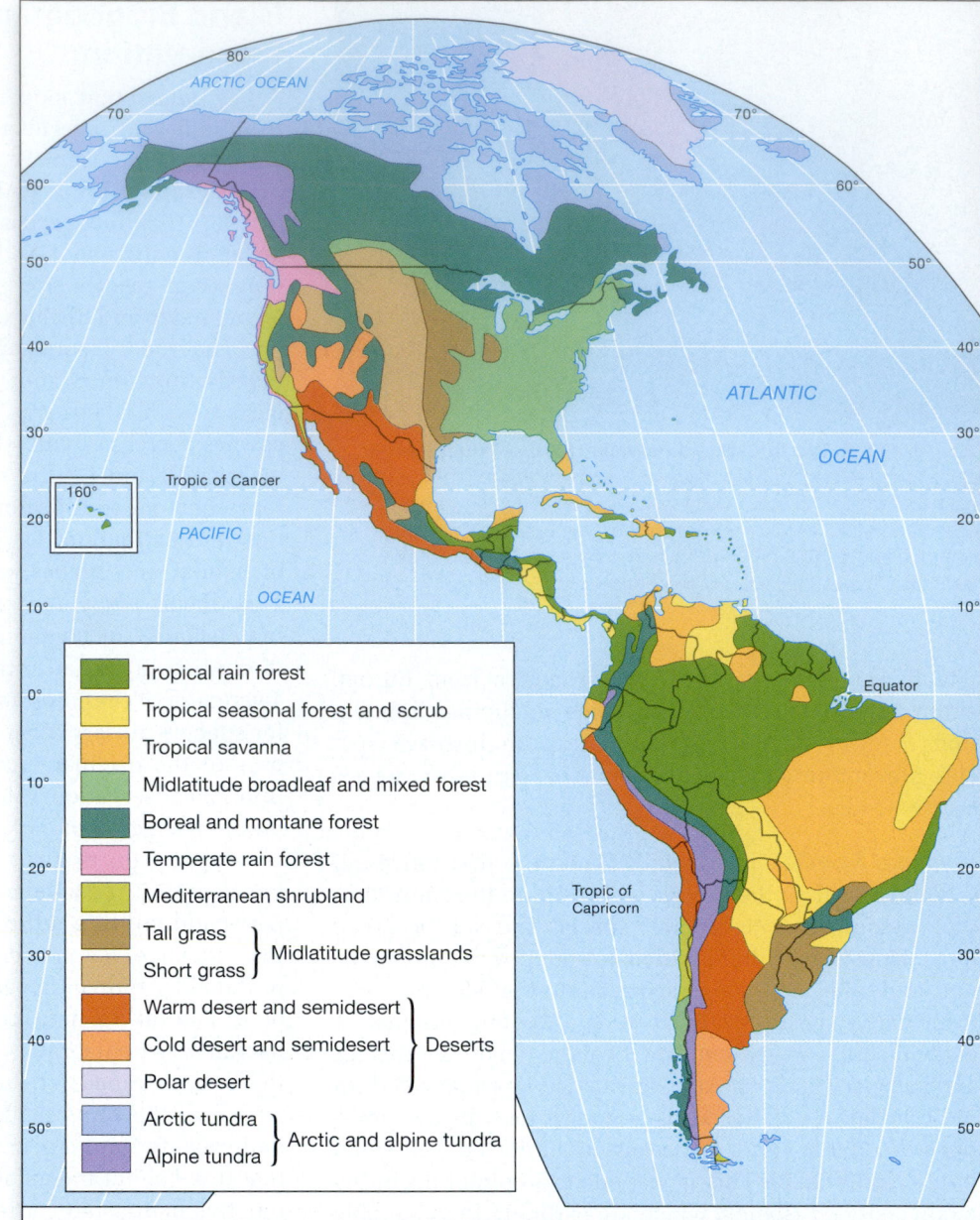

Figure 20.10 **The 10 major global terrestrial biomes.**

Legend:
- Tropical rain forest
- Tropical seasonal forest and scrub
- Tropical savanna
- Midlatitude broadleaf and mixed forest
- Boreal and montane forest
- Temperate rain forest
- Mediterranean shrubland
- Tall grass } Midlatitude grasslands
- Short grass }
- Warm desert and semidesert } Deserts
- Cold desert and semidesert }
- Polar desert
- Arctic tundra } Arctic and alpine tundra
- Alpine tundra }

Tropical Rain Forest Biome

Distribution

- Tropical rain forest climate
- Amazon region of South America; the Pacific coast of Ecuador and Colombia; Venezuela; and the east coast of Central America; equatorial regions of Africa; eastern Madagascar; parts of Southeast Asia, including Indonesia and New Guinea; parts of India and Australia

Vegetation characteristics and growth forms

- Thick, continuous, multilayered vegetation canopy
- Broadleaf evergreen trees, lianas, epiphytes, tree ferns, palms

Environmental factors

- Consistent year-round daylength (12 hours)
- Consistently warm temperatures ranging from 21° to 30°C (70° to 86°F) all year; average annual temperatures about 25°C (77°F)
- Abundant precipitation totaling 180–400 cm (71–157 in.) annually, with more than 6 cm (2.4 in.) each month
- Moisture surpluses all year
- Soils mainly Oxisols with some Ultisols

Human impacts

- Forest removal for ranching, agriculture, development
- Climate change

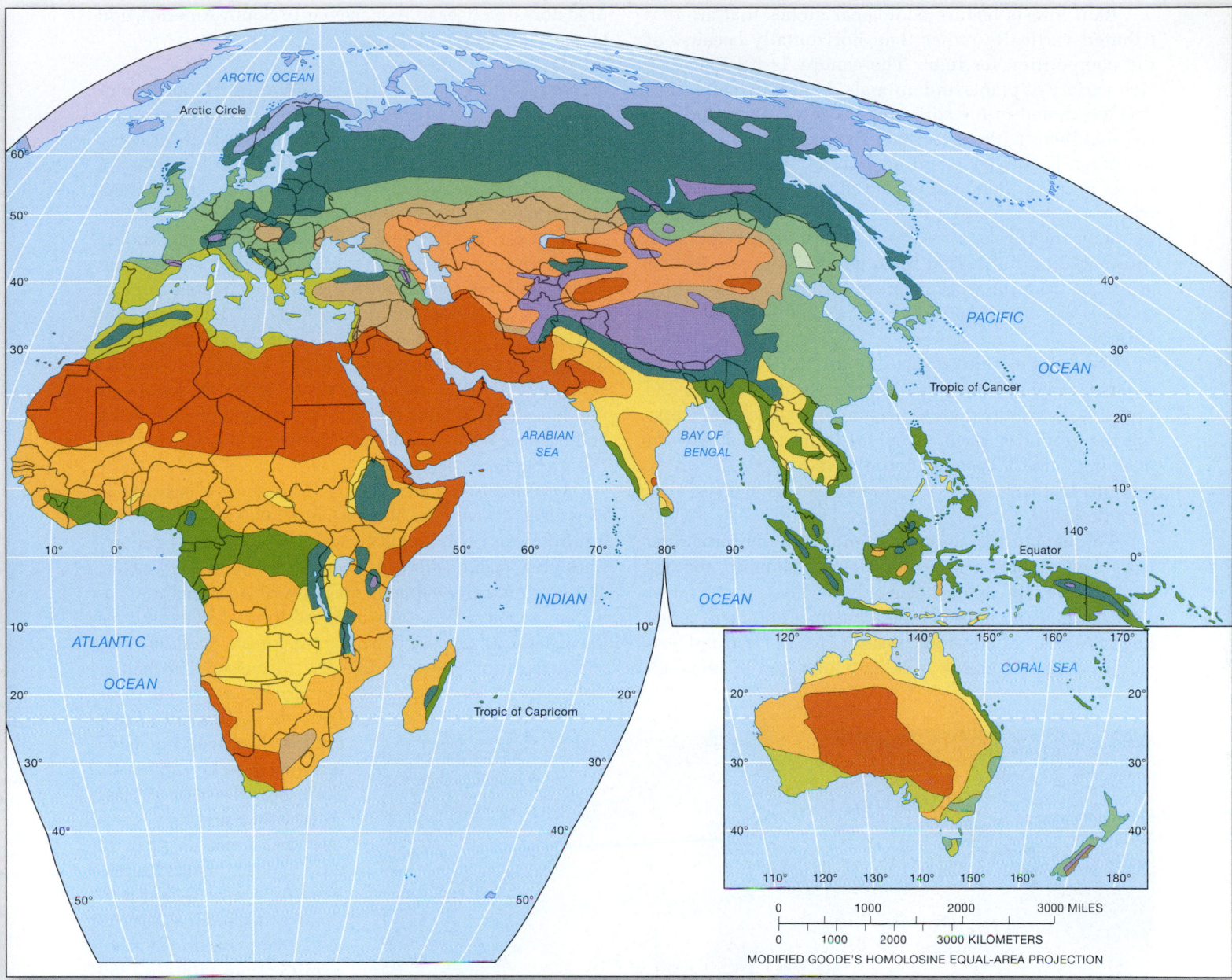

MODIFIED GOODE'S HOMOLOSINE EQUAL-AREA PROJECTION

Tropical Rain Forest

The lush biome covering Earth's equatorial regions is the **tropical rain forest**, which is host to the most diverse collection of plants and animals on the planet. Tropical rain forests occupy about 7% of the world's total land area but represent approximately 50% of Earth's species and about half of its remaining forests. Rainforest species evolved during the long-term residence of the continental plates near equatorial latitudes.

The largest tract of tropical rain forest occurs in the Amazon region, where it is called the *selva*. The cloud forests of western Venezuela are high-elevation tropical rain forests, perpetuated by high humidity and cloud cover. Although this biome is stable in its natural state, undisturbed tracts of rain forest are becoming increasingly rare; deforestation is perhaps the most pervasive human impact.

Rain Forest Flora and Fauna The structure of a rain forest includes four levels, illustrated in Geosystems in Action 20. The upper level, called the *overstory*, or *emergent layer*, is not continuous, but features the crowns of the tallest trees, which rise above the continuous *canopy* beneath. Biomass in a rain forest is concentrated in the dense mass of overhead leaves in these two upper levels. Beneath the canopy is the *understory*, made up of shade-tolerant shrubs, herbs, and small trees. The *forest floor* receives only about 1% of the sunlight arriving at the canopy. This lowest level of vegetation includes seedlings and ferns on a litter-strewn ground surface in deep shade. The high humidity, odors of mold and rotting vegetation, strings of thin roots and vines dropping down from above, windless air, and echoing sounds of life in the trees together create a unique environment.

Rain forests feature ecological niches that are distributed vertically rather than horizontally because of the competition for light. The canopy is filled with a rich variety of plants and animals. Lianas (woody vines that are rooted in the soil) stretch from tree to tree, entwining them with cords that can reach 20 cm (8 in.) in diameter. Epiphytes, such as orchids, bromeliads, and ferns, flourish there, supported physically, but not nutritionally, by the structures of other plants. On the forest floor, the trunks of rainforest trees are covered with thin bark and buttressed by large, wall-like flanks that grow out from the trees to brace the trunks. These buttresses form angular hollows that are habitat for various animals.

The animal and insect life of the rain forest is diverse, ranging from animals living exclusively in the upper stories of the trees to decomposers (bacteria) working the ground surface. *Arboreal* (from the Latin word meaning "tree") species, those dwelling in the trees, include sloths, monkeys, lemurs, parrots, and snakes (**Figure 20.11**).

Throughout the canopy are multicolored birds, tree frogs, lizards, bats, and a rich insect community that includes more than 500 species of butterflies. On the forest floor, animals include pigs (the bushpig and giant forest hog in Africa, wild boar and bearded pig in Asia, and peccary in South America), small antelope, and mammalian predators (the tiger in Asia, jaguar in South America, and leopard in Africa and Asia).

Deforestation of the Tropics Clearing of Earth's old-growth tropical rain forest to make way for agriculture has occurred for thousands of years, but with growing population, economic development, and globalization, the scale of deforestation has increased. For the past several decades, tropical forests have been cleared at alarming rates for farming, fuel wood, cattle ranching, timber export, and most recently, palm oil production. By continent, total rainforest losses are now estimated at more than 50% in Africa, more than 40% in Asia, and 40% in Central and South America. Tropical deforestation is threatening native rainforest species, including potential sources of valuable pharmaceuticals and new foods—so much is still unknown and undiscovered. Forest clearing and burning release millions of metric tons of carbon into the atmosphere each year.

Worldwide, an area nearly the size of Wisconsin is cleared each year (169,000 km², or 65,000 mi²), and about a third more is disrupted by selective cutting of canopy trees that occurs along the edges of deforested areas. The economically valuable varieties of trees include mahogany, ebony, and rosewood. Additional commodities harvested and exported from rain forests include beef, soybeans, rubber, and coffee. As discussed in Chapter 18, farmers use fire to clear land for subsistence agriculture; however, intensive farming quickly exhausts the productivity of tropical soils, which are then generally abandoned in favor of newly burned lands (unless fertility is maintained artificially by chemical fertilizers). Many rainforest trees require from 100 to 250 years to reestablish after a major disturbance.

Mobile MG
Field Trip
The Cloud Forest
of Monteverde

https://goo.gl/bRb2R5

◄**Figure 20.11** **Arboreal monkeys in the Amazon rain forest.** Black-capped squirrel monkeys spend the majority of their time in the rainforest canopy, feeding on insects, fruits, and seeds. [Anna Kucherova/ Alamy.]

Tropical Seasonal Forest and Scrub Biome

Distribution
- Tropical monsoon and tropical savanna climates
- Parts of Brazil, Paraguay, and Argentina; Australia; southern Africa; central Africa extending west to east from Angola through Zambia into parts of Tanzania and Kenya; portions of India; and Southeast Asia, from interior Myanmar through northeastern Thailand

Vegetation characteristics and growth forms
- Plants adapted to a dry season
- Broadleaf evergreen and deciduous trees; acacias and other thorn trees
- Open areas of shrubs and grasses ranging to seasonal forests with dense undergrowth

Environmental factors
- Variable, mostly warm temperatures all year, with average annual temperatures greater than 18°C (64°F)
- Annual precipitation totaling from 130 to 200 cm (51 to 79 in.), with more than 40 rainy days during the four driest months
- Seasonal moisture surpluses and deficits
- Soils mainly Oxisols, Ultisols, Vertisols (in India), and some Alfisols

Human impacts
- Forest removal for agriculture
- Climate change

Tropical Seasonal Forest and Scrub

At the margins of the world's rain forests are areas of seasonal changes in precipitation, characterized by the **tropical seasonal forest and scrub** biome. These are regions of lower and more erratic rainfall than occurs in the equatorial zone. Vegetation in this biome is adapted to climatic conditions with a distinct dry season. The shifting intertropical convergence zone (ITCZ) affects precipitation regimes, bringing moisture with the high Sun of summer and then a season of dryness with the low Sun of winter. This shift produces a seasonal pattern of moisture deficits, which affects vegetation leaf loss and flowering.

The tropical seasonal forest and scrub biome includes seasonal forests as well as scrub woodland and thorn forest. The term *semideciduous* applies to many broadleaf trees that lose some of their leaves during the dry season. *Scrub vegetation* consists of low shrubs and grasses with adaptations to semiarid conditions. *Thorn forest* includes thorny trees and shrubs that shed their leaves during the dry season.

Overall, the tropical seasonal forest and scrub is a varied biome that occupies a transitional area from wetter to drier tropical climates. Natural vegetation ranges from tropical deciduous forests to open woodlands to thorn forests to semiarid scrub vegetation. The deciduous forests have an average height of 15 m (50 ft) with a discontinuous canopy. Local names for these communities include the *Chaco* (or *Gran Chaco*) in southeastern Brazil, Paraguay, and northern Argentina (**Figure 20.12**); the *brigalow* scrub of Australia; and the *dornveld* of southern Africa.

The trees throughout most of this biome make poor lumber, but some, especially teak, may be valuable for fine cabinetry and furniture. In addition, some of the plants with dry-season adaptations produce usable waxes, such as the carnauba wax produced by the Brazilian palm tree. Animal life includes the koalas and cockatoos of Australia and the antelope, large cats, anteaters, rodents, and ground-dwelling birds in other examples of this biome. Worldwide, humans use these areas for ranching. In Africa, this biome includes numerous wildlife parks and preserves.

(a) Trumpet trees are dry-season deciduous trees that are common in the seasonal forest and scrub of Paraguay.

(b) Cattle ranching is common in the Gran Chaco region.

▲**Figure 20.12 Tropical seasonal forest and scrub, Gran Chaco, Paraguay.**
[(a) ImageBroker/Alamy. (b) Universal Images/Alamy.]

E arth's tropical rain forests are a vast reservoir of biodiversity. The rain forest's layered structure reflects intense competition for sunlight and space among numerous species of trees and other plants (GIA 20.1). During the past several decades, humans have cleared over half of Earth's old-growth rain forests for agriculture, cattle ranching, timber export, and palm oil production (GIA 20.2). In Brazil, deforestation decreased from 2004 to 2012 (GIA 20.2c), but in Africa, Indonesia, and other parts of South America, rain forest losses continue to increase.

20.1a VERTICAL STRUCTURE OF A RAIN FOREST

The structure of a tropical rain forest includes the overstory (also known as the emergent layer), the middle canopy, the understory, and the forest floor, shown below. Long vines called lianas, rooted in the soil, connect these layers, while dead leaves form litter on the deeply shaded forest floor.

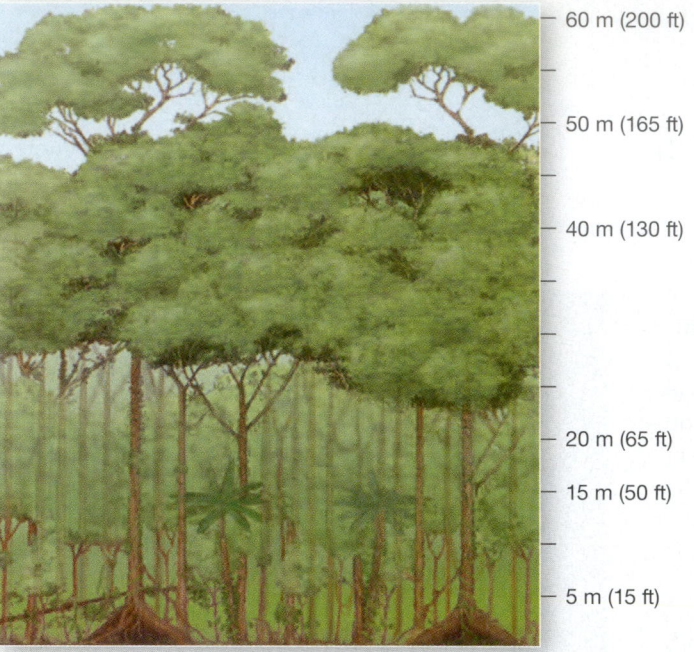

60 m (200 ft)

50 m (165 ft)

Overstory, or Emergent Layer:
The overstory, or emergent layer, consists of the tallest trees, whose tops "emerge" from the main canopy, jutting above the surrounding forest.

40 m (130 ft)

Middle canopy:
Formed of the interlocking crowns of mature trees, the middle canopy is home to a variety of animals and plants.

20 m (65 ft)

15 m (50 ft)

Understory:
Between the middle canopy and the forest floor, the understory consists of shade-tolerant shrubs and trees and woody vines that climb up tree trunks toward sunlight.

5 m (15 ft)

Forest floor:
The forest floor is a deeply shaded area of ferns and litter of dead leaves and other plant material.

20.1b RAINFOREST SOIL

Rainforest soil is poor in nutrients. Most soil nutrients have been taken up to help form the biomass of trees and other rainforest organisms. These nutrients are recycled rapidly as plant and animal remains decay on the forest floor and are reabsorbed by tree roots.

Leaf litter covers the rainforest floor, seen here with a typical buttressed tree trunk and lianas in the background.

Animation (MG)
Plant Productivity in a Warming World

https://goo.gl/N5Zgdz

MasteringGeography™

Visit the Study Area in MasteringGeography™ to explore rain forests.

Visualize: Study a video of plant productivity in a warming world.

Assess: Demonstrate understanding of rain forests (if assigned by instructor).

Animation (MG)
Amazon Deforestation

https://goo.gl/dvgpZa

20.2 AMAZON RAIN FOREST DESTRUCTION

In Brazil, the vast Amazon rain forest is being cleared to make way for agriculture and ranching, and for selective timber export, some illegal, of species such as mahogany. Roads that penetrate undeveloped areas increase the habitat fragmentation that hastens biodiversity losses. Satellite images show the changes in one area between 2000 and 2009. During roughly the same time span, Brazil lost rain forest equal in area to all of the New England states plus New Jersey.

2000

Madeira River

Reservoir behind Samuel Dam, Jamari River

BR364

Aerial view of deforestation along highway BR364.

20.2a True-color image of Rondônia in western Brazil in 2000 shows deforestation along highway BR364, the main artery of the region.

2009

BR364

BR429

20.2b The same region in 2009. Note the increased amount of deforested land and the branching pattern of feeder roads.

20.2c **Deforestation in Brazil since 1994.** Law enforcement and new environmental policies helped reduce deforestation from 2004 to 2012. Rainforest destruction rose sharply during the first half of 2015 in response to forest code revisions that relax environmental protections, in addition to a weakened Brazilian currency that makes agricultural exports more profitable. [UNEP, after D. Nepstad et al., 2014, "Slowing Amazon deforestation through public policy and interventions in beef and soy supply chains," *Science*, 344 (6188): 1118–1123.]

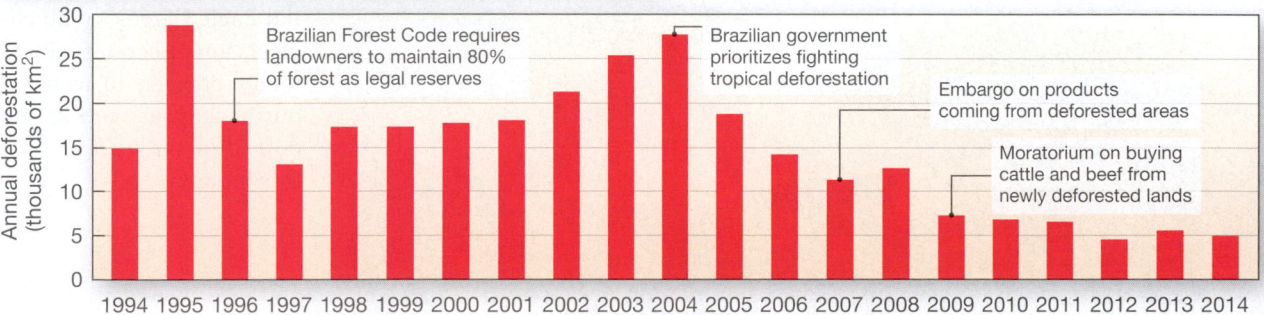

Brazilian Forest Code requires landowners to maintain 80% of forest as legal reserves

Brazilian government prioritizes fighting tropical deforestation

Embargo on products coming from deforested areas

Moratorium on buying cattle and beef from newly deforested lands

Annual deforestation (thousands of km²)

Year

GEOquiz

1. Describe: What are the characteristics of the four main layers of the rain forest?

2. Infer: How does the physical structure of the rain forest help to account for the great variety of organisms found there?

3. Analyze: Refer to the satellite images in GIA 20.2 to compare conditions in the area between the Madeira River and highway BR364 in 2000 and in 2009. How might these changes have affected wildlife populations? Explain.

4. Predict: Identify an area of rain forest on the 2009 satellite image in GIA 20.2b that is likely to be deforested in the near future and explain how and why the area will change.

Tropical Savanna Biome

Distribution

- Tropical savanna climate
- Sahel region across Africa; Australia; India; and South America, mainly in Venezuela and Brazil

Vegetation characteristics and growth forms

- Clumped grasses, scrub vegetation, scattered thorn trees
- Trees with flattened crowns
- Vegetation adapted to drought, fire, and herbivory (grazing)

Environmental factors

- Variable, mostly warm temperatures all year with no cold weather limitations
- Annual precipitation totaling from 9 to 150 cm (3.5 to 59 in.) annually, with a seasonal trend
- Tending toward seasonal moisture deficits
- Soils mainly Alfisols, Ultisols, and Oxisols

Human impacts

- Hunting and poaching
- Overgrazing and desertification

Tropical Savanna

The **tropical savanna** biome consists of large expanses of grassland, either treeless or interrupted by scattered trees and shrubs (**Figure 20.13**). Tropical savannas receive precipitation during approximately 6 months of the year, when they are influenced by the shifting ITCZ. The rest of the year they are under the drier influence of shifting subtropical high-pressure cells. This is a transitional biome between the tropical seasonal forests and the semi-arid tropical steppes and deserts.

Shrubs and trees of the savanna biome are adapted to drought, grazing by large herbivores, and fire. Most species are *xerophytic*, or drought resistant, with various adaptations to help them conserve moisture during the dry season—for example, small, thick leaves or waxy leaf surfaces (other xerophytic adaptations are discussed with the desert biomes). In the vast savannas of east Africa, a common tree is the acacia, with its flat top, thorny stems, and small leaves that reduce moisture loss.

Savanna vegetation is maintained by fire, both a natural and a human-caused disturbance in this biome.

During the wet season, grasses flourish, and as rainfall diminishes, this thick growth provides fuel for fires, which are often intentionally set to maintain the open grasslands. Hot-burning dry-season fires kill trees and seedlings and deposit a layer of nutrient-rich ash over the landscape. These conditions foster the regrowth of grasses, which again grow vigorously as the wet season returns, sprouting from extensive underground root systems that are an adaptation for surviving fire disturbance. In northern Australia, the aboriginal people are credited with creating and maintaining many of the region's tropical savannas; as the traditional practice of setting annual fires declines, many savannas are reverting to forest.

Africa has the largest area of tropical savanna on Earth, including the famous Serengeti Plains of Tanzania and Kenya. Local names for tropical savannas include the *Llanos* in Venezuela, stretching along the coast and inland east of the Andes, and the *Pantanal* of southwestern Brazil.

Particularly in Africa, savannas are the home of large land mammals—zebra, giraffe, buffalo, gazelle, wildebeest, antelope, rhinoceros, and elephant. These animals graze on savanna grasses, while others (lion, cheetah) feed upon the grazers themselves. Birds include the Common Ostrich, Martial Eagle (largest of all eagles), and Secretary Bird. Many species of venomous snakes, as well as the crocodile, are present in this biome.

◄**Figure 20.13 Elephants and acacias in the tropical savanna of southern Africa.** [Franz Aberham/Stockbyte/Getty Images.]

Midlatitude Broadleaf and Mixed Forest Biome

Distribution

- Humid subtropical and humid continental (hot-summer) climates
- Large areas across North America, Europe, and Asia; scattered areas of Australia and New Zealand

Vegetation characteristics and growth forms

- Mixed broadleaf and needleleaf trees
- Broadleaf deciduous trees, losing leaves in winter
- Pines of U.S. South and East adapted to fire

Environmental factors

- Temperate with a cold season
- Annual precipitation totaling from 75 to 150 cm (29 to 59 in.) annually
- Water budgets show a seasonal pattern with summer-maximum precipitation and potential evapotranspiration
- Soils mainly Ultisols with some Alfisols

Human impacts

- Forest removal for agriculture and development

Midlatitude Broadleaf and Mixed Forest

Moist continental climates support a mixed forest in areas of warm to hot summers and cool to cold winters. This **midlatitude broadleaf and mixed forest** biome includes several distinct communities in North America, Europe, and Asia. In the United States, relatively lush evergreen broadleaf forests occur along the Gulf of Mexico. To the north are the mixed deciduous broadleaf and needleleaf trees associated with sandy soils and frequent fires—pines (longleaf, shortleaf, pitch, loblolly) predominate in the southeastern and Atlantic coastal plains. In areas of this region protected from fire, broadleaf trees are dominant. Into New England and westward in a narrow belt to the Great Lakes, white and red pines and eastern hemlock are the principal conifers, mixed with broadleaf deciduous oak, beech, hickory, maple, elm, chestnut, and many others (**Figure 20.14**).

These mixed stands contain valuable timber, and logging has altered their distribution. Native stands of white pine in Michigan and Minnesota were removed before 1910, although reforestation sustains their presence today. In northern China, these forests have almost disappeared as a result of centuries of harvest. The forest species that once flourished in China are similar to species in eastern North America: oak, ash, walnut, elm, maple, and birch. This biome is quite consistent in appearance from continent to continent and at one time represented the principal vegetation of the humid subtropical (hot-summer) regions of North America, Europe, and Asia.

A wide assortment of mammals, birds, reptiles, and amphibians is distributed throughout this biome. Representative animals (some migratory) include red fox, white-tailed deer, southern flying squirrel, opossum, black bear, and a great variety of birds, including Tanager and Cardinal. To the west of this biome in North America are the rich soils and midlatitude climates that favor grasslands, and to the north is the gradual transition to the poorer soils and colder climates that favor the coniferous trees of the northern boreal forests.

(a) Aerial view of agricultural fields bordering the mixed forest of Elm-Lappwald Nature Park, Lower Saxony, Germany.

(b) Great Smoky Mountains National Park in the southern Appalachian Mountains contains one of the largest remaining tracts of old-growth forest in North America, including nearly 100 native tree species and over 200 species of birds.

(c) Great Smoky Mountains is home to 66 mammal species, including black bears, shown here in Cades Cove in Tennessee.

▲**Figure 20.14 Mixed broadleaf forest, Germany and the United States.** [(a) LOOK Die Bildagentur der Fotografen/Alamy. (b) Sean Lema/Shutterstock. (c) Simon Crumpton/Alamy.]

Boreal and Montane Forest Biome

Distribution

- Humid continental (mild summer), subarctic, and highland climates
- Boreal forest: In North America, stretching from the east coast of Canada and the Atlantic Provinces westward to the Canadian Rockies and portions of Alaska; in Eurasia, stretching from northern Europe across the entire extent of Russia through Siberia; not present in South America
- Montane forest: High elevations on mountains worldwide

Vegetation characteristics and growth forms

- Needleleaf conifers, mostly evergreen pine, spruce, fir
- Deciduous needleleaf trees, such as Russian larch

Environmental factors

- Short summer, cold winter
- Annual precipitation totaling from 30 to 100 cm (12 to 39 in.) annually
- Moderate precipitation, low potential evapotranspiration; no moisture deficits
- Soils mainly Spodosols, Histosols, Inceptisols, Alfisols; moist soils, some waterlogged and frozen in winter

Human impacts

- Climate change
- Logging
- Fire suppression

(a) European larch in autumn foliage in the Alps near Chamonix, France, with the Mont Blanc Massif in the distance.

(b) Gray wolves in the montane forest of Montana.

▲**Figure 20.15 Flora and fauna of the boreal and montane forest biome.**
[(a) ImageBroker/Alamy. (b) Design Pics Inc./Alamy.]

Boreal and Montane Forest

The distribution of the **boreal forest** biome, also known as the *northern needleleaf forest*, coincides with microthermal climates that have a cold winter season and also some summer warmth. The northern, less densely forested part of this biome, transitional to the arctic tundra biome, is called the *taiga*. The needleleaf forests at high elevations on mountains worldwide are the **montane forests**.

Boreal forests of pine, spruce, fir, and larch occupy most of the subarctic climates on Earth that are dominated by trees. Although these forests have similar vegetation life forms, individual species vary between North America and Eurasia. The larch is one of only a few needleleaf trees that drop needles in the winter months (**Figure 20.15a**). Larches are also found in North America.

This biome also occurs at high elevations at lower latitudes, such as in the Sierra Nevada, Rocky Mountains, Alps, and Himalayas. Douglas fir and white fir grow in the western mountains of the United States and Canada. Economically, these forests are important for lumber in the southern margins of the biome and for pulpwood throughout the middle and northern portions. Present logging practices and the sustainability of these yields are issues of increasing controversy.

Representative fauna in this biome include wolf, elk, moose (the largest member of the deer family), bear, lynx, beaver, wolverine, marten, small rodents, and migratory birds during the brief summer season (**Figure 20.15b**). Birds include hawks and eagles, several species of grouse, Pine Grosbeak, Clark's Nutcracker, and several species of owls. About 50 species of insects particularly adapted to the presence of coniferous trees inhabit the biome.

Temperate Rain Forest

The lush forests in wet, humid regions make up the **temperate rain forest** biome. These forests of broadleaf and needleleaf trees, epiphytes, huge ferns, and thick undergrowth correspond generally to marine west coast climates (occurring along middle- to high-latitude west coasts), with precipitation approaching 400 cm (160 in.) per year, moderate air temperatures, summer fog, and an overall maritime influence.

The tallest trees in the world occur in this biome—the coast redwoods of the California and Oregon coasts. These trees can exceed 1500 years in age and typically range in height from 60 to 90 m (200 to 300 ft), with some exceeding 100 m (330 ft). Virgin stands of other representative trees, such as Douglas fir, spruce, cedar, and hemlock, have been reduced by timber harvests to a few remaining valleys in Oregon and Washington—less than 10% of the original forest that existed when Europeans first arrived. Most forests in this biome are secondary-growth forests, having regrown from a major disturbance, usually human-caused (**Figure 20.16a**).

The biome is home to bear, badger, deer, wild pig, wolf, bobcat, fox, and numerous bird species, including the Northern Spotted Owl (**Figure 20.16b**). In the 1990s, this owl became a symbol for the conflict between species-preservation efforts and the use of resources to fuel local economies. In 1990, the U.S. Fish and Wildlife Service listed the owl as a "threatened" species under the U.S. Endangered Species Act, citing the loss of old-growth forest habitat as the primary cause for its decline. The next year, logging practices in areas with spotted owl habitat were halted by court order. The ensuing controversy pitted conservationists against loggers and other forest users, with the end result being large-scale changes in forest management throughout the Pacific Northwest.

Later research by the U.S. Forest Service and independent scientists noted the failing health of temperate rain forests and suggested that timber-management plans balance resource use with ecosystem preservation. Sustainable forestry practices emphasize the continuing health and productivity of forests into the future and are increasingly based on a multi-use ethic that serves local, national, and global interests.

(a) Old-growth Douglas fir, redwoods, cedars, and a mix of deciduous trees, ferns, and mosses in the Gifford Pinchot National Forest, Washington. Only a small percentage of these old-growth forests remain in the Pacific Northwest.

(b) The Northern Spotted Owl is an "indicator species" representing the health of the temperate rainforest ecosystem.

▲Figure 20.16 **Temperate rain forest.** [(a) Bobbé Christopherson. (b) Zuma Press, Inc./Alamy.]

Mediterranean Shrubland Biome

Distribution
- Mediterranean dry-summer climate
- California; Mediterranean region of Europe; Chile; parts of Australia

Vegetation characteristics and growth forms
- Shrubs and grasses adapted to drought
- Chaparral woodlands adapted to fire
- Sclerophyllous shrubs and trees (Australian eucalyptus forest)

Environmental factors
- Hot, dry summers and cool winters
- Annual precipitation totaling from 25 to 65 cm (10 to 26 in.) annually
- Summer deficits, winter surpluses
- Soils mainly Alfisols and Mollisols

Human impacts
- Removal for development and agriculture
- Fire suppression

Mediterranean Shrubland

The **Mediterranean shrubland** biome, also referred to as a temperate shrubland, occupies temperate regions that have dry summers, generally corresponding to the Mediterranean climates. The dominant shrub formations that occupy these regions are low growing and able to withstand hot-summer drought. The vegetation is *sclerophyllous* (from *sclero*, for "hard," and *phyllos*, for "leaf"). Most shrubs average a meter or two in height, with deep, well-developed roots; leathery leaves; and uneven low branches.

Typically, the vegetation varies between woody shrubs covering more than 50% of the ground and grassy woodlands covering 25%–60% of the ground. In California, the Spanish word *chaparro* for "scrubby evergreen" gives us the name *chaparral* for this vegetation type (**Figure 20.17a**). This scrubland includes species such as manzanita, toyon, red bud, ceanothus, mountain mahogany, blue and live oaks, and the dreaded poison oak.

This biome is located poleward of the shifting subtropical high-pressure cells in both hemispheres. The stable high pressure produces the characteristic dry-summer climate and establishes conditions conducive to fire. The vegetation is adapted for rapid recovery after fire—many species are able to resprout from roots or burls after a burn or have seeds that require fire for germination (**Figure 20.17b**).

In the Mediterranean shrubland of southern California, invasive species have altered plant community dynamics in this fire-adapted ecosystem. Although the native vegetation is adapted for wildfire, non-native species often are able to colonize burned areas more efficiently; thus exotic plants are changing the successional processes in this biome. The establishment of non-natives leads to thick undergrowth, providing more fuel for fires that are increasing in frequency. Native vegetation is adapted for fires that occur at intervals of 30 to 150 years; the increase in fire frequency with climate change puts these species at a disadvantage. More frequent fires in the region combine with the increasing numbers of non-native species to cause the conversion of southern California's shrubland to grassland.

A counterpart to the California chaparral in North America is the *maquis* of the Mediterranean region of Europe, which includes live and cork oak trees (the source of cork) as well as pine and olive trees. In Chile, this biome is known as the *mattoral*, and in southwestern Australia, it is *mallee scrub*. In Australia, the bulk of the *Eucalyptus* species are sclerophyllous in form and structure in whichever area they occur.

The Mediterranean climates are home to commercial agriculture, including subtropical fruits, vegetables, and nuts, with many food types (e.g., artichokes, olives, almonds) produced only in these climates. Animals include several types of deer, coyote, wolf, bobcat, various rodents and other small animals, and various birds. In Australia, this biome is home to Malleefowl, a ground-dwelling bird, and numerous marsupials.

(a) Chaparral vegetation, southern California.

(b) Fire-adapted chaparral sends out sprouts from roots a few months after a wildfire in the San Jacinto Mountains, southern California.

▲**Figure 20.17 Mediterranean chaparral and fire adaptations.** [Bobbé Christopherson.]

Midlatitude Grassland Biome

Distribution

- Humid subtropical and humid continental (hot-summer) climate zones
- North America; Ukraine; the *Pampas* of Argentina and Uruguay

Vegetation characteristics and growth forms

- Tallgrass prairies and shortgrass steppes, highly modified by human activity
- Adapted to fire

Environmental factors

- Temperate continental temperature patterns
- Annual precipitation totaling from 25 to 75 cm (10 to 29 in.) annually
- Balance between soil-moisture utilization and recharge; irrigation and dry farming in drier areas
- Soils mainly Mollisols and Aridisols; major areas of commercial grain farming

Human impacts

- Removal for agriculture, ranching, and development

▲**Figure 20.18 Protected grasslands in the United States.** Buffalo Gap National Grassland in western South Dakota is one of 20 protected national grasslands (see http://www.fs.fed.us/grasslands/). [Jason Patrick Ross/Shutterstock.]

Midlatitude Grassland

Of all the natural biomes, the **midlatitude grassland** is the most modified by human activity. This biome includes the world's "breadbaskets"—regions that produce bountiful grain (wheat and corn), soybeans, and livestock (hogs and cattle). In these regions, the only naturally occurring trees are deciduous broadleaf trees along streams and other limited sites. These regions are called grasslands because of the predominance of grasslike plants before human intervention (Figure 20.10 shows the natural location of this biome). In North America, tallgrass prairie vegetation once grew to heights of 2 m (6.5 ft) in the eastern Great Plains, with shortgrass steppes in the drier lands farther west.

Few patches of the original prairies (tall grassland) or steppes (short grassland) remain within this biome (**Figure 20.18**). In the prairies alone, the natural vegetation was reduced from 100 million hectares (250 million acres) down to a few areas of several hundred hectares each. In most regions where these grasslands were the natural vegetation, human development of them was critical to territorial expansion.

This biome is the home of large grazing animals, including deer, pronghorn, and bison (**Figure 20.19a**). Gophers, prairie dogs, ground squirrels, Turkey Vultures, grouse, and Prairie Chickens are common, as are grasshoppers and other insects. Predators include the coyote, badger, and birds of prey—hawks, eagles, and owls.

The black-footed ferret, a member of the weasel family, is a predator that has recently come back from the edge of extinction (**Figure 20.19b**). Once numbering in the tens of thousands and ranging throughout the grasslands from Canada to northern Mexico, this species was down to 18 individuals by 1986, a result of introduced diseases and habitat destruction. Today, after years of captive breeding, reintroduction, and habitat preservation, the black-footed ferret population has reached an estimated 1000 in the wild, including self-sustaining populations in three U.S. states and at least one Canadian province. The species remains listed as endangered, but its promising future exemplifies a conservation success story.

▼**Figure 20.19 Bison and black-footed ferrets in grasslands.** [(a) Michael Wheatley/Getty Images. (b) Wendy Shattil/Alamy.]

(a) Bison graze in the grasslands near the Rocky Mountain Front, Waterton National Park, Alberta, Canada.

(b) Black-footed ferrets, once close to extinction, are now bred in captivity and then reintroduced to their natural habitat. Ferrets have been successfully released in eight states, including Colorado (shown here).

Desert Biome

The desert biomes cover more than one-third of Earth's land area and are divided into warm, cold, and polar desert biomes..

Warm Desert and Semidesert, Cold Desert and Semidesert

Distribution

- Warm desert: Arid desert climates (precipitation is less than one-half of water demand)
- Cold desert: Semiarid steppe climates (precipitation is greater than one-half of water demand)

Vegetation characteristics and growth forms

- Grasses, shrubs, and trees adapted to dry conditions
- Xerophytes include cacti, creosote bush, and acacia trees

Environmental factors

- Average annual temperature around 18°C (64°F)
- Annual precipitation totaling 2–25 cm (0.8–9.8 in.)
- Chronic moisture deficits, irregular precipitation events
- Soils mainly Aridisols and Entisols

Human impacts

- Increased drought with climate change
- Human development and desertification

Polar Desert

Distribution

- Ice sheet and ice cap climates

Vegetation characteristics and growth forms

- Mosses and lichens, adapted to drought, cold, and wind

Environmental factors

- Warmest months less than 10°C (50°F)
- Annual precipitation less than 25 cm (9.8 in.)
- Gelisols or soils absent

Deserts

We subdivide the desert biomes into **warm desert and semidesert**, caused by the dry air and low precipitation of subtropical high-pressure cells, and **cold desert and semidesert**, which tend toward higher latitudes, where subtropical high pressure affects climate for less than 6 months of the year. A third subdivision, Earth's **polar deserts**, occurs in high-latitude regions, including most of Antarctica and Greenland, with very cold, dry climates. Vegetation, sparse in the predominantly ice- and rock-covered polar deserts, is mainly lichens and mosses.

Desert vegetation includes numerous **xerophytes**, plants that have adapted to dry conditions. For example, cacti and other desert plants known as *succulents* have thick and fleshy tissues that store water during dry periods. Other adaptations of xerophytes include

- long taproots to access groundwater (mesquite trees);
- shallow, spreading root systems to maximize water uptake (palo verde trees);
- small leaves to minimize surface area for water loss (acacia);
- waxy leaf coatings to retard water loss (creosote bush); and
- leaf drop during dry periods (ocotillo).

A number of xerophytic plants have also developed spines, thorns, or bad-tasting tissue to discourage herbivory.

Some desert plants are *ephemeral*, or short-lived, an adaptation that takes advantage of a short wet season or even a single rainfall event in desert environments. The seeds of desert ephemerals lie dormant on the ground until a rainfall stimulates the seed germination. Seedlings grow rapidly, mature, flower, and produce large numbers of new seeds, which are then dispersed long distances by wind or water. Seeds then go dormant until the next rainfall event. Some plants that grow along desert washes produce seeds that require seed coat scarification—abrasion of the surface—for the seed to take up water and germinate. A flash flood flowing down a desert wash can provide the tumbling, churning action that breaks open the seed coat, as well as the moisture for seed germination.

The vegetation of the Sonoran Desert of southern Arizona is an example of the warm desert biome (**Figure 20.20**). This landscape features the unique saguaro cactus, which grows to many meters in height and up to 200 years in age if undisturbed. First blooms do not appear until it is 50 to 75 years old. In cold deserts, where precipitation is greater and temperatures are colder, characteristic vegetation includes grasses and woody shrubs, such as sagebrush. Succulents that hold large amounts of water, such as the saguaro cactus, cannot survive in cold deserts that experience consecutive days or nights with freezing winter temperatures.

The faunas of both warm and cold deserts are limited by the extreme conditions and include only a few resident large animals. Camels, which still remain in the wild in the Gobi Desert of central Asia,

◀**Figure 20.20 Saguaro cacti in the Sonoran Desert.** Saguaro cacti in bloom in Arizona with the Superstition Mountains in the distance. [Anton Foltin/Shutterstock.]

▲**Figure 20.21 Bat-eared fox, Botswana, Africa.** The bat-eared fox is found in the deserts and savannas of south and east Africa. The large ears are to detect sounds of termites, its main food, and for thermoregulation, helping the animals dissipate heat. The foxes are nocturnal in the summer, during the hottest temperatures, and diurnal during the winter months. [Blaine Harrington III/Alamy.]

are well adapted to the extreme daily temperature range of cold deserts as well as limited water availability. These animals can lose up to 30% of their body weight in water without harm (for humans, a 10%–12% loss is dangerous). Desert bighorn sheep are another large animal, occurring in scattered populations in mountains and canyons in the U.S. Southwest and northern Mexico.

Other representative desert animals are the ring-tailed cat, kangaroo rat, lizards, scorpions, and snakes. Most of these animals become active only at night, when temperatures are lower (**Figure 20.21**). In addition, various birds have adapted to desert conditions and available food sources—for example, roadrunners, thrashers, ravens, wrens, hawks, grouse, and nighthawks.

Arctic and Alpine Tundra Biome

Distribution
- Tundra and subarctic cold-winter climates
- Arctic tundra: Extreme northern regions of North America and Eurasia; scattered islands near Antarctica
- Alpine tundra: High elevations above tree line on mountains worldwide

Vegetation characteristics and growth forms
- Few trees
- Dwarf shrubs, stunted sedges, mosses, lichens, and short grasses

Environmental factors
- Seasonal variation in daylength
- Warmest months >10°C (>50°F); only 2 or 3 months above freezing
- Annual precipitation totaling from 15 to 180 cm (6 to 71 in.) annually
- Permafrost soils, mainly Gelisols, Histosols, and some Entisols

Human impacts
- Resource extraction
- Climate change

Arctic and Alpine Tundra

The **arctic tundra** biome occurs mainly in regions bordering the Arctic Ocean and generally north of the 10°C (50°F) isotherm for the warmest month. Daylength varies greatly throughout the year, seasonally changing from almost continuous day to continuous night. This area, except for a few portions of Alaska and Siberia, was covered by ice during all of the Pleistocene glaciations.

This biome corresponds to climates with long, cold winters and short, cool summers. The growing season lasts only 60–80 days, and even then frosts can occur at any time. Roots can penetrate only to the depth of thawed ground, usually about a meter (3 ft). These regions have been warming with recent climate change, affecting species and ecosystems.

Arctic tundra vegetation consists of low, ground-hugging herbaceous plants such as sedges, mosses, arctic meadow grass, and some woody species such as dwarf willow (**Figure 20.22**). Owing to the short growing season, some perennials form flower buds one summer and open them for pollination the next. Animals of the tundra biome include musk ox, caribou, reindeer, rabbit, Ptarmigan, lemming, and other small rodents, which are important food for the larger carnivores—the wolf, fox, weasel, Snowy Owl, polar bear, and, of course, mosquito. The tundra is an important breeding ground for geese, swans, and other waterfowl.

▼**Figure 20.22 Arctic tundra.** [(a) All Canada Photos/Alamy. (b) Efrain Padro/Alamy.]

(b) Rocky arctic tundra landscape near the Hoffellsjokul Glacier in Vatnajokull National Park, Iceland.

(a) Bearberry leaves turn bright red in early fall in the arctic tundra landscape of Yukon, Canada, above the Arctic Circle.

Alpine tundra is similar to arctic tundra, but it can occur at high elevations in the lower latitudes. This biome usually occurs above the tree line (the elevation above which trees cannot grow), which shifts to higher elevations closer to the equator. Alpine tundra communities occur in the Andes near the equator, the White Mountains and Sierra of California, the American and Canadian Rockies, the Alps, and Mount Kilimanjaro of equatorial Africa as well as in mountains from the Middle East to Asia.

Alpine tundra features ground-hugging grasses and herbs, lichens, mosses, and low-growing woody shrubs, such as willows and heaths. In many alpine locations, plants have forms that are shaped by frequent winds. Alpine tundra can also experience permafrost conditions. Characteristic fauna include mountain goats, Rocky Mountain bighorn sheep, elk, and voles (**Figure 20.23**).

Vegetation of the tundra biome is slow-growing, has low productivity, and is easily disturbed. Hydroelectric projects, mineral exploitation, and even tire tracks leave marks on the landscape that persist for hundreds of years. With rising population and energy demand, the region will face even greater challenges from the environmental impacts of petroleum resource development.

▲**Figure 20.23** **Alpine ibex, Switzerland.** Alpine ibex live in the steep, rocky terrain above snowline in the European Alps, browsing on alpine tundra vegetation. Hunting in the early 1900s reduced populations of this wild goat, which has since rebounded into its former range. [blickwinkel/Alamy.]

Aquatic Biomes and Marine Sanctuaries

Human activities have affected freshwater and marine biomes in ways roughly similar to terrestrial biomes. Coastal ocean waters, in particular, continue to deteriorate from pollution and habitat degradation, as well as unsustainable fishing practices. Declines in aquatic species, such as the precipitous drop of the herring population in the Georges Bank fishing area of the Atlantic in the 1970s, highlight the need for an ecosystem approach to understanding and managing these international waters.

The U.S. National Marine Sanctuary System includes 13 protected marine sanctuaries and two marine national monuments. In 2016, the federal government expanded Papahānaumokuākea Marine National Monument, which includes the islands and atolls of the Hawaiian Island chain extending northwest of the main Hawaiian Islands, making it the largest contiguous fully protected conservation area protected by the U.S. government (see http://www.papahanaumokuakea.gov/). Papahānaumokuākea includes extensive coral reefs, shallow water environments important to endangered green sea turtles and Hawaiian

monk seals, and an area of land used by about 14 million seabirds for breeding and nesting.

Anthropogenic Biomes

Even in many of the most pristine ecosystems on Earth, evidence of early human settlement exists. Today, we are the most powerful biotic agent on Earth, influencing all ecosystems on a planetary scale. Scientists are measuring ecosystem properties and building elaborate computer models to simulate the evolving human–environment experiment on our planet—in particular, the shifting patterns of environmental factors (temperatures and changing frost periods; precipitation timing and amounts; air, water, and soil chemistry; and nutrient redistribution) wrought by human activities.

Anthropogenic biomes result from ongoing human interaction with ecosystems, linked to land-use practices such as agriculture, forestry, and urbanization (shown in the Human Denominator 20 and in Figure 20.21 on page 605). The most extensive anthropogenic biome is rangelands, covering about 32% of Earth's ice-free land; croplands, forested lands, and wildlands each cover about 20%, and settlements take up about 7%. The concept of anthropogenic biomes does not replace terrestrial biome classifications but instead presents another perspective for classification.

GEOreport **20.1**   Plant communities survive under glacial ice

Glacial retreat has exposed communities of bryophytes (nonflowering, spore-producing plants, such as mosses) that were frozen into the glacial ice formed during the Little Ice Age about 400 years ago. Recently, scientists collected and dated samples of these communities in the Canadian Arctic. They also successfully cultured the plants in a laboratory, using a single cell of the exhumed material to regenerate the entire original organism. Thus, bryophytes can survive long periods of burial under thick glacial ice and, under the right conditions, potentially recolonize a landscape after glaciation.

BIOMES IMPACT HUMANS

- Natural plant and animal communities are linked to human cultures, providing resources for food and shelter.
- Earth's remaining undisturbed ecosystems are becoming a focus for tourism, recreation, and scientific attention.

HUMANS IMPACT BIOMES

- Invasive species, many introduced by humans, disrupt native ecosystems.
- Tropical deforestation is ongoing, with more than half of Earth's original rain forest already cleared.

20a

Residential rain-fed mosaic. Prince Edward Island, Canada. [All Canada Photos/Alamy Stock Photo.]

20b

Urban settlement. London, England. [Justin Kase z12z/Alamy Stock Photo.]

20c

Irrigated village. Satpara, Pakistan. [Dave Stamboulis/Alamy.]

Settlements
- ● Urban
- ● Dense settlement
- ● Rice villages
- ● Irrigated villages
- ● Cropland and pastoral
- ● Pastoral villages
- ● Rain-fed villages
- ● Rain-fed mosaic villages

Croplands
- ● Residential irrigated cropland
- ● Residential rain-fed mosaic
- ● Populated irrigated cropland
- ● Populated rain-fed cropland
- ● Remote cropland

Rangelands
- ● Residential rangelands
- ● Populated rangelands
- ● Remote rangelands

Forested lands
- ● Populated forest
- ● Remote forest

Wildlands
- ● Wild forest
- ● Sparse trees
- ● Barren or ice-covered

Map courtesy of Erle Ellis, University of Maryland, Baltimore County, and Navin Ramankutty, McGill University/NASA; available at: http://earthobservatory.nasa.gov/IOTD/view.php?id=40554.

20e

Remote rangelands. Northern Chile. [Independent Picture Service/Alamy.]

20d

Populated forest. Raja Ampat Islands, Indonesia. [Images & Stories/Alamy.]

ISSUES FOR THE 21ST CENTURY

- Management of species and ecosystems must become a priority to avoid extinctions and loss of diversity.
- Shifting of species distributions in response to environmental factors will continue with ongoing climate change.
- Population control and global education (including education for women and disadvantaged minorities in all countries) are critical for sustaining natural and anthropogenic biomes.

QUESTIONS TO CONSIDER

1. Which regions on the map of anthropogenic biomes have the largest expanses of wildlands? What explains the distribution of remaining wildlands?
2. Among these biomes, how would you classify the area in which you live?

KEY**LEARNING**concepts**review**

Locate the world's biogeographic realms and *discuss* the basis for their specification.

The interplay of evolutionary and abiotic factors within Earth's ecosystems determines biodiversity and the distribution of plant and animal communities. A **biogeographic realm** (p. 582) is a major geographic region in which certain groups of associated plant and animal species evolved. This recognition laid the groundwork for understanding communities of flora and fauna known as biomes.

1. What is a biogeographic realm?
2. What are the zoological realms? What is Wallace's line?

Explain the basis for grouping plant communities into biomes and *list* the major terrestrial biomes on Earth.

A **biome** (p. 583) is a large, stable, terrestrial or aquatic ecosystem classified according to the predominant vegetation type and the adaptations of particular organisms to that environment. Biomes carry the name of the dominant vegetation because it is the most easily identified feature. The six main terrestrial vegetation classifications are forest, savanna, grassland, shrubland, desert, and tundra. Within these general groups, biome designations are based on more-specific growth forms; for example, forests are subdivided into rain forests, seasonal forests, broadleaf mixed forests, and needleleaf forests. Ideally, a biome represents a mature community of natural vegetation. A boundary transition zone between adjoining ecosystems is an **ecotone** (p. 584).

3. Define biome. What is the basis for the designation?
4. Name and describe the transition zone between two ecosystems.

Explain the potential impact of non-native species on biotic communities, using several examples, and *discuss* strategies for biodiversity conservation based on principles of biogeography.

Native species are those that occur naturally in a particular biome resulting from evolutionary and environmental factors. Some native species are also **endemic species** (p. 586), meaning that they live in only one geographic location on Earth. Communities, ecosystems, and biomes can be affected by species that are introduced from elsewhere by humans, either accidentally or intentionally. After arriving in the new ecosystem, some non-native species may disrupt native ecosystems and become **invasive species** (p. 586).

Efforts are under way worldwide to set aside and protect remaining representative sites within most of Earth's principal biomes. Principles of **island biogeography** (p. 587) used in the study of isolated ecosystems are important in setting up wildlife reserves and establishing ecological corridors. Island communities are special places for study because of their spatial isolation and the relatively small number of species present.

5. Give several examples of invasive species described in the text, and describe their impact on natural systems.
6. Describe the theory of island biogeography. How has this theory become important for preserving biodiversity?

Summarize the characteristics of Earth's 10 major terrestrial biomes and *locate* them on a world map.

Earth's major natural terrestrial biomes include:

tropical rain forest (p. 589)
tropical seasonal forest and scrub (p. 591)
tropical savanna (p. 594)
midlatitude broadleaf and mixed forest (p. 595)
boreal forest (p. 596) and **montane forest** (p. 596)
temperate rain forest (p. 597)
Mediterranean shrubland (p. 598)
midlatitude grassland (p. 599)

The desert and arctic and alpine tundra biomes are split into subgroups:

warm desert and semidesert (p. 600)
cold desert and semidesert (p. 600)
polar desert (p. 600)
arctic tundra (p. 601)
alpine tundra (p. 602)

Vegetation of Earth's deserts and semideserts includes numerous **xerophytes** (p. 600), plants that have adapted to dry conditions by evolving mechanisms to prevent water loss.

In reality, few undisturbed biomes exist in the world, for most have been modified by human activity. The new concept of **anthropogenic biomes** (p. 602) considers the impacts of human settlement, agriculture, and forest practices on vegetation patterns.

7. Describe the role of fire in the tropical savanna biome and in the midlatitude broadleaf and mixed forest biome.
8. In which biome do we find Earth's tallest trees? Which biome is dominated by small, stunted plants, lichens, and mosses?
9. What type of vegetation predominates in the Mediterranean dry-summer climate? Describe the adaptations necessary for these plants to survive.
10. What are some adaptations of xerophytes?

MasteringGeography™

GEO**SPATIAL** ANALYSIS

Invasive Species

Invasive plant species cause damage to ecosystems by competing with native plant species. Where the invasive plant populates a field or pasture they pose problems for agriculture.

Activities

Go to the Early Detection and Distribution Mapping System (EDD MapS) website at https://www.eddmaps.org/. Click on "Distribution Maps."

1. How many invasive species are monitored on this web site?

2. Click on each species type to determine if the invaders are plants, insects, diseases, or wildlife?

Click on the "Plants" and then on "Canada thistle" (Cirsium arvense). All of the data are loaded when the numbers on the map stop fluctuating (may take a few minutes).

3. How many "positive infestations" are noted? Characterize the distribution. How many treated areas are designated? How many regions are no longer finding (rated "negative") the Canada thistle?

4. Approximately what percentage of the United States has a problem with Canada thistle?

5. Click on "States," then "Counties." Is the Canada thistle located in your state? County? If not, what is the closest state and county where the Canada thistle is reported? (Zoom in and hover over the county to see its name.)

Near the top of the page click on "Species Information" located underneath "Invasive Plant Atlas."

6. What is the ecological threat associated with the Canada thistle?

7. Using the images provided, have you seen this species in your area?

8. Is the Canada thistle regulated in your state?

9. Which states rate the Canada thistle as a troublesome or common weed in one or more crops?

Go back to the "Distribution Maps" page showing the list of all invasive species. Find an invasive species that is found in your county. Some widely distributed invasives that may occur include: tree-of-heaven (ailanthus), Japanese or bush honeysuckle, purple loosestrife, European common reed (phragmites), and tamarisk. You can go directly to the county map by clicking on "County" under "View."

10. Which invasive species is found in or near your county? Is this species a plant, insect, disease, or wildlife?

11. Have any reported observations been submitted? If so, how many?

12. Click on "Species Information" near the top of the page. In general terms, what does this invasive species look like? What is the ecological threat associated with this species, if any?

▲**Figure 20.24 Freeway through the Puerto Rican rain forest.** Humans are Earth's most powerful agent of geomorphic and biotic change. The human denominator influences all biomes and all Earth systems.
[Bobbé Christopherson.]

A | Maps in This Text and Topographic Maps

Maps in This Text

Geosystems uses several map projections to present different types of data: for example, Goode's homolosine, Robinson, and Miller cylindrical. **Goode's homolosine projection** is an interrupted world map designed in 1923 by Dr. J. Paul Goode of the University of Chicago and first used in the Rand McNally *Goode's Atlas* in 1925. This equal-area map projection (**Figure A.1**) is a combination of two oval projections, which together make the projection excellent for mapping spatial distributions when interruptions of oceans or continents do not pose a problem.

In the Goode's homolosine projection, two equal-area projections are cut and pasted together to improve the rendering of landmass shapes. A *sinusoidal projection* is used between 40° N and 40° S latitude. Its central meridian is a straight line; all other meridians are drawn as sinusoidal curves (based on sine-wave curves), and parallels are evenly spaced. A *Mollweide projection*, also called a *homolographic projection*, is used from 40° N latitude to the North Pole and from 40° S latitude to the South Pole. Its central meridian is a straight line; all other meridians are drawn as elliptical arcs, and parallels are unequally spaced—farther apart at the equator, closer together poleward. This technique of combining two projections preserves areal size relationships.

Examples of the Goode's homolosine projection in *Geosystems* include the world climate maps in Chapter 9, the continental shield map in Chapter 12 (Figure 12.2), the world karst map in Chapter 13 (Figure 13.18), the world loess deposits map in Chapter 15 (Figure 15.13), and the terrestrial biomes map in Chapter 20 (Figure 20.10).

This text also uses the **Robinson projection**, designed by Arthur Robinson in 1963. This projection is neither equal area nor true shape, but is a compromise between the two (**Figure A.2**). The North and South Poles appear as lines slightly more than half the length of the equator; thus, higher latitudes are exaggerated less than on other oval and cylindrical projections.

Examples of the Robinson projection in *Geosystems* include the latitudinal geographic zones map in Chapter 1 (Figure 1.14), the daily net radiation map in Chapter 2 (Figure 2.13), the world temperature range map in Chapter 4 (Figure 4.31), and the maps of lithospheric plates and volcanoes and earthquakes in Chapter 11 (Figures 11.25 and 11.27).

The **Miller cylindrical projection** is another compromise map used in this text (**Figure A.3**). This projection, which today frequently appears in world atlases, was first developed by Osborn Miller and presented by The American Geographical Society in 1942. This projection is neither true shape nor true area, but is a compromise that avoids the severe scale distortion of the Mercator. Examples of the Miller cylindrical projection in *Geosystems* include the world time zone map in Chapter 1 (Figure 1.18), global temperature maps in Chapter 4 (Figures 4.29 and 4.30), and the two global pressure maps in Chapter 5 (Figure 5.12).

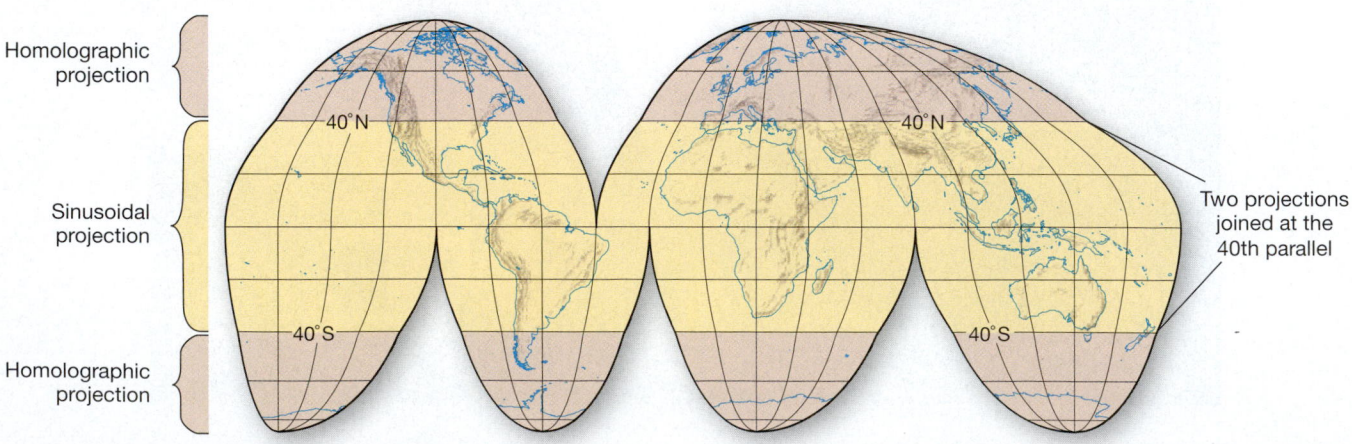

Homolographic projection

Sinusoidal projection

Homolographic projection

40°N   40°N

40°S   40°S

Two projections joined at the 40th parallel

Figure A.1 Goode's homolosine projection.
An equal-area projection.

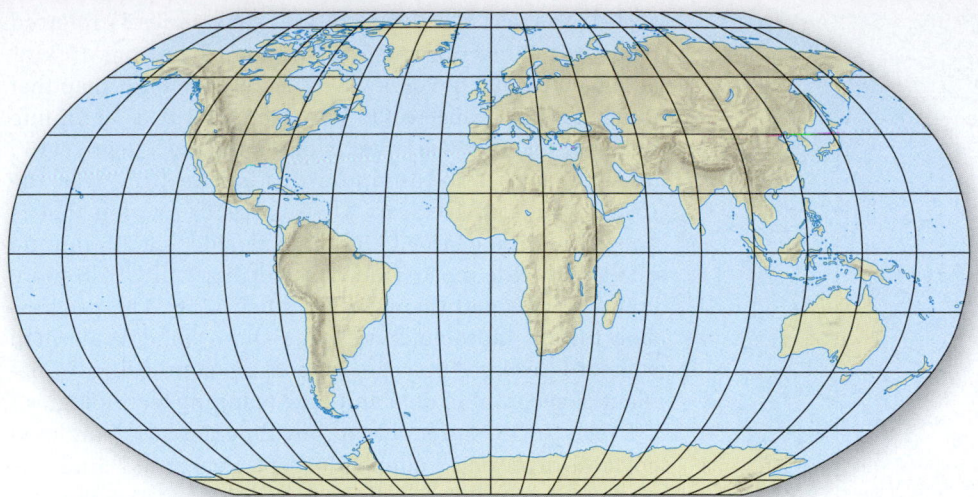

Figure A.2 **Robinson projection.**
A compromise map projection between equal area and true shape.

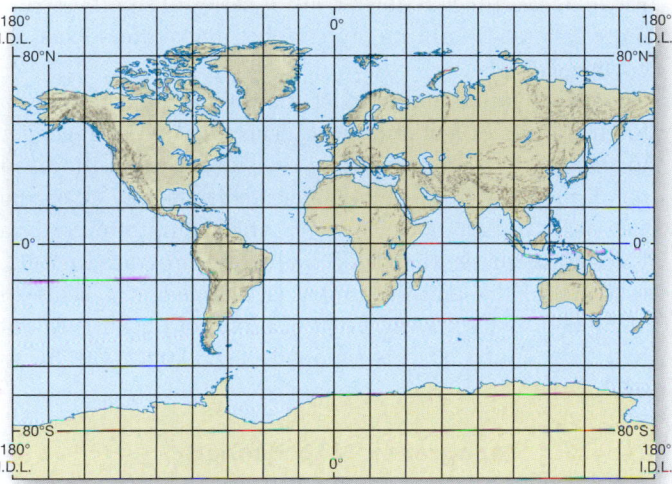

Figure A.3 **Miller cylindrical projection.**
A compromise map projection between equal area and true shape.

Quadrangles and Topographic Maps

The westward expansion across the vast North American continent demanded a land survey for the creation of accurate maps. Maps were needed to subdivide the land and to guide travel, exploration, settlement, and transportation. In 1785, the Public Lands Survey System began surveying and mapping government land in the United States. In 1836, the Clerk of Surveys in the Land Office of the Department of the Interior directed public-land surveys. The Bureau of Land Management replaced the Land Office in 1946. The actual preparation and recording of survey information fell to the U.S. Geological Survey (USGS), also a branch of the Department of the Interior (see http://www.usgs.gov/pubprod/maps.html).

In Canada, Natural Resources Canada conducts the national mapping program. Canadian mapping includes base maps, thematic maps, aeronautical charts, federal topographic maps, and the National Atlas of Canada, now online in its sixth edition (see http://atlas.nrcan.gc.ca/).

Quadrangle Maps

The USGS depicts survey information on quadrangle maps, so called because they are rectangular maps with four corner angles. The angles are junctures of parallels of latitude and meridians of longitude rather than political boundaries. These quadrangle maps utilize the Albers equal-area projection from the conic class of map projections.

The accuracy of conformality (shape) and scale of this base map is improved by the use of not one, but two, standard parallels. (Remember from Chapter 1 that standard lines are where the projection cone touches the globe's surface, producing greatest accuracy.) For the conterminous United States (the "lower 48"), these parallels are 29.5° N and 45.5° N latitude (noted on the Albers projection shown in Figure 1.19). The standard parallels shift for conic projections of Alaska (55° N and 65° N) and for Hawai'i (8° N and 18° N).

Because a single map of the United States at 1:24,000 scale would be more than 200 m wide (more than 600 ft), some system had to be devised for dividing the map into a manageable size. Thus, a quadrangle system using latitude and longitude coordinates was developed. Note that these maps are not perfect rectangles because meridians converge toward the poles. The width of quadrangles narrows noticeably as you move north (poleward).

Quadrangle maps are published in different series, covering different amounts of Earth's surface at different

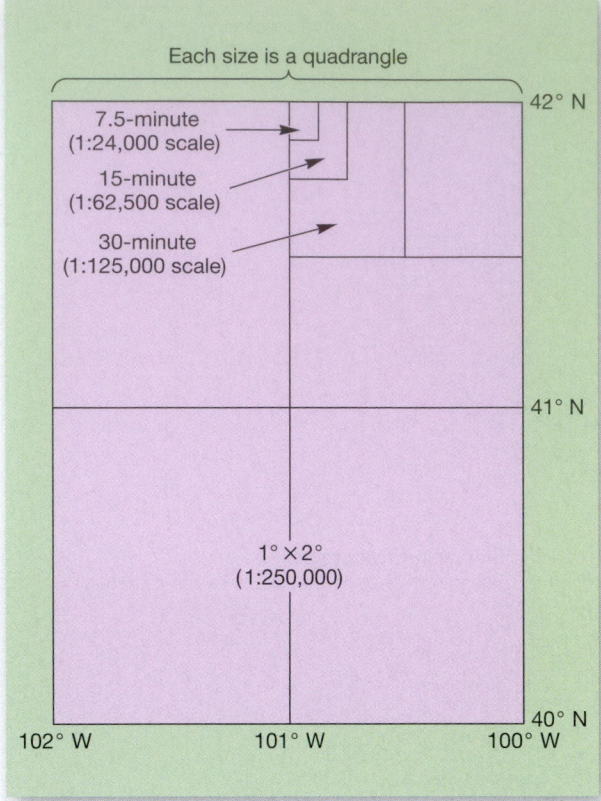

Figure A.4 Quadrangle system of maps used by the USGS.

scales. You see in **Figure A.4** that each series is referred to by its angular dimensions, which range from 1° × 2° (1:250,000 scale) to 7.5′ × 7.5′ (1:24,000 scale). A map that is one-half of a degree (30′) on each side is a 30-minute quadrangle, and a map that is one-fourth of a degree (15′) on each side is a 15-minute quadrangle (this was the USGS standard size from 1910 to 1950). A map that is one-eighth of a degree (7.5′) on each side is a 7.5-minute quadrangle, the most widely produced of all USGS topographic maps and the standard since 1950. The progression toward more-detailed maps and a larger-scale map standard through the years reflects the continuing refinement of geographic data and new mapping technologies.

The USGS National Mapping Program has completed coverage of the entire country (except Alaska) on 7.5-minute maps (1 in. to 2000 ft, a large scale). It takes 53,838 separate 7.5-minute quadrangles to cover the lower 48 states, Hawai'i, and the U.S. territories. A series of smaller-scale, more general 15-minute topographic maps offers Alaskan coverage.

In the United States, most quadrangle maps remain in English units of feet and miles. The eventual changeover to the metric system requires revision of the units used on all maps, with the 1:24,000 scale eventually changing to a scale of 1:25,000. However, after completing only a few metric quads, the USGS halted the program in 1991. In Canada, the entire country is mapped at a scale of 1:250,000, using metric units (1.0 cm to 2.5 km). About half the country also is mapped at 1:50,000 (1.0 cm to 0.50 km).

Topographic Map Symbols

The most popular and widely used quadrangle maps are *topographic maps* prepared by the USGS. An example of such a map is a portion of the Cumberland, Maryland, quad shown in **Figure A.5**. You will find several topographic maps throughout *Geosystems* because they portray landscapes effectively.

Figure A.6 shows the standard symbols and colors used on USGS topographic maps: black for human constructions, blue for water

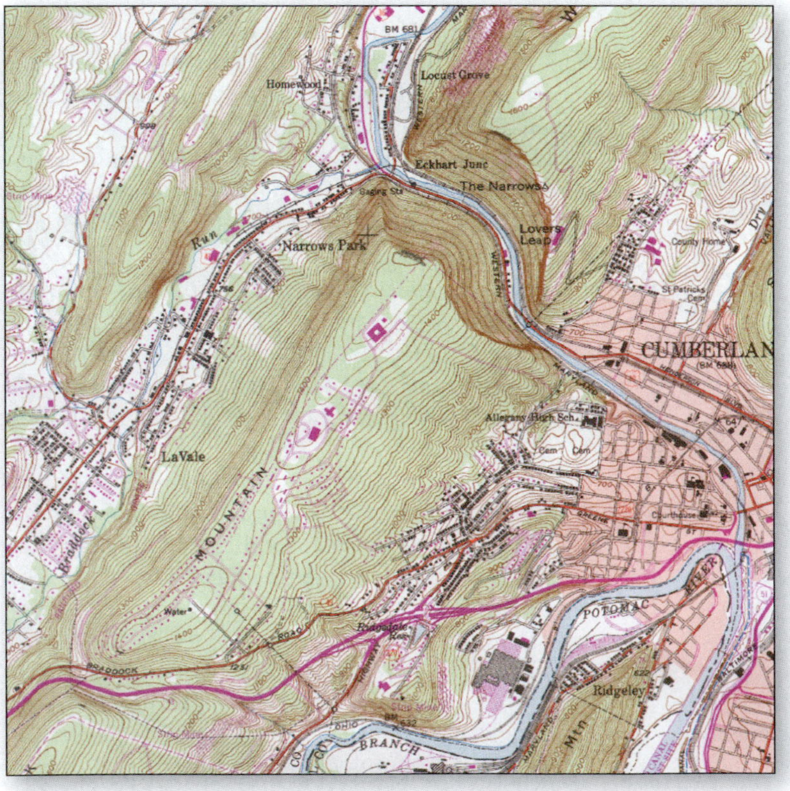

Figure A.5 An example of a topographic map from the Appalachians.
Cumberland, MD, PA, WV 7.5-minute quadrangle topographic map prepared by the USGS. In the *Applied Physical Geography*, 10/e lab manual, this topographic map is accessible through Google Earth so that you can see the topography in 3D, viewing it at any angle or scale you choose.

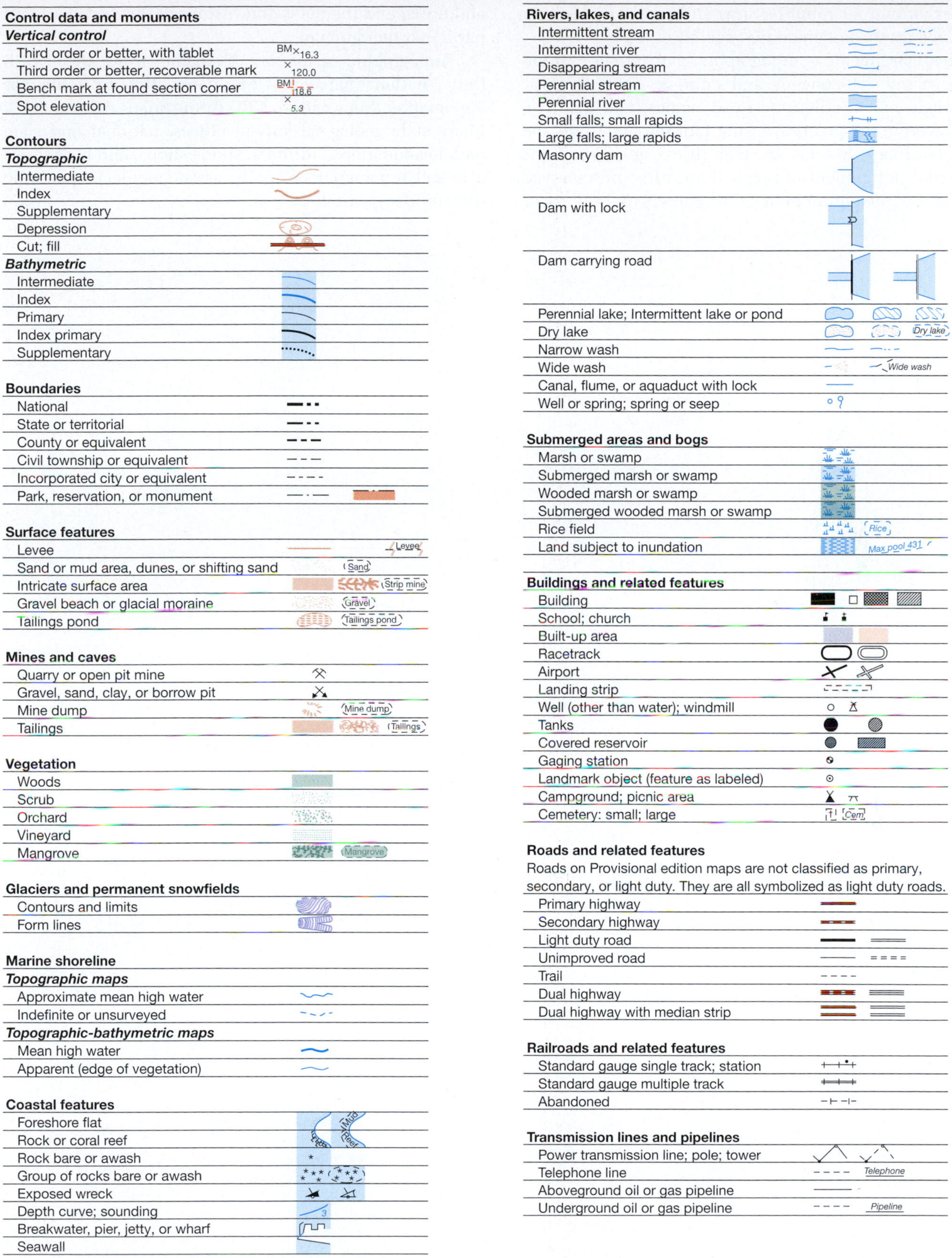

Control data and monuments

Vertical control

Third order or better, with tablet	BM ×16.3
Third order or better, recoverable mark	×120.0
Bench mark at found section corner	BM ×118.6
Spot elevation	×5.3

Contours

Topographic

Intermediate	
Index	
Supplementary	
Depression	
Cut; fill	

Bathymetric

Intermediate	
Index	
Primary	
Index primary	
Supplementary	

Boundaries

National	
State or territorial	
County or equivalent	
Civil township or equivalent	
Incorporated city or equivalent	
Park, reservation, or monument	

Surface features

Levee	Levee
Sand or mud area, dunes, or shifting sand	(Sand)
Intricate surface area	(Strip mine)
Gravel beach or glacial moraine	(Gravel)
Tailings pond	(Tailings pond)

Mines and caves

Quarry or open pit mine	
Gravel, sand, clay, or borrow pit	
Mine dump	(Mine dump)
Tailings	(Tailings)

Vegetation

Woods	
Scrub	
Orchard	
Vineyard	
Mangrove	(Mangrove)

Glaciers and permanent snowfields

Contours and limits	
Form lines	

Marine shoreline

Topographic maps

Approximate mean high water	
Indefinite or unsurveyed	

Topographic-bathymetric maps

Mean high water	
Apparent (edge of vegetation)	

Coastal features

Foreshore flat	Mud
Rock or coral reef	Reef
Rock bare or awash	*
Group of rocks bare or awash	
Exposed wreck	
Depth curve; sounding	3
Breakwater, pier, jetty, or wharf	
Seawall	

Rivers, lakes, and canals

Intermittent stream	
Intermittent river	
Disappearing stream	
Perennial stream	
Perennial river	
Small falls; small rapids	
Large falls; large rapids	
Masonry dam	
Dam with lock	
Dam carrying road	
Perennial lake; Intermittent lake or pond	
Dry lake	Dry lake
Narrow wash	
Wide wash	Wide wash
Canal, flume, or aquaduct with lock	
Well or spring; spring or seep	

Submerged areas and bogs

Marsh or swamp	
Submerged marsh or swamp	
Wooded marsh or swamp	
Submerged wooded marsh or swamp	
Rice field	Rice
Land subject to inundation	Max pool 431

Buildings and related features

Building	
School; church	
Built-up area	
Racetrack	
Airport	
Landing strip	
Well (other than water); windmill	
Tanks	
Covered reservoir	
Gaging station	
Landmark object (feature as labeled)	
Campground; picnic area	
Cemetery: small; large	Cem

Roads and related features

Roads on Provisional edition maps are not classified as primary, secondary, or light duty. They are all symbolized as light duty roads.

Primary highway	
Secondary highway	
Light duty road	
Unimproved road	
Trail	
Dual highway	
Dual highway with median strip	

Railroads and related features

Standard gauge single track; station	
Standard gauge multiple track	
Abandoned	

Transmission lines and pipelines

Power transmission line; pole; tower	
Telephone line	Telephone
Aboveground oil or gas pipeline	
Underground oil or gas pipeline	Pipeline

Figure A.6 Standardized topographic map symbols used on USGS maps.
English units still prevail, although a few USGS maps are in metric units. [USGS.]

features, brown for relief features and contours, pink for urbanized areas, and green for vegetation.

The margins of a topographic map contain information about its concept and content, including the quadrangle name, adjoining quad names, and quad series and type; the position in the latitude-longitude and other coordinate systems; the map title, legend, magnetic declination (alignment of magnetic north), and compass information; the datum plane; the symbols used for roads and trails; and the dates and history of the survey of that particular quadrangle.

Topographic maps are available from the USGS (http://nationalmap.gov/ustopo/index.html) or Centre for Topographic Information, NRC (http://maps.nrcan.gc.ca/). Many state geological survey offices, national and state park headquarters, outfitters, sports shops, and bookstores also sell topographic maps to assist people in planning their outdoor activities.

The Köppen Climate Classification System

Over a century ago, German climatologist and botanist Wladimir Köppen (1846–1940) designed a system for classifying climate that is still today the most widely used in teaching and research. The Köppen system is based on empirical data that are standardized and readily available. The classification uses average monthly temperatures, average monthly precipitation, and total annual precipitation to define each climate region. The system is most useful for identifying general climate patterns rather than for delineating precise climate boundaries (remember that climate boundaries are zones of gradual change, not abrupt transitions). The emphasis on general trends is especially important given the small scales used on world maps.

After initial publication of his system, Köppen collaborated with German climatologist Rudolph Geiger (1894–1981) to modify the climate zones, producing the *Köppen–Geiger climate classification*, first mapped in 1923. This map was revised numerous times until Geiger's last version in 1961.

In 2007, a team of Australian scientists published a comprehensive update of the Köppen–Geiger climate map, using 70 years of temperature and precipitation data from thousands of stations worldwide. We present this map in Figure B.1. On the world climate map in Chapter 9, Figure 9.3, we present the same map with the addition of the genetic, or causative, factors for each climate type (and without the Köppen lettering system). For additional maps and detailed information, see M. C. Peel, B. L. Finlayson, and T. A. McMahon, "Updated World Map of the Köppen–Geiger Climate Classification," *Hydrology and Earth System Sciences* 11 (2007): 1633–1644 (available at http://www.hydrol-earth -syst-sci.net/11/1633/2007/hess-11-1633-2007.pdf).

The Köppen Climate Types

The Köppen system uses capital letters (A, B, C, D, E) to designate primary climatic categories from the equator to the poles. Each category includes two or three subcategories with more specific climatic conditions. The guidelines for each of these categories and subcategories are in the margin of **Figure B.1**.

Four of the primary climates are based mainly on temperature characteristics:

A Tropical climates (rain forest, monsoon, and savanna)
C Mesothermal climates (humid subtropical, marine west coast, and Mediterranean)
D Microthermal climates (humid continental and subarctic)
E Polar climates (tundra and ice cap/ice sheet)

Only one primary climate is based mainly on moisture characteristics:

B Dry climates (deserts and semiarid steppes)

Within each capital letter climate category, additional lowercase letters designate specific temperature and precipitation conditions. For example, in a tropical rain forest (*Af*) climate, the *A* tells us that the average coolest month is above 18°C (64.4°F), and the *f* indicates that the weather is constantly wet, with the driest month receiving at least 6 cm (2.4 in.) of precipitation. (The designation *f* is from the German *feucht*, for "moist.") The map shows the distribution of the *Af* climate along the equator and equatorial rain forest.

In a *Dfa* climate, the *D* means that the average warmest month is above 10°C (50°F), with at least 1 month falling below 0°C (32°F); the *f* says that at least 3 cm (1.2 in.) of precipitation fall during every month; and the *a* indicates a warmest summer month averaging above 22°C (71.6°F). Thus, a *Dfa* climate is a humid continental hot-summer climate category within the microthermal category.

Highland climates, abbreviated *H* and discussed in Chapter 9, were not part of the Köppen climate classification until the 1953 revision by Geiger and German climatologist Wolfgang Pohl. Because the 2007 update in Figure B.1 is based on the Köppen–Geiger system, it does not include the highland climate type. However, many modern climate classification schemes include highland climates to represent the effects of altitude in mountain ranges at all latitudes.

Köppen Guidelines and Map

Take a few minutes to examine the climate classifications on the map in Figure B.1 and the criteria and considerations for each principal climate category in the colored boxes. Remember that the modified Köppen–Geiger system does not consider winds, temperature extremes, precipitation intensity, quantity of sunshine, cloud cover, or net radiation.

As a way to work through the climate types and distributions, first check the margin boxes for a primary climate type and examine its subcategories. Then check the distribution of that climate on the map. As a next step, consider the causal elements that produce this climate; refer to Chapter 9—Figure 9.3 and the colored boxes summarizing each major climate category— for help.

Figure B.1 World climates and their classification guidelines according to the Köppen system.

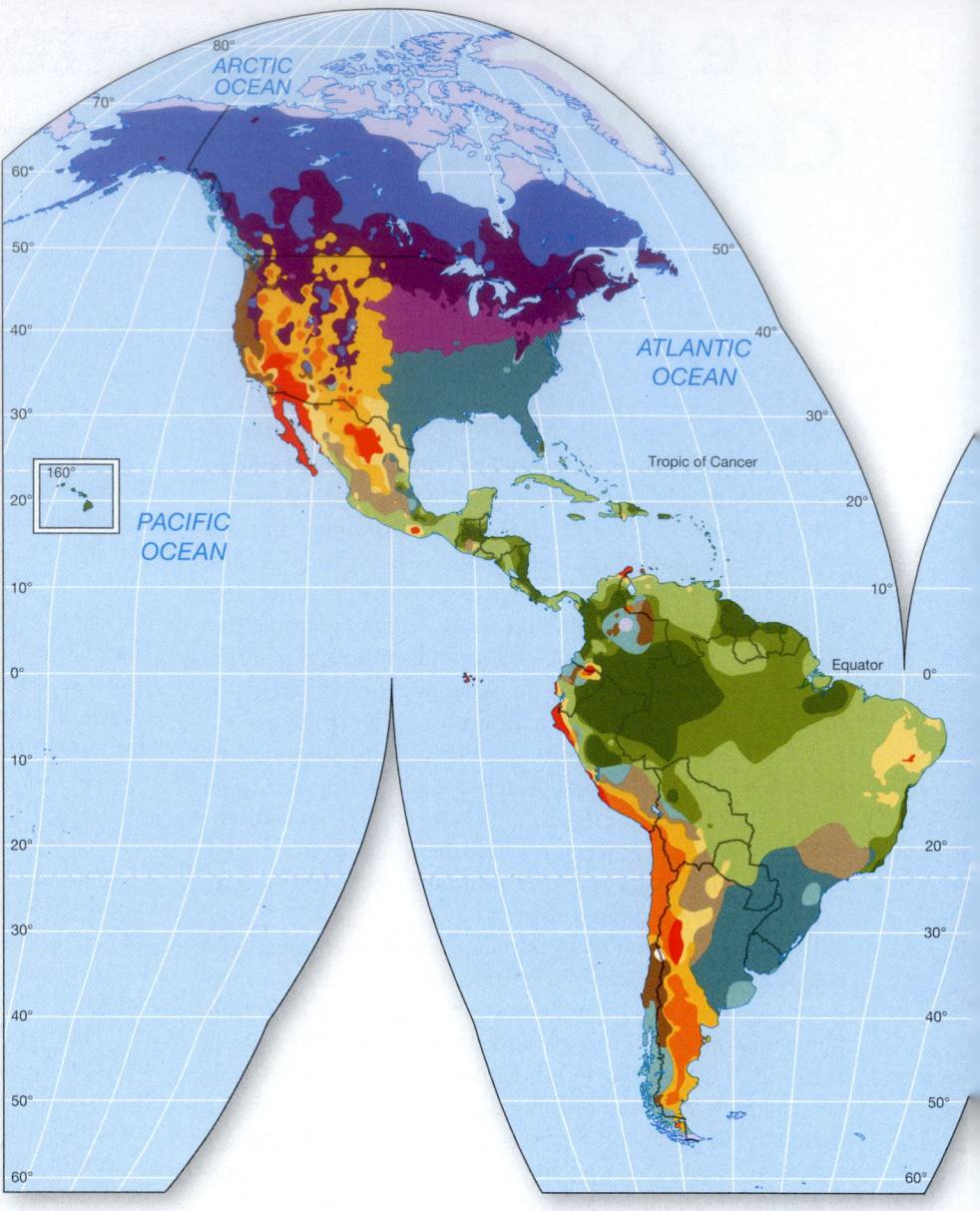

Köppen Guidelines
Tropical Climates—A

Consistently warm with all months averaging above 18°C (64.4°F); annual water supply exceeds water demand.

Af—Tropical rain forest
f = All months receive precipitation in excess of 6 cm (2.4 in.).

Am—Tropical monsoon
m = A marked short dry season with 1 or more months receiving less than 6 cm (2.4 in.) precipitation; an otherwise excessively wet rainy season. ITCZ 6–12 months dominant.

Aw — Tropical savanna
w = Summer wet season, winter dry season; ITCZ dominant 6 months or less, winter water-balance deficits.

Mesothermal Climates—C

Warmest month above 10°C (50°F); coldest month above 0°C (32°F), but below 18°C (64.4°F); seasonal climates.

Cfa — Humid subtropical, moist all year
Cwa, Cwb, Cwc—Humid subtropical, winter dry
f = Year-round precipitation.
w = Dry winter; wettest summer month with 10 times more precipitation than driest winter month.
a = Hot summer; warmest month above 22°C (71.6°F).
b = Warmest month below 22°C (71.6°F) with 4 months above 10°C.
c = 1–3 months above 10°C.

Cfb, Cfc—Marine west coast, mild-to-cool summer
f = Year-round precipitation.
b = Warmest month below 22°C (71.6°F) with 4 months above 10°C.
c = 1–3 months above 10°C.

Csa, Csb — Mediterranean dry summer
s = Pronounced dry summer with 70% of winter precipitation.
a = Hot summer with warmest month above 22°C (71.6°F).
b = Mild summer; warmest month below 22°C.

Microthermal Climates—D

Warmest month above 10°C (50°F); coldest month below 0°C (32°F); cool-to-cold conditions; snow climates. In Southern Hemisphere, occurs only in mountains.

Dwa, Dfa, Dsa—Humid continental, hot summer
Dwb, Dfb, Dsb—Humid continental, mild summer
w = Dry winter.
f = Year-round precipitation.
s = Dry summer.
a = Hot summer; warmest month above 22°C (71.6°F).
b = Mild summer; warmest month below 22°C (71.6°F).

Dwc, Dfc, Dsc—Subarctic, cool summer
Dwd, Dfd, Dsd—Subarctic, cold winter
w = Dry winter.
f = Year-round precipitation.
s = Dry summer.
c = 1–4 months above 10°C.
d = Coldest month below −38°C (−36.4°F), in Siberia only.

Arid and Semiarid Climates—B

Potential evapotranspiration* (natural moisture demand) exceeds precipitation (natural moisture supply) in all B climates. Subdivisions based on precipitation amount and mean annual temperature.

Arid Climates:
BWh — Hot low-latitude desert
BWk — Cold midlatitude desert
BW = Precipitation less than 1/2 natural moisture demand.
h = Mean annual temperature >18°C (64.4°F).
k = Mean annual temperature <18°C.

Semiarid climates:
BSh—Hot low-latitude steppe
BSk—Cold midlatitude steppe
BS = Precipitation more than 1/2 natural moisture demand, but not equal to it.
h = Mean annual temperature >18°C.
k = Mean annual temperature <18°C.

Polar Climates—E

Warmest month below 10°C (50°F); always cold; ice climates.

ET—Tundra
Warmest month 0–10°C (32–50°F); precipitation exceeds small potential evapotranspiration demand;* snow cover 8–10 months.

EF—Ice cap and ice sheet
Warmest month below 0°C (32°F); precipitation exceeds a very small potential evapotranspiration demand in the polar regions.

*Potential evapotranspiration is the amount of water that would evaporate or transpire if it were available—the natural moisture demand in an environment; see Chapter 8.

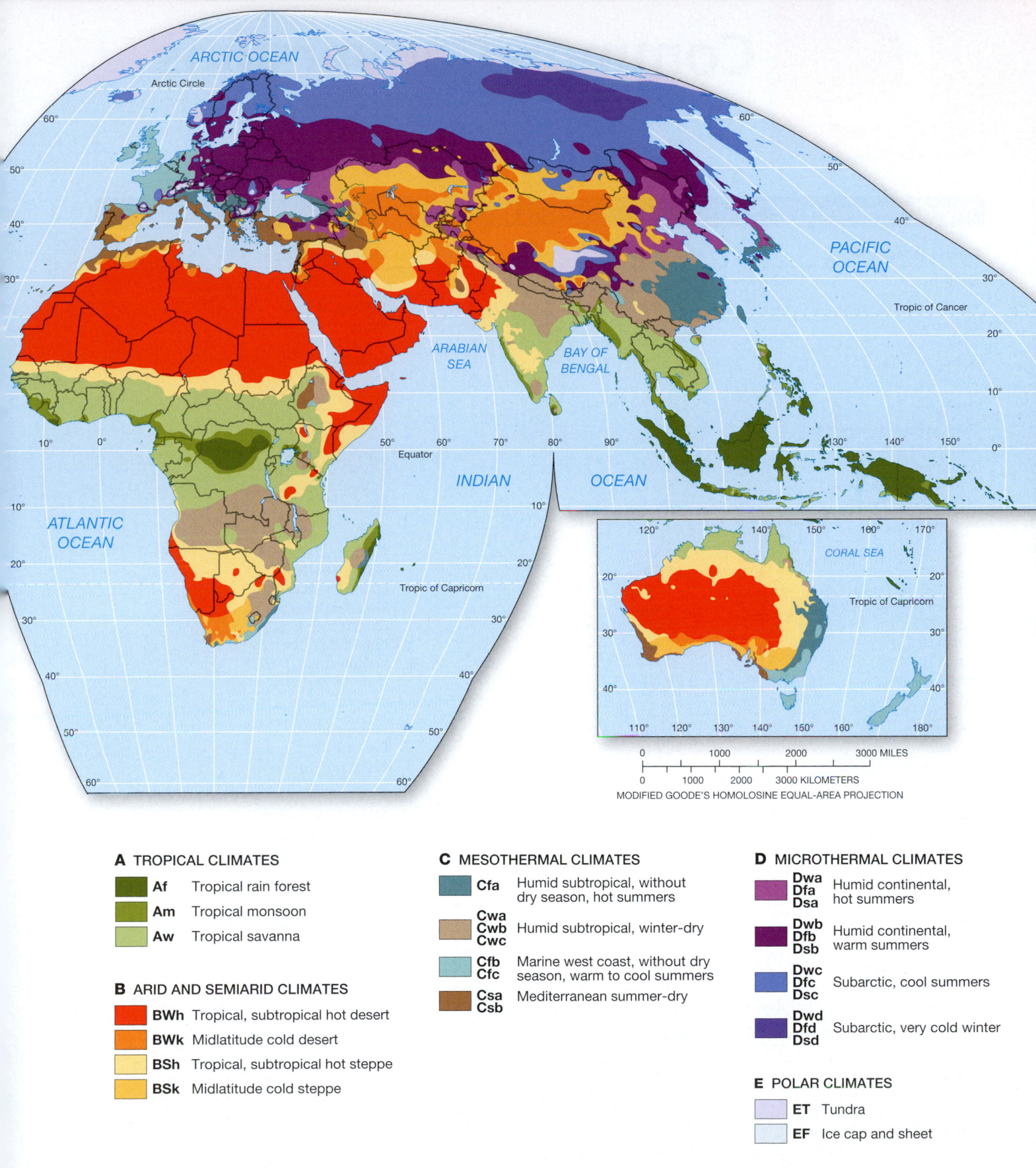

MODIFIED GOODE'S HOMOLOSINE EQUAL-AREA PROJECTION

A TROPICAL CLIMATES

	Af	Tropical rain forest
	Am	Tropical monsoon
	Aw	Tropical savanna

B ARID AND SEMIARID CLIMATES

	BWh	Tropical, subtropical hot desert
	BWk	Midlatitude cold desert
	BSh	Tropical, subtropical hot steppe
	BSk	Midlatitude cold steppe

C MESOTHERMAL CLIMATES

	Cfa	Humid subtropical, without dry season, hot summers
	Cwa **Cwb** **Cwc**	Humid subtropical, winter-dry
	Cfb **Cfc**	Marine west coast, without dry season, warm to cool summers
	Csa **Csb**	Mediterranean summer-dry

D MICROTHERMAL CLIMATES

	Dwa **Dfa** **Dsa**	Humid continental, hot summers
	Dwb **Dfb** **Dsb**	Humid continental, warm summers
	Dwc **Dfc** **Dsc**	Subarctic, cool summers
	Dwd **Dfd** **Dsd**	Subarctic, very cold winter

E POLAR CLIMATES

	ET	Tundra
	EF	Ice cap and sheet

C Common Conversions

Metric to English

Metric Measure	Multiply by	English Equivalent
Length		
Centimeters (cm)	0.3937	Inches (in.)
Meters (m)	3.2808	Feet (ft)
Meters (m)	1.0936	Yards (yd)
Kilometers (km)	0.6214	Miles (mi)
Nautical mile	1.15	Statute mile
Area		
Square centimeters (cm^2)	0.155	Square inches (in.^{2})
Square meters (m^2)	10.7639	Square feet (ft^2)
Square meters (m^2)	1.1960	Square yards (yd^2)
Square kilometers (km^2)	0.3831	Square miles (mi^2)
Hectare (ha) (10,000 m^2)	2.4710	Acres (a)
Volume		
Cubic centimeters (cm^3)	0.06	Cubic inches (in.^{3})
Cubic meters (m^3)	35.30	Cubic feet (ft^3)
Cubic meters (m^3)	1.3079	Cubic yards (yd^3)
Cubic kilometers (km^3)	0.24	Cubic miles (mi^3)
Liters (l)	1.0567	Quarts (qt), U.S.
Liters (l)	0.88	Quarts (qt), Imperial
Liters (l)	0.26	Gallons (gal), U.S.
Liters (l)	0.22	Gallons (gal), Imperial
Mass		
Grams (g)	0.03527	Ounces (oz)
Kilograms (kg)	2.2046	Pounds (lb)
Metric ton (tonne) (t)	1.10	Short ton (tn), U.S.
Velocity		
Meters/second (mps)	2.24	Miles/hour (mph)
Kilometers/hour (kmph)	0.62	Miles/hour (mph)
Knots (kn) (nautical mph)	1.15	Miles/hour (mph)
Temperature		
Degrees Celsius (°C)	1.80 (then add 32)	Degrees Fahrenheit (°F)
Celsius degree (C°)	1.80	Fahrenheit degree (F°)
Additional water measurements:		
Gallon (Imperial)	1.201	Gallon (U.S.)
Gallons (gal)	0.000003	Acre-feet

1 cubic foot per second per day = 86,400 cubic feet = 1.98 acre-feet

Additional Energy and Power Measurements

1 watt (W) = 1 joule/s

1 joule = 0.239 calorie

1 calorie = 4.186 joules

1 W/m^2 = 0.001433 cal/min

697.8 W/m^2 = 1 cal/cm^{2}min^{-1}

1 W/m^2 = 2.064 cal/cm^{2}day^{-1}

1 W/m^2 = 61.91 cal/cm^{2}month^{-1}

1 W/m^2 = 753.4 cal/cm^{2}year^{-1}

100 W/m^2 = 75 kcal/cm^{2}year^{-1}

Solar constant:

1372 W/m^2

2 cal/cm^{2}min^{-1}

English to Metric

English Measure	Multiply by	Metric Equivalent
Length		
Inches (in.)	2.54	Centimeters (cm)
Feet (ft)	0.3048	Meters (m)
Yards (yd)	0.9144	Meters (m)
Miles (mi)	1.6094	Kilometers (km)
Statute mile	0.8684	Nautical mile
Area		
Square inches (in.^{2})	6.45	Square centimeters (cm^2)
Square feet (ft^2)	0.0929	Square meters (m^2)
Square yards (yd^2)	0.8361	Square meters (m^2)
Square miles (mi^2)	2.5900	Square kilometers (km^2)
Acres (a)	0.4047	Hectare (ha)
Volume		
Cubic inches (in.^{3})	16.39	Cubic centimeters (cm^3)
Cubic feet (ft^3)	0.028	Cubic meters (m^3)
Cubic yards (yd^3)	0.765	Cubic meters (m^3)
Cubic miles (mi^3)	4.17	Cubic kilometers (km^3)
Quarts (qt), U.S.	0.9463	Liters (l)
Quarts (qt), Imperial	1.14	Liters (l)
Gallons (gal), U.S.	3.8	Liters (l)
Gallons (gal), Imperial	4.55	Liters (l)
Mass		
Ounces (oz)	28.3495	Grams (g)
Pounds (lb)	0.4536	Kilograms (kg)
Short ton (tn), U.S.	0.91	Metric ton (tonne) (t)
Velocity		
Miles/hour (mph)	0.448	Meters/second (mps)
Miles/hour (mph)	1.6094	Kilometers/hour (kmph)
Miles/hour (mph)	0.8684	Knots (kn) (nautical mph)
Temperature		
Degrees Fahrenheit (°F)	0.556 (after subtracting 32)	Degrees Celsius (°C)
Fahrenheit degree (F°)	0.556	Celsius degree (C°)
Additional water measurements:		
Gallon (U.S.)	0.833	Gallons (Imperial)
Acre-feet	325,872	Gallons (gal)

Additional Notation

Multiples		Prefixes	
$1,000,000,000 = 10^9$	giga	G	
$1,000,000 = 10^6$	mega	M	
$1,000 = 10^3$	kilo	k	
$100 = 10^2$	hecto	h	
$10 = 10^1$	deka	da	
$1 = 10^0$			
$0.1 = 10^{-1}$	deci	d	
$0.01 = 10^{-2}$	centi	c	
$0.001 = 10^{-3}$	milli	m	
$0.000001 = 10^{-6}$	micro	μ	

GLOSSARY

Terms that appear as **boldfaced** within the text are listed below, followed by a specific definition relevant to the term's usage in the chapter.

A

Aa (12) Rough, jagged basaltic lava with sharp edges. This texture is caused by the loss of trapped gases, a slow flow, and the development of a thick skin that cracks into the jagged surface.

Ablation (17) Loss of glacial ice through melting and evaporation, sublimation, or the calving of blocks of ice at the glacier's toe.

Abrasion (14, 15, 17) A type of erosion that breaks up rock particles and wears away bedrock, accomplished by the rolling and grinding of particles carried in a stream, removed by wind in a "sandblasting" action, or imbedded in glacial ice.

Absorption (4) Assimilation and conversion of radiation from one form to another in a medium. In the process, the temperature of the absorbing surface is raised, thereby affecting the rate and wavelength of radiation emitted from that surface.

Active layer (17) A zone of seasonally frozen ground that exists between the subsurface permafrost layer and the ground surface. The active layer is subject to consistent daily and seasonal freeze–thaw cycles. (*See* Permafrost, Periglacial.)

Actual evapotranspiration (AE) (8) The actual amount of evaporation and transpiration occurring at any given location; derived in the water balance by subtracting the deficit from potential evapotranspiration (PE).

Adhesion (6) The attraction of molecules of one kind for molecules of another kind; in water, adhesion causes capillary action in which water moves upward against gravity as water molecules stick to the molecules of other substances, such as paper, glass, or soil.

Adiabatic (6) Pertaining to the change in temperature of a vertically moving parcel of air—cooling by expansion as it rises or heating by compression as it sinks—occurring without any exchange of heat between the air parcel and the surrounding environment.

Advection (4) Horizontal movement of air or water from one place to another. (*Compare* Convection.)

Advection fog (6) Active condensation formed when warm, moist air moves laterally over cooler water or land surfaces, causing the lower layers of the air to be chilled to the dew-point temperature.

Aerosols (3) Small particles of dust, soot, and pollution suspended in the air.

Aggradation (14) The general building of a land surface because of deposition of material; opposite of degradation. When the sediment load of a stream exceeds the stream's capacity to carry it, the stream channel accumulates material through this process.

Air (3) A simple mixture of gases (N, O, Ar, CO_2, and trace gases) that is naturally odorless, colorless, tasteless, and formless, blended so thoroughly that it behaves as if it were a single gas.

Air mass (7) A distinctive, homogeneous body of air that has taken on the moisture and temperature characteristics of its source region.

Air pressure (3, 5) Pressure produced by the motion, size, and number of gas molecules in the air and exerted on surfaces in contact with the air. (*See* Atmospheric pressure.)

Albedo (4) The reflective quality of a surface, expressed as the percentage of reflected insolation out of the total incoming insolation; a function of surface color, angle of incidence, and surface texture.

Aleutian low (5) *See* Subpolar low.

Alfisols (18) A soil order in the Soil Taxonomy. Moderately weathered forest soils, with productivity dependent on specific patterns of moisture and temperature; rich in organics. Most widespread of the soil orders.

Alluvial fan (15) Fan-shaped fluvial landform at the mouth of a canyon; generally occurs in arid landscapes with intermittent streamflow. (*See* Bajada.)

Alluvial terraces (14) Level areas composed of alluvium that appear as topographic steps above a stream, produced by erosion as the stream downcuts into its floodplain after stream rejuvenation. (*See* Alluvium.)

Alluvium (14) General descriptive term for clay, silt, sand, gravel, or other unconsolidated rock and mineral fragments transported by running water and deposited as sorted or unsorted sediment on a streambed, floodplain, delta.

Alpine glacier (17) A glacier confined in a mountain valley or walled basin, consisting of three subtypes: valley glacier (within a valley), cirque glacier (forming at the head of a valley), and piedmont glacier (valley glaciers that coalesce at the base of a mountain range, spreading freely over nearby lowlands). (*Compare* Ice sheet).

Alpine tundra (20) A biome occurring at high elevations above treeline in mountains outside of the Arctic region; characterized by dwarf shrubs and low, ground-hugging herbaceous plants. (*See* Arctic tundra.)

Altocumulus (6) Middle-altitude clouds composed of ice and water that occur in several forms: patchy rows, wave patterns, a "mackerel sky," or lens-shaped "lenticular" clouds.

Andisols (18) A soil order in the Soil Taxonomy. Volcanic soils derived from volcanic parent materials in areas of volcanic activity.

Anemometer (5) A device that measures wind speed using cups that are pushed by the wind. A vane anemometer measures wind speed and direction using a wind vane with an attached propeller. (*See* Wind vane.)

Aneroid barometer (5) A device that measures air pressure using a partially evacuated, sealed cell. (*See* Air pressure.)

Angle of repose (13) The angle at which a slope is inclined and beyond which downslope movement (slope failure) will occur. It is the limit of steepness on a slope, measured from a horizontal plane, and depends on the size, texture, and water content of the slope materials.

Antarctic Circle (2) At 66.5° S latitude, the northernmost parallel (in the Southern Hemisphere) that experiences a 24-hour period of darkness in winter or daylight in summer.

Antarctic high (5) A consistent high-pressure region centered over Antarctica; source region for an intense polar air mass that is dry and associated with the lowest temperatures on Earth.

Anthropogenic biome (20) A recent term for a biome modified by human activity; for example, by land-use practices related to agriculture, forestry, and urbanization.

Anticline (12) Arch-shaped, upward fold in which rock strata slope downward from the axis, or central ridge, of the fold. (*Compare* Syncline.)

Anticyclone (5) A dynamically or thermally caused area of high atmospheric pressure with descending and diverging airflows that rotate clockwise in the Northern Hemisphere and counterclockwise in the Southern Hemisphere. (*Compare* Cyclone.)

Aphelion (2) The point of Earth's greatest distance from the Sun in its elliptical orbit; reached on July 4 at a distance of 152,083,000 km (94.5 million mi); variable over a 100,000-year cycle. (*Compare* Perihelion.)

Aquifer (8) A subsurface body of permeable rock or sediments through which water can flow in amounts adequate for wells and springs.

Arctic amplification (4) The tendency for polar latitudes, especially the north polar region, to experience enhanced warming of air and water temperatures relative to the rest of Earth; the phenomenon results in part from the presence of snow and ice and related positive feedback loops.

Arctic Circle (2) At 66.5° N latitude, the southernmost parallel (in the Northern Hemisphere) that experiences a 24-hour period of darkness in winter or daylight in summer.

Arctic tundra (20) A biome in the northernmost portions of North America and northern Europe and Russia, featuring low, ground-level herbaceous plants, dwarf shrubs, and few trees. (*See* Alpine tundra.)

Arête (17) A sharp ridge that divides two cirque basins. Derived from "knife edge" in French, these form serrated ridges in glaciated mountains.

Aridisols (18) A soil order in the Soil Taxonomy. Desert soils typical of dry climates that are low in organic matter and dominated by calcification and salinization; the largest soil order in terms of area.

Artesian water (8) Pressurized groundwater that rises in a well or a rock structure above the local water table; may flow out onto the ground without pumping. (*See* Potentiometric surface.)

Artificial levee (14) Human-built earthen embankments along river channels, often constructed on top of natural levees.

Asthenosphere (11) Region of the upper mantle just below the lithosphere; the least rigid portion of Earth's interior and known as the plastic layer, flowing very slowly under extreme heat and pressure.

Atmosphere (1) The thin veil of gases surrounding Earth, which forms a protective boundary between outer space and the biosphere; generally considered to extend out about 480 km (300 mi) from Earth's surface.

Atmospheric pressure (3) The pressure exerted by the weight of air in Earth's atmosphere; an average force at sea level of 1 kg/cm^3 (14.7 lb/in^2). Normal sea-level pressure, as measured by the height of a column of mercury (Hg), is expressed as 1013.2 millibars, 760 mm of Hg, or 29.92 inches of Hg.

Atmospheric stability (6) The tendency of the atmosphere to either encourage or discourage vertical air movement; stable air parcels resist upward displacement, while unstable air parcels rise until they reach an altitude where the surrounding air has a similar temperature and density.

Aurora (2) A spectacular glowing light display in the ionosphere, stimulated by the interaction of the solar wind with principally oxygen and nitrogen gases and few other atoms at high latitudes; called *aurora borealis* in the Northern Hemisphere and *aurora australis* in the Southern Hemisphere.

Autumnal equinox (2) *See* September equinox.

Axial parallelism (2) The condition in which Earth's axis maintains the same alignment relative to the plane of the ecliptic and to Polaris, the North Star, and other stars throughout its entire orbit around the Sun; essentially, Earth "remains parallel to itself."

Axial tilt (2) Earth's axis tilts 23.5° from a perpendicular to the plane of the ecliptic (plane of Earth's orbit around the Sun).

Axis (2) An imaginary line, extending through Earth from the geographic North Pole to the geographic South Pole, around which Earth rotates.

Azores high (5) A subtropical high-pressure cell that forms in the Northern Hemisphere in the eastern Atlantic (*see* Bermuda high); associated with warm, clear water and large quantities of sargassum, a seaweed characteristic of the Sargasso Sea.

B

Badlands (15) Rugged terrain of slopes dissected by rills and gullies in arid and semiarid regions; usually in shales and siltstones that are easily eroded by overland flow from intense rainfall events.

Bajada (15) A continuous apron of coalesced alluvial fans, formed along the base of mountains in arid and semiarid climates. (*See* Alluvial fan.)

Barchan dune (15) A type of dune formed with tips pointing downwind, usually in areas with limited sand supply and little or no vegetation.

Barrier beach (16) Narrow, long, depositional feature generally composed of sand that forms offshore roughly parallel to the coast. (*See* Barrier island.)

Barrier island (16) A long, narrow offshore deposit of sand or sediment running parallel to the coastline and separated from it by a sound, inlet, or lagoon. (*See* Barrier beach.)

Barrier spit (16) A depositional landform that develops when transported sand or gravel in a barrier beach or island is deposited in long ridges that are attached at one end to the mainland and partially cross the mouth of a bay.

Basalt (11) A common fine-grained, extrusive igneous rock, comprising the bulk of the ocean-floor crust, lava flows, and volcanic forms; gabbro is its intrusive form.

Base flow (8) The portion of streamflow that consists of groundwater.

Base level (14) The level below which a stream cannot erode its valley; the ultimate base level is sea level.

Basin and Range Province (13) A large region of the U.S. West and Mexico recognized for its roughly parallel north-south-trending basins and mountain ranges, few permanent streams, and interior drainage.

Batholith (11) A large intrusive igneous body made up of multiple plutons that converge to form an expansive mass. (*See* Pluton.)

Bay barrier (16) An extensive barrier spit of sand or gravel that encloses a bay, cutting it off completely from the ocean and forming a lagoon; produced by littoral drift and wave action; sometimes referred to as a baymouth bar. (*See* Barrier spit, Lagoon.)

Beach (16) The relatively narrow strip along a coastline where sediment is reworked and deposited by waves and currents.

Beach drift (16) Material, such as sand, gravel, and shells, that is moved by the longshore current in the effective direction of the waves.

Bed load (14) Coarse materials that are dragged along the bed of a stream by traction or by the rolling and bouncing motion of saltation; involves particles too large to remain in suspension. (*See* Traction, Saltation.)

Bedrock (13) The rock of Earth's crust that lies below the soil and regolith, and is sometimes exposed at the surface as an outcrop.

Bergschrund (17) This forms when a crevasse or wide crack opens along the headwall of a glacier; most visible in summer when covering snow is gone.

Bermuda high (5) A subtropical high-pressure cell that forms in the western North Atlantic. (*See* Azores high.)

Biodiversity (19) Short for biological diversity, the variety of life on Earth or in a particular habitat or ecosystem. Includes species diversity (the number and variety of different species), genetic diversity (the amount of genetic variation within these species), and ecosystem diversity (the number and variety of ecosystems, habitats, and communities on a landscape scale).

Biogeochemical cycle (19) One of several circuits of continuously cycling chemical elements and materials (carbon, oxygen, nitrogen, phosphorus, water) through Earth's living and nonliving systems.

Biogeographic realm (20) A geographic region, sometimes called an ecozone, where a group of associated plant and animal species evolved; a broad geographical classification scheme.

Biogeography (19) The study of the distribution of plants and animals and related ecosystems; the geographical relationships with their environments over time.

Biomass (19) The total mass of living organisms on Earth or per unit area of a landscape; also the weight of the living organisms in an ecosystem.

Biome (20) A large-scale, stable, terrestrial or aquatic ecosystem classified according to the predominant vegetation type and the adaptations of particular organisms to that environment.

Biosphere (1) That area where the atmosphere, lithosphere, and hydrosphere function together to form the context within which life exists; an intricate web that connects all organisms with their physical environment.

Boreal forest (20) A biome composed mainly of needleleaf trees (pine, spruce, fir, and larch), sometimes called the northern needleleaf forest. Occurs mainly in microthermal climates in North America, from the east coast of Canada westward to Alaska, and Eurasia, from Siberia westward across the entire extent of Russia to the European Plain.

Brackish (16) Descriptive of seawater with a salinity of less than 30 parts per thousand (ppt), or 30‰; for example, the Baltic Sea. (*See* Salinity.)

Braided stream (14) A stream carrying a high sediment load that becomes a maze of interconnected channels. Braiding often occurs with a reduction of discharge that reduces a stream's transporting ability or with an increase in sediment load.

Breaker (16) The point where a wave's height exceeds its vertical stability and the wave breaks as it approaches the shore.

Brine (16) Seawater with a salinity greater than 50 parts per thousand (ppt), or 50‰; for example, brine pools on the ocean floor in the Red Sea. (*See* Salinity.)

Butte (15) A steep-sided landform that forms from the weathering and mass wasting of a mesa. The height of a butte is greater than its width. (*See* Mesa.)

C

Calcification (18) The accumulation of calcium carbonate or magnesium carbonate in the B and C soil horizons in arid and semiarid deserts and grasslands; the process forms an illuviated calcic horizon.

Caldera (12) An interior sunken portion of a composite volcano's crater; usually steep-sided and circular, sometimes containing a lake; also can be found in conjunction with shield volcanoes.

Calving (17) The process in which pieces of ice break free from the terminus of a tidewater glacier or ice sheet to form floating ice masses (icebergs) where glaciers meet an ocean, bay, or fjord.

Capillary water (8) Soil moisture, most of which is accessible to plant roots; held in the soil by cohesion of water molecules and adhesion between water molecules and soil. (*See also* Field capacity, Hygroscopic water, Wilting point.)

Carbon monoxide (CO) (3) An odorless, colorless, tasteless combination of carbon and oxygen produced by the incomplete combustion of fossil fuels or other carbon-containing substances.

Carbon sink (10) An area in Earth's atmosphere, hydrosphere, lithosphere, or biosphere where carbon is stored; also called a *carbon reservoir*.

Carbonation (13) A chemical weathering process in which weak carbonic acid (water and carbon dioxide) reacts with minerals that contain calcium, magnesium, potassium, and sodium (especially limestone), transforming them into carbonates.

Carnivore (19) A secondary consumer that principally eats meat for sustenance. (*Compare* Herbivore.)

Cartography (1) The making of maps and charts; a specialized science and art that blends aspects of geography, engineering, mathematics, graphics, computer science, and artistic specialties.

Cation-exchange capacity (CEC) (18) The ability of soil colloids to exchange cations between their surfaces and the soil solution; a measured potential that indicates soil fertility. (*See* Soil colloid, Soil fertility.)

Cellular respiration (19) The process by which plants oxidize carbohydrates to derive energy for their operations; essentially, the reverse of the photosynthetic process; releases carbon dioxide, water, and heat energy into the environment. (*Compare* Photosynthesis.)

Chaparral (20) Dominant shrub formations of *Mediterranean* (dry summer) climates; characterized by sclerophyllous scrub and short, stunted, tough forests; derived from the Spanish *chaparro*; specific to California. (*See* Mediterranean shrubland.)

Chemical weathering (13) Decomposition and decay of the constituent minerals in rock through chemical alteration of those minerals. Processes include hydrolysis, oxidation, carbonation, and solution.

Chinook wind (7) North American term for a warm, dry, downslope airflow characteristic of the rain-shadow region on the leeward side of mountains. (*See* Rain shadow.)

Chlorofluorocarbons (CFCs) (3) Synthetic molecules containing chlorine, fluorine, and carbon that, when exposed to ultraviolet light, undergo chemical reactions that break down ozone molecules in the atmosphere.

Chlorophyll (19) A light-sensitive pigment that resides within chloroplasts (organelles) in leaf cells of plants; the basis of photosynthesis.

Cinder cone (12) A volcanic landform of pyroclastics and scoria, usually small and cone-shaped and generally not more than 450 m (1500 ft) in height, with a truncated top.

Circle of illumination (2) The division between light and dark on Earth; a day–night great circle.

Cirque (17) A scooped-out, amphitheater-shaped basin at the head of a valley glacier in a mountain region; an erosional landform.

Cirrus (6) Wispy, filamentous ice-crystal clouds that occur above 6000 m (20,000 ft); appear in a variety of forms, from feathery hairlike fibers to veils of fused sheets.

Classification (9) The process of ordering or grouping data or phenomena in related classes; results in a regular distribution of information; a taxonomy.

Climate (9) The consistent, long-term behavior of weather over time, including its variability; in contrast to weather, which is the condition of the atmosphere at any given place and time.

Climate change science (10) The interdisciplinary study of the causes and consequences of changing climate on Earth.

Climate feedback (10) A process that either amplifies or reduces a climatic trend toward either warming or cooling.

Climatic region (9) An area designated by broadly similar weather statistics, especially temperature and precipitation.

Climatology (9) The scientific study of climate and its variability, including long-term weather patterns over time (at least 30 years) and space. Also includes the causal factors that produce Earth's diverse climatic conditions and climate regions; as well as the effects of climate change on human society and culture.

Climograph (9) A graph that plots daily, monthly, or annual temperature and precipitation values for a selected station; may also include additional weather information.

Closed system (1) A system that is shut off from the surrounding environment, so that it is entirely self-contained in terms of energy and materials; Earth is a closed material system. (*Compare* Open system.)

Cloud (6) An aggregate of tiny water droplets and ice crystals suspended in the air and great enough in volume and concentration to be visible.

Cloud droplet (6) A tiny water droplet, typically 0.02 mm in diameter, that constitutes the initial composition of clouds. Cloud droplets form as rising air cools to the dew-point temperature, becomes saturated, and condenses on cloud-condensation nuclei in the lower atmosphere. (*See* Cloud-condensation nuclei.)

Cloud-albedo forcing (4) The cooling effect on Earth's surface temperatures caused by the increase in albedo (reflectivity) of clouds as they reflect insolation.

Cloud-condensation nuclei (6) Microscopic particles—such as dust, soot, or ash—necessary as matter on which water vapor condenses to form cloud droplets; giant cloud condensation nuclei, such as sea salt, have a diameter greater than 0.01 mm.

Cloud-greenhouse forcing (4) The warming effect on Earth's surface temperatures, known as greenhouse warming, caused by the insulating effect of clouds as they delay outgoing longwave (infrared) radiation.

Cohesion (6) The attraction of molecules for other molecules of the same kind, such as occurs between water molecules as a result of hydrogen bonding. Cohesion causes beading of water on hydrophobic surfaces and surface tension that allows a steel needle to float on a water surface.

Col (17) Formed by two headward-eroding cirques that reduce an arête (ridge crest) to form a high pass or saddlelike depression.

Cold desert and semidesert (20) A type of desert biome usually found at higher latitudes than warm deserts. Interior location and rain shadows produce these cold deserts in North America.

Cold front (7) The leading edge of an advancing cold air mass; identified on a weather map as a line marked with triangular spikes pointing in the direction of frontal movement. (*Compare* Warm front.)

Collision–coalescence process (6) The process by which raindrops form in clouds with temperatures above freezing. Updrafts of rising air force the condensation of water vapor onto cloud-condensation nuclei, which then move aloft, mixing and colliding to form raindrops that eventually fall under their own weight.

Community (19) A convenient biotic subdivision within an ecosystem; formed by interacting populations of animals and plants in an area.

Composite volcano (12) A volcano formed by a sequence of explosive volcanic eruptions; steep-sided, conical in shape; sometimes referred to as a stratovolcano, although composite is the preferred term. (*Compare* Shield volcano.)

Conduction (4) The slow molecule-to-molecule transfer of heat through a medium, from warmer to cooler portions.

Cone of depression (8) The depressed shape of the water table around a well after active pumping. The water table adjacent to the well is drawn down by the water removal.

Confined aquifer (8) An aquifer that is bounded above and below by impermeable layers of rock or sediment. (*See* Artesian water, Unconfined aquifer.)

Constant isobaric surface (5) An elevated surface in the atmosphere on which all points have the same pressure, usually 500 mb. Along this constant-pressure surface, isobars mark the paths of upper-air winds.

Consumer (19) Organism in an ecosystem that depends on producers (organisms that use carbon dioxide as their sole source of carbon) for its source of nutrients; also called a *heterotroph*. (*Compare* Producer.)

Consumptive use (8) A use that permanently removes water from a stream or water environment and makes it unavailable for further use. (*Compare* Nonconsumptive use.)

Continental divide (14) A ridge or elevated area that separates drainage on a continental scale; specifically, that ridge in North America that separates drainage to the Pacific on the west side from drainage to the Atlantic and Gulf on the east side and to Hudson Bay and the Arctic Ocean in the north.

Continental drift (11) A proposal by Alfred Wegener in 1912 stating that Earth's landmasses have migrated over the past 225 million years from a supercontinent he called Pangaea to the present configuration; the basis for plate tectonics theory. (*See* Plate tectonics.)

Continental shield (12) Generally, old, low-elevation heartland regions of continental crust; various cratons (granitic cores) and ancient mountains are exposed at the surface.

Contour lines (1) Isolines on a topographic map that connect all points at the same elevation relative to a reference elevation.

Convection (4) Transfer of heat from one place to another through the physical movement of air; involves a strong vertical motion. (*Compare* Advection.)

Convectional lifting (7) Air passing over warm surfaces gains buoyancy and lifts, initiating adiabatic processes.

Convergent lifting (7) Air flowing from different directions forces lifting and displacement of air upward, initiating adiabatic processes.

Coordinated Universal Time (UTC) (1) The official reference time in all countries, formerly known as Greenwich Mean Time; now measured by primary standard atomic clocks; the legal reference for time in all countries and broadcast worldwide.

Coral (16) A simple marine animal with a cylindrical, saclike body that includes a stomach with a single mouth opening. Hard corals secrete calcium carbonate to form a hard external skeleton. Corals live symbiotically with nutrient-producing single-celled organisms (zooxanthellae) that live within the coral tissues. (*See* Coral reef, Coral bleaching.)

Coral bleaching (16) The process whereby changes in environmental conditions cause corals to expel their symbiotic partners, single-celled zooxanthellae, and turn white. Corals can recover if conditions return to normal, but prolonged environmental stress causes corals to die.

Coral reef (16) A ridge or mound of marine rock that forms over long time periods from the deposition of calcium carbonate by living organisms, mainly corals but also algae and shellfish.

Core (11) The deepest inner portion of Earth, representing one-third of its entire mass; differentiated into two zones—a solid-iron inner core surrounded by a dense, molten, fluid metallic-iron outer core.

Coriolis force (5) The apparent deflection of moving objects (wind, ocean currents, missiles) from travelling in a straight path, in proportion to the speed of Earth's rotation at different latitudes. Deflection is to the right in the Northern Hemisphere and to the left in the Southern Hemisphere; maximum at the poles and zero along the equator.

Counterradiation (4) Within the Earth–atmosphere energy balance, the heat emitted from the atmosphere toward Earth's surface, a total amount that is more energy than is absorbed at the surface from insolation.

Crater (12) A circular surface depression formed by volcanism; built by accumulation, collapse, or explosion; usually located at a volcanic vent or pipe; can be at the summit or on the flank of a volcano.

Crevasse (17) A vertical crack that develops in a glacier as a result of friction between valley walls, or tension forces of extension on convex slopes, or compression forces on concave slopes.

Crust (11) Earth's outer shell of crystalline surface rock, ranging from 5 to 60 km (3 to 38 mi) in thickness from oceanic crust to mountain ranges. Average density of continental crust is 2.7 g/cm³, whereas oceanic crust is 3.0 g/cm³.

Cryosphere (1, 17) The frozen portion of Earth's waters, including ice sheets, ice caps and fields, glaciers, ice shelves, sea ice, and subsurface ground ice and frozen ground (permafrost).

Cumulonimbus (6) A towering, precipitation-producing cumulus cloud that is vertically developed across altitudes associated with other clouds; frequently associated with lightning and thunder and thus sometimes called a *thunderhead*.

Cumulus (6) Bright and puffy cumuliform clouds up to 2000 m (6500 ft) in altitude.

Cyclogenesis (7) An atmospheric process that describes the birth of a midlatitude cyclone, usually along the polar front. Also refers to strengthening and development of a midlatitude cyclone along the eastern slope of the Rockies, other north–south mountain barriers, and the North American and Asian east coasts. (*See* Midlatitude cyclone, Polar front.)

Cyclone (5) A dynamically or thermally caused area of low atmospheric pressure with ascending and converging airflows that rotate counterclockwise in the Northern Hemisphere and clockwise in the Southern Hemisphere. (*Compare* Anticyclone; *see* Midlatitude cyclone, Tropical cyclone.)

D

Daylength (2) Duration of exposure to insolation, varying during the year depending on latitude; an important aspect of seasonality.

Daylight saving time (1) Time is set ahead 1 hour in the spring and set back 1 hour in the fall in the Northern Hemisphere. In the United States and Canada, time is set ahead on the second Sunday in March and set back on the first Sunday in November—except in Hawai'i, Arizona, and Saskatchewan, which exempt themselves.

Dead zone (19) Low-oxygen conditions and limited marine life caused by excessive nutrient inputs in coastal oceans and lakes.

Debris avalanche (13) A high-speed flow of rock and debris, sometimes fluidized by ice in steep mountain regions. A type of mass movement classified as a flow; may become a debris flow as it moves downslope. (*See* Debris flow.)

Debris flow (13) A type of mass movement that flows downslope in a slurry of unconsolidated material, specifically a mixture of water and sediment that is mainly gravels, boulders, and other rock fragments coarser than sand, but also includes mud, silt, and sand. (*Compare* Mudflow.)

December solstice (2) The time when the Sun's declination is at the Tropic of Capricorn, at 23.5° S latitude, December 21–22 each year. The day is 24 hours long south of the Antarctic Circle. The night is 24 hours long north of the Arctic Circle. (*Compare* June solstice.)

Declination (2) The latitude that receives direct overhead (perpendicular) insolation on a particular day; the subsolar point migrates annually through 47° of latitude between the Tropics of Cancer (23.5° N) and Capricorn (23.5° S).

Decomposers (19) Bacteria and fungi that digest organic debris outside their bodies and absorb and release nutrients in an ecosystem. (*See* Detritivores.)

Deficit (8) In the water balance, a natural water shortage; the amount of unmet (unsatisfied) potential evapotranspiration (PE). (*See* Potential evapotranspiration.)

Deflation (15) A process of wind erosion that removes and lifts individual particles, literally blowing away unconsolidated, dry, or noncohesive sediments.

Degradation (14) The process occurring when sediment is eroded along a stream, causing channel incision.

Delta (14) A depositional plain formed where a river enters a lake or an ocean; named after the triangular shape of the Greek letter delta, Δ.

Dendroclimatology (10) The study of past climates using tree rings. The dating of tree rings by analysis and comparison of ring widths and coloration is *dendrochronology*.

Denudation (13) A general term that refers to all processes that cause degradation of the landscape: weathering, mass movement, erosion, and transport.

Deposition (14) The process whereby weathered, wasted, and transported sediments are laid down by gravity, wind, water, and ice.

Depositional coastline (16) A coastline formed by depositional processes, usually in a region where land is subsiding because of tectonic plate movement and long-term changes in sea level; also called an emergent coastline. (*Compare* Erosional coastline.)

Derecho (7) A destructive windstorm characterized by strong linear winds in excess of 93 kmph (58 mph) and a damage path at least 386 km (240 mi) long; associated with thunderstorms and bands of showers crossing a region.

Desalination (8) In a water resources context, the removal of organics, debris, and salinity from seawater through distillation or reverse osmosis to produce potable water.

Desert pavement (15) On arid landscapes, a surface formed when wind deflation and sheetflow remove smaller particles, leaving residual pebbles and gravels to concentrate at the surface; an alternative sediment-accumulation hypothesis explains some desert pavements; resembles a cobblestone street. (*See* Deflation, Sheetflow.)

Desertification (18) The expansion of deserts worldwide, related principally to poor agricultural practices (overgrazing and inappropriate agricultural practices), improper soil-moisture management, erosion and salinization, deforestation, and the ongoing climatic change; an unwanted semipermanent invasion into neighboring biomes.

Detritivores (19) Detritus feeders and decomposers that consume, digest, and destroy organic wastes and debris. *Detritus feeders*—worms, mites, termites, centipedes, snails, crabs, and even vultures, among others—consume detritus and excrete nutrients and simple inorganic compounds that fuel an ecosystem. (*Compare* Decomposers.)

Dew-point temperature (6) The temperature at which a given mass of air becomes saturated, holding the maximum amount of water vapor possible. Any further cooling or addition of water vapor results in active condensation.

Differential weathering (13) The effect of different resistances in rock, coupled with variations in the intensity of physical and chemical weathering.

Diffuse radiation (4) The downward component of scattered incoming insolation from clouds and the atmosphere.

Digital cartography (1) The practice of making maps using data collected and presented in a virtual image on a computer or mobile device; usually relies on GPS technology. (*See* Cartography.)

Discharge (14) The measured volume of flow in a river that passes by a given cross section of a stream in a given unit of time; expressed in cubic meters per second or cubic feet per second.

Dissolved load (14) Materials carried in chemical solution in a stream, derived from minerals such as limestone and dolomite or from soluble salts.

Drainage basin (14) The basic spatial geomorphic unit of a river system; distinguished from a neighboring basin by ridges and highlands that form divides, marking the limits of the catchment area of the drainage basin.

Drainage density (14) A measure of the overall operational efficiency of a drainage basin, determined by the ratio of combined channel lengths to the unit area.

Drainage pattern (14) A distinctive geometric arrangement of streams in a region, determined by slope, differing rock resistance to weathering and erosion, climatic and hydrologic variability, and structural controls of the landscape.

Drawdown (8) *See* Cone of depression.

Drought (8) An extended period of dry conditions caused by lower precipitation and higher temperatures than normal.

Drumlin (17) A depositional landform related to glaciation that is composed of till (unstratified, unsorted) and is streamlined in the direction of continental ice movement—blunt end upstream and tapered end downstream with a rounded summit.

Dry adiabatic rate (DAR) (6) The rate at which an unsaturated parcel of air cools (if ascending) or heats (if descending); a rate of 10 C° per 1000 m (5.5 F° per 1000 ft). (*See* Adiabatic; *compare* Moist adiabatic rate.)

Dune (15) A depositional feature of sand grains deposited in transient mounds, ridges, and hills; extensive areas of sand dunes are ergs, or sand seas.

Dust dome (3) A dome of airborne pollution associated with every major city; may be blown by winds into elongated plumes downwind from the city.

Dynamic equilibrium (1) Fluctuating operations in a system demonstrate a trend over time, a change in average conditions.

Dynamic equilibrium model (13) The balancing act between tectonic uplift and erosion, between the resistance of crust materials and the work of denudation processes. Landscapes evidence ongoing adaptation to rock structure, climate, local relief, and elevation.

E

Earth systems science (1) The science that seeks to understand Earth as an interacting set of physical, chemical, and biological systems.

Earthquake (12) A sharp release of energy that sends waves travelling through Earth's crust at the moment of rupture along a fault or in association with volcanic activity. The moment magnitude scale (formerly the Richter scale) estimates earthquake magnitude; intensity is described by the Mercalli scale.

Ebb tide (16) Falling or lowering tide during the daily tidal cycle. (*Compare* Flood tide.)

Ecological niche (19) The function, or operation, of a life form within a given ecological community.

Ecological succession (19) The process whereby different and usually more complex assemblages of plants and animals replace older and usually simpler communities; communities are in a constant state of change as each species adapts to changing conditions. Ecosystems do not exhibit a stable point or successional climax condition as previously thought. (*See* Primary succession, Secondary succession.)

Ecology (19) The science that studies the relations between organisms and their environment and among various ecosystems.

Ecosystem (19) A self-regulating association of living plants and animals and their nonliving physical and chemical environments.

Ecotone (20) A boundary transition zone between adjoining ecosystems that may vary in width and represent areas of tension as similar species of plants and animals compete for the resources. (*See* Ecosystem.)

Effusive eruption (12)   A volcanic eruption characterized by low-viscosity basaltic magma and low-gas content, which readily escapes. Lava pours forth onto the surface with relatively small explosions and few pyroclastics; tends to form shield volcanoes. (*See* Shield volcano, Lava, Pyroclastics; *compare* Explosive eruption.)

El Niño–Southern Oscillation (ENSO) (5)   Sea-surface temperatures increase, sometimes more than 8 C° (14 F°) above normal in the central and eastern Pacific, replacing the normally cold, nutrient-rich water along Peru's coastline. Pressure patterns and surface ocean temperatures shift from their usual locations across the Pacific, forming the Southern Oscillation.

Elastic-rebound theory (12)   A concept describing the faulting process in Earth's crust, in which the two sides of a fault appear locked despite the motion of adjoining pieces of crust, but with accumulating strain, they rupture suddenly, snapping to new positions relative to each other, generating an earthquake.

Electromagnetic spectrum (2)   All the radiant energy produced by the Sun placed in an ordered range, divided according to wavelengths.

Eluviation (18)   The removal of finer particles and minerals from the upper horizons of soil; an erosional process within a soil body. (*Compare* Illuviation.)

Endemic species (20)   Plant or animal species that occupy only one geographic location on Earth. (*Compare* Invasive species.)

Endogenic system (11)   The system internal to Earth, driven by radioactive heat derived from sources within the planet. In response, the surface fractures, mountain building occurs, and earthquakes and volcanoes are activated. (*Compare* Exogenic system.)

Entisols (18)   A soil order in the Soil Taxonomy. Specifically lacks vertical development of horizons; usually young or undeveloped. Found in active slopes, alluvial-filled floodplains, and poorly drained tundra.

Environmental lapse rate (3)   The actual rate of temperature decrease with increasing altitude in the lower atmosphere at any particular time under local weather conditions; may deviate above or below the average lapse rate of 6.4 C° per km, or 1000 m (3.5 F° per 1000 ft). (*Compare* Lapse rate.)

Eolian (16)   Relating to, caused by, or carried by wind; Eolian processes refer to the erosion and deposition of materials by wind; also spelled *aeolian*.

Epicenter (12)   The location on Earth's surface directly above the focus of an earthquake. (*See* Focus.)

Epipedon (18)   The diagnostic soil horizon that forms at the surface; not to be confused with the A horizon; may include all or part of the illuviated B horizon.

Equal area (1, Appendix A)   A trait of a map projection; indicates the equivalence of all areas on the surface of the map, although shape is distorted. (*See* Map projection.)

Equatorial low (5)   A thermally caused low-pressure area that almost girdles Earth, with air converging and ascending all along its extent; also called the *intertropical convergence zone (ITCZ)*.

Erg (16)   An extensive area of sand and dunes, also called a *sand sea*; from the Arabic word for "dune field."

Erosion (14)   Denudation by wind, water, or ice, which dislodges, dissolves, or removes surface material.

Erosional coastline (16)   A rugged, high-relief, tectonically active coastline formed by erosional processes as land is uplifted or exposed by changes in sea level. (*Compare* Depositional coastline.)

Esker (17)   A sinuously curving, narrow deposit of coarse gravel that forms along a meltwater stream channel, developing in a tunnel beneath a glacier.

Estuary (14)   The point at which the mouth of a river enters the sea, where freshwater and seawater are mixed; a place where tides ebb and flow.

Eustasy (8)   Refers to worldwide changes in sea level that are related not to movements of land, but rather to changes in the volume of water in the oceans.

Eutrophication (19)   The gradual enrichment of water bodies that occurs with nutrient inputs, either natural or human-caused.

Evaporation (8)   The movement of free water molecules away from a wet surface into air that is less than saturated; the phase change of water to water vapor.

Evaporation fog (6)   A fog formed when cold air flows over the warm surface of a lake, ocean, or other body of water; forms as the water molecules evaporate from the water surface into the cold, overlying air; also known as steam fog or sea smoke.

Evapotranspiration (8)   The merging of evaporation and transpiration water loss into one term. (*See* Potential evapotranspiration, Actual evapotranspiration.)

Evolution (19)   A theory that single-cell organisms adapted, modified, and passed along inherited changes to multicellular organisms. The genetic makeup of successive generations is shaped by environmental factors, physiological functions, and behaviors that created a greater rate of survival and reproduction and were passed along through natural selection.

Exfoliation (13)   The physical weathering process that occurs as mechanical forces enlarge joints in rock into layers of curved slabs or plates, which peel or slip off in sheets; also called *sheeting*.

Exogenic system (11)   Earth's external surface system, powered by insolation, which energizes air, water, and ice and sets them in motion, under the influence of gravity. Includes all processes of landmass denudation. (*Compare* Endogenic system.)

Exosphere (3)   An extremely rarefied outer atmospheric halo beyond the thermopause at an altitude of 480 km (300 mi); probably composed of hydrogen and helium atoms, with some oxygen atoms and nitrogen molecules present near the thermopause.

Explosive eruption (12)   A violent and unpredictable volcanic eruption, the result of magma that is thicker (more viscous), stickier, and higher in gas and silica content than that of an effusive eruption; tends to form blockages within a volcano; produces composite volcanic landforms. (*See* Composite volcano; *compare* Effusive eruption.)

Extinction (19)   The point at which the last individual of a species dies; the end of an organism or group of organisms.

Extrusive igneous rock (11)   A rock that solidifies and crystallizes from a molten state as it extrudes onto the surface, such as basalt.

F

Faulting (12)   The process whereby displacement and fracturing occur between two portions of Earth's crust; usually associated with earthquake activity.

Feedback loop (1)   Created when a portion of system output is returned as an information input, causing changes that guide further system operation. (*See* Negative feedback, Positive feedback.)

Field capacity (8)   Water held in the soil by hydrogen bonding against the pull of gravity, remaining after water drains from the larger pore spaces; the available water for plants. (*See* Available water, Capillary water.)

Fire ecology (19)   The study of fire as a natural agent and dynamic factor in community succession.

Firn (17)   Snow of a granular texture that is transitional in the slow transformation from snow to glacial ice; snow that has persisted through a summer season in the zone of accumulation.

Firn line (17)   The elevation on a glacier above which winter snow and ice remain intact throughout the summer melt season but below which summer melting occurs.

Fjord (17)   A drowned glaciated valley, or glacial trough, along a seacoast.

Flash flood (14)   A sudden and short-lived local high streamflow that fills a channel; can occur in any environment, but often associated with arid and semiarid washes.

Flood (14)   A high water level that overflows the natural riverbank along any portion of a stream.

Flood basalt (12)   A type of effusive eruption that occurs when magma flows out from elongated fissures onto the surface and cools into extensive sheets of basaltic lava; associated with hot spots and continental rift valleys. (*See* Basalt.)

Flood tide (16)   Rising tide during the daily tidal cycle. (*Compare* Ebb tide.)

Floodplain (14)   A flat, low-lying fluvial landform composed of alluvium along a stream or river channel, created by and subject to recurrent flooding.

Fluvial (14)   Stream-related processes; from the Latin *fluvius* meaning "river."

Focus (12)   The location below Earth's surface where the motion of seismic waves that cause an earthquake begins; also called the *hypocenter*.

Fog (6)   A cloud, generally stratiform, in contact with the ground, with visibility usually reduced to less than 1 km (3300 ft).

Folding (12)   The bending and deformation of beds of rock strata subjected to compressional forces.

Food chain (19)   The circuit along which energy flows from producers (plants), which manufacture their own food, to consumers (animals); a one-directional flow of chemical energy, ending with decomposers.

Food web (19)   A complex network of interconnected food chains. (*See* Food chain.)

Formation class (20)   The dominant vegetation type extending across a region.

Freezing nuclei (6)   Tiny atmospheric particles upon which water vapor deposits (changes phase from vapor to solid) to form ice crystals.

Friction force (5)   The effect of drag by the wind as it moves across a surface; may be operative through 500 m (1600 ft) of altitude. Surface friction slows the wind and therefore reduces the effectiveness of the Coriolis force.

Frost action (13)   A powerful mechanical force produced as water expands up to 9% of its volume as it freezes. Water freezing in a cavity in a rock can break the rock if it exceeds the rock's tensional strength.

Frost wedging (13)   The physical weathering process driven by frost action, or freeze–thaw action, that breaks rocks apart; a type of physical weathering.

Funnel cloud (7)   The visible swirl extending from the bottom side of a cloud, which may or may not develop into a tornado. A tornado is a funnel cloud that has extended all the way to the ground. (*See* Tornado.)

Fusion (2)   The process of forcibly joining positively charged hydrogen and helium nuclei under extreme temperature and pressure; occurs naturally in thermonuclear reactions within stars, such as our Sun.

G

Gelisols (18)   A soil order in the Soil Taxonomy, added in 1998, describing cold and frozen soils at high latitudes or high elevations.

General circulation model (GCM) (10)   Complex, computerized climate model used to assess past climatic trends and their causes and to project future changes in climate.

Geodesy (1)   The science that determines Earth's shape and size through surveys, mathematical means, and remote sensing. (*See* Geoid.)

Geographic information system (GIS) (1)   A computer-based data processing tool or methodology used for gathering, manipulating, and analyzing geographic information to produce a holistic, interactive analysis.

Geography (1)   The science that studies the relationships among natural systems, geographic areas, human culture, and the interdependence of all of these over space.

Geoid (1)   A word that describes Earth's shape; literally, "the shape of Earth is Earth-shaped." A theoretical surface at sea level that extends through the continents; deviates from a perfect sphere.

Geologic cycle (12)   A general term characterizing the vast cycling that proceeds in the lithosphere. It encompasses the hydrologic cycle, tectonic cycle, and rock cycle.

Geologic time scale (11)   A depiction of eras, periods, and epochs that span Earth's history; shows both the sequence of rock strata and their absolute dates, as determined by methods such as radioactive isotopic dating.

Geomagnetic reversal (11)   A polarity change in Earth's magnetic field. With uneven regularity, the magnetic field fades to zero and then returns to full strength, but with the magnetic poles reversed. Reversals have been recorded nine times during the past 4 million years.

Geomorphic threshold (13)   The threshold up to which landforms change before lurching to a new set of relationships, with rapid realignments of landscape materials and slopes.

Geomorphology (11)   The science that analyzes and describes the origin, evolution, form, classification, and spatial distribution of landforms.

Geostrophic wind (5)   A wind moving between areas of different pressure along a path that is parallel to the isobars. It is a product of the pressure gradient force and the Coriolis force. (*See* Isobar, Pressure gradient force, Coriolis force.)

Geothermal energy (11)   The energy in steam and hot water heated by subsurface magma near groundwater. Geothermal energy literally refers to heat from Earth's interior, whereas *geothermal power* relates to specific applied strategies of geothermal electric or geothermal direct applications. This energy is used in Iceland, New Zealand, Italy, and northern California, among other locations.

Glacial drift (17)   The general term for all glacial deposits, both unsorted (till) and sorted (stratified drift).

Glacial ice (17)   A hardened form of ice, very dense in comparison to normal snow or firn.

Glacier (17)   A large mass of dense, perennial ice resting on land, formed from the accumulation and recrystallization of snow, which then flows slowly under the pressure of its own weight and the pull of gravity.

Glacier surge (17)   The rapid forward movement of a glacier at speeds much faster than normal.

Gleization (18)   A process of humus and clay accumulation in cold, wet climates with poor drainage.

Global carbon budget (11)   The exchange of carbon between sources and sinks in Earth's atmosphere, hydrosphere, lithosphere, and biosphere.

Global dimming (4)   The decline in sunlight reaching Earth's surface due to pollution, aerosols, and clouds.

Global Positioning System (GPS) (1)   Latitude, longitude, and elevation are accurately calibrated using a handheld instrument that receives radio signals from satellites.

Goode's homolosine projection (Appendix A)   An equal-area projection formed by splicing together a sinusoidal and a homolographic projection.

Graben (12)   Pairs or groups of faults that produce downward-faulted blocks; characteristic of the basins of the interior western United States. (*Compare* Horst; *see* Basin and Range Province.)

Graded stream (14)   An idealized condition in which a stream's load and the landscape mutually adjust. This forms a dynamic equilibrium among erosion, transported load, deposition, and the stream's capacity.

Gradient (14)   The drop in elevation from a stream's headwaters to its mouth, ideally forming a concave slope.

Granite (11)   A coarse-grained (slow-cooling) intrusive igneous rock of 25% quartz and more than 50% potassium and sodium feldspars; characteristic of the continental crust.

Gravitational water (8)   That portion of surplus water that percolates downward from the capillary zone, pulled by gravity to the groundwater zone.

Gravity (2)   The mutual force exerted by the masses of objects that are attracted one to another and produced in an amount proportional to each object's mass.

Great circle (1)   Any circle drawn on a globe with its center coinciding with the center of the globe. An infinite number of great circles can be drawn, but only one parallel of latitude—the equator—is a great circle. (*Compare* Small circle.)

Greenhouse effect (4)   The process whereby radiatively active gases (carbon dioxide, water vapor, methane, and CFCs) absorb and emit the energy at longer wavelengths, which are retained longer, delaying the loss of infrared to space. Thus, the lower troposphere is warmed through the radiation and re-radiation of infrared wavelengths. The approximate similarity between this process and that of a greenhouse explains the name.

Greenhouse gases (4)   Gases in the lower atmosphere that delay the passage of longwave radiation to space by absorbing and reradiating specific wavelengths. Earth's primary greenhouse gases are carbon dioxide, water vapor, methane, nitrous oxide, and flourinated gases, such as chlorofluorocarbons (CFCs).

Greenwich Mean Time (GMT) (1) Former world standard time, now reported as Coordinated Universal Time (UTC). (*See* Coordinated Universal Time.)

Ground ice (17) The subsurface water that is frozen in regions of permafrost. The moisture content of areas with ground ice may vary from nearly absent in regions of drier permafrost to almost 100% in saturated soils.

Groundwater (8) Water beneath the surface that is beyond the soil-root zone; a major source of potable water.

Groundwater mining (8) Pumping an aquifer beyond its capacity to flow and recharge; an overuse of the groundwater resource.

Gulf Stream (4) A strong, northward-moving, warm current off the east coast of North America, which carries its water far into the North Atlantic.

H

Habitat (19) A physical location to which an organism is biologically suited. Most species have specific habitat parameters and limits. (*Compare* Niche.)

Hail (7) Ice pellets formed when graupel (small snow pellets) circulates within a cloud, moving repeatedly above and below the freezing level, adding layers of ice. Eventually the graupel forms hail that falls to the ground when it becomes too heavy to stay aloft.

Heat (4) The flow of kinetic energy from one body to another because of a temperature difference between them.

Heat wave (4) A prolonged period of abnormally high temperatures, usually, but not always, in association with humid weather.

Herbivore (19) The primary consumer in a food web, which eats plant material formed by a producer (plant) that has photosynthesized organic molecules. (*Compare* Carnivore.)

Heterosphere (3) A zone of the atmosphere above the mesopause, from 80 km (50 mi) to 480 km (300 mi) in altitude; composed of rarefied layers of oxygen atoms and nitrogen molecules; includes the ionosphere.

High tide (16) The maximum height of the daily tide cycle, occurring twice each day. (*Compare* Low tide.)

Histosols (18) A soil order in the Soil Taxonomy. Formed from thick accumulations of organic matter, such as beds of former lakes, bogs, and layers of peat.

Homosphere (3) A zone of the atmosphere from Earth's surface up to 80 km (50 mi), composed of an even mixture of gases, including nitrogen, oxygen, argon, carbon dioxide, and trace gases.

Horn (17) A pyramidal, sharp-pointed peak that results when several cirque glaciers gouge an individual mountain summit from all sides.

Horst (12) Upward-faulted blocks produced by pairs or groups of faults; characteristic of the mountain ranges of the interior of the western United States. (*See* Graben, Basin and Range Province.)

Hot spot (11) An individual point of upwelling material originating in the asthenosphere, or deeper in the mantle; tends to remain fixed relative to migrating plates; some 100 are identified worldwide, exemplified by Yellowstone National Park, Hawai'i, and Iceland.

Human–Earth relationships (1) One of five traditional themes of geographic teaching and research focusing on connections between humans and their environment.

Humidity (6) Water vapor content of the air. The capacity of the air for water vapor is mostly a function of the temperature of the air and the water vapor.

Humus (18) A mixture of organic debris in the soil worked by consumers and decomposers in the humification process; characteristically formed from plant and animal litter deposited at the surface.

Hurricane (7) A tropical cyclone that is fully organized and intensified in inward-spiraling rainbands; ranges from 160 to 960 km (100 to 600 mi) in diameter, with wind speeds in excess of 119 kmph (65 knots, or 74 mph); a name used specifically in the Atlantic and eastern Pacific. (*Compare* Typhoon.)

Hydration (13) A chemical weathering process involving water that is added to a mineral, which initiates swelling and stress within the rock, mechanically forcing grains apart as the constituents expand. (*Compare* Hydrolysis.)

Hydraulic action (14) The erosive work accomplished by the turbulence of water; causes a squeezing and releasing action in joints in bedrock; capable of prying and lifting rocks.

Hydric soil (18) A soil that is saturated for long enough periods to develop anaerobic, or "oxygen-free," conditions. Hydric soils are characteristic of wetlands.

Hydrograph (14) A graph of stream discharge (in m³/s or cfs, ft³/s) over a period of time (minutes, hours, days, years) at a specific place on a stream.

Hydrologic cycle (8) A simplified model of the flow of water, ice, and water vapor from place to place. Water flows through the atmosphere and across the land, where it is stored as ice and as groundwater. Solar energy empowers the cycle.

Hydrology (14) The science of water, including its global circulation, distribution, and properties—specifically water at and below Earth's surface.

Hydrolysis (13) A chemical weathering process in which minerals chemically combine with water; a decomposition process that causes silicate minerals in rocks to break down and become altered. (*Compare* Hydration.)

Hydropower (8) Electricity generated using the energy of moving water, usually flowing downhill through the turbines at a dam; also called *hydroelectric power.*

Hydrosphere (1) An abiotic open system that includes all of Earth's water.

Hygroscopic water (8) That portion of soil moisture that is so tightly bound to each soil particle that it is unavailable to plant roots; the water, along with some bound capillary water, that is left in the soil after the wilting point is reached. (*See* Wilting point.)

I

Ice age (17) A cold episode, with accompanying glaciations, that has repeated roughly every 200 to 300 million years since the late Precambrian Era (1.25 billion years ago); includes the most recent episode during the Pleistocene Epoch.

Ice cap (17) A roughly circular glacier covering an area less than 50,000 km² (19,300 mi²), completely burying the underlying landscape.

Ice field (17) The least extensive form of a glacier, with mountain ridges and peaks visible above the ice; less than an ice cap or ice sheet.

Ice sheet (17) A continuous mass of unconfined ice, covering at least 50,000 km² (19,500 mi²). The bulk of glacial ice on Earth covers Antarctica and Greenland in two ice sheets (*Compare* Alpine glacier.)

Icelandic low (5) *See* Subpolar low-pressure cell.

Igneous rock (11) One of the basic rock types; it has solidified and crystallized from a hot molten state (either magma or lava). (*Compare* Metamorphic rock, Sedimentary rock.)

Illuviation (18) The downward movement and deposition of finer particles and minerals from the upper horizon of the soil; a depositional process. Deposition usually is in the B horizon, where accumulations of clays, aluminum, carbonates, iron, and some humus occur. (*Compare* Eluviation; *see* Calcification.)

Inceptisols (18) A soil order in the Soil Taxonomy. Weakly developed soils that are inherently infertile; usually, young soils that are weakly developed, although they are more developed than Entisols.

Industrial smog (3) Air pollution associated with coal-burning industries; it may contain sulfur oxides, particulates, carbon dioxide, and exotics.

Infiltration (8) Water access to subsurface regions of soil moisture storage through penetration of the soil surface.

Inselberg (15) An isolated remnant of resistant rock that is a product of weathering and erosion.

Insolation (2) Solar radiation that is incoming to Earth systems.

Instream use (8) Uses of streamflow while it remains in the channel, without being removed.

Interception (8) A delay in the fall of precipitation toward Earth's surface caused by vegetation or other ground cover.

Internal drainage (14) In regions where rivers do not flow into the ocean, the outflow is through evaporation or subsurface gravitational flow. Portions of Africa, Asia, Australia, and the western United States have such drainage.

International Date Line (IDL) (1) The 180° meridian, an important corollary to the prime meridian on the opposite side of the planet; established by an 1884 treaty to mark the place where each day officially begins.

Intertropical convergence zone (ITCZ) (5) See Equatorial low.

Intrusive igneous rock (11) A rock that solidifies and crystallizes from a molten state as it intrudes into crustal rocks, cooling and hardening below the surface, such as granite.

Invasive species (20) Species introduced from elsewhere by humans, either accidentally or intentionally, that are able to take over niches already occupied by native species.

Ionosphere (3) A layer in the atmosphere above 80 km (50 mi) where gamma, X-ray, and some ultraviolet radiation is absorbed and converted into longer wavelengths and where the solar wind stimulates the auroras.

Island biogeography (20) A theory and conceptual model for understanding species distributions on islands and the effects of fragmented habitat in conservation biogeography. The theory summarizes three patterns: (1) the number of species increases with island area, (2) the number of species decreases with island isolation (distance from the mainland), and (3) the number of species on an island represents an equilibrium between the rates of immigration and extinction.

Isobar (5) An isoline connecting all points of equal atmospheric pressure.

Isostasy (11) A state of equilibrium in Earth's crust formed by the interplay between portions of the less-dense lithosphere and the more-dense asthenosphere and the principle of buoyancy. The crust depresses under weight and recovers with its removal—for example, with the melting of glacial ice. The uplift is known as isostatic rebound.

Isotherm (4) An isoline connecting all points of equal temperature.

Isotope analysis (10) A technique for long-term climatic reconstruction that uses the atomic structure of chemical elements, specifically the relative amounts of their isotopes, to identify the chemical composition of past oceans and ice masses.

J

Jet contrails (4) Condensation trails produced by aircraft exhaust, particulates, and water vapor can form high cirrus clouds, sometimes called *false cirrus clouds.*

Jet stream (5) The most prominent movement in upper-level westerly wind flows; irregular, concentrated, sinuous bands of geostrophic wind, travelling at 300 kmph (190 mph).

Joint (13) A fracture or separation in rock that occurs without displacement of the sides; increases the surface area of rock exposed to weathering processes.

June solstice (2) The time when the Sun's declination is at the Tropic of Cancer, at 23.5° N latitude, June 20–21 each year. The night is 24 hours long south of the Antarctic Circle.

The day is 24 hours long north of the Arctic Circle. (*Compare* December solstice.)

K

Kame (17) A depositional feature of glaciation; a small hill of poorly sorted sand and gravel that accumulates in crevasses or in ice-caused indentations in the surface.

Karst topography (13) Distinctive topography formed in a region of chemically weathered limestone with poorly developed surface drainage and solution features that appear pitted and bumpy; originally named after the Krs Plateau in Slovenia.

Katabatic winds (5) Regional-scale, gravity-driven winds that develop on elevated plateaus or highlands and flow downslope; known worldwide by many local names.

Kettle (17) Forms when an isolated block of ice persists in a ground moraine, an outwash plain, or a valley floor after a glacier retreats; as the block finally melts, it leaves behind a steep-sided hole that frequently fills with water.

Kinetic energy (3) The energy of motion in a body; derived from the vibration of the body's own movement and stated as temperature.

Köppen–Geiger climate classification (Appendix B) An empirical classification system that uses average monthly temperatures, average monthly precipitation, and total annual precipitation to establish regional climate designations.

L

Lacustrine deposit (17) Lake sediments that form terraces, or benches, along former lake shorelines and often mark lake-level fluctuations over time.

Lagoon (16) An area of coastal seawater that is virtually cut off from the ocean by a bay barrier or barrier beach; also, the water surrounded and enclosed by an atoll.

Land and sea breezes (5) Winds along coastlines created by different heating characteristics of land and water surfaces—onshore (toward land) sea breezes occur in the afternoon and offshore (toward the sea) land breezes occur at night.

Landfall (7) The location along a coast where a storm moves onshore.

Landslide (13) A sudden rapid downslope movement under the influence of gravity of a cohesive mass of soil, regolith, or bedrock; often used as a catch-all term for mass-movement material that falls, slides, flows.

Land–water heating difference (4) Differences in the degree and way that land and water heat, as a result of contrasts in transmission, evaporation, mixing, and specific heat capacities. Land surfaces heat and cool faster than water and have continentality, whereas water provides a marine influence.

Lapse rate (3) The rate of temperature decrease with increasing altitude in the lower atmosphere; the average lapse rate is 6.4 C° per km, or 1000 m (3.5 F° per 1000 ft). (*Compare* Environmental lapse rate.)

Latent heat (6) Heat energy that is "hidden" within the structure of water's physical states—ice, water, or water vapor—and when absorbed or released during a phase change does not produce a change in temperature. Heat energy is absorbed as the latent heat of melting, vaporization, or sublimation. Heat energy is released as the latent heat of freezing, condensation and deposition.

Latent heat of condensation (6) The heat energy released to the environment in a phase change from water vapor to liquid; under normal sea-level pressure, 540 calories are released from each gram of water vapor that changes phase to water at boiling, and 585 calories are released from each gram of water vapor that condenses at 20°C (68°F).

Latent heat of sublimation (6) The heat energy absorbed (680 calories for one gram of ice) in the phase change from ice to water vapor—no liquid phase. The change from water vapor to ice is deposition, which releases a comparable amount of heat.

Latent heat of vaporization (6) The heat energy absorbed from the environment in a phase change from liquid to water vapor at the boiling point; under normal sea-level pressure, 540 calories must be added to each gram of boiling water to achieve a phase change to water vapor.

Lateral moraine (17) Debris transported by a glacier that accumulates along the sides of the glacier and is deposited along these margins.

Laterization (18) A pedogenic process operating in well-drained soils that occurs in warm and humid regions; typical of Oxisols. Plentiful precipitation leaches soluble minerals and soil constituents. Resulting soils usually are reddish or yellowish.

Latitude (1) The angular distance measured north or south of the equator from a point at the center of Earth. A line connecting all points of the same latitudinal angle is a parallel. (*Compare* Longitude.)

Lava (11) Magma that issues from volcanic activity onto the surface; the extrusive rock that results when magma solidifies. (*See* Magma.)

Life zone (19) A zonation by altitude of plants and animals that form distinctive communities. Each life zone possesses its own temperature and precipitation relations.

Lightning (7) Flashes of light caused by tens of millions of volts of electrical charge heating the air to temperatures of 15,000°C to 30,000°C.

Limestone (11) The most common chemical sedimentary rock (nonclastic); it is lithified calcium carbonate; very susceptible to chemical weathering by acids in the environment, including carbonic acid in rainfall.

Limiting factor (19) The physical or chemical factor that most inhibits biotic processes, through either lack or excess.

Liquefaction (12) The process whereby ground shaking, usually from an earthquake, disrupts and loosens the structure of the soil, causing it to flow.

Lithification (11)   The compaction, cementation, and hardening of sediments into sedimentary rock.

Lithosphere (1, 11)   Earth's crust and that portion of the uppermost mantle directly below the crust, extending down about 70 km (45 mi). Some sources use this term to refer to the entire Earth.

Littoral drift (16)   Transport of sand, gravel, sediment, and debris along the shore; a more comprehensive term that considers *beach drift* and *longshore drift* combined.

Littoral zone (16)   A specific coastal environment; that region between the high-water line during a storm and a depth at which storm waves are unable to move sea-floor sediments.

Loam (18)   A soil that is a mixture of sand, silt, and clay in almost equal proportions, with no one texture dominant; an ideal agricultural soil.

Location (1)   One of five traditional themes of geographic teaching and research, focusing on the absolute and relative positions of people, places, and things on Earth's surface.

Loess (15)   Large quantities of fine-grained clays and silts left as glacial outwash deposits; subsequently blown by the wind great distances and redeposited as a generally unstratified, homogeneous blanket of material covering existing landscapes; in China, loess originated from desert lands.

Longitude (1)   The angular distance measured east or west of a prime meridian from a point at the center of Earth. A line connecting all points of the same longitude is a meridian. (*Compare* Latitude.)

Longshore current (16)   A current that forms parallel to a beach as waves arrive at an angle to the shore; generated in the surf zone by wave action, transporting large amounts of sand and sediment. (*See* Beach drift.)

Low tide (16)   The minimum height of the daily tide cycle, occurring twice each day. (*Compare* High tide.)

M

Magma (11)   Molten rock from beneath Earth's surface; fluid, gaseous, under tremendous pressure, and either intruded into existing crustal rock or extruded onto the surface as lava. (*See* Lava.)

Magnetosphere (2)   Earth's magnetic force field, which is generated by dynamo-like motions within the planet's outer core; deflects the solar wind flow toward the upper atmosphere above each pole.

Mangrove swamp (16)   A wetland ecosystem between 30° N and 30° S; tends to form a distinctive community of mangrove plants. (*Compare* Salt marsh.)

Mantle (11)   An area within the planet representing about 80% of Earth's total volume, with densities increasing with depth and averaging 4.5g/cm³; occurs between the core and the crust; is rich in iron and magnesium oxides and silicates.

Map (1, Appendix A)   A generalized view of an area, usually some portion of Earth's surface, as seen from above at a greatly reduced size. (*See* Scale, Map projection.)

Map projection (1, Appendix A)   The reduction of a spherical globe onto a flat surface in some orderly and systematic realignment of the latitude and longitude grid.

March equinox (2)   The time around March 20–21 when the Sun's declination crosses the equator (0° latitude) and all places on Earth experience days and nights of equal length. (*Compare* September equinox.)

Mass movement (13)   The downslope movement of a body of material (soil, sediment, or rock) propelled by the force of gravity; also called mass wasting.

Mass wasting (13)   Gravitational movement of nonunified material downslope; also called mass movement.

Maunder Minimum (10)   A solar minimum (a period with little sunspot activity and reduced solar irradiance) that lasted from about 1645 to 1715, corresponding with one of the coldest periods of the Little Ice Age. Although this event suggests a causal effect between decreased sunspot numbers and cooling temperatures in the North Atlantic region, research has repeatedly refuted this hypothesis.

Mean sea level (MSL) (16)   The average of tidal levels recorded hourly at a given site over a long period, which must be at least a full lunar tidal cycle.

Meandering stream (14)   The sinuous, curving pattern common to graded streams, with the energetic outer portion of each curve subjected to the greatest erosive action and the lower-energy inner portion receiving sediment deposits. (*See* Graded stream.)

Medial moraine (17)   Debris transported by a glacier that accumulates down the middle of the glacier, resulting from two glaciers merging their lateral moraines; forms a depositional feature following glacial retreat.

Mediterranean shrubland (20)   A biome dominated by the *Mediterranean* (dry summer) climate and characterized by sclerophyllous scrub and short, stunted, tough forests. (*See* Chaparral.)

Megathrust earthquake (12)   A powerful earthquake that occurs along a subduction zone; the most powerful earthquakes on Earth.

Mercator projection (1, Appendix A)   A true-shape projection, with meridians appearing as equally spaced straight lines and parallels appearing as straight lines that are spaced closer together near the equator. The poles are infinitely stretched, with the 84th north parallel and 84th south parallel fixed at the same length as that of the equator. It presents false notions of the size (area) of midlatitude and poleward landmasses, but presents true compass direction. (*See* Rhumb line.)

Mercury barometer (5)   A device that measures air pressure using a column of mercury in a tube; one end of the tube is sealed, and the other end is inserted in an open vessel of mercury. (*See* Air pressure.)

Meridian (1)   A line designating an angle of longitude. (*See* Longitude.)

Mesa (15)   Flat-topped landforms with steep slopes on all side that are elevated above the surrounding landscape; characteristic landform of the U.S. West and Southwest.

Mesocyclone (7)   A large, rotating atmospheric circulation, initiated within a parent cumulonimbus cloud at midtroposphere elevation; generally produces heavy rain, large hail, blustery winds, and lightning; may lead to tornado activity.

Mesosphere (3)   The upper region of the homosphere from 50 to 80 km (30 to 50 mi) above the ground; designated by temperature criteria; atmosphere extremely rarified.

Metamorphic rock (11)   One of three basic rock types, it is existing igneous and sedimentary rock that has undergone profound physical and chemical changes under increased pressure and temperature. Constituent mineral structures may exhibit foliated or nonfoliated textures. (*Compare* Igneous rock, Sedimentary rock.)

Meteorology (7)   The scientific study of the atmosphere, including its physical characteristics and motions; related chemical, physical, and geological processes; the complex linkages of atmospheric systems; and weather forecasting.

Microclimatology (7)   The study of local climates at or near Earth's surface or up to that height above the Earth's surface where the effects of the surface are no longer determinative.

Midlatitude broadleaf and mixed forest (20)   A biome in humid continental climates in areas of warm-to-hot summers and cool-to-cold winters; relatively lush stands of broadleaf forests trend northward into evergreen conifer stands.

Midlatitude cyclone (8)   An organized area of low pressure, with converging and ascending airflow producing an interaction of air masses; migrates along storm tracks. Such lows or depressions form the dominant weather pattern in the middle and higher latitudes of both hemispheres.

Midlatitude grassland (20)   A biome so named for the predominance of grasslike plants, although deciduous broadleaf trees appear along streams and other limited sites; the biome most modified by human activity, mainly agriculture.

Mid-ocean ridge (12)   A submarine mountain range that extends more than 65,000 km (40,000 mi) worldwide and averages more than 1000 km (600 mi) in width; centered along seafloor spreading centers. (*See* Seafloor spreading.)

Milankovitch cycles (10)   The consistent orbital cycles—based on the irregularities in

Earth's orbit around the Sun, its rotation on its axis, and its axial tilt—that relate to climatic patterns and may be an important cause of glacials and interglacials. Milutin Milankovitch (1879–1958), a Serbian astronomer, was the first to correlate these cycles to changes in insolation that affected temperatures on Earth.

Milky Way Galaxy (2) A flattened, disk-shaped mass in space estimated to contain up to 400 billion stars; a barred-spiral galaxy; includes our Solar System.

Miller cylindrical projection (Appendix A) A compromise map projection that avoids the severe distortion of the Mercator projection. (*See* Map projection.)

Mineral (11) An element or combination of elements that forms an inorganic natural compound; described by a specific formula and crystal structure.

Mirage (4) A refraction effect when an image appears near the horizon where light waves are refracted by layers of air at different temperatures (and consequently of different densities).

Model (1) A simplified version of a system, representing an idealized part of the real world.

Mohorovičić discontinuity, or Moho (11) The boundary between the crust and the rest of the lithospheric upper mantle; named for the Yugoslavian seismologist Mohorovičić a zone of sharp material and density contrasts.

Moist adiabatic rate (MAR) (6) The rate at which a saturated parcel of air cools in ascent; a rate of 6 C° per 1000 m (3.3 F° per 1000 ft). This rate may vary, with moisture content and temperature, from 4 C° to 10 C° per 1000 m (2 F° to 6 F° per 1000 ft). (*See* Adiabatic; *compare* Dry adiabatic rate.)

Mollisols (18) A soil order in the Soil Taxonomy; humus-rich, usually alkaline soils with high organic content. Earth's most important agricultural soils.

Moment magnitude (M) scale (12) An earthquake magnitude scale. Considers the amount of fault slippage, the size of the area that ruptured, and the nature of the materials that faulted in estimating the magnitude of an earthquake—an assessment of the seismic moment.

Monsoon (5) Seasonally shifting winds produced by changing atmospheric pressure systems that cause an annual cycle of regional precipitation regimes, ranging from a wet season to a dry season; affects India, Southeast Asia, Indonesia, northern Australia, portions of Africa, and the U.S. Southwest. From the Arabic word *mausim,* meaning "season."

Montane forest (20) A biome characterized mainly by needleleaf forest (conifers and deciduous needleleaf trees such as larch) associated with high elevations in mountains at all latitudes. (*See* Boreal forest.)

Moraine (17) Marginal glacial deposits (lateral, medial, terminal, ground) of unsorted and unstratified material.

Mountain and valley breezes (5) Local winds produced when mountain air cools rapidly at night and heats up rapidly during the day. As valley slopes heat up during the day, air moves upward, creating low pressure and an upslope valley breeze. At night, valley slopes lose heat, and the cooler, denser air subsides downslope, producing a nighttime mountain breeze.

Movement (1) One of five traditional themes of geographic teaching and research, focusing on migration, communication, and the interaction of people and processes across space.

Mudflow (13) Fluid downslope flows of material of smaller size and higher water content than a debris flow.

N

Natural levee (14) A long, low ridge that forms on both sides of a stream in a developed floodplain; a depositional product (coarse gravels and sand) of river flooding.

Neap tide (16) Unusually low tidal range produced during the first and third quarters of the Moon, with an offsetting pull from the Sun. (*Compare* Spring tide.)

Negative feedback (1) Feedback that tends to slow or dampen responses in a system; promotes self-regulation in a system; far more common than positive feedback in living systems. (*See* Feedback loop; *compare* Positive feedback.)

Net primary productivity (19) The net photosynthesis (photosynthesis minus respiration) for a given community; considers all growth and all reduction factors that affect the amount of useful chemical energy (biomass) fixed in an ecosystem.

Net radiation (NET R) (4) The net all-wave radiation available at Earth's surface; the final outcome of the radiation balance process between incoming shortwave insolation and outgoing longwave energy.

Nickpoint (knickpoint) (14) The point at which the longitudinal profile of a stream is abruptly broken by a change in gradient; for example, a waterfall, rapids, or cascade.

Nimbostratus (6) Rain-producing, dark, grayish stratiform clouds characterized by gentle drizzle.

Nitrogen dioxide (NO_2) (3) A noxious (harmful) reddish-brown gas produced in combustion engines; can be damaging to human respiratory tracts and to plants; participates in photochemical reactions and acid deposition.

Noctilucent cloud (3) A rare, shining band of ice crystals that may glow at high latitudes long after sunset; formed within the mesosphere, where cosmic and meteoric dust act as nuclei for the formation of ice crystals.

Nonconsumptive use (8) A use that removes or diverts water from the immediate stream environment, followed by the subsequent return of that water to the same supply.

Normal fault (12) A type of geologic fault in rocks. Tension produces strain that breaks a rock, with one side moving vertically relative to the other side along an inclined fault plane. (*Compare* Reverse fault.)

O

Occluded front (7) In a cyclonic circulation, the overrunning of a surface warm front by a cold front and the subsequent lifting of the warm air wedge off the ground; initial precipitation is moderate to heavy.

Omnivore (19) A consumer that feeds on both producers (plants) and consumers (meat)—a role occupied by humans, among other animals. (*Compare* Consumer, Producer.)

Open system (1) A system with inputs and outputs crossing back and forth between the system and the surrounding environment. Earth is an open system in terms of energy. (*Compare* Closed system.)

Orogenesis (12) The process of mountain building that occurs when large-scale compression leads to deformation and uplift of the crust; literally, the birth of mountains.

Orographic lifting (7) The uplift of a migrating air mass as it is forced to move upward over a mountain range—a topographic barrier. The lifted air cools adiabatically as it moves upslope; clouds may form and produce increased precipitation.

Outgassing (8) The release of trapped gases from rocks, forced out through cracks, fissures, and volcanoes from within Earth; the terrestrial source of Earth's water.

Outwash plain (17) Area of glacial stream deposits of stratified drift with meltwater-fed, braided, and overloaded streams; occurs beyond a glacier's morainal deposits.

Overland flow (8) Surplus water that flows across the land surface toward stream channels. Together with precipitation and subsurface flows, it constitutes the total runoff from an area.

Oxbow lake (14) A lake that was formerly part of the channel of a meandering stream; isolated when a stream eroded its outer bank, forming a cutoff through the neck of the looping meander (*see* Meandering stream). In Australia, known as a billabong (the Aboriginal word for "dead river").

Oxidation (13) A chemical weathering process in which oxygen dissolved in water oxidizes (combines with) certain metallic elements to form oxides; most familiar is the "rusting" of iron in a rock or soil (Ultisols, Oxisols), which produces a reddish-brown stain of iron oxide.

Oxisols (18) A soil order in the Soil Taxonomy. Tropical soils that are old, deeply developed, and lacking in horizons wherever well drained; heavily weathered, low in cation-exchange capacity, and low in fertility.

Ozone layer (3) *See* Ozonosphere.

Ozonosphere (3) A layer of ozone occupying the full extent of the stratosphere (20 to 50 km, or 12 to 30 mi, above the surface); the region of the atmosphere where ultraviolet wavelengths of insolation are extensively absorbed and converted into heat.

P

Pacific high (5) A high-pressure cell that dominates the Pacific in July, retreating southward in the Northern Hemisphere in January; also known as the *Hawaiian high*.

Pacific Ring of Fire (11) A tectonically and volcanically active region encircling the Pacific Ocean; also known as the *circum-Pacific belt* or the "ring of fire."

Pahoehoe (12) Basaltic lava that is more fluid than aa. Pahoehoe forms a thin crust that forms folds and appears "ropy," like coiled, twisted rope.

Paleoclimatology (10) The science that studies past climates and the causes of variations in climate throughout historic and geologic time.

Paleolake (17) An ancient lake, such as Lake Bonneville or Lake Lahonton, associated with past wet periods when the lake basins were filled to higher levels than today.

Pangaea (11) The supercontinent formed by the collision of all continental masses approximately 225 million years ago; named in the continental drift theory by Wegener in 1912. (*See* Plate tectonics.)

Parallel (1) A line, parallel to the equator, that designates an angle of latitude. (*See* Latitude.)

Parent material (13) The unconsolidated material, from both organic and mineral sources, that is the basis of soil development.

Particulate matter (PM) (3) Dust, dirt, soot, salt, sulfate aerosols, fugitive natural particles, or other material particles suspended in air.

Paternoster lake (17) One of a series of small, circular, stair-stepped lakes formed in individual rock basins aligned down the course of a glaciated valley; named because they look like a string of rosary (religious) beads.

Patterned ground (17) Areas in the periglacial environment where freezing and thawing of the ground create polygonal forms of arranged rocks at the surface; can be circles, polygons, stripes, nets, and steps.

Pedogenic regime (18) A specific soil-forming process keyed to a specific climatic regime; for example, laterization, calcification, and salinization.

Pedon (18) A soil profile extending from the surface to the lowest extent of plant roots or to the depth where regolith or bedrock is encountered; imagined as a hexagonal column; the basic soil sampling unit.

Percolation (8) The process by which water permeates the soil or porous rock into the subsurface environment.

Periglacial (17) Cold-climate processes, landforms, and topographic features along the margins of glaciers, past and present; periglacial characteristics exist on more than 20% of Earth's land surface; includes permafrost, frost action, and ground ice.

Perihelion (2) The point of Earth's closest approach to the Sun in its elliptical orbit, reached on January 3 at a distance of 147,255,000 km

(91,500,000 mi); variable over a 100,000-year cycle. (*Compare* Aphelion.)

Permafrost (17) Forms when soil or rock temperatures remain below 0°C (32°F) for at least 2 years in areas considered periglacial; criterion is based on temperature and not on whether water is present. (*See* Periglacial.)

Permeability (8) The ability of water to flow through soil or rock; a function of the texture and structure of the medium.

Peroxyacetyl nitrate (PAN) (3) A pollutant in photochemical smog formed from photochemical reactions involving nitric oxide (NO) and volatile organic compounds (VOCs).

Phase change (6) The change in state among the solid, liquid, and gas phases of water (ice, water, and water vapor). Each phase change involves the absorption or release of latent heat. (*See* Latent heat.)

Photochemical smog (3) Air pollution produced by vehicle emissions through interaction of ultraviolet light, nitrogen dioxide, and hydrocarbons; produces ozone and Peroxyacetyl nitrate through a series of complex photochemical reactions.

Photosynthesis (19) The process by which plants produce their own food from carbon dioxide and water, powered by solar energy. The joining of carbon dioxide and hydrogen in plants, under the influence of certain wavelengths of visible light; releases oxygen and produces energy-rich organic material, sugars, and starches. (*Compare* Cellular respiration.)

Physical geography (1) The science concerned with the spatial aspects and interactions of the physical elements and process systems that make up the environment: energy, air, water, weather, climate, landforms, soils, animals, plants, microorganisms, and Earth.

Physical weathering (13) The breaking up and disintegrating of rock without any chemical alteration; sometimes referred to as *mechanical* or *fragmentation weathering*.

Pioneer community (19) The initial plant community in an area; usually is found on new surfaces or those that have been stripped of life, as in beginning primary succession, and includes lichens, mosses, and ferns growing on bare rock.

Place (1) One of five traditional themes of geographic teaching and research, focused on the characteristics that make each location unique; no two places on Earth are alike.

Plane of the ecliptic (2) A plane (flat surface) intersecting all the points of Earth's orbit.

Planetesimal hypothesis (2) Proposes a process by which early protoplanets formed from the condensing masses of a nebular cloud of dust, gas, and icy comets; a formation process now being observed in other parts of the galaxy.

Plate tectonics (11) The conceptual model and theory that encompass continental drift, seafloor spreading, and related aspects of crustal movement; accepted as the foundation of crustal tectonic processes. (*See* Continental drift.)

Playa (15) An area of salt crust left behind by evaporation on a desert floor, usually in the middle of a desert or semiarid bolson or valley; intermittently wet and dry.

Pluton (11) A mass of intrusive igneous rock that has cooled slowly in the crust; forms in any size or shape. The largest partially exposed pluton is a batholith. (*See* Batholith.)

Podzolization (18) A process occurring in the soils of cool, moist climates that forms a highly leached soil with strong surface acidity produced by the decomposition of acid-rich leaf litter from evergreen trees.

Point bar (14) In a stream, the inner portion of a meander, where sediment fill is redeposited. (*Compare* Undercut bank.)

Polar desert (20) A type of desert biome found at higher latitudes than cold deserts, occurring mainly in the very cold, dry climates of Greenland and Antartica.

Polar easterlies (6) Variable, weak, cold, and dry winds moving away from the polar region; an anticyclonic circulation.

Polar front (5) A significant zone of contrast between cold and warm air masses; roughly situated between 50° and 60° N and S latitude.

Polar high (5) Weak, anticyclonic, thermally produced pressure systems positioned roughly over each pole; that over the South Pole is the region of the lowest temperatures on Earth. (*See* Antarctic high.)

Pollutants (3) Natural or human-caused gases, particles, and other substances in the troposphere that accumulate in amounts harmful to humans or to the environment.

Polypedon (18) The identifiable soil in an area, with distinctive characteristics differentiating it from surrounding polypedons that form the basic mapping unit; composed of many pedons. (*See* Pedon.)

Porosity (8) The spaces, or voids, between particles in a material such as soil or rock.

Positive feedback (1) Feedback that amplifies or encourages responses in a system. (*Compare* Negative feedback; *see* Feedback loop.)

Potential energy (1) Energy that is stored (either due to composition or to position) and therefore has the capacity to accomplish work under the right conditions.

Potential evapotranspiration (PE) (8) The amount of moisture that would evaporate and transpire under optimum moisture conditions where adequate precipitation and soil moisture are present. PE is the total water demand, which if not satisfied results in a deficit, or moisture shortage. (*Compare* Actual evapotranspiration.)

Potentiometric surface (8) A pressure level in a confined aquifer, defined by the level to which water rises in wells; caused by the fact that the water in a confined aquifer is under the pressure of its own weight. This surface can extend above the surface of the land, causing water to rise above the water table in wells in confined aquifers. (*See* Artesian water.)

Precipitation (8)   Rain, snow, sleet, and hail, occurring when condensed water droplets or ice crystals in a cloud become large enough to fall with gravity. In the water balance, the moisture supply (P).

Pressure gradient force (5)   Causes air to move from an area of higher barometric pressure to an area of lower barometric pressure due to the pressure difference.

Primary succession (19)   Succession that occurs among plant species in an area of new surfaces created by mass movement of land, cooled lava flows and volcanic eruption landscapes, or surface mining and clear-cut logging scars; exposed by retreating glaciers, or made up of sand dunes, with no trace of a former community.

Prime meridian (1)   An arbitrary meridian designated as 0° longitude, the point from which longitudes are measured east or west; established at Greenwich, England, by international agreement in an 1884 treaty.

Process (1)   A set of actions and changes that occur in some special order; analysis of processes is central to modern geographic synthesis.

Producer (19)   Organism (plant) in an ecosystem that uses carbon dioxide as its sole source of carbon, which it chemically fixes through photosynthesis to provide its own nourishment; also called an *autotroph*. (*Compare* Consumer.)

Proxy method (10)   Information about past environments that can be used to reconstruct climates that extend back further than our present instrumentation allows. Examples are carbon isotope analysis and tree ring dating. Also called a *climate proxy*.

Pyroclastic (12)   An explosively ejected rock fragment launched by a volcanic eruption; sometimes described by the more general term *tephra*.

R

Radiation fog (6)   Formed by radiative cooling of a land surface, especially on clear nights in areas of moist ground; occurs when the air layer directly above the surface is chilled to the dew-point temperature, thereby producing saturated conditions.

Radiative forcing (10)   The amount by which some perturbation causes Earth's energy balance to deviate from zero; a positive forcing indicates a warming condition, a negative forcing indicates cooling; also called *climate forcing*.

Radioactive isotope (10)   An unstable isotope that decays, or breaks down, into a different element, emitting radiation in the process. The unstable isotope carbon-14 has a constant rate of decay known as a *half-life* that can be used to date plant material in a technique called *radiocarbon dating*.

Rain gauge (9)   A weather instrument; a standardized device that captures and measures rainfall.

Rain shadow (7)   The area on the leeward slope of a mountain range where precipitation receipt is greatly reduced compared to the windward slope on the other side. (*See* Orographic lifting.)

Reflection (4)   The portion of arriving insolation that is returned directly to space without being absorbed and converted into heat and without performing any work. (*See* Albedo.)

Refraction (4)   The bending effect on electromagnetic waves that occurs when insolation enters the atmosphere or another medium; the same process disperses the component colors of the light passing through a crystal or prism.

Region (1)   One of five traditional themes of geographic teaching and research, defined as an area with uniform physical or human characteristics.

Regolith (13)   Partially weathered rock overlying bedrock, whether residual or transported.

Relative humidity (6)   The ratio of water vapor actually in the air (content) to the maximum water vapor possible in air (capacity) at that temperature; expressed as a percentage. (*Compare* Vapor pressure, Specific humidity.)

Relief (12)   Elevation differences in a local landscape; an expression of local height differences of landforms.

Remote sensing (1)   Information acquired from a distance, without physical contact with the subject—for example, photography, orbital imagery, and radar.

Respiration (19)   *See* Cellular respiration.

Reverse fault (12)   Compressional forces produce strain that breaks a rock so that one side moves upward relative to the other side; also called a *thrust fault*. (*Compare* Normal fault.)

Revolution (2)   The annual orbital movement of Earth about the Sun; determines the length of the year and the seasons.

Rhumb line (1)   A line of constant compass direction, or constant bearing, that crosses successive meridians at the same angle; appears as a straight line only on the Mercator projection.

Richter scale (12)   An open-ended, logarithmic scale that estimates earthquake amplitude magnitude; designed by Charles Richter in 1935; now replaced by the moment magnitude scale. (*See* Moment magnitude scale.)

Robinson projection (Appendix A)   A compromise (neither equal area nor true shape) oval projection developed in 1963 by Arthur Robinson.

Roche moutonnée (17)   A glacial erosion feature; an asymmetrical hill of exposed bedrock; displays a gently sloping upstream side that has been smoothed and polished by a glacier and an abrupt, steep downstream side.

Rock (11)   An assemblage of minerals bound together, or sometimes a mass of a single mineral.

Rock cycle (11)   A model representing the interrelationships among the three rock-forming processes: igneous, sedimentary, and metamorphic; shows how each can be transformed into another rock type.

Rockfall (13)   Free-falling movement of debris from a cliff or steep slope, generally falling straight or bounding downslope.

Rossby wave (5)   An undulating horizontal motion in the upper-air westerly circulation at middle and high latitudes.

Rotation (2)   The turning of Earth on its axis, averaging about 24 hours in duration; determines day–night relation; counterclockwise when viewed from above the North Pole and from west to east, or eastward, when viewed from above the equator.

S

Salinity (16)   The concentration of natural elements and compounds dissolved in solution, as solutes; measured by weight in parts per thousand (ppt or ‰) in seawater.

Salinization (18)   A pedogenic process that results from high potential evapotranspiration rates in deserts and semiarid regions. Soil water is drawn to surface horizons, and dissolved salts are deposited as the water evaporates.

Salt marsh (16)   A wetland ecosystem characteristic of latitudes poleward of the 30th parallel. (*Compare* Mangrove swamp.)

Saltation (14)   The transport of sand grains (usually larger than 0.2 mm, or 0.008 in.) by stream or wind, bouncing the grains along the ground in asymmetrical paths.

Saturation (6)   The point at which air is holding the maximum amount of water vapor possible at that temperature, and beyond which point any addition of water vapor will cause net condensation; also known as *saturation equilibrium*, the point at which evaporation and condensation are in balance. (*See also* Dew-point temperature.)

Saturation vapor pressure (6)   The vapor pressure, expressed in millibars, of saturated air (air that is carrying the maximum possible amount of water vapor for the current temperature).

Scale (1)   The ratio of the distance on a map to that in the real world; expressed as a representative fraction, graphic scale, or written scale.

Scattering (4)   Deflection and redirection of insolation by atmospheric gases, dust, ice, and water vapor; the shorter the wavelength, the greater the scattering; thus, skies in the lower atmosphere are blue.

Scientific method (1)   An approach that uses applied common sense in an organized and objective manner; based on observation, generalization, formulation, and testing of a hypothesis, ultimately leading to the development of a theory.

Seafloor spreading (11)   As proposed by Hess and Dietz, the mechanism driving the movement of the continents; associated with upwelling flows of magma along the worldwide system of mid-ocean ridges. (*See* Mid-ocean ridge.)

Secondary succession (19)   Succession that occurs among plant species in an area where vestiges of a previously functioning community are present; an area where the natural community has been destroyed or disturbed, but where the underlying soil remains intact.

Sediment (11) Rock particles of varying sizes, from coarse gravels to fine-grained silts, eroded and deposited by gravity, water, wind, or ice.

Sediment transport (14) The movement of solid particles (sediment), typically by the action of gravity or the movement of a fluid, such as water, in which the sediment is entrained.

Sedimentary rock (11) One of the three basic rock types; formed from the compaction, cementation, and hardening of sediments derived from other rocks. (*Compare* Igneous rock, Metamorphic rock.)

Seismic wave (11) The shock wave sent through the planet by an earthquake or underground nuclear test. Transmission varies according to temperature and the density of various layers within the planet; provides indirect diagnostic evidence of Earth's internal structure.

Seismograph (12) A device that measures seismic waves of energy transmitted throughout Earth's interior or along the crust (also called a seismometer).

Seismometer (12) An instrument used to detect and record the ground motion during an earthquake caused by seismic waves traveling through Earth's interior to the surface; the instrument records the waves on a graphic plot called a *seismogram*.

Sensible heat (4) Heat that can be measured with a thermometer; a measure of the concentration of kinetic energy from molecular motion.

September equinox (2) The time around September 22–23 when the Sun's declination crosses the equator (0° latitude) and all places on Earth experience days and nights of equal length. (*Compare* March equinox.)

Sheetflow (14) Surface water that moves downslope in a thin film as overland flow; not concentrated in channels larger than rills.

Shield volcano (12) A symmetrical mountain landform built from effusive eruptions (low-viscosity magma); gently sloped and gradually rising from the surrounding landscape to a summit crater; typical of the Hawaiian Islands. (*Compare* Effusive eruption, Composite volcano.)

Single-cell thunderstorm (7) An isolated, short-lived thunderstorm fueled by the rapid upward movement of warm, moist air.

Sinkhole (13) Nearly circular depression created by the weathering of karst landscapes with subterranean drainage; also known as a *doline* in traditional studies; may collapse through the roof of an underground space. (*See* Karst topography.)

Sleet (7) Ice pellets that form as raindrops fall through a layer of subfreezing air near the ground and freeze.

Slipface (15) On a sand dune, formed as dune height increases above 30 cm (12 in.) on the leeward side at an angle at which loose material is stable—its angle of repose (30° to 34°).

Slope (13) A curved, inclined surface that bounds a landform.

Small circle (1) A circle on a globe's surface that does not share Earth's center—for example, all parallels of latitude other than the equator. (*Compare* Great circle.)

Snowline (17) A temporary line marking the elevation where winter snowfall persists throughout the summer; seasonally, the lowest elevation covered by snow during the summer.

Soil (18) A dynamic natural body made up of fine materials covering Earth's surface in which plants grow, composed of both mineral and organic matter.

Soil colloid (18) A tiny clay and organic particle in soil; provides a chemically active site for mineral ion adsorption. (*See* Cation-exchange capacity.)

Soil creep (13) A persistent mass movement of surface soil where individual soil particles are lifted and disturbed by the expansion of soil moisture as it freezes or by grazing livestock or digging animals.

Soil fertility (18) The ability of soil to support plant productivity when it contains organic substances and clay minerals that absorb water and certain elemental ions needed by plants through adsorption. (*See* Cation-exchange capacity.)

Soil horizons (18) The various layers exposed in a pedon; roughly parallel to the surface and identified as O, A, E, B, C, and R (bedrock).

Soil porosity (18) The total volume of space within a soil that is filled with air, gases, or water (as opposed to soil particles or organic matter).

Soil profile (18) A vertical section of soil extending from the surface to the deepest extent of plant roots or to regolith or bedrock.

Soil science (18) Interdisciplinary science of soils. Pedology concerns the origin, classification, distribution, and description of soil. Edaphology focuses on soil as a medium for sustaining higher plants.

Soil Taxonomy (18) A soil classification system based on observable soil properties actually seen in the field; published in 1975 by the U.S. Soil Conservation Service and revised in 1990 and 1998 by the Natural Resources Conservation Service to include 12 soil orders.

Soil-moisture recharge (8) Water entering available soil storage spaces.

Soil-moisture storage (8) The retention of moisture within soil. In the water balance, this is the savings account that can accept deposits (soil-moisture recharge) or allow withdrawals (soil-moisture utilization) as conditions change.

Soil-moisture utilization (8) The extraction of soil moisture by plants for their needs; efficiency of withdrawal decreases as the soil-moisture storage is reduced.

Soil-moisture zone (8) The area of water stored in soil between the ground surface and the water table. Water in this zone may be available or unavailable to plant roots, depending on soil texture characteristics.

Solar constant (2) The amount of insolation intercepted by Earth on a surface perpendicular to the Sun's rays when Earth is at its average distance from the Sun; a value of 1372 W/m^2; averaged over the entire globe at the thermopause.

Solar wind (2) Clouds of ionized (charged) gases emitted by the Sun and travelling in all directions from the Sun's surface. Effects on Earth include auroras, disturbance of radio signals, and possible influences on weather.

Solifluction (13) In polar regions and at high elevations, the downslope movement of saturated soil during the summer months after seasonal thaw has occurred.

Solum (18) The A, E, and B horizons within a pedon, together considered the true definable soil within that soil profile. (*See* Pedon.)

Spatial analysis (1) The examination of phenomena across space, or area; a key unifying approach across all of geographic science.

Specific heat (4) The increase of temperature in a material when energy is absorbed; water has a higher specific heat (can store more heat) than a comparable volume of soil or rock.

Specific humidity (6) The mass of water vapor (in grams) per unit mass of air (in kilograms) at any specified temperature. The maximum mass of water vapor that a kilogram of air can hold at any specified temperature is termed its maximum specific humidity. (*Compare* Vapor pressure, Relative humidity.)

Speed of light (2) Specifically, 299,792 kilometers (186,282 miles) per second, or more than 9.4 trillion kilometers (5.9 trillion miles) per year—a distance known as a light-year; at light speed, Earth is 8 minutes and 20 seconds from the Sun.

Speleothem (10) A calcium carbonate mineral deposit in a cave or cavern, such as a stalactite or stalagmite, that forms as water drips or seeps from rock and subsequently evaporates, leaving behind a residue of calcium carbonate that builds up over time.

Spheroidal weathering (13) A chemical weathering process in which the sharp edges and corners of boulders and rocks are weathered in thin plates that create a rounded, spheroidal form.

Spodosols (18) A soil order in the Soil Taxonomy. Occurs in northern coniferous forests; best developed in cold, moist, forested climates; lacks humus and clay in the A horizon, with high acidity associated with podzolization processes.

Spring tide (16) The highest tidal range, which occurs when the Moon and the Sun are in conjunction (at new Moon) or in opposition (at full Moon) stages. (*Compare* Neap tide.)

Squall line (7) A zone slightly ahead of a fast-advancing cold front where wind patterns are rapidly changing and blustery and precipitation is strong.

Stability (6) The condition of a parcel of air with regard to whether it remains where it is or changes its initial position. The parcel is stable if it resists displacement upward and unstable if it continues to rise.

Star dune (15) A type of sand dune with multiple slipfaces produced by winds that come from varying directions; the dune form that attains the largest size.

Stationary front (7) A frontal area of contact between contrasting air masses that shows little horizontal movement; winds in opposite directions on either side of the front flow parallel along the front.

Steady-state equilibrium (1) The condition that occurs in a system when the rates of input and output are equal and the amounts of energy and stored matter are nearly constant around a stable average.

Steppe (9) A regional term referring to the vast semiarid grassland biome of Eastern Europe and Asia; the equivalent biome in North America is shortgrass prairie, and in Africa, it is the savanna. Steppe in a climatic context is considered too dry to support forest, but too moist to be a desert.

Stomata (19) Small openings on the undersides of leaves through which water and gasses pass.

Storm surge (7) A large quantity of seawater pushed inland by the strong winds associated with a tropical cyclone.

Storm tracks (7) Seasonally shifting paths followed by migrating low-pressure systems.

Stratified drift (17) Sediments deposited by glacial meltwater that appear sorted; a specific form of glacial drift. (*Compare* Till.)

Stratigraphy (11) A science that analyzes the sequence, spacing, geophysical and geochemical properties, and spatial distribution of rock strata.

Stratocumulus (7) A lumpy, grayish, low-level cloud, patchy with sky visible, sometimes present at the end of the day.

Stratosphere (3) That portion of the homosphere that ranges from 20 to 50 km (12.5 to 30 mi) above Earth's surface, with temperatures ranging from $-57°C$ ($-70°F$) at the tropopause to $0°C$ ($32°F$) at the stratopause. The functional ozonosphere is within the stratosphere.

Stratus (7) A stratiform (flat, horizontal) cloud generally below 2000 m (6500 ft).

Strike-slip fault (12) Horizontal movement along a fault line—that is, movement in the same direction as the fault; also known as a *transcurrent* fault. Such movement is described as right lateral or left lateral, depending on the relative motion observed across the fault. (*See* Transform fault.)

Subduction zone (11) An area where two plates of crust collide and the denser oceanic crust dives beneath the less dense continental plate, forming deep oceanic trenches and seismically active regions.

Sublimation (6) The phase change of ice, a solid, directly to water vapor, a gas. The opposite process is deposition, in which water vapor changes directly to ice.

Subpolar low (5) A region of low pressure centered approximately at 60° latitude in the North Atlantic near Iceland and in the North Pacific near the Aleutians as well as in the Southern Hemisphere. Airflow is cyclonic; it weakens in summer and strengthens in winter. (*See* Cyclone.)

Subsolar point (2) The only point receiving perpendicular insolation at a given moment—that is, the Sun is directly overhead. (*See* Declination.)

Subtropical high (5) One of several dynamic high-pressure areas covering roughly the region from 20° to 35° N and S latitudes; responsible for the hot, dry areas of Earth's arid and semiarid deserts. (*See* Anticyclone.)

Sulfate aerosols (3) Sulfur compounds in the atmosphere, principally sulfuric acid; principal sources relate to fossil fuel combustion; scatter and reflect insolation.

Sulfur dioxide (SO_2) (3) A colorless gas detected by its pungent odor; produced by the combustion of fossil fuels, especially coal, that contain sulfur as an impurity; can react in the atmosphere to form sulfuric acid, a component of acid deposition.

Summer solstice (2) *See* June solstice.

Sun altitude (2) The angular distance between the horizon (a horizontal plane) and the Sun (or any point in the sky).

Sunspots (2) Magnetic disturbances on the surface of the Sun, occurring in an average 11-year cycle; related flares, prominences, and outbreaks produce surges in solar wind.

Supercell thunderstorm (7) A severe thunderstorm with a deep, persistently rotating updraft that can produce heavy rain, large hail, and tornadoes.

Surface creep (15) A form of eolian transport that involves particles too large for saltation; a process whereby individual grains are impacted by moving grains and slide and roll.

Surface runoff (8) Surplus water that flows across the ground surface toward stream channels when soils are saturated or when the ground is impermeable; also called *overland flow*.

Surplus (8) In terms of the water balance, the condition that occurs when all water demands are met and extra water remains; often takes the form of surface runoff that feeds lakes and streams and recharges groundwater.

Suspended load (14) Fine particles held in suspension in a stream. The finest particles are not deposited until the stream velocity nears zero.

Sustainability science (1) An emerging, integrated scientific discipline based on the concepts of sustainable development related to functioning Earth systems.

Swell (16) Regular patterns of smooth, rounded waves in open water; can range from small ripples to very large waves.

Syncline (13) A trough-shaped downward fold in which rock strata slope toward the central axis of the fold. (*Compare* Anticline.)

System (1) Any ordered, interrelated set of materials or items existing separate from the environment or within a boundary; energy transformations and energy and matter storage and retrieval occur within a system.

T

Talus slope (13) Formed by angular rock fragments that cascade down a slope along the base of a mountain; poorly sorted, cone-shaped deposits.

Tarn (17) A small mountain lake, especially one that collects in a cirque basin behind risers of rock material or in an ice-gouged depression.

Temperate rain forest (20) A major biome of lush forests at middle and high latitudes; occurs along narrow margins of the Pacific Northwest in North America, among other locations; includes the tallest trees in the world.

Temperature (4) A measure of sensible heat energy present in the atmosphere and other media; indicates the average kinetic energy of individual molecules within a substance.

Temperature inversion (3) A reversal of the normal decrease of temperature with increasing altitude; can occur anywhere from ground level up to several thousand meters; functions to block atmospheric convection and thereby trap pollutants.

Terminal moraine (17) Eroded debris that is dropped at a glacier's farthest extent.

Terrane (12) A migrating piece of Earth's crust, dragged about by processes of mantle convection and plate tectonics. Displaced terranes are distinct in their history, composition, and structure from the continents that accept them.

Thermal equator (4) The isoline on an isothermal map that connects all points of highest mean temperature.

Thermocline (16) A transitional layer in the midlatitude oceans extending to a depth of about 1000 m (3300 ft) that lacks the motion of the surface and within which temperature changes rapidly with depth.

Thermohaline circulation (5) Deep-ocean currents produced by differences in temperature and salinity with depth; Earth's deep currents.

Thermopause (2, 3) A zone approximately 480 km (300 mi) in altitude that serves conceptually as the top of the atmosphere; an altitude used for the determination of the solar constant.

Thermosphere (3) A region of the heterosphere extending from 80 to 480 km (50 to 300 mi) in altitude; contains the functional ionosphere layer.

Threshold (1) A moment in which a system can no longer maintain its character and lurches to a new operational level, which may not be compatible with previous conditions.

Thrust fault (12) A reverse fault where the fault plane forms a low angle relative to the horizontal; an overlying block moves over an underlying block.

Thunder (7) The violent expansion of suddenly heated air, created by lightning discharges, which sends out shock waves as an audible sonic bang.

Tide (16) A pattern of twice-daily oscillations in sea level produced by astronomical relations among the Sun, the Moon, and Earth; experienced in varying degrees around the world. (*See* Neap tide, Spring tide.)

Till (17) Direct ice deposits that appear unstratified and unsorted; a specific form of glacial drift. (*Compare* Stratified drift.)

Till plain (17) A large, relatively flat plain composed of unsorted glacial deposits behind a terminal or end moraine. Low-rolling relief and unclear drainage patterns are characteristic.

Tombolo (16) A landform created when coastal sand deposits connect the shoreline with an offshore island outcrop or sea stack.

Topographic map (Appendix A) A map that portrays physical relief through the use of elevation contour lines that connect all points at the same elevation above or below a vertical datum, such as mean sea level.

Topography (12) The undulations and variations of Earth's surface, including slope and relief; portrayed on topographic maps.

Tornado (7) An intense, destructive cyclonic rotation, developed in response to extremely low pressure; generally associated with mesocyclone formation.

Traction (14) A type of sediment transport that drags coarser materials along the bed of a stream. (*See* Bed load.)

Trade winds (5) Winds from the northeast (in the northern hemisphere) and southeast (in the southern hemisphere) that converge in the equatorial low-pressure trough, forming the intertropical convergence zone.

Transform fault (12) A type of geologic fault in rocks. An elongated zone along which faulting occurs between mid-ocean ridges; produces a relative horizontal motion with no new crust formed or consumed; strike-slip motion is either left or right lateral. (*See* strike-slip fault.)

Transmission (4) The passage of shortwave and longwave energy through space, the atmosphere, or water.

Transparency (4) The quality of a medium (air, water) that allows light to easily pass through it.

Transpiration (8) The movement of water vapor out through the pores in leaves; the water is drawn by the plant roots from soil-moisture storage.

Tropic of Cancer (2) At 23.5° N latitude, the parallel that marks the farthest north the subsolar point migrates during the year. (*See* Tropic of Capricorn, June solstice.)

Tropic of Capricorn (2) At 23.5° S latitude, the parallel that marks the farthest south the subsolar point migrates during the year. (*See* Tropic of Cancer, December solstice.)

Tropical cyclone (7) A rotating low-pressure storm system originating in the tropics, with strong winds, thunderstorms, heavy rain, and storm surge; characterized by closed isobars and circular organization. (*See* Hurricane, Typhoon.)

Tropical rain forest (20) A lush biome of tall broadleaf evergreen trees and diverse plants and animals, roughly between 23.5° N and 23.5° S. The dense canopy of leaves is usually arranged in three levels.

Tropical savanna (20) A biome containing large expanses of grassland interrupted by trees and shrubs; a transitional area between the humid rain forests and tropical seasonal forests and the drier, semiarid tropical steppes and deserts.

Tropical seasonal forest and scrub (20) A biome on the margins of the rain forests, occupying regions of lesser and more erratic rainfall; the site of transitional communities between the rain forests and tropical grasslands.

Tropopause (3) The top zone of the troposphere defined by temperature; wherever −57°C (−70°F) occurs.

Troposphere (3) The home of the biosphere; the lowest layer of the homosphere, containing approximately 90% of the total mass of the atmosphere; extends up to the tropopause; occurring at an altitude of 18 km (11 mi) at the equator, at 13 km (8 mi) in the middle latitudes, and at lower altitudes near the poles.

True shape (1) A map property showing the correct configuration of coastlines; a useful trait of conformality for navigational and aeronautical maps, although areal relationships are distorted. (*See* Map projection; *compare* Equal area.)

Tsunami (16) A seismic sea wave, travelling at high speeds across the ocean, formed by sudden motion in the seafloor, such as a sea-floor earthquake, submarine landslide, or eruption of an undersea volcano.

Typhoon (7) A tropical cyclone that occurs in the western Pacific; same as a hurricane except for location. (*Compare* Hurricane.)

U

Ultisols (18) A soil order in the Soil Taxonomy. Features highly weathered forest soils, principally in the humid subtropical climatic

classification. Increased weathering and exposure can degenerate an Alfisol into the reddish color and texture of these Ultisols.

Unconfined aquifer (8) An aquifer that has a permeable layer of rock or sediment above and an impermeable layer of rock or sediment beneath. (*Compare* to Confined aquifer.)

Undercut bank (14) In streams, a steep bank formed along the outer portion of a meandering stream; produced by lateral erosive action of a stream; sometimes called a *cutbank*. (*Compare* Point bar.)

Uniformitarianism (11) An assumption that physical processes active in the environment today are operating at the same pace and intensity that has characterized them throughout geologic time; proposed by Hutton and Lyell.

Upslope fog (6) Forms when moist air is forced to higher elevations along a hill or mountain and is thus cooled. (*Compare* Valley fog.)

Upwelling (5) In the oceans, the upward movement of cold, nutrient-rich water from great depth to replace surface water that is swept away by surface divergence or by offshore winds; occurs along the west coasts of North and South America.

Urban heat island (4) An urban microclimate that is warmer on average than areas in the surrounding countryside because of the interaction of solar radiation and various surface characteristics.

V

Valley fog (7) The settling of cooler, more dense air in low-lying areas; produces saturated conditions and fog. (*Compare* Upslope fog.)

Vapor pressure (7) That portion of total air pressure that results from water vapor molecules, expressed in millibars (mb). At a given dew-point temperature, the maximum capacity of the air is termed its saturation vapor pressure.

Vascular plant (19) A plant having internal fluid and material flows through its tissues; almost 270,000 species exist on Earth.

Ventifact (15) A piece of rock etched and smoothed by eolian erosion—that is, abrasion by windblown particles.

Vernal equinox (2) *See* March equinox.

Vertisols (18) A soil order in the Soil Taxonomy. Features expandable clay soils; composed of more than 30% swelling clays. Occurs in regions that experience highly variable soil moisture balances through the seasons.

Volatile organic compounds (VOCs) (3) Compounds, including hydrocarbons, produced by the combustion of gasoline and from cleaning and paint solvents; react with nitric oxides to produce photochemical smog.

Volcano (12) A mountainous landform at the end of a magma conduit, which rises from below the crust and vents to the surface.

Magma rises and collects in a magma chamber deep below, erupting effusively or explosively and forming composite, shield, or cinder-cone volcanoes.

W

Warm desert and semidesert (20) A desert biome caused by the presence of subtropical high-pressure cells; characterized by dry air and low precipitation.

Warm front (7) The leading edge of an advancing warm air mass, which is unable to push cooler, passive air out of the way; tends to push the cooler, underlying air into a wedge shape; identified on a weather map as a line marked with semicircles pointing in the direction of frontal movement. (*Compare* Cold front.)

Water budget (8) A water accounting system for an area of Earth's surface using inputs of precipitation and outputs of evapotranspiration (evaporation from ground surfaces and transpiration from plants) and surface runoff. Precipitation "income" balances evaporation, transpiration, and runoff "expenditures"; soil moisture storage acts as "savings" in the budget.

Water table (8) The upper surface of groundwater; that contact point between the zone of saturation and the zone of aeration in an unconfined aquifer. (*See* Zone of aeration, Zone of saturation.)

Water withdrawal (8) Sometimes called *offstream use*, the part of the surplus in the water budget that is removed from the natural water supply, used for various purposes, and then returned to the water supply.

Waterspout (7) An elongated, funnel-shaped circulation formed when a tornado exists over water.

Wave (16) An undulation of ocean water produced by the conversion of solar energy to wind energy and then to wave energy; energy produced in a generating region or a stormy area of the sea.

Wave cyclone (7) *See* Midlatitude cyclone.

Wave refraction (16) A bending process that concentrates wave energy on headlands and disperses it in coves and bays; the long-term result is coastal straightening.

Wave-cut platform (16) A flat or gently sloping, tablelike bedrock surface that develops in the tidal zone where wave action cuts a bench that extends from the cliff base out into the sea.

Wavelength (2) A measurement of a wave; the distance between the crests of successive waves. The number of waves passing a fixed point in 1 second is called the frequency of the wavelength.

Weather (7) The short-term condition of the atmosphere, as compared to climate, which reflects long-term atmospheric conditions and extremes. Temperature, air pressure, relative humidity, wind speed and direction, daylength, and Sun angle are important measurable elements that contribute to the weather.

Weathering (13) The processes by which surface and subsurface rocks disintegrate, dissolve, or are broken down. Rocks at or near Earth's surface are exposed to physical and chemical weathering processes.

Westerlies (5) The predominant surface and aloft wind-flow pattern from the subtropics to high latitudes in both hemispheres.

Western intensification (5) The piling up of ocean water along the western margin of each ocean basin, to a height of about 15 cm (6 in.); produced by the trade winds that drive surface currents westward along the equator.

Wetland (8) An area that is permanently or seasonally saturated with water and characterized by vegetation adapted to hydric soils; highly productive ecosystem with an ability to trap organic matter, nutrients, and sediment.

Wilting point (8) That point in the soil-moisture balance when only hygroscopic water and some bound capillary water remain. Plants wilt and eventually die after prolonged stress from a lack of available water.

Wind (5) The horizontal movement of air relative to Earth's surface; produced essentially by air pressure differences between locations.

Wind vane (5) A weather instrument used to determine wind direction; winds are named for the direction from which they originate.

Winter solstice (2) *See* December solstice.

X

Xerophyte (20) A plant that has adapted to survive in dry conditions, usually by evolving mechanisms to access water, store water, or prevent water loss.

Y

Yardang (15) A streamlined rock structure formed by deflation and abrasion; appears elongated and aligned with the most effective wind direction.

Z

Zone of aeration (8) A zone above the water table where soil and rock are less than saturated and some pore spaces contain air rather than water.

Zone of saturation (8) A groundwater zone below the water table in which all pore spaces are filled with water.

INDEX

World – Physical

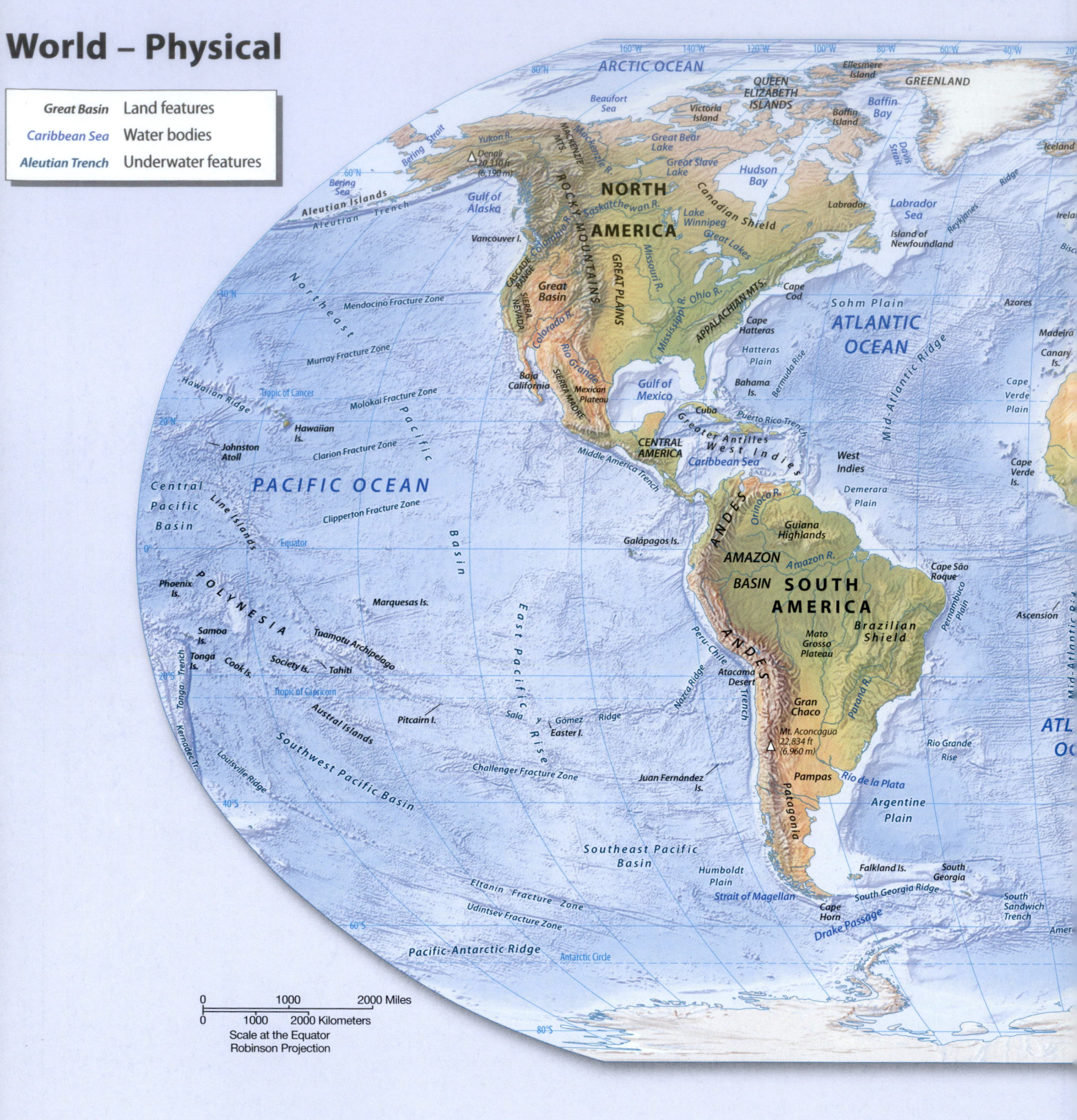

ARCTIC OCEAN

QUEEN ELIZABETH ISLANDS
GREENLAND
Ellesmere Island
Baffin Bay
Baffin Island
Iceland
Beaufort Sea
Victoria Island
Great Bear Lake
Hudson Bay
Davis Strait
Ireland
Yukon R.
Denali 20,310 ft (6,190 m)
MACKENZIE MTS.
Great Slave Lake
Labrador
Labrador Sea
Island of Newfoundland
Reykjanes Ridge
Bering Strait
Bering Sea
Gulf of Alaska
ROCKY MOUNTAINS
Saskatchewan R.
Canadian Shield
Lake Winnipeg
Great Lakes
NORTH AMERICA
Aleutian Islands
Aleutian Trench
Vancouver I.
CASCADE RANGE
Columbia R.
Missouri R.
Azores
Northeast
Mendocino Fracture Zone
Great Basin
SIERRA NEVADA
GREAT PLAINS
Mississippi R.
Ohio R.
APPALACHIAN MTS.
Cape Cod
Sohm Plain
ATLANTIC OCEAN
Madeira Is.
Canary Is.
Murray Fracture Zone
Colorado R.
Cape Hatteras
Hatteras Plain
Bermuda Rise
Mid-Atlantic Ridge
Hawaiian Ridge
Tropic of Cancer
Molokai Fracture Zone
SIERRA MADRE
Rio Grande
Baja California
Mexican Plateau
Gulf of Mexico
Bahama Is.
Cape Verde Plain
Hawaiian Is.
Clarion Fracture Zone
Middle America Trench
CENTRAL AMERICA
Cuba
Greater Antilles
Puerto Rico Trench
West Indies
West Indies
Cape Verde Is.
Johnston Atoll
Pacific
Caribbean Sea
PACIFIC OCEAN
Central Pacific Basin
Line Islands
Clipperton Fracture Zone
Galápagos Is.
ANDES
Orinoco R.
Guiana Highlands
Demerara Plain
Basin
Equator
AMAZON
Amazon R.
Cape São Roque
Phoenix Is.
POLYNESIA
Marquesas Is.
BASIN
SOUTH AMERICA
Brazilian Shield
Pernambuco Plain
Ascension
Samoa Is.
Tuamotu Archipelago
East Pacific Rise
Mato Grosso Plateau
Mid-Atlantic Ridge
Tonga Is.
Cook Is.
Society Is.
Tahiti
ANDES
Atacama Desert
Tonga Trench
Austral Islands
Tropic of Capricorn
Pitcairn I.
Sala y Gómez Ridge
Easter I.
Gran Chaco
Paraná R.
Rio Grande Rise
ATL OC
Kermadec Trench
Southwest Pacific Basin
Challenger Fracture Zone
Juan Fernández Is.
Mt. Aconcagua 22,834 ft (6,960 m)
Pampas
Rio de la Plata
Louisville Ridge
Patagonia
Argentine Plain
Southeast Pacific Basin
Humboldt Plain
Falkland Is.
South Georgia
Eltanin Fracture Zone
Strait of Magellan
South Georgia Ridge
South Sandwich Trench
Udintsev Fracture Zone
Cape Horn
Drake Passage
Amer
Pacific-Antarctic Ridge
Antarctic Circle